THE MOST TRUSTED NAME IN TRAVEL

Frommer's®

ITALY 2027

19th Edition

By Donald Strachan, Elizabeth Heath, Michelle Schoenung, Stephen Brewer, Stephen Keeling

FrommerMedia LLC

Frommer's Italy 2027, 19th Edition

Published by:
FrommerMedia LLC

ISBN 978-1-62887-673-4 (paper), 978-1-62887-674-1 (ebk)

Editorial Director: Pauline Frommer
Editor: Holly Hughes
Production Editor: Erin Geile
Compositor: Lissa Auciello Brogan
Cartographer: Andy Dolan
Photo Editor: Meghan Lamb
Indexer: Cheryl Lenser
Cover Designer: Dave Riedy

Front cover photo: Galleria Vittorio Emanuele II in Milan. © Pyty / shutterstock.com

Back cover photo: View of Positano. © Ragemax / Shutterstock

For information on our other products or services, see www.frommers.com.

FrommerMedia LLC also publishes its books in a variety of electronic formats. Some content that appears in print may not be available in electronic formats.

Manufactured in Malaysia

5 4 3 2 1

HOW TO CONTACT US

In researching this book, we discovered many wonderful places—hotels, restaurants, shops, and more. We're sure you'll find others. Please tell us about them, so we can share the information with your fellow travelers in upcoming editions. If you were disappointed with a recommendation, we'd love to know that, too. Please write to: Support@FrommerMedia.com

FROMMER'S RATINGS SYSTEM

Every hotel, restaurant and attraction listed in this guide has been ranked for quality and value. Here's what the hearts mean:

♥ Recommended
♥♥ Highly Recommended
♥♥♥ A must! Don't miss!

AN IMPORTANT NOTE

The world is a dynamic place. Hotels change ownership, restaurants hike their prices, museums alter their opening hours, and buses and trains change their routings. And all of this can occur in the several months after our authors have visited, inspected, and written about these hotels, restaurants, museums, and transportation services. Though we have made valiant efforts to keep all our information fresh and up-to-date, some few changes can inevitably occur in the periods before a revised edition of this guidebook is published. So please bear with us if a tiny number of the details in this book have changed. Please also note that we have no responsibility or liability for any inaccuracy or errors or omissions, or for inconvenience, loss, damage, or expenses suffered by anyone as a result of assertions in this guide.

CONTENTS

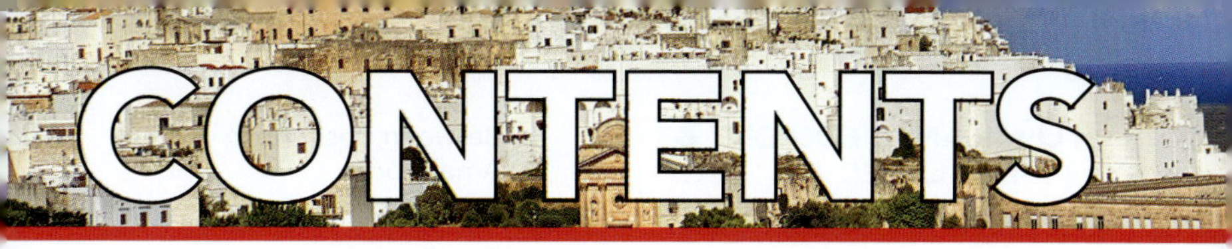

LIST OF MAPS

VATICAN CITY
Via di Belvedere
Borgo Vittorio
Piazza Adriana
Castel Sant'Angelo
Via della Conciliazione
Piazza Pio XII

ABOUT THE AUTHORS

Stephen Brewer has been savoring Italian pleasures ever since he sipped his first cappuccino while a student in Rome many years ago. He has written about Italy for many magazines and guidebooks and remains transported in equal measure by Bolognese cooking, Tuscan hillsides, the Bay of Naples, and the streets of Palermo.

A longtime contributor to Frommer's guides and Frommers.com, **Elizabeth Heath** writes about travel from her hilltop village of Allerona, Umbria. Her work has appeared in *The Washington Post*, *National Geographic*, *Travel + Leisure*, and many other titles. She has degrees in fine arts and humanities and completed doctoral coursework in anthropology and archaeology, when her studies led her to Italy. Since moving here in 2009, Liz has written extensively about traveling and living in Italy. She is the founder of Villaggio Tours (villaggiotours.com), a family-run small-group tour company offering immersive experiences in her home region of Umbria, and the co-owner of Six Keys Guesthouse (sixkeysumbria.com) in Allerona.

Stephen Keeling has been traveling to Italy since 1985 (when a serving of gelato was 1,000 lire), and covering his favorite nation for Frommer's since 2007. He has written for *The Independent*, *Daily Telegraph*, various travel magazines, and numerous travel guides. Stephen resides in New York City.

Michelle Schoenung is an American journalist and translator in Milan who relocated to the Belpaese in 2000 for what was to be a yearlong adventure. More than two decades later, she is pleased that Milan has evolved into a much more international and cosmopolitan metropolis, shedding its image as merely being a foggy northern Italian business hub. Her writings and translations have appeared in magazines and books in the United States, Italy, and beyond. In her free time, she enjoys exploring Italy's less-known villages and loves a good Piedmontese red wine.

Donald Strachan has written about Italy and European travel for publications worldwide, including *National Geographic Traveller*, *The Guardian*, *Telegraph*, and CNN.com. He is author or co-author of several recent Frommer's guides, including *Frommer's Rome, Florence & Venice* and *Frommer's Amsterdam Day by Day*. He lives in London, England.

1

THE BEST OF ITALY

By Donald Strachan

For the first timer or the perennial visitor, Italy always has something irresistible. Just think the word "Italy" and you can already see the noble stones of ancient Rome and the temples of Sicily; the wine hills of Tuscany and Piedmont; the ruins of Pompeii; the food of Parma and Bologna; the secret canals and crumbling palaces of Venice. For centuries, visitors have come here looking for their own slice of *la dolce vita*. For the most part, they have found it.

Nowhere felt the impact of the Renaissance quite like its birthplace, **Florence,** whose vast repository of art includes works left by Botticelli, Leonardo da Vinci, Masaccio, Michelangelo, and many, many others. Much of the "known world" was once ruled from **Rome,** a city supposedly founded by twins Romulus and Remus in 753 B.C.E. There is no place with more artistic treasures—not even **Venice,** an impossible floating city whose beauty and history were shaped by trade along the Silk Road, and with Byzantine and Islamic empires of the east.

But Italy is so much more than these three distinct cities. Long before Italy was a country, it was a loose grouping of city-states. Centuries of alliance and rivalry left a legacy of art and architecture in **Verona,** where Shakespearean romance rubs alongside an intact Roman arena; and in **Mantua,** which blossomed during the Renaissance under the Gonzaga dynasty. **Padua**'s revolutionary Giotto paintings are within easy reach of Venice, too. In **Siena,** ethereal art and Gothic palaces survive, barely altered since their 1300s heyday.

More than a millennium earlier, the eruption of Vesuvius in C.E. 79 preserved **Pompeii** and **Herculaneum** under volcanic ash. They remain the best places to conjure up daily Roman life. The buildings of ancient Greece still stand at **Paestum,** in Campania, and at sites on **Sicily,** the Mediterranean's largest island. Cave-dwellings, frescoed rupestrian churches, and even a rock cathedral are hewn into the cliffs of **Matera,** in the unspoiled Basilicata region.

The corrugated, vine-clad hills of the **Chianti** and the cypress-studded, emerald-green expanses of the **Val d'Orcia** serve up iconic images of **Tuscany.** Adventurous walkers of all ages can hike between the coastal villages of the **Cinque Terre** or the headlands of the **Amalfi Coast,** where you can roam untroubled by the 21st century, if you pick the right season. Whether it's seafood in **Puglia,** pizza in **Naples,** pasta in **Bologna,** pesto in **Genoa,** or the red Barolo and Barbaresco wines of **Piedmont,** your tastebuds enjoy their own adventure. For shoppers,

PREVIOUS PAGE: **Amalfi's elegant clifftop Hotel Santa Caterina, with its terraced gardens and seaside pool.**

Hiking between the colorful coastal villages of the Cinque Terre.

Milan and Florence are centers of world fashion. Welcome to *la bella Italia.*

ITALY'S best AUTHENTIC EXPERIENCES

- **Dining Italian style:** In Italy, no pastime is more cherished than eating—even better, eating outdoors with a view of a medieval church or vineyard. And forget any idea of a single "Italian" cuisine: Each region and city has its own beloved recipes, handed down over generations. *Buon appetito!*
- **Exploring Rome's working food markets:** Testaccio's reborn historic market is a culinary and cultural treat, where local chefs and feisty *signore* compete for the best *pomodori, mozzarella di bufala,* and *trippa* (tripe). Savor delicious

Lingering over a meal at a street cafe in Rome.

street food as you soak up a genuine neighborhood south of the Aventine Hill. See p. 154.

- **Catching an opera at Verona's Arena:** Summer means opera under the stars. The setting for Italy's largest and most famous outdoor festival is the ancient Arena di Verona, a site grand enough to accommodate enough elephants for a showpiece *Aïda*. See p. 464.
- **Feeling the modern pulse of historic Bologna:** The youthful exuberance of Bologna, Europe's oldest university town, reveals itself amid medieval palaces and squares; 25 miles of portico-covered sidewalks; and best of all, markets, shops, and restaurants that dish up arguably Italy's best food. See chapter 8.
- **Slowing down to the Italian pace:** Nothing happens quickly here: Linger over a glass of wine in the Tuscan hills, slurp a gelato made with seasonal Sicilian fruit, enjoy the *passeggiata* (evening walk) just like the locals. It is easy to see how and why the Slow Food movement started here.

ITALY'S most memorable RESTAURANTS

- **Burro e Acciughe** (Florence): You can't get much farther from the coast anywhere south of the Apennine mountains, but the sourcing and culinary creativity here marks it out as a standout seafood specialist. See p. 219.
- **Taverna San Giuseppe** (Siena): A brick-vaulted room from the 12th century is a characterful setting for hand-rolled *pici* with a *ragù* of *cinghiale* (wild boar), ricotta-filled *gnudi,* and other expert takes on Tuscan comfort food. See p. 244.

Luscious tortellini is the signature dish at Da Nello al Montegrappa in Bologna.

- **Ristorante da Nello al Montegrappa** (Bologna): In the heart of a city devoted to food, these cozy paneled subterranean rooms have been a favorite spot since 1948. Signature *tortellini Montegrappa,* in a cream-and-meat sauce, provides a sample of the kitchen's traditional ways, all the better when washed down with a wine from the surrounding Colli Bolognesi. See p. 367.
- **Wistèria** (Venice): Part of a wave of contemporary restaurants opening in Venice, this place features innovative riffs on traditional *cicchetti* and seafood from the lagoon and farther out in the Adriatic. See p. 451.
- **Mimì alla Ferrovia** (Naples): Veteran waiters in bow ties and white jackets serve up old-fashioned charm at this beloved institution. Mimì creates culinary art from fried street food, market-fresh fish, and other Neapolitan favorites. See p. 615.

ITALY'S unforgettable FLAVORS

- **Sicilian sweets:** Italy's largest island is a haven for sweet tooths. Begin the day with a granita-filled brioche; liven up your mid-morning espresso with a ricotta-stuffed *cannolo;* end a meal with a *biancomangiare.* Sicily's *pasticcerie* are justly famous.
- ***Bistecca alla fiorentina:*** The ultimate carnivores' sharing plate is usually at least 1.2kg (almost 3 lb.) of prime Chianina beef on the bone. It's flame-grilled—briefly—and best accompanied by simple sides such as stewed Tuscan beans or potatoes roasted with rosemary. Dig in at **Mario** (p. 217), **La Gratella** (p. 216), and all over Florence.
- **The humble artichoke:** One of the joys of visiting Italy—especially Rome—in winter and early spring is sampling artichokes every way: as a pizza topping; in traditional Roman dishes like *carciofi alla romana* or *alla giudia;* or carpaccio style, with just a splash of oil, a grind of pepper, and some shavings of hard cheese. *Delizioso!*

Tempting sweets at a bakery shop in Taormina, Sicily.

- ***Cicchetti* and a spritz:** Tapas-like small plates, usually at a bar, are a Venetian tradition. A spritz made with Aperol and sparkling prosecco wine from Veneto completes the *cicchetti* experience.

- ***Vino rosso:*** If you are not by a lake or the sea, chances are the wine you're sipping is red. There is so much variety: near-black Primitivo from Puglia, robust reds from the Langhe in Piedmont, or the elegance of a great Tuscan Chianti Classico or Brunello di Montalcino.
- **Neapolitan pizza:** Leaving aside whether it was really invented in Naples, pizza Margherita finds its ultimate expression around Spaccanapoli and in the Quartieri Spagnoli. Prepared dough spends a few seconds in wood-burning furnaces—enough to aerate the crusts around a gorgeous puddle of molten mozzarella and San Marzano tomato.
- **A coffee *al banco:*** Italians—especially city dwellers—don't linger in a piazza sipping their morning cappuccino. For them, *un caffè* is a pit stop: They stand at the counter (*al banco*), throw back the bitter elixir, and continue on their way, reinforced by a hit of caffeine. Taking your coffee Italian-style costs less, often less than half the sit-down price.

ITALY'S most charming HOTELS

- **Villa Spalletti Trivelli** (Rome): Recent upgrades have only enhanced the unique experience of staying in a neoclassical mansion in the middle of the capital. Opulence plus impeccable, understated service comes at a price, of course. When our lottery numbers come up, we will be booking a long stay here. See p. 133.
- **Santa Caterina** (Amalfi): Amid fragrant citrus groves above the sea, Santa Caterina is not outrageously posh, just magically transporting. Ceramic tiles, a smattering of antiques, sea-view terraces, a garden path leading to a private beach—it's worth the splurge. Shoulder-season rates and special offers bring prices down. See p. 674.
- **Palazzo Tolomei** (Florence): A palace where Raphael once stayed—perhaps even giving its owners a painting to make rent—sounds grand indeed. You won't be disappointed. Its Renaissance layout and baroque redecoration from the 1600s are intact. See p. 208.
- **Butera 28 Apartments** (Palermo): You easily settle into the Sicilian capital when the duchess of Palma is your host, at a seaside palace where guest quarters are spacious apartments bursting with character and family heirlooms. Adding literary cachet is the fact that this was the final home of Giuseppe Tomasi di Lampedusa, author of the Italian literary classic *The Leopard.* See p. 764.
- **Donna Camilla Savelli** (Rome): Not every hotel can claim baroque pioneer Francesco Borromini as its architect. Yet this converted convent—a small community of nuns still lives here—bears his signature style, especially an elegant staircase, vaulted lounge corridor,

The farmhouse kitchen at welcoming Agriturismo La Bruciata, just outside Montepulciano.

and peaceful cloister, now a delightful setting for breakfast or aperitivo. It's a wee bit pricier than many Trastevere neighbors, but a definite upgrade. See p. 136.

- **Palazzo dei Dondoli** (Lecce): An early-20th-century townhouse at the edge of old Lecce is an elegant (and great value) retreat in a city that's all about grace. Stylish quarters surround a lush courtyard where you quickly get a taste for Puglia's outdoor lifestyle. See p. 742.
- **Agriturismo La Bruciata** (Montepulciano): All the ingredients of a perfect Tuscan stay come together in these stone houses on a sunny hillside. Accommodations are spacious; breakfasts and dinners are homegrown and homemade; and the welcome is as bright as the flower garden. See p. 253.

ITALY'S most vibrant NEIGHBORHOODS

- **San Frediano, Florence:** Most Florentines have abandoned their *centro storico* to the visitors, but the Arno's Left Bank in San Frediano has plenty of local action after dark. Dine at **iO** (p. 220), slurp a gelato by the river at **La Carraia** (p. 222), and sip cocktails or a whisk(e)y at **Love Craft** (p. 226).
- **Garibaldi/Porta Nuova, Milan:** Milan's newest neighborhood has risen from abandoned railway yards to become a thriving mix of old and current: Beside a gate from the days when Milan was a walled city are boutique stores, fashionable cafes, and modern landmarks like Italy's tallest skyscraper and the Bosco Verticale (Vertical Forest) buildings. See chapter 10.

Across the river from tourist Florence, the Oltrarno and San Frediano neighborhoods give you a feel for the Florence locals know and love.

- **Kalsa, Palermo:** Settled a thousand years ago, the city's old Arab quarter is a warren of art-filled palaces and ornate churches, set along alleyways that open to banyan-shaded squares and breezy seaside promenades. This being Sicily, food is at the forefront—at pastry shops, *friggitorie* (fried-food stalls), and family trattorias. See chapter 15.
- **Centro Storico, Rome:** Ancient walls form the foundations—and in many cases, the first floors—of many buildings in Rome's UNESCO-protected old center. Pieces of ancient columns, inscriptions, and marble fragments here and there, form a mosaic-like cityscape that spans three millennia. See chapter 4.
- **Sasso Barisano & Sasso Caveoso, Matera:** Inhabited for more than 3,000 years, clusters of dwellings carved into limestone cliffs create one of Italy's weirdest urban spectacles. The primitive, earth-hued assemblage of homes, churches, and monasteries pile one atop the other along a jumble of stepped streets. You can stay or dine here, too. See p. 520.

ITALY'S most peaceful LANDSCAPES

- **Gran Paradiso National Park** (Valle d'Aosta): Outside the August peak season, you could wander for hours without meeting a soul.

With this mountain region's four towering peaks in constant view, trek for miles up valleys and across wildflower meadows, then linger over steaming bowls of the local specialty, *carbonade con polenta* (beef stewed with juniper berries and red wine, served with cornmeal). See p. 547.

- **Umbria:** With fine wines, fêted produce (including game and olive oil), and centuries-old art and architecture, Tuscany's under-visited neighbor is often called "Italy's green heart." Wander off the beaten track to unspoiled Spello; explore vine-carpeted hillsides on the Strada del Sagrantino wine trail; or find solitude in medieval Gubbio, where St. Francis himself lodged in peace. See chapter 7.
- **The Val d'Orcia** (Tuscany): Supremely photogenic hills are carpeted with olive groves, vineyards, and wheat fields, topped with castles and ancient towns like Pienza and Montalcino. These otherworldly landscapes foster quiet contemplation at the isolated Abbey of Sant'Antimo and yield Brunello wines so superior that sipping them is an equally spiritual experience. See p. 256.
- **Sicily's west coast:** Beyond the clamor of Palermo's markets and the glamor of Taormina is another Sicily. Go west, where salt marshes are a stopover for migrating birds: The maquis and coastline of the Zingaro reserve are off-limits to motor vehicles. Even the towns—from mountaintop Erice to seaside Mazara del Vallo—are a world removed. See chapter 15.

The unspoiled Umbrian hill town of Spello.

ITALY'S best MUSEUMS

- **Vatican Museums** (Rome): The 100 galleries of the Musei Vaticani are loaded with papal treasures accumulated over centuries. Musts include the Sistine Chapel, ancient Greek and Roman sculptures like *Laocoön* and *Belvedere Apollo*, and room upon room of Raphael frescoes (among them his *School of Athens*). See p. 81.
- **Galleria degli Uffizi** (Florence): This U-shaped High Renaissance building designed by Giorgio Vasari—once administrative headquarters, or *uffizi* (offices), for Tuscany's dukes—is now the crown jewel of Europe's fine-art museums and holds the world's greatest collection of Renaissance paintings. See p. 179.

Taking time to admire a Giotto at the Uffizi Gallery in Florence.

- **Accademia** (Venice): Another of Europe's great museums houses an unequaled array of Venetian paintings, exhibited chronologically from the 13th to the 18th century. Walls are hung with art by Bellini, Carpaccio, Giorgione, Titian, and Tintoretto. See p. 421.
- **Museo Archeologico Nazionale** (Naples): Come here to see mosaics and frescoes from Pompeii and Herculaneum—the original "Cave Canem" ("Beware of the Dog") mosaic, Villa of the Papyri frescoes—and much more, including the "Farnese Bull." See p. 601.
- **Museo Egizio** (Turin): A dazzling refit has doubled the size and reconfigured the space of Turin's Egyptology museum, the world's oldest and the finest collection of artifacts outside Cairo. See p. 529.
- **Galleria Borghese** (Rome): Some of the very best of Rome's preeminent baroque sculptor, Gian Lorenzo Bernini, is here, inside a glittering palace originally built for one of his patrons, alongside works by Caravaggio, Raphael, and many others. See p. 112.
- **Museo dell'Opera del Duomo** (Florence): With icons of sculpture in marble and bronze, modern multimedia curation, and a creative layout, this collection is the homage that two great Florentines—Ghiberti and Brunelleschi—fully deserve. See p. 178.

ITALY'S iconic ARCHITECTURE

- **Brunelleschi's dome** (Florence): It took the genius of Filippo Brunelleschi to raise a vast dome over the gaping hole in Florence's cathedral roof. Although rejected for a commission to cast the Baptistery doors, Filippo didn't sulk: He became the city's greatest architect instead, creating one of Europe's most recognizable landmarks. See p. 179.
- **Beehive towns of the southeast** (Puglia): In the hinterlands of the Adriatic coast, storybook *trulli* dwellings enchant travelers to Alberobello and the Valle d'Itria. Once you're here, a bonus: the mazelike "white cities" of Ostuni, Martina Franca, Locorotondo, and Cisternino. See chapter 14.
- **The Gothic center of Siena** (Tuscany): Shell-shaped Piazza del Campo stands at the heart of one of Europe's best-preserved medieval cities. Steep, canyonlike streets, icons of Gothic architecture like the Palazzo Pubblico, and Madonnas painted on gilded altarpieces transport you back to a time before the Renaissance. See p. 234.
- **Pompeii** (Campania): When Mt. Vesuvius blew its top in C.E. 79, Pompeii was buried under molten lava and ash, ending the lives of perhaps 35,000 citizens and suspending the city in a time capsule. Today, still in the menacing shadow of the volcano, you can coax this poignant ghost town into life with little imagination. See p. 629.
- **Valley of the Temples, Agrigento** (Sicily): Seven Greek temples by the sea were built to impress, and their honey-colored columns and

Piecing together fragments of the past in Pompeii.

pediments still do. Seeing these romantic ruins—some, like the Temple of Concordia, beautifully preserved; others, like the Temple of Juno, timeworn but proud—is an experience never forgotten. See p. 805.

ITALY'S best FREE THINGS TO DO

- **Watching the sun rise over the Roman Forum:** A short stroll from the Capitoline Hill down Via del Campidoglio to Via di Monte Tarpeo brings you to a perfect outlook: a terrace behind the Michelangelo-designed square, an ideal photo op when the sun rises behind the Temple of Saturn, illuminating the archaeological complex below in pink-orange light. See p. 91.
- **Basking in the lights of the Renaissance:** At dusk, make the steep climb to the ancient church of San Miniato al Monte, Florence. Sit down on the steps and watch the city begin to twinkle. See p. 200.
- **Driving the Chiantigiana:** This fabled road—technically, unromantically the SR222—rises, winds, and sinks amid the Chianti hills between Florence and Siena, traversing iconic landscapes that are home to some of Italy's most celebrated vineyards and velvety, ruby-red wines. See chapter 6.
- **Discovering you're hopelessly lost in Venice:** You haven't experienced Venice until you have turned a corner, convinced you're on the way to somewhere, only to find yourself smack against a canal with no bridge. Shrug, smile, and give the maze of city streets another try, because getting lost here is a pleasure. See chapter 9.
- **Hiking the Sentiero degli Dei** (Amalfi Coast): You'll appreciate the name as you plunge through heavenly scenery with the bluest ocean glimmering far below and the island of Capri a phantom on the horizon. These paths follow mountainsides and headlands—perfect antidotes to this coastline's overdose of glitz and glamor. See p. 663.
- **Surrendering to the madness of a Palermo market:** In Sicily's capital—a crossroads between Europe, Africa, and Asia for 2,000 years—the colorful street theater is a vignette of a culture that feels part Middle Eastern, part European. See p. 771.

It's a pleasure to get lost among the narrow streets and side canals of Venice.

best UNDISCOVERED ITALY

- **Byzantine art up close:** Unless you plan on living for another century or two, you will never again have the chance to see the 10 million mosaics of Florence's Baptistery ceiling from just inches away. While a major restoration is underway, small groups may ascend the scaffolding for this closer look. Book now. See p. 176.
- **Genoa's UNESCO center:** Don't be fooled by the rough, industrial exterior: Genoa has Italy's largest *centro storico,* with architecture to rival Venice. A restored old port, the Palazzo Reale, and the palaces of Strada Nuova are just a few highlights. With a new high-speed rail connection opening in 2026, getting here from Milan will be quicker than ever. See chapter 11.
- **The canals of Treviso:** Venice's inland neighbor has canals of its own, and much thinner crowds, even in peak season. Visit an atmospheric old fish market and churches decorated by Tommaso da Modena. See p. 465.
- **The old, old stones of Puglia:** Remains of a once-thriving Roman trading center are scattered across Puglia's coastal plains at Egnazia. Notable spots include a segment of the Trajan Way and the Tomb of the Pomegranates, its huge doors bearing ancient handles and hinges that still function. "Built to last" and then some. See p. 725.
- **The *sagre* of Piedmont:** This northern Italian region flies under the radar for many visitors. As a consequence, many traditions remain

Colorful medieval pageantry is all part of the festivities at Alba's annual white truffle fair.

undisturbed, including a packed calendar of local festivals (*sagre*). Gather to celebrate hyperlocal foods, wine, chocolate—or the king among tubers at Alba's white truffle fair each autumn. See p. 543.

ITALY'S best ACTIVE ADVENTURES

- **Flying in the Lucanian Dolomites** (Basilicata): Villagers in Castelmezzano and Pietrapertosa, on adjacent mountainsides, have linked themselves in a novel way: You can glide, via zipline, from one village to another. The Flight of the Angel is a thrill or a heartstopper, depending on your taste. See p. 721.
- **Touring Ferrara on two wheels:** Join bike-mad *Ferraresi* as they zip along narrow, cycle-friendly lanes that snake through the old center, past Castello Estense and the Renaissance elegance of Palazzo Schifanoia. You can even bike a circuit around the medieval walls. See p. 374.
- **Floating through the Alps on the Monte Bianco Skyway:** In Italy's far northwestern corner, a cable car from Courmayeur scales Europe's tallest mountain: Monte Bianco ("Mont Blanc" to the French), flanked by perilous glaciers and jagged granite peaks,

The Volo dell'Angelo (Flight of the Angel) zipline joins two mountain villages in Basilicata.

standing 4,810m (15,780 ft.) high on the border of France and Italy. On a clear day, the view is unforgettable. See p. 549.

- **Hiking the Cinque Terre** (Liguria): For sheer beauty, we love the 3-mile path from Corniglia to Vernazza and a 2-mile section from Vernazza to Monterosso, but the entire Cinque Terre area is rewarding to hike, especially off-season. Narrow paths skirt terraced vineyards and olive and lemon groves hover over the sapphire Mediterranean Sea. See p. 579.

ITALY'S best FOR FAMILIES

- **Climbing Pisa's wonky tower** (Tuscany): Are we walking up or down? Pleasantly disoriented kids are bound to ask as you spiral your way to a rooftop-viewing balcony atop one of the world's most famous pieces of botched engineering. See p. 302.
- **The beaches of Puglia and Basilicata:** Many of Italy's best sands are in the southeast, often reached via an easy, signposted track through coastal forest. Even the prettiest may be empty outside high season. Try Torre Guaceto, north of Brindisi; Porto Selvaggio or Punta della Suina, close to Gallipoli; or coves along the remote Maratea coast. See chapter 14.

Italian families know that the "heel" of Italy's boot has many of Italy's best beaches.

- **Exploring beneath Naples:** There's more to Naples than you can see at ground level. Head under its maze of streets to explore remains of ancient Greek and Roman cities, creepy catacombs used for early Christian burials, and tunnels where Neapolitans hid from an 1884 cholera epidemic and World War II bombs. See p. 606.
- **Taste-testing every artisan gelateria:** When it comes to Italian ice cream, choose carefully—Smurf-blue or bubblegum-pink flavors are a sure sign of color enhancers, and beware ice crystals and fluffy heaps which betray additives and pumped-in air. Authentic *gelaterie* produce good stuff from scratch daily, with fresh seasonal produce; look for a short, all-natural ingredient list posted proudly for all to see. Check "Where to Eat" and "Gelato" sections in individual chapters.

2

ITALY IN CONTEXT

By Donald Strachan

This chapter provides historical and cultural background to help you understand what makes Italy tick. Many stereotypes you hear about this extraordinary country are accurate. Food and soccer are a religion; children are fussed over wherever they go; the North–South divide is alive and well; and (alas) bureaucracy is a frustrating feature of daily life for families and businesses—much less so for visitors. Some stereotypes, however, are wide of the mark: Not every Italian you meet will be open and effusive. Every now and then—but rarely in the South—they do taciturn pretty well, too. Keep reading and we'll fill in some more of the gaps for you.

One important fact to remember is that, for a land so steeped in history—3 millennia and counting—Italy has not been *a nation* for long. In 2026 Italy celebrated its 165th birthday. Prior to 1861, the political map of the peninsula was in constant flux. War, alliance, invasion, and disputed successions caused that map to change color as often as a chameleon in a bag of M&Ms. Republics, city-states, emirates, dukedoms, kingdoms, and theocracies roll on and off the pages of Italian history with regularity. In many regions, you'll hear languages and dialects other than Italian. Identities are often expressed regionally rather than nationally.

This chaotic history explains why your Italian experience will differ wildly if you visit, say, Turin in the northwest rather than Matera in the southeast. (And why you should visit both if you can.) The architecture is different; the food is different; legends and important historical figures are different. And the people are different: While the North–South schism is most often written about, cities as close together as Florence and Siena feel very dissimilar. Milan to Naples is just over 4 hours by train, but you will experience them like two different worlds. Our aim in this chapter is to help you understand why.

ITALY TODAY

Italy's post-Covid bounce-back has been rapid. Walking the streets of Florence or Rome today, you could be forgiven for forgetting all about the pandemic. Bars and restaurants are full; hotels enjoy a booking boom that is unrelenting. Cafe chatter has returned to the plight of the local soccer team or Mt. Etna's latest fireworks. In May 2025, the country waited in unison for the white smoke signifying the conclave's election of a Chicago native to head the Catholic Church, as Pope Leo XIV.

FACING PAGE: **Florence's Bargello Museum is a treasure trove of Renaissance sculpture.**

Pandemic aftershocks are still visible in politics, however. Covid-19 caused repeated government crises, which culminated in the collapse of a unity government in 2022. The election that followed was a triumph for the Fratelli d'Italia (FdI), a nationalist and socially conservative political party. FdI's controversial but canny leader, Giorgia Meloni, became Italy's first female prime minister. She now dominates an occasionally fractious right-wing coalition, in part thanks to her unexpected caution in government—certainly when compared to her pre-election firebrand populism. Government actions have been a mixed bag, with a much-criticized clampdown on rights of protest, controversial abortion measures, re-affirmation of a commitment to fight climate change, efforts to reduce energy bills, and attempts to bridge differences between Europe and the U.S. on crises in Ukraine and Israel.

The country's main challenge, as ever, is economic. In a difficult international climate, the outlook for Italy appears moderately optimistic. Without being spectacular, economic growth has broadly tracked the Eurozone average since the pandemic. Tourism numbers set new records, inflation remains low, and government finances are healthier than they've been for over a decade: A substantial national debt has, at least for now, stopped growing. Italy has taken the first small steps on a bumpy road to recovery—and bouncing back is critical for an economy which needs and draws visitors from every corner of the globe.

THE MAKING OF ITALY

Prehistory to the Rise of Rome

Among early inhabitants of the Italian peninsula, the **Etruscans** left the most extensive legacy. Archaeologists debate exactly where they came from; inscriptions they left behind (often on graves in *necropoli*) are too bland to be of much help. Whatever their origins, within 2 centuries of appearing around 800 B.C.E., they had subjugated the lands now known as Tuscany (so named to reflect that heritage), northern Lazio, and Campania, and the so-called **Villanovan** tribes who already lived there.

The **Latins,** who were based at Rome, were eventually conquered by the Etruscans around 600 B.C.E. These new overlords introduced gold tableware and jewelry, bronze urns and terra-cotta statuary, and the art and culture of Greece and Asia Minor; they also made Rome the government seat of Latium. "Roma" is an Etruscan name, and Rome's early, perhaps mythical kings had Etruscan names: Numa, Ancus, even Romulus.

Etruscan rule began to wane after the **Roman Revolt** around 509 B.C.E., which expelled Rome's Etruscan kings. By 250 B.C.E. Romans and their allies had vanquished or assimilated the Etruscans, wiping out their language and religion. However, many of the former rulers' manners and beliefs remained and became integral to what we now understand as "Roman culture."

The Valley of the Temples in Agrigento, Sicily, is a Greek archaeological site.

Meanwhile, the **Greeks**—who predated both the Etruscans and the Romans—had built powerful colonial outposts in the South, notably in Naples, founded as Greek "Neapolis." Remains of a Greek *àgora,* or market square, survive below **San Lorenzo Maggiore** (p. 604) in the old center of the city. The Greeks also left stone monuments above ground, including at the **Valley of the Temples,** Agrigento, Sicily (p. 805).

To see remnants of Etruscan civilization, Rome's **Museo Nazionale Etrusco** (p. 111) and the Etruscan collection in Rome's **Vatican Museums** (p. 81) are a logical starting point. Florence's **Museo Archeologico** (p. 194) houses one of the greatest Etruscan bronzes yet unearthed, the "Arezzo Chimera." Further fine Etruscan collections are in **Volterra,** Tuscany (p. 285) and **Orvieto,** Umbria (p. 342). Tombs litter the countryside of southern Tuscany and northern Lazio—Alice Rohrwacher's charming 2023 movie *La Chimera* is set in the world of 1980s Etruscan tomb-robbers. Mary Beard's excellent book *SPQR* is packed with insight on the rise of ancient Rome.

The Roman Republic: ca. 509–27 B.C.E.

After the Roman Republic was established around 509 B.C.E.—precise dating is impossible—the Romans continued to increase their power by conquering neighboring communities in the highlands and forming alliances with other Latins in the lowlands. They gave to their allies, and then to conquered peoples, partial or complete Roman citizenship with a corresponding obligation of military service. This further increased Rome's power and reach. Citizen colonies were set up as settlements of Roman farmers or military veterans, including both **Florence** and **Siena.**

The culture of the Roman Republic was stern, characterized by belief in the gods, the necessity of learning from the past, strength of the family, education through reading and public service, and most importantly obedience. The all-powerful Senate presided as Rome defeated rival powers one after another and came to rule the Mediterranean. The Punic Wars with **Carthage** (in modern-day Tunisia) in the 3rd century B.C.E. were a temporary stumbling block, as Carthaginian general **Hannibal** (247–182 B.C.E.) conducted a devastating campaign across the Italian peninsula, crossing the Alps with elephants and winning bloody battles by the shore of Lago Trasimeno, in Umbria, and at Cannae, in Puglia. Ultimately, however, Rome prevailed.

No figure was more towering during the late Republic, or more instrumental in its collapse into Empire (see below), than **Julius Caesar,** the charismatic conqueror of Gaul—"the wife of every husband and the husband of every wife," according to scurrilous rumors reported by 1st-century historian Suetonius. After defeating the last resistance of the Pompeiians in 45 B.C.E., he came to Rome and was made dictator and consul for 10 years. Conspirators, led by Marcus Junius Brutus, stabbed him to death at the Theater of Pompey on March 15, 44 B.C.E., the "Ides of March." The site, now Largo di Torre Argentina, is an Instagram hotspot these days. (Not for the history; ruins there are home to a photogenic feral cat colony.)

Statue of Julius Caesar, charismatic leader of Rome.

The conspirators' motivation was to restore the power of the Republic and topple dictatorship. But they failed: **Mark Antony,** a Roman general, assumed control. He made peace with Caesar's willed successor, **Octavian,** and after the Treaty of Brundisium dissolved the Republic, found himself married to Octavian's sister, Octavia. This marriage, however, didn't prevent him from also marrying Cleopatra in 36 B.C.E. A furious Octavian gathered the legions and defeated Antony at the **Battle of Actium** on September 2, 31 B.C.E. Cleopatra fled to Egypt, followed by Antony, who committed suicide in disgrace a year later. Cleopatra, unable to seduce his successor and retain her rule of Egypt, reputedly followed suit with the help of an asp (Egyptian cobra). The permanent end of the Republic was nigh.

Many standing buildings around ancient Rome date to periods after the Republic fell, but parts of the **Forum** (p. 91) were built during the Republic, including the **Temple of Saturn.** The adjacent **Capitoline Hill** and **Palatine Hill** have been sacred religious and civic places since the earliest days of Rome. Rome's best artifacts from the Republican era are inside the **Musei Capitolini** (p. 94).

The Roman Empire in Its Pomp: 27 B.C.E.–C.E. 395

Born Gaius Octavius in 63 B.C.E., and later known as Octavian, **Augustus** became the first Roman emperor in 27 B.C.E. and reigned until C.E. 14. His autocratic rule ushered in the so-called *Pax Romana,* 2 centuries of peace.

In Rome you can still see the remains of the **Forum of Augustus** (p. 90) and admire his statue in the **Vatican Museums** (p. 81).

By now, Rome ruled the entire Mediterranean world, either directly or indirectly. All political, commercial, and cultural pathways led to Rome, a sprawling city set on seven hills: the Capitoline, Palatine, Aventine, Caelian, Esquiline, Quirinal, and Viminal. It was during this period **Virgil** wrote his epic poem *The Aeneid,* which supplied a grandiose founding myth for the great city and its empire; in this era **Ovid** composed erotic poetry and **Horace** wrote his *Odes.*

Under the emperors, Rome expanded its territory but also reached new heights of extravagance. Without the checks and balances once provided by the Senate and legislatures, success led to corruption. These centuries witnessed a steady decay in the ideals and traditions on which Rome was founded. The army became a fifth column of unruly mercenaries, and for every good emperor (Augustus, Claudius, Trajan, Vespasian, and Hadrian, to name a few), there were several cruel, debased, or incompetent tyrants (Caligula, Nero, Caracalla, and many others).

After Augustus died (by poison, perhaps), his widow, **Livia**—a shrewd operator who had divorced her first husband to marry Augustus—used intrigues and poisonings to set up her son, **Tiberius,** as ruler. A series of murders and purges ensued, and Tiberius, who ruled during Pontius Pilate's trial and crucifixion of Christ, was eventually murdered in his late seventies. Top-level murders were common; a short time later, **Domitian** (ruled C.E. 81–96) became so obsessed with the possibility of assassination, he had his palace walls covered in reflective mica to see behind himself at all times. He was murdered anyway.

EARLY ROMAN emperors

Caligula (r. C.E. 37–41): Young emperor whose reign of cruelty and terror ended when he was assassinated by his own Praetorian guard.

Nero (r. C.E. 54–68): The last emperor of the Julio-Claudian dynasty and another cruel megalomaniac. He killed his own mother and was blamed—probably unfairly—for starting the Great Fire of Rome (C.E. 64).

Vespasian (r. C.E. 69–79): First emperor of the Flavian dynasty, who built the Colosseum (p. 88) and lived as husband-and-wife with a freed slave, Caenis.

Domitian (r. C.E. 81–96): Increasingly paranoid authoritarian and populist who fixated on the idea he would be assassinated—and was proved right.

Trajan (r. C.E. 98–117): Virtuous soldier–ruler who presided over the moment when Rome was at its geographically grandest scale; he also rebuilt much of the city.

Hadrian (r. C.E. 117–138): Humanist, general, and builder who redesigned the Pantheon (p. 103) and added the Temple of Venus and Roma to the Forum.

Marcus Aurelius (r. C.E. 161–180): Philosopher-king, and last of the so-called Five Good Emperors, whose statue is in the Musei Capitolini (p. 94).

Rome, Cradle of the Christian Church

Probably about a decade after the death of Jesus, the Christian church was founded in Rome as a separate religion from Judaism, continuing to gain followers despite early (and enthusiastic) persecution by the Romans. The best way today to relive the early Christian era is to walk along the **Via Appia Antica** (p. 120), just outside Rome's ancient walls and declared a UNESCO World Heritage Site in 2024. A church on the Appian Way marks the spot where the disciple Peter, fleeing Roman persecution, is said to have received a pivotal vision of Christ; the nearby **Catacombs** (p. 121), the first cemeteries of the Christian community of Rome, house the remains of early popes and martyrs.

Excesses ruled the day—at least, if you believe the biased contemporary chroniclers: **Caligula** supposedly committed incest with his sister, Drusilla, appointed his horse to the Senate, lavished money on egotistical projects, and proclaimed himself a god. Caligula's successor, his uncle **Claudius,** was poisoned by his final wife—who was also his niece, Agrippina the Younger—to secure the succession of **Nero,** her son by a previous marriage. Nero's thanks were to later murder not only his mother but also his own wife (Claudius's daughter) and his rival, Claudius's 13-year-old son, Britannicus. An enthusiastic persecutor of Christians, Nero committed suicide with the cry, "What an artist I destroy!"

By the 3rd century, rivalry and corruption had become so prevalent that 23 emperors ruled in 73 years. Few, however, were as twisted as **Caracalla** (r. C.E. 198–217), who, to secure control, had his brother Geta slashed to pieces while Geta was in the arms of their mother, former empress Julia Domna.

Constantine the Great, who became emperor in C.E. 306, made Constantinople (or Byzantium) the new capital of the Empire in 330, moving administrative functions away from Rome altogether, partly because of the growing menace of barbarian attacks. Constantine was the first Christian emperor, allegedly converting after he saw the "True Cross" in a dream, accompanied by the words, "IN THIS SIGN YOU SHALL CONQUER." He defeated rival emperor Maxentius and his followers at the **Battle of the Milvian Bridge** (C.E. 312), a victory memorialized by Rome's triumphal **Arco di Costantino (Arch of Constantine;** p. 86) and reimagined in Piero della Francesca's iconic 15th-century frescoes in **Arezzo** (p. 266). Constantine formally ended the persecution of Christians with the **Edict of Milan** (C.E. 313).

During the Imperial period, Rome flourished in architecture—advancing in size and majesty far beyond earlier cities built by the Greeks. **Classical orders** were simplified into forms of column capital: **Doric** (a plain capital), **Ionic** (a capital with a scroll), and **Corinthian** (a capital with flowering acanthus). Much of this advance was thanks to a new form of concrete and fine-tuning of the arch, used with a logic, rhythm, and ease never before seen. Many of these monumental buildings still stand, notably **Trajan's Column** (p. 90), the **Colosseum** (p. 88), and Hadrian's **Pantheon** (p. 103). Elsewhere in Italy, Verona's massive **Arena** (p. 464) bears witness to crowds the brutal sport of gladiatorial combat would draw. Three **Roman cities** have been preserved, with street plans and, in some cases, even buildings intact: doomed **Pompeii** (p. 635) and its neighbor **Herculaneum** (p. 631), both buried by Vesuvius's cataclysmic C.E. 79 eruption, and Rome's ancient seaport, **Ostia Antica** (p. 158). At Herculaneum, one of Rome's greatest writers perished, **Pliny the Elder** (C.E. 23–79). It is thanks to him, his nephew **Pliny the Younger,** satirist **Juvenal,** and historians **Tacitus, Suetonius, Cassius Dio,** and **Livy** that knowledge of ancient Roman life and events was not lost.

Surviving Roman **art** had a major influence on the painters and sculptors of the Renaissance (p. 29). In Rome itself, look for the marble bas-reliefs (sculptures that project slightly from a flat surface) on the **Arco di Costantino** (p. 86), the sculpture and mosaic collections at the **Palazzo Massimo alle Terme** (p. 114), and the gilded equestrian statue of Marcus Aurelius at the **Musei Capitolini** (p. 94). In Florence, the **Uffizi** (p. 179) displays Medici rulers' vast collection of Roman statuary. Naples's **Museo Archeologico Nazionale** (p. 601) houses the world's most extraordinary collection of Roman art, preserved for centuries under the lava at Pompeii.

The Fall of the Empire Through the "Dark Ages"

The Eastern and Western sections of the Roman Empire split in C.E. 395, leaving the Italian peninsula without support it once received from east of the Adriatic. When the **Goths** moved toward Rome in the early 5th century, citizens in the provinces, who had grown to hate the bureaucracy set up by Emperor **Diocletian,** initially welcomed the invaders. And then mass pillage began.

Byzantine mosaics in Ravenna.

Rome was first sacked by **Alaric I,** king of the Visigoths, in C.E. 410. The populace made no attempt to defend their city, other than trying in vain to buy him off (a tactic that worked 3 years earlier); most people fled to the hills. The feeble Western emperor **Honorius** hid out the entire time in **Ravenna** (p. 381), which in C.E. 402 he'd declared the new capital of the Western Roman Empire.

More than 40 troubled years passed until **Attila the Hun** invaded Italy to besiege Rome. While Attila

cuisine AROUND THE COUNTRY

Italians know how to cook—just ask any Italian. But be sure to leave plenty of time: Once Italians start talking food, they do not pause for breath. Yet Italy doesn't have one national "Italian" cuisine; it's more a loose grouping of regional cuisines that share a few staples, notably pasta, bread, tomatoes, and pig meat cured in many ways. On visit to a to **Rome,** you'll encounter local specialties such as *saltimbocca alla romana* (literally "jump-in-the-mouth"—thin slices of veal with sage, cured ham, and cheese) and *carciofi alla romana* (artichokes cooked with herbs, such as mint and garlic), plus a dish that's become ubiquitous, *spaghetti alla carbonara*—pasta coated in a silky sauce made with egg, *Pecorino Romano* (ewe's milk cheese), and cured pork (*guanciale*, or cheek, if it's following tradition). For reasons of historical migration, a strong current of Jewish cuisine also runs through Roman cooking.

To the north, in **Florence** and **Tuscany,** seasonal ingredients are served simply. A major component of almost any savory dish is the local olive oil, prized for low acidity. The typical Tuscan pasta is wide, flat *pappardelle*, generally tossed with a game sauce such as *lepre* (hare) or *cinghiale* (boar). Tuscans are fond of their own strong ewe's milk *Pecorino* cheese, made most famously around the Val d'Orcia town of Pienza. Meat is usually the centerpiece of the *secondo:* A *bistecca alla fiorentina* is the classic main dish, a T-bone-like cut of meat big enough to share (and almost always flame-grilled rare). An authentic *fiorentina* should come only from the white Chianina breed of cattle. Sweet treats are also good here, particularly Siena's *panforte* (a dense sticky cake); *biscotti di Prato* (hard almond-flour biscuits for dipping in dessert wine, also known as *cantuccini*); and the *miele* (honey) of Montalcino.

Emilia-Romagna is the country's gastronomic center. Rich in produce, its school of cooking first created many pastas now common around Italy: *tagliatelle*, *tortellini*, and *cappelletti* (made in the shape of "little hats"). Pig also comes to the table in several ways, including in Bologna's *mortadella* (finely ground spiced pork, often studded with pistachios) and deliciously sweet *prosciutto di Parma* (cured ham), served in paper-thin slices. The distinctive cheese *Parmigiano Reggiano* is made by hundreds of small producers in the provinces of Parma and Reggio Emilia.

Probably the most famous dish of **Lombardy** is *cotoletta alla milanese* (veal cutlet dipped in egg and

was dissuaded from attacking, thanks largely to a peace mission headed by Pope Leo I in C.E. 452, relief was short-lived: In C.E. 455 **Gaiseric,** king of the Vandals, sailed from Carthage in North Africa to carry out a 2-week sack of unparalleled thoroughness. The empire of the West lasted only another 20 years; finally, in C.E. 476, sacks and chaos ended a once-mighty city, and Rome itself was left to the popes, though still ruled nominally from Ravenna by an Exarch from Byzantium (aka Constantinople).

Although little detailed history of Italy in the immediate post-Roman period is known—and few buildings survive—the growth of the Christian church undoubtedly created a new society. We have Christianity, along with the influence of Byzantium, to thank for Italy's next great artistic style: the **Byzantine.** Painting and mosaic work in this era were stylized breadcrumbs and fried in olive oil)—German speakers call it *Wienerschnitzel*. *Osso buco* is another Lombard classic: braised shin of veal cooked in a *ragù*. **Piedmont** and Turin's iconic dish is *bagna càuda*—literally "hot bath" in the Piedmontese language, a sauce made with olive oil, garlic, butter, and anchovies, into which you dip raw vegetables. Piedmont is also the spiritual home of *risotto*, specifically Vercelli, a town surrounded by rice paddies.

Contemporary **Venice** is rarely celebrated for its cuisine, but its fresh seafood is usually excellent and figures heavily in the Venetian diet. Grilled fish is often served with red radicchio, a bitter leaf that thrives around nearby Treviso. Two more classic Venetian dishes are *fegato alla veneziana* (liver and onions) and *risi e bisi* (rice and peas). **Liguria** also turns toward the sea for its inspiration, as reflected by its version of bouillabaisse, *burrida*. The region's most famous food is *pesto alla genovese*, made with fresh basil, hard cheese, olive oil, and crushed pine nuts, and used to dress pasta, fish, and many more local dishes.

So many Neapolitans moved to the New World that the cookery of **Campania**—including pizza and spaghetti with clam sauce—is familiar to North Americans. Mozzarella is the local cheese, the finest being *mozzarella di bufala,* made with milk from water buffalo (first introduced to Campania from Asia in the Middle Ages). Mixed fish fries (*fritto misto*) are a staple of many a lunch table, and genuine Neapolitan pizza is in a class of its own. The cuisine of **Basilicata** and **Puglia** is founded on peasant simplicity: pasta, often made without egg, tossed with oil and seasonal vegetables such as broccoli rabe (*cime di rapa*) or garbanzo beans (*ceci*). The region is known for sweet, piquant Senise peppers and spicy or fennel-spiked Lucanica sausage. A whole *burrata* (an unctuous sphere of young mozzarella cheese and cream) is one indulgent Puglian starter, picnic staple, or pasta accompaniment.

Sicily's distinctive cuisine features strong flavors and aromatic sauces deeply influenced by North Africa. One staple is *pasta con le sarde* (with pine nuts, wild fennel, spices, chopped sardines, and olive oil). Fish is good and fresh almost everywhere (local swordfish is a standout). Classic desserts include *cannoli,* sweet cylindrical pastry cases filled with ricotta and candied fruit or chocolate. Sicilian *gelato* and homemade pastries are among the best in Italy.

and static, but also ornate and ethereal. The most accomplished examples of Byzantine art are found in the churches of **Ravenna** (p. 382). Later buildings in the Byzantine style include Venice's **Basilica di San Marco** (p. 410).

The Middle Ages: 9th Century to 14th Century

A ravaged Rome entered the Middle Ages, its population scattered. A modest number of residents continued to live in the swamps of the **Campus Martius.** The Seven Hills—now without water because invaders cut the aqueducts—stood abandoned and crumbling.

The pope turned toward Europe, where he found a powerful ally in **Charlemagne,** king of the Franks. In C.E. 800, Pope Leo III crowned him

ALL ABOUT *vino*

Italy is the second-largest **wine**-producing country in the world, just behind France; as early as 800 B.C.E. the Etruscans were vintners, and in 2023, the country produced more wine than the U.S. and Chile combined. However, only in 1965 were laws enacted to guarantee consistency in Italian winemaking. Quality wines are labeled **"DOC"** (Denominazione di Origine Controllata). If you see **"DOCG"** on a label (the "G" means *garantita*), this denotes an even higher-quality wine region (at least in theory). **"IGT"** (Indicazione Geografica Tipica) indicates a more general wine zone—for example, "Umbria"—but still with mandatory quality control. Excellent low-intervention **natural wines** (red, white, and orange), including from previously unheralded regions like **Emilia-Romagna,** are finding their way onto many modern wine lists.

Tuscany: Tuscan red wines rank with some of the world's finest. **Sangiovese** is the prince of grapes here, and **Chianti** from the hills south of Florence is the most widely known Sangiovese wine. The premium zone is **Chianti Classico,** where a lively ruby-red wine develops a bouquet of violets. The Tuscan south houses two even finer DOCGs: mighty, robust **Brunello di Montalcino,** a garnet-colored red and ideal partner for roasts or game; and almost purple **Vino Nobile di Montepulciano,** which has a rich, velvet body. End a meal with the Tuscan dessert wine called **vin santo,** which is often accompanied by hard *biscotti* to dunk into your glass.

Veneto & Lombardy: Reds around Venice and the Lakes vary from light, lunchtime-friendly **Bardolino** to **Valpolicella,** which can be particularly intense if grapes are partly dried before fermentation to make an **Amarone.** White, Garganega-based **Soave** has a pale amber color and a velvety flavor; **Lugana** at its best has a sparkle of gold and a rich, dry structure. **Prosecco** is the classic Italian sparkling white, the base for both a Bellini and a spritz—you're doing it wrong if you use champagne!

Piedmont: The finest reds in Italy may hail from the misty, vine-clad slopes of Piedmont, particularly those from the late-ripening **Nebbiolo** grape in the Langhe hills south of Alba. The big names—with big flavors and big price tags—are **Barbaresco** (brilliant ruby red with a delicate flavor) and **Barolo** (also brilliant ruby red, gaining finesse when it mellows into a velvety old age).

The South & Sicily: From the volcanic soil around Vesuvius, the wines of **Campania** have been admired for centuries: Homer praised **Falerno,** straw yellow in color. The key DOCG wines from Campania these days are **Greco di Tufo** (a mouth-filling, full white) and **Fiano di Avellino** (subtler and more floral). The wines of **Sicily**—once called a "paradise of the grape"—were also extolled by the ancients, and table wines here are improving rapidly. Sicily is the home of **Marsala,** a fortified golden wine often served with dessert; it also makes a great sauce for veal, chicken, or pork. **Puglia**'s blockbuster is the inky-red, plummy **Primitivo.**

emperor. This didn't mark Rome's return to the big time, however: Charlemagne ruled his empire from Aachen, now northwest Germany. And although Charlemagne pledged allegiance to the Church and made the pope the final arbiter in most religious and cultural matters, he also set Western Europe on a course of bitter opposition to papal meddling in affairs of state.

In the Middle Ages, Venice was a powerful maritime republic.

The successor to Charlemagne's empire was a political entity known as the **Holy Roman Empire** (C.E. 962–1806). The new Empire defined the end of the Dark Ages but ushered in a long period of bloody warfare. Magyars from Hungary invaded northeastern Lombardy and, in turn, were defeated by increasingly powerful **Venice,** which, having defeated its naval rival **Genoa** in the 1380 Battle of Chioggia, reigned over most of the eastern Mediterranean. Venetian merchants ruled a republic that lasted a millennium and built a city of imposing architecture such as the **Doge's Palace** (p. 414). The Lion of St. Mark—symbol of Venice's dominion—appears as far away as **Bergamo** (p. 497), close to Milan.

Meanwhile, **Rome** during the Middle Ages was a quaint backwater. Narrow lanes with overhanging buildings filled areas that were once showcases for imperial power. The forums, mercantile exchanges, temples, and theaters of the Imperial era slowly disintegrated. It remained the seat of the Roman Catholic Church, and its state was almost completely controlled by priests, who aggressively expanded church influence and acquisitions. An endless series of power struggles ensued. Between 1378 and 1417, competing popes—one in Rome, another **"antipope"** in Avignon—made simultaneous claims to St. Peter's legacy. In 1409–15, there were three—a third "pope" ruled from **Pisa.**

Down in **Sicily,** the **Normans,** from northern France, gained military control from the Arabs in the 11th century, dividing the island from the rest of Italy and altering forever its ethnic makeup. The reign of **Roger II of Sicily** (ruled C.E. 1130–54) was notable for religious tolerance, the multiracial nature of his court, and distinctive architecture. The **Palazzo dei Normanni** (p. 761) in Palermo, and nearby **Monreale** (p. 772), are just two of many great projects from Sicily's Norman era.

In the mid-14th century, the **Black Death** ravaged Europe. Western history's deadliest pandemic killed perhaps a third of Italy's population. The unique preservation of Tuscan towns like **San Gimignano** (p. 277) and **Siena** (p. 229) owes much to the fact they never fully recovered after the devastation of the 1348–49 plague. Despite such setbacks, Italian **city-states** grew wealthy from Crusader booty, trade, and banking. The **Florin,** a gold coin minted in Florence, became the first truly international currency for centuries and dominated trade all over the European continent.

The medieval period marks the start of building in stone on a mass scale. Flourishing from C.E. 800 to 1300, **Romanesque** architecture took inspiration and rounded arches from ancient Rome. Architects built large churches with wide aisles to accommodate the masses. Pisa's **Campo dei Miracoli** (1153–1360s; p. 299) is typical of the Pisan-Romanesque style, with stacked arcades of mismatched columns on the cathedral's facade (and wrapped around the **Leaning Tower of Pisa**) and blind arcading set with diamond-shaped lozenges. The influence of Arab architecture is clear; Pisa was a city of seafaring merchants.

Monreale's cathedral, a dazzling example of Sicily's Norman architecture.

Romanesque **sculpture** was fluid but still far from naturalistic. Often wonderfully childlike in narrative simplicity, works frequently mix biblical scenes with the myths and motifs of local pagan traditions that were incorporated into medieval Christianity. Among Italy's greatest surviving examples of Romanesque sculpture are 48 relief panels on the bronze doors of the **Basilica di San Zeno Maggiore** in Verona (p. 464). The exterior of Parma's **Baptistery** (p. 390) has Romanesque friezes by Benedetto Antelami (1150–1230).

As the appeal of Romanesque and Byzantine faded, the **Gothic** style flourished from the 13th to the 15th centuries. In architecture, Gothic was characterized by flying buttresses, pointed arches, and delicate stained-glass windows. These engineering developments freed architecture from the heavy, thick walls of the Romanesque and allowed ceilings to soar, walls to thin, and windows to proliferate.

Although religion remained dominant in the Gothic age, many secular buildings also arose, including palaces designed to show off the prestige of various ruling regimes and families. Siena's civic **Palazzo Pubblico** (p. 237) and many great buildings in **Venice** (see chapter 9) date from this period. **San Gimignano** (p. 277), in Tuscany, has a preserved Gothic center. Milan's **Duomo** (p. 475) is one of Europe's supreme Gothic cathedrals.

Painters such as **Cimabue** (1251–1302) and **Giotto** (1266–1337) in Florence, **Pietro Cavallini** (1259–ca. 1330) in Rome, and **Duccio di Buoninsegna** (ca. 1255–1319) in Siena lifted art from its Byzantine rigidity and set it on the road to realism. Giotto's finest work is his fresco cycle at Padua's **Cappella degli Scrovegni** (p. 462); he was a harbinger of the approaching Renaissance, which would forever change art and architecture. Duccio's 1311 *Maestà,* now in Siena's **Museo dell'Opera Metropolitana** (p. 239),

A statue of Dante in Florence.

influenced Sienese painters for centuries. Ambrogio Lorenzetti painted the greatest civic frescoes of the Middle Ages—his *Allegories of Good and Bad Government* in Siena's **Palazzo Pubblico** (p. 237)—before he succumbed to the Black Death, along with almost every significant Sienese artist of his generation.

The medieval period saw the birth of literature in the Italian language, which was a written version of the **Tuscan dialect**—primarily because the great writers of the age were Tuscans. Florentine **Dante Alighieri** wrote his *Divine Comedy* in the 1310s and Boccaccio's *The Decameron*—a kind of *Canterbury Tales* narrated by nobles fleeing the Black Death in Florence—appeared in the 1350s. A fun black-comedy series of the same name, released in 2024 on Netflix, is loosely based on Boccaccio's original.

Renaissance & Baroque Italy

The story of Italy from the dawn of the Renaissance in the early 15th century to the "Age of Enlightenment" in the 17th and 18th centuries is as fascinating and complicated as the rise and fall of the Roman Empire.

During this period, **Rome** underwent major physical change. The old centers of culture reverted to pastures and fields—cows grazed on the crumbling Forum—and great churches and palaces were built with the stones of Ancient Rome. The city's construction boom did more damage to ancient temples than any barbarian sack: Rare marbles were stripped from Imperial baths and used as altarpieces or sent to lime kilns for "recycling." So enthusiastic was several popes' destruction of Imperial Rome, it's a genuine miracle anything is left.

Milan (p. 470) was a glorious Renaissance capital, particularly under the Sforza dynasty and Ludovico "Il Moro" (1452–1508), a patron of Leonardo da Vinci. Smaller but still significant centers of power included the Gonzaga family's **Mantua** (p. 501) and the Este clan's **Ferrara** (p. 373).

Around 1400, however, the most significant power in Italy was the city where the Renaissance began: **Florence** (see chapter 5). Slowly but surely, the **Medici** family rose to become the most powerful of the city's ruling oligarchy, usurping the powers of trade guilds and republicans. They reformed law and commerce, expanded the city's power by taking control of neighbors such as **Pisa,** and sparked a "renaissance," or rebirth, in painting, sculpture, and architecture. Christopher Hibbert's *The Rise* *and Fall of the House of Medici* is the most readable account of the era. Netflix's *Medici: Masters of Florence* and *The Magnificent* serve up a sensationalized, fictionalized, but not entirely inaccurate "history" of power plays in the Renaissance city.

Under the patronage of the Medici (as well as other powerful Florentine families), innovative young painters and sculptors pursued expressiveness and naturalism. **Donatello** (1386–1466) cast the first freestanding nude since antiquity (a bronze now in Florence's **Museo Nazionale del Bargello;** see p. 183). **Lorenzo Ghiberti** (1378–1455) labored for 50 years on two sets of doors for Florence's **Baptistery** (p. 172), the most famous of which were dubbed the "Gates of Paradise" (now magnificently displayed in Florence's **Museo dell'Opera,** p. 178). **Masaccio** (1401–28) produced the first painting to realistically portray linear perspective, on a nave wall of **Santa Maria Novella** (p. 191).

Next followed a brief period known as the **High Renaissance.** The epitome of Renaissance Man, Florentine **Leonardo da Vinci** (1452–1519) painted his *Last Supper,* now in Milan's **Santa Maria delle Grazie** (p. 483), and an *Annunciation* (1481), hanging in Florence's **Uffizi** (p. 179) alongside countless Renaissance masterpieces from such iconic painters as Paolo Uccello, Sandro Botticelli, and Piero della Francesca. **Raphael** (1483–1520) produced a sublime body of work in his short lifetime (37 years). Skilled in sculpture, painting, and architecture, **Michelangelo** (1475–1564) has come to represent the apogee of Renaissance: His giant *David* at the **Galleria dell'Accademia** (p. 193) in Florence is the world's most famous statue, and his **Sistine Chapel** frescoes lure millions to the **Vatican Museums** (p. 81) in Rome. The father of the Venetian High Renaissance was **Titian** (1485–1576), known for mastery of color and tone. Venice (see chapter 9) has a rich trove of Titian's work, along with works by earlier Venetian masters **Gentile Bellini** (1429–1507), **Giorgione** (1477–1510), and **Vittore Carpaccio** (1465–1525).

Titian's *The Descent of the Holy Ghost* in Santa Maria della Salute in Venice.

As in painting, Renaissance **architecture** stressed proportion, order, classical inspiration, and mathematical precision. **Filippo Brunelleschi** (1377–1446), in the early 1400s, grasped the concept of "perspective" and provided artists

A Growing Taste for Beer

Italy will always be known, and adored, for its wine. But one gastronomic trend to watch for as you travel is the popularity of **artisanal beer,** especially among young Italians. Although supermarket shelves are stacked with mainstream brands like Peroni and Moretti, smaller stores and bars increasingly offer craft brews (known as *birre artigianali*). Italy had fewer than 50 breweries in 2000; according to brewers' association **Unionbirrai** (unionbirrai.it), more than 1,300 were operating by 2023, with the greatest concentration in the North but rapid growth in the South. Look for Unionbirrai's official seal on the label of genuine craft products. You'll even find these beers on the hallowed shelves of some wine merchants. **Zero-** and **low-alcohol beers,** plus gluten-free brews, are increasingly available.

with ground rules for creating the illusion of 3-D on a flat surface. (Ross King's *Brunelleschi's Dome* tells the story of his greatest achievement, crowning Florence's cathedral with its massive dome.) Even **Michelangelo** took up architecture late in life, designing the Laurentian Library (1524) and New Sacristy (1524–34) at Florence's **Medici Chapels** (p. 189) before moving south to complete the soaring dome of Rome's **St. Peter's Basilica** (p. 78). The third great Renaissance architect—and most influential of them all—**Andrea Palladio** (1508–80) worked in a classical mode of columns, porticoes, pediments, and other ancient-temple-inspired features. His masterpieces include fine churches in Venice. The "Palladian" style of many U.S. capitol buildings is named for him.

In time, the High Renaissance evolved into the **baroque.** Stuccoes, sculptures, and paintings were designed to complement each other—and the space itself—to create a unified whole. The baroque movement's spiritual home was Rome, and its towering figure was **Gian Lorenzo Bernini** (1598–1680), the greatest baroque sculptor, an accomplished architect, and a more-than-decent painter, too. Among many fine, flowing sculptures, you'll find his best in Rome's **Galleria Borghese** (p. 112) and **Santa Maria della Vittoria** (p. 116). Baroque architecture is especially prominent in the South: in the churches and devotional architecture of **Naples** (p. 595) and in **Siracusa** (p. 789), Sicily. Under the Savoy dynasty, **Turin** (p. 523) was remodeled by the baroque architecture of **Guarino Guarini** (1624–83) and **Filippo Juvarra** (1678–1736). In music, the most famous of the baroque composers is Venetian **Antonio Vivaldi** (1678–1741), whose *Four Seasons* is among the most performed classical compositions of all time.

In painting, many baroque artists mixed a kind of super-realism, based on using everyday people as models and bold contrasts of light and dark—a technique called *chiaroscuro*—with compositional complexity and explosions of dynamic fury, movement, and color. The period produced many fine painters, notably **Caravaggio** (1571–1610). Among his masterpieces are a *St. Matthew* cycle (1599) in Rome's **San Luigi dei**

A flamboyant fresco by Giambattista Tiepolo, perhaps the finest of Italy's rococo painters, in Milan's Palazzo Clerici.

Francesi (p. 102) and *The Acts of Mercy* in **Pio Monte della Misericordia** (p. 602), Naples. The baroque era also had an outstanding female painter in **Artemisia Gentileschi** (1593–1652): Her brutal *Judith Slaying Holofernes* (1620) hangs in Florence's **Uffizi** (p. 182).

Frothy **rococo** art was the baroque taken to ornate extremes and had few serious proponents in Italy. **Giambattista Tiepolo** (1696–1770), arguably the best of the rococo painters, specialized in ceiling frescoes and canvases with cloud-filled heavens of light. He worked extensively in Venice and the northeast. For rococo building—more a decorative than an architectural movement—look no further than Rome's **Spanish Steps** (p. 109) or the **Trevi Fountain** (p. 109).

At Last, a United Italy: The 1800s

By the 1800s, the glories of the Renaissance were a fading memory. From Turin to Naples, chunks of Italy had changed hands many, many times—between the Austrians, the Spanish, and the French, among autocratic thugs and enlightened princes, between the noble and the merchant classes. The 19th century witnessed the final collapse of many Renaissance city-states. The last of the Medici, Gian Gastone, had died in 1737, leaving Tuscany in the hands of foreign Lorraine and Habsburg princes.

French emperor **Napoleon** brought an end to a millennium of republican government in **Venice** in 1797 and installed puppet or client rulers across the Italian peninsula. During the **Congress of Vienna** (1814–15), which followed Napoleon's defeat by an alliance of British, Prussians, and Dutch, Italy was once again divided.

Political unrest became a fact of life, some of it spurred by the industrialization of the North and some by the activity of insurrectionists like **Giuseppe Mazzini** (1805–72). Europe's year of revolutions, **1848,** rocked Italy, too, with violent uprisings in Lombardy and Sicily. After decades of political machination, growing nationalism, and intrigue, and thanks to the efforts of statesman **Camillo Cavour** (1810–61) and rebel general **Giuseppe Garibaldi** (1807–82), the Kingdom of Italy was proclaimed in 1861; **Vittorio Emanuele II** of Savoy became its first monarch. Initially the capital was Turin (1861–65), seat of the victorious Piedmontese. Indeed, many modern revisionist histories consider Italian unification as more of a Piedmontese annexation, a theme explored in one of the country's iconic novels, *The Leopard*, published a century later (see box, p. 34). Later followed a brief period when the capital was Florence (1865–71).

The establishment of the kingdom, however, didn't mean Italy was completely unified yet: Latium (including Rome) was still under papal control and Venetia was held by Austria. This was partially resolved in 1866, when Venetia joined the rest of Italy after the **Seven Weeks' War** between Austria and Prussia. Then, in 1871, Rome became the capital of this newly formed country, after the city was taken on September 20, 1870. Present-day **Via XX Settembre** is the very street up which patriots advanced after breaching the city gates. The **Risorgimento**—the "resurgence," Italian unification—was complete.

Political heights in Italy seemed to correspond to historic depths in art and architecture. Among few notable practitioners of this era, the most well-known is Venetian **Antonio Canova** (1757–1822), Italy's major neoclassical sculptor, who became notorious for portraying both Napoleon

Rebel general Guiseppe Garibaldi, a pivotal figure in Italy's unification.

and his sister Pauline as mythical nudes. His best work is in Rome's **Galleria Borghese** (p. 112). Tuscany also bred a late-19th-century precursor to French Impressionism, the **Macchiaioli** movement; see their works in the "modern art" galleries at Florence's **Palazzo Pitti** (p. 199).

As art hit a low note, **music** was experiencing its Italian golden age. It's **opera** for which the 19th century is largely remembered. *Bel canto* composer **Gioachino Rossini** (1792–1868) was born in Pesaro, in the Marches, and found fame in 1816 with *The Barber of Seville*. The reputation of **Gaetano Donizetti** (1797–1848), a prolific native of Bergamo, was assured when his *Anna Bolena* premiered in 1830. Both were later overshadowed by **Giuseppe Verdi** (1813–1901), whose arias from such operas as *Rigoletto* and *La Traviata* took on profound national symbolism, and have since become some of the most whistled tunes on the planet. At the turn of the century, the dominant Romantic movement gave way to the *verismo* ("realism") of composer **Giacomo Puccini** (1858–1924), whose operas *La Bohème* (1896), *Tosca* (1900), *Madama Butterfly* (1904), and the unfinished *Turandot* (1924) still pack houses worldwide. He's celebrated with a museum and opera festival in **Lucca** (p. 297).

The 20th Century: Two World Wars & One *Duce*

In 1915, Italy entered **World War I** on the side of the Allies. They joined the British Empire (including Canada, Australia, and New Zealand), Russia, France, Japan, and later the United States to help defeat Germany, the Ottoman Empire, and Italy's traditional enemy to the north—now known as the Austro-Hungarian Empire—and so to "reclaim" Trentino and Trieste. (Mark Thompson's *The White War* tells the story of Italy's catastrophic campaign.) In the aftermath of the wartime carnage, Italians suffered further with rising unemployment and horrendous inflation. As in Germany, deep political crisis led eventually to dictatorship.

THE A-LIST OF italian novels IN ENGLISH

- Alessandro Manzoni, *The Betrothed* (1827)
- Giovanni Verga, *Mastro Don Gesualdo* (1889)
- Alberto Moravia, *The Conformist* (1951)
- Giuseppe Tomasi di Lampedusa, *The Leopard* (1958)
- Elsa Morante, *History: A Novel* (1974)
- Italo Calvino, *If on a Winter's Night a Traveler* (1979)
- Umberto Eco, *Foucault's Pendulum* (1988)
- Amara Lakhous, *Clash of Civilizations Over an Elevator in Piazza Vittorio* (2006)
- Elena Ferrante, *Neapolitan Quartet* (2012–15)
- Donatella di Pietrantonio, *A Girl Returned* (2019)

On October 28, 1922, **Benito Mussolini,** who started his Fascist Party in 1919, saw that the country was ripe for change. He gathered 30,000 Black Shirts for his **March on Rome.** Inflation was soaring and workers had called a general strike. Rather than recognize a state under siege, **King Victor Emmanuel III** (r. 1900–46) proclaimed Mussolini as the new leader. Thousands of dissidents, including political philosopher **Antonio Gramsci** (1891–1937), were thrown in jail, or worse. In 1929, "Il Duce"—a moniker Mussolini attached to his personality cult from 1925—also defined the divisions between the Italian government and the pope by signing the Lateran Treaty, which granted political, territorial, and fiscal autonomy to the microstate of **Vatican City.** During the Spanish Civil War (1936–39), Mussolini's support for General Franco's Fascists, who had staged a coup against the elected government of Spain, helped seal an Axis alliance between Italy and Nazi Germany. Despite a mutual distrust (even dislike) between Hitler and Mussolini, Italy was inexorably and disastrously sucked into **World War II.**

Deeply unpleasant though their politics were, the Fascist regime did sponsor some remarkable **Rationalist architecture,** at its best in Rome's planned satellite community, **EUR** (p. 118). Important public buildings from the Fascist 1930s include the huge, ornate **Milano Centrale** train station (1931) and Florence's **Santa Maria Novella station** (1934), a striking modernist statement in local sandstone. Today memorials at both stations remember Jews who were sent from there to their deaths in Nazi Germany after Italy's 1943 surrender to the Allies left most of northern and central Italy under direct Nazi occupation.

After defeat in World War II, Italy's people voted to end the monarchy and establish the First Republic—overwhelmingly so in northern and central Italy, which outvoted a southern royalist majority. Italy quickly succeeded in rebuilding its economy, in part because of U.S. aid under the **Marshall Plan** (1948–52). By the 1960s, as a member of the European Economic Community (founded by the **Treaty of Rome** in 1957), Italy had become one of the world's leading industrialized nations, and prominent in the manufacture of automobiles and office equipment. Fiat (from Turin), Ferrari (from Emilia-Romagna), and Olivetti (from northern Piedmont) were known around the globe.

The postwar Italian **movie industry** was celebrated for innovative directors, beginning with Roberto Rossellini (1906–77). His *Rome, Open City* (1945) was filmed literally amid the city's wartime ruins. **Federico Fellini** (1920–93) burst onto the scene with a highly individual style, beginning with *La Strada* (1954) and later such classics as *The City of Women* (1980). His *La Dolce Vita* (1961) seems to define an era in Rome. The gritty "neorealism" of **Pier Paolo Pasolini** (1922–75) is conveyed most vividly in *Accattone* (1961), which he wrote and directed.

The country was plagued, however, by economic inequality, including between an industrially prosperous North and the depressed South. During the late 1970s and early 1980s, Italy was also rocked by domestic

Milano Centrale train station, an ornate example of 1930s public architecture.

terrorism: These were the so-called **Anni di Piombo** (Years of Lead), during which extremists of the left and right bombed and assassinated with impunity. Conspiracy theories became an Italian staple diet; everyone from a shadow state to Masonic lodges to the CIA was accused of involvement in what became, in effect, an undeclared civil war. The most notorious incidents were the kidnap and murder of Prime Minister **Aldo Moro** in 1978 and the **Bologna station bombing,** which killed 85 in 1980. You'll find a succinct account of these murky years in Tobias Jones's book *The Dark Heart of Italy.* Netflix's 2025 *Monster of Florence* dramatizes the hunt for a notorious serial murderer in the hills around the city—and captures some of the period's opaque, conspiratorial spirit.

Into the 21st Century

Resonant events in recent Italian history have touched on religion, too. As much of the world watched and prayed, Pope John Paul II died in April 2005, at the age of 84, ending a reign of 26 years. A doctrinal hardliner next took the papal throne as Pope Benedict XVI. He was succeeded by relatively liberal Pope Francis in 2013, after Benedict became the first pope since the 1400s to resign the office. The story of this extraordinary handover was fictionalized in the 2019 movie *The Two Popes*.

On the back of a severe economic crisis early in the 21st century—whose effects are still reflected in elevated levels of government debt—immigration has become a persistent national issue. Italy's population is aging, and the youth vacuum is filled by immigrants, especially those from Eastern Europe, notably Romania and Albania. The plight of migrant refugees from Syria and North Africa through the 2020s added yet another layer of complexity to Italy's relationship with *stranieri* (foreigners). Italy does not have a "melting pot" history: Tensions were inevitable, and discrimination is a daily fact of life for many minorities (although you are unlikely to experience it overtly as a visitor). Change is coming: More than a decade ago, Cécile Kyenge became Italy's first government minister of African descent. But it is coming too slowly for many, and anti-migrant sentiment is gleefully stoked by populist politicians.

While others arrive, a "brain drain" continues to push young Italians abroad to seek opportunity. The problem is especially ingrained in rural communities and on the islands, where the old maxim, "It's not what you know, it's who you know," applies more strongly than ever. It was in this unstable national context—and accompanying political turmoil—that the coronavirus pandemic hit in early 2020.

WHEN TO GO

The best months for traveling in much of Italy are from **April to June** and **mid-September to October:** Temperatures are usually comfortable, rural colors are rich, and crowds aren't too intense (except around Easter). May and June usually usher in peak hotel prices in Rome and Florence. From July through early September, the country's holiday spots teem with visitors. **August,** however, is the worst month in many places: Not only does it get uncomfortably hot and muggy, but seemingly the entire country goes on vacation for at least 2 weeks (many Italians take off the entire month). Family-run restaurants and shops are often shuttered, except at the spas, beaches, mountains, and islands, where most Italians take their holidays. Paradoxically, you will have some urban places almost to yourself if you visit in August—Turin and Milan in particular feel apocalyptically deserted, and even excellent hotels there are heavily discounted. (Florence and Rome are no longer quiet, as they once were, alas.) Be aware that many fashionable urban restaurants and nightspots close for the whole month.

From **late October to Easter,** many attractions operate on shorter winter hours and hotels occasionally close for renovation or redecoration, although this inconvenience is much less likely if you visit a city. Between November and February, beach resorts become padlocked ghost towns and family-run restaurants everywhere take a week or two off.

Weather

It's warm all over Italy in **summer;** it can be extremely hot in the South and almost everywhere without a sea breeze. Landlocked cities in Tuscany and Umbria, and on the plains of Veneto, Lombardy, and Emilia-Romagna, feel stifling during a July or August hot spell—and near-unbearable in what appear now to be regular annual heat waves. Higher temperatures (measured in Italy in degrees Celsius) usually begin everywhere in May, often lasting until early October. **Winters** in the north of Italy are cold, with rain, fog, and snow. A biting wind whistles over the mountains into Milan, Turin, Venice, and sometimes even Florence. In Rome and the

South, the weather is warm (or at least, warm-ish) almost all year, averaging 10°C (50°F) in winter. But even here chilly snaps are possible, including occasional freezing temperatures and snow. The rainiest months pretty much everywhere are October and November. But as recent spring floods in Emilia-Romagna reminded everyone, these are only general patterns—even more so, in a world where the climate seems already to be in flux.

Italy's Average Daily High Temperature & Monthly Rainfall

ROME

	JAN	FEB	MAR	APR	MAY	JUNE	JULY	AUG	SEPT	OCT	NOV	DEC
TEMP. (°C)	13	13	16	19	23	27	29	30	26	22	18	14
TEMP. (°F)	56	56	61	66	73	81	84	86	79	72	64	57
RAINFALL (IN.)	3.2	2.8	2.7	2.6	2	1.3	.6	1	2.7	4.5	4.4	3.8

FLORENCE

	JAN	FEB	MAR	APR	MAY	JUNE	JULY	AUG	SEPT	OCT	NOV	DEC
TEMP. (°C)	11	12	16	20	25	29	32	32	27	22	15	11
TEMP. (°F)	52	54	61	68	77	84	90	90	81	69	59	52
RAINFALL (IN.)	1.9	2.1	2.7	2.9	3	2.7	1.5	1.9	3.3	4	3.9	2.8

VENICE

	JAN	FEB	MAR	APR	MAY	JUNE	JULY	AUG	SEPT	OCT	NOV	DEC
TEMP. (°C)	8	9	13	17	23	26	29	29	24	19	13	8
TEMP. (°F)	46	48	56	63	73	79	84	84	75	66	56	46
RAINFALL (IN.)	2.3	.1	2.2	2.5	2.7	3	2.5	3.3	2.6	2.7	3.4	2.1

Public Holidays

Offices, government buildings (but usually not tourist offices), and stores in Italy are generally closed on: January 1 (*Capodanno,* or New Year); January 6 (*La Befana,* or Epiphany); Easter Sunday (*Pasqua*); Easter Monday (*Pasquetta*); April 25 (*Festa della Liberazione,* or Liberation Day); May 1 (*Festa del Lavoro,* or Labor Day); June 2 (*Festa della Repubblica,* or Republic Day); August 15 (*Ferragosto,* or the Assumption of the Virgin); November 1 (All Saints' Day); December 8 (*L'Immacolata,* or the Immaculate Conception); December 25 (*Natale,* Christmas Day); and December 26 (*Santo Stefano,* or St. Stephen's Day). Businesses may also close for the annual celebration day dedicated to their specific local saint (for example, on Jan 31 in San Gimignano, Tuscany).

SUGGESTED ITALY ITINERARIES

By Donald Strachan

3

Italy is so vast and full of treasures, it's easy to be tempted to pack too much into limited time. You can't even skim the surface of this country in 1 or 2 weeks—so relax, and don't try. If you're a first-time visitor with scarce touring time, we suggest zeroing in on the classic cities: Rome, Florence, and Venice could be packed into 1 very busy week, better yet in 2.

How can you accomplish that? Well, for starters, Italy has well-maintained highways (called *autostrade*). You'll pay a toll (p. 830), but it's much quicker to drive on them than to trust your limited time to minor roads, which can be *much* slower going.

You'll also find one of the most efficient high-speed rail networks in Europe. Rome, Bologna, Florence, Naples, and Milan are key hubs; for example, from Rome's Termini station, Florence can be reached in only 95 minutes. If you're city-hopping between Rome, Florence, and Venice, you need never rent a car, because the key routes are served by frequent quick trains that take you center-to-center and can be very affordable if you follow our ticket-buying advice (p. 832). Of course, you may feel more comfortable traveling in your own rented vehicle than a train carriage; see p. 829 for car rental tips. Be warned, however: Traffic around cities can be infuriating.

The following itineraries introduce many of our favorite places. During the pandemic, many museums restricted visitor numbers with compulsory advance booking. Some of these measures remain with a new purpose: to keep crowds manageable at popular sites. You should certainly reserve ahead for any place your heart is set on. Organize each day around your must-sees.

Occasionally the pace of our itineraries may be a bit breathless for some visitors, so consider skipping a stop to enjoy some downtime. You're on vacation, after all. You can also use any itinerary as a jumping-off point to develop your own custom-made adventure. *Buon viaggio!*

ITALY'S REGIONS IN BRIEF

Although bordered on the northwest by France, on the north by Switzerland and Austria, and on the northeast by Slovenia, Italy is mostly surrounded by sea. It isn't enormous; the peninsula's slender boot shape gives the impression of a much larger area. Here's a brief rundown of the cities and regions covered in this guide. See the inside front cover for a map of Italy by region.

ROME & LATIUM The region of **Latium ("Lazio"** in Italian) is dominated by **Rome,** capital of both an ancient empire and modern Italy. Much

PREVIOUS PAGE: **The Grand Canal in Venice.**

The rolling green hills of Tuscany.

of the Mediterranean (and beyond) was once ruled from here, starting when Romulus and Remus are said to have founded Rome in 753 B.C.E. No place has more artistic monuments, or a bigger buzz.

FLORENCE, TUSCANY & UMBRIA **Tuscany** is one of Italy's most culturally and politically influential regions. The development of Italy without Tuscany is unthinkable. In fact, today's Italian language is essentially an update of medieval Florentine dialect. Nowhere in the world is the impact of the Renaissance still felt more fully than in **Florence,** a repository of artworks by Masaccio, Leonardo da Vinci, Michelangelo, Raphael, and many others. The main Tuscan destinations beyond Florence are the compact provincial cities of **Lucca, Pisa,** and especially **Siena,** Florence's great historical rival, as well as the **Chianti** winelands. Neighboring **Umbria** is a land of rolling green hills and olive groves, where the pace of life is sedate. It too has outstanding art and architecture sites in **Perugia, Assisi,** and the ancient Etruscan capital of **Orvieto.**

BOLOGNA & EMILIA-ROMAGNA Italians don't agree on much, but one national consensus is that the food in **Emilia-Romagna** is Italy's best. The regional capital, **Bologna,** also has museums, churches, and a fine university founded in the Middle Ages. Among the region's other cities, none has a nobler heritage than **Ravenna,** with Byzantine mosaics dating to a time when it was capital of the declining Western Roman Empire.

VENICE & THE VENETO Northeastern Italy is one of Europe's great treasures, encompassing **Venice** (one of the world's most unusual cities) and the surrounding **Veneto** region. Aging, decaying, and slowly sinking into the lagoon, Venice is so alluring we're tempted to say: Visit even if you have to skip everywhere else. Also recommended are the art cities of the Venetian Arc: **Verona,** with Shakespearean romance and an intact Roman amphitheater hosting a famous summer opera festival; and **Padua,** with iconic Giotto paintings on the walls of its Scrovegni Chapel.

LOMBARDY, PIEDMONT & THE LAKES Flat, fertile, and prosperous, **Lombardy** is dominated by **Milan,** home to Leonardo's *Last Supper,* the La Scala opera house, shopping, and some major museums. You'll also find nearby **Bergamo**—a charming small city—and **Mantua,** as well as the photogenic lakes of **Como** and **Garda.** In Piedmont's largest city, **Turin**—home of the Fiat empire—the best-known sight is the Sacra

Sindone (Holy Shroud), which some Christians believe is the cloth in which Christ's crucified body was wrapped.

LIGURIA Encompassing most of the **Italian Riviera,** the region of **Liguria** offers the major historical seaport of **Genoa,** glittering ports such as **Portofino,** and Italy's best coastal hiking, between the villages of the **Cinque Terre.**

CAMPANIA, PUGLIA & BASILICATA **Campania** incorporates the alluring anarchy of **Naples,** renowned ruins at **Pompeii** and **Herculaneum,** and the elegant beauty of **Capri** and the **Amalfi Coast.** In **Basilicata,** the city of **Matera** is peppered with cave dwellings—the *Sassi*—inhabited almost continuously since the Paleolithic Era. **Puglia** (sometimes called "Apulia" in English) is home to the conical *trulli* houses of **Alberobello** and the Valle d'Itria, and the baroque architecture of **Lecce**—sometimes nicknamed (a little ambitiously) "the Florence of the South."

SICILY The largest island in the Mediterranean Sea, **Sicily** has a unique mix of bloodlines and architecture from medieval Normandy, Aragonese Spain, Moorish North Africa, Ancient Greece, Phoenicia, and Rome. Cars, street markets, and fashionable people clog the lanes of its capital, **Palermo.** Areas of ravishing beauty and eerie historical interest include the coastal towns of **Syracuse** (Siracusa in Italian) and **Taormina,** and the ruins at **Agrigento** and **Selinunte.**

THE BEST OF ITALY IN 8 DAYS: ROME, FLORENCE & VENICE

Let's be realistic: It's impossible to see this country properly in a week. However, a fast, efficient rail network along the Rome–Florence–Venice line makes it surprisingly easy to see some of the best that these three very different, but equally enticing cities have to offer. Our weeklong itinerary treads familiar highlights. But there's a reason these are the country's most visited sights: They provide memories that last a lifetime.

DAYS 1–3: Rome: Capital, Ancient & Modern ♥♥♥

You could spend forever in the Eternal City, but 3 days is enough for a taste. Two essential areas should be your focus on a short stay. The first is the legacy of Imperial Rome, with the **Forum, Campidoglio,** and **Colosseum** (p. 88). Bookend **DAY 1** with the Forum and Colosseum (one first, the other last) to avoid the busiest times; the same ticket is good for both. Sights there are almost exclusively outdoors. On **DAY 2,** tackle **St. Peter's Basilica** and the **Vatican Museums** (p. 76), with a collection unlike any other in the world (including, of course, Michelangelo's **Sistine Chapel**). On **DAY 3,** it's a toss-up: Choose between visiting the underground catacombs of the **Via Appia Antica** (p. 120) or wandering the ***centro storico*** (p. 100) and

the **Tridente** (p. 106) for Piazza Navona, the Pantheon, the Spanish Steps, the Trevi Fountain, and more. Spend your evenings in the bars of **Campo de' Fiori** or **Monti** (p. 157) and the restaurants of **Trastevere** (p. 149) or **Testaccio** (p. 151). Toward the end of your third day, catch a late train to Florence. ***Tip:*** You will save money if you book rail tickets in advance: Walk-up fares are much more expensive than advance tickets on the high-speed network. However, only fully flexible fares are fully refundable. We suggest booking (and paying upfront) only when your travel plans are set; see p. 832 for more rail travel advice.

Florence's landmark bridge, the Ponte Vecchio.

DAYS 4 & 5: Florence: Cradle of the Renaissance ♥♥♥

You have 2 whole days to explore the city of Giotto, Leonardo, Botticelli, and Michelangelo. Start **DAY 4** with their masterpieces at the **Uffizi** (p. 179; prebook tickets, weeks or even months ahead if possible), followed by the **Duomo** complex (p. 177): Scale Brunelleschi's dome (again, reservations are essential), and follow up with a visit to the **Battistero di San Giovanni,** the revamped **Museo dell'Opera del Duomo,** and **Campanile di Giotto.** Start **DAY 5** with *David* at the **Accademia** (p. 193; another essential advance reservation). For the rest of your time, get to know the intimate murals of **San Marco** (p. 194), paintings hanging at the **Palazzo Pitti** (p. 199), and Masaccio's revolutionary frescoes in **Santa Maria Novella** (p. 191) and/or the **Cappella Brancacci** (p. 201). For evening drinks and dining, you'll find lively bars and affordable, creative restaurants clustered in neighborhoods just beyond the historic center—around the San Lorenzo market, east of the center close to Santa Croce, and south of the Arno, in San Frediano make great options for wandering. Leave to explore Venice on the morning of **DAY 6.**

DAYS 6–8: Venice: City That Defies the Sea ♥♥♥

Ride into the heart of Venice on a *vaporetto* (water bus), taking the **Grand Canal,** the world's greatest thoroughfare. Begin the sightseeing at **Piazza San Marco** (p. 410). The **Basilica di San Marco** is right there, and after exploring it, visit the nearby **Palazzo Ducale** (Doge's Palace; p. 414) before walking over the **Bridge of Sighs.** Begin your evening with the classic Venetian *aperitivo,* an Aperol spritz, followed by *cicchetti* (Venetian tapas) before a late dinner. Make **DAY 7** all about the city's unique art: the **Gallerie dell'Accademia** (p. 421), the modern **Peggy Guggenheim Collection** (p. 422), and **San Rocco**

(p. 425). Catch the morning train on **DAY 8** back to Rome or onward to Milan's airports.

THE BEST OF ITALY IN 2 WEEKS

It's still difficult to see the top sights of Italy—and to see them properly—in just 2 weeks. But this itinerary gets you to many of the best. You go beyond the well-trodden (and spectacular) Rome–Florence–Venice trail to include the southern region of Campania, notably Pompeii, which has Europe's most precious Roman ruins. Additional stops in the center and north are Pisa (for the Leaning Tower and more) and Verona (city of lovers since Romeo met Juliet).

DAYS 1–3: Rome ♥♥♥

Follow the itinerary suggested in "The Best of Italy in 8 Days," above. On your third day take a late afternoon train to Naples, where you'll be based for the next 2 nights.

DAY 4: Naples ♥♥

Spend a full day taking in the major attractions of urban Naples, the historic "capital" of southern Italy. Pore over an unparalleled collection of ancient artifacts at the **Museo Archeologico Nazionale** (p. 601), then enjoy Titian, Caravaggio, and more at the **Museo e Real Bosco di Capodimonte** (p. 607). After dark, wander **Spaccanapoli**—the old center's main east–west thoroughfare—or the lively **Spanish Quarter,** off Via Toledo, then make a date with a **pizzeria:** Neapolitans claim pizza was invented here. It's certainly a Neapolitan artform. After dinner, stroll the **Mergellina** boardwalk for sea breezes and views across the Bay of Naples.

DAY 5: Pompeii ♥♥ & Sorrento ♥

Ride the Circumvesuviana train from Porta Nolana Station to spend a day wandering Europe's best-preserved Roman ruins at **Pompeii** (p. 629), 24km (15 miles) southeast of Naples. Pack water and lunch, because onsite services aren't great. Buried for almost 2,000 years after Vesuvius erupted in C.E. 79, Pompeii is one of the great archaeological treasures of Europe, including the patrician Casa dei Vettii and the frescoed Villa dei Misteri. Continue by local train to the pretty seaside town of **Sorrento** (p. 644), where you will lodge for 2 nights (you may leave luggage at Pompeii Scavi Station while you tour the ruins). This side trip (including **DAY 6,** below) is also straightforward by rental car: We recommend arranging pickup outside Naples' city center, where driving will be a hair-raising experience.

DAY 6: The Amalfi Coast ♥♥

On the morning of **DAY 6,** take a bus along the **Amalfi Drive,** of which Nobel laureate André Gide said: "[There is] nothing more beautiful on this earth." The drive twists around a precipitous coastline to the southern resorts of **Positano** (p. 660) and **Amalfi** (p. 670), either of which makes an idyllic stopover to extend your stay. Allow at least 4 hours for a round-trip back to Sorrento, because it can be slow-moving and you will want to linger.

DAYS 7 & 8: Florence ♥♥♥

Connect from Sorrento by rail to Naples' Stazione Centrale (1 hr.), then onward via an early high-speed train to Florence (journey time: 3 hr.). For the first 2 days, follow the itinerary suggested in "The Best of Italy in 8 Days," above. You'll be staying in Florence for 4 nights in total.

DAY 9: Siena ♥♥♥

It's just over an hour to Siena on the *rapida* bus from Florence (p. 229). Leave early and set out immediately on arrival for **Piazza del Campo,** the shell-shaped main square, including its art-filled **Museo Civico** (inside the **Palazzo Pubblico;** p. 237). Squeeze in a look at the **Duomo** (p. 236) and **Museo dell'Opera Metropolitana,** where you'll find Sienese master Duccio's giant *Maestà* painting. Pick an outdoor table on the Campo for an early evening drink and then head to a restaurant in Siena's atmospheric backstreets. Eat an early dinner: The last bus back to Florence usually departs around 8:45pm (7:10pm on Sun).

DAY 10: Pisa ♥♥

Most trains between Florence and Pisa take around an hour. On arrival, hop aboard bus no. 1+ outside Pisa Centrale Station, alighting at the "Torre di Pisa" stop for the **Campo dei Miracoli** ("Field of Miracles"). This architectural set-piece is one of the most photographed slices of real estate on the planet—and home to the **Leaning Tower** (p. 302). Visit the **Duomo,** with its Arab-influenced Pisan-Romanesque facade; the **Battistero** with a carved pulpit and crazy acoustics; and the rest of the piazza's monuments and museums on the same combination ticket. Book a slot ahead of time if you want to climb the Leaning Tower. For dining *alla pisana,* head away from the touristy piazza

Pisa's iconic Leaning Tower.

to a warren of streets around the market square, **Piazza delle Vettovaglie** (p. 300). Finish your visit with a stroll along a handsome promenade beside the **River Arno.** The last train back to Florence usually leaves at 10:30pm (although 9:30pm is often the final fast service).

DAYS 11 & 12: Venice ♥♥♥

Set your alarm clock for an early start: It takes around 2 hours to reach Venice from Florence aboard the high-speed train. Follow the itinerary suggested in "The Best of Italy in 8 Days," p. 42. You'll be staying in Venice for 3 nights.

DAY 13: Verona ♥♥♥

Book round-trip tickets ahead of time for a high-speed Frecciarossa train between Venice and Verona—the journey is just 1 hour, 10 minutes, compared with more than 2 hours for local train service. Although he likely never set foot in the place, Shakespeare placed the world's most famous love story, *Romeo and Juliet,* here. Wander **Piazza dei Signori** and take in another square, **Piazza delle Erbe,** before visiting the **Arena di Verona** (p. 464), the world's best-preserved gladiatorial arena, which hosts monumental open-air operas all summer. Head back to Venice for the night. Fast trains usually run until 10pm.

DAY 14: Milan ♥♥

Prebook a fast train connection between Venice and Milan, a journey of between 2¼ and 2½ hours. The most bustling city in Italy isn't only about industry and commerce. Milan has one of Europe's finest Gothic cathedrals, the **Duomo** (p. 475), two great art collections at the **Pinacoteca Ambrosiana** (p. 482) and the **Pinacoteca di Brera** (p. 482), and Leonardo's fading but magnificent ***Last Supper*** (p. 483; prebook as far ahead as possible). Stay overnight here if you are flying home or onward: Milan is one of Europe's major airline hubs.

ITALY FOR FAMILIES

Italy is probably the friendliest family vacation destination in Europe. Practically, it presents few challenges. If you're traveling by rental car with young children, be sure to request safety car seats ahead of time. Let the rental company know the age of your child and they will arrange for a seat to comply with local regulations. Rail travelers should remember that reduced-price family fares are available on much of the high-speed network; ask when you buy your tickets or use a booking agent.

As you tour, don't hunt for "child-friendly" restaurants or special kids' menus. There is always plenty available for little ones anywhere you dine, sometimes even dishes that aren't offered to grown-ups. Never be afraid to ask if you have a fussy eater in the family. Pretty much any request is met with a smile. Many of our favorite places to eat have outdoor tables—if that's your preference, don't hesitate to ask.

Perhaps the main issue for travelers with children is spacing your museum visits so you get to see the masterpieces without having young kids suffer a meltdown after one saint painting too many. You **often must book** major museum targets ahead of arrival; leave plenty of time between them if you are traveling with young children. And remember to punctuate every day with a **gelato** stop. Italy has the world's best ice cream, and soya milk flavors are available for anyone with an intolerance. End your trip in Venice, which for many kids is every bit as magical as a Disney park: It's a city. That floats. (Kinda.)

DAY 1: Rome's Ancient Outdoors ♥♥♥

History is on your side here: The wonders of **ancient Rome** (p. 86) should appeal as much to kids (of almost any age) as to adults. There are gory tales to tell at the **Colosseum** (p. 88), where the bookshop has guides aimed at kids. After that, they can let off steam wandering the **Roman Forum** and the usually much quieter **Palatine Hill** (p. 91). (The roadside ruins of the **Imperial Forums** can be viewed at any time.) Cap the afternoon by exploring the **Villa Borghese** (p. 111), a large park in the heart of Rome where you can rent bikes. At dinner, find crispy crusts at an authentic Roman **pizzeria.**

DAY 2: Rome: Living History ♥♥♥

Head early to **St. Peter's Basilica** (p. 78). The kids will find it spooky wandering the Vatican grottoes, and few can resist climbing up to Michelangelo's dome at 114m (375 ft.). After a timeout for lunch, begin your assault on the **Vatican Museums** and **Sistine Chapel** (p. 76). Even if your kids don't like museums, they may gawp at the grandeur. Later in the day, head for the **Spanish Steps** (a spot for upscale souvenir shopping; see p. 154) before wandering to the **Trevi Fountain** (p. 109). Let the kids toss coins into the fountain, which is said to ensure a return to Rome—perhaps when they are older and can fully appreciate the city's artistic attractions.

DAY 3: Rome: Underground ♥♥♥

Literal, physical layers of history survive below the city streets. Kids will love exploring the catacombs of the **Via Appia Antica** (p. 120), the first cemetery of Rome's Christian community, where the devout practiced their faith in secret during periods of persecution. After descending through the layers—and centuries—under **San Clemente** (p. 96), eat more **pizza** before you leave the city. Rome's pizzerias are matched only by those in Naples, to the south, and our next recommended stops all lie to the north. Leave on a late afternoon train to Florence: Tickets on high-speed trains include an allocated seat, so you all sit together.

DAYS 4 & 5: Florence ♥♥♥

Florence is usually thought of as a grown-up city, but there's enough to fill 2 family days. A bonus: Much of the center is traffic-free. With multiple nights here, renting an apartment gives you space to spread out—see p. 208 for apartment-rental suggestions. Close to the Duomo,

The Colosseum brings ancient Rome to life for kids.

Residence Hilda (p. 212) is a small, family-friendly hotel with large, apartment-style rooms and kitchenettes.

Begin with the city's monumental main square, **Piazza della Signoria,** an open-air museum of statues. The **Palazzo Vecchio** (p. 186) dominates one side; you can tour it with special family-friendly guides, including docents dressed as Cosimo I de' Medici and Eleonora di Toledo. Turn a visit to the famed **Uffizi Gallery** (p. 179) into a treasure trail by arriving with pictures or names of key artworks to hunt down (see their website). On the second morning, kids will delight in climbing to the top of Brunelleschi's dome on the **Duomo** (p. 177) for a classic panorama. Book an early slot, when the weather is cooler, because parts of the ancient staircase to the top are not well ventilated. If kids and adults have still more energy to burn, climb the 414 steps up to the **Campanile di Giotto** (p. 176), run around in the **Giardino di Boboli** (p. 198), and cross the **Ponte Vecchio** (p. 187) at dusk. With older, sporty children, you could add another day here, to allow time to see the Chianti hills on two wheels (see p. 170 for bike-rental info).

DAY 6: Pisa ♥♥

If your kids are 7 or under, consider skipping **Pisa** (p. 297): Eight is the minimum age to climb up the bell tower of Pisa's cathedral, aka the **Leaning Tower.** Older kids enjoy the hyperreal monuments of the **Campo dei Miracoli** and learning about the city's Galileo links: The scientist was born here and supposedly discovered his law of pendulum motion while watching a swinging lamp inside the **Duomo.** Take the kids to taste a local specialty, *cecina,* a pizza-like garbanzo-bean flatbread served warm. Your daylong visit complete, whiz up the coast on the fast train to Genoa. There are luggage storage facilities (*deposito bagagli*) around Pisa Centrale Station.

DAYS 7 & 8: Genoa & the Riviera di Levante ♥♥

The industrial city-seaport of Genoa is home to one of Italy's most popular family attractions: The **Acquario di Genova** (p. 558) is Europe's largest aquarium, where you can take a trip around the world's oceans. It requires a half-day to see properly, so reserve an early entry slot, and then head out to the **Riviera di Levante** (p. 569), a coastline of pretty ports and rocky coves east of the city. Our favorite base around here is romantic **Portofino** (p. 575), where you can easily enjoy a second day in Liguria beside an azure sea, dining on fish or filling up with *pesto al basilico,* a classic Ligurian pasta dish loaded with basil. Nearby **Santa Margherita Ligure** (p. 573) is a budget-friendlier alternative to Portofino, just a ferry-hop away, with an easy rail link, a fine promenade, and a laid-back vibe.

DAYS 9 & 10: Lake Garda ♥♥

Slow down for a couple of days by Italy's biggest inland lake, perhaps basing yourself at photogenic **Sirmione** (p. 513). Take a ferry trip, hire a pedal boat or kayak, eat simple grilled fish, and ease into lakeside life. In Sirmione you can scramble on the ramparts of the **Castello Scaligero,** then ride the little train out to Roman ruins at the **Grotte di Catullo,** a villa supposedly inhabited by the Roman poet Catullus (ca. 84 B.C.E.–ca. 54 B.C.E.). For active families with more time to spend, **Riva del Garda** (p. 515), close to the lake's northernmost point, is one of Europe's major windsurfing and sailboarding centers; many European Olympians have trained here.

DAYS 11–13: Venice ♥♥♥

In Venice, the fun begins the moment you arrive and take a *vaporetto* along the **Grand Canal.** Head straight for **Piazza San Marco** (p. 410), where children delight in riding the elevator up the great **Campanile.** Catch the mosaics inside the **Basilica di San Marco,** which dominates the square. At the **Palazzo Ducale,** cross the infamous **Bridge of Sighs.** As in Florence, make time for some art: Prioritize the **Gallerie dell'Accademia** (p. 421) and **San Rocco,** where kids can imagine the episodic Tintoretto paintings as a picture book or comic. In summer, save time for the beach at **Lido** (p. 432) and perhaps for getting a different angle on Venice's canals, from the seat of a **gondola** (p. 408).

ITALY FOR FOOD & WINE LOVERS

Italy has one of Europe's great cuisines—or rather, make that *several* of Europe's great cuisines (some claim that Italy has 50 distinct culinary traditions). This nation's history as a collection of independent city-states and fiefdoms left a diverse legacy in food. Each regional cuisine is committed to its own local produce and artisanal specialties, with treasured recipes handed down through generations. Fans of Stanley Tucci's CNN show *Searching for Italy* will be familiar with this backstory. (And if you haven't seen it, you certainly should.)

Italy is also the world's biggest wine producer. Although much is undistinguished (if perfectly drinkable) table wine, many icons of world wine hail from here. Our itinerary takes in three of the great Italian red wine areas: **Montepulciano,** whose noble wine was known to the Ancient Etruscans; **Chianti,** the first legally defined wine zone anywhere in the world; and **Piedmont,** whose robust reds Barolo and Barbaresco command top prices at restaurants everywhere.

DAYS 1 & 2: Rome ♥♥♥

The restaurants of Italy's capital offer cuisines from every corner of the peninsula (and far beyond). The **Trastevere, Monti,** and **Testaccio** neighborhoods are great for dining and drinks after dark (see pp. 157–158 for suggestions). While here, sample traditional Roman dishes like pasta with *cacio e pepe* (sheep's milk cheese and black pepper);

spaghetti alla carbonara (similar but enriched with egg yolk plus added *guanciale,* cured pork cheek) or *alla gricia* (also with *guanciale* and *Pecorino* cheese, but no egg); *saltimbocca alla romana*—literally, "jump in the mouth," a veal cutlet with prosciutto and sage; and *coda alla vaccinara* (stewed oxtail with tomatoes and celery). **Gelato** is either Florentine or Sicilian in origin, depending on who you ask, but in Rome you'll find lots of the country's tastiest (p. 143). The city also has some of Italy's best craft beer bars (p. 157). You'll need a rental car for your next leg. Collect it on your second afternoon and head north to Tuscany, to leave almost a full day at your next stop.

DAY 3: Montepulciano ♥♥♥

Begin with a walk up the handsome, steep Corso from the town gate to **Piazza Grande,** monumental heart of the *comune,* where you'll find the Palazzo Comunale (climb to the terrace for a panorama of the surrounding winelands) and Cattedrale. Oenophiles should head to the **Enoliteca Consorzio del Vino Nobile di Montepulciano,** where you can taste vintages from small producers and seek advice for nearby wineries to visit. End the evening at **Acquacheta** (p. 255), with a menu that's all about beef—*"bistecca numero uno"* is how

Contucci winemaker Adamo once described it to us. Other local delicacies include sheep's milk cheese, *Pecorino di Pienza*. You can even take along your own favorite bottle to wash it all down.

DAYS 4 & 5: The Chianti ♥♥♥

Pick a base close to **Greve in Chianti** (p. 248) to lodge at the heart of Tuscany's largest quality wine region. Sangiovese grape–based Chianti is a diverse wine: Chianti Classico denotes grapes from the original (and most consistent) growing zone, and tasting opportunities abound at wineries such as **Castello di Volpaia** (p. 247). Book ahead if you require a tour anywhere. The Chianti is also famed for its butchers, where you can buy everything from cuts of fresh beef (ideal if you're lodging in a villa) to *salumi* made from a local breed of pig, the *Cinta Senese*. **Falorni** (p. 248), in Greve, is outshone perhaps only by **Dario Cecchini** (p. 247), in nearby Panzano. Also look for Tuscan extra virgin olive oil. Squeezed from the first pressing of olives harvested in November, this "green gold" is famed for its low acidity. It is among Italy's best.

DAYS 6 & 7: Bologna ♥♥

You have arrived in Italy's gastronomic capital. You can leave the rental car here; it's easy to continue onward by train, if you wish. The agricultural plains of Emilia-Romagna are Italy's breadbasket. So much of the produce we think of as typical "Italian food" hails from here: cured prosciutto and *Parmigiano-Reggiano* cheese from Parma and Reggio nell'Emilia; aged balsamic vinegar from Modena; mortadella sausage and *tortellini* (filled pasta) from Bologna itself. Many producers scattered around the hills of Emilia-Romagna lead the way in Italy's **natural wine** movement. Foodies should also browse Bologna's markets, the **Mercato delle Erbe** and the **Quadrilatero,** a warren of lanes with enticing food shops. Make a dinner reservation at a restaurant specializing in classic Bolognese cooking; see p. 366 for our picks.

DAYS 8 & 9: Turin ♥♥

Snowcapped alpine peaks line the horizon north and west of the Piedmontese capital (p. 523). The cooking in Italy's northwest reflects the heartier and hardier mountain folk who live on the city's doorstep. Nearby **Vercelli** is Italy's rice capital—this town is ringed by paddy fields—and *risotto* tastes its creamy best here. There's also a noticeable Ligurian current in Torinese food: Basil-based pesto is superb, and the local slice-on-the-go isn't pizza but *farinata,* garbanzo bean–flour flatbread dusted with rosemary and/or pepper. The **Langhe Hills** (p. 544), south of the city, are famed for blockbuster red wines and white truffles. Sweet vermouth was also invented in Turin; the classic local labels are slightly bitter **Punt e Mes** ("point and a half"

Bologna's Quadrilatero is full of enticing food shops.

in Piedmontese), **Cocchi di Torino,** and vanilla-rich **Carpano Antica Formula.**

HISTORIC CITIES OF THE NORTH

Often overshadowed by Rome and Florence, the cities of northern Italy make an excellent itinerary for returning visitors. Each city on our tour has a center with refined architecture and a history of independence—as well as struggle with, and eventual subjection to, the great regional powers, often Venice. The itinerary's logical starting point is Milan, air gateway to Italy. Spend a day there, collect your rental car or rail tickets—all train connections on this tour are easy—and set off early. The endpoint is Venice, where we recommend you extend your stay by as many days as you can; see chapter 9 for full coverage of the city.

DAYS 1 & 2: Milan ♥♥ & Turin ♥♥

See Milan under "The Best of Italy in 2 Weeks," p. 48. Spend **DAY 2** on a day trip by train to **Turin** (p. 523). The city of Fiat and football (meaning "soccer") has a handsome baroque center, the finest Egyptian artifacts collection outside of Cairo at the **Museo Egizio** (p. 529), and views of the Alps from the top of the **Mole Antonelliana** tower (p. 528). It also has a food culture every bit as refined as Bologna's; Turin is the city of vermouth and on the doorstep of the Piedmont wine-growing region, so you will not go thirsty. You can complete a rail journey between the cities in as little as 45 minutes: There's no need to relocate your base from Milan if you prefer not to change lodgings.

DAY 3: Bergamo ♥♥

Whether you arrive by train or car, alight in the **Lower Town** (Città Bassa) and ascend to the **Upper Town** (Città Alta) in style, on the century-old funicular railway. **Piazza Vecchia** (p. 498) is the architectural heart of the Upper Town. Among its arcades you'll find the Romanesque **Basilica di Santa Maria Maggiore** and the Renaissance **Cappella Colleoni,** with a frescoed ceiling by Venetian rococo painter Tiepolo. You should also make time for the **Accademia Carrara** (p. 498), which has an exceptional collection of northern Italian paintings. Bergamo was the birthplace of *bel canto* composer Donizetti and has a lively arts program (largely opera). You needn't relocate from your Milan base: Bergamo is another easy day trip from Milan (50 min. by train), although it makes a serene overnight stop, too.

DAY 4: Verona ♥♥

A visit to northern Italy's most renowned small city (p. 463) is less about ticking off sights than soaking up the elegance of a place eternally associated with Shakespeare's doomed lovers, Romeo and Juliet. If you're here in summer, make straight for the box office at the **Arena di Verona;** Italy's most intact Roman amphitheater hosts monumental outdoor opera productions, which you will not want to miss. Last-minute tickets are often available; see *Aïda* if you can, the opera which inaugurated the festival in 1913 and is still most associated with the Arena. You should also see the **Basilica di San Zeno Maggiore,** one of Italy's most important Romanesque churches. Use Verona as a base for 2 nights and visit Mantua (below) as a day trip.

DAY 5: Mantua ♥♥♥

Landlocked it may be, but the Renaissance city of Mantua (Mantova in Italian; p. 501) is almost completely, romantically surrounded by lakes fed by the River Mincio. Just 45 minutes from Verona by train, Mantua owes its grandeur to the Gonzaga family, who filled piazzas and palaces with art by the greatest masters of the period, notably

Juliet's Balcony in Verona is an irresistible photo op.

Mantegna. One day is just enough to visit architect L. B. Alberti's **Basilica di Sant'Andrea,** the frescoed **Palazzo Ducale,** and the Room of Giants inside **Palazzo Te.**

DAYS 6 & 7: Venice ♥♥♥

Follow the itinerary suggested in "The Best of Italy in 8 Days," p. 42. Use Venice as a base for your last 5 nights, seeing Padua, Ferrara, and Treviso on day excursions.

DAY 8: Padua ♥♥

Design your day around a prebooked time slot to see the most historically significant paintings in northern Italy, Giotto's frescoes in the **Cappella degli Scrovegni** (p. 462). The **Basilica di Sant'Antonio** is the final resting place of St. Anthony of Padua, the second-most eminent Franciscan after St. Francis himself.

DAY 9: Ferrara ♥♥

Like Mantua, this small, stately city owes its grandeur to one despotic family—in this case, the Este dukes, who held sway from the 1200s to the 1500s, ruling the city from their moated **Castello Estense** (p. 374). Elsewhere in the center, check out the elaborate exterior of a Gothic-Romanesque **Duomo;** the **Palazzo dei Diamanti,** another

Este creation, named for 9,000 diamond-shaped stones adorning its facade; and **MEIS,** a national museum dedicated to the long cultural history of Jews and Judaism in Italy. Ferrara is under an hour by high-speed train from Venice.

DAY 10: Treviso ♥♥

It's not far (half-hour by train) from Venice to its small northern neighbor, which the powerful Venetians dominated for over 450 years from the 14th century onward. They left a rich architectural legacy—plus canals, of course. The pace here is sedate. You'll have ample time to survey the greatest hits of painter **Tomaso da Modena,** at the churches of **Santa Lucia** and **San Nicoló,** and the **Museo di Santa Caterina** (p. 467), before sauntering over to **Piazza dei Signori,** the medieval city's pretty heart, to enjoy a glass of local prosecco sparkling wine.

ITALY'S ANCIENT RUINS

Italy itself isn't old: As a unified country, it only just passed the 160-year mark. But the peninsula is rightly considered a cradle of European civilization. Michelangelo and the Renaissance, Gothic architecture, even the Byzantine mosaics of Ravenna: These are relatively recent moments in Italian time. Even the Romans were not the first civilization to leave a mark here. Several ancient buildings still standing owe their construction to expats from Classical Greece. ***Note:*** Ancient sites may have cramped or poorly ventilated underground areas and uneven pathways.

DAYS 1–4: Sicily ♥♥♥

As Greek Syracuse, modern-day **Siracusa** (p. 788) was one of the cultural hotspots of the ancient Mediterranean: Dramatist Aeschylus was a visitor and lyric poet Sappho was exiled here toward the end of the 7th century B.C.E. A ruined Doric **Temple of Apollo** stands in town, and the **Area Monumentale della Neapolis** (p. 792) has a Greek theater still used to stage dramas each summer. Our suggestion: Fly into Catania, 67km (41 miles) north of Siracusa, which is well connected by air with Rome (1 hr., 15 min. flight), then rent a car to cross the island and make your base in Sicily's southwest for at least half your time here, to tour coastal **Selinunte** (p. 819), **Segesta** (p. 776), the Valley of the Temples at **Agrigento** (p. 805), and the mosaics of the **Villa Romana del Casale** in Piazza Armerina (p. 804). Return to Siracusa and fly back from Catania to Rome.

DAYS 5–7: Rome ♥♥♥

Rome is the biggest brand name when it comes to ancient, archaeological ruins. Rome was the epicenter of a republic and empire that for centuries ruled most of Europe and the Levant, plus much of North Africa and the Middle East, too. Spend **DAY 5** walking

outdoors amid ancient Rome's civic and spiritual heart, the **Forum** (p. 91); the same ticket gets you into the **Colosseum** (p. 88). Between visits to those two, it makes sense to see the **Imperial Forums, Trajan's Markets,** and the city's best artifact collection at the **Musei Capitolini** (p. 94). Rome's museums display an array of relics dug up over the centuries: Add the ancient collections of the **Vatican Museums** (p. 81) and the busts and Roman art at **Palazzo Massimo alle Terme** (p. 114) to your list for **DAY 6.** The outdoor ruins of Rome's former seaport, **Ostia Antica** (p. 158), stand a short train journey from the city—a comfortable half-day round-trip for **DAY 7.** On the way back into the city, jump off at the Circo Massimo Metro stop to visit the **Terme di Caracalla** (p. 96) baths complex, and to admire for one last time the view of the **Palatine Hill** from the Circus Maximus. You could probably spend a month here just looking at the remnants of ancient Rome and its empire.

DAYS 8–10: Naples & Campania ♥♥

Ancient Naples—established as a fishing port, Parthenope, then refounded as Neapolis in the 6th century B.C.E.—was a key settlement in Magna Graecia, or "Greater Greece." Reminders of the ancient world lie below Naples's *centro storico:* Visit the excavations under **San Lorenzo Maggiore** (p. 604) to see remains of the Greek *agora* (market) and a later Roman Forum. Day trips to the Roman towns of **Pompeii** and **Herculaneum** (p. 629) reveal haunting artifacts preserved for centuries under ash and lava after Vesuvius's cataclysmic eruption in C.E. 79; visit Naples' **Museo Archeologico Nazionale** (p. 601) to see wall art from Pompeii and Roman statuary, including the *Toro Farnese.* Another day trip heads west of Naples to the amphitheater at **Pozzuoli** (p. 623), third-largest in the Roman world. Leave Naples on the high-speed Frecciarossa or Italo service late on **DAY 10** to get to Florence, just under 3 hours by rail.

An ancient statue in the haunting ruins of Pompeii.

DAYS 11 & 12: Florence ♥♥

Florence's Renaissance heyday, in the 1400s and 1500s, dominates much of the center's art and architecture. However, the **Museo Archeologico** (p. 194) displays relics from a civilization that predated the Romans: the Etruscans. While other visitors zero in on Michelangelo & co., you may have the *Arezzo Chimera* and many other precious Etruscan objects to yourself. You can also visit parts of a Roman theater uncovered below the **Palazzo Vecchio** (p. 186; temporarily closed). A 20-minute bus journey from Florence gets you to **Fiesole** (p. 202), now an outsize village but with a preserved Roman theatre, a stretch of Etruscan wall, and an archaeological area where you can roam freely among old stones—testaments to its much grander distant past.

DAY 13: Verona ♥♥

It seems harsh to label the **Arena di Verona** (p. 464) a "ruin." This city's enormous amphitheater is the best preserved in Italy and still in regular use. Come in summer—and book ahead—for the chance to experience one of Europe's most atmospheric outdoor opera festivals.

ROME

By Elizabeth Heath

4

It's easier than ever to be a visitor to Rome. With the coronavirus pandemic and the Papal Jubilee now a few years in the past, many positive effects still resonate—the pandemic's forced closures and no-contact rules finally pulled Rome into the digital age, and the 2025 Jubilee Year saw extensive clean-ups, renovations, and improvements. Yes, it's still crowded, but lines move more quickly, and advance booking rules mean fewer bottlenecks. Despite frequent strikes and service outages, public transportation is mostly efficient and reliable.

Despite these much-needed technological advancements, Rome is still Rome—a timeless city where the ancient, the modern and the merely antique blend in an often chaotic, always spellbinding urban mosaic. This is, after all, the city that once ruled the Western world, and even the partial, scattered ruins of Rome's empire are among the most overpowering sights on earth. To walk the Roman Forum, to view the Colosseum, the Pantheon, and the Appian Way: These are some of the most memorable, instructive, and illuminating experiences in all of travel. Across the Tiber River, St. Peter's and the Holy See loom large—both for their physical imprint on the city and for how they shaped the history and culture of Rome, Italy, Europe, and much of the Western world.

As a visitor to Rome, you will be constantly reminded of its extraordinary history. Yet this is no city stuck in a time warp—Rome is a living, breathing metropolis whose residents just happen to live, work, dine out, and relax among ancient ruins, medieval piazzas, Renaissance palaces, and baroque fountains. Discover the city's ancient wonders, but don't just seek out old Rome—find the innovative bistro or the modern art exhibit. Get lost in the maze of streets of Rome's *centro storico,* and stumble upon its monuments, moments, and simpler pleasures.

Walk the streets of Rome, and the city will be yours.

DON'T LEAVE ROME WITHOUT . . .

Exploring the World's Smallest Country. Vatican City is just .2 square miles, but it packs a lot into that tiny space. From one of the finest museums on the planet to its largest Catholic church and the architectural

 PREVIOUS PAGE: **Zipping past the Colosseum on a Vespa.**

masterwork that is St. Peter's Square, your trip isn't complete without at least a day spent here. See p. 76.

Gazing over the Roman Forum and Palatine from the Capitoline Hill Terraces at Night. Yes, explore the ruins by day too, but after dark—as spotlights cast dramatic glows over solitary columns and crumbling arches—the view is truly, disarmingly spectacular, and more than a wee bit romantic. See p. 92.

Lingering over Dinner. Take time to unwind at a typical Roman trattoria, with a steady and wonderfully affordable flow of wine and delicious food. Make one special meal the full Italian dining experience, and order antipasto, pasta, and meat courses—and dessert, of course. See p. 138.

Shopping like a Local at the Lively Mercato di Testaccio. No other market in the city has such a strong sense of community, coupled with the chance to sample real Roman street food. See p. 154.

Plan Ahead to Visit the Past . . .

We've always encouraged readers to buy tickets in advance for the attractions they really want to see; that advice is even more pertinent now. During the tentative post-pandemic days, many attractions switched to **advance ticketing** to limit crowds, and they've retained these crowd control systems, which ultimately give visitors a better experience. We've indicated where advance reservations are required or recommended, but the takeaway is this: If an attraction is one of your must-sees, book ahead.

ESSENTIALS

Arriving

BY PLANE Most flights arrive to Terminal 3 of Rome's **Leonardo da Vinci International Airport (FCO;** adr.it; ✆ **06-65951**), popularly known as **Fiumicino,** 30km (19 miles) from the city center. (If you're arriving from other European cities, you might land at Ciampino Airport, discussed below.) As you exit baggage claim in Terminal 3, you'll see a **tourist information desk** to the right, staffed daily from 8:30am to 8pm. There are several ***cambio*** (currency exchange) desks in the pre- and post-security areas, but it's just as easy, and probably less expensive, to withdraw cash from an ATM (*bancomat*) in the airport or even once you're in the city. ***Pro tip:*** Only use ATMs clearly affiliated with a bank, and avoid the standalone kiosks that at best charge exorbitant fees and at worst, will skim your card info. See p. 836 for tips on using Italian ATMs.

Exiting to the right from baggage claim and customs, follow signs marked TRENI (look for the yellow train icon) to find the **airport train station,** about a 10-minute walk. ***Pro tip:*** If you have a lot of bags and opt for the train, grab a free luggage cart when you get to baggage claim. Heading towards the train station, you'll see an elevator on your right, though there

Train or Taxi?

Whether to take the airport shuttle train or a taxi into Rome from FCO depends on your budget and your tolerance for schlepping. If you're traveling solo and/or traveling light, the train is the most economical option for getting into the city and takes about the same time as a taxi. If you've got a lot of bags, however, bear in mind that the train is a bit of a long walk from the Arrivals terminal—and that, once your train arrives at Termini station, you'll still have to walk, or take the Metro, a bus, or a taxi to your destination. (See "By Train," below, for more on Termini station options.) Bottom line? If there are three or more in your party or you're carrying lots of luggage, we say go for a taxi.

may be a line. Otherwise, you'll have to ditch the luggage cart and take the escalator.

From the station, catch the delightfully named **Leonardo Express** for a 32-minute ride to Rome's main station, **Stazione Termini.** The shuttle runs every 15 minutes (every 30 min. at off-peak hours) from 5:38am to 11:35pm for 14€ one-way (free for kids 12 and under). You can buy tickets from one of several machines (machines take cash or credit, and you can opt for instructions in English) or at the Trenitalia window near the tracks. You can also buy e-tickets at trenitalia.com or use the Trenitalia mobile app. I like to use the app and purchase my ticket right after I land. But if you purchase ahead, be sure to allow enough time for getting through passport control and baggage claim, which can be quite time-consuming. You're allowed to miss the train time you purchased and catch the next one—after that, you have to buy a new ticket.

A **taxi** from Fiumicino airport to the city costs a flat-rate 55€ for the 35-minute to 1-hour trip, depending on traffic. Note that the flat rate applies from the airport to central Rome and vice versa, but only if your location is inside the Aurelian Walls (most hotels are). Otherwise, standard metered rates apply, which can bump the fare higher. There are also surcharges for large luggage, Sunday and holiday rides, more than four passengers, and rides after 10pm and before 6am.

If you arrive at **Ciampino Airport** (**CIA;** adr.it/ciampino; ✆ **06-65951**), you can take a **Terravision** bus (terravision.eu; ✆ **06-4880086;** first bus 8:45am, last bus 11:40pm) to Stazione Termini. This takes about 45 minutes and costs 7€. (Note that the timetable for buses fluctuates based on current flight schedules.) A **taxi** from Ciampino costs a flat rate of 40€, provided you're going to a destination within the old Aurelian Walls.

From either airport, ride-sharing service **Uber** is available—sort of. Because of licensing laws (and strong resistance from Rome's taxi unions), only Uber Lux, Van, or Black services are offered, and they're much more expensive than a taxi. You can use the Uber app to order a taxi, but from the airports, there are few advantages to doing so.

BY TRAIN OR BUS Trains and buses (including trains from the airport) arrive in the center of old Rome at **Stazione Termini,** Piazza dei

ROMA & OMNIA passes

If you plan to do some serious sightseeing in Rome (and why else would you be here?), the **Roma Pass** (www.romapass.it) is worth considering. For either 38€ (a 2-day pass) or 62.90€ (a 3-day pass), you get free entry to the first one or two museums or archaeological sites you visit; "express" entry to the Colosseum; discounted entry to all other museums and sites; free use of the city's public transport network (bus, Metro, tram, and railway lines, not including transfers to Fiumicino Airport); free use of P.Stop bathrooms (turismoroma.it/en/page/pstop); and a free map.

The free transportation perk with the Roma Pass is not insignificant, if only because it saves you the hassle of buying digital farecards or paper tickets. In any case, do some quick math: One major museum or attraction entrance costs 13€ to 22€, and each ride on public transportation is 1.50€. Discounts to other sites range from 20% to 50%. If you plan to visit lots of sites and dash around the city on public transport, it's probably worth the money.

A glaring disadvantage of the Roma Pass is that it does not include access to the Vatican Museums or the paid areas of St. Peter's. That's where the **Omnia Card** comes in. The 72-hour card combines all the benefits of the Roma Pass with skip-the-line entry to the Vatican Museums and St. Peter's, an audioguide to St. Peter's, a hop-on-hop-off bus pass, and admission to other Vatican properties. At 149€, it's an investment, but worth it if you want to take in all the heavy hitters of Rome and the Vatican. If you just want express entrance to the Vatican Museums and St. Peter's, there's also a 24-hour Omnia Card (69€) that does not include Roma Pass benefits. The cards can be purchased online at omniavaticanrome.org and picked up at one of four Omnia Card offices in the city, including at St. Peter's Square.

You can buy Roma Passes online (www.romapass.it) and activate them on the Roma Pass app; you can also order in advance by phone, with a credit card, at ✆ **06-060608.** Roma Passes are also sold directly at most Tourist Information Points and at some museums and ATAC subway ticket offices. Note that physical cards are still available at press time, but the move seems to be towards digital-only passes.

Note: Roma Pass holders intending to visit the Colosseum **must reserve timed entry.** We find the easiest way to do this is as follows: At the bottom of the Roma Pass website, go to the FAQ page and click Reservations, then question 5.1. Follow the link to Ticketing Colosseo and reserve your timed entry—then purchase your Roma Pass once you're certain your dates are available. Note that other sites included on the Roma Pass may also require advance booking; check individual websites for the latest on opening hours and Roma Pass reservation requirements.

Cinquecento. This is the train, bus, and transportation hub for all of Rome, and it is surrounded by many hotels, especially budget choices.

The station is filled with services. Currency exchange windows and ATMs are located on the platform level, as well as on floor -1 (subway level). **Informazioni Ferroviarie** (in the outer hall) dispenses info on rail travel to other parts of Italy. There are two **tourist information booths,** plus baggage services, clean public toilets (1€), and snack bars.

To get from Termini to your accommodation in Rome, you have several options. If you're taking the **Metropolitana** (subway), follow the illuminated red-and-white M signs. To catch a city bus, go straight through the outer hall and enter the sprawling bus lot of **Piazza dei Cinquecento.** (See p. 71 for more information about getting around Rome by public transportation.) You will also find a line of **taxis** parked out front. Note that taxis charge a 2€ supplement for any fares originating at Termini, plus 1€ for each bag in the trunk. Use one of the official taxi queues located in front of the station or on Via Marsala; don't go with a driver who approaches you or get into any cab where the meter is "broken." You should be able to pay with a credit or debit card in any official taxi, but confirm this before getting in.

Some trains only go as far as **Roma Tiburtina** station, which is outside the historic center. From here, commuter trains and the Metro connect to Termini, or you can grab a taxi in front of the station.

BY CAR From the north or south, the main access route is the **Autostrada A1,** which runs from Milan to Naples via Bologna, Florence, and Rome. At 754km (469 miles), it is the longest Italian *autostrada* and the "spinal cord" of Italy's road network. All the *autostrade* connect with the **Grande Raccordo Anulare** (**GRA**), a ring road encircling Rome, channeling traffic into and around the congested city. ***Tip:*** Long before you reach the GRA, study your route carefully to see what part of Rome you plan to enter. Route signs along the ring road tend to be confusing.

Warning: If you must drive a car into Rome, return your rental car immediately on arrival, or at least get yourself to your hotel, park your car, and leave it there until you leave the city. Seriously think twice before driving in Rome—the traffic, as well as the scarce parking options, are nightmarish. Most of central Rome is a **Zona Traffico Limitato** (**ZTL**), off-limits to nonresidents. This is rigorously enforced by cameras, and you will almost certainly be fined; the ticket might arrive at your home address months after your trip.

Visitor Information

Information, maps, and the **Roma Pass** (p. 65) are available at six Tourist Information Points around the city maintained by **Roma Capitale** (turismoroma.it/en). Each kiosk keeps its own hours and none are exactly the same, but you can reliably find them open after 9:30am and before 6pm (some open earlier and stay open later). Note that the ones at Termini provide info only and do not sell any tickets or Roma Passes.

City Layout

The bulk of what you'll want to visit—ancient, Renaissance, and baroque Rome (as well as the train station)—lies on the east side of the **Tiber River** (Fiume Tevere), which curls through the city. However, several important landmarks are on the other side: **St. Peter's Basilica** and the **Vatican, Castel Sant'Angelo,** and the colorful **Trastevere** neighborhood. Even if those last sights are slightly farther afield, Rome has one of the most compact and walkable city centers in Europe.

That doesn't mean you won't get lost from time to time. While most of us rely on Google maps or similar smartphone tools, satellite signals don't always reach Rome's narrow streets, and those digital maps can get you terribly turned around. Most hotels hand out a pretty good paper version of a city map, which is good to rely on for backup.

Rome's Neighborhoods in Brief

Much of Rome's historic core does not fall under neighborhood classifications that would mean much to visitors. Instead, when describing a location, the frame of reference is usually the nearest large monument or square, like St. Peter's or Piazza di Spagna. Street numbers usually run consecutively, with odd numbers on one side and evens on the other. However, in Centro, the numbers sometimes run up one side and then back down on the other side (so #50 could potentially be opposite #308).

St. Peter's Square is the spiritual heart of Vatican City.

VATICAN CITY & PRATI **Vatican City** is technically a sovereign state, although in practice it is just another part of Rome. The **Vatican Museums, St. Peter's,** the **Vatican Gardens** and papal apartments take up most of the land area. If you plan to spend most of your time exploring Vatican City sights, or if you just want to stay outside the city center, **Prati,** a middle-class neighborhood east of the Vatican, has a smattering of affordable hotels, shopping streets, and some excellent places to eat.

CENTRO STORICO & THE PANTHEON One of the most desirable and busiest areas of Rome, the ***centro storico*** (historic center) is a maze of narrow streets and cobbled alleys dating from the Middle Ages, filled with churches and palaces built during the Renaissance and baroque eras, as well as countless hotels and Airbnb rentals. The only way to explore it is by foot. Its heart is elegant **Piazza Navona,** built over Emperor Domitian's stadium and bustling with overpriced sidewalk cafes and restaurants, street artists and musicians (licensed or otherwise), and milling crowds. Nearby, the area around the ancient Roman **Pantheon** is abuzz with crowds, restaurants, and nightlife. South of Corso Vittorio Emanuele is the lively square of **Campo de' Fiori,** home to the famous produce market. West of Via Arenula lies the old Jewish **Ghetto,** with several good restaurants and a few interesting hotels.

Rome's Neighborhoods & Top Attractions

Appian Way & the Catacombs **25**
Basilica di San Clemente **21**
Basilica di San Giovanni in Laterano **22**
Baths of Caracalla **24**
Baths of Diocletian **15**
Castel Sant'Angelo **3**
Colosseum **20**
ETRU (National Etruscan Museum) **1**
Galleria Borghese **13**
Imperial Forums **18**
Museum & Crypt of the Capuchin Friars **14**
Palazzo Massimo alle Terme **16**
Pantheon **9**
Piazza del Popolo **2**
Piazza Navona **8**
Roman Forum **19**
San Paolo Fuori le Mura **23**
Santa Cecilia in Trastevere **7**
Santa Maria in Trastevere **6**
Santa Maria Maggiore **17**
Sistine Chapel **4**
Spanish Steps **11**
St. Peter's Basilica **5**
Trevi Fountain **10**
Vatican Museums **4**
Villa Borghese **12**

Galleria Borghese
National Gallery of Modern Art
Piazza di Siena
VILLA BORGHESE/ PARIOLI
See "Tridente & Via Veneto" map
VIA VENETO
Spanish Steps
PIAZZA BARBERINI
Trevi Fountain
Palazzo del Quirinale
National Roman Museum
Termini Station
Teatro dell'Opera
Santa Maria Maggiore
See "Around Termini" map
SAN LORENZO
Palazzo Venezia
Vittorio Emanuele Monument
Capitoline Museums
ANCIENT ROME
Roman Forum
Colosseum
Golden House of Nero
San Pietro in Vincoli
PALATINE HILL
Circus Maximus
San Giovanni in Laterano
See "Ancient Rome, Monti & Celio" map
AVENTINE HILL
Baths of Caracalla
Information
City walls
Metro A
Metro B
Metro C
(under construction)
Railway
0 1/4 mi
0 250 m

ANCIENT ROME, MONTI & CELIO Although no longer the heart of the city, this is where Rome began, with the **Colosseum, Palatine Hill, Roman Forum, Imperial Forums,** and **Circus Maximus.** For more of a neighborhood feel, stay in **Monti** (Rome's oldest *rione,* or quarter, located north of the Colosseum) or **Celio** (southeast of the Colosseum). Monti especially has good dining and plenty of nightlife. Just beyond the Circus Maximus, the **Aventine Hill** is now a posh residential quarter with great city views. Note that most of the restaurants right near the Colosseum should be skipped.

TRIDENTE & THE SPANISH STEPS The most upscale part of Rome, full of expensive hotels, designer boutiques, and chic restaurants, lies north of Rome's center. It's called the Tridente, because Via di Ripetta, Via del Corso, and Via del Babuino form a trident leading down from **Piazza del Popolo.** The star here is unquestionably **Piazza di Spagna,** which attracts Romans and tourists alike (though mostly the latter) to linger at its celebrated **Spanish Steps.** (Just don't snack on the steps! See p. 108.) Some of Rome's priciest shopping streets, including **Via Condotti,** fan out from here.

VIA VENETO & PIAZZA BARBERINI In the 1950s and early 1960s, the tree-lined boulevard **Via Veneto** was the swinging place to be, the haunt of la dolce vita celebrities and paparazzi. Luxury hotels, cafes, and restaurants still cluster here, although the restaurants are mostly overpriced tourist traps. To the south, Via Veneto ends at **Piazza Barberini** and the magnificent **Palazzo Barberini,** begun in 1623 by Carlo Maderno and later completed by Bernini and Borromini.

VILLA BORGHESE & PARIOLI Bordered by the green spaces of the **Villa Borghese** to the south and the **Villa Glori** and **Villa Ada** to the north, **Parioli** is Rome's most elegant residential section, a setting for excellent restaurants, museums, and public parks. That said, along with Pinciano, just to its south, this is not exactly central and not the best base if you plan to depend on public transportation.

AROUND STAZIONE TERMINI For many visitors, their first glimpse of Rome is the main train station and the unappealing **Piazza dei Cinquecento** out front. A lot of affordable hotels are in this area (as well as several less-affordable ones), and the location is convenient, near the city's transportation hub and not far from ancient Rome.

The restful green space of Villa Borghese.

Hotels on the Via Marsala side often occupy floors of a *palazzo* (palace), with clean and decent, sometimes even charming, rooms. The once-seedy neighborhoods on either side of Termini (Esquilino and Tiburtino) have slowly been cleaning up.

TRASTEVERE In a Roman shift of the Latin *Trans Tiber,* Trastevere means "across the Tiber." Since the 1970s, when expats and other bohemians made their base here, this once-medieval working-class district has been gentrifying and is most definitely on the tourist map. Yet Trastevere retains its colorful appeal, with dance clubs, offbeat shops, pubs, and little *trattorie* and wine bars. Trastevere has places to stay—mostly rather quaint rentals and Airbnbs—and excellent restaurants and bars, too. The area centers on the ancient churches of **Santa Cecilia** and **Santa Maria in Trastevere.**

TESTACCIO & SOUTHERN ROME Once home to slaughterhouses and Rome's port on the Tiber, the working-class neighborhood of **Testaccio** was built around one strange feature: a huge, compacted mound of broken amphorae and terra-cotta roof tiles, begun under Emperor Nero in C.E. 55 and added to over the centuries. Houses were built around the mound; caves were dug into its mass to store wine and foodstuffs. Now known for its authentic Roman restaurants, Testaccio is also one of Rome's liveliest areas after dark. Stay here if you want a taste of a real Roman neighborhood, but bear in mind that you're a bus, tram, or subway ride from most tourist sights.

THE APPIAN WAY Farther south and east, the 2,300-year-old **Via Appia Antica** road once extended from Rome to Brindisi on the southeast coast. This is one of the most archaeology-rich areas of Rome, great for a day trip, but not a convenient place to stay. Its most famous sights are the **Catacombs,** the underground cemeteries of early Christians and patrician families.

Getting Around Rome

Central Rome is perfect for exploring on foot, with sites of interest often clustered together. Much of the inner core is traffic-free, so you will need to walk whether you like it or not. ***Tip:*** Wear sturdy, comfortable walking shoes. In the most tourist-trod parts of the city, be ready to cope with crowds, uneven cobblestones, heavy traffic, and narrow (if any) sidewalks.

BY SUBWAY The **Metropolitana** (**Metro**) is managed by **ATAC** (atac.roma.it; ✆ **06-57003**), which also runs the city's buses, trams, and urban trains. The Metro operates daily from 5:30am to 11:30pm (Fri and Sat until 1:30am). A big red M indicates the entrance to the subway. The Metro is usually much faster than surface transportation but study a map first: It's often just as easy to walk between two points. The Metro has three lines: **Line A** (orange) runs southeast to northwest via Termini, Barberini, Spagna, and several stations in Prati near the Vatican; **Line B** (blue) runs north to south via Termini and stops at the Colosseum; and a third, **Line C** (green), will ultimately run from Monte Compatri in the southeast to Clodio/Mazzini (just beyond the Ottaviano stop on Line A) and include several stops in the *centro storico.* Work on the line has been painstakingly slow, largely because crews working underground keep stumbling upon new archaeological finds that have to be researched and excavated, but the dazzling new Colosseo/Fori Imperiali station finally opened in late 2025. The station connects the B and C lines while displaying artifacts and ruins discovered during construction, including some of 28 ancient wells. Just another daily commute in Rome!

Tickets are 1.50€ and are available via Tap & Go (see box, below), from *tabacchi* (tobacco shops), many newsstands, and vending machines at all stations; booklets of tickets are also available at newsstands, *tabacchi,* and in some terminals. You can also buy a daily or weekly **pass** (see "By Bus & Tram," below). To open the subway barrier, insert your ticket or tap in using your phone or card. If you have a **Roma Pass** (p. 65), touch it against the yellow dot and the gates will open. Tickets, which are valid for 100 minutes from the first time they're used, can be used to transfer to buses, trams, and urban trains. See the Metro map on the tear-out map in this guide.

BY BUS & TRAM For 1.50€ you can ride to most parts of Rome on buses or trams, although it can be slow going in all that traffic, and buses are often very crowded. A ticket is valid for 100 minutes, during which time you can ride on many buses and trams, as well as the Metro, using the same ticket. Tickets are sold in *tabacchi,* at newsstands, and at bus stops, but there are seldom ticket-issuing machines on the vehicles themselves. Note that if you switch from a bus or tram to Metro within your 100-minute ticket time, you must revalidate your ticket before boarding the subway. If you're using Tap & Go, remember to tap out of one vehicle before you transfer to another.

Go Ticketless with Tap & Go or Moovit

Skip the hassle of buying a transit ticket and ride paperless on Rome's Metro, buses and trams using Tap & Go. Any credit/debit card or smartphone equipped for contactless payment should work, and no registration is necessary—simply tap in at the turnstile or bus/tram entrance and tap out when you exit. Once you're tapped in, you can ride for up to 100 minutes on all public transport methods on a single 1.50€ fare. The ATAC system is also fully integrated with **Moovit,** the international urban mobility app, so users can plan their journeys, track real time schedules, buy tickets, and access other transportation methods all within the app.

You can buy **special timed passes:** A 24-hour (ROMA24H) ticket is 8.50€; a 48-hour ticket is 15.00€; a 72-hour ticket costs 22€; and a 7-day ticket is 29€. These passes make sense only if you plan to make several public transportation trips in a single day, considering it takes six rides for that 8.50€ pass to be a bargain.

Bus information booths at Piazza dei Cinquecento, in front of Stazione Termini, offer advice on routes. Buses and trams stop at areas marked

Walk or Ride?

Rome is such a walkable city that getting around on foot is half the fun. And public transportation doesn't necessarily save that much time. For example, walking from Piazza Venezia to Piazza di Santa Maria in Trastevere takes about 25 minutes at a leisurely pace; it takes 12 minutes via bus and tram, but that doesn't include potential time spent waiting for the bus or tram to show up. My take? On a nice day and for relatively short distances, enjoy the stroll. On the other hand, if you want to save your steps (maybe for a marathon tour of the Vatican Museums), then head to the nearest Metro, tram, or bus stop.

fermata. Signs will display the numbers of the buses that stop there and a list of all stops along each bus route, making it easier to scope out your destination; digital displays at most stops show how soon the next bus or tram will arrive. Generally, buses run daily from 5:30am to midnight. From midnight until dawn, special night buses (look for the "N" in front of the bus number) run only on main routes. In the wee hours, it's best to take a taxi; if you can't find one, call for one (see "By Taxi," below).

BY TAXI If you've reached your walking limit, don't feel like waiting for a bus, or need to get someplace in a hurry, taking a taxi in Rome is reasonably affordable compared with other major world cities. Just don't count on hailing a taxi on the street, which is basically impossible. Instead, have your hotel call one, or if you're at a restaurant, ask the waiter or cashier to dial for you. If you want to phone for yourself, try the **city taxi service** at ✆ **06-0609** (Italian only) or one of the following **radio taxi numbers,** which may or may not have English-speaking operators on duty: ✆ **06-6645, 06-3570,** or **06-4994.** You can also text a taxi at ✆ **366-6730000** by typing the message "Roma [address]" (assuming you know the address in Italian). Taxis on call incur a surcharge of 3.50€. Otherwise, available cabs wait at taxi stands around the city, including at Piazza Venezia (east side), Piazza di Spagna, the Colosseum, Corso del Rinascimento (Piazza Navona), Largo Argentina, the Pantheon, Piazza del Popolo, Piazza Risorgimento (near St. Peter's), and Piazza Belli (Trastevere). We always have luck finding a cab at Piazza di San Pantaleo on Corso Vittorio Emanuele II.

Taxis are required by law to accept credit cards, but it's still best to confirm this before getting in. Between 6am and 10pm, the meter begins at 3€ (Sat–Sun 4.50€); it starts at 6.50€ between 10pm and 6am. The meter adds 1.10€ per kilometer up to 11€, after which it's 1.30€ to 1.60€ per kilometer, depending on the length of the ride.

The main smartphone app for official city taxis is **itTaxi** (ittaxi.it), which is run by Rome's largest taxi company, **3570** (3570.it/services). You can pay directly from the app using a credit card or PayPal. Popular throughout Europe, the **FreeNow** (formerly MyTaxi) app offers Uber-like convenience for ordering and prepaying a cab. **Uber** is currently available in Rome in a limited capacity only.

Rome's Key Bus Routes

First, know that any map of the Roman bus system will likely be outdated before it's printed. Second, take extreme caution when riding Rome's busiest buses—where tourists are frequent targets of pickpockets. Bus no. 64, a favorite of visitors because of its route through the historic districts, is also a particular favorite of Rome's petty thieves, earning it such nicknames as the "Pickpocket Express" and "Wallet Eater."

Although routes may change, a few reliable bus routes have remained valid for years in Rome:

- **40 (Express):** Stazione Termini to the Vatican by Via Nazionale, Piazza Venezia and Piazza Pia, by Castel Sant'Angelo
- **64:** The "tourist route" from Termini, along Via Nazionale and through Piazza Venezia and along Via Argentina to Piazza San Pietro in the Vatican
- **75:** Stazione Termini to the Colosseum
- **H:** Stazione Termini via Piazza Venezia and the Ghetto to Trastevere via Ponte Garibaldi

BY CAR All roads may lead to Rome, but you don't want to drive on them once you get here. If you must drive into the city, call or e-mail ahead to your hotel to find out the best route into Rome from wherever you are starting out. You will want to get rid of your rental car as soon as possible or park it in a garage and leave it there until you depart Rome.

If you want to **rent a car** to explore the countryside around Rome or drive to another city, you'll save money if you reserve before leaving home (see p. 829 in chapter 16). If you decide to book a car here, most major car rental companies have desks inside Stazione Termini. Note that rental cars in Italy may be smaller than what you're used to, particularly in trunk space. Make sure you consider both luggage size and the number of people when booking your vehicle.

[Fast FACTS] ROME

Banks In general, banks are open Monday to Friday 8:30am to 1:30pm and 2:30 or 2:45 to 4pm. Note that many banks do not offer currency exchange.

Business Hours Most Roman shops open at 10am or earlier and close at 7pm from Monday to Saturday. Smaller shops close for 1 or 2 hours at lunch and may remain closed Monday morning and Saturday afternoon. Many restaurants are closed for *riposo* (rest) 1 day per week, usually Sunday or Monday.

Dentists **Studi Dentistici Mazzei & Co.,** Via Napoleone III, 58 (a few blocks from Termini Station; studimazzei.com/mazzei-dental-clinic; ✆ **06-4440656**), offers multilingual staff and emergency service.

Doctors Call the U.S. Embassy at ✆ **06-46741** for a list of English-speaking doctors. You'll find English-speaking doctors at the privately run **Salvator Mundi International Hospital,** Viale delle Mura Gianicolensi 67 (in the Gianicolo neighborhood; upmc.it/en/locations/salvator-mundi; ✆ **06-588961**). The **International Medical Center** is on 24-hour duty at Via Firenze 47 (near Piazza della Repubblica; imc84.com; ✆ **06-4882371**). **Medi-Call**

Italia, Via Cremera 8 (medi-call.it; ✆ **06-8840113**), can arrange for a qualified doctor to make a house call at your hotel or anywhere in Rome.

Emergencies Call ✆**112** to be connected to the police, request an ambulance, or report a fire.

Newspapers & Magazines The biweekly English-language expat magazine ***Wanted in Rome*** (wantedinrome.com) lists current events and shows.

Pharmacies Easily recognizable by their neon green or red cross signs, *farmacie* are generally open 8:30am to 1pm and 4 to 7:30pm, though some stay open later. All closed pharmacies have signs in their windows indicating the nearest open pharmacy.

Police Dial ✆ **112.**

Safety Walking alone at night is usually fine anywhere in the *centro storico.* Violent crime is virtually nonexistent in Rome's touristed areas, though pickpocketing is common. Purse snatching happens on occasion, often by perps speeding by on scooters; keep your purse on the wall side of your body with the strap across your chest. Other pickpockets dress like typical businesspeople, so always be suspicious of anyone who tries to "befriend" you in a tourist area. Thieves will also strike where you may least expect it, such as in crowded paid areas like the Colosseum or Vatican Museums.

EXPLORING ROME

Rome's ancient monuments are a constant reminder that this was one of the greatest centers of Western civilization. In the heyday of the Empire, all roads led to Rome, with good reason. It was one of the first cosmopolitan cities, importing food, textiles, slaves, gladiators, great art, and even citizens from the far corners of the known world. Despite its brutality and corruption, Rome left a legacy of law, art, architecture, and engineering—and a canny lesson in how to conquer enemies by absorbing their cultures.

But ancient Rome is only part of the spectacle. The Vatican has had a tremendous influence on making the city a tourism center. Although Vatican architects in the Renaissance stripped down much of the city's ancient glory, looting ruins (the Forum especially) for their precious marble, they created more treasures and occasionally incorporated the old into the new—as Michelangelo did when turning Diocletian's Baths complex into a church. And in the years that followed, Bernini adorned the city with baroque wonders, especially his glorious fountains.

Arrivederci, Long Lines

It used to be that going to Rome's three biggest attractions—the Colosseum, the Vatican Museums, and St. Peter's Basilica—meant waiting in long, long lines. Now, thanks to advance ticket sales for timed entry, there's no reason to wait in excessively long lines for the Colosseum or the Vatican Museums. (See individual listings for more details.) And in 2026, as part of the 400th anniversary of St. Peter's Basilica, the Vatican will roll out a new online reservation system, which should drastically reduce wait times there.

St. Peter's & the Vatican

The world's smallest sovereign state, **Vatican City** is a truly tiny territory, comprising little more than St. Peter's Basilica, the Vatican Museums, and the walled headquarters of the Roman Catholic Church. While there are no border controls, the city-state's 800 inhabitants (mostly clergymen and Swiss Guards) have their own radio station, daily newspaper, pharmacy and petrol pumps, postal service, and head of state—the pope. The pope had always exercised a high degree of political independence from the rest of Italy, formalized by the 1929 Lateran Treaty between Pope Pius XI and the Italian government to create the Vatican. The city is still protected by the flamboyantly uniformed (their outfits allegedly designed by Michelangelo) Swiss Guards, a tradition dating from when the Swiss, known as brave soldiers, were often hired out as mercenaries for foreign armies. Today the Vatican remains the center of the Roman Catholic world, the home of the pope—and the resting place of St. Peter. **St. Peter's Basilica** is obviously one of the highlights, but the only part of the Apostolic Palace itself that you can visit independently is the **Vatican Museums,** the world's biggest and richest museum complex.

On the left side of Piazza San Pietro, the **Vatican Tourist Office** (vatican.va; ✆ **06-69882019;** Mon–Sat 8:30am–6:30pm) sells maps and guides that will help you make sense of the treasures in the museums; it also accepts reservations for tours of the Vatican Gardens. Adjacent to the

Making the Most of a Day in Vatican City

Most Vatican visitors allot a day to see its two major sights, **St. Peter's Basilica** and the **Vatican Museums** (including the Sistine Chapel). We recommend starting with the museums. **Pre-order** tickets for the earliest time slot (from 9am) available the day you wish to visit. Plan to devote several hours to seeing the collection highlights (p. 76).

Next, grab a quick late lunch, either in the museum cafeteria (warning: the food is disappointing) or at a nearby sandwich shop or pizza joint. The streets leading from the museum exit to St. Peter's Basilica are lined with cheap eateries—mostly mediocre, but they'll do in a pinch. (See p. 139 for some notably good options.)

Once you enter **St. Peter's Square,** head to the basilica's entry line (a new online reservation system launched in 2026). From the time you enter, you'll need at least 1 hour for even the most cursory tour in the crowded basilica.

By now it'll be late afternoon, and you've got two options: Visit the **Vatican Grottoes,** burial place of dozens of popes, or climb the 551 steps (320 if you take the elevator) to the top of the **dome of St. Peter's.** Note that the dome and grottoes are open April to September until 6pm, October to March until 5pm. If you've still got energy, head to nearby **Castel Sant'Angelo** (p. 80)—the view of Rome from the castle's roof is a perfect way to cap off your marathon Vatican day.

Want more time at the Vatican Museums? Arrive at St. Peter's early in the morning to get in line before it opens at 7am; that way you can tour the basilica before the crowds show up. Then head to a late morning appointment at the museums and spend the rest of the day there.

information office, the **Vatican Post Office** sells special Vatican postage stamps (Mon–Sat 8:30am–6pm).

The only entrance to St. Peter's for tourists is through one of the glories of the Western world: Bernini's 17th-century **St. Peter's Square** (Piazza San Pietro). As you stand in the huge piazza, you are in the symbolic arms of the Church—an ellipse partly enclosed by a majestic **Doric-pillared colonnade.** Stand in the marked marble discs embedded in the pavement near the fountains to see all the columns lined up in a striking optical/geometrical play. Straight ahead is the facade of St. Peter's itself and to the right, above the colonnade, the dark brown buildings of the **papal apartments** and the Vatican Museums. In the center of the square stands a 4,000-year-old

Egyptian obelisk, created in the ancient city of Heliopolis on the Nile Delta and appropriated by the Romans under Emperor Augustus. Flanking the obelisk are two 17th-century **fountains.** The one on the right (facing the basilica), by Carlo Maderno, who designed the facade of St. Peter's, was placed here by Bernini himself; the other is by Carlo Fontana.

Basilica di San Pietro (St. Peter's Basilica) ♥♥♥ CHURCH St. Peter's is the holiest shrine of the Catholic Church, built on the site of St. Peter's tomb by the greatest Italian artists of the 16th and 17th centuries. The line on the right side of the piazza funnels you into the basilica (from where you can access the underground grottoes) or the dome. Whichever you opt for first, you must be **properly dressed**—a rule that is very strictly enforced.

The grand interior of St. Peter's Basilica.

In Roman times, the Circus of Nero, where Peter is said to have been crucified, was just to the left of where the basilica is today. He was allegedly buried here in C.E. 64, and in C.E. 324 Emperor Constantine commissioned a church to be built over Peter's tomb. That structure stood for more than 1,000 years. The present basilica, mostly completed in the 1500s and 1600s, is predominantly High Renaissance and baroque. Inside, the massive scale is almost too much to absorb, showcasing some of Italy's greatest artists: Bramante, Raphael, and Michelangelo. In a church of such grandeur—overwhelming in its detail of gilt, marble, and mosaic—you can't expect much subtlety. It is meant to be overpowering.

Going straight into the basilica, the first thing you see on the right side of the nave—the longest nave in the world, as clearly marked in the floor along with other cathedral measurements—is the chapel containing Michelangelo's graceful ***Pietà*** **♥♥♥**. Created in the 1490s when the artist was still in his 20s, it clearly shows his genius for capturing the human form. (The sculpture has been kept behind reinforced glass since an act of vandalism in the 1970s.) Note the lifelike folds of Mary's

St. Peter's: Dress the Part

St. Peter's has a hard-and-fast dress code that makes no exceptions: **Men and women in shorts, above-the-knee skirts, or bare shoulders** are not admitted to the basilica, period, and **hats should be off.** I've occasionally seen guards handing out disposable cloaks for the scantily clad, but don't count on that: Cover up or bring a shawl. The same holds for the Roman Necropolis, the Vatican Museums, and churches elsewhere in the city.

robes and her youthful features; although she would've been middle-aged at the time of the Crucifixion, Michelangelo portrayed her as a young woman to convey her purity. A few yards past the *Pietà* is a chapel housing the **tomb of Pope John Paul II.**

Farther inside the nave, Michelangelo's dome is a mesmerizing space, rising high above the supposed site of St. Peter's tomb. With a diameter of 41.5m (136 ft.), the dome is Rome's largest, supported by four bulky piers decorated with reliefs depicting the basilica's key holy relics: St. Veronica's handkerchief (used to wipe the face of Christ); the lance of St. Longinus, which pierced Christ's side; and a piece of the True Cross. The fourth relic, St. Andrew's skull, is now in Patras, Greece. Under the dome, a twisty-columned **baldacchino ♥♥** by Bernini shelters the papal altar. The ornate 29m-high (96-ft.) canopy was created in part, so it is said, from bronze stripped from the Pantheon. Bernini sculpted the face of a woman on the base of each pillar; starting with the face on the left pillar (with your back to the entrance), circle the entire altar to see the progress of expressions from the agony of childbirth through to the fourth pillar, where the woman's face is replaced with that of her newborn baby.

Just before reaching the dome, on the right, the devout stop to touch or kiss the well-worn foot of the 13th-century **bronze of St. Peter ♥**, attributed to Arnolfo di Cambio. (Note that the statue is sometimes cordoned off.) Elsewhere the church is decorated by more of Bernini's lavish sculptures, including his monument to Pope Alexander VII in the south transept, its winged skeleton writhing under heavy marble drapes.

An entrance off the nave leads to the Sacristy and the **Historical Museum** (Museo Storico) or **treasury ♥**, which is chock-full of richly jeweled chalices, reliquaries, and copes (a liturgical cape or shawl), as well as the late-15th-century bronze tomb of Pope Sixtus IV by Pollaiuolo.

An entrance to the left of the baldacchino leads down to the **Vatican grottoes ♥♥**, with their tombs of the popes, both ancient and modern. There, behind a glass wall, is what is considered to be the tomb of St. Peter.

After you leave the grottoes, you find yourself in a courtyard and ticket line for the grandest sight in the basilica: the climb to **Michelangelo's dome ♥♥♥**, about 114m (375 ft.) high. You can walk all the way up or take the elevator as far as it goes (this saves you 231 steps). At this first stop, you can walk on the roof of the basilica (where there's also a restroom, a snack bar, and a gift shop) and also around the interior of the drum of the dome, which offers a bird's-eye view of the basilica below. After that, you *still* have 320 stairs to go to reach the very top. (Claustrophobes take note: The last part of the climb is up a very narrow spiral staircase.) At the top, you'll have a scintillating view over the rooftops of Rome and even the Vatican Gardens and papal apartments. The elevator down drops you in the basilica interior, near the front entrance, or you can descend via a spiral ramp, its walls lined with inscriptions recalling famous visitors to the dome.

Visits to the **Necropolis Vaticana** ♥♥ and St. Peter's tomb itself are restricted to 250 persons per day on guided tours (90 min.). Booking requests are accepted via an online form, and it's best to apply well in advance of your trip dates. The entrance to the necropolis is to the left of the stairs up from the basilica; you'll have to show proof of reservation to get past the Swiss Guards. Note that the Necropolis is not suitable for claustrophobes, and children under the age of 10 are not permitted.

Piazza San Pietro. www.basilicasanpietro.va. ✆ **06-69881662.** Free admission to Basilica (including grottoes). Timed entrance 7€. Necropolis Vaticana (St. Peter's tomb) 20€. Stairs to the dome 17€ adults, 10€ ages 7–18; elevator (part-way) to the dome 22€ adults, 14€ ages 7–18; sacristy (with Historical Museum) 17€ adults, 10€ ages 7–18. Free for children 7 and under. All include entrance to St. Peter's with audioguide. **Basilica:** Daily 7am–7:10pm. **Dome:** Daily 7:30am–6pm (Oct–Mar until 5pm). ***Note:*** Basilica may not open until noon or 1pm on Wed when papal audience is in square. **Sacristy/museum:** Daily 7:30am–6:30pm. **Grottoes:** Daily 9am–6pm (Oct–Mar until 5pm). Metro: Ottaviano/San Pietro, then a 10-min. walk; or bus 40, 46, or 62 to Piazza Pia/Transpontina, then a 10-min. walk.

Castel Sant'Angelo ♥♥ CASTLE/PALACE Over the years, this bulky cylindrical fortress on the Vatican side of the Tiber has had many lives: as the mausoleum tomb of Emperor Hadrian in C.E. 138; as a papal

papal AUDIENCES

When the pope is in Rome, he gives a public audience every Wednesday beginning at 9:30am. If you want to get a good seat near the front, arrive early and prepare to wait—security begins to let people in between 7 and 7:30am, but the line starts much earlier. Audiences take place in the Paul VI Hall of Audiences, although sometimes St. Peter's Basilica and St. Peter's Square are used to accommodate a large attendance in the summer. You can check on the pope's appearances and the ceremonies he presides over, including celebrations of Mass, on the Vatican website (vatican.va). Anyone is welcome, but you must first obtain a **free ticket;** without a reservation you can try the Swiss Guards by the Bronze Doors located just after security at St. Peter's (summer 8am–8pm and winter 8am–7pm). You can pick up tickets here up to 3 days in advance, subject to availability.

If you prefer to reserve a place in advance, visit **vatican.va/various/prefettura/index_en.html** to download a request form, which must be submitted via fax or e-mail. Tickets can be picked up at the office just inside the Bronze Doors from 3 to 7pm on the preceding day or on the morning of the audience from 7am.

At noon on Sundays, the pope speaks briefly from his study window and gives his blessing to visitors and pilgrims gathered in St. Peter's Square (no tickets required for this). From about mid-July to mid-September, the Angelus and blessing historically takes place at the pope's summer residence at **Castel Gandolfo,** some 26km (16 miles) out of Rome. Under Pope Francis, the residence, gardens, and villas of the castle were opened to visitors as a museum, and new Pope Leo XIV, the first American to wear the miter, has continued the practice. The area is accessible via Metro and bus and, depending on the whims of the Vatican, a seasonal train service from Roma San Pietro station.

residence in the 14th century; as a castle, where in 1527 Pope Clement VII hid from the looting troops of Charles V; and as a military prison from the 17th century on. Consider renting an audioguide at the entrance to fully appreciate its various manifestations.

From the entrance, a stone ramp (*rampa elicoidale*) winds to the upper terraces, where you can see amazing views of the city and enjoy a coffee at the outdoor cafe. The sixth floor features the **Terrazza dell'Angelo,** crowned by a florid 18th-century statue of the Archangel Michael. It's famous to opera fans—the last act of Puccini's *Tosca* is set here.

From here you can walk back down through five floors. On levels 3 to 5 you'll see the Renaissance apartments used by some of Rome's most infamous popes, including Alexander VI, the Borgia pope. Below the apartments are the grisly dungeons (**Le Prigioni**) that served as torture chambers in the medieval period (Cesare Borgia made great use of them). The castle is connected to St. Peter's Basilica by **Il Passetto di Borgo,** a walled passage built in 1277 by Pope Nicholas III, used by popes who needed to make a quick escape to the fortress in times of danger. Il Passetto is periodically open to the public, and worth booking if it's available on the day of your visit (10€ additional).

Lungotevere Castello 50. castelsantangelo.com. ✆ **06-32810.** Admission 20€ adults, free for ages 17 and under. Daily 9am–7:30pm. Bus: 23, 40, 62, 280, 982 (to Piazza Pia).

Vatican Museums & the Sistine Chapel ♥♥♥ MUSEUM Nothing else in Rome quite lives up to the awe-inspiring collections of the **Musei Vaticani (Vatican Museums)**, a 15-minute walk from St. Peter's out of the north side of Piazza San Pietro. It's a vast treasure store of art from antiquity and the Renaissance gathered by the Roman Catholic Church through the centuries, filling a series of ornate papal palaces, apartments, and galleries leading to one of the world's most beautiful interiors, the justly celebrated **Cappella Sistina (Sistine Chapel)**. Obviously, one trip is not enough to see everything here. Below are previews of the main highlights, showstoppers, and masterpieces (in alphabetical order).

Note: The Vatican dress code also applies to its museums (no sleeveless blouses, no miniskirts, no shorts, no hats allowed), though it tends to be less rigorously enforced than at St. Peter's.

APPARTAMENTO BORGIA ♥ Created for Pope Alexander VI (the infamous Borgia pope) between 1492 and 1494, these rooms were frescoed with biblical and allegorical scenes by Umbrian painter Pinturicchio and his assistants. Look for what is thought to be the earliest European depiction of Native Americans, painted little more than a year after Columbus returned from the New World and Alexander had "divided" the globe between Spain and Portugal.

COLLEZIONE D'ARTE CONTEMPORANEA ♥ Spanning 55 rooms of almost 800 works, these galleries contain the Vatican's concession to modern art. There are some big names, and themes usually have a spiritual and religious component: Van Gogh's *Pietà, after Delacroix* is here, along with Francis Bacon's eerie *Study for a Pope II*. You will also see works by Paul Klee (*City with Gothic Cathedral*), Siqueiros (*Mutilated Christ No. 467*), Otto Dix (*Road to Calvary*), Gauguin (*Religious Panel*), and Chagall (*Red Pietà*), and a room dedicated to Georges Rouault.

MUSEI DI ANTICHITÀ CLASSICHE ♥♥♥ The Vatican maintains four classical antiquities museums, the most important being the **Museo Pio Clementino ♥♥♥**, crammed with Greek and Roman sculptures in the small Belvedere Palace of Innocent VIII. At the heart of the complex lies the Octagonal Court, where highlights include the sculpture of the Trojan priest ***Laocoön*** **♥♥♥** and his two sons locked in a doomed struggle with sea serpents, dating from around 40 B.C.E., and the exceptional ***Belvedere Apollo*** **♥♥♥** (a 2nd-c. Roman reproduction of a Greek work from the 4th c. B.C.E.), the symbol of classic male beauty and a possible inspiration for Michelangelo's *David.* Look for the impressive gilded bronze statue of ***Hercules*** (late C.E. 2nd c.) in the Rotonda, and the **Hall of the Chariot,** containing a magnificent sculpture of a chariot combining Roman originals and 18th-century work by Francesco Antonio Franzoni.

The **Museo Chiaramonti ♥** occupies the long loggia that links the Belvedere Palace to the main Vatican palaces, jam-packed on both sides with more than 800 Greco-Roman works, including statues, reliefs, and sarcophagi. In the **Braccio Nuovo ♥** (New Wing), a handsome neoclassical extension sumptuously lined with colored marble, lies the colossal statue of the ***Nile*** **♥**, the ancient river portrayed as an old man with his 16

Strategies for Visiting the Vatican Museums

The sheer size of the collections and vast crowds mean that seeing one of the greatest museums of art in the world isn't a leisurely, or even necessarily pleasant, experience. Visitors tend to get herded through room after room of galleries as they make their way to the Sistine Chapel, and lack of descriptive labels means they often don't know what they're looking at. Here are some tips to make sense of it all:

- Book **timed-entry tickets** in advance through the Vatican Museums.
- Do some research in advance and decide which collections you most want to see.
- Once you're in the museum, take a few minutes to review the galleries map and plan out your visit.
- If your priority is to see the Sistine Chapel, follow signs for the "Percorso Breve" (short itinerary) to the Cappella Sistina.

For a deeper experience, consider a breakfast or after-hours visit (p. 85) or springing for a private tour of the collections. These are a great way to get the most out of a visit, especially if you have limited time. They're also the only way to visit the **Vatican Gardens.** Booking online is mandatory; visit **tickets.museivaticani.va** for information. See "Organized Tours" (p. 123) for info on private companies offering Vatican tours.

children, most likely a reproduction of a long-lost Alexandrian Greek original.

The **Museo Gregoriano Profano ♥♥**, built in 1970, houses more Greek sculptures looted by the Romans (some from the Parthenon), mostly funerary stelae and votive reliefs, as well as some choice Roman pieces, notably the restored mosaics from the floors of the public libraries in the **Baths of Caracalla** (p. 96).

MUSEO ETNOLOGICO ♥♥ Founded in 1926, the Ethnological Museum is an astounding assemblage of artifacts and artwork from cultures around the world, from ancient Chinese coins and notes to plaster sculptures of Native Americans and ceremonial art from Papua New Guinea.

MUSEO GREGORIANO EGIZIO ♥♥♥ Nine rooms are packed with plunder from Ancient Egypt, including sarcophagi, mummies, pharaonic statuary, votive bronzes, jewelry, cuneiform tablets from Mesopotamia, inscriptions from Assyrian palaces, and Egyptian hieroglyphics.

MUSEO GREGORIANO ETRUSCO ♥♥ The core of this collection is a cache of rare Etruscan art treasures dug up in the 19th century, dating from between the 9th and the 1st centuries B.C.E. The Romans learned a lot from the Etruscans, as the highly crafted ceramics, bronzes, silver, and gold on display attest. Don't miss the **Regolini-Galassi tomb** (7th c. B.C.E.), unearthed at Cerveteri. The museum is housed within the *palazzettos* of Innocent VIII (reigned 1484–92) and Pius IV (reigned 1559–65), the latter adorned with frescoes by Federico Barocci and Federico Zuccari.

PINACOTECA ♥♥♥ The great painting collections of the popes are displayed in the Pinacoteca, including work from all the big names in Italian art, from Giotto and Fra' Angelico to Perugino, Raphael, Veronese, and Crespi. Early medieval work occupies Room 1, with the most intriguing piece a keyhole-shaped wood panel of the *Last Judgment* by Niccolò e Giovanni, dated to the late 12th century. **Giotto** takes center stage in Room 2, with the *Stefane chi Triptych* (six panels) painted for the old St. Peter's Basilica between 1315 and 1320. **Fra' Angelico** dominates Room 3, his *Stories of St. Nicholas of Bari* and *Virgin with Child* justly praised (check out the Virgin's microscopic eyes in the latter piece). Carlo Crivelli features in Room 6, and decent works by Perugino and Pinturicchio grace Room 7, but most visitors press on to the **Raphael salon ♥♥♥** (Room 8), where you can view five paintings by the Renaissance master. The best are the *Coronation of the Virgin,* the *Madonna of Foligno,* and the vast *Transfiguration* (completed shortly before his death). Room 9 boasts Leonardo da Vinci's ***St. Jerome with the Lion*** **♥♥**, as well as Giovanni Bellini's *Pietà*. Room 10 is dedicated to Renaissance Venice, with Titian's *Madonna of St. Nicholas of the Frari* and Veronese's *Vision of St. Helen* being paramount. Don't skip the remaining galleries: Room 11 contains Barocci's *Annunciation,* while Room 12 is really all about one baroque masterpiece, Caravaggio's ***Deposition from the Cross*** **♥♥**.

Raphael's masterful fresco *School of Athens.*

STANZE DI RAFFAELLO ♥♥♥ In the early 16th century, Pope Julius II hired the young Raphael and his workshop to decorate his personal apartments, on the second floor of the Pontifical Palace. Completed between 1508 and 1524, the **Raphael Rooms** now represent one of the great artistic spectacles inside the Vatican.

The **Stanza dell'Incendio** served as the pope's high court room and later, under Leo X, a dining room. Most of its lavish frescoes have been attributed to Raphael's pupils. Leo X commissioned much of the work here, which explains the themes (past popes named Leo). Note the intricate ceiling, painted by Umbrian maestro Perugino, Raphael's first teacher.

Raphael is the main focus in the **Stanza della Segnatura,** originally used as a papal library and private office; here you'll find the awe-inspiring ***School of Athens*** **♥♥♥** fresco, depicting primarily Greek classical philosophers such as Aristotle, Plato, and Socrates. Many of the figures are thought to be based on portraits of Renaissance artists, including Bramante (on the right as Euclid, drawing on a chalkboard), Leonardo da Vinci (as Plato, the bearded man in the center), and Raphael himself (in the lower-right corner with a black hat). On the wall opposite stands the equally magnificent *Disputa del Sacramento,* where Raphael used a similar technique; Dante Alighieri stands behind the pontiff on the right, and Fra' Angelico poses as a monk (which in fact, he was) on the far left.

The **Stanza di Eliodoro,** where the pope held private audiences, was painted by Raphael immediately after he did the Segnatura. His aim here was to flatter his papal patron, Julius II: The pope is depicted driving Attila from Rome, symbolizing Julius II's mission to push the French out of Italy. Finally, the **Sala di Costantino,** used for papal receptions and official ceremonies, was completed by Raphael's students after his death, but based on his designs and drawings. It's a jaw-dropping space, commemorating four major episodes in the life of Emperor Constantine.

SISTINE CHAPEL ♥♥♥ Michelangelo labored for 4 years (1508–12) to paint the ceiling of the Sistine Chapel; it is said he spent the entire time on his feet, paint dripping into his eyes. Could he have imagined that more than 500 years later, his magnum opus would still be considered one of the greatest accomplishments in Western art? Today, the world's most famous fresco is as vibrantly colorful and filled with roiling life as it was in 1512. And the chapel is still of central importance to the Catholic Church: This is where the Papal Conclave elects new popes, most recently in 2025 with the installation of Leo XIV.

The *Creation of Adam,* at the center of the ceiling, is one of the best known and most reproduced images in history, the outstretched hands of God and Adam—not quite touching—an iconic symbol of not just the Renaissance but the Enlightenment that followed. Nevertheless, it is somewhat ironic that this is Michelangelo's best-known work: The artist always regarded himself as a sculptor first and foremost.

Tip: The ceiling **frescoes** are obviously the main showstoppers, but staring up at them tends to take a heavy toll on the neck. To relieve your neck (and your tired feet), make your way to one of the benches that line both long sides of the gallery. As soon as someone gets up, grab a seat so you can gaze upward in relative comfort.

Commissioned by Pope Julius II in 1508 and completed in 1512, the ceiling frescoes primarily depict nine scenes from the Book of Genesis (including the famed *Creation of Adam*), from the *Separation of Light and Darkness* at the altar end to the *Great Flood* and *Drunkenness of Noah.* Surrounding these main frescoes are paintings of 12 people who prophesied the coming of Christ, from Jonah and Isaiah to the Delphic Sibyl. Once you have admired the ceiling, turn your attention to the altar wall. At the age of 60, Michelangelo was summoned to finish the chapel decor 23 years after he finished the ceiling work. Apparently saddened by leaving Florence and depressed by the morally bankrupt state of Rome at that time, he painted these dark moods in his *Last Judgment,* where he included his own self-portrait on a sagging human hide held by St. Bartholomew (who was martyred by being flayed alive).

Keys, Please

For an extraordinary experience, available only a select number of days each year, join a Vatican Museums head Key Master in opening the doors of the museum galleries, including the Sistine Chapel, and turning on the lights. The tour begins at 6am, hours before the museums open to the public and when its hundreds of galleries are still dark and silent. It's truly a once-in-a-lifetime experience. On the **Get Your Guide** website (getyourguide.com), search for the **"Vatican: Alone in the Sistine Chapel—The Key Master's Tour"** for the latest dates.

Yet the Sistine Chapel isn't all Michelangelo. The southern wall is covered by a series of astonishing paintings completed in the 1480s: *Moses Leaving to Egypt* by Perugino, the *Trials of Moses* by Botticelli, *The Crossing of the Red Sea* by Cosimo Rosselli (or Domenico Ghirlandaio), *Descent from Mount Sinai* by Cosimo Rosselli (or Piero di Cosimo), Botticelli's *Punishment of the Rebels,* and Signorelli's *Testament and Death of Moses.* On the right-hand northern wall are Perugino's *The Baptism of Christ,* Botticelli's *The Temptations of Christ,* Ghirlandaio's *Vocation of the Apostles,* Perugino's *Delivery of the Keys,* and Cosimo Rosselli's *The Sermon on the Mount* and *Last Supper.* On the eastern wall, originals by Ghirlandaio and Signorelli were painted over in the 1570s by Hendrik van den Broeck's *The Resurrection* and Matteo da Lecce's *Disputation over Moses.*

Vatican City, Viale Vaticano (walk around Vatican walls from St. Peter's Square). www.museivaticani.va. ✆ **06-69884676. Advance booking with timed entrance is required.** Admission 25€ adults, 13€ ages 7–18, free for children 6 and under; 2-hr. tours of Vatican Gardens 40€. Mon–Sat 8am–7pm, last Sun every month (free admission) 9am–2pm. Closed Jan 1 and 6, Feb 11, Mar 19, Easter, May 1, June 29, Aug 15, Nov 1, Dec 8, and Dec 25–26. Metro: Ottaviano or Cipro–Musei Vaticani. Buses 23 and 492 to Bastioni di Michelangelo (3-min. walk from entrance), or buses 590, 982, and 19 tram to Piazza del Risorgimento (10-min. walk from entrance).

The Colosseum, Forum & Ancient Rome

THE MAJOR SIGHTS OF ANCIENT ROME

Your sightseeing experience will be enhanced if you know a little about the history and rulers of ancient Rome: See p. 18 for a brief rundown.

Arco di Costantino (Arch of Constantine) ♥♥ MONUMENT

The triumphal arch next to the Colosseum was erected by the Senate in C.E. 315 to honor Constantine's defeat of Maxentius at the Battle of the

The ruins of the Colosseum.

Ancient Rome, Monti & Celio

HOTELS
Duca d'Alba 22
The Glam 26
Inn at the Roman Forum 17
Lancelot 30

ATTRACTIONS
Arco di Costantino 15
Basilica di San Clemente 28
Basilica di San Giovanni in Laterano 31
Case Romane del Celio 14
Circus Maximus 11
Colosseum 16
Domus Aurea (Nero's Golden House) 27
Domus Romane di Palazzo Valentini 2
Fori Imperiale 4
Foro Romano & Palatine Hill 8
Musei Capitolini 7
Museo della Forma Urbis 13
Museo Nazionale del Palazzo di Venezia 1
Museum of the Imperial Forums & Trajan's Markets 3
San Pietro in Vincoli 20
Santa Maria in Aracoeli 6
Santa Maria in Cosmedin 10
Terme di Caracalla 12
Vittoriano 5

RESTAURANTS
Fatamorgana 21
InRoma al Campidoglio 9
La Barrique 25
La Bottega del Caffè 23
La Taverna dei Fori Imperiali 18
Li Rioni 29
Maharajah 24
Taverna Romana "Monti 79" 19

Strategies for Seeing Ancient Rome

Even though they're all included in the same admission fee, the ruins of the **Colosseum, Roman Forum,** and **Palatine Hill** are quite a lot to take in on a single day, particularly in the heat of the Roman summer. But if a day is all you have budgeted, buy your tickets well in advance so that you can choose the earliest morning entry to the Colosseum. Then you'll have the rest of the day for the Forum and Palatine Hill. Since the standard ticket is good for 24 hours, you could also plan to enter the Colosseum by, say, 10am on Day 1, then enter the Forum and Palatine Hill by 10am on Day 2. If you've got more time and interest, buy the 2-day Full Experience ticket (24€), which also gets you access to the arena floor of the Colosseum (p. 89).

Milvian Bridge (C.E. 312). Many of the reliefs have nothing whatsoever to do with Constantine or his works, but they tell of the victories of earlier Antonine rulers (lifted from other, long-forgotten memorials).

The arch marks a period of great change in Western history. Converted to Christianity by a vision on the eve of battle, Constantine ended the centuries-long persecution of the Christians, during which many followers of the new religion had been put to death. Although Constantine didn't ban paganism (which survived officially for another half century or so), he espoused Christianity himself and began the process that ended in the conquest of Rome by the Christian religion.

Btw. Colosseum and Palatine Hill. Metro: Colosseo. Bus: 51, 85, 87, 118. Tram: 3.

Circus Maximus ♥ HISTORIC SITE Now mostly a long, oval-shaped field, the once-grand Circo Massimo was plundered by medieval and Renaissance builders in search of marble and stone—it's a far cry from its *Ben-Hur*–esque heyday. What the Romans called a "circus" was a large arena ringed by tiers of seats and used for sports or spectacles. At one time, 300,000 Romans could assemble here, while the emperor observed the games from his box high on the Palatine Hill. The last games were held in C.E. 549 on the orders of Totila the Goth, who had seized Rome twice. Afterwards, Circus Maximus was never used again, and the demand for building materials reduced it, like so much of Rome, to a great dusty field, now used mostly for big-name rock concerts. An archaeological area at its eastern end (closest to the Metro station) offers insights into how the space once functioned. A 40-minute virtual reality tour (13€, including site admission) does a lot to contextualize the site. ***Tip:*** If you're crunched for time, bypass the Circus Maximus and instead take in the emperor's-eye views of the arena from atop the Palatine Hill.

Btw. Via dei Cerchi and Via del Circo Massimo. sovraintendenzaroma.it (search "Circo Massimo," then translate); see circomaximoexperience.it for VR tour. ✆ **060608.** Archaeological area 5€. Tues–Sun 9:30am–7pm summer (last entrance 6pm), to 5pm winter. Metro: Circo Massimo. Bus: 81, 118, 160.

Colosseum ♥♥♥ ICON No matter how many pictures you've seen, your first view of the Flavian Amphitheater (the Colosseum's original name) is likely to amaze you with its sheer size and ruined grandeur. While you're still outside its massive walls, take time to walk completely around its 500m (1,640-ft.) circumference. It doesn't matter where you start, but do the circle. Look at the various stages of ruin; note the different column styles on each level. Mere photos could never convey its physical impact.

Vespasian ordered the construction of the elliptical bowl in C.E. 72; it was inaugurated by Titus in C.E. 80. Built for gladiatorial contests and wild animal fights, the stadium could hold as many as 87,000 spectators by some counts; seats were sectioned on three levels, dividing the people by social rank and gender. Some 80 entrances allowed massive crowds to be seated and dispersed within a few minutes. When the Roman Empire fell, however, the abandoned arena was eventually overgrown. Much of the travertine that once sheathed its surfaces was used for palaces like the nearby Palazzo Venezia and Palazzo Cancelleria.

Different parts of the amphitheater, including the **Arena Floor and Underground,** as well as the upper tiers or **Attics,** are accessible depending on which ticket you have. Of the several different options, the two pertinent to most visitors are the 24-hour (also called Regular) and Full Experience tickets. Regular tickets (18€) are good for 24 hours from their first activation and include admission to the Colosseum, Roman Forum, and Palatine Hill. Full Experience tickets (24€, valid for 48 hr. from first activation) add the Arena Floor, but not the Underground or Attics, which are available with different tickets. We know, it's confusing. In recent years, archaeological areas of the Palatine and Forum known as the SUPER sites (and normally closed to visitors) are accessible via the full ticket. If you're really interested in the mechanics of the Colosseum, guided educational tours of the Underground (32€) include explanations of the complex system of ramps, elevators, and trap doors that unleashed onto the arena floor the gladiators, wild animals, and array of theatrical effects. The **Passage of Commodus,** a newly restored secret tunnel used by the notorious son and heir of Marcus Aurelius, opened to visitors in late 2025. At press time, access was limited to a few days a week, and only to holders of Full Experience tickets.

Though the pre-ticketing system has eliminated the long line to enter, you still must go through security screening and **present photo ID,** which can take up to an hour on busy days. **Roma Pass holders** must reserve in advance a time to enter the Colosseum, either online or by calling **© 06-39967575,** *or* in person at one of the Forum/Palatine ticket offices the day you wish to enter. Reservations are free, but do not include the Arena Floor, Underground, or Attics.

Piazzale del Colosseo. colosseo.it/en. © **06-39967700.** Admission 18€ pre-purchased online, includes Roman Forum & Palatine Hill; Full Experience ticket including Arena Floor, and SUPER sites of the Palatine 24€. Free for ages 17 and under; 2€ booking fee applies. Daily 8:30am–dusk (as early as 4:30pm in winter, as late as 7:15pm Mar–Aug). Last entry 1 hr. before closing. Metro: Colosseo. Bus: 51, 75, 85, 87, 118. Tram: 3.

Ancient Rome, Recreated in 3D

The ruins of ancient Rome require a lot of imagination, as it's admittedly hard to picture what the Colosseum, Pantheon, and Forum of Trajan looked like at their apex. But a new app is changing that, and in a way that feels surprisingly authentic. **Portyl,** available on Android or IOS, is an interactive augmented reality app that recreates Rome's ancient sites as they once were, complete with sounds, animation, and even a parade of elephants. Created with gaming technology, the results could be cheesy but are not, thanks in large part to precision 3D scans, meticulous attention to detail, and the input of expert Roman archaeologists. For adults, and especially for kids who might tire of all those piles of bricks and stone, the app brings Rome to life in riveting fashion.

Fori Imperiale (Imperial Forums) ♥ RUINS Begun by Julius Caesar to relieve overcrowding in Rome's older forums, the Imperial Forums were, at the time of their construction, flashier, bolder, and more impressive than anything that had come before them in Rome. They conveyed the unquestioned authority of the emperors at the height of their absolute power.

Mussolini, feeling his regime was more important than the ancient one, issued the controversial orders to cut through centuries of debris and buildings to carve out Via dei Fori Imperiali, linking the Colosseum to the 19th-century monuments of Piazza Venezia. Excavations under his Fascist regime uncovered countless archaeological treasures, but most ruins more recent than imperial Rome were destroyed.

The best view of the Forums is from the railings on the north side of Via dei Fori Imperiali; begin where Via Cavour joins the boulevard. Closest to the junction are the remains of the **Forum of Nerva,** built by the emperor whose 2-year reign (C.E. 96–98) followed the assassination of the paranoid Domitian. You'll be struck by how much the ground level has risen in 19 centuries. The only really recognizable remnant is a wall of the Temple of Minerva with two fine Corinthian columns. The next along is the **Forum of Augustus** ♥♥, built to commemorate Emperor Augustus's victory over Julius Caesar's assassins, Cassius and Brutus, in the Battle of Philippi (42 B.C.E.). Continuing along the railing, you'll see the vast, multilevel semicircle of **Trajan's Markets** ♥♥, essentially an ancient shopping mall whose arcades were once stocked with merchandise from the far corners of the Roman world. You can visit the part that has been transformed into the **Museum of the Imperial Forums & Trajan's Markets** (p. 95).

In front of the Markets, the **Forum of Trajan** ♥♥ was built between C.E. 107 and 113, designed by Greek architect Apollodorus of Damascus (who also laid out the adjoining market). Many fragments and pedestals still bear legible inscriptions, but more interesting is the great Basilica Ulpia, whose gray marble columns rise roofless into the sky. This forum was once regarded as one of the architectural wonders of the world. Beyond the Basilica Ulpia is **Trajan's Column** ♥♥♥, in magnificent condition, with an intricate bas-relief sculpture depicting Trajan's victorious campaign in Dacia (modern Romania).

The **Forum of Julius Caesar ♥♥**, the first of the Imperial Forums to be built, lies on the opposite side of Via dei Fori Imperiali, adjacent to the Roman Forum. This was the site of the stock exchange as well as the Temple of Venus.

Along Via dei Fori Imperiali. 24-hr. Colosseum ticket includes entrance to the grounds of the Imperial Forums, or you can view them from street level. Metro: Colosseo. Bus: 51, 75, 85, 87, 118.

Foro Romano (Roman Forum) & Palatino (Palatine Hill) ♥♥♥

RUINS Traversed by the **Via Sacra ♥** (Sacred Way), the main thoroughfare of ancient Rome, the Roman Forum flourished as the center of religious, social, and commercial life in the days of the Republic, before it gradually lost prestige (but never spiritual draw) to the Imperial Forums (see above). You'll see ruins and fragments, partially intact columns, and monumental arches, and you'll feel the rush of history here. That any semblance of the Forum remains today is miraculous: It was used for years as a quarry (as was the Colosseum) and eventually became a cow pasture. Excavations in the 19th century and later in the 1930s began to bring to light one of the world's most historic spots.

You can spend at least a morning wandering the ruins of the Forum. Enter via the gate on Via dei Fori Imperiali, at Via della Salara Vecchia. There's another entrance near the Colosseum close to the Arch of Titus, though our itinerary assumes you'll enter at the Via Salara Vecchia. Turn right at the bottom of the entrance slope to walk west along the old Via Sacra toward the arch. Just before it on your right is the large brick **Curia Iulia ♥♥**, the main seat of the Roman Senate, built by Julius Caesar, rebuilt by Diocletian, and consecrated as a church in C.E. 630.

The triumphal **Arch of Septimius Severus ♥♥** (C.E. 203) is the next important sight, displaying time-bitten reliefs of the emperor's victories in

The ruins of the Foro Romano offer a window into life in ancient Rome.

THREE free views TO SAVOR FOR A LIFETIME

The Forum from the Campidoglio Standing on Piazza del Campidoglio, outside the Musei Capitolini (p. 94), walk around the right or left side of the Palazzo Senatorio to terraces overlooking the best panoramas of the Roman Forum, with the Palatine Hill and Colosseum as a backdrop. At night, the ruins look even more haunting when the Forum is dramatically floodlit.

The Whole City from the Janiculum Hill From many vantage points in the Eternal City, the views are panoramic. But one of the best spots for a memorable vista is the Janiculum Hill (*Gianicolo*) above Trastevere. Laid out before you are Rome's rooftops, peppered with domes ancient and modern. From up here, you will understand why Romans complain about the 19th-century Vittoriano (p. 99)—it's a gigantic white shock in a sea of rose- and honey-colored stone. Walk 50 yards north of the balcony where all the tour buses stop, and you'll get a slightly better angle from the Belvedere 9 Febbraio 1849. Views from the 1612 Fontana dell'Acqua Paola are also splendid, especially at night.

The Aventine Hill & the Priori dei Cavalieri di Malta The mythical site of Remus's original settlement, the Aventine (*Aventino*) is now a leafy residential neighborhood blessed with some magical views. From Via del Circo Massimo, walk through the gardens along Via di Valle Murcia, and keep walking in a straight line. Along your right side, the Giardino degli Aranci (Orange Tree Garden) offers views over the dome of St. Peter's. When you reach Piazza dei Cavalieri di Malta, look through the keyhole of the Priory gate (on the right) for a "secret" view of the Vatican.

what are now Iran and Iraq. During the Middle Ages, Rome became a provincial backwater, and frequent flooding of the Tiber helped bury (and thus preserve) most of the Forum. Some bits did still stick out above ground, including the top half of this arch, which was used to shelter a barbershop! Just to the left of the arch, you can make out the remains of a cylindrical lump of rock with some marble steps curving off it. That round stone was the **Umbilicus Urbus,** considered the center of Rome and of the entire Roman Empire; the curving steps are those of the **Imperial Rostra** ♥, where great orators and legislators stood to speak and the people gathered to listen. Nearby, a much-photographed trio of fluted columns with Corinthian capitals supports a bit of architrave from the corner of the **Temple of Vespasian and Titus** ♥♥. (Emperors were routinely turned into gods upon dying.) Head to your left toward the eight Ionic columns marking the front of the **Temple of Saturn** ♥♥ (rebuilt in 42 B.C.E.), which housed the first treasury of Republican Rome. It was also the site of one of the Roman year's biggest annual blowout festivals, the December 17 feast of Saturnalia, which, after a bit of tweaking, Christians now celebrate as Christmas. Turn left to start heading back east, past the worn steps and stumps of brick pillars outlining the enormous **Basilica Julia** ♥♥, built by Julius Caesar. Farther along, on the right, are the three

Corinthian columns of the **Temple of the Dioscuri ♥♥♥**, dedicated to the Gemini twins, Castor and Pollux. Forming one of the most photogenic sights of the Roman Forum, a trio of columns supports an architrave fragment. The founding of this temple dates from the 5th century B.C.E.

Beyond the bit of curving wall that marks the site of the little round **Temple of Vesta** (rebuilt several times after fires started by the sacred flame within), you'll find the reconstructed **House of the Vestal Virgins** (C.E. 3rd–4th c.), home of the consecrated young women who tended the sacred flame. Chosen from patrician families to serve a 30-year-long priesthood, these women were among Rome's most venerated citizens, with unique powers such as the ability to pardon condemned criminals. The cult was quite serious about the "virgin" part of the job description—if a Vestal was found to have broken her vow of chastity, she was buried alive, because it was forbidden to shed a Vestal's blood. (Her amorous accomplice was merely flogged to death.) The overgrown rectangle of their gardens is lined with broken, heavily worn statues of senior Vestals on pedestals.

The path dovetails back to Via Sacra. Turn right, walk past the so-called Temple of Romulus, and then left to enter the massive brick remains of the 4th-century **Basilica of Constantine and Maxentius ♥♥** (Basilica di Massenzio). These were Rome's public law courts, and their architectural style was adopted by early Christians for their houses of worship (the reason so many ancient churches are called "basilicas").

Return to the path and continue toward the Colosseum. Veer right to the Forum's second great triumphal arch, the extensively rebuilt **Arch of Titus ♥♥** (C.E. 81). One relief depicts the looting of treasures from Jerusalem's temple—look closely and you'll see a menorah among the booty. The war that this arch glorifies ended with the expulsion of Jews from the colonized Judea, signaling the beginning of the Jewish Diaspora throughout Europe. You can exit behind the Arch to continue to the Colosseum, or head up to the Palatine Hill.

Above the Forum looms the **Palatine Hill ♥♥** (Palatino), where Romulus, after eliminating his twin brother Remus, founded Rome around 753 B.C.E. After a gradual climb to the top of the hill, visitors are presented with a sprawling, mostly crowd-free archaeological garden, with some shady spots for cooling off in summer. The Palatine was where the first settlers built their huts under the direction of Romulus; in later years, it became a patrician residential district that attracted such citizens as Cicero. In time, however, the area was gobbled up by imperial palaces and drew an infamous roster of tenants, such as Livia (some of the frescoes in the House of Livia are in miraculous condition), Tiberius, Caligula (murdered here by members of his Praetorian Guard), Nero, and Domitian. A museum houses some of the most important

Famine in the Forum

While you'll find a few water fountains on the Palatine and in the Forum, there is no place to eat, other than some vending machines near the Domus Tiberiana. If you're making a day of it, pack some snacks.

finds from hill excavations. Portions of the **houses of Augustus ♥♥ and his wife Livia ♥♥** are open to those who purchase the Full Experience ticket, which also includes other Palatine sites not normally open to the public. Only the ruins of the Palatine's grandeur remain today, but it's worth the climb for the panoramic views of the Roman and Imperial Forums, as well as the Capitoline Hill, the Colosseum, and Circus Maximus. You can also enter from here and do the entire tour in reverse.

Forum entrance on Via dei Fori Imperiali at Via della Salara Vecchia. Palatine Hill entrance at Via di San Gregorio 30 (south of the Colosseum). colosseo.it/en. ✆ **06-39967700.** Admission 18€ pre-purchased online (includes Colosseum); Full Experience ticket 24€. Free for ages 17 and under; 2€ booking fee applies. Daily 9am–dusk (as early as 4:30pm in winter and as late as 7:15pm Mar–Aug). Last entry 1 hr. before closing. Metro: Colosseo. Bus: 51, 75, 85, 87, 118. Tram: 3.

Musei Capitolini (Capitoline Museums) ♥♥ MUSEUM The masterpieces here are considered Rome's most valuable (recall that the Vatican Museums are *not* technically in Rome). They certainly were collected early: This is the oldest public museum *in the world.* Try and schedule adequate time, as there's much to see.

First stop is the courtyard of the **Palazzo dei Conservatori** (the building designed by Michelangelo, on the right of the piazza if you enter via the ramp from Piazza Venezia). It's scattered with gargantuan stone body parts—the remnants of a massive 12m (39-ft.) statue of the emperor Constantine, including his colossal head, hand, and foot. It's nearly impossible to resist posing for a photo next to the giant finger.

On the *palazzo*'s ground floor, the unmissable works are in the first series of rooms. These include ***Lo Spinario*** (Room 3), a lifelike bronze of

The Capitoline Museums display a wealth of classical statuary.

a young boy digging a splinter out of his foot that was widely copied during the Renaissance; and the ***Lupa Capitolina*** (Room 4), a bronze statue of the famous she-wolf that suckled Romulus and Remus, the mythical founders of Rome. Scholars disagree on the date of the statue: It was long thought to be from around 500 B.C.E., but recent analysis suggests it may be from the 1100s. What is certain is that the twins were not on the original statue but were added in the 15th century. Room 5 has Bernini's famously pained portrait of ***Medusa,*** even more compelling when you see its writhing serpent hairdo in person.

Before heading upstairs, go toward the newer wing at the rear, which houses the original equestrian **statue of Marcus Aurelius** ♥♥♥, dating to around C.E. 180—the piazza outside, where it stood from 1538 until 2005, now has a copy. There's a giant bronze head from a statue of Constantine (ca. C.E. 337) and the foundations of the original Temple of Jupiter, which stood on the Capitoline Hill since its inauguration in 509 B.C.E.

The second-floor **picture gallery** ♥ is strong on baroque oil paintings. Highlights include Caravaggio's *John the Baptist* and *The Fortune Teller* (1595) and Guido Reni's *St. Sebastian* (1615).

A tunnel takes you under the piazza to the other part of the Capitoline Museums, the **Palazzo Nuovo,** via the **Tabularium** ♥♥. Built in 78 B.C.E. to house ancient Rome's city records, it was later used as a salt mine and then as a prison. Here, the moody *galleria lapidaria* houses a well-executed exhibit of ancient portrait tombstones and sarcophagi, many of their poignant epitaphs translated into English, and provides access to one of the best balcony **views** ♥♥♥ in Rome: along the length of the Forum toward the Palatine Hill.

Much of the Palazzo Nuovo is dedicated to statues excavated from the forums below and brought in from outlying areas like Hadrian's Villa in Tivoli (p. 161). If you're running short on time, head straight for Room 3 and the 1st-century ***Capitoline Venus*** ♥♥, modestly covering up after a bath, and, in Rooms 4 and 5, a chronologically arranged row of distinct, expressive busts of Roman emperors and their families. Another favorite is the beyond handsome ***Dying Gaul*** ♥♥, a Roman copy of a lost ancient Greek work. Lord Byron considered the statue so moving that he mentioned it in his poem *Childe Harold's Pilgrimage.*

Piazza del Campidoglio 1. museicapitolini.org. ✆ **060608.** Admission 15€ (more during special exhibits) adults, 9.50€ ages 7–18, free for children 6 and under; 15.50€ for 7-day ticket that includes Centrale Montemartini. Daily 9:30am–7:30pm. Last entry 1 hr. before closing. Bus: 40, 44, 60, 63, 64, 70, 118, 160, 170, 628, 716 or any bus that stops at Piazza Venezia.

Museo dei Fori Imperiali (Museum of the Imperial Forums) & Mercati di Traiano (Trajan's Markets) ♥♥ RUINS/MUSEUM

Built on three levels, Emperor Trajan's Market housed 150 shops and commercial offices—think of it as the world's first shopping mall. Grooves still evident in the thresholds allowed merchants to slide doors shut and lock up for the night. You're likely to have the covered, tunnel-like market halls mostly to yourself—making the ancient past feel all the more present in this overlooked site. The Museum of the Imperial Forums occupies a converted section of the market, and excellent visual displays help you imagine what these grand public squares and temples used to look like. All in all, it's home to 172 marble fragments from the Fori Imperiali, as well as remnants from the Forum of Augustus and Forum of Nerva.

Via IV Novembre 94. mercatiditraiano.it. ✆ **060608.** Admission 15€ adults (more during special exhibits), 9.50€ ages 6–25, free for children 5 and under. Daily 9:30am–7:30pm. Last admission 1 hr. before closing. Bus: 40, 60, 64, 70, 170.

Terme di Caracalla (Baths of Caracalla) ♥♥ RUINS Built during the reign of the despotic Emperor Caracalla, the Baths of Caracalla were completed in C.E. 217, the same year as his assassination. The richness of decoration has faded, but the massive brick ruins and the mosaic fragments that remain give modern visitors an idea of the complex's scale and grandeur. In their heyday, the baths sprawled over 11 hectares (27 acres) and included hot, cold, and tepid pools, as well as a *palestra* (gym) and changing rooms. A museum in the tunnels below the complex—built over an even more ancient *mithraeum,* a worship site of an eastern cult—explores the hydraulic and heating systems (and slave power) needed to serve 8,000 or so Romans per day. Summer operatic performances here are an ethereal treat (p. 156).

Via delle Terme di Caracalla 52. museiitaliani.it (search for "Caracalla"). ✆ **06-57174520.** Admission 8€ (13€ with special exhibits) adults, free for ages 17 and under. Tues–Sun 9am–dusk (as early as 4:30pm or as late as 7:15pm). Last entry 1 hr. before closing. Bus: 118 or 628. Metro: Circo Massimo.

OTHER ATTRACTIONS NEAR ANCIENT ROME

Basilica di San Clemente ♥♥ CHURCH A perfect example of how layers of history overlap in Rome, this 12-century Norman church, full of beautiful Byzantine mosaics, hides much more. Down in its eerie grottos are frescoes and mosaic floors from its previous incarnations as a 4th-century Christian church and a temple dedicated to the pagan deity Mithras—and below that, the foundations of a Roman house from the 1st century, where early Christians worshipped in secret. Listen for the rush of water from an ancient channel that still runs through the ruins.

Via San Giovanni in Laterano (at Piazza San Clemente). basilicasanclemente.com. ✆ **06-7740021.** Free admission to Basilica; excavations 10€ (advance booking recommended), 5€ ages 18–26, free for ages 17 and under. Mon–Sat 9am–12:30pm and 2–6pm; Sun noon–6pm. Last entry 30 min. before closing. Metro: Colosseo. Bus: 51, 85, 87, 117. Tram: 3.

Basilica di San Giovanni in Laterano ♥♥ CHURCH This church, not St. Peter's, is officially the cathedral of the diocese of Rome; the pope celebrates Mass here on certain holidays. Though it was built in 314 by Constantine, only parts of the original baptistery remain; what you see today is an 18th-century facade by Alessandro Galilei (note signs of damage from a 1993 terrorist bomb) and an interior by Borromini, built for

NERO'S golden HOUSE

After the Great Fire of C.E. 64, charismatic, despotic Emperor Nero staged a land grab to facilitate construction of his *Domus Aurea,* or Golden House, a massive gilded villa complex covering all or parts of the Palatine, Esquiline, and Caelian hills, displaying a level of ostentation and excess unheard of even among past emperors. After his death by noble suicide in C.E. 68, a campaign to erase all traces of Nero from the imperial city ensured that the palace was stripped of its gold, marble, jewels, mosaics, and statuary, then intentionally buried under millions of tons of rubble. It remained buried until the Renaissance, when young artists, including Raphael, descended into its "grottos" (actually the vaulted ceilings) to study the fanciful frescoes—the term grotesque (*grotto-esque*) comes from here. Later excavations revealed the scale and richness of the villa, but also subjected it to catastrophic moisture damage. The Domus Aurea is open for tours—but only if you time your trip well and plan ahead. **Guided tours** (colosseo.it/en/area/the-domus-aurea; 26€ adults, 8€ ages 17 and under) of the underground site are currently offered on Friday, Saturday, and Sunday, only with advance reservations. The tour includes a spectacular **virtual reality experience ♥♥♥** that in itself is worth the visit. The site closes sporadically during the year. ***Tip:*** Frustratingly, online resellers snap up all the English-language tour tickets as soon as they're available. The only sure way to get tickets is to wait online for the exact moment sales open—which is 30 days to the minute before the tour time and date—and be ready to pounce. Otherwise, you'll have to find tickets through an online travel agency.

Pope Innocent X. In a misguided redecoration long ago, frescoes by Giotto were apparently destroyed; remains attributed to Giotto, discovered in 1952, are displayed against the first inner column on the right.

Across the street is the **Santuario della Scala Santa** (Palace of the Holy Steps), Piazza San Giovanni in Laterano 14 (✆ **06-7726641**), a set of 28 marble steps supposedly brought from Jerusalem by Constantine's mother, Helen. Though some historians say the stairs might date only from the 4th century, legend claims these were the stairs Christ climbed at Pontius Pilate's villa the day he was sentenced to death. Today pilgrims from the world over come here to climb the steps on their knees.

Piazza San Giovanni in Laterano 4. ✆ **06-69886433.** Free admission. Daily 7am–6:30pm. Metro: San Giovanni.

Case Romane del Celio ♥♥ RUINS Beneath the 5th-century Basilica of SS. Giovanni e Paolo lies a fascinating archaeological site: a complex of Roman houses of different periods—a wealthy family's townhouse from the 2nd century and a 3rd-century apartment building for artisans. According to tradition, the latter was the home of two Roman officers, John and Paul (not the Apostles), who were beheaded during the reign of Julian the Apostate (361–63) for refusing to serve in a military campaign. They were later made saints, and their bones were said to have been buried here. The two-story construction also contains a small museum with finds from the site and fragmentary 12th-century frescoes. ***Note:*** We recommend visiting the basilica, if it's open, as well as the nearby **Museo della Forma Urbis** (see below).

Piazza Santi Giovanni e Paolo 13 (entrance on Clivo di Scauro). caseromanedelcelio.it/en. ✆ **06-70454544.** Admission 10€ adults, 8€ children 6–14, 2€ ages 5 and under. Thurs–Mon 10am–1pm; 3pm–6pm. Last entry 1 hr. before closing. Metro: Colosseo or Circo Massimo. Bus: 75, 81, 118. Tram: 3.

Domus Romane di Palazzo Valentini ♥♥♥ RUINS/EXHIBIT All too often in Italy, archaeological sites are presented with little context, and it's difficult for untrained eyes to really understand what they're seeing. Not so at Palazzo Valentini, possibly Rome's best-presented ancient site. Visitors descend underneath a Renaissance *palazzo* and peer through a glass floor into the remains of several upscale Roman homes. Through innovative 3D projections, the walls, ceilings, floors, and fountains of these once-grand houses spring to life, offering a captivating look at lives of the ancient rich and possibly famous.

Via Foro Traiano 85 (near Trajan's Column). palazzovalentini.it. ✆ **06-22761280.** Admission 16.50€ adults, 9.50€ children 6–14, 1.50€ children 5 and under. Wed–Mon 10am–7pm timed entrance (6pm in winter), with guided tours in English several times daily; reservations suggested. Last entry 5:30pm (4:30pm in winter). Metro: Colosseo. Bus: 40, 63, 70, 81, 83, 87, or any bus to Piazza Venezia. Tram: 8.

Museo della Forma Urbis ♥♥ MUSEUM If you've made the trek to the fairly out-of-the-way Case Romane del Celio (see above), then it's definitely worth stopping at this small museum and open-air archaeological park inaugurated in 2024. The museum contains the remaining fragments of the Forma Urbis, known to scholars as the Marble Map—the enormous scale map of 3rd-century Rome, carved into marble slabs. Though little remains of the incredibly detailed ancient map, the museum re-creates the entire map under a glass floor. The adjacent park contains tomb monuments, temple fragments, and engravings.

Entrance at Viale del Parco del Celio 20-22 or Clivo di Scauro 4. sovraintendenzaroma.it/content/il-museo-della-forma-urbis. ✆ **060608.** Admission 11€ adults, 6.50€ ages 6–25, free for children 5 and under; free to enter park. Museum Tues–Sun 10am–7pm (to 4pm in winter); last entry 1 hr. before closing. Park daily 7am–dusk. Metro: Colosseo or Circo Massimo. Bus: 75, 81, 118. Tram: 3.

Museo Nazionale del Palazzo di Venezia ♥ MUSEUM Best remembered today as Mussolini's Fascist headquarters in Rome, the palace was built in the 1450s as the Rome outpost of the Republic of Venice—hence the name. Today, several of its rooms house an eclectic mix of European paintings and decorative and religious objects spanning centuries; highlights include Giorgione's enigmatic *Double Portrait* and some early Tuscan altarpieces. Given the many museum options in Rome, we'd save this one for a rainy day.

Via del Plebiscito 118. vive.cultura.gov.it/en/palazzo-venezia. ✆ **06-69994211.** Admission 18€ adults, 5€ ages 18–25, free for ages 17 and under, valid for 7 days; includes entrance to the Vittoriano monument (p. 99). Daily 9:30am–7:30pm. Bus: 30, 40, 46, 62, 64, 70, 87, or any bus to Piazza Venezia. Tram: 8.

San Pietro in Vincoli (St. Peter in Chains) ♥♥ CHURCH Founded in the 5th century to house the chains (*vincoli*) that supposedly bound St. Peter in Jerusalem (preserved under glass below the main altar), this lovely church is mainly worth visiting to see one of the world's most famous sculptures: **Michelangelo's *Moses* ♥♥**, carved for the tomb of Pope Julius II. Michelangelo never completed the 44 magnificent figures planned for the tomb, but this "minor" figure he did complete now numbers among his masterpieces.

Piazza San Pietro in Vincoli 4A. ✆ **06-97844952.** Free admission. Daily 8am–12:30pm and 3–7pm. Metro: Colosseo or Cavour. Bus: 75, 117.

Santa Maria in Aracoeli ♥♥ CHURCH This plain-on-the-outside church is worth the climb for its splendid interior. According to legend, Augustus ordered a temple erected on this spot on the Capitoline Hill, where a sibyl foretold the coming of Christ. The current church, built for the Franciscans in the 13th century, boasts a coffered Renaissance ceiling and the tomb of Giovanni Crivelli carved by the great Renaissance sculptor Donatello. The **Cappella Bufalini ♥** (first chapel on the right) was frescoed by Pinturicchio with scenes of the life and death of St. Bernardino of Siena. A chapel behind the altar contains the **Santo Bambino,** a wooden figure of the Baby Jesus that's venerated every Christmas Eve. The long flight of stairs leading up to the church was built in 1348 to celebrate the end of the Black Plague.

Scala dell'Arcicapitolina 12. ✆ **06-69763838.** Free admission. Daily 9am–12:30pm; 3–6:30pm. Bus: 30, 40, 46, 62, 64, 70, 87, or any bus to Piazza Venezia.

Santa Maria in Cosmedin ♥ CHURCH People line up outside this ancient church not for great art treasures (though it's worth a peek inside), but for the ***Mouth of Truth,*** a large disk on the wall of the portico. As Gregory Peck demonstrated to Audrey Hepburn in the film *Roman Holiday*, the mouth is supposed to chomp down on the hands of liars. It may have been an ancient drain cover, though one hypothesis says it was a so-called talking statue, where anonymous notes were left to betray wrongdoers. Our take? Save this hokey photo op until you've seen everything else you want to see in Rome.

Piazza della Bocca della Verità 18. ✆ **06-6787759.** Free admission. Daily 9:30am–6pm (5pm winter). Bus: 30, 44, 81, 83, 85, 87, 118, 160, 628, 715.

All Roads Lead to . . . Piazza Venezia

Love it or loathe it, the massive Vittoriano monument at Piazza Venezia is a helpful landmark for visitors to get their bearings, and almost every bus line convenient to tourists stops here. Streets fanning out from the piazza lead to Termini Station, the Colosseum, the Trevi Fountain, and across the Tiber to the Vatican and Trastevere.

Vittoriano (Altare della Patria) ♥ MONUMENT It's impossible to miss the white marble Vittorio Emanuele monument dominating Piazza

Venezia. Built in the late 1800s to honor the first king of a united Italy, this flamboyant (and widely disliked) landmark has been compared to everything from a wedding cake to a Victorian typewriter, its harsh white color glaring in a city of honey-gold tones. An eternal flame burns at the Tomb of the Unknown Soldier. For a panoramic city view, take a glass elevator to the **Terrazza delle Quadrighe** ♥ (Terrace of the Chariots).

Piazza Venezia. vive.cultura.gov.it/en. ✆ **06-6780664.** Admission 18€ adults, 5€ ages 18–25, free for ages 17 and under, valid for 7 days; includes admission to Palazzo Venezia; p. 98). Daily 9:30am–7:30pm (last entry 6:45pm). Bus: 30, 40, 46, 62, 64, 70, 87, or any bus to Piazza Venezia.

Centro Storico & the Pantheon

Just across the Tiber from the Vatican and Castel Sant'Angelo lies the true heart of Rome, the ***centro storico,*** or "historic center," the triangular wedge of land that bulges into a bend of the river. Although the area was outside the Roman city, it came into its own during the Renaissance, and today its streets and alleys are crammed with piazzas, elegant churches, and lavish fountains, all buzzing with scooters and people. It's a wonderful area in which to wander and get lost.

PIAZZA NAVONA & NEARBY ATTRACTIONS

Rome's most famous square, **Piazza Navona** ♥♥♥, is a gorgeous baroque gem, lined with cafes and restaurants and often full of tourists, street artists, and pigeons. Its long oval shape follows the contours of the old ruined Roman Stadium of Domitian, where chariot races once took place, made over in the mid–17th century by Pope Innocent X. The twin-towered facade of 17th-century **Sant'Agnese in Agone** lies on the piazza's western side, while the **Fontana dei Quattro Fiumi** ♥♥♥ (Fountain of the Four Rivers) opposite is one of three great fountains in the square and a typically exuberant creation by Bernini, topped with an Egyptian obelisk. The four stone personifications below symbolize the world's greatest rivers: the Ganges, Danube, de la Plata, and Nile. It's fun to try to figure out which is which. (***Hint:*** The figure with the shroud on its head is the Nile, so represented because the river's source was unknown at the time.) At the south end is Bernini's **Fontana del Moro** (Fountain of the Moor) and the 19th-century **Fontana di Nettuno** (Fountain of Neptune).

Art lovers should make the short walk from the piazza to **Santa Maria della Pace** ♥♥ on Arco della Pace, a 15th-century church given the usual baroque makeover by Pietro da Cortona in the 1660s. The real gems are inside, beginning with Raphael's ***Four Sibyls*** ♥♥ fresco, above the arch of the Cappella Chigi, and the **Chiostro del Bramante** ♥ (Bramante cloister), built between 1500 and 1504 and the Renaissance master's first work in the city. The church is normally open daily from 9:30am to 6:30pm, while the cloister opens daily 10am to 8pm (Sat–Sun until 9pm); admission to the church and cloister is free (www.chiostrodelbramante.it). ***Tip:*** Waiters from Piazza Navona's many overpriced restaurants lie in

ATTRACTIONS

Campo de' Fiori **29**
Fontana delle Tartarughe **35**
Galleria Doria Pamphilj **23**
Jewish Museum of Rome & Great Synagogue **37**
Palazzo Altemps **5**
Palazzo Farnese **30**
Palazzo Spada **32**
The Pantheon **18**
Piazza Navona **15**
Sacred Area of Largo Argentina **34**
San Luigi dei Francesi **16**
Sant'Agnese in Agone **14**
Santa Maria della Pace **8**
Santa Maria sopra Minerva **21**

HOTELS

Albergo Santa Chiara **20**
Chapter Roma **39**
citizenM Roma Isola Tiberina **38**
Coronari Palace **6**
Damaso Hotel **27**
Hotel L'Orologio **25**
Mimosa **19**
Raphael **7**
Residenza in Farnese **31**
Singer Palace **22**

RESTAURANTS

Alfredo e Ada **10**
Antica Hostaria Romanesca **28**
Antico Forno Roscioli **33**
Casa Coppelle **4**
Da Baffetto **12**
Frigidarium **13**
Gelateria del Teatro **9**
Il Bacaro **3**
La Campana **1**
La Vecchia Locanda **24**
L'Insalata Ricca **26**
Nonna Betta **36**
Pietro al Pantheon **17**
Pipero Roma **11**
Retrobottega **2**

wait, hoping to woo passing tourists. While the setting is unmatchable, you'll find far better meals on the side streets off the piazza.

Palazzo Altemps ♥♥ MUSEUM Inside this 15th-century *palazzo,* today a branch of the National Museum of Rome, is one of the city's most charming museums housing some of its most famous private and public art collections. Much of it was once part of the famed **Boncompagni Ludovisi Collection,** created by Cardinal Ludovico Ludovisi (1595–1632) and sold at auction in 1901. Among the highlights is the ***Ludovisi Ares*** **♥♥**, a handsome 2nd-century copy of an earlier Greek statue of Mars (Ares to the Greeks). Equally renowned is the ***Ludovisi Gaul*** **♥**, a marble depiction of a Gaulish warrior plunging a sword into his chest rather than become a slave of Rome; looking backward defiantly, he supports a dying woman with his left arm. Also worth a look is the ***Ludovisi Throne,*** a sculpted block of white marble, thought to date from the 5th century B.C.E., depicting Aphrodite rising from the sea.

Piazza di Sant'Apollinare 46. museonazionaleromano.beniculturali.it. ✆ **06-39967700.** Admission 15€ (valid for 1 week, also includes Palazzo Massimo and the Baths of Diocletian); free for ages 17 and under. Tues–Sun 9:30am–7pm. Last entry 1 hr. before closing. Bus: 70, 81, 87, 492, 628.

San Luigi dei Francesi ♥♥ CHURCH For a painter of such stratospheric standards as Caravaggio, it is impossible definitively to name his "masterpiece." However, the ***Calling of St. Matthew*** **♥♥♥**, in the far-left chapel of Rome's French church, must be a candidate. Done in Caravaggio's distinct *chiaroscuro* (extreme light and shade) style, the panel dramatizes the moment Jesus and Peter "called" Matthew, a customs officer, to join them. Around the same time (1599–1602) Caravaggio also painted the other two St. Matthew panels in the Cappella Contarelli, including one depicting the saint's martyrdom. Other church highlights include Domenichino's masterful *Histories of Saint Cecilia* fresco cycle. Scan the QR code at the entrance for a free audioguide in English.

Via di Santa Giovanna d'Arco 5. saintlouis-rome.net. ✆ **06-688271.** Free admission. Mon–Fri 9:30am–12:45pm; Sat 9:30am–noon; Sun noon–12:45pm, plus daily 2:30–6:30pm. Bus: 30, 70, 81, 87, 492, 628.

THE PANTHEON & NEARBY ATTRACTIONS

The Pantheon stands on **Piazza della Rotonda,** a lively square with outdoor cafes and great people-watching.

Galleria Doria Pamphilj ♥♥ ART MUSEUM One of the city's finest rococo palaces, the Palazzo Doria Pamphilj is still privately owned by the aristocratic Doria Pamphilj family, but their stupendous art collection is open to the public. The *galleria* winds through their old apartments, with paintings displayed floor-to-ceiling among antique furniture and richly decorated walls. The strong Dutch and Flemish collection includes Pieter Bruegel the Elder's *Battle in the Port of Naples,* and his son Jan Brueghel the Elder's *Earthly Paradise with Original Sin.* Among the best Italian works are two Caravaggio paintings, the moving *Repentant Magdalene* and his wonderful *Rest on the Flight into Egypt,* hanging near Titian's *Salome with the Head of St. John.* There's also Raphael's *Double Portrait,* an *Annunciation* by Filippo Lippi, and a *Deposition from the Cross* by Vasari. The gallery's real treasures occupy a special room: Bernini's bust of the Pamphilj ***Pope Innocent X*** ♥, and Velázquez's **enigmatic painting** ♥♥ of the same man. Make sure you grab a free audioguide at the entrance—it's colorfully narrated by Prince Jonathan Doria Pamphilj himself, who recalls roller-skating in the *palazzo* as a child. Reservations required. Via del Corso 305 (just north of Piazza Venezia). doriapamphilj.it. ✆ **06-6797323.** Admission 17€ adults, 1€ children 12 and under. Mon, Tues, Thurs 9am–7pm; Fri–Sun 10am–8pm; last entry 1 hr. before closing. Bus: 64 or any to Piazza Venezia.

The Pantheon ♥♥♥ HISTORIC SITE Stumbling onto Piazza della Rotunda from the dark warren of streets surrounding it will likely leave you agape, marveling at one of ancient Rome's great buildings—the only one that remains intact. The Pantheon ("Temple to All the Gods") was first built in 27 B.C.E. by Marcus Agrippa but was entirely reconstructed by Hadrian in the early 2nd century C.E. This remarkable building, 43m (142 ft.) wide and 43m (142 ft.) high, is among the architectural wonders of the world, even today. Hadrian himself is credited with the basic plan: a perfect sphere resting in a cylinder. There are no visible arches or vaults holding up the dome; instead they're sunk into the concrete of the building's walls. The ribbed dome outside is a series of cantilevered bricks.

Animals were once sacrificed and burned in the center, with the smoke escaping through the only means of light, the oculus, an opening at

With its perfectly cantilevered dome, the Pantheon is one of the architectural wonders of the world.

the top 5.5m (18 ft.) in diameter. The interior was richly decorated, with white marble statues ringing the central space in its niches. Nowadays, apart from the jaw-dropping size of the space, the main items of interest are the tombs of two Italian kings (Vittorio Emanuele II and his successor, Umberto I) and the artist **Raphael** (fans still bring him flowers), with its poignant epitaph. Since the 7th century, the Pantheon has been used as a Catholic church, the **Santa Maria ad Martyres,** also known as Santa Maria della Rotonda. ***Tip:*** It's best to buy tickets online, as only a limited number of tickets are sold on a walk-up basis. If you opt to try walk-up, skip the longer line at the cash-only machine and go to the credit card line to get in faster.

Piazza della Rotonda. museiitaliani.it. ✆ **06-68300230.** Admission 5€ adults, free for ages 17 and under. Daily 9am–7pm (last entry 6:30pm). Bus: 30, 40, 62, 64, 81, 87, or 492 to Largo di Torre Argentina.

Santa Maria sopra Minerva ♥♥ CHURCH Just 1 block behind the Pantheon, Santa Maria sopra Minerva is Rome's most significant Dominican church and the only major Gothic church downtown. The facade is in Renaissance style (the church was begun in 1280 but worked on until 1725), but inside, the arched vaulting is pure Gothic. The main art treasures here are the *Statua del Redentore* (1521), a statue of Christ by **Michelangelo** (just to the left of the altar), and a wonderful fresco cycle in the **Cappella Carafa** (on the right before the altar), created by Filippino Lippi between 1488 and 1493 to honor St. Thomas Aquinas. Devout Catholics flock to the tomb of **Saint Catherine of Siena** under the high altar—the room where she died in 1380 was reconstructed by Antonio Barberini in 1637 (far left corner of the church). **Fra' Angelico,** the Dominican friar and painter, also rests here, in the **Cappella Frangipane e Maddaleni-Capiferro.** In the piazza outside the church, a small obelisk sits on a delightful elephant statue by **Bernini.**

Piazza della Minerva 42. santamariasopraminerva.it/en. ✆ **06-69920384.** Free admission. Daily 9am–noon, 4–7pm.

CAMPO DE' FIORI

The southern section of the *centro storico,* **Campo de' Fiori** is another neighborhood of narrow streets, small piazzas, and ancient churches. Its main focus is the piazza of **Campo de' Fiori ♥♥** itself, where a touristy open-air market runs daily (with fewer vendors on Sun) from early morning until midday, selling a colorful array of fruits, vegetables, and spices as well as loads of cheap T-shirts and handbags. (Keep an eye on your valuables here.) From the center of the piazza rises a statue of the severe-looking monk **Giordano Bruno,** a reminder that heretics were occasionally burned at the stake here: Bruno was executed by the Inquisition in 1600—today, he gazes toward the Vatican. Curiously, this is the only piazza in Rome that doesn't have a church in its perimeter.

Built from 1514 to 1589, the **Palazzo Farnese ♥**, on Piazza Farnese just south of the Campo, was designed by Sangallo and Michelangelo, among others, and was an astronomically expensive project for the time. Its famous residents have included a 16th-century member of the Farnese family, plus Pope Paul III, Cardinal Richelieu, and the former Queen Christina of Sweden, who moved to Rome after abdicating. During the 1630s, when the heirs couldn't afford to maintain the *palazzo,* it was inherited by the Bourbon kings of Naples and purchased by the French government in 1874; the French Embassy is still located here, so the building is mostly closed to the public. Tours in English are currently held on Mondays and Tuesdays and cost 15€. A 5pm Tuesday tour (20€) includes the Roman ruins in the palace basement. Reservations are mandatory (visite-palazzofarnese.it).

Palazzo Spada/Galleria Spada ♥♥ MUSEUM Built around 1540 for Cardinal Gerolamo Capo di Ferro, Palazzo Spada was purchased by the eponymous Cardinal Spada in 1632, who then hired Borromini to restore it—most of what you see today dates from that period. Its ornate facade, covered in high-relief stucco decorations in the Mannerist style, is the finest of any building from 16th-century Rome. The State Rooms are closed (the Italian Council of State still meets here), but the richly decorated **courtyard and corridor ♥♥**, where Borromini created a masterful illusion of perspective (*la prospettiva di Borromini*), and the four rooms of the **Galleria Spada** are open to the public. Inside you will find some absorbing paintings, such as the *Portrait of Cardinale Bernardino Spada* by Guido Reni, Titian's *Portrait of a Violinist,* and minor works from Parmigianino, Pietro Testa, and Gianni Battista Gaulli.
Piazza Capo di Ferro 13. galleriaspada.beniculturali.it. ✆ **06-6874893.** Admission 6€ adults, free for ages 17 and under. Wed–Mon 8:30am–7:30pm. Bus: 23, 280, tram 8, or any bus to Largo di Torre Argentina.

THE JEWISH GHETTO

Across Via Arenula, Campo de' Fiori merges into the old **Jewish Ghetto ♥♥**, established near the Tiber River by a Papal Bull in 1555, which required that all the Jews in Rome live in one area. Walled in, overcrowded, prone to floods and epidemics, and set on some of the worst land in the city, it was an extremely grim place to live. After the Ghetto was abolished in 1882, its walls were finally torn down, and the area was largely reconstructed. In the waning years of World War II, Nazis sent more than 1,000 Roman Jews to concentration camps; only a handful returned. Look for the inscribed bronze "stumbling stones" that remember Holocaust victims in front of their former homes.

Today, **Via Portico d'Ottavia** forms the heart of a small but flourishing Jewish Quarter; Romans and tourists flock here for the Roman-Jewish and Middle Eastern food for which the area is known. Head north on winding Via di S. Ambrogio to toss a coin in the **Fontana delle Tartarughe ♥**, a beloved Renaissance fountain. The turtles, added in the 1600s, are thought to be by Bernini.

Museo Ebraico di Roma (Jewish Museum of Rome) ♥♥ MUSEUM On the premises of the Great Synagogue of Rome, the Museo Ebraico di Roma chronicles the history of not only Roman Jews but Jews from all over Italy. Displays include works of 17th- and 18th-century Roman silversmiths, precious textiles from all over Europe, and a number of parchments and marble carvings that were saved when the ghetto's original synagogues were demolished. Museum admission includes a guided English-language tour of the **Great Synagogue of Rome** (Tempio Maggiore), built from 1901 to 1904 in an eclectic style evoking Babylonian and Persian temples. Attacked by terrorists in 1982, the synagogue is now heavily guarded by *carabinieri,* a division of the Italian police, armed with machine guns.

Via Catalana. museoebraico.roma.it/en. ✆ **06-6840061.** Admission 12€ adults, free for children 10 and under. Apr–Sept Sun–Thurs 10am–6pm and Fri 10am–4pm; Jan 21–Mar, Oct Sun–Thurs 10am–5pm and Fri 9am–2pm (Nov 1–Jan 20 closes 4 or 4:30pm Mon–Thurs; last entry 3:15pm). Closed on Jewish holidays.

Sacred Area of Largo Argentina ♥ ARCHAEOLOGICAL SITE In the middle of a transportation hub just north of the Jewish Ghetto, Largo Argentina contains the ruins of four Republican-era temples dating from the 4th to 2nd centuries B.C.E. Apart from being a well-loved cat sanctuary for Rome's strays, the site is most famously the approximate scene of Julius Caesar's assassination on the Ides of March, 44 B.C.E. Long visible only from street level, the site is now accessible to the public, thanks to a restoration funded by Bulgari. Archaeology buffs will appreciate the up-close access; for everyone else, the street level views suffice.

Ticket office at Torre del Papito, Piazza dei Calcarari. sovraintendenzaroma.it. ✆ **06-0608.** Admission 7€ adults, 4€ ages 6–25, free for children 5 and under. Tues–Sun 9:30am–dusk. Bus: 23, 280, tram 8, or any bus to Largo di Torre Argentina.

The Tridente & the Spanish Steps

The northern half of central Rome is known as the **Tridente,** thanks to the trident shape formed by three roads—Via di Ripetta, Via del Corso, and Via del Babuino—leading down from **Piazza del Popolo.** The area around **Piazza di Spagna** and the **Spanish Steps** was once the artistic quarter of the city, attracting English poets Keats and Shelley, German author Goethe, and film director Federico Fellini (who lived on Via Margutta). A few historic shops and cafes are still here (p. 154), but between the soaring rents and the throngs of tourists and shoppers, you're unlikely to see many artists left.

PIAZZA DEL POPOLO

Elegant **Piazza del Popolo ♥♥** is haunted with memories. Legend has it that the ashes of Nero were enshrined here, until 11th-century residents began complaining to the pope about his imperial ghost. The **Egyptian obelisk** dates from the 13th century B.C.E.; it was brought to Rome from Heliopolis during Augustus's reign (it once stood at the Circus Maximus).

Tridente & Via Veneto

ATTRACTIONS
- ETRU (National Etruscan Museum) 4
- Galleria Borghese 2
- Galleria Nazionale d'Arte Antica 28
- Galleria Nazionale d'Arte Moderna 4
- Keats-Shelley House 15
- MAXXI (National Museum of the XXI Century Arts) 5
- Museo dell'Ara Pacis 10
- Museo e Cripta dei Frati Cappuccini 30
- Palazzo del Quirinale 25
- Piazza Barberini 29
- Piazza del Popolo 8
- Santa Maria del Popolo 7
- Spanish Steps 17
- SS. Vincenzo e Anastasio 23
- Trevi Fountain 22
- Trinità dei Monti 18
- Vicus Caprarius 24
- Villa Borghese 32

RESTAURANTS
- Al Ceppo 1
- Babington's Tea Rooms 16
- Colline Emiliane 27
- Imàgo 19
- Pic Nic 3
- ViVi 1

HOTELS
- Condotti Selection 13
- The Inn at the Spanish Steps 14
- La Lumière 11
- La Residenza 31
- Maison Roma Piazza di Spagna | UNA Esperienza 9
- Palazzo Dama 6
- Palazzo Talìa 21
- Panda 12
- Parlamento 20
- Villa Spalletti Trivelli 26

Valadier, Napoleon's architect, designed the current piazza in the early 19th century. Standing astride the three roads that form the "trident" are almost-twin baroque churches, **Santa Maria dei Miracoli** (1681) and **Santa Maria di Montesanto** (1679). The standout church, however, is at the piazza's northern curve: the 15th-century **Santa Maria del Popolo ♥♥**, with its splendid baroque facade modified by Bernini between 1655 and 1660. Inside, look for Raphael's mosaic series, the *Creation of the World* adorning the interior dome of the **Cappella Chigi** (second chapel on the left). Pinturicchio decorated the main choir vault with frescoes such as the *Coronation of the Virgin*. The **Cappella Cerasi** (to the left of the high altar) contains gorgeous examples of baroque art: an altarpiece painting of *The Assumption of the Virgin* by Carracci, and on either side two great works by Caravaggio, *Conversion on the Road to Damascus* and *The Crucifixion of Saint Peter*.

MAXXI (National Museum of the XXI Century Arts) ♥ MUSEUM Ten minutes north of Piazza del Popolo by tram, leave the Renaissance far behind at MAXXI, a masterpiece of contemporary architecture designed by the late, great Zaha Hadid. The museum is divided into two sections, MAXXI art and MAXXI architecture, primarily serving as a venue for temporary exhibitions of contemporary work in both fields (although it does have a small permanent collection). Built in a dynamic design of bending and overlapping oblong tubes, the building is worth a visit in its own right.

Via Guido Reni 4a. maxxi.art/en. ✆ **06-3201954.** Admission 15€ adults (14€ online), 12€ (11€ online) for ages 18–25, free for ages 17 and under. Tues–Sun 11am–7pm. Metro: Flaminio, then tram 2.

Museo dell'Ara Pacis ♥♥ MUSEUM Set in a stunning ultra-modern building, the templelike marble Altar of Peace was erected in 9 B.C.E. to honor soon-to-be-Emperor Augustus's success in subduing tribes north of the Alps. For centuries the monument was lost to memory; signs of its existence surfaced in the 16th century, but it wasn't until the 1930s that it was fully excavated. Even so, it lay virtually abandoned after World War II until a true restoration began in the 1980s. The exhibit complex provides context, with interactive displays in English. ***Note:*** While closed at press time, the hulking **Mausoleum of Augustus** is right next door to the Ara Pacis Museum.

Lungotevere in Augusta. arapacis.it/en. ✆ **06-060608.** Admission 14€ adults, free for children 5 and under. Daily 9:30am–7:30pm (last entry 6:30pm). Metro: Spagna. Bus: 30, 70, 81, 87, 119, 280, 492, 628, 913.

No Swimming, Sitting, or Picnicking Allowed

In an effort to keep tourists from littering the city's monuments, or soaking their feet and even swimming (yes, it happens) in its famous fountains, visitors are no longer permitted to picnic or even sit on the Spanish Steps or linger at the edge of the Trevi and other landmark fountains. You can stop long enough for a photo or coin toss, but don't plan on getting comfortable (or taking a dip).

Tourists gather on the Spanish Steps.

PIAZZA DI SPAGNA

The undoubted highlight of Tridente is **Piazza di Spagna,** which attracts hordes of tourists to admire its celebrated **Spanish Steps** ♥♥ (Scalinata della Trinità dei Monti), the widest stairway in Europe. The Steps are especially enchanting in early spring, when thousands of blooming azaleas frame the scene. At their foot lies "Fontana della Barcaccia," a fountain shaped like an old boat, the work of Pietro Bernini, father of sculptor and fountain-master Gian Lorenzo Bernini.

Built from 1723 to 1725, the monumental stairway of 135 steps and the square take their names from the Spanish Embassy (it used to be headquartered here) but were actually funded almost entirely by the French. That's because the **Trinità dei Monti** church at the top was under the patronage of the Bourbon kings of France at the time. The stately baroque facade of the 16th-century Trinità dei Monti perches photogenically at the top of the Steps, behind yet another Roman obelisk, the "Obelisco Sallustiano." It's worth climbing up just for the views.

Fontana di Trevi (Trevi Fountain) ♥♥ MONUMENT As you elbow your way through the crowds around the Trevi Fountain, it's hard to believe that this little piazza was nearly always deserted before 1950, when it began "starring" in films: *Roman Holiday* (1953), *Three Coins in the Fountain* (1954), and the iconic scene in Fellini's 1960 masterpiece *La Dolce Vita*. To this day, thousands of euros' worth of coins are tossed into the fountain daily. The area is always jam-packed with tourists and selfie-stick hawkers, so keep your eye (and hands) on your belongings. Completed in 1762, this glorious baroque fountain centers on the triumphant figure of Neptune, standing on a shell chariot drawn by winged steeds and

Two Bucks in the Fountain...

Tossing a coin in the Trevi Fountain will cost you more than just the value of said coin. As of early 2026, the City of Rome will charge tourists 2€ each to descend the steps in front of the Trevi Fountain and launch a coin. The measure, intended to help with crowd control, is controversial, and may or may not be a permanent change. At press time, the new fee had just been announced, so we'll see how smoothly (or not) the roll-out goes.

led by a pair of tritons. Allegorical figures in the side niches represent good health and fertility. On the southwestern corner of the piazza, the church of **SS. Vincenzo e Anastasio** has a strange claim to fame: Within it are the relics (hearts and intestines) of several popes. In an alley nearby, **Vicus Caprarius—the City of Water** ♥ (vicus caprarius.com; ✆ **339-7786192;** 8€ adults, 1€ ages 14–17, free for children 13 and under; reservations suggested) is a privately run archaeological area comprised of several underground levels of ancient development, including an upscale home and part of the Acquedotto Vergine, the aqueduct that still feeds the Trevi. ***Note:*** At press time, daytime access to the fountain is only via the central staircase, and only for up to 400 visitors at a time. So expect a wait during peak hours. After 9pm, access is unregulated.

The Trevi Fountain.

Piazza di Trevi. Metro: Barberini. Bus: 52, 62-63, 80, 83, 85, 160, 492.

Keats-Shelley House ♥ MUSEUM At the foot of the Spanish Steps is the 18th-century house where the Romantic English poet John Keats died of consumption on February 23, 1821, at age 25. Since 1909, it has been a library established in honor of Keats and fellow poet Percy Bysshe Shelley, who drowned off the coast of Viareggio with a copy of Keats' works in his pocket. Mementos range from kitsch to extremely moving. The apartment where Keats spent his last months, tended by his close friend Joseph Severn, displays a death mask of Keats as well as the "deadly sweat" drawing by Severn. Both Keats and Shelley are buried in their beloved Rome, at the Protestant cemetery near the Pyramid of Cestius, in Testaccio.

Piazza di Spagna 26. keats-shelley-house.org. ✆ **06-6784235.** Admission 7€ adults, 5€ seniors and children ages 6–18, free for children 5 and under. Mon–Sat 10am–1pm and 2–6pm. Metro: Spagna.

Palazzo del Quirinale ♥♥ HISTORIC SITE Once the palace of popes and the King of Italy, since 1946 the Quirinale has been the official residence of the President of Italy, but parts of it are open to the public. Although it can't compare to Rome's major artistic showstoppers (there's little art or furniture in the rooms), the palace's baroque and neoclassical walls and ceilings are quite a spectacle. Few rooms anywhere are as impressive as the richly decorated 17th-century **Salone dei Corazzieri,** the **Sala d'Ercole** (once the apartments of Umberto I but completely rebuilt in 1940), and the tapestry-covered 17th-century **Sala dello Zodiaco.** Despite its Renaissance origins, the *palazzo* is rich in associations with ancient emperors and deities. The colossal statues of the "Dioscuri," Castor and Pollux, which now form part of the fountain in the piazza, were found in the nearby Baths of Constantine; in 1793 Pius VI had an ancient Egyptian obelisk moved here from the Mausoleum of Augustus. The sweeping view of the city from the piazza, which crowns the highest of the seven ancient hills of Rome, is itself worth the trip.

Piazza del Quirinale. palazzo.quirinale.it/palazzo.html. ✆ **06-39-96-7557.** Admission 2.50€ for an 80-min. tour following one of three themed itineraries. Reservations mandatory. Tues–Wed and Fri–Sun 9:30am–4pm. Closed Aug. Metro: Barberini. Bus: 53, 60, 62-63, 70, 71, 80, 83, 85, 492.

Villa Borghese & Parioli

Villa Borghese ♥♥, just northeast of the Tridente, is not actually a villa but a large park, 6km (3¾ miles) in circumference. Cardinal Scipione Borghese created the park in the 1600s; Umberto I, King of Italy, acquired it in 1902 and presented it to the city of Rome. The greenbelt is crisscrossed by roads, but there are plenty of green spaces to enjoy. On a sunny weekend, it's a pleasure to stroll here and see Romans at play. The park has a few casual cafes and food vendors (**Pic Nic ♥♥** is a solid choice; see p. 147); you can also rent bikes, surrey bikes, or Segways here. In the northeast part of the park, you'll find a **zoo** and the **Galleria Borghese ♥♥♥** (see below). The neighborhoods to the north, Parioli and Pinciano, are elegant enclaves for those wishing to stay outside the crowded city center (p. 125).

ETRU: Museo Nazionale Etrusco (National Etruscan Museum) ♥♥♥ MUSEUM The great Etruscan civilization was one of Italy's most advanced, although it remains enigmatic, in part because of its centuries-long rivalry with Rome. Rome definitively conquered the Etruscans by the 3rd century B.C.E., and though they adopted certain aspects of Etruscan culture, including religious practices, engineering innovations, and gladiatorial combat, gradual Romanization eclipsed virtually all the Etruscans' achievements.

Bernini's *Rape of Persephone* in the Galleria Borghese.

Housed in the handsome Renaissance Villa Giulia, built by Pope Julius III between 1550 and 1555, ETRU, the National Etruscan Museum, is the best place in Italy to learn about the Etruscans, thanks to its precious artifacts, sculptures, vases, monuments, tools, weapons, and jewels, the vast majority from tombs. Fans of ancient history could spend several hours here, but for those with less time, the most striking attraction is the stunning **Sarcofago degli Sposi** ♥♥ (Sarcophagus of the Spouses), a late-6th-century-B.C.E. terra-cotta funerary monument featuring a life-size bride and groom lounging at a banquet in the afterlife (Paris's Louvre has a similar monument). Equally fascinating are the **Pyrgi Tablets,** gold-leaf inscriptions in both Etruscan and Phoenician from the 5th century B.C.E., and the **Apollo of Veii,** a huge painted terra-cotta statue dating to the 6th century B.C.E.

Piazzale di Villa Giulia 9. museoetru.it. ✆ **06-3226571.** Admission 13€. Tues–Sun 8:30am–7:30pm; last entry 6:30pm. Bus: 982. Tram: 2, 19.

Galleria Borghese ♥♥♥ ART MUSEUM On the far northeastern edge of the Villa Borghese, the Galleria Borghese occupies the former Villa Borghese Pinciana, built between 1609 and 1613 for Cardinal Scipione Borghese, an early patron of Bernini and an astute collector of work by Caravaggio. Today the gallery displays much of his collection and a lot more besides, making it one of Rome's great art treasures. It's also one of Rome's most pleasant sights to tour, thanks to the limited number of people allowed in at a time.

The ground floor is a **sculpture gallery** par extraordinaire, housing Canova's famously risqué statue of Paolina Borghese, sister of Napoleon and wife of the reigning Prince Camillo Borghese. (When asked if she was uncomfortable posing nude, she reportedly replied, "No, the studio was heated.") The genius of Bernini reigns supreme in the following rooms, with his *David* (the face of which is thought to be a self-portrait) and ***Apollo and Daphne*** ♥♥, both seminal works of baroque sculpture, as is his stunningly lifelike ***The Rape of Persephone*** ♥♥♥. Caravaggio is represented by several paintings: the *Madonna of the Grooms*, the shadowy *St. Jerome,* and the haunting ***David Holding the Head of Goliath*** ♥♥. Upstairs lies a rich collection of paintings, including Raphael's graceful *Deposition* and his sinuous *Lady with a Unicorn*. There's also a series of self-portraits by Bernini, and his lifelike busts of Cardinal Scipione and Pope Paul V. One of Titian's best, ***Sacred and Profane Love*** ♥♥, lies in one of the final rooms.

Important: No more than 360 visitors at a time are allowed on the ground floor, and no more than 90 on the upper floor, during set 2-hour windows. **Reservations are essential** and can be made through the museum website. Roma Pass holders need to reserve an entry time by calling ✆ **06-32810** (Mon–Fri 9am–6pm, Sat 9am–1pm) or e-mailing romapass@tosc.it. English labeling in the museum is minimal. Guided tours in English cost an extra 8€, or opt for an audioguide.

Piazzale del Museo Borghese 5 (off Via Pinciana). galleriaborghese.beniculturali.it. ✆ **06-32810.** Admission 18€ adults, 4€ ages 18–25, free for ages 17 and under. Audioguides 5€. Tues–Sun 9am–7pm. Bus: 52, 53, 61, 89, 160, 490, 495, 590, 910. Tram: 3 or 19.

Galleria Nazionale d'Arte Moderna (National Gallery of Modern Art) ♥ ART MUSEUM Housed in the monumental Bazzani Building constructed in 1911, this "modern" art collection ranges from neoclassical and Romantic paintings and sculpture to 20th-century works. Quality varies, but fans should seek out van Gogh's *Gardener* and *Portrait of Madame Ginoux* in Room 15, the handful of Impressionists in Room 14 (Cézanne, Degas, Monet, and Rodin), and Klimt's *Three Ages of Woman* in Room 16. Surrealist and Expressionist works by Miró, Kandinsky, and Mondrian appear in Room 22, and Pollock's *Undulating Paths* and Calder's *Mobile* hold court in Room 27. One of Warhol's *Hammer and Sickle* series is tucked away in Room 30. Viale delle Belle Arti 131. lagallerianazionale.com. ✆ **06-322981.** Admission 17€ adults, free for ages 17 and under. Tues–Sun 9am–7pm. Metro: Flaminio. Bus: 61, 89, 160, 490, 495. Tram: 3 or 19.

Take a Break at ViVi

Museum cafes tend to the mundane, but not so at **ViVi ♥**, the health food bistro that now has a branch inside Galleria Borghese (vivi.it/store/galleria-borghese). Scrumptious pastries, avocado toast, generous poke bowls (the Mango Tango is my favorite), salads, sandwiches, and more are on offer, all locally sourced, organic, and sustainable. Now only if the service was as bright and cheerful as the food and setting, they'd be onto something.

Via Veneto & Piazza Barberini

Piazza Barberini lies at the foot of several streets, among them Via Barberini, Via Sistina, and Via Vittorio Veneto. It would be a far more pleasant spot were it not for the traffic swarming around its principal feature, Bernini's **Fountain of the Triton ♥♥** (Fontana del Tritone). For almost 4 centuries, this figure sitting in a vast open clam has been blowing water from his triton. To one side of the piazza is the aristocratic facade of the **Palazzo Barberini,** named after one of Rome's powerful families; inside is the **Galleria Nazionale d'Arte Antica ♥♥♥** (see below). The Barberini reached their peak when a son was elected pope as Urban VIII; he encouraged Bernini and gave him patronage.

As you walk up **Via Vittorio Veneto,** look for the small fountain on the right corner of Piazza Barberini—it's another Bernini, the **Fountain of the Bees ♥** (Fontana delle Api). At first they look more like flies, but they're the bees of the Barberini, the crest of that powerful family complete with the crossed keys of St. Peter above them. (Keys were always added to a family crest when a member was elected pope.)

Galleria Nazionale d'Arte Antica (National Gallery of Ancient Art) ♥♥♥ ART MUSEUM On the southern side of Piazza Barberini, the grand **Palazzo Barberini** houses the Galleria Nazionale d'Arte Antica, which despite the "ancient" in its title is a trove of Italian art mostly from the early Renaissance to late baroque periods. Some of the art on display is wonderful, but the building itself is the main attraction, a baroque masterpiece begun by Carlo Maderno in 1627 and completed in 1633 by Bernini, with additional work by Borromini (notably a whimsical spiral staircase). The **Salone di Pietro da Cortona** in the center is the most captivating space, with a trompe l'oeil ceiling frescoed by da Cortona, a depiction of *The Triumph of Divine Providence*. The museum's most intriguing works include Raphael's *La Fornarina*, a baker's daughter thought to have been the artist's lover (look for Raphael's name on her bracelet); paintings by Tintoretto and Titian (Room 15); a Holbein portrait of English King Henry VIII (Room 16); and a couple of typically unsettling El Grecos in Room 17. Caravaggio dominates room 20 with the justly celebrated *Judith and Holofernes* and *Narcissus*.

The *Triumph of Divine Providence*, a captivating ceiling fresco in the Galleria Nazionale d'Arte Antica.

Via delle Quattro Fontane 13. barberinicorsini.org. ✆ **06-4814591.** Admission 15€, valid for 20 days, also includes Palazzo Corsini; free for ages 17 and under. Tues–Sun 10am–7pm; last entry 6pm. Metro: Barberini. Bus: 53, 61–63, 80, 81, 83, 160, 492, 590.

Museo e Cripta dei Frati Cappuccini (Museum and Crypt of the Capuchin Friars) ♥♥ RELIGIOUS SITE/MUSEUM One of the most mesmerizingly macabre sights in all Christendom, this otherwise restrained (and exhaustive) museum dedicated to the Capuchin order ends with a series of six chapels in the crypt, adorned with the skulls and bones of more than 3,700 Capuchin brothers and woven into works of art. Some of the skeletons are intact, draped with Franciscan habits; others form lamps and ceiling friezes. The experience is both spooky and meditative. The entrance is halfway up the first staircase on the right of the church of the Convento dei Frati Cappuccini, completed in 1630 and rebuilt in the early 1930s. With all due respect to the friars, we suggest moving quickly through the museum to get to the crypts. ***Note:*** Because this site is within a church, it maintains a strict dress code: no short pants or skirts and no bare arms—and no photos. We don't recommend this experience for kids under 10 or so.

Via Vittorio Veneto 27. museoecriptacappuccini.it. ✆ **06-88803695.** Admission 11.50€ adults, 8€ ages 17 and under. Daily 9:30am–1:30pm (last entry 1:30pm), 2:30–6:30pm; last entry 5:30pm. Metro: Barberini. Bus: 52, 53, 61, 63, 80, 83, 160, 590.

Around Stazione Termini

Palazzo Massimo ♥♥ MUSEUM A third of Rome's assortment of ancient art can be found at this branch of the Museo Nazionale Romano;

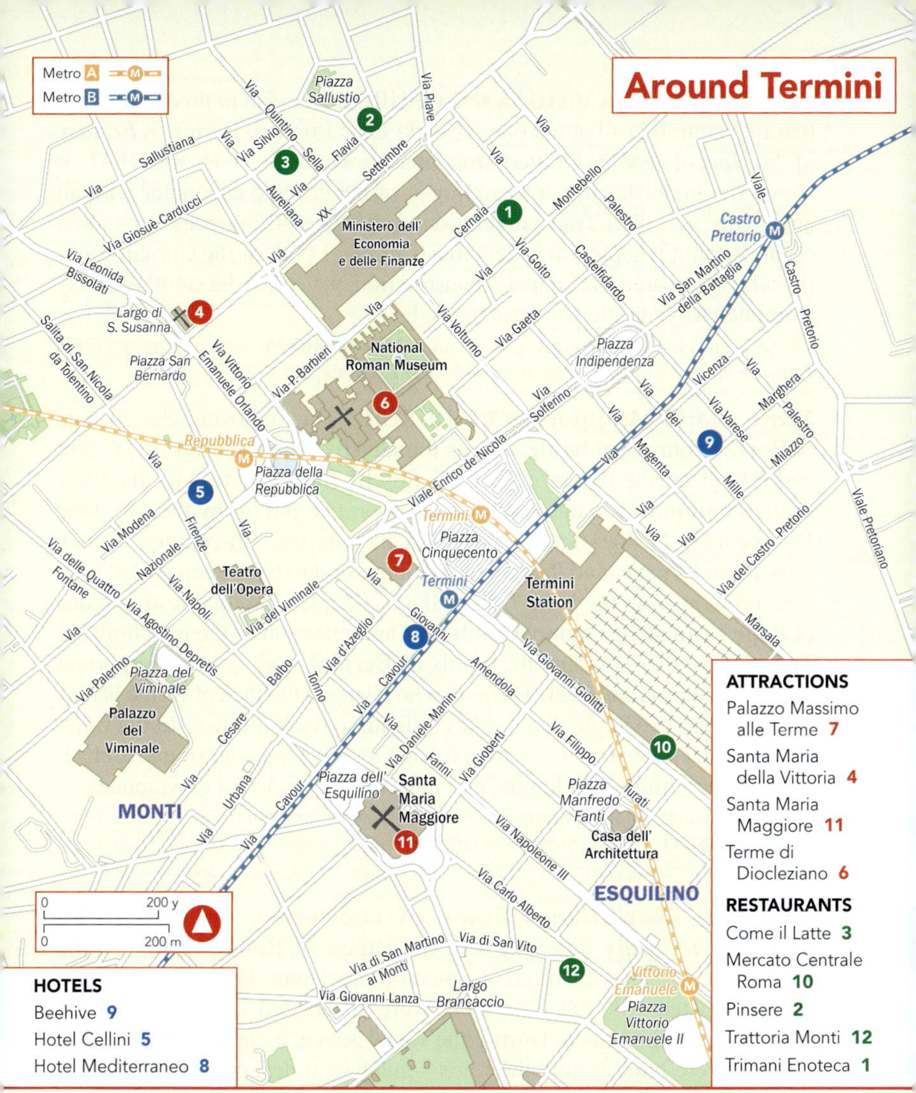

among its treasures are a major coin collection, extensive maps of trade routes (with audio and visual exhibits on the network of traders over the centuries), and a vast sculpture collection that includes portrait busts of emperors and their families, as well as mythical figures like the Minotaur and Athena. The real draw is on the second floor, where you can see some of Rome's oldest **frescoes** ♥♥; they depict an entire garden, complete with plants and birds, from the Villa di Livia a Prima Porta. (Livia was the wife of Emperor Augustus and was deified after her death in C.E. 29.) Largo di Villa Peretti. museonazionaleromano.beniculturali.it/palazzo-massimo. ✆ **06-39967700.** Admission 15€ (1-week pass also includes Palazzo Altemps and the Baths of Diocletian); free for ages 17 and under. Tues–Sun 9:30am–7pm; last entry 1 hr. before closing. Metro: Termini or Repubblica. Bus: 40, 64, or any bus that stops at Termini.

Santa Maria della Vittoria ♥♥ CHURCH A visit to this pretty little baroque church is all about one artwork: Gian Lorenzo Bernini's ***Ecstasy of St. Teresa*** ♥♥♥. Crafted from marble between 1644 and 1647, it shows the Spanish saint at the moment of her ecstatic encounter with an angel (the so-called Transverberation), who gleefully pierces her with a spear. Bernini's depiction is deliciously erotic. Look for the Cornaro family, who sponsored the chapel's construction, watching the saint's ecstasy from their voyeuristic perch on the right.

Via XX Settembre 17 (at Largo S. Susanna). ✆ **06-42740571.** Free admission. Daily 9am–noon and 4–6pm. Metro: Repubblica. Bus: 61, 62, 85, 492, 590.

Santa Maria Maggiore ♥♥ CHURCH This imposing church, one of Rome's four papal basilicas, was founded by Pope Liberius in C.E. 358 and rebuilt on the orders of Pope Sixtus III from 432 to 440. Its 14th-century **campanile** is the city's loftiest. Don't be put off by the overdone 18th-century facade: Treasures within include the 5th-century Roman mosaics in its nave, and the coffered ceiling, said to have been gilded with gold brought from the New World. Since 2025, it's the final resting place of **Pope Francis;** his humble tomb is an apt reflection of the man himself. The church also contains the **tomb of Bernini,** Italy's most important baroque sculptor/architect. The man who changed the face of Rome is buried in a tomb so simple that it takes a sleuth to track it down (to the right, near the altar). The basilica is free, though tours of its underground archaeological area, mosaiced loggia, and museums are ticketed experiences.

Piazza di Santa Maria Maggiore. www.basilicasantamariamaggiore.va/en.html. ✆ **06-69886841.** Free admission; tickets for various guided tours available on website. Daily 7am–7pm. Metro: Termini or Cavour. Bus: 16, 70, 71, 75, 360, 590, 649, 714.

Terme di Diocleziano (Baths of Diocletian) ♥♥ MUSEUM/RUINS Originally this spot held the largest of Rome's baths, dating back to C.E. 298 and the reign of Emperor Diocletian. The vast baths once accommodated 3,000 at a time but were abandoned in the 6th century after the Goth invasions. During the Renaissance, a church, cloister, and convent were built around the ruins—much of it designed by Michelangelo, no less. Today the entire hodgepodge is part of the Museo Nazionale Romano; it's a compelling museum stop that's usually quieter than the city's blockbusters. Exhibits include statuary and a large collection of inscriptions and other stone carvings from the Roman and pre-Roman eras. Since 2022, the **Museo dell'Arte Salvata** ♥♥ (Museum for Rescued Art) occupies one hall of the baths and mounts changing exhibits that reveal the massive scale and history of art and artifact looting, dubious museum acquisitions, and items recovered by Italy's highly effective Carabinieri Unit for the Protection of Cultural Heritage.

Viale E. di Nicola 78. museonazionaleromano.beniculturali.it/terme-di-diocleziano. ✆ **06-39967700.** Admission 15€ (1-week pass also includes Palazzo Altemps and Palazzo Massimo alle Terme) including 2€ booking fee; free for ages 17 and under. Tues–Sun 9:30am–7pm; last entry 1 hr. before closing. Metro: Termini or Repubblica. Bus: 66, 82, 85, 590, 910, or any bus to Termini.

A TRIO OF churches IN TRASTEVERE

Before Trastevere became bohemian and cool, it was a working-class neighborhood, separated by the Tiber from central Rome. Step into the shadowy calm of any of these neighborhood churches to get a glimpse of the old Trastevere. Admission is always free, and they're open daily, though they may close at lunchtime.

On Piazza Santa Maria, the heart of Trastevere, ornate **Santa Maria in Trastevere ♥♥** is one of Rome's oldest churches, founded around C.E. 350. The pride of the neighborhood, it's spectacular inside and out, with a Romanesque brick bell tower, colorful frescoes, mosaics, and loads of recycled ancient marbles. Look for Cavallini's 1293 mosaics of the *Life of the Virgin Mary* in the apse.

From there, Via di San Francisco a Ripa angles southeast to the church of **San Francesco d'Assisi a Ripa ♥**, so named because it's built over a convent where St. Francis stayed in 1219 when he came to Rome to see the pope (his simple cell is preserved inside). A Bernini treasure is tucked into the last chapel on the left: the "Tomb of Beata Ludovica Albertoni" (1675), commemorating a noblewoman who dedicated her life to the city's poor.

Next, follow Via Anicia northeast to **Santa Cecilia in Trastevere ♥♥** (Piazza Santa Cecilia; benedettinesantacecilia.it), a still-functioning convent with a peaceful courtyard garden. Tradition holds that St. Cecilia herself once lived on this site; the church's altar has an exquisite marble sculpture of St. Cecilia (ca. 1600) carved by Stefano Maderno. The basilica and Roman-era ruins underneath can be visited Monday to Saturday, 10am to 12:30pm and 4 to 6pm, and Sunday from 11:30am. The partial remains of a *Last Judgment* by Pietro Cavallini (ca. 1293), a masterpiece of Roman medieval painting, can be visited only in the morning.

Trastevere

Galleria Nazionale d'Arte Antica in Palazzo Corsini ♥ PALACE/ART MUSEUM Palazzo Corsini first found fame—or more accurately, notoriety—as the home of Queen Christina of Sweden, a Catholic convert who moved to Rome after abdicating the Swedish throne in 1654. (She was famously described as "Queen without a realm, Christian without a faith, and a woman without shame," referring to her open bisexuality.) Several other big names stayed in this beautiful palace, from Michelangelo to Napoleon's mother, Letizia. Today one wing houses a moderately interesting museum, with a lot of the runoff from Italy's national art collection. Worth a look is Caravaggio's *St. John the Baptist* (1606) and panels by Luca Giordano, Fra' Angelico, and Poussin; otherwise the palace history is more interesting than the museum itself.

Via della Lungara 10. barberinicorsini.org. ✆ **06-68802323.** Admission 15€ adults, valid for 20 days, also includes Palazzo Barberini; free for ages 17 and under. Tues–Sun 10am–7pm; last entry 6pm. Bus: 23 or 280.

Villa Farnesina ♥ HISTORIC HOME Originally built for Sienese banker Agostino Chigi in 1511, this elegant villa was acquired by the Farnese family in 1579. With two such wealthy Renaissance patrons, it's hardly surprising that the interior decor is top drawer. Architect Baldassare Peruzzi began the decoration, with frescoes and motifs rich in myth and symbolism. He was later assisted by Sebastiano del Piombo, Sodoma, and, most notably, Raphael. Raphael's **Loggia of Cupid and Psyche ♥♥** was frescoed to mark Chigi's marriage to Francesca Ordeaschi—though his assistants did much of the work. The ornamental gardens are perfumed and colorful in spring and summer.

Via della Lungara 230. villafarnesina.it. ✆ **06-68077268.** Admission 12€ adults, 10€ seniors, 7€ ages 10–18; free for children ages 9 and under. Guided tours 16€. Tues–Sat 9am–2pm; 2nd Sun of month 9am–5pm. Bus: 23, 125, 280.

Testaccio & Southern Rome

Centrale Montemartini ♥♥ MUSEUM The renovated boiler rooms of Rome's first thermoelectric plant now house a grand collection of Roman and Greek statues, creating a unique juxtaposition of classical and industrial archaeology. The 19th-century powerhouse was the first public plant to produce electricity for the city. Striking installation spaces include the vast boiler hall, a 1,000-sq.-m (10,764-sq.-ft.) room where ancient statues share space with a complex web of pipes, masonry, and -metal walkways. Equally striking is the Hall of Machines, where two towering turbines stand opposite the reconstructed pediment of the **Temple of Apollo Sosiano ♥♥**, which illustrates a famous Greek battle. Unless you run across a school group, this place is never crowded, and it provides an intimate look at the ancient world, despite the cavernous setting.

Via Ostiense 106. www.centralemontemartini.org/en. ✆ **06-0608.** Admission 11€ (higher during special exhibitions); 15.50€ for 7-day ticket that includes Musei Capitolini, 6.50€ ages 6–25, free for children 5 and under. Tues–Sun 9am–7pm; last entry 1 hr. before closing. Metro: Garbatella. Bus: 23 or 769.

MACRO Testaccio/Mattatoio ♥ MUSEUM The Testaccio outpost of Rome's contemporary art museum and performance space is housed—appropriately for this former meatpacking neighborhood—in a converted slaughterhouse (*mattatoio* in Italian). Its edgy exhibits are a mix of installations, visuals, events, and special viewings. It's only open when there's

Mussolini's City of the Future

South of the city center, the outlying **EUR suburb ♥** (the acronym stands for *Esposizione Universale Romana*) was designed and purpose-built by Mussolini in the Fascist era to stage the planned World's Fair of 1942—canceled, due to World War II. Today, EUR's mix of rationalist and classical-inspired elements will enthuse anyone with a serious interest in architecture. Perfect symmetry and sleek marble-lined avenues house a number of museums, corporate headquarters, and office agglomerates, easily connected to the *centro storico* by Metro (Line B). We keep hoping that the **Museum of Roman Civilization** (museociviltaromana.it), closed indefinitely for renovation, will reopen one of these days: It's known for its huge scale model of Rome at the time of Emperor Constantine.

Trastevere & Testaccio

ATTRACTIONS
Centrale Montemartini 25
Galleria Nazionale d'Arte Antica in Palazzo Corsini 3
MACRO Testaccio 23
San Francesco d'Assisi a Ripa 16
San Paolo Fuori le Mura 25
Santa Cecilia in Trastevere 15
Santa Maria in Trastevere 8
Villa Farnesina 4

RESTAURANTS
Antico Arco 1
Biscottificio Artigiano Innocenti 13
Checchino dal 1887 22
Dar Poeta 5
Fior di Luna 10
Flavio al Velavevodetto 21
Food Factory Trastevere 9
Osteria Cacio e Pepe 6
Osteria degli Amici 20
Osteria La Gensola 11
Pizzeria Remo A Testaccio 18
Porto Fluviale 24
Spirito DiVino 14
Trattoria Perilli 19

HOTELS
Arco del Lauro 12
Donna Camilla Savelli 2
Hotel San Francesco 17
Santa Maria 7

something on. Make an early evening visit before going out to dinner in Testaccio.

Piazza Orazio Guistiniani 4. mattatoioroma.it. ✆ **06-671070400.** Free admission. Tues–Sun 2–8pm; last entry 1 hr. before closing. Metro: Piramide. Bus: 23, 75, 83, 170, 280, 716. Tram: 3, 8.

San Paolo Fuori le Mura ♥♥ CHURCH The giant Basilica of St. Paul, whose origins date from the time of Constantine, is Rome's fourth great patriarchal church. It was erected over the tomb of St. Paul the Apostle and is the second-largest church in Rome after St. Peter's. The basilica caught fire in 1823 and was rebuilt—hence the relatively modern look. Inside, translucent alabaster windows illuminate a forest of single-file columns and mosaic medallions (portraits of the various popes). Its most important artistic treasure is a 12th-century marble candelabrum by Vassalletto, who's also responsible for the remarkable cloisters containing twisted pairs of columns enclosing a rose garden. Miraculously, the baldacchino by Arnolfo di Cambio (1285) wasn't damaged in the fire; it now shelters the tomb of St. Paul.

Via Ostiense 190 (at Piazzale San Paolo). basilicasanpaolo.org. ✆ **06-69880800.** Free admission to Basilica; cloisters 4€. Basilica daily 7am–6:30pm; cloisters 9am–5:30pm. Metro: Basilica di San Paolo. Bus: 23, 769, 792.

Via Appia Antica (Appian Way) & the Catacombs

Of all the roads that led to Rome, **Via Appia Antica** (begun in 312 B.C.E.) was the most famous. It stretched all the way to the seaport of Brindisi, through which trade with Greece and the East funneled. According to Christian tradition, it was along the Appian Way that an escaping St. Peter encountered a vision of Christ, causing him to go back into the city to face martyrdom. Monuments and ancient tombs of patrician Roman families—burials were forbidden within the city walls as early as the 5th century B.C.E.—line the road's initial stretch in Rome. Below ground are miles of tunnels hewn of the soft *tufa* stone, which hardens on exposure to the air.

These tunnels, or catacombs, were where early Christians buried their dead. A few are open to the public, so you can wander through tunnels whose walls are gouged out with tens of thousands of burial niches, now mostly empty, including small niches made for children. Early Christians referred to each chamber as a *dormitorio*—they believed the bodies were only sleeping, awaiting resurrection (which is why they could not observe the traditional Roman practice of cremation). In some you can still see the remains of early Christian art. The obligatory guided tours feature occasionally biased history, plus a dash of sermonizing, but the guides are very knowledgeable.

The **Appia Antica park** is a popular Sunday picnic site for Roman families, following the half-forgotten pagan tradition of dining in the

A Noble Survivor

Of all the monuments on the Appian Way itself, the most impressive is the **Tomb of Cecilia Metella ♥**, within walking distance of the catacombs. The cylindrical tomb, clad in travertine and topped with a marble frieze, honors the wife of one of Julius Caesar's military commanders from the republican era. Why such an elaborate tomb for a figure of relatively minor historical importance? Other mausoleums may have been even more elaborate, but Cecilia Metella's earned enduring fame simply because her tomb has remained while the others have decayed. Part of the reason is its symbiotic relationship with the early-14th-century **Castle Caetani** attached to the rear. For centuries, the tomb survived being plundered for building materials because of the castle, which was built to guard the road and collect tolls; in later eras, the castle was spared because it was attached to the romantic ruin of the tomb. Admission to the tomb (8€–12€) includes access to other sites in the archaeological park. It's open from 9am to dusk. See **parco archeologicoappiaantica.it** for more info (Italian only).

presence of one's ancestors on holy days. Via Appia Antica is closed to cars on Sundays, left for the picnickers, walkers, and cyclists. See **parco appiaantica.it** for more, including downloadable maps.

To reach the catacombs area, take bus no. 218 from the San Giovanni Metro stop or the 118 from Colosseo or Circus Maximus. ***Tip:*** The 118 runs more frequently than the 218 and deposits you closer to the catacombs, but it runs less frequently on Sundays. If you are in a hurry, take a taxi (p. 73).

Catacombe di Domitilla ♥♥♥ RELIGIOUS SITE/TOUR The oldest of the catacombs is the hands-down winner for most enjoyable experience. Groups are relatively small (in part because the site is not directly on the Appian Way), and guides are entertaining and personable. The catacombs—Rome's longest at 17km (11 miles)—were built below land donated by Domitilla, a noblewoman of the Flavian dynasty who was exiled from Rome for practicing Christianity. They were rediscovered in 1593, after a church abandoned in the 9th century collapsed. The visit begins in the sunken church founded in C.E. 380, the year Christianity became Rome's state religion.

There are fewer "sights" here than in the other catacombs, but this is the only catacomb where you'll still see bones; the rest have emptied their tombs to rebury the remains in inaccessible lower levels. Elsewhere in the tunnels, 4th-century frescoes contain some of the earliest representations of Saints Peter and Paul. Notice the absence of crosses: It was only later that Christians replaced the traditional fish symbol with the cross. During this period, Christ's crucifixion was a source of shame to the community, as he'd been killed like a common criminal.

Via delle Sette Chiese 282. domitilla.info. ✆ **06-5110342.** Admission 10€ adults, 7€ ages 6–14, free for children 5 and under. Wed–Mon 9am–noon and 2–5pm. Closed mid-Dec to mid-Jan. Bus: 714, 716, 160 or 670.

Catacombe di San Callisto (Catacombs of St. Callixtus) ♥♥

RELIGIOUS SITE/TOUR "The most venerable and most renowned of Rome," said Pope John XXIII of the San Callisto funerary tunnels. These catacombs are often packed with tour-bus groups, but the tunnels are phenomenal. They're the first cemetery of Christian Rome, the burial place of 16 popes in the 3rd century. They bear the name of the deacon St. Callixtus, who served as pope from C.E. 217–22. The network of galleries on four levels reaches a depth of about 20m (65 ft.), the deepest in the area. There are many sepulchral chambers and almost half a million tombs of early Christians.

Entering the catacombs, you see the most important crypt, that of nine popes. Some of the original marble tablets of their tombs are preserved. Also commemorated is St. Cecilia, patron of sacred music (her relics were moved to her church in Trastevere during the 9th c.; see p. 117). Farther on are the Cubicles of the Sacraments, with 3rd-century frescoes.

Via Appia Antica 110–26. catacombe.roma.it. ✆ **06-5130151.** Admission 10€ adults, 7€ ages 7–15, free for children 6 and under. Thurs–Tues 9am–noon and 2–5pm. Closed mid-Jan to mid-Feb. Bus: 118, 218.

Catacombe di San Sebastiano (Catacombs of St. Sebastian) ♥

RELIGIOUS SITE/TOUR Today the tomb and relics of St. Sebastian are in the ground-level basilica, but his original resting place was in the catacombs beneath it. Sebastian was a senior Milanese soldier in the Roman army who converted to Christianity and was martyred during Emperor Diocletian's persecutions, which were especially brutal in the first decade of the 4th century. From the reign of Valerian to that of Constantine, the bodies of Saints Peter and Paul were also hidden in the catacombs, which were dug from the soft volcanic rock (*tufa*). The church was built in the 4th century and remodeled in the 17th. In the tunnels and mausoleums are mosaics and graffiti, along with many other pagan and Christian objects. Four Roman tombs with their frescoes and stucco fairly intact were found here in 1922 after being buried for almost 2,000 years.

Via Appia Antica 136. catacombe.org. ✆ **06-7850350.** Admission 10€ adults, 7€ ages 6–15, free for children 5 and under. Tues–Sun 9:15am–5:15pm. Closed Dec. Bus: 118, 218.

See the City as It Wakes Up

Tour guide, art historian, and runner Isa Calidonna, the force behind **ArcheoRunning** (archeorunning.com), leads early-morning **running and walking tours** of the city, including options that explore Trastevere, the Appian Way, and Villa Borghese. With frequent stops for Calidonna's engaging history lessons, there's time to catch your breath before setting off again. Having the streets, bridges, and piazzas of Rome to yourself in the early morning hours is a glorious treat.

Especially for Kids

Seeing Rome with kids doesn't demand an itinerary redesign, as the very best parts of the city for kids—ruins, subterranean worlds, and gelato—are aspects you'd want to explore anyway. And despite what you have heard

ORGANIZED tours

Forget the flag-waving guides leading herds of dazed travelers around monuments. A better class of professionally guided tours delivers insider expertise, focused themes, and personal attention, plus perks such as skipping entry lines and visiting after hours. For **food tours and cooking classes** in Rome, see p. 140.

One of the leading tour operators in Rome, **Context Travel** ♥ (contexttravel.com; ✆ **800/691-6036** in the U.S., or 06-96727371) uses historians, art historians, and archaeologists to lead small-group walking tours around Rome's monuments, museums, and piazzas, as well as culinary walks and excellent family programs. Vatican tours start around 100€ per person, and ancient Rome walking tours begin around 60€. More in-depth or private experiences cost significantly more.

The affable team at **The Roman Guy** (theromanguy.com; ✆ **06-342-8761859**) provides knowledgeable guides who explain thousands of years of history in an engaging, informal way. They offer small-group (most about 15 people) tours of the Colosseum, Vatican Museums, and the Catacombs, food tours of Trastevere, and other options. Prices run from about 50€ per person to much more for exclusive VIP access and/or private excursions.

Walks of Italy (walksofitaly.com; ✆ **06-95583331**) also runs excellent guided tours of Rome starting from 49€; more in-depth explorations of the Colosseum, Vatican Museums, and Forum go for 60€ to 150€.

Enjoy Rome (enjoyrome.com; ✆ **06-4451843**) offers a number of "greatest hits" walking tours, plus an early-evening tour of the Jewish Ghetto and Trastevere; its bus excursion to the catacombs and Appian Way visits an ancient aqueduct that most Romans, let alone tourists, never see. Tours start at 45€ per person; entrance fees are included with some (but not all) tours.

Golf-cart tours have existed in Rome for several years, and while we imagine they are loathed by residents, there's simply no other way to cover so much ground in Rome and absorb so much information in such a short amount of time. As with any tour, knowledgeable and passionate guides make all the difference. We've had good experiences with the folks at **Biga Tours** (bigatours.com; 100€ for a 2½-hr. highlights tour), **Turtle Tours** (turtletourrome.com; 160€ for a 3-hr. private tour) and **My Best Tour** (mybesttour.com; from 110€ for a 3-hr. tour).

The team at **Through Eternity** (througheternity.com; ✆ **06-7009336**) are art historians and architects; what sets them apart is their theatrical delivery, helped along by the dramatic scripts that many of the guides follow. It can be a lot of fun, but it's not for everyone. A 3-hour tour of the Vatican at St. Peter's is 139€; many other tours start at 60€.

Tour broker **Get Your Guide** (getyourguide.com) offers a range of options in Rome, including the usual ancient Roman suspects, as well as guided tours of Galleria Borghese (highly recommended) and day trips to Pompeii and Tivoli.

For something completely different, artist Kelly Medford runs **Sketching Rome Tours** (sketchingrometours.com), 2½-hour small-group drawing and painting lessons in some of Rome's prettiest corners. Supplies are provided, and no artistic talent is required (75€ per person).

about its famous seven hills, much of the center is mercifully flat, and pedestrian- (if not always stroller-) friendly.

Food is pretty easy too: Roman **pizzas** are some of the best in the world—see "Where to Eat" (p. 138) for our favorites. Ditto the ice cream, or *gelato* (p. 143). Restaurants in any price category will be happy to serve simple *pasta al pomodoro* (pasta with tomato sauce), and kids are welcomed virtually everywhere, including late in the evening.

The city is shorter on green spaces than many European cities, but the landscaped gardens of the **Villa Borghese** have plenty of room for kids to let off steam. Pack a picnic or rent some bikes (p. 111). The **Parco Appia Antica** (parcoappiaantica.it) is another favorite, especially on a Sunday or holiday when the old, cobbled road is closed to traffic. The park's **catacombs** (p. 120) are eerie enough to intrigue young minds.

Museums, of course, are trickier. My then 10-year-old was enthralled during our guided tour of the Galleria Borghese but could not get out of the crowded Vatican Museums fast enough—it's not much fun when you can't see over the backs of all those adults. You can probably get kids fired up more easily for the ancient stuff. Make the bookshop at the **Colosseum** (p. 88) an early stop; it has a good selection of guides aimed at under-12s, themed on gladiators and featuring funny or cartoonish material. The **Musei Capitolini** (p. 94) invites kids to hunt down some of the collection's treasures, highlighted on a free leaflet—it'll buy you a couple of hours to admire the exhibits and perhaps see them from a new and unexpected angle. The multiple levels below **San Clemente** (p. 96) and the **Case Romane del Celio** (p. 97) are another draw.

Also build in some time to throw a coin in the **Trevi Fountain** (p. 109), and to enjoy watching the feral cats relaxing amid the ruins of **Largo di Torre Argentina.** A cat sanctuary here provides basic healthcare to Rome's stray felines.

Aspiring young gladiators may want to spend 2 hours at the **Rome Gladiator School** (romegladiatorschool.com; 120€ per person, with discounts for multiple participants), where they can prepare for a duel in a reasonably authentic way.

Several of the tour operators listed on p. 123 offer family-oriented tours with special activities and perks for younger travelers.

WHERE TO STAY IN ROME

Hotels in Rome's *centro storico* are often overpriced and disappointing, and all too often the grand exteriors and lobbies of historic buildings give way to bland modern rooms. Our selections here made the cut because they offer unique experiences, highly personalized service, or extreme value—and in a few cases, all of the above.

Room rates vary wildly throughout the year, and the exact same room that sells for 180€ in the off season may cost 500€ or more in high season. Yet last-minute deals are not unheard of if a hotel has empty beds to fill. Always **book directly with the hotel**—you'll usually get a better rate and the chance to build some rapport with reception staff.

Breakfast at all but the highest echelon of hotels is often a continental buffet with coffee, fruit, bread, pastries, cereals, yogurt, and cheese. It's not

> **A Note on a Notte in Rome**
>
> The Rome City Council applies a "sojourn" tax of 4€ to 10€ (depending on hotel class) per person, per night. Many hotels will request this fee in cash upon check-in or check-out; this is perfectly normal. Children ages 10 and under are exempt.

always included in the rate, but we note when it is in the listing information after each hotel review below. If you are budgeting and breakfast is a payable extra, skip it and go to a nearby cafe-bar, where a *caffè e cornetto* (espresso and croissant) will cost you just a few euros.

Though most Roman hotels now have **air-conditioning** (a must during the stifling summer months), some budget options and vacation rentals still do not. If you're not sure, double-check directly with the hotel.

Around Vatican City & Prati

What used to be a rather dull area to stay in has gotten more appealing in recent years, thanks to several good restaurants and a quieter vibe than the busy *centro storico*. But do know that it's well removed from the ancient sites and not really geared to nightlife. If the main purpose of your visit centers on the Vatican, or you don't mind a hike into the city center, you'll be fine here, and you will be joined by thousands of other pilgrims, nuns, and priests. These hotels are on the map on p. 77.

MODERATE

Mama Shelter Roma ♥ The Rome installment of the trendy, affordable-ish design hotel chain is certainly the most interesting lodging in this corner of the city—an otherwise nondescript residential area northwest of the Vatican Museums. Rooms are small, busy, and perhaps a little too self-consciously hip, but definitely on-brand. Buzzy perks include a roof deck; a restaurant, bar, and pizzeria; and an indoor pool—the latter a real rarity in Rome.

Via Luigi Rizzo 20. mamashelter.com/roma. ✆ **06-94538900.** 217 units. 130€–350€ double. Metro: Cipro. **Amenities:** Restaurant; bar; pizzeria; roof terrace; indoor pool; fitness room; free Wi-Fi.

QuodLibet ♥♥♥ The name is Latin for "what pleases," and well, everything pleases us here. This upscale B&B boasts spacious, colorful rooms, gorgeous artwork and furnishings, and generous breakfasts (served on the roof terrace, which also offers evening bar service). All the rooms are set on the fourth floor of an elegant building, so it's quieter than many other places. It's located just a 10-minute walk from the Vatican Museums and a block from the Metro. Charming, conscientious hosts possess a deep knowledge of Rome and what will interest visitors. A top pick, even if prices have gone up quite a bit—especially in high season.

Via Barletta 29. www.quodlibetroma.com. ✆ **347-335-5160.** 7 units. 160€–600€ double. Rates include breakfast. Min. stay required some periods. Metro: Ottaviano. **Amenities:** Roof terrace; free Wi-Fi.

Residenza Paolo VI ♥♥ Literally across the street from Vatican City limits, Residenza Paolo can legitimately claim it's "steps from St. Peter's." Taking breakfast on the rooftop terrace is a special treat, as this narrow strip overlooks St. Peter's Square—if your timing's right, you'll see the pope blessing crowds on Sunday. (There's bar service on the terrace from 4pm onward.) The rooms have old-world charm, featuring tile or hardwood floors, heavy drapes, rugs, and quality beds, though standard guest rooms can be a bit "cozy."
Via Paolo VI 29. residenzapaolovi.com. ✆ **06-684870.** 35 units. 130€–400€ double. Rates include breakfast. Metro: Ottaviano (15-min. walk). Bus: 64. **Amenities:** Bar; room service; free Wi-Fi.

Bold patterns lead the Anna Fendi–designed decor at Villa Laetitia.

Villa Laetitia ♥♥♥ This elegant hotel overlooking the Tiber River is the work of Anna Fendi of the Roman fashion dynasty. Thanks to her design aesthetic, the rooms are anything but traditional, despite the 1911 villa setting surrounded by tranquil gardens. The eclectic decor features bold patterns on the beds and floors, and modern art on the walls. Splurge for the black-and-white Giulio Cesare suite, with its round leather bed and blissful garden views. Standard rooms are on the snug side, but most have kitchenettes. It's worth noting that the hotel is a 20-minute walk to *centro storico* and thus perhaps not the best choice for first-timers to Rome. **Enoteca la Torre** is the two-Michelin-starred restaurant located in the hotel. ***Tip:*** Check for great last-minute rates on the hotel website.
Lungotevere delle Armi 22–23. villalaetitia.com. ✆ **06-3226776.** 20 units. 215€–450€ double. Rates include breakfast. Metro: Lepanto. **Amenities:** Restaurant; bar; babysitting; bike rentals; fitness room; room service; free Wi-Fi.

INEXPENSIVE

Rome Armony Suites ♥♥♥ A warning: Rome Armony Suites is almost always booked up months in advance, so if you're interested, book early. Why so popular? The answer starts with service; owner Luca is a charming, sensitive host, especially helpful with first-time visitors to Rome. Rooms are big, clean, and modern, with private baths, minimalist decor, Nespresso machines, air-conditioning, safes, and a fridge in each unit. The owners also rent an apartment, Trevi Armony, through Airbnb, with direct views of the famous fountain.
Via Orazio 3. romearmonysuites.com. ✆ **348-8843565.** 5 units. 85€–180€ double. Breakfast 20€ per person. Metro: Lepanto. **Amenities:** Free Wi-Fi.

Ancient Rome, Monti & Celio

Not many hotel rooms on earth have a view of a 2,000-year-old amphitheater, so there's a definite "only in Rome" feeling to lodging on the edge of the ancient city (see map on p. 87). The negative to staying in this area—and it's a big minus—is that the streets adjacent to those ancient monuments have little life outside tourism. There's a lot more going on in **Monti,** Rome's oldest "suburb" (only 5 min. from the Forum), which is especially lively after dark. **Celio** has more of a neighborhood vibe quite separate from tourism.

EXPENSIVE

The Inn at the Roman Forum ♥♥ This small hotel is tucked down a medieval lane on the edge of Monti, with the forums of several Roman emperors as neighbors. Rooms are tastefully plush, with colorful silks, rich textures, and spacious bathrooms. The posh fifth-floor Master Garden Rooms have private patios surrounded by flowers and greenery, and a luxury apartment with a kitchen sleeps up to six people. The hotel's small **roof lounge** has views of the Campidoglio, and for archaeology buffs there's an ancient Roman *cryptoporticus* behind the lobby—hands down the most atmospheric place in Rome to enjoy an espresso or a glass of wine.

Via degli Ibernesi 30. theinnattheromanforum.com. ✆ **06-69190970.** 21 units. 250€–600€ double. Rates include breakfast. Metro: Cavour. **Amenities:** Bar; roof terrace; concierge; room service; free Wi-Fi.

MODERATE

Duca d'Alba ♥♥ Located on one of the main drags of hip Monti, with all the nightlife and authentic dining you'll need, Duca d'Alba strikes a fine balance between old-world gentility and 21st-century amenities. Rooms in the main building are snug and contemporary, with modern furniture and gadgetry and smallish bathrooms. Annex rooms are slightly less expensive and a bit more classic in decor, with terra-cotta floors, oak and cherry furniture, and soundproofed street-facing rooms. Second-floor rooms are the brightest. Overall, this remains a solidly affordable choice in a neighborhood where hotel prices are steadily climbing.

Via Leonina 14. hotelducadalba.com. ✆ **06-484471.** 27 units. 95€–230€ double. Metro: Cavour. **Amenities:** Bar; free Wi-Fi.

The Glam ♥♥ A decidedly modern vibe pervades at this boutique-y hotel, well located right on busy Via Nazionale, within walking distance of Termini Station, the Colosseum and Forum, Trevi Fountain, and just about everything else you'll want to see in central Rome. Art-filled rooms are cool and functional, if a little impersonal, but a welcoming staff and a complimentary minibar with soft drinks and snacks more than compensates. Terrazza Monti, the rooftop restaurant and glorious open-air bar and terrace, is the setting for breakfast and a popular nighttime gathering spot.

Via Nazionale 82. theglamhotelroma.it. ✆ **06-99345430.** 59 units. 185€–450€ double. Most rates include breakfast. Metro: Repubblica or Cavour. **Amenities:** Bar; restaurant; roof terrace; free minibar; free Wi-Fi.

INEXPENSIVE

Lancelot ♥♥♥ Expect warmth and hospitality from the minute you walk in the door. The staff, many of whom have been here for years, are the heart and soul of Lancelot and the reason why the hotel has so many repeat guests. Room decor is simple and inviting; most units are spacious, immaculately kept, and light-filled, thanks to large windows. Bathrooms are small but serviceable. Sixth-floor rooms have private terraces overlooking ancient Rome—well worth springing for. The 1938 building retains vestiges of its Art Deco past, most felt in the cantilevered marble staircase and chandelier-lit common areas for meeting other travelers, *A Room with a View*–style. Unusual for Rome, Lancelot also has limited private parking—but you'll need to book it in advance.

Via Capo d'Africa 47. lancelothotel.com. ✆ **06-70450615.** 60 units. 150€–225€ double. Rates include breakfast. Metro: Colosseo. Bus: 53, 75, 85, 87, 118. Tram: 3. **Amenities:** Restaurant; bar; free Wi-Fi.

The Centro Storico & Pantheon

There's nothing like an immersion in the atmosphere of Rome's lively Renaissance heart, though you'll pay dearly for a room among the city's most archetypal streets and piazzas. Since many of *centro*'s characteristic streets are pedestrian-only, expect to do a lot of walking, but that's a reason many visitors come here in the first place—to wander and discover the glory that was and is Rome. Many restaurants and cafes are an easy walk from the hotels here. See map p. 101.

EXPENSIVE

Chapter Roma ♥♥ Stylish and irreverent, this design hotel is in step with the evolving character of the Jewish Ghetto, where modern art galleries and concept stores are springing up next to traditional kosher restaurants. Rooms range from small to party-size, and all have wood floors, an industrial-chic vibe, original artworks, and Marshall speakers; all but the smallest have bars stocked with pricey booze and mixers. We appreciate the eco-friendly bath amenities and absence of tiny plastic bottles. The millennial vibe is strong in the lobby bar and adjacent **Market** cafe, which serves smoothies, wraps, and salads. A seasonal rooftop restaurant serves margaritas and Mexican food.

Via di S. Maria De' Calderari 47. chapter-roma.com. ✆ **06-89935351.** 42 units. 170€–520€ double. Bus: 40, 64 (to Largo Argentina). Tram: 8. **Amenities:** 2 restaurants; bars; cafe; free Wi-Fi.

Raphael ♥♥♥ This ivy-covered palace just off Piazza Navona is an ideal choice for a special occasion stay, with luxurious rooms, enthusiastic staff, and a roof terrace with spectacular views across Rome. It's a gorgeous hotel, highlighted by 20th-century artwork inside, including Picasso ceramics and paintings by Miró, Morandi, and de Chirico scattered around the property. Standard rooms are all decorated in Victorian style, with antique furnishings and hardwood floors; the Richard Meier–designed

Chapter Roma brings an industrial-chic vibe to the Jewish Ghetto.

executive suites blend modern and Asian design and feature oak paneling, contemporary art, and Carrara marble. The commitment to green practices here never feels preachy or performative, and the haute organic vegetarian/vegan restaurant will leave even skeptical carnivores convinced. Largo Febo 2, near Piazza Navona. raphaelhotel.com. ✆ **06-682831.** 51 units. 295€–800€ double. Bus: 40, 64, 70. **Amenities:** Restaurant; bar; babysitting; concierge; room service; free Wi-Fi.

Singer Palace ♥♥ Thanks to an extremely faithful remodel and impeccable attention to detail, the former European headquarters of the Singer Corporation (of sewing-machine fame) retains its stylish Art Deco touches, including a stunning cantilevered staircase and original wood inlays, all reimagined in a boutique five-star. The location is a busy one, just off the main thoroughfare of Corso Cavour, but the entrance is on a side street, and well-insulated windows keep the elegant, compact rooms mostly quiet. A rooftop bar and restaurant is the setting for fancy cocktails and a menu that, despite the chic setting, sticks to Roman classics. Via Alessandro Specchi 10. singerpalacehotel.com. ✆ **06-6976161.** 30 units. 425€–800€ double. Bus: 64, 85, 492. **Amenities:** Restaurant; bar; roof terrace; concierge; room service; free Wi-Fi.

MODERATE

Albergo Santa Chiara ♥♥ You're *this* close to the Pantheon when you book at this reliable, welcoming three-star. Rooms, while not long on character, are bright and offer the basic comforts; some sleep up to five, making Santa Chiara an attractive option for families. The lobby-level bar and patio make a nice place to relax with a spritz after a long day in the crowded streets of Rome. Breakfast here is kind of ho-hum; if it's not included in the rate, you might be better off at a nearby bar-cafe. Note that prices are usually on the low end of those shown below. Via Santa Chiara 21. albergosantachiara.com. ✆ **06-6872979.** 96 units. 160€–340€ double. Bus: 30, 40, 46, 64, 70. **Amenities:** Bar; free Wi-Fi.

citizenM Roma Isola Tiberina ♥♥ In a city surging with each-pricier-than-the-next five-star hotels, the 2023 debut of this reasonably affordable hotel was a welcome event, especially given its great location in a modern building on the edge of the Jewish Ghetto. Rooms are true to the chain's concept—small, tech-rich, and anonymous, but also quiet, comfortable, and highly functional. In the large, colorful lobby and bar area, guests are welcome to park for the day for co-working, impromptu meetings, and casual meals. You don't get much of a sense of being in Rome here, but you do have the best of the city right around the corner. A high-quality breakfast is offered with a surcharge.

Lungotevere de' Cenci, 5–8. citizenm.com. ✆ **06-85871180.** 162 units. 150€–430€ double. Bus: H, 63, 75. Tram: 8. **Amenities:** Bar; restaurant; lounge; roof terrace; free Wi-Fi.

Coronari Palace ♥♥ Just a few steps from Piazza Navona, the well-equipped Coronari Palace offers 16 rooms featuring modular furnishings and wood laminate floors; three junior suites have terraces. While some bathrooms are on the snug side, they're sleek and well-designed, most with enough counter/sink space for a toiletry bag. The seasonal Coronari Terrace rooftop bar invites guests to enjoy a pleasant evening gazing over the terra-cotta rooftops of Rome. There are no surprises here, just clean, up-to-date facilities, good prices (for central Rome), and amicable staff.

Via dei Coronari 231. coronaripalace.com. ✆ **06-68309541.** 16 units. 165€–350€ double; min. stay required some periods. Rates include breakfast. Bus: 40, 64. **Amenities:** Roof terrace; free Wi-Fi.

Damaso Hotel ♥♥ Consistently rated as one of Rome's top hotels, this upscale three-star in a 19th-century *palazzo* punches above its weight class. Cheerful, well-thought-out rooms and sleek marble bathrooms make the most of their small dimensions, though rooms overlooking busy Corso Vittorio Emanuele II may be a touch noisy. A tempting breakfast buffet is offered in a wood-clad dining room that converts to a cocktail bar at night, and the rooftop terrace brings the views.

Piazza della Cancelleria 62. hoteldamaso.it. ✆ **06-45503061.** 39 units. 150€–400€ double. Rates include breakfast. Min. stay required some periods. Bus: 42, 62, 64, 916. **Amenities:** Bar; roof terrace; lounge; free Wi-Fi.

Hotel L'Orologio ♥♥ Despite being relatively new to the market, this sleek four-star feels like it's been here a long time—maybe because it occupies a historic *palazzo* just steps from the Largo Argentina archaeological site. The lovely mid-century modern lobby also lends a vintage air. Rooms are small and well-organized, if a little dark and anonymous, and showers have excellent water pressure. Two things stand out here: the extremely welcoming staff and a stunner of a rooftop terrace, where breakfast and evening *aperitivo* are served with a glorious view of the Rome skyline.

Corso Vittorio Emanuele II 110. hotelorologioroma.com. ✆ **06-6865019.** 43 units. 202€–600€ double. Rates include breakfast. Bus: 46, 62, 64, 81, 916. **Amenities:** Rooftop terrace, bar; free Wi-Fi.

The rooftop terrace at Hotel L'Orologio.

INEXPENSIVE

Mimosa ♥♥ This budget stalwart in the heart of the *centro storico* enjoys great word of mouth, so book early. Recently renovated rooms are colorful and bright, with private bathrooms and air-conditioning—neither a given at this price point. Larger units are suitable for families with small children. Being this close to the Pantheon at these prices (mostly on the low end of the scale below) is hard to beat.

Via di Santa Chiara 61. hotelmimosa.net. ✆ **06-68801753.** 11 units. 85€–250€ double. Bus: 40, 64, 70 to Largo di Torre Argentina. **Amenities:** Free Wi-Fi.

Residenza in Farnese ♥♥ Set in a 15th-century mansion across the street from the Palazzo Farnese, this little gem is within stumbling distance of Campo de' Fiori but still reasonably quiet. Rooms vary in size and are eclectic and artsy, with tiled floors and a vaguely Renaissance theme. The complimentary breakfast spread is downright generous; many guests cite it as a highlight of their stay. ***Tip:*** Prices are usually on the low end of the range shown, and last-minute rates are often even lower.

Via del Mascherone 59. residenzafarneseroma.it. ✆ **06-68210980.** 31 units. 98€–250€ double. Rates include breakfast. 2-night min. many weekends. Bus: 40, 64. **Amenities:** Bar; roof terrace; concierge; room service; free Wi-Fi.

Tridente, the Spanish Steps & Via Veneto

The heart of the city is a great place to stay if you're a serious shopper or enjoy the romantic nostalgia of the Spanish Steps and Trevi Fountain. But expect to part with a lot of extra euros for the privilege. Some of Rome's most legendary luxury hotels are in this area, including **Hotel Hassler** (hotelhasslerroma.com), **Hotel d'Inghilterra** (collezione.starhotels.com), and **Hotel de Russie, Hotel de la Ville** (both roccofortehotels.com), as well as **Bulgari Hotel Roma** (www.bulgarihotels.com)—any of which we heartily recommend if you've got the cash to splash. Here, we list some rare bargains in this most elegant area of Rome, plus a few worthy splurges. See map p. 107 for locations.

EXPENSIVE

The Inn at the Spanish Steps ♥♥♥ Set in one of Rome's most desirable locations on the famed Via dei Condotti shopping street, this hotel is the epitome of luxe. Rooms are fantasias of design and comfort, some with parquet floors and cherubim frescoes on the ceiling, others decked out with wispy fabrics draping canopied beds; upgraded units have swoon-worthy views of Piazza di Spagna. The rooftop terrace provides beautiful views, to be enjoyed at breakfast—with its generous buffet spread—or for evening cocktails.

Via dei Condotti 85. theinnatthespanishsteps.com/en. ✆ **06-69925657.** 24 units. 160€–500€ double. Metro: Spagna. **Amenities:** Bar; babysitting; concierge; roof terraces; room service; free Wi-Fi.

Palazzo Dama ♥♥ Hidden in plain sight just 2 blocks from Piazza del Popolo, this swanky five-star in a Liberty-era villa is full of surprises, not the least of which is an outdoor pool surrounded by a garden of lemon and olive trees. Rooms and suites are done in Art Deco style, with soothingly elegant color schemes, premium Acqua di Parma toiletries, and large windows, many offering views of the pool or the Tiber. The hotel's PACIFICO restaurant serves Peruvian-Japanese specialties, and there are indoor and outdoor cocktail bars. A basement-level wellness area features saunas, a whirlpool, and treatment rooms.

Lungotevere Arnaldo da Brescia 2. palazzodama.com. ✆ **06-89565272.** 29 units. 248€–750€ double. Metro: Flaminio. **Amenities:** Restaurant; 2 bars; outdoor pool; garden; spa; room service; babysitting; free Wi-Fi.

Ceiling frescoes and parquet floors add drama to rooms at the Inn at the Spanish Steps.

Palazzo Talìa ♥♥ A late 2024 entry on Rome's crowded luxury hotel landscape, Palazzo Talìa occupies a 1600s palace that for centuries served as an elite private school for wealthy Roman offspring. Remodeled with a mix of original architectural details and bold modern interiors imagined by Italian film director Luca Guadagnino, the result is a sumptuous space that manages to feel intimate, despite its palatial dimensions. A basement-level spa with a heated pool is a delightful haven in the center of the city, as is the courtyard garden. The Trevi Fountain is a coin's throw away.
Largo del Nazareno 25. palazzotalia.com/en. ✆ **06-692521.** 26 units. 634€–990€ double. Rates include breakfast. Metro: Barberini or Spagna. **Amenities:** Bar; restaurant; concierge; garden; room service; spa w/indoor pool; free Wi-Fi.

Villa Spalletti Trivelli ♥♥♥ This really is an experience rather than a hotel, an early-20th-century neoclassical villa remodeled into an exclusive 14-room guesthouse, where lodgers mingle in the gardens or the great hall, as if invited by an Italian noble for the weekend. There is no key for the entrance door; ring a bell and a staff member will open it for you, often offering you a glass of prosecco as a welcome. Rooms feature elegant antiques and embroidered bed linens, with sitting areas or separate lounges. And the minibar? All free, all day. A rooftop lounge boasts Jacuzzis, a complimentary bar, and light fare; on site there is a sizeable modern wellness oasis for those who want extra pampering.
Via Piacenza 4. villaspalletti.it. ✆ **06-48907934.** 14 units. 451€–985€ double. Rates include breakfast. Metro: Barberini. **Amenities:** Restaurant; bar; concierge; exercise room; roof terrace; room service; Jacuzzis; sauna; free Wi-Fi.

MODERATE

La Lumière ♥ You won't be checking in for chic design or innovation—this traditional hotel just off Via dei Condotti smacks of old-school comforts, from rooms with matchy-matchy color schemes, wood floors, and warm lighting to the glassed-in roof terrace or open-air patio where breakfast and evening *aperitivo* are served. For all but the highest season and holidays, it's a winner on the price/location ratio.
Via Belsiana 72. lalumieredipiazzadispagna.com. ✆ **06-69380806.** 10 units. 150€–500€ double. Rates include breakfast. Metro: Spagna. **Amenities:** Bar; roof terrace; free Wi-Fi.

La Residenza ♥ Considering its location just off Via Veneto, this hotel—hosting guests since 1936—is a smart deal. Classic but updated rooms retain a touch of Art Deco appeal and are all relatively spacious, with a couple of easy chairs or a small couch in addition to a desk. Families with children are especially catered to—quad rooms and junior suites on the top floor feature a separate kids' alcove with two sofa beds, and there's an outdoor terrace with patio furniture. The excellent breakfast buffet includes quality charcuterie and cheeses, homemade breads, and pastries.
Via Emilia 22–24. hotel-la-residenza.com. ✆ **06-4880789.** 27 units. 125€–360€ double. Rates include breakfast. Metro: Barberini. **Amenities:** Bar; babysitting; cafe; terrace; room service; free Wi-Fi.

Maison Roma Piazza di Spagna | UNA Esperienza ♥♥ Down a blink-and-you'll-miss-it passageway off pretty Via Margutta, this hotel is set in a former friary—the altar has been converted into the lobby bar that doubles as the breakfast area. Upstairs, modern rooms are compact but comfortable, with parquet floors, premium bedding, and a range of pillow choices; welcome extras include bathrobes, slippers, and a coffee set-up. We don't love the institutional feel of the hallways, but rooms this nice, at this price point, in *this* neighborhood are a real rarity. The Spanish Steps are just around the corner, and there's great shopping on Via del Babuino and nearby side streets.

Via Margutta 56. www.unaitalianhospitality.com. ✆ **06-328711.** 46 units. 180€–400€ double. Rates include breakfast. Metro: Spagna. **Amenities:** Bar; courtyard; free Wi-Fi.

Parlamento ♥♥ Set on the top floors of a 17th-century *palazzo,* this is one of the best moderately priced deals in the area. Rooms are pleasantly fresh and modern, with wood floors and monochromatic color schemes. Breakfast is served on the rooftop terrace, where you can also chill with a glass of wine in the evening. The Trevi Fountain, Spanish Steps, and the Pantheon are all within a 5- to 10-minute walk.

Via delle Convertite 5 (at Via del Corso). hotelparlamento.it. ✆ **06-69921000.** 19 units. 150€–300€ double. Rates include breakfast. Min. stay required some periods. Metro: Spagna. **Amenities:** Bar; roof terraces; concierge; room service; free Wi-Fi.

INEXPENSIVE

Condotti Selection ♥ This cozy cluster of hotels and rental rooms can be a tremendously good deal depending on when you stay and how far out you book. For your money you'll get a clean, unpretentious room, though the common areas aim higher, with marble floors, antiques, tapestries, and a Venetian-glass chandelier. Standard rooms are tight; you'll get a bit more space and modernity in the nearby annex rooms. Budget-priced "petite" rooms measure less than 9.3 sq. m (100 sq. ft). Overall it's worth considering for its proximity to the Spanish Steps. Breakfast is an add-on.

Via Mario de' Fiori 37. hotelcondotti.com. ✆ **06-6794661.** 16 units. 88€–320€ double. Metro: Spagna. **Amenities:** Bar; babysitting; free Wi-Fi.

Panda ♥ Panda has long been popular among budget travelers, so it books up quickly. Rooms are spare, but not without some old-fashioned charm, like the characteristic Roman terra-cotta floor tiles, and the odd frescoed ceiling or exposed beam—and they do have air-conditioning. Most rooms are a bit cramped, but for these prices in this neighborhood they remain a very, very good deal. Outside your doorstep are several great cafes and wine bars where you can start the day with espresso and end with a nightcap. ***Tip:*** With its budget single rooms with shared baths, Panda is a fine pick for solo travelers. A breakfast voucher is good for the bar a couple of doors down.

Via della Croce 35. hotelpanda.it. ✆ **06-6780179.** 28 units (8 w/shared bath). 107€–330€ double w/bath. Metro: Spagna. **Amenities:** Free Wi-Fi.

Around Termini

Known for its concentration of cheap hotels, the Termini area (see map, p. 115) is about the only part of the center where you can still score a high-season double for under 100€—though that's getting tougher and tougher. It's also seen a growing number of more upscale hotels, particularly in the zone northwest of the station. Streets close to the train station are hardly picturesque, and parts of the neighborhood are a little sketchy. Still, it's very convenient to most of Rome's top sights, and a hub for Metro lines, buses, and trams.

MODERATE

Hotel Cellini ♥♥ It's tradition all the way at Cellini, a modest, refined hotel around the corner from Piazza della Repubblica. Antique-styled rooms are proudly 19th century, with thick walls (so no noise from your neighbors), solid furnishings, and handsome parquet floors, yet also offer modern comforts like memory-foam mattresses and air-conditioning. Bathrooms come with Jacuzzi tubs or jetted showers. Service is top-notch and wonderfully personal.

Via Modena 5. hotelcellini.com/en. ✆ **06-47825204.** 10 units. 135€–290€ double. Most rates include breakfast. Metro: Repubblica. **Amenities:** Concierge; room service; free Wi-Fi.

Hotel Mediterraneo ♥♥♥ Within sight of Termini station, this upscale hotel offers vintage Art Deco style, along with a team of long-time employees who warmly evoke a bygone era of service. Freshly renovated rooms are large and well-equipped, with bathrooms of grand proportions; suites are downright palatial; and seven top-floor units have terraces with sweeping views. Read about the hotel's interesting World War II–era history as you linger over cocktails in its Wes Anderson-y bar. Sister properties **Atlantico** and **Massimo D'Azeglio,** located next door and across the street, respectively, offer lower room prices and share some amenities with Mediterraneo. The area, while safe and convenient, lacks a neighborhood feel, but you're just a short walk from buzzy Monti.

Via Cavour 15. romehotelmediterraneo.it. ✆ **06-4884051.** 245 units. 190€–495€ double. Rates include breakfast. Metro: Termini. **Amenities:** Restaurant; bar; concierge; gym; roof terrace; room service; free Wi-Fi.

INEXPENSIVE

Beehive ♥♥♥ Conceived as part hostel and part hotel, the Beehive is an utterly cheerful lodging experience, run by eco-minded American owners and offering rooms for a variety of budgets. Options range from fancy-for-the-price private rooms with ensuites and TVs to economical rooms with shared bathrooms, as well as both mixed and female-only dorms, all with air-conditioning. All are decorated with flair, adorned with artwork or flea-market treasures. A garden offers trees and secluded space for reading and relaxing.

Via Marghera 8. the-beehive.com. ✆ **06-44704553.** 20 units. 85€–150€ double; 35€–65€ dorm beds. Metro: Termini or Castro Pretorio. **Amenities:** Cafe; garden; lounge; free Wi-Fi.

Trastevere

This was once an "undiscovered" neighborhood—but those days are long over. Being based here does give some degree of escape from the busy *centro storico,* though Trastevere's narrow streets can be packed to the gills in the evenings, as this boho section of Rome (see map on p. 119) is chock-full of bars, shops, and restaurants.

MODERATE

Donna Camilla Savelli ♥♥♥ Set at the northeastern edge of Trastevere at the foot of the Janiculum Hill, this walled complex, part of which still operates as a convent, is a tranquil refuge. Rooms, many of which are former nuns' cells, are well-equipped if a wee bit creaky, but the real attractions are the grand common areas, including a vaulted corridor, cloister, and stairway designed by baroque architect Borromini. In fine weather, there is no place better for pre-dinner drinks than the enclosed garden, set in the former cloister. Request a tour of the property, where a staff member will point out the Borromini-designed features and lead you to the hotel's Roman crypt. ***Note:*** A separate annex offers comfortable budget rooms (priced from 150€) but fewer amenities.

Via Garibaldi 27. donnacamillasavelli.com. ✆ **06-588861.** 99 units. 260€–500€ double. Bus: H, 64, or 75. **Amenities:** Bar; restaurant; garden; terraces; free Wi-Fi.

Donna Camilla Savelli, in a converted convent, is a tranquil refuge.

Hotel San Francesco ♥♥ Lying at the edge of Trastevere, close to the Porta Portese gate, this hotel has a local feel that has disappeared from much of the neighborhood. All rooms are bright, with color-washed walls and modern tiling. Doubles can be fairly small, but the bathrooms are quite roomy. The grand piano in the lobby adds a touch of old-time charm; a top-floor garden with a cocktail bar overlooks terra-cotta rooftops and pealing church bell towers. Breakfast is top-notch here, so it's worth booking a rate that includes it. ***Tip:*** Book a "charity room" and the hotel will match your 2€ donation to help Rome's shelter dogs.

Via Jacopa de' Settesoli 7. www.hotelsanfrancesco.net. ✆ **06-48300051.** 24 units. 140€–240€ double. Most rates include breakfast. Bus: H, 44, or 75. Tram: 3 or 8. **Amenities:** Bar; bike rentals; free Wi-Fi.

Santa Maria ♥♥♥ Hidden behind an ivy-covered wall, the lovely Santa Maria is built around a 16th-century cloister, now a relaxing courtyard fragrant with orange trees. Cheerful rooms, some with exposed brick walls and beamed ceilings, are mostly on the ground floor. Free breakfast and loaner bikes, a roof garden, and a cocktail bar (which does a very nice evening *aperitivo*) all make this charmer a standout in hotel-deprived Trastevere. ***Tip:*** Several spacious, multi-bed rooms are a fine option for families or groups of friends.

Vicolo del Piede 2. htlsantamaria.com. ✆ **06-5894626.** 20 units. 140€–305€ double. Rates include breakfast. Tram: 8. Bus: 23, 280, H. **Amenities:** Bar; courtyard; loaner bikes; free Wi-Fi.

INEXPENSIVE

Arco del Lauro ♥♥ Hidden in Trastevere's snaking alleyways, this serene little B&B occupies the ground floor of a shuttered pink *palazzo*. Bright rooms have wood floors, plush beds, and simple decor, with a mix of modern and period furnishings. Rooms can't be defined as large, but they all feel spacious thanks to lofty wood ceilings. Breakfast is at a nearby cafe (with a surcharge); coffee and snacks are available around the clock.

Via Arco de' Tolomei 29. arcodellauro.it. ✆ **346-2443212.** 6 units. 95€–160€ double. Min. stay required in high season. Bus: 23, 280, H. Tram: 8. **Amenities:** Free Wi-Fi.

Apartments & Rentals

Rental apartments have some great virtues for travelers: They're often cheaper than standard facilities, and they let you save money by preparing at least some of your own meals. For locals, however, the conversion of apartments to short-term rentals means that long-time tenants face eviction and the character of neighborhoods changes. Recently, there's been significant backlash, with self-styled Robin Hood vigilantes gluing shut lockboxes of vacation rentals. A nationwide law passed in 2024 outlawed lockboxes and requires that a property owner or their representative be physically present to check in guests. Don't be surprised if you're not greeted warmly by your neighbors, who are sick of the revolving door of transient guests in their apartment buildings.

Nonetheless, Rome has thousands of rental units. Goliath booking sites **Airbnb** and **Vrbo**—platforms that allow individuals to rent their own apartments to guests—will often be cheaper than apartments rented through local agencies, like those listed below. However, the big companies' units won't always be vetted, and sometimes you're on your own if something goes wrong. If you decide to rent through one of the agencies below, know that it is standard practice for them to collect 30% of the total rental amount upfront to secure a booking. When you get to Rome and check in, the balance of your rental fee is often payable in cash only. Upon booking, the agency should provide you with detailed "check-in" procedures. ***Tip:*** Make sure you ask for a few numbers to call in case of an emergency. Beyond that, most apartments come with information sheets that list neighborhood shops and services.

RECOMMENDED AGENCIES **Cities Reference** (citiesreference.com/en/rome; ✆ **06-48903612**) offers no-surprises property descriptions (with helpful and diplomatic tags like "better for young people") and even includes the eco-footprint for each apartment. You can expect transparency and responsiveness from the straightforward staff. **Rental in Rome** (rentalinrome.com; ✆ **06-3220068**) has the widest selection of mid-range and luxury apartments in the *centro storico* (less expensive ones, too), plus an alluring website with video clips of the apartments.

Monasteries & Convents

Staying in a convent or a monastery can be a great bargain. But remember, these are religious houses, which means the decor is most often stark and the rules inflexible. Cohabitating is almost always frowned upon—though marriage licenses are rarely required—and unruly behavior is not tolerated (so no roaring in after too much vino at dinner). Plus, there's usually a curfew. Most rooms in convents and monasteries do not have private bathrooms; ask when making your reservation in case some are available. If, however, you're planning a low-key trip to Rome and can live with these parameters, convents and monasteries are an affordable and often fascinating option. The place to start is **monasterystays.com**, which lays out all your monastic options for the Eternal City.

WHERE TO EAT IN ROME

Rome remains a top destination for food lovers and today offers more dining diversity than ever. Though many of its *trattorie* haven't changed their menus in a quarter of a century (for better or worse), the city has an increasing number of creative spots with chefs willing to revisit tradition.

Restaurants generally serve lunch between 12:30 and 2:30pm and dinner between 7:30 and 10:30pm. At all other times, most restaurants are closed—though a new generation is moving toward all-day dining, with limited service at "in-between" mid-afternoon times.

If you have your heart set on any of these places below, we seriously recommend *reserving ahead of arrival.* Hot tables go quickly, especially on high-season weekends—often twice: once for the early-dining tourists, and then again for locals, who dine later, typically around 9pm.

A ***servizio*** (tip or service charge) is almost always added to your bill or included in the price. Sometimes it's marked on the menu as *coperto e servizio* or *pane e coperto* (bread, cover charge, and service). You can leave extra if you wish—a couple of euros as a token—but in general, big tipping is not the norm (although, contrary to advice from some sources, Italian waitstaff will *not* be offended if you overtip). If you have questions about an item on your bill, don't hesitate to ask for an explanation.

Near Vatican City

For restaurant locations, see map p. 77. The path leading from the Vatican Museums to St. Peter's Basilica is something of a gauntlet of bad food—overpriced tourist traps set for dazed crowds that have just wandered out of the museum and need sustenance before tackling the basilica. Fortunately, a handful of very fine inexpensive options are near the Vatican. **Duecento Gradi** ♥♥ is a top-notch *panino* joint with lots of yummy choices, right across from the Vatican walls at Piazza Risorgimento 3 (duecentogradi.it; ✆ **06-39754239;** Sun–Thurs 10am–2am, Fri–Sat 11am–5am). Around the corner, in a friendly hole-in-the-wall at Via Dei Gracchi 7, **Pinsa 'Mpò!** ♥♥ serves light and crispy *pinsa* pizzas with organic ingredients and gourmet toppings, most priced around 5€ (✆ **06-88980716;** Mon–Sat 10:30am–9pm).

EXPENSIVE

Taverna Angelica ♥♥ MODERN ITALIAN/SEAFOOD In a sea of mediocre restaurants near St. Peter's, Angelica serves surprisingly good and fairly priced (though not cheap) fare. Main courses might include *tortelli* (a type of large ravioli) with venison and sea urchin, or whitefish with shallots, orange, and hazelnuts. The aptly titled "I trust Luca" tasting menus put you in the hands of the chef for six or eight courses. Save room for the delicious, non-run-of-the-mill desserts (the dark chocolate tart with sea salt is our current champion). Reservations are required.

Piazza A. Capponi 6. instagram.com/taverna_angelica. ✆ **06-6874514.** Main courses 20€–45€; tasting menus from 65€–110€. Tues–Wed 7:30–11pm; Thurs–Sun 12:30–3pm and 7:30–11pm. Closed 10 days in Aug. Metro: Ottaviano.

Seafood is a menu standout at Taverna Angelica.

deep dives INTO ROME'S CUISINE

Travel is inextricably linked to eating new and different foods, and perhaps nowhere is eating as important as it is in Italy. Numerous food tours and cooking classes offer a taste of Rome's culinary variety, from morning market tours to street food crawls to day-long cooking classes where you leave with new recipes and skills to try out at home. In addition to all that eating, drinking, and cooking, tours offer historical context and a more intimate look at Roman life as it relates to food. Here are a few of our favorite ways to sample the vibrant, storied cuisine of the Eternal City:

The **Roman Food Tour** (foodtourrome.com) limits its offerings to a handful of well-thought-out tours, including to the Prati and Trionfale areas, where you're far more likely to run into local shoppers and diners than competing tour groups. The 4-hour tours start at 99€—use the discount code "Romesaver" for 10% off.

Eating Europe (eatingeurope.com) and **Devour Tours** (devourtours.com) offer in-depth small-group food and wine tours in Rome, particularly of Testaccio and Trastevere. Guides connect Rome's culinary culture to the city's history and traditions, and guests leave with their curiosity (and hunger) sated. Tours from 69€.

Run by a trio of food experts, including American **Eleonora Baldwin,** a TV foodie celebrity in Italy, **Casa Mia Tours** (casamiatours.com) offers private tours of Rome's markets and neighborhoods, with plenty of sampling along the way. They also do private cooking classes and dinners with locals. Prices range from 160€ per person for a cooking class to 390€ for a 3-hour private food tour for two.

MODERATE

Bonci Pizzarium ♥♥♥ PIZZA Celebrity chef Gabriele Bonci has always had a cult following in the Eternal City, and as his doughy empire has expanded worldwide, you can expect long lines at his pizzeria. No matter—it's worth waiting (and walking 10 min. west of the Vatican Museums) for some of the best pizza you'll ever taste, sold by the slice or by weight. His ingredients are fresh and organic, the crust perfect, and toppings often out-of-the-ordinary, such as roasted zucchini with stracciatella or spicy 'nduja sausage with burrata. There's a good choice of Italian craft IPAs and wheat beers and wines by the glass. Only a handful of stand-up tables are inside, with benches outside for seating, and reservations aren't taken.

Via della Meloria 43. bonci.it. ✆ **06-39745416.** Pizza 16€–48€ per kilo. Mon–Sat 11am–10pm; Sun 11am–3pm and 5–10pm. Metro: Cipro.

Il Sorpasso ♥♥ ITALIAN/SMALL PLATES This innovative, ultra-friendly bistro is a breath of fresh air among the touristy eateries in this neighborhood. In addition to daily specials, the menu offers a range of small plates ideal for sharing, as well as pastas, salads, and a nice selection of cured meats and cheeses from the Norcia area of Umbria. Located equidistant from the Vatican Museums and St. Peter's, it's a great option for those looking for a sit-down meal, but one that won't last for hours.

Via Properzio 31. sorpasso.info. ✆ **06-89024554.** Small plates and pastas 6€–24€. Mon–Sat 8:30am–1am. Metro: Ottaviano.

Ancient Rome, Monti & Celio

For restaurant locations, see map p. 87. For a cappuccino, a quick bite, or *aperitivo* snacking, head to the epicenter of Monti, **La Bottega del Caffè** ♥ (✆ **06-4741578**), on lively Piazza Madonna dei Monti, open from 8am to the wee hours. When we hanker for something other than Italian food, we head to **Maharajah** ♥♥, an elegant Northern Indian eatery at Via dei Serpenti 124 (maharajah.it; ✆ **06-4747144**).

MODERATE

InRoma al Campidoglio ♥ ITALIAN Once a club for Rome's film industry, InRoma sits on a cobbled lane opposite the Palatine Hill. Though the place rests heavily on its cinematic laurels, it still serves up mostly authentic Roman and regional cuisine. Meals might start with *caprese di bufala affumicata* (tomatoes and smoked buffalo mozzarella) followed by classic pasta carbonara—they claim to do the best in Rome—or a main course of *saltimbocca* (veal cutlets wrapped with prosciutto and sage). Opt for a sidewalk table with a view to remember.

Via dei Fienili 56. inroma.eu. ✆ **06-69191024.** Main courses 14€–28€. Daily 12:30–3pm and 7:30–10pm. Bus: H, 64, 75, 81, 83, 160, 170, 628.

La Barrique ♥♥ MODERN ROMAN At this cozy, contemporary *enoteca* (wine bar with food), the kitchen knocks out fresh farm-to-table fare that complements the well-chosen wine list. The atmosphere is lively and informal, with rustic place settings and friendly service—as any proper *enoteca* should be. The menu offers classic comfort food, like meatballs in tomato sauce or beef stew, plus lighter fare like poached pompano with baked fennel. Vegetarians will find plenty of options.

Via del Boschetto 41B. labarriquevinoecucina.wordpress.com. ✆ **06-47825953.** Main courses 10€–18€. Mon–Sat 12:45–2:30pm and 7:30–11pm; Sun 12:30–10pm. Metro: Cavour.

La Taverna dei Fori Imperiali ♥♥ TRADITIONAL ROMAN Nostalgia is heady at this classic eatery near the Roman Forum, now in its fourth generation of serving hearty Roman specialties in a cozy, crowded, noisy dining room lined with photos of famous guests, where the host makes the rounds, greeting old friends and making new ones. Stick to the usual Roman suspects, or try them with a twist, such as *cacio e pepe* with truffles or a vegetarian carbonara. Daily specials are almost always interesting here, and if you've still got room for dessert, you won't regret sticking a spoon into a dish of creamy *zabaione* or the ricotta cheesecake.

Via della Madonna dei Monti 9. latavernadeiforiimperiali.com. ✆ **06-6798643.** Main courses 14€–22€. Daily 12:30–3pm and 7–10pm. Metro: Cavour.

Taverna Romana "Monti 79" ♥♥ TRADITIONAL ROMAN The scenery at this homey trat is so on-brand for Rome that it's practically archetypal—the wooden chairs, paper tablecloths, and bad lighting are entirely free of artifice. The food, too, is as comforting as you'd expect, with generous portions of Roman specialties like *carciofi alla romana* (herb-seasoned artichokes), pasta *alla gricia* (with tomato, pork cheek, and Pecorino cheese), *saltimbocca alla romana* perfumed with sage and white wine, oxtail stew, and many plates where offal is the protagonist. It's all served by staff who know they're delivering the real deal.

Via della Madonna dei Monti 79. ✆ **06-4745325.** Main courses 11€–18€. Daily 12:30–3pm and 7–11pm. Metro: Cavour.

INEXPENSIVE

Li Rioni ♥♥ PIZZA This fab neighborhood pizzeria is close enough to the Colosseum to be convenient, but just distant enough to avoid the dreaded "touristy" label that applies to so much dining in this part of town. Roman-style pizzas baked in the wood-stoked oven are among the best in town, with perfectly crisp crusts. There's also a bruschetta list (from around 4€) and a range of salads. Outside tables can be cramped, but there's plenty of room inside. If you want to eat late, booking is essential or you'll be fighting with hungry locals for a table. ***Tip:*** After visiting the Colosseum or the Basilica of San Clemente, stop for an *aperitivo,* then head here at 7 for an early (and cheap) pizza dinner.

Via SS. Quattro 24. lirioni.it. ✆ **06-70450605.** Pizzas 9€–14€. Wed–Mon 7pm–midnight. Closed 2 weeks Aug. Metro: Colosseo. Bus: 51, 85, 87. Tram: 3 or 8.

Centro Storico & the Pantheon

For restaurant locations, see map on p. 101. Vegetarians (or anyone who wants a break from meat and carbs) looking for big salads can find them at **L'Insalata Ricca** ♥, Largo dei Chiavari 85 (✆ **06-68803656;** daily 11am–midnight).

EXPENSIVE

Casa Coppelle ♥♥♥ MODERN FRENCH AND ITALIAN The long-standing rivalry between French and Italian cuisine is deliciously resolved in this elegant dining room near Piazza Navona. Helmed by Omar, a Roman, and Rachelle, from France, the menu draws from the classics of both cultures, so expect French onion soup, seafood risotto, and Roman-style artichokes vying for your attention, all served with modern flair. Dinners here are delightfully romantic, especially the tasting menu experiences.

Piazza delle Coppelle 49. casacoppelle.com. ✆ **06-68891707.** Main courses 17€–38€, tasting menus 90€–160€. Tues–Sun 6:30pm–midnight. Closed Mon. Bus: 52, 53, 70, 71.

Pipero Roma ♥♥ MODERN ITALIAN This Michelin-starred, long-established foodie haven occupies chic digs opposite the Chiesa Nuova, in a setting that's as sophisticated as the plates paraded forth from the

GETTING YOUR FILL OF gelato

Don't leave town without trying one (or several) of Rome's outstanding **ice cream parlors.** But choose your gelato carefully: Don't buy close to the tourist-packed piazzas, and don't be dazzled by vats of brightly (and artificially) colored, air-pumped gelato. The best gelato is made only from natural ingredients, which impart a natural color—if the pistachio gelato is bright green, move on. Take your cone (*cono*) or small cup (*coppetta*) and stroll as you eat—sitting down on the premises is usually more expensive. The recommended spots below are generally open mid-morning to late, sometimes after midnight on summer weekends. Cones and small cups cost between 2.50€ and 5€—at these prices you can eat it twice a day!

Not far from Piazza Navona, **Gelateria del Teatro ♥♥**, Via dei Coronari 65/66 (✆ **06-45474880**), is a perennial favorite for both traditional and unexpected flavors, which rotate seasonally, including a dark chocolate infused with red wine from Sicily, or sage and raspberry. In Monti, fabulous (and gluten-free) **Fatamorgana ♥♥♥**, Piazza degli Zingari 5 (gelateriafatamorgana.com; ✆ **06-86391589;** Metro: Cavour; other locations across Rome), is the place to try inventive flavors like delicate lavender and chamomile, or zingy avocado, lime, and white wine.

Two exceptions to the rule about avoiding gelato in touristy areas: venerable **Old Bridge Gelateria ♥**, Viale Bastioni di Michelangelo (gelateriaoldbridge.com; ✆ **328-411-9478**), which delights customers lined up for the Vatican Museums; and, near Piazza Navona, **Frigidarium ♥♥♥**, Via del Governo Vecchio 112 (frigidarium-gelateria.com; ✆ **334-995-1184**), whose intense and creamy flavors will make you weep with joy. Have a *coppetta* of mango and coconut for me.

In the Termini area, tiny but sleek **Come il Latte ♥♥♥**, Via Silvio Spaventa 24 (✆ **06-42903882;** Metro: Repubblica or Castro Pretorio), turns out artisan gelatos in flavors ranging from salted caramel to mascarpone and crumbled cookies; fruit flavors change according to season.

Trastevere's best artisan gelato, **Fior di Luna ♥♥♥**, Via della Lungaretta 96 (fiordiluna.com; ✆ **06-64561314;** bus H or 780; tram 8), is made with natural and Fair Trade produce. Star flavors are the incredibly rich chocolates, spiked with fig or orange, and an absolutely perfect pistachio.

kitchen. The focus here is on 3- to 10-course tasting menus, with options like an elevated take on carbonara, mussels in clear broth, and desserts that may feature lychee fruit, rosewater, and other delicate flavors. The small, precious servings will either dazzle you or drive you nuts with their pretension—it's better to make that decision before you book a table.

Corso Vittorio Emanuele II 250. piperoroma.it. ✆ **06-68139022.** Tasting menus 100€–220€. Tues–Fri noon–3pm and 7–11pm; Mon, Sat 7–11pm. Closed Sun. Bus: 40, 46, 62, 64, 916.

MODERATE

Antica Hostaria Romanesca ♥ ROMAN It's very easy to eat badly on Campo de' Fiori, which makes this authentic spot with ringside seats on the piazza such a pleasant surprise. Romanesca does dependable, old-school Roman fare at fair prices, including a gloriously juicy *pollo e* *peperoni* (stewed chicken with peppers) and *abbacchio scottadito,* lamb chops hot off the grill, as well as reliably good classic Roman pastas. Locals snatch up the tables after 9pm, so a reservation is advised. Look for the daily blackboard specials—they'll reflect whatever looked good in the market that day.

Campo de' Fiori 40 (east side of square). facebook.com/anticahostariaromanesca. ✆ **06-6864024.** Main courses 13€–18€. Daily noon–3pm and 7–11pm. Bus: 40, 64, 70. Tram: 8.

Sidewalk tables are prized seats at Il Bacaro.

Il Bacaro ♥♥ MODERN ITALIAN Set on a hidden backstreet near the Pantheon, this is a romantic and low-key respite from the traffic and tourist crush. Delicious *primi* and *secondi* include spaghetti with butter, anchovies and herbed breadcrumbs, or grilled octopus with zucchini cream and walnuts. Desserts are of the creamy and fluffy variety, including the obligatory tiramisu. The wine list features well-priced varietals from all over Italy, including a couple dozen by the glass. Try to get a prized sidewalk table on a balmy summer evening.

Via degli Spagnoli 27 (near Piazza delle Coppelle). ilbacaroroma.com. ✆ **06-6872554.** Main courses 16€–28€. Daily noon–3pm and 7pm–midnight. Bus: 70, 71.

La Campana ♥♥♥ ROMAN/ITALIAN Family atmosphere and a classic Roman elegance prevail in Rome's oldest restaurant (feeding guests since 1518). The atmosphere is convivial yet refined, with a lovely mix of regulars and tourists. A broad selection of *antipasti* is displayed on a long table at the entrance, and the daily menu features authentic *cucina romana* that's heavy on offal. You'll also find classics like *cacio e pepe,* plus myriad vegetarian choices. The wine list includes interesting local labels, the staff and service are impeccable, and prices are fair.

Vicolo della Campana 18/20. ✆ **06-6875273.** Main courses 12€–22€. Tues–Sun 12:30–3pm and 7:30–11pm. Metro: Spagna. Bus: 70.

La Vecchia Locanda ♥♥ ROMAN If you have boxes to tick, this friendly, unpretentious tavern will grab your attention: a snug, rustic dining room, a lower cantina level lined with wine bottles and dotted with Roman ruins, and a comfort food menu with all the usual suspects. Look for reliably tasty charcuterie platters, carbonara, *amatriciana,* or *cacio e pepe,* and stellar desserts. It also has a nice range of seafood choices.

Vicolo Sinibaldi 2. ✆ **06-68802831.** Main courses 13€–20€. Mon–Sat 6:45–11pm. Bus: 30, 40, 46 or any to Largo Argentina. Tram: 8.

Nonna Betta ♥♥ ROMAN/JEWISH The history is palpable at Nonna Betta, where images of the 19th-century Rome Ghetto line the walls. Traditional dishes include delicious *carciofi alla giudia:* deep-fried artichokes served with small morsels like battered cod filet, stuffed and fried zucchini flowers, carrot sticks, or whatever vegetable is in season. Don't forego the *baccalà* with onions and tomato or the zucchini carbonara. Middle Eastern specialties such as falafel and hummus are on the menu, and all desserts are homemade, including a stellar cake with pine nuts. In keeping with kosher law, meat and dairy are on separate menus and never combined in recipes, making this a great choice for vegetarians.
Via del Portico d'Ottavia 16. nonnabetta.it. ✆ **06-68806263.** Main courses 13€–18€. Wed–Mon 12:15–3pm and 6:30–10pm. Bus: 40, 64, 170. Tram 8.

Pietro al Pantheon ♥ ROMAN "I want to eat there!" my guest, a first-timer to Rome, pointed, without ever looking at the menu at this atmospheric trattoria a block off the Pantheon. And truthfully, if we awarded stars just for ambience, Pietro merits at least three. While there are no culinary marvels here, you'll find well prepared staples like bruschetta, supplì, pastas, and meats (though pizzas are forgettable), all in a charmingly cluttered candlelit setting that looks like something out of a movie. We prefer the inside dining room to the crowded streetside terrace.
Via dei Pastini 125. ✆ **06-6789940.** Main courses 10€–18€. Daily noon–10:30pm. Bus: 63, 83, 160.

Retrobottega ♥♥♥ MODERN ROMAN Fresh, modern, and progressive, the somewhat misnamed Retrobottega is a jolting contrast to the well-worn streets and predictable trattorias surrounding it. This culinary laboratory, founded by a team of young, accomplished chefs, is an intimate but convivial choice. Most seats surround the open kitchen, and customers interact directly with the chefs as their food is prepared. The handful of daily offerings focus on local, seasonal, responsibly sourced ingredients and unexpected pairings, like tortelli with savoy cabbage, Parmigiano broth, and bay leaf oil, or pork prepared with a confit of Jerusalem artichokes and salted lemon. Breakfast offers upgraded takes on *caffè* and cornetto.
Via d'Ascanio 26A. retro-bottega.com. ✆ **06-68136310.** Main courses 19€–33€; breakfast items 3€–14€. Tues–Sun 8:30am–11:30pm; Mon dinner only. Bus: 40, 70, 85.

Pietro al Pantheon is an atmospheric find just a block from the Pantheon.

INEXPENSIVE

Alfredo e Ada ♥♥ ROMAN A daily chalkboard menu is the norm here, which speaks to the freshness and simplicity of this ultimate comfort-food destination, now in its third generation of family ownership. Look for classic trattoria fare like eggplant Parmigiana, excellent carbonara, and Roman-style tripe or oxtail stew. The whole place oozes character, with shared tables, scribbled walls, and the house wine poured from a tap in the wall. There are only a handful of tables, so it's best to make a reservation or get here early. This sort of place is increasingly rare in Rome—enjoy it while you can.

Via dei Banchi Nuovi 14. ✆ **06-6878842.** Main courses 10€–18€. Tues–Sat noon–3pm and 7–10pm. Closed Aug. Bus: 40, 64.

Antico Forno Roscioli ♥♥♥ BAKERY Some places merit all the hype they get. Three generations of Rosciolis have been running this celebrated bakery since the 1970s, though bread has been made here since at least 1824. Today it's the home of the finest crusty sourdough in Rome, assorted cakes, and addictive pastries and biscotti, as well as exceptional Roman-style *pizza bianca* and *pizza rossa* sold by weight. This is largely a takeout joint with limited seating, and the wider range of pizza toppings is only available from noon to 2:30pm. Around the corner is the wonderful **Roscioli restaurant and *salumeria* deli** at Via dei Giubbonari 21 and, at Piazza Benedetto Cairoli 16, **Roscioli Caffè,** which offers breakfast treats, cappuccino, and palate-pleasing panini.

Via dei Chiavari 34. anticofornoroscioli.it. ✆ **06-6864045.** Pizza from 5€ (sold by weight). Daily 7:30am–8pm. Bus: 40, 85, 492, or any to Largo Argentina. Tram: 8.

Da Baffetto ♥♥ PIZZA You don't come to Baffetto for cheerful service or even for comfort—tables are cramped and you might wind up sharing one with strangers. You come for the gloriously authentic Roman pizza: crisp-crusted and dispatched quickly from the wood oven. This place is dirt-cheap and immensely popular with locals. If there's a line out the door, take heart: They shuffle people in and out of here quickly, and a lot of folks are in line for takeaway. After dinner, pop next door to **Frigidarium ♥♥♥** (p. 143) for a gelato.

Via del Governo Vecchio 114. ✆ **06-6861617.** Pizza 8€–15€. Wed–Mon 12:30–3:30pm, 6pm–midnight. Closed Tues and first 2 weeks of Aug. Bus: 40, 64, 70, 492.

Tridente, the Spanish Steps & Via Veneto

For restaurant locations, see map p. 107. The historic cafes near the Spanish Steps are saturated with history but, sadly, tend to be overpriced tourist traps, where mediocre slices of cake or even a cup of coffee or tea will cost 5€. Nevertheless, you may want to pop into the celebrated **Babingtons Tea Rooms** (babingtons.com; ✆ **06-6786027;** Wed–Mon noon–10pm), established in 1893 at the foot of the Spanish Steps by a couple of English *signore.* Sadly, **Antico Caffè Greco,** Rome's oldest bar, which opened in 1760, closed in 2025 after a long legal battle with its landlords, though at press time there were murmurs of a possible reopening. In the heart of the Villa Borghese park, on Piazzale delle Canestre, **Pic Nic ♥♥ (✆ 06-855-7493;** daily 9am–7pm) is a great spot for lunch or a snack.

EXPENSIVE

Al Ceppo ♥♥ MARCHIGIANA/ROMAN The setting of this Parioli dining institution is an elegant 19th-century parlor, with dark wood furnishings, chandeliers, fresh flowers, family portraits on the walls, and an open kitchen with a wood-stoked hearth. The menu features regional dishes from the owners' home, the Le Marche region northeast of Rome: fish stews, fresh seafood, and grilled meats, all artfully prepared and presented, along with pastas both hearty and delicate. It's reason enough to head north to explore Parioli's many charms.

Via Panama 2 (near Piazza Ungheria). ristorantealceppo.com. ✆ **06-8419696.** Main courses 24€–50€. Tues–Sun 12:30–3pm and 7:30–11pm; Mon 7:30–11pm. Closed last 2 weeks Aug. Bus: 223, 360, 910. Tram: 3 or 19.

Imàgo ♥♥♥ INTERNATIONAL If you're lucky enough to score one of just twelve tables at this sixth-floor, Michelin-starred hotel restaurant, the views of Rome are jaw-dropping, as the old city glows pink as the sun goes down. The food is equally breathtaking and painstakingly presented. Chef Andrea Antonini's seasonal menus reinterpret Italian cuisine, borrowing heavily from international culinary traditions, which may mean amberjack crudo with citrus and fennel pollen, Roman artichoke with hazelnut and aged pecorino, or a delicate tortellini in crystalclear consommé. Reservations are essential; jackets required for men.

In Hotel Hassler, Piazza della Trinità dei Monti 6. imagorestaurant.com. ✆ **06-69934726.** Tasting menus 210€–220€, beverages excluded. Tues–Sat 7–10:30pm. Closed first 2 weeks of Jan. Metro: Spagna.

The expert chefs at Imàgo make sure the food is just as outstanding as that knockout view.

MODERATE

Colline Emiliane ♥♥♥ EMILIANA-ROMAGNOLA This family-owned restaurant tucked in an alley beside the Trevi Fountain has been serving traditional Emilia-Romagna dishes since 1931. Service is excellent and so is the food: Classics include *tortelli di zucca* (pumpkin ravioli in butter sauce) and magnificent *tagliatelle alla Bolognese,* the mother of all Italian comfort foods. The *secondi* menu is heavy on beef, nearly all of it served with mashed potatoes. Save room for the walnut-and-caramel cake or lemon meringue pie. Reservations are essential.

Via degli Avignonesi 22 (off Piazza Barberini). collineemiliane.com. ✆ **06-4817538.** Main courses 15€–23€. Tues–Sat 12:45–2:45pm and 7:30–10:45pm, Sun 12:45–2:45pm. Closed Aug. Metro: Barberini.

Around Termini

4

For restaurant locations, see map p. 115. Mostly catering to dazed travelers toting wheeled suitcases, restaurants around Termini don't have to be good to bring in business. The following are some of our favorite exceptions to that norm.

MODERATE

Trattoria Monti ♥♥ REGIONAL/MARCHE Word is definitely out on this cozy, plain-Jane trattoria near Termini station. You will remember for the rest of your life the *tortello al rosso d'uovo,* a large, delicate ravioli filled with spinach, ricotta, and egg yolk—the one everyone posts videos of on social media. You also may discover a few new favorites among the territory's underappreciated wines. Vegetarians take heart: Four or five non-meat main courses are always available.

Via di San Vito 13A (at Via Merulana). ✆ **06-4466573.** Main courses 13€–24€. Tues–Sat 1–2:45pm and 8–10:45pm. Metro: Cavour or Vittorio Emanuele. Bus: 360, 714. Tram: 5 or 14.

Trimani Enoteca ♥ MODERN ITALIAN This small bistro and well-stocked wine bar (with a 20-page wine list!) attracts wine lovers and after-workers in a modern, relaxed ambience, accompanied by smooth jazz. The refined main courses might include smoked trout with orange mayonnaise, or a simple grilled filet with potatoes. The wines-by-the-glass list changes daily. If you just want a snack to accompany your vino, cheese and salami platters range from 10€ to 20€. Organized wine tastings here are great fun, too. The selection at Trimani's vast wine shop next door boggles the oenophile mind.

Via Cernaia 37B. trimani.com. ✆ **06-4469630.** Main courses 15€–24€. Mon–Sat 9am–8:30pm. Closed 2 weeks mid-Aug. Metro: Repubblica or Castro Pretorio.

INEXPENSIVE

Mercato Centrale Roma ♥♥ GOURMET MARKET This ambitious, three-story gourmet dining hall and street food hub is the best place to dine in Termini Station, with top-notch purveyors of everything from gourmet pizza to chocolate to truffles, plus a wine bar and a high-end restaurant. The space is inviting, if a little chaotic. Even if you don't have a train to catch, it's worth having lunch or a quick snack here if you're in the area. ***Tip:*** Walk through the hall and check out all the offerings, then snag a table and have members of your party take turns going to order food. If you have a train to catch, be sure to allow extra time to get to the market, on the Via Giovanni Giolitti side of the station.

Via Giovanni Giolitti 36 (in Termini Station). mercatocentrale.it/roma. ✆ **06-46202900.** Daily 7am–midnight. Metro: Termini.

Pinsere ♥♥ PIZZA *Pinsa* is an ancient Roman preparation: an oval focaccia made with a blend of four organic flours and olive oil that's left to rise for 2 to 3 days. The result is a crispy, feather-light, single-portion snack perfect for a light lunch. This friendly, small bakery always has an assortment of *pinse* ready to pop in the oven. Favorites come with pureed pumpkin, smoked cheese, and pancetta; classic tomato, basil, and *bufala;* or the surprising combo of ricotta, fresh figs, raisins, pine nuts, and honey. There are a few tables under a gazebo out front, otherwise plan to eat standing up at an inside counter, or take it to go. ***Note:*** Pinsere is closed on weekends.

Via Flavia 98. ✆ **06-42020924.** *Pinse* 5€–7.50€. Mon–Fri 10am–9pm. Metro: Castro Pretorio. Bus: 38, 66, 90, 223.

Trastevere

For restaurant locations, see map p. 119. On Piazza di San Cosimato, **Food Factory Trastevere ♥♥** (✆ **06-58340297**) serves traditional snacks like *supplì* (fried stuffed rice croquettes) as well as a daily menu of filling favorites. Hearts and tastebuds soar at **Biscottificio Artigiano Innocenti ♥♥**, Via della Luce 21 (✆ **06-5803926**), where Stefania and her family have been turning out delicate handmade cookies and cakes since the 1920s.

EXPENSIVE

Antico Arco ♥♥♥ CREATIVE ITALIAN This well-known address for new Italian cuisine consistently delivers exquisite dishes made with the finest local and seasonal ingredients—like a blond onion flan with Parmesan zabaglione and saffron, black truffle carbonara, or a beef fillet with yellow tomatoes and buffalo mozzarella, all accompanied by excellent wine and top-notch service. A full meal here makes a special night out (reservations essential), but you can also just come to the restaurant's wine bar for *vino* and finger food—it pairs nicely with rapturous *centro storico* views from the nearby terraces of the Janiculum Hill. ***Tip:*** It's a 15-minute walk uphill from Trastevere, but the climb is gradual and pleasant.

Piazzale Aurelio 7 (at Via San Pancrazio). anticoarco.it. ✆ **06-5815274.** Main courses 22€–35€. Wed–Mon noon–midnight. Bus: 75, or tram 3 or 8, then 15-min. walk.

Spirito DiVino ♥♥♥ ROMAN/SLOW FOOD In a medieval synagogue atop a 2nd-century street (which you can visit on a cellar tour), the

Catalani family does exceptional modern cuisine using only organic ingredients. Dishes such as an appetizer of chicken liver pate with apple jelly, or rigatoni with lamb ragu, as well as ancient Roman cuisine (like *maiale alla mazio,* a favorite pork dish of Julius Caesar's), are as warm and comforting as the ambience. Finish with almond and chocolate cake served with banana and chile pepper.

Via dei Genovesi 31 (at Vicolo dell'Atleta). ristorantespiritodivino.com. ✆ **06-5896689.** Main courses 14€–26€. Mon–Sat 7–11:30pm. Bus: H, 75. Tram: 8.

MODERATE

Osteria Cacio e Pepe ♥ ROMAN This neighborhood stalwart is an ultra-traditional trattoria, complete with paper tablecloths, a TV showing the game, the owner chatting up clients, and a crowd of patrons—admittedly many of them tourists—waiting to be seated. Start with cheapo plates of fried tidbits, from rice *suppli* to cod to vegetables, then move on to the namesake pasta *cacio e pepe* or other classic Roman pasta dishes—and be ready for hearty portions. For *secondi*—if you have room left—consider *saltimbocca alla romana* (veal cutlets with sage and ham) or grilled meats, all reasonably priced. There's even pizza for the kids.

Vicolo del Cinque 15. osteriacacioepepe.it. ✆ **06-89572853.** Main courses 13€–26€. Daily noon–2am. Bus: H. 75. Tram: 8.

Osteria La Gensola ♥♥♥ SEAFOOD/ROMAN Considered one of the best seafood destinations in Rome, this warm and welcoming family-run restaurant feels like a true Trastevere home; decor is cozy, with soft lighting and a life-size wood-carved tree in the middle of the main dining room. Fish lovers come for heavenly *spaghetti alle vongole* (with fresh clams), grilled or fried calamari, sea bass ravioli, and other traditional Roman plates with a marine twist. The grill churns out succulent beefsteaks as well, but we really do come to La Gensola for the seafood. Reservations are a must on weekends.

Piazza della Gensola 15. osterialagensola.it. ✆ **06-58332758.** Main courses 14€–27€; many fish dishes priced by weight. Daily 12:30–3pm and 7:30–11:30pm. Bus: 75, 85, 170, H. Tram: 8.

INEXPENSIVE

Dar Poeta ♥ PIZZA Ranking among the best pizzerias in Rome, "the poet" is a fine place to enjoy a classic Roman pizza *margherita* (tomato sauce, mozzarella, and fresh basil) or a more creative combo like the *Dar Poeta,* with mozzarella, zucchini, soft ciauscolo salami, garlic, and chili. They also serve bruschetta, cold-cut platters, and entree salads. On a sultry summer night, dining at one of the wobbly sidewalk tables is a quintessential Trastevere experience; though if the wait is too long, you can also order takeout.

Vicolo del Bologna 45. darpoeta.com. ✆ **06-5880516.** Pizzas 7€–13€. Daily noon–midnight. Bus: 75, H.

Testaccio

The slaughterhouses of Rome's old meatpacking district (see map on p. 119) have been transformed into art venues, markets, and the museum **MACRO ♥** (p. 118), but restaurants here still specialize in (though are not limited to) meats from the *quinto quarto* (the "fifth quarter")—the leftover parts of an animal after slaughter, typically offal like sweetbreads, tripe, tails, and other goodies you won't find on most American menus. This is an area to eat *cucina romana*—either in the restaurants below or from street-food stalls in the **Nuovo Mercato di Testaccio ♥♥♥** (p. 154). Food-themed tours of Rome invariably end up here.

EXPENSIVE

Checchino dal 1887 ♥♥ ROMAN Often mischaracterized as an offal-only joint, this establishment, opened in 1887 across from Rome's now-defunct abattoir, is a special-night-out type of place, serving wonderful *bucatini all'amatriciana* and veal saltimbocca—as well as hearty plates of oxtail, sweetbreads, intestines, livers, and other odd bits. Checchino is a pricier choice than most restaurants in this area, but Romans from all over the city keep coming back when they want the real thing. Despite its meat-centric leanings, Checchino has several meat-free pasta and soup options, and they will also make gluten-free pasta.
Via di Monte Testaccio 30 (at Via Galvani). checchino-dal-1887.com. ✆ **06-5746316.** Main courses 13€–26€. Wed–Sun 12:30–3pm and 7:30–11pm. Closed Aug and part of Dec–Jan. Metro: Piramide.

MODERATE

Flavio al Velavevodetto ♥ ROMAN Flavio's plain dining room is burrowed out of the side of Rome's most unusual "hill": a large mound made from amphorae discarded during the Roman era (p. 71). Food-lovers come here for classic Roman pastas like *cacio e pepe* and *amatriciana,* plus *quinto quarto* (nose-to-tail) main courses at fair prices. Hearty dishes like *polpette al sugo* (meatballs in red sauce), *coda alla vaccinara* (oxtail), and fried calamari and anchovies are good for sharing. Though justly famous, Flavio may be coasting on reputation just a wee bit.
Via di Monte Testaccio 97–99. ristorantevelavevodetto.it. ✆ **06-5744194.** Main courses 13€–20€. Daily noon–3pm and 7:30–11pm. Metro: Piramide.

Osteria degli Amici ♥♥ MODERN ROMAN On the corner of nightclub central and the hill of broken amphorae, this intimate, friendly *osteria* with a sleek dining room serves traditional Roman classics and creative variations. Claudio and Alessandro base their menu on their combined experience in famous kitchens around the world, with presentations that are more sophisticated than is typical for this part of town. Our favorites include a creamy burrata swimming in gazpacho, a just-spicy-enough spaghetti with garlic, oil, and chili pepper, and seared yellowfin tuna marinated with soy sauce and panzanella. Leave room for a homemade dessert—they're all good.

Via Nicola Zabaglia 25. osteriadegliamiciroma.it. ✆ **06-5781466.** Main courses 12€–26€. Wed–Mon 12:30–2:30pm and 8pm–midnight. Metro: Piramide.

Porto Fluviale ♥ MODERN ITALIAN This multifunctional restaurant—part trattoria, part street-food stall, part pizzeria—can accommodate pretty much whatever you fancy. The decor is vaguely industrial, with a daytime clientele of families and professionals on lunch break; the vibe gets younger after dark. From the various menus, dozens of inexpensive small plates allow you to sample the kitchen's range. Several pastas and main courses are available in half-portions, and the meat kebabs are served with dramatic flair. Both the locale and the menus are highly kid-friendly, and the Sunday brunch is a good bargain.

Via del Porto Fluviale 22. portofluviale.com. ✆ **06-5743199.** Small plates 3€–7€; main courses 11€–28€; Sun brunch 25€ (13€ for kids). Daily 10:30am–2am. Metro: Piramide.

Trattoria Perilli ♥♥ ROMAN Dine elbow-to-elbow with locals and enjoy the old-school atmosphere at this beloved institution of Roman *ristorazione.* With zero pretense, Perilli's formally attired waitstaff serve unadulterated renditions of Roman classics. The menu is small and the dishes reliable, from pasta standbys like a spinach and ricotta ravioli that my Italian mother-in-law would approve of, to grilled meats and that most English of Italian desserts, *zuppa inglese* (literally "English soup," or trifle). It's a fun and reasonably affordable place for a four-course meal of *antipasto, primo, secondo,* and *dolce.* Reservations recommended.

Via Marmorata 39 (at Via Galvani). perilliatestaccio.com. ✆ **06-5742415.** Main courses 15€–25€. Tues–Sat 12:30–3pm and 7:30–11:15pm; Sun 12:30–3pm. Metro: Piramide. Bus: 75. Tram: 3.

INEXPENSIVE

Pizzeria Remo A Testaccio ♥♥ PIZZA Mentioning "Testaccio" and "pizza" in the same sentence elicits one typical response from locals: Remo, a Roman institution. In the summer especially, come early or be prepared to wait for a table. Every crisp-crusted, perfectly foldable pizza is made for all to see behind open counters. The most basic ones (margherita and marinara) start at around 7€. If it's too crowded on a summer evening, order your pizza to go and eat it in the park across the street.

Piazza Santa Maria Liberatrice 44. ✆ **06-5746270.** Pizzas 6€–10€. Mon–Sat 7pm–1am. Bus: 75. Tram: 3, 8.

ROME SHOPPING

As in major cities everywhere, the Rome shopping landscape continues to grow more and more homogenous, as long-time, family-run shops finally give up the ghost, their storefronts filled by multinational fast fashion chains or cheap souvenir vendors.

That said, Rome is still a magnet for high-end shoppers, foodies, lovers of antiques, and those in search of the arcane. In our limited space below we've summarized streets and areas known for their shops. Keep in mind that the monthly rent on the famous streets is very high, and those costs are passed on to you. Note that **sales** usually run twice a year, starting in January and July, with savings of anywhere from 30% to 70%.

Top Shopping Streets & Areas

AROUND PIAZZA DI SPAGNA Most of Rome's haute couture and seriously upscale shopping fans out from the bottom of the Spanish Steps. **Via Condotti** is probably Rome's poshest shopping street, where you'll find Prada, Gucci, Bulgari, and the like. A few more down-to-earth stores have opened, but it's still largely a playground for the super-rich. Neighboring **Via Borgognona** also has chic, ultra-expensive merchandise, but thanks to its pedestrian-only access and handsome baroque and neoclassical facades, it offers a nicer window-browsing experience. Shops are more densely concentrated on **Via Frattina,** the third of this trio of upscale streets. Chic boutiques for adults and kids rub shoulders with ready-to-wear fashion, high-end chains, and a few tourist tat vendors. It's usually crowded with shoppers who appreciate the lack of motor traffic.

CAMPO DE' FIORI Though the campo itself is now chockablock with restaurants, the streets leading up to it, notably **Via dei Giubbonari** and **Via Dei Baullari,** offer edgy and often one-of-a-kind fashions. Boutiques go in and out of business with dizzying frequency, but something interesting is always popping up. Off Piazza Farnese, **Via di Monserrato** has a stretch of quirky shops, especially **Chez Dédé** at no. 35 (chezdede.com), with its pleasing mix of collectibles and bespoke housewares and accessories.

MONTI Rome's most fashion-conscious central neighborhood has a pleasing mix of artisan retailers, vintage boutiques, and honest, everyday stores frequented by locals, with not a brand name in sight. Roam the length of **Via del Boschetto** for one-off fashions, designer ateliers, and unique homewares. In fact, you can roam in every direction from the spot where Via del Boschetto meets **Via Panisperna.** Turn on nearby **Via Urbana** or **Via Leonina,** where boutiques jostle for space with cafes that are ideal for a break or light lunch.

VIA COLA DI RIENZO The commercial heart of the Prati neighborhood, this long street runs straight from the Tiber to Piazza Risorgimento. It's known for stores selling a variety of merchandise at reasonable prices, from jewelry to fashionable clothing, bags, and shoes. Among the most prestigious is the historic Roman perfume store (with products for men and women), **Bertozzini Profumeria dal 1913,** at no. 192 (bertozzini dal1913.it). Department store **Coin** is at no. 173 (with a large supermarket in the basement); the largest branch of gourmet food store **Castroni** is at no. 196 (castronicoladirienzo.com).

VIA DEI CORONARI An antiques-lover's souk. If you're shopping, or just window-shopping for antiques, art, or vintage-style souvenir prints, then spend an hour walking the length of this pretty, pedestrian-only street. At Via dei Coronari 218, **Manufactus** (manufactus.it) sells hand-crafted leather goods and stationery.

VIA DEL CORSO With less of a glamour quotient (and less-stratospheric prices) than Via Condotti or Via Borgognona, Via del Corso boasts affordable styles aimed at younger consumers. Occasional gems are scattered amid international shops selling jeans and sportswear. The most interesting stores are toward the Piazza del Popolo end of the street (**Via del Babuino** has a similar profile). Or turn at Largo Chigi towards Via del Tritone, and run a retail gauntlet that includes **Rinascente,** a high-end department store, **Hugo BOSS, Sephora,** and other familiar names. The farther south you walk (toward the Vittoriano monument), the narrower the sidewalks—and generally, the tackier the stores.

VIA DEL GOVERNO VECCHIO We love everything about this pretty street that winds parallel to Corso Vittorio Emanuele II, including its two venerable vintage shops, **Omero e Cecilia** (at no. 110) and **Cinzia** (no. 45). Via del Governo Vecchio also has great places to eat and drink, particularly on the end closest to Piazza di San Pantaleo.

VIA MARGUTTA This beautiful, tranquil street is home to numerous art stalls and artists' studios—Federico Fellini used to live here—though a lot of stores these days tend to offer the same sort of antiques and mediocre paintings. You have to shop hard to find real quality. A definite highlight is **Bottega del Marmoraro** at no. 53b, the whimsical studio of master stone carver Sandro Fiorentini.

Rome's Best Markets

Campo de' Fiori ♥ Central Rome's food market, running since at least the 1800s, is no longer the place to find a produce bargain (though the fruit and veg displays are dazzling). It tends to attract more tourists than locals, but it's still a genuine slice of Roman life in one of its most attractive squares. The market runs daily 7am to 1 or 2pm, with fewer produce vendors on Sunday. Campo de' Fiori. No phone. Bus: 40, 64, 170. Tram: 8.

Nuovo Mercato di Testaccio ♥♥♥ Traditional food and produce stalls meet street-food central in this modernist, sustainably powered market building. It's the best place for produce shopping and a terrific stop for a lunch of *suppli* (fried rice balls) and craft beer (**Food Box ♥♥**, Box 66), or a meat- and sauce-stuffed panini (**Mordi e Vai ♥♥**, Box 15). There are also clothing and kitchenware stalls. The market runs Monday to Saturday 7am to 3:30pm. Btw. Via Luigi Galvani and Via Aldo Manuzio (at Via Benjamin Franklin). mercatoditestaccio.it. No phone. Metro: Piramide.

Porta Portese ♥ Trastevere's vast weekly flea market stretches all the way from the Porta Portese gate along Via di Porta Portese to Viale di

Trastevere. You'll have to wade through a lot of junk (and a sea of humanity—hold tight to your belongings), but there are good stalls for vintage housewares, clothing, and collectibles. It runs Sundays from dawn until midafternoon. Via di Porta Portese. No phone. Tram: 8.

ENTERTAINMENT & NIGHTLIFE

Several English-language outlets offer current information about nightlife and cultural events in Rome. ***Wanted in Rome*** (wantedinrome.com) has listings of opera, rock, and English-language cinema showings, and gives an insider look at expat Rome. ***Romeing*** (romeing.it) is worth consulting, especially for contemporary arts and culture. As blogs go, we like the soup-to-nuts approach of Elyssa Bernard's **Romewise** (romewise.com) and the insider tips in Rome-based travel writer Laura Itzkowitz's Substack newsletter **The New Roman Times** (newromantimes.substack.com).

Unless you're dead set on making the Roman nightclub circuit, try what might be a far livelier and less expensive option—sitting late into the evening on **Piazza della Rotonda** (the Pantheon), **Piazza del Popolo,** or one of Rome's other piazzas, all for the (admittedly inflated) cost of a prosecco or a Campari and soda. If you're a clubber who likes it loud and late, jump in a cab to **Monte Testaccio** or **Via del Pigneto** and bar-hop wherever your fancy takes you. In Trastevere, there's always a bit of life on **Via del Politeama** where it meets **Piazza Trilussa.** In the *centro storico,* a nice *aperitivo-cena* scene unfolds along **Via del Governo Vecchio.**

Performing Arts & Live Music

Rome's music scene doesn't have the same vibrancy as Florence's (p. 225) nor the high-quality opera of **La Scala** in Milan (p. 496) or **La Fenice** in Venice (p. 417). Still, classical music fans are well catered to here. In

Rome, Illuminated

When the sun goes down, Rome's palaces, ruins, fountains, and monuments are bathed in a theatrical white light. During your stay in Rome, be sure to make time for a memorable evening stroll past the solemn pillars of old temples or the cascading torrents of Renaissance fountains glowing under the blue-black sky. The **Fountain of the Naiads** (Fontana delle Naiadi) on Piazza della Repubblica, the **Fountain of the Tortoises** (Fontana della Tartarughe) on Piazza Mattei, the **Fountain of Acqua Paola** (Fontanone) at the top of the Janiculum Hill, and the **Trevi Fountain** (p. 109) are particularly beautiful at night. The **Capitoline Hill** (or Campidoglio) is magnificently lit after dark, its Renaissance facades glowing like jewel boxes. The view of the Roman Forum seen from the rear of Piazza del Campidoglio is perhaps the grandest in Rome (see "Three Free Views to Savor for a Lifetime," p. 92). Across the Tiber, the Vatican's **Piazza San Pietro** (p. 76) is impressive at night without the crowds. The combination of illuminated architecture, baroque fountains, and sidewalk shows makes **Piazza Navona** (p. 100) even more delightful at night.

addition to the major venues featured below, look for concerts and one-off events in churches and salons around the city. For a calendar of opera and ballet staged by the **Opera in Roma** association at enchanting venues across the city, check **operainroma.com**. The **Pontificio Instituto di Musica Sacra** regularly runs classical music and operatic evenings.

Alexanderplatz Jazz Club ♥♥ Alexanderplatz has been the home of Rome's jazz scene since the early 1980s. If there's a good act in the city, you will find it here. Live music 7 nights a week. Via Ostia 9. alexanderplatzjazz.com. ✆ **06-39742171.** Cover usually 10€. Metro: Ottaviano.

Auditorium–Parco della Musica ♥♥ This multipurpose arts center, designed by Renzo Piano, brings a refreshing breath of modernity to Rome. The schedule features lots of aging rockers and eclectic singer-songwriter acts, as well as traditional orchestras. Great cafes and a bookstore on-site, too. Viale Pietro de Coubertin 30. auditorium.com. ✆ **06-80241281.** Metro: Flaminio, then Tram 2. Bus: 910.

Teatro dell'Opera di Roma ♥♥ Here you'll find marquee operas such as *Aida* and *Rigoletto*; classical concerts from top-ranked orchestras; and such ballets as *Giselle*, *Swan Lake*, and *The Nutcracker*. In summer the action moves outdoors for unforgettable open-air operatic performances at the ruined **Baths of Caracalla** (p. 96). Piazza Beniamino Gigli 1 (at Via del Viminale). operaroma.it. ✆ **06-4817003** (box office). Tickets 25€–150€. Metro: Repubblica.

Cafes

Remember: In Rome and everywhere else in Italy, if you just want to drink a quick coffee and bolt, walk up to *il banco* (the bar), order *"un caffè, per favore"* or *"un cappuccino,"* and stay at the bar. They will make it for you to drink on the spot. (Note that in many small bars, you pay for your coffee at the cash register first, then take your receipt to the bar to order.) It will usually cost more (at least double) to sit down to drink it—if you're in high-traffic, touristy areas, outdoor table service is the most expensive way to go. Even in the heart of the city center, a short coffee *al banco* should cost about 1€; add around .30€ for a *cappuccino*. Expect to pay up to five times that price if you sit outdoors on a marquee piazza. Most cafes in the city serve a decent cup of coffee, but here's a small selection of places worth hunting down.

With its shabby-chic interior and namesake fig tree backdrop to charming outdoor seating, **Bar del Fico ♥**, Piazza del Fico 26 (bardelfico.com; ✆ **06-68808413**), is one of Rome's most beloved *aperitivo* spots and a coveted see-and-be-seen nightlife destination. **Sant'Eustachio il Caffè ♥♥**, Piazza Sant'Eustachio 82 (santeustachioilcaffe.it; ✆ **06-68802048**), roasts its own Fair Trade Arabica beans and draws a friendly crowd a few deep at the bar. (Unless you ask, the coffee comes with sugar.) Debate still rages among Romans as to whether the city's best cup of coffee is served here or at **Tazza d'Oro ♥**, near the Pantheon (Via degli Orfani 84; tazzadorocoffeeshop.com; ✆ **06-6789792**).

Wine Bars, Cocktail Bars & Craft Beer Bars

The tradition of *aperitivo* (happy hour) provides great insight into the particular ways of real Romans. It started in hard-working northern cities like Milan, where you'd go to a bar after leaving the office and, for the price of one drink, enjoy one or more plates of high-quality food—often with cheese, cured meats, bruschetta, and pasta salad. Luckily for Rome, the custom trickled down here, and now the city is filled with casual little places to drop in for a drink (from 6 or 7pm on) and eat to your heart's content. *Aperitivo* spreads vary in quantity and quality, but generally you'll pay anywhere from 8€ to 12€ per person for a drink and buffet. All the places listed here are fine for families, too—Italian kids love *aperitivo* (minus the alcohol, of course). Look for signs in the window and follow your nose. The **Monti** neighborhood is a good place to begin.

Ai Tre Scalini ♥ This little *bottiglieria* (wine bar) is the soul of Monti. It has a traditional menu, as well as a wine list sourced from across Italy. Arrive early or call for a table: This place is usually jammed. Via Panisperna 251. aitrescalini.org. ✆ **06-48907495.** Metro: Cavour.

Cielo Rooftop ♥♥♥ On the top floor of luxury Hotel de la Ville, Cielo offers breathtaking views down the Spanish Steps and of the sun setting behind St. Peter's. Cocktails are elaborate, served with a nice selection of aperitivo snacks. They don't take reservations, so get here early. Via Sistina, 69. roccofortehotels.com. ✆ **06-97793716.** Metro: Spagna.

Drink Kong ♥♥ The aesthetic here is King Kong conquers Tokyo while posting it to TikTok. But it's the innovative cocktails that have repeatedly earned Drink Kong a slot in the prestigious World's 50 Best Bars list. Piazza di S. Martino Ai Monti 8. drinkkong.com. ✆ **06-23488666.** Metro: Cavour.

Freni e Frizioni ♥♥♥ Trastevere's "Brakes and Clutches" is a former mechanics' garage turned delightfully grungy nighttime hotspot and has been steadily creeping up the World's 50 Best Bars list. On the adjacent square, an effervescent crowd lounges against stone walls and parked *motorini.* Via del Politeama 4–6 (near Piazza Trilussa). freniefrizioni.com. ✆ **06-45497499.** Bus: H. Tram: 8.

La Bottega del Caffè ♥ Beers, wine, cocktails, *aperitivo*—there's a little of everything at one of Monti's busiest neighborhood bars. Piazza Madonna dei Monti 5. ✆ **06-64741578.** Metro: Cavour.

Ma Che Siete Venuti A Fà ♥♥ This Trastevere beer pub takes its brews seriously, with 16 often obscure and constantly changing microbrews on tap at any given time, plus scores of bottled beers. This place is divey good fun, as is the rest of the bar-lined street it sits on. Via Benedetta 25. football-pub.com. ✆ **06-42918213.** Bus: H. Tram: 8.

Open Baladin ♥♥ If anyone ever tells you that Italians don't do good beer, send them to this bar near the Ghetto. Forty taps line the bar, with beers from its own Piedmont brewery and across Italy. Via degli Specchi 5–6. baladin.it/en/open-baladin-roma. ✆ **06-6838989.** Bus: 40, 64, 70. Tram: 8.

An alfresco cocktail and nibbles at Salotto42.

4

Salotto42 ♥♥ It's all fancy cocktails and well-chosen wines at this über-hip bookbar opposite the columned facade of 2nd-century Hadrian's Temple (near the Pantheon). A classy after-dinner stop, it also does shared plates, fresh juices, smoothies, and infused teas. Piazza di Pietra 42 (off Via del Corso). salotto42.it. ✆ **06-6785804.** Bus: 64, 85, 492.

Stravinskij Bar ♥ An evening at this award-winning cocktail bar inside one of Rome's most famous grand hotels is always a regal affair. Mixology, ingredients, and canapés are all top-notch. Inside Hotel de Russie, Via del Babuino 9. ✆ **06-32888874.** Metro: Spagna.

Vale la Pena Pub ♥♥ This way-casual, tongue-in-cheek beer pub, part of a nonprofit that works to reduce recidivism, offers beer from its own microbrewery, made by inmates from Rome's Rebibbia prison. It fits like a glove in the working-class Tuscolano district. Via Eurialo 22. economia carceraria.com. ✆ **06-87606875.** Metro: Furio Camillo.

SIDE TRIPS FROM ROME

Ostia Antica ♥♥

24km (15 miles) SW of Rome

The ruins of Rome's ancient port are a must-see for anyone who can't make it to Pompeii (p. 629). It's an easier day trip with smaller crowds and a similar theme: the chance to wander around the preserved ruins of an ancient Roman settlement that has been barely touched since its abandonment.

Ostia, at the mouth of the Tiber, was the port of Rome, the gateway for riches from the far corners of the Empire. Founded in the 4th century B.C.E., it became a major port and naval base under two later emperors, Claudius and Trajan. A prosperous city developed, full of temples, baths, theaters, and patrician homes. Flourishing between the 1st and 3rd centuries, Ostia survived until around the 9th century before it was abandoned, becoming little more than a malaria bed, a buried ghost city fading into

history. A papal-sponsored commission launched a series of digs in the 19th century, but the major work of unearthing was carried out under Mussolini's orders from 1938 to 1942. The city is only partially dug out today, but it's believed that all the chief monuments have been uncovered. ***Note:*** Ostia is a mostly flat site, but the Roman streets underfoot are clad in giant basalt cobblestones—wear comfortable walking shoes. Archaeology enthusiasts, especially those with their own car, might want to visit some of the other sites in the area, including the remains of the Imperial Harbors and the vast Necropolis of Porto.

ESSENTIALS

ARRIVING Take the Metro to Piramide, changing lines there for the Lido train to Ostia Antica. Departures to Ostia run every half hour; the trip is 25 minutes and included in the price of a Metro single-journey ticket or **Roma Pass** (p. 65). It's just a 5-minute walk to the excavations from the Metro stop: Exit the station, walk over the footbridge, and continue straight until you reach the car park. The ticket booth is to the left.

VISITOR INFORMATION The site is open Tuesday to Sunday from 8:30am. Closing time is at dusk, which ranges from 7pm in spring/summer to 4:30pm in fall/winter; check at **ostiaantica.cultura.gov.it** or call

✆ **06-56350215.** The ticket office closes 1 hour before the ruins close. Admission is 18€ (free for ages 12 and under) and is valid for 8 days, offering access to all the sites within the broader Ostia Antica Archaeological Park. The inexpensive map on sale at the ticket booth is a wise investment.

PARKING The car park, on Viale dei Romagnoli, costs a few euros per day, but it is fairly small. Arrive early if you're driving.

EXPLORING OSTIA ANTICA

The principal monuments are all labeled. On arrival, visitors first pass the *necropoli* (burial grounds, always outside the city gates in Roman towns and cities). The main route follows the giant cobblestones of the **Decumanus** ♥ (the main street) into the heart of Ostia. The **Piazzale delle Corporazioni** ♥♥ is like an early version of Wall Street: This square contained nearly 75 corporations, the nature of their businesses identified by the patterns of preserved mosaics. Nearby, Greek dramas were performed at the **Teatro,** built in the early days of the Empire. The theater as it looks today is the result of much rebuilding. Every town the size of Ostia had a **Forum** ♥. Here the layout is still intact: A well-preserved **Capitolium** (once the largest temple in Ostia) faces the remains of the 1st-century **Temple of Roma and Augustus.** Elsewhere in the grid of streets are the ruins of the **Thermopolium** ♥♥, which was a bar; its name means "sale of hot drinks." An *insula* (a Roman block of apartments), **Casa Diana** ♥, remains, its rooms arranged around an inner courtyard. The **Terme di Nettuno** ♥ was a vast baths complex; climb the building at its entrance for an aerial view of its well-preserved mosaics.

WHERE TO EAT IN OSTIA ANTICA

There is no real need to eat by the ruins—a half-day here should suffice, and Ostia is within easy reach of Rome's city center. Picnicking on-site is prohibited, though you might want to pack a snack and a refillable water bottle. If you crave a sit-down meal, trattoria **Arianna al Borghetto** ♥, Via del Forno 11 (✆ **06-56352956**), is a 5-minute walk from the archaeological park entrance. There's also a snack and coffee bar on-site.

Tivoli & the Villas ♥♥♥

32km (20 miles) E of Rome

Perched high on a hill east of Rome, ancient Tivoli has always been a place of retreat from the city. In Roman times it was known as Tibur, a retirement town for the wealthy; during the Renaissance it again became the playground of the rich, who built their country villas here. You need a full day to do justice to the gardens and villas that remain—especially if Villa Adriana is on your list, as indeed it should be—so set out early.

ESSENTIALS

ARRIVING Tivoli is 32km (20 miles) east of Rome on Via Tiburtina, about an hour's drive with traffic (the Rome–L'Aquila *autostrada,* A24, is usually faster). If you don't have a car, you can take one of several daily direct trains from Termini or Tiburtina to Tivoli station. Villa d'Este is in Tivoli itself, close to the train station; to get to Villa Adriana you'll need to catch a regional bus from town.

EXPLORING TIVOLI & THE VILLAS

Villa Adriana ♥♥♥ HISTORIC SITE/RUINS Globe-trotting Emperor Hadrian spent the last 3 years of his life in grand style. Less than 6km (3¾ miles) from Tivoli, between 118 and 134 C.E., he built one of the greatest estates ever conceived, filling acre upon acre with architectural wonders he'd seen in his travels. Hadrian erected theaters, baths, temples, fountains, gardens, and canals, filling palaces and temples with sculptures, some of which now rest in the museums of Rome. In later centuries, barbarians, popes, and cardinals, as well as anyone who needed a slab of marble, carted off much that made the villa so spectacular. But enough of the fragmented ruins remain to inspire a real sense of awe. The most outstanding remnant is the **Canopo** ♥♥♥, a re-creation of the Egyptian town of Canopus with its famous Temple of the Serapis. The ruins of a rectangular area, **Piazza d'Oro,** are still surrounded by a double portico. Likewise, the **Edificio con Pilastri Dorici** (Doric Pillared Hall) remains, its pilasters with bases and capitals holding up a Doric architrave. The apse and the ruins of some magnificent vaulting are found at the **Grandi Terme** (Great Baths), while only the north wall remains of the **Pecile** ♥, known as the *Stoà Poikile di Atene* or Painted Porch, which Hadrian discovered in Athens and had reproduced here. The best is saved for last—the **Teatro Marittimo** ♥♥♥, a circular theater in ruins, its central building enveloped by a canal spanned by small swing bridges.

Largo Marguerite Yourcenar 1, Tivoli. villae.cultura.gov.it. ✆ **0774-382733.** Admission 15€ adults, free for ages 17 and under. Daily 8:15am–sunset. Bus: 4 from Tivoli.

Villa d'Este.

Villa d'Este ♥♥ PARK/GARDEN Like Hadrian centuries before, Cardinal Ippolito d'Este of Ferrara in the mid-16th century ordered this villa built on a Tivoli hillside. The dank Renaissance structure, with its second-rate paintings, is not that interesting; the big draw for visitors are the **spectacular gardens** ♥♥♥, designed by Pirro Ligorio. As you descend the cypress-studded garden slope, you're rewarded with everything from lilies to gargoyles spouting water, torrential streams, and waterfalls. The loveliest fountain is the

Fontana dell Ovato ♥♥, by Ligorio. Nearby is the most spectacular engineering achievement: the **Fontana dell'Organo Idraulico ♥♥** (Fountain of the Hydraulic Organ), dazzling with music and water jets in front of a baroque chapel (the fountain "plays" every 2 hr. from 10:30am). The moss-covered **Fontana dei Draghi** (Fountain of the Dragons), also by Ligorio, and the so-called **Fontana di Vetro** (Fountain of Glass), by Bernini, are also worth seeking out, as is the main promenade, lined with 100 spraying fountains. The garden is worth hours of exploration, but it involves a lot of walking, with some steep climbs.

Piazza Trento 5, Tivoli. villae.cultura.gov.it. ✆ **0774-332920.** Admission 15€ adults, free for ages 17 and under. Tues–Sun 8:45am to 1 hr. before sunset; Mon from 2pm. Bus: Cotral service from Ponte Mammolo (Roma–Tivoli); bus stops near the entrance.

Villa Gregoriana ♥ PARK/GARDEN Villa d'Este dazzles with artificial glamour, but Villa Gregoriana relies more on nature. Originally laid out by Pope Gregory XVI in the 1830s, its main highlight is the panoramic waterfall of Aniene, with the trek to the bottom studded with grottoes and balconies that open onto the chasm. The only problem is that if you do make the full descent, you might need a helicopter to pull you up again (the climb back up is fierce). From one of the belvederes is a view of the **Temple of Vesta** on the hill.

Largo Sant'Angelo, Tivoli. fondoambiente.it/luoghi/parco-villa-gregoriana/visita. ✆ **0774-332650.** Admission 10€, 3€ ages 6–18, free for children 5 and under. Late Mar to mid-Dec daily 9:30am–dusk (from 9am in summer); closed mid-Dec to late Mar. The park is a 5-min. walk from Tivoli train station.

WHERE TO EAT IN TIVOLI

Tivoli's gardens make for a pleasant picnic place, but if you crave a sit-down meal, **Taverna Quintilia,** Vicolo Todini 4 (tavernaquintilia.it; ✆ **0774-314686**), specializes in seafood but has plenty of land-based options. It's just a few minutes' walk from Villa d'Este.

FLORENCE

By Donald Strachan

5

Florence (*Firenze* in Italian) may be relatively small, but over the centuries it has packed a major punch in European history and culture. Its center—which you can comfortably navigate on foot—evokes this illustrious past and overflows with monuments from the city's golden age. In the 14th and 15th centuries, Florence's achievements in art and architecture, science, literature, and even banking were unmatched. The rest of Europe looked on with envy.

This was the birthplace of the Renaissance movement in art and the hometown of its leading lights: Michelangelo, Brunelleschi, Leonardo da Vinci, Giotto, Galileo, Donatello, and many others. Florence built up a store of riches that still dazzles—including the **Uffizi Gallery,** heaving with masterpieces; an ingenious domed Cathedral; Michelangelo's ***David;*** and any number of decorated halls, palaces, and chapels. These treasures still represent some of the best humankind can achieve. Florence remains a must-visit for every first-time traveler to Italy, and a must-return destination for anyone with a passion for painting, sculpture, and architecture.

DON'T LEAVE FLORENCE WITHOUT . . .

Seeing Michelangelo's *David.* Rarely does an icon of art live up to its reputation as this one does. See p. 193.

Touring the Uffizi. Yes, everyone does it, but for good reason: The Uffizi has the best Renaissance art collection on earth. See p. 179.

Getting into Leather. A long-standing mecca for leather goods, the Florence area has hundreds of jacket-, boot-, and bag-makers. Browse the street stalls of San Lorenzo Market (p. 224) for a deal, the higher-end offerings at Santa Croce's leather school (p. 224), or Benheart (p. 222) for craftsmanship.

Roaming the Dome. Allot plenty of time to explore Piazza del Duomo, Florence's cathedral square dominated by Brunelleschi's dome—which you can experience from the inside, the outside, and up on top. See p. 177.

Feasting on *Bistecca alla Fiorentina.* Thick, juicy steak prepared over a wood-burning grill: The city's succulent signature dish makes carnivores very happy indeed.

Shopping & Dining on the Left Bank. Buy from fifth-generation artisans in family workshops around the Oltrarno neighborhood, then hit the restaurants and lively bars of San Frediano.

 PREVIOUS PAGE: **Pedicab drivers wait for passengers in Piazza del Duomo.**

ESSENTIALS

Arriving

BY PLANE Most international travelers reach Florence via the airports in Rome (p. 63) or Milan (p. 470), proceeding onward to Florence via train (see below). There are also direct international flights into Pisa's **Galileo Galilei Airport** (p. 298), 97km (60 miles) west of Florence; several budget airlines fly here from European cities. Between 7 and 12 daily **Sky Bus Lines** buses (bus.caronnatour.com; ✆ **366/126-0651** [WhatsApp only]) connect Florence with Pisa Airport in just over 1 hour (15€ adults; 9€ children 2–11). Florence drop-off/pickup is at the Guidoni tram stop near Florence Airport (see below), except during the night, when the bus runs to/from Florence's main rail station. Enter your phone number during booking to confirm a seat booking via WhatsApp.

A growing number of European airlines—including British Airways, Air France, Austrian, Iberia, KLM, Swiss, and Vueling—serve Florence's super-convenient **Amerigo Vespucci Airport** (**FLR;** firenze-airport.it/en; ✆ **055/306-15**), sometimes called **Peretola,** just 5km (3 miles) northwest of downtown. A modern **tram line** (**T2**) is the most cost-efficient way to reach the center from there (1.70€ each way; you can pay on board with a tap; see "Getting Around Florence," below). Trams depart every 5 to 11 minutes, 5am to midnight. Journey time to Florence's rail station is 20 minutes. **Taxis** line up outside the arrivals terminal: Exit and turn immediately to the right to find the rank. They charge a regulated flat rate of 31€ for the 15-minute journey to the city center (33€ holidays, 35€ after 10pm; extra 1.20€ per bag).

BY TRAIN Most travelers arrive in Florence by train. This is Tuscany's rail hub, with regular connections to all Italy's major cities. To get here from Rome, take a high-speed **Frecciarossa** or **Frecciargento** train (1½ hr.; trenitalia.com) or rival high-speed trains operated by **Italo** (italotreno.it). High-speed trains run from Venice (2 hr.) via Padua and Bologna, and also direct from Rome's Fiumicino Airport. On high-speed trains, you must sit in your reserved seat.

Most Florence-bound trains roll into **Stazione Santa Maria Novella,** Piazza della Stazione, which you'll see abbreviated as **S.M.N.** The station is an architectural masterpiece, albeit one dating to Italy's Fascist period rather than the Renaissance. It lies on the northwestern edge of the city's compact historic center, a 10-minute walk from the Duomo and a brisk 15-minute walk from Piazza della Signoria and the Uffizi.

BY CAR The **A1** ***autostrada*** runs north from Rome past Arezzo to Florence and continues to Bologna. Unnumbered **superhighways** run to and from Siena (the *SI-FI raccordo*) and Pisa (the so-called *FI-PI-LI*). To reach Florence from Venice, take the A13 southbound, then switch to the A1 at Bologna.

Driving *to* Florence is easy; the problems begin once you arrive. Almost all cars are banned from the historic center for much of the time; only residents or merchants with special permits are allowed into this clearly marked, camera-patrolled *zona a traffico limitato* (ZTL). You can enter the ZTL to drop off baggage at your hotel or go direct to a prebooked parking garage (either can organize temporary ZTL permission when provided with your license plate, preferably in advance, but also on arrival in a pinch). Usual ZTL hours are Monday to Friday 7:30am to 8pm, Saturday 7:30am to 4pm, with an extension from 11pm to 3am on Thursday to Saturday evenings April through October. It's a real hassle, so only rent a car if you're leaving town to visit somewhere that is not on the rail network. **Day-trippers** coming by car should park and ride the tram: From the south, use the "Drive and Tramway" lot at the Villa Costanza tram terminus (A1 exit Villa Costanza; parcheggiovillacostanza.it); arriving from the north, head for Parcheggio T2 Guidoni, beside the Guidoni stop on tram line T2. You can park all day at either car park for a few euros.

If you do drive into the center, your best bet for overnight or longer-term parking is one of the city-run garages. The best deal—better than most hotels' garage rates—is at the **Parterre parking lot** under Piazza Libertà at Via del Ponte Rosso 4 (✆ **055/5030-2209**). Open around the clock, it costs 2€ per hour or 15€ per day. Find more info on parking at **fipark.com/parcheggi**.

Don't park your car overnight on the street without local knowledge. If you're ticketed and towed, the fine is hefty, plus the headaches to retrieve the car are beyond description and a near-impossible task on weekends. If this happens to you, start by calling the vehicle removal department (**Recupero Veicoli Rimossi**) at ✆ **055/422-4142.** One more reason ***you should not drive in Florence.***

Advance Reservations for the Uffizi, Accademia & More

As soon as you set a date for your visit to Florence, start thinking about reservations for the **Uffizi** and the **Accademia** museums—it's the best way to avoid spending time in line, and last-minute walk-ups are either discouraged or pointless at the top museums. (Buying a combo ticket—see "Discount Tickets for Florence," p. 173—is the only other smart strategy.) Book via the museum's own website (see p. 183): **Uffizi** tickets always stipulate a timed entry and are bookable at **tickets.uffizi.it** or by calling ✆ **055/035-4135.** For the Accademia (essential) and a range of smaller museums (usually not required), book at the **official portal: b-ticket.com/b-ticket/firenzemusei**. Do not buy from elsewhere, and especially not from street vendors. If you arrive in town without reservations, you can also book for the Accademia by phone (✆ **055/294-883**) or in person at official ticket agents **Dear Guests,** Via Ricasoli 105 (dearguests.com). To prebook timed admission slots at city-run museums such as the Palazzo Vecchio or Cappella Brancacci (rarely required), visit the **Florence Welcome Center** (p. 167) or the ticketing hub at **ticketsmuseums.comune.fi.it**.

Visitor Information

TOURIST OFFICES Opened in 2024, the **Florence Welcome Center** is the biggest and most convenient tourist office. It is opposite Florence's main rail terminus at Piazza della Stazione 5. With your back to the tracks, take the left exit and then bear right—it's across the tram tracks and road junction ahead. The office is open daily 9am to 7pm (off-season Sun until 5:30pm) and provides useful advice in English, the latest opening hours, tickets for city-owned museums, and free street maps. A second, smaller central office, at Via Cavour 1R, 2 blocks north of the Duomo, is open Monday through Saturday 9am to 7pm and Sunday 9am to 2pm. An information kiosk in the Arrivals Hall at Florence airport is open daily 9am to 7pm (off-season Sun until 5:30pm). One central **phone number covers all tourist assistance: ✆ 055/000** (Mon–Sat 9am–7pm, Sun 9am–2pm). English is spoken.

Locating Addresses: The Red & the Black

The address system in Florence has a split personality. Private homes, some offices, and hotels are numbered in black (or blue), but businesses, shops, and restaurants are numbered independently in red. (That's the theory anyway. In reality, the division between black and red numbers isn't so clear-cut.) The result is that 1, 2, 3 (black) addresses march up the block numerically oblivious to their 1R, 2R, 3R (red) neighbors. You might find doorways on one side of a street numbered 1R, 2R, 3R, 1, 4R, 2, 3, 5R. The color codes occur only in the old sections of town. Outlying neighborhoods didn't bother with this confusing system.

WEBSITES The official Florence tourism website, **feelflorence.it**, contains up-to-date information, including on local events. ***Tip:*** In the "Organize Your Trip" section of the site, you should download a printable PDF with opening hours for city sights; the document is updated daily. For disabled travelers, ideas, advice, and dedicated resources are at **feelflorence.it/en/without-barriers**. The **Feel Florence app** is available for Android and Apple mobile devices. For one-off exhibitions, inspiration, and culture, **Art Trav** (arttrav.com) is an essential English-language blog. For more Florence info, go to **frommers.com/destinations/florence**.

City Layout

Florence is a smallish city, sitting on the Arno River and petering out rather quickly to olive-planted hills to the north and south, but extending farther west and east along the Arno valley with suburbs and light industry. It has a compact center and is best negotiated on foot. No two major sights are more than a 25-minute walk apart, and most hotels and restaurants in this chapter are in the relatively small ***centro storico*** (historic center), a tangle of medieval streets and squares where visitors spend most of their time. The bulk of Florence, including the majority of sights, is north of the river, with the **Oltrarno,** an old working artisans' neighborhood, hemmed in between the Arno and hills on the south side.

Florence Neighborhoods in Brief

THE DUOMO The area surrounding Florence's gargantuan cathedral is as central as you can get. The Duomo itself is halfway between the two monastic churches of Santa Maria Novella and Santa Croce, as well as at the midpoint between the Uffizi Gallery and the Ponte Vecchio to the south and San Marco and the Accademia (home of Michelangelo's *David*) to the north. A tangle of medieval streets south of the Duomo—little changed since Dante lived here in the late 1200s—heads toward **Piazza della Signoria** (see below). Southwest of the Duomo, **Piazza della Repubblica** lies in an even older part of town, in parts still laid out in its Roman-era grid, although the square itself, which was "modernized" in the 19th century, chafes architecturally with the rest of the center and has become a bit of a tourist trap. Overall, the Duomo neighborhood is one of the most hotel-heavy parts of town. But beware: Some hotels and many restaurants here rely on their location rather than on quality.

The iconic red dome of Florence's Duomo stands at the city's heart.

PIAZZA DELLA SIGNORIA & PONTE VECCHIO The city's civic heart is also prime territory for museum hounds—the Uffizi, Palazzo Vecchio, and Bargello sculpture collection are all nearby. A few blocks northward from the Ponte Vecchio have a selection of mainstream and chain stores but unappealing modern buildings, thanks to post–World War II reconstruction. This neighborhood is stiflingly crowded in peak season—**Via Por Santa Maria** is one street to avoid—but in rare moments when it's empty of tour groups, some of its lanes remain the romantic heart of medieval Florence. As in the Duomo neighborhood, be *very* choosy when picking a restaurant (or even an ice cream shop!) around here.

SAN LORENZO & THE MERCATO CENTRALE Centered on the Medici family church of **San Lorenzo,** this wedge of streets between the train station and the Duomo is market territory. The vast indoor **Mercato Centrale** food hall is here, along with the **San Lorenzo street market,** where stalls groan under the weight of leather goods and other souvenirs. It's a colorful but rarely quiet area, with many reasonably priced hotels, bars, and some very good, affordable dining.

SANTA TRÍNITA This piazza is just north of the river at the south end of Florence's high-end shopping mecca, **Via de' Tornabuoni.** It's a quaint, well-to-do, and still medieval neighborhood—and if you're an upscale-shopping fiend, there's no better place to be. Many excellent restaurants hide in the lanes between here and Santa Maria Novella.

SANTA MARIA NOVELLA Bounding the western edge of the *centro storico,* this neighborhood has two characters: a bland, busy zone around the train station and a grander area south of it. In general, the rail-station area is noisy and lacks medieval atmosphere, but it does have more budget hotel options than any other quarter, especially along **Via Faenza** and its tributary streets. Try to avoid staying on noisy, traffic-clogged **Via Nazionale.** The situation improves dramatically as you head south toward the river, where **Piazza Santa Maria Novella** has several stylish hotels, mostly mid-priced and up. Way up.

SAN MARCO & SANTISSIMA ANNUNZIATA On the northern edge of the *centro storico,* you'll find **Piazza San Marco** and **Piazza Santissima Annunziata,** the most architecturally unified square in the city. The neighborhood is home to Florence's university, the **Accademia,** the San Marco paintings of Fra' Angelico, and quiet streets with some hotel gems. It's not a long walk from the heart of the action, yet just far enough to escape any crowds.

SANTA CROCE Few tourists roam east beyond **Piazza Santa Croce,** so if you want to feel a bit Florentine, head here. The streets around the **Mercato di Sant'Ambrogio** have an appealing feel and get lively after dark, especially **Via Pietrapiana, Borgo La Croce,** and the northern end of **Via de' Macci.** Some of the city's best restaurants and bars are in this area. There are fewer hotels, but apartment rentals are everywhere.

THE OLTRARNO, SAN NICCOLÒ & SAN FREDIANO "Across the Arno" is an old artisans' neighborhood, still dotted with workshops. It began as working-class overflow from the medieval city and later became a chic area for aristocrats to build palaces with country views. The largest of these, the **Pitti Palace,** today houses a set of paintings second only to the Uffizi in scope. The Oltrarno's tree-shaded hub, **Piazza Santo Spirito,** is lined with bars and close to great restaurants and nightlife. West of here, the neighborhood of **San Frediano** is ever more fashionable; it's a bistro- and bar-hopping nirvana, with a mix of locals and visitors. **San Niccolò,** at the foot of Florence's southern hills, also has popular bars. South of the Arno doesn't (yet) have a vast hotel range, but here you can eat and drink better, at better prices, than in the *centro storico,* which in any case is only a short walk away.

Getting Around Florence

Florence is a **walking** city. You can stroll between the two top sights, Piazza del Duomo and the Uffizi, in 5 minutes or so. The hike from the most northerly major museums, San Marco and the Accademia, to the most southerly, the Pitti Palace, takes less than 25 minutes for most. From Santa Maria Novella eastward to Santa Croce is a flat 20- to 30-minute walk. But beware: **Flagstones,** some of them uneven, are everywhere. Wear sensible shoes with good padding and foot support.

BY BUS & TRAM You will rarely need Florence's efficient **AT bus system** (at-bus.it; ✆ **800/14-24-24** in Italy) since the center is so compact. Bus tickets cost 1.70€ and are good for 90 minutes, irrespective of how many changes you make (even if you switch to a tram). Tickets are sold at some *tabacchi* (tobacconists) and automatic machines, but the easiest solution is to pay contactless with a tap. You tap once every time you board; payment calculations are automated. The machines accept debit and credit cards, as well as Apple/Google Pay. You need one payment method per traveler (don't tap twice with one card). ***Note:*** If you have a paper ticket, you must validate it in the onboard machine to avoid a fine. Since traffic is restricted in most of the center, buses make runs on principal streets only, except for four lines (C1–4) that trundle about the *centro storico* and Oltrarno. These tiny electric buses often have very little luggage space: Don't rely on them to/from your accommodations. The most useful routes to outlying areas are no. 7 (for Fiesole) and nos. 12 and 13 (for Piazzale Michelangiolo); it's a standard *urbano* fare (1.70€) for either destination. Buses run from 6am until 9:30 or 10pm daily, with a limited night service on a few key routes.

Trams (firenzetramvia.it) run from 5am until after midnight (until 2am Fri–Sat). Route T1 connects Careggi and the Fortezza via Santa Maria Novella station with the Opera di Firenze, Cascine Park, and Florence's southwestern suburbs. Line T2 connects the rail station and San Marco with Peretola airport. Work on a new line (T3) began in 2025. **Moovit** (moovitapp.com) is a useful app for planning public transportation trips around the city and surrounding areas.

BY TAXI Taxis aren't cheap, and with the city so small and a one-way system forcing drivers to take convoluted routes, they aren't an economical way to get about the old center. However, they may be useful in shuttling you and your bags between the train station and a hotel. Taxis charge 3.80€ to start the meter (which rises to 6.10€ Sun or to 7.70€ 10pm–6am), plus 1.10€ per bag or for a fourth passenger. Well-used taxi stands are outside the train station, at Piazza Ognissanti, in Piazza San Marco, and in Piazza Santa Croce; otherwise, call **Radio Taxi SOCOTA** at ✆ **055/4242** (hail a cab by WhatsApp on ✆ **334/662-2550**), **Radio Taxi COTAFI** at ✆ **055/4390,** or **ItTaxi** at ✆ **055/3131.**

BY BICYCLE Florence had already begun expanding its network of marked cycle lanes before Covid, and the project has accelerated since. Ask for a dedicated cycle lane map at the Welcome Center (p. 167). It's simple to use the app-powered, dockless **bike-sharing** scheme **Ridemovi** (ridemovi.com). When you've downloaded the app and registered, you're good to go: Simply scan the QR code and ride. The Ridemovi fleet includes standard city bikes, e-scooters, and e-bikes. All payments are handled inside the app, which also offers discounted prices for bulk ride-time purchases (for example, 45 total e-bike minutes for 10€ instead of .30€ per minute). Bikes are plentiful, and the app makes it easy to see where you may not park.

The surviving private bike-rental specialists—a better bet for full-day rentals—are mostly located around San Lorenzo and San Marco, including **Florence by Bike,** Via San Zanobi 54R (florencebybike.it; ✆ **055/488-992**), which rents city, touring, and mountain bikes for adults and kids (from around 30€ per day) as well as e-bikes (around 45€). Reservations are essential (and sometimes discounted). They provide helmets, lights, and route maps for rides into the hills north and south of the center. Make sure to use a lock (one will be provided): Bike theft is depressingly common.

BY CAR Trying to drive in the *centro storico* is a frustrating, useless exercise, and unauthorized cars are fined if they enter the limited traffic zone (ZTL) without paying. You need a permit to do anything beyond dropping off and picking up bags at your hotel. **Park your vehicle in one of the lots outside the centro** and pound the sidewalk. (See "By Car" under "Arriving," p. 165.)

[FastFACTS] FLORENCE

Business Hours Hours mainly follow the Italian norm (p. 836), although most larger and/or central shops stay open through the traditional midday *riposo* or nap.

Doctors & Dentists Tourist-oriented **Medical Service Firenze,** at Via Roma 4 (medicalservice.firenze.it; ✆ **055/475-411**), is generally open Monday to Friday 11am to noon, 1 to 3pm, and 5 to 6pm; and Saturday 11am to noon and 1 to 3pm. **All visits should be arranged in advance by phone;** call in the morning. A similar rule operates at **Dr. Stephen Kerr,** who has an office at Piazza Mercato Nuovo 1 (dr-kerr.com; ✆ **335/836-1682**), usually open Monday to Friday 10am to 12:20pm and 2 to 4:20pm. His consultation fee is 95€.

Hospitals The most central hospital is **Santa Maria Nuova,** a block northeast of the Duomo on Piazza Santa Maria Nuova (uslcentro.toscana.it), with a 24-hour emergency room (*pronto soccorso*). Dial ✆ **112** in any emergency.

Left Luggage On platform 16 at Santa Maria Novella Station, you can leave luggage at **KiPoint** (kibag.it), open daily 7am to 9pm; the cost is 8€ per item for the day, and you can pay in advance online. Cheaper (1€/hr.; 6€/day) but less convenient for anyone catching a train is **Left Luggage Florence,** Via de' Boni 5R (leftluggageflorence.com; ✆ **334/700-7714**).

Mail Florence's **main post office** at Via Pellicceria 3 (✆ **055/273-6481**), off the southwest corner of Piazza della Repubblica, is open Monday to Friday 8:20am to 7:05pm and Saturday 8:20 to 11:15am.

Pharmacies A 24-hour pharmacy (also open Sun and state holidays) is in **Stazione Santa Maria Novella** (✆ **055/216-761;** ring the bell across from the taxi rank 11pm–7am). On holidays and at night, look for a sign in any pharmacy window telling you which ones are open locally, or check **feelflorence.it/en/farmacieh24**.

Police To report a crime or loss of passport, call the municipal police on ✆ **055/328-3333.** Lost property might find its way to the *Ufficio oggetti trovati:* ✆ **055/334-802.**

Safety As in any city, pickpockets are a risk in Florence; they are often light-fingered youngsters hanging around the train station. Otherwise it's a safe city, but steer clear of the Cascine Park after dark. In the wee hours when nightlife is finished, avoid the quietest areas like the Oltrarno south of Santo Spirito and the backstreets beyond Santa Croce.

EXPLORING FLORENCE

Opening times can change without notice, especially at city churches. Local tourist staff updates a list of opening hours daily at **feelflorence.it**. We **strongly advise** downloading their free PDF or collecting it from any tourist office (p. 167). In the listings below we list opening times that *usually* apply. You should, alas, treat these as provisional. Note that last admission everywhere is usually between 30 and 45 minutes before the official closing time.

Italy's national **"First Sundays"** program (cultura.gov.it/domenicalmuseo), when admission to state museums is free on the first Sunday of the month, usually operates in Florence between October and March. Check with the tourist office or individual museum websites. It can be both a blessing and a curse: Big hitters like the Uffizi are mobbed, so aim for the many niche state museums instead.

Piazza del Duomo

The cathedral square is always lively: filled with tourists, hawkers, and caricature artists during the day, strolling pedestrians in the early evening, and international students strumming guitars on the Duomo steps at night. The piazza's vivacity amid the glittering facades of the cathedral and the Baptistery doors sustain this as an eternal Florentine sight.

Battistero ♥♥♥ CHURCH In choosing a date to mark the beginning of the Renaissance, art historians often seize on 1401, the year Florence's powerful wool merchants' guild held a contest for the commission to design the **North Doors ♥♥** of the Baptistery to match its Gothic **South Doors ♥♥**, cast 65 years earlier by Andrea Pisano. The era's foremost Tuscan sculptors each cast a bas-relief bronze panel depicting their vision of the "Sacrifice of Isaac." Twenty-two-year-old Lorenzo Ghiberti, competing against Donatello, Jacopo della Quercia, and Filippo Brunelleschi, won. He spent the next 21 years casting 28 bronze panels and building his doors. The restored originals of all the Baptistery portals are now inside the **Museo dell'Opera del Duomo** (p. 178).

The result so impressed the merchants' guild—not to mention the public and Ghiberti's fellow artists—that they asked him in 1425 to do the **East Doors ♥♥♥**, facing the Duomo, this time giving him artistic freedom to realize his Renaissance ambitions. Twenty-seven years later, just

discount **TICKETS FOR FLORENCE**

It may seem odd to label the **Firenzecard** (firenzecard.it) a "discount" ticket, since it costs a substantial 85€. Is it a good buy? For a busy, museum-packed trip, a Firenzecard is a really good value, particularly as individual museum prices have edged up in recent years. If you expect to see only one or two major highlights, skip it.

The details: This card (valid for 72 hr.) allows one-time entrance to around 60 sites, including the Uffizi, Accademia, Cappella Brancacci, Palazzo Pitti, San Marco, and Palazzo Vecchio, plus a host of excellent smaller museums and the city's main fee-charging churches (Santa Croce, Santa Maria Novella, and San Lorenzo). In fact, most of what we recommend in this chapter *except the Duomo complex* is included with the card, even sites in Fiesole (p. 202). A Firenzecard gets you into "fast track" lines where they exist and includes prebooking fees—a saving of 4€ for the Uffizi and Accademia. However, those two, the Palazzo Vecchio, and the Brancacci **require Firenzecard holders to prebook** timed admission (see the "Museums" section at firenzecard.it/en). Once your 72 hours expire, it's also free to activate **Firenzecard Restart** within 12 months. This gives you 48-hour access to any of the sites *you haven't yet visited.* Activation can only be done on a smartphone.

Important: First, **only buy a Firenzecard from the official website.** Some city passes with similar names do not offer equivalent benefits. Second, **don't buy a Firenzecard for kids:** With a full-priced card you can take family members ages 17 and under for free. Companions 17 and under join the express queue with you and pay only the "reservation fee" at national museums (4€ at the Uffizi, for example). Those 17 and under also earn free admission to city museums (such as the Palazzo Vecchio). Private museums and sights have their own payment rules, but this will not add up to 85€ per child. Not even close.

Not included on the Firenzecard are sites on the cathedral square. The **Brunelleschi Pass** gets you into everything here—including climbing the dome—and costs 30€ (12€ ages 7–14), valid for 3 days. However, to ease crowding, only 1,800 of these comprehensive tickets are sold per day. If your heart is set on seeing the view from the top, **reserve a time slot as early as you can.** It is **obligatory** when you buy this pass. The cheaper **Giotto Pass** covers everything except the dome (Baptistery, Campanile, and revamped Museo dell'Opera; 20€/7€). With this pass only, you **must** prebook a time slot for the Campanile. The **Ghiberti Pass** excludes the Campanile (15€/5€). The cathedral is always free to visit. See **duomo.firenze.it/en** for details and to buy tickets. In Florence, you can also buy from the ticket office opposite the Baptistery's North Doors, at Piazza San Giovanni 9. In peak season, the 1,800 slots to climb the dome quickly sell out: Plan ahead. **Do not buy "skip the line" or other tickets for Brunelleschi's dome on the street.** These are not valid and you will be turned away. It is compulsory to leave backpacks and other luggage at the storage facility next to the Museo dell'Opera, at Piazza del Duomo 38R.

Another value option for art lovers is the **PassePartout 5 Days** ticket. It covers the Uffizi (including time slot), Pitti Palace, and Boboli Garden for 40€. You can combine this with a Piazza del Duomo ticket, above, for a highlights-only (yet still culture-packed) visit at a lower cost than a Firenzecard. The ticket is available online.

These are the only discount tickets we would recommend you consider.

- Battistero **14**
- Campanile di Giotto **15**
- Cappelle Medicee **10**
- Cenacolo di Sant'Appollonia **2**
- Chiostro dello Scalzo **1**
- Duomo (Cattedrale di Santa Maria del Fiore) **16**
- Galleria degli Uffizi (Uffizi Gallery) **21**
- Galleria dell'Accademia **4**
- Giardino di Boboli **30**
- HZERO **13**
- MAF Museo Archeologico Nazionale **6**
- Museo dell'Opera del Duomo **17**
- Museo Nazionale del Bargello **18**
- Museo Novecento **12**
- Orsanmichele **22**
- Palazzo Davanzati **23**
- Palazzo Medici-Riccardi **8**
- Palazzo Pitti **29**
- Palazzo Vecchio **20**
- Piazzale Michelangiolo **31**
- Ponte Vecchio **25**
- San Lorenzo **9**
- San Marco **3**
- San Miniato al Monte **32**
- Santa Croce **19**
- Santa Felicita **26**
- Santa Maria del Carmine **28**
- Santa Maria Novella **11**
- Santo Spirito **27**
- Santa Trínita **24**
- Santissima Annunziata **5**
- Spedale degli Innocenti **7**

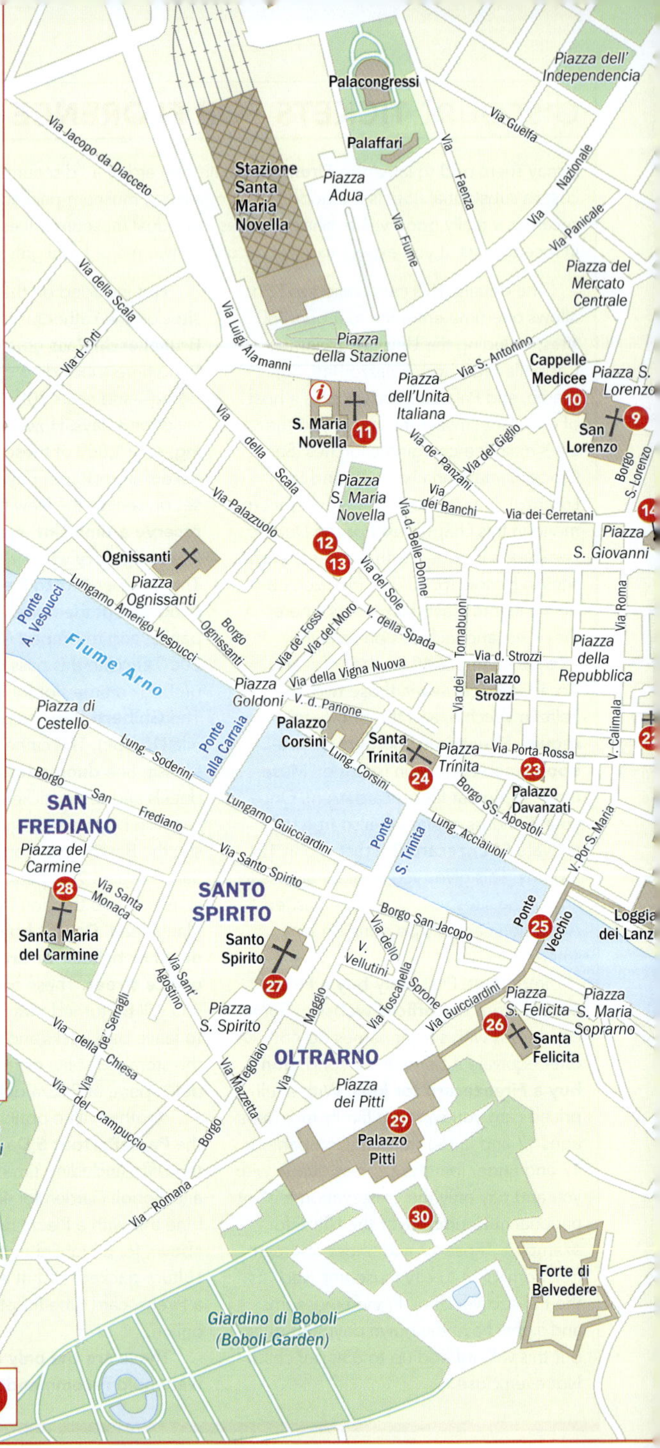

Florence Attractions

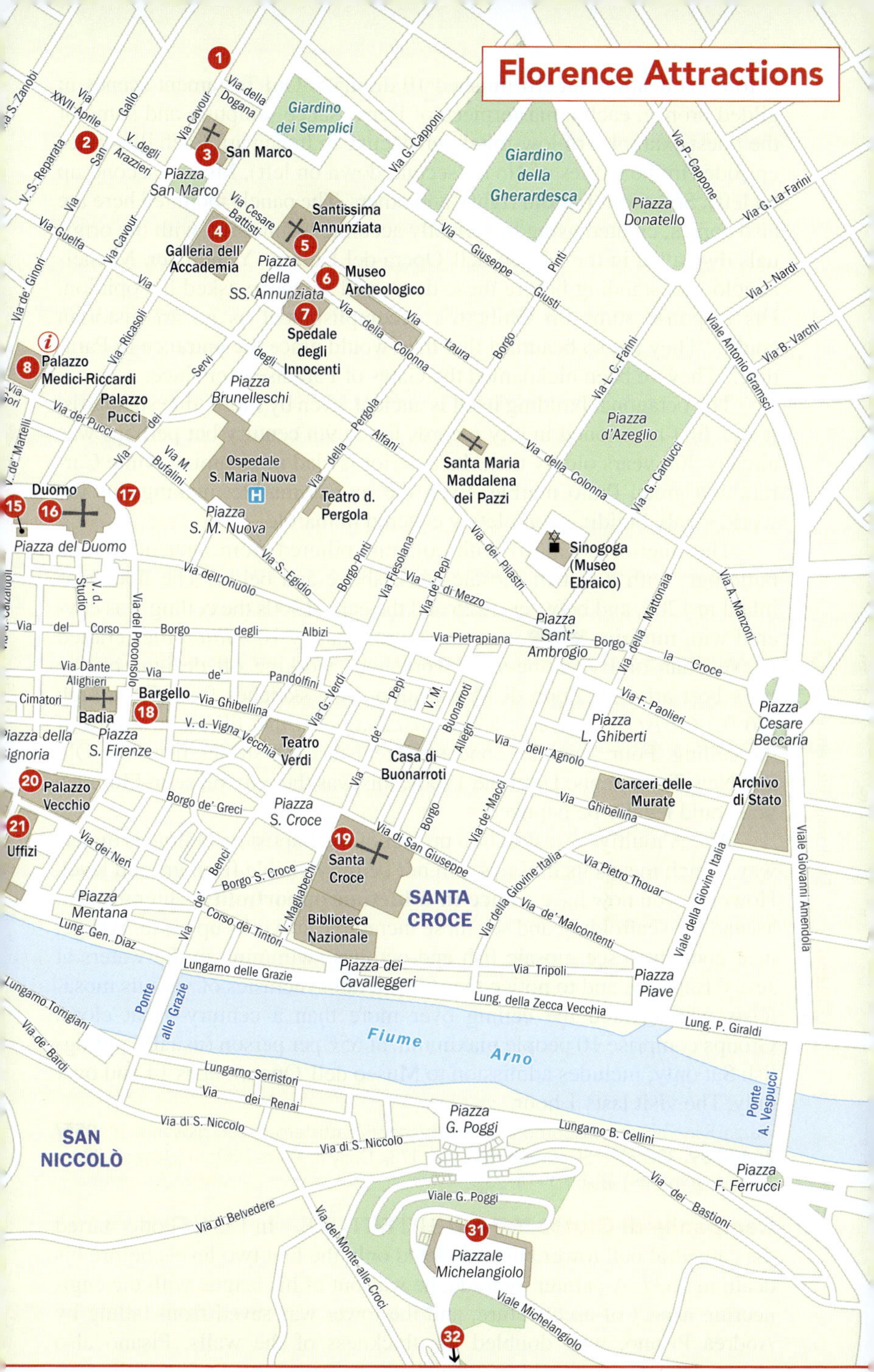

before his death, Ghiberti finished 10 dramatic Old Testament scenes in gilded bronze, each a masterpiece of Renaissance sculpture and some of the finest examples of low-relief perspective in Italian art. Each illustrates episodes in the stories of Noah (second down on left), Moses (second up on left), Solomon (bottom right), and others. The panels mounted here are also copies, created using historically accurate techniques, with the originals displayed in the Museo dell'Opera del Duomo. Years later, Michelangelo was standing before these doors and someone asked his opinion. His response sums up Ghiberti's accomplishment as no art historian could: "They are so beautiful that they would grace the entrance to Paradise." They've been nicknamed the Gates of Paradise ever since.

The octagonal building itself is ancient, even by Florentine standards. It was first mentioned in city records in the 9th century but perhaps was already 300 years old by then. Its exterior is clad in gleaming white Carrara and green Prato marble. Even the roof is marble, making this the world's only building completely covered in marble.

The interior is ringed with columns pilfered from ancient Roman buildings, with a riot of mosaic-work above and below. The floor was inlaid in 1209, and between 1225 and the early 1300s the ceiling was covered with **mosaics ♥♥♥**, most of approximately 10 *million* tiles crafted by Venetian or Byzantine-style workshops working off designs by the era's best artists. Coppo di Marcovaldo drew sketches for a 7.8m-high (26-ft.) *Christ in Judgment* and a *Last Judgment* that fills over a third of the ceiling. Four separate, concentric registers tell stories from the Old and New Testaments. Until the 1700s, this was the only place in Florence you could legally be baptized.

Tip: A multiyear restoration project of the Baptistery ceiling is underway, which means its mosaics will not be fully visible from ground level. However, you now have a **once-in-a-lifetime opportunity**—literally—to ascend the scaffolding and see these incredible artworks up close. You get near enough to see mosaic fish and octopus swimming in the waters at Jesus' Baptism, and to notice the stylistic idiosyncrasies of various mosaicists who created the ceiling over more than a century—that close. Groups comprise 10 people maximum, at 65€ per person (usually in English Sat only; includes admission to Museo dell'Opera); ages 14 and over only. The visit lasts 1 hour.

Piazza San Giovanni. duomo.firenze.it/it/scopri/battistero-di-san-giovanni. ✆ **055/264-5789.** 30€/20€/15€ combo ticket (p. 173). Daily 8:30am–7:30pm (closes 1:30pm 1st Sun of month). Bus: C1, 14, 23.

Campanile di Giotto ♥♥ ARCHITECTURE In 1334, Giotto started the cathedral bell tower but completed only the first two levels before his death in 1337. A painter by trade, he was out of his league with the engineering aspect of architecture, and the tower was saved from falling by Andrea Pisano, who doubled the thickness of the walls. Pisano also changed the design to add statue niches—he even carved a few of the statues himself—before quitting the project in 1348. Francesco Talenti finished the job between 1350 and 1359. The **reliefs** and **statues** in the lower levels—by Andrea Pisano, Donatello, Luca della Robbia, and others—are all copies; weatherworn originals are housed in the Museo dell'Opera (p. 178). If you are fit, we recommend climbing the 414 steps to the top; the **view** ♥♥ is memorable as you ascend and offers one of the city's best close-ups of Brunelleschi's dome. If dome tickets are sold out, the Campanile is a worthy substitute.

Piazza del Duomo. duomo.firenze.it/it/scopri/campanile-di-giotto. ✆ **055/264-5789.** 30€/20€ combo ticket (p. 173). Daily 8:15am–6:45pm. Bus: C1, 14, 23.

Duomo (Cattedrale di Santa Maria del Fiore) ♥♥ CATHEDRAL

By the late 13th century, Florence was feeling peevish. Archrivals Siena and Pisa had flamboyant new cathedrals while it was saddled with a tiny 5th- or 6th-century cathedral dedicated to St. Reparata. So, in 1296, the city hired Arnolfo di Cambio to design a new Duomo; he raised the facade and the first few bays before his death (around 1310). Work continued under the auspices of the Wool Guild and architect Francesco Talenti, who expanded the planned size and finished up to the drum of the dome. Over the centuries, many designs for the unfinished facade were offered and rejected. For one lavish Medici wedding, the family even commissioned a temporary facade in papier-mâché. The permanent one is a neo-Gothic design by Emilio De Fabris, added from 1871 to 1887.

The Duomo's most distinctive feature is its enormous **dome** ♥♥♥ (or *cupola*), which dominates the skyline and has become the symbol of Florence itself. The raising of this dome was no mean architectural feat, tackled by Filippo Brunelleschi between 1420 and 1436 (see "A Man & His Dome," p. 179). The largest dome in the world in its time, it remains the widest ever built in brick. You can climb up between its two shells for one of the classic panoramas across the city—something not recommended for claustrophobes or anyone with no head for heights. Booking a time slot to climb the dome is **compulsory.** Book as far ahead as you can in peak seasons: Only 1,800 people may make the climb daily.

The Duomo's ornate neo-Gothic exterior.

Restored in 2022, two optical-illusion **equestrian "statues"** ♥ decorate the north wall—of English soldier Sir John Hawkwood, painted in 1436 by Paolo Uccello, beside Niccolò da Tolentino by Andrea Del Castagno—elevating these two

Murder in the Duomo

The cathedral's spartan interior was the setting for one of the most dramatic episodes in the history of Florence: the so-called Pazzi Conspiracy, the attempted assassination of the Medici brothers on Easter Sunday, 1478. Giuliano de' Medici was murdered, but a wounded Lorenzo barricaded himself into a sacristy (no one is certain which of the two) and escaped. Revenge was exacted in grisly fashion. Plotters including the powerful Pazzi family and the Archbishop of Pisa were found and hanged from the windows of the Palazzo Vecchio.

mercenaries to a status they perhaps did not deserve. The remains and mosaic floors of old **Santa Reparata** ♥ are in the crypt. English Mass is held Saturdays at 5pm.

Tip: The cathedral is an impressive space, for sheer scale alone. However, **it is *not* worth waiting in line for an hour or more to go inside,** especially on a short visit to Florence. Better uses of your time abound, so if the queue looks epic, move on.

Piazza del Duomo. duomo.firenze.it. ✆ **055/264-5789.** Free admission to Duomo; cupola via 30€ Brunelleschi Pass (p. 81). Church Mon–Sat 10:15am–3:45pm. Cupola Mon–Fri 8:15am–6:45pm; Sat 8:15am–4:30pm; Sun 12:45–4:30pm. Bus: C1, 14, 23.

Museo dell'Opera del Duomo ♥♥♥ MUSEUM Florence's majestic, modern Cathedral Museum shows off Italy's second-largest collection of devotional art after the Vatican (p. 81). But at heart, it's an homage to two Florentine geniuses: Lorenzo Ghiberti and Filippo Brunelleschi.

The location is significant, as this was once the workshop where Michelangelo sculpted his *David.* Today the prize exhibits are the original **Gates of Paradise** ♥♥♥ cast by Lorenzo Ghiberti in the early 1400s (see Battistero, p. 172), displayed as the centerpiece of an extraordinary, life-size re-creation of the early 1400s piazza, complete with a reimagined version of the cathedral's Gothic-era facade. Ghiberti's Baptistery **North Doors** ♥♥♥ have also been moved inside, scrubbed to reveal rose gold below years of soot and dirt. In 2019, Pisano's **South Doors** ♥♥♥ joined them to complete an unparalleled set of bronze relief sculptures.

Also on the ground floor, restored in 2021, is Michelangelo's ***Bandini Pietà*** ♥♥ that nearly wasn't. Early in the process he told students this Pietà was to stand at his tomb, but when he found an imperfection in the marble, he began attacking it with a hammer (look at Christ's left arm). The master never returned to the work, but students later repaired the damage. The figure of Nicodemus was untouched, legend has it, because it was a self-portrait of the artist—a Michelangelo myth that, for once, is probably true.

In a **multimedia section** ♥♥ dedicated to Brunelleschi, films, displays, and models explain the engineering process behind his dome. Exhibits include original equipment and machines he invented or used. A **roof terrace** ♥ provides a photo op and a closeup of his extraordinary achievement. Elsewhere are works by Donatello (including a restored

Magdalen ♥), Andrea del Verrocchio, and Luca della Robbia, and a restored early Giotto ***Madonna*** ♥ damaged by the 1993 Uffizi car bomb. Piazza del Duomo 9 (behind cathedral). duomo.firenze.it. ✆ **055/264-5789.** 30€/20€/15€ combo ticket (p. 173). Daily 8:30am–7pm. Closed 1st Tues of month. Bus: C1, 14, 23.

Around Piazza della Signoria & Santa Trínita

Galleria degli Uffizi (Uffizi Gallery) ♥♥♥ ART MUSEUM Welcome to the summit: There is no collection of Renaissance art on the planet to match the Uffizi Gallery. For this reason, **you must reserve a timed admission slot** as soon as you can. Despite its crowds and other inconveniences, the Uffizi is always a must-see. But take one piece of advice from someone who has been *at least* 20 times: **Do not try to take it all in one visit.** Jump around, follow your interests, draw inspiration from the text below about my highlights, but also look out for your own.

A MAN & HIS dome

Filippo Brunelleschi, a diminutive man whose ego was as big as his talent, managed in his arrogant, quixotic, and brilliant way to invent Renaissance architecture. Having been beaten by Lorenzo Ghiberti in the contest to cast the **Baptistery** doors (p. 172), Brunelleschi decided he would rather be Florence's top architect than its second-best sculptor and took off for Rome to study its ancient buildings. On returning to his home city, he combined gray *pietra serena* stone, quarried near Fiesole, with smooth white plaster to create airy arches, vaults, and arcades with perfect classical proportions, in his own variant on the ancient orders of architecture. He designed **Santo Spirito** (p. 202), the **Spedale degli Innocenti** (p. 196), a chapel at **Santa Croce** (p. 197), and a new sacristy for **San Lorenzo** (p. 191). But his greatest achievement was erecting the dome over Florence's cathedral.

The Duomo—at that time the world's largest church—had already been built, but nobody had figured out how to cover the daunting space over its crossing. No one was even sure they could create a dome that would hold up under its own weight. Brunelleschi insisted he knew how, and once granted the commission, revealed his ingenious plan, probably inspired by study of Rome's **Pantheon** (p. 103). He built the dome in two shells, the inner one thicker than the outer, both shells thinning as they neared the top, thus leaving the center hollow and removing a good deal of the weight. He also planned to construct the dome from giant vaults with ribs crossing them and dovetailed the stones making up the actual fabric of the dome. In this way, the walls of the dome would support themselves as they were erected. In the process of building, Brunelleschi found himself as much an engineer as an architect, designing winches and hoists to carry the materials (plus food and drink) faster and more efficiently up to the level of the construction work. Reputedly, only one person died during construction—a drunken worker who fell.

His finished work speaks for itself, 45m (148-ft.) wide at the base and 90m (295-ft.) high. The marble lantern—which Brunelleschi did not live to see dropped into place in 1446—serves as the structure's keystone. For his achievement, Brunelleschi was accorded the rare honor of burial inside Florence's cathedral.

It's not a "one bite" museum. You will spot those who are trying: After about Room 15, they have the vacant stare of a *Walking Dead* extra. Don't be that zombie.

WHAT WILL YOU SEE? Some 80-plus rooms and marble corridors—built in the 16th century as the Medici's private offices, or *uffici*—packed with famous paintings, among them Botticelli's *Birth of Venus,* Leonardo da Vinci's *Annunciation,* Michelangelo's *Holy Family,* and many, many more. In recent years the museum has become *much* better at making use of its under- or un-occupied spaces. You will often stumble across a temporary and/or contemporary art installation. Take time, take a detour. Also note that the curators like to tinker. The precise location of some artworks does change (although the first 35 rooms or so appear to be set for now); the PDF map at **uffizi.it/gli-uffizi** should be current.

BEFORE THE RENAISSANCE **Room A4** kicks off the Gothic style of painting born in the Middle Ages. Compare Cimabue's *Santa Trínita Maestà,* painted around 1290, with his student Giotto's ***Ognissanti Madonna*** ♥♥♥, done in 1310. Both paintings have a similar subject and setting, but Giotto transformed Cimabue's iconlike Byzantine style into something human. Giotto's Madonna looks like she's sitting on a throne, her clothes emphasizing the curves of her body, whereas Cimabue's Madonna and angels float in space, like portraits on coins, with stiff positions. The room's third great Madonna, Duccio's sinuous, ethereal ***Rucellai Madonna*** ♥♥ (1285), became a founding work for the Sienese School of painters.

Room A5 showcases the Sienese School at its peak, with Simone Martini's dazzling ***Annunciation*** ♥♥♥ (1333) slathered in gold ground and Ambrogio Lorenzetti's *Presentation at the Temple* (1342). Tragically, the Black Death of 1348 wiped out this entire generation of Sienese painters (along with half of Siena's population). **Rooms A6–A7** show Florentine painting at its most decorative, in a pre-Renaissance style now termed International Gothic. The iconic work, Gentile da Fabriano's ***Procession of the Magi*** ♥♥♥ (1423), depicts the line to meet newborn Jesus, full of decorative and comic elements. It's even longer than the line waiting to enter the Uffizi.

THE BIRTH OF A REBIRTH Painting begins to change noticeably with **Piero della Francesca** (and his contemporaries). The unflattering profiles of the Duke Federico da Montefeltro of Urbino and his duchess, painted in oil around 1473, are the centerpieces of **Room A9.** Piero's subjects are portrayed in a starkly realistic way: The duke exposes his warts and crooked nose, which was broken in a tournament. This focus on earthly, rather than Christian, elements draws from the secular teachings of Ancient Greece and Rome, and is made more vivid by a depiction (on the back) of the couple riding chariots driven by the humanistic virtues of faith, charity, hope, and modesty (for her) and prudence, temperance, fortitude, and justice (for him). Humanism became a key motif of

The Uffizi Gallery displays an incredible collection of Renaissance art.

Renaissance thought, writing, and imagery. The same room displays works by **Filippo Lippi** from the mid-15th century. The best backstory belongs to his ***Madonna and Child with Two Angels*** ♥♥, painted around 1465. The work was a celebrity scandal. The woman who modeled for Mary was said to be Filippo's lover—would-be nun Lucrezia Buti, whom he spirited away from a convent before she took her vows—and the child looking toward the viewer, a product of their union. (That son, Filippino Lippi, would also become a painter of some renown.) Note the background, with distant mountains on one side and water on the other framing the portrait of a woman's face; Leonardo da Vinci stole the configuration 40 years later for his *Mona Lisa.* Also here is Paolo Uccello's ***Battle of San Romano*** (1435), essentially an experiment in the technique of painting perspective—with crazy results.

YOU'VE SEEN THESE SOMEWHERE BEFORE **Rooms A11** and **A12** (one connected space, despite the numbering) are devoted to the works of Filippo Lippi's student (and his son Filippino's teacher) Sandro Filipepi, better known by his nickname "Little Barrels," or **Botticelli.** Botticelli's 1485 ***Birth of Venus*** ♥♥ hangs like a billboard you have passed a thousand times. Venus's pose is taken from classical statues, while the winds Zephyr and Aura blowing her to shore, and the muse welcoming her, are based on tales from Roman poet Ovid's *Metamorphoses.* Botticelli's 1478 ***Primavera*** ♥♥♥, its dark, bold colors a stark contrast to filmy, pastel *Venus,* defies definitive interpretation. But again it features Venus (center), alongside Mercury, with the winged boots, the Three Graces, and the goddess Flora. Botticelli had a phenomenal eye for botanical detail.

The **Tribuna** ♥♥, next along the corridor (**A16**), is an architectural oddity, a timeout from the timeline. An ornate octagonal room added on the orders of Grand Duke Francesco I, its centerpiece is the ***Medici Venus*** ♥♥, a Greek marble crafted in the 1st century B.C.E. Botticelli copied her pose for his Venus. The **Map Terrace (A14)** shows the now-unified territory of Tuscany divided up between the city-states of Florence, Siena, and Lucca.

PANORAMIC PAUSE To cross to the Uffizi's west wing, you pass picture windows with **views of the Arno River ♥♥** to one side and a perfect Renaissance perspective of the Uffizi piazza to the other—plus an often overlooked Roman sculpture gallery most museums would kill for.

PEAK RENAISSANCE This wing showcases two true heavyweights from the period known as the **High Renaissance. Room A35** displays Leonardo da Vinci's magnificent, unfinished ***Adoration of the Magi* ♥♥♥**, with much of the artist's line drawing still visible, beside an ***Annunciation* ♥♥♥**. In the latter, completed in the early 1470s while young Leonardo was still a student in Verrocchio's workshop, his ability to orchestrate the viewer's eye is already masterful: The line down the middle of the brick corner of the house draws your glance to Mary's delicate fingers, which themselves point along the top of a stone wall to the angel's two raised fingers. Those, in turn, draw attention to the mountain between the two parallel trees dividing Mary from the angel, representing the gulf between the worldly and the spiritual. Its apparently warped perspective was in fact painted intentionally, to be viewed from the lower right. (Test for yourself.)

Room A38 is dedicated to another two masters of the Italian High Renaissance. In Michelangelo's 1505–08 ***Holy Family* ♥♥**, the twisting shapes of Mary, Joseph, and Jesus recall those in the Sistine Chapel for their sculpted form and punchy colors. Among several Uffizi Raphaels, his enchanting ***Madonna of the Goldfinch* ♥♥♥**—painted around the same time—has a background landscape and aerial perspective inspired by Leonardo and Botticelli.

DOWNSTAIRS: THE PIANO NOBILE The layout here has been overhauled in the last decade to better showcase art that followed the High Renaissance, from Italy and the rest of Europe. The bodily torsion and tensions of Michelangelo's painting and sculpture inspired the next generation of Florentine painters, known as the **Mannerists ♥♥**. Andrea del Sarto, Rosso Fiorentino, and Pontormo (**Room D12**) are among the highlights of rooms dedicated to the Cinquecento (1500s). **Room D23** shows off Titian's reclining nude, ***Venus of Urbino* ♥♥♥**. It is the highlight of the Uffizi's **Venetian Renaissance collection ♥♥**, which also includes Tintoretto and Giorgione. It's no coincidence that the edge of the curtain, the angle of her hand and leg, and the line splitting the floor and bed all intersect at the forbidden part of Venus's body.

The final big-hitters hang in the **Sale Seicento** (1600s Rooms): paintings by Caravaggio, notably his crazed ***Medusa* ♥♥♥** (**Room E4**) self-portrait and an enigmatic ***Bacchus* ♥♥**. These rooms also explore 17th-century artists who imitated his *chiaroscuro* (bright light and dark shadows) style. Greatest among them was Artemisia Gentileschi, a rare female painter from this period. Her ***Judith Slaying Holofernes* ♥♥** (ca. 1612; **Room E4**) is one of the bloodiest paintings in the gallery.

Vasari's Corridor

An enclosed passage along the top of the Ponte Vecchio is part of the **Corridoio Vasariano** ♥♥ (Vasari Corridor), a private, above-ground "tunnel" running between the Palazzo Vecchio (p. 199) and Palazzo Pitti (p. 199), including along the top of the Ponte Vecchio. Duke Cosimo I found the idea of mixing with the hoi polloi distressing—and assassination was a real risk—so he commissioned Vasari to design his VIP commute in 1565. Almost a half-mile long, it was built in less than 5 months. The duke's former secret passageway was later hung with the world's best collection of artists' self-portraits. The corridor was closed for restoration work for almost a decade but fully reopened in 2025 **for 45-minute accompanied visits only.** It's open during Uffizi hours, with pre-bookable slots between 10:15am and 4:35pm. Access is from inside the Uffizi, so you must also buy an Uffizi ticket; it costs 18€ extra per adult to add Corridor access. Your timed entry into the Uffizi should be booked 2 hours before Corridor access. Keep an eye on **uffizi.it/corridoio-vasariano** because availability may change.

Tip: If you find yourself flagging (it happens to us all), a **coffee shop** at the far end of the upper floor's west wing can help. Prices are in line with the piazza below, plus you get a close-up of the Palazzo Vecchio's facade from its terrace. Fully refreshed, you can return to discover works by many great artists we haven't space to cover here: Cranach, Rembrandt, and Dürer from northern Europe; Spaniards Velazquez, El Greco, and Goya; Bellini and Mantegna; Bernini and Barocci; and Masaccio, Bronzino, Parmigianino, and Veronese. There is nowhere like the Uffizi—in Italy or anywhere else in the world.

Piazzale degli Uffizi. uffizi.it. ✆ **055/035-4135.** Admission 29€ adults (prebooked timed slot after 4pm 20€), free for ages 17 and under (2€ booking fee). Tues–Sun 8:15am–6:30pm (in summer, Tues or Fri sometimes 'til 9:30pm). Bus: C1, C2.

The Bargello Museum's wide-ranging sculpture collection includes Donatello's bronze *David* (probably actually a statue of the god Mercury).

Museo Nazionale del Bargello (Bargello Museum) ♥♥♥

MUSEUM The Bargello Museum is the most important museum anywhere for Renaissance **sculpture**—yet it's often quieter than other museums in the city. Originally the city's prison, torture chamber, and place of execution, the Bargello has survived fire, flood, sieges, and more in its 800-year lifespan. It now stands as a three-story museum containing some of the best of Michelangelo, Donatello, and Ghiberti, as well as their most successful Mannerist successor, Giambologna.

In the ground-level Michelangelo room, scope out the variety of his craft, from a whimsical 1497 ***Bacchus*** ♥♥ to a severe, unfinished *Brutus* of 1539. *Bacchus,* created when Michelangelo was just 22, genuinely looks drunk, leaning back a little too far, his head off-kilter, with a cupid about to bump him over. Nearby is Giambologna's twisting ***Mercury*** ♥, taking flight propelled by the breath of Zephyr. Cellini's ***Cosimo I*** ♥, created about the same time as his *Perseus* (p. 185), casts this Florentine Grand Duke cosplaying an Imperial Roman general.

Upstairs, on an open-air loggia, is an "aviary" of bronze birds that once decorated the Medici family's Villa di Castello. Minutely observed and intricately cast, they were completed in the mid-16th century by Giambologna, Ammannati, and others. An adjacent vaulted hall features some of Donatello's most accomplished sculpture, including his original *Marzocco* (from outside the Palazzo Vecchio; p. 186), and ***St. George*** ♥, from a niche at Orsanmichele (see below). His bronze ***David*** ♥♥♥ (which some think might be the god Mercury), done around 1440, was Italy's first freestanding nude sculpture after Roman times. The classical detail of Donatello's sculptures, as well as their naturalistic poses and reflective mood, is the essence of the Renaissance style.

Side by side on the back wall are the contest entries submitted in 1401 by Ghiberti and Brunelleschi for the Baptistery doors commission. With the ***Sacrifice of Isaac*** ♥♥ as their biblical theme, both displayed innovative use of perspective. Ghiberti won, perhaps because of his composition's greater balance. Brunelleschi could have ended up a footnote in art history, but instead he gave up the chisel and turned to architecture instead (see "A Man & His Dome," p. 179).

Faded 1330s frescoes by Giotto and his workshop—the last known works by the master—decorate the **Cappella della Maddalena** ♥♥, where prisoners would await their execution. On the opposite wall, painted imaginings of Paradise and Hell were heavily influenced by Dante's ***Divine Comedy,*** published a decade earlier.

Via del Proconsolo 4. bargellomusei.it. ✆ **055/064-9440.** Admission 10€ adults, free for ages 17 and under. Wed–Mon 8:15am–6:50pm. Closed 2nd and 4th Sun of each month. Bus: C2.

Orsanmichele ♥♥ CHURCH/MUSEUM This bulky structure halfway down Via dei Calzaiuoli looks more like a Gothic warehouse than a church—which is exactly what it was, built as a granary and grain market in 1337. After a miraculous image of the Madonna appeared on a column inside, its lower level was turned into a shrine and chapel. The city's merchant guilds each decorated a Gothic tabernacle around the outside with a statue of their patron saint. Masters such as Ghiberti, Donatello, Verrocchio, and Giambologna all cast or carved masterpieces to set here (those remaining are mostly copies, including Donatello's *St. George*). Reopened in 2024 after restoration, the dark interior has an elaborate Gothic stone **Tabernacle** ♥♥ (1349–59) by Andrea Orcagna, which protects a

PIAZZA DELLA signoria

When the Guelph party came out on top after a medieval political struggle with the Ghibellines, they razed part of Florence's old center to build a new palace for civic government. It's reputed that the Guelphs ordered architect Arnolfo di Cambio to build what we now call the **Palazzo Vecchio** (p. 186) in the corner of this space to make sure not an inch would sit on Ghibelline land. (This odd legend was probably fabricated to explain Arnolfo's off-center architecture.) At any rate, the L-shaped space around the *palazzo* became the new civic center of town, **Piazza della Signoria ♥♥♥**, named after the city's ruling oligarchy (the "Signoria"). Today, it's an outdoor sculpture gallery, teeming with tourists and ringed by outdoor cafes. If you want to catch the square at its serene best, arrive by 8am and have it to yourself.

The statuary on the piazza is particularly beautiful, starting on the left (as you face the Palazzo Vecchio) with Giambologna's 1594 equestrian statue of Grand Duke Cosimo I. To its right is one of Florence's favorite sculptures to hate, the **Fontana del Nettuno** (Neptune Fountain; 1560–75), created by Bartolomeo Ammannati as a tribute to Cosimo's naval ambitions. (Florentines have dubbed it "Il Biancone," or "Big Whitey.") A **porphyry plaque** on the ground in front of the fountain marks the site where puritanical monk Savonarola held his Bonfire of the Vanities. With fiery apocalyptic preaching, he whipped Florentines into a frenzy. Hundreds filed into this piazza, arms loaded with their "decadent" possessions to throw it all on the flames.

To the right of Neptune, a raised platform fronting the Palazzo Vecchio was known as the *arringheria*, from which soapbox speakers would lecture to crowds (and from where we get our word *harangue*). On its far left is a copy (original in the Bargello) of Donatello's *Marzocco*, symbol of the city, a Florentine lion resting its raised paw on a shield emblazoned with the *giglio* (lily). To its right is another Donatello replica, *Judith Beheading Holofernes*. Farther down is a man who needs little introduction, Michelangelo's ***David,*** a 19th-century copy of the famous original, now in the Accademia (p. 193). Near enough to David to look truly ugly in comparison is Baccio Bandinelli's lumpy *Hercules and Cacus* (1534).

At the piazza's south end, the **Loggia dei Lanzi ♥♥♥** (1376–82) is named after the Swiss Guard of lancers (*lanzi*) whom Cosimo de' Medici stationed here. (It's also called the Loggia della Signoria or the Loggia dell'Orcagna, after its designer Andrea Orcagna.) At front left stands Benvenuto Cellini's masterpiece in bronze, ***Perseus*** **♥♥♥** (1545), holding up the severed head of Medusa. On the far right is Giambologna's ***Rape of the Sabines*** **♥♥**. You must walk all the way around to appreciate the dynamism, catching the action and artistry of its spiral design from different angles. The subject matter is a controversial tale from Roman mythology—a mass abduction—though this was only fixed after the sculpture was complete. Giambologna himself only intended it to showcase his skill. Talk continues about moving the statue indoors, safe from the elements . . . but for now, it's still here.

luminous 1348 *Madonna and Child* painted by Giotto's student Bernardo Daddi, to which miracles were ascribed during the Black Death of 1348–50. Upstairs, airy museum rooms house many of the original sculptures that adorned the exterior niches. Among the treasures are a trio of bronzes: Ghiberti's *St. John the Baptist* (1412–16), the first life-size bronze of the

Renaissance; Verrocchio's *Incredulity of St. Thomas* (1483); and Giambologna's *St. Luke* (1602). Climb up one more floor, to the top, for an unforgettable 360-degree **panorama** ♥♥♥ of the city.

Via Arte della Lana 1. bargellomusei.it/musei/orsanmichele. ✆ **055/238-8610.** Admission 8€ adults, free for ages 17 and under. Mon and Wed–Sat 8:30am–6:30pm; Sun 8:30am–1:30pm (Sun church closes at noon). Bus: C2.

Palazzo Davanzati ♥♥ HISTORIC HOME Restored in 2022, one of the city's best-preserved 14th-century palaces offers a glimpse of domestic life during the medieval and Renaissance period. It was originally built for the Davizzi family in the mid-1300s, then bought by the Davanzati clan in 1558; the latter's family tree, dating back to the 1100s, is emblazoned on ground-floor courtyard walls. Painted wooden ceilings and murals have aged well (even surviving World War II damage). The emphasis here is not on decor, however, but on insights into the medieval life of a noble Florentine family: feasts and festivities in the **Sala Madornale;** a private internal well that secured the water supply when things in Florence got sticky; and magnificent 14th-century bedchamber frescoes recounting, comic-strip style, *The Chatelaine of Vergy,* a medieval morality tale. The palace has surprising American connections: In 1916, a New York auction of its furnishings launched a "Florentine style" trend in U.S. interior design, and 2 years later, the set for the Met Opera premiere of Puccini's *Gianni Schicchi* was based on Palazzo Davanzati interiors.

Via Porta Rossa 13. bargellomusei.it/musei/palazzo-davanzati. ✆ **055/064-9460.** Admission 6€ adults, free for ages 17 and under. Fri–Sun 1:15–6:50pm; Tues–Thurs 8:15am–1:50pm. Also closed 1st, 3rd, and 5th Sun of each month. Bus: C2.

Palazzo Vecchio ♥♥ PALACE The core of this fortresslike town hall was constructed from 1299 to 1302 to designs by Arnolfo di Cambio, master builder of Gothic Florence. Home to centuries of Florentine government, the palace is still city hall. When Duke Cosimo I and his Medici family moved to the *palazzo* in 1540, they redecorated. Michelozzo's 1453 **courtyard** ♥♥♥ was left architecturally intact but frescoed by Vasari with scenes of Austrian cities, to celebrate the 1565 marriage of Francesco I de' Medici and Joanna of Austria. A grand staircase leads up to the **Sala dei Cinquecento** ♥♥, named for a 500-man assembly that met here in the pre-Medici days of the Florentine Republic. It's also the site of the greatest fresco cycle that ever

Vasari's frescoes in the Palazzo Vecchio courtyard.

wasn't: Leonardo da Vinci was commissioned in 1503–05 to paint one long wall with a scene celebrating Florence's victory at the 1440 Battle of Anghiari. Always trying new methods and materials, he decided to mix wax into his pigments. Leonardo had finished painting part of the wall, but it wasn't drying fast enough, so he brought in braziers stoked with hot coals to hurry the process. As onlookers watched in horror, wax in the fresco melted under the heat and colors ran to a puddle on the floor. The search for what remains of his work continues; some hope emerged in 2012 with discovery of pigments similar to those used by Leonardo in a cavity behind the current wall. Michelangelo was also supposed to paint a fresco on the opposite wall, but never got past preparatory drawings before Pope Julius II called him to Rome to paint the Sistine Chapel. Vasari and his assistants covered the bare walls from 1563 to 1565 with deferential frescoes exalting Cosimo I and his regime's military victories against Pisa (near wall) and Siena (far wall). Opposite the door you enter, Michelangelo's statue of ***Victory*** ♥, carved from 1533 to 1534, was for Pope Julius II's tomb but later donated to the Medici.

The first series of rooms on the upper floor is the **Quartiere degli Elementi,** frescoed with allegories and mythological characters, again by Vasari. Crossing the balcony overlooking the Sala dei Cinquecento, you enter the **Apartments of Eleonora di Toledo** ♥, decorated for Cosimo's Spanish wife. Her **private chapel** ♥♥♥ is a masterpiece of mid-16th-century fresco painting by Bronzino. Under the coffered ceiling of the **Sala dei Gigli** is Ghirlandaio's fresco of *St. Zenobius Enthroned,* with figures from Republican and Imperial Rome, and Donatello's original ***Judith and Holofernes*** ♥ bronze (1455), one of his final works. In the palace basement the **Scavi del Teatro Romano** ♥ are remnants of Roman Florentia's theater, upon which the medieval palace was built.

Visitors can also climb the **Torre di Arnolfo** ♥♥, the palace's crenelated tower. If you can bear small spaces and 218 steps, views from the top of this medieval skyscraper and the palace battlements are sublime. The 95m (312-ft.) Torre is closed during bad weather. The minimum age to climb up is 6; ages 17 and under must be accompanied by an adult. ***Tip:*** A **completely free** exhibit off the ground-floor courtyard, **Tracce di Firenze** ♥♥ shows how Florence has (and hasn't) changed via historical maps, paintings, and other images, from walled medieval city to the 20th century, including (thankfully unrealized) dreams to turn its center into a little Paris of wide boulevards and neoclassical blocks.

Piazza della Signoria. ticketsmuseums.comune.fi.it. ✆ **055/276-8325.** Palazzo 12.50€ (17.50€ w/exhibition); Torre 12.50€ adults, free for ages 17 and under. Palazzo: Fri–Wed 9am–7pm; Thurs 9am–2pm. Torre: Fri–Wed 9am–5pm; Thurs 9am–2pm. Bus: C1, C2.

Ponte Vecchio ♥ ARCHITECTURE The oldest and most famous bridge across the Arno, the Ponte Vecchio was built in 1345–50 by Taddeo Gaddi to replace an earlier version. Overhanging shops have lined a bridge here since at least the 12th century. In the 16th century, it was home to butchers, until Duke Ferdinand I moved into the Palazzo Pitti across the river. He couldn't bear the stench, so evicted the meat cutters and moved in goldsmiths, silversmiths, and jewelers, who occupy it to this day.

In 1944 the Ponte Vecchio's fame saved it from the Nazis, who had orders to blow up all bridges before retreating as Allied forces advanced. They couldn't bring themselves to reduce this span to rubble, so instead blew up the ancient buildings on either end to block it off. Less discriminating was the **Great Arno Flood** of 1966, which severely damaged the stores. A private night watchman saw waters rising alarmingly and called many goldsmiths at home. They rushed to remove valuable stock before it was washed away. ***Tip:*** The Ponte Vecchio is a busy bottleneck for people crossing the river. If you are not comfortable in crowds, take another bridge, any of which will be much quieter.

Via Por Santa Maria/Via de'Guicciardini. Bus: C3, C4.

Catch a Contemporary Exhibition at the Strozzi

The Renaissance **Palazzo Strozzi ♥♥**, Piazza Strozzi (palazzostrozzi.org; ✆ **055/264-5155**), Florence's major space for international contemporary art exhibitions, has had its own 21st-century rebirth. Hit shows in recent years include Bill Viola's "Electronic Renaissance" in 2017 and a Helen Frankenthaler retrospective in 2025. There's usually plenty going on around each show, including talks, late Thursday openings, and downloadable activities for kids. Admission to headline exhibitions is usually around 15€, with a small discount if you show an admission ticket from **San Marco** (p. 194).

Santa Trínita ♥♥ CHURCH Behind Bernardo Buontalenti's late–16th-century facade lies a dark church, rebuilt in the 1300s but originally founded by the Vallombrosan religious order before 1177. The third chapel on the right has remains of 14th-century frescoes of the *Madonna Enthroned* by Spinello Aretino, discovered beneath an icon of the International Gothic painting style in the next chapel along, the **Cappella Bartolini Salimbeni ♥♥**: Lorenzo Monaco's 1424 *Scenes from the Life of the Virgin* frescoes. This chapel's iron gate is also contemporaneous (ca. 1420). In the right transept, Ghirlandaio frescoed the **Cappella Sassetti ♥♥** in 1485 with a cycle on the *Life of St. Francis,* setting all the scenes against Florentine backdrops peopled with portraits of contemporary notables. His *Francis Receiving the Order from Pope Honorius* (in the lunette) takes place under an arcade on the north side of Piazza della Signoria; you'll recognize the Loggia dei Lanzi in the middle, and on the left, the Palazzo Vecchio (the Uffizi hadn't yet been built). Take a 2€ coin for chapel lighting.

Tip: The south end of the piazza leads to the **Ponte Santa Trínita ♥♥♥**, Florence's most graceful bridge. In 1567, Ammannati built this span for the wedding of Cosimo II, and set it with four statues of the seasons. After the Nazis blew up the bridge in 1944, it was rebuilt and everything was reset in place—save the head on Spring, which remained lost until a team dredging the river in 1961 found it by accident. If you want to photograph the Ponte Vecchio, head here at dusk.

Piazza Santa Trínita. ✆ **055/216-912.** Free admission. Mon–Sat 8am–noon and 4–6:15pm; Sun 8:15–10:45am and 4–6:15pm. Bus: C3, C4, 6, 11.

Around San Lorenzo & the Mercato Centrale

The church of San Lorenzo was once lost behind the leather and souvenir stalls of Florence's **San Lorenzo Street Market** (p. 224), until a decade ago, when the carts were moved into adjacent streets. A bustle of commerce characterizes this neighborhood centered on this tourist market and the **Mercato Centrale,** a showcase for Italian street food (p. 224).

Cappelle Medicee (Medici Chapels) ♥♥ MONUMENT Michelangelo built San Lorenzo's **Sagrestia Nuova** ♥♥ (New Sacristy) between 1519 and 1533 (finished by Vasari in 1556), as a monument to Lorenzo the Magnificent and his generation of relatively enlightened Medici; it was built in harmony with Brunelleschi's Old Sacristy inside San Lorenzo itself (p. 191). (Architectural note: The dome's windows taper as they near the top to fool you into thinking the dome is higher.) Michelangelo was supposed to produce three tombs here (perhaps four) but ironically finished only the two less important ones. So, Lorenzo de' Medici—wise ruler of the city, poet of note, grand patron of the arts, moneybags behind much of the Renaissance, and star of his own Netflix miniseries (*The Magnificent*)—ended up with a mere inscription of his name next to his brother Giuliano's on a plain marble slab against the entrance wall. They did get one Michelangelo sculpture to decorate their slab, an unfinished ***Madonna and Child*** ♥. On the left wall of the sacristy, Michelangelo's ***Tomb of Lorenzo*** ♥ commemorates the duke of Urbino (Lorenzo the Magnificent's grandson), whose seated statue symbolizes the contemplative life. Below him on the tomb's curves stretch a pair of sculptures, *Dawn* (female) and *Dusk* (male). Observing them, one wonders if Michelangelo perhaps hadn't seen many naked women.

Of the two Medici Chapels, the 17th-century Capella dei Principi is a riot of multicolored marble, while the 16th-century Sagrestia Nuova is more harmonious.

In contrast, when work got underway in 1604 on the adjacent **Cappella dei Principi** (Chapel of the Princes), it was to become one of Italy's most arrogant memorials, a mausoleum for the grand dukes, whose ranks include many decrepit tyrants. The Cappella dei Principi is a monolith of cut marble and semi-precious stones—jasper, alabaster, mother-of-pearl, agate, and the like—slathered onto walls and ceiling with little regard for composition or chromatic unity. Ducal funds poured into this monstrosity until Gian Gastone de' Medici drank himself to death in 1737, without an heir. Teams were still finishing the floor in 1962. It was restored in 2019; judge for yourself.

Piazza Madonna degli Aldobrandini. bargellomusei.it. ✆ **055/238-8602.** Admission 9€ adults, free for ages 17 and under. Wed–Mon 8:15am–6:50pm. Bus: C1, 14, 23.

Palazzo Medici-Riccardi ♥♥ HISTORIC HOME/ART MUSEUM Built by Michelozzo in 1444 for Medici "godfather" Cosimo il Vecchio, this is the prototype Florentine *palazzo,* on which the more overbearing Strozzi and Pitti were modeled. It remained the Medici private home until Cosimo I (not the same guy) officially declared his power as duke by moving to the Palazzo Vecchio, Florence's civic nerve center. A door off Michelozzo's grand Renaissance courtyard leads up a staircase to the **Cappella dei Magi** ♥♥♥, the oldest chapel to survive inside a private Florentine palace. Its walls are covered with dense and colorful Benozzo Gozzoli **frescoes** ♥♥♥ (1459–63), classics of the International Gothic style. The walls depict an extended *Journey of the Magi* to see the Christ child, who's being adored by Mary in the altarpiece. Ever more sections of the palace have been opened to the public, including the **Sculpture Gallery** and **Mirror Gallery** ♥♥, a riotous concoction of gilding with a baroque ceiling painted in the 1680s by Luca Giordano.

Via Cavour 3. palazzomediciriccardi.it. ✆ **055/276-0552.** Admission 15€ adults (10€ Nov–Feb), free for ages 17 and under. Thurs–Tues 9am–7pm. Bus: C1, 14, 23.

Courtyard of the Medici-Riccardi palace, the model for many a Florentine *palazzo.*

San Lorenzo ♥♥ CHURCH A rough brick anti-facade fronts what is most likely the oldest church in Florence, founded in C.E. 393. It was the Medici family's parish church; Cosimo il Vecchio, whose wise behind-the-scenes rule made him popular with Florentines, is buried in front of the high altar. A plaque marking the spot is inscribed PATER PATRIAE, "Father of the Homeland." Off the left transept, the **Sagrestia Vecchia ♥♥** (Old Sacristy) is one of Brunelleschi's purest pieces of early Renaissance architecture. The focal sarcophagus contains the remains of Cosimo il Vecchio's parents, Giovanni di Bicci de' Medici and Piccarda Bueri. A side chapel is decorated with a star map showing the night sky above Florence in 1442—a scene that also features, precisely, in Brunelleschi's Pazzi Chapel in Santa Croce (p. 198).

On the wall of the main church's left aisle, Bronzino's 1568 fresco of the ***Martyrdom of San Lorenzo* ♥♥** depicts the poor saint being roasted on a grill in Rome. Two **bronze nave pulpits ♥♥**, depicting the *Passion* and *Resurrection*, were Donatello's final works.

Piazza San Lorenzo. sanlorenzofirenze.it. ✆ **055/214-042.** Admission 9€ adults, free for ages 11 and under. Mon–Sat 10am–5:30pm (last entry 4:30pm). Bus: C1.

Near Piazza Santa Maria Novella

Two squat obelisks in **Piazza Santa Maria Novella ♥♥**, resting on tortoises crafted by Giambologna, once served as turning posts for "chariot" races held here between the 16th and mid–19th century. Down-at-heel just a couple of decades ago, this neighborhood now has some of Florence's priciest hotels.

Museo Novecento ♥♥ MUSEUM Inaugurated a decade ago, this museum covers 20th-century Italian art in a multitude of media. Crowds are often sparse—let's face it, you're in Florence to experience the 1400s, not the 1900s. But this is no reflection on the collection's quality, which expertly encompasses 100 years of visual arts. Exhibits include works by major names such as De Chirico and Futurist Gino Severini; Florence's role in fashion; and Italy's relationship with the European avant-garde. In a top-floor room, a 20-minute movie-clip montage shows Florence through the lens of the century's filmmakers, from Arnaldo Ginna's 1916 *Vita Futurista* to *A Room with a View* and *Tea with Mussolini.*

Piazza Santa Maria Novella 10. museonovecento.it/en. ✆ **055/276-8224.** Admission 9.50€ adults, free for ages 17 and under. Fri–Wed 11am–8pm. Bus: 6, 11.

Santa Maria Novella ♥♥♥ CHURCH Of all Florence's major churches, this home of the Dominican order is the only one with a contemporaneous **facade ♥♥**. The lower Romanesque half was started in the 1300s by architect Fra' Jacopo Talenti. Renaissance architect Leon Battista Alberti finished the facade, adding a classically inspired top that not only chimed seamlessly with the lower half, but also created a Cartesian plane of perfect geometry. Inside, Masaccio's ***Trinità* ♥♥♥** (ca. 1425) was the first painting ever to use linear mathematical perspective.

Florentine citizens and artists flooded in to see the fresco's unveiling, many in awe that it seemed to punch a hole into space, creating a chapel out of a flat wall. The painting was restored in 2024. Frescoes by Filippino Lippi and others fill the **transept.** The **Sanctuary ♥♥** behind the main altar was painted after 1485 by Ghirlandaio with the help of apprentices, probably including a young Michelangelo. The left wall is covered with a cycle on the *Life of the Virgin* and the right has a *Life of St. John the Baptist,* works that are also snapshots of the era's fashions, stuffed with portraits of the Tornabuoni family who commissioned them.

The convent cloisters are accessible on the same admission ticket. The **Chiostro Verde ♥♥** (Green Cloister) was partly frescoed between 1431 and 1446 by Paolo Uccello, a Florentine painter who became obsessed with the mathematics behind perspective. His Old Testament scenes include *Universal Deluge,* which ironically was badly damaged by the Great Arno Flood of 1966. Off the cloister, the **Spanish Chapel ♥♥** is complex Dominican propaganda, frescoed in the 1360s by Andrea di Bonaiuto. One of the oldest parts, the **Chiostro dei Morti ♥♥♥** (Cloister of the Dead), with low-slung vaults decorated by Andrea Orcagna and others, was also damaged in 1966. Visitors can access the **Chiostro Grande** (Florence's largest cloister) and papal apartments frescoed by Florentine Mannerist painter, Pontormo. Allow at least 90 minutes to explore this complex.

Piazza Santa Maria Novella/Piazza della Stazione 4. smn.it. ✆ **055/219-257.** Admission 7.50€ adults (10€ during exhibition), 5€ ages 11–18, free for children 10 and under. Mon–Sat 9am–5pm (Fri from 11am); Sun 1–5pm. Bus: C2, 6, 11.

Near San Marco & Santissima Annunziata

Cenacolo di Sant'Apollonia ♥♥ MUSEUM Andrea del Castagno (1421–57) learned his trade in the city prison, painting portraits of condemned men, and the influence of this apprenticeship is apparent on the disciples' faces in his version of ***The Last Supper,*** the first of many painted in Florence during the Renaissance. This giant fresco, completed around 1447, covers an entire wall in this former convent refectory. Judas is banished to the far side of a communal table. Castagno's *Crucifixion, Deposition,* and *Entombment* complete the sequence.

Via XXVII Aprile 1. cultura.gov.it/luogo/cenacolo-di-sant-apollonia. ✆ **055/238-8608.** Admission 5€. Daily 8:30am–1:50pm. Closed 2nd, 4th, and 5th Sun of each month plus the Mon following the 1st and 3rd Sun. Bus: C1, 6, 14, 17, 23, 31, 32.

Chiostro dello Scalzo ♥♥ MUSEUM Opening times here can be erratic, but for art lovers it rewards the short detour from San Marco. Between 1509 and 1526 painter Andrea del Sarto frescoed a cloister belonging to a religious fraternity dedicated to St. John the Baptist, who is the theme of an unusual monochrome (*grisaille*) fresco cycle. Follow the story counterclockwise from right of the main door. The cloister shines a light on del Sarto's development—work here spans almost his entire career. Compare the *Baptism of Christ* (1509) with the contorted, muscular Mannerism of his *Beheading of the Baptist* (1523), on your left as you walk in. The cloister is usually blissfully empty, too.

Via Cavour 69. cultura.gov.it/luogo/chiostro-dello-scalzo. ✆ **055/238-8604.** Admission 5€. Daily 8:30am–2pm; closed 1st, 3rd, and 5th Sun of each month plus the Mon following the 1st and 3rd Sun. Bus: C1, 14, 17, 23, 31, 32.

Galleria dell'Accademia ♥♥♥ ART MUSEUM The Accademia's star exhibit, ***David*** **♥♥♥**—"Il Gigante"—is much larger than you imagine, looming 4.8m (16 ft.) on top of a 1.8m (6-ft.) pedestal. He hasn't faded with time, either; the marble still gleams as if it were unveiling day in 1504. Viewing the statue is a pleasure in the bright and spacious room custom-designed for him after his move to the Accademia in 1873, following 300 years of pigeons perching on his head in Piazza della Signoria. (Replicas now take the abuse there, and at Piazzale Michelangiolo; a spot high on the northern flank of the Duomo, for which he was originally commissioned, stands empty.)

But the Accademia is not only about David: A stellar supporting cast of Renaissance works complements him. Michelangelo's unfinished ***Prisoners*** **♥♥** statues are a contrast to David, their rough forms struggling to emerge from the raw stone. Michelangelo famously explained how he tried to free the sculpture within every block, and you can appreciate the brute physicality of his technique here. **Renaissance rooms** showcase devotional paintings by Perugino, Filippino Lippi, and Paolo Uccello, as well as a preparatory model for the ***Rape of the Sabines*** **♥♥** from the Loggia dei Lanzi (p. 185)—one of the world's oldest 1:1 scale models. Medieval rooms extend upstairs to showcase medieval Florentine art from 1370 onward, including Giotto and Andrea Orcagna. Also reopened after restoration, the **Plaster Cast Gallery** (***Gipsoteca***) **♥♥** displays over 400

Michelangelo's *David* at the Accademia.

casts in a fresh, "studio" style, many by 19th-century sculptor Lorenzo Bartolini.

Via Ricasoli 58–60. galleriaaccademiafirenze.it. ✆ **055/294-883.** Admission 16€ adults, free for ages 17 and under (prebooking required, online or via office opposite at Via Ricasoli 105R). Tues–Sun 8:15am–6:50pm. Bus: C1, 6, 14, 17, 23, 31, 32.

MAF Museo Archeologico Nazionale (Archaeological Museum) ♥ MUSEUM If you can force yourselves away from the Renaissance, rewind a millennium or two at one of the most important archaeology museums in central Italy, with particular strength in Etruscan art and artifacts. You'll need a little patience, however. The collection inside 17th-century Palazzo della Crocetta is not easy to navigate, although you will quickly find the **"Arezzo Chimera"** ♥♥♥, a bronze figure of a mythical lion-goat-serpent dating to the 4th century B.C.E., perhaps the most important bronze sculpture to survive from the Etruscan era. It is displayed alongside the ***Arringatore*** ♥, a life-size bronze of an orator dating to the 1st century, just as Etruscan culture was being subsumed by ancient Rome. On the top floor is the ***Idolino*** ♥, a lithe and slightly mysterious bronze. The museum collection is strong on Etruscan-era *bucchero* pottery and funerary urns and Egyptian relics, including several sarcophagi displayed in a series of eerie galleries. A vast collection of gems, cameos, and intaglio were gathered by generations of Medici and Lorraine dukes. Some pieces date back many centuries B.C.E. With many travelers so focused on the city's medieval and Renaissance sights, you may have this museum almost to yourself.

Piazza Santissima Annunziata/Via della Colonna. maf.cultura.gov.it. ✆ **055/23-575.** Admission 8€ adults, free for ages 17 and under. Mon–Sat 8:30am–2pm, open until 7pm Tues and Thurs; also open 1st Sun of month 8:30am–2pm. Bus: 6, 8, 14, 17, 23, 31, 32.

San Marco ♥♥♥ MUSEUM Showcasing the work of Fra' Angelico, Dominican monk and Florentine painter in the International Gothic style, this is the most important collection in the world of his altarpieces and painted panels, residing in a deconsecrated 13th-century convent, once home to the multitasking artist-monk. Seeing it all in one place helps you appreciate how his decorative impulses and the sinuous lines of his figures place his work right on the cusp of the Renaissance. The most moving and unusual is his ***Annunciation*** ♥♥♥, a postcard favorite, but a close second are intimate frescoes of the life of Jesus—painted not on one giant wall, but scene by scene in monks' small cells that honeycomb the upper floor. The idea was that these scenes, painted by Fra' Angelico and his assistants, would aid in prayer and contemplation. The final cell on the left corridor belonged to firebrand preacher Savonarola, who briefly incited the people of the most art-filled city in the world to burn their "decadent" paintings, illuminated manuscripts, and anything else he felt was a worldly betrayal of Jesus's ideals. (*Game of Thrones* fans may spot parallels with the High Sparrow.) In Savonarola's cell are his rosary, chair, and what's

At the former convent of San Marco, the hallways, cloisters, and even monks' cells are decorated with masterpieces by Fra' Angelico.

left of the clothes he wore. An anonymous painted panel shows the day in 1498 when he was burned at the stake outside the Palazzo Vecchio, having run afoul of Signoria, pope, and populace.

There's much more Fra' Angelico art secreted around the Michelozzo-designed cloisters, including a ***Crucifixion*** ♥♥ in the Chapter House. The former Pilgrims' Hospice is now a gallery dedicated to Angelico and his contemporaries; look especially for his ***Tabernacolo dei Linaioli*** ♥♥, painted for the linen workers' guild, and a seemingly weightless ***Deposition*** ♥♥.

Piazza San Marco 3. museitoscana.cultura.gov.it/luoghi_della_cultura/museo_di_san_marco. ✆ **055/238-8608.** Admission 11€ adults, free for ages 17 and under. Tues–Sun 8:30am–1:50pm. Tram: T2; Bus: C1, 6, 14, 17, 23, 31, 32.

Santissima Annunziata ♥♥ CHURCH The story of this church begins humbly, in 1233, when seven Florentine nobles had a spiritual crisis, gave away their possessions, and retired to the forest to contemplate divinity. In 1250, they returned to what were fields outside the city walls and founded a small oratory, proclaiming themselves Servants of Mary (the "Servite Order"). Over the years, thanks to a miraculous painting (more on that later), the oratory grew into a grand basilica, enlarged by Michelozzo (1444–81) and later redecorated in unrestrained baroque style.

Visitors enter through the **Chiostro dei Voti** (Votive Cloister), which is today the church's main art draw, decorated with some of the city's finest **Mannerist frescoes** ♥♥ (1465–1515), once again vibrant after a 5-year restoration. Rosso Fiorentino provided an *Assumption* (1513) and Pontormo the *Visitation* (1515) just to the right of the door. Their master, Andrea del Sarto, contributed a *Birth of the Virgin* (1513), in the far-right corner, one of his finest works. To the right of the door into the church is a damaged but still fascinating *Procession of the Magi* (1514) by del

Sarto, who included a giraffe and a self-portrait (front right, looking out from under his blue hat).

The church interior is a flamboyant affair, smothered in multicolored marble and topped with a gilded coffered ceiling. In a side chapel to the left of the entrance, an ornate tabernacle houses a small 14th-century painting of the *Annunciation.* Why such a grandiose setting? According to legend, a friar who was painting the picture became vexed that he couldn't make the Madonna's face as beautiful as she should be and went to take a nap. When he awoke, he found an angel had completed the face for him. This miraculous painting became an object of cult worship, and a once-humble church was changed forever.

On **Piazza Santissima Annunziata** ♥♥ outside, flanked by elegant Brunelleschi porticos, an equestrian statue of Grand Duke Ferdinand I was Giambologna's last work, cast in 1608 by his student Pietro Tacca after his death; Tacca also did the two fountains of fantastical "mermonkeys." ***Tip:*** You can stay right on this sublime piazza, at one of our favorite hotels, the **Loggiato dei Serviti** (p. 211).

Piazza Santissima Annunziata. ✆ **055/266-181.** Free admission. Cloister: Daily 7am–12:45pm and 4–5pm. Church: Daily 4–5pm. Bus: 6, 8, 14, 17, 23, 31, 32.

Spedale degli Innocenti ♥♥ MUSEUM/ARCHITECTURE Originally funded by the silk guild, the "Nocenti" opened in 1419 and ever since has been one of the world's leading childcare organizations. (Their Institute still works with UNICEF.) Its landmark building was designed by Brunelleschi himself, with elegant Renaissance loggias on the facade and surrounding its interior "Women's" and "Men's" **courtyards** ♥. Inside, a three-floor museum has multimedia exhibits tracing the history of the place and the personal stories of many who benefited from its care. The Institute also has a fine **art collection,** including Renaissance works by Botticelli and Ghirlandaio, displayed in a top-floor gallery alongside original painted ceramic roundels by Della Robbia, which elegantly completed Brunelleschi's facade. As you leave, notice the little grated window on the north wall of the main loggia. Here, for centuries, babies were delivered anonymously to the orphanage's care.

Piazza Santissima Annunziata 13. istitutodeglinnocenti.it. ✆ **055/203-7122.** Admission 9€ adults, free for children 10 and under. Daily 9:30am–7pm. Bus: 6, 8, 14, 17, 23, 31, 32.

Around Piazza Santa Croce

Piazza Santa Croce is like any grand Florentine square—an open space ringed with souvenir and leather shops and thronged with tourists. Once a year (in late June) it's covered with dirt as violent Renaissance-style "soccer" is played on the piazza in a tournament known as **Calcio Storico Fiorentino** ♥♥♥. From late November until a few days before Christmas, you'll also find Florence's main festive market, the **Weihnachtsmarkt**—a fun, if boilerplate, German-style affair.

Michelangelo's tomb, designed by Vasari, in the church of Santa Croce.

Santa Croce ♥♥♥ CHURCH The vast Gothic interior of this church is best known as a **mausoleum ♥♥** of famous Florentines, even though **Dante** is not actually interred below his grandiose 19th-century memorial. (Exiled from Florence during his lifetime, he's buried in Ravenna; p. 382.) Starting from the main door, immediately on the right is the Vasari-designed tomb of the most venerated Renaissance master, **Michelangelo Buonarroti,** who died in Rome in 1564 at the age of 89. The pope wanted him buried in the Eternal City, but canny Florentines snuck his body home. Farther along are the tombs of philosopher and statesman **Niccolò Machiavelli** (who left us the word *Machiavellian*) and *bel canto* composer **Gioacchino Rossini.** Directly opposite Michelangelo is heretical scientist **Galileo Galilei** and two berths along, a modest memorial to Italian-American nuclear physicist, **Enrico Fermi.**

Building work on this center of Florence's Franciscan universe began in 1294 under Gothic master Arnolfo di Cambio, whose instructions were to build a rival to the Dominicans' Santa Maria Novella across the city. Santa Croce wasn't consecrated until 1442, and even then remained faceless until a neo-Gothic facade was added in 1857.

The right transept is richly decorated with frescoes. The **Cappella Castellani ♥** was painted with stories of four saints' lives by Agnolo Gaddi. His father, Taddeo Gaddi—one of Giotto's closest followers—decorated the **Cappella Baroncelli ♥** (1328–30) at the transept's end. Its frescoes depict scenes from the *Life of the Virgin* and include an *Annunciation to the Shepherds,* the first night scene in Italian fresco. Giotto himself painted the two chapels to the right of the high altar. Whitewashed over in the 17th century, they were uncovered in the 1800s and inexpertly restored. The more famous **Cappella Bardi ♥♥♥** appeared in the movie *A Room with a View.* Key panels, featuring episodes in the life of St.

Francis, include the *Trial by Fire Before the Sultan of Egypt* on the right wall; and one of Giotto's best-known works, the *Death of St. Francis,* in which monks weep and wail with convincing pathos. The image of Cimabue's damaged 13th-century wooden **Crucifix ♥♥**, now hanging in the **Sacristy,** became a global symbol of the 1966 Great Arno Flood.

Outside in the cloister is the **Cappella Pazzi ♥♥♥**, one of Filippo Brunelleschi's architectural masterpieces, faithfully finished after his death in 1446, more than 30 years before every Pazzi would become *persona non grata* after a failed coup against the Medici (p. 178). Giuliano da Maiano probably designed the chapel's porch, set with glazed terra cottas by Luca della Robbia. The chapel is one of Brunelleschi's signature pieces, decorated with his trademark *pietra serena* gray stone. It is the defining example of early Renaissance architecture. This art-stuffed complex demands 2 hours of your time to see properly.

Piazza Santa Croce. santacroceopera.it. ✆ **055/246-6105.** Admission 10€ adults (family tickets available), 6€ ages 12–17, free for children 11 and under. Mon–Sat 9:30am–5pm; Sun 12:30–5:45pm. Bus: C2, C3, 14, 23.

The Oltrarno, San Niccolò & San Frediano

Giardino di Boboli (Boboli Garden) ♥♥ GARDEN/ART The Boboli Garden behind the Pitti Palace is one of the earliest and finest Renaissance gardens, laid out mostly between 1549 and 1656 with box hedges in geometric patterns, groves of ilex (holm oak), dozens of statues, and rows of cypress. Just above the entrance through the courtyard of the Palazzo Pitti is an oblong **amphitheater** modeled on Roman circuses, with a **granite basin** from Rome's Baths of Caracalla and an **Egyptian obelisk ♥** of Ramses II. In 1589 this was the setting for the wedding reception of Ferdinand de' Medici and Christine of Lorraine. For the occasion, the family commissioned entertainment from Jacopo Peri and Ottavio Rinuccini, who decided to set a classical story entirely to music and called it *Dafne*—the world's first opera. (Their follow-up hit, *Euridice,* performed here in 1600, is the earliest opera whose score survives.) At the south end of the park, the **Isolotto ♥♥** is a dreamy island in a pond full of huge goldfish, with Giambologna's *L'Oceano* sculptural composition at its center. At the north end, around the end of the Pitti Palace, are fake caverns filled with statuary, attempting to invoke a classical sacred grotto. The most famous, the **Grotta Grande ♥**, was created by Giorgio Vasari, Bartolomeo Ammannati, and Bernardo Buontalenti between 1557 and 1593. Dripping with phony stalactites, it's set with replicas of Michelangelo's unfinished *Prisoners* statues. You can usually get inside on the hour (but not every hour) for 15 minutes.

Enter via Palazzo Pitti. uffizi.it/giardino-boboli. ✆ **055/238-8791.** Admission 10€ adults; joint ticket for Boboli and Pitti (see below) 22€ adults; free for ages 17 and under. June–Aug daily 8:15am–7:10pm; Apr–May and Sept closes 6:30pm; Mar and Oct closes 5:30pm; Nov–Feb closes 4:30pm. Closed 1st and last Mon of month. Bus: C3, C4, 11.

Palazzo Pitti ♥♥ MUSEUM/PALACE Although built by and named after a rival of the Medici in the 1450s—the merchant Luca Pitti—the gigantic Pitti Palace soon came into Medici hands. It was the Medici family's principal home from the 1540s and continued to house Florence's rulers until 1919. The Pitti contains five museums, including one of the world's best collections of Raphael canvases. Out back are elegant Renaissance gardens, the **Boboli** (see above).

In the rooms of the Pitti's **Galleria Palatina ♥♥**, paintings are displayed like cars in a parking garage, stacked on walls above each other following the Enlightenment style of exhibition. Rooms are alternately dimly lit or garishly bright; this is how many great art treasures were once seen and enjoyed. For the casual browser, it can be a frustrating experience; but for art lovers, gems abound, including some of the best efforts of Titian, Raphael, and Rubens. One room here holds enough for a fine art museum in many other cities.

Key works in the **Sala di Prometeo** (Prometheus Room) include Filippo Lippi's tondo (round painting) ***Madonna and Child*** **♥** (1452), which looks suspiciously like another portrait of Lippi's nun-turned-lover, Lucrezia Buti (see Uffizi, p. 181). Two giant canvasses of the *Assumption of the Virgin,* both by Mannerist painter Andrea del Sarto, dominate the **Sala dell'Iliade** (Iliad Room). Here you will also find another Biblical woman painted by Artemisia Gentileschi, *Judith,* and panels by Annibale Carracci and Rosso Fiorentino. The **Sala di Saturno ♥♥** (Saturn Room) overflows with Raphaels; and in the **Sala di Giove** (Jupiter Room) is his sublime, naturalistic portrait of ***La Velata*** **♥♥**, as well as ***The Three Ages of Man*** **♥**. The current attribution of the latter is Venetian Giorgione, though that has been disputed. Keep digging to unearth Allori, Bronzino, Rubens, and more.

At the **Appartamenti Reali** (Royal Apartments) you get a feeling for the conspicuous consumption of the Medici Grand Dukes and their successors, the Austrian and Belgian Lorraine dynasty—and see some notable paintings in their original, ostentatious setting. Italy's first king lived here for several years during the country's 19th-century unification process—when Florence was the second national capital after Turin, between 1865 and 1871, until Rome was finally conquered and the court moved there. Much of the gilded stucco, fabrics, and general decoration is in thunderously poor taste.

The Pitti's "modern" gallery, the **Galleria d'Arte Moderna ♥**, has a broad collection of 19th-century Italian paintings with a focus on Romanticism, Neoclassical works, and the **Macchiaioli ♥**, a school of Italian painters who worked in an "impressionistic style" chronologically before the French Impressionists. Highlights hunters: Head straight for major works of the latter, in Sala 18 through 20, where Maremma landscapes by **Giovanni Fattori ♥♥** (1825–1908) and Telemaco Signorini (1835–1901) hang. The Pitti's two lesser museums—the **Museo della Moda e del Costume** (Fashion Collection, revamped in 2024) and **Museo degli Argenti**

(Museum of Silverware)—have specialist historical interest and combine to prove that wealth and taste do not always go hand in hand. One thing you will notice in the fashion galleries is how much smaller locals were a few centuries ago. In 2022, another Medici private collection was opened to the public as the **Museum of Russian Icons ♥**, the oldest such collection in the Western world.

Piazza Pitti. uffizi.it/palazzo-pitti. ✆ **055/294-883.** Admission 16€ adults (joint ticket for Pitti and Boboli, see above, 22€), free for ages 17 and under. Tues–Sun 8:15am–6:30pm. Bus: C3, C4, 11.

Piazzale Michelangiolo ♥♥ VIEW This pedestrianized, panoramic piazza is on the itinerary of every tour bus—for good reason. The balustraded terrace was laid out in 1869 to give a sweeping **vista ♥♥♥** of the Renaissance city, spread out in the valley below and backed by the hills of Fiesole beyond. You'll snap the classic shot of the Florence skyline from here. A bronze replica of *David* points directly at his original home, outside the Palazzo Vecchio.

Viale Michelangelo. Bus: 12, 13.

San Miniato al Monte ♥♥ CHURCH High atop a hill, its gleaming white-and-green marble facade visible from the city below, San Miniato is one of few truly ancient churches of Florence to survive the centuries virtually intact. The current building took shape in 1013, under the auspices of the powerful Arte di Calimala guild, whose symbol, a bronze eagle clutching a bale of wool, perches on the **facade ♥♥**. Above the central window is a 13th-century mosaic of *Christ Between the Madonna and St. Minias* (a motif repeated in the apse). Restored in 2025, the interior has a few Renaissance additions, but they blend well with the overall medieval aspect—an airy, stony space with a raised choir at one end, painted wooden ceiling trusses, and tombs interspersed with inlaid marble zodiac symbols paving the floor.

Below the choir is an 11th-century **Crypt ♥♥** with remains of frescoes by Taddeo Gaddi. Off to the right of the raised choir is the sacristy, which Spinello Aretino covered in 1387 with elaborate frescoes depicting the ***Life of St. Benedict* ♥♥**. Off the left of the nave is the 15th-century **Cappella del Cardinale del Portogallo ♥♥**, a collaborative effort by Renaissance artists to honor a Portuguese humanist, Cardinal Jacopo di Lusitania. It's worth timing your visit to come here when the Benedictine monks are celebrating Vespers in Gregorian chant (usually 6:30pm). Around the back of the church is San Miniato's monumental **cemetery ♥♥**, whose paths are lined with tombs and mausoleums built in elaborate pastiches of every generation of Florentine architecture. It's a peaceful, often deserted spot, soundtracked only by birdsong and the occasional toll of a church bell.

Via Monte alle Croci. sanminiatoalmonte.it. ✆ **055/234-2731.** Free admission. Mon–Sat 9:30am–1pm and 3:30pm until dusk; Sun 3–5:30pm. Bus: 12, 13.

Santa Felicita ♥♥ CHURCH Greek sailors who lived in this neighborhood in the 2nd century brought Christianity to Florence, and this little church was probably the second to be established in the city, its first iteration rising in the late 4th century. The interior was largely remodeled in the 1730s. Its star artworks are in the first chapel on the right, Brunelleschi-designed **Cappella Barbadori-Capponi ♥♥**, with paintings by Mannerist master Pontormo (1525–27). Pontormo's ***Deposition* ♥♥** and frescoed *Annunciation* are rife with his garish color palette of oranges, pinks, golds, lime greens, and sky blues, and exhibit his trademark surreal sense of figure.

Piazza Santa Felicita. terrediflorentia.it/partner/chiesa-di-santa-felicita. ✆ **055/213-018.** Free admission (1€ to illuminate chapel lights). Mon–Sat 9:30am–12:30pm and 3:30–5:30pm. Bus: C3, C4.

Santa Maria del Carmine ♥♥♥ CHURCH Following a 1771 fire that destroyed everything but the transept chapels and sacristy, this Carmelite church was almost entirely reconstructed in high baroque style. To see the much older **Cappella Brancacci ♥♥♥** in the right transept, you enter through the cloisters and pay admission. The frescoes here were commissioned by an enemy of the Medici, Felice Brancacci, who in 1424 hired Masolino and Masaccio to decorate it with a *Life of St. Peter.* Masolino probably worked out the cycle's scheme and painted a few scenes before taking off for 3 years to serve as court painter in Budapest. Masaccio kept painting, quietly creating the early Renaissance's greatest frescoes. Masaccio eventually left for Rome in 1428, where he died at age 27; the cycle was completed between 1480 and 1485 by Filippino Lippi. It looks better than ever after a 3-year project to install new lighting was completed in 2025.

Skip the main church of Santa Maria del Carmine and head instead for its older chapel, the Cappella Brancacci, to see the marvelous frescoes.

Masolino painted *St. Peter Preaching,* the upper panel to the left of the altar, and the two top scenes on the right wall, which shows his fastidious, decorative style in a long panel of *St. Peter Healing the Cripple* and *Raising Tabitha,* and his *Adam and Eve.* Contrast this first man and woman, about to take the snake's bait, with Masaccio's ***Expulsion from the Garden* ♥♥♥**, opposite it.

5

FLORENCE | Exploring Florence

Masolino's figures are highly posed, expressionless models, while Masaccio's Adam and Eve burst with intense emotion. The top scene on the left wall, Masaccio's ***Tribute Money*** ♥♥, showcases his use of linear perspective. The scenes to the right of the altar are Masaccio's as well; the ***Baptism of the Neophytes*** ♥♥ is another of his masterpieces.

Piazza del Carmine. ticketsmuseums.comune.fi.it. ✆ **055/276-8224.** Admission 10€ adults, free for ages 17 and under; reservations recommended in high season. Mon and Wed–Sat 10am–5pm; Sun 1–5pm. Bus: C4, 36, 37.

Santo Spirito ♥♥ CHURCH One of Filippo Brunelleschi's masterpieces of architecture, this 15th-century church doesn't look like much from the outside. No proper facade was ever added. But the **interior** ♥♥ is a marvelous High Renaissance space—an expansive landscape of proportion and mathematics in classic Brunelleschi style, with coffered ceiling, lean columns with Corinthian capitals, and the stacked perspective of arched arcades. Late Renaissance and baroque paintings are scattered throughout, but the best stuff lies in the transepts, especially the **Cappella Nerli** ♥, with a late-15th-century panel by Filippino Lippi. The church's extravagant baroque altar has a ciborium inlaid in *pietre dure* around 1607—and frankly, it looks a bit silly amid the restrained elegance of Brunelleschi's interior. A side entrance admits you to the **Sacristy** to see a crucifix carved from lime wood that has, controversially, been attributed to Michelangelo, as well as Santo Spirito's 17th-century cloister and refectory. ***Tip:*** **Piazza Santo Spirito** ♥ is one of the focal points of the Oltrarno, ringed with cafes and outdoor tables. Sometimes a few farmers sell fresh fruits and vegetables on the square.

Piazza Santo Spirito. basilicasantospirito.it. ✆ **055/210-030.** Free admission; 2€ Sacristy and cloister. Mon–Tues and Thurs–Sat 10am–1pm and 3–6pm; Sun 11:30am–1:30pm and 3–6pm. Bus: 11.

A Side Trip to Fiesole ♥♥

Although it's only a short distance from Florence, **Fiesole** has a proud status as an independent municipality. In fact, this hilltop village high above Florence predates its big neighbor in the valley by centuries.

Etruscans from Arezzo probably founded a town here in the 6th century B.C.E., on the site of a Bronze Age settlement. This *Faesulae* became the most important Etruscan regional center, and although it eventually became a Roman town—conquered in 90 B.C.E., its inhabitants built a theater and adopted Roman customs—it retained a bit of otherness. Its place in late Roman history was ensured when, in C.E. 406, Ostrogoth King Radagaisus was defeated and executed near Fiesole, after an unsuccessful siege of Florence. Following later barbarian invasions, it became part of Florence's administrative district in the 9th century yet continued to struggle for self-government. Medieval Florence settled things in 1125 by attacking and razing the entire settlement, save the cathedral and bishop's palace.

Fiesole Essentials

To get to Fiesole, take bus no. 7 from Piazza Libertà (p. 170 for bus ticket instructions). A scenic 20-minute ride through the greenery above Florence takes you to Fiesole's main square, **Piazza Mino.** The **tourist office** is at Via Portigiani 3 (fiesoleforyou.it; ✆ **055/596-1311**). Hours are changeable, but it's usually open 10am to 1pm and 3 to 6pm: daily in April and May, Friday through Monday June to September, and Friday to Sunday March and October (closing at 5pm). November through February is low season, when typical hours are Saturday and Sunday only from 10am to 3pm.

Fiesole's sights offer a single admission ticket, costing 12€ adults, 8€ for ages 7 to 18; a family ticket (2 adults and up to 4 children) is 24€. Prices are 2€ per person lower without the Museo Bandini, which is fine to skip unless you're an ardent art lover, and anyway only opens Friday through Sunday. For more information, visit **museidifiesole.it** or call ✆ **055/596-1293.** The **Firenzecard** (p. 173) is valid in Fiesole.

An oasis of cultivated greenery still separates Fiesole from Florence. Even with the big city so close, Fiesole preserves the character of a Tuscan small town—making it a perfect escape from the city's bustle. It stays relatively cool in summer, and while you sit at a sidewalk cafe on Piazza Mino, sipping an iced cappuccino, the Uffizi lines seem distant indeed.

San Francesco ♥♥ MONASTERY/MUSEUM The very summit of the town is occupied by a tiny monastery. Its 14th-century church has been largely overhauled, but at the end of a small nave hung with devotional works—Piero di Cosimo and Cenni di Francesco are both represented—is a fine *Crucifixion and Saints* altarpiece by Neri di Bicci. Off the cloisters is a quirky little **Ethnographic Museum,** stuffed with objects picked up by Franciscan missionaries, including an Egyptian mummy, Chinese jade, and ceramics. Entrance to the church's painted, vaulted **crypt** is through the museum. To reach San Francesco, you will climb a sharp hill. Pause close to the top, where a balcony provides perhaps the best **view ♥♥♥** of Florence and the wine hills of the Chianti beyond. Via San Francesco 13. fratifiesole.it. ✆ **055/59-175.** Free admission (donation requested). Mon–Sat 10am–noon and 2–5pm; Sun 2–5pm. Bus: 7.

Teatro Romano ♥♥ RUINS Fiesole's archaeological area is a romantically overgrown scattering of columns, broken friezes, and other ancient remnants. It is also dramatically sited, terraced into a hill with views over the olive groves and forests north of Florence. Beyond a **Roman Theater ♥♥♥** (which seated 1,500 in its day), three rebuilt arches mark the remains of C.E.-1st-century **baths.** Near the arches, a cement balcony over the far edge of the archaeological park gives a good view of a remaining stretch of Fiesole's 4th-century-B.C.E. **Etruscan walls.** At the other end of the park from the baths, the floor and steps of a 1st-century-B.C.E. **Roman Temple** were built atop a 4th-century-B.C.E. Etruscan one dedicated to Minerva. To the left are oblong **Lombard tombs** from the C.E.

7th century, when this part of Fiesole was a necropolis. A small on-site **Archaeological Museum** displays finds uncovered around Fiesole.

Via Portigiani 1. museidifiesole.it/en. ✆ **055/596-1293.** Admission with Fiesole single admission (p. 203). Apr–Sept daily 9am–7pm; Mar and Oct daily 10am–6pm; Nov–Feb Wed–Mon 10am–3pm. Bus: 7.

Organized Tours

To really get under the surface of Florentine history, art, and culture, book a themed culture tour with **Context Travel ♥♥** (contexttravel.com/cities/florence). Led by academics and other experts on anything from the gastronomic to the archaeological and the artistic, these insightful tours, limited to six people, generally cost around $170 per person. The quality of Context's walks is unmatched, well worth the above-average cost. Private tours start from around $350.

Food tours are booming. A few hours in city markets, or in the company of street vendors or a pro chef, gives you an insight into traditions and trends in Florentine cooking. The glass-fronted Arclinea kitchens upstairs at the Mercato Centrale host the **Lorenzo de' Medici Cooking School ♥** (cucinaldm.com; ✆ **334/304-0551**), where 2-hour small-group courses (80€–85€; ages 14 and older) teach the skills to create dishes such as fresh pasta, seasonal soups and risottos, bread, or Italian meat and fish courses. You must enroll by 1pm the day before the class. **Eating Europe** (eatingeurope.com/florence) offers themed small-group tours (79€–115€) covering gelato-making, Oltrarno foodie haunts, and more. They can also customize a Florence food experience for you. Offbeat offerings from **Curious Appetite ♥♥** (curiousappetitetravel.com) include Negroni making, *aperitivo,* and a four-stop "dinner crawl." Prices range from $129 to $165 per person, which includes food and drink.

Truescany ♥♥ (truescany.com; ✆ **055/093-5928**) specializes in trips farther afield in fully equipped Mercedes vans (including Wi-Fi, use of iPad, complimentary bottle of prosecco) with an English-speaking driver. It operates full- and half-day private and group food and wine tours into the Chianti hills—by day or night—plus visits to the Ferrari and Lamborghini factories, a Tuscan movie location tour, and trips to the Cinque Terre (p. 578).

Especially for Kids

You have to put in a bit of work (and reserve ahead) to reach some of Florence's best views. But the climbs, up claustrophobic medieval staircases, are a favorite with many kids. The cupola of **Santa Maria del Fiore** (p. 177), the **Palazzo Vecchio**'s Torre di Arnolfo (p. 187), and the **Campanile di Giotto** (p. 176) are perfect for any youngster who has a head for heights.

Kids (of any age) who are nuts about trains will be entranced by **HZERO ♥♥**, Piazza degli Ottaviani 2R (hzero.com; ✆ **055/283-619**), a near-1km-long miniature model railway with 70 trains that run through accurate landscapes covering 280 sq. m (over 300 sq. ft.). Although adult admission may seem a little steep (14€), child discounts (8€) and family tickets make this a more affordable way to spend an hour or two together lost in your imagination. Open Wednesday through Monday 10am to 7pm.

The best museum activities are run by **Mus.e** ♥♥ (musefirenze.it; ✆ **055/054-1450**), a program that offers child's-eye tours in English around the Palazzo Vecchio, led by guides in period costumes. Lively, affordable activities focus on life at the ducal court, including "The Turtle and the Snail," pitched at children ages 4 to 7. Programs cost 5€ per person; book online or at the desk next to the Palazzo Vecchio ticket booth.

Cycling ♥♥ is a pleasure in the riverside **Parco delle Cascine** (p. 170 for bike-rental advice). Tourist offices can provide a map of the best family cycling routes around the city. The terrain is mostly flat. And remember you are in the **gelato** capital of the world. At least one multi-scoop gelato per day is the minimum recommended dose; see p. 221. This is not just any old ice-cream.

Tip: For more ideas and the latest advice, ask at a Florence tourist office for the up-to-date version of its **Firenze for Families** mini-guidebook.

WHERE TO STAY IN FLORENCE

Despite a fast-growing stock of hotel beds, it remains difficult to find a high-season double you'd want to sleep in for less than around 120€. **Rates also vary wildly by season:** A double at 300€ in June might cost 85€ in February. Sadly, once-attractive August deals have dried up; Florence no longer gets much quieter in its hottest month. Rooms almost everywhere are smaller than the North American norm. Most hotels mid-price and up have smart TVs where you can log into your own streaming accounts like Netflix, Prime, or Apple TV.

Florence's city government adds a tourist levy of 3.50€ to 8€ **per person per night,** depending on the hotel's official star rating, for the first 7 nights of any stay. It is payable on departure and is not included in quoted rates. Children below age 12 are exempt from the tax. Airbnb and holiday rentals are **not** exempt.

Peak hotel season is Easter through early July, September through October, and Christmas through January 6. May, June, and September are very popular; January and February are the months to grab a bargain—haggle if you come then, especially for a multi-night stay. **Booking direct** via phone, e-mail, or the hotel's website is often key to unlocking the lowest rates and/or complimentary extras. Always ask for a discount if you plan to stay more than 3 consecutive nights.

To help you decide in which area you'd like to base yourself, consult "Florence Neighborhoods in Brief," p. 168. For first-time visitors, there's no good reason to stay outside the center and/or Oltrarno. Some hotels offer babysitting services, but almost always "on request"—at least a couple days' notice is advisable. ***Note:*** We include parking information in listings, below, only for those places that offer it.

HOTELS
Alessandra 8
Antica Dimora Johlea 22
Burchianti 14
Davanzati 9
Grand Hotel Minerva 13
Il Guelfo Bianco 20
La Maison du Sage 33
Loggiato dei Serviti 24
Palazzo dal Borgo 12
Palazzo Tolomei Residenza d'Epoca 19
Ponte Vecchio Suites 7
Relais Hotel Centrale 15
Residence Hilda 25
Residenza della Signoria 28
Riva Lofts 1
Villa Tortorelli 37

RESTAURANTS
3dddì 35
Brac 32
Burro e Acciughe 3
Coquinarius 26
Da Rocco 36
Da Tito 23
Da' Vinattieri 27
Formaggioteca Terroir 34
Gelateria dei Neri 31
Gelateria della Passera 6
I Fratellini 29
iO: Osteria Personale 2
La Carraia 4
La Gratella 16
Mangiando Mangiando 23
Mario 18
Mercato Centrale 17
Ostaria dei Centopoveri 11
Osteria dell'Enoteca 5
Osteria di Giovanni 10
SandwiChic 21
Vini e Vecchi Sapori 30

Florence Hotels & Restaurants

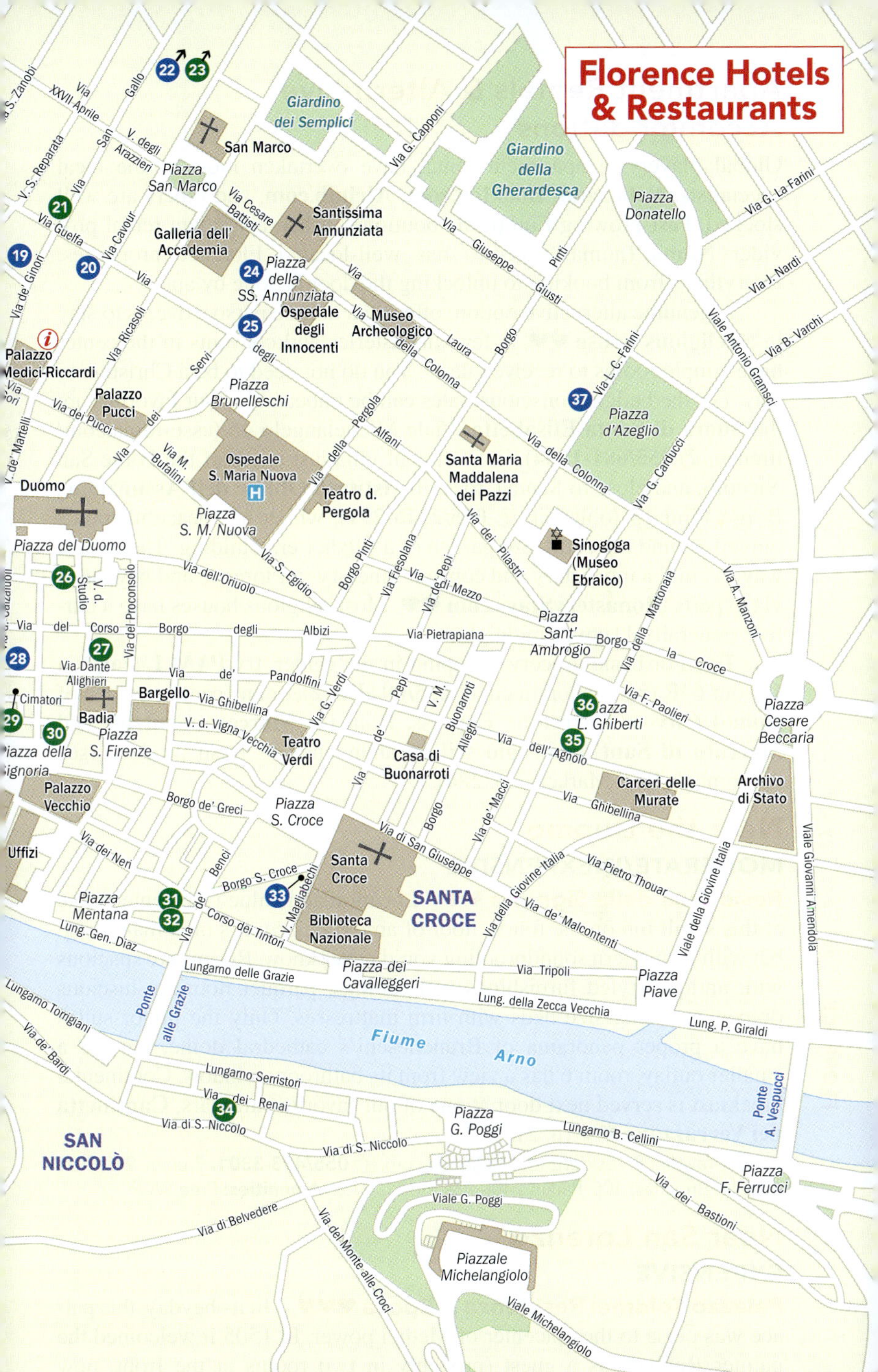

Apartment Rentals & Alternative Accommodations

Global players in apartment rental have overtaken most of the local specialists. **Vrbo.com**, **Booking.com**, **Airbnb.com**, and others are well stocked. Fast-growing European "boutique" urban apartment rental provider **Numa** (numastays.com) has well-located Florence properties. Everything from booking to unlocking the door is done by app.

A genuine alternative option, offering a unique perspective, is to stay in a **religious house** ♥♥. A few monasteries and convents in the center have simple rooms to receive guests: You do not need to be a Christian to stay. For the budget-conscious, rates can be unbeatable. Our favorites are the **Suore di Santa Elisabetta,** Viale Michelangelo 46 (csse-roma.com/firenze; ✆ **055/681-1884**), in a colonial villa just south of the Ponte San Niccolò; and close to Santa Croce, the **Istituto Oblate dell'Assunzione,** Borgo Pinti 15 (oblate.it; ✆ **055/2346-291**), which has peaceful rooms ranged around the courtyard garden of a Medici-era building. The easiest way to build a monastery and convent itinerary in Florence and beyond is via experts **MonasteryStays.com** ♥♥. Most religious houses have a curfew, generally 11pm or midnight.

5

Tip: For basic grocery shopping in the center, try **PAM Local,** Via Cavour 64R (pampanorama.it; ✆ **055/0944-672**), or any central branch of **Conad City** or **Carrefour Express.** Both the **Mercato Centrale** and **Mercato di Sant'Ambrogio** sell an abundance of fresh produce (see "Florence's Best Markets," p. 224).

Near the Duomo

MODERATE/INEXPENSIVE

Residenza della Signoria ♥♥ Location and value take center stage at this small inn on the fourth floor of an old palace. It's on a main drag, but with its modern soundproofing you'd never know. Rooms are spacious with antique-styled furnishings and ceilings, parquet flooring, luscious drapes, and king-size beds with firm mattresses. Only the junior suites have a proper panorama of Brunelleschi's cathedral dome, but for a smaller outlay, room 6 has a view from its bathroom window. Continental breakfast is served next door at one of our favorite cafe-bars, **Cantinetta dei Verrazzano** ♥♥ (p. 217).

Via dei Tavolini 8. residenzadellasignoria.com. ✆ **055/493-3301.** 7 units. 99€–299€ double. Breakfast 10€. Parking 40€–45€. Bus: C1, C2. **Amenities:** Free Wi-Fi.

Near San Lorenzo

EXPENSIVE

Palazzo Tolomei Residenza d'Epoca ♥♥♥ In its heyday, this palace was close to the epicenter of Medici power. In 1505 it welcomed the painter Raphael as a guest (probably in two rooms at the front, now Barocco 1 and 2). Guest rooms are large, with Renaissance wooden ceilings, terra-cotta floors, free minibar, and Nespresso machines. Modern fittings—leather sofas, soft mattresses, and florid crystal chandeliers—chime perfectly with a 17th-century baroque redecoration, complete with ceiling frescoes by Alessandro Gherardini. The lower floor has opulent public rooms, just like when it was the *piano nobile* of the family palazzo. These days you'll find a music room, art books, a welcoming host, and probably an open bottle of Tuscan red wine. Book direct for deals—perhaps free late checkout or a discounted rate.

Via de' Ginori 19. palazzotolomei.it. ✆ **055/292-887.** 8 units. 219€–549€ double. Rates include breakfast. Bus: C1. **Amenities:** Concierge; free Wi-Fi.

MODERATE

Il Guelfo Bianco ♥♥ Decor in this former noble Florentine home retains an authentic *palazzo* feel, with the bonus of full hotel service and a thorough renovation from 2023. No two units are the same—stone walls this thick cannot be knocked through—and several have antiques integrated into the design schemes. Grand rooms at the front have Renaissance coffered ceilings and extra space; it's well worth around 20% extra to stay in these Superior units. Families: Every Junior Suite here has a sofa bed.

Via Cavour 29. ilguelfobianco.it. ✆ **055/288-330.** 46 units. 110€–320€ double. Rates include breakfast. Parking 35€–40€. Bus: C1, 14, 23. **Amenities:** Free Wi-Fi.

Relais Hotel Centrale ♥♥ Noticeable touches lift this place above its neighbors in a hotel-heavy part of town. Service is warm and efficient—far outstripping what you'd expect in this price bracket. The breakfast buffet is supplemented by an a la carte menu of eggs, smoothies, and specialty coffees, also available in your room at no extra charge. High ceilings admit lots of natural light in the unfussy guest rooms, which are spread over three floors of the palace: It's worth paying extra for a deluxe room on a higher floor for a view across rooftops to the Medici Chapels.

Via dei Conti 3. hotelcentralefirenze.it. ✆ **055/215-761.** 36 units. 180€–490€ double. Rates include breakfast. Valet parking 38€. Bus: C2, C4, 14. **Amenities:** Bar; bike rental; concierge; free Wi-Fi.

INEXPENSIVE

Burchianti ♥♥ This friendly *pensione* (between a guesthouse and a hotel) has been in business for over a century. Its rooms range over several floors of a historic palace once owned by the King of Italy, now shared with residences and a couple of B&B-style lodgings. High ceilings in guest rooms give an airy feel; decor is in the traditional Florentine style, with terracotta parquet floors, dark wood furniture, and in several rooms, restored 17th-century frescoes. In-room gadgetry is limited, but then you likely didn't come to Florence to watch TV. The top-floor Panoramic Suite—beyond the reach of the elevator, alas—costs way less than you'd think for a stunning close-up of Michelangelo's San Lorenzo cupola.

Via del Giglio 8. hotelburchianti.it. ✆ **055/212-796.** 11 units. 80€–250€ double. Bus: C2, C4, 14. **Amenities:** Babysitting (prebooking essential); concierge; free Wi-Fi.

Near the Ponte Vecchio

MODERATE

Alessandra ♥♥♥ Another typical Florentine *pensione* that transports you to the age of the gentleman and lady traveler. Decor has grown organically and with regular renovation since it opened as a hotel in 1950; Alessandra is a place for evolution, not revolution. A pleasing mix of styles is the result—some rooms have carved headboards, gilt frames, and gold damask; others have eclectic postwar furniture, like a midcentury period movie set. A couple have views of the Arno, while front-side rooms overlook Borgo SS. Apostoli, one of the center's most atmospheric streets. **Le Stanze di Alessandra,** five more rooms across the street with contemporary decor—including two mini-apartments—have a separate website (residenzaalessandra.com).

Borgo SS. Apostoli 17. hotelalessandra.com. ✆ **055/283-438.** 27 units. 140€–300€ double. Breakfast 13€. Parking 31€. Bus: C2, 6. Closed a few days around Christmas, plus late Jan–Feb. **Amenities:** Free Wi-Fi.

Davanzati ♥♥ Although installed in a historic building, the Davanzati never rests on medieval laurels: There is an iPad with cellular data for free guest use, movies to stream, and new energy-efficient air-conditioning. Rooms (many renovated in 2025) are decorated in the Tuscan style, with color-washed walls, cool tiled floors, and half-canopy beds. Room 100 is probably the best family room in Florence, full of nooks, crannies, and split levels that give both adults and kids their own space. Free daily afternoon tea and *aperitivo* from 6:30pm are all part of the family welcome.

Via Porta Rossa 5 (on Piazza Davanzati). hoteldavanzati.it. ✆ **055/286-666.** 27 units. 79€–450€ double. Rates include breakfast and *aperitivo*. Valet parking 35€–40€. Bus: C2, 6. **Amenities:** Bar; concierge; free Wi-Fi.

Near Santa Maria Novella

EXPENSIVE

Grand Hotel Minerva ♥♥♥ The second you step inside this hotel, Florence's hectic energy melts away. Poet Henry Wadsworth Longfellow stayed in lodgings on this site, on what is now one of Florence's most prestigious squares. I doubt the service was anywhere near the refined standard set here today. Art-filled public spaces give way to subtly stylish rooms in soothing cream tones, natural wood, tan leather, and travertine bathrooms. Each one is well soundproofed against neighbors and outdoor noise. A major bonus from April to October: a rooftop pool with panoramic sundeck, cocktail bar, and evening *aperitivo* service.

Piazza Santa Maria Novella 16. grandhotelminerva.com. ✆ **055/27-230.** 97 units. 300€–995€ double. Rates include breakfast. Parking 45€. Bus: C2, C4, 13. **Amenities:** Restaurant; 2 bars; concierge; gym; pool; free Wi-Fi.

MODERATE

Palazzo dal Borgo ♥♥ High ceilings and spacious rooms—especially second-floor Superior units—are typical of a Florentine noble palace.

A room with a view at the Grand Hotel Minerva.

This building was just that: Built in the 1500s, it was converted into a hotel in the early 1900s, leaving many original ceiling frescoes and architectural features intact. For an extra-silent night, request a room overlooking its interior courtyard or the church of Santa Maria Novella, which is out back. A breakfast buffet is served in a quaint bar or outside among the citrus trees. The location provides maximum convenience for the rail station and airport tram.

Via della Scala 6. hotelpalazzodalborgo.it. ✆ **055/216-237.** 34 units. 99€–299€ double. Rates include breakfast. Parking 30€–40€. Bus: C2, 6, 11, 37. **Amenities:** Bar; concierge; free Wi-Fi.

Near San Marco & Santissima Annunziata

MODERATE

Antica Dimora Johlea ♥♥ There's a neighborhood feel to the streets around this *dimora* (traditional home) guesthouse, which means evenings are lively and Sundays are quiet (although it's only a 7-min. walk to San Lorenzo). Standard-size rooms are snug; upgrade to an Executive if you need space, but there is no difference in the decor, a mix of Florentine and earthy boho with silk drapes and other natural materials. The terrace has knockout views over rooftops to the dome and hills beyond. It is pure magic at dusk, when a scent of lavender floats on the breeze.

Via San Gallo 80. antichedimorefiorentine.it. ✆ **055/463-3292.** 6 units. 100€–250€ double. Parking 15€–25€. Bus: C1, 1, 8, 10. **Amenities:** Bar; free Wi-Fi.

Loggiato dei Serviti ♥♥♥ This city icon was restyled in 2023 with a light touch that did not sacrifice why we have always loved it: A stay evokes Florence as experienced by the travelers of the Grand Tour. For starters, the building is a genuine Renaissance landmark, built by

Sangallo the Elder in the 1520s. A sense of grandeur and unconventional luxury permeates common areas and rooms with vintage ambience. No unit is small. However, spring for a Deluxe to enjoy a room with a view of this perfect piazza (no. 4 is the only one with a balcony).

Piazza Santissima Annunziata 3. loggiatodeiservitihotel.it. ✆ **055/289-592.** 37 units. 180€–350€ double. Rates include breakfast. Bus: C1, 6, 14, 19, 23, 31, 32. **Amenities:** Concierge; free Wi-Fi.

Residence Hilda ♥♥♥ With no hint of the Renaissance, these spacious, luxe mini-apartments are all bright-white decor and designer furnishings, with natural wood flooring, hypoallergenic mattresses, Starck chairs, and modern gadgetry. Each is spacious and soundproofed against Florence's perma-noise. An efficient heating/cooling system makes this place a good choice for the temperature-sensitive. Every unit has a minikitchen, equipped for preparing a simple meal, ideal if you have kids in tow; they'll even arrange grocery delivery. Unusual for apartments, all are bookable by the single night—some guests stay for a year.

Via dei Servi 40. residencehilda.com. ✆ **055/288-021.** 12 units. 135€–410€ for 2- to 4-person apt. Breakfast (at cafe opposite) 7€–12€. Parking 30€–35€. Bus: C1, 6, 14, 19, 23, 31, 32. **Amenities:** Airport transfer; babysitting; concierge; free Wi-Fi.

5

Near Santa Croce

MODERATE

La Maison du Sage ♥♥♥ In case you've wondered, this is what "going all in" on Art Deco looks like. There's light walnut-wood and geometry wherever you look inside this converted Liberty villa: on chairs and tables, beds and bookcases. King rooms are harmonious, bright, and spacious; plumbing and power-showers are modern and efficient; complimentary in-room refreshments are generous. The location practically overlooks Santa Croce's Pazzi Chapel, while being just away from the main walking route back to the busiest parts of the center.

Via Magliabechi 7. lamaisondusage.com. ✆ **055/094-8343.** 27 units. 150€–480€ double (2-night min. on peak weekends). Breakfast 20€. Parking 35€–55€. Bus: C2, C3, 14, 23. **Amenities:** Bar; concierge; free Wi-Fi.

Villa Tortorelli ♥♥ Peace, quiet, and a hotel pool are scarce resources in central Florence, but not totally out of the question. Set amid trees—and in the same neighborhood as the Four Seasons (at fraction of the price)—Liberty-style Villa Tortorelli has them all, plus a terrace overlooking a walled garden to domes of Florence's cathedral and synagogue. Inside the guest rooms are *trompe l'oeil* painted cornices and architraves and (real) Murano glass chandeliers. Bright bathrooms have huge mirrors and concealed lighting. Check-in by PIN can feel a bit isolating or superconvenient, depending on your taste.

Piazza Massimo D'Azeglio 39. villatortorelli.com. ✆ **351/535-4357.** 12 units. 80€–420€ double. Rates include breakfast. Parking 25€. Bus: 6, 12, 13, 14, 17, 23, 31, 32. **Amenities:** Pool (Apr–Oct); free Wi-Fi.

Oltrarno

MODERATE

Ponte Vecchio Suites ♥♥♥ A calm, contemporary nest on one of the south bank's most evocative medieval streets—and with Piazza della Signoria only a 5-minute walk away. Rooms are spacious, all with modern furnishings and large bathrooms; a few suites can accommodate families with children in comfort. Soundproofing is immaculate, making it an ideal choice for light sleepers (Florence can be a noisy city). Both staff service and the daily buffet breakfast exceed expectations. Book direct for the best price and free extras like daily soft-drink refills.

Via de' Belfredelli 9. pontevecchiosuites.com. ✆ **055/217-379.** 14 units. 200€–450€ double. Rates include breakfast. Parking 32€–39€. Bus: C3, C4. **Amenities:** Bar; concierge; spa; free Wi-Fi.

Plunge pool at Riva Lofts.

Beyond San Frediano

MODERATE

Riva Lofts ♥♥♥ The traditional Florentine alarm call—traffic and tourism—is replaced by birdsong when you awake in one of these stylish rooms by the Arno. A former artisan workshop, Riva had a refit to earn its "loft" label: mellow colors, laminate flooring, floating staircases, marble bathrooms with rainfall showers, and clever integration of natural materials such as original wooden ceilings. The center is a 30-minute walk, or hop on one of Riva's vintage-style bikes and cycle along the river. Further standout features are a shaded garden—where you can often dine on contemporary Tuscan food at their bistro, Riva-K—and an outdoor plunge pool.

Via Baccio Bandinelli 98. rivalofts.com. ✆ **055/713-0272.** 12 units. 150€–550€ double. Rates include breakfast. Parking 15€. Tram: T1. **Amenities:** Restaurant (Wed–Sun); bar; bike rental (free); pool; free Wi-Fi.

WHERE TO EAT IN FLORENCE

Florence is well supplied with restaurants, but in the most touristy areas around the Duomo, Piazza della Signoria, Piazza della Repubblica, and

Ponte Vecchio, you must choose carefully: Many eateries are of below-average quality or charge high prices, sometimes both. Alas, that online review that flags up a secret little place around here known only to savvy locals **is just not true.** The highest concentration of excellent *ristoranti* and *trattorie* are north of **Santa Croce** and across the river in **San Frediano.** There's also much improved but still visitor-oriented dining around **San Lorenzo.** Bear in mind that restaurant menus can change weekly or even daily. The city has become **gluten-savvy** and **alternate milks** (soy, almond, occasionally oat; *latte di soia, mandorla, avena*) are often available. If you have a food intolerance, just ask.

Reservations are strongly recommended if your heart is set on somewhere specific, especially at dinner on weekends. You can book at many Florence restaurants, including several of our favorites below, using **The Fork** (thefork.it) or **Quandoo** (quandoo.it) restaurant reservation services.

Near the Duomo

MODERATE

Coquinarius ♥♥ MODERN TUSCAN This long-standing Frommer's favorite has a traditional cellarlike interior and a menu that enhances the best flavors of the Chianti hills, just south of the city, with modern Spanish influences. A light appetizer such as swordfish carpaccio with fennel and pink grapefruit or Cantabrian anchovy filet leaves room for a heartier *secondo*. Classic Tuscan stuffed rabbit or pigeon pairs perfectly with a full-bodied bottle of Chianti Classico red.

Via delle Oche 11R. coquinarius.it. ✆ **055/230-2153.** Main courses 20€–26€. Mon–Sat noon–3pm and 7pm–midnight; Sun 7pm–midnight. Bus: C1, 14, 23.

Tagliatelle with guinea fowl ragù at Coquinarius.

INEXPENSIVE

I Fratellini ♥♥ SANDWICHES This hole-in-the-wall has been serving food to go since 1875. Here's the drill: Choose a filling, pick a drink, then eat your fast-filled roll on the move. There are around 30 combos to choose from, including the usual Tuscan meats and cheeses—porchetta, Pecorino, prosciutto—and flamboyant options such as fennel-spiked salami with

creamed cheese or *bresaola* (air-dried beef) and arugula. A *calice* (small glass) of wine to wash it down costs from 2€. Lunchtime lines can be long, including at their *schiacciata* (Tuscan flatbread) hatch next door.
Via dei Cimatori 38R (at corner of Via Calzaiuoli). ✆ **055/239-6096.** Sandwich 6€; *schiacciata* 7€–8€. Daily 10am–5pm. Bus: C1, C2.

Near Piazza della Signoria

MODERATE

Vini e Vecchi Sapori ♥♥♥ TUSCAN The daily menu here rarely strays far from classic seasonal Florentine flavors: bruschetta with tomatoes ripened in the Tuscan sun; salami with late-summer figs; pumpkin-flower pasta; and plenty of meat: stewed in a *peposo* (Tuscan beef stew); stuffed and roasted rabbit; and of course flame-grilled cuts of veal, pork, and beef. The place is cramped and lively, with super-friendly service and a genuine Florentine vibe. As the best (and best-value) restaurant in this part of the city, it is always packed, so reservations are a must: Call ahead (you may get lucky and they pick up), or better still, go in person the day you arrive.
Via dei Magazzini 3R. facebook.com/osteriavinievecchisapori. ✆ **055/293-045.** Main courses 14€–26€. Mon–Sat noon–2:30pm and 7–10:30pm. Bus: C2.

Near Santa Maria Novella

MODERATE

Osteria di Giovanni ♥♥♥ MODERN TUSCAN If only every Tuscan restaurant in town was this good. Family-run Osteria di Giovanni is always buzzing, so make a reservation even in low season. Meat is a specialty, both traditional (the *bistecca alla fiorentina* with roast potatoes is legendary) and modern interpretations like *faraona all'arancia* (guinea hen stewed with a slightly sweet orange). Only the very brave should attempt a full *primo/secondo/dolce,* since portions are large. The steep cover charge (4€) is actually a value deal, because it includes a couple of tasty snacks and all the mineral water you can drink.
Via del Moro 22. osteriadigiovanni.com. ✆ **055/284-897.** Main courses 25€–29€. Mon–Sat 7–10:30pm. Closed 10 days around New Year. Bus: C3, 6, 11, 13, 14, 36, 37.

INEXPENSIVE

Ostaria dei Centopoveri ♥♥ TUSCAN/TRADITIONAL ITALIAN This place offers one of Florence's best lunch deals: Appetizer, main, water, and a large glass of wine for 12€. Their classic Italian menu of Tuscan-accented flavors has something for everyone—even pizzas (dinner only). Crowd-pleasing appetizers include caprese salad and bruschetta, either classic (tomato and basil) or adventurous (*lardo di Colonnata,* thinly sliced, cured pork fat that melts in your mouth). The strongest mains are the stews (wild boar, osso buco) and grilled meats or

Talking Tripe

New York has the hot dog. London has pie and mash. Florence has . . . cow's intestine in a sandwich. The city's traditional street food, *lampredotto* (the cow's fourth stomach) stewed with tomatoes, made a big comeback over the last decade, including on some fine-dining menus. The best places to sample it affordably are the city's *trippai*, tripe vendors who sell from food trucks. The most convenient vendors are in **Piazza de' Cimatori** and on **Via de' Macci** at Piazza Sant'Ambrogio. **Da' Vinattieri ♥♥**, Via Santa Margherita 6R, also offers counter service. A hearty, nutritious lunch should cost 6€ to 8€. Most are open Monday through Saturday, but close in August, when Florentines flee their city.

Mediterranean fish, such as sea bream. A long Tuscan wine list goes beyond the usual Chianti, with Super-Tuscans, Maremma labels, and more. The ambience is bustling and noisy, without airs.

Via Palazzuolo 31R. centopoveri.it. ✆ **055/218-846.** Main courses 10€–22€. Daily noon–3pm and 7–11pm. Closed 2 weeks mid-Aug. Bus: C3, 6, 11, 13, 14, 36, 37.

Near San Lorenzo

Florence's best sandwich bar, **SandwiChic ♥♥♥**, Via San Gallo 3R (facebook.com/sandwichic; ✆ **055/281-157**), keeps things simple, with freshly baked bread and expertly sourced ingredients such as Tuscan cured meats, preserved vegetables, and savory condiments. Try the likes of *finocchiona* (salami spiked with fennel), Pecorino cheese, and *crema di porri* (a creamy leek relish). Sandwiches cost around 9€. It's open 11am to 6pm daily except Saturday.

This neighborhood's proximity to the food market has nurtured several excellent **steakhouses,** where local tradition makes it almost compulsory to **order steak cooked rare.** Many places won't even ask your preference.

MODERATE

La Gratella ♥♥ FLORENTINE It doesn't look much—a workers' canteen on a nondescript side street—but looks don't matter when you can source and cook meat like this. With the market in close proximity, the unsurprising star of the show is the *fiorentina.* This large T-bone-like cut is flame-grilled on the bone and brought to the table over coals. It is sold by weight and made for sharing; expect to pay around 80€ for enough to feed three, or two big appetites, with simple Tuscan sides like *fagioli all'uccelletto* (beans stewed with tomato). They are happy to cater to celiacs and have kid-friendly dishes, too.

Via Guelfa 81R. lagratella.it. ✆ **055/211-292.** Main courses 17€–28€. Daily noon–2:30pm and 7–11pm. Bus: 6, 11, 14.

CAFÉ CULTURE alla fiorentina

Although they're often overpriced tourist spots (especially around **Piazza della Repubblica**), Florence's few remaining high-toned piazza cafes are fine if you want to sit outdoors and people-watch. If you pick one overpriced sidewalk cafe in Florence, make it **Rivoire** ♥ (rivoire.it; ✆ **055/214-412**) in the Piazza della Signoria. Steep prices (7€ a cappuccino) pay your rent for one of the prettiest slices of real estate on the planet

A cozier central option, without the view, **Cantinetta dei Verrazzano** ♥♥, Via dei Tavolini 18R (verrazzano.com/la-cantinetta-in-firenze; ✆ **055/268-590;** closed Sun), is decked out with antique wooden wine cabinets, in genuine *enoteca* style. Wines come from the first-rate Verrazzano estate, in Chianti (p. 248). Light breakfast and morning cappuccino are a delight.

At Piazza Santa Maria Novella 12R, **Cortese Café '900** ♥♥ (cortesecafe.com; ✆ **055/024-1691;** closed Thurs) was the original location for Vito Cortese's revolutionary raw-food pastries, vegan and made without refined sugar: They're pure indulgence. You'll easily find a nondairy *cappuccino* these days, but his homemade almond milk is really something.

The moment you enter Procacci ♥♥, Via Tornabuoni 64R (procacci1885.it; ✆ **055/211-656**), you're hit with the perfume of Procacci's specialty: *panini tartufati,* brioche rolls spread with truffle butter. It's also a wine-bar every evening.

Inside a Michelucci-designed modernist building at Via dello Sprone 5R, on-trend **Ditta Artigianale** ♥♥ (dittaartigianale.com; ✆ **055/045-7163**) offers a bit of everything. The highlight is fantastic coffee from its own small-batch roastery in Arezzo, founded a decade ago. There's daily brunch, too, both here and at their other central branches.

The Cantinetta dei Verrazzano.

INEXPENSIVE

Mario ♥♥♥ FLORENTINE Though firmly on the tourist trail, this market workers' trattoria remains utterly Florentine—an experience as much as a meal. It clings to an ethos adopted when the burners first fired up 70 years ago: The food is simple, hearty, and traditionally served at communal tables. If you prebook, which is essential (e-mail 1953@trattoriamario.com), they hold your slot for just 5 minutes. Without reservations, arrive early, "check in," and if you're lucky you'll be offered seats

when they come free; lingering is discouraged. A typical meal might be *passato di fagioli* (bean puree soup) followed by traditional Tuscan beef pot roast, *stracotto,* or *maialino al forno* (roast piglet). *Fiorentina* is the favorite dinner choice—and priced lower than at many neighboring spots.
Via Rosina 2R. trattoriamario.com. ✆ **055/218-550.** Main courses 9€–20€. Mon–Sat noon–3pm; Fri also 7–10pm (except July). Closed Aug. Bus: C1.

Mercato Centrale ♥ MODERN ITALIAN The upper floor of Florence's produce market is a bustling shrine to modern street food. Indeed, it's become a little too bustling in recent years: A visit here trades convenience for comfort. There's no questioning the food, however. Counters sell dishes from all over Italy (and beyond): pasta, vegetarian and vegan fare, fresh fish, Chianina burgers, Florentine boiled beef dripping in its juices, and much more. Or just stop by for a drink and soak up the buzz: There's a beer bar and a superb enoteca.
Piazza Mercato Centrale. mercatocentrale.com/florence. ✆ **055/239-9798.** Dishes 6€–20€. Daily 9am–11pm (Fri–Sat until midnight). Bus: C1.

Near San Marco

MODERATE

5

Da Tito ♥♥♥ FLORENTINE Every night feels like a party at one of central Florence's most genuine neighborhood trattorias. (It's usually packed: Reserve ahead, including by e-mail at least a day in advance.) The dishes are classic Florentine, with a few modern Italian curveballs: Start, perhaps, with a seasonal treat like raw artichokes with shaved Grana Padano cheese or, in summer, *risotto con piselli e guanciale* (rice with fresh peas and cured pork cheek) before going on to a traditional grill such as *lombatina di vitella* (veal chop steak). The neighborhood location, a 10-minute walk north of San Lorenzo, and a mixed clientele keep quality consistent. We've never been disappointed.
Via San Gallo 112R. trattoriadatito.com. ✆ **055/472-475.** Main courses 15€–25€. Daily 12:30–3pm and 7–11pm. Bus: C1, 1, 8, 10.

Mangiando Mangiando ♥♥ TUSCAN Tastes of rural Chianti reign in this small brick-vaulted dining room on the edge of the center, a second location of a popular restaurant in Greve (p. 248). The seasonal Tuscan cuisine is simple and flavor-led, in dishes such as potato gnocchi with Chianti saffron and Parmesan cream, or *crostini* with chicken livers. Meat dishes lean into classics from the Tuscan countryside, starring pigeon, guinea hen, Casentino pork, and of course beef, flame-grilled to perfection, as long as you like it rare. There's an important focus on details, too: homemade pasta, home-baked bread using traditional grains, and condiments from the Chianti, including luscious, low-acidity extra virgin olive oil.
Via Agnolo Poliziano 7R. mangiandomangiando.it. ✆ **055/493-5302.** Main courses 16€–28€. Mon–Fri noon–2:30pm and 7–9:30pm; Sat 7–10pm. Bus: 1, 11, 12, 13, 20.

Near Santa Croce

MODERATE

Brac ♥♥ VEGETARIAN/VEGAN An artsy cafe-bookshop for most of the day, this is also one of Florence's best spots for vegetarian and vegan food (brunch, lunch, *aperitivo,* or dinner). A *piatto unico* works out best for hungry diners: one combo plate with three different dishes from the menu, perhaps avocado carpaccio; *agnolotti* (pasta parcels) with red onion, plum, and a pine-nut cream; plus a *pane carasau* (Sardinian flatbread) with Datterini tomatoes and egg. The courtyard atmosphere is intimate, yet singletons won't feel out of place. Dinner reservations are a must.

Via dei Vagellai 18R. libreriabrac.net. ✆ **055/094-4877.** Main courses 12€–20€. Daily noon–midnight (kitchen closes midafternoon). Bus: C1, C3, 23.

INEXPENSIVE

Da Rocco ♥♥ TUSCAN In business for 4 decades, this small trattoria inside Sant'Ambrogio Market serves one of our favorite no-frills lunches. Behind a takeout counter is an enclosed seating area with snug booths. Hearty dishes of lasagne, roast meats like *coniglio* (rabbit), and *peposo* (spicy Tuscan beef stew) are plenty filling, especially if you pair one with a side like roast peppers or lightly fried spinach. Fish dishes appear on Fridays. Service is friendly but brisk: Lingering is gently discouraged to keep the regular lunchtime lines moving.

Mercato di Sant'Ambrogio. www.daroccotrattoria.com. ✆ **339/838-4555.** Main courses 9€–10€. Mon–Sat 11:30am–2:30pm. Bus: C2, C3, 14, 23.

3dddì ♥♥♥ PIZZA There's no such thing as an "authentic" Florentine pizza, so take license here to cut loose with toppings and forget tradition. (***Warning:*** *Do not attempt this in Naples.*) You're served pizzas vaguely in the Naples style, with thin base, mozzarella puddle, and aerated crusts. The mirrored, whitewashed, and curves-everywhere interior suits contemporary combos like Parma ham and Puglian burrata or "white pizza" (no tomato) with Gorgonzola, pumpkin cream, and Italian sausage. Gluten- and/or cheese-free pies available. They also do takeout: Send a WhatsApp to order.

Piazza Ghiberti 10R. 3dddipizzeria.it. ✆ **349/890-0467.** Pizza 7€–15€. Mon–Sat 7pm–midnight. Bus: C2, C3, 14, 23.

In the Oltrarno & San Frediano

EXPENSIVE

Burro e Acciughe ♥♥♥ SEAFOOD This fish-lovers' paradise serves no meat and looks after vegetarians well. Choose from a range of dishes that let flavors shine: the eponymous Cantabrian anchovies with warm buttered bread; a choice of tartares dressed with citrus and daikon; left-field combinations such as lukewarm egg with intense katsuobushi-style fish flakes; and grilled fresh catch. Even the basket of homemade focaccia and sweet *pane nero* is memorable; ditto the wine list. Online reservations (25€ deposit required) are recommended: There are only 15 tables.

Via dell'Orto 35R. burroeacciughe.com. ✆ **055/045-7286.** Main courses 24€–30€. Tues–Sun 7–11pm; Sat–Sun also 12:30–2:30pm. Bus: C4, 36, 37.

iO: Osteria Personale ♥♥♥ CONTEMPORARY TUSCAN There's a "grown-up hipster" atmosphere here, with the minimalist whitewashed brick interior and young, attentive, enthusiastic staff. But a fine dining ethos is ingrained, too: Many ingredients familiar to Tuscan cooking are combined in a fresh way with global influences. The menu is short—iO is better for adventurous rather than fussy eaters—but there are always seafood, meat, and vegetarian dishes, perhaps smoked risotto with mackerel, strawberry, and bay leaf, or pigeon with apple and peanuts in a light tamarind sauce. Reservations are advised; this place's reputation has only grown since we first championed it 15 years ago.

Borgo San Frediano 167R. io-osteriapersonale.it. ✆ **055/933-1341.** Main courses 24€–28€; tasting menus 52€–68€. Mon–Sat 7:30–10pm. Closed 10 days in Jan and most of Aug. Bus: C3, 6, 13.

MODERATE

5

Formaggioteca Terroir ♥♥♥ CHEESE Is this a wine bar or a restaurant? I guess it depends where you place cheese among the major food groups. Personally, I can't think of many things better than skipping all the preliminaries and moving straight to the six-part cheese course. The huge range includes goat, cow, and ewe varieties, of French and Italian origin (but note, as is normal in Europe, many will be from unpasteurized "raw" milk). Our advice: Tell them any no-no's and let them choose what's in optimum condition. Bread, wine, and maybe a little fruit jam are the only sides you need.

Via dei Renai 19. formaggiotecaterroir.it. ✆ **055/215-901.** Platters 14€–26€. Mon–Wed 4:30–10:30pm; Thurs–Sat 11:30am–11pm; Sun 12:30–10pm. Bus: C4, 23.

Osteria dell'Enoteca ♥♥♥ MODERN TUSCAN Run by experienced wine-bar owners, this place majors in reasonably priced, elegant dining. Traditional flavors dominate, although combinations are often modern, in such dishes as poached egg yolk "affogato," floating in a Pecorino cheese cream with wild mushrooms, or oven-roasted pigeon with Swiss chard. Portions are not large, so cut loose and order three courses. There is no wine list; an English-speaking waiter leads you to a chiller stocked with boutique labels—strong on Tuscan as well as Langhe/Piedmont reds. The dining room itself is refined, with slate floors, stripped brick, and soft jazz. This is the place for a romantic meal that won't blow your budget. Reservations recommended.

Via Romana 70R. osteriadellenoteca.com. ✆ **055/228-6018.** Main courses 18€–24€. Wed–Mon 7–10:30pm; Fri–Sun also noon–2:30pm. Closed 3 weeks Feb. Bus: 11.

Osteria dell'Enoteca's version of the Tuscan classic *bistecca*.

Gelato

Florence has a fair claim to being the birthplace of gelato and has some of the world's best *gelaterie*—but many poor imitations, too. Steer clear of spots around major attractions with air-fluffed mountains of ice cream and flavors so full of artificial colors they glow in the dark. If you can see the Ponte Vecchio or Piazza della Signoria from the front door of the gelateria, you may want to move on. Walk a block, or duck down a side street, to find a genuine gelato artisan. Trust us, you'll taste the difference. Opening hours tend to be discretionary: On warm evenings, many places stay open beyond 11pm; closures during a bad spell of winter weather are possible.

Gelateria dei Neri ♥♥ A large range of fruit, white, and chocolate flavors, but nothing overly elaborate. If the seasonal ricotta and fig flavor is offered, you are in luck. There's also a restroom. Via dei Neri 9R. facebook.com/gelateriadeneri. ✆ **055/210-034.** Cone from 3€. Closed Mon and mid-Dec to mid-Feb. Bus: C1, C2, C3, 23.

Gelateria della Passera ♥♥♥ The milk-free water ices here are intensely flavored, with moderate sweetness that doesn't overpower the taste. Try the likes of pink grapefruit or jasmine tea gelato. Via Toscanella 15R (at Piazza della Passera). gelateriadellapassera.it. ✆ **055/614-2071.** Cone from 2.80€. Closed Mon. Bus: C4, 11.

La Carraia ♥♥♥ It's packed with locals late into the evening on summer weekends—for good reason. The range is vast, the quality high. Piazza N. Sauro 25R. gelaterialacarraia.it. ✆ **055/280-695.** Cone from 2.50€. Bus: C3, C4, 6, 11, 12, 36, 37. Closed Jan.

FLORENCE SHOPPING

After Milan, Florence is **Italy's top shopping city**—beating even Rome. Here's what to buy: leather, designer fashion, shoes, marbleized paper and other stationery, hand-embroidered linens, Tuscan wines including Chianti, handmade jewelry, *pietre dure* (known also as "Florentine mosaic," inlaid semiprecious stones), and antiques. Artisans practicing their individual traditions have occupied many locations around the city for decades, even centuries. These workshops and stores are recognized and protected as ***Botteghe Storiche.*** Look for the official mark on the door or window; see **attivitastoriche.destinationflorence.com/en** for more details. ***Note:*** It is illegal to knowingly buy fake goods anywhere in the city (and yes, a "Louis Vuitton" bag at 10€ counts as *knowingly*). You may be served a hefty on-the-spot fine if caught.

Traditionally, Florentine **shopping hours** are Monday through Saturday from 9:30am to noon or 1pm and 3 or 3:30 to 7:30pm. Increasingly, **larger shops and those in tourist areas stay open on Sunday and through the midafternoon *riposo,*** or "nap." Some small or family-run places close Monday mornings instead of Sundays.

Top Shopping Streets & Areas

AROUND SANTA TRÍNITA *Haute couture* lines both sides of elegant **Via de' Tornabuoni,** with an extension along **Via della Vigna Nuova** and other surrounding streets. Here you'll find the cream of Italian and Florentine fashion names, like **Gucci ♥** (at no. 73R–81R; gucci.com; ✆ **055/264-011**), **Pucci ♥♥** (at no. 22R; pucci.com; ✆ **055/265-8082**), and **Ferragamo ♥♥♥** (inside medieval Palazzo Spini Ferroni at no. 2; ferragamo.com; ✆ **055/292-123**), where they also house the fascinating **Ferragamo Museum ♥♥** (museo.ferragamo.com/en; daily 10:30am–7:30pm; 10€, free ages 17 and under). Florence-headquartered leather specialist **Benheart ♥♥**, Via della Vigna Nuova 85R (benheart.it; ✆ **055/239-9483;** also at Via dei Calzaiuoli 78R), sells up-to-the-minute clothing, footwear, and accessories. You can even create your own belt with a choice of leather and buckles. Benheart isn't cheap, but the quality is first-rate. A Florence branch of quality thrift store **Humana Vintage ♥**, Via delle Belle Donne 4R (humanavintage.it), adds another dimension to the neighborhood.

AROUND VIA ROMA & VIA DEI CALZAIUOLI These are some of Florence's busiest streets, packed with mostly mainstream storefronts. Here you'll find major department store **La Rinascente ♥**, Piazza della

Repubblica (rinascente.it; ✆ **055/219-113**), alongside European fashion brands such as Longchamp, Patrizia Pepe, and Zara. **La Feltrinelli RED,** Piazza della Repubblica 26 (lafeltrinelli.it; ✆ **199/151-173**), is the center's best bookstore. Online couture sales sensation **LuisaViaRoma** ♥ (luisa viaroma.com) has its flagship store here, at Via Roma 21R.

AROUND SANTA CROCE One-of-a-kind stores flourish in the eastern part of the center, with a scattering of independent fashions. **Borgo degli Albizi** and its tributary streets are worth roaming—**Sabatini** ♥ (at no. 75R; ✆ **055/234-0240**) is a go-to for good-value casual footwear. Across the street, **Marzotto** ♥♥ (at 86R; cartafiorentinafirenze.com; ✆ **055/234-0726**) is a treasure cave of affordable Florentine stationery. It's been in business since 1890.

THE OLTRARNO Many specialist artisans inhabit stores and workshops close to the Ponte Vecchio and Piazza Santo Spirito (see below). Along **Borgo San Jacopo** you'll also find a refreshing range of fashion boutiques for men and women, stocking smaller, stylish labels.

Crafts & Artisans

Florence has a long-standing reputation for craftsmanship. Although display windows along touristed streets are stuffed with cheap, mass-produced imports, if you search around you will find handmade, top-quality items.

5

FLORENCE | Florence Shopping

Il Torchio ♥♥ This small Oltrarno workshop sells hand-bound notebooks and marbleized paper. Bespoke designs available. Via de' Bardi 17. legatoriailtorchio.com. ✆ **320/970-7319.** Closed Sat, Sun, and early Jan. Bus: C1, C3, C4.

Madova ♥♥♥ For more than a century, this has been the city's best retailer of handmade leather gloves, lined with silk, cashmere, or lambswool. You'll pay between 55€ and 90€ a pair. Madova is the real deal, even so close to the Ponte Vecchio. Via Guicciardini 1R. madova.com. ✆ **055/239-6526.** Closed Sun. Bus: C3, C4.

Marioluca Giusti ♥♥ The boutique of this renowned Florentine designer sells only his trademark acrylic crystal. The range includes colorful reinventions of cocktail and wine glasses, jugs, and tumblers—every piece lightweight, tough, and chic. Via della Spada 20R. mariolucagiusti.it. ✆ **055/214-583.** Bus: 6, 11, 13. Also at Via della Vigna Nuova 88R.

Officina Profumo-Farmaceutica di Santa Maria Novella ♥♥♥ A shrine to scents and skincare, this is Florence's historic herbal pharmacy, with roots in the 17th century, when it was founded by the Dominican monks of Santa Maria Novella. Nothing is cheap, but the perfumes, cosmetics, moisturizers, and other products are handmade from the finest natural ingredients and packaged exquisitely. Via della Scala 16. smnovella.com. ✆ **055/216-276.** Bus: C2, 6, 11, 37.

Parione ♥ This Florentine stationer celebrated its 100th birthday in 2023. It stocks notebooks, marbleized paper, fine pens, and souvenirs like wooden music boxes and playing cards with 17th-century designs. Via dello Studio 11R. parione.it. ✆ **055/215-030.** Closed Sun. Bus: C1.

Scuola del Cuoio ♥♥ Florence's leading leather school and workshop is an open house for visitors. You can watch trainee leatherworkers and gilders at work (Mon–Fri), breathe in the aromas of cowhide and glue, splash out on a handmade jacket, and visit the small store to buy portable items like wallets, belts, and bags. Via San Giuseppe 5R (behind Santa Croce). scuoladelcuoio.it/en. ✆ **055/244-534.** Nov–Mar closed Sun. Bus: C2, C3, 14, 23.

Leather artisan at the Scuola del Cuoio.

Florence's Best Markets

Mercato Centrale ♥♥♥ The center's main market stocks the usual fresh produce, and you can browse (and taste) cheese, salami and cured hams, Tuscan wines, takeout food, sweets, and much more. This is picnic-making heaven; they'll also vacuum-pack items for transporting home. It runs Monday to Saturday until 2pm (until 5pm Sat for most of the year). Upstairs is street-food nirvana, all day, every day; see p. 218. Btw. Piazza del Mercato Centrale and Via dell'Ariento. mercatocentrale.it/firenze. No phone. Bus: C1.

Mercato di San Lorenzo ♥ The city's tourist street market is a fun place to pick up T-shirts, marbleized paper, a leather-bound notebook, or another city souvenir. Wallets, purses, bags, and jackets are popular with international visitors—be sure to assess the workmanship, which can be variable, and haggle shamelessly. This busy market runs daily; watch for pickpockets. Via dell'Ariento and Via Rosina. No phone. Bus: C1.

ENTERTAINMENT & NIGHTLIFE

Florence has several listings publications, including **Informacittà** (informacitta.net), strong on theater, concerts, and one-off markets. Younger and hipper **Zero** (zero.eu/en/firenze) is hot on the latest eating, drinking, offbeat lifestyle, and edgy nightlife. ***Firenze Spettacolo*** (firenze spettacolo.it), an Italian-language monthly sold at newsstands (2€), is the city's most comprehensive listing of nightlife, arts, and entertainment. It has an English-language section.

If you prefer to wander and see what grabs you, you will find tourist-oriented action in bars around the city's main squares, many with outside piazza seating. For something livelier—and with a more local feel—crawl **Borgo San Frediano** or across town, the northern end of Via de' Macci, into Via Pietrapiana and especially **Borgo La Croce.** The bars of **San Niccolò** are often lively too, with a mixed clientele of tourists and locals hovering around outdoor tables.

Arts & Live Music

Florence does not have the traditional music cachet of Milan, Venice, Naples, or Rome, but it has two symphony orchestras and a fine music school in Fiesole, as well as a modern **opera house** (see below). The theaters are respectable, and most major touring companies make stops. Buy tickets to cultural events online at **Box Office,** Via delle Vecchie Carceri 1 (boxofficetoscana.it).

Many classical and chamber music performances are sponsored by the **Amici della Musica** (amicimusicafirenze.it; ✆ **055/607-440**), so check its website to see what's on. The venue is often **Teatro Niccolini** or historic **Teatro della Pergola;** prices range from 10€ to 25€ for adults.

La Cité ♥♥ A cafe/bookshop by day, after dark this place becomes a casual wine-bar and small-scale live-music venue. The lineup is eclectic, with offbeat or world music. One night, it's forró or swing, the next Italian folk or chanteuse. Borgo San Frediano 20R. lacitelibreria.info. ✆ **055/210-387.** Bus: C3, C4, 6, 11, 12, 36, 37.

Teatro Maggio Musicale Fiorentino ♥♥ This vast opera house, concert hall, and arts complex seats up to 1,800 in daring postmodernist surrounds. Its program incorporates opera, ballet, and orchestral music. Each May and June it hosts the **Maggio Musicale Fiorentino,** one of Italy's most prestigious music festivals. Piazzale Vittorio Gui. maggiofiorentino.com. ✆ **055/277-9309.** Tickets 15€–130€. Tram: T1.

Wine Bars, Cocktails & Craft Beer

Birreria Art. 17 ♥♥ Grungy and friendly, with 10 taps of top-ranked Italian craft beers, including their own brews, plus a fridge bulging with bottles from across Europe. Around 6€ a pint. Via Borgo La Croce 64R. articolo17birreria.it. ✆ **055/234-6694.** Bus: C2, C3.

Il Santino ♥♥♥ Tiny sibling of a long-standing popular restaurant, Il Santo Bevitore next door, this snug wine bar sources niche labels from across Italy and serves exquisite "Florentine tapas" (11€–15€) to munch while you sip. Via Santo Spirito 60R. ilsantino.shop. ✆ **055/230-2820.** Bus: C3, C4, 6, 11, 12, 36, 37.

Love Craft ♥♥♥ The bar is the star at this snazzy little spot dedicated to everything whiskey (and whisky): Around 300 labels are displayed altarlike on the backlit shelves. Global blends and single malts, cocktails (not just whiskey), and flights are all well-priced (around 11€). Borgo San Frediano 24R. lovecraftfirenze.it. No phone. Bus: C3, C4, 6, 11, 12, 36, 37.

Manifattura ♥♥♥ Clientele skews young and casual at this creative cocktail bar in the old center. Drinks are mixed with Italian spirits only, so expect plenty of invention—and lots of gin, vermouth, and bitter Italian liquors, plus seasonal takes on Florence's icon, the Negroni. Piazza San Pancrazio 1R. manifatturafirenze.it. No phone. Bus: 6, 11.

Mayday ♥♥ A Florence original, this laid-back bar offers signature cocktails commemorating famous Tuscans, iconic hangouts, and events in 20th-century history. It's delightfully decked out like a mismatched junk store, with everything from old school desks to low-watt lamps hanging from the ceiling. Via Dante Alighieri 16R. maydayclub.it. ✆ **055/238-1290.** Closed Sun–Mon. Bus: C1, C2.

Vineria Sonora ♥♥♥ Busy wine bar specializing in natural producers (sparkling, red, white, orange), with a long list by the glass. Turn it into a memorable casual dinner with artisanal cold cuts, cheese, anchovies, or a seasonal organic salad. Via degli Alfani 39R. vineriasonora.it. ✆ **333/199-9093.** Bus: 6, 14, 17, 23, 31, 32.

Zanobini ♥♥ This stacked wine merchant has a small counter where you can sit and sip, surrounded wall-to-wall by bottles. Wines by the glass from 3€; closed Sunday. Via Sant'Antonino 47R. lelame.com. ✆ **055/239-6850.** Bus: C1.

6

TUSCANY

By Stephen Brewer

Even for Italians from other parts of the peninsula, Tuscany is the epitome of everything that's good about their country: beguiling landscapes carpeted with vineyards, delicious food and wine, evocative medieval churches and castles, and some of the greatest art and architecture of the Renaissance—including the Leaning Tower of Pisa, Piero della Francesca's frescoes in Arezzo, and Ambrogio Lorenzetti's *Allegories* in Siena's Palazzo Pubblico. Even a short visit inundates a traveler with an embarrassment of riches.

Soaking up culture is certainly part of the allure, and the pleasures of the palate are equally appealing. Even a simple meal can seem like a work of art in places as bountiful as the Valdichiana and Val d'Orcia. Somehow it only makes sense that full-bodied red wines should come from towns as appealing as Montepulciano and Montalcino, and character-filled whites from proud little San Gimignano. Then there's all that iconic scenery, in landscapes like the rolling fields and pointy cypresses of the Crete Sienese or the vineyards of Chianti. Art, scenery, food, wine—you may come to agree that all the good things in life come together in Tuscany.

DON'T LEAVE TUSCANY WITHOUT . . .

Getting into Hill Town Life. Panoramic views, cobblestone squares, friendly cafes: These are the charms of everyday life in a Tuscan hill town, ready to be savored in Cortona, Montepulciano, Volterra, San Gimignano, and Montalcino.

Fresco Gazing in Siena. Domenico di Bartolo and others left behind detailed scenes of medieval life in the former hospital Santa Maria della Scala, founded in the 11th century, and the characters seem to reach across the centuries and speak to us.

Basking in Some of the World's Most Beautiful Landscapes. Open your senses to the beauties of the Tuscan countryside as you drive through the famous Chianti vineyards between Siena and Florence, or along the meandering roads of the Val d'Orcia between Pienza and Montalcino.

Enjoying Fine Wines. You've seen the vines; now sample the wines. Tuscany's bounty, of course, includes famous Chianti, Brunello di Montalcino, and Vino Nobile di Montepulciano, but don't stop there—almost every town has its own trademark vintages, from San Gimignano's Vernaccia to Cortona's Syrah.

PREVIOUS PAGE: **The towers of San Gimignano rise above the Tuscan countryside.**

SIENA ♥♥♥

70km (43 miles) S of Florence, 232km (144 miles) N of Rome

Florence's longtime rival, this medieval city of rose-colored brick seems to have come out on top in terms of grace and elegance. With steep, twisting stone alleys and proud churches, palaces, and crenellated public buildings draped across three gentle hillsides, Siena is for many admirers the most beautiful town in Italy. At the city's heart is a ravishing piazza, and from the heights rises a magnificent duomo of striped marble.

The city trumpets the she-wolf as its emblem, a holdover from its days as Saena Julia, the Roman colony founded by Augustus about 2,000 years ago (though the official Sienese myth has the town founded by the sons of Remus, younger brother of Rome's legendary forefather). Civic projects and artistic prowess reached their greatest heights in the 13th and 14th centuries, when artists invented a distinctive Sienese style as banking and a booming wool industry made Siena one of the richest Italian republics. Then, in 1348, the Black Death killed more than half of the population, decimating the social fabric and devastating the economy. Siena never recovered, and much of the city has barely changed since, inviting you to slip into the rhythms and atmosphere of the Middle Ages.

Well, not entirely, because Siena is also a vibrant university town and home to 50,000 residents. This is a place to take in the beauty around you, indulge in excellent food and wine and pasta, and enjoy Italian life at its best.

Essentials

ARRIVING

BY TRAIN Siena's **train station** is at Piazza Roselli, about 3km (1¾ miles) north and far below the city center. Trains connect Siena with **Florence** (usually 90 min.); trains to and from Rome (3–4 hr.) require a change in Chiusi-Chianciano Terme. To get into town, take the **no. 7 or 10 bus** to Piazza Gramsci (buy your ticket, 1.70€, at the newsstand in the station, from machines at the bus stop, or with contactless card or device). Don't take the buses that stop in front of the station, but go into the big brick shopping center across the street and take the escalator to the underground bus stop. Be sure to ask *"Piazza Gramsci?"* when you board, or you may end up in a far-flung district. You can also take a series of escalators up toward town from the top floor of the shopping center—these are poorly marked in places, but as long as you're going up you're moving in the right direction. You will be deposited onto Via Vittorio Emanuele II; turn left to reach the Porta Camollia, then follow Via Camollia into the city center. It becomes Via Montanini, then Via Banchi di Sopra as it heads up to the Piazza del Campo. ***Note:*** Siena's train station does not have a baggage storage office, though there is one at the bus station on Piazza Gramsci (see below).

Pistoia
Fornacelle
Agliana
Prato
Pescia
Montecatini Terme
Monsummano Terme
Sesto Fiorentino
Poggio a Caiano
Lucca
Capannori
San Rocco
Torre del Lago
Artimino Prato
Vinci
Parco Naturale Tenuta di S. Rossore
Arno
Montelupo
Empoli
Tavarnuzz
Calci
Pisa
Ginestra Fiorentina
San Miniato
Parco Naturale Tenuta di Tombolo
San Casciano in Val di Pesa
Marina di Pisa
Pontedera
Montespertoli
Pesa
Ponsacco
Castelfiorentino
TUSCANY
Tavarnelle Val di Pesa
Montaione
Elsa
Livorno
Barberino Val d'Elsa
Gambassi Terme
Casciana Terme
San Gimignano
Poggibonsi
Ris. Naturale Castevecchio
Castellina Marittima
Era
Colle di Val d'Elsa
Volterra
Roncolla
Montecatini Val di Cecina
Rosignano Solvay
Riparbella
Riserva Naturale di Berignone
Vada
Casole d'Elsa
Cecina
Pomarance
Colline Metallifere
Bibbona
Riserva Naturale di Monterufoli
Radicondoli
Larderello
Marina di Bibbona
Bólgheri
Ris. Statale Cornocchia
Ris. Statale Palazzo
Riserva Naturale di Caselli
Castenuovo di Val di Cecina
Ris. Naturale Cornate e Fosini
Donoratico
Terme di Bagnolo
Chiusdino
Abbazia di San Galga
Castagneto Carducci
Monterotondo Marittimo
Monticiano
Ligurian Sea
San Vincenzo
Cornia
Ris. Naturale La Pietra
Suvereto
Massa Marittima
Campiglia Marittima
Roccatederighi
Venturina Terme
Golfo di Baratti
Roccastrada
Populonia
Ribolla
Gavorrano
Piombino
Follonica
Scarlino
Golfo di Follonica
Isola d'Elba
Vetulonia
A1
A11
A12
SS1
E80
SS22

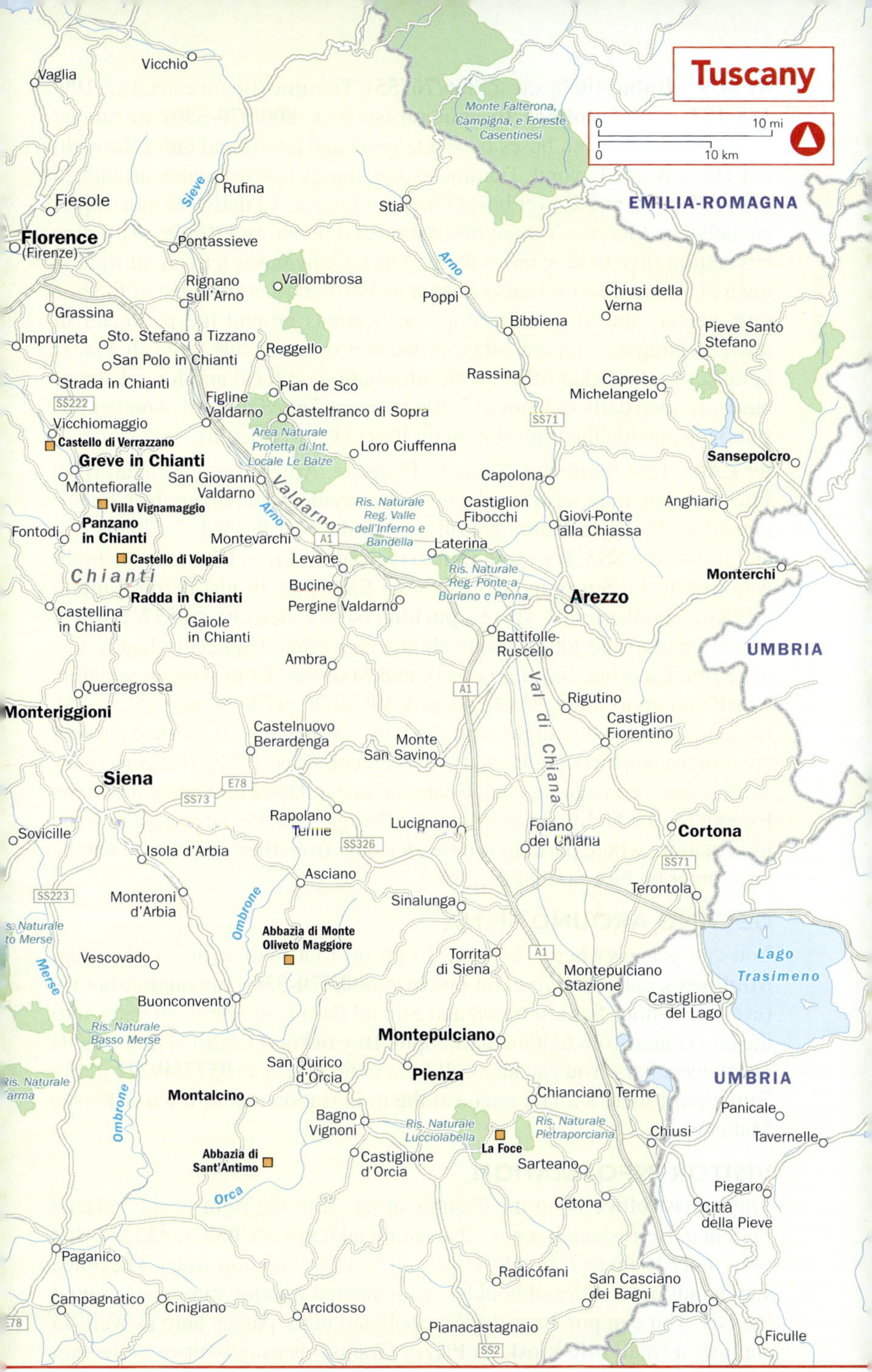
Tuscany
0 10 mi
0 10 km
EMILIA-ROMAGNA
UMBRIA
UMBRIA
Monte Falterona, Campigna, e Foreste Casentinesi
Vaglia
Vicchio
Fiesole
Florence (Firenze)
Rufina
Stia
Pontassieve
Rignano sull'Arno
Vallombrosa
Poppi
Chiusi della Verna
Bibbiena
Pieve Santo Stefano
Grassina
Impruneta
Sto. Stefano a Tizzano
San Polo in Chianti
Reggello
Rassina
Caprese Michelangelo
Strada in Chianti
Pian de Sco
Figline Valdarno
Castelfranco di Sopra
Vicchiomaggio
Castello di Verrazzano
Area Naturale Protetta di Int. Locale Le Balze
Loro Ciuffenna
Sansepolcro
Greve in Chianti
San Giovanni Valdarno
Montefioralle
Capolona
Villa Vignamaggio
Valdarno
Ris. Naturale Reg. Valle dell'Inferno e Bandella
Castiglion Fibocchi
Anghiari
Panzano in Chianti
Fontodi
Montevarchi
Giovi-Ponte alla Chiassa
Laterina
Castello di Volpaia
Levane
Chianti
Ris. Naturale Reg. Ponte a Buriano e Penna
Monterchi
Bucine
Radda in Chianti
Pergine Valdarno
Arezzo
Castellina in Chianti
Gaiole in Chianti
Battifolle-Ruscello
Ambra
Val di Chiana
Quercegrossa
Rigutino
Monteriggioni
Castelnuovo Berardenga
Castiglion Fiorentino
Monte San Savino
Siena
Rapolano Terme
Lucignano
Foiano della Chiana
Cortona
Sovicille
Isola d'Arbia
Asciano
Terontola
Monteroni d'Arbia
Sinalunga
Abbazia di Monte Oliveto Maggiore
Torrita di Siena
Vescovado
Montepulciano Stazione
Lago Trasimeno
Castiglione del Lago
Buonconvento
Ris. Naturale Basso Merse
Montepulciano
San Quirico d'Orcia
Pienza
Chianciano Terme
Montalcino
Bagno Vignoni
Ris. Naturale Lucciolabella
Ris. Naturale Pietraporciana
La Foce
Chiusi
Panicale
Tavernelle
Abbazia di Sant'Antimo
Castiglione d'Orcia
Sarteano
Piegaro
Cetona
Città della Pieve
Paganico
Radicófani
San Casciano dei Bagni
Campagnatico
Cinigiano
Arcidosso
Fabro
Pianacastagnaio
Ficulle
Arno
Sieve
Ombrone
Merse
Orca
A1
SS71
SS222
SS73
E78
SS326
SS223
SS2

BY BUS **Itabus** (itabus.it; ✆ **866/76755**), **Tiemme** (tiemmespa.it; ✆ **199/168-182**), and **Autolinee Toscane** (at-bus.it; ✆ **800/570-530**) are among the operators that run buses between Siena and towns and cities throughout Tuscany and beyond. Tiemme express buses (*corse rapide;* around 25 daily; 75 min.) and slower buses (*corse ordinarie;* 14 daily; 95 min.) operate between Florence's main bus station and Siena, and Rome's Tiburtina bus station (five to nine buses daily; 3 hr.). Many buses let you off right in town at Piazza Gramsci (also known as Via Tozzi), at the edge of the historic center, and also make stops at locations around the perimeter of town. A luggage storage office is located in an arcade beneath Piazza Gramsci, and a ticket office, with information on local and long-distance buses, is open daily 6:30am to 7:30pm (opens 7am Sat–Sun). Another bus station is outside the train station on Piazza Carlo Rossetti.

BY CAR Fast roads link Siena to Florence, Arezzo, and Perugia; from **Florence** you may wish to take the more scenic route, down the Chiantigiana SS222. From **Rome** get off the A1 north at the Val di Chiana exit and follow the SS326 west for 50km (31 miles). From **Pisa** take the highway toward Florence and exit onto the SS429 south just before Empoli (100km/62 miles total). There's **parking** (sipark.siena.it; ✆ **0577/228711**) in well-signposted lots just outside the city gates. Especially handy lots are Santa Caterina, San Francesco, and Stazione, from which escalators whisk you up to town. Most charge 1.50€ to 2€ per hour, and 25€ to 35€ for a full day and overnight. You can park for free at well-marked parking areas in the outskirts, connected to the center by bus (1.20€, from machines at the stops); convenient choices are the one at Due Ponti (near the Siena Est exit for the highways to Rome and Perugia) and the large garage at the train station, where parking is only 2€ a day; from there you can reach the city center by bus, taxi, or escalator.

GETTING AROUND SIENA

You can get anywhere you want to go on foot, with a bit of climbing. **Minibuses,** called *pollicini* (at-bus.it; ✆ **800/570-530**), run quarter-hourly (every half-hour Sat afternoon and Sun all day) from the main gates into the city center from 6:30am to 8:30pm. Buy tickets (1.50€) at newsstands or *tabacchi* bars. You can also call for a radio **taxi** at ✆ **0577/49222** (daily 7am–9pm); there's a taxi queue at the train station and in town at Piazza Matteotti.

VISITOR INFORMATION

The **tourist office** is on the Campo, at no. 7, to the right of the Palazzo Pubblico (terresiena.it or visitsienaofficial.it/en; ✆ **0577/292222**). It's open daily 10am to 7pm (closes at 5pm Nov through mid-Mar). The office staff hands out a series of booklets with themed walking itineraries around the city. You can purchase the Acropoli and other passes here as well. In summer a small **info kiosk** on Piazza Gramsci is usually open daily 9am to 6pm.

ATTRACTIONS

Archivo di Stato **24**
Casa di Santa Caterina **4**
Duomo **19**
Museo Civico/ Palazzo Pubblico **23**
Museo dell'Opera Metropolitana **20**
Pinacoteca Nazionale **27**
San Domenico **2**
Santa Maria della Scala **18**

RESTAURANTS

Antica Osteria da Divo **16**
Enoteca Italiana **1**
Gastronomia Morbidi **7**
Gino Cacino di Angelo **25**
The Irishman **9**
Kopakabana **10**
La Prosciutteria **29**
Liberamente **21**
L'Osteria dei Rossi **8**
Osteria La Chiacchera **5**
Osteria La Sosta di Violante **31**
Pier Pettinaio Ristorante a Siena **11**
Pizzicheria di De Miccoli Bruno **22**
Pretto Prosciutteria **12**
Taverna San Giuseppe **28**
Te Ke Voi? **13**

HOTELS

Campo Regio Relais **6**
Casacenti **15**
Fonte Gaia Experience **14**
Hotel Alma Domus **3**
Il Battistero **17**
Palazzo Bulgarini **30**
Palazzo Ravizza **26**
Santa Caterina **32**

Exploring Siena

The heart of Siena is the sloping, scallop-shell-shaped **Piazza del Campo** (Il Campo). Laid out in the 1100s on the site of the Roman forum, the welcoming expanse is a testament to the city's civic achievements, anchored by a crenellated town hall, the **Palazzo Pubblico** (1297–1310). The herringbone brick pavement is divided by white marble lines into nine sections representing the city's medieval ruling body, the Council of Nine. A 19th-century replica of Jacopo della Quercia's 14th-century fountain, the **Fonte Gaia,** is on one side of the square (some of the restored, but badly eroded, original panels are in Santa Maria della Scala; see p. 240). The dominant public monument is the slender 100m-tall (328-ft.) brick **Torre del Mangia** (1338–48), named for a slothful bell ringer nicknamed Mangiaguadagni or "profit eater." (An armless statue of him is in the courtyard of Palazzo Pubblico.) From the platform atop the tower's 503 steps, the undulating Tuscan hills seem to rise and fall to the ends of the earth. Tower admission is 10€, family ticket 25€ for 2 adults and 2 children 11 to 18, free for children 10 and under (cumulative admission with Museo Civico 15€, with Museo Civico and Santa Maria della Scala 20€, 40€ family ticket). Visitors can enter every 45 minutes from 10am on (last entry Mar–Oct 6:15pm, last entry Nov–Feb 3:15pm).

Siena's main streets run toward the Campo from seven gates in the old city walls. To follow in the footsteps of medieval pilgrims who stopped in Siena while walking the Via Francigena holy road between Canterbury and Rome, enter the city through **Porta Camollia,** where the phrase COR

The Palazzo Pubblico anchors Siena's Piazza del Campo.

A DAY AT THE races

On the evenings of July 2 and August 16, Siena's **Palio delle Contrade** (ilpalio.org) transforms the Piazza del Campo into a racetrack, with spectators squeezing through the city's narrow alleyways to watch. This aggressive bareback horse race involves 10 of Siena's 17 *contrade* (districts), chosen by lot to participate, and is preceded by a showy flag-waving ceremony and parade. The race itself is over in just 2 minutes. Frenzied celebrations greet the winner (which may be a riderless horse, as a *contrada* is not disqualified if the jockey falls off on one of the tight corners), and the day is rounded off with communal feasts in each district.

To witness the event from the cordoned-off public view section in the middle of the Campo, you'll end up standing for hours in the sun—you'll need to arrive at least 5 hours before race time and, while vendors are on hand with refreshments, there are no toilet facilities. To view the Palio in relative comfort, reserve a spot in one of the temporary stands operated by the bars and shops in front of which they're erected. Getting a seat on one of these stands, for at least 300€, involves making arrangements with an establishment or a travel agent as long as a year in advance. Another option is to share a terrace or even a window with one of the aristocratic occupants of the apartments overlooking the campo—for one of these perches, expect to pay 800€ per person. Among the travel agents handling such arrangements is self-proclaimed Palio expert **Jacopo della Torre** (jacopodellatorre.com). Palio Tours (paliotours.com/palio-di-siena; ✆ **305/905-1109**) arranges grandstand seating, viewing of the horse blessing and historical parade, a place at the Contrada dinner, and 3 nights' accommodation on packages that begin at 1,500€ a person.

Otherwise, you may want to settle for the trial races, also held in the Campo on June 29 and 30 and August 13 and 14. Trial races aren't as fast and furious as the real thing, but they're just as photogenic and fun to watch, and they include the presentation of the chosen horses and their assignment to the *contrade*. Events begin at 7am, with trial races at 7:45pm in June and 7:15pm in August.

MAGIS TIBI SENA PANDIT ("Siena opens her heart to you") is carved over the arch. As you walk along Via Camollia, note the simple-fronted church of **San Pietro alla Magione,** once a pilgrim's hospice. Farther down, the street widens into a little piazza and you'll pass the imposing Gothic **Palazzo Salimbeni,** the fortress-home of a wealthy banker-merchant clan and, since 1472, headquarters of the Monte die Paschi, one of the world's oldest banks. Flanking Palazzo Salimbeni are a Mannerist palace on the left and a Renaissance palace on the right, bringing together the city's historic styles. Up the street (now called Banca di Sopra) is **Palazzo Tolomei,** home of the Salimbenis' bitterest banking rivals—the competition took a bloody turn when the Salimbenis stabbed 18 Tolomeis to death with roasting spits. Via di Citta flows to the right off Banca di Sopra and skirts the **Campo,** then rises toward the **Duomo,** passing the elegant, arcaded **Palazzo Chigi Saracini** (Via di Citta 89). In September 1260, during the Battle of Montaperti—the bloodiest European skirmish of the Middle

A Glimpse at Medieval Recordkeeping

Tucked into the 1469 Florentine Renaissance-style Palazzo Piccolomini off the northeast corner of the Campo at Via Banchi di Sotto 52, Siena's official archives, **Archivo di Stato** (visitsiena official.it/en/state-archive; ✆ **0577/247145**), display such historic documents as Boccaccio's will and Jacopo della Quercia's contract for designing the Fonte Gaia fountain. The intriguing "Tavolette di Biccherna" is a remarkable set of wooden covers made in the 1200s for the city's account books; they're painted with religious scenes, vignettes of daily working life, and important events in Siena's history. Sadly, these relics of medieval Siena are on view only on Saturday mornings from 10 to 11:30am. Admission is free.

Ages—the Sienese successfully fought Florentine forces on a ridge outside the city walls, and a drummer in the palace tower tapped out ongoing reports to citizens inside the walls.

As you walk the streets of Siena, look for the little plaques on the corners. They denote which of the city's 17 *contrade* (districts) you are in, and each depicts the district's symbol—Civetta (Little Owl), Lupa (She-Wolf), and so on. Any Sienese can tell you which animal or mythological creature represents which district, and you'll see them on *contrade* flags flying all over the city.

Duomo ♥♥♥ CATHEDRAL Much of the artistic greatness of Siena comes together in this black-and-white-marble cathedral, a magnificent showcase of Italian Gothic architecture begun in the 12th century. You're likely to come away with a great appreciation for the Pisanos, father and son. Nicola was the principal architect of the church, until he fell out of favor with the group overseeing construction; young Giovanni did much of the carving on the facade, where an army of prophets and apostles appears around three portals (most of the originals are now in the Museo dell'Opera Metropolitana; see p. 239). Both worked on the pulpit, with sumptuously sculpted scenes of the life of Christ, the prophets, and evangelists.

The Duomo of Siena.

Beneath the pulpit spreads flooring of 59 etched and inlaid marble and mosaic panels (1372–1547), a showpiece for 40 of Siena's medieval and Renaissance artistic luminaries. Most prolific among them was Domenico Beccafumi, born into a local peasant family and adopted by his lord, who saw the boy's talent for drawing. Beccafumi studied in Rome but returned to Siena and spent much of his career designing 35 scenes for the flooring (from 1517–47); his richly patterned images are a repository of Old Testament figures. Matteo di Giovanni, another Sienese, did a gruesome Slaughter of the Innocents—a favorite theme of the artist, whose fresco of the same scene is in Santa Maria della Scala (p. 240). Most of the panels are protected by cardboard overlays and are usually uncovered only in July and from mid-August to mid-October.

Umbrian Renaissance master Bernardino di Betto (better known as Pinturicchio, or Little Painter, because of his stature) is the star in the **Libreria Piccolomini,** entered off the left aisle. Cardinal Francesco Piccolomini built the library in 1487 to house the illuminated manuscripts of his famous uncle, a popular Sienese bishop who later became Pope Pius II (served 1458–64) and is also known for designing the town of Pienza (p. 240), the first planned city in Europe. Cardinal Piccolomini himself later became Pope Pius III—for a mere 18 days, before dying in office—and is commemorated in the Duomo just outside the library entrance with the magnificent Piccolomini Altarpiece, created by artists including Michelangelo; his depiction of St. Paul in the first niche on the right is said to be a self-portrait. Pinturicchio's frescoes depict 10 scenes from Pope Pius II's life, including an especially dramatic departure for the Council of Basel as a storm rages in the background.

In the **Baptistery** (not a separate building but beneath the choir), the great early Renaissance trio of Sienese and Florentine sculptors—Jacopo della Quercia, Lorenzo Ghiberti, and Donatello—crafted the gilded bronze panels of the baptismal font. Donatello wrought the dancing figure of Salome in the *Feast of Herod,* and della Quercia did the statue of St. John that stands high above the marble basin. The subterranean **Cripta** displays fragments of colorful 13th-century frescoes discovered during excavation work beneath the Duomo in 1999.

Piazza del Duomo. operaduomo.siena.it. ✆ **0577/283048.** Cathedral only 7€, 10€ when floor is uncovered. **Opa Si Pass** (includes Duomo, Libreria Piccolomini, Museo dell'Opera Metropolitana, Baptistery, Cripta, and cathedral rooftops) 20€, purchased online (recommended) or from ticket office at Piazza del Duomo 14/8. Mar–Oct Mon–Sat 10am–7pm, Sun 9:30–6pm (rooftops closed early Jan to Feb).

Museo Civico/Palazzo Pubblico ♥♥♥ MUSEUM Presiding over the Piazza del Campo, and topped by the soaring Torre del Mangia, this great Gothic-style town hall houses some of the city's finest artistic treasures. Siena's medieval governors, the Council of Nine, met in the **Sala della Pace,** and to help ensure they bore their duties responsibly, Ambrogio Lorenzetti frescoed the walls with what has become the most important piece of secular art to survive from medieval Europe. His 1338 *Allegory of Good and Bad Government and Their Effects on the Town and Countryside* provides not only a moral lesson but also a remarkable visual record of Siena and the nearby countryside as it appeared in the 14th century. Probably not by accident, the good-government frescoes are nicely illuminated by natural light, while scenes of bad government are cast in shadow (and have deteriorated over the years). In a panorama on the good side of the room, the towers, domes, and rooftops of Siena appear much as they do today, with horsemen, workers, and townsfolk going about their daily affairs; in the countryside, genteel lords on horseback overlook bountiful fields. On the bad-government side, streets are full of rubble, houses are collapsing, and soldiers pillage; beyond the walls, fields are barren and villages are ablaze.

Among other frescoes in the *palazzo* is Sienese painter Simone Martini's greatest work, and his first, a *Maestà* (Majesty), finished in 1315 (he went over it again in 1321), in the **Sala del Mappamondo.** He shows the Virgin Mary as a medieval queen beneath a royal canopy, surrounded by a retinue of saints, apostles, and angels. The work not only introduces a secular element to a holy scene but also adds a sense of three-dimensional depth and perspective that came to the fore in Renaissance painting. Mary's presence here in the halls of civil power reinforces the idea of good government, with the Virgin presiding as a protector of the city. Just opposite is another great Martini work (though the attribution has been called into question), the *Equestrian Portrait of Guidoriccio da Fogliano,*

SIENA'S scholarly SAINT

Catherine di Benincasa (1347–80), one of 25 children of a wealthy Sienese cloth dyer, had her first vision of Christ when she was 5 or 6 and vowed to devote her life to God. She took a nun's veil but not the vows; she "mystically" wed Christ when she was 21 and became known for helping the poor and infirm. She founded a woman's monastery outside Siena and promoted "the total love for God" and a stronger church; she also acted as an envoy for the pope and wrote spiritual treatises. Frequent fasting eventually took such a toll on her health that she died at age 33. She was canonized as St. Catherine of Siena in 1461 by Pope Pius II, himself a native of the city, and, along with St. Francis, she is a co-patron saint of Italy, as well as the patron of nurses and firefighters (so anointed because of her statement, "Be who God meant you to be, and you will set the world on fire").

The stark, cavernous church of **San Domenico** in Piazza San Domenico (free admission; daily 7:30am–6:30pm, from 8:45am Sun) houses Catherine's venerated head and her thumb, preserved in a heavily frescoed baroque chapel. A scene of the saint in ecstasy is by Il Sodoma, so named for his predilections, which might account for the presence of well-built young men in extremely tight-fitting clothing. Another fresco is by Francesco Vanni and shows Catherine performing an exorcism, one of her many talents. Her family home, the **Santuario Casa di Santa Caterina,** Costa di Sant'Antonio (✆ **0577/44177;** free admission; daily 9am–2:30pm and 3–5pm), has been preserved as a shrine; the former kitchen is now an oratory with a spectacular 16th-century majolica-tiled floor.

a depiction of a proud mercenary riding past a castle that's said to be one of the world's first realistic landscape paintings.

Palazzo Pubblico, Piazza del Campo. museocivico.comune.siena.it. ✆ **0577/292-226.** Museo Civico 10€ adults, 9€ ages 11–19, free for children 10 and under; family ticket 25€ for 2 adults and 2 children 11–18. Cumulative ticket with Santa Maria della Scala 14€; with Torre del Mangia 15€; with Torre del Mangia and Santa Maria della Scala 20€; family ticket with Torre del Mangia and Santa Maria della Scala 40€. Daily 10am–7pm (Nov–Feb closes 6pm). Bus: A (pink), B.

Museo dell'Opera Metropolitana ♥♥ MUSEUM Work on expanding the Duomo had just begun when the Black Death killed more than half the city's inhabitants in 1348. Construction never resumed, partly because it was discovered that the foundations could not support the massive structure. The aborted nave of the so-called New Duomo has now been repurposed to house many of the church's treasures. Here you can see the glorious-if-worse-for-wear statues by Giovanni Pisano that once adorned the facade, as well as a 30-sq.-m (323-sq.-ft.) stained-glass apse window from the late 1280s, with nine colorful panels depicting the Virgin Mary, Siena's four patron saints, and the four biblical Evangelists.

Upstairs is the *Maestà* by Duccio di Buoninsegna, an altarpiece that was declared a masterpiece when it was unveiled in 1311 and carried in a procession from the painter's workshop to the Duomo's altar. As a contemporary wrote, "All honorable citizens of Siena surrounded said panel with candles held in their hands, and women and children followed humbly behind." The front depicts the Madonna and Child surrounded by saints and angels, while the back once displayed 46 scenes from the lives of Mary and Christ. In 1711 the altarpiece was dismantled, and pieces are now in collections around the world. What remains here shows the genius of Duccio, who slowly broke away from a one-dimensional Byzantine style to imbue his characters with nuance, roundness, and emotion.

The **Facciatone,** a walkway atop the would-be facade of the "New Duomo," is the city's second-most popular viewpoint, with a stunning perspective of the cathedral across the piazza and sweeping views over the city's rooftops to Siena's favorite height, the Torre del Mangia towering over the Campo.

Piazza del Duomo 8. operaduomo.siena.it. ✆ **0577/283048.** Opa Si Pass (includes Duomo, Libreria Piccolomini, Museo dell'Opera Metropolitana, Baptistery, Cripta, and cathedral rooftops) 20€, purchase online (recommended) or from ticket office at Piazza del Duomo 14/8. Apr–Oct daily 9:30am–7:30pm; Nov–Mar daily 10:30am–5:30pm.

Pinacoteca Nazionale ♥♥ ART MUSEUM While the greatest works of Sienese art have long since been dispersed to museums around the world, these adjoining palaces provide an overview of the city's major artists, especially those of the 12th through the 16th centuries. What you'll notice is that while the Renaissance was flourishing in Florence, Siena held to its old ways—these works are rich in Byzantine gold and Eastern styling. Duccio (of the famous *Maestà* in the Museo dell'Opera; see

p. 239) is represented by *Madonna and Child with Saints,* in which a placid, otherworldly-looking Mary holds a very wise-looking infant Jesus. Simone Martini (painter of Siena's other great *Maestà,* in the Museo Civico; see p. 237) did the wonderful *Agostino Novello* altarpiece, depicting St. Augustine performing all sorts of heroic deeds, such as flying over boulders to save a monk trapped in a ravine. There are some charming landscapes by Ambrogio Lorenzetti (artist of the *Allegory of Good and Bad Government* in the Palazzo Pubblico; see p. 237), including the almost surreal *Castle on the Lake,* an architectural fantasy reminiscent of the 20th-century works of Giorgio di Chirico. His brother Pietro's *Madonna of the Carmelites,* an altarpiece created for the Carmelite church in Siena, shows the Virgin and Child in a distinctly medieval setting, in a Sienese landscape complete with horsemen and planted hillsides. Domenico Beccafumi's sketches for his Duomo floor panels are on the first floor.

Via San Pietro 29. pinacotecanazionalesiena.it. ✆ **0577/281-161.** Admission 6€ adults, 2€ ages 12–17, free for children 11 and under; family ticket 10€ for 2 adults and 2 children 12–17. Tues–Sat 9am–7pm; Sun–Mon 9am–1:30pm.

Santa Maria della Scala ♥♥♥ MUSEUM One of Europe's first hospitals, founded around 1090, raised abandoned children, took care of the infirm, fed the poor, and lodged pilgrims who stopped in Siena on their way to and from Rome. These activities are recorded in scenes in the **Sala del Pellegrinaio** (Pilgrims' Hall), where colorful depictions of patients and healers from the Middle Ages looked down upon rows of hospital beds as recently as the 1990s. These are some of the finest secular works of the Middle Ages, color-rich 15th-century frescoes by Domenico di Bartolo and others, showing surgeons dressing a leg wound or holding a flask of urine to the light, or caregivers offering fresh clothing to an indigent young man. One of Bartolo's panels encapsulates an orphan's lifetime experience at the hospital, as he pictures infants being weaned, youngsters being taught by a stern-looking schoolmistress, and a young couple being wed (young women raised in the hospital were given dowries). As these activities transpire, a dog and cat scuffle, foundlings climb ladders toward the Virgin Mary, and wealthy benefactors stand on Oriental carpets.

You'll also see other frescoes and altarpieces commissioned by the hospital as it acquired considerable wealth over the centuries. One gallery houses some original panels from Jacopo della Quercia's 14th-century fountain in the Piazza del Campo, the Fonte Gaia. In the cellars is the dark and eerie **Oratorio di Santa Caterina della Notte,** where St. Catherine (p. 238) allegedly passed her nights in prayer.

Piazza del Duomo 2. santamariadellascala.com. ✆ **0577/292-615.** Admission 9€ adults, 6.50€ ages 12–19, family ticket 18€ for 2 adults and 2 children ages 12–19, free for children 11 and under. With Museo Civico/Palazzo Pubblico 14€; with Torre del Mangia and Museo Civico/Palazzo Pubblico 20€. Mid-Mar to Oct daily 10am–7pm; Nov to mid-Mar Mon and Wed–Fri 10am–5pm and Sat–Sun 10am–7pm.

Where to Stay in Siena

Many hotels have discount arrangements with garages outside the city center; 25€ per day is standard. If you plan on driving to a hotel to unload, check to make sure it is not in a restricted zone that is off-limits to non-resident drivers or for which you need written permission to enter.

EXPENSIVE

Campo Regio Relais ♥♥♥ A *Room with a View* ambience pervades this stylish old house a 10-minute walk from the Campo. Two of the beautifully appointed rooms have spectacular views up a hillside crowned with the Duomo, one from its own sun-filled terrace, and all guests enjoy the same vista from an inviting sitting room/bar/breakfast room that also opens to a terrace. Lush fabrics and elegant furnishings enhance the old-fashioned *pensione* atmosphere, and amenities include an honesty bar, library, attentive service, and an excellent breakfast.

Via della Sapienza 25. camporegio.com. ✆ **0577/222073.** 6 units. 160€–240€ double. Rates include breakfast. **Amenities:** Library; free Wi-Fi.

Il Battistero ♥♥ Only a brief stroll from the Campo, this character-filled small *palazzo,* once home to a pope, adds quiet sophistication to Siena's medieval charm, blending old tilework and rough-hewn beams with contemporary furnishings and modern art. Individually designed rooms and suites, some with terrace, overlook the baptistery or across rooftops to San Domenico. Along with a welcoming guest lounge/library and a cozy bistro/cafe, a wine shop stocked with top vintages from throughout Tuscany is at one end of the reception hall, with an atmospheric tasting cellar below.

Piazza San Giovanni 12. battisterosiena.com. ✆ **057/288921.** 7 units. 145€–170€ double. Rates include breakfast. **Amenities:** Bar/restaurant; free Wi-Fi.

MODERATE

Casacenti ♥♥♥ Host Stefano Centi has converted a family apartment into a welcoming bed-and-breakfast inn with the feel of a private home. Rooms are spacious, airy, and nicely furnished. All have hardwood floors, beamed ceilings, and beautifully done bathrooms, and several open to sweeping views across the rooftops to the countryside beyond. The Duomo and other sights are just outside the door, as is the escalator to the Santa Caterina parking lot, making this an especially good choice if you're traveling by car.

Via di Vallepiatta 6, Siena. casacenti.it. ✆ **339/215-6827.** 4 units. 85€–140€ double. Rates include breakfast. Closed Jan and early Feb. **Amenities:** Free Wi-Fi.

Fonte Gaia Experience ♥♥♥ Maurizio and Glenda's homey little guesthouse is reason enough to settle down in Siena for a while. Their attention to detail shows up in the tasteful decor, excellent lighting and mattresses, and common areas that include a kitchenette stocked with home-baked goods and a comfortable communal lounge that adds a lot of

bonus space to the already roomy accommodations. The Campo is a short (uphill) walk away, and shops and restaurants are just outside the door.
Via Fontebranda 50. fontegaiaexperience.com. ✆ **331/645-2982.** 2 units. 120€–140€ double. Rates include breakfast. **Amenities:** Lounge; free Wi-Fi.

Palazzo Ravizza ♥♥♥ Generations of travelers have fallen under the spell of this 17th-century Renaissance *palazzo,* where high ceilings, oil paintings, highly polished antiques, and the gentle patina of age all suggest an era of grand travel. A large garden in the rear is a popular cocktail spot for guests and Sienese alike. All the rooms are different, though most have wood beams and a surfeit of period detail, including some frescoes and coffered ceilings, and furnishings throughout are comfortable and traditionally stylish. While this wonderful old place has the aura of a country hideaway, it's right in the city center, just a few streets below the Piazza del Campo—and it even has its own private parking lot, easily reached from Porta San Marco.
Pian dei Mantellini 34 (near Piazza San Marco). palazzoravizza.it. ✆ **0577/280462.** 35 units. 85€–155€ double. Rates include breakfast. Free parking. Closed early Jan to Feb. Bus: A (green, yellow). **Amenities:** Bar; babysitting; concierge; room service; free parking; free Wi-Fi.

Santa Caterina ♥♥ Just outside the Siena walls—literally so, as this is the first house after Porta Romana—this homey old inn feels as if it's in the countryside, yet it's only a 10-minute walk from Piazza del Campo. Have breakfast or a drink under the trees in good weather in the large, shady garden; inside is a snug little bar, a well-upholstered lounge, and a glass-enclosed breakfast room. Most of the cozy rooms, with wood-beamed ceilings, simple wood furnishings, and old prints on the walls, face the back, where wide-sweeping views over the rolling hills seem to go on forever. One choice room has a little balcony; a few others are bi-level, with bedrooms snuggled beneath the eaves. Ask for a rear-facing room or you'll miss that wonderful view.
Via Enea Silvio Piccolomini 7. hscsiena.it. ✆ **0577/221105.** 22 units. 80€–150€ double. Rates include breakfast. Bus: A (red) or 2. **Amenities:** Babysitting; bikes; concierge; garden; free Wi-Fi.

INEXPENSIVE

Hotel Alma Domus ♥♥ This modern redo of the former drying rooms of a medieval wool works is run by the nuns of St. Catherine, who provide homey and spotless lodgings with a slightly contemporary flair. Set into the hillside below San Domenico basilica, near the Fontebranda (the oldest and most picturesque of the city's fountains), the place has the quiet air of a retreat, along with a great perk: city-view balconies in the more expensive rooms. Less expensive rooms do not come with views or air-conditioning. Breakfast is included, but it's a bit basic; you may prefer to walk up the hill and enjoy a cappuccino in the Campo.
Via Camporegio 37. hotelalmadomus.it. ✆ **0577/44177.** 28 units. 60€–95€ double. Rates include breakfast. Bus: A (red). **Amenities:** Free Wi-Fi.

Palazzo Bulgarini ♥♥ The converted *piano nobile* salons of an old palace aren't as opulent as they once were—furnishings are a bit dated, and some better lighting would be welcome—but enough of the grandeur remains to elicit a gasp or two as you enter one of the six enormous guest rooms embellished with marble fireplaces and ceiling frescoes. Unchanged over the centuries are the stunning views from the rear rooms over the countryside, a surprise given the city-center location. Prices are very reasonable, especially for accommodations so genuinely palatial.
Via Pantaneto 93. bbpalazzobulgarini.com. ✆ **0577/152-4466.** 6 units. 60€–105€ double. Rates include breakfast. Bus: A (pink). **Amenities:** Free Wi-Fi.

Where to Eat in Siena

While a drink or meal on the Campo can be an expensive and less-than-satisfying experience, a pleasant exception is friendly **Liberamente,** Piazza del Campo 7 (✆ **0577/274733**), where drinks are well-priced and usually come with generous nibbles. **The Irishman,** Via dei Rossi 115 (instagram.com/theirishmansiena; ✆ **0577/557137**), is an amiable pub with Irish beers and sophisticated Italian cocktails. An atmospheric place to taste some top Tuscan wines is the **Enoteca Italia,** tucked away in the Medici fortress at the edge of town (enotecaitalianasiena.it; ✆ **0577/160-7520**).

For the best panini in Siena (plus generous cheese and meat platters) step into **Gino Cacino di Angelo,** behind a huge flowering vine at Piazza Mercato 31 (ginocacinodiangelo.blogspot.com; ✆ **0577/553-855**). Another popular fast-food stop, **Te Ke Voi?** (tekevoi.com; ✆ **0577/40139**)—translation: Whaddaya Want?—is a pleasant, bustling room on Vicolo San Pietro, one of the narrow, sloping alleyways leading into the Campo; pasta, pizza, and burgers are dispensed from a self-service counter, along with wine and beer. For a quick meal, step into bright little **Pretto Prosciutteria** for sandwiches, delicious bruschetta, and generous platters of hams and cheeses, near the Campo at Via dei Termini 4 (instagram.com/prettoprosciutteria; ✆ **0577/289089**); or **La Prosciutteria,** on the corner of Via Magalotti and Via Pantaneto (laprosciutteria.com; ✆ **0577/42026**), where you can quite literally pig out on a platter of Tuscan hams or a *porchetta* sandwich, served on tables out front or in a series of ornate rooms. **Pizzacheria di De Miccoli Bruno,** Via di Città (facebook.com/antica pizzicheriachigiana; ✆ **0577/289164**) is another popular sandwich stop, with ham, boar, and local cheeses served on rustic bread. At **Gastronomia Morbidi,** Via Banca di Sopra 75, a busy deli and gourmet shop, you can stock up on cheeses, hams, and pastries, enjoy a glass of wine or a cocktail, or partake of the buffet (morbidi.com; ✆ **0577/280268**).

Every Italian city has a favorite *gelateria,* and Siena's is **Kopakabana,** Via de' Rossi 52–54 (gelateriakopakabana.it; ✆ **0577/284124**), with flavors that include *panpepato,* based on the peppery Sienese cake.

Taste Siena (sienafoodtour.com) gives an excellent introduction to Sienese cuisine on walks with stops for breakfast, pasta tastings, artisanal cheeses, wine, and other specialties, and a lot of lively insight into the history and cultural life of the city. Tours run daily, last 3 hours, and cost 95€, food and beverages included; two-person minimum.

EXPENSIVE

Antica Osteria da Divo ♥♥ CONTEMPORARY SIENESE An otherworldly assemblage of brick vaulting, exposed timbers, walls of bare rock, and even some Etruscan tombs is the setting for innovatively refined, uniquely Sienese dishes such as *pici alla lepre* (thick spaghetti in hare sauce), *sella di cinghiale* (saddle of wild boar braised in Chianti), or a breast of guinea fowl (*faraona*) roasted with balsamic vinegar. Service is outstanding, and the intimate spaces are beautifully candlelit at night.
Via Franciosa 25–29. osteriadadivo.com. ✆ **0577/284381.** Main courses 20€–35€. Wed–Mon noon–2:30pm and 7–10:30pm. Closed 2 weeks Jan–Feb. Bus: A (green, yellow).

MODERATE

Osteria La Sosta di Violante ♥♥♥ SIENESE This warm, friendly, rose-hued room is only a 5-minute walk from Piazza del Campo but far enough off the beaten track to seem like a getaway (after all, *sosta* means "rest" or "break," as in "take a break"). The surroundings attract a mostly neighborhood crowd that counts on the kitchen for excellent preparations of *pappardelle, pici,* and other Tuscan pastas in rich sauces. Grilled Florentine steaks are another specialty, and so are many vegetarian choices, including delicious *frittelle di pecorino* (Pecorino cheese fritters with pear sauce) and a cauliflower (*cavolfiore*) soufflé. The restaurant's name refers to Violante, the Bavarian-born 18th-century duchess who, after her Medici husband died from syphilis, became a beneficent governor of Siena; she divided the city into its present-day *contrade* (districts).
Via di Pantaneto 115. lasostadiviolante.it. ✆ **0577/43774.** Main courses 14€–22€. Mon–Sat 12:30–3pm and 7:15–10:30pm. Bus: A (pink).

Pier Pettinaio Ristorante a Siena ♥♥ SIENESE Italian celebs whose photos hang alongside etchings and paintings are among generations of diners who have enjoyed this wonderfully old-world, cavernous, vaulted dining room that radiates hospitality from every brick. Among the Sienese the premises are best known as just "Guido," for founder Guido Borri, who set up shop here in 1935. Waiters in crisp jackets and ties make a special occasion of meals that might include one of the house-made pastas—*pici fatti al cacio e pepe* (with cheese and pepper) is a house classic—followed by one of several variations of grilled Tuscan beef.
Vicolo Beato Pier Pettinaio 7. ristorantepierpettinaio.it. ✆ **0577/280-042.** Main courses 14€–24€. Tues–Sun 12:30–2:30pm and 7:30–10:30pm.

Taverna San Giuseppe ♥♥♥ TUSCAN/GRILL A long, brick vaulted room from the 12th century is the setting for meals many travelers long remember as among the best they've had in Italy. The hospitable staff works hard to make diners feel at home, and they are justly proud of the Tuscan classics they bring out of the kitchen. *Pici,* the thick local pasta, with a ragù of *cinghiale* (wild boar), is surprisingly delicate, while ricotta-filled *gnudi* almost float off the plate. Meals often begin with a complimentary glass of Prosecco and might end with a dessert on the house, bookends to an experience that in its entirety seems like a treat. Dinner reservations are a must.

Via G. Dupré 132. tavernasangiuseppe.it. ✆ **0577/42286.** Main courses 15€–30€. Daily noon–2:30pm and 7–9:30pm. Closed mid- to late Jan and Thurs and Sun in Feb and Mar. Bus: A (red).

INEXPENSIVE

L'Osteria dei Rossi ♥♥ TUSCAN One of Siena's neighborhood treasures is this simple tile-floored, wood-beamed room where straightforward local cuisine is expertly prepared and served at extremely reasonable prices. Truffles occasionally appear in some special preparations, but for most of the year the short menu sticks to the classics—*pici al cinghiale* (pasta with wild boar sauce), tripe (*trippa*) stew, and thick steaks, accompanied by *fagioli bianchi* (white beans) and *patate fritte* (fried potatoes). Service can be brusque but efficient.

Via dei Rossi 79–81 (near San Francesco). ✆ **0577/287-592.** Main courses 9€–22€. Mon–Sat 12:30–3pm and 7–10:30pm and Sun 12:30–3pm. Bus: A (red).

Osteria La Chiacchera ♥♥ SIENESE This rustic room halfway along a steep alleyway is tiny but satisfies big appetites with large portions of *ribollita* (hearty bread and vegetable soup), *salsicce e fagioli* (sausage and white beans), or *tegamata di maiale* (a Sienese pork casserole). Good weather provides a unique dining experience on the street out front, where the legs of tables and chairs have been cut to accommodate the steep slope.

Costa di Sant'Antonio 4 (near San Domenico). osterialachiacchera.it. ✆ **0577/280-631.** Main courses 9€–21€. Daily noon–3pm and 6–11pm. Bus: A (red).

Siena Shopping

Siena is famous for its *panforte,* a sweet, dense cake made from candied fruits, nuts, and honey that was created by city bakers in the Middle Ages and is still sold in shops all over town. Each shop has its own recipe, with the most popular varieties being sweet Panforte Margherita and bitter Panforte Nero. Try a slice at **Drogheria Manganelli,** Via di Città 71–73 (drogheriamanganelli.it; ✆ **0577/280002**), which has made its own *panforte* and soft *ricciarelli* almond cookies since the 19th century. Some Sienese would send you just as enthusiastically to the venerable **Pasticceria Nannini,** just off the Campo at Via Banchi di Sopra 24 (en.nannini dolciecaffe.com; ✆ **0577/236009**), or **Il Magnifico,** Via dei Pelligrini 27 (ilmagnifico.siena.it; ✆ **0577/281-106**). The **Consorzio Agrario Siena,** Via Pianigiani 9 (www.consorziagrariditalia.it; ✆ **0577/2301**), showcases

FEEL THE magic AROUND SIENA

If the Disney empire were to set up shop in Tuscany, it would have some ready-made stage sets near Siena. **Monteriggioni ♥♥**, 14km (8½ miles) northwest of Siena along the SS2, is one of the most perfectly preserved fortified villages in all of Italy. The town was once a Sienese outpost, where soldiers were posted in towers to keep an eye out for Florentine troops—an image that Dante once likened to the circle of Titans guarding the lowest level of Hell. All 14 towers have survived, and you can climb up for a view (5€; Apr–Sept daily 9:30am–1:30pm and 2–7:30pm, Oct daily 9:30am–1:30pm and 2–5pm, Nov to early Jan daily 10am–1:30pm and 2–4:30pm [until 5pm Dec 26–Jan 6], mid-Jan to Mar Fri–Mon 10am–1:30pm and 2–4:30pm). A walk from one end of Monteriggioni to the other takes about 5 minutes—as you pass, note the garden plots along the walls, which once kept townsfolk nourished in times of siege. The **tourist office** is at Piazza Roma 23, 53035 Monteriggioni (monteriggioniturismo.it; ✆ **0577/304810**). Siena city buses 130A and 130R run out to Monteriggioni every hour, or you can hike out along a 20km (12-mile) stretch of the Via Francigena (viefrancigene.org), the medieval pilgrimage route that crossed Europe between Canterbury, England, and Rome.

The enchanting **Abbey of San Galgano ♥♥** (fondazionesangalgano.it; ✆ **577/049-305**), in a grassy meadow on the banks of the River Merse, has a "Sword in the Stone" backstory. Galgano, born in Siena in 1148, was pursuing his career as a knight when he had a vision of the archangel Michael, who led him to a circular temple outside the village of Montesiepi, where he met the Twelve Apostles. Moved by the vision, Galgano went off to Montesiepi, drove his sword into a stone to renounce his knighthood, and built a round stone hermitage. After his death in 1182, his simple dwelling was expanded into a spectacular rotunda, which became the center of a community of Cistercian monks. Great church builders, the brothers oversaw the construction of the cathedral in Siena as well as the Gothic Abbey of San Galgano down the hill, now an evocative ruin—you can prowl around the skeletal nave, admiring the high arches, carved capitals, and stone settings for long-vanished stained-glass windows. The saint's tomb is up the hill in the hermitage; though his body long ago went missing, his sword remains in the stone, with only its handle protruding. The abbey and hermitage are outside the village of Chiusdino, about 40km (25 miles) southwest of Siena via S73. Admission is 6€ adults, 5€ ages 17 and under, families of 2 adults and 2 children 17€; it's open daily 9am to 7pm (until 8pm July–Aug, closes 6pm Nov and Apr), closed December to March.

local wines, cheeses, pasta, pastry, and an appetizing selection of cheese- and ham-topped focaccia slices, all from small Tuscan producers.

Authentic Sienese ceramics feature only three colors: black, white, and the reddish-brown "burnt sienna," or *terra di Siena.* **Ceramiche Artistiche Santa Caterina,** Via di Città 74–76 (✆ **0577/283098**), sells high-quality pieces, courtesy of Maestro Marcello Neri and his son, Fabio.

A huge **market,** where vendors sell clothing, household items, and fresh produce and other food, surrounds the walls of the Fortezza on Wednesdays, from 8:30am to 1:30pm.

A Side Trip into the Chianti ♥♥♥

For many visitors to Italy, heaven on earth is the 167 sq. km (64 sq. miles) of land between Florence and Siena, known as the Chianti. Traversing the gentle hillsides on the SR222, a twisting, picturesque route known as the Chiantigiana, is a classic drive of about 60km (37 miles) through landscapes smothered in vineyards and olive groves, punctuated by woodland, and peppered with *case coloniche*—stone farmsteads with trademark square dovecotes protruding from the roofs. The region famously produces Chianti Classico wines, made from the Sangiovese grapes that grow on the hillsides. Visiting wineries and tasting these velvety, ruby-red Classicos at the source is a compelling reason to visit (but make sure a designated driver accompanies you on the tastings).

You'll need a car to get the most out of the route, but from Siena's train station you can get as far as Radda by four-times-a-day bus service, for a quick taste of the countryside; the trip takes an hour, and round-trip fare is about 10€; you'll find schedules at **tiemmespa.it**.

First stop for wine lovers is **Gaiole in Chianti ♥♥**, a little hamlet 30km (18 miles) north of Siena that surrounds a triangular square and is the start of the annual October L'Eroica, a gravel bike race. Just outside Gaiole is the Castello di Brolio, not only home to the oldest winery in the world, established in 1141, but also where Barone Bettino Ricasoli concocted the blend for Chianti Classico wines in the mid-19th century. Castagnoli, a tiny hamlet 6km (4 miles) south of Gaiole, surrounds a fortress and provides what might be the region's best views, across miles of forests and terraced vineyards.

Radda in Chianti, 10km (6 miles) west of Gaiole, is an important wine center that retains its medieval street plan and a bit of its walls. The center of town is the 15th-century **Palazzo del Podestà,** studded with the mayoral coats of arms of past *podestà.* **Casa Porciatti** will give you a taste of traditional salami and cheeses at its *alimentari* on Piazza IV Novembre 1 at the gate into town (casaporciatti.it; ✆ **0577/738234**). **Castellina in Chianti ♥♥**, 11km (7 miles) west of Radda, is a pretty little village clustered around a castle. A particularly atmospheric street is Via delle Volte, an underground passageway in the town walls with defensive outlooks that provide views over the countryside.

Seven kilometers (41⁄3 miles) north of Radda on a secondary road is the **Castello di Volpaia ♥♥** (volpaia.com; ✆ **0577/738066**), a Florentine holding that was buffeted by Sienese attacks from the 10th to 16th centuries. The still-impressive central keep houses an enoteca for tastings and sales, plus award-winning olive oils and farm-produced vinegars. Back on the Chiantigiana (SR222), the next town is hilltop **Panzano in Chianti ♥♥**, 13km (8 miles) north of Radda, known for its embroidery, ruined castle, and a celebrity butcher, Dario Cecchini. At his shop **Antica Macelleria Cecchini ♥♥**, Via XX Luglio 11 (dariocecchini.com; ✆ **055/852020**), the flamboyant Cecchini entertains visitors with classical music, product

Castello di Volpaia.

samples, sometimes even poetry recitations; in adjacent dining rooms he serves a five-course, beef-heavy tasting menu (50€ per person, including wine) at 12:30 and 7:30pm daily; reservations advised, vegetarian version available.

Outside of Panzano, heading toward Greve, take a well-marked detour to follow a cypress-lined lane up to the pretty hamlet of **Lamole,** for expansive views over the countryside. Then backtrack and continue on to **Greve in Chianti** ♥♥♥, 9km (5½ miles) north of Panzano on the SR222, the center of the wine trade and the unofficial capital of Chianti. The central **Piazza Matteotti** is a rough triangle surrounded by a mismatched patchwork arcade—each merchant had to build the stretch in front of his own shop. Greve hosts Chianti's annual September wine fair; naturally, the town has dozens of wine shops. One of the best is the **Enoteca Bottega del Chianti Classico** ♥♥, Piazzetta Santa Croce 8 (✆ **055/853297**). At **Antica Macelleria Falorni** ♥♥, Piazza Matteotti 69–71 (falorni.it; ✆ **055/854363**), established in 1806, a cornucopia of *prosciutti* and dozens of other cured meats hang above display cases and tables where you can enjoy the products on tasting platters, in sandwiches, and other light meals (daily 9am–7:30pm). **Montefioralle** ♥♥, an atmospheric village just beyond the outskirts of Greve, is partially enclosed within a double circuit of walls and surrounds a castle keep; it's said that Amerigo Vespucci, the explorer who lent his name to the New World, was born here in a modest house on the main street.

The **Castello di Verrazzano** ♥♥ (verrazzano.com; ✆ **055/854243**), 6km (4 miles) northwest of Greve, is another significant stop for Americans: the ancestral home of the Verrazzano family, where Giovanni Verrazzano, the first European to lay eyes on what would come to be named New York harbor, was born in 1485. The estate has been making wine since at least 1170; free tastings are offered daily at the roadside shop.

Tours of the gardens and cellars run Monday through Friday (prebooking essential); a rustic farmhouse inn, **Foresteria Casanova,** offers rooms from 145€.

From here it's 30km (18 miles) to Florence, or 50km (30 miles) back to Siena on the Chiantigiana—allow a little over an hour without stops for the return trip.

WHERE TO STAY IN THE CHIANTI REGION

B&B Grano e Lavanda ♥♥ This charming little inn is tucked away in a centuries-old *palazzo* right in the center of Greve, steps off Piazza Matteotti, and provides a delightful base for exploring the surrounding countryside and wine villages. Nicely furnished rooms overlook the town and the welcoming hills beyond, as does a terrace off the cozy shared lounge, where breakfast is served. Along with a surfeit of beams and other traditional Tuscan charm, guest quarters are equipped with excellent bathrooms and showers and soothing lighting. Gracious host Luca is on hand with advice and recommendations.

Via Cesare Battisti 5. granoelavanda.com. ✆ **331/5326723.** 4 rooms, 1 apt. 80€–120€ double. Rates include breakfast. **Amenities:** Free Wi-Fi.

Castello Vicchiomaggio ♥♥ A castle converted to a Renaissance manor, complete with a crenellated tower, has hosted such luminaries as Leonardo da Vinci; modern-day visitors enjoy a stay on a working wine estate set amid world-acclaimed vineyards. Large, character-filled apartments in the manor are in turrets and salons along twisting staircases and corridors, each filled with old-fashioned furnishings that are more homey than grand. An adjacent priory has been converted into six comfortable suites that surround a communal lounge. All share a shady formal garden and a swimming pool that hangs over the vineyards.

Via Vicchiomaggio, Greve in Chianti. vicchiomaggio.it. ✆ **055/854079.** 12 units. 170€–240€ double. Rates include breakfast. Minimum stay required some periods. **Amenities:** Restaurant; pool; free Wi-Fi.

Palazzo Leopoldo ♥♥ One of the grandest palaces in Radda in Chianti dates to the 15th century and was redone as a noble residence in the 18th century. Guest rooms open off vaulted salons and have chunky beams, colorful frescoes, and comfy traditional furnishings to offer a satisfyingly historic, slightly regal ambience at very good value. Breakfast is served in the 18th-century kitchens, while a sunny terrace overlooks the nearby hills. A hedonistic **spa** is tucked beneath pleasant but slightly less atmospheric lodgings in an adjoining house.

Via Roma 33, Radda in Chianti. palazzoleopoldo.it. ✆ **0577/735605.** 22 units. 110€–195€ double. Most rates include breakfast. **Amenities:** Restaurant; bar; pool; spa; free Wi-Fi.

Villa le Barone ♥♥♥ The Count and Countess Aloisi de Larderel are your hosts at this estate set amid the hills outside Panzano. Rooms in the manor house are appropriately grand and furnished with family antiques, while those in several converted cottages and barns are charmingly rustic but no less comfortable, and they all share extensive, view-filled grounds, gardens, and several welcoming lounges. Excellent meals are served in a charming outbuilding that once housed the estate's olive press.

Via San Leolino. Panzano in Chianti. villalebarone.com. ✆ **055/852621.** 28 units. 200€–300€ double. Rates include breakfast. Closed Nov–Mar. **Amenities:** Restaurant; bar; pool; tennis courts; free Wi-Fi.

MONTEPULCIANO ♥♥

67km (41 miles) SE of Siena, 124km (77 miles) SE of Florence, 186km (116 miles) N of Rome

Sipping a delicious ruby wine in a friendly hill town is a good reason to trek across the beautiful Tuscan countryside. There are few better places to aim for than Montepulciano, with its medieval alleyways, Renaissance palaces, and famous violet-scented, orange-speckled Vino Nobile di Montepulciano. You'll earn your libation with some serious exercise, because Montepulciano's steep streets give new meaning to the notion of a "hill town."

Montepulciano is also a good base for exploring other hill towns, especially nearby **Pienza** (p. 257) and **Montalcino** (p. 260), and for other excursions into the enchantingly beautiful Val d'Orcia region (p. 256).

Essentials

ARRIVING Driving is the best method: From Siena, the most scenic route is south through the Val d'Orcia on the SS2 to San Quirico d'Orcia, where you get the SS146 east through Pienza to Montepulciano. A dozen or so well-marked parking lots surround the town. Convenient lots are P8, at the top of the town next to the fortress, and P1, at the bottom of town just outside Porta al Prato. Rates are about 1.50€ to 2€ an hour; pay at a machine and put the ticket on the dashboard or use the EasyPark app.

Buses operated by **Autolinee Toscane** (at-bus.it; ✆ **800/142242**) run from Siena several times a day (2½ hr.), often with a change in Buonconvento. Montepulciano is served by **train,** with frequent service from Siena and Florence, but the station is about 15km (9 miles) outside town, with infrequent bus connections on **Autolinee Toscane;** a taxi into town will cost about 25€. Another option is to travel by train to Sinalunga and to transfer there to one of the frequent buses operated by **Autolinee Toscane,** or to Chiusi with a transfer to a Tiemme bus (tiemmespa.it; ✆ **199/168182**).

GETTING AROUND Montepulciano's Corso is very steep. For those not up to the climb, little green electric *pollicini* buses connect the junction just below the Porta al Prato and Piazza Grande in about 8 minutes. Tickets cost 1.40€ each way (buy them on the bus or at *tabacchi*) and run every 20 minutes.

VISITOR INFORMATION Montepulciano's **tourist office** is off the P1 parking lot just below Porta al Prato at Piazza Don Mizzoni 1

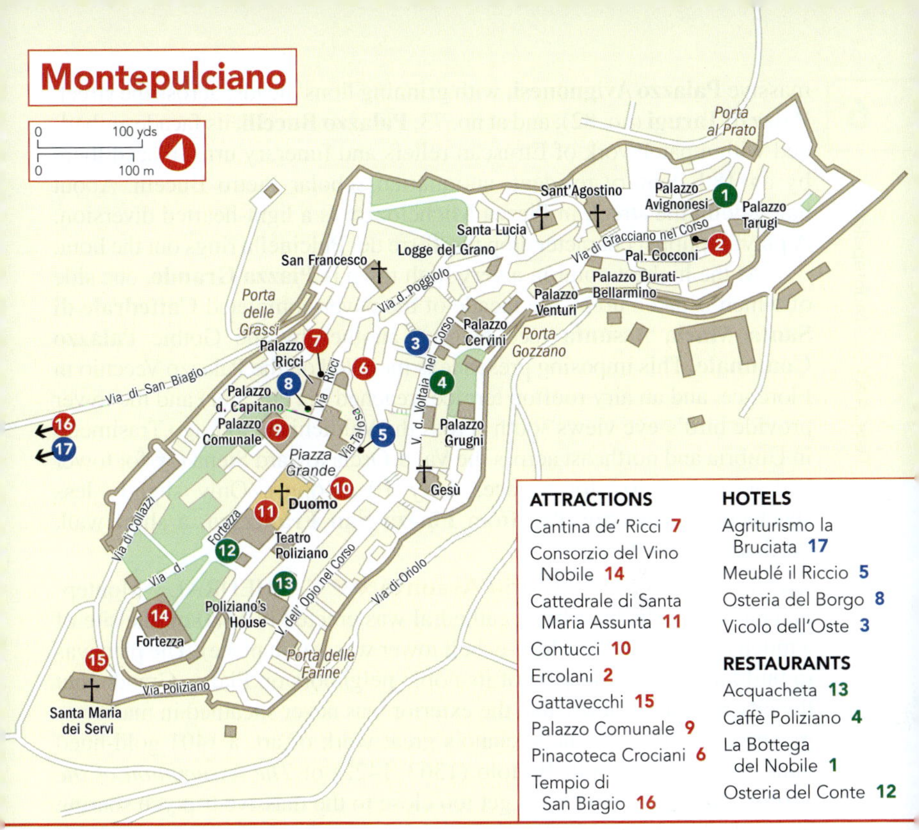

(prolocomontepulciano.it; ✆ **0578/757341**). It's open Monday through Saturday 10am to 1pm and 2 to 5pm and Sundays 10am to 1pm. Another office at Piazza Grande 7 (stradavinonobile.it; ✆ **0578/717484**) represents the Strada del Vino Nobile di Montepulciano e dei Sapori della Valdichiana Senese—that is, vineyards and other sights in the countryside around Montepulciano; it's a good place to learn about wine touring and smaller nearby towns. The office is open Monday to Friday 9:30am to 1:30pm and 2:30 to 6pm, Saturday 10am to 1pm and 2 to 5pm, and Sunday 10am to 1pm.

The climb up Montepulciano's main street will seem like a piece of cake after you witness the annual **Bravio delle Botte** on the last Sunday in August, when residents of the town's 8 *contrade* (districts) compete by pushing barrels all the way up to Piazza Grande; the race is preceded by a parade with much medieval finery on display.

Exploring Montepulciano

It's all uphill from **Porta al Prato,** where the Medici crest (five balls) above the gate hint at Montepulciano's long association with Florence. It's a steep climb up the Corso (the street name changes several times), but along the way you can see some impressive palaces—at no. 91, the massive **Palazzo Avignonesi,** with grinning lions' heads; across the street, **Palazzo Tarugi** (no. 82); and at no. 73, **Palazzo Bucelli,** its facade embedded with a patchwork of Etruscan reliefs and funerary urns, placed there by an 18th-century resident, antiquarian scholar Pietro Bucelli. About halfway up the street, in Piazza Michelozzo, is a light-hearted diversion: A playful puppet character atop the Torre del Pulcinella rings out the hour.

At the highest point in a very high town is **Piazza Grande,** one side of which is taken up by the facade of the never-completed **Cattedrale di Santa Maria Assunta** (see below), another by the Gothic **Palazzo Comunale.** This imposing presence is modeled on the Palazzo Vecchio in Florence, and an airy rooftop terrace (reached via elevator) and the tower provide bird's-eye views south across the Valdichiana to Lago Trasimeno in Umbria and northeast across the Val d'Orcia toward Siena (5€ for tower and terrace, 2.50€ for terrace; daily 10am–6pm). Only slightly less spectacular views are also from **Piazza San Francesco,** a short walk north along Via Ricci.

Cattedrale di Santa Maria Assunta ♥♥ CATHEDRAL Montepulciano's homely, bare-brick cathedral was erected in 1680 on the site of a much earlier church (a 15th-c. bell tower was left in place). The plan was to build a landmark worthy of its noble neighbors on Piazza Grande, but the city ran out of funds, and the exterior was never sheathed in marble as planned. Inside is Montepulciano's great work of art, a 1401 gold-hued altarpiece by Taddeo di Bartolo (1363–1422) of *The Assumption of the Virgin with Saints.* You can't get too close to the massive triptych soaring above the high altar, which is a shame, because the charm lies in the detail of its many various panels. The main sections show the death of the Virgin, with the apostles by her bedside; her ascension into Heaven, as the apostles survey her empty tomb; and the Virgin's coronation in heaven. Piazza Grande. No phone. Free admission. Daily 9am–12:30pm and 3:15–7pm.

Pinacoteca Crociani ♥♥ MUSEUM A few years ago this unassuming little collection found itself in possible possession of a blockbuster masterpiece when it was suggested that its painting *Portrait of a Gentleman* was done by Caravaggio, the wildly popular art star of the late 16th and early 17th centuries. Many art historians remain skeptical, though a nifty digital display next to the painting makes a compelling case for the provenance. Other showpieces are blue-and-white glazed ceramic sculptures by Renaissance master Andrea della Robbia and a transcendently glowing portrait of Montepulciano's patron saint, St. Agnes, by Domenico Beccafumi, who did much of the flooring in Siena's Duomo (p. 236). Via Ricci 10. museocivicomontepulciano.it. ✆ **0578/717300.** Admission 6€, 4€ ages 16–18, free for ages 15 and under. Apr Wed–Mon 10am–6pm; May–Oct Wed–Mon 10am–7pm; Nov–Mar Sat–Sun 10am–6pm.

Tempio di San Biagio ♥♥ CHURCH This intriguing church just outside the town walls, completed in 1534, is the masterwork of Antonio

WINE TASTING IN montepulciano

The cellars of the **Gattavecchi** *cantine* (wineries), Via di Collazzi 74 (toppetta.it/en/gattavecchi; ✆ **0578/757110**), have been in use since before 1200, originally by the friars of the adjacent church Santa Maria dei Servi. Older still is the tiny room at the bottom, probably an Etruscan tomb. Gattavecchi's Vino Nobile is top-notch, as is the 100% Sangiovese Parceto. Tasting is free.

Cavernous cellars at **Cantina de' Ricci,** Via di Collazzi 7 (cantinadericci.it; ✆ **0578/757166**), seem to spread beneath half of Montepulciano, with the main cellar, soaring 60 feet high, filled with centuries-old oak barrels. The cantina is open daily, with tastings (glasses from 2€) at the end of the tour. **Contucci** (contucci.it; ✆ **0578/757006**), in the 11th-century cellars of a historic palace in Piazza Grande, has a fine range of Vino Nobile wines; it's open for free tastings daily. **Ercolani,** Via Gracciano nel Corso 80/82 (ercolanimontepulciano.it; ✆ **0578/716-764**), ages its Vino Nobiles and Vin Santos in labyrinthine underground passages they rightfully call the "Underground City" and show off as part of a tasting. The **Consorzio del Vino Nobile di Montepulciano** (consorziovinonobile.it) occupies view-filled quarters in the Fortezza di Montepulciano, a 5-minute walk beyond Piazza Grande, and offers tastings from local wineries. If you're heading into the country for some wine touring, staff here can provide maps. Across the corridor, the **Strada del Vino Nobile** office (stradavinonobile.it; ✆ **0578/717484**) will help you arrange a wine itinerary.

Tours of Tuscany (toursoftuscany.it; ✆ **3492/804365**) runs several day-long tours of the Tuscan wine regions, including one around Montalcino and Montepulciano, with tastings, lunch in a centuries-old wine cellar, a walk through Pienza, and other highlights; the price (120€) includes pickup and drop-off in Siena or Florence or other points.

da Sangallo the Elder. Best known for fortresses and other military defenses, here Sangallo broke out of the mold to create a beautiful travertine church on the plan of a Greek cross, with the four arms of equal length radiating from a central dome. Since the church is in the countryside with no other buildings nearby, it's easy to admire its classical unity. The interior is as refined as the exterior.

Via di San Biagio. tempiosanbiagio.it. ✆ **0577/286-300.** Admission 5€ adults, free for children 5 and under. Apr–Sept daily 10am–1:30pm and 2–6:30pm; Oct and late Mar daily 10:30am–1:30pm and 2–6pm; Nov to mid-Mar Sat–Sun 10:30am–1:30pm and 2–5pm (Sun from 11:30am); Dec 26–Jan 8 daily 10:30am–1:30pm and 2–5pm (Sun from 11:30am).

Where to Stay in Montepulciano

Agriturismo la Bruciata ♥♥♥ A farmhouse poised on the edge of the Val d'Orcia just outside Montepulciano is an ideal base for a Tuscan getaway, a great spot for walking, touring wineries, or just lounging on the lawns next to the pools, soaking in the views and enjoying the hospitality of the Duchini family. Spacious, handsomely outfitted apartments have

A guest room at Agriturismo la Bruciata, just outside Montepulciano.

kitchens, terraces, and fireplaces for the chilly months, while fruits and vegetables from the family farm show up on the lavish breakfast buffet, at the welcome dinner (prepared weekly for guests and on request), and in the cooking classes that host Laura and her mother offer guests.

Via del Termine 9, Poggiano, 2km (1 mile) south of Montepulciano. agriturismolabruciata.it. ✆ **0578/757704.** 11 units. 650€–1,100€ a week, nightly rates on request. **Amenities:** Bar; dining room; kitchens; 2 pools; free Wi-Fi.

Meublé il Riccio ♥♥♥ This atmospheric 800-year-old *palazzo* near Piazza Grande, passed down through the innkeeper's family, lays on the charm—in the arcaded, mosaic-tiled courtyard, the antiques-and-art-filled salon and breakfast room, the comfy lounge, and the rooftop terrace overlooking the landscapes of the Valdichiana. A suite matches the surroundings with palatial expanses and a terrace of its own, while other rooms make up for the lack of view with their character and comfort. Carved wooden *ricci* (hedgehogs) make an appearance in all rooms. Ivana and Giorgio Caroti are on hand to dispense advice and make restaurant reservations, serving up delicious homemade pastries at breakfast and drinks throughout the day.

Via di Tolosa 21. ilriccio.net. ✆ **0578/757713.** 10 units. 140€–155€ double. Breakfast 10€. **Amenities:** Bar; free Wi-Fi.

Osteria del Borgo ♥♥ In good weather this homey restaurant serving Tuscan specialties spills out of a 13th-century dining room into a view-filled patio with views across the rolling Val d'Orcia countryside, making this a favorite spot for a drink or meal (open Wed–Mon noon–2:15pm and 7–9:15pm; main courses 14€–35€). Upstairs are four bright, large rooms, with wood beams, exposed brickwork, stylishly traditional furnishings, and, from some, panoramic views across the valley; others look onto Piazza Grande. They share a terrace high atop the town and valley.

Via Ricci. osteriadelborgo.it. ✆ **0578/716799.** 4 units. 130€–300€ double. Rates include breakfast and parking. 2-night minimum stay. **Amenities:** Restaurant; free Wi-Fi. Closed Jan to mid-Mar.

Vicolo dell'Oste ♥♥ Tuscan chic prevails in this house on a narrow lane off the Corso, just below Piazza Grande. Wood-beamed ceilings set off the comfortable furnishings, and some rooms have such deluxe touches as large Jacuzzis; others include simple kitchens. While there are no communal spaces, breakfast is served in a nearby cafe, and innkeepers Giuseppe and Luisa are at hand to take care of your needs.

Via delle Oste. vicolodelloste.it. ✆ **0578/758393.** 5 units. 90€–140€ double. Rates include breakfast. **Amenities:** Free Wi-Fi.

Where to Eat in Montepulciano

With a local wine that pairs especially well with hearty sauces and red meat, it's no accident that menus in Montepulciano rely heavily on game, beef from the Valdichiana, and thick pastas like hand-rolled *pici.* Aside from the town's many tasting rooms (see box p. 253), you can also drink wine and taste local salami and cheeses, as well as excellent pastries and desserts, in an atmospheric old cafe, the venerable, late-19th-century **Caffè Poliziano,** on the Corso (No. 27; caffepoliziano.it; ✆ **0578/758615**).

Acquacheta ♥♥♥ SOUTHERN TUSCAN/GRILL If you're craving steak, head for this cellar eatery's rustic, hearth-warmed vaulted dining room, where meat is sold by weight and brought to your table for your approval by a cleaver-wielding chef before it goes onto the grill. A choice of mix-and-match pastas and sauces are also available, as are hearty salads. It's essential to make a reservation.

Via del Teatro 22. facebook.com/OsteriaAcquacheta. ✆ **0578/717086.** Main courses 12€–40€ (steak by weight). Wed–Mon 12:30–3pm and 7:30–10:30pm. Closed mid-Jan to mid-Mar.

La Bottega del Nobile ♥♥ TUSCAN At this appealing tasting room/restaurant, the upper floor is part cafe and part wine shop, representing the region's best producers. In the brick-walled cellars below, an affable young staff serves thick Tuscan steaks, pork roasts, and hearty sauces atop *pici,* and eagerly pairs the right wine to complement each dish.

Corso 95. labottegadelnobile.it. ✆ **0578/757016.** Main courses 18€–24€ (steak by weight). Thurs–Mon 12:30–2:30pm and 7:30–9:30pm.

Osteria del Conte ♥♥ SOUTHERN TUSCAN A trek to the top of town is rewarded with a delicious meal in this simple room off Piazza Grande, overseen by a mother-and-son team who provide home cooking and warm hospitality. Put yourself in their hands with the set menu, which includes a huge platter of cheese, salami, and other starters, a steak, and wine, or choose from the a la carte selection—the *pici all'aglione*

The Valdichiana: The Big Valley

Montepulciano, Cortona, and Arezzo nestle on the flanks of the Valdichiana (or Val di Chiana), a wide swath of farmland running north–south for some 100km (62 miles) through central Italy. Etruscans settled the valley 2,500 years ago, leaving behind remnants of their sophisticated civilization in Cortona, Chiusi, and other centers of their 12-city confederation. These days the valley supplies some of Italy's most prized beef, *bistecca alla fiorentina,* from Chianina cattle, along with stunning views from Cortona and other hill towns overlooking the green and golden landscape. You can shoot through the valley on the A1 *autostrada* or on fast trains between Rome and Florence, but for a nice close-up look, opt for the scenic 33km (20-mile) drive between Cortona and Montepulciano.

(handmade spaghetti with garlic sauce) is a standout, and lamb and steaks are grilled to order.

Via di San Donato 19. osteriadelconte.it. ✆ **0578/756062.** Main courses 12€–25€; set menu 42€. Tues–Sun 12:30–2:30pm and 7:30–10pm.

Montepulciano Shopping

You may leave town with more than wine in your shopping bags. The Mazzetti family has been crafting copper in Montepulciano since the end of the 19th century, and Cesare and his craftspeople display their pots, pans, and other beautiful wares in the **Bottega del Rame** at Via dell'Opio nel Corso 64 (rameria.com; ✆ **0578/758753**); an adjacent museum shows off some of the family's prized pieces.

INTO THE VAL D'ORCIA

Montepulciano sits at the edge of the Val d'Orcia, a beautiful landscape of vineyards and wheat fields through which cypress-shaded roads lead to hilltop villages. Renaissance artists captured these scenes as a background for their paintings, and you probably won't be able to resist joining the ranks of photographers who have followed suit with countless shots of pointy cypresses on golden hillsides that are some of the most iconic images of Italy.

From Montepulciano, SS146 heads west across the valley through a string of appealing towns (see below). Another route, SP88, drops 11km (7 miles) south to **La Foce,** an extensive and storied estate that encompasses farmlands and beautiful Renaissance gardens (lafoce.com; ✆ **0578/69101;** guided tours 10€, Wed at 3, 4:30, and 6pm, and Sun at 11:30am and 3 and 4:30pm). The remarkable **Rocca di Radicofani**—a fortress atop a 914-m (3,000-ft.) summit commanding views across much of southern Tuscany from the stone town of Radicofani—is another 30km (19 miles) south.

Wherever you drive in the Val d'Orcia, you will probably be in sight of the volcanic dome of **Monte Amiata,** reaching 1,732m (5,682 ft.), making it the second-highest volcano in Italy, after Mount Etna in Sicily (p. 782).

Pienza ♥♥♥

14km (9 miles) W of Montepulciano, 55km (34 miles) SE of Siena

A 20-minute drive west of Montepulciano on the SS146 leads to one of the Val d'Orcia's most appealing towns, where shops sell the local products: *pecorino* (sheep's milk cheese), honey, and, of course, wine (the Val d'Orcia has its own wine designation, Orcia DOC reds and whites). Little Pienza has a unique noble heritage, dating to the mid-15th century, when it was rebuilt by humanist Pope Pius II and architect Bernardo Rossellino to be the ideal Renaissance town. Piazzas and palaces, spaces and perspectives, were designed to reflect Renaissance ideals of rationality and humanism, and to instill the populace with notions of peace and harmony. Rossellino's budget was 10,000 florins, and he spent 50,000, but Pius was so pleased with the transformation of his birthplace that he scrapped the town's name (Corsignano) and renamed it after himself. Pius died soon thereafter, and most of his plans for palaces, churches, piazzas, and well-ordered streets were never realized.

Park in one of the well-marked paid lots outside the town walls (1.25€ first hour, 1€ each following hour) and follow the main street, **Corso Rossellino,** through the center of the little town to the splendid **Piazza Pio II.** This focal point of Pius's town-planning dream is a Renaissance stage set of architectural perfection, flanked by the two main buildings of Pius's ambitious dream: the **Duomo** and the pope's residence,

Pienza was designed to be the ideal Renaissance city.

Palazzo Piccolomini. If you follow the little lane to the left of the square you'll come to a walkway with extensive views over the surrounding landscape. Pienza's **tourist office** is on Piazza Dante Alighieri (ufficio turisticodipienza.it; ✆ **0578/748359;** Mon–Tues and Thurs 10am–1pm, Fri–Sun 10am–1pm and 3–6:30pm).

Duomo ♥♥ CATHEDRAL This light-drenched *domus vitrea* (literally "house of glass") fulfilled Pius's notion that the church should symbolize enlightenment. The exterior represents Renaissance ideals of unity with a facade of three blind arches, atop which the pope immodestly placed his coat of arms. The interior was in part inspired by his travels in Germany, where he admired hall churches, lit by tall windows. For all of its perfection, the structure showed a serious flaw almost as soon as it was completed—the hillside on which it is built is unstable, and the foundations are slowly shifting (as you walk toward the rear, you'll notice that the floor slightly slopes).

Piazza Pio II. ✆ **0578/749059.** Free admission. Daily 7am–1pm and 2:30–7pm.

Palazzo Piccolomini ♥♥ HISTORIC SITE Pope Pius had to have a residence worthy of his lofty status, of course, and his dining room, bedroom, library, and other chambers are appropriately regal. The stuffy rooms remained home to the pope's descendants until 1968. Linger in the *palazzo*'s hanging garden and on the triple-decked loggia to take in the views over the Val d'Orcia. With a setting like this, it's easy to see why Pius II, born Silvio Piccolomini into an impoverished branch of a noble Sienese family, wanted to return to this humble town of his birth after an eventful life as a humanist scholar, itinerant diplomat, and pope from 1458 to 1464.

Piazza Pio II. palazzopiccolominipienza.it. ✆ **0577/286300.** Admission 7€ adults, free for children 4 and under. Wed–Mon 10am–4:30pm.

WHERE TO STAY & EAT IN & AROUND PIENZA

Dopolavoro La Foce ♥♥ La Foce, 19km (11 miles) southeast of Pienza, is the creation of Iris and Clemente Origo, who in the 1920s began reworking an extensive estate with farmlands and employing dozens of families, for whom they built housing and a school. The former social hall is now a rustic restaurant, with a beautiful warm-weather terrace, serving grilled meats and other Tuscan fare, much of it (including the accompanying wines) produced on the estate. While there, visit the beautiful Renaissance gardens the Ortigias created, open by appointment Wednesdays 3, 4:30, and 6pm and Sunday (and Thurs in Apr only) 11:30am and 3 and 4:30pm; admission is 10€, children under 12 free. A visit to La Foce might inspire you to read Iris Origo's engrossing World War II memoir, *War in Val D'Orcia.*

Strada della Vittoria 90, Pienza. dopolavorolafoce.it. ✆ **0578/754025.** Main courses 16€–28€. Daily noon–3pm and 7–11pm.

Fonte Berusi ♥♥♥ Accommodations in rural Tuscany don't get much more appealing than these large one- and two-room apartments in old farm buildings on an olive estate just outside Pienza. Color-rich, character-filled living and sleeping spaces open to vine-draped terraces and sunny patios; the Il Cortile apartment has a wood-burning stove, a nice amenity for an autumn or early-spring stay. Guests share the extensive grounds and pool, along with a book-lined living room filled with artworks by Eduardo and his son Andrea, who, along with daughter-in-law Manuela, are the attentive resident proprietors.

Podere Fonte Bertusi. fontebertusi.it. ✆ **0578/748-077.** 8 units. 170€–290€ double. Rates include breakfast. Closed Jan to mid-Mar. **Amenities:** Pool; free Wi-Fi.

La Bandita Townhouse ♥♥ This luxurious guesthouse brings 21st-century style to Pienza with huge, loftlike guest quarters that seem better suited to New York or Berlin (the elevator is the only one for miles around). Amid design-magazine staples like steel frame beds, distressed leather armchairs, and slinky divans, you can enjoy such luxuries as slipping effortlessly from a supremely comfortable mattress into a deep tub perched right alongside. Timeless pleasures include honey-colored stone walls and garden views over the surrounding countryside. The in-house **Bandita Townhouse Caffe** (Tues–Sun 12:30–2:30pm and 7:30–10:30pm, Mon 7:30–10:30pm; main courses 16€–36€), decked out with retrofitted furnishings from a 1950s-era Florence school, presents innovative takes on local cuisine, with offerings that include rich pastas as well as hamburgers made from the best Valdichiana beef.

Corso il Rossellino. la-bandita.com. ✆ **0578/749-005.** 12 units. 385€–465€ double. Rates include breakfast. **Amenities:** Restaurant; bar; free Wi-Fi.

La Casa di Adelina ♥♥♥ Monticchiello, a walled village 10km (6 miles) east of Pienza, is a storybook assemblage of piazzas and stone towers, and adding to the charm are these four rooms and an apartment in a grand old house on the central square. All are full of antiques, family heirlooms, and vintage-modern and contemporary pieces. Guests share a large, beamed lounge where a fire burns in the stove on chilly evenings and a breakfast with homemade pastries is served by affable host Francesco. With a couple of shops and places to eat, the village is a good base for exploring the Val d'Orcia.

Piazza San Martina 3, Monticchiello. lacasadiadelina.eu. ✆ **0578/755167.** 5 units. 115€–125€ double. 2- and 3-night min. some periods. Rates include breakfast. Usually closed 2 weeks Feb. **Amenities:** Lounge; free Wi-Fi.

Trattoria da Fiorella ♥♥ TUSCAN An old stable is now an unusual and inviting dining room, with just eight or so tables on the main floor and a few on a balcony above. In this almost theatrical setting the two friendly proprietors/brothers give the town's famous pecorino cheese the star treatment: *crespelle al forno ripiene con zucchini e pecorino fresco,* baked crepes filled with zucchini and young Pecorino cheese; *verdure grigliata* *con pecorino,* a nice assortment of vegetables topped with shaved cheese; and mixed Pecorinos with honey and walnuts. Several hearty homemade pastas, some with sauces of *cinghiale* (wild boar), and grilled steak and pork also show off Tuscan flavors.

Via Condotti 11. ✆ **0578/749045.** Main courses 10€–18€. Thurs–Sat and Mon–Tues noon–2pm and 7–9pm; Sun noon–2pm

Trattoria Latte di Luna ♥♥ TUSCAN Home-cooked meals here are a lunchtime treat in Pienza, prepared by mom in the kitchen and served by dad and daughter in the yellow stucco dining room, off a little square at one end of the town's main street. *Pici all'aglione* (with spicy tomato-and-garlic sauce) or *zuppa di pane* (a local variant on *ribollita,* with more cabbage) are stellar starters, followed by wild boar or suckling pig in season or grilled steaks any time. The dessert of choice is the house-made *semifreddo* flavored with walnuts and seasonal fruits and berries.

Via San Carlo, next to Porta al Ciglio. ✆ **0578/748606.** Main courses 8€–16€. Wed–Mon 11:30am–3:30pm; Sat–Sun until 4pm (sometimes open summer evenings).

Montalcino ♥♥

23km (14 miles) W of Pienza; 28km (17 miles) W of Montepulciano; 40km (25 miles) S of Siena

The road from Pienza to Montalcino crosses the Val d'Orcia's most beautiful scenery, and some of the best views are around the attractive walled town of **San Quirico d'Orcia ♥♥**. A favorite of photographers is the sight of the Vitaleta chapel surrounded by cypresses, on a hillside that comes into view just as you're driving into San Quirico. It's also worth stopping in San Quirico to visit the **Horti Leoni,** formal gardens next to the honey-colored **Collegiata dei Santi Quirico e Giulitta,** laid out around 1580 with geometric box hedges and shady holm oaks that once provided shade to pilgrims on the Via Francigena for whom San Quirico was a rest stop (free admission; daily 8am–sunset).

Montalcino presents a warm welcome as you approach from the Ombrone River valley below, its medieval houses clinging higgledy-piggledy to precipitous alleys beneath prickly towers. A circuit of walls encloses a warren of narrow streets that fan out from the Piazza del Popolo, where a slender clock tower soars above the Palazzo dei Priori and a Gothic loggia that at times still serves as a marketplace. Of course, if you know wine, you're aware that the town's real calling card is Brunello di Montalcino, one of the world's most acclaimed reds, of which the town produces more than 3.5 million bottles a year, along with 3 million of its lighter-weight cousin Rosso di Montalcino. The **tourist office** is at Costa del Municipio 1 (✆ **0578/757341;** daily 9am–1pm, May–Sept 2–6pm).

Montalcino was known as the "Republic of Siena at Montalcino" for housing Sienese refugees after Florence conquered Siena in 1555; after Montalcino fell to Florence in 1559, it more or less languished until the

1960s, when the world began noticing that the local Sangiovese grapes yielded a wine to be reckoned with. The town's Sienese connections come to light in the **Civic and Diocesan Museum of Sacred Art,** in the former convent of St. Augustine at Via Racasoli 1 (orodimontalcino.it; ✆ **0577/286300**). In rooms opening off the cloisters are some notable works by Simone Martini, Ambrogio Lorenzeti, and other Sienese masters. Admission costs 10€, 8€ children 6 to 12, under 6 free (open Apr–Oct daily 10am–6:30pm, Nov–Feb Sat–Sun 10:30am–5pm, Mar Fri–Sun 10:30am–5pm), which includes entry to the adjacent Tempio di Brunello wine museum.

La Fortezza ♥♥ HISTORIC SITE Built in 1361, this castle's moment arrived when the Sienese holed up here for 4 years after their city's final defeat by Florence in 1555 (ironically, the fortress had only recently been expanded and strengthened by Florence's Medici dukes). You can wander round the pentagonal walls and scale a ladder to the highest turret for a view across hills and dales all the way to Siena—but do so before you enjoy a wine tasting (accompanied by local cheeses and salami) in the

SAMPLING THE vino

Brunello di Montalcino is one of Italy's mightiest reds, a ruby-red wine that exudes the smell of damp earth and musky berries and tastes of dark, sweet fruits and dry vanilla. Brunello can hold its own with the rarest *bistecca alla fiorentina* and is also the perfect accompaniment to game, pungent sauces, and aged cheeses. Although Montalcino has produced wine for centuries, its flagship Brunello is a recent development, born in the late 19th century. Brunello di Montalcino was the first wine, in 1980, to receive a designation of Denominazione di Origine Controllata e Garantita (DOCG), the highest classification of Italian wines. By regulation Brunello must be made from 100% Sangiovese grapes and aged for at least 4 years, part of that time in oak barrels. Rosso di Montalcino, which has a slightly less stringent Denominazione di Origine Controlla (DOC) classification, is made from 100% Sangiovese grapes from younger vines and aged for a minimum of 6 months.

A 19th-century pioneer of Montalcino wines was Ferrucci Biondi Santi, who in 1888 founded Montalcino's most popular drinking spot, **Fiaschetteria Italiana,** Piazza del Popolo 6 (✆ **0577/849043**). Patrons have included England's King Charles II.

Montalcino's wine consortium **Consorzio del Vino Brunello di Montalcino,** Piazza Cavour 8 (consorziobrunellodimontalcino.it; ✆ **0577/848246**), can provide info on local wines and steer you to vineyards that are open to the public. **Poggio Antico,** 4.5km (3 miles) south of Montalcino off SP14 toward Grosetto (poggioantico.com; ✆ **0577/84804;** daily 10am–6pm), gives informative tours in English, an excellent introduction to Brunello and other wines of the region, as well as tastings, for 40€. **Sasso di Sole,** 10km (6 miles) northeast of Montalcino (sassodisole.it; ✆ **0577/834-303**), produces Brunello and Rosso di Montalcino as well as wines of the Orcia DOC and welcomes guests at tastings and tours of the vineyards and cellars, from 20€ to 38€.

on-premises enoteca, with one of the region's most extensive wine selections.

Piazzale Fortezza. ✆ **0577/849211.** Admission 4€ adults, 2€ ages 6–17, free for children 5 and under. Tastings from 25€. Ramparts daily 9am–sunset; enoteca daily 9am–8pm.

WHERE TO STAY & EAT IN MONTALCINO

Albergo-Hotel Il Giglio ♥♥♥ Here's just the sort of homey old-fashioned inn you'd expect to find along the medieval lanes of Montalcino. Tall, arched windows look across the Val d'Orcia, a fireplace glows in the cooler months, and the town's Brunello is dispensed from a small lobby bar and in the excellent restaurant. In the rooms upstairs, armchairs are poised to take in the same sweeping views, and beds with wrought-iron headboards are tucked into alcoves.

Via Soccorso 5, Montalcino. gigliohotel.com. ✆ **0577/848167.** 12 units. 180€–190€ double. Rates include breakfast. **Amenities:** Restaurant; bar; free Wi-Fi.

Castello Banfi ♥♥ WINERY One of Tuscany's leading wine producers houses guests in stylish luxury, in a repurposed little *borgo* pressed against the castle walls. What were once peasant cottages are now extraordinarily luxurious suites and rooms fitted with stylish traditional furnishings, sumptuous fabrics, and rare antiques, plus the latest tech gadgetry. Along with polished, attentive service, guests enjoy such amenities as a pool, secluded rose garden, two excellent restaurants, and an enoteca. Also on the estate is the Podere Collupino farmhouse, with five large apartments that provide a much more informal experience; furnishings are comfortably rustic, terraces overlook miles of vineyards, and the kitchens are stocked with estate wines and breakfast provisions.

Castello di Poggio alle Mura, Montalcino. castellobanfiwineresort.it. ✆ **0577/877700.** 14 borgo units, 5 apts. Borgo units 670€–1,340€ double; apts 300€. Rates include breakfast. Il Borgo closed mid-Nov to late Mar; farmhouse closed Dec–Jan. **Amenities:** 2 restaurants; bar; pool (borgo suites only); free Wi-Fi.

Around Montalcino

Montalcino lies at the southern edge of a landscape of gentle clay hills known as the Crete Senesi, literally "the clays of Siena." Roads through the region rise and fall across stark, lonely golden rolling hills planted with wheat, fava beans, and sunflowers. There's an especially scenic route from Siena to Montalcino on the S438, passing the Abbazia di Monte Oliveto Maggiore (see below) and the pretty hillside village of **San Giovanni d'Asso.** The faster, and only slightly less scenic, route on SS2 passes through the charming and pretty town of **Buonconvento** (the name derives from Latin for "happy place"). Just off the SS715, about 20km (13 miles) east of Siena and 40km (25 miles) north of Montalcino, the thermal spa town of **Rapolano Terme** offers several lavish bathing establishments including **San Giovanni Terme Rapolano** (termesangiovanni.it; ✆ **0577/724030**), with five thermal pools set in lush gardens overlooking the Crete

Senesi landscapes. A soak begins at 20€, and the park is open daily 9am to 8pm (until 10pm on Sun).

Abbazia di Monte Oliveto Maggiore ♥♥♥ RELIGIOUS SITE The most famous of Tuscany's rural monasteries is set in the scarred hills of the Crete Senesi, 22km (13 miles) northeast of Montalcino. The Olivetan order, founded by a group of wealthy Sienese businessmen who wanted to devote themselves to the contemplative life, built this red-brick monastic complex in the early 15th century. What draws most visitors today is one of the masterpieces of High Renaissance narrative painting, a 36-scene **fresco cycle** by Luca Signorelli and Sodoma illustrating the Life of St. Benedict. Signorelli started the job in 1497, before skipping town to work on Orvieto's Duomo, where he created his masterpiece *Last Judgment* (p. 343). Antonio Bazzi, who arrived in 1505 and finished the cycle by 1508, is better known as "Il Sodoma," probably a reference to his predilection for young men, although he was married at least three times and had as many as 30 children. Look for his self-portrait in scene 3—he's the richly dressed fellow with flowing black hair, accompanied by two pet badgers, a chicken, and a raven. To follow the cycle's narrative, start in the back left-hand corner, with a scene of the young Benedict, astride a spirited white horse, leaving his parents' home to study in Rome. The scenes' precise details of medieval life are especially appealing: Check out the

Resident monks file past the famous frescoes at the Abbazia di Monte Oliveto Maggiore.

hot spot: THE VAL D'ORCIA

Bagno Vignoni, 5km (3 miles) south of San Quirico d'Orcia, is little more than a group of houses surrounding one of the most memorable *piazze* in Tuscany. Instead of paving stones you'll find a steaming pool of mineral water, created when the Medici harnessed the hot sulfur springs percolating from the ground. Even St. Catherine of Siena (p. 238) relaxed here with a sulfur cure.

To see the springs in their more natural state, as Roman legionnaires did, take the second turnoff on the curving road into town and pull over after about a kilometer (½ mile), where on your right you see a tiny sulfurous mountain where the waters bubble up in dozens of tiny rivulets. You can also look down on the spectacle from the Parco di Mulino at the edge of town. From both vantage points, there's a good view of the fairytale **Rocca d'Orcia,** the 11th-century stronghold of the Aldobrandeschi clan, formidable toll collectors along the Via Francigena pilgrim road.

Should you wish to partake of the waters, head to the **Albergo de Terme,** Piazza del Moretto 12 (termedibagnovignoni.it; ✆ **0577/887150**), or the pools at the **Hotel Posta Marcucci** (postamarcucci.it; ✆ **0577/887112**).

construction crews in scene 11, and the harlots smuggled into a monastery in scene 19 (allegedly, the abbot made Sodoma add clothing to the nudes he'd first painted). Also inside the church are gorgeous choir stalls crafted in intarsia in 1505 by the monk Giovanni da Verona, showing city scenes with remarkably detailed perspective.

SP 451, Strada di Monte Oliveto, Asciano. monteolivetomaggiore.it. ✆ **0577/707258.** Free admission. Daily 9:30am–12:20pm and 2:30–5:40pm (Nov to mid-Mar until 4:40). From Montalcino, take SP45 north to Buonconvento, then SP451 northeast.

Abbazia di Sant'Antimo ♥♥♥ RELIGIOUS SITE This exquisite Romanesque abbey of pale-yellow travertine and alabaster nestles serenely in a valley amid vines and olive groves at the foot of the village of Castelnuovo dell'Abate, 9km (6 miles) south of Montalcino on SP55. Legend has it that the first stone here was laid on the order of Charlemagne in C.E. 781, after an angel cured his plague-stricken entourage on a journey from Rome. Near the entrance is a charming medieval relief of the Madonna and Child, and carvings of mythological animals and geometric designs surround the doors. Inside the columned interior, the carving continues: On the right side is an intricate depiction of Daniel in the lion's den. In the chapel, 15th-century frescoes by Giovanni di Asciano show scenes from the life of St. Benedict, rich in earthy detail (one scene features two blatantly amorous pigs).

Via Della Badia di Sant'Antimo, Castelnuovo dell'Abate. antimo.it. ✆ **0577/286300.** Free admission; video guides 3€ and 6€. Apr–Sept daily 10am–6:30pm; Oct daily 10am–6pm; Nov–Mar daily 10:30am–5pm.

AREZZO ♥♥

53km (32 miles) NE of Montepulciano

This lively little city on the eastern flanks of the Valdichiana is not as popular as some of its Tuscan neighbors, but get past the fairly unremarkable 20th-century perimeter—much of it built atop the rubble left by Allied bombings in World War II—and you'll find an enticing medieval city of cobbled streets and art-filled churches. Famous natives include Giorgio Vasari (author of the gossipy Renaissance-era *Lives of the Artists*), painter Piero della Francesca (from nearby Sansepolcro), the poet Petrarch (1304–74), and actor and director Roberto Benigni, who filmed parts of his 1999 classic *La Vita è Bella* (*Life Is Beautiful*) here.

Essentials

ARRIVING Arezzo is just off the A1 autostrada, putting it within easy reach of Florence and Rome by **car.** There's frequent **bus** service (at-bus.it) to and from Siena, and Arezzo is on a main north–south **train** line, with frequent service to and from Florence and Rome. If you are just hopping off the train or bus to see the Piero della Francesco frescoes in the Basilica di San Francesco (well worth the stopover), you can leave your bags in the tobacco shop in the station by making reservations and paying in advance (7€) at **Kibag** (kibag.it). Two easy-to-reach underground parking garages near the historic center are **Parcheggio Piazza del Popolo,** at Piazza del Popolo 1, 2€ an hour for the first 2 hours, 2.50€ an hour after that; and **Parcheggio Piazza della Misericordia,** at Via Garibaldi 143, 1.50€ an hour (✆ **393/921-3276**).

VISITOR INFORMATION The main **Arezzo Tourist Office** is on Piazza Grande at Via Giorgio Vassari 13 (discoverarezzo.com; ✆ **0575/377468**) and is usually open daily 10am to 6pm. The town also operates a smaller infopoint across from the Duomo on Piazza della Libertà, usually open 10am to 6pm. Every Saturday at 4pm, the office leads a tour of notable

Treasure Hunters & Knights

Arezzo's famous **antiques fair** takes over the Piazza Grande and adjoining streets the first Sunday of each month and the preceding Saturday. More than 500 vendors come from around Italy to sell an appealing array of old furniture, silver, oil paintings, and other wares, at very good prices.

The **Giostra del Saracino** (giostradelsaracinoarezzo.it), a jousting contest between the four districts of the town, turns the clock back to medieval times twice a year in June and September. A lively procession through the streets to the accompaniment of trumpets and drums ends in Piazza Grande, where jousters on colorfully bedecked horses wield their lances against armor-plated dummies.

churches, palaces, and squares (15€, children 6–13 5€, 5 and under free), an excellent introduction to the city.

Exploring Arezzo

Arezzo's medieval core centers on the charmingly lopsided **Piazza Grande.** An elegant loggia by Giorgio Vasari anchors one side of the piazza, while the rest of the space drapes casually across the slope, with slanting cobblestones and an irregular shape. The Duomo crowns the hilltop, while next to it the green expanse of the Parco del Prato, with airy views of the countryside, surrounds a ruined 16th-century fortress. Near the Duomo, at Via dell'Oro 28, **Casa Petrarca** (museiarezzo.it/casa-petrarca; ✆ **331/565-0036**) preserves the home of Arezzo-born Francesco Petrarch, the early Renaissance poet and scholar; it's now an academic institution with a fine collection of medieval manuscripts and historic coins on display. Admission is 5€ adults, 3€ students and ages 17 and under; it's open daily 9:30am to 6:30pm (Oct–Mar Sat–Sun only, 10:30am–5:30pm).

Basilica di San Domenico ♥♥ CHURCH Within this stunningly plain Gothic church from 1275 is one of Arezzo's many art treasures, a crucifix by Cimabue (1240–1302). The painter's lifelike portrayals were a break from the flat Byzantine style of his time, and he's considered to have led the way into the Renaissance. Cimabue was a nickname that means "bull-headed." He was famously arrogant and haughty and is mentioned in Dante's *Divine Comedy* as repenting for his pride. Supposedly Cimabue was so averse to disapproval that he would destroy any of his works that attracted criticism. Fortunately this crucifix, one of the great masterpieces of the Middle Ages, was not one of them.

Piazza San Domenico. ✆ **0575/22906.** Free admission. Mon–Sat 10am–1pm and 2–7pm; Sun 12:30–7pm.

Basilica di San Francesco ♥♥♥ CHURCH Piero della Francesca's *Legend of the True Cross* is reason enough to come to Arezzo. One of the greatest artists of the Renaissance painted one of the world's greatest fresco cycles, in a league with the Sistine Chapel, between 1452 and 1466. The 10 panels are remarkable for their grace, narrative detail, compositional precision, perfect perspective, depth of humanity, and dramatic light effects—"the most perfect morning light in all Renaissance painting," wrote art historian Kenneth Clark. The full religious significance of the story may escape you, but with stalwart knights and fair ladies, the scenes seem like a medieval romance. The beauty is in the details: heaving bosoms, pouty lips, and dreamy eyes, along with some wonderful ancient and medieval finery. You may have seen these frescoes in the film *The English Patient,* when Kip hoists Hana up to them by means of ropes and pulleys and we see her delight and wonder as she comes face to face with

Piero della Francesca's masterful fresco cycle in Arezzo's Basilica di San Francesco.

Piero's colorful ladies and gents. You'll feel the same, even when earthbound and jostling for a good look with your co-viewers.

Piazza San Francesco. museiarezzo.it/affreschi-di-piero-della-francesca. ✆ **0575/20059.** Church: Free admission. Della Francesca cycle: 9€ adults, 5€ students and ages 12–16, free for children 11 and under; timed-entry tickets (30 min.) only; reservations required by phone, website, or in person. Mon–Tues and Thurs–Sat 9am–7pm (until 6pm Nov–Mar); Sun 1–6pm (until 5:30pm Nov–Mar).

Casa di Vasari ♥♥ HISTORIC HOUSE Giorgio Vasari was born in Arezzo in 1511, just as the Renaissance was flowering all around him. Though he never achieved the greatness of many of the other artists working around him, Vasari helped define the period in his writings and may have even coined the term "Renaissance" for the creative period that led Europe out of the Dark Ages. An architect as well an artist—he designed the Galleria degli Uffizi in Florence (p. 179)—Vasari is best known for *Lives of the Most Excellent Painters, Sculptors and Architects,* a rather juicy account of the great masters, many of whom Vasari knew personally. He settled down here in his hometown in 1540 and set about frescoing the walls and ceilings of his gracious house with classical themes and portraits. In the Room of Celebrities, Vasari painted portraits of Michelangelo, Andrea del Sarto, and other notable contemporaries, surrounding himself with the cultural greats of his day. Vasari's copious correspondence,

LEGEND OF THE true cross

Piero della Francesca based his great Arezzo frescoes on a story from Jacopo da Varazze's 1260 *Golden Legend*, a compilation of saintly lore that was a wildly popular medieval bestseller.

As the story goes, Seth, son of Adam, planted on his father's grave the seeds from the apple tree that had led to his parents' fall from Eden; timbers from the tree were eventually made into a bridge. Many years later, the much-mythologized Queen of Sheba was crossing the bridge and recognized that the wood had special significance. She predicted to Solomon, king of Israel, that a savior would one day be hung from the timbers and cause the downfall of the Jewish nation. Solomon prudently had the wood buried but Romans inevitably discovered the beams and used them to crucify Christ.

Two centuries later, Roman emperor Constantine the Great saw the cross in a vision, emblazoned the image on his army's shields, defeated his co-emperor Maxentius, and converted to Christianity. His mother, Helen, went in search of the true cross in Jerusalem. Fragments of the Cross became popular religious relics. It's a convoluted story, but in the hands of Piero della Francesca, the twists and turns become riveting.

including 17 letters from Michelangelo, is sometimes on view. Part of the beautiful garden remains, and like the rest of the house provides a glimpse of a cultured Renaissance lifestyle.

Casa di Vasari: Via XX Settembre 55. museiarezzo.it/museo-casa-vasari. ✆ **0575/409040.** Admission 7€ adults, 5€ students and ages 17 and under. Mon and Wed–Sat 9am–7:30pm; Sun 9am–1:30pm.

Duomo di Arezzo (Cattedrale dei Santi Pietro e Donato) ♥♥ CATHEDRAL As you step inside the coldly stark interior of this big, austere Gothic hall, the first thing to catch your eye will be the stained-glass windows by Guillaume de Marcillat (1470–1529), a French master summoned to Rome to work for the popes, who spent the last 10 years of his life in Arezzo creating these seven magnificent windows depicting Biblical scenes. Beneath these colorful tableaux are some other fine works: a robust Mary Magdalene portrayed in a fresco by Piero Della Francesca in an arch near the sacristy door; stone-carved battle scenes on the tomb of Guido Tarlati, an Aretine bishop who died in 1327; and in the chapel on the left near the entrance, a series of terra cottas by Andrea della Robbia showing the Assumption, the Crucifixion, and a Madonna and Child.

Piazza del Duomo. ✆ **0575/23991.** Free admission. Daily 6:30am–7pm.

Santa Maria della Pieve ♥♥ CHURCH Most great churches are intended to draw the eye heavenward, but few achieve the effect quite as dramatically as this 12th-century arched facade. Three stacked arcades of beige stone subtly narrow as they rise above a five-arched lower floor and the street below; above it all rises a bell tower with five rows of windows. The effect is all the more powerful since the church sits on a slope. Inside is an altarpiece by Pietro Lorenzetti, a Sienese artist who perished in the Black Death in 1348 and whose best-known works are frescoes in the lower church of the Basilica of San Francesco in Assisi (p. 326). Remains of the town's patron saint, Donato, a 4th-century bishop of Arezzo, are here, too, in a beautiful gold reliquary.

Corso Italia 7. ✆ **0575/377678.** Free admission. Daily 8am–noon and 3–6:30pm.

Where to Stay in Arezzo

B&B Antiche Mura ♥♥♥ This tall, narrow house dating from the 1200s is tucked into the town walls just a few steps below the Duomo. Rock outcroppings, stone walls, glass walkways over ancient foundations, and an old olive press celebrate the heritage, while sleek, simple furnishings, bright white walls, and splashes of color reflect the modern sensibility of the hosts, siblings Patrizio and Barbara. Each room is named and styled after a famous woman in literature or the movies, from Madame Bovary's period decor to the sensual reds in the Marilyn Monroe room.

Piaggia di Murello 35. antichemura.it. ✆ **0575/20410.** 6 units. 65€–80€ double. Breakfast 5€. Free parking nearby. **Amenities:** Free Wi-Fi.

Graziella Patio Hotel ♥♥ Decor in this old palace a stone's throw from the church of San Francesco is based on the travel essays of the late Bruce Chatwin, and his presence adds romance and drama to the hotel's many comforts. The Colonial India room, with bright yellow walls and a four-poster bed, seems distinctly suited to the palatial surroundings, and the Moroccan room, with beautiful glazed-tile walls, is as colorful as the town's famous frescoes. Three especially extravagant rooms are on a

PAY HOMAGE TO piero

Piero della Francesco, whose *Legend of the True Cross* graces Arezzo's Basilica di San Francesco, was a visionary whose figures appear as vivid, thriving beings even 500 years after he committed them to canvas. The master's *Madonna del Prato* hangs in the little museum in **Monterchi,** 28km (16 miles) east of Arezzo on SS73. The painting is rare in Italian art in that it depicts a heavily pregnant Virgin Mary—she holds her hand against her side to support her belly, and if you happen to be in the same condition, the 7€ admission fee is waived (madonnadelparto.it; ✆ **0575/70713;** Mar–Sept daily 9am–1pm and 2–7pm, Oct–Feb 10am–1pm and 2–5pm). **Sansepolcro,** 15km (9 miles) farther north on SS73, houses another of Piero's great works, a 1468 *Resurrection of Christ* that British writer Aldous Huxley called "the greatest picture." In World War II, a British officer demanded that shelling of the town cease lest the painting be damaged, and the transcendent work remains in the **Museo Civico** (www.museocivicosansepolcro.it; ✆ **0575/732218;** 8€ adults, 3€ ages 11–18, free for children 10 and under; daily 10am–1pm and 2:30–6pm).

lower floor that opens to a hidden garden: One has a hot tub the size of a small swimming pool, and another has a huge sunken bathtub reached by a staircase behind the bed.

Via Cavour 23. hotelpatio.it. ✆ **0575/401962.** 10 units. 130€–150€ double. Rates include breakfast. **Amenities:** Spa services; free Wi-Fi.

Vogue Hotel ♥♥ With a name like this, a hotel had better be stylish, and these good-size and gracious rooms deliver on the promise, bringing comfort and sophistication to a centuries-old palace with rich fabrics, fine carpets, and handsome wood furnishings. Stone walls and beams accent rooms where huge soaking tubs are placed behind glass headboards, enormous showers have windows, and sitting areas are set into alcoves. Some rooms also provide a timeless view of the town's towers and rooftops, and all the sights are just steps away.

Via Guido Monaco 54. voguehotel.it. ✆ **0575/24361.** 26 units. 90€–135€ double. Rates include breakfast. **Amenities:** Bar; free Wi-Fi.

Where to Eat in Arezzo

Even in the rain, **Vasari Café** (✆ **0575/21945**) under the loggia on Piazza Grande is a prime spot to enjoy a pre-dinner glass of wine or aperitif while watching the comings and goings on the square. Good stops for a casual meal are **Dal Moro,** Via Cavour 68 (instagram.com/dalmoro.arezzo; ✆ **0575/043-208**), with creative sandwiches and a huge selection of local cheeses and cold cuts, and **Gastronomia il Cervo** (✆ **380/767-2553**), a food shop on Piazza San Francesco with a welcoming dining room upstairs. **Cremì,** Corso Italia 100 (✆ **333/976-6336**), dishes up the best artisan gelato in town, along with crepes with a choice of sweet fillings.

Antica Fonte ♥♥ TUSCAN Chef/owner Lucca sticks to Arezzo favorites in an attractive room at the edge of the historic center. That means down-to-earth Tuscan classics: homemade *pici* topped with thick sauces, *pasta patata* (a potato-stuffed ravioli), and rich stews and grilled meats—each carefully paired with choices from a cellar well stocked with wines from Tuscany and around the world.

Via Porta Buia 18. antica-fonte.eatbu.com. ✆ **0575/28038.** Main courses 10€–18€. Daily 12:30–3pm and 7:30–11pm.

Antica Osteria l'Agania ♥♥♥ TUSCAN Two floors of plain, brightly lit dining rooms bustle with locals. Pastas are homemade from organic ingredients, produce is market fresh, and the meat is from local farms. Daily specials on the ever-changing menu may include such local favorites as *trippa* (tripe) or eggs topped with fresh asparagus or *tartufo* (dried truffles), especially tasty when accompanied with a local Pinot Grigio, along with the house grappa to put the perfect finish on a meal.

Via Mazzini 10. agania.com. ✆ **0575/295-381.** Main courses 8€–12€. Wed–Sun noon–2:30pm and 7–10:30pm.

CORTONA ♥♥♥

34km (22 miles) S of Arezzo; 31km (19 miles) NE of Montepulciano

Draped across a green mountainside above terraced olive groves, austere-looking Cortona is a steep medieval city, where cut-stone staircases take the place of many streets. In recent years, the book and film *Under the Tuscan Sun* have brought more appreciative fans to town, but Cortona's appeal is timeless, and somber lanes and stage-set piazzas have survived the wave of popularity. Among the attractions are the chance to enjoy Tuscan hill-town life, some significant art treasures, and romantic, misty views over the wide Valdichiana.

Palazzo Comunale in Cortona.

Essentials

ARRIVING Cortona is on **rail** lines that run between Florence to the north and Perugia, Chiusi, and Rome to the south. The Camucia/Cortona train station (✆ **0575/603018**) is 5km (3 miles) below Cortona in the workaday town of Camucia, where many services are located as well. **Buses** run from here up to Piazza Garibaldi in Cortona about hourly. You can buy a ticket at Bar Stazione (1.50€) or pay on the bus.

VISITOR INFORMATION You'll find a **tourist office** at Piazza Signorelli 9, in the courtyard beyond the Museo dell'Accademia Etrusca ticket office (cortonaweb.net; ✆ **0575/637223;** daily 10am–6pm). Several paid-parking areas are just outside the city walls, including ones at Piazzale del Mercato and Porta Colonia, where you'll pay about 1€ an hour, and you can also park for free at designated spots around the city walls.

Exploring Cortona

Via Nazionale, known as the Rugapiana ("flat street," since it's the only one in town that even comes close to fitting that description), runs west–east through the medieval town from Piazza Garibaldi to **Piazza della Repubblica,** presided over by a stern city hall loaded with towers, a stone staircase, and wooden balconies. The northern corner of the square leads into **Piazza Signorelli,** named for the town's famous Renaissance artist, Luca Signorelli (1445–1523). This piazza was once the headquarters of

Cortona's Florentine governors, whose coats of arms adorn the Casali Palace (now home to the excellent Etruscan museum; see p. 273). From here, streets lead down to the **Piazza del Duomo** and a treasure trove of art in the **Museo Diocesano** (Diocesan Museum; p. 274). Other streets climb steeply uphill from Via Nazionale through the upper town to the **Basilica di Santa Margherita** (✆ **0575/605064**), where the embalmed body of the namesake patron—to which the centuries have not been terribly kind—lies in full view in a lavish 14th-century tomb above the main altar. Margaret, the former mistress of a lord from Montepulciano, was a follower of St. Francis who devoted her life to caring for the sick and poor. Admission is free; the church is open daily 7am to 7:30pm (slightly shorter hours in winter). On the climb up, you can admire 15 modern mosaics depicting the Stations of the Cross by Cortona's Futurist artist Gino Severini (1883–1966).

Even higher is the hilltop **Fortezza di Girifalco** (fortezzadelgirifalco.it; ✆ **0575/637235;** admission 5€, 3€ seniors and students), defenses built over ancient foundations in 1556 on the orders of Duke Cosimo di Medici, under whom Cortona was a prosperous city; aside from housing a military garrison, the keep, bastions, and vaulted galleries have served as an orphanage and a World War II German radio headquarters. Today the fort hosts cultural events and has an excellent wine bar. Admission to the fortress is 5€ (open daily 10am–8pm mid-June to Aug, closes at 6 or 7pm spring and fall; open Sat–Sun only Nov to mid-Mar, 10am to 5 or 6pm). From Piazza Signorelli you can stay on level ground and walk east along Via Nazionale to airy **Piazza Garibaldi** and just beyond into public gardens with views south to Lago Trasimeno in Umbria and west across the Valdichiana to Montepulciano.

Church of San Francesco ♥♥ CHURCH This simple Romanesque church with its wood-raftered ceiling is the second Franciscan church ever built (the first, in St. Francis' hometown of Assisi, was begun around 1228, while this one dates to 1245). The church houses the tomb of Brother Elias of Cortona, who administered the Franciscan Order after Francis's death in 1226, as well as three precious relics of St. Francis himself—his tunic, his manuscript of the New Testament, and a cushion he often used. On the high altar is the Reliquary of the Holy Cross, an ornate 10th-century ivory tablet said to contain a fragment of Christ's cross, presented to Elias by the Byzantine Emperor in 1244. The artist Luca Signorelli, who died in Cortona in 1523, is believed to be buried in the crypt.
Via Berrettini. ✆ **0575/402-7226.** Free admission. Daily 9am–12:30pm and 3–4:30pm.

Eremo le Celle ♥♥♥ RELIGIOUS SITE St. Francis passed through Cortona in 1211, on his way to a mountainside hermitage 3km (2 miles) outside of town. Francis' companion Brother Elias then took up residence in one of the caves and redid the place into a bona fide monastery, which it remains to this day, home to a small community of monks and a place of solitary retreat for the religious. The honey-colored stone dwellings, forest paths, bubbling streams, and simple, rock-hewn chapels are bucolic and humbling, and the walk out from town is a delight. From Piazza Mazzini, outside Porta Colonia, walk northeast (to the right as you leave the gate) for about 500 feet to a gravel road on the left that skirts olive groves high above the baroque church of Santa Maria Nuova. At the entrance to a villa garden you will come to a fork; follow the road on the right to the Celle. If driving, follow SP34 northeast to a well-marked exit about 3km (2 miles) outside of town.

Localita Cappuccini 1. ✆ **0575/603362.** Donations welcome. Daily 7am–7pm (until 5pm in winter).

MAEC, Museo dell'Accademia Etrusca e Della Città di Cortona ♥♥ MUSEUM Cortona was one of the 12 cities of the Etruscan confederation, and so many artifacts from that era were discovered nearby that an Etruscan Academy was founded in 1727. The collection is still housed in the Palazzo Casali, a 13th-century mansion built for the city's governors. The lower galleries tackle the Etruscan and Roman history of Cortona, with lots of gold from excavated tombs and the enigmatic Cortona Tablet, a 200-word document inscribed in bronze. On the sprawling upper floors, the most intriguing object is a one-of-a-kind oil lamp, a large chandelier from the late 4th century B.C.E. decorated with human heads, allegorical figures, and a few virile Pans playing their pipes, all surrounding a leering Gorgon's head on the bottom. The museum also houses a small but worthy collection of sarcophagi and other Egyptian artifacts, and a couple of galleries are devoted to the work of painter Gino Severini (1883–1966). A Cortona native who embraced the European art movements of the early 20th century, Severini made his reputation in Paris and Rome but remained tied to his humble origins in his hometown. Several Etruscan tombs and the remains of a Roman villa, still being excavated, litter the Parco Archeologico, outside the hamlet of Sodo in the valley below town.

A detail from an ornate Etruscan chandelier at MAEC, Museo dell'Accademia Etrusca e Della Città di Cortona.

Piazza Signorelli 9. cortonamaec.org. ✆ **0575/637235.** Museum: 12€ adults, 8€ children 6–12, free for children 5 and under; 15€ and 10€ with Parco Archeologico. Apr–Oct daily 10am–7pm; Nov–Mar Tues–Sun 10am–5pm.

Museo Diocesano ♥♥♥ MUSEUM Almost every work in this small collection in the former Gesù church is a masterpiece. Pride of place, however, belongs to Fra' Angelico and Luca Signorelli. The Fra' Angelico gem is a splendid 1436 altarpiece of *The Annunciation,* graced by his mastery of perspective and command of detail—notice the angel's precious garment embroidered in gold, the Virgin's elaborate robes, and the carpet of wildflowers (the new Eden) on which her house sits. Luca Signorelli, who was born in Cortona around 1450 and whose masterpiece is the fresco cycle in Orvieto's duomo (p. 343), is represented by a vividly detailed *Deposition* originally painted for Cortona's cathedral in 1502. The painter instilled his figure of Christ with so much realism and passion that legend claims he modeled it on his own son, who'd died of the plague that same year. Signorelli's *Communion of the Apostles* (1512) in the same room shows the artist's strong sense of architectural space. Notice Judas in the foreground, hiding the communion host in his purse—ashamed of his imminent betrayal, he can't swallow it.

Via Mura del Duomo. cortonatuseibellezza.it. ✆ **0575/877-3610.** Admission 8€ adults, 6€ children ages 6–12, free for children 5 and under. Apr–Oct daily 10:30am–6:30pm, Nov–Mar Fri–Sun 10am–5pm. Duomo (adjacent) Apr–Oct daily 8am–7:30pm, Nov–Mar daily 8:30am–6:30pm.

Where to Stay in Cortona

Some of Cortona's most reasonably priced accommodations are in a convent and retreat house, **Villa Santa Margherita,** just a few minutes' walk from the town center at Viale Cesare Battisti 17 (villasantamargherita cortona.it; ✆ **0575/082440**). Spartan but pleasant doubles begin at about 105€.

Casa Zeni ♥♥♥ You'll take to hill-town life easily in one of these charming, stone-walled apartments in a meticulously restored medieval house in the center of town. Apartments sleep from three to six guests in great style, with contemporary furniture that blends well with rustic tile floors and wood-beamed ceilings. Amenities include kitchens, washer/dryers, superb beds, and beautifully equipped bathrooms. Hosts Silvia and Cristian provide caring hospitality and a wealth of handy advice.

Via Maccari 21. casazeni.com. ✆ **338/830-7737.** 3 units. 95€–140€ double. 2-night min. stay; discounts for stays of 1 week or longer. Rates include breakfast at nearby cafe. **Amenities:** Free Wi-Fi.

Hotel Italia ♥♥ This 15th-century palace is not as grand as the neighboring San Michele (see below), but the hospitality hits the same high notes. Piazza Signorelli is just steps away, and the relaxed ambience suits Cortona's small-town pace. Spacious rooms are plain but atmospheric, with tasteful rustic wood furnishings, beamed ceilings, and other architectural flourishes. Only a few have views, but guests can enjoy panoramic vistas from the top-floor breakfast room or the roof terrace.

Via Ghibellina 5–7. hotelitaliacortona.com. ✆ **0575/630254.** 17 units. 90€–110€ double. Rates include breakfast. **Amenities:** Free Wi-Fi.

Hotel San Michele ♥♥ In this 15th-century *palazzo* in the center of town, the salons and high-ceilinged guest rooms, a few frescoed and paneled, recall Cortona's prosperous and noble past. Tile-floored rooms are appealingly, rather grandly furnished; some have views over the valley below, a choice few, including tower suites, from their own terraces. A roof terrace with the same vistas is open to all guests, as is a decidedly medieval-looking courtyard. The San Michele also operates **Villa Borgo San Pietro** (borgosanpietro.com; ✆ **0575/612402**), 4km (2½ miles) outside town in San Pietro a Cegliolo, with a countrified take on grand living—14 rooms and five apartments set amid 7 acres of olive trees and lavender, with a swimming pool (from 120€ a night, closed mid-Oct to mid-Apr).

Via Guelfa 15. hotelsanmichele.net. ✆ **0575/604348.** 42 units. 120€–130€ double. Rates include breakfast. Closed Nov to mid-Mar. **Amenities:** Bar; free Wi-Fi.

Monastero di Cortona ♥♥ A flourishing monastery in the 15th century, this walled compound clinging to a hillside high up in town has now been transformed into a tranquil and luxurious getaway, full of frescoes, loggias, and vaulted ceilings; plush furnishings transform the small but elegant quest quarters into luxurious havens. A lavish spa is tucked away in a Roman-era cistern, and a gemlike garden with a plunge pool hangs above the valley below. On the premises are the Gli Affreschi restaurant, awash in frescoes, and the more informal Osteria di Santo; shops and other restaurants are a short downhill walk away.

Via del Salvatore. monasterodicortona.com. ✆ **0575/178-5839.** 36 units. 330€-470€ double. Rates include breakfast. Closed Dec to mid-Mar. **Amenities:** 2 restaurants, bar, spa, pool; free Wi-Fi.

Relais Il Falconiere ♥♥ When Riccardo Baracchi inherited a farm from his grandmother, he and his wife, Sylvia, created a stylish and sophisticated retreat, with antiques-filled rooms scattered among a villa and stone farmhouses. Beamed ceilings and terra-cotta floors befit the rural setting, with a pool and gardens amid 20 acres of olive groves and vineyards. A luxurious spa with a walled garden enhances the sense of relaxation. Sylvia oversees one of the best restaurants in the area, serving refined Tuscan food in the refitted lemon house.

San Martino (3km/2 miles north of Cortona). ilfalconiere.it. ✆ **0575/612616.** 15 units. 380€–440€ double. Rates include breakfast. Closed Mid-Nov to Mar. **Amenities:** Restaurant; bar; 2 swimming pools; spa; free Wi-Fi.

Spend Time in a Tuscan Kitchen

Chef Ryan Hanley (cookingclassestuscany.com; ✆ **388/100-3342**) teaches Tuscan cooking in his home kitchen just below Cortona in Pergo; the 3- to 4-hour-long lunch or dinner sessions end with a leisurely meal accompanied by local wines. Ryan also prepares four-course lunches and dinners, served at his house or yours, and he and his Arezzo-born wife, Debora, lead tours of vineyards around Cortona and across the valley near Montepulciano. Classes are 195€ a person; meals 75€ a person; tour prices vary.

6 | Cortona | TUSCANY

Where to Eat in Cortona

A walk through town usually includes a stop at **Molesini,** Piazza della Repubblica 3 (molesini-market.com; ✆ **0575/62544**), a wine shop with a good selection from Cortona vineyards, where Syrah grapes are producing increasingly sophisticated yields. **Enoteca Enotria,** Via Nazionale 81 (✆ **0575/603595**), sells wine by the glass and sandwiches, making the rustic room a popular hangout well into the late evening. **Il Solco,** Via Guelfa 1, is a friendly spot for a cocktail or glass of wine.

Osteria al Teatro ♥♥♥ TUSCAN Chef Emiliano Rossi and his staff lay on the charm in three character-filled, candlelit rooms brimming with antiques and old prints. All the good things of the palate come together in these amiable surroundings: excellent wines from a vast cellar, including many Cortona vintages, and a thoughtful and innovative menu, which presents beef from the Valdichiana in many different ways (look for truffle pairings in season). End the meal with a carving board of house-made chocolate (not available in warmer months).

Via Maffei 2. osteria-del-teatro.it. ✆ **0575/630556.** Main courses 12€–24€. Thurs–Tues 12:30–2:30pm and 7:30–9:30pm.

Ristorante la Loggetta ♥♥ TUSCAN/GRILL You would probably be happy eating canned spaghetti while savoring the outlook over the Piazza della Repubblica from this restaurant's namesake loggia, or for that matter, dining under the enchanting stone-and-brick vaults inside. It's a moot point, because the food here is very well done, nicely served, and hits a high point with beef from the Valdichiana in a rich red-wine reduction. If you're a Conan O'Brien fan, enjoy a clip of his visit to la Loggetta with his producer Jordan Schlansky (youtube.com/watch?v=N7hlIbJkvUQ).

Piazza di Pescheria. laloggetta.com. ✆ **0575/630575.** Main courses 9€–28€. Thurs–Tues noon–2:30pm and 7–11pm. Closed Jan.

Trattoria Dardano ♥♥ TUSCAN/GRILL Cortonans (including the *carabinieri* from their headquarters across the street) come to these welcoming rooms for meat roasted over a charcoal fire, with the emphasis on *bistecca alla fiorentina* from cattle raised in the valley below town (generally considered the best beef in Italy). *Pollo* (chicken), *anatra* (duck), *maiale* (pork), and *faraona* (guinea hen) also go onto the flames. The heaping platters are usually preceded by *crostini neri* (little black toasts), with chicken liver, some local salami, and often *ribollita,* the thick Tuscan soup, all accompanied by local wine.

Via Dardano 24. trattoriadardano.com. ✆ **0575/601944.** Main courses 8€–18€. Thurs–Tues noon–3pm and 6:30–11pm.

Cortona Shopping

Cortona produces its own distinctive ceramics, in warm, creamy yellows and pleasant greens. You'll find these handsome wares at **Terrabruga,** Via Nazionale 54 (terrabruga.com; ✆ **0575/605099**), which ships its finely crafted tableware anywhere. **Il Pozzo** ("the Old Well") is a treasure trove of well-curated photography and art by local artists, alongside leather goods, handcrafted paper, and much more, shown off in historic surroundings at Via Nazionale 10/12 (✆ **0575/603730**). From a swanky showroom in a medieval olive mill at Vicolo Corazzi 17, off Piazza della Repubblica, **DelBrenna** (delbrennajewelry.com; ✆ **0575/630640**) sells distinctive jewelry, including signature chains embellished with gemstones and ancient coins, as well as handmade shoes.

SAN GIMIGNANO ♥♥

42km (26 miles) NW of Siena, 52km (32 miles) SW of Florence

In the 12th and 13th centuries, more than 70 towers rose above the tile roofs of San Gimignano, built partly to defend against outside invaders but mostly as status symbols for San Gimignano's powerful families. A dozen towers remain, and as you approach across the rolling countryside, they give the town the look of a fantasy kingdom—lending credence to such nicknames as "Manhattan of the Middle Ages" and "City of Beautiful Towers." Once inside the gates, the Manhattan reference seems all too apt, with visitors shoulder-to-shoulder in its narrow lanes, obliterating the medieval aura you've come to savor. Almost everyone traveling the hill-town circuit makes a stop here, while bus tours pour in from Siena and Florence, and Italians arrive on weekend outings. If you want to be swept back to the Middle Ages, you're best visiting midweek in off-season, or late on weekday afternoons after the buses have pulled out. Aside from a surfeit of medieval atmosphere, you'll also enjoy some especially pleasing frescoes and other works of art.

Essentials

ARRIVING San Gimignano does not have a train station, but dozens of daily **trains** run between Siena and Florence and **Poggibonsi,** from where more than 30 buses make the 25-minute run to San Gimignano Monday through Saturday; only six buses run on Sunday.

It's more convenient to travel to San Gimignano on buses operated by **Autolinee Toscana** (at-bus.it). They run hourly (fewer on Sun) for most of the day from **Florence** (50 min.) to Poggibonsi and Colle di Val d'Elsa; many immediately connect with buses to San Gimignano (20–25 min. farther). From **Siena** there are 10 daily direct buses to San Gimignano (a 1¼ hr. journey) Monday through Saturday; on Sunday you'll have to connect in Poggibonsi.

Arriving by **car,** take the Poggibonsi Nord exit off the **Florence-Siena** highway or the SS2. San Gimignano is 12km (7½ miles) from Poggibonsi. Parking is tight, and the *centro storico* is off-limits to most vehicles. Read signs carefully, since many spots are reserved for residents, and some only allow parking for 1 hour. The most convenient parking is at **Parcheggio P2 Montemaggio,** outside the Porta San Giovanni (3€ first hour, 2.50€ second hour, 2€ each successive hour, 15€ a day; comune.sangimignano.si.it/it/page/p2-montemaggio). You can easily walk into town from here.

VISITOR INFORMATION The **tourist office** at Piazza Duomo 1 (sangimignano.com; ✆ **0577/940008**) is open daily 10am to 1pm and 3 to 7pm (Nov–Feb 10am–1pm and 2–6pm). From March through October and 2 weeks in December, guided walks (20€) of the town depart from outside the office Monday through Saturday at 10:30am and 5pm (sometimes also 9:30pm in summer) and Sunday at 5pm. The office also leads walks in the hills around town at varying times, depending on demand, with fees from 20€ to 25€, depending on the walk. The office books accommodations.

Exploring San Gimignano

You'll see the town at its lively best if you come on a Thursday or Saturday morning, when the interlocking **Piazza della Cisterna** and **Piazza del Duomo** fill with market stalls. Piazza della Cisterna is named for the well at its center that for centuries was a repository for rainwater channeled from rooftops—a reliable source of water that could not be contaminated by events outside the city walls. For a little more solitude, head up from the Duomo to the well-marked **Rocca e Parco di Montestaffoli,** filling the shell of the town's 14th-century fortress, where you can find greenery and views of town and countryside, all the better from the little tower in the far corner. Another refreshing vantage point, with views for miles across the rolling countryside, is the walkway atop the **town walls,** a circuit of about 1½ miles. You can access it from any of the four gates; **Porta delle Fonti,** at the east end of town, is an especially scenic entry point, as just outside the portal are romantically arched medieval fountains. Step into **San Gimignano 1300** (Via Costarella 3; sangimignano1300.com; ✆ **327/4395165;** free admission) for an enchanting look at how the town appeared in medieval times—not much different actually. The detailed ceramic model shows the town with many more towers still standing.

Piazza della Cisterna in San Gimignano.

Chiesa di Sant'Agostino ♥♥ CHURCH An especially appropriate presence in this 13th-century church at the north end of town is St. Sebastian, the "saint who was martyred twice." As a stop along trade routes and the Via Francigena pilgrimage trail, San Gimignano was decimated by the plague time and again; this gave residents a special fondness for the 3rd-century Saint Sebastian, who also was prone to repeated bad fortune. In 1464, after surviving yet another plague, the town hired Florentine painter Benozzo Gozzoli to paint a thankful scene. As the fresco shows, when Sebastian first proclaimed his faith, the emperor Diocletian ordered that he be taken to a field and shot full of arrows. Sebastian miraculously survived and was nursed back to health, but he tempted fate again by haranguing Diocletian as he passed in royal procession; the emperor had him bludgeoned to death on the spot. Gozzoli also frescoed the choir behind the main altar with scenes from the life of St. Augustine, a worldly scholar who, faced with the decision to give up his concubine, famously prayed, "Grant me continence and chastity but not just yet." The scenes are rich in landscape and architectural detail.

Piazza Sant'Agostino, 10. conventosantagostino.it. ✆ **0577/904313.** Free admission. Apr–Oct daily 9am–noon and 3–7pm; Nov–Mar daily 9am–noon and 3–6pm (opens 10:30am Sun).

Collegiata di Santa Maria Assunta ♥♥ CHURCH San Gimignano's main church is awash in frescoes. To the left of the main door, a gruesome *Last Judgment* by Sienese artist Taddeo di Bartolo (1410) shows mean-looking little devils taunting tortured souls. (Bartolo allegedly modeled some of the characters after townsfolk who rubbed him the wrong way.) Much of the nave is covered in flat, two-dimensional frescoes of the Sienese school—a comic-strip-like Poor Man's Bible, illustrating familiar stories for the illiterate faithful. The left wall is frescoed with scenes from the Old Testament (look for the panel showing the pharaoh and his army being swallowed by the Red Sea), and the right wall features the New Testament (a very shifty-looking Judas receives his 30 pieces of silver for betraying Christ). The best frescoes in the church are in the tiny **Cappella di Santa Fina,** where Domenico Ghirlandaio decorated the walls with airy scenes of the life of Fina—a local girl who, though never officially canonized, is one of San Gimignano's patron saints. Little Fina was so devout that when she fell ill with paralysis, she refused a bed and lay instead on a board, never complaining even when worms and rats fed off her decaying flesh. As you'll see in one of the panels, St. Gregory foretold the exact day (his feast day, Mar 12) when Fina would die. She expired right on schedule and began working miracles immediately—all the bells in town rang spontaneously at the moment of her death, and yellow violets sprang from her pallet.

Piazza del Duomo. duomosangimignano.it. ✆ **0577/286-300.** Admission 10€ adults, 8€ ages 6–18, or 15€ (12€ ages 6–17) with Palazzo Comunale, Torre Grossa, and church of San Lorenzo in Ponte; free for children 5 and under. Mon–Fri 10am–7:30pm, Sat 10am–5pm, Sun 12:30–7:30pm (Nov–Mar closes daily 5pm).

Palazzo Comunale & Torre Grossa ♥♥ MUSEUM The late-13th-century home of the city government, also known as Palazzo del Popolo, is topped with San Gimignano's tallest tower, the aptly named Torre Grossa (Big Tower), finished in 1311. Your reward for a climb to the top will be views of the cityscape and rolling countryside of the Val d'Elsa. (***Tip:*** Save your knees and enjoy the same outlook for free by making the gentler 5-min. climb uphill from Piazza del Duomo to the ruined Rocca.) Inside the *palazzo*'s **Camera del Podestà** (Room of the Mayor) are San Gimignano's most famous frescoes, Memmo di Filippuccio's *Scenes of Married Life*. In one scene, a couple takes a bath together, and in the other, the scantily clad fellow climbs into bed beside his naked wife; on the opposite wall, a young man is seduced and robbed by several women and Aristotle cavorts with a courtesan, suggesting the cycle was meant to show the dangerous power of lust over reason and contentment. The *Coppo di Marcovaldo Crucifix*, in the adjoining painting gallery, is an astonishingly touching work in which a vulnerably human figure of Christ is surrounded by six intricate little scenes of the Crucifixion. The artist, Coppo, was a Florentine soldier who was captured by the Sienese; they soon realized what a treasure they had in him and put him to work. His masterpieces show a transition from flat Byzantine style to more varied texture and three-dimensionality. The head of St. Fina (see the Collegiata; p. 279) is kept in the **Tabernacle of Santa Fina** (1402), painted with scenes of the teenage saint's ability to heal wounds and other miracles. Taddeo di Bartolo (see his terrifying *Last Judgment* in the Collegiata; p. 279) painted the *Life of St. Gimignano* for this room. St. Gimignano was a 5th-century bishop of Modena who miraculously spared the little

Civic Art

Towers and medieval ambience aside, you'll also discover that San Gimignano is full of frescoes and other art—in churches, public buildings, and even outdoors. In **Piazza Pecori,** reached through the archway to the left of the Collegiata's facade, is a fresco of the *Annunciation,* possibly painted in 1482 by the Florentine Domenico Ghirlandaio, who also painted the Santa Fina frescoes in the Collegiata (p. 279). The door to the right of the tourist office leads into a courtyard of the **Palazzo del Commune,** where Taddeo di Bartolo's 14th-century *Madonna and Child* is flanked by two works on the theme of justice by Sodoma. The simple 13th-century **church of San Lorenzo in Ponte** (Via Santo Stefano 8) features several frescoes depicting the life of St. Benedict (in one scene, he almost gives in to temptation and accepts a loaf of poisoned bread); entry to this church is included in cumulative tickets that also include the Collegiata and Palazzo Comunale (see above). **Galleria Continua** adds contemporary art to the mix, showcasing well-known and emerging artists in a rambling complex that includes a former cinema, a tower, a cellar, and an old apartment (Via Del Castello 11; galleriacontinua.com; ✆ **0577/943134;** free admission; daily 10am–1pm and 2–7pm).

town then known as Silvia from a barbarian attack. The grateful citizenry changed their town's name to honor the saint, who is depicted cradling his namesake town in his lap, towers and all.

Piazza del Duomo. sangimignanomusei.it. ✆ **0577/286300.** Admission 10€ adults, 8€ ages 6–17 (also includes church of San Lorenzo in Ponte), or 15€ (12€ ages 6–17) with Collegiata; free for children 5 and under. Apr–Oct daily 10am–7:30pm; Nov–Mar Mon–Fri 11am–5:30pm, Sat–Sun 11am–6pm.

Where to Stay & Eat in San Gimignano

San Gimignano's slightly peppery, dry white wine, **Vernaccia di San Gimignano,** is the only DOCG white in Tuscany, and has quite a provenance, too: It's cited in Dante's *Divine Comedy.* A relaxing place to sip a glass or two is **diVinorum,** former stables with a small terrace at Via degli Innocenti 5 (divinorumwinebar.com; ✆ **0577/907192**). Combine a glass with a choice of panini and focaccia, along with some pastas and meat courses, at **Dal Toscano Sapori e Tradizione,** in tranquil Vicolo dell'Oro (✆ **338/347-1107**). At the famous **Gelateria Dondoli ♥**, Piazza della Cisterna 4 (gelateriadondoli.com; ✆ **0577/942244**), master gelato maker Sergio offers creative combinations like refreshing Champelmo, with sparkling wine and pink grapefruit, and *crema di Santa Fina,* made with saffron and pine nuts. The shop also conducts 2-hour gelato-making classes in the morning, booked through the website with prices on request.

Chiribiri ♥♥ ITALIAN This tiny, vaulted cellar, with a welcoming patio almost next to the walls, seems more serious about what it sends out of the kitchen than do many of the more expensive, more touristic spots in the center of town. Ravioli with pumpkin, white beans, and sage; beef in Chianti; wild boar stew; and other Tuscan classics are done very well and served without fuss in convivial surroundings.

Piazzetta della Madonna 1. ✆ **0577/941948.** Main courses 8€–14€. Daily 11am–4pm and 6–10pm.

Hotel La Cisterna ♥♥ The ivy-clad entrance on the town square has been a welcoming sight in San Gimignano for centuries, and quarters that once housed pilgrims on the Via Francigena now accommodate guests in rooms that vary considerably in size and outlook. Some smaller ones overlook a courtyard, and many larger ones open to balconies with views that extend for miles. Furnishings are simply and unobtrusively traditional Tuscan, with wrought-iron bedsteads offset with flourishes like arches, tile floors, and stone walls. The **restaurant** (main courses 13€–28€; daily noon–3pm and 7–9:45pm) and terrace, along with a view-filled, glassed-in dining room upstairs, serve Tuscan food better than you'd expect, given the large tour groups that often pile in for lunch.

Piazza della Cisterna 24. hotelcisterna.it. ✆ **0577/940328.** 48 units. 130€–180€ double. Rates include breakfast. Closed Jan to mid-Mar. **Amenities:** Restaurant; bar; free Wi-Fi.

Hotel l'Antico Pozzo ♥♥♥ When this 15th-century *palazzo* was a convent, the namesake "ancient well" served a grim purpose—young novices were dangled over the depths when they resisted *droit de seigneur*, the feudal rights of noblemen to have their way with young women living on their lands. The present incarnation is more enlightened, being all about taste, elegance, and comfort. Reached by a broad stone staircase (or an elevator), many of the character-filled rooms are beamed and frescoed and have nice views of the town and Rocca. All beautifully decorated, with classic furnishings that sometimes include canopied beds, along with fine prints and other appointments. A grassy garden is in the rear.
Via San Matteo 87. anticopozzo.com. ✆ **0577/942014.** 18 units. 120€–130€ double. Rates include breakfast. **Amenities:** Bar; free Wi-Fi.

Osteria delle Catene ♥♥ TUSCAN A medieval room accented with contemporary art is a welcoming setting for Tuscan classics that begin with thick *ribollita* and move through some innovative pastas that include *penne al porro* (stubby pasta quills in cheesy leek sauce), then onto hearty main courses such as *salsicce con fagioli all'uccelletto* (grilled sausage with beans stewed with tomatoes). The local hams and cheeses are carefully curated, as is a wine list of standout local Vernaccias.
Via Mainardi 18. osteriadellecatene.it. ✆ **0577/941966.** Main courses 15€–35€. Daily 11:30am–11pm.

VOLTERRA ♥♥

29km (18 miles) SW of San Gimignano, 50km (31 miles) W of Siena

You'll see Volterra, rising 540m (1,772 ft.) above the valley below, long before you arrive. In the words of British novelist D.H. Lawrence, the town perches "on a towering great bluff that gets all the winds and sees all the world." Lawrence came here to study relics of the Etruscans; Volterra, originally known as Velathri, was one of the largest cities in the Etruscan confederation. While many visitors come here to see Etruscan bronzes and alabaster urns, if you're a fan of Stephanie Meyer's teen vampire trilogy *Twilight,* you might also come to see the hometown of the Volturi vampire coven. Whatever brings you to Volterra, you'll soon find a richly atmospheric place that's more focused on day-to-day life than on plying the tourist trade.

Essentials

ARRIVING Driving is the easiest way to get here: Volterra is on the SS68 about 30km (19 miles) from the Colle di Val d'Elsa exit on the Florence-Siena highway. From San Gimignano, head southwest on the road to Castel di San Gimignano, where you can pick up the SS68. You can park for free in a large lot below Porta Fiorentina, but you will pay a price—a climb up 350 steps to town. The well-marked La Dogana underground garage off Piazza Martiri della Libertà is handier, just a short walk from central Piazza dei Priori, and charges 2€ an hour.

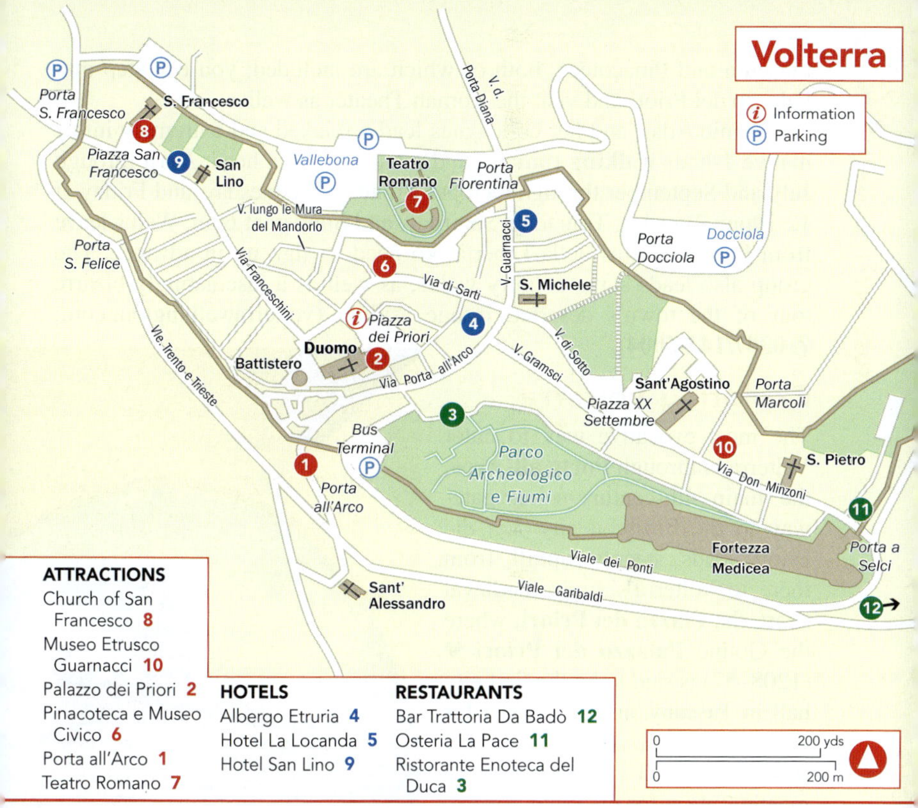

From **Siena,** some 16 daily **Tiemme buses** (tiemmespa.it; ✆ **199/168182**) make the 20- to 30-minute trip to **Colle di Val d'Elsa,** from which there are four daily buses to Volterra (50 min.). From **San Gimignano,** first take a bus to Poggibonsi (20 min.), then link up with those Colle di Val d'Elsa buses to Volterra. From **Florence,** take one of five daily buses (three on Sun) to Colle di Val d'Elsa and transfer there (2½–3 hr. total). From **Pisa,** take the train to Pontedera and change there for a bus operated by **Consorzio Pisano Trasporti** (**CPT;** pisa.cttnord.it; ✆ **800/570-530**) or **Autolinee Toscana** (at-bus.it; ✆ **800/142242**), depending on the time; total trip time is about 2 to 2½ hours. You can also take one of the **trains** that run six times a week from Pisa to Saline (1½ hr.) and transfer there to one of the hourly CPT buses that run up to Volterra (15 min.).

VISITOR INFORMATION Volterra's helpful **tourist office,** Piazza dei Priori 20 (volterratur.it; ✆ **0588/87257**), offers information and free hotel reservations. It's open daily 9:30am to 1pm and 2 to 6pm (until 7pm Aug–Sept). The office rents an audioguide (5€ for a handset) for an hourlong walk around town, providing some good tidbits about churches, palaces, and Etruscan and Roman remains along the way. The office's **Volterra Card** is worth the 15€ even if you're planning to see only the Etruscan museum and Pinacoteca, both of which are included; you can step into Palazzo dei Priori and visit the Roman Theater as well.

Annie Adair and her colleagues lead a relaxed and extremely informative 1-hour **walking tour** around town for 20€ a head, April through July and September through October Monday, Wednesday, and Friday at 12:30pm; Tuesday, Thursday, Saturday, and Sunday at 6pm. Walks leave from Piazza Martiri della Libertà; no need to sign up in advance. The group also leads some country walks, as well as a fascinatingly bizarre tour of the town's deserted insane asylum (volterrawalkingtour.com; ✆ **0347/143-5004**).

Exploring Volterra

Volterra's Gothic town hall, the Palazzo dei Priori.

The most evocative way to enter Volterra is through **Porta all'Arco,** the main 4th-century-B.C.E. gateway to the Etruscan city. Via die Priori leads steeply uphill from there to Volterra's stony medieval heart, the **Piazza dei Priori,** where the Gothic **Palazzo dei Priori** ♥ (1208–57) is said to be the first city hall in Tuscany, and the model for Florence's Palazzo Vecchio; the frescoed council chamber is still a meeting place for the town government. A skull and crossbones outside the main hall handily sums up the medieval view of righteousness: "REMEMBER DIVINE JUDGEMENT AND YOU WILL NOT SIN FOR ALL ETERNITY." Magistrates meted out justice within the stately chamber, sometimes wasting no time in leveling sentences—guilty parties were promptly thrown from the mullioned windows. Two stone lions flanking the somber facade are symbols of the Florentines, who conquered Volterra in the early 14th century; inscribed in the stone are hatch marks marking the "canna volteranna," the city's medieval unit of measure with which goods were assessed and taxed. The squat tower in the eastern corner is festooned with a little pig (*porcellino*), hence its name, **Torre del Porcellino.** The beast is actually a boar, a symbol of strength for medieval residents—not only because of its robust heft but also because boars were plentiful in the surrounding woods and the mainstay of their diet (pasta with *ragù di cinghiale* and grilled boar are still menu favorites). The council chamber and bell tower are open daily 10am to 6:30pm (early Nov through mid-Mar Tues–Fri 10am–4pm and Sat–Sun 10am–6:30pm);

admission is 10€, 8€ seniors and ages 6 to 16 (free for children 5 and under), included with the Volterra Card.

Inside the modest-looking **Duomo ♥**, or Cattedrale di Santa Maria Assunta, around the corner (Piazza dei Priori; animadivolterra.it; ✆ **0588/88261**) is a life-size *Deposition from the Cross*, carved in wood around 1228 by anonymous Pisan masters and painted in bright colors. With their fluidity and emotional expressiveness, the figures look surprisingly contemporary. The Duomo is open 10am to 6pm daily (late Nov through Feb open Fri–Sun only); 8€ admission includes an audioguide plus entry to the Battistero and adjacent 12th-century hospital of Santa Maria Maddalena, now an art gallery.

The **church of San Francesco ♥**, across town and just inside the Porta San Francesco, is worth the walk for one reason: Halfway up the right aisle is the Cappella Croce del Giorno, frescoed with the *Legend of the True Cross* in medieval Technicolor by Cenni di Francesco in 1410. Cenni's version of this popular medieval tale pales in comparison to Piero della Francesca's take on the legend in Arezzo (p. 266), but his attempt is quite compelling and shows a knack for reproducing the dress and architecture of his era, with golden backgrounds, flattened space, and elongated figures with elegant features. The church is open daily 8:30am to 12:30pm and 3:30 to 6pm; admission is free.

Museo Etrusco Guarnacci ♥♥♥ MUSEUM Volterra's remarkable collection of Etruscan artifacts is a joyful celebration of the farmers, seafarers, and miners who flourished between the Tiber and Arno rivers from about 800 B.C.E. until their assimilation by Rome in the C.E. 1st century (the name "Tuscany" is derived from "Etruscan"). The bulk of the holdings are row after row of **Etruscan funerary urns,** most from the 3rd century B.C.E., but some from as early as the 7th century B.C.E. Note the elaborately carved lids, with finely dressed characters lounging with wine cups to offer to the gods, or horse and carriage rides into the underworld. One of the finest, the Urna degli Sposi, is a striking portrait of a husband and wife, somewhat dour-faced and full of wrinkles, together in death as in life. The Etruscans also crafted bronze sculptures, and one of the finest is a lanky young man with a beguiling smile known as the *Ombra della Sera* (Shadow of the Evening)—so called because the elongated shape looks like a shadow stretched in evening light.

Via Don Minzoni 15. comune.volterra.pi.it. ✆ **0588/86347.** Admission 10€ or free with the Volterra Card (p. 283), free for children 5 and under. Mid-Mar to early Nov daily 9am–7pm; Nov to mid-Mar Tues–Fri 10am–4pm and Sat–Sun 10am–6:30pm.

Pinacoteca e Museo Civico ♥♥ MUSEUM While much of Volterra preserves the Etruscan, Roman, and medieval past, the town's worthy painting gallery transports you to the Renaissance. Room 4 has a remarkably intact 1411 polyptych of the *Madonna with Saints* signed by Taddeo di Bartolo. (The fellow in the red cape and beard in the tiny left tondo is the original Santa Claus, St. Nicholas of Bari.) In room 11 is *Christ in*

Glory with Saints (1492), the last great work of Florentine master Domenico Ghirlandaio. If you look hard, you can spot a giraffe being led along the road—an exotic animal that had only recently been acquired by the Medici for their menagerie. In room 12 hangs a remarkably colored *Annunciation* (1491) by Luca Signorelli—note the great rush of feeling as the archangel bursts through the doorway to announce the news to Mary. In the same room is a *Deposition* (1521) by 26-year-old Rosso Fiorentino, a red-headed (and reportedly hot-headed) Florentine painter, who ended up going to France to work at the Chateau Fontainebleau. Painted in his odd color palette of flat grays and reds, it unusually portrays this solemn scene of Christ being taken off the cross as a frantic swirl of action, with sashes flapping in the wind and workers scurrying up and down ladders.
Via del Sarti 1. comune.volterra.pi.it. ✆ **0588/87580.** Admission 10€ or free with the Volterra Card (p. 283); includes adjacent Ecomuseo dell'Alabastro (p. 287); free for children 5 and under. Mid-Mar to Nov daily 9am–7pm; Nov to mid-Mar Tues–Fri 10am–4pm and Sat–Sun 10am–6:30pm.

Porta all'Arco ♥♥♥ HISTORIC GATE Volterra's greatest landmark is this huge and magnificent gate built by the Etruscans as early as the 3rd century B.C.E. in their 7km (4-mile) circuit of city walls. The round arch contains a keystone that the Romans later incorporated into much of their architecture. On the outside are mounted three basalt heads—features worn away by well over 2,000 years of wind and rain—said possibly to represent the Etruscan gods Tinia (Jupiter), Uni (Juno), and Menrva (Minerva). The gateway almost didn't survive World War II, when retreating German troops decided to blow it up to block the Allied advance through the city. Volterrans dug up the surrounding paving stones and temporarily plugged the opening, convincing the Germans not to destroy a gate that no one could pass through anyway.
Porta all'Arco. No phone. Free admission.

Volterra walking tours explore local landmarks like the huge Porta all'Arco, built by the Etruscans.

Teatro Romano (Roman Theater) ♥♥ ARCHAEOLOGICAL SITE Take a stroll along Via Lungo le Mure, a walkway atop the medieval ramparts, to overlook the impressive remains of Volterra's Roman theater and baths, some of the best-preserved Roman remains in Tuscany. They remained buried for centuries, until the 1950s, when

crafty VOLTERRANS

The Etruscans made good use of the easily mined local stone, a translucent calcium sulfate known as **alabaster**—witness the hundreds of alabaster sarcophagi in the Guarnacci museum (p. 285). Alabaster became a major industry in Volterra again at the end of the 19th century, when the material was much in demand for lampshades with the advent of electric lighting. Today local artisans work alabaster into a mind-boggling array of objects, from fine art pieces to some remarkable kitsch.

Plaques around town denote the workshops of some of the best traditional artisans, where you will find only handworked items. Via Porta all'Arco has several fine workshops, including internationally known **Paolo Sabatini ♥♥**, at no. 45 (italia-sumisura.it/en/azienda/paolo-sabatini; ✆ **0588/81515**), whose alabaster sculptural pieces often combine wood and stone. The large **Rossi Alabastri ♥** shop (rossialabastri.com; ✆ **0588/86133**) at Piazzetta della Pescheria shows off some especially distinctive lighting pieces, as well as alabaster bowls, fruits, and all sorts of other easily portable items. At **alab'Arte ♥**, Via Don Minzoni 18 (alabarte.com; ✆ **340/718189** or 340/981-6908), Roberto Cini and Giorgio Finazzo create sculptural pieces of museum quality—in fact, they are often called upon to help restore sculptures in churches and museums around Italy.

You'll find the work of many local artisans at the **Società Cooperativa Artieri Alabastro,** Piazza dei Priori 5 (artierialabastro.it; ✆ **0588/86135**), a sales showroom for smaller workshops. To learn more about the town's alabaster industry, visit the **Ecomuseo dell'Alabastro,** Piazzetta Minucci 2 (comune.volterra.pi.it; ✆ **0588/87580;** admission 8€ or included with the Volterra Card; mid-Mar to early Nov daily 9:30am–7pm, early Nov to mid-Mar Tues–Fri 10am–4pm and Sat and Sun 10am–6:30pm).

Alabaster isn't the only craft in town. **Fabula Etrusca ♥**, Via Lungo le Mura del Mandorlo 10 (fabulaetrusca.it; ✆ **0588/87401**), sells intricate handmade jewelry based on original Etruscan designs. For prints created from hand-engraved zinc plates—another local specialty—visit **L'Istrice,** Via Porta all'Arco 23 (laboistrice.it; ✆ **0347/726-9888**).

Enrico Fiumi of the Museo Etrusco Guarnacci unearthed them with the assistance of patients from the town's huge, now defunct insane asylum. The theater dates back to the 1st century B.C.E., though parts of it were torn up for building materials during the construction of the medieval walls. The view from up here is the best way to see it all, and for free, but if you do want to wander among the stones, an entrance is on Viale Francesco Ferrucci.

Viale Francesco Ferrucci. comune.volterra.pi.it/aree_archeologiche. ✆ **0588/86050.** Admission 10€ or free with the Volterra Card (p. 283), free for children 5 and under. Mid-Mar to early Nov Tues–Fri 10am–4pm and Sat–Sun 10am–6:30pm.

Where to Stay in Volterra

Staying within Volterra's city walls can be a transporting experience, especially in the quiet of the evening when the city seems to drift back into the Middle Ages. Choices are fairly limited, so book ahead, especially if you're planning a visit between May and September. If you're using public transport, Volterra is not a terribly convenient base for touring, but if you have a car, Pisa, Lucca, San Gimignano, Siena, and many other Tuscan towns are within fairly easy reach.

Albergo Etruria ♥♥ The lounge is a homey touch, but the real attraction of this cozy lodging is the roof garden, where the greenery is backed by the town's brick towers and tile rooftops. Parts of an Etruscan wall enhance the historic character of the old house, yet rooms are up-to-date and filled with comfortable, attractive furniture handpicked by the friendly owners. The Piazza dei Priori is only a few steps away.
Via Matteotti 32. albergoetruria.it. ✆ **0588/87377.** 18 units. 95€–105€ double. Rates include breakfast. Parking 15€. **Amenities:** Free Wi-Fi.

Hotel La Locanda ♥♥ A location just inside the town walls makes this converted convent a good choice if traveling by car, because free parking is just steps away. High-ceilinged rooms are done in soothing pastels, a few have massage showers and whirlpool tubs, and most show off a patch or two of exposed stone and timber. The main sights are an easy walk away, and a quiet terrace at the back offers a breath of fresh air.
Via Guarnacci 24. hotel-lalocanda.com. ✆ **0588/81547.** 18 units. 110€–120€ double. Rates include breakfast. **Amenities:** Restaurant; bar; free Wi-Fi.

Hotel San Lino ♥♥ There's a utilitarian ring to the hallways and some guest rooms here, probably because for many centuries the 13th-century *palazzo* served as a cloistered convent. The enclosed gardens are still in place, and a little terrace looks across miles of countryside. There's also a small pool, the only one inside the city walls and reason enough to stay here in the summer. Some rooms are merely functional, while others bring the decor and comfort up a notch. The best rooms overlook the garden and sweeping landscapes beyond.
Via San Lino 6 (near Porta San Francesco). hotelsanlino.net. ✆ **0588/85250.** 44 units. 115€–125€ double. Rates include breakfast. **Amenities:** Restaurant; bar; pool; free Wi-Fi.

Where to Eat in Volterra

Bar Trattoria Da Badò ♥♥♥ TUSCAN Owner Giacomo's mom, Lucia, is in the kitchen of this favorite in the San Lazzero neighborhood, just outside the walls. She prepares a few daily choices that often include *zuppa volterrana* (bread and vegetable soup) and *baccalà rifatto* (pan-fried salted codfish stewed with tomatoes), along with *pappardelle alla lepre* (wide fettuccine with rabbit sauce) and other hearty pastas well suited to the homey, stone-arched surroundings. Lucia also makes the jams that fill her delicious homemade tortes. A **cafe** in front serves coffee and pastries all day.
Da Bado. Borgo San Lazzero 9. ✆ **0588/80402.** Main courses 8€–18€. Thurs–Tues 12:30–2:30pm and 7:30–10pm.

Osteria La Pace ♥♥ VOLTERRAN/TUSCAN No restaurant in Volterra can boast of such a long provenance, serving since 1600 and in the hands of the same family since 1939. The old brick walls and vaults look just as they must have 400 years ago, and the kitchen follows suit with its versions of Volterra classics such as tagliatelle with chestnuts and mushrooms and a hearty stew of wild boar.
Via Don Giovanni Minzoni 29. osteria-lapace.com. ✆ **0588/86511.** Main courses 10€–24€. Thurs–Tues 10am–3pm and 6:30pm–midnight.

Ristorante Enoteca del Duca ♥♥ MODERN TUSCAN At Volterra's finest restaurant, you can choose either the elegant high-ceilinged dining room, a bottle-lined enoteca, or a pretty patio out back to enjoy innovative and refined takes on Tuscan classics. All the salami and cheeses are from local producers, *lavagnette* (homemade egg pasta) comes with a sauce of celery and Pecorino pesto, and local beef is grilled to perfection. Some of the wines come from the owners' vineyards.
Via di Castello 2. ✆ **0588/81510.** Main courses 15€–25€. Thurs–Tues noon–3pm and 7–10pm (Fri–Sun only some winter months).

LUCCA ♥♥♥

72km (45 miles) W of Florence

Lucca is the "other" Tuscan town, a bit off the beaten track, but the Etruscans were here as early as 700 B.C.E., and the Romans after them. The city flourished as a silk center in the Middle Ages. Later, a beautifully preserved circuit of 16th- and 17th-century walls (designed in part, allegedly, by Leonardo da Vinci) ensured centuries of peace and prosperity. No doubt such a long and colorful history inspired the romantic operas of Lucca native son Giacomo Puccini (1858–1924), composer of *Tosca*, *Madame Butterfly*, and *La Bohème*. Lucca can seem like a stage set, and it's easy to look at the tiered facade of the church of San Michele and hear the strains of Puccini's aria *O Mio Bambino Caro*.

Essentials

ARRIVING Lucca is on the Florence-Viareggio **train** line, with about 30 trains daily (fewer on Sun) connecting with **Florence** (75–90 min.). A similar number of trains make the short hop to/from **Pisa** (30 min.). The **station** is a short walk south of Porta San Pietro, an entrance to the walled city. You can stash your bags at **Tourist Center Lucca,** on the piazza in front of the station (touristcenterlucca.com; ✆ **0583/494401**), open daily 10am to 6m; the cost per bag is 5€ a day. This is handy if you want to stop in Lucca on your way west to Pisa, the Cinque Terre, or Liguria.

By **car,** the A11 runs from Florence past Prato, Pistoia, and Montecatini before hitting Lucca. Inside the walls, you'll usually find a pay-parking space underground at **Mazzini** (enter from the east, through the Porta Elisa, and take an immediate right); above-ground parking areas surround

Get in the Saddle

The popular way to get around Lucca, you'll soon learn, is via bike. Enjoy the medieval lanes and squares on foot, but equip yourself with two wheels for a ride on the **Passeggiata della Mura,** atop the medieval walls. You can do so in style on one of the neon-green or Barbie-pink models from **Antonio Poli** at Piazza Santa Maria 42 (biciclettepoli.com; ✆ **0583/493787;** daily 8:30am–7:30pm, closed Sun mid-Nov to Feb and Mon mornings year-round). On the same street, bikes are also available from **Cicli Bizzarri,** Piazza Santa Maria 32 (ciclibizzarri.net; ✆ **0583/496682;** daily 8:30am–12:30pm and 2–7:30pm). The going rates are 5€ an hour, 20€ for the day; 10€ an hour for e-bikes.

the other gates as well, with rates from 1€ an hour; go to parcheggilucca.it.

Autolinee Toscana (at-bus.it; ✆ **800/142242**) service runs hourly from Florence (70 min.) and from Pisa (50 min.) to Lucca.

GETTING AROUND A set of *navette* (electric **minibuses**) whiz down the city's peripheral streets, but the flat center is easily traversed on foot. Taxis line up at the train station (✆ **0583/494-989**), Piazzale Verdi (✆ **0583/581305**), and Piazza Napoleone (✆ **0583/491-646**). To get around like a Lucchese, rent a bike—see box to the left for rental information.

VISITOR INFORMATION There's a **tourist office** on Piazzale Verdi next to Porta San Donato (turismo.lucca.it; ✆ **0583/538150;** daily 9:30am–6:30pm, Nov–Mar until 4:30pm). Another office is outside the train station on Piazza Curtatone (✆ **0583/442213;** Wed–Sat 9:30am–1:30pm, Tues and Thurs 2:30–5:30pm; hours can vary).

SPECIAL EVENTS For a few days at the end of October, the city is taken over by costumed attendees of the **Lucca Comics & Games** convention (luccacomicsandgames.com).

Exploring Lucca

Lucca has many remarkable architectural landmarks, but the first you'll notice are the incredibly intact city walls—more than 4km (2½ miles) of them, with 11 bastions and six gates; some stretches are 18m (59 ft.) wide. Topping the walls, the tree-shaded **Passeggiata delle Mura** can be circumnavigated on foot or by bike (see "Get in the Saddle," above), as you peer across Lucca's rooftops toward the hazy mountains. A stretch near the northeast corner of the walls overlooks the baroque gardens of the **Palazzo Pfanner,** a 17th-century nobleman's home. You can tour a few rooms of the palace and stroll in the gardens, but the formal plantings and an exquisite external staircase are just as impressive when viewed from the walls (palazzopfanner.it; ✆ **0583/95215;** 10€ adults, 8€ seniors and ages 12–16, under 12 free; garden 8€ adults, 6.50€ seniors and ages 12–16; Apr–Nov daily 10am–6pm).

The most curious feature of Lucca's street plan is **Piazza dell'Anfiteatro,** near the north end of Via Fillungo, the main shopping street. This semicircle of handsome medieval houses stands atop what

were once the grandstands of a C.E. 1st- or 2nd-century Roman amphitheater; some of the little alleys leading into the square from surrounding, elliptical Via dell'Anfiteatro are the original entrances to the theater, with portions of their marble archways still visible. Nearby, **Torre Guinigi** (Via Sant'Andrea 41; ✆ **0583/48090**) rises from the 14th-century palace of one of Lucca's most powerful families; the tower is topped with a little grove of seven holm oaks, typical of the gardens that once flourished atop hundreds of similar tower houses around the city. Climb the 230 steps for a spectacular view of Lucca's skyline, the snowcapped Apuan Alps, and the rolling green valley of the River Serchio (8€ adults, 6.50€ seniors and ages 6–12, free for children 5 and under; daily 9:30am–7pm, Apr–May closes 6:30pm, Oct and Mar closes 5:30pm, Nov–Feb closes 4pm).

The facade of the **Basilica di San Frediano,** Piazza San Frediano (✆ **349/844-0290;** free admission), is embellished with a two-story-tall 13th-century mosaic depicting the Apostles watching Christ's ascent to heaven. San Fernando faces east, so the facade is a glittering spectacle when the mosaics catch the morning sun. If you want to step inside to see a lavishly frescoed chapel, the church is open daily from 9am to 4:30pm (Sat until 5pm). As you stroll around town, especially along the main shopping street, **Via Fillungo,** notice how many shopfronts display Art

Nouveau signs etched in glass, adding a modern grace note to the city's medieval atmosphere. A splendid exception is the Renaissance cabinetry of fine wood and glass in front of **Carli,** at no. 95, a gold and silver shop founded in 1651.

Cattedrale di San Martino ♥♥ CATHEDRAL Completed in 1070 to house one of the most renowned artifacts in Christendom, the Volto Santo (more on that below), Lucca's ornate Duomo does justice to its prized procession. On the facade, three arches open to a deep portico sheathed in marble; above it rise three tiers of arcaded loggias supported by dozens of little columns, each different. Legend has it that the Lucchese commissioned many artists to carve the columns, with the promise of hiring the best to do them all; they used all the entries and never paid anyone. A pair of binoculars will help you pick out the elaborate details of figures, animals, vines, and patterns in the loggias and on the portico. St. Martin, the former Roman soldier to whom the cathedral is dedicated, figures prominently—look for the statue of him ripping his cloak to give half to a beggar. A labyrinth is carved into the wall of the right side of the portico, for the faithful to make a figurative pilgrimage to the center of the maze, as if to Jerusalem, before entering the church. A Latin inscription reads, "This is the labyrinth built by Daedalus of Crete; all who entered therein were lost, save Theseus, thanks to Ariadne's thread."

Inside, the handsome sweep of inlaid pavement and the high altar are the work of 15th-century Lucca native Matteo Civitali. He also designed the **Tempietto,** an octagonal, freestanding chapel of white-and-red marble in the left nave, where the famous **Volto Santo** is kept—a venerable crucifix said to have been carved by Nicodemus, the man who helped remove

A crucifix WITH A MIND OF ITS OWN

Throughout the medieval era, the legend of the **Volto Santo** attracted pilgrims to Lucca from throughout Europe. Tradition claimed that when Nicodemus, a follower of Christ, was carving this crucifix, he did not complete the face, fearing he could not do the holy visage justice. He fell asleep, and when he awoke, a beautiful face had miraculously been carved on the crucifix.

Nicodemus stashed the Volto Santo crucifix in a cave for safekeeping; centuries later, an 8th-century Italian bishop on pilgrimage to the Holy Land discovered it (apparently the location had come to him in a dream). The bishop put the crucifix adrift in a boat, which magically washed up in northern Italy, where the relic somehow got into a driverless wagon pulled by two oxen and arrived in Lucca. The crucifix was first placed in the basilica of San Frediano but had other ideas and transported itself to the cathedral.

On May 3 and September 13 to 14, the Lucchese walk in a candlelit procession from San Frediano to the cathedral, where the famous carving awaits them, dressed in gold and wearing a gold crown.

A statue of the composer Giacomo Puccini outside his birthplace in Lucca.

Christ's body from the cross. (See "A Crucifix with a Mind of Its Own," p. 292). The cathedral's other great treasure is the **Tomb of Ilaria Carretto Guinigi,** the wife of Lucca ruler Paolo Guinigi, who died in 1405 at the age of 26; she lives on, accompanied by a little dog (a sign of her faithfulness) in a beautiful image carved by Jacopo della Quercia, the Sienese sculptor whose work heavily influenced Michelangelo (p. 357). An unseen presence is that of the great composer Giacomo Puccini, who was born nearby in 1858 and sang in the church choir. Among the gold and other treasures in the cathedral museum are some exquisite textiles, a legacy of the city's onetime role as a center of the silk trade.

Piazza San Martino. museocattedralelucca.it. ✆ **0583/490530.** Admission 5€ adults, 3€ ages 6–14, free for children 5 and under; campanile 3€; museum 4€; combined ticket (cathedral, campanile, museum, and nearby church of Saints Giovanni and Reparata) 10€, 8€ ages 6–25 and seniors, children 5 and under free, families 20€. Mon–Fri 10am–5pm; Sat 9:30am–6pm; Sun noon–5pm. Campanile and cathedral museum Mon–Fri 10am–5pm; Sat–Sun 10am–6pm.

Museo Casa Natale di Giacomo Puccini ♥♥ MUSEUM Walking around Lucca, a Puccini aria could pop into your head at any moment, but the maestro comes most vividly to life in **Piazza Cittadella,** where in the guise of a bronze statue he sits, legs crossed, in an armchair. Puccini was born around the corner at 9 Corte San Lorenzo and lived there until he left for Milan in his early 20s. The modest-yet-comfortable rooms display some of his scores, random pieces of heavy furniture, and, most notably, the piano on which he often composed.

9 Corte San Lorenzo. puccinimuseum.org. ✆ **0583/584028.** Admission 9€ adults, 7€ ages 17 and under. Apr–Sept daily 10am–7pm; Feb–Mar and Oct Wed–Mon 10am–5pm; Nov–Jan Mon–Fri 10am–2pm and Sat–Sun 10am–5pm.

San Michele in Foro ♥♥ CHURCH The magnificent facade of the Cattedrale di San Martino is matched, maybe even outdone, by the delicately stacked arches and arcades of this 12th-century church, which rises above the site of Lucca's Roman forum. The show begins just above the main portal, where St. Michael slays a dragon; above that two lions flank a rose window. Then begin four soaring tiers of little columns, inlaid with intricate carvings and topped with human heads, flowers, and animals;

above each row is a frieze on which carved animals jump and run. The two narrow top tiers are capped by a bronze-winged statue of **St. Michael the Archangel,** flanked by two trumpeting cohorts. Lucchese claim to see a distinct glow emanating at sunset from St. Michael's right hand, created by a sapphire that, according to legend, he wears on his finger. The interior is rather dull by comparison, although in the right transept is a fine painting of *Sts. Roch, Sebastian, Jerome, and Helen* by Filippino Lippi. Born of a notorious relationship between the painter Fra Filippo Lippi and a young nun, Lucrezia Buti, Filippino became one of the most accomplished painters of the late 15th century.

Piazza San Michele. ✆ **0583/53576.** Free admission. Daily 9am–6pm.

Where to Stay in Lucca

Rentals in the countryside around Lucca include **Bertolli Villas** ♥ (bertollivillas.com; ✆ **335/776-7610**) in San Colombano Alto, 11km (7 miles north), where two stylishly comfortably houses on an olive estate are set in beautiful gardens and have private pools; 1,600€ to 3,300€ for six guests for 7 nights.

EXPENSIVE

Grand Universe Lucca ♥♥♥ Lucca's most luxurious lodgings occupy a revamped *palazzo* next to the city's opera house, Teatro del Giglio, with a sweep of glamorous lounges, a cantina set amid Roman ruins in the cellar, and upstairs, chic contemporary-style rooms done with rich upholstery and silks that pay homage to Lucca's historic textile trade. Above it all is a view-filled rooftop champagne bar. A nearby palace houses the even-more sumptuous suites and apartments of the Grand Universe La Residenza.

Piazza del Giglio. granduniverselucca.com. ✆ **058/340041.** 55 units. 200€–300€ double; La Residenza 350€–600€ double. Rates include breakfast. **Amenities:** Restaurant; 3 bars; free Wi-Fi.

MODERATE

Alla Corte degli Angeli ♥♥ In this beautifully restored pink *palazzo* just off Via Fillungo, the main shopping street, colorful murals incorporate a different flower in each room, and rich draperies and upholstered headboards pick up on the themes. A scattering of antique pieces and excellent lighting enhance the stylish comfort. Bathrooms are good-size, and some have both showers and hydromassage tubs. Rooms on an upper floor are filled with sunlight—third-floor Paolina, with two exposures, is an especially bright choice.

Via degli Angeli 23 (off Via Fillungo). allacortedegliangeli.com. ✆ **0583/469204.** 21 units. 110€–250€ double. Rates include breakfast. Closed 2 weeks Jan. **Amenities:** Bikes; concierge; free Wi-Fi.

Hotel Palazzo Alexander ♥♥ Stepping into this 12th-century palace tucked into medieval streets is like walking onto an operatic stage set,

and the feeling certainly doesn't let up as you settle into rooms named after Puccini operas and done with gilded and polished wood, reproduction antiques, old prints, and plush fabrics. *Putti* (cherubs) grin down from frescoed ceilings, and some of the especially charming suites have vaulted and beamed ceilings that put a luxury spin on Rodolfo's *La Bohème* garret. Meanwhile, marble baths, Jacuzzi tubs in some rooms, excellent beds and fine linens, and other amenities are thoroughly up to date.
Via Santa Giustina 28. hotelpalazzoalexander.it. ✆ **0583/583571.** 9 units. 85€–230€ double. Rates include breakfast. Closed Jan and Feb. **Amenities:** Bar; free Wi-Fi.

San Luca Palace Hotel ♥♥ A sense of tasteful, old-world comfort begins in the downstairs hall and sitting room and continues into the large guest rooms, with parquet floors and well-coordinated fabrics and draperies. Among the inviting flourishes are small "reading" alcoves with day beds in many rooms. This old palace just inside the walls also has plenty of practical conveniences, including an easy-to-reach location (parking is adjacent) just a short stroll from the sights and train station. There's no in-house restaurant, but a bar off the lobby serves light snacks.
Via San Paolino 103 (off Piazza Napoleone). sanlucapalace.com. ✆ **0583/317446.** 26 units. 80€–220€ double. Rates include breakfast. **Amenities:** Bar; free Wi-Fi.

INEXPENSIVE

B&B Arena di Lucca ♥♥♥ Hosts Alex and Livia make sure the guests in their old apartment, a parcel of prime real estate overlooking the Piazza dell'Anfiteatro, feel as if they have come for a stay in a family home. Terra-cotta floors, oil paintings, and comfy sofas and chairs fill the shared lounge, while two high-ceilinged rooms also face the lively scene below from small balconies; two other rooms look onto the atmospheric Via dell'Anfiteatro. The hosts serve a large breakfast by the kitchen hearth.
Via dell'Anfiteatro 16. bbarenalucca.com. ✆ **0389/948355.** 4 units. 90€–120€ double. Rates include breakfast. **Amenities:** Free Wi-Fi.

Corte Meraviglia ♥♥ Accommodations at this price rarely come with such atmospheric surroundings, a gracious old palace on the back lanes not far from the Piazza dell'Anfiteatro. Decor in the lounge and well-equipped rooms tucked away on a couple of floors is comfortably shabby chic, and they share a shady terrace that opens to extensive gardens. Ceiling fans and thick walls stand in for air-conditioning. Friendly host Paolo serves a light breakfast and is a welcoming presence.
Gia Via Nuova 63, Lucca. cortemeraviglia-lucca.com. ✆ **339/778-6914.** 4 units. 59€–115€ double. Rates include breakfast. **Amenities:** Garden; free Wi-Fi.

Where to Eat in Lucca

Lucca's highly regarded extra-virgin olive oil appears on every restaurant table. An atmospheric 19th-century pastry shop, **Taddeucci ♥**, Piazza San Michele 34 (buccellatotaddeucci.it; ✆ **0583/494933**), is famous for *buccellato,* a Lucca specialty—a ring-shaped sweet bread flavored with raisins and fennel seeds that sustained Roman legionnaires. For a fortifying snack, stop by **Amedeo Giusti** ♥, Via Santa Lucia 18 (✆ **0583/496285**), where focaccia with many different toppings emerges piping-hot from the oven. Sample Lucca's excellent DOC wines at **Enoteca Vanni** ♥, Piazza San Salvatore 7 (enotecavanni.com; ✆ **0583/491902**). The atmospheric **Antica Bottega di Prospero** ♥, Via Santa Lucia 13 (✆ **0583/494875**), amply proves the sophistication of Lucca's palate—it's stocked with local olive oils, preserved vegetables, and an array of dried beans and grains.

EXPENSIVE

Buca di Sant'Antonio ♥♥ LUCCHESE Quietly formal service (with waiters in bow ties) and a welcoming glass of prosecco nicely accent a meal of traditional Lucchese dishes enjoyed beneath a canopy of hanging copper pots. The menu changes regularly but always includes fresh house-made pastas such as *tordelli Lucchese* (ravioli-like pockets stuffed with beef and pork) and other local specialties like *farro alla garfagnana* (spelt or barley soup) and *coniglio in umido* (rabbit stew). A house dessert is the town's *buccellato* (sweet bread).

Via della Cervia 3 (just west of Piazza San Michele). bucadisantantonio.com. ✆ **0583/55881.** Main courses 15€–25€. Tues–Sat 12:30–2:30pm and 7:30–10pm.

Ristorante All'Olivo ♥♥ LUCCHESE/SEAFOOD This is where the Lucchese come for fish. Taking a seat in one of its four comfortable and elegant little rooms—one with a fireplace, another a covered garden—definitely elevates a meal to a special occasion. Seafood is brought in daily from the nearby Tuscan port of Viareggio and appears in a bounty of pastas, grilled platters, a nice choice of *antipasti di mare,* and a simply prepared catch of the day. Hearty roasts, grilled Tuscan steaks, and several vegetarian pasta dishes are also on the menu.

Piazza San Quirico 1. ristoranteolivo.it. ✆ **0583/493129.** Main courses 15€–35€. Daily 12:30–3:30pm and 7:30–11:30pm.

MODERATE

Osteria San Giorgio ♥♥ LUCCHESE/TUSCAN This neighborhood favorite on a quiet street near the Piazza dell'Anfiteatro has a courtyard out front and comfortably informal rooms decorated with old photos. Tuscan steaks are on a menu that leans heavily toward traditional Lucchese dishes: hearty *farro alla Lucchese* (a soup made with spelt, a barley-like grain cooked al dente), *coniglio stufato con olive taggiasche e uva* (rabbit stew with olives and grapes), and a local seafood favorite, *baccalà alla griglia con ceci* (grilled cod with chickpeas).

Via San Giorgio 26. osteriasangiorgio.com. ✆ **0583/953233.** Main courses 9€–18€. Tues–Sun noon–3pm and 7–10:30pm.

INEXPENSIVE

Trattoria Da Giulio ♥♥♥ LUCCHESE/TUSCAN The family at this local favorite has been feeding the neighborhood since 1945, and it seems like everyone is on a first-name basis with the busy staff that dashes between the tables in the three brightly lit rooms. A long menu of local classics includes *salsicce con fagioli all'ucelletto* (sausage with beans in tomato sauce and sage); *tagliatelle alla contadina,* with fresh tomatoes, basil, and oregano; and *cavallo* (horsemeat, served minced and raw, *tartara*). Excellent house wines are available by the pitcher.

Via delle Conce 25. trattoriadagiulio.it. ✆ **0583/55948.** Main courses 9€–13€. Mon–Sat noon–2:30pm and 7–10:30pm.

Trattoria Da Leo ♥♥ LUCCHESE/TUSCAN This pleasantly old-fashioned room with plastic-draped tablecloths has been serving local classics for 50 years, and the *arrosto di maialino con patate* (roast piglet and potatoes), *coniglio alla contadina* (roast rabbit), and other authentic Lucchese fare remain as good as ever. You'll get a proper taste of local specialties on one of the good-value set menus.

Via Tegrimi 1 (just north of Piazza San Salvatore). trattoriadaleo.webnode.it. ✆ **0583/492236.** Main courses 9€–12€. Set menus 20€ and 24€. Mon–Sat noon–3pm and 7:30–10pm; Sun noon–3pm.

Lucca Entertainment & Nightlife

Every evening at 7pm from April through October, the church of San Giovanni (Piazza di San Giovanni) hosts an opera recital or orchestral concert honoring hometown composer Giacomo Puccini, in a series called **Puccini e la sua Lucca** (puccinielasualucca.com). Tickets are 30€ (25€ for those 22 and under). Just try listening to *Nessun Dorma* in this lovely church in the composer's hometown without chills running up your spine. Lago di Massaciuccoli is the backdrop for the summer **Puccini Festival ♥♥** in nearby Torre del Lago, where the composer built a villa (puccinifestival.it; ✆ **340/8106042**); tickets for operas and concerts can be purchased online in advance (20€–175€).

PISA ♥♥

85km (53 miles) south of Lucca, 76km (47 miles) W of Florence

It's ironic that one of the most famous landmarks in a country that has given Western civilization much of its greatest art and architecture is in fact an engineering failure. Built on sandy soil too unstable to support so much heavy marble, Pisa's famous tower began to lean even while it was still under construction. Eight centuries later, the Leaning Tower puts Pisa on the map. Seeing the tower, maybe climbing it, and touring other landmarks on the Piazza del Duomo is probably why you come to this city near Tuscany's northwestern coast.

Pisa began as a seaside settlement around 1000 B.C.E. and was expanded into a naval trading port by the Romans in the 2nd century B.C.E. By the 11th century, the city had grown into one of the peninsula's most powerful maritime republics. In 1284, however, Pisa's battle fleet was destroyed by Genoa's navy at Meloria (off Livorno), forcing Pisa's long slide into twilight. Florence took control in 1406 and, despite a few small rebellions, stayed in charge until Italian unification in the 1860s.

Pisa is lively and cosmopolitan, soaked in medieval and Renaissance ambience, and home to a university founded in 1343, one of Europe's oldest. Pisa is an easy day trip from Florence or nearby Lucca.

Essentials

ARRIVING Around 25 trains run daily between **Lucca** and Pisa (25–35 min.); from **Florence,** 50 daily trains make the trip (60–90 min.). Trains pull into **Pisa Centrale** station, though on the Lucca line, day-trippers can get off at **San Rossore station,** a few blocks west of Piazza del Duomo and the Leaning Tower. **Left Luggage Pisa,** at the east end of Centrale's platform one (leftluggagetuscany.com), is open daily 8am to 7pm; the cost per bag is 4€ per hour, 10€ per day. This is handy if you want to stop in Pisa for a look at the tower on your way to somewhere else—if you're on the way from Genoa to Florence, for instance. The office also allows customers to recharge their electronic devices for free.

There's a Florence–Pisa fast **highway** along the Arno valley. Take the SS12 or SS12r from Lucca. Parking anywhere near the Duomo is not easy. Best bet is the Pietrasantina lot, in the northwest corner of the city and well-marked as you exit the autostrada at Pisa Nord; it's free, within walking distance of the Duomo, and also connected by frequent shuttle-bus service (1€ on the bus or at the I in the lot). For details on parking locations and charges, see **pisamo.it**.

Tuscany's main international airport, **Galileo Galilei** (**PSA;** pisa-airport.com), just 3km (2 miles) south of the center, is served by many European carriers, with service to and from London, Paris, Amsterdam, Frankfurt, and other international hubs. The automated **PisaMover** tram runs every 5 to 8 minutes from 6am to midnight (until 1am June–Sept) for the 5-minute trip between the airport terminal and Pisa Centrale station; the fare is 6.50€ (pisa-mover.com). Buy tickets from machines at the stops. A metered **taxi** ride to the station or Piazza del Duomo costs 10€ to 15€ (drivers accept credit cards).

GETTING AROUND **CPT** (pisa.cttnord.it; ✆ **800/570-530**) runs the city's **buses.** The LAM Rossa bus runs from Pisa Centrale station to the Piazza del Duomo (fare 1.70€; buy tickets at newsstands and tobacco shops or from machines at some stops, or pay onboard with a contactless card or device). It's also an easy and pleasant 25-minute walk from the station to the Duomo on a route that will take you through the heart of the medieval city. Head north from the station on Corso Italia toward the river, and from the other bank follow Borgo Stretto to Via Dini and through Piazza Cavalieri toward the Piazza del Duomo.

Taxis can be found on Piazza della Stazione and Piazza del Duomo. Call a radio taxi at ✆ **050/541600.**

VISITOR INFORMATION The main **tourist office** is near the Leaning Tower on Piazza del Duomo (turismo.pisa.it; ✆ **050/550100**); it's open daily 10am to 6pm (until 4pm some winter months). Another office is near the river on Piazza XX Settembre and is open Monday through Friday 8:30am to 1:30pm. You can pick up a basic map (with few street names) for free or a detailed one for 3€.

Exploring Pisa

On a grassy lawn wedged into the northwest corner of the city walls, medieval Pisans created one of the most dramatic squares in the world. Often dubbed **Piazza dei Miracoli** (Square of Miracles) or **Campo dei Miracoli** (Field of Miracles), **Piazza del Duomo** ♥♥♥ is lined with elegant buildings that epitomize the Pisan-Romanesque style. A subtle part of the appeal, aside from the beauty of the white marble-sheathed buildings, is the spatial geometry: If you were to look at an aerial photo of the square and draw connect-the-dot lines between the doors and other focal points, you'd come up with all sorts of perfect triangles and tangential lines. Less subtle are the visitors posing for photos angled to make it seem they're propping up the leaning tower.

Aside from immersing yourself in these spectacles, take a little time to see the rest of the city, where much of the historic center is a well-preserved slice of the Middle Ages and Renaissance. From the Duomo, walk south on Via Santa Maria and turn left onto Via dei Mille to reach **Piazza dei Cavalieri,** the seat of government when Pisa was one of the world's most powerful maritime republics. Dominating the square is a statue of Cosimo I Medici, a reminder that Florence conquered Pisa in the early 1500s, after which the city never regained its might or glory. Follow Via Ulisse Dini to **Borgo Stretto,** a lively shopping street; just off the street in **Piazza delle Vettovaglie,** a fish and vegetable market fills a Renaissance loggia every morning except Sunday.

As you reach the river, pause in the middle of **Ponte di Mezzo** to look at the *palazzo*-lined banks; in the Middle Ages this graceful span, rebuilt many times, was lined with shops like the Ponte Vecchio in Florence. Tidily wedged onto the south bank, downstream from the bridge, the exquisite **Chiesa di Santa Maria della Spina** was wrought by Pisa's leading Gothic sculptors, including Giovanni Pisano. From the south side of the bridge, shop-lined **Corso Italia** passes a graceful Florentine loggia and continues to the central train station.

At Corso Vittorio Emanuele II, a slight detour to the west brings you to Via Zandonai and an unexpected sight: Shortly before his death in 1990, New York street artist Keith Haring painted the giant **Tuttomondo** mural on the theme of "peace and harmony," filling it with his trademark Pop Art figures.

Visiting the Campo dei Miracoli

Admission to the **Leaning Tower** and the **cathedral** is 20€. It costs 8€ to enter the cathedral and any one of the Campo's other sights: the **Baptistery, Camposanto,** the **Museo delle Sinopie,** or the **Museo Opera.** Admission to all of these sights except the Tower is 11€, or 27€ with the Tower (free for children 10 and under). Admission to the Tower is by timed entry only and space is limited; visitors are encouraged to purchase tickets in advance at **opapisa.it**.

Baptistery ♥♥ CHURCH Italy's largest baptistery (104m/341 ft. in circumference), begun in 1153 and capped with a Gothic dome in the 1300s, is built on the same unstable soil as the Leaning Tower—the first thing you notice is a decided tilt towards the cathedral. But it's the Baptistery's unadorned interior that is of greatest interest: Art historians consider this to be where the Renaissance, with its emphasis on classical style, first began to flower, in the pulpit created by sculptor Nicola Pisano (1255–60). Pisano had studied ancient Roman works that the Pisan navy brought back from Rome as booty, and the classical influence on his work is obvious—note the nude Roman god Hercules taking his place next to statues of St. Michael and St. John the Baptist (who is bathed in ethereal light on June 24, when the sun shines through a strategically placed opening in the walls to illuminate the saint on the feast of his birth). In scenes of the life of Christ, figures wear tunics and Mary wears the headdress of a Roman matron. Roughly once an hour or so, one of the guards will stand near the middle of the structure and sing, and the sound will reverberate melodically (the performer deserves a small tip). These acoustics are no accident—studies show that the baptistery was designed in such a way to amplify sounds to mimic a perfectly tuned pipe organ.

Piazza del Duomo. opapisa.it. ✆ **050/835-011.** For prices, see box p. 300. Apr–Sept daily 9am–8pm; Oct and Mar 9am–7pm; Nov–Feb 9am–6pm.

Camposanto ♥♥ CEMETERY Pisa's cemetery, where the city's aristocracy was buried until the 1800s, was begun in 1278, when Crusaders began shipping back dirt from Golgotha (the mount where Christ was crucified). Giovanni di Simone (architect of the Leaning Tower) enclosed the field in a marble cloister, and the walls were covered by magnificent 14th- and 15th-century frescoes. These were mostly destroyed by Allied bombings in World War II, but you can see renderings of them in the Museo delle Sinopie across the square. Roman sarcophagi, used as funerary monuments, fared better (84 of these survive), as did the huge chains that medieval Pisans used to protect their harbor, which now hang on the cemetery walls.

Piazza del Duomo. opapisa.it. ✆ **050/835-011.** For prices, see box p. 300. Daily Apr–Sept 9am–8pm; Oct and Mar 9am–7pm; Nov–Feb 9am–6pm.

The Leaning Tower of Pisa becomes more meaningful when seen as part of the entire cathedral complex, the beautiful Campo dei Miracoli.

Cattedrale ♥♥ CATHEDRAL Pisa's magnificent white marble cathedral will forever be associated with native son Galileo Galilei (1564–1642), a founder of modern physics. Bored during church services, he discovered the law of perpetual motion (a pendulum's swings always take the same amount of time) by watching the swaying of a bronze chandelier now known as the "Lamp of Galileo." (It's also said that Galileo dropped two wooden balls of differing sizes from the Leaning Tower; they hit the ground at the same time, thus proving that gravity exerts the same force on objects no matter what they weigh.) The exuberant cathedral, with its intricate tiers of arches and columns, is remarkable in its own right as a prime example of Pisan Romanesque architecture, which was heavily influenced by Pisa's trading contact with the Arab world. Giovanni Pisano, whose father, Nicola, sculpted the pulpit in the Baptistery, created the pulpit here (1302–11), covering it with scenes from the New Testament. They're now considered a masterpiece of Gothic sculpture, but 16th-century restorers deemed them too old-fashioned and packed them away in crates; they were reassembled, rather clumsily, in 1926.
Piazza del Duomo. opapisa.it. ✆ **050/835011.** For prices, see box p. 300. Daily Apr–Sept 9am–8pm; Oct and Mar 9am–7pm; Nov–Feb 9am–6pm.

Leaning Tower of Pisa ♥♥♥ ICON Construction began on the bell tower of Pisa Cathedral in 1173. Three stories into the job, it became apparent the structure was leaning distinctly, whereupon architects Guglielmo and Bonanno Pisano called off the work. A century later, Giovanni di Simone resumed the job, having quite literally gone back to the drawing board—he tried to compensate for the tilt by making successive layers taller on one side than the other, thus giving the tower a slight banana-like curve but not slowing the lean. Over the centuries engineers have poured concrete into the foundations and tried other solutions, all in vain. By the late 20th century the tower was in such serious danger of collapse that it was braced with cables while crews removed more than 70 tons of earth from beneath the structure, allowing it to slightly right itself as it settled. With a lean of only 4m (13 ft.), compared to a precarious 4.6m (15 ft.) before the fix, the tower has been deemed stable and safe to climb once again. But before you do, take time to notice just how lovely the multicolor marble tower is, with eight arcaded stories that provide a mesmerizing sense of harmony as you look up its height.

The only way to climb the tower is to book a visit in the office on the north side of the piazza—or, for peak season, book online well in advance. Visits are limited to 30 minutes, and you must be punctual for your slot or you'll lose your chance to climb the 293 steps. Children 7 and under are not permitted to climb the tower, and those 8 to 18 need to be accompanied by an adult (children 8–12 must hold an adult's hand at all times).
Piazza del Duomo. opapisa.it. ✆ **050/835011.** For prices, see box p. 300. Apr–Sept daily 9am–8pm; Oct and Mar 9am–7pm; Nov–Feb 9am–6pm.

Where to Stay in Pisa

Most visitors come to Pisa on a day trip, often from Florence, which helps keep hotel prices down but also limits quality options. The low season for most hotels in Pisa is August.

Novecento ♥♥ These small, simple rooms set around a courtyard in an old villa are modestly done, with a few contemporary touches that include upholstered headboards set against colored accent walls. A lush garden is filled with lounge chairs, and off to one side is the best room in the house, a self-contained, cottagelike unit. Pisa's Botanical Garden is just up the street, and the Duomo is a 10-minute walk away.

Via Roma 37. hotelnovecento.pisa.it. ✆ **050/500323.** 14 units. 100€–120€ double. Rates include breakfast. **Amenities:** Free Wi-Fi.

Palazzo Cini ♥♥♥ Everything you need in Pisa is within an easy walk of these five extremely comfortable, tastefully designed rooms in a 19th-century palace—shops and the train station are around the corner, and the Piazza del Duomo is a pleasant stroll across town. The stylishly elegant rooms, some outfitted with huge tubs and a few tucked under beamed ceilings, share a lounge, terrace, and a garden full of exotic plantings.

12 Via Alessandro Manzoni 12. palazzocinilux.com. ✆ **050/501125.** 5 units. 115€–250€. Rates include breakfast. **Amenities:** Lounge; garden; free Wi-Fi.

Royal Victoria Hotel ♥♥♥ The gracious Piegaga family has been hosting travelers since the days of the 19th-century Grand Tour, and their high-ceilinged guest rooms and fern-filled parlors ooze old-world charm. Little has changed since Charles Dickens stayed here—guests requiring spas, high-tech gadgetry, chic designer style, or even the latest plumbing (or air-conditioning in some rooms) should look elsewhere. The rest of us will delight in front-room views of the Arno, an airy upper-floor terrace for cocktails, Art Deco tile work, marble mantelpieces, frescoes, and all the other trappings that only get better with age.

Lungarno Pacinotti 12. royalvictoria.it. ✆ **050/940111.** 40 units. 80€–130€ double. Rates include breakfast. **Amenities:** Bar; free Wi-Fi.

Where to Eat in Pisa

Any visit to Pisa should include a stop for a coffee and pastry at **Caffè dell'Ussero ♥♥♥**, one of Italy's oldest literary cafe-bars, doing a brisk business since 1775 from the ground floor of riverside Palazzo Agostini, Lungarno Pacinotti 27 (ussero.com; ✆ **34/906-7286**). For pizza or *cecina* (a flatbread made of chickpea flour and served warm), stop in at **Il Montino ♥♥**, in the historic center a block or so west of Borgo Stretto at Vicolo del Monte 1 (pizzeriailmontino.it; ✆ **050/598695**). At the end of Borgo Stretto, at no. 11 in the riverside Piazza Garibaldi, is Pisa's most popular gelato shop, **La Bottega del Gelato ♥♥** (bottegadelgelatopisa.it; ✆ **050/575467**).

Il Campano ♥♥ PISAN A meal in these simply furnished brick-and-stone rooms in an 18th-century tower house tends to be a leisurely event—the kitchen makes the Tuscan classics to order, as it has been doing for past 100 years. Aside from robust *pappardelle alla lepre* (homemade pasta with hare sauce), *tagliata di scamerita di maiale* (grilled pork chops), and Florentine steaks, the menu also usually includes fresh fish and seafood, and it's all accompanied by a huge selection of wine.

Via Cavalca 19. ilcampano.com. ✆ **050/580585.** Main courses 10€–24€. Daily 7–11pm; Sat–Tues also 12:30–3pm.

Osteria dei Cavalieri ♥♥♥ PISAN Set in plain, vaulted rooms dating to the 12th century, the "Restaurant of the Knights" serves superb Tuscan cooking that honors the Slow Food principles of fresh and local. Being Pisa, this means seafood (*tagliolini* with razor clams or a classic *baccalà,* dried cod lightly battered and fried), hearty meat choices such as grilled steaks or *pappardelle* with rabbit sauce, and robust vegetable soups. The three set menus—fish, vegetable, and meat—are a very good value.

Via San Frediano 16. osteriacavalieri.pisa.it. ✆ **050/580858.** Main courses 16€–19€; set menus 37€–39€. Thurs–Sat and Mon–Tues 12:15–2:15pm and 7:45–10:30pm; Wed 7:45–10:30pm.

Trattoria Sant'Ombrono ♥♥♥ Pisans on the lookout for authentic Tuscan cooking at fair prices know just where to go and they crowd these rooms, which are as non-fussy as the cooking (reservations are essential, especially for dinner). The daily-changing, handwritten menu is likely to include such classics as *tagliatelle al ragù d'anatra* (tagliatelle with duck ragù) or a local favorite, *trippa pisana* (Pisan-style tripe, simmered with pancetta in white wine). Friendly service enhances the meal, as does an excellent choice of local wines, many by the glass.

Piazza Sant'Ombrono 6. instagram.com/trattoria_s.omobono. ✆ **050/540847.** Main courses 8€–12€. Daily 12:30–2:30pm and 7:30–10pm.

7

UMBRIA & THE MARCHES

By Stephen Brewer

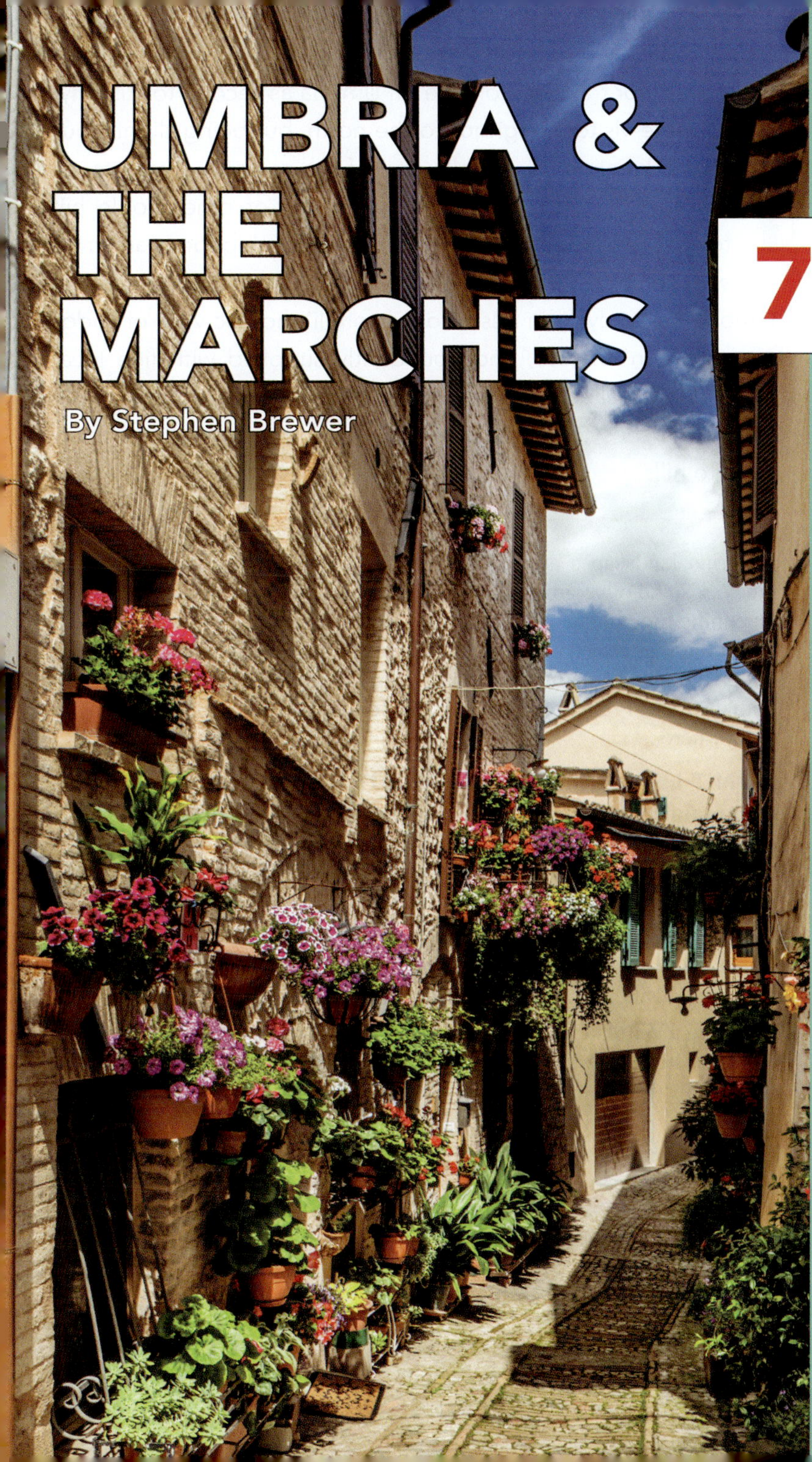

It's easy for travelers to write off Umbria as second to Tuscany, its more-visited neighbor to the north, but being slightly out of the limelight is actually one of the region's great assets. Perugia, Spoleto, Gubbio, and dozens of other noble hill towns are a little quieter than their Tuscan neighbors, and a bit easier to enjoy. They are filled with art treasures, from Giotto's famous fresco cycle in Assisi to Signorelli's horrific view of Judgment Day in Orvieto, and abundantly supplied with fine local wines and excellent food. Even less visited are the rugged valleys of the Marches to the east, where charming towns like Urbino cling to hillsides in relative isolation.

Umbrian landscapes are most memorably green, a picturesque mix of vineyards and olive groves, fertile valleys, and deep forests, edged by the Apennine mountains. As the nation's only region that does not touch the sea or another country, it is aptly referred to as the "green heart of Italy." Umbria is also sometimes called *la terra dei santi* (land of the saints), in homage to St. Francis of Assisi and his followers, reminders of whom are everywhere.

DON'T LEAVE UMBRIA WITHOUT . . .

Communing with the Spirit of St. Francis. The kindly saint is still a presence in medieval Assisi and Gubbio, where he lived and performed miracles, as well as in the region's forested hills and mist-shrouded valleys.

Getting Vertigo While Crossing Spoleto's Ponte Delle Torri. High above the Tessino river gorge, this majestic medieval span leads off a scenic 4-mile walk through Umbrian forests and olive groves.

Scenting a Whiff of Brimstone in Orvieto. Luca Signorelli's masterpiece, his Last Judgment fresco cycle in the Duomo, delivers all the spine-tingling thrill of a horror movie—it may literally put the fear of God in you!

Finding Your Inner Renaissance Courtier in Urbino. As you stroll through the palace of the Duke of Montefeltro—model for Castiglione's 1507 bestseller *Book of the Courtier*—the ghosts of the Renaissance's highest ideals of art and thought still seem very much present.

 PREVIOUS PAGE: **A flower-lined street in the hill town of Spello.**

PERUGIA ♥♥

164km (102 miles) SE of Florence, 176km (109 miles) N of Rome

Perugia may be Umbria's capital and the largest city between Florence and Rome, but this is still a medieval hill town at heart. In the historic center, strung out along ridges high above the Tiber valley, ancient alleys drop precipitously off **Corso Vannucci,** the cosmopolitan shopping promenade, and Gothic palaces rise above stony piazzas. The city produced and trained some of Umbria's finest artists, whose works fill the city's excellent art gallery. Thousands of students from Perugia's two universities impart a youthful energy, and Perugia's most famous product, chocolate, adds a sweet note to the city's appeal.

A fresco of St. Francis in Assisi's Basilica di San Francesco.

Essentials

ARRIVING Trains connect Perugia and **Rome** (2–3 hr.; many trains require a change at Terontola) and **Florence** (2¼ hr.; some trains also require a change at Terontola) every couple of hours. In addition, hourly trains run to **Assisi** (20–30 min.), **Spoleto** (1¼ hr.), and other Umbrian towns. Limited high-speed Frecciarossa service connects Perugia with Florence (about 1½ hr.) and **Milan** (about 4 hr.). The main station, Perugia Fontivegge, is a few kilometers southwest and below the town center at Piazza Vittorio Veneto (✆ **147/888088**) but is well connected with buses to/from Piazza Italia (1.50€; 2€ if bought on bus; www.fsbusitalia.it). Perugia's seven-stop, 3km (2-mile) long "minimetro" also makes the run from the station up to stops in the center (1.50€; buy tickets from machines). A few trains arrive and depart from Stazione Sant'Anna, in Piazzale Bellucci, operating on routes between Perugia and **Sansepolcro** (with stops in Umbertide, Citta del Castello, and other small towns to the north) and between Perugia and **Terni** (with stops in Deruta, Todi, and other towns to the south). For tickets and information, go to www.fsbusitalia.it (✆ **075/963-7001**).

SULGA lines (sulga.eu; ✆ **075/500-9641**) operates four buses a day to and from Rome (2½ hr.), three also stop at Rome's Fiumicino airport,

Deruta, Todi, and Assisi. Direct **BusItalia** buses (www.fsbusitalia.it; **© 075/963-7001**) run six times daily between Perugia and Assisi (50 min.), Gubbio (70 min.), and Todi (75 min.). The main Perugia bus station is in Piazza Partigiani, connected by escalator to Piazza Italia in the *centro storico*.

Perugia is well connected by **road** to Siena (a little over an hour on the free Raccordo), Rome (about 2 hr. via the A1 autostrada), and Assisi, Spoleto, and other Umbrian towns. While much of the *centro storico* is off-limits to nonresident drivers, well-marked parking lots are situated at the base of the hills over which old Perugia sprawls, with elevators and escalators to take you up to the center. Some of the most convenient parking is at the underground pay lot at **Piazza Partigiani,** from which escalators ascend to Piazza Italia with some amazing underground scenery along the route (see box p. 314). Parking rates (sabait.it) are 2€ to 2.40€ an hour, or from 13.50€ to 23€ per day. Some hotels issue a card that lets you park for 8€ a day, leaving and entering as you wish.

Perugia's small **Umbria Aeroporto Internazionale San Francisco d'Assisi** (**PEG;** airport.umbria.it; **© 075/592141**), 10km (6 miles) east of the city, serves some inter-European flights, including **Ryanair** (ryanair.com) service between Perugia and London Stansted. Ryanair also operates flights between Perugia and Cagliari, Catania, Palermo, as well as many other European airports in summer. Infrequent buses connect the airport with the Perugia bus and train station and historic center (30–40 min.; 5€). Taxis to or from the airport cost around 25€.

VISITOR INFORMATION The **tourist office** at Piazza Matteotti 18 (turismo.comune.perugia.it; **© 075/573-6458**), open daily 9am to 6pm, provides a fairly useless map for free and a good one for 1€. For 10 days in July, **Umbria Jazz** (umbriajazz.it) showcases entertainers at the Arena Santa Giuliana and other venues around town.

THE CITY OF *cioccolato*

Perugia is a chocoholic's paradise. **Perugina,** with a sweet-scented shop at Corso Vannucci 101 (**© 075/573-4760**), has been making candy here since 1907 and now pumps out 120 tons a day of the sweet stuff, including 1½ million Baci (kisses), its gianduja-and-hazelnut bestseller. Perugia also hosts a weeklong **Eurochocolate Festival** (eurochocolate.com) in October. Perugina's **Casa di Cioccolato** (perugina.com) guides 90-minute tours through its highly mechanized factory on the city outskirts, with a stop in a chocolate museum and a tasting at the end; the company also teaches chocolate-making classes. Tours run Monday, Tuesday, and Thursday to Saturday 9am to 1pm and 2 to 5:30pm, they cost 10€ (9€ seniors and ages 13–17, 5€ kids 6–12, free for children 5 and under). Classes run 3 to 4 hours and cost 44€ to 75€. Casa di Cioccolato is outside the historic center at Viale San Sisto, San Sisto.

Umbria
0 10 mi
0 10 km
Urbino
Ponte di Trajano
Fermignano
Pieve Santo Stefano
Urbania
Metauro
Mercatello sul Metauro
Caprese Michelangelo
Piobbico
Pergola
Sansepolcro
Apennines
Cagli
Anghiari
San Giustino
Arcevia
Selci Lama
Cantiano
Monterchi
Città di Castello
Pietralunga
Sassoferrato
Scheggia
E45
Morra
Montone
Fabriano
Trestine
Gubbio
TUSCANY
Osteria del Gatto
Umbertide
Monte Urbino
MARCHE
Cortona
Gualdo Tadino
Tiber
SS71
SS3
Terontola
Passignano sul Trasimeno
Monte Tezio
UMBRIA
Camerino
Monte Pennino
Valfabbrica
Lago Trasimeno
Magione
Topino
Serravalle di Chienti
Corciano
Perugia
Nocera Umbra
Castiglione del Lago
San Feliciano
Petrignano
Assisi
Monte Subasio
Lago di Chiusi
Bastia Umbra
Rivotorto
Torgiano
Chiascio
SS77
Panicale
Chiusi
Spello
Deruta
Tavernelle
Cannara
Città della Pieve
Piegaro
Visso
Foligno
Gualdo Cattaneo
Bevagna
Chiana
Marsciano
Montefalco
Montegabbiano
Collazzone
Trevi
A1
E45
Bastardo
Campello sul Clitunno
Fabro
San Venanzo
Ficulle
Castel Ritaldi
Monte Castello di Vibio
Norcia
Ponterio
Nera
Monte Peglia
Madonna di Lugo
Massa Martana
Todi
Paglia
Castel Viscardo
SS448
Cáscia
Fontanelle di Bardano
Spoleto
Lago di Corbara
Orvieto
Acquasparta
Castel Giorgio
Baschi
Castell dell'Aquila
Ferentillo
Guardea
Bolsena
San Gemini
Tiber
Montefranco
Bagnoregio
Lugnano in Teverina
Leonessa
Lago di Bolsena
Terni
Torreorsina
Amelia
Piediluco
SS2
Posta
Montefiascone
Lago di Piediluco
Narni
Marta
Giove
SS71
A1
Antroloco
Orte
SS3
Calvi dell'Umbria
Rieti
Monti Sabini
Viterbo
Magliano Sabina
LAZIO
Lago di Vico
Vetralla
Tiber
Civita Castellana

Exploring Perugia

Perugia's main public square, **Piazza Italia,** hangs like a balcony over the hillside at one end of the old town. Among the somber, formidable banks and government buildings fronting the piazza you'll see the imposing porticoes of the Provincia d'Umbria, the provincial offices, to your left as you face the airy, view-filled end of the square. A favorite game in town is to stand in a corner of one of the huge arches, place a companion in the corner diagonally across, and whisper—even the softest murmur travels as if transmitted over a phone. From Piazza Italia the sophisticated **Corso Vannucci** flows north to **Piazza IV Novembre,** presided over by the massive Palazzo dei Priori (home of the Galleria Nazionale dell'Umbria; p. 312) and the city's cathedral, a stark presence with its unfinished exterior. The square's focal point is the elaborate **Fontana Maggiore,** with its carved panels and figures depicting saints, prophets, ancient Roman figures, signs of the zodiac, and biblical scenes (look for the temptation of Adam and Eve); it was crafted by Nicola Pisano and his son Giovanni between 1275 and 1278. Elegant as it is, the fountain also served as the city's main source of fresh water.

Perugia's Piazza IV Novembre and the Fontana Maggiore.

It's especially entertaining to stroll up the Corso in the early evening, when the wide pavement becomes the stage for one of Italy's most lively and decorous evening *passeggiate.* Anywhere you walk in Perugia, however, an upward glance reveals a tower, an arch, or a Renaissance facade decorated with marble figures. An especially scenic walk is along **Via dell'Acquedotto,** north of Piazza IV Novembre, following the 13th-century aqueduct constructed to bring water into the city to the Fontana Maggiore. As the narrow way crosses a ravine, an airy panorama of the old city and green hills unfolds. On the other side is the Borgo Sant'Angelo, seat of the University of Perugia. At the top of the neighborhood is the 14th-century **Cassero di Porta Sant'Angelo,** a gate topped by a massive watchtower, and nearby is another remarkable remnant of early Perugia, **San Michele Arcangelo,** a round, plain early Christian church from the 5th century (free admission, open daily 9am–7pm).

It's a short but steep climb from Piazza IV Novembre east up to the **Arco dei Gigli,** also known as Porta Sole, one of the gates in the Etruscan

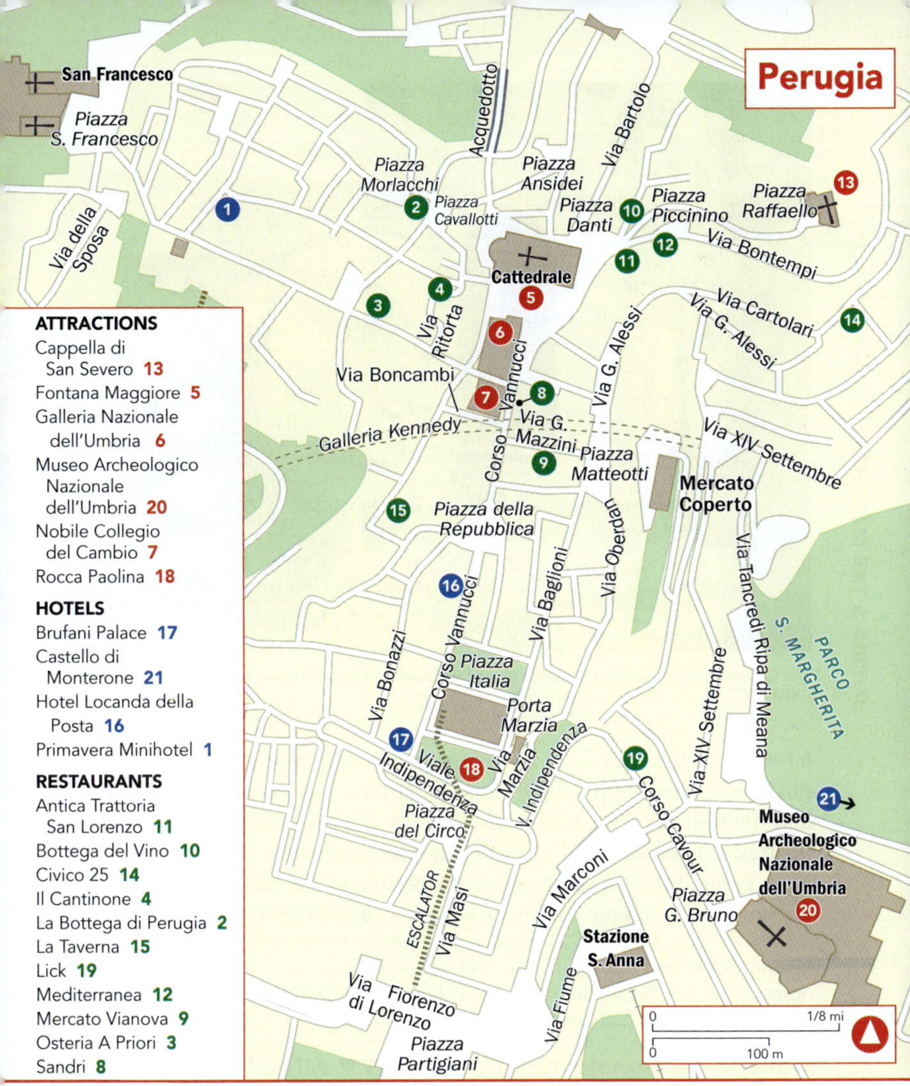

walls that once enclosed the city. Your reward is a view over the old town and valley below.

Cappella di San Severo ♥♥ CHURCH Don't be fooled by the modest 18th-century exterior; the 14th-century chapel inside contains a real treasure. Before young Raphael Sanzio made a name for himself in Florence and Rome, he settled briefly in Perugia, where in 1504 he painted the first of many frescoes that would make him famous in his own lifetime (and vault him into the triumvirate of great Renaissance masters, with da Vinci and Michelangelo). Unfortunately only the upper half of his *Holy Trinity* remains here, and that is damaged. The work seems touchingly modest compared to the complex *School of Athens* and other works he

The Cappella di San Severo contains one of Raphael's earliest frescoes and a bust of the young artist.

later did for the Vatican. As energetic in life as he was in his work, Raphael ran a huge workshop, had dozens of patrons, was in line to be a cardinal, and died on his 37th birthday, allegedly after a lustful session with his mistress. After Raphael's death, his then-septuagenarian teacher, Perugino, painted the six saints along the bottom of the fresco.

Piazza Raffaello. turismo.comune.perugia.it. ✆ **075/573/947-1766.** Admission 4€ adults, 2€ ages 18–25, 1€ children 7–14, free for children 6 and under. Apr daily 10am–1:30pm and 2:30–6pm; May and Sept–Oct Tues–Sun 10am–1:30pm and 2:30–6pm; June–July Tues–Sun 10am–6pm; Aug daily 10am–6pm; Nov–Mar Tues–Sun 11am–1:30pm and 2:30–5pm.

Galleria Nazionale dell'Umbria ♥♥♥ MUSEUM Seven or so centuries of Umbrian art are on the top floors of the crenellated Palazzo dei Priori, where a ruling council of powerful merchants and guilds met in medieval times. It's only fitting that the museum spotlights native son Perugino, who was born nearby in Città della Pieve and spent much of his career working in Perugia (he also studied alongside Leonardo da Vinci in Florence and executed frescoes in the Sistine Chapel in Rome). Perugino's altarpieces are full of delicate landscapes, sweet Madonnas, and grinning Christ Childs that reveal his spare, precise style. Their divine beauty seems ironic, given that Perugino was openly anti-religion and had a fairly turbulent life: He was arrested in Florence for assault and barely escaped exile; he sued Michelangelo for defamation of character; and more than once he was censured for reusing images. He persevered, and worked prodigiously until his death at age 73, leaving a considerable fortune.

The museum's other showpiece is Piero della Francesca's *Polyptych of Perugia*, painted for the city's church of Sant'Antonio in 1470. Its symmetry and realistic dimensions reflect the artist's other occupation as a mathematician; at the same time, his figures are robustly human. Della Francesca works sheer magic at the top of the piece, in a scene of the Annunciation, where an angel appears to Mary in a brightly lit cloister to tell her she will be the mother of the son of God; the illusion of pillars leading off into the distance behind her is regarded as one of the greatest examples of perspective in Renaissance art.

Palazzo dei Priori, Corso Vannucci 19. gallerianazionaledellumbria.it. ✆ **075/574-1247.** Admission 10€ adults, free for ages 17 and under. Daily 8:30am–7:30pm (closed Mon Nov–June).

Museo Archeologico Nazionale dell'Umbria ♥♥ MUSEUM Etruscans are the stars of this collection set in the former church, convent, and cloisters of San Domenico. Most riveting are the stories of everyday life that emerge in stone on the large tombs from around the Tuscan/Umbrian region, which 2,500 years ago was the heartland of a 12-city Etruscan confederation. A man with scales in hand, perhaps an architect, stands in front of a town gate; a young couple kisses; workers harvest grapes. One of the most fascinating pieces, the Sarcophagus dello Sperandio, was discovered in 1843 in the tomb of a warrior, surrounded by iron weapons. On one side, three men recline on a divan, enjoying a banquet as a slave serves them; in another long relief, men, women, and animals (including heavily laden pack animals and collared dogs) follow one another in a procession, possibly a ceremonial parade or migration. It's believed the sarcophagus was fashioned in Chiusi and brought to Perugia by wagon along a rough ancient track. The Cippo di Perugia, from the 3rd century B.C.E., is the longest piece of Etruscan script ever found: It's a land contract between two families, proof that real estate has always been a sound investment.

Piazza Giordano Bruno 10. musei.umbria.beniculturali.it. ✆ **075/572-7141.** Admission 5€. Tues–Sun 8:30am–7:30pm (closed 3rd Sun of the month).

Nobile Collegio del Cambio ♥♥ MUSEUM The cubicles and fluorescent lighting of modern office life will seem even more banal after you visit the frescoed meeting rooms of Perugia's Moneychanger's Guild, one of the best-preserved "office suites" of the Renaissance. Perugino was hired in 1496 to fresco the Sala dell'Udienza (Hearing Room), perhaps with the help of his young student Raphael. The images merge religion (scenes of the Nativity and Transfiguration) with classical references (female representations of the virtues) and, most riveting of all, glimpses of 15th-century secular life.

Palazzo dei Priori, Corso Vannucci 25. collegiodelcambio.it. ✆ **075/572-8599.** Admission 6€. Mon–Sat 9am–1pm and 2:30–5:30pm.

Perugia's Medieval Underground

Beneath Piazza Italia, layers of history are displayed—literally. Around 1530, after the Perugians rebelled against Pope Paul III over a tax on salt (to this day, Perugian bread is salt-free), the Pope demolished more than a quarter of the city in retribution and built his own castle, **Rocca Paolina,** atop the ruins. After Italian unification in 1860, locals ripped the castle to pieces and built Piazza Italia on top of that. Today, the vaults of the Pope's fort and even older relics of medieval dwellings and streets are in full view beneath the piazza. You can clamber through doorless entrances, climb the remains of stairways, walk through empty rooms, and wander at will through the brick maze. Enter the underground city (free admission; daily 6:15am–1:45am) from the escalators that connect Piazza Italia to the lower town's Piazza Partigiani, with its car park and bus station. Guides lead 30-minute tours of the underground departing from the cathedral hourly from 10am to 7pm Monday through Friday (every half hour on weekends); cost is 12€ adults, 10€ seniors 76 and older, 7€ for ages 6 to 17, and free for children 5 and under; guides speak English. Buy tickets in advance at **isolasanlorenzo.it**.

Where to Stay in Perugia

Brufani Palace ♥♥ Built in 1883 to host English travelers on the Grand Tour, Perugia's bastion of luxury commands one side of Piazza Italia and overlooks the valley below. The premises have not changed too much in the intervening years, except that the large, traditionally furnished rooms are now equipped with lavish marble bathrooms and lots of other amenities, including comfortable lounge chairs and sofas. Fires burn in big stone hearths in the dining room and lounges; a swimming pool has been carved out of subterranean brick vaults, with see-through panels exposing Etruscan ruins beneath; and a large rooftop terrace is a perfect spot for a sunset glass of wine.

Piazza Italia 12. sinahotels.com. ✆ **075/573-2541.** 94 units. 200€–260€ double. Rates include breakfast. **Amenities:** Restaurant/bar; babysitting; concierge; exercise room; indoor pool; room service; free Wi-Fi.

Castello di Monterone ♥♥♥ In the 19th century, the Piceller family of musicians, artists, and archaeologists made this 13th-century stronghold their home, creating lounges surrounding massive fireplaces and a beautiful cloister garden dotted with ancient artifacts. These days the many nooks and crannies have been converted to utterly charming guest rooms embellished with wide beams, stone walls, handcrafted iron and wood furniture, and large marble bathrooms. Adding to the ambience is a library tucked off a landing, a cozy lounge bar in the old hall, a swimming pool surrounded by lawns, and a roof terrace on the old battlements. Though the castle nestles on a rural hillside, the center of Perugia is only 10 minutes away.

Strada Monteville 3. castellomonterone.com. ✆ **075/572-4214.** 14 units. 110€–180€ double (2-night min. stay some periods). Rates include breakfast. Closed Feb–Mar. **Amenities:** Restaurant; bar; pool; free Wi-Fi.

Medieval remnants add character to guest rooms at Castello di Monterone.

Hotel Locanda della Posta ♥♥ Perugia's oldest hotel has hosted the likes of Goethe and Hans Christian Andersen, and cherubs still smile down on modern guests from the frescoed ceilings in the lounges (as well as in one of the larger suites) as they did on them. Most guest rooms are contemporary and minimalist, out of character with the surroundings but very well done, with views over the tile-roofed town taking center stage in most. Among modern touches are enormous marble showers, larger than the bathrooms in many hotels. The hotel has another 15 similarly stylish rooms in the Bank, an annex down the street.

Corso Pietro Vannucci 97, Perugia. locandadellapostahotel.it. ✆ **075/572-8925.** 24 units. 140€–240€ double. Some rates include breakfast. Parking (25€ fee). **Amenities:** Room service; spa; free Wi-Fi.

Primavera Minihotel ♥♥ It's well worth the climb up three flights of stairs to this aerie with tall windows framing views of rooftops and the green valley below. Rooms surround a welcoming lounge/breakfast room (breakfast costs extra), except for the best room in the house—a large rooftop double with a terrace. Some are furnished with Art Nouveau pieces, others with traditional rustic furnishing and Deruta pottery, and all have lots of timber, stone, and other architectural details. Piazza della Repubblica and the center of town are just up some twisty streets, and an escalator puts the hotel within easy reach of Parking Pellini.

Via Vincioli 8. primaveraminihotel.it. ✆ **075/572-1657.** 8 units. 100€–120€ double. Closed mid-Jan to mid-Feb. **Amenities:** Free Wi-Fi.

Where to Eat in Perugia

Perugia's youthful student population ensures a wealth of pizza and *panini* (sandwiches). Most popular among cheap *pizzerie* is **Mediterranea ♥**, at Piazza Piccinino 11 (✆ **075/572-4021**). Pizzas cost 5€ to 12€ (daily 12:30–2:30pm and 7:30–10:30pm, Sat until 11pm). Top choice for a panino is **La Bottega di Perugia ♥**, Piazza Francesco Morlacchi 4 (facebook.com/labottegadiperugia; ✆ **075/573-2965**), where the young proprietors pride themselves on using only local Umbrian hams, greens, and other ingredients; panini cost about 4€ and can be washed down with wine or beer (Mon–Wed 11am–10:30pm, Thurs 11am–11pm, Fri–Sat 11am–11:30pm, Sun 11am–9pm). Opened in 1860, the venerable **Sandri ♥** is Perugia's

GO jump IN THE LAKE

Lago Trasimeno, Italy's fourth-largest lake, washes up against the Tuscany-Umbria border between Cortona and Perugia. The shallow waters can't compete with the beauty of Como and other lakes up north (chapter 10), but Trasimeno is nonetheless a refreshing splash of blue amid olive groves and sunflower fields. **Passignano,** on the northern shore 30km (18 miles) northwest of Perugia, is a good stop for a stroll along the shoreline promenade and a gelato or a sunset aperitivo at **Bar del Sole,** Via Aganoor Pompili (✆ **340/504-5309**). At **Castiglione del Lago,** on the western shore 50km (30 miles) west of Perugia, you can swim from a pebbly beach or cycle on shoreline paths; rent bikes (10€ half a day, 15€ a day) at **Cicli Valentini,** Via Firenze 68/B (ciclivalentini.it; ✆ **333/967-8327;** Mon–Sat 9am–1pm and 3:30–8pm). An especially pleasant way to explore the lakeshore is on an e-bike (40€ a day).

From either town, 30-minute ferry trips run hourly across the lake to picturesque **Isola Maggiore,** a nice place to take a dip in the cool waters, or to buy lace from the few local women who carry on the long-standing tradition. Stepping ashore on Isola Maggiore, you'll be following in the footsteps of St. Francis, who spent Lent of 1213 here. Allegedly, the saint even charmed the local fish—when Francis threw a pike given to him by a fisherman back into the lake, the creature swam alongside his savior until the saint gave him a special blessing.

oldest and most esteemed *pasticceria,* serving coffee, pastry, and light meals in Art Deco surrounds at Corso Vannucci 32 (✆ **075/572-4112;** Tues–Sun 7:30am–8pm). The name says it all at **Lick** ♥, Corso Cavour 40 (✆ **075/572-6917**), which dishes up gelato in such unusual variations as Gorgonzola cheese and basil with prosecco (Thurs–Tues noon–8pm; closed Jan).

Antica Trattoria San Lorenzo ♥♥ MODERN ITALIAN Everything here is local, right down to the Perugian-made pottery on the candlelit tables. Chef/owner Simone Ciccotti sources his ingredients from producers in the nearby countryside, then invents dishes that emphasize those flavors, such as a "muffin" of caramelized onions and foie gras, or a *millefeuille* of grilled vegetables with smoked mozzarella. You know you're in good hands because the restaurant's namesake does double duty as a patron saint of Perugia and the patron saint of chefs.
Piazza Danti 19a. anticatrattoriasanlorenzo.com. ✆ **075/527-1956.** Main courses 15€–30€. Daily 12:30–2:30pm and 7–11pm.

Bottega del Vino ♥♥ UMBRIAN In a snug, vintage-photo-lined room right off Piazza IV Novembre you can choose from wines by the glass along with a nice assortment of Umbrian hams and cheeses, perfect for an evening *aperitivo.* The small lunch and dinner menus include salads and a couple of pastas, as well as a dish or two of the day—such as a steak or roasted leg of lamb. Live jazz often plays into the wee hours.
Via del Sole 1. labottegadelvino.net. ✆ **075/571-6181.** Main courses 8€–16€. Tues–Sat noon–2pm and 7pm–midnight. Closed Jan.

Il Cantinone ♥♥ UMBRIAN/PIZZA Even a pizza seems like a meal fit for a medieval courtier when you dine in this softly lit, stone-walled, brick-vaulted 14th-century cantina in a hidden courtyard around the corner from Piazza Maggiore. Also on offer are such hearty dishes as homemade tagliatelle with duck ragù or wild boar sauce, locally sourced Valdichiana beef topped with black truffles, and other Umbrian specialties that befit the distinctively Old Perugia surroundings.

Via Ritorta. ristoranteilcantinoneperugia.com. ✆ **075/573-4430.** Main courses 8€–22€. Wed–Sun 12:30–2:30pm and 7:30–10:30pm.

La Taverna ♥♥♥ UMBRIAN A tiny courtyard down a flight of steps from Corso Vannucci fills with tables in warm weather, while inside, barrel-vaulted ceilings shimmer with candlelight in the evening. The service and Chef Claudio's cooking are similarly warm and down-to-earth. Everything, from bread to pasta to desserts, is made in-house and typically Umbrian: pappardelle with a hearty ragù, *caramelle rosse al Gorgonzola* (beet ravioli with Gorgonzola), and meats seasoned with fresh herbs.

Via delle Streghe 8 (near Piazza Repubblica). ristorantelataverna.com. ✆ **075/572-4128.** Main courses 14€–30€. Daily noon–2:30pm and 7–10:30pm (until 11pm Fri–Sat).

Osteria A Priori ♥♥♥ UMBRIAN You'll pass through a wine shop and climb a flight of stairs to reach this welcoming brick-vaulted room with contemporary wood furnishings, where the emphasis is on Umbrian products and age-old recipes. The staff will eagerly walk you through the daily menu and suggest wine pairings with such specialties as slowly cooked beans (*fagiolina*) paired with eggs and onions and slow-roasted pork shank (*stinco di maiale*) served with crisp potatoes.

Via dei Priori 39. osteriaapriori.it. ✆ **075/572-7098.** Main courses 9€–18€. Mon–Sat 12:30–2:30pm and 7:30–10pm.

Cocktail Hour in Perugia

Top spot for a cocktail in good weather is **Punto Di Vista,** Viale Indipendenza (facebook.com/Puntodiview; ✆ **333/843-2929**) with a panoramic terrace from which the views seem to extend across all of Umbria. You can also sip stylish cocktails at **Mercato Vianova,** Via Giuseppe Mazzini 15 (instagram.com/mercatovianova; ✆ **075/573-04450;** Thurs–Sun noon–3pm and 6pm–1:30am, Wed 7:30pm–1:30am), while **Civico 25** serves from an extensive list of wines by the glass, along with excellent food, at Via della Viola 25 (civico25.com; ✆ **075/571-6376;** Thurs and Mon–Tues 7:30–10:30pm, Fri–Sat 7:30–11pm).

Perugia Shopping

At **Museo Atelier Giuditta Brozzetti,** in a former church at Via Tiberio Berardi 5/6 (brozzetti.com; ✆ **075/40236**), Marta Cucchia oversees a centuries-old family weaving business, based on age-old techniques. The studio/shop (Mon–Fri 8:30am–12:30pm, other times by appointment) offers pillows, runners, and other textiles for sale or on custom order. One-day courses are available, in English, in hand-weaving, lacemaking, and embroidery. At the **Studio Moretti Caselli,** the focus is on stained glass—the Moretti family has been crafting exquisite pieces since 1849. Splendid examples as well as vintage tools are on display at their workshop/museum in a 15th-century house at Via Fatebenefratelli 2 (studiomoretti caselli.it; ✆ **340/776-5594**). Guided tours are by appointment Monday through Saturday 9am to 1pm and cost 5€.

Deruta, a little hill town 20km (12 miles) south of Perugia via SS3bis, has been known for its ceramics since the Middle Ages, and today some 300 studios line the streets. The Perugia tourist office can give you a list of shops; trains run frequently (see above). Deruta products are displayed in Perugia on the overflowing shelves at **Bettini Ceramiche Maiolica Deruta Perugia,** Via Ulisse Rocchi (terrecottederuta.com; ✆ **075/971-0550;** Mon and Wed–Sat 10am–1pm and 2–7pm, Tues 10am–7pm).

GUBBIO ♥♥

39 km (24 miles) NE of Perugia

Perhaps the most medieval-looking town in Italy, Gubbio presents itself to the world with a crenellated skyline backed by darkly forested mountains. At this old hill town's stony heart, the severe red-brick expanse of Piazza Grande dramatically drops away on its south side to soul-soothing views of misty hills and a sweeping valley.

When it comes to St. Francis lore, beautiful Gubbio gets overshadowed by **Assisi** (p. 323), yet it was here that the saint performed one of his most popular miracles—taming a wolf that was terrorizing the citizens (see **Taverna del Lupo** on p. 321)—and it was here that the wealthy young Francis first cast off his finery and put on a rough monk's habit, forsaking his worldly goods. Gubbio is also associated with another holy presence, Don Matteo, the priest detective of a wildly popular Italian TV series set in the town, though filming has moved to **Spoleto** (p. 334).

Essentials

ARRIVING If you're **driving,** a handy place to park is below the old town in Piazza 40 Martiri, named for citizens killed by the Nazis for aiding partisans during World War II. You'll pay about 1.10€ an hour and .40€ each successive hour between 8am and 8pm. Gubbio is not served directly by **train,** though Fossato di Vico, 18km (11 miles) south, is on the Rome–Ancona line, with trains arriving about every 2 hours. Buses operated by **BusItalia** (www.fsbusitalia.it; ✆ **075/963-7001**) run from the station for the 35-minute trip to Gubbio usually at least hourly. Eight or nine daily BusItalia buses also run between Gubbio and Perugia (70 min.); buses arrive at Piazza 40 Martiri. From here it's an easy, level walk to an elevator at the junction of Via Repubblica and Via Baldassini that will take you up to Piazza Grande (at the junction of Via Repubblica and Via

Baldassini; daily 9am–7:30pm). Alternatively, from Piazza 40 Martiri a free shuttle bus runs to Piazza Grande and other stops in the upper town (www.fsbusitalia.it; every 15 min. 7:30am–7:30pm).

VISITOR INFORMATION The **tourist office,** Via della Repubblica 15 (comune.gubbio.pg.it; ✆ **075/922-2027**), is open daily 9am to 7pm. Staffers hand out maps and sell a handy walking guide (1€).

SPECIAL EVENTS Aside from the springtime **Festa dei Ceri** (see Monte Ingino on p. 320), Gubbio's biggest event is lighting the **world's largest Christmas tree** on the slopes in December. Lights are laid out to form a shape 650m (2,130 ft.) high and 335m (1,100 ft.) wide at the base. The pope often does the honors of lighting the tree, using a computer in the Vatican palace. The town seems especially medieval the **last weekend in May,** when Eugubian *balestrieri,* or crossbow competitors, line up in Piazza Grande to face off with competitors from Sansepolcro in Tuscany.

Exploring Gubbio

Start your explorations on hillside **Piazza Grande.** After marveling at the airy view over the valley below, turn around to admire the rambling **Palazzo Ranghiasci** behind you, on the north side. The facade's resemblance to an 18th-century neoclassical British country house is no accident: A nobleman of the time married an English lady and brought her back to Gubbio, where she languished, homesick, then ran away. To lure his wife back, the heartbroken duke commissioned an architect to rebuild the front of his palace in the latest British fashion, but to no avail—she never returned. Note that one of the Greek-style columns has been clumsily

Festa dei Ceri celebrations outside the Palazzo dei Consoli in Gubbio.

replaced with bricks, a patch job after the Allies lobbed a shell into the piazza to dislodge Nazi occupiers at the end of World War II. Next, head for the **Fountain of the Madmen** in Largo Bargello, a short walk west of the piazza along Via Consoli, but approach with care—it's said that if you circle the monument three times you are sure to go mad. Many of the surrounding houses have a narrow door next to the main entrance, raised above street level and known as a **Porta dei Morti,** or "Door of the Dead." It's said that the deceased were removed through them, but it's more likely they provided a safe vantage point from which to see who was at the main entrance.

Steep, narrow lanes switchback up the hill to Gubbio's sturdy **Duomo** and fortresslike **Palazzo Ducale** at the top of the town, where church and state could keep an eye on the citizens below (you may also reach the Duomo and *palazzo* on an elevator off the east side of Piazza Grande). In 1472, Duke Federico da Montefeltro commissioned for his palace the **Gubbio Studiolo,** a glorious room decorated with wood inlay; to see this treasure nowadays, however, you'd have to go to the Metropolitan Museum of Art in New York City. What remains in the formal, painting-hung salons is less inspiring, though the classically proportioned Renaissance courtyard is beautiful (musei.umbria.beniculturali.it; admission 5€; Tues–Sun 8:30am–7:30pm). As you approach the palace on Via Federico da Montefeltro, through a gate you'll see the **Botte dei Canonici** (Canon's Barrel), a humongous vessel capable of holding more than 5,000 gallons of wine. Monks in the monastery above, or so the story goes, could serve themselves by dipping a ladle through a trapdoor in the ceiling.

Gubbio's first-century **Roman Theater** (musei.umbria.beniculturali.it) is on level ground at the foot of the Upper Town, where some rows of overgrown seating are ringed by a semicircle of archways. The site is open Tuesday and Friday 8:30am to 1:30pm, Wednesday and Thursday 2:10 to 7:30pm, and weekends 8:30 to 7:30pm. Admission is 3€.

Monte Ingino ♥♥ PARK/GARDEN On an open-air funicular, **Funivia Colle Eletto** (funiviagubbio.it; ✆ **075/927-3881**), you hop into a moving basket to be whisked about 6 minutes to the top of this 908m (2,980-ft.) summit for stupendous Umbrian views. In the May 15 **Corso dei Ceri** (ceri.it), teams race up the mountainside on foot carrying 15ft.-long wooden battering rams called *ceri,* or "candles." The race is part of the Festa dei Ceri festivities honoring St. Ubaldo, the bishop who allegedly smooth-talked Frederick Barbarossa out of sacking the town in the 1150s. Ubaldo's corpse is up here, too, in a glass casket at the Basilica di Sant'Ubaldo, a 5-minute walk from the funicular stop.

Funicular leaves from Via San Girolamo. Round trip 7€ adults, 5€ kids 4–13, children 3 and under free. June daily 9:30am–1:15pm and 2:30–7pm; July–Aug daily 9am–8pm; early Sept daily 9:30am–7pm; late Sept Mon–Sat 9:30am–1:15pm and 2:30–7pm, Sun 9am–7pm; Oct daily 10am–1:15pm and 2:30–6pm; Nov–Feb Thurs–Tues 10am–1:15pm and 2:30–5pm; Mar daily 10am–1:15pm and 2:30–5:30pm (until 6pm Sun); Apr–May daily 10am–1:15pm and 2:30–6:30pm (until 7pm Sun).

Museo del Palazzo dei Consoli ♥♥ MUSEUM The former home of the town government is a solidly Gothic-looking palace, with crenellations, a tower, and an imposing stone staircase that sweeps up from Piazza Grande. The main hall, where the medieval commune met, houses the town museum, which has one stand-out artifact: The seven **Eugubine Tables.** Inscribed on bronze from 200 to 70 B.C.E. these are Umbria's equivalent of the Rosetta Stone, the only existing record of the ancient Umbri language transposed in Etruscan and Latin letters. A local farmer turned up the tablets while plowing his fields in 1444; city officials convinced him to sell them for 2 years of grazing rights. ***Tip:*** Look for the secret corridor from the back of the ceramics room to the Pinacoteca upstairs, via the medieval toilets.

Piazza Grande. palazzodeiconsoli.it. ✆ **075/927-4298.** Admission 12€ adults, 3€ ages 6–18, free for children 5 and under. Mon–Fri 10am–1pm and 3–6pm; Sat–Sun 10am–6pm.

Where to Stay & Eat in Gubbio

Grotta dell'Angelo ♥♥ ITALIAN/UMBRIAN A barrel-vaulted dining room where locals have been gathering for the past 700 years or so is the place to sit in winter, while warm-weather dining is on a vine-shaded terrace. Wherever you eat, enjoy the homemade gnocchi, followed by sausages and other meats roasted over the open fire—the whole roast chicken stuffed with fennel is especially delicious. Hotel rooms upstairs are similarly homey (55€–70€ double; breakfast 6€).

Via Gioia 47. grottadellangelo.it. ✆ **075/927-1747.** Main courses 9€–16€. Wed–Mon 12:15–2pm and 7:30–9:30pm. Closed Jan 7–Feb 7.

Hotel Relais Ducale ♥♥ These were once the palace annexes of the Montefalco dukes, the great Renaissance powerbrokers. Now they open off Piazza Grande and house extremely comfortable guest rooms that are scattered over several levels, with highly polished floors and well-tended traditional furnishings befitting the royal surroundings. Some have barrel vaulting or open to terraces, and all are within easy reach of patios and shady nooks. Proprietors Daniela and Sean offer lots of personal attention; they'll even pick you up at the train station in Fossato di Vico.

Via Galeotti 19. relaisducale.com. ✆ **075/922-0157.** 30 units. 85€–115€ double. Rates include breakfast. **Amenities:** Bar; room service; free Wi-Fi.

Taverna del Lupo ♥♥ UMBRIAN Around 1220, or so the story goes, a ferocious wolf (*lupo*) menaced the good people of Gubbio, devouring them the moment they stepped outside the town gates. St. Francis, then living a monkish life of contemplation in Gubbio, went to the beast's lair, tamed him, and led him back into the marketplace, where townsfolk agreed to feed him in return for good behavior. A charming fresco depicting Francis and the wolf is one of many artworks on the stone walls of these former cellars, where legend says the animal often popped in for a meal. These days diners count on the refined surroundings for

specialties like homemade tagliatelle with truffles or the kitchen's famous *faraona al ginepro,* guinea hen roasted with juniper berries.
Via Ansidei 21. tavernadellupo.it. ✆ **075/927-4368.** Main courses 15€–32€; tasting menu 45€. Daily noon–3pm and 7–10pm. Closed Jan 7–Feb 7.

A Side Trip to Urbino ♥♥

One of the steepest hill towns in Italy, Urbino is a time capsule of the Renaissance, a storybook compilation of towers, domes, and red-tile roofs. Though its glory days wound down 500 years ago, this remote hill town is still prosperous and lively, thanks to Urbino's prestigious university. The 66km (40-mile) drive or bus trip (autolineecurcio.it) northeast from Gubbio through mountainous terrain on the SS3 takes a leisurely hour or so, and the landscape en route is stunning: rippling hills carpeted with fields and forests, topped with the occasional walled village. Stash your car in the large parking lot at Borgo del Mercatale (1.50€ per hour, 12€ a day), and then hit the steep cobblestone streets on foot.

Aside from the scenic hills, Urbino's main draw is art: The city is the birthplace of Raphael, Renaissance painter of glorious frescoes, and home to the outstanding collection of Duke Federico da Montefeltro.

Casa Raffaello (Raphael's Birthplace) ♥♥ MUSEUM One of the great artists of the High Renaissance (you can see his work at Cappella di San Severo in Perugia [p. 311] and his best efforts at the Vatican [p. 84]) was born in Urbino in 1483. His earliest known work, a modest boyhood fresco, *Madonna and Child,* hangs on one of the walls here in his childhood home. Compare this modest effort to his *Portrait of a Young Woman,* in the nearby Palazzo Ducale (see above), which shows the genius of his mature style. The museum also holds works by Raphael's lesser-known father, Giovanni Santi, a court painter to the duke.
Via Rafaello 57. casaraffaello.com. No phone. Admission 4€, ages 15 and under free. Mon–Sat 9am–1pm and 3–7pm (9am–2pm only Nov–Feb), Sun 10am–1pm and 3–6pm.

Galleria Nazionale delle Marche Palazzo Ducale di Urbino ♥♥♥ MUSEUM Wise and worldly Duke Federico da Montefeltro (1422–82) paced the halls of this palace and contemplated his vast holdings from the study window, all the while dreaming up some of the most enlightened ideals of the Renaissance. One of the palace's most enchanting rooms is that study, beautifully paneled with intarsia depicting classical and humanistic writers as well as great religious thinkers. The duke famously came up with the concept of *sprezzatura,* the ideal of maintaining grace under pressure. Duke Federico and his son, Guidobaldo, oversaw a court so enlightened that Baldassare Castiglione set his 1507 bestseller, *Book of the Courtier,* in the palace's Hall of Vigils. Father and son were patrons of some of the great artists of their day, whose works now hang in the salons and staterooms. *Ideal City,* attributed to Piero della Francesca, perfectly evokes the dukes' enlightened ideas; della Francesca's *Flagellation,* another palace treasure, is one of the Renaissance's finest accomplishments in

Intricate intarsia wood paneling graces the Duke of Montefeltro's study, now part of the Galleria Nazionale delle Marche Palazzo Ducale di Urbino.

perspective. Another achievement in perspective, Paolo Uccello's *Miracle of the Profaned* reveals 15th-century anti-Semitic propaganda in its depiction of a Jewish pawnbroker attempting to cook the sacred communion wafer (believed to transform into the body of Christ during the Eucharist), as blood seeping under his door attracts bailiffs.

Piazza Duca Federico. gallerianazionalemarche.it. ✆ **0722/322625.** Admission 12€ adults, ages 17 and under free. Tues–Sun 8:30am–7:15pm.

WHERE TO EAT IN URBINO

Taverna degli Artisti ♥♥ ITALIAN These vaulted underground rooms, one with colorful frescoes, are the place to try an Urbino favorite, *strozzapreti con salmone, asparagi, e funghi:* thick, elongated pasta with a creamy sauce of salmon, asparagus, and mushrooms (the name *strozzapreti* is an old term meaning "priest choker," from an anticlerical wish among the poor that well-fed priests would choke on their pasta). The other pastas and pizzas are excellent, too.

Via Bramante 52. tavernadegliartistiurbino.it. ✆ **0722/2676.** Main courses 8€–20€. Tues–Sun 12:30–2:30pm and 7:30–11pm; Mon 10am–2pm.

ASSISI ♥♥♥

27km (17 miles) E of Perugia, 175km (109 miles) SE from Florence, 175km (109 miles) NE from Rome

St. Francis is still working miracles: His birthplace remains a transporting Umbrian hill town despite a steady onslaught of visitors. Many pilgrims come to pay homage to Francis at the Basilica di San Francisco, and

WORLD'S favorite saint

For Christian pilgrims, the magic of Assisi is all about **St. Francis,** one of the patron saints of Italy (along with Catherine of Siena; see p. 238). Founder of one of the world's largest monastic orders, Francis is generally considered to have been just about the holiest person to walk the earth since Jesus.

Born to a wealthy merchant, Francis was a spoiled young man of his time, until he did an about-face in his early 20s and dedicated himself to a life of poverty. Known for his humility and love of animals, he also is said to have invented Christmastime crèche scenes, all of which have helped ensure his legend. Francis traveled as far as Egypt (in an unsuccessful attempt to convert the sultan and put an end to the Crusades), but he is most associated with the gentle countryside around Assisi, where he spent months praying and fasting in lonely hermitages.

almost as many are drawn by Giotto's frescoes celebrating the life of the saint. You'll find a blend of romance and magic in Assisi's honey-colored stone, quiet lanes, and mists that rise and fall over the Val di Spoleto below town. With this saintly presence and pleasing ambience, Assisi is an essential stop on any Umbrian tour.

Essentials

ARRIVING About 20 trains run daily from **Perugia** (25–30 min.). From **Florence** (2–3 hr.), trains run almost hourly, though some require a transfer at Terontola; hourly trains run from Rome, most requiring a change in Foligno (2 hr. or more with connection). Trains arrive in the modern valley town of Santa Maria degli Angeli, about 5km (3 miles) from Assisi, with bus connections up to Assisi every 30 minutes; buy tickets at the bar in the station for 1.30€ or pay 1.50€ exact change on the bus; the stop in Piazza Matteotti leaves you about a 5-minute downhill walk away from Piazza del Comune. **A taxi** ride from the station up to town costs 15€ to 20€. You can stash your luggage at the station bar for 4€ a bag; it's open 6:30am to 7:30pm.

By **car,** Assisi is 18km (11 miles) east of Perugia, off the SS75bis. The center's steep streets are off-limits to nonresident drivers. The best strategy is to **park** in Piazza Matteotti (2€ per hour; sabait.it), keep walking west, and finish at the basilica; it's all downhill and a fairly gentle uphill walk on the return. A dependable alternative is the Mojano, a multistory garage (2€ hr.) halfway up the hill from Piazza Giovanni Paolo II to Porta Nuova. From there, escalators whisk you into the center of town. Other well-marked garages and lots surround the town.

At least six daily **BusItalia** buses (www.fsbusitalia.it; ✆ **075/963-7001**) connect **Perugia** with Assisi (50 min.); five buses a day run between Assisi and **Gubbio** (1¾ hr.). At least two buses a day run between Assisi and **Rome's** Tiburtina train station (3 hr.; sulga.it and www.fsbusitalia.it).

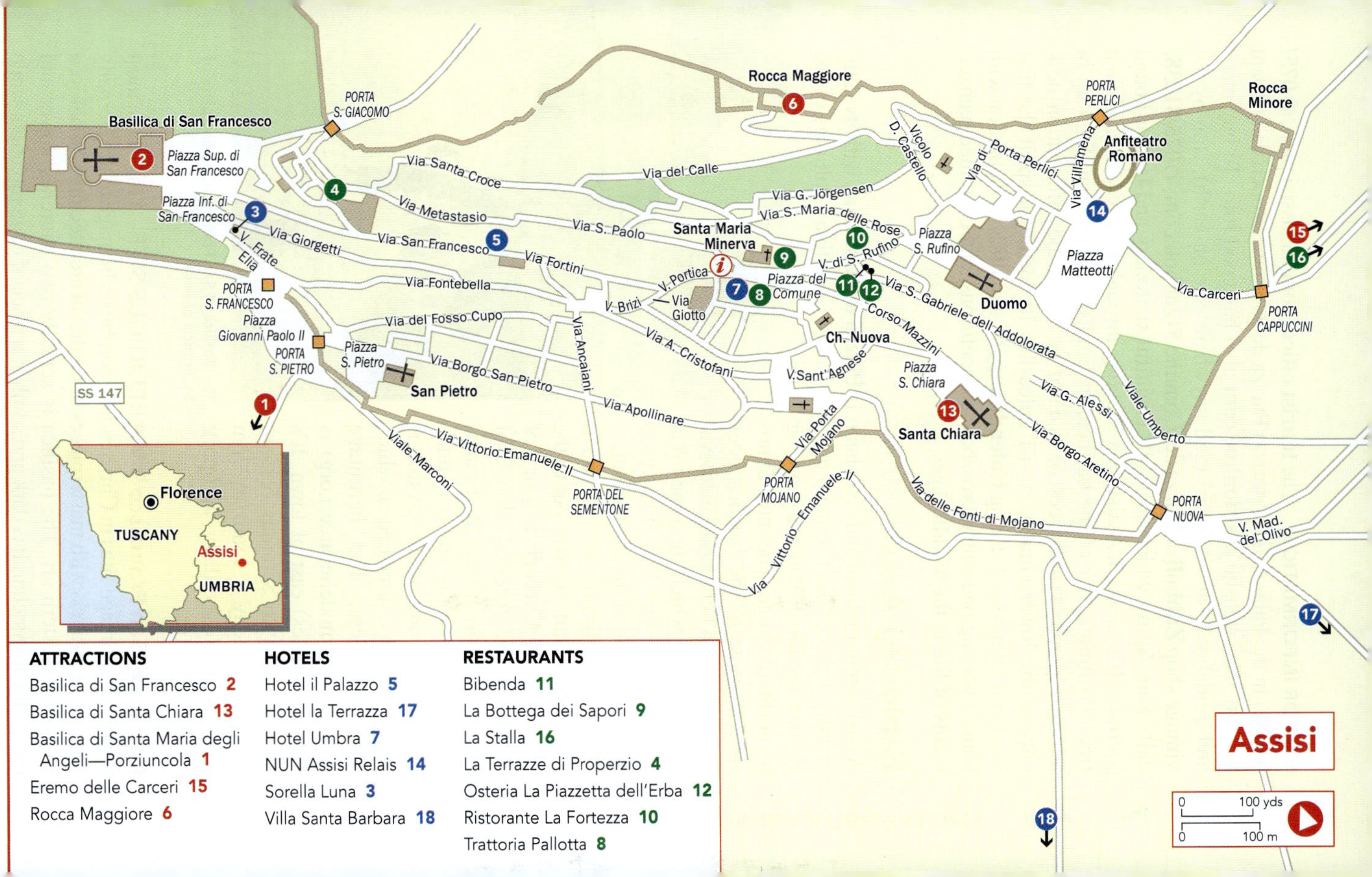
Assisi
0 100 yds
0 100 m
ATTRACTIONS
Basilica di San Francesco 2
Basilica di Santa Chiara 13
Basilica di Santa Maria degli Angeli—Porziuncola 1
Eremo delle Carceri 15
Rocca Maggiore 6
HOTELS
Hotel il Palazzo 5
Hotel la Terrazza 17
Hotel Umbra 7
NUN Assisi Relais 14
Sorella Luna 3
Villa Santa Barbara 18
RESTAURANTS
Bibenda 11
La Bottega dei Sapori 9
La Stalla 16
La Terrazze di Properzio 4
Osteria La Piazzetta dell'Erba 12
Ristorante La Fortezza 10
Trattoria Pallotta 8
Basilica di San Francesco
Piazza Sup. di San Francesco
Piazza Inf. di San Francesco
PORTA S. GIACOMO
Rocca Maggiore
PORTA PERLICI
Rocca Minore
Anfiteatro Romano
Piazza Matteotti
Duomo
Piazza S. Rufino
Santa Maria Minerva
Piazza del Comune
Ch. Nuova
Piazza S. Chiara
Santa Chiara
San Pietro
Piazza S. Pietro
PORTA S. FRANCESCO
Piazza Giovanni Paolo II
PORTA S. PIETRO
PORTA DEL SEMENTONE
PORTA MOJANO
PORTA NUOVA
PORTA CAPPUCCINI
SS 147
Via Santa Croce
Via Metastasio
Via San Francesco
Via Giorgetti
V. Frate Elia
Via Fontebella
Via del Fosso Cupo
Via Borgo San Pietro
Via Vittorio Emanuele II
Viale Marconi
Via Ancaiani
Via Fortini
Via S. Paolo
Via del Calle
Via G. Jörgensen
Via S. Maria delle Rose
V. Portica
V. Brizi
Via Giotto
Via A. Cristofani
Via Apollinare
V. Sant'Agnese
Via Porta Mojano
V. di S. Rufino
Via S. Gabriele dell'Addolorata
Corso Mazzini
Via G. Alessi
Viale Umberto
Via Borgo Aretino
Via delle Fonti di Mojano
V. Mad. del Olivo
Via Carceri
Via Villamena
Via di Porta Perlici
Vicolo D. Castello
Florence
TUSCANY
Assisi
UMBRIA

VISITOR INFORMATION The **tourist office** (comune.assisi.pg.it; ✆ **075/81381**) in the Palazzo dei Priori on Piazza del Comune is open daily 10am to 5pm. The website **assisionline.com** also has good info. To buy maps and guidebooks about Assisi (and anywhere else on earth), stop by the vintage shop **Zubboli** at Piazza del Comune 5 (zubboli.com; ✆ **075/81238;** daily 8am–8pm), which also sells beautiful stationery and leather-bound journals. If you are in Assisi on a Monday through Friday you can join a free, 75-minute tour of the basilica, in English, with a friar. Sign up in advance at info@sanfrancescoassisi.org or ask at the information desk outside the lower church. Assisi unleashes its medieval spirit the first weekend after May 1 during **Calendimaggio,** a multiday celebration with banner-waving pageantry, crossbow competitions, and costumed reenactments of life in the Middle Ages.

Exploring Assisi

Assisi's geographical and civic heart is **Piazza del Comune,** with its 13th-century Palazzo del Capitano and the stately Corinthian columns of the Roman Tempio di Minerva guarding its northern fringe. The most atmospheric route to the basilica goes downhill from here along medieval Via Portica, which becomes Via Fortini and Via San Francesco before arriving at the main event.

Some pilgrims like to end a visit with a walk or drive out to the **Eremo delle Carceri,** a series of caves on the forested slopes of Monte Subasio where St. Francis would retire to pray and commune with nature; one of the grottos is equipped with a stone bed on which the saint slept. The hermitage (santuarioeremodellecarceri.org) is 4km (2½ miles) east of town. It's open Monday to Saturday 6:15am to 7pm, Sunday 7:15am to 7pm (Nov–Mar closes daily at 6pm); admission is free.

The Basilica di San Francesco, resting place of St. Francis of Assisi.

Basilica di San Francesco ♥♥♥ RELIGIOUS SITE One of the most popular pilgrimage sites in Christendom combines homage to the eternally popular St. Francis with masterpieces of medieval architecture and beloved works of Western art. The basilica is actually two churches, lower and upper; the lower church is dark and somber, a place of contemplation, while the upper church soars into light-filled Gothic vaults, instilling a sense of celebration. This assemblage was begun soon after the saint's death in 1226, under the guidance of Francis's savvy and worldly colleague Brother Elias. Set on a steeply sloping site just outside the city walls, previously used for executions and known as the Hill of Hell, the lower church was completed in 1230, the upper church in 1280. Today the presence of Francis, patron saint of Italy, and his credo, "For it is in giving that we receive," still seems to permeate the soft gray stones. These frescoed spaces move the devout to tears and art lovers to fits of near-religious ecstasy.

THE LOWER CHURCH Entered off Piazza Inferiore di San Francesco (the lower of the two squares abutting the church), the basilica's bottom half is first and foremost a crypt, housing the stone **sarcophagus of St. Francis,** surrounded by four of his disciples. An almost steady stream of the faithful files past the monument, many on their knees. The dimly lit atmosphere is enlivened by many rich frescoes, including Simone Martini's action-packed *Life of St. Martin* in the **Cappella di San Martino** (1322–26). Martini displays a flair for boldly patterned fabrics and familiarity with detailed manuscript illumination. Martini was, like St. Martin, a knight, which may have influenced his depictions of the saint—a Roman soldier—being invested, ripping his cloak to share it with a beggar, and renouncing chivalry and weaponry in favor of doing good deeds. The imagery is not out of keeping with Francis, who as a youth dreamed of being a soldier. Giotto and his assistants frescoed the **Cappella della Santa Maria Maddalena** with the *Life of St. Mary Magdalene* (1303–09). An incredibly moving cycle of *Christ's Passion* (1316–19) by Pietro Lorenzetti includes a hauntingly humane *Deposition*, in which the young Sienese artist depicts a gaunt Christ and sorrowful Mary, displaying a naturalism and emotion not before seen in painting.

THE UPPER CHURCH Entering the light-filled interior of the Upper Church, you'll first encounter **scenes of the New Testament** by Cimabue, the last great painter of the Byzantine style. Some critics say only the faded, vaguely surreal *Crucifixion* (1277) is his, the rest being by his assistants. In any case, it's ironic he's here at all: The artist was infamous for his stubborn, difficult character (in the *Divine Comedy,* Dante places him in Purgatory among the proud, adding that "Cimabue thought to hold the field of painting, and now Giotto hath the cry"). And it's Giotto who famously holds court in this church, with his 28-part fresco cycle ***The Life of St. Francis,*** completed in the 1290s. Even nonreligious viewers love the scenes of the saint removing his clothing to renounce material possessions, marrying poverty (symbolized by a woman in rags), and preaching to the birds (the subject of ubiquitous postcards on sale). Assisi itself stars in the panel in which a humble man spreads his cloak before Francis—the sturdy palaces of Piazza del Comune are a recognizable backdrop.

Piazza Superiore di San Francesco. ✆ **075/819001.** Free admission. Lower church: Mon–Sat 6am–6:30pm, Sun 10:30am–4:30pm; Upper church 8:30am–6:45pm (until 5:45pm in winter), Sun 1–6:45pm (until 5:45pm in winter).

Basilica di Santa Chiara ♥♥ CHURCH One of the first followers of St. Francis was a young woman, Chiara (Clare, in English), daughter of a count and countess, who was so swept away by the teachings of the zealot that she allowed him to cut her hair and dress her in sackcloth. She founded the order of the Poor Dames (now known as Poor Clares), whose members continue to renounce material possessions. Her remains lie in this vast, stark church on full view, her face covered in wax. Also in this church, the **Oratorio del Crocifisso** houses the venerated 12th-century crucifix from which the figure of Christ allegedly spoke to St. Francis, asking him to rebuild his church (the institution had by then become mired in corruption and warfare). As Clare lay ill on Christmas Eve 1252, she allegedly voiced regrets that she would not be able to attend services in the new Basilica di San Francisco. Suddenly, in a vision, she saw and heard the Mass clear as a bell and in color, a miracle for which in 1958 she was named the patron saint of television.

Piazza Santa Chiara. assisisantachiara.it. ✆ **075/812282.** Free admission. 6:30am–noon and 2–6:45pm (5:45pm in winter).

Basilica di Santa Maria degli Angeli—Porziuncola ♥♥ CHURCH The seventh-largest church in Christendom sits on the plains below Assisi, on ground that's been hallowed since St. Francis died in 1226 in a simple infirmary cell, the Cappella del Transito, to one side of the present-day basilica. Beginning in 1569, pilgrim huts and friar cells were cleared to make room for this massive edifice, a century in the making. A soaring domed nave surrounds the well-preserved and heavily frescoed **Porziuncola** ("little portion"), a chapel that's been on this site since the 9th century, where Francis renounced his worldly goods to live among the poor, establishing the Franciscan order. Outside is the **rose garden** where Francis communed with turtle doves and asked them to be one with God.

Piazza della Porziuncola, Santa Maria degli Angeli. porziuncola.org. ✆ **075/805-1430.** Free admission to basilica; museum 4€, 3€ ages 11–18, 10 and under free. Daily 6:15am–12:30pm and 2:30pm–7:30pm; museum Thurs–Tues 9am–1pm and 2:30–5pm.

> **Dress Appropriately**
>
> San Francesco and Santa Chiara have a strict dress code. Entrance is forbidden to those wearing shorts or miniskirts or showing bare shoulders. You also must remain silent and cannot take photographs in the Upper Church of San Francesco.

Rocca Maggiore ♥♥ CASTLE This civic show of might built of bleached yellow stone is perched atop a steep hillside high above Assisi. The views across the Umbrian plains below are wonderful, and you can enjoy them from the grounds without paying admission to see the dull displays of costumes and weapons in the restored keep and soldiers' quarters.

Piazzale delle Libertà Comunali, at the ends of Via della Rocca, Via del Colle, and Vicolo San Lorenzo off Via Porta Perlici. visit-assisi.it. ✆ **075/8138680.** Admission 8€ adults, 6€ seniors and ages 8–18, free for children 7 and under. Daily 10am–7pm (closes 8pm June–Aug, 5pm Nov–Feb).

Where to Stay in Assisi

Especially from Easter to fall, never show up in Assisi without a hotel reservation. Don't even *think* of showing up without a reservation on **church holidays** or the **Calendimaggio** in early May. At these times you may wind up stuck overnight in one of the bus-pilgrimage facilities 4km (2½ miles) away in Santa Maria degli Angeli.

Hotel il Palazzo ♥♥♥ Stonework and vaulted ceilings show off this refined palace's 12th-century origins, but decor throughout is stylishly contemporary. Original artwork hangs in the hallways, a solid buffet breakfast is served in a grotto-like breakfast room, and guests can relax in an inviting lounge and courtyard. All the rooms are soothingly done, with ample workspace and armchairs, but the standouts are the light-filled superiors with wide-sweeping valley views.

Via San Francesco. hotelilpalazzo.it. ✆ **075/816841.** 13 units. 110€–140€ double. Most rates include breakfast (10€). **Amenities:** Lounge; free Wi-Fi.

Assisi draws spiritual pilgrims as well as tourists.

Hotel la Terrazza ♥♥ The best of two worlds come together here in the countryside just outside the town walls—the basilica and other sights are a 20-minute walk away, while an on-site pool, garden, and green surroundings provide a break from Assisi's stony streets and squares. The nicest rooms are in a low-slung outbuilding facing lawns on one side and balcony views of the valley on the other, but those in a hotel section also open to gardens or balconies. Room decor is functionally comfortable, enlivened with colorful reproductions of Giotto's basilica murals over the beds to instill dreams of doing saintly deeds.

Via Fratelli Canonichetti 1. laterrazzahotel.it. ✆ **075/812368.** 40 units. 110€–140€ double. Rates include breakfast. **Amenities:** Restaurant; bar; pool; spa; free Wi-Fi.

Hotel Umbra ♥♥ Assisi lodgings just don't get any homier than the Laudenzi family's traditional little inn, down a tiny alley from Piazza del Comune. A gate opens into a shady patio, and beyond are comfortable guest rooms with vaulted ceilings, fresco fragments, and other historic remnants, all nicely furnished with old-fashioned armoires and dressers. Views over rooftops to the valley below unfold through the tall windows, from airy public terraces and a few private ones.

Via Degli Archi 6 (off west end of Piazza del Comune). hotelumbra.it. ✆ **075/812240.** 24 units. 125€–160€ double. 2-night minimum stay some periods. Rates include breakfast. Closed mid-Jan to Easter. **Amenities:** Babysitting; concierge; room service; free Wi-Fi.

NUN Assisi Relais ♥♥ A contemporary redo of a centuries-old convent offers handsome guest quarters with all-white surfaces and bursts of color, accented with stone walls and arches and boldly turned out with Eames chairs, laminate tables, and high-tech lighting. A two-level suite with a hanging sleeping loft is focused on a massive 13th-century fresco of saints in the wilderness. Downstairs are pleasures the former tenants could never have dreamed of: two pools, sauna and steam room, and a state-of-the-art spa.

Eremo delle Carceri 1A. nunassisi.com. ✆ **075/815-5150.** 18 units. 580€–720€ double. Rates include breakfast. Closed Jan to mid-Feb. **Amenities:** Restaurant; bar; concierge; indoor pools; room service; sauna; steam room; spa; free Wi-Fi.

Sorella Luna ♥♥ A renovated 15th-century palace does justice to the positive, harmony-seeking nature of namesake Clare (Sorella Luna), the follower of St. Francis whose church is on the other end of town. A flower-filled terraced garden and glassed-in atriums lead to bright guest rooms, in which stone walls and wood beams offset contemporary furnishings and tiled modern baths. The Basilica di San Francisco is just down the street.

Via Frate Ella 5. hotelsorellaluna.it. ✆ **075/816194.** 13 units. 125€–140€ double. Rates include breakfast. Closed Jan–Feb. **Amenities:** Free Wi-Fi.

Villa Santa Barbara ♥♥♥ If you have a car, consider visiting Assisi from smaller nearby towns, like the appealing wine village of Montefalco (see box p. 333), about half an hour south. This 16th-century estate outside town will make you feel like a guest in a gracious Italian villa. Airy, light-filled bedrooms are comfortably equipped with armchairs, king-size beds, antiques, and large marble-sheathed bathrooms. Palm-shaded gardens surround the pool, and welcoming lounges are filled with books and pottery. Dinners are served in a vaulted room glistening with terra-cotta tiles. Locanda San Luca (just east of Montefalco). hotelvillasantabarbara.com. ✆ **0742/399-402.** 34 units. 180€–200€ double. Rates include breakfast. Closed Nov–Mar. **Amenities:** Restaurant; bar; pool; free Wi-Fi.

Where to Eat in Assisi

Assisi's restaurants serve a local flatbread called *torta al testo,* often grilled and split and stuffed with cheeses, sausages, and vegetables (spinach is popular). Another Umbrian classic is *porchetta,* roasted pork stuffed with garlic and herbs; it's often served with *torta al testo.* **La Bottega dei Sapori,** a wine and food shop on Piazza del Comune (no. 34; ✆ **075/812-204**), serves platters of local meats and cheese and a delicious *porchetta* sandwich, accompanied by excellent wines. Seating is limited, but they'll fix a snack plate for you to take back to your hotel. They also ship wines. **Bibenda,** an atmospheric wine cellar off Piazzetta dell'Erba at Vicolo Nepis 9 (bibendaassisi.it; ✆ **075/815-5176**), pairs Umbrian wines with small plates of local cheeses and salami. Popular in these parts are full-bodied, honey-colored whites made from Grechetto grapes grown in the nearby Montefalco vineyards (p. 333).

La Stalla ♥♥ GRILL/UMBRIAN A 15-minute walk into the countryside will work up an appetite for a hearty meal in these rustic stone-walled rooms, converted from livestock stalls. Begin with the *assaggini di torta al testo,* samplers of flatbread stuffed with cheese, meat, and vegetables, then move through a selection of pastas to ample servings of grilled steak, chicken, pork, and sausage skewers, accompanied by grilled potatoes. House wines complement the meals, served on a terrace in good weather. Santuario della Carceri 24, 1.5km (about 1 mile) from center, direction Eremo. fontemaggio.it. ✆ **075/813636.** Main courses 9€–18€. Thurs–Mon 12:30–2:30pm and 7:30–10pm; Tues–Wed 7:30–10pm. Closed Jan–Feb.

La Terrazze di Properzio ♥♥♥ UMBRIAN The award for best view and most romantic dining experience goes to these attractive stone-walled rooms opening onto a terrace that seems to float above the valley. Lofty as the setting is, the menu focuses on such down-to-earth Umbrian classics as fried artichokes, pasta carbonara, and boar stew. Reserve a terrace table.

Via Metastasio 13. facebook.com/ilbardiroccoecracra. ✆ **075/816868.** Main courses 9€–24€. Tues–Sun 12:30–2:30pm and 7:30–10pm. Closed Jan to mid-Feb.

Osteria La Piazzetta dell'Erba ♥♥ UMBRIAN The arched room and flower-filled terrace facing a market square seem in keeping with this postcard-perfect hill town, but the kitchen breaks from tradition with Asian takes on Umbrian classics. Even a stalwart Umbrian *costolette di maiale* (baked pork ribs) gets a fresh twist with a honey yogurt sauce, while tartares of salmon and tuna, *tataki di tonno* (a Japanese method of quick searing marinated tuna), and sushi, *maki* rolls, and poke bowls add a taste of the sea to the meat-heavy local cuisine.

Via San Gabriele dell'Addolorata 15b. osteriapiazzettadellerba.it. ✆ **075/815352.** Main courses 18€–24€. Tues–Sun 12:30–2:30pm and 7:30–10pm.

Ristorante La Fortezza ♥♥ UMBRIAN In the Chiocchetti family's plain, stone-walled dining room, the focus is on authentic Umbrian home cooking. The many specialties include *cannelloni all'Assisiana* (fresh pasta sheets wrapped around a veal ragù, all baked under *Parmigiana*) and *coniglio in salsa di mele* (rabbit roasted in a wine-apple sauce). The service is as warm and comforting as the surroundings and the food. Seven homey rooms are tucked onto the upper floors (75€–90€ double).

Vicolo della Fortezza (just off Piazza del Comune). ✆ **352/785-3163.** Main courses 9€–18€. Tues–Sat 11:30am–3pm and 7–11pm; Sun 11am–3pm. Shorter hours some winter months.

Trattoria Pallotta ♥♥ UMBRIAN All the warmth of Assisi comes to the fore in this Assisi dining institution, serving since 1860, where beamed, tiled, and charmingly furnished rooms are tucked under the arches off Piazza del Comune. The food is satisfyingly Umbrian—homemade pastas with rich sauces, roasted rabbit, and grilled filets, with many specials changing with the seasons.

Piazza del Comune. trattoriapallotta.it. ✆ **075/815-5273.** Main courses 12€–22€. Wed–Mon noon–2:30pm and 7–9:30pm.

A Side Trip to Spello ♥♥

14km (9 miles) S of Assisi

It's a short trip down SS75 from Assisi to this beguilingly pretty, walled hill town of pink and honey-colored stone on the flanks of Monte Subasio. Roman Spello, known as Hispellum, comes to the fore in the **Villa of Mosaics ♥♥**, Via Paolina Schicchi Fagotti 7, where excavations have revealed exquisite mosaic flooring in rich colors, depicting birds, wild animals, mythical creatures, and scenes of grape harvests and other prosaic events. Admission is 8€ and the villa is open Monday and Wednesday to Friday 10:30am to 1:30pm and 3 to 7pm, Saturday and Sunday 10:30am to 7pm (Oct–Apr closes 5:30pm, also closed 1:30–3pm weekends). A millennium and a half later Pinturicchio—"The Little Painter"—created one of Umbria's great masterpieces here, color-saturated frescoes of the life of Christ in the Cappello Baglioni (see below). And, speaking of color-saturated, on the Feast of Corpus Cristi (June 19), the town stages the **Infiorata,** laying a mile-long carpet of fresh flowers fashioned into biblical scenes along the streets. The **tourist office** in Piazza Matteotti

CLIMBING HIGHER: more hill towns

For sheer picturesqueness, few Umbrian hill towns can match proud **Todi** ♥♥, 45km (28 miles) southwest of Spello. At the top of the town is one of the finest squares in Umbria, an assemblage of 12th- to 14th-century palaces and the Duomo, with belvederes that provide soaring views of the rolling Umbrian countryside and Tiber Valley below.

Montefalco ♥♥, 18km (11 miles) southwest of Spello on SR316, tops a hill above the Valle Umbra, with the five-sided Piazza del Commune at the highest point in town. Surrounding vineyards yield Grechetto whites and Sagrantino reds; the **Strada del Sagrantino** wine trail office, Piazza del Comune 17 (stradadelsagrantino.it; ✆ **0742/378490**), can set you up with maps and winery-tour info. Art lovers come here for a charming mid-15th-century fresco cycle of the life of St. Francis by Florentine master Benozzo Gozzoli, in the **Museo di San Francesco,** Via Ringhiera Umbra 6 (museomontefalco.it; ✆ **0742/379598;** admission 10€ adults, free for kids 13 and under; Apr–Oct daily 10:30am–6pm [June–Aug to 7pm], Nov–Mar Wed–Sun 10:30am–1pm and 2:30–5pm).

Rather than clinging to a hillside, **Bevagna** ♥♥, 8km (5 miles) north of Montefalco on SP443, nestles on the floor of the Valle Umbra beside the River Teverone. The river courses through a picturesque mill race not far from a meadow where Saint Frances is said to have preached to the birds. Inside sturdy gates, Bevagna seems firmly locked into the Middle Ages, with the simply ornamented churches of **San Michele Arcangelo** and **San Silvestro** facing each other across Piazza Silvestri (both usually open 9am–1pm and 4–7pm). The mosaic floor of a ruined bath complex on Via Terme Romana, with a swirl of octopi and other sea creatures, is a reminder of the town's prosperity as a Roman outpost on the Via Flaminia; the ruins are part of the **Museo Civico,** Corso Giacomo Matteotti 70 (bevagnacultura.com; ✆ **0742/194-4966;** admission 8€ adults, 5€ ages 6–14, free for children 5 and under; Apr–Dec daily 10am–1pm and 3–6pm [Aug until 6:30pm, Nov–Dec until 5pm], Jan–Mar Sun 11am–1pm and 3–5pm).

(comune.spello.pg.it; ✆ **0742/301009**) is open daily 9:30am to 12:30pm and 3:30 to 5:30pm.

Cappella Baglioni ♥♥♥ CHURCH/MUSEUM Spello's powerful Baglioni family decided to use this side chapel in the Santa Maria Maggiore church to generate some good press, and maybe some goodwill with the Almighty. Troilo Baglioni commissioned Pinturicchio to paint scenes from the boyhood of Christ after the infamous Red Wedding in June 1500, when one branch of the family turned against the other in a murderous bloodbath (the incident was portrayed in an episode of *Game of Thrones*). The color-filled frescoes are enchanting, filled with rich architectural detail and Umbrian landscapes, with some sly cynical commentaries (note the church treasurer with bursting money bags witnessing the Annunciation). Pinturicchio himself appears in a portrait in the Annunciation scene, and Troilo Baglioni shows up in the Disputation in the Temple.

Piazza Matteotti. No phone. Admission 3€. Tues–Sun 9:30am–12:30pm and 3–5:30pm.

SPOLETO ♥♥

63km (39 miles) SE of Perugia

Spoleto feels like the center of the cultured world in June, when the **Festival dei Due Mondi** (aka **Spoleto Festival**) draws performers and audiences from all over the globe. For most of the year, though, Spoleto is just another appealing Umbrian hill town, a pleasant warren of steep streets and airy piazzas lined with artifacts from the Roman past and prosperous Middle Ages, including one of Italy's most beautifully situated cathedrals.

Essentials

ARRIVING Spoleto is a main **rail** station on the Rome-Ancona line, and 16 daily trains from **Rome** stop here (about 1½ hr.). From **Perugia,** take one of the 20 daily trains to Foligno (25 min.) to transfer to this line for the final 20-minute leg. From outside the station, take bus A, B, or C to the Posterna stop, where you can get on the moving walkway (see below) to stops in the Upper Town. Buses (www.fsbusitalia.it) run about every 20 to 30 minutes and the fare is 1.30€; buy a ticket at a *tabacchi* or newsstand, or pay 2€ on the bus. From the station it's a level 15-minute walk to Piazza della Vittoria on the edge of the old town.

By **car,** approach town on the old Roman Via Flaminia, now the SS3. Three lots/garages (www.fsbusitalia.it) are at the base of the hill: Spoletosfera, Posterna, and Ponzianina are all connected to sights in the old town above via escalators, moving sidewalks, and elevators. Parking is 1.80€ the first hour and 1.40€ per subsequent hour up to 14€ for the day; take a ticket upon entering and pay in a machine upon leaving. Hotels can help arrange long-term parking.

VISITOR INFORMATION The **information center** is at Largo Francesco Ferrer 7 (comune.spoleto.pg.it; ✆ **0743/220773;** Mon–Sat 9am–1:30pm and 2:30–6pm, Sun 9am–1pm). The office hands out useful booklets on the town's sights and an excellent map. The **Spoleto Card,** valid for 7 days, provides admission to the Casa Romana, Rocca, Teatro Romana, and several other sights; the cost is 12€, while separate admission to just those three sights would come to 14.50€; the card is available at participating sights.

GETTING AROUND It's an easy 10-minute walk south from Piazza della Vittoria at the edge of the old town along Via Interna delle Mura to the Posterna parking garage, where you can get on the **moving walkway** (Percorso Meccanizzato) that runs deep beneath the historic center. Its upper terminus, at **Piazza Campello,** is near the Duomo and the Rocca; other exits along the way connect via elevator to most of the important sights in town. A similar system of escalators runs up the hill from the Ponzianina parking lot to the Rocca, with exits at the Duomo and other sights, and another connects the Spoletosfera parking garage with Piazza

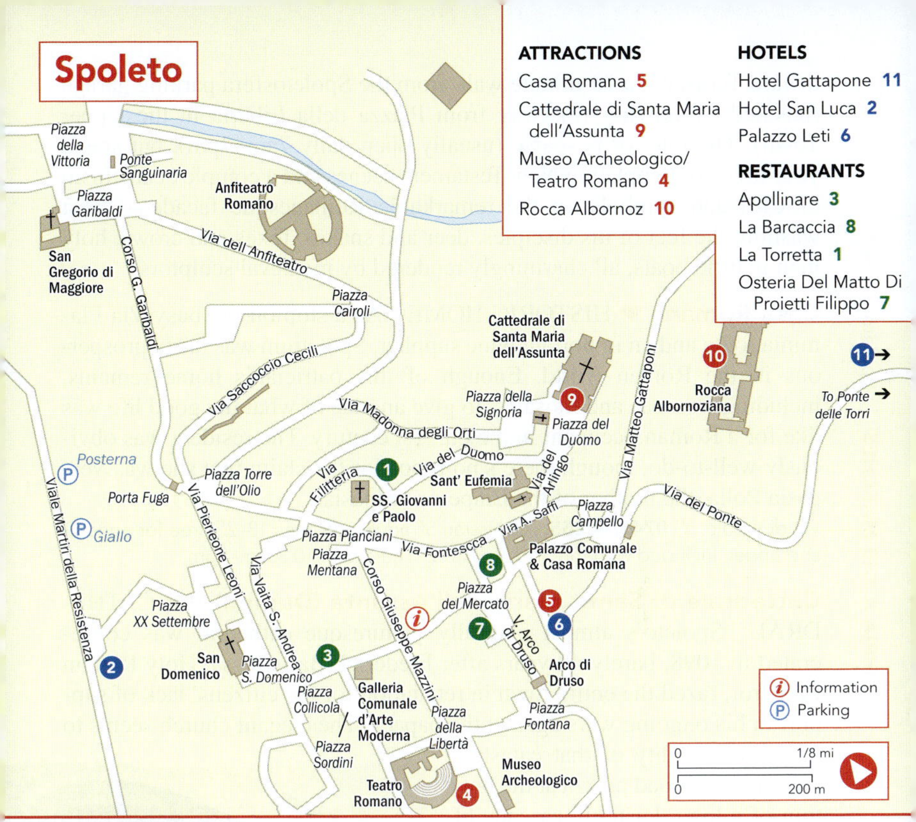

della Libertà. **Piazza del Mercato,** the probable site of the old Roman forum, is a bustling spot in the Upper Town lined with grocers and fruit vendors' shops.

Exploring Spoleto

While the upper town is the main attraction, before you head uphill, stop by the imposing 11th-century Romanesque church of **San Gregorio di Maggiore** ♥, Piazza della Vittoria (✆ **0743/44140;** free admission; daily 8am–noon and 4–6pm). The church's namesake saint was killed at the nearby amphitheater in C.E. 304, along with some 10,000 other lesser-known martyrs; their bones reside beneath the altar. Pop into the Cappella degli Innocenti, on the left side of the portico, to see a fresco depicting Spoleto as it looked in the 16th century (little has changed since then). Across the piazza, a gated staircase, open most mornings, leads down to a platform where you can view **Ponte Sanguinario,** a 1st-century travertine bridge 24m (79 ft.) long and 4.5m (15 ft.) wide, which over the centuries was buried in sediment from the stream it once crossed.

Another worthwhile stop outside the town walls is the remarkable 12th-century church of **San Pietro Extra Moenia** ♥, off the busy SS3 toward Terni; it's a 10-minute walk from the Spoletosfera parking garage (reached by moving walkway from Piazza della Libertà in the Upper Town). The interior is sparse (usually open daily 7am–7pm), but spend your time contemplating New Testament scenes and a complex catechism of Christian symbols on the remarkable Romanesque facade—Christ washing the feet of his disciples, deer and snakes, foxes and crows, holy men in little boats, all charmingly rendered by medieval sculptors.

Casa Romana ♥ HISTORIC HOME As a stop on the busy Via Flaminia route and an important wine supplier, Spoletium was fairly prosperous in the Roman world. Enough of this patrician's home remains, including frescoes and mosaics, to give an idea of what the good life was like for a Roman occupant in the C.E. 1st century. The resident was obviously well-to-do, though there's no proof for the claim that she was Vespasia Polla, the mother of the Emperor Vespasian.

Via di Visiale. ✆ **0743/40255.** Admission 5€ adults, 3€ ages 18–25, free for ages 17 and under. Included with the Spoleto Card. Thurs–Sun 10:30am–5pm.

Cattedrale di Santa Maria dell'Assunta (Duomo) ♥♥ CATHEDRAL Spoleto's almost playfully picturesque cathedral was consecrated in 1098, barely 40 years after Frederick Barbarossa, Holy Roman Emperor, razed the entire town in retaliation for the citizens' lack of support in his ongoing wars against the papacy. The elegant church seems to defy the brutality of that catastrophe, set in a broad piazza at the bottom of a long, leisurely cascade of steps. White marble and golden mosaics on the dazzling facade are framed against a gentle backdrop of a forested hillside. Inside, the apse is graced with frescoes of the *Life of the Virgin,* largely from the brush of Filippo Lippi, an ordained priest who shirked his duties and was eventually given permission to paint full-time. Though he was a favorite of the Medicis, he was chronically impoverished, supposedly because he spent so much money on women. The commission to come to Spoleto must have been a plum for the artist, then close to 60. His engaging scenes of the Virgin being visited by the Archangel and holding her sweet-looking infant betray nothing of the turbulence in his life—he was fighting to

Filippo Lippi's engaging frescoes in Spoleto's Duomo.

get dispensation to marry a young nun, Lucrezia Buti, who had borne his son, Filippino Lippi (who would soon match his father's greatness as a painter). Both Lippis appear in the Dormition of the Virgin scene, Filippo wearing a white habit with young Filippino, as an angel, in front of him. Filippo died before he completed the frescoes; his assistants finished the work. The cause of his death was suspected to be poison, perhaps administered by Lucrezia's family or yet another paramour. He is buried beneath a monument on the right side of the transept, which his son Filippino designed. The **Cappella delle Reliquie** (Reliquary Chapel), on the left aisle, holds a rare treasure—a letter written and signed by St. Francis. (Assisi has his only other bona fide signature.) The seasonal Art of the Spirit tour, with an audioguide, also visits the nearby Church of Sant'Eufemia and Diocesan Museum and explores the cathedral's upper galleries and campanile.

Piazza del Duomo. duomospoleto.it. ✆ **0743/218620.** Free admission. Art of the Spirit Tour 12€, 8€ ages 7–11 and adults with Spoleto Card, children 6 and under free. Cathedral: daily 8:30am–7pm (Nov–Mar until 6pm). Art of the Spirit Tour: Apr–Oct Mon–Sat 11am–5pm, Sun 1–5pm. Church of Sant'Eufemia and Diocesan Museum: 9€. Apr–Oct daily 10am–1:30pm and 2:30–6pm; Nov–Mar Sat–Sun 10am–5pm.

Museo Archeologico/Teatro Romano ♥ MUSEUM/RUINS Spoleto had the good fortune to flourish through the Dark Ages and the Middle Ages, and as the city prospered most of the Roman town was quarried or built over. In 1891 it was discovered that the monastery of St. Agata had been built atop this splendid ancient theater. Thoroughly restored in the 1950s, the theater is an evocative performance venue, often used during the Spoleto Festival. Much of the original orchestra flooring is intact, as is an elaborate drainage system (installed for flushing out the blood of slain animals and martyrs). Busts and statuary that once adorned the theater are on display in the adjoining Museo Archeologico. ***Tip:*** You can view the theater for free from the east end of Piazza della Libertà.

Via di Sant'Agata 18A. musei.umbria.beniculturali.it. ✆ **0743/223277.** Admission 4€ adults, 2€ ages 18–25, ages 17 and under free. Included with the Spoleto Card. Thurs–Sun 8:30am–7:30pm.

Rocca Albornoz ♥♥ CASTLE Cardinal Albornoz, a power-hungry zealot tasked with rebuilding and strengthening the papal states, arrived in Spoleto in the mid-14th century and commissioned the Umbrian architect Matteo Gattapone to build a fortress. The site was perfect—atop a high hill above the town and virtually impregnable. The walled-and-moated castle became famous in the 20th century as one of Italy's most secure prisons, where members of the Red Brigades terrorist organization were routinely incarcerated. The current occupant of the fortress is the **Museo Nazionale del Ducato di Spoleto,** a somewhat numbing collection of sarcophagi, mosaics, and statuary. There's also a highly reputable school here that trains students in the craft of restoring books and manuscripts, but that's off-limits to the public. You can walk around the Rocca grounds, no admission fee required, to enjoy spectacular views of the town and Umbrian countryside, and it's an easy trip up to these heights, via a series of escalators and elevators.

Piazza Campello. musei.umbria.beniculturali.it. ✆ **0743/224952.** Admission 7.50€. Included with the Spoleto Card. Wed–Mon 10am–5:30pm.

Walks Around Spoleto

Climbing Spoleto's steep streets is exercise in itself. If you want to stretch your legs a bit more, try the fairly easy, well-marked scenic walk that makes a circuit from Piazza Campello around the base of the **Rocca** (p. 337) then, with a vertigo-inducing bang, crosses the **Ponte delle Torri ♥♥♥**, a 232m-long (760-ft.) aqueduct built in the 13th century on Roman foundations. The arches span a deep, verdant gorge of the Tessino River, 90m (295 ft.) below. From the bridge's far side, the trail follows a forested hillside then descends into the valley and the bottom of town. The only equipment you'll need is a pair of comfortable walking shoes and a camera.

Spoleto's Big Bash

Over 3 weeks from the end of June through early July, the **Spoleto Festival dei Due Mondi** (festivaldispoleto.com) stages world-class drama, music, and dance in such evocative spaces as the open-air restored Roman theater and the piazza fronting the Duomo. A secondary **Spoleto d'Estate** season (comune.spoleto.pg.it) runs from just after the festival through September.

Some of the most scenic cross-country trekking is on and around the **Plains of Castelluccio ♥♥♥**, outside the walled town of **Norcia,** a pretty drive of 40km (25 miles) west of Spoleto along SS685. These three upland plateaus are beautiful at any time, but especially from May into July, when they are ablaze with wildflowers. Just to the north are the upland forests and lakes of **Parco Nazionale dei Monti Sibillini** (sibillini.net). Norcia was severely damaged in a 2016 earthquake and many of its buildings are still being restored, but it's a lively, friendly town, with shops and restaurants specializing in *norcineria,* sausages made from wild boar and hams.

Where to Stay in Spoleto

Accommodations are tight during the Spoleto Festival; reserve by March if you want to find a room. Whether arriving by car or public transport, ask for explicit directions on how to reach your hotel—navigating the Upper Town, built on many different hillside levels, can be a challenge.

Hotel Gattapone ♥♥ From the street, this hideaway beneath the Rocca Albornoz looks like a relatively modest 19th-century villa. But step inside and there's a 1960s Antonioni-film feel to the place: polished wood, free-floating staircases, and leather couches facing windows overlooking the Ponte delle Torri and green Monteluco hillsides. Guest rooms have slightly dated but well-maintained contemporary furnishings mixed with traditional pieces, and large, view-filled windows. Some guests comment that the air-conditioning is vintage, too. Travelers with mobility issues should know there's no elevator, and rooms and lounges are set on several levels.

Via del Ponte 6. hotelgattapone.it. ✆ **0743/223447.** 15 units. 100€–130€ double. Rates include breakfast. **Amenities:** Bar; free Wi-Fi.

Hotel San Luca ♥♥♥ A 19th-century tannery at the bottom of the old city next to the Roman walls lends itself well to a welcoming hotel. A book-lined lounge, where canaries chirp in an antique cage and a fire crackles in cold months, faces a large courtyard, and so do many rooms; others overlook a rose garden to the side. The unusually large quarters are all different, a mix of traditional and contemporary pieces with a smattering of antiques, plus extremely large and well-equipped marble bathrooms. Sights and restaurants are within easy reach, many via the moving walkway from nearby Posterna, and the attentive staff will map out a route that involves the least amount of climbing. The in-house garage is a real rarity in Spoleto.

Via Interna delle Mura 21. hotelsanluca.com. ✆ **0743/223399.** 35 units. 95€–140€ double. Rates include breakfast. Parking 15€. Closed Jan–Feb. **Amenities**: Bar; babysitting; bikes; concierge; room service; free Wi-Fi

Palazzo Leti ♥♥♥ An entrance through a Renaissance garden that opens to the Tessino gorge announces that this beautifully restored 13th-century palace of the Leti family is an exceptional place. Views of the gorge and green Monteluco hills are the focal point of most rooms, though a few overlook a medieval alley that has its own charm. All rooms have period furniture and rich fabrics, plus couches and armchairs in the larger rooms and wood beams, granite hearths, and vaulted ceilings throughout. Anna Laura and Gianpaolo, who restored the palace from a dilapidated pile, are a friendly presence and provide all sorts of helpful advice.

Via degli Eremiti 10. palazzoleti.com. ✆ **0743/224930.** 12 units. 120€–130€ double. Rates include breakfast. Closed Dec to early Mar. **Amenities:** Bar; bikes; spa; free Wi-Fi.

Where to Eat in Spoleto

A nice spot for an aperitivo is **Caffè degli Artisti ♥**, Piazza del Mercato 32 (✆ **0743/225071**), where your drink comes with a view of the comings and goings in the lively square. **Prosciutteria del Corso ♥**, near Piazza della Libertà at Corso Mazzini 73, makes delicious sandwiches from local meats and cheeses (✆ **0743/224014;** daily noon–3pm and 7pm–midnight). **Gelateria Crispini ♥**, Viale Trento e Trieste 29 (gelaticrispini.it; ✆ **0743/235015;** daily 1–8pm, from 3pm Sun), serves some of Umbria's best gelato, notably the pistachio and "bread and chocolate" flavors.

Apollinare ♥♥♥ UMBRIAN The low wood ceilings, stone walls, and beams are traditional holdovers from a 12th-century Franciscan monastery, while the adventurous menu puts a fresh twist on local ingredients and traditional recipes: *Strangozzi* (the local long, rectangular wheat pasta) is topped with a pungent sauce of cherry tomatoes and mint; herb-roasted rabbit is served with black olive sauce; and pork filet mignon is topped with a sauce of Pecorino cheese and pears soaked in Rosso di Montefalco.

Via Sant'Agata 14 (near Piazza della Libertà). ristoranteapollinare.it. ✆ **0743/223256.** Main courses 25€–35€. Wed–Mon 12:30–2pm and 7:30–10pm. Closed Feb.

La Barcaccia ♥♥ UMBRIAN Despite the name (the "Old Boat"), these brightly lit rooms are set on dry land near the top of the town—and, except for some Adriatic fish choices, the menu is firmly landlocked in Umbrian classics. This is the place to enjoy *strangozzi alla spoletina,* peppery tomato sauce served atop thick *strangozzi* (from "string") pasta that's said to resemble the laces of Roman sandals. A good choice of vegetarian dishes includes *scamorza,* a cow's milk cheese similar to mozzarella, baked with radicchio.

Piazza Fratelli Bandiera 4. ristorantelabarcaccia.it. ✆ **0743/225082.** Main courses 9€–18€. Daily 11am–3pm and 6–10pm.

La Torretta ♥♥♥ UMBRIAN In two welcoming rooms in a medieval tower, brothers Stefano and Elio Salvucci extend a genuine welcome and a nice selection of Umbrian dishes. Delicious starters such as *tris di antipasti al tartufo estivo* (trio of truffle-based appetizers) and *zuppa di farro* (spelt soup with sausage) pave the way for beautifully seasoned pork or beef grilled over a wood fire.

Via Filitteria 43. trattorialatorretta.com. ✆ **0743/44954.** Main courses 12€–30€. Mon, Wed–Sat 12:30–2:30pm and 7:30–10pm; Sun 12:30–2:30pm.

Osteria del Matto di Proietti Filippo ♥♥ UMBRIAN You'll put yourself in the hands of friendly Filippo Proietti when you walk in the door of this charmingly eclectic and old-fashioned room off the market square. He brings you whatever the kitchen is preparing that day, five or six courses, always including a pasta or two and many appetizers, along with a meat or fish course, and dessert. House wine is a little extra, and excellent, and grappa usually follows. The total will rarely be much more than 35€ a person.

Piazza del Mercato 3. ✆ **0743/225506.** Prix-fixe menu with wine about 35€. Wed–Mon noon–2:30pm and 7–9:30pm.

ORVIETO ♥♥

87km (54 miles) W of Spoleto, 86km (53 miles) SW of Perugia

Walking through the streets of Orvieto, you might be pleased to discover that nothing much has changed in the past 500 years. Adding to the magic is what might be Italy's most beautiful cathedral, with a facade covered in dazzling mosaics and statuary and rising above an airy piazza. The final coup de grace is the fact that the entire town is set atop a volcanic

outcropping some 315m (1,033 ft.) above the green countryside. This impenetrable perch ensured that Etruscan "Velzna" was among the most powerful members of the *Dodecapoli* (Etruscan confederation of 12 cities), and the lofty setting continues to make Orvieto seem a world apart.

Essentials

ARRIVING Fourteen **trains** on the **Rome–Florence** line stop at Orvieto daily (1 hr., 45 min. from Florence; 1 hr., 20 min. from Rome). From **Perugia,** take the train to Terontola (16 trains daily) to transfer to the line heading south toward Rome, for a total trip time of 1½ hours. From **Spoleto,** hourly trains connect through **Orte,** for a total trip time of just over 2 hours. Orvieto makes a convenient stopover on a train trip between Rome and Florence; you can store bags at the Welcome Point (orvietoviva.com) behind the train station in the Piazza della Pace (5€ per large bag for 4 hr., 15€ for 24 hr.; open 9am–5pm). Orvieto's **station** is in the valley, in Orvieto Scalo, but right across the street from the station, a **funicular** (orvietoviva.com; 1.30€; every 10 min. from 7:15am–8:30pm [holidays from 8am]) ascends to hilltop Orvieto. It's an easy, level 15-minute walk from the upper terminus to the Duomo and other sights in the historic center, and a free shuttle bus runs to and from Piazza Duomo.

Orvieto is easy to reach by **car:** It's right off the A1. A main link to the rest of Umbria is the SS448 to Todi (40 min.) for the E45 between Perugia and Terni. You can drop off your car at the large free parking lot behind the train station off Piazza della Pace and take the funicular up to town, but if you want to get a bit closer, a lot and garage at Campo della Fiera, just outside the Porta Romana, is connected by an elevator/escalator system up to Piazza San Giovanni or Piazza Ranieri. Parking at Campo della Fiera and at other lots on the perimeter of the upper town costs 1.50€ an hour; a lot next to the Duomo costs 2€ an hour.

VISITOR INFORMATION The **tourist office** is opposite the Duomo at Piazza Duomo 24 (✆ **0763/341772**). It's open Monday to Friday 9am to 1pm and 3 to 6pm, Saturday and Sunday 10am to 7pm. You'll find a lot of information about the town at orvietoviva.com. Orvieto hosts the **Umbria Jazz Winter Festival** in December and January.

Exploring Orvieto

Life in Orvieto transpires on and around animated **Corso Cavour,** cutting through the center of town. If you take the funicular up from the lower town, you'll begin your walk through Orvieto at the eastern end of the street. In the very center of town rises the **Torre del Moro,** a 13th-century show of civic might and clock tower that provides views across all the territory the medieval city controlled, stretching east to the Apennines and west to the Mediterranean. To enjoy those views today, you'll take an elevator and then climb up 171 steps (3.80€, 3€ seniors; daily May–Aug 10am–8pm, Mar–Apr and Sept–Oct 10am–7pm, Nov–Feb 10:30am–4:30pm). Just to the north is **Piazza del Popolo,** where the Capitano del Popolo (Captain of the People) ruled from the formidable, crenellated Palazzo del Popolo. Market stalls fill the square on Thursday and Saturday mornings. **Via del Duomo** leads south from the tower to Orvieto's masterwork, one of the most celebrated cathedrals in Italy (see below).

Orvieto's other great wonder is the volcanic plug upon which the city sits. To look at the city's tufa foundations, take a hike along the ***rupe,*** a path that encircles the base of the cliff. (The tourist office can supply a map.) A landmark along the north side of the path is the **Necropoli Etrusca del Crocifisso del Tufo** (Etruscan Necropolis), where ancient Etruscan tombs lie in a gridlike pattern in subterranean caverns (musei.umbria.beniculturali.it; ✆ **0763/343611;** admission 2€; Wed and Fri 9am–7pm, Thurs and Sat 9am–3pm, Sun 9am–6pm). Many of the jewelry, ceramics, and other finds are in the town's two small archaeological collections on Piazza Duomo: The **Museo Archeologico Nazionale** (orvietoviva.com; ✆ **0763/341039**) is open Tuesday through Sunday 8:30am to 7:30pm and admission is 5€; the **Museo Claudio Faina di Orvieto** (museofaina.it; ✆ **0763/341511**) is open Wednesday through Monday 9:30am to 6pm April through September and 10am to 5pm October through March; admission is 7€, 11€ with Duomo. For views across the surrounding countryside, stroll along the high ramparts that fringe the edges of town. Some of the most accessible are on the west side, just past Sant'Agostino church.

Duomo ♥♥♥ CATHEDRAL Orvieto's pièce de résistance is a mesmerizing assemblage of spikes and spires, mosaics and marble statuary—and that's just the facade. The rest of the bulky-yet-elegant church is banded in black and white stone and seems to perch miraculously on the edge of the cliffs that surround the town. The church is wider at the front than at the back, designed to create the optical illusion upon entering that the nave is longer than it actually is. The facade has been compared to a medieval altarpiece, and it reads like an illustrated catechism. On the four broad marble panels that divide the surface, Sienese sculptor and architect Lorenzo Maitani (who more or less designed the church) and others carved scenes from the Old and New Testament. On the far left is the story of creation, with Eve making an appearance from Adam's rib; on the far right, Christ presides over the Last Judgment, as the dead shuffle out of their sarcophagi to await his verdict. Prophets and apostles surround a huge rose window, and Mary appears in lush mosaics inlaid in fields of gold.

The ornate facade of Orvieto's Duomo.

CAPPELLA DEL CORPORALE In 1263, a Bohemian priest, Peter of Prague, found himself doubting transubstantiation, the sacrament in which the communion bread, or host, is transformed into the body of Christ during mass. He went to Rome to pray on St. Peter's tomb that his faith be strengthened and, stopping in Bolsena, just below Orvieto, was saying Mass when the host began to bleed, dampening the corporal, or altar cloth. Pope Urban IV had the cloth brought to him in Orvieto, and a few decades later, Pope Nicholas IV ordered the cathedral built to house the relic. Frescoes in the chapel tell the story of the miracle, and the exquisite enamel reliquary that once held the cloth remains in place.

CAPPELLA SAN BRIZIO The cathedral's other treasure is one of the Renaissance's greatest fresco cycles. The themes are weighty—temptation, salvation, damnation, resurrection—yet the scenes are rich in everyday humanity. These frescoes allegedly inspired Michelangelo, who came to Orvieto and filled sketchbooks before starting the Sistine Chapel. Fra' Angelico (see p. 194) began the series in 1447; Luca Signorelli (p. 271) completed the works, which are considered his masterpiece, in 1504. Both artists appear, dressed in black in the lower left corner, in a magnificent panel of the *Sermon of the Antichrist,* in which the devil coaxes a Christ impostor to lure the faithful to damnation. Signorelli looks handsome and proud, with his long blond hair; a mistress who jilted him is shown receiving funds from a money lender (for prostitution services, some conject). To the right of the altar is *The Entrance to Hell* and *The Damned in Hell,* in which devils torment their victims, bodies writhe in agony, and a man raises his fists to curse God as he sees Charon crossing the Styx for him. Signorelli gets revenge on his ex-mistress again—she's the terrified blonde on the back of a leering winged devil. For something a little more uplifting, look at the *Elect in Heaven,* where the saved look quite content in their assurance of eternal salvation.

Piazza del Duomo. opsm.it. ✆ **0763/341-167.** Admission 8€, 11€ with Claudio Faina; free for children 10 and younger. Apr–Sept Mon–Sat 9:30am–7pm, Sun 1–5:30pm; Mar and Oct Mon–Sat 9:30am–6pm, Sun 1–5:30pm; Nov–Feb Mon–Sat 9:30am–5pm, Sun 1–4:30pm.

Orvieto Underground ♥♥ HISTORIC SITE More than 1,200 artificial and natural caverns have been found in the *pozzolana* (a volcanic stone powdered to make cement mix) and tufa rock upon which Orvieto rests. Guided tours explore 15m (45 ft.) below Santa Chiara convent, reached by a steep climb up and down 55 steps, along a narrow rock-hewn passage. Over centuries the caverns have been used as Etruscan houses, water wells, ceramic ovens, pigeon coops, and cold storage (the temperature is a constant 14°C/58°F). Medieval citizens considered the tunnels safe refuges in times of siege, and residents took shelter in them during World War II Allied bombings, but most unwisely—a direct hit would have annihilated the soft rock. For a quicker look at the city's underside, step into **Pozzo della Cava,** where a self-guided tour reveals a series of caverns beneath a medieval house.

Piazza Duomo 23. orvietounderground.it. ✆ **0763/344-891.** Guided tours only: 10€ adults, 8€ students and seniors, free for children 5 and under. Tours (45 min.–1 hr.) daily; timing of English-language tours varies, but usually 11am, 12:15, 2:30, 4 and 5:15pm. Reservations recommended in summer. **Pozzo della Cavo:** Via della Cava 28 (pozzodellacava.it; ✆ **0763/342373**); admission 4€ adults, 2.50€ seniors and children 6 and under; Tues–Sun 9am–8pm.

Pozzo di San Patrizio (St. Patrick's Well) ♥ HISTORIC SITE Orvieto's position atop a rocky outcropping made the city a perfect redoubt in time of siege, but with one big drawback—a lack of water. When Pope Clement VII holed up in Orvieto in 1527 to avoid turbulence in Rome, he hired Antonio Sangallo the Younger, one of the designers of St. Peter's in Rome, to dig a new well. Sangallo's design was unique: a shaft 53m (175-ft.) deep and 14m (45-ft.) wide, accessible via a pair of wide spiral staircases that form a double helix, lit by 72 internal windows. Mule-drawn carts could descend on one ramp and come back up the other.

You can climb down, too, though it's a 496-step trek down and back up, and there's nothing at the bottom but, well, a well. A few steps up and down is all you need to get the idea. The name refers to St. Patrick's Purgatory, a pilgrimage site in Ireland where Christ allegedly showed St. Patrick a cave and told him it was an entrance to hell. The well entrance is in a view-filled public garden at the edge of town.

Viale San Gallo (near funicular stop on Piazza Cahen). liveorvieto.com. ✆ **0763/343768.** Admission 6€ adults, 4.50€ seniors, students, and ages 17 and under. May–Aug daily 9am–7:30pm; Mar–Apr and Sept–Oct daily 9am–7pm; Nov–Feb daily 10am–4:30pm.

Where to Stay in Orvieto

The upper town has few places to stay, so book ahead—especially on weekends, when Romans flock to Orvieto for a small-town getaway.

B&B Orvieto Sant'Angelo 42 ♥♥ From the moment you step into the stone-floored foyer you'll feel right at home in Giulia Donato's pretty house on a narrow street off the Corso. In a lounge/breakfast room, a couch and chairs surround a huge hearth, and up a stone staircase are high-ceilinged guest rooms, two large doubles and a suite-size triple. Bathrooms are spacious (with deep tubs in the larger rooms), beds are luxurious, and handsome traditional pieces complement highly polished floors and mellow old beams and stones. Top-floor rooms come with a perk: little step-out balconies looking across rooftops to the distant hills.

Via Sant'Angelo 42. bborvieto.com. ✆ **0763/341-959.** 3 units. 70€–100€ double. Rates include breakfast. **Amenities:** Lounge; free Wi-Fi.

Hotel Duomo ♥♥ These quarters just a few steps from the Duomo (viewable from some rooms with a lean out the window) have modern built-in wood furnishings and excellent lighting and plenty of quirky decor. A local artist, Livio Orazio Valentini, hung his surrealistic paintings in the hallways, lounges, and rooms, complementing them with colorful upholstery and carpets. He also created the sculptural light fixtures hanging over many of the desks. The homey bohemian ambience is topped off with a pleasant garden to one side of the hotel.

Vicolo dei Maurizio 7. orvietohotelduomo.com. ✆ **0763/341-887.** 18 units. 120€–160€ double. Rates include breakfast. **Amenities:** Free Wi-Fi.

Palazzo Piccolomini ♥♥ Two restored 16th-century *palazzos,* one with a tower, show off stones and vaults in the subterranean breakfast room and frescoes in the salons. Guest rooms are contemporary, with wood and tile floors, dark furnishings, and crisp white walls with soothing neutral-tone accents. Some rooms have sitting areas or open to terraces, or are two-level; rooms on the upper floors look over rooftops to the countryside far below.

Piazza Ranieri 36. palazzopiccolomini.it. ✆ **0763/341-743.** 32 units. 130€–150€ double. Rates include breakfast. **Amenities:** Restaurant; babysitting; concierge; room service; Wi-Fi (free in public areas).

Six Keys Guesthouse offers medieval hill-town character just outside Orvieto.

Six Keys Guesthouse ♥♥♥ A stay in this beautifully restored 15th-century house in the pretty hilltop village of Allerona surrounds you with the pleasant rhythm of small-town Umbrian life, yet Orvieto is only a short drive or train ride away. Wood beams, stone walls, and handmade terra-cotta tiles make the most of the character-rich surroundings, while a tasteful mix of traditional and contemporary furnishings are geared to comfort and convenience, with such thoughtful touches as USB ports next to the excellent beds and complimentary wine and snacks. Hosts Elizabeth and Paolo also run Villaggio Tours (villaggiotours.com), geared to small-group immersive travel in Umbria and beyond, so they are just the folks to help you get the most out of the region.
Via Nuova 9, Allerona (17km/11 miles NW of Orvieto). sixkeysumbria.com. ✆ **334/398-3057.** 6 units. 90€–100€ double. **Amenities:** Lounge; free Wi-Fi.

Where to Eat in Orvieto

Orvieto restaurants do a brisk business in summer and on weekend evenings, when it's best to reserve a table. Orvieto's favorite pasta is *umbrichelli,* a slightly chewy spaghetti rolled out unevenly by hand, similar to the *pici* of southern Tuscany. To sample a glass of Orvieto Classico (accompanied by a panino), drop by the **Cantina Foresi ♥**, Piazza Duomo 2 (www.cantinaforesi.it; ✆ **0763/341-611**). Ask to see the small, moldy cellar carved directly into the tufa. **Bar Montanucci ♥**, Corso Cavour 23 (barmontanucci.com; ✆ **0763/341262**), is a popular spot for snacks and drinks, with fun wooden sculptures, a large rear terrace, and a huge selection of chocolates, some house-made. **Bartolomei Oleoteca ♥**, Corso Cavour 49 (oleoteca.oleificiobartolomei.it; ✆ **0763/344540**), a cafe specializing in local dishes, sells its own olive oils and such delicacies as olive paste and roasted artichokes in oil. **Gastronomia Aronne ♥♥**, Corso Cavour 101 (✆ **0763/340014**), elevates a light meal into a gourmet indulgence, with excellent meat and cheese platters, sandwiches, pastas, and other well-prepared fare in a light-filled shop/dining room.

Capitano del Popolo ♥♥♥ UMBRIAN Chef/proprietor Valentina Santanicchio grew up on a farm outside Orvieto, and she combines a passion for cooking with a commitment to locally grown ingredients. In a dining room with vintage '50s cabinets and tables topped with crisp linens and fresh flowers, Valentina presents her *carbonara* and other pastas, along with spicy boar ragùs, roast duck, and other Umbrian classics that have won the praise of many fans, among them actor Stanley Tucci, who featured Valentina on his show *Searching for Italy*.

Piazza del Popolo 7–9. capitanodelpopolo.com. ✆ **320/928-7474.** Main courses 10€–25€. Daily 12:30–3pm and 7:30–10pm.

Le Grotte del Funaro ♥♥ UMBRIAN A thousand years ago, a *funaro* (ropemaker) had his workshop in these grottoes carved into the cliff's tufa; you can almost see him at work in the shadowy recesses of the rooms. Take a seat outside in good weather or better yet—so you don't miss the ambience inside—ask for one of the few window seats; most are in atmospheric subterranean chambers. You'll dine well on grilled meats, the house specialty (try a *grigliata mista* of suckling pig, lamb, sausage, and yellow peppers), or excellent pizzas.

Via Ripa Serancia 41 (near Porta Maggiore). grottedelfunaro.com. ✆ **0763/343-276.** Main courses 10€–22€; pizza 7€–10€. Tues–Sun 12:15–2:30pm and 7–10:30pm. Closed 1 week in July.

Mezza Luna ♥♥ UMBRIAN When booking your Orvieto hotel room, ask them to reserve a table for you at this small, vaulted room behind a vine-covered entrance on a side street. Reserving in advance is the only way you're likely to eat here, because for more than 40 years proprietor Averino has been serving what many people consider the best carbonara they've ever eaten—and that attracts customers from the ends of the earth. The kitchen also prepares some other excellent pastas and grilled meat, but don't miss out on the standout attraction.

Via Ripa Serancia 5. facebook.com/lamezzalunapizzeria. ✆ **0763/341-234.** Main courses 7€–12€. Tues–Sat 12:30–2pm and 7:15–8:30pm.

Orvieto's Liquid Gold

The plains and low hills around Orvieto grow the grapes—Verdello, Grechetto, and varietals of Trebbiano and Malvasia—that produce one of Italy's great wines, a pale straw-colored DOC white called **Orvieto Classico.** Well-rounded and fragrant (often with a hint of crushed almonds), the wine goes well with lunch or a light dinner. Most Orvieto Classico is *secco* (dry), but you can also find *abboccato* (semidry/semisweet), *amabile* (medium sweet), and *dolce* (sweet) varieties. To visit a winery, pick up the "Strada dei Vini" brochure at the Orvieto tourist office.

Trattoria la Palomba ♥♥♥ UMBRIAN This is the kind of warm and welcoming place where you'll want to linger in the homey dining room for a long lunch or leisurely evening dinner. Black Umbrian truffles top many of the homemade pastas, most notably *umbrichelli al tartufo,* tossed with egg yolk and Parmigiano. The signature dish, *palomba* (wild dove), is roasted in a delicious sauce of capers, rosemary, olives, and a hint of anchovies. Any of the meat dishes, including beef in a red wine sauce, are similarly satisfying. It's essential to reserve, especially on weekends.

Via Cipriano Manente 16. instagram.com/trattorialapalomba. ✆ **0763/343395.** Main courses 10€–22€. Thurs–Tues 12:30–2:15pm and 7:30–9:30pm.

Orvieto Shopping

Orogami ♥, Via del Duomo 14/16 (orogami.com; ✆ **0763/344206**), sells a distinctive line of gold jewelry, including playful pieces like a medallion replicating the Duomo's rose window. The showroom of internationally acclaimed ceramicist **Marino Moretti ♥♥**, Via del Duomo 55 (marino moretti.it; ✆ **0763/361663**), sells tiles, dinnerware, and other modern takes on traditional designs. **L'Orvietan ♥**, Via del Duomo 74 (lorvietan.com; ✆ **0763/341060**), sells the town's famous elixir, an herbal amaro and onetime cure-all concocted in 1603 (a production lab around the corner can also be visited). Gifted shoemaker **Federico Badia ♥♥** hand-fashions made-to-order shoes, purses, bags, and belts in his workshop at Corso Cavour 223 (federicobadiashoes.com).

BOLOGNA & EMILIA-ROMAGNA

By Stephen Brewer

8

Many travelers zip through this northernmost stretch of central Italy as they hurry along the well-worn path between Florence and Venice or Milan. That's good news for those who choose instead to slow down a bit. Emilia-Romagna's appealing towns and cities are a little less crowded and more engaged in everyday Italian life than more popular stops on the Italian tourism circuit, and along with treasure troves of art and culture, the region has an almost hedonistic devotion to fine food.

Each of the region's main towns has its own distinct character. Bologna is one of Europe's largest remaining medieval enclaves, with art-filled palaces and imposing piazzas, yet it also has an animated street life revved up by students at Europe's oldest university. Ferrara is a time capsule of the Renaissance, and Ravenna seems to be entirely covered in glittering Byzantine mosaics. Parma proudly shows off its musical heritage, its art treasures, and its famous hams and cheeses.

DON'T LEAVE BOLOGNA & EMILIA-ROMAGNA WITHOUT . . .

Immersing Yourself in the Middle Ages. Bologna is one of the world's best-preserved medieval holdovers, an atmospheric set piece with palaces, towers, and 25 miles of centuries-old porticos.

Enjoying Some of the Best Food in Italy. Even other Italians agree: Emilia-Romagna is the culinary heart of the country, with Parma's hams and cheeses setting a delectable gold standard.

Biking Around Ferrara. The city's palace- and convent-lined streets are delightfully flat for easy pedaling, and you can even ride atop the old city walls.

Marveling at Ravenna's Mosaics. Saturated in color, the intricate mosaics blanketing Ravenna's churches and mausoleums have awed travelers since the city's 5th-century heyday.

BOLOGNA ♥♥♥

119km (71 miles) N of Florence, 378km (234 miles) N of Rome, 151km (94 miles) SW of Venice

It's easy to love a city so enamored of food that it's nicknamed *La Grassa* (the Fat); so devoted to scholarship (home of Europe's oldest university, founded in 1088) that it's called *La Dotta* (the Learned); and so noted for

 PREVIOUS PAGE: **Heading into Piazza Maggiore, the centerpiece of Bologna's historic center.**

Fresh produce for sale in the Quadrilatero, Bologna's medieval heart.

its fiery liberal politics that it's known as *La Rossa* (the Red), a name that is also said to refer to the city's red-tile roofs. Nonetheless, there are plenty of other reasons to like Bologna. The lively city of more than a million residents is built around one of Europe's largest and best-preserved medieval cores, an attractive swath of palaces, towers, quirky museums, and art-filled churches, and its grand piazzas and narrow lanes are easily traversed on foot. In the Quadrilatero, the medieval town center, shop windows brim with the region's famous hams and cheeses. You don't even have to carry an umbrella in Bologna, because 25 miles of sidewalks are covered with handsome loggias.

Essentials

ARRIVING

BY PLANE The international **Aeroporto Guglielmo Marconi (BLQ;** bologna-airport.it; ✆ **051/647-9615**), 6km (3¾ miles) north of the city center, is served by many of the main European airlines, including British Airways and Ryanair. The airport does not accommodate transatlantic flights, so travelers from the U.S. will make connections in London or another European hub. The **Marconi Express** automated tram (marconi express.it) links the airport and main rail station (Stazione Centrale) in just 7 minutes and runs daily every 7 minutes between 5:40am and midnight. One-way fare is 12.80€, round-trip 23.30€, payable with tickets dispensed from machines near the platform or with contactless card or device. A taxi from the airport into the city center costs about 20€.

BY TRAIN Bologna is well connected to nearby cities by train, making it easy to explore the region without a car. Frequent high-speed trains operated by **Trenitalia** (trenitalia.com) and **Italo** (italotreno.it) from Florence (trip time about 30 min.), Milan (about 1 hr.), Venice (1 hr., 40 min.), Rome (2 hr., 20 min.), and Naples (3 hr., 50 min.) arrive at **Stazione Centrale,** Piazza Medaglie d'Oro 2 (✆ **892-021**). Slower and less expensive trains also run on these routes. A staffed luggage storage facility operated by **KiBag** (kibag.it) on the ground floor, open daily 7am to 9pm, stores baggage for 8€ per piece a day; it also has a porter service for 8€ a bag. As you leave the station through the main entrance and walk into Piazza delle Medaglia d'Oro, notice the clock to the right: It is permanently stopped at

10:25am, the precise time on August 2, 1980, when a bomb exploded in a waiting room, killing 85 people and injuring more than 200; it was later determined that a neo-fascist group had planted the device.

Bus nos. A, 25, and 30 run between the station and Piazza Maggiore, Bologna's historic center; taxi trips into the center cost around 6€. However, it's an easy, level 15-minute walk from the station to Piazza Maggiore down lively, shop-lined Via dell'Indipendenza, mostly under covered loggias.

BY CAR If you're driving from Florence, head north on A1 until you reach the outskirts of Bologna, where signs direct you to the city center. From Milan, take A1 southeast. From Venice or Ferrara, follow A13 southwest. From Rimini, Ravenna, and towns along the Adriatic, cut west on A14. See the note on p. 362 about driving and parking in Bologna; if you have a choice, it's much easier to visit Bologna without a car.

VISITOR INFORMATION The **Bologna Welcome tourist office** (bologna welcome.com; © **051/658-3111**), on Piazza Maggiore in the Palazzo del Podestà, is open Monday to Saturday 9am to 7pm and Sunday 10am to 5pm. Helpful staff hand out free city maps, bus maps, and guides to what's happening around the city. The office's daily 2½-hour

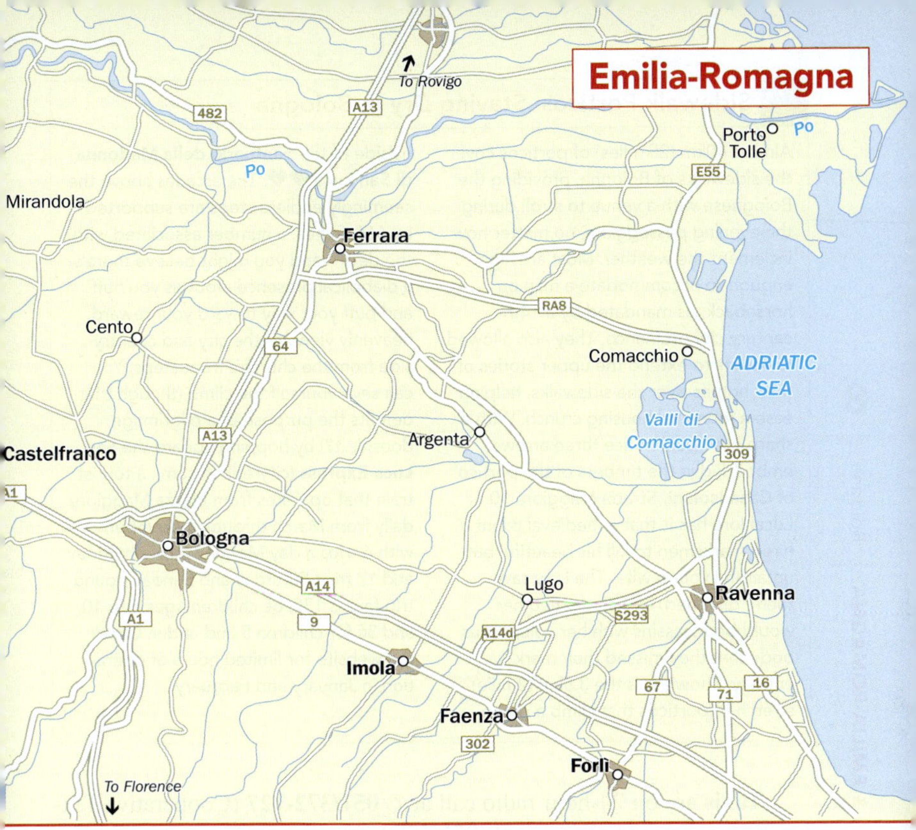

English-language Discover Bologna **walking tour** is an excellent, informative introduction to the city (18€; leaves from Bologna Welcome Office in Piazza Maggiore daily, twice daily Fri–Sun). The tour is included on the excellent-value (35€) **Bologna Welcome Card,** which includes free admission to museums and attractions, including such must-see sights as the Museo Medievale, Museo Morandi, the church of Santa Maria della Vita, and the Tagliavani music collection.

GETTING AROUND Central Bologna is easy to cover **on foot;** most of the major sights are around Piazza Maggiore. **City buses,** operated by **TPER** (Trasporto Passeggeri Emilia-Romagna; tper.it), leave for most points from the train station or from Piazza Nettuno or Piazza Maggiore in the city center. Single-ride rickets (2.30€), valid for 1 hour, can be bought at many booths and *tabacchi* in Bologna; a **day ticket,** valid until midnight on the day of validation, costs 9€; a carnet of 10 tickets costs 19€. Once on board, you must validate your ticket or you'll be fined up to 150€. You can use contactless payment on some buses. Many buses also have machines that sell single-ride tickets for 2.50€, exact change required. A TPER office, with English-speaking staff offering info and selling tickets, is outside the train station entrance in Piazza Medaglie d'Oro (Mon–Sat 6am–7pm, Sun 7am–7pm).

Sidewalk Porticos: Staying Dry in Bologna

Almost 40km (25 miles) of porticos cover the sidewalks of Bologna, providing the Bolognese with a venue to stroll during the evening *passeggiata*, no matter how inclement the weather. Most are high enough to accommodate a man on horseback, as mandated by a 14th-century city ordinance. They also allowed residents to extend the upper stories of their homes over the sidewalks, helping ease a medieval housing crunch. With a sharp eye you'll notice three arrows embedded in the timbers of the portico of **Casa Isolani,** Strada Maggiore 10. Local lore has it that a medieval count hired marksmen to kill his beautiful but unfaithful young wife. The lady saw them, disrobed, and so dazzled her would-be assassins with her voluptuous body that they missed their mark entirely. Showiest is the 3.5km (2-mile) stretch of porticos that climb a green hillside to the **Santuario della Madonna di San Luca ♥♥**. The arcades above the seemingly endless steps are supported by 666 arches, a number associated with the devil—and you might believe there's a diabolical presence afoot as you huff and puff your way toward your reward, heavenly views of the city and countryside from the church's front steps. You can save yourself the climb (though that defeats the purpose of a pilgrimage, doesn't it?) by hopping aboard the **San Luca Express** (cityredbus.com), a tourist train that operates from Piazza Maggiore daily from March through December, with 6 trips a day Monday through Friday and 12 trips Saturday and Sunday; round-trip fare is 13€, 6€ children ages 6 to 10, and 3€ for children 5 and under. Check the website for limited hours of operation in January and February.

Taxis are on 24-hour radio call at ✆ **051/372-727** (Cooperativa Taxisti Bolognesi; cotabo.it) or ✆ **051/4590** (Consorzio Autonomo Taxisti; taxibologna.it). The meter starts at 3.40€ (6.10€ at night) and goes up 1.25€ per kilometer.

Exploring Bologna

A huge statue of a virile Neptune presides over the center of Bologna, the sweeping expanse of **Piazza Maggiore.** At one end looms the enormous, though never completed, **Basilica di San Petronio** (p. 357); crenellated 12th- and 13th-century *palazzi* occupy the other sides, including, on the northeast, the **Palazzo di Rei Enzo.** In the long-running feud between the Ghibellines (who supported the Holy Roman Empire) and the Guelphs (supporters of the pope), Enzo—the illegitimate son of German Emperor Frederick II, and king of Sardinia—sided with the Ghibellines at the wrong time. He was imprisoned in this palace for 23 years until his death, though he didn't exactly languish in a dungeon—he was known for his lavish feasts and romantic conquests, and almost escaped once (his blond hair, protruding from a basket, gave him away).

Rising high above the square is the **Torre dell'Orologio ♥♥**, an impressive cap atop the formidable **Palazzo d'Accursio,** seat of Bologna's municipal offices. An ascent to the parapet provides a bird's-eye view over the city's towers, domes, and medieval rooftops and comes with

HOTELS

Albergo delle Drapperie 26
Art Hotel Commercianti 22
Art Hotel Orologio 20
Casa Bertagni 11
Hotel Accademia 8
Hotel Corona D'Oro 1890 14
Hotel il Guercino 3
Hotel Metropolitan 4
Hotel Porta San Mamolo 31
Hotel Roma 21
Hotel Touring 30

RESTAURANTS

All'Osteria Bottega 29
Caminetto d'Oro 5
Enoteca Italiana 6
Gelatauro 33
Il Rovescio 1
Ristorante da Nello al Montegrappa 17
Sorbetteria 32
Trattoria Anna Maria 9
Trattoria Bertozzi 1
Trattoria da Me 1
Trattoria dal Biassanot 7

ATTRACTIONS

Basilica di San Domenico 28
Basilica di San Petronio 23
Basilica di Santo Stefano 27
Church of Santa Maria della Vita 25
Fontana di Nettuno 18
Museo Civico Medievale 16
Museo d'Arte Moderna di Bologna (MAMbo) 2
Museo per la Memoria di Ustica 2
Palazzo dell'Archiginnasio 24
Palazzo Fava 15
Palazzo Magnani-Salem 13
Pinacoteca Nazionale di Bologna 10
San Giacomo Maggiore 12
Torre dell'Orologio 19

a look at frescoed salons filled with the city's art collections. With the closing of the Asinelli tower (p. 358), this is the best view over Bologna you are going to get. It's open daily, mid-May through mid-September 10am to 8:20pm (the rest of the year, it closes at 6:20pm); admission is 10€ adults, 5€ children ages 4 to 12, free for children 3 and under and with Bologna Welcome Card.

Most of the city's sights are within an easy walk from the piazza. Just to the east of the square rise the **Due Torri** (p. 358), Bologna's iconic leaning towers, presiding over the atmospheric **Piazza della Mercanzia,** a marketplace from Roman times through the Middle Ages. The poet Dante, exiled from his native Florence, sat in cafes on this piazza and

Public Indecency

Bologna's famous **Fontana di Nettuno ♥♥♥** (Neptune Fountain), in Piazza del Nettuno, was designed in 1566 by the Flemish artist Giambologna, who gave the naked sea god many rippling muscles and surrounded him with erotic cherubs and sirens spouting water from their breasts. When the papal legate who occupied the piazza's Palazzo d'Accursio protested that the spectacle was indecent, Giambologna got his revenge: If you approach the statue from its rear right side, you'll notice that the left arm is positioned in such a way to suggest an indecently large . . . well, walk around the statue and see for yourself. Giambologna fled to Florence when the legate vowed to have the artist's arms cut off as punishment.

watched beautiful women stroll by. From the square, little lanes dive southwest into the **Quadrilatero,** the old quarter of food shops (p. 365); Via Santo Stefano leads south to the basilicas of **Santo Stefano** (p. 358) and **San Domenico** (below), and Via Zamboni heads northeast past the **Jewish Ghetto,** established in the 16th century and now a quiet enclave of tall houses on little lanes, into the **university district.** The University of Bologna, founded in 1088 and said to be the oldest university in continuous operation in the world, does not have a campus but occupies old *palazzos* and other buildings on streets surrounding **Piazza Verdi.** More than 90,000 students infuse the neighborhood with a lot of youthful energy, along with coffeeshops, bars, inexpensive eateries, and nightlife spots.

Basilica di San Domenico ♥♥ CHURCH Spanish-born St. Dominic, founder of the Dominican order and patron saint of astronomers, rests forever in a shrine designed by the 13th century's greatest sculptor, Nicola Pisano. Raised in wealth, Dominic aligned himself with the poor as a young student. To feed the starving, he sold his belongings, including his manuscripts, saying, "Would you have me study off these dead skins, when men are dying of hunger?" In Bologna he encouraged his followers "to have charity, to guard their humility, and to make their treasure out of poverty." The saint traveled from one end of Europe to the other preaching his doctrine of charity, poverty, and humility and died in 1221 in Bologna on a bed of sackcloth; now he lies beneath elaborate carvings depicting his colorful life, the work of Arnolfo di Cambio. In the 15th century, Nicolo di Bari added a canopy, carved with images of saints and evangelists, and was so proud of his work that he changed his name to Nicolo di Arca. A young Michelangelo, arriving in Bologna in 1495 when his patrons, the Medici, were expelled from Florence, added transcendent renderings of two other Bologna saints, Petronius and Proculus (who appears to be the prototype for his *David*). Bologna-born Guido Reni topped off the shrine in 1615 with a ceiling fresco depicting Dominic entering heaven.

Piazza San Domenico 13. sandomenicobologna.it. ✆ **051/640-0411.** Free admission. Mon–Sat 7am–1pm and 3:30–6pm; Sun 3:30–8pm. Bus: A, 16, 30, 38, 39, 59.

Basilica di San Petronio ♥♥ CHURCH The massive church honoring Bologna's patron, the 5th-century bishop Petronio, was begun in 1390, designed to be larger than St. Peter's in Rome. Then papal powers cut off funding and the basilica remains unfinished—the formidable brick walls were never sheathed in marble as intended and transepts are severely truncated (look down either side of the church to see where extensions end abruptly in the surrounding streets). Among the few flourishes are a magnificent **central doorway** surrounded by Old and New Testament figures rendered in marble by Jacopo della Quercia of Siena (where he designed the Fonte Gaia for the Campo; see p. 234). Michelangelo claimed that della Quercia's rendering of the *Creation of Adam* here inspired his *Genesis* in the Sistine Chapel. The head of the namesake saint is enshrined in the **Capella di San Petronio,** while in the **Cappella dei Magi** ♥♥♥ (also known as Cappella Bolognini), the fourth on the left as you enter, Giovanni da Modena's fresco cycle, painted between 1408 and 1420, depicts Petronio's life. Scenes of Hell from Dante's *Inferno* include a startling image of Satan eating and excreting doomed souls and Mohammed being devoured by devils (Al-Qaeda operatives and other terrorists in recent years have tried to blow up the church in retaliation). If you visit the church around noon, look for a shadow falling on a meridian line in the left aisle, indicating the day of the year; it's the world's longest sundial,

The marble cladding stops partway up the outside walls of the massive but unfinished Basilica di San Petronio.

70m (231 ft.) long, designed by famed 17th-century astronomer Giovanni Domenico Cassini.

Piazza Maggiore. basilicadisanpetronio.org. ✆ **051/231415.** Free admission; Cappella dei Magi 5€; 3€ over 65 and ages 11–18; children 10 and under free. Basilica: Daily 8:30am–1pm and 2:30–6pm. Cappella dei Magi: Daily 8:30am–1:15pm and 2:30–5:15pm. Bus: A, 11, 13, 14, 17, 18, 19, 20, 25.

Basilica di Santo Stefano ♥♥♥ CHURCH Bologna's most storied religious site is actually four churches, a stone maze of medieval apses, romantic porticos, and courtyards awash in legend. Petronio, the 5th-century bishop of Bologna, allegedly founded the church on the remains of a Roman temple to the earth goddess Isis. He was originally laid to rest here in the **Church of the Sepulcher,** where pregnant Bolognese women would circle his tomb 33 times—once for every year of Christ's life—stopping at every turn to crawl through a low door to say a prayer before the saint's remains (his body has been since been reunited with his head in the Basilica di San Petronio; see above); prostitutes were allowed to perform the same ritual as an act of purification once a year at Easter. The mothers-to-be moved on to the **Church of the Trinity** to pray before a fresco depicting a very pregnant Madonna stroking her belly. The **Church of Vitale and Agricola** is devoted to two other popular Bolognese saints and the city's first Christian martyrs, the 4th-century nobleman Agricola and his devoted slave; a cross near the tomb is said to be the one Agricola was holding when he was crucified, though it dates from much later. Similarly, a marble basin in the **Cortile di Pilato** (Courtyard of Pilate), alleged to be the one in which Pontius Pilate washed his hands after condemning Christ to death, actually dates to the 8th century; a statue atop a nearby column pays homage to the rooster who crowed three times when Peter

Leaning Towers & Medieval Waterways

It's been estimated that in the 12th and 13th centuries as many as 180 stone towers rose above Bologna's rooftops, reaching heights of up to 100m (330 ft.). Probably built as places of refuge in times of war, they were also proof of a family's wealth—it took enormous expense to erect such towers, carefully crafted with successively thinner layers of masonry on the upper levels. Some 22 towers remain; the most famous are **Le Due Torri,** two slender medieval skyscrapers just east of Piazza Maggiore. The **Garisenda** rises 49m (162 ft.) and leans about 3m (10 ft.) from perpendicular; the **Asinelli** stands 102m (334 ft.) tall and inclines almost 2.5m (8 ft.). Garisenda has been off-limits for years and, amid growing concerns of instability, Asinelli also has been closed to visitors, leaving the **Torre dell'Orologio** (p. 354) as the best option. Structural tests and engineering efforts for Asinelli may continue for some time. Other medieval remnants are the few remaining stretches of the **canals** that once diverted waters from the Rena and Savena rivers to course through the city and power silk works and mills, along with providing transport for goods and people. In your wanderings, keep an eye out for windows on Via Piella, Via Oberdan, and Via Malcontenti that open to sections that have not been built over.

denied knowing Jesus. It's said that Dante used to sit in the Romanesque **cloister** and reflect during his exile in Bologna. He might have found inspiration for the hellish scenes of the *Divine Comedy* while looking at the carved capitals atop the pillars, with their grotesque imagery of swiveling heads and men crushed beneath boulders.

Via Santo Stefano 24. santostefanobologna.it. ✆ **051/223-256.** Free admission. Tues–Sun 7:30am–12:30pm and 2:30–7pm. Bus: 11, 13, 90, 96.

Museo Civico Medievale ♥♥ MUSEUM Displayed in the salons of the magnificently medieval Palazzo Ghisilardi Fava, the treasures here bring the Bologna of the Middle Ages vividly to life. You'll find rare illuminated manuscripts and intriguing artifacts such as a courtesan's dainty shoe, but most illuminating are the statues showing off the haircuts and clunky headgear of the times, and the ordinary funeral slabs that provide such telling glimpses as a relief of a supine professor with his hands resting on a book, as if he has fallen asleep while reading.

Via Manzoni 4. museibologna.it/arteanticaen. ✆ **051/219-3930.** Admission 6€ adults, 2€ seniors and students 18–25, free for ages 17 and under. Included with Bologna Welcome Card. Tues and Thurs 10am–2pm; Wed and Fri 2–7pm; Sat–Sun 10am–7pm. Bus: A, 11, 20, 27, 28.

Museo d'Arte Moderna di Bologna (MAMbo) ♥♥ MUSEUM This is the city's showcase for the avant-garde, with an emphasis on post–World War II art. The standout is a museum within a museum, the **Museo Morandi ♥♥♥**, exhibiting a collection of works by Bolognese painter/printmaker Giorgio Morandi (1890–1964), who once said, "What interests me most is expressing what's in nature, in the visible world," an understatement given his deceptively straightforward still lifes, which seem almost abstract in their minimalism. Morandi's studio has been reconstructed here, and you can also visit his **apartment** at Via Fondazza 36 (✆ **051/649-6653;** by appointment; free admission), converted to stark galleries where his personal effects and the vases, utensils, and other objects he painted are on view. In the larger museum, one standout piece is Renato Guttuso's *I Funerali di Togliatti* (1972), awash in red flags, as the painting depicts the funeral of the leader of the communist party, surrounded by images of left-wing luminaries.

Via Don Minzoni 14. mambo-bologna.org. ✆ **051/649-6611.** Admission 6€ adults, 4€ students and ages 6–17, children 5 and under free. Included with Bologna Welcome Card. Tues–Wed 2–7pm; Thurs 2–8pm; Fri–Sun 10am–7pm. Bus: A, 11, 20, 27, 28.

Palazzo dell'Archiginnasio ♥♥ HISTORIC SITE It's no accident that one of the grander buildings of Bologna University, completed in 1563, is adjacent to the basilica of San Petronio. Pope Pius IV ordered this central hall for the university faculties to be built here to prevent the basilica from expanding, so it wouldn't surpass in size St. Peter's in Rome. Corridors and staircases decorated with family crests lead to the **Teatro Anatomico ♥♥♥**, a handsome spruce-paneled lecture hall with tiers of wood benches surrounding a marble slab for med-school dissections. Apollo, god of medicine, gazes down from the ceiling, and statues of Hippocrates and other august physicians line the walls; the doctor holding a nose is Gaspare Tagliacozzi, a pioneer of rhinoplasty (aka "nose job"), a procedure much in demand in an era when noses were routinely cut off for punishment. Look for the secret panel, through which a church inquisitor spied on classes to make sure dissections followed church protocol—only during Lent and in one continuous session (often 2 full days) to preserve the bodies, and all organs had to remain *in situ* and intact, ready for Judgment Day. Piazza Galvani. archiginnasio.it. ✆ **051/276811.** Admission 10€ w/audioguide, 12€ guided tour. Mon–Sat 9am–7pm. Bus: A or 29B.

In the university's grand Palazzo dell'Archiginnasio, students pass along corridors decorated with family crests.

Pinacoteca Nazionale di Bologna ♥♥ MUSEUM Beginning in the late 18th century, the former St. Ignatius monastery began to house altarpieces and other works gathered from religious institutions throughout Bologna. Among the great works is Raphael's *St. Cecilia in Ecstasy* (Gallery 15), in which the saint, patron of music, is portrayed holding a lute, rapturously listening to a heavenly choir. **Guido Reni** (1575–1642), born and buried in Bologna, dominates Gallery 24 with his *Massacre of the Innocents*, in which two muscular, knife-wielding soldiers set upon a group of screaming women and children. Gallery 23 features Bologna's **Carracci family**—brothers Agostino and Annibale and their cousin Lodovico—who opened a famous academy in Bologna in the 1580s. Agostino's masterpiece is *The Communion of St. Jerome*, but the work for which he became best known was his copy of *I Modi* (The Way), a highly erotic series of engravings (not here). Annibale was the greater and more passionate painter, known for his realistic renderings of human features, as you'll see in his darkly moving *Mocking of Christ*. He was famous for his photographic memory: When still a child, he and his father were set upon by robbers, and young Annibale drew the thieves with such precision that they were soon apprehended and the Carraccis' money returned. Via delle Belle Arti 56. pinacotecabologna.cultura.gov.it. ✆ **051/420-9411.** Admission 12€ adults, 2€ ages 18–25, ages 17 and under free. Included with Bologna Welcome Card. Tues–Sun 9am–7pm. Bus: 20, 28, 36, 37, 89, 93, 94, 99 (to Porta San Donato).

San Giacomo Maggiore ♥♥ CHURCH Facing one of Bologna's most welcoming squares, this Romanesque landmark is fronted with an elegant Renaissance portico. In its present form the church was largely funded by Bologna's most powerful 15th-century family, the Bentivoglios, who were constantly plotting and being plotted against. Many are laid to rest in the Cappella Bentivoglio, decorated in vivid frescoes by Lorenzo Costa, who came to Bologna in the 1480s before moving on to great fame in Mantua (p. 501). *Madonna Enthroned* depicts Giovanni II Bentivoglio kneeling with his wife next to the Madonna, as his family gives thanks for the unmasking of a conspiracy against them. Anton Galeazzo Bentivoglio, who fell out of favor with the papacy and was beheaded in 1435, lies in a tomb designed by Jacopo della Quercia in San Petronio (p. 357). For an eerie thrill, follow the left-side chapels about halfway down until you come to a terrifyingly realistic effigy of the corpse of Christ, complete with lash marks, oozing wounds, and plenty of blood.

Piazza Rossini, Via Zamboni. facebook.com/agostinianibologna. ✆ **051/225-970.** Free admission. Mon–Fri 7:30am–12:30pm and 3:30–6pm; Sat and Sun 8:30am–12:30pm and 3–6:30pm. Bus: C.

YET MORE ART to explore

The Carraccis are the stars of the Pinacoteca Nazionale (p. 360), but their masterpiece, the *Founding of Rome* fresco cycle, is in the **Palazzo Magnani-Salem,** Via Zamboni 20 (✆ **051/296-2503;** free admission; hours vary but usually Wed 10am–1:30pm and 2:30–6pm and second Sat of month). The Carraccis also decorated the first floor of **Palazzo Fava ♥♥**, Via Manzoni 2, with colorful renditions of Jason and the Argonauts and other mythical scenes. A gentle portrait of Medea bathing next to a stream is considered to be the first female nude since classical times. The palace hosts temporary art exhibitions, so hours and admission fees can vary (genusbononiae.it; ✆ **051/1993-6305;** admission usually 14€; usually Tues–Sun 10am–7pm).

Aside from his carvings on the tomb of St. Dominic (p. 356), Niccolò dell'Arca's other great work in Bologna is *Compianto sul Cristo Morto* (Lamentation over the Dead Christ) in the **Church of Santa Maria della Vita ♥♥♥**, Via Clavature 8 (genusbononiae.it; ✆ **051/230260;** admission 8€, free with Bologna Welcome Card; daily 10am–6:30pm). These life-size terra-cotta figures depicting Christ being taken from the cross are some of the most humane and moving religious images you'll ever see, the expressions on the faces of the lamenters etched in grief.

Of more recent vintage is a haunting installation by Christian Boltanski, **Museo per la Memoria di Ustica ♥♥**, outside the city center in the Bolognina neighborhood at Via di Saliceto 3/22, commemorating the crash of a Bologna–Palermo flight off the Sicilian island of Ustica on June 27, 1980. Wreckage of the DC-9, allegedly shot down by an Italian military missile when mistaken for a Libyan spy plane, is accompanied by lighting and sound effects—victims are represented by 81 lights blinking off and on against the black ceiling while from 81 speakers come snippets of heartbreakingly ordinary conversation (museomemoriaustica.it; ✆ **051/377-680;** free admission; Thurs–Fri 9:30am–1:30pm and Sat–Sun 10am–6:30pm).

The nearby **Holocaust Memorial,** at the northern end of Ponte Matteotti, consists of two 10m-tall (30-ft.) steel blocks that face each other to form a dark chasm.

CABINETS OF curiosity

Life was precarious in the Middle Ages, and the medieval mindset never forgot that we are, in the end, just flesh and blood. For a grisly reminder of this, head to **Chiesa della Santa ♥♥**, Tagliapietre 19, where the body of St. Catherine—a 15th-century nun who's the city patron and protector of artists—sits on a golden throne in a side chapel. The faithful claim Catherine has remained miraculously intact since her death, but the blackened, leathery flesh stretched over skeletal features suggests otherwise. To enter the little sanctuary, adorned with the saint's violin and other relics, ring the bell next to a wooden door on the left in the church vestibule (daily 9am–noon and 3–7pm).

There's a similarly creepy vibe to the human anatomy and natural history exhibits in the University of Bologna's **Musei di Palazzo Poggi ♥♥**, Via Zamboni 33, where a wonderful 16th-century assemblage of what was thought to be all the living organisms on earth is on display. Along with fossils and an (alleged) unicorn tusk, you'll see anatomically correct wax models of humans in various states of flaying that helped medieval physicians advance medicine from folk practice to science (museopalazzopoggi.unibo.it; ✆ **051/20-99610;** admission 8€, 5€ seniors and ages 19–26, free for 18 and under; Tues–Fri 10am–4pm, Sat–Sun 10am–6pm).

On a lighter note, the frescoed salons of the Palazzo Sanguinetti, Strada Maggiore 34, are home to the **Museo Internazionale e Biblioteca della Musica ♥♥**, filled with scores, libretti, and musical instruments from the 16th century on, including an utterly charming re-creation of a lute-maker's studio (museibologna.it/musica; ✆ **051/275-711;** admission 5€, free with Bologna Welcome Card; Tues–Thurs 11am–1:30pm and 2:30–6:30pm, Fri 10am–1:30pm and 2:30–7pm, Sat–Sun 10am–7pm). Music lovers should also check out the harpsichords, pianos, and other early instruments that fill the beautiful former church of St. Colombano, Via Parigi 5, all part of the **Collezione Tagliavani ♥♥♥** (genusbononiae.it; ✆ **051/1993-6366;** admission 7€, free with Bologna Welcome Card; Wed–Sun 11am–6pm).

Where to Stay in Bologna

Bologna normally hosts four to six major trade fairs a year, which dramatically affect hotel room rates; check the calendar at bolognafiere.it to see if anything's scheduled for the time you wish to visit. Rate ranges below do not reflect the sky-high prices during fairs, when you're better off staying elsewhere in Emilia-Romagna. Bologna has many short-term rental apartments, many appearing on **Airbnb.com** and **Vrbo.com**.

Important note: Parts of central Bologna (Via Ugo Bassi, Via Rizzoli, and Via dell'Indipendenza) are closed to cars almost entirely, and large parts of the central city are entirely off-limits to traffic on Sundays. Other areas are closed to cars without special permits daily 7am to 8pm (including Sun and holidays). If your hotel is in a limited traffic zone, you will be allowed to drive in to unload your bags and park, but only if you've first registered with the police. (When booking a room, present your car registration number, which the hotel will then provide to the police to ensure you are not fined for driving in a restricted area.) If you're planning to drive into Bologna, ask about these restrictions when booking, and also ask where to find nearby parking facilities.

EXPENSIVE

Art Hotel Commercianti ♥♥♥ You can't stay any closer to San Petronio than this atmosphere-rich 11th-century *palazzo,* which once served as town hall then housed university professors. In the best rooms and suites you can lie in bed, sit on a leafy terrace, or even soak in a deep tub while admiring the church's exquisite brickwork and statuary. Plenty of exposed timbers and fresco fragments suggest the medieval provenance. Three generations of the Orsini family have added artwork, plush armchairs, couches, and other beautiful furnishings, along with their polished and attentive service, to create one of the city's most inviting inns. A morning buffet is served beneath vaulted arches that show off the hotel's 13th-century origins.

Via de' Pignattari 11. art-hotel-commercianti.it. ✆ **051/745-7511.** 34 units. 250€–320€ double. Rates include breakfast. Parking 30€. Bus: 11, 13, 20, 30. **Amenities:** Bar; babysitting; bikes; room service; free Wi-Fi.

Art Hotel Orologio ♥♥ This tall, narrow old house has been an inn for a couple of centuries and takes its name from the nearby Torre dell'Orologio. The comfy surroundings are full of nooks and crannies, and no two guest rooms are the same. Most of the traditionally furnished rooms have soothing, deep-hued wall coverings, and many have nice touches like little writing alcoves. The higher you get, the more likely your room or suite has a glimpse of nearby Piazza Maggiore, or at least a tower or dome or two. The lively market streets of the Quadrilatero (p. 365) and many other city sights are just steps away.

Via 4 Novembre 10. art-hotel-orologio.it. ✆ **051/745-7411.** 33 units. 190€–410€ double. Rates include breakfast. Parking 30€. Bus: 11, 13, 20, 30. **Amenities:** Bar; room service; free Wi-Fi.

Hotel Corona D'Oro 1890 ♥♥♥ A favorite stopover for visitors to the city since the 1860s, this character-rich old *palazzo* in the shadow of the Due Torri was once the residence of a medieval noble family. Today, comfortable guest rooms surround a glass-domed lobby fashioned out of a courtyard, which is especially welcoming in the evening when *cicchetti* (snacks) are laid out to accompany cocktails from the bar. Rooms, soothingly done in soft hues, are comfortably up to date but retain old-world ambience.

Via Guglielmo Oberdan 12. hco.it. ✆ **051/745-7611.** 40 units. 210€–500€ double. Most rates include breakfast (35€). Parking 30€. Bus: A, 11, 20, 27, 28. **Amenities:** Restaurant; bar; garage; free Wi-Fi.

MODERATE

Casa Bertagni ♥♥♥ Guido Carlo Vincenzi has converted his family residence in the university district into a charming and welcoming

guesthouse. Its attractive, eclectically decorated rooms, each named after one of the seven virtues, have been a favorite of visiting writers, artists, and politicians for the past 30 years. The quirky charm extends to the luxuriant garden, and restaurants and shops are just outside the gate.
G.B. De Rolandis 7. casabertagni.it. ✆ **3463/239-8931.** 7 units. 150€–300€ double. Parking 25€. Bus: A, 11, 20, 27, 28. **Amenities:** Garden; free Wi-Fi.

Hotel Accademia ♥♥ One of a few hotels in the university district, the Accademia is surrounded by lively clubs, bars, and affordable student-oriented *osterie.* Its large, high-ceilinged guest rooms are attractively up to date, with polished floors, blond furniture, muted colors, and shiny bathrooms. The colorful street life can be a late-night curse for some; if this bothers you, ask for a room facing the courtyard.
Via delle Belle Arte 6. hotelaccademia.com. ✆ **051/232-318.** 28 units. 135€–175€ double. Rates include breakfast. Parking 25€. Bus: A, 11, 20, 27, 28. **Amenities:** Bikes; free Wi-Fi.

Hotel Metropolitan ♥♥♥ Just a few steps off Via dell'Indipendenza, this stylish haven is an oasis of calm and comfort where soothing whites and neutral shades offset Indonesian antiques and other Asian pieces. All rooms have large mosaic-tiled bathrooms, many have small sitting rooms, and several have terraces. In addition to a rooftop terrace, five airy two-room suites open onto a leafy roof garden. Piazza Maggiore and most city sights are an easy walk away. The hotel also offers modern, well-equipped apartments nearby; rates range from 115€ to 400€ per day.
Via Dell'Orso 6. hotelmetropolitan.com. ✆ **051/229-393.** 50 units. 115€–380€ double. Rates include breakfast. Parking 20€. Bus: A, 11, 20, 27, 28. **Amenities:** Restaurant; bar; babysitting; room service; free Wi-Fi.

Hotel Porta San Mamolo ♥♥ Most of these rather romantic rooms, only a 15-minute walk from Piazza Maggiore, surround a leafy courtyard, bringing a sense of the surrounding countryside into the heart of Bologna. Nice-sized, tile-floored rooms are done in soothing creams and warm golds and reds, with stylishly contemporary furnishings offset by exposed beams, vaulted ceilings, and other architectural details. A few rooms have large terraces; others open directly into the garden. Breakfast is served in an airy pavilion that seems summery even during the gray Bolognese winter.
Vicolo del Falconi 6–8. hotel-portasanmamolo.it. ✆ **051/583056.** 43 units. 130€–315€ double. Rates include breakfast. Parking 20€. Bus: 29B or 52. **Amenities:** Bikes; room service; free Wi-Fi.

Hotel Touring ♥♥ A rooftop terrace overlooking tile roofs and domes to the hills that surround Bologna is perfect for a few hours of quiet relaxation, an *aperitivo,* or even a soak in the hot tub. Guest rooms are all geared to quiet comfort, too, done in soothing cream colors and functional furnishings, and those on the third and fourth floors have a great amenity:

city-view terraces or balconies. A ground-floor reading room warmed by a fireplace is a perfect hideout in cooler weather.

Via De' Mattuiani 1/2. hoteltouring.it. ✆ **051/584-305.** 135€–330€ double. Rates include breakfast. Parking 25€. Bus 30 or A. **Amenities:** Bar; free Wi-Fi.

INEXPENSIVE

Albergo delle Drapperie ♥♥ This centuries-old guesthouse is smack in the middle of the bustling market streets and steps from Piazza Maggiore. Top-floor rooms, the largest and best, have vaulted ceilings, wooden beams, gables, window seats that double as extra beds, and other atmospheric touches. Lower-floor rooms are smaller and furnished with not much more than beds, though they're enlivened with homey iron bedsteads and the occasional fresco or coffered ceiling. You'll have to do

A moveable feast IN THE QUADRILATERO

On a warren of medieval lanes behind Piazza Maggiore, the **Quadrilatero ♥♥♥** is the gastronomic epicenter of Bologna, packed with greengrocers, fishmongers, and venerable gourmet shops. At **Tamburini,** Via Caprarie 1 (tamburini.com; ✆ **051/234726**), a selection of pastas, meats and fish, soups and salads, vegetables, and sweets can be taken away or enjoyed in-house, accompanied by 200 wines by the glass. **La Baita Vecchia Malga,** Via Pescherie Vecchie 3A (vecchiamalga.com; ✆ **051/223940**), lets you choose from a dizzying selection of hams and cheeses and enjoy them in a busy mezzanine dining room. At **Salumeria Simoni,** Via Drapperie 5/2A (salumeriasimoni.it; ✆ **051/231880**), you can stock up (or dine in) on cheese and meat, sandwiches, and other dishes, while next-door **Gilberto,** Via Drapperie 5 (drogheriagilberto.it; ✆ **051/223925**), sells balsamic vinegars, oils, chocolates, and other local specialties. Founded in 1880, nearby **Atti,** Via Caprarie 7 (paoloatti.com; ✆ **051/220425**), is renowned for pasta and pastries.

Part of an international chain, **Bologna Eataly,** Via degli Orefici 19 (eataly.it; ✆ **051/095-2820**), sells cookbooks, cheeses, hams, and other products, as well as prepared foods and wine that can be consumed picnic-style at indoor and outdoor tables. The covered marketplace across the way has been converted into the **Mercato di Mezzo ♥**, Via Clavature (✆ **051/232919**), a food hall housing small bars and food stands; in the evenings many offer snacks to accompany drinks. **Osteria del Sole ♥**, Vicolo Ranocchi 1D (osteriadelsole.it; ✆ **348/225-6887;** closed Sun), is an invitingly rundown room with a provenance (serving since 1465) and a novel twist on the BYO policy—you bring the food from neighboring shops and they supply the wine for 2.50€ a glass.

Venture a few blocks west of the Quadrilatero to find Bologna's central food market, **Mercato delle Erbe ♥**, at Via Ugo Bassi 25 (mercatodelleerbe.eu; stores Mon–Sat 7am–7:30pm; restaurants Mon–Sat noon–2:30pm and 7pm–midnight, Sun 11am–3pm). Aside from produce, fish, and other food vendors, the hall has fast-food outlets with a couple of clamorous dining areas.

Just a short walk north from the Quadrilatero, **Sfoglia Rina ♥**, Via Castiglione 5b (sfogliarina.it; ✆ **051/9911710**), offers a changing menu of the city's traditional tagliatelle and tortellini, freshly made and topped with ragù and other signature sauces, served at communal tables or packaged for takeaway.

some climbing to reach any of these rooms, as well as the lobby and breakfast room. The Drapperie also rents out apartments in a nearby building; contact for rates.

Via Drapperie 5. albergodrapperie.com. ✆ **051/223-955.** 21 units. 100€–250€ double. Rates include breakfast. Bus: A, 11, 20, 27, 28. **Amenities:** Free Wi-Fi.

Hotel Il Guercino ♥♥ In Bolognina, a middle-class neighborhood just outside the city center, a welcoming courtyard sets the tone for colorful lounges hung with prints by the namesake artist and comfortable guest rooms with a warm, bohemian air; the superiors on the top floor come with a terrace. The location just behind the train station is a plus for exploring the region, and the surrounding bars and restaurants, many run by immigrants from Eastern Europe, North Africa, and Asia, lend a friendly neighborhood vibe. Prime sightseeing is a half-hour walk away or an easy ride on one of the hotel bikes.

Via Luigi Serra 7, Bologna. guercino.it. ✆ **051/369893.** 85€–140€ double. Rates include breakfast. Bus 30, 35, or 90. **Amenities:** Fitness room; spa; free bikes; free Wi-Fi.

Hotel Roma ♥♥ What this old Bologna fixture lacks in chic style it makes up for with plenty of old-school hospitality and a wonderful location just off Piazza Maggiore. Downstairs lounges and a small bar are gracious and welcoming, and the no-nonsense guest rooms upstairs are large and pleasantly done with brass beds and gleaming wooden floors; many open to small terraces overlooking the surrounding streets. The excellent in-house restaurant, **C'era Una Volta**—which translates as "Once Upon a Time"—offers Bolognese classics.

Via Massimo d'Azeglio 64. hotelroma.biz. ✆ **051/226-322.** 86 units. 120€–185€ double. Rates include breakfast. Parking 20€. Bus: 11, 13, 20, 30. **Amenities:** Restaurant; bar; bikes; room service; free Wi-Fi.

Where to Eat in Bologna

As capital of Italy's most productive agricultural region, Bologna has been a food center for centuries. Specialties include locally raised beef, cured pork (especially prosciutto, salami, and mortadella), fresh pastas, and hearty sauces; Bologna denies any association with the Americanized sandwich meat that was named after the city. See p. 365 for details on the food shops of the **Quadrilatero** neighborhood.

A Street of Cheap Eats

For an inexpensive meal, head to **Via del Pratello,** west of Piazza Maggiore near the basilica of San Francesco; low-cost osterias, bars, and no-frills take-out shops line the narrow street. **Capra e Cavoli ♥**, at no. 58c (capraecavolibologna.it; ✆ **342/775-7553**), and **Pasta Fresca Naldi ♥**, at no. 69 (pastafrescanaldi.it; ✆ **051/523288**), prepare delicious pastas, including *tortellini alla panna,* to match those from the finest kitchens in town. **MozzaBella ♥**, at no. 65 (✆ **051/550506**), transforms pizza slices into gourmet concoctions.

Artisan Gelato, Bologna Style

Run by three brothers, **Gelatauro ♥♥**, Via San Vitale 98 (instagram.com/gelatauro; ✆ **051/230049**), is known for its organic gelato, including a divine concoction made from Sicilian oranges. **Sorbetteria Castiglione ♥** (lasorbetteria.it) makes more than 100 decadently rich flavors as well as some classic tastes without milk and sugar, dispensing them from shops at Via Castiglione 44 (✆ **051/095-0772**) and Via Saragozza 83 (✆ **051/093568**). Gelato aficionados can visit the **Gelato Museum ♥** (gelatomuseum.com; ✆ **051/650-5306**), attached to the Carpigiani factory, a producer of gelato-making machines in outlying Anzola Emilia, for tours, tastings, and gelato-making classes, from 10€. Bus 87 to Anzola leaves from Piazza XX Settembre in front of the train station and stops in front of Carpigiani.

EXPENSIVE

All'Osteria Bottega ♥♥♥ BOLOGNESE/ITALIAN In this unassuming storefront, the simple tables are covered with butcher paper, and pride of place belongs to the bright red meat slicer and the meats and cheeses on display. These find their way into *affettati misti* (mixed cold cuts) and delicious pastas, followed by roast rabbit, veal cutlets, and other hearty main courses. On hand to enthuse about the daily offerings, owner Danielle Minarelli will guide you through one of your most memorable meals in Italy. Reservations recommended, especially for dinner.
Via Santa Caterina 51. osteriabottega.it. ✆ **051/585111.** Main courses 16€–30€. Tues–Sat 12:30–2:30pm and 8–10:30pm. Bus: 11 or 13.

Caminetto d'Oro ♥♥ BOLOGNESE/ITALIAN Despite the sleekly contemporary look of its formal dining room and more casual bistro to the side, the Caratti family has been feeding Bologna for 90 years, from premises that were once a bakery. A decades-old oven is still used to bake their own delicious breads, which are all made, along with the pasta, using wheat flour from a mill near Modena. The *tagliatelle al ragù* here is renowned and a favorite of many performers and theatergoers from nearby Arena del Sole. This is also one of the best places in town for a steak, with T-bones from local Romagnola cattle seared on soapstone.
Via de' Falegnami 4. caminettodoro.it. ✆ **051/263494.** Main courses 12€–28€. Tues–Sat 12:30–2:30pm and 7:30–10:30pm. Bus: C.

Ristorante da Nello al Montegrappa ♥♥ BOLOGNESE These cozy paneled subterranean rooms just off Piazza Maggiore have been a favorite dining spot since 1948. Crisply uniformed waiters lead you through specialties that include the house signature dish, *tortellini Montegrappa,* served in a cream-and-meat sauce. *Funghi porcini* and truffles appear in many of the classics, including a fragrant veal scallopine in truffle sauce. Meals should begin with a platter of buttery prosciutto and

At Ristorante da Nello al Montegrappa, a cook deftly shapes the signature *tortellini Montegrappa.*

end with a selection of local cheeses, washed down with one of the wines from nearby vineyards. To ensure a table, reserve for dinner.

Via Montegrappa 2. ristorantedanello.com. ✆ **051/236331.** Main courses 16€–35€. Tues–Sun noon–2:30pm and 7–10:30pm. Closed 2 weeks Jan/Feb and all of Aug. Bus: A, 11, 20, 27, 28.

MODERATE

Il Rovescio ♥♥ BOLOGNESE/VEGETARIAN The name of this rustic-looking little room just off bar- and *osterie*-lined Via del Pratello (p. 366) translates roughly as "upside down" or "backward," and you're likely to find some unusual takes on traditional Bolognese cuisine. All the food is locally sourced, and the menu changes frequently to reflect what's in season. A rarity in meat-loving Bologna, there are many vegetarian choices, such as grilled radicchio on a bed of polenta, or crepes filled with caramelized squash. Rovescio operates an evenings-only **bio-pizzeria** next door, where only organically grown ingredients are used.

Via Pietralata 28. rovescio.it. ✆ **051/523-545.** Main courses 13€–20€. Tues–Sun 12:30–2:30pm (Sat–Sun until 3pm) and 7:30–10:30pm (Fri–Sat until 11pm). Bus: C, 11, 13.

Trattoria Bertozzi ♥♥ BOLOGNESE An unassuming neighborhood favorite just west of the historic center enjoys citywide acclaim for friendly service, overseen by on-the-scene proprietors Fabio and Alessandro and their close-to-perfection takes on *tortellini in brodo, tagiliatelle al ragù,* braised lamb chops, and other classic dishes. Homemade cakes are just as winning.

Via Andrea Costa 84/2. trattoriabertozzibologna.it. ✆ **051/614-1425.** Main courses 14€–25€. Fri, Sat, and Mon 12:30–2:30pm and 7:30–10pm; Tues–Thurs 7:30–10pm. Bus: 14, 21, 61, 89.

Trattoria da Me ♥♥♥ MODERN BOLOGNESE Chef Elisa Rusconi became a TV star with her cooking show *4 Ristoranti*, then returned to her Bologna roots to revamp the simple trattoria her grandparents opened in the 1930s. Warm and welcoming shabby-chic surroundings do the old-fashioned premises justice, while Elisa's menu puts a delicious twist on Bolognese favorites, including pumpkin tortellini with beets and bacon, a cheese board that includes some memorable cheese gelati, and the town's best *cotoletta alla Bolognese,* a pounded veal chop with prosciutto and Parmigiano-Reggiano. Many regulars would dine nowhere else, so reserve for dinner.

Via San Felice 50. trattoriadame.it. ✆ **051/555486.** Main courses 15€–25€. Tues–Sun 12:30–2:30pm and 7:30–10pm (Sat–Sun from noon). Bus: 36, 37, 39.

Trattoria dal Biassanot ♥♥♥ EMILIAN The wood beams, lace tablecloths, warm service, and other grace notes of this welcoming bistro (the name roughly means "night owl") do justice to expertly prepared Bolognese classics. Light-as-a-feather *tagliatelle* with ragù has a reputation as one of the best in a city that's famous for the dish, but all of the handmade pastas and succulent sauces are excellent. For a taste of the city's famous pastas, try three with Biassanot's Tris Bologna offering. Reservations are a must at this popular spot.

Via Piella 16a. dalbiassanot.it. ✆ **051/230644.** Main courses 15€–25€. Mon–Sat noon–2:15pm and 7–10:15pm. Closed Aug. Bus: 19, 27, 94.

INEXPENSIVE

Trattoria Anna Maria ♥♥ BOLOGNESE Photographs of Sophia Loren, Marcello Mastroianni, and legions of other celebrity patrons line the walls of these high-ceilinged, welcoming rooms, but everyone in Bologna knows that the real star is Anna Maria, who has been serving her freshly made pasta for 35 years. *Tortellini in brodo,* parcels of pasta filled with minced pork and floating in chicken broth, and tagliatelle with a hearty ragù sauce are her signature dishes, but the lasagnas are memorable, too. Anna Maria will likely find her way to your table at some point during your meal to make sure you've eaten every bite, but that won't be an issue.

Via Bella Arti 17/A. trattoriannamaria.com. ✆ **051/266894.** Main courses 12€–15€. Tues–Sun 12:30–3pm and 7:30–11pm. Bus: 11, 13, 20, 29B, 30, 38, 39.

Bologna Shopping

Shopping in Bologna often revolves around food; see p. 365 for some recommended gourmet stops. U.S. travelers should remember that you are allowed to bring Parmigiano and other hard cheese home, as long as it's wrapped and labeled from the shop, but not prosciutto or most other meats. Olive oil and vinegar are okay, too, but any container over 3½ ounces will have to go into your checked luggage. See p. 837 for more info.

Diving Deeper into the Local Food Scene

Tours with **Italian Days ♥♥** (italiandays.it; ✆ **338/421-6659**) venture into Bologna markets and food shops for a 4-hour introduction to the city's culinary richness (about 100€) or into the countryside to visit top producers of Parmigiano-Reggiano, prosciutto, and balsamic vinegar. These full-day country tours include breakfast, lunch, many tastings, discourses on the aging and certification processes, and hospitality as delectable as the food (from 200€). At **Salotto di Penelope ♥♥**, Via San Felice 116 (ilsalottodipenelope.it; ✆ **051/649-3627**), the engaging Barbara and Pietro lead half-day workshops in preparing gnocchi, tagliatelle, and tortelloni as well as the city's classic ragù, in which carrot, onion, and celery are combined with minced beef, wine, and a dab of tomato paste and simmered for hours. Lessons and the accompanying lunch or dinner are laced with lively tips on techniques and shopping and dining in Bologna. Classes are about 120€.

Bologna also has many famous chocolatiers. **Majani ♥♥**, Via de' Carbonesi 5 (majani.it; ✆ **051/234302**), claims to be Italy's oldest sweets shop, making confections since 1796. **Roccati ♥♥**, Via Clavature 17A (roccaticioccolato.com; ✆ **051/261964**), is run by a husband-and-wife team who make the *gianduja* (hazelnut and cognac-filled chocolate) their ancestors once concocted for the princes of Savoy.

An old-fashioned throwback, **Drogheria dalla Pioggia ♥**, Via Galleria 27 (facebook.com/DrogheriaDallaPioggia; ✆ **051/223-754**), is a neighborhood shop (*drogheria* means "grocery") stuffed floor to ceiling with cookies, candy, oil, wine, and other essentials. **Galleria Cavour ♥**, off Piazza Maggiore at Via Farini 14, is an Aladdin's cave of another sort, housing outlets of many of Italy's finest clothing and accessory shops.

It also only stands to reason that this youth-oriented city is awash in bohemian chic, and the place to seek out some stylish vintage fashion is **La Leonarda ♥♥**, Via San Leonarda 2/2A (✆ **340/936-8884**), with an ever-changing selection of secondhand apparel that might include finds from top Italian designers; proceeds go to an organization that aids the homeless.

Entertainment & Nightlife

The 200-plus-year-old **Teatro Arena del Sole,** Via dell'Indipendenza 44 (bologna.emiliaromagnateatro.com; ✆ **051/291-0911**), stages theater and dance productions. **Teatro Comunale,** Largo Respighi 1 (tcbo.it; ✆ **051/529995**), inaugurated in 1763, is the city's main venue for opera and classical music.

Bologna's large student population keeps bars, clubs, and *osterie* busy. Many are clustered near the university on Via Zamboni and Via delle Belle Arti. Bolognese of all stripes, even those who plan to turn in early, stop at bars all over town for an *aperitivo,* when a glass of wine or a cocktail comes with snacks.

Camera a Sud ♥ Three shabby-chic rooms in the Jewish ghetto are part coffeehouse, part wine bar, and popular any time of day. Via Valdonica 5. cameraasud.net. ✆ **051/095-1448.** Daily noon–1am (Sun–Mon until midnight).

Cantina Bentivoglio ♥♥ You'll hear some of the best jazz in Bologna in the cellars of this 16th-century *palazzo* near the university. Select from more than 500 labels that fill the wine racks. Via Mascarella 4B. cantina bentivoglio.it. ✆ **051/265-416.** Daily 8pm–1am; Sun also noon–3pm.

Enoteca Italiana ♥♥♥ No place in Bologna serves a better selection of regional and Italian wines, accompanied by ham, cheese, and a wide choice of gourmet goods to eat on the premises or take away. Via Marsala 2/B. enotecaitaliana.it. ✆ **051/235-989.** Mon–Sat 9am–9:30pm.

Le Stanze ♥♥ Cocktails are served in the heavily frescoed salons and 17th-century chapel of an aristocratic palace. Via del Borgo di San Pietro. lestanzecafe.it. ✆ **051/228-767.** Tues–Thurs 6pm–midnight; Fri–Sat 6pm–1:30am; Sun noon–10pm.

Nu Lounge Bar ♥♥ Hip young professionals check out each other (and themselves in the huge mirrors) while enjoying martinis under the porticos in the Quadrilatero. Via dei Musei 6. nuloungebar.com. ✆ **051/222-532.** Daily 5:30pm–2am (Fri and Sat until 3am).

Side Trip to Modena ♥♥

45km (28 miles) NW of Bologna

By all appearances, residents of this elegant little city, only a half-hour train ride from Bologna, excel at whatever pursuit they undertake. The city is famous for cars (see box p. 372); for hams and cheeses, like its neighbors in Emilia-Romagna; and for balsamic vinegar, *aceto balsamico,* made from grape must. You will taste the dark, intense elixir at just about any meal around town, and sample a wide variety at such specialty shops as **La Consertia 1966,** Piazza Giuseppe Mazzini 9 (✆ **393/802-7841**), or on a walk through **Mercato Albinelli,** the covered market at Via Albinelli 13.

At the city center is the showiest creation of all, the 12th-century **Duomo ♥♥♥** (visitmodena.it; ✆ **059/216078**), probably the finest creation of Romanesque architecture, above which towers a slightly leaning bell tower, the **Ghirlandina.** Around 1110, the sculptor Wiligelmo surrounded the main Duomo entrance with a fearsome medieval bestiary depicting the temptation-ridden perils of our mortal journey, offset with poignant depictions of Adam and Eve, Noah's Ark, and other scenes from the Old Testament to suggest the path to redemption. On the northern side, the Porta della Pescheria (Fish Market doorway) is framed with a charming assemblage of scenes of the 12 months (an old crone huddles in front of a fire in February) and knights-on-steeds tales from Arthurian legend.

NIRVANA FOR sports car geeks

Prosperous **Modena,** 40km (25 miles) northwest of Bologna, lies in the center of the La Terra dei Motori, the "Land of Motors." A car enthusiast who's been patiently traipsing through museums and churches might be delighted to learn that all of Italy's famed sports-car manufacturers are located here and open to the public.

Maserati, founded in Bologna in 1914, is now based in Modena, and 20 vintage models are parked permanently at the **Collezione Umberto Panini** at Via dell'Aeroporto 140B (visitmodena.it). Highlights include a rare Maserati Tipo 6CM from the 1930s and a Maserati A6G/54 from the 1950s. The collection is open daily, 9:30am to 1pm and 2:30 to 6pm; admission is 15€, 12€ ages 66 to 75 and 8 to 17; free for visitors over 75 and under 8. In Maranello, 18km (11 miles) south of Modena, **Museo Ferrari Maranello,** Via Dino Ferrari 43, pays homage to the magnificent cars that Enzo Ferrari began turning out in 1929; vintage and current models are on display. More Ferraris, and the engines that power them, are on display at the **Museo Enzo Ferrari,** Via Paolo Ferrari 85, Modena. Both museums have the same website and phone number (musei.ferrari.com; ✆ **0536/943-204**). Each museum charges 32€ June through August, 27€ September through May, 24€ and 22€ seniors, 12€ and 9€ ages 6 to 18; combined ticket 42€ June through August, 38€ September through May; 18€ and 12€ ages 6 to 18; free for children 5 and under. Both are open daily April to May and September through October 9:30am to 7pm; June through Aug 9am to 7pm; and November through March 9:30am to 6pm.

The **Museo Lamborghini** (lamborghini.com; ✆ **051/681-7611**), at Via Modena 12 in the company's hometown of Sant' Agata Bolognese, between Bologna and Modena, is open daily October to April 9:30am to 6pm and May to September 9:30am to 7pm. Visits cost 18€ (14€ seniors); and 23€ (19€ seniors) with a guide. A museum visit with a tour of the factory is 90€ (86€ seniors).

It's possible to do the pilgrimage by public transport, but not easily, and you certainly couldn't do the whole circuit in a day. As an alternative, **MotorStars** (motorstarstour.com; ✆ **059/921-667**) provides a wide range of tours, with transport from Bologna plus lunch; prices vary with the museums and factories visited and start at 280€.

Motorcycle buffs don't even need to leave Bologna: The **Ducati Museum** is at Via Antonio Cavalieri Ducati 3 (ducati.com; ✆ **051/641-1311**). The museum is open daily 9am to 6pm and admission is 17€; tours of the factory, including the museum, are 32€.

Admission to the duomo is free (Mon 7am–12:30pm and 3:30–7pm; Tues–Sun 7am–7pm); timed admission to the Ghirlandina is 6€, 4€ seniors and ages 13–26, under 13 free (daily 9:30am–7pm; closes 6:30pm Oct–Mar).

A treasure trove of Italian painting (including Boticelli's transcendent *Madonna and Child*) is in **Galleria Estense ♥♥**, Largo Porta Sant'Agostino 337, the legacy of the Este dukes who ruled the city from the 14th through 18th centuries (gallerie-estensi.beniculturali.it; ✆ **059/439-5711;** admission 8€; 2€ ages 18–25; under 18 free; Tues–Sun 10am–6pm).

FERRARA ♥♥

52km (32 miles) NE of Bologna, 100km (62 miles) SW of Venice

It's not that quiet, elegant Ferrara hasn't had some big moments. For almost 4 centuries, the powerful Este family controlled this city on the Po River, and painters, composers, and poets under their patronage made Ferrara one of Europe's great capitals of culture. Lucrezia Borgia, notorious femme fatale of the Renaissance, arrived by ceremonial barge in 1502 to marry Prince Alfonso Este, and they and the other Estes built pleasure pavilions and gardens and expanded their holdings into the Addizione, a model Renaissance city crisscrossed with straight palace-lined avenues. By the end of the 16th century, however, the Estes were gone and Ferrara has looked pretty much the same ever since. That, of course, is the appeal. Ferrara is essentially a time capsule, and the Estes' castle and palaces, the city's encircling walls, and proud old convents and churches serve as a backdrop for everyday life in this attractive provincial city. If you're in Venice and feeling overwhelmed by the crowds, a day trip to this quiet beauty (just an hour south by train or car) might be a soothing tonic.

Essentials

ARRIVING Ferrara is on the main **train** line between Bologna and Venice, with service to and from both cities twice an hour (30–45 min. from Bologna; 1–1½ hr. from Venice). Ravenna is an hour away, with hourly departures all day. From the train station it's an easy 20-minute walk to the Duomo, but you can also take the frequent no. 1 or 9 bus to Piazza Travaglio (fare 1.90€; buy your ticket at the bus office inside the train station or at a tobacco shop; tper.it). You may also rent a **bike** at the station and get around the way most locals do (p. 374).

If you have a **car** and are coming from Bologna, take A13 north. From Venice, take A4 southwest to Padua and continue on A13 south to Ferrara. A convenient parking spot close to the historic center is Parcheggio Centro Storico off Via Darsena, where daytime rates are 1€ an hour up to a maximum of 6€ for the day between 7:30am and 8pm, and .50€ up to a maximum of 2€ between 8pm and midnight.

VISITOR INFORMATION The helpful **tourist office** is inside the Castello Estense, Piazza del Castello (www.ferraraterraeacqua.it; ✆ **0532/419190**). It's open Monday to Saturday 9am to 6pm, Sunday 9:30am to 5:30pm.

Exploring Ferrara

The **Castello Estense** is at the center of town, just north of the Piazza della Cattedrale, where you'll find the **Cattedrale San Giorgio Martire** and the **Loggia dei Merciai,** a charmingly ramshackle portico sheltering medieval merchant stalls. Just beyond are the twisting lanes of the medieval town, including the city's most atmospheric stretch of cobblestones, the narrow **Via delle Volte,** darkened with arched, upper-story passageways that once

From Streets & Squares to the Po Delta

Ferrara is known in Italy as a *città della bicicletta* because just about everyone in town, regardless of age, gets around on two wheels. The flat streets and squares lend themselves to easy pedaling, and the medieval walls are topped with trees, lawns, and a wide path that's ideal for cycling. Many hotels offer guests free use of bikes, or you can rent them from the lot outside the train station (2.50€/hr., 10€/day). If you want to go a bit farther afield, well-marked bike paths lead east to **Po Delta Park.** At the heart of the delta and park is **Comacchio** (42km/25 miles east of Ferrara; frequent bus connections at tper.it), a small town laced with canals lined with some impressive landmarks that include the Tre Ponti, a massive brick bridge that crosses the intersection of several canals. Comacchio is a base for excursions by boat and bike through lagoons and salt flats and is adjacent to a string of Adriatic beaches; info on excursions at ferrarainfo.com.

linked merchants' houses with their riverside warehouses. North from the Castello, **Corso Ercole I d'Este,** flanked by beautiful *palazzi,* leads into the Renaissance city and past **Palazzo dei Diamanti** to the city walls.

The Ferrara tourist card, **MyFe,** covers all the attractions listed here, except for MEIS and the Monastero di Sant'Antonio in Polesine. At a cost of 20€ for 2 days, 22€ for 3 days, and 25€ for 6 days, the card offers substantial savings compared to individual admissions. It's available from the tourist office and most museum ticket offices.

Casa Romei ♥♥ PALACE Ambitious 15th-century financier Giovanni Romei worked his way up in the Este administration, capping off his rise by marrying the daughter of an Este duke. He built this palatial townhouse between 1440 and 1450, commissioning lavish frescoes for salons surrounding a vast interior courtyard. Though the Estes carted off most of the furnishings when they left Ferrara in 1598, the Sala delle Sibille, with its original terra-cotta fireplace, coffered wooden ceiling, and images of the sibyls (classical Greek prophetesses) provides an idea of the comfortable lifestyle the occupants enjoyed. Scattered around the place are frescoes and sculptures from churches and chapels around the city.

Via Savonarola 30. casaromei.cultura.gov.it. ✆ **0532/234130.** Admission 5€, 2€ ages 18–25, 17 and under free. Included with MyFe Card. Sun–Wed 8:30am–2pm; Thurs–Sat 2–7:30pm. Bus: 11.

Castello Estense ♥♥ CASTLE With its moat, hefty brick walls, drawbridges, heavy gates, and four sturdy towers, the domain of the Este family still suggests power and might. Niccolò II d'Este ordered the castle built in 1385 as a refuge after some of his subjects, restless after a series of tax increases, tore one of his officials to pieces. A long, elevated gallery links the castle to the family's earlier residence, now the Palazzo Municipale, next door (wander into the double courtyard for a look at the monumental staircase). Duke Niccolò d'Este III forever made the castle a place of infamy when, in 1425, he used a contrivance of mirrors to catch his

20-year-old wife, Parisina d'Este, *in flagrante delicto* with his illegitimate son, Ugolino. He promptly had the pair taken to the dungeons and beheaded; Robert Browning tells the story in his poem "My Last Duchess." (Ironically, Niccolò himself boasted of sleeping with 800 women; a popular rhyme of the time was "left and right of the river Po, everywhere there are children by Niccolò.") Young Lucrezia Borgia, with a reputation for adultery, incest, and poisoning, arrived in 1502 as the wife of Duke Alfonso d'Este, who kept his half-brother, Giulio, in the dungeons for 53 years for plotting to overthrow him; the old boy allegedly created quite a stir when he re-emerged onto the streets in half-century-old finery. For all their perfidy, the Estes hosted one of the finest courts in Europe and cultivated Renaissance arts and humanities. Their refined tastes come to the fore in the frescoed **Salone dell'Aurora** (the Salon of Dawn) and **Salone dei Giochi** (the Salon of Games), and an *orangerie* that continues to flourish on terraces high above the city. Take a walk up the innovative ramplike spiral staircase ascending from the courtyard that allowed the dukes to ride their horses right up to their quarters.

Largo Castello. castelloestense.it. ✆ **0532/299-233.** Admission 12€ adults, 10€ 65 and older, 5€ ages 11–17, free for children 11 and under, included with MyFe Card. Wed–Mon 10am–6pm. Bus: 1, 7, 9, 11, 21.

Lucrezia Borgia: a Woman Misjudged?

Five hundred years after their Renaissance heyday, the Borgias are still one of history's most dysfunctional families. Lucrezia, born into the clan in 1480, was the illegitimate daughter of Cardinal Rodrigo Borgia (soon to be Pope Alexander VI). By the time she was 20, she had a child, allegedly fathered by her brother Cesare, and had been married twice—one husband fled for his life when the Pope decided Lucrezia needed a more politically useful alliance, another was strangled as he lay recovering from knife wounds (both attacks arranged by Cesare). No wonder Lucrezia got a chilly reception when she arrived in Ferrara in 1500 as the new bride of Duke Alfonso d'Este. However, she soon proved herself to be a brilliant conversationalist and generous patron of the arts. While she is said to have carried on a passionate affair with the poet Pietro Bembo, she was also a loving wife and attentive mother, dying just before her 39th birthday after giving birth to her fifth child.

Cattedrale San Giorgio Martire ♥♥ CATHEDRAL The faithful did not even have to step beyond the magnificent porch of Ferrara's 12th-century cathedral to understand that salvation is a pretty dicey affair. In exquisite carvings above the entryway, the dead creep out of their tombs as an angel weighs their sins and good deeds on a scale. As if to prove the odds are against them, the devil tugs on the evil side so the scale skews toward sin. The saved, gloriously robed and crowned, proceed toward Heaven, where they are welcomed into the lap of Abraham; the damned slouch down to hell to be tormented by sneering demons. In the vast interior, redone in baroque style after an 18th-century fire, a fresco by Guercino (the "squinter") depicts the martyrdom of St. Lawrence. When Roman authorities demanded that Lawrence, an early church deacon, turn over the ecclesiastic treasures, he brought them the poor, saying they constituted the wealth of the church. As punishment Lawrence was tied to a spit and burned over a fire. After the good-natured saint roasted for a while, he allegedly said, "I'm well done, turn me over," a wisecrack that has made him the patron saint of cooks and chefs. The cathedral museum, housed in the former San Romano church and monastery opposite the cathedral, is well stocked with canvases by Ferrara's leading 15th-century painter of the Este court, Cosmé Tura.

Piazza della Cattedrale. cattedralediferrara.it. ✆ **0532/207-449.** Church: Free admission; Mon–Sat 7:30–noon and 3:30–7pm. Church museum: Admission 6€; Tues–Sun 9:30am–1pm and 3–6pm.

Monastero di Sant'Antonio in Polesine ♥♥ CHURCH The Estes weren't all about worldly goods and power. In the early 13th century the aristocratic lady who would become Saint Beatrice d'Este entered this tranquil convent near the city walls when her groom-to-be died of battle wounds just before their wedding day. Over the years Este money paid for improvements that included a colorful fresco cycle by the school of Giotto in the nun's chapel—the charming images include an exuberant Christ climbing a ladder onto the cross, where two spike-wielding tormentors await, and a gentle-looking Virgin fluttering her hands to ascend to Heaven. Ring the bell to enter, and a nun will emerge to show off the frescoes (in Italian). She'll also invite you to return for 5pm vespers, where you'll hear the cloistered order sing Gregorian chants from behind a grill.

Vicolo del Gambone. monasterosantantonioinpolesine.org. ✆ **0532/64068.** Free admission (donations welcome). Mon–Sat 9:30–11:30am and 3:15–4:45pm. Bus 2 to XX Settembre Ghisiglieri stop.

Palazzina Marfisa d'Este ♥♥ A 16th-century resident of this well-preserved brick villa was Marfisa d'Este. a granddaughter of Lucrezia Borgia. Marfisa allegedly used to ride through the streets of Ferarra on moonlit nights in a carriage pulled by wolves, and she is said to have enjoyed entertaining young men in her elegant salons before murdering them. Legends aside, the beautifully preserved villa and large garden in the Renaissance quarter east of the Castello are a remarkable remnant of a long-vanished aristocratic lifestyle.

Corso Giovecca 170. museiferrara.it/palazzina-marfisa-deste. ✆ **0532/244-949.** Admission 6€, over 65 3€, included with MyFe Card. Tues–Sun 9:30am–1pm and 3–6pm.

Palazzo dei Diamanti ♥♥ MUSEUM The facade of the Estes' most remarkable residence consists of 8,500 spiky diamond-shaped white marble blocks and creates an architectural spectacle, shimmering in the light and seemingly constantly in movement. The *palazzo* stands at the intersection of two monumental avenues that were the main thoroughfares of the Addizione that Ercole d'Este laid out in the late 15th century, doubling the size of Ferrara and making the city a Renaissance showplace. On the first floor of the *palazzo,* the **Pinacoteca Nazionale** provides a handy overview of the School of Ferrara, especially the trio of old masters who flourished under the Estes—Cosmé Tura, Francesco del Cossa, and Ercole de' Roberti. Pride of place belongs to Tura's *Martyrdom of St. Maurelius*, in which the saint, an early bishop of Ferrara, calmly kneels as his

The Jews of Ferrara

Ferrara's Jewish heritage dates to the Middle Ages, when a Jewish community flourished under the Este control of the city. The sad fate of Ferrara's socially prominent 20th-century Jews is the subject of Giorgio Bassani's novel *The Garden of the Finzi-Contini*, brought evocatively to the screen in director Vittorio de Sica's 1970 film. **MEIS—National Museum of Italian Jewry and the Shoah,** in a former prison at Via Piangipane 81, displays manuscripts and other artifacts from Ferrara and elsewhere in Italy, as well as video and multimedia exhibits on the Jewish-Italian experience from the Roman era through the rise of Christianity; on Jews in the Renaissance; and on the Holocaust experience in Italy (meis.museum; ✆ **0532/769-137;** admission 11€, 9€ for ages 6–18, free for children 5 and under; Tues–Sun 10am–6pm).

executioner swings a sword above his neck and some nattily attired soldiers gather cheerfully around.

Corso Ercole d'Este 21. palazzodiamanti.it. ✆ **0532/244949.** Pinacoteca 8€ adults, 2€ students 18–25, free for ages 17 and under, included with MyFe Card. Tues–Sun 10am–6pm. Bus: 3C or 4C.

Palazzo Schifanoia ♥♥♥ PALACE The Estes retreated for leisure to this pleasure palace enlarged by Duke Borso d'Este between 1450 and 1471. Schifanoia translates roughly as "chasing away tedium," and the concept comes to the fore in the **Salone dei Mesi** (Salon of the Months), where a mesmerizing cycle of frescoes once represented the 12 months. Only a few remain intact, each divided into three horizontal bands: The lower bands show scenes from the daily life of courtiers and people, with Duke Borso frequently making an appearance astride a horse; the middle bands illustrate zodiac signs; and upper sections depict gods and goddesses associated with each sign. In the frescoes, a collaboration by the masters of the Ferrarese school of painting (Francesco del Cossa, Ercole de' Roberti, and Cosmé Tura), characters seem to come alive and step out of the scenes (one figure actually does and perches on the edge of the frame as if he's about to jump into the room). Men ride horses and run footraces, harvesters pick grapes, women do needlework and play lutes. The artists even dug some skeletons out of the Este closet: In a mythical scene depicting Mars and Venus caught in a net as they make love, their clothing laid beside the bed suggests a decapitated man and woman—a sly reference to the fate of Ugolino and Parisina d'Este (see Castello Estense on p. 374).

Via Scandiana 23. museiferrara.it/museo-schifanoia-e-museo-lapidario. ✆ **0532/244949.** Admission 12€ adults, 9€ seniors and ages 18–30, free for kids 17 and under, included with MyFe Card. Tues–Sun 10am–7pm. Bus: 1, 7, 9, or 21.

Frescoes in the Palazzo Schifanoia's Salone dei Mesi.

Where to Stay in Ferrara

Hotel Annunziata ♥♥ The setting, across from Castello Estense, is medieval and Casanova spent the night here when the place was a simple inn. But once inside the doors, you'll feel like you've been transported from old Ferrara into a Milanese showroom for contemporary style. The white color scheme strays into grays and beige here and there, even the occasional burst of red or orange, but for the most part this place is all about sleek lines, soothing neutrals, and minimalist calm. In large and bright guest rooms (the best with castle views), high-tech lighting and snowy linens contrast with wood floors and the occasional timbered ceiling, and the bathrooms are large and well-equipped. Six stylish apartments with kitchenettes are in a 14th-century annex.

Piazza Repubblica 5. annunziata.it. ✆ **0532/201111.** 27 units. 80€–110€ double. Rates include breakfast. Bus: 1, 7, 9, 11, 21. **Amenities:** Restaurant; bar; babysitting; bikes; room service; free Wi-Fi.

Hotel de Prati ♥♥ At this welcoming inn near the Castello, a refined old-world air is enhanced by the gracious service provided by the de Prati family, who have been running the place for three generations. Timbered beams and old archways show off the house's centuries-old origins, while the bright, quiet rooms are furnished with polished antiques, wrought-iron bedsteads, and colorful paintings by local artists.

Via Padiglioni 5. hoteldeprati.com. ✆ **0532/241905.** 28 units. 95€–115€ double. Most rates include breakfast. Bus: 3C or 4C. **Amenities:** Bikes; free Wi-Fi.

Locanda Borgonuovo ♥♥♥ This lovely old house, converted from a 17th-century convent and just down a cobblestone street from the Castello, could set the gold standard for B&Bs everywhere. The four rooms are furnished with family pieces, including some serious antiques, and share a flowery courtyard; one especially large double has an extra bed and a kitchenette. An excellent breakfast is served in the family living room, and gracious host Filippo lends bikes and dispenses advice about the best ways to enjoy Ferrara. The *locanda* also houses guests in a few one- and two-bedroom apartments in an adjoining building.

Via Cairoli 21. borgonuovo.com. ✆ **0532/211100.** 80€–105€ double. Rates include breakfast. Bus: 4C or 7. **Amenities:** Bikes; free Wi-Fi.

Where to Eat in Ferrara

You'll get a good intro to Ferrara's iconic foods, many dating from the Renaissance, on a stroll down **Via Cortevecchia,** a narrow brick lane near the cathedral, and through the food stalls of the **Mercato Comunale,** at the corner of Via Santo Stefano and Via del Mercato. Traditional *salumerias* sell the city's famous *salama da sugo,* handmade sausages of pork and spices that are often boiled for 8 hours and served atop mashed potatoes or pumpkin. This sausage and mash was a favorite of Lucrezia Borgia, whose golden locks are said to have inspired *coppia ferrarese,* sourdough bread stretched into intertwining rolls; the name derives from the fact that the bread resembles two sets of legs ("the couple"). The pastas to try are *cappellacci di zucca,* round pasta stuffed with pumpkin or squash and served *al burro e salvia* (with butter and sage sauce) or *al ragù* (with meat sauce), and *pasticcio,* also known as *maccheroni alla ferrarese;* this favorite of the d'Este family is a rich pie with a sweet or salty crust filled with short, macaroni-like pasta, pork and liver ragù, wild mushrooms, and a creamy, nutmeg-infused bechamel sauce.

Ai Tri Scalin ♥♥ FERRARESE Locals pack into this simple, half-paneled room near the city walls at mealtimes (best to reserve for dinner) to enjoy the age-old dishes their grandmothers used to make. That means lots of meat: Grilled *salama da sugo,* the city's famed sausages, are preferred starters, followed by *pasticcio* (see above). *Cotechino,* boiled sausage, is served with a rich salami sauce, and lamb chops or steaks are seasoned with green peppercorns and grilled. The dessert of choice is *tenerina,* the city's own version of chocolate cake, similar to a brownie, with a crunchy crust and creamy interior.
Via Darsena 50. ✆ **0532/760331.** Main courses 9€–18€. Tues–Sat 11am–3pm and 7pm–midnight; Sun 11am–3pm. Bus: 2.

Enoteca Al Brindisi ♥♥ FERRARESE It would be easy for this paneled, wood-beamed drinking hall to rest on its laurels, since the premises date to 1435 and Brindisi is probably the oldest wine bar in the world. Titian was a regular, Copernicus is said to have lived upstairs while studying for his degree in 1503, and it seems as if some of the dusty bottles stacked above the cramped tables have been around ever since. Some of the regulars look like they've been around awhile, too. Waiters take earnest pride in recommending wines, accompanied by a short menu of *cappellacci di zucca* (squash ravioli) and a few other local specialties.
Via Adelardi 11. albrindisi.net. ✆ **0532/473744.** Main courses 8€–18€. Wed–Sun 11am–11pm. Bus: 11.

Osteria del Ghetto ♥♥ FERRARESE/SEAFOOD From a simple storefront on the narrow cobblestone lanes of Ferrara's centuries-old Jewish ghetto, a staircase leads to two homey upstairs rooms enlivened with colorful murals. Dishes show off traditional Ferrarese cuisine and some Middle Eastern and Jewish influences, as well as a passion for fish—including rich fish soup, *spaghetti alle vongole,* grilled octopus, pan-fried anchovies, a fresh catch of the day, and other choices to tempt you away from the region's meat-heavy staples.
Via Vittoria 26/28. ✆ **0532/764936.** Main courses 8€–18€. Tues–Sun noon–2:30pm and 7:30–10:30pm. Bus: 2.

Trattoria Da Noemi ♥♥♥ FERRARESE The surroundings date to 1400, with a pleasant old-world decor that befits the gracious service and honest cooking that namesake Noemi introduced in 1958 and that her daughter and two grandsons ensure are still hallmarks The menu of

Ferrarese classics introduces you first and foremost to *cappellacci di zucca,* the city's signature dish, little pockets of light egg pasta stuffed with roasted butternut squash with hints of nutmeg and Parmigiano. Most of the meat-heavy *secondi* feature local beef grilled over a wood fire. The house *semifreddo,* a delicious half-frozen custard with pistachio and walnuts or mint, is the perfect finish.

Via Ragno 31. trattoriadanoemi.it. ✆ **0532/769070.** Main courses 9€–24€. Thurs–Mon 12:30–2:30pm and 7:30–10:30pm. Bus: 2 or 11.

RAVENNA ♥♥

74km (46 miles) SE of Bologna, 145km (90 miles) S of Venice,

It's hard to believe that Ravenna was the epicenter of the Western World for a brief spell. It was the capital of the Western Roman Empire from C.E. 402 to C.E. 476 and for several centuries after that was a major center of Ostrogoth and Byzantine cultures. These rulers and fathers of the early Christian church blanketed Ravenna's churches and monuments in glittering mosaics to create an artistic legacy that rivals the splendors of Venice and Istanbul. The poet Dante, who's buried here, described Ravenna's mosaics as "the sweet color of Oriental sapphires." Set amid the marshy landscapes of Emilia-Romagna's coastal plain, this once powerful city is a bit off the beaten path but well worth the effort to reach.

Essentials

ARRIVING With hourly **trains** that take only 1 hour, 20 minutes from Bologna, Ravenna can easily be visited on a day trip. There's also frequent service from Ferrara (1 hr., 15 min.), which has connections to Venice. The train station is a 10-minute walk from the center at Piazza Bernini (✆ **892-021**). If you have a **car** and are coming from Bologna, head east along A14. From Ferrara, take the S16.

Bicycles and alfresco cafes line Ravenna's Piazza del Popolo.

GETTING AROUND If you need to take a local **bus** (you will only need to do so to visit the Basilica di Sant'Apollinare in Classe; see p. 384), buy tickets (1.50€; startromagna.it) in advance from bars or *tabacchi* or pay on board with a contactless card or device. Ravenna is flat and well-suited to biking, and many hotels offer **bikes** for guests to use. You can pedal farther afield to the beaches around Marina di Ravenna (12km/7 miles) or into Po Delta Park (p. 374). Among many shops that rent bikes and e-bikes is **V.E.R.A. Bike Rental,** Piazza Farini 1 (velostazione.ra.it; ✆ **345/718-7028**), from 5€ for 3 hours.

VISITOR INFORMATION The **tourist office** at Piazza San Francesco (turismo.ravenna.it; ✆ **0544-35755**) offers a good map and attraction tickets and also books accommodations. The office is open Monday, Wednesday, Friday, and Saturday 8:30am to 7pm and Tuesday and Thursday 9:30am to 10pm.

Exploring Ravenna

To visit almost all of Ravenna's main sights (with the exception of the Basilica di Sant'Apollinare in Classe), you'll need to purchase the **Ravenna inclusive ticket.** The card costs 10.50€ (9.50€ for students, free for children 10 and under) and is valid for 7 days, with one entry per monument; admission to the Neonian Baptistery and Mausoleum of Galla Placidia costs an additional 2€. You can purchase tickets at ravenna mosaici.it, at the monuments, or at the Ravenna museum ticket office in Piazza Arcivescovado (✆ **0544/541-688**), open daily 9am to 7pm (Nov–Apr 10am–5pm).

Ravenna's elegant, Venetian-looking **Piazza del Popolo** was laid out in the late 15th century, when Venice ruled the city. From here you can easily walk to all of the sights, with the exception of Sant'Apollinare in Classe (p. 384), for which you'll want to take a bus or drive. In a quiet corner off Via Dante Alighieri is the **tomb of Dante,** author of the *Divine Comedy,* who settled in Ravenna in 1318 and died here of marsh fever on September 14, 1321. This simple marble monument is inscribed with a harsh reprimand to the Florentines, who still clamor for the body's return: "Here in this corner lies Dante, exiled from his native land, born to Florence, an unloving mother." Admission is free; open daily 10am to 6:30pm (Oct–Mar closes 4pm).

The mosaic-rich interior of the Basilica di San Vitale.

Basilica di San Vitale ♥♥♥

CHURCH The emperor Justinian (who never visited Ravenna and ruled instead from Constantinople) completed this octagonal church—richly ornamented with intensely green, blue, and gold mosaics—in 540 as a symbol of his power. Endowed with a halo to indicate his

HOTELS

Albergo Cappello **8**
Casa Masoli **7**
Hotel Centrale Byron **10**
Hotel Diana **6**
M Club **2**

RESTAURANTS

Ca' de Ven **12**
La Bella Venezia **9**
Osteria del Tempo Perso **5**
Ristorante Alexander **15**

ATTRACTIONS

Basilica di Sant'Apollinare in Classe **16**
Basilica di Sant'Apollinaire Nuovo **14**
Basilica di San Vitale **3**
Battistero Neoniano (Neonian Baptistery) and Museo Arcivescovile **11**
Dante's Tomb **13**
Domus of the Stone Carpets **1**
Mausoleo di Galla Placidia **4**

role as head of church and state, Justinian is portrayed standing next to a clean-shaven Christ, perched atop the world, flanked by saints and angels. Looking on are Justinian's two most important adjuncts, his empress, Theodora, and a bald Maximianus, bishop of Ravenna. Theodora's presence suggests her immense influence and rapacious rise to power. Born into the circus, she became a famous actress and courtesan known for her beauty. As Justinian's wife, she wielded such power that in 532, not long before this church was completed, she ordered that 30,000 insurgents be gathered up, brought to the Hippodrome in Constantinople, and slaughtered.

Via San Vitale 17. ravennamosaici.it. ✆ **0544/215-193.** Included in Ravenna inclusive ticket (p. 382). Daily Mar–Oct 9am–7pm; Nov–Feb 10am–5pm.

Basilica di Sant'Apollinare in Classe ♥♥ CHURCH What is now a landlocked suburb was at one time the seaport of the capital of the Western Roman Empire. This huge 6th-century church, dedicated to St. Apollinare, the first bishop of Ravenna, befits the city's onetime importance. Apollinare allegedly landed in Ravenna sometime in the 2nd century and converted the locals. A dazzling mosaic shows him in prayer, surrounded by lambs (his flock) against a background of rocks, birds, and plants, including the pines that still grow outside the church. (Lord Byron used to ride here with his Ravennese mistress, Teresa Guiccioli.) Above Apollinare is a scene of the Transfiguration, when Christ became radiant with light; he is represented as a golden cross on a starry blue background, while Peter, James, and John, the three disciples who witnessed the event, are shown as lambs. Some especially touching mosaics on the right of the church shows three Old Testament figures who made sacrifices to God: Abel, Melchizedek, and Abraham. The church is in the town of Classe, about 6km (3¾ miles) south of Ravenna.

Via Romea Sud 224, Classe. turismo.ra.it. ✆ **0544/473-569.** Admission 5€ adults, 2€ ages 18–25, free for ages 17 and under. Mon–Sat 8:30am–7:30pm. Bus: 4 from train station or Piazza Caduti.

Basilica di Sant'Apollinare Nuovo ♥♥ CHURCH The church that Emperor Theodoric built in the first part of the 6th century for followers of Arianism, a Christian sect, seems to be in perpetual motion. On the left side of the nave, reserved for women, 22 female saints and martyrs approach Mary and the Christ child as they receive gifts from the Three Magi. On the right side, 26 male martyrs led by St. Martin approach a bearded Christ. Above these processions are 26 charmingly rendered scenes from the life of Christ, including one of Christ standing on the shore and calling to Peter and Andrew in their small fishing boat, asking them to be his disciples. Mosaics near the door provide a picture-postcard view of the old city, including Theodoric's palace and the port city of Classe. Look for the detached hand and forearm wrapped around a

underground TREASURES

In 1993, archeologists found a Roman palace beneath the church of Sant'Eufemia—14 rooms and three courtyards carpeted in colorful mosaics, with scenes of dancers, lute players, and frolicking forest animals. The so-called **Domus of the Stone Carpets** ♥♥, Via Barbiani 16 (domusdeitappetidipietra.it; ✆ **0544/32512**), evokes a lavish lifestyle at the very end of the Roman empires. The mosaics are on view Tuesday to Sunday 10am to 5pm; admission is 6€. Descend into the 5th-century crypt of the **Basilica of San Francesco** ♥, Piazza San Francesco (free admission; daily 8am–1pm and 4–7pm) for an eerie sight: As groundwater has seeped into the crypt, mosaics on the submerged floor can be seen shimmering in the light.

column of Theodoric's palace—it was once part of a portrait of Theodoric's court that was removed when the church became a Catholic basilica.

Via di Roma. ravennamosaici.it. ✆ **0544/541-688.** Included in Ravenna inclusive ticket (p. 382). Daily Mar–Oct 9am–7pm; Nov–Feb 10am–5pm.

Battistero Neoniano (Neonian Baptistery) ♥♥ CHURCH Ravenna's oldest monument was erected by Bishop Ursus around 400, to accompany a basilica (long since destroyed) on the site of an ancient Roman bath. The eight sides of this octagonal structure represent the 7 days of the week, as set out in Genesis, plus the day of the Resurrection, when Christ gave mankind eternal life. Intensely colored blue, green, and gold mosaics spread over the dome show John the Baptist baptizing Christ in the River Jordan, surrounded by the Twelve Apostles carrying crowns as a sign of celestial glory. Many of the marble panels in the walls were taken from the Roman bathhouse. Note that the baptistery was originally at street level, which has risen more than 3m (10 ft.) over the intervening centuries. The adjacent **Museo Arcivescovile** is set in what was the private oratory of the 5th-century bishops of Ravenna. A mosaic in the chapel portrays Christ in a way he is rarely seen elsewhere, as a victorious warrior in battle garb standing on a snake. The museum is a warren of cramped little galleries, but make sure you locate one item in particular: a 6th-century bishops' throne that just may be the finest bit of ivory work in the world.

Piazza del Duomo. ravennamosaici.it. ✆ **0544/215-201.** Included in Ravenna inclusive ticket (p. 382). Daily Mar–Oct 9am–7pm; Nov–Feb 10am–5pm.

Mausoleo di Galla Placidia ♥♥ MONUMENT One of the most powerful women of the Byzantine world, Galla Placidia was the daughter and granddaughter of Roman emperors, sister of one ruler of the Western Roman Empire and widow of another. Captured by the Visigoths during the sack of Rome in 410, she married King Athaulf, moved with his barbarian hordes to Barcelona, was traded back to the Romans for grain when Athaulf was murdered, and then married co-emperor Constantius, with whom she had a son, Valentinian III. When Constantius died and Valentinian became emperor at the age of 6, Galla acted as regent, ruling the Western world for 12 years. Though she's most likely buried in Rome, her mausoleum here is spectacular, crowned with a dome decorated with mosaics in vivid hues of peacock blue, moss green, Roman gold, eggplant purple, and burnt orange. Their simple spirituality is striking—doves drink from fountains, as the devout are nourished by God; lambs surround a purple-robed Christ, as the Heavenly king is surrounded by the faithful; and 570 tiny gold stars, suggesting life eternal, twinkle in the cupola. Soft light filtered by alabaster infuses everything with otherworldly luminosity.

Via Benedetto Fiandrini. ravennamosaici.it. ✆ **0544/541-688.** Included in Ravenna inclusive ticket (p. 382). Daily Mar–Oct 9am–7pm; Nov–Feb 10am–5pm.

Where to Stay in Ravenna

Albergo Cappello ♥♥ An old palace in the center of town retains enough damask, Murano chandeliers, stone fireplaces, and impressive old furnishings to make any guest feel like an aristocrat. (One former high-born inhabitant was Francesca da Polenta, whose story Dante told in his *Divine Comedy*—her husband caught her with her lover and strangled them both.) Most of the seven large, high-ceilinged rooms are suites that open off salons on the *piano nobile,* while a few less grand but similarly character-filled quarters are tucked into a wing in the rear. Breakfast is served in a morning room downstairs amid a charming bestiary of forest creatures; a handsome wood-beamed **wine bar** serves well into the night. Via IV Novembre 41. albergocappello.it. ✆ **0544/212-114.** 7 units. 140€–160€ double. Rates include breakfast. **Amenities:** Restaurant; wine bar; free Wi-Fi.

Casa Masoli ♥♥♥ An 18th-century *palazzo* near the city center exudes a familial and slightly bohemian ambience, like the home of an arty aunt and uncle. Two splendid suites at the front of the house are especially grand and cavernous—one retains the original brick vaulting, another frescoes and a marble tub—but high ceilings, tall windows, and wood-veneered bathrooms lend all the rooms a dose of grandeur; back rooms face a garden. Scattered antiques, comfy lounge chairs and couches, and framed lithographs are friendly touches, and a generous breakfast buffet with lots of homemade fare is served in a frescoed salon. Via Girolamo Rossi 22. casamasoli.it. ✆ **0544/217-682.** 7 units. 80€–190€ double. Rates include breakfast. **Amenities:** Free Wi-Fi.

At Casa Masoli, bohemian touches enliven the grand rooms of an 18th-century *palazzo*.

Hotel Centrale Byron ♥♥ From 1819 to 1821, the British poet Lord Byron shared a nearby palace with his lover, Contessa Teresa Guiccioli, her husband (who was 40 years her senior), and a bestiary of pets that included peacocks and ducks, and Ravenna has been milking the story ever since. One of several establishments in town named for the Romantic poet, this is a lot less evocative than its name suggests, but it is wonderfully located, a stone's throw from most sights, a few steps from Piazza

del Popolo, and an easy stroll from the train station. Constant updating has given the rooms a contemporary look and lots of comfort.
Via IV Novembre 14. hotelsravenna.it. ✆ **0544/212-225.** 54 units. 85€–120€ double. Most rates include breakfast. Closed part of Jan–Feb. **Amenities:** Bar; room service; free Wi-Fi.

Hotel Diana ♥♥ Slightly off the beaten path at the quiet edge of the city center, but an easy stroll from the sights, these large, light, and eclectically homey rooms are enlivened with bright colors and attractive prints (and many have extremely large bathrooms). The staff shares recommendations with genuine enthusiasm, and a generous buffet breakfast is served on a large, glass-enclosed patio. This is a handy base if you're traveling by car, with several easy-to-reach garages nearby.
Via Girolamo Rossi 47. hoteldiana.ra.it. ✆ **0544/39164.** 33 units. 85€–120€ double. Rates include breakfast. **Amenities:** Bikes; free Wi-Fi.

M Club ♥♥♥ It's easy to settle comfortably into these bright and distinctively decorated upper-floor quarters at the edge of the historic center, facing Hadrian's Gate across the square out front or a quiet garden in back. Sharing a couple of inviting lounges, the nicely outfitted rooms are crisscrossed with heavy beams and filled with a tasteful mix of antiques, oil paintings, French and Italian prints, and family memorabilia. The suite has a monastery table long enough to host a banquet.
Via Baracca. m-club.it. ✆ **333/955-6466.** 5 units. 110€–130€ double. Rates include breakfast. Closed 2 weeks late Jan/early Feb. **Amenities:** Bikes; free Wi-Fi.

Where to Eat in Ravenna

Ravenna's **Mercato Coperto** (near the center of town on Piazza Andrea Costa) houses shops, bars, and restaurants. **Gastronomia Marchesini,** an elegant food store at Via Mazzini 2/6 (ristorantemarchesiniravenna.it; ✆ **0544/212309**), is a good place to buy regional hams and cheeses, and it operates a reasonably priced self-service restaurant upstairs and a full-service restaurant above that. **Profumo di Piadina,** 24 Via Cairoli (profumodipiadina.it; ✆ **333/292-8079**), tops warm-from-the oven *piadina* (flatbread) with prosciutto, creamy *squacquerone* (cheese), and other locally produced ingredients that you can eat on the go or enjoy at one of the few tables.

Ca' de Ven ♥♥♥ ROMAGNOLA A 16th-century guesthouse and former spice warehouse with frescoed ceilings and lots of paneling and exposed timbers makes a character-filled stop for lunch or a light dinner. The emphasis here is on *piadina,* the local flatbread, served with a dozen or so fillings or, even better, by itself warm from the oven with a selection of cured meats and *squacquerone,* a delicate soft cheese. There's also a huge selection of wine by the glass. At lunch and in early evening you'll rub elbows at communal tables with what seems like half the population of Ravenna, so enjoy the atmosphere and ignore the often-brusque service.

Via Corrado Ricci 24. cadeven.it. ✆ **0544/30163.** *Piadine* about 6€; main courses 10€–20€. Tues–Sun 11am–2:30pm and 6:30–10:30pm (until 10pm on Sun).

La Bella Venezia ♥♥ ROMAGNOLA Cream-colored walls and light, starched tablecloths in this small room off the Piazza della Popolo create the scene for elegant, old-world dining. Despite the name, the menu is typically and deliciously Romagnolese, and the kitchen is much respected for its *cappelletti alla romagnolu*, cap-shaped pasta stuffed with a meal's worth of ingredients: ricotta, roasted pork loin, chicken breast, and nutmeg, served with meat sauce. Other homemade and memorable pastas include simple ravioli with butter and sage and risotto with fresh seasonal vegetables.

Via IV Novembre 16. ristorantebellavenezia.it. ✆ **0544/212-746.** Main courses 10€–22€. Tues–Fri 11am–3pm and 7pm–midnight, Sat and Mon 7pm–midnight. Closed part of late Jan.

Osteria del Tempo Perso ♥♥ SEAFOOD/ROMAGNOLA Ravenna is no longer a port, but the sea is close enough to supply fresh seafood for an innovative menu, accompanied by soft jazz in warm-hued rooms lined with books and wine bottles. It would be a shame not to indulge in at least one seafood course, maybe the *spaghetti con bocconcini di spade,* with savory chunks of swordfish, or a hefty fritto misto. *Tortelloni di zucca* (pumpkin-filled pasta) and other land-based local favorites are expertly done, too.

Via Gamba 12. osteriadeltempoperso.it. ✆ **0544/215-393.** Main courses 15€–30€. Daily 12:30–2:30pm and 7:30–10:30pm.

Ristorante Alexander ♥♥ ITALIAN/SEAFOOD In this former church that was later converted to a movie house, vintage film posters hang beneath ancient beams in a vast, double-height hall—a blend of sacred and profane that makes a sophisticated setting for refined cooking. Ravenna's proximity to the sea comes to the fore in fresh fish and in nice combinations like fusilli with tuna and pork or calamari couscous; meat dishes lean toward some unusual local preparations, such as veal cheeks with potato and lemon puree. Service is friendly and attentive, as soft jazz and mellow renditions of movie themes float through the space.

Via Bassa del Pignataro 8. ristorantealexander.it. ✆ **0544/212-967.** Main courses 19€–26€, 5-course set menu fish 58€, meat 56€. Tues–Sun 12:30–2:30pm and 7:30–10:30pm.

PARMA ♥♥

97km (60 miles) NW of Bologna, 121km (75 miles) SE of Milan

This prosperous and elegant little city on the Roman Via Emilia, about an hour north of Bologna, delivers a slice of the good life. Residents are surrounded by art-filled palaces and churches bestowed upon them by the

HOTELS

B&B Al Battistero d'Oro **5**

Hotel Button **10**

Hotel Torino **8**

Palazzo Dalla Rosa Prati **7**

RESTAURANTS

Enoteca Fontana **12**

Gallo d'Oro **11**

La Greppia **4**

Trattoria del Tribunali **13**

ATTRACTIONS

Battistero (Baptistery) and Duomo **6**

Camera di San Paolo **3**

Museo Casa Natale Arturo Toscanini **1**

Palazzo della Pilotta: Galleria Nazionale **2**

Teatro Regio **9**

Renaissance Farnese family and later Marie-Louise, wife of Napoleon. They enjoy the music of their own Giuseppe Verdi in a grand opera house, and when it comes to food, Parma has given the world some of the finest hams and cheeses ever. You can easily fill a very satisfying day or two here, enjoying beautiful monuments, listening to music, stepping in and out of tempting food shops, and sitting down to some memorable meals.

Essentials

ARRIVING Parma is served by the Milan-Bologna **rail** line, with two or three trains arriving from Milan (trip time: 1 hr. on fast trains, 1½ hr. on less-expensive slower trains). From Bologna, trains depart for Parma every 30 minutes or so (the trip takes a little under an hour). There are a few direct trains a day from Florence (2 hr.); most journeys require a change in Bologna. For information and schedules, go to trenitalia.com. You might also pass through Parma to connect with a train to La Spezia on the west coast, and from there to the Cinque Terre and other places along the Italian Riviera. Whatever your destination, hop off the train long enough to see the beautiful Duomo and Baptistery. Stash your bags in one of several locations around the station through **Nannybag** (nannybag.com), from 5€ per bag per day.

If you are coming by **car** from Bologna, drive northwest along A1. Note that **driving in the historic center is restricted**—from October through March it's off-limits to cars entirely on Thursdays, and cars are not allowed within the ring roads on the first Sunday of the month, December excluded. Don't drive into the old city without first contacting your hotel—without a special pass you'll be fined 90€. Outside the restricted area, you can park on the street wherever you see blue lines (purchase a ticket from curbside machines) or aim for the official parking lots: Goito, Toschi, Duc, Dus, and Via Abbeveratoia (around 1€–1.70€ per hour), with free shuttle service to the city center.

GETTING AROUND Parma is bike-friendly, with rentals available from the large stand operated by **Cicleterria** outside the train station in Piazzale Carlo Alberto dalla Chiesa (✆ **0521/281-979**). Rates are 1.50€ an hour, 8€ an hour for an electric bike. Bus no. 15 (1.70€, buy ticket at newsstands or use the contactless card machines onboard; tep.pr.it) makes a handy run from the train station to Teatro Regio and the historic center, though the walk is only about 10 minutes.

VISITOR INFORMATION The **tourist office** at Piazza Garibaldi 1 (parmawelcome.it; ✆ **0521/218-889**) is open daily 9am to 7pm.

Exploring Parma

It's easy to explore Parma on foot, since most of the sights surround Piazza del Duomo and Palazzo della Pilotta, an easy walk from the train station.

Battistero (Baptistery) and Duomo ♥♥♥ CATHEDRAL The moment you walk into the Piazza del Duomo, you're in for some visual storytelling. To one side rises the elegant **baptistery,** primarily the work of Italy's great Romanesque master Benedetto Antelami and begun in 1196. The octagonal structure has four open loggias and tiers of 16 slender columns—all playing off the number eight, the sign of the Resurrection. Alternating bands of white and pink marble represent purity and the blood of Christ; carvings above the entrance are scripture in stone (look for the sequence depicting King Herod pulling his beard in rage, Salome dancing, and St. John losing his head). Inside, colorful 13th-century frescoes depict the zodiac, the months and seasons, and the life of Christ with a wealth of medieval iconography.

Colorful medieval frescoes cover the interior of the octagonal Battistero, part of Parma's elegant Duomo complex.

Two stone lions guard the entrance to the adjacent **Duomo,** one crushing a serpent (the devil), the other a lamb (symbol of sacrifice) under their paws. Inside are two of Parma's greatest treasures. Correggio, the master of light and color, spent 8 years painting the cupola, and after finishing in 1530, he took his payment in a sack full of small change, went home, and died of fever at the age of 40. His *Assumption of the Virgin* is a sea of free-floating angels and billowing clouds amid which a leggy Christ tumbles out of the celestial light to meet the outstretched arms of his ascending mother. A contemporary compared the effect to a "hash of frogs' legs," and Charles Dickens commented that this was a scene that "no operative surgeon gone mad could imagine in his wildest delirium." Church authorities supposedly approached Titian to redo the dome, and he replied that the work was so masterful that they should have filled the structure with gold and presented it to Correggio. The other highlight is in the transept to the right: a somber bas-relief of *The Deposition from the Cross* by Antelami, creator of the baptistery next door. A melancholy Christ stretches his elongated arms over two groups—Mary and pious converts to one side, and the unenlightened on the other, including a group of Roman soldiers playing cards.

Piazza del Duomo 1. piazzaduomoparma.com. ✆ **0521/235-886.** Cathedral: Free admission. Battistero: 12€ adults with Museo Diocesano, 10€ students, free for children 12 and under. Cathedral: Daily 7:45am–7:20pm; Battistero and Museo Diocesano: Daily 10am–6pm.

Camera di San Paolo ♥♥ CONVENT San Paolo was one of many well-endowed convents where wealthy women who did not marry could spend their lives in relative comfort. Around 1519, the cultured abbess Giovanna di Piacenza wanted to fresco her private dining room and had the means to hire Correggio, who created vivid mythological scenes, cherubs, astrological references, and an image of Diana, goddess of the hunt. The frescoes may have sparked conversation for the intellectuals who frequently gathered at the abbess's table, though the significance of the images remains a mystery. Church authorities later sealed off the chamber—with no religious subjects and so many bare-bottomed *putti,* it was deemed profane.

Via Melloni 3 (off Strada Garibaldi). ✆ **0521/533-221.** Admission 8€ adults, 6€ ages 18–25, free for ages 17 and under. Wed–Mon 9:30am–5:30pm (Sat–Sun until 6:30pm).

Palazzo della Pilotta: Galleria Nazionale ♥♥ MUSEUM Like many Italian cities, Parma became a great center of the Renaissance under one ruling family—in this case, the Farneses, whose members included popes, cardinals, and the dukes of Parma. They began their fortresslike Palazzo della Pilotta in the 1580s and remained there until the last heiress, Elisabetta, married King Philip of Spain and decamped for Madrid in 1714. The Hapsburg princess Marie-Louise (1791–1847)—Napoleon's second wife and a great-niece of Marie Antoinette—was awarded the duchy a century later, and she set about gathering art treasures from the city in the palace the Farneses had left empty; she also collected works from villas and churches throughout Italy, confiscated when her husband marched down the peninsula. Badly bomb-damaged in World War II, the restored palace now houses the Galleria Nazionale. It's not surprising that the Vienna-born duchess's collection would include such northern artists as Hans Holbein, Brueghel, and van Dyck, but Parma artists steal the show. Correggio's *Madonna della Scodella* [with a Bowl] portrays Joseph as an elderly man and Mary as a young woman gazing adoringly at her infant son; his *St. Jerome with the Madonna and Child* also represents age, youth, and love—a gentle ode to tenderness. (Napoleon supposedly wanted to cart these prize paintings off to the Louvre, but Marie-Louise insisted they remain in Parma.) The alluring *Turkish Slave*, by the city's own Parmigiano, portrays a well-kept young woman dressed in gold-threaded finery; everything about her—turban, cheeks, eyes, breasts—is beautifully rounded. *La Scapigliata* (aka the "Female Head") is unfinished yet is one of the most celebrated paintings by Leonardo da Vinci. The palace's other treasure is the **Teatro Farnese,** a wooden theater the Farneses had built, along the lines of Palladio's theater at Vicenza, to impress the Medicis, and still in use today.

Piazzale della Pilotta 15. complessopilotta.it. ✆ **0521/233-309.** Admission 18€ adults, 2€ ages 18–25, free for ages 17 and under; includes Teatro Farnese. Tues–Sun 9am–7pm.

NEAR PARMA

Castello di Torrechiara ♥♥ CASTLE One of Italy's most beautiful castles is on a hilltop above the lush agricultural valleys outside Parma. Soldier and courtier Count Pier Maria Rossi built the castle as a fortress, installing massive walls, towers, and a drawbridge, and also as a love nest where he could rendezvous with his mistress, Milanese noblewoman Bianca Pellegrini. The two sojourned on view-filled loggias and in heavily frescoed salons, all beautifully intact to provide a glimpse at a late-medieval/early Renaissance luxe lifestyle. A hamlet clustered around the walls has a couple of shops and eateries. Buses run from Parma's station almost hourly, with a stop at Torrechiara (fare 3.40€). From there it's a 10- to 15-minute uphill climb to the main gate.

Torrechiara, 18km (11 miles) S of Parma on SP665. castellideIducato.it. ✆ **0521/355-821.** Admission 8€, 2€ ages 18–25, free for ages 17 and under. Tues–Fri 9am–3pm; Sat–Sun 11am–5pm.

Where to Stay in Parma

B&B Al Battistero d'Oro ♥♥♥ It's easy to slip into the Parma good life in this elegant 19th-century house just behind the Duomo, where Patrizia Valenti's sprawling and tasteful apartment surrounds a courtyard. The hostess puts up her guests in a delightful ground-floor room with a private entrance and two large bedrooms off a back corridor, welcoming them also into her bright and handsomely furnished living room and

HITTING THE high NOTES

Besides collecting art in the Palazzo della Pilotta (p. 391), Duchess Marie-Louise also enriched Parma's cultural life in 1829 by building the **Teatro Regio ♥♥**, Via Garibaldi 16, near Piazza della Pace (teatroregioparma.it; ✆ **0521/203-911**). Still considered one of the world's finest music theaters, the house hosts an opera season that rivals Milan's. Particularly favored are the operas of **Giuseppe Verdi,** composer of *Il Trovatore* and *Aïda*, who was born outside Parma in 1813 and later lived with his mistress, soprano Giuseppina Strepponi, in nearby Busseto. Their villa, set on lush parklike grounds, is owned by descendants and only occasionally open to the public; check with the tourist office in Parma for details. Each October, Parma celebrates the **Verdi Festival,** with concerts and performances in the Teatro Regio and other venues.

Parma's other musical genius, **Arturo Toscanini,** the great 20th-century orchestral conductor, was born in Parma in 1867. His birthplace, **Museo Casa Natale Arturo Toscanini ♥**, Via Rodolfo Tanzi 13, now displays his scores, photos, and other personal effects (museotoscanini.it; ✆ **0521/031769;** free admission; Wed–Sun 10am–6pm).

polished dining room, where she serves a delicious breakfast. Patrizia is on hand to dispense advice on getting the most out of her native Parma.
Strada Sant'anna 22. albattisterodoro.com. ✆ **338/490-4697.** 3 units. 140€–150€ double. Rates include breakfast. **Amenities:** Free Wi-Fi.

Hotel Button ♥♥ The Cortesa family has been welcoming guests to this converted 17th-century *palazzo* for more than 40 years, providing lots of advice and dispensing excellent coffee from the small lobby bar. You might be charmed by the extra-large rooms and old-fashioned ambience in the public areas (as we are) or find the place to be a bit stuffy and out of date. Regardless, you can't quibble with the excellent location in the heart of old Parma just off Piazza Garibaldi.
Borgo delle Salina 7. hotelbutton.it. ✆ **0521/208039.** 40 units. 70€–110€ double. Rates include breakfast. **Amenities:** Bar; babysitting; free Wi-Fi.

Hotel Torino ♥♥ A couple of handsome lounges off the lobby and a sprightly, patio-like breakfast room do justice to one of Parma's best lodging locations, just down the street from Piazza del Duomo. Guest rooms are all soothing with muted tones and neutral furnishings, but they range in size. Standard doubles are snug and some of the singles feel like ship cabins, but furnishings are streamlined with lots of handy built-ins for stashing gear. A few larger units are in a handsomely redone annex next door. Parking in a small garage beneath the hotel is 15€ a night.
Borgo Angelo Massa. hotel-torino.it. ✆ **0521/281046.** 47 units. 85€–105€ double. Rates include breakfast. **Amenities:** Bar; free Wi-Fi.

Palazzo Dalla Rosa Prati ♥♥♥ The Marquis Dalla Rosa Prati and his family have converted one wing of their sprawling palace to seven

WELCOME TO THE food valley

Parma has been distinguished as a UNESCO Creative Center of Gastronomy, a nod to the Parmigiano cheese, hams and other cured meats, and balsamic vinegar produced in surrounding farms and factories in what is known as the Food Valley. Among cured meats, pride of place belongs to *culatello di Zibello*, the haunch of the pig that is slightly salted, stuffed in a pig bladder, and cured in drying rooms in low-lying plains near the Po and Parma rivers. The region enjoys a microclimate that provides just the right conditions for curing meats and is legally designated under the protection of DOP (Denominazione Origine Protetta), with stringent rules for production.

Paying homage to the region's gastronomic output are 25 so-called **Museums of Taste** (winefoodemiliaromagna.com) that include the **Museo del Parmigiano Reggiano ♥** in Soragno, the **Museo del Prosciutto di Parma ♥** in Langhirano, and the **Museo del Balsamico ♥** in Spilamberto.

You can visit local producers on tours with **Maestro** (maestrotravelexperience.com), from 15€. The **Consorzio del Parmigiano Reggiano,** Via Gramsci 26 (parmigianoreggiano.com; ✆ **0521/292-7000**), can also help you plan visits to local producers. Among them is **Caseificio San Pier Damiani,** Strada Gazzano 35/A (sanpierdamiani.com; ✆ **521/645181**), where in a 2-hour visit (25€) you can see cheese production from curd to ready-to-age wheel.

You may also see and taste local products in town at the attractive and aromatic **Salumeria Garibaldi ♥**, Via Garibaldi 42 (specialitadiparma.it; ✆ **0521/235606**), and **La Prosciutteria ♥**, Strada Farini 9 (silvanoromaniparma.it; ✆ **0521/234-188**).

handsomely furnished rooms and suites, many with kitchenettes and some with views onto Piazza del Duomo; another section is broken into 10 large apartments. In the suites, huge wooden bedsteads, massive armoires, and other polished antiques complement the largely 18th-century surroundings. Apartments have one or two bedrooms, generous space to spread out, and full kitchens.

Strada al Duomo 7. palazzodallarosaprati.it. ✆ **0521/386429.** 17 units. 95€–135€ double. Some rates include breakfast. **Amenities:** Free Wi-Fi.

Where to Eat in Parma

Bar and cafes line **Via Farini,** which cuts a swath through the old town south of Piazza Garibaldi. The top stop for a quick meal is **Enoteca Fontana ♥,** Via Farini 24 (✆ **0521/286037**), for morsels of Parmigiano drizzled with balsamic vinegar from Modena, slices of prosciutto, and *crostini,* pieces of bread topped with everything from pesto to chicken livers (Tues–Sat noon–2:30pm and 8–10pm).

Gallo d'Oro ♥ PARMIGIANA Parma's formidable food scene becomes decidedly relaxed at this bric-a-brac-filled trattoria just off Piazza Garibaldi. A local crowd appreciates the old traditions: Lambrusco, a slightly sparkling red, is the wine of choice, and *cavallo* (horse) and *coniglio* (rabbit) are served a few different ways. Less adventurous eaters can enjoy *tortelli ripieni* (pasta stuffed with cheese and vegetables), *ravioli alla zucca* (pumpkin), and a long list of other homemade pastas. Borgo della Salina 3. gallodororistorante.it. ✆ **0521/208-846.** Main courses 9€–18€. Daily noon–midnight.

La Greppia ♥♥♥ PARMIGIANA/ITALIAN Looking toward the window at one end of the simple dining room, you'll see into the kitchen and notice that the kitchen crew is mostly female. In their hands you'll be treated to exquisite dishes, some of which you may never have encountered before. Pears poached in red wine with a dense cream sauce is the house antipasto; handmade pastas are often filled with the freshest local vegetables; and the *secondi* menu features duck breast, filets of beef and sucking pig, and other regional favorites. The homemade *tortas,* filled with marmalade and a miraculous mélange of other ingredients, are irresistible.

Via Garibaldi 39. lagreppiaparma.com. ✆ **0521/233-686.** Main courses 13€–28€. Fri–Wed noon–2:30pm and 7–10:30pm.

Sumptuous pasta dishes head out to the dining room at La Greppia.

Trattoria del Tribunale ♥♥ PARMIGIANA/ITALIAN In two floors of dining rooms, stretching beyond counters hung with hams, menu choices range from delicious pastas, such as *tortelli* (pasta pockets) stuffed with pumpkin or ricotta, to steaks simmered in Barolo and veal stuffed with Parmigiano. You may also be tempted to try such distinctly local fare as horsemeat hash. A veteran staff never seems too flustered to be friendly. It's a good idea to reserve, especially on weekend nights.

Vicolo Politi 5. trattoriadeltribunale.it. ✆ **0521/285-527.** Main courses 9€–22€. Daily noon–3pm and 7–11pm.

NEAR PARMA

Al Vedel ♥♥♥ EMILIA-ROMAGNAN A simple village tavern established in 1780 has expanded into several elegant dining rooms, and below them are the cellars of Podere Cadassa, where some of the region's most prized *culatello di Zibello* (from the haunch of the pig) is aged. That delicacy is the starter of choice, along with other cured meats and local cheeses. Chef-proprietor Enrico Bergonzi proudly shows off the *culatello* operation to his guests, and he and his staff produce many seasonal variations of local favorites, such as wintertime tortellini filled with *mostarda.* Via Vodele 68, Colorno (about 20km/12 miles N of Parma). poderecadassa.it. ✆ **0521/816169.** Main courses 16€–28€; set menus 65€ and 80€. Wed–Sun noon–2:30pm and 7:30–10:30pm. Closed mid- to late Feb.

Hostaria d'Ivan ♥♥♥ EMILIA-ROMAGNAN A trip out to this welcoming inn, in a farm hamlet near the River Po, is an immersion course in all that's good about the region's cooking. *Culatello,* the choicest cut of prosciutto, and Parmigiano, aged for several years, are produced on nearby farms; the duck, roasted with herbs, comes from marshes along the riverbanks. On request, you can dine in the "salametherapy room," where cured meats hang from the ceiling, and a meal in the simply furnished dining room, overlooking a small garden, is just as memorable. Four cozy bedrooms are tucked under the eaves at the top of the house (115€ double).

Via Villa 24, Fontanelle di Roccabianca (25km/15 miles NW of Parma via SP10). hostariadaivan.it. ✆ **0521/870-113.** Main courses 13€–18€. Wed 7:30–10pm; Thurs–Sun noon–3pm and 7:30–10pm.

VENICE

By Stephen Keeling

9

No other place in the world looks quite like Venice. This vast, floating city of grand *palazzi,* elegant bridges, gondolas, and canals is a magnificent spectacle, truly magical when approached by sea for the first time, when its golden domes and soaring bell towers seem to rise straight from the water. While it can sometimes appear that Venice is little more than an open-air museum where tourists always outnumber locals—by a large margin—it is still surprisingly easy to lose the crowds. Indeed, the best way to enjoy Venice is simply to get lost in its labyrinth of narrow, enchanting streets, stumbling upon a quiet *campo* (square), market stall, or cafe far off the beaten track, where even the humblest medieval church might contain masterful work by Tiepolo, Titian, or Tintoretto.

The origins of Venice—known as "La Serenissima" ("the most serene") for centuries—are as muddy as parts of the lagoon it now occupies, but most histories begin with the arrival of refugees from Attila the Hun's invasion of Italy in the mid-5th century (though the official foundation date is C.E. 421). The mudflats were gradually built over and linked together, channels and streams eventually becoming canals. By the 11th century, Venice had emerged as a major independent trading city, and by the 13th century its seaborne empire (which included Crete, Corfu, and Cyprus) was held together by a huge navy and commercial fleet. Despite being embroiled with wars against the Turks and rival Italian city Genoa, the next few centuries were golden years for Venice, when booming trade with the Far East funded much of its grand architecture and art. Although it remained an outwardly rich city, by the 1700s the good times were over, and in 1797 Napoleon dissolved the Venetian Republic without a shot (handing it over to the Austrians shortly afterward). You'll gain a sense of some of this history touring **Piazza San Marco** and **St. Mark's Basilica,** or by visiting the **Accademia,** one of Italy's great art galleries. But only when you wander the back *calli* (streets) will you encounter the true, living, breathing side of Venice, still redolent of those glory days.

DON'T LEAVE VENICE WITHOUT . . .

Getting Lost. So sublime is the city's lineup of architectural eye candy that Venice simply invites aimless wandering. Stroll beyond the (surprisingly

PREVIOUS PAGE: **A gondola ride, though expensive, is truly as romantic an experience as it looks.**

Venice Orientation

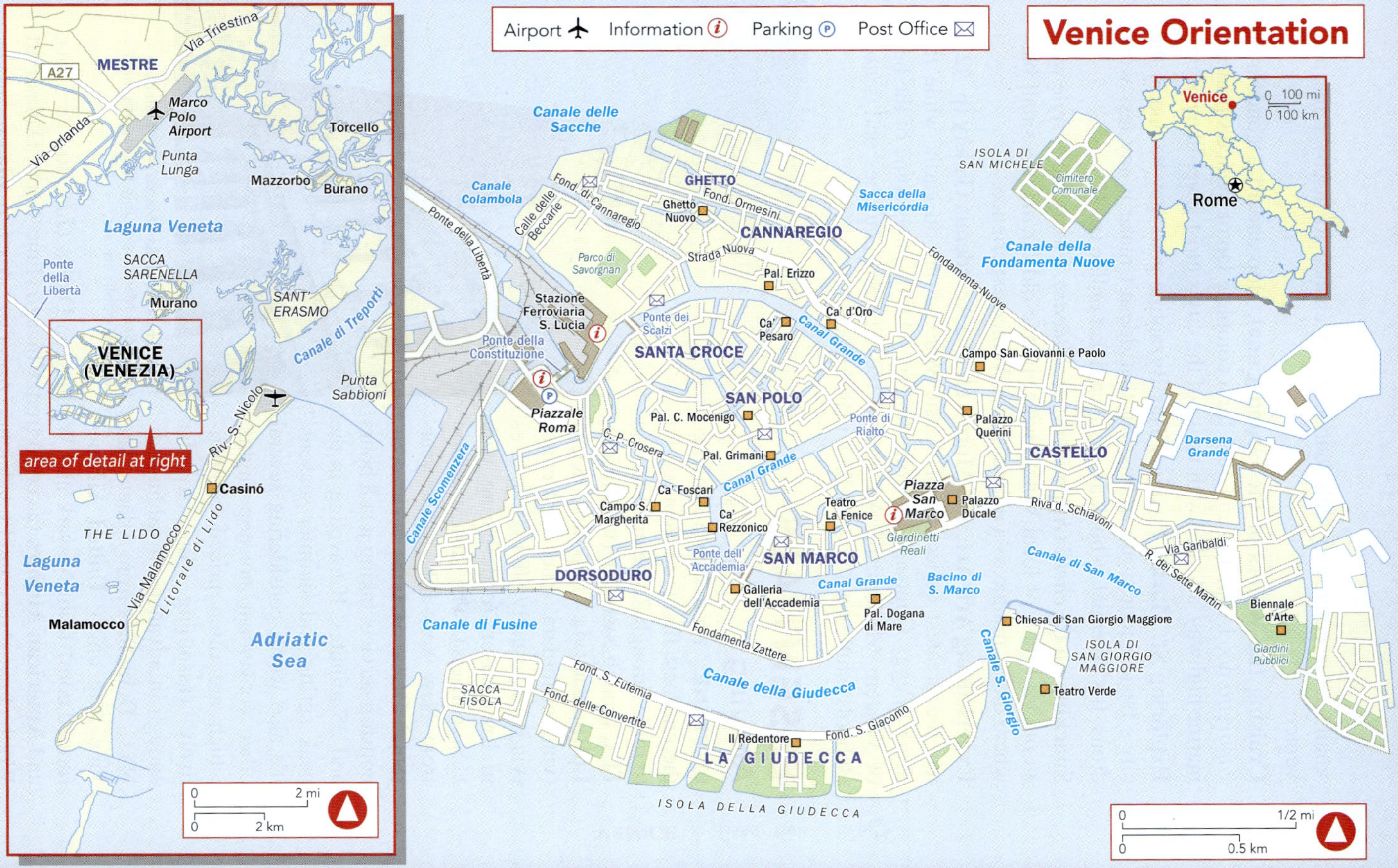

small) areas congested with tourists for a chance to discover the real Venice.

Cruising the Waters of the Grand Canal. Hop aboard a gondola or *vaporetto* no. 1 (pp. 408 and 403) for a complete lap of Venice's primary marine highway, adorned with views of the city's most jewel-like *palazzi.*

Exploring St. Mark's Basilica. This Byzantine gem may be one of the city's busiest tourist attractions, but that doesn't make it any less wondrous. It's essential to book an advance ticket online (p. 410).

Snacking on *Cicchetti* (Appetizers) at a *Bàcaro.* Eating tapas-style with an *ombra* (glass of local Veneto wine) in age-old *bàcari,* the small bars where locals mingle, is a quintessential Venice experience.

Experiencing Art, Art, and More Art. The Accademia Gallery (p. 421) has the greatest collection of classic Venetian art on earth, while the nearby Peggy Guggenheim Collection (p. 422) displays some of the best of Western Modernism. All around the city are churches and *scuole* (schools) stuffed with compelling masterpieces.

ESSENTIALS

Arriving

BY PLANE From North America, the cheapest flights to Venice tend to route through Rome or Milan via **ITA,** though **Swissair** (via Zurich), **Lufthansa** (via Frankfurt), **KLM** (via Amsterdam), and **Air France** (via Paris) usually offer cheap fares in low season (codesharing with U.S. carriers). The fastest option from New York-JFK is the year-round **Delta Airlines** (delta.com) nonstop service, taking just 8 hours and 25 minutes. If traveling in the peak spring and summer seasons, it's also worth considering several other convenient nonstop flights, which are often priced competitively (assuming you buy far enough in advance): in addition to NYC, **Delta** flies from Atlanta (late June–Aug only); **United Airlines** (united.com) from Newark and Washington-Dulles (June to late Sept); and **American Airlines** (aa.com) from Chicago (June–Sept), Dallas/Fort Worth (June–Aug), and Philadelphia (Apr–Oct). **Air Canada** (aircanada.com) also offers nonstop flights from Montréal and Toronto in the

The Campanile di San Marco rises high over Piazza San Marco, possibly the world's most beautiful public square.

summer. For those already in Europe, numerous budget airlines serve Venice, offering rock-bottom prices. No-frills **easyJet** (easyjet.com) flies nonstop from Amsterdam, Berlin, London-Gatwick, Manchester, and Paris, while **Ryanair** (ryanair.com) flies from Barcelona, Dublin, Edinburgh, and London-Stansted, with many more flights routed through nearby **Treviso Airport** (a 1-hr. bus ride to Venice; see trevisoairport.it).

Flights land at the **Aeroporto di Venezia Marco Polo (VCE)**, 7km (4¼ miles) north of the city on the mainland (veneziaairport.it; ✆ **041/2609260**). There are several alternatives for getting into town. The cheapest is by **bus,** though this is not recommended if you have heavy luggage; buses can't drive into Venice itself, so you'll have to walk to or from the final stop, Piazzale Roma, to the nearby ***vaporetto*** (water bus) stop for the final connection to your hotel. (See "The *Vaporetto* Lowdown," p. 403.) It's rare to find porters who'll help with luggage, so pack light. The **ATVO airport express bus** (www.atvo.it; ✆ **0421/594672**) runs between Piazzale Roma and the airport about every 30 minutes, costing 10€ (18€ round-trip); the trip takes about 20 minutes (the bus has free Wi-Fi). Buy tickets online in advance, at the automatic ticket machines in the baggage claim area, or at the Public Transport ticket desks in the Arrivals Hall (daily 8am–midnight). The local **ACTV bus no. 5** (actv.avmspa.it; ✆ **041/2424**) also costs 10€, takes a bit longer (around 25 min.), has slightly less space for luggage, and runs two to four times an hour depending on the time of day; on the plus side you can buy the combined ACTV and "Rete Unica" ticket for 18€ (valid for 90 min.), which includes your first *vaporetto* ride at a slight discount. Buy tickets via the **AVM Venezia Official App** or at machines just outside the airport terminal. Alternatively, you can ride these buses by paying with your contactless credit card on embarking (one-way only). They don't take cash.

It's also possible to take a **land taxi** (radiotaxivenezia.com; ✆ **041/5964**) from the airport to Piazzale Roma (where you get the *vaporetto*) for a fixed 40€ (35€ to Mestre). While this is more convenient and a bit faster (15 min.) than the bus, it still doesn't take you to your hotel (unless you're staying right by Piazzale Roma)—you are better off spending the extra euros on water transport.

The most evocative and traditional way to arrive in Venice is by sea. For 18€ (32€ round-trip), **Alilaguna** (alilaguna.it; ✆ **041/2401701**) operates a large *motoscafo* (shuttle boat) service from the airport boathouse (a short, covered walk from the terminal; you can also buy tickets at the Public Transport desks in the Arrivals Hall) with two primary routes. The **Linea Blu** (blue line) runs almost every 30 minutes from 5:20am to 12:20am, stopping at Murano (10€) and the Lido before arriving, after about 1 hour and 15 minutes, in Piazza San Marco (San Zaccaria). The **Linea Arancio** (orange line) runs almost every 30 minutes from 8:35am to 11:05pm, taking 1 hour and 13 minutes to arrive at San Marco (Santa Maria del Giglio), but gets there through the Grand Canal, which is much more spectacular and offers the possibility of getting off at one of the stops along the way. This might be more convenient to your hotel and could save you from having to take another means of transportation. If you arrive at Piazza San Marco and your hotel isn't in the area, you'll have to make a connection at the *vaporetto* launches. (If you're booking a hotel in advance, be sure to get specific advice on how to get there.) Your ticket includes one main bag and one hand luggage—it's 4€ for each additional bag.

A good alternative is the **Venice Shuttle** (venicelink.com; daily 8am–10:30pm; minimum two people for reservations), a shared water taxi (carrying six to eight people) that will whisk you from the airport directly to many hotels and most major locations in the city for 32€ (add 6€ after 8pm). You must reserve online in advance.

A **private water taxi** (20–30 min. to/from the airport) is the most convenient option but costly—there is a 150€ to 170€ fee (discounted rates at venicelink.com) for up to four passengers with one bag each (plus 10€ more for each extra person up to a maximum of 10, 5€ for each extra suitcase, and another 15€ for arrivals 10pm–7am). It's worth considering if you're pressed for time, have an early flight (water taxis run 24 hr.), are carrying a lot of luggage (a Venice no-no), or can split the cost with a friend or two. The taxi may be able to drop you off at the front (or side) door of your hotel, or as close as it can maneuver given your hotel's location (check with the hotel before arriving). Your taxi captain should be able to tell you before boarding just how close you can get. Try **Consorzio Motoscafi Venezia** (motoscafivenezia.com/it; ✆ **041/5222303** or **041/2406712**) or **Venezia Taxi** (veneziataxi.it; ✆ **041/723112**).

BY TRAIN Trains from Rome (4 hr.), Milan (2½ hr.), Florence (2¼ hr.), and all over Europe arrive at the **Stazione Venezia Santa Lucia.** To get there, all must pass through a station marked Venezia-Mestre. Don't be confused: Mestre is a charmless industrial city that's the last major stop on the mainland (some trains also stop at the next station, Venezia Porto Marghera, before continuing to Venice proper). Occasionally trains end in Mestre, in which case you have to catch one of the frequent 10-minute shuttles connecting with Venice; it's inconvenient, so when you book your ticket, confirm that the final destination is Venezia Santa Lucia.

BY BUS Although rail travel is more convenient and commonplace, Venice is serviced by long-distance buses from all over mainland Italy and some international cities. The final destination is Piazzale Roma, where you'll need to pick up *vaporetto* no. 1 or no. 2 (see box p. 403) to connect you with stops in the heart of Venice and along the Grand Canal. **Eurolines** (eurolines.eu) buses drop off on the adjacent island of **Tronchetto,** which is a much longer walk from the action. Buses stop at the Tronchetto **People Mover** station where a light railway takes you to Piazzale Roma in just 3 minutes (1.50€ one-way), though you will most likely need onward transportation from there. *Vaporetto* line 2 does stop at Tronchetto: Facing the water, boats depart left to the train station and Grand Canal, right to San Marco.

THE *vaporetto* LOWDOWN

Whether you're arriving by train, bus, or car, your first challenge upon arriving in Venice will be to take a *vaporetto* (water bus) to your final destination. The *vaporetto* is the seagoing streetcar of Venice, going to all parts of the city. Here's how to do it right.

Finding the right boat is a little easier if you're arriving by bus or car, because you'll be in Piazzale Roma, the **route no. 1** *vaporetto* terminus, and all these boats will be going the right direction. (See "By *Vaporetto*," p. 407, for information on tickets.) Exiting the train station, however, you'll find the Grand Canal immediately in front of you, with the docks for a number of *vaporetti* lines to your left and right. Head to the booths to your left, near the bridge, to buy tickets, then head for the docks farther to your right.

The most useful routes are the two lines plying the Grand Canal: the **no. 2 express** (from bay "B"), which stops only at the San Marcuola, Rialto Bridge, San Tomà, San Samuele, and Accademia before hitting San Marco (30 min. total); and the slower **no. 1** (from bay "E"), which makes 13 stops before arriving at San Marco (a 36-min. trip). Both leave every 10 minutes or so, but before 9am and after 8pm, the no. 2 sometimes stops short at Rialto, meaning you'll have to disembark and hop on the next no. 1 or 2 that comes along to continue to San Marco.

Word to the wise: The *vaporetti* go in two directions from the train station. Those heading left go down the Grand Canal toward San Marco—which is the (relatively) fast and scenic way. The no. 2 route heading right also eventually gets you to San Marco (at the San Zaccaria stop) but takes more than twice as long because it goes the long way around Dorsoduro (this line serves mainly commuters). As for the no. 1 line going to the right from the train station, it will go only one more stop before it hits its terminus at Piazzale Roma. **Make sure the *vaporetto* you get on is heading to the left from the train station.** Departing from **Piazzale Roma, make sure no. 2 is going to the right** (the no. 1 will only go right).

BY CAR The only wheels you'll see in Venice are those attached to luggage. **No cars are allowed,** or more to the point, no cars could drive through the narrow streets and over the footbridges—even the police, fire department, and ambulance services use boats. You can drive across the Ponte della Libertà from Mestre (on the mainland) to Venice, but you can go no farther than Piazzale Roma at the Venice end, where many garages eagerly await your euros (and in high season are often full). The **Autorimessa Comunale garage** (avm.avmspa.it; ✆ **041/2727301**) charges 35€ for a 24-hour period, while **Garage San Marco** (garagesanmarco.it; ✆ **041/5232213**) costs 45€ for 24 hours (25€ up to 5 hr.). From Piazzale Roma, you can catch *vaporetti* lines 1 and 2 (see box above), which go down the Grand Canal to the train station and, eventually, Piazza San Marco. Cheaper (and in some cases free) parking is available on the adjacent island of **Tronchetto** (see "By Bus," above), first right as you cross the Ponte della Libertà.

tourist tax: **NEW START FOR VENICE?**

Pre-Covid, Venice was attracting an astounding 30 million visitors a year or around 80,000 visitors per day—dwarfing the population of just 50,000. The 2020 lockdown resulted in less pollution and crystal-clear canals for the first time in decades. Though most Venetians recognize the importance of tourism to the local economy, few want to return to the pre-lockdown bad old days of overtourism. Organizations such as the **Venetian Heritage Foundation** (venetianheritage.org), **Venezia NON è Disneyland** (facebook.com/VeneziaNONDisneyland), and **Save Venice** (savevenice.org) have called for more restrictions, including on Airbnb apartments in Venice, and support for cheaper long-term rentals to encourage locals to move back from the mainland.

In a move widely applauded, large **cruise ships were banned** from the inner lagoon in August 2021 (with ships diverted to the ports of Marghera, Fusina, or even Ravenna, 2 hr. by road from Venice), though smaller cruise ships under 25,000 gross register tonnage can still dock in the city.

In 2024, **tour groups in Venice** were limited to 25 people (with loudspeakers banned), while local police now strictly enforce the ban on swimming in canals with a 450€ fine and expulsion from the city (over 1,000 tourists were booted out in 2025).

And to encourage "slow tourism" and longer stays—as opposed to "*mordi e fuggi*," or "hit-and-run" tourism—the city also introduced **entry fees for day-trippers** ages 14 and over in 2025. A 5€ day-trip tax is now applied every Friday through Sunday (and on holidays) from **April through July** (enforced 8:30am–4pm). Day-trippers must make an online booking at **cda.ve.it/it** just to *enter* Venice (entry is monitored via electronic entry points). Visitors who fail to make reservations up to 4 days in advance pay more: 10€. You are exempt if you have accommodations booked in Venice. So far, it seems that the tax has completely failed to rein in overtourism, though it has raised a fair chunk of extra revenue for the city. Check the city's information website (**comune.venezia.it**) for the latest.

Visitor Information

TOURIST OFFICES The most central **Venezia Unica information office** lies in the arcade at the western end of Piazza San Marco (Calle Larga de l'Ascensione 71F), near Museo Correr (✆ **041/2424;** daily 9am–7pm). Offices are also at Piazzale Roma (kiosk near Ponte della Costituzione; daily 7am–7pm), the train station (opposite platforms 2 and 3; daily 7am–7pm), and in the arrivals hall at Marco Polo Airport (daily 8am–7pm). These offices do not offer free maps—they cost 3€. See also **veneziaunica.it**.

Live Venice (live-venice.it) is another useful website, while monthly magazine ***VeNews*** (venezianews.it; 3€ or 4.50€ during the Biennale) is sold at city newsstands (in English and Italian).

City Layout

Even armed with the best map or a hefty smartphone data plan, expect to get a little bit lost in Venice, at least some of the time (GPS directions can be unreliable here). View it as an opportunity to stumble upon Venice's most intriguing corners. Keep in mind as you wander hopelessly among the *calli* (streets) and *campi* (squares) that Venice wasn't built to make sense to those on foot, but rather to those plying its canals.

Venice lies 4km (2½ miles) from terra firma, connected to the mainland at Mestre by the Ponte della Libertà, which leads to Piazzale Roma. Snaking through the city like an inverted *S* is the **Grand Canal,** the wide main artery. Central Venice refers to the built-up block of islands in the lagoon's center, the six main *sestieri* (districts) that make up the bulk of the tourist city. Greater Venice includes all the inhabited islands of the lagoon—central Venice plus Murano, Burano, Torcello, and the Lido.

Venice Neighborhoods in Brief

SAN MARCO The most visited, and most central, *sestiere* is anchored by the magnificent Piazza San Marco and St. Mark's Basilica to the south and the Rialto Bridge to the north. This has been the commercial, religious, and political heart of the city for more than a millennium. Unfortunately, ever-rising rents have persuaded most locals to look for housing in other neighborhoods, but the area is flush with first-class hotels—see p. 435 for suggestions on where to stay in the heart of Venice without going broke.

CASTELLO Just east of Piazza San Marco, Castello's tony waterside esplanade Riva degli Schiavoni follows the Bacino di San Marco (St. Mark's Basin), skirting Venice's most congested area to the north and east. Riva degli Schiavoni is often thronged, but if you head farther east in the direction of the Arsenale or inland away from the *bacino,* the crowds thin out. Here you'll find such major sights as Campo SS. Giovanni e Paolo and the Scuola di San Giorgio.

DORSODURO Residential Dorsoduro, the largest of the *sestieri,* lies across the Accademia Bridge from San Marco. Home to the Accademia and Peggy Guggenheim museums, it was known as an artists' haven until rising rents forced many residents to relocate. Come here for good neighborhood restaurants, a charming gondola boatyard, lively Campo Santa Margherita, and the sunny canalside quay of Zattere.

SAN POLO This mixed bag of residential corners and tourist sights stretches northwest of the Rialto Bridge to the church of Santa Maria dei Frari. At the foot of the bridge, you'll find the bustling Rialto Market. Some of the city's best restaurants flourish here alongside some of its worst tourist traps. Spacious Campo San Polo is the main piazza.

A Note on Addresses

Within each *sestiere* is a most original system of numbering the *palazzi,* using one continuous string of 6,000 or so numbers. The format for addresses in this chapter is, where possible, the number with the actual street or *campo* on which you'll find that address. But official mailing addresses (and what you'll see written down in most places) are simply the *sestiere* name followed by the building number, which isn't especially helpful—for example, San Marco 1471 may not necessarily be found close to San Marco 1473. Many buildings aren't numbered at all.

SANTA CROCE North and northwest of the San Polo district and across the Grand Canal from the train station, Santa Croce stretches all the way to Piazzale Roma. Less lively than San Polo but just as authentic, it feels light-years away from San Marco; its little-visited eastern section is a great place for curious visitors to explore. Quiet, lovely Campo San Giacomo dell'Orio is its heart.

CANNAREGIO On the same side of the Grand Canal as San Marco and Castello, Cannaregio stretches north and east from the train station to include the old Jewish Ghetto. One-quarter of Venice's ever-shrinking population of 50,000 lives here. Many one-star hotels are clustered about the train station—not a dangerous neighborhood but not known for its charm, either. Strada Nova is Cannaregio's main thoroughfare, leading to the Rialto bridge.

LA GIUDECCA Across the Giudecca Canal from Piazza San Marco and Dorsoduro, tranquil La Giudecca is a residential island where you'll find a youth hostel and a few hotels (including the deluxe Cipriani).

LIDO DI VENEZIA This slim, 11km-long (6¾-mile) island, the only spot in the Venetian lagoon where cars circulate, is the city's beach, fronting the open sea. It's also home of the annual Venice Film Festival.

Getting Around Venice

Aside from traveling by boat, the only way to explore Venice is by walking—and by getting lost repeatedly. You'll navigate many twisting streets whose names change constantly and don't appear on any map, and streets that may very well simply end in a blind alley or spill abruptly into

Vaporetti can be useful for exploring Venice, though you'll see plenty by simply walking.

a canal. You'll also cross dozens of footbridges. Treat getting bewilderingly lost in Venice as part of the fun, and budget more time than you'd think necessary to get wherever you're going.

STREET MAPS & SIGNAGE The map sold by the tourist office (3€) and free maps provided by most hotels (and Alilaguna) don't always show—much less name or index—all the *calli* (streets) and pathways of Venice. Pick up a more detailed map (ask for a *pianta della città* at news kiosks—especially those at the train station and around San Marco or most bookstores). The best is the highly detailed **Touring Club Italiano map,** available in a variety of forms (folding map from 8.50€) and scales. If using your phone, note that GPS directions can be unreliable in Venice, though Google Maps has much improved in recent years (and has added its "streetview" option).

As you wander, look for the yellow signs (well, *usually* yellow) whose destinations and arrows direct you toward five major landmarks: **Ferrovia** (the train station), **Piazzale Roma** (the parking garage and bus station), **Rialto** (one of four bridges over the Grand Canal), **San Marco** (the city's main square), and the **Accademia** (museum and the southernmost Grand Canal bridge).

BY *VAPORETTO* The various *sestieri* are linked by a comprehensive *vaporetto* (water bus/ferry) system of about a dozen lines operated by the **Azienda del Consorzio Trasporti Veneziano (ACTV;** actv.avmspa.it; ✆ **041/5287886**). Transit maps are available at the tourist office and most ACTV ticket offices, but it's also worth downloading the AVM Venezia Official App if you have a smartphone. It's easier to get around the center on foot; the *vaporetti* mostly serve the Grand Canal, outskirts, and outer islands. The crisscross network of small canals is the province of delivery vessels, gondolas, and private boats.

A ticket for 75 minutes of travel (after validation) on a *vaporetto* is a steep 9.50€, while a 24-hour travel card is 25€. Most lines run every 10 to 15 minutes from 7am to midnight, and then hourly until morning. Most *vaporetto* docks have timetables posted. You can buy tickets on the app, at Venezia Unica offices, authorized retailers that display the ACTV/Venezia Unica sticker in town, and usually at the dock itself, though not all of these have machines or kiosks that sell tickets. If you haven't bought a travel card (see "Venice Discounts," p. 418) or tickets beforehand, you'll have to settle up with the conductors onboard. Look for them immediately on boarding—they won't come looking for you—or you risk a stiff on-the-spot fine of at least 61€. No excuses accepted. Also available are travel cards for 48 hours (35€), 72 hours (45€), and 1 week (65€). If you're planning to stay in Venice for a week or more and intend to use the *vaporetto* service a lot, it makes sense to pick up a **Venezia Unica city pass** (see "Venice Discounts," p. 418), with which you can buy *vaporetto* tickets for just 1.50€. You **must validate** all tickets at the machines at the docks

CRUISING THE canals

A leisurely cruise along the **Grand Canal** ♥♥♥ (p. 414) from Piazza San Marco to the train station (Ferrovia)—or the reverse—is one of Venice's must-dos. It's the world's most unusual Main Street, a watery boulevard whose *palazzi* have been converted into condos. Lower water-lapped floors are now deserted, but the higher floors are still coveted by the city's titled families, who have inhabited these glorious residences for centuries; others have become the dream homes of privileged expats, drawn as irresistibly as the romantic Venetians-by-adoption who preceded them—Richard Wagner, Henry James, Robert Browning, and Lord Byron among them.

As much a symbol of Venice as the winged lion, the **gondola** ♥♥♥ is one of Europe's great traditions, incredibly expensive but truly as romantic as it looks (detractors who write it off as too touristy have most likely never tried it). The official fixed rate is 90€ for a 30-minute gondola tour for up to five passengers from 9am to 7pm. The rate bumps up to 110€ from 7pm to 4am (for 35 min.), and it's 45€ for every additional 20 minutes (55€ at night). That's not a typo: 165€ for a not-quite-1-hour evening cruise. ***Tip:*** Although the price is fixed by the city, a good negotiator at the right time of day (when business is slow) can sometimes grab a small discount for a shorter ride. And at these ridiculously inflated prices, there is no need to tip the gondolier. You might also find **discounts online.**

Aim for late afternoon before sundown, when the light does its magic on the canal reflections (and bring a bottle of prosecco and glasses). If the price is too high, ask visitors at your hotel or others lingering about at the gondola stations if they'd like to share it. Though the price is "fixed," before setting off you should establish with the gondolier the cost, time, and route (back canals are preferable to the trafficked and often choppy Grand Canal). If you'd prefer to arrange a boat in advance, contact the local gondola specialists, **Agenzia Gondolieri Travel** (gondolieritravel.com; ✆ **041/2410085**).

And what of the **serenading gondolier** immortalized in film? Frankly, you're better off without, but if warbling is de rigueur for you, here's the scoop: An ensemble of accordion player and tenor is so expensive that it's shared among several gondolas traveling together. A number of tour operators (and online brokers, such as viator.com) book evening serenades for around 50€ per person.

Venice has 10 gondola stations, including Piazzale Roma, the train station, and Piazza San Marco (Traghetto Gondole Molo or Bacino Orseolo). There are also a number of smaller stations, with *gondolieri* in striped shirts standing alongside their sleek 11m (36-ft.) black wonders looking for passengers. They all speak enough English to communicate the necessary details. Remember, if you just want a quick taste of being in a gondola, you can take a cheap *traghetto* across the Grand Canal.

before boarding (tap your ticket, or your smartphone for the app, on the validator pad and wait for the green light).

BY *TRAGHETTO* Just four bridges span the Grand Canal, and to fill in the gaps, *traghetti* skiffs (oversize gondolas rowed by two standing *gondolieri*) cross the Grand Canal at several intermediate points. Stations were traditionally located at the end of streets named Calle del Traghetto and indicated by a yellow sign with the black gondola symbol. These days only a handful operate regularly, primarily at San Tomà, Santa Maria del

Giglio, and Santa Sofia (check with a local if in doubt). The fare is 2€ cash, which you hand to the gondolier when boarding. Most Venetians cross standing up. Try the Santa Sofia crossing (Mon–Sat 7:30am–7pm, Sun 9am–7pm; Oct–Mar last crossing 6pm), which connects the Ca' d'Oro and the Pescheria fish market, on the Grand Canal just north of the Rialto Bridge—the gondoliers expertly dodge water traffic at this point of the canal, where it's the busiest and most heart-stopping.

BY WATER TAXI *Taxi acquei* (water taxis) charge high prices and aren't for visitors watching their euros. Trips in town are likely to cost at least 60€ to 90€, depending on distance, time of day, and whether you've booked in advance or just hired on the spot. Each trip includes allowance for up to four to five pieces of luggage—beyond that there's a surcharge of 3€ to 5€ per piece (rates differ slightly according to company and how you reserve your trip). Plus there's a 15€ supplement for service from 10pm to 7am, and a 5€ charge for taxis on-call. Those rates cover up to four people; if any more squeeze in, it's another 5€ to 10€ per extra passenger (maximum 10 people). Taking a water taxi from the train station to Piazza San Marco or any area hotels costs around 90€ (the Lido is around 100€), while fixed fees to the airport range from 150€ to 170€ (for up to four people). Taxis to Burano or Torcello will be at least 160€. Note that only taxi boats with a yellow strip are the official operators sanctioned by the city. You can book trips with **Consorzio Motoscafi Venezia** online at **motoscafivenezia.it** or call ✆ **041/5222303.** Six water-taxi stations serve key points in the city: the Ferrovia, Piazzale Roma, the Rialto Bridge, Piazza San Marco, the Lido, and Marco Polo Airport.

[Fast FACTS] VENICE

Doctors & Hospitals The **Ospedale Civile Santi Giovanni e Paolo** (aulss3.veneto.it; ✆ **041/5294111**), on Campo Santi Giovanni e Paolo in Castello, has English-speaking staff and provides 24/7 emergency service (*vaporetto* Ospedale).

Emergencies For general emergency, call ✆ **112.** To call the local police, dial ✆ **113;** for an ambulance, ✆ **118;** for a fire ✆ **115.**

Internet Access Venice offers citywide Wi-Fi through the **Wi-Fi Venezia** (veneziaunica.it) network of 200 hotspots. Buy packages online (5€/24 hr., 15€/3 days, or 20€/7 days); access codes are then sent via e-mail.

Mail The most convenient post offices are **Venezia Centro** at Calle de la Acque, San Marco (✆ **041/2404149;** Mon–Fri 8:20am–7:05pm); **Venezia 4** at Calle de l'Ascension 1241, off the west side of Piazza San Marco (✆ **041/2446711;** Mon–Fri 8:20am–1:35pm); and **Venezia 3** at Campo San Polo 2022 (✆ **041/5200315;** Tues and Thurs 8:20am–1:35pm).

Police Dial ✆ **113.**

Safety Generally speaking, Venice is one of Italy's safest cities. Be aware of pickpocketing on crowded *vaporetti*, particularly on tourist routes where passengers are more intent on the passing scenery than on watching their bags. Venice's often deserted back streets are virtually crime-free, but take the usual precautions at night.

EXPLORING VENICE

Venice is notorious for changing and extending the opening hours of its museums and, to a lesser degree, its churches (often due to special events or strikes). Before you begin exploring Venice's sights, check online or ask at the tourist office for specific museum and church hours.

San Marco

Basilica di San Marco (St. Mark's) ♥♥♥ CATHEDRAL One of the grandest, and certainly the most exotic of all cathedrals in Europe, **Basilica di San Marco** is a treasure heap of Venetian art and all sorts of booty garnered from the eastern Mediterranean. Legend has it that **St. Mark,** on his way to Rome in the C.E. 1st century, was told by an angel his body would rest near the lagoon that would one day become Venice. Hundreds of years later, the city fathers were looking to replace their original patron St. Theodore with a saint of high stature, someone more in keeping with their lofty aspirations. In 828 the prophecy was fulfilled when Venetian merchants stole the remains of St. Mark from Alexandria in Egypt (supposedly the body was packed in pickled pork to avoid the attention of the Muslim guards). Today the high altar's green marble canopy on alabaster columns is believed to cover the remains of St. Mark and continues to be the focus of the basilica, at least for the faithful.

Modeled on Constantinople's Church of the Twelve Apostles, the original shrine of St. Mark was consecrated in 832, but in 976 the church burned down. The present incarnation was completed in 1094, then extended and embellished over the years; it served as the doge's personal

The magnificent Basilica di San Marco.

St. Mark's Tickets: Online Only

Since 2025 it has been mandatory to buy tickets to St. Mark's in advance (up to 45 days ahead) via the official booking website **tickets.basilicasanmarco.it**; you must select a specific time slot as well. Tickets are not refundable or changeable, but this guarantees relatively swift entry (though you still line up for the security check). In theory it is possible to buy entry tickets online when you arrive in Venice, but these are often sold out two days in advance. ***Note:* There is no longer a ticket office at the church entrance and you cannot buy tickets on-site.**

Note also that the standard 10€ ticket only includes a basic one-way walking route around the main church—you must pay extra for the Pala d'Oro, museum, or terrace. At all times the guards at St. Mark's entrance are serious about forbidding entry to anyone in **inappropriate attire:** shorts, sleeveless shirts, cropped tops, and skirts above the knee. Note also that you cannot enter the basilica with luggage. Photos and filming inside are permitted, for private use only.

church. Today, San Marco looks more Orthodox cathedral than Roman Catholic church, with a cavernous interior gilded with Byzantine mosaics added over 7 centuries, covering every inch of ceiling and pavement.

For a closer look at the most remarkable ceiling mosaics and a better view of the carpet–like patterns of the pavement mosaics, it's worth it to pay the admission to go upstairs to the **Museo di San Marco** (enter in the atrium at the principal entrance); this was originally the women's gallery, or *matroneum,* and includes access to the outdoor **Loggia dei Cavalli.** Here you can admire a panoramic view of the piazza below and replicas of the celebrated ***Triumphal Quadriga,*** four gilded bronze horses dating from the C.E. 2nd or 3rd century; the Roman originals were moved inside in the 1980s for preservation. (The word *quadriga* actually refers to a car or chariot pulled by four horses, though in this case there are only the horses.) The horses were transported to Venice from Constantinople in 1204, along with lots of other loot from the Fourth Crusade.

The basilica's greatest treasure is the altarpiece known as the **Pala d'Oro** (Golden Altarpiece), a Gothic masterpiece encrusted with over 2,000 precious gems and 83 enameled panels. It was created in 10th-century Constantinople and embellished by Venetian and Byzantine artisans between the 12th and 14th centuries. Second to the Pala d'Oro in importance is the 10th-century ***Madonna di Nicopeia,*** a bejeweled icon also purloined from Constantinople and exhibited in its own chapel. Worth a visit as well is the **Tesoro** (Treasury), a collection of crusaders' plunder from Constantinople and other relics amassed over the years. Much of the loot has been incorporated into the interior and exterior of the basilica in the form of marble, columns, capitals, and statuary.

Guided tours in English (1 hr.) normally run daily at 2:45pm from April to early November, and at 1:45pm (Fri–Sun) the rest of the year (with an additional tour at 10:45am Mon–Sat year-round)—well worth

Basilica di San Marco **22**
Basilica SS. Giovanni e Paolo **26**
Campanile di San Marco **21**
Galleria Giorgio Franchetti alla Ca' d'Oro **11**
Gallerie dell'Accademia **8**
Giardini **24**
Ghetto Venezia **1**
Il Redentore **10**
Museo Ebraico di Venezia **2**
Palazzo Ducale **23**
Peggy Guggenheim Collection **9**
Piazza San Marco **19**
Punta della Dogana **17**
Rialto Bridge **13**
San Giorgio Maggiore **18**
San Sebastiano **6**
Santa Maria della Salute **16**
Santa Maria Gloriosa dei Frari **3**
Scala Contarini del Bovolo **14**
Scuola di San Giorgio degli Schiavoni **25**
Scuola Grande dei Carmini **5**
Scuola Grande di San Rocco **4**
Squero di San Trovaso **7**
Teatro La Fenice **15**
T Fondaco dei Tedeschi **12**
Torre dell'Orologio **20**

Venice Attractions

considering if you'd like to get a better understanding of the Basilica's treasures. Book tours (45.50€) online at **venetoinside.com**. Alternatively, audioguides are available at the counter just beyond the entrance turnstile (included).

Piazza San Marco. basilicasanmarco.it. ✆ **041/2708311.** Basilica 10€; Basilica plus Museo di San Marco (includes Loggia dei Cavalli) 20€; Basilica plus Pala d'Oro 20€; Basilica, Museo, and Pala d'Oro 30€. Basilica, Tesoro, and Pala d'Oro Mon–Sat 9:30am–5:15pm (last access 4:45pm), Sun 2–5:15pm. Museo di San Marco daily 9:30am–5:15pm (last access 4:45pm). *Vaporetto:* San Marco.

Campanile di San Marco ♥♥♥ ICON An elevator whisks you to the top of this 97m (318-ft.) brown-brick bell tower where you get awe-inspiring views of St. Mark's cupolas. With a gilded angel atop its spire, it is the highest structure in the city, offering a pigeon's-eye panorama that includes the lagoon, neighboring islands, and the red rooftops and church domes of Venice. Originally built in the 9th century, the bell tower was reconstructed in the 12th, 14th, and 16th centuries, when the pretty marble loggia at its base was added by Jacopo Sansovino. It collapsed unexpectedly in 1902, miraculously hurting no one except a cat. Nine years later it was rebuilt exactly as before, using most of the same materials—even one of the five historical bells that it still uses today. As with the Basilica (see above), you **must buy tickets in advance** from **tickets.basilicasanmarco.it** (you cannot buy tickets on site). ***Tip:*** If you have limited time, the view from the bell tower of **San Giorgio Maggiore ♥♥** (p. 429) is much better (you get a wider panorama of the whole city) and is half the price, though you'll need to take a *vaporetto* to get there.

Piazza San Marco. basilicasanmarco.it. ✆ **041/2708311.** Admission 15€. Daily mid-Mar to early Nov 9:30am–9:15pm (last access 8:45pm), early Nov to mid-Mar 9:30am–7:15pm (last access 6:45pm); closed Jan. *Vaporetto:* San Marco.

Canal Grande (Grand Canal) ♥♥♥ LANDMARK A leisurely cruise along the "Canalazzo" from Piazza San Marco to the Ferrovia (train station), or the reverse, is one of Venice's (and life's) must-do experiences (see box p. 403). Hop on the **no. 1 *vaporetto*** in the late afternoon (try to get one of the coveted outdoor seats in the prow), when the weather-worn colors of the former homes of Venice's merchant elite are warmed by the soft light and reflected in the canal's rippling waters, and the busy traffic of delivery boats, *vaporetti,* and gondolas that fills the city's main thoroughfare has eased somewhat (if it's too busy at that time, get on the boat first thing in the morning to beat the crowds).

Best stations to start/end a Grand Canal tour: Ferrovia (train station) or Piazzale Roma on northwest side of canal; Piazza San Marco on southeast side. Tickets 9.50€.

Palazzo Ducale ♥♥♥ PALACE The pink-and-white marble Gothic-Renaissance **Palazzo Ducale** (Doge's Palace), residence of the doges who ruled Venice for more than 1,000 years, stands between the Basilica di San Marco and the sea. A symbol of prosperity and power, the original was destroyed by a succession of fires, with the current building started in

Grand Canal gondoliers and Rialto Bridge.

1340, extended in the 1420s, and redesigned again after a fire in 1483. If you want to understand something of this magnificent place, the history of the 1,000-year-old maritime republic, and the intrigue of the government that ruled it, take the **Secret Itineraries tour ♥♥♥** (see box p. 416). Failing that, at least download the MUVE app audioguide to help make sense of it all (the app is free, but you need to activate the palace audioguide at the museum for 5€). Unless you can tag along with an English-speaking tour group, you may otherwise miss out on the importance of much of what you're seeing.

The 15th-century **Porta della Carta** (Paper Gate) opens onto a splendid inner courtyard with a double row of Renaissance arches (today, visitors enter through a doorway on the lagoon side of the palace). The self-guided route through the palace begins in the main courtyard, where the **Museo dell'Opera** contains assorted bits of masonry preserved from the *palazzo*'s exterior. Beyond here, the first major room you'll come to is the spacious **Sala delle Quattro Porte** (Hall of the Four Doors), with a worn ceiling by Tintoretto. The **Sala dell'Anticollegio,** where foreign ambassadors waited to be received by the doge and his council, is covered in four works by Tintoretto, including *Mercury & the Three Graces* and ***Bacchus and Ariadne*** **♥♥**, the latter deemed one of his best by some critics. The Tintorettos are outshone, however, by Veronese's ***Rape of Europa*** **♥♥**, one of the *palazzo*'s finest paintings. The highlight of the adjacent **Sala del Collegio** (the Council Chamber itself) is the spectacular cycle of **ceiling paintings ♥♥**, a Veronese masterpiece completed between 1575 and 1578. Next door lies the most impressive of the interior rooms, the richly adorned **Sala del Senato** (Senate Chamber), with Tintoretto's ceiling painting *The Triumph of Venice*. After passing again through the Sala delle Quattro Porte, you'll enter the Veronese-decorated **Stanza del Consiglio dei Dieci** (Room of the Council of Ten), where justice was dispensed and decapitations ordered by the Republic's dreaded security police. Formed in the 14th century to deal with emergency situations, the Ten became more powerful than the Senate. In the **Sala della Bussola** (Compass Chamber), notice the **Bocca dei Leoni** (Lion's Mouth), a slit in the wall into which secret denunciations and accusations of enemies of the state were placed for quick action by the much-feared Council.

The main sight on the next level down—indeed, the main sight in the entire palace—is the **Sala del Maggior Consiglio** (Great Council Hall). This enormous space is animated by Tintoretto's huge ***Paradiso*** ♥♥ at the far end of the hall above the doge's seat. Measuring 7×23m (23×75 ft.), it is said to be the world's largest oil painting; together with Veronese's gorgeous ***Il Trionfo di Venezia*** ♥♥ (*The Triumph of Venice*) in the oval panel on the ceiling, it affirms the power emanating from the council sessions held here. Tintoretto also did the portraits of the 76 doges encircling the top of this chamber. Note that the picture of the Doge Marin Falier, who was convicted of treason and beheaded in 1355, has been blacked out—Venice has never forgiven him. Tours culminate at the enclosed **Ponte dei Sospiri** (Bridge of Sighs), built in 1600, which connects the Ducal Palace with the grim **Palazzo delle Prigioni** (Prison). The bridge took its current name in the 19th century—Lord Byron popularized it in his epic poem *Childe Harold's Pilgrimage*, romantically imagining the prisoners' final breath of resignation upon viewing the outside world one last time. Some cells still have the original graffiti of past prisoners, many of them locked up interminably for petty crimes.

San Marco, Piazza San Marco. palazzoducale.visitmuve.it. ✆ **041/2715911.** Admission 35€ (reduced to 30€ if purchased 30 days in advance online), 15€ students and seniors. Included in **Museum Pass** (p. 418). For **Secret Itineraries** guided tour in English, see box below. Daily Apr–Oct 9am–7pm (last entrance 6pm), Nov–Mar 9am–6pm (last entrance 5pm). *Vaporetto:* San Marco.

secrets OF THE PALAZZO DUCALE

The **Itinerari Segreti** ♥♥♥ (Secret Itineraries) guided tours of the Palazzo Ducale are a must-see for any visit to Venice of more than 1 day. The tours offer an unparalleled look into the world of Venetian politics over the centuries and are the only way to access the otherwise restricted quarters and hidden passageways of this enormous palace, such as the doges' private chambers and the torture chambers where prisoners were interrogated. The tour must be reserved in advance online (muve.vivaticket.it), by phone (✆ **041/4273-0892**), or in person at the ticket desk. Tours often sell out at least a few days ahead, especially from spring through fall. Tours in English are daily at 10am, 11:30am and 1pm, and cost 40€ adults; 20€ ages 6 to 14, seniors, and students aged 15 to 25. There are also tours in Italian at 11am and 12:30pm, and French at 10:30am and noon. The tour lasts about 75 minutes.

Rialto Bridge ♥♥♥ ICON This graceful arch over the Grand Canal, linking the San Marco and San Polo districts, normally teems with tourists browsing overpriced boutiques. Until the 1800s it was the only bridge across the Grand Canal, originally built as a pontoon bridge at the canal's narrowest point. The 1444 incarnation was the first to include shops, interrupted by a drawbridge in the center. In 1592, the current graceful stone span was finished with the designs of Antonio da Ponte, who beat out Sansovino, Palladio, and Michelangelo with plans that called for a single, vast, 28m-wide (92-ft.) arch to allow trading ships to pass.

Ponte del Rialto. *Vaporetto:* Rialto.

Scala Contarini del Bovolo ♥♥ LANDMARK/VIEW Part of a *palazzo* built in the late 15th century, this multi-arch spiral staircase was artfully restored in 2016, featuring a belvedere with fabulous views of Venice. Halfway up, the **Sala del Tintoretto** (Tintoretto Room) contains the rare portrait of Lazzaro Zen, an African who converted to Christianity in Venice in 1770, as well as a preparatory painting by Tintoretto of his monumental *Paradise* (the final version is in the Palazzo Ducale). You can buy **timed entry tickets** in advance at ticketlandia.com.

Corte Contarini del Bovolo 4299. gioiellinascostidivenezia.it. ✆ **041/309-6605.** Admission 9€ adults, 7€ seniors and ages 12–26, free for children 11 and under. Daily 10am–6pm (Nov–Feb 9:30am–5:30pm). *Vaporetto:* Rialto.

T Fondaco dei Tedeschi ♥♥ PALAZZO This 16th-century *palazzo* was converted into a posh department store in 2016 but was sadly closed in 2025 after a lease dispute. Its **Rooftop Terrace** featured Venice's greatest view—it may reopen in the future (check with the tourist office).

Calle de Fontego dei Tedeschi, Ponte di Rialto, San Marco. *Vaporetto:* Rialto.

Teatro La Fenice ♥♥♥ OPERA HOUSE One of Italy's most famous opera houses (it ranks third after La Scala in Milan and San Carlo in Naples), La Fenice was originally completed in 1792 but has been rebuilt twice after devastating fires in 1837 and in 2004. Self-guided tours take in the opulent main theater, ornate side rooms, the gilded "royal box," and a small exhibit dedicated to soprano Maria Callas. For tickets to performances, see p. 459.

Campo San Fantin 1965, San Marco. teatrolafenice.it (buy tour tickets on-site or in advance at festfenice.com). ✆ **041/2424.** Admission 12€ adults, 9€ seniors, 7€ ages 7–26, free for children 6 and under. Daily 9:30am–6pm, but check festfenice.com for current monthly schedule. *Vaporetto:* Giglio.

Torre dell'Orologio ♥♥ MONUMENT As you enter the magnificent **Piazza San Marco,** this Renaissance clock tower is one of the first things you see, standing on the north side, the centerpiece of the stately white **Procuratie Vecchie** (the ancient administration buildings for the Republic). With its distinctive blue face ringed by astrological symbols, the tower was built between 1496 and 1506; the clock mechanism still keeps perfect time. On the top, two bronze figures, known as "Moors"

VENICE discounts

Venice offers a somewhat bewildering range of passes and discount cards. For short stays, we recommend buying an **ACTV travel card** (p. 401) and combining that with one of the first two passes listed below. The more complex Venezia Unica card scheme is recommended if you intend to stay up to 7 days and do a lot of sightseeing. The **Venezia Unica website** (veneziaunica.it) is a one-stop shop for most of the passes listed below.

The **Museum Pass** (**MUVE**) grants admission to all city-run museums over a 6-month period, and also lets you skip ticketing lines, a useful perk in high season. The pass covers the museums of St. Mark's Square—Palazzo Ducale, Museo Correr, Museo Archeologico Nazionale, the Biblioteca Nazionale Marciana (it's 30€–35€ to visit just these museums with a San Marco Museum Pass)—as well as the Museo di Palazzo Mocenigo (Costume Museum), Ca' Rezzonico, Ca' Pesaro, the Museo del Vetro (Glass Museum) on Murano, and the Museo del Merletto (Lace Museum) on Burano. The Museum Pass is available online (visitmuve.it) or at any participating museum. It costs 50€ adults and 25€ students under 26, kids ages 6 to 14, and seniors over 65. It's a good deal, as the Doge's Palace alone will set you back 35€; visit two more of the larger museums (for example, Palazzo Mocenigo [15€] or Ca' Pesaro [15€]) and you've made a decent saving.

The **Chorus Pass** (chorusvenezia.org) grants admission to almost every major church in Venice, 19 in all, for 15€ (10€ for students 12–25), for up to 1 year. For 30€, the **Chorus Pass Family** gives you the same perks for two adults and their children 17 and under. Most churches charge 3.50€ admission, which means you'll need to visit more than four to make this pass worthwhile.

The **Venezia Unica card** (venezia unica.it) combines the above passes, transport, discounts, and even Internet access on one card via a "made-to-order" online system, where you choose the services you want—it can be confusing, so make sure you understand what you're buying before paying (and read the small print). The 7-day City Pass (if available) is usually the best value (though these do *not* include transport). You can also buy various transportation packages from Venezia Unica (1-, 2-, 3- and 7-day ACTV passes [25€–65€], for example, which cover all vaporetto and bus travel, or just Wi-Fi access [from 5€ for 24 hr.]).

For visitors between ages 6 and 29, the **Rolling Venice** card (also available at veneziaunica.it) costs just 6€. Valid through the end of the year in which you buy it, it entitles the bearer to significant (20%–30%) discounts at participating restaurants (cardholder's meal only) and discounted ACTV travel cards (27€ for 3 days), along with discounts in museums, stores, hotels, and bars across the city (it comes with a thick booklet listing everywhere you're entitled to get discounts).

because of the dark color of the bronze, pivot to strike the hour. Visits inside are by 1-hour guided tour only (included in admission), recommended only for those interested in the clock's history.

Piazza San Marco. torreorologio.visitmuve.it. ✆ **848/082000** or 041-42730892. Tour 15€ adults, 11€ ages 6–14 and students 15–25; children 5 and under not allowed. Ticket also good for Museo Correr, Museo Archeologico Nazionale, and Biblioteca Nazionale Marciana (but not Palazzo Ducale). Tours in English 11am (Mon, Fri, Sun), noon (Tues–Thurs), 2pm (Mon–Wed, Fri–Sat), 4pm (Fri–Sat); must reserve in advance online. *Vaporetto:* San Marco.

Castello

While the highlight of this neighborhood is the huge **Santi Giovanni e Paolo** (see below), within a few minutes' walk from here are two more magnificent Renaissance churches: **Santa Maria Formosa ♥♥** (3.50€; Mon–Sat 10:30am–5pm), on Campo Santa Maria Formosa, and **San Zaccaria ♥♥**, at Campo San Zaccaria (free admission; daily 10am–6pm), which contains Giovanni Bellini's exceptional **San Zaccaria Altarpiece ♥♥**. Pay 3.50€ to enter San Zaccaria's side chapels for Tintoretto's *Birth of Saint John the Baptist*, the Golden Chapel with frescoes by Andrea del Castagno, and the creepy flooded crypt, which houses the bodies of eight doges. Several attractions lie on the far eastern side of Castello. For folks with a deep interest in maritime history (others can skip it), there's the sprawling **Museo Storico Navale di Venezia ♥♥**, Riva San Biasio 2148 (munav.it; 16€, or 26€ including submarine *Enrico Dandolo*; Wed–Mon 10am–6pm, Nov–Mar until 4pm). Nearby is the **Ponte del Paradiso ♥♥** and the famous twin-towered entrance to the **Arsenale** (only open during the Biennale).

Basilica SS. Giovanni e Paolo ♥♥ CHURCH Built by the Dominican order from the 13th to the 15th century, this massive Gothic church is an unofficial Pantheon where 25 doges are buried (a number of tombs are

COME HELL OR high water

During the tidal *acqua alta* (high water) floods, Venice's lagoon rises until it engulfs the city, leaving up to 1.5 to 1.8m (5–6 ft.) of water in the lowest-lying streets. Piazza San Marco, as the lowest point in the city, goes first. As many as 60 floods a year have been recorded since they first started keeping track in the late 1700s. One of the most devastating was in 1966, though the second-highest occurred in November 2019, and they seem to be getting worse—in 2021 flooding affected the city in August, much earlier than usual.

The good news is that the long-delayed **Modulo Sperimentale Elettromeccanico,** or **MOSE** project (mosevenezia.eu), began operating in October 2020. A complex system of 78 hydraulic gates, MOSE now protects the lagoon from the worst of the flooding. It's controversial because of its environmental impact—keeping the gates closed for long periods could result in parts of the lagoon becoming stagnant, for example. Note also, MOSE is only activated to block tides of more than 130cm (4 ft., 3 in.), which means light flooding is still likely to occur (St. Mark's Square starts to flood at around 80cm/2 ft., 7½ in.).

Significant *acqua alta* can begin as early as late September or October but usually takes place November to March (there is no way to predict them in advance). The waters usually recede after just a few hours—there is no need to get wet and the city doesn't shut down. Walkways are set up along the main routes, but if you intend to wander around, do as the locals do and buy rubber wading boots, available from most stores from 20€ (for about 10€, souvenir shops and stands in Piazza San Marco also sell disposable knee-high plastic waterproof slippers, good for a couple of days).

part of the unfinished facade). The church, commonly known as Zanipolo in Venetian dialect, is also home to many artistic treasures. The brilliantly colored ***Polyptych of St. Vincent Ferrer*** (ca. 1465), attributed to a young Giovanni Bellini, is in the right aisle. You'll also see the mummified foot of St. Catherine of Siena—considered a holy relic—encased in glass near here. Visit the **Cappella del Rosario ♥♥**, through a glass door off the left transept, to see three restored ceiling canvases and one oil painting by Paolo Veronese, *The Assumption of the Madonna*.

Anchoring the large and impressive *campo* outside the church, a popular crossroads for this area of Castello, is the **statue of Bartolomeo Colleoni ♥♥**, the Renaissance *condottiere* (mercenary) who defended Venice's interests at the height of its power until his death in 1475. The 15th-century sculpture by the Florentine Andrea Verrocchio is considered one of the world's great equestrian monuments.

Campo Santi Giovanni e Paolo. santigiovanniepaolo.it. ✆ **041/5235913.** Admission 3.50€. Daily 7:30am–7pm; open to tourists Mon–Sat 9am–6pm, Sun noon–6pm. *Vaporetto:* Rialto.

Scuola di San Giorgio degli Schiavoni ♥♥♥ MUSEUM One of the most mesmerizing spaces in Europe, the tiny main hall of this *scuola* once served as a meeting house for Venice's Dalmatian community (Dalmatia is a region of Croatia—*Schiavoni* means "Slavs"). Venetian *scuole,* or schools, were guilds that brought together merchants and craftspeople from certain trades or similar religious devotions. Built beside its sister church, San Giovanni di Malta, in the early 16th century, the scuola is most famous for the awe-inspiring **cycle of paintings** on its walls, created by Renaissance master Vittore Carpaccio between 1502 and 1509. The paintings depict the lives of the Dalmatian patron saints George (of dragon-slaying fame), Tryphon, and Jerome; in the upper hall (Sala dell'Albergo) is Carpaccio's masterful *Vision of St. Augustine*.

Calle dei Furlani 3259A. scuoladalmatavenezia.com. ✆ **041/5228828.** Admission 6€. Cash only. Mon and Wed–Sun 10am–5:30pm (last entry 5pm). *Vaporetto:* Rialto.

The Biennale

Venice hosts the latest in contemporary art and sculpture from dozens of countries during the prestigious **Biennale d'Arte ♥♥♥** (labiennale.org; ✆ **041/5218711**), one of the world's top international art shows. It fills the pavilions of the **Giardini** (public gardens) at the east end of **Castello,** and at the **Arsenale,** as well as other spaces around the city from April to November in even years (2026, 2028 and so on). Sites are usually open Tuesday through Sunday 10am to 6pm; tickets cost around 30€ to 45€ (16€–20€ students and ages 26 and under). The **Biennale Architettura** (international architecture exhibition) takes place in alternate years (2027, 2029, and so on).

Dorsoduro

Art aficionados should head to the eastern tip of Dorsoduro and the 17th-century Dogana di Mare (Customs House), transformed by architect

Tadao Ando into a beautiful exhibition space dubbed the **Punta della Dogana,** Fondamenta della Dogana alla Salute 2 (pinaultcollection.com). Don't miss also the church of **San Pantalon** (sanpantalon.it) with its stupendous ceiling fresco painted by Giovanni Antonio Fumiani between 1680 and 1704 (free entry).

Gallerie dell'Accademia ♥♥♥ MUSEUM Along with San Marco and the Palazzo Ducale, the Accademia is one of the city's highlights, a magnificent collection of European art and Venetian painting from the 14th to the 18th centuries. Visitor numbers are always capped, so online advance reservations are essential. In general, the least crowded times are when it opens and around 2 hours before closing.

There's a lot to take in here, so buy a catalog in the store, as these contain detailed descriptions of the core paintings and plenty of context—the audioguides are a little muddled and not worth 6€. Note also that one of the museum's prize holdings, Da Vinci's iconic **Vitruvian Man ♥♥♥** (*L'Uomo Vitruviano*), is an extremely fragile ink drawing and rarely displayed in public; check the website before you visit, as exhibitions featuring the work are rare but well-publicized.

Rooms are laid out in rough chronological order, though renovations and closures mean some rooms may be off-limits when you visit (call ahead to check on specific paintings or check the website, updated monthly). The following artworks should be on display somewhere in the museum, though locations may change (again, check the website for the latest).

Veronese's enormous *Feast in the House of Levi* is just one highlight of the Gallerie dell'Accademia's collection of masterpieces.

Visits normally begin upstairs on the second floor, where room 1 (the grand meeting room of the Scuola Grande della Carità) displays a beautiful collection of lavish medieval and early Renaissance art, primarily religious images and altarpieces dating from 1300 to 1450. The giant canvases in room 2 include Carpaccio's *Presentation of Jesus in the Temple* and works by Giovanni Bellini (Bellini is also the focus of rooms 3, 4, and 5). Room 7 features the unsettling, surreal paintings of Hieronymus Bosch, while Giorgione's *The Tempest* and *The Old Woman* are in Room 8. Paolo Veronese's mammoth ***Feast in the House of Levi*** ♥♥ dominates Room 10, while other vast Veronese canvases make up the rest of the space. Room 11 contains work by another Venetian legend, Tintoretto, including ***The Miracle of the Slave*** ♥♥, along with several paintings by Tiepolo, the master of 18th-century Venetian art, and Titian's last painting, a *Pietà* intended for his own tomb. A reassembled ceiling painted by Giorgio Vasari in 1542 is the star of room 13, with room 14 dedicated to the Bassano family of painters. Tintoretto's *Madonna of the Treasurers* is in room 15. One of Annibale Carracci's *Saint Francis* paintings dominates room 16.

Room 20 is usually filled by Gentile Bellini's cycle of ***The Miracles of the Relic of the Cross*** ♥♥, painted around 1500. Room 21 normally contains a monumental cycle of nine paintings by Carpaccio illustrating the ***Story of St. Ursula*** ♥♥; most of these continue to undergo restoration, with *Arrival in Cologne* the only one likely to be displayed for some time (rooms 18–23 are likely to be closed until 2027). Finally, room 24 is adorned with Titian's ***Presentation of the Virgin,*** actually created between 1534 and 1538 specifically to hang in this space.

Downstairs, the beautifully renovated ground-floor galleries mostly cover the late 17th to 19th centuries, with a collection of lesser-known baroque and romantic works by the likes of Bernardo Strozzi, Pietro Longhi, Francesco Guardi, and Canaletto. Delicate paintings by Tiepolo share space with his large tondo ***Feast of the Cross*** in gallery 2, along with Veronese's ***Venice Receives Homage from Hercules and Ceres.*** Sculpture galleries (featuring the work of Antonio Canova and Andrea Palladio) are also on this level.

Campo della Carità 1050, at foot of Accademia bridge. gallerieaccademia.it. ✆ **041/5200345.** 20€ adults, 15€ ages 26–35 on Fri 5:15–7pm, 2€ for EU citizens ages 18–25; free for kids 17 and under. Prices may change during temporary exhibitions. Daily 9am–7pm (Mon until 2pm). *Vaporetto:* Accademia.

Peggy Guggenheim Collection ♥♥♥ MUSEUM It's one of the best museums in Italy covering American and European art of the 20th century, but you might find the experience a little jarring, given its location in a city so heavily associated with the High Renaissance and the baroque. Nevertheless, art aficionados will find some fascinating work here, and the main galleries occupy Peggy Guggenheim's wonderful former home, the 18th-century "unfinished" Palazzo Venier dei Leoni, right on the Grand Canal. Guggenheim purchased the mansion in 1949 and lived here, on and off, until her death in 1979 (the history of this once-derelict palace is wonderfully brought to life in Judith Mackrell's *The Unfinished Palazzo*). Today the entire villa has been converted into galleries. Highlights include Picasso's extremely abstract *Poet* and his gentler *On the Beach*, several works by Kandinsky (*Landscape with Red Spots No. 2* and *White Cross*), Miró's expressionistic *Seated Woman II*, Klee's mystical *Magic Garden*, and some unsettling works by Max Ernst (*The Kiss*, *Attirement of the Bride*), who was briefly married to Guggenheim in the 1940s. Also look for Magritte's *Empire of Light*, Dalí's *Birth of Liquid Desires*, and a couple of gems from Pollock (who was especially championed by Guggenheim): his early *Moon Woman*, which recalls Picasso, and *Alchemy*, a more typical "poured" painting. The Italian Futurists are also well represented here, with a rare portrait from Modigliani (*Portrait of the Painter Frank Haviland*). Adjacent buildings added later to the complex (serving as temporary exhibition space, a cafe, and shop) are connected to the main building by the pleasantly shady **Nasher Sculpture Garden;** Guggenheim is buried in the corner, marked by a simple headstone. Free presentations on aspects of the collection are given daily in the museum galleries or garden (check the website for times). Guided tours can be arranged in advance and cost 95€ to 135€, for a group of up to 20 people. ***Tip:*** It's not a good idea to visit the Guggenheim and St. Mark's on the same day—it's a fairly long walk between the two. We also don't advise seeing it on the same day as the Accademia, even though they're only 10 minutes apart; the artistic overload could prove too much for even the most avid art aficionado.

Fondamenta Venier dai Leon 704. guggenheim-venice.it. ✆ **041/2405411.** Tickets (advance purchase online recommended) 16€ adults, 14€ 70 and over, 9€ students 10–26, free for children 9 and under. Audioguide 7€. Mon and Wed–Sun 10am–6pm (last entry 5pm). *Vaporetto:* Accademia (walk around left side of Accademia, take first left, and follow signs).

San Sebastiano ♥♥♥ CHURCH Lose the crowds as you make a pilgrimage to the parish church of **Paolo Veronese,** home to some of his finest work. Veronese painted the coffered nave ceiling with the florid *Scenes from the Life of St. Esther*. In the 1560s he also decorated the organ shutters and panels in the chancel with scenes from the life of St. Sebastian. Although Veronese is the main event here, don't miss Titian's sensitive *St. Nicholas* (just inside the church on the right). Veronese's sepulchral monument (with bust by Mattia Carneri) is to the left of the altar. The real highlight is the sacristy (go through the door under the organ), a tiny jewel box of a room adorned with more wonderful Veronese paintings of the *Coronation of the Virgin* and the *Four Evangelists*.

Campo San Sebastiano. chorusvenezia.org. ✆ **041/2750462.** Admission 3.50€. Mon–Sat 10:30am–5pm. *Vaporetto:* San Basilio.

Santa Maria della Salute ♥♥ CHURCH The church of the Virgin Mary of Good Health, known as "La Salute," is a jewel of baroque architecture, proudly reigning over a landmark point almost directly across from the Piazza San Marco, where the Grand Canal empties into the lagoon. The first stone was laid in 1631 after the Senate decided to honor the Virgin Mary for delivering Venice from a plague that had killed around 95,000 people. It was built from the revolutionary plans of a young, relatively unknown architect, Baldassare Longhena, who dedicated the next 50 years of his life to overseeing its progress (he would die 5 years before its completion). Today the dome of the church is an iconic presence on the Venice skyline, recognized for its exuberant exterior of volutes, scrolls, and more than 125 statues. The most revered image inside is the **Madonna della Salute,** a rare, black-faced sculpture of Mary brought back as war booty from Candia in Crete in 1670. The otherwise sober interior is enlivened by the **sacristy** (6€ entry), with a number of important ceiling paintings and portraits by **Titian.** On the right wall of the sacristy is Tintoretto's ***Marriage at Cana*** ♥♥♥, considered one of his best paintings. It's also possible to climb 150 steps up the dome (the Cupola) for 8€ (usually late Mar–Sept Thurs–Sun 10am–5pm, but check the website) for a unique panorama of the city from the south.

Campo della Salute 1. basilicasalutevenezia.it. ✆ **041/5225558.** Free admission to church; sacristy 6€; plus cupola 13€. Daily Apr–Oct 9am–noon and 3–5:30pm; Nov–Mar 9:30am–12:30pm and 3–5:30pm. **Sacristy:** Apr–Oct Tues 2–3:30pm and 4:40–5:30pm, Wed–Fri 10am–12:30pm, 2–3:30pm, and 4:40–5:30pm, Sat 10am–12:30pm and 2–5:30pm, Sun 10–10:30am and 2–5:30pm; Nov–Mar Tues–Fri 10am–noon, 3–3:30pm, and 4:40–5:30pm, Sat 10am–noon and 2–5:30pm, Sun 10–10:30am and 2–5:30pm. *Vaporetto:* Salute.

Scuola Grande dei Carmini ♥♥♥ CHURCH The former Venetian base of the Carmelites, finished in the 18th century, is now a shrine of sorts to **Giambattista Tiepolo,** who painted the ceiling of the upstairs hall between 1739 and 1744. It's a magnificent sight. Tiepolo's elaborate rococo interpretation of *Simon Stock Receiving the Scapular* is now fully restored, along with various panels throughout the building.

Campo San Margherita 2617. scuolagrandecarmini.it. ✆ **041/5289420.** Admission 10€, 7€ for 65 and above. Daily 10am–5pm. *Vaporetto:* San Basilio.

Squero di San Trovaso ♥♥ HISTORIC SITE One of the most intriguing sights in Venice is this small *squero* (boatyard), which first opened in the 17th century on the narrow Rio San Trovaso (not far from the Accademia Bridge). It is surrounded by Tyrolean-looking wooden structures (a rarity in this city of stone) that are home to the multigenerational owners and

Gondolas are built and repaired at the Squero di San Trovaso boatyard in Dorsoduro.

original workshops for traditional Venetian boats. Aware that they themselves have become a tourist sight, the gondoliers don't mind if you watch them at work from across the narrow Rio di San Trovaso, but don't try to invite yourself in.

Dorsoduro 1097 (on the Rio San Trovaso). *Vaporetto:* Zattere.

San Polo & Santa Croce

Santa Maria Gloriosa dei Frari ♥♥ CHURCH Known simply as "i Frari," this immense 14th-century Gothic basilica built by the Franciscans is the largest church in Venice after San Marco. It houses a number of important artworks, including two Titian masterpieces: the ***Assumption of the Virgin*** **♥♥** over the main altar, painted when the artist was in his late 20s, and *Virgin of the Pesaro Family* in the left nave, for which Titian's wife posed for the figure of Mary (she died soon afterward in childbirth). Don't miss Giovanni Bellini's ***Madonna & Child*** **♥♥** over the altar in the sacristy, of which novelist Henry James wrote, "It is as solemn as it is gorgeous." The grand **mausoleum of Titian** is on the right as you enter the church, opposite an incongruous pyramid-shaped 18th-century monument to sculptor **Antonio Canova**—designed by Canova himself, this was originally supposed to be Titian's tomb.

Campo dei Frari. basilicadeifrari.it. ✆ **041/2728611.** Admission 5€, 3€ ages 65 and over, 2€ students 12–29, free for children 11 and under. Audioguide 2€. Easter–Oct Mon–Fri 9am–7:30pm (last entry 7pm); Sat 9am–6pm (last entry 5:30pm); Sun 1–6pm (last entry 5:30pm); Nov–Easter Mon–Sat 9am–6pm (last entry 5:30pm), Sun 1–6pm (last entry 5:30pm). *Vaporetto:* San Tomà (walk straight on Calle del Traghetto, turn right and immediately left across Campo San Tomà; walk straight on Ramo Mandoler then Calle Larga Prima, turn right at beginning of Salizada San Rocco).

Scuola Grande di San Rocco ♥♥♥ MUSEUM Like many medieval saints, French-born San Rocco (St. Roch) died young, but thanks to his work healing the sick in the 14th century, his cult became associated with the power to cure the plague and other serious illnesses. When his body was brought to Venice in 1485, this *scuola* began to reap the benefits, and by 1560, the current complex was completed. Work soon began on more than 50 paintings by **Tintoretto,** and today the *scuola* is primarily a shrine to the masterful Venetian artist. You enter at the **Sala Terrena** (Ground Floor Hall), where the paintings were created between 1583 and 1587, led by one of the most frenzied *Annunciations* ever made. The *Flight into Egypt* here is undeniably one of Tintoretto's greatest works. Upstairs is the **Sala Superiore** (Great Upper Hall), where Old Testament scenes cover the ceiling. The paintings around the walls, based on the New Testament, are generally regarded as a master class of perspective, shadow, and color. In the **Sala dell'Albergo,** an entire wall is adorned by Tintoretto's mind-blowing *Crucifixion* (as well as his *Glorification of St. Roch,* on the ceiling, the painting that actually won him the contract to paint the *scuola*). Way up in the loft, the **Tesoro** (Treasury) is a tiny space dedicated primarily to gold reliquaries containing venerated relics such as

The ceilings and walls of the Scuola Grande di San Rocco are covered in paintings by Tintoretto, one of Venice's greatest artists.

the fingers of St. Peter and St. Andrew, and one of the thorns that crowned Christ during the crucifixion.

Campo San Rocco 3052, adjacent to Campo dei Frari. scuolagrandesanrocco.org/home-en. ✆ **041/5234864.** Admission 12€ adults, 10€ over 70, 8€ students 18–26, 3€ ages 8–18, free for children 7 and under. Audioguide 5€. Daily 9:30am–5:30pm (last entry 5pm). *Vaporetto:* San Tomà (walk straight on Calle del Traghetto, turn right and immediately left across Campo San Tomà; walk straight on Ramo Mandoler, Calle Larga Prima, and Salizada San Rocco, which leads into the *campo* of the same name—look for crimson sign behind Frari Church).

Cannaregio

Galleria Giorgio Franchetti alla Ca' d'Oro ♥♥ MUSEUM A magnificent *palazzo* overlooking the Grand Canal, the "golden house" was built between 1428 and 1430 for the noble Contarini family. Baron Giorgio Franchetti bought the place in 1894, and it now serves as an atmospheric gallery for his exceptional art collection (mostly early Renaissance Italian and Flemish). The highlight is Paduan artist Andrea Mantegna's ***St. Sebastian*** **♥♥**, displayed in its own marble side chapel. Mantegna's third and final painting of the saint, created around 1490, this painting is quite different from the other two (in Vienna and Paris); this bold, deeply pessimistic work has none of Mantegna's usual background details to detract from the saint's suffering. Don't miss the three panels from Carpaccio's *Stories of the Virgin* series on the second floor. Note that until a major restoration project is complete sometime in 2027, parts of the museum are liable to be closed.

Strada Nuova 3932. museiveneto.cultura.gov.it. ✆ **041/520-0345.** Admission 3€ during restoration, free for children 17 and under. Free audioguide available online. Tues–Sun 10am–7pm (last entry 6:30pm). *Vaporetto:* Ca' d'Oro.

Ghetto Venezia ♥♥ MUSEUM/SYNAGOGUE The various historic attractions of the old Jewish quarter are grouped together under the **Ghetto Venezia** umbrella, with tickets available online or in person at the ticket office just off the main square (Campo del Ghetto Nuovo), where there's also a small exhibition on the history of Jewish Venice. You can opt for guided or slightly cheaper self-guided tours: the latter comes with an informative online audioguide, but you'll need your smartphone and roaming service to access it. The two cover the same sites, but you'll learn a bit more with the guided option. Note that although you can see many of the Jewish sites for free from the outside, you must have a ticket to enter the synagogues and the tranquil Secret Garden of the Spanish Synagogue. Tours begin in the Campo del Ghetto Nuovo, with stops at a 15th-century well, bronze "stolpersteine" on cobblestones (commemorating victims of the Holocaust), and various monuments; the highlights are the quarter's five historic synagogues. You can currently visit the interiors of two. The **Levantine** (Scuola Levantina), founded in 1540s but rebuilt in the 17th century, is still used by the local Jewish community in winter; its main hall is a small but gorgeous space with a richly carved wooden *teva* (pulpit). The **Great Spanish Synagogue** (Scuola Spagnola) has an even more spectacular baroque interior that resembles a Venetian theater, with Dutch chandeliers, giant red curtains, and silver lamps. This was the last synagogue built here (circa 1580s), established by Sephardic Jews and still the main place of worship today. The Canton, German, and Italian synagogues are undergoing various stages of restoration that should also be

il ghetto & THE JEWS OF VENICE

Jews began settling in Venice in great numbers in the 15th century, and the Republic soon came to value their services as moneylenders, physicians, and traders. In 1516, however, fearing their growing influence, the Venetians forced the Jewish population to live on an island with an abandoned foundry (*ghetto* is old Venetian dialect for "foundry"), and drawbridges were raised to enforce a nighttime curfew.

By the end of the 17th century, as many as 5,000 Jews lived in the Ghetto's cramped confines. Napoleon tore down the Ghetto gates in 1797, but it wasn't until the unification of Italy in 1866 that Jews achieved equal status.

Il Ghetto remains the spiritual center for Venice's ever-diminishing community of Jewish families, with two working synagogues and a Chabad House; it's said that anywhere from 450 to 2,000 Jews live in all of Venice and Mestre, though very few now live in the Ghetto. Aside from its historic interest, this is also one of the less touristy neighborhoods in Venice and makes for a pleasant and scenic place to stroll.

Venice's first kosher restaurant, **Gam Gam ♥**, opened here in 1996, at 1122 Ghetto Vecchi on the canal (gamgamkosher.com; ✆ **366/2504505**), close to the Guglie *vaporetto* stop. Owned and run by Orthodox Jews, it is open Sunday to Thursday noon to 10pm, Friday noon to 2 hours before Shabbat (sunset), and Saturday from 1 hour after Shabbat until 11pm (excluding summer).

The baroque Great Spanish Synagogue, a highlight of Ghetto Venezia tours.

complete in 2027 (depending on funding)—until then you can only view their exteriors. Note that the **Jewish Museum** (Museo Ebraico di Venezia) has been closed for restoration since 2021 with no opening date announced—check the website for the latest.

Campo del Ghetto Nuovo. ghettovenezia.com. ✆ **041/715359.** Self-guided tours 12€ adults, 10€ ages 6–26 (plus 2€ if purchased online); guided tours 15€ adults, 13€ ages 6–26 (plus 2€ if purchased online); free for children 5 and under. Sites open Sun–Thurs 10am–7:30pm, Fri 9am–5pm. Tours in English hourly Sun–Thurs 10am–5pm, Fri 9am–4pm. Closed Jewish holidays. *Vaporetto:* Guglie.

Giudecca

Il Redentore ♥♥ CHURCH Perhaps the greatest masterpiece of Andrea Palladio, the great Renaissance architect from nearby Padua, Il Redentore was commissioned by Venice to give thanks for being delivered from the great plague (1575–77), which claimed over a quarter of the population (some 46,000 people). The doge established a tradition of visiting this church by crossing a long pontoon bridge made of boats from the Dorsoduro's Zattere on the third Sunday of each July, a tradition that survived the demise of the doges and remains one of Venice's most popular festivals (Festa del Redentore on third Sun in July). The interior is done in austere but elegant Palladian style. Artworks tend to be workshop pieces (from the studios or schools of Tintoretto and Veronese), but a fine *Baptism of Christ* by Veronese himself is in the sacristy (accessed through a door in the last chapel on the right).

Campo del Redentore. ✆ **041/275-0462.** Admission 3.50€. Mon–Sat 10:30am–5pm. *Vaporetto:* Redentore.

San Giorgio Maggiore

Sitting on the little island of San Giorgio Maggiore across from Piazza San Marco are a handful of intriguing sights, not least its namesake church, another Palladio masterpiece. Next door to the church and designed by Selldorf Architects, the stylish **Stanze del Vetro** (lestanzedel vetro.org; usually free) hosts traveling exhibitions dedicated to the art of glassmaking (it's usually closed between shows, so check the website for the latest). At the nearby **Fondazione Giorgio Cini** (visitcini.com; from 15€), you can tour the galleries of the old San Giorgio Monastery, plus the foundation's Borges Labyrinth, its 10 "Vatican Chapels," and the 1950s Teatro Verde.

San Giorgio Maggiore ♥♥ CHURCH Palladio designed this magnificent church in 1565 and it was completed in 1610. To impose a classical front on the traditional church structure, Palladio designed two interlocking facades, with repeating triangles, rectangles, and columns harmoniously proportioned. The main altar is flanked by two epic paintings by Tintoretto, *The Fall of Manna,* to the left, and the more noteworthy ***The Last Supper*** **♥♥** to the right, famous for its chiaroscuro. Accessed by free guided tour only (usually Apr–Oct; reservations essential at visite@abbaziasangiorgio.it), the adjacent **Cappella dei Morti** (Chapel of the Dead) contains Tintoretto's *Deposition*, and the **Coro Notturno** (upper chapel) contains Carpaccio's *St. George Killing the Dragon*. To the left of the choir is an elevator that you can take to the top of the 1791 campanile—for a charge of 8€, cash only—to experience an unforgettable view of the island, the lagoon, and the Palazzo Ducale and Piazza San Marco across the way.

San Giorgio Maggiore. ✆ **041/5227827.** Free admission. Daily Apr–Oct 9am–7pm; Nov–Mar 8:30am–6pm. *Vaporetto:* Take Giudecca-bound *vaporetto* no. 2 on Riva degli Schiavoni (San Marco/San Zaccaria) and get off at first stop, San Giorgio Maggiore.

Exploring Venice's Islands

Venice shares its lagoon with four other principal islands: **Murano, Burano, Torcello,** and the **Lido.** Guided tours of the first three are available (30€–45€ for 3–4 hr.), but while these can be informative, unless you are very short of time you'll enjoy exploring the islands in far more leisurely fashion on your own, easily done using the *vaporetti.* Line nos. 4.1 and 4.2 make the journey to **Murano** from Fondamente Nove (north side of Castello). For **Murano, Burano,** and **Torcello,** Line no. 12 departs Fondamente Nove every 30 minutes; for Torcello, change to the Line 9 shuttle boat from Burano, timed to match arrivals from Venice (it zips between the two islands every 15 min. or so). The islands are small and easy to navigate, but check the schedule for island-to-island departures and plan your return so that you don't spend most of your day waiting for connections.

Vaporetto line nos. 1, 2, 5.1, 5.2, and LN cross the lagoon to the **Lido** from the San Zaccaria–Danieli stop near San Marco. Note that the Lido becomes chilly, windswept, and utterly deserted October to April.

MURANO ♥♥

The island of Murano has long been famous throughout the world for the products of its glass factories. The illuminating **Museo del Vetro ♥♥** (Museum of Glass), Fondamenta Giustinian 8 (museovetro.visitmuve.it; ✆ **041/739586**), charts the history of the island's glassmaking and is definitely worthwhile if you intend to purchase a lot of glassware, providing plenty of background so you know what you're buying in the stores outside. It's normally open daily 10am to 5pm (to 6pm Apr–Oct); admission is 15€ adults, 7.50€ ages 6 to 14 and students 25 and under; it's also included in the Museum Pass (p. 418).

Dozens of *fornaci* (kilns) offer free (or cheap) shows of mouth-blown glassmaking, almost invariably hitched to a hard-sell tour of the factory outlet store. Once you're on the island, you can't miss these places; they're pretty much of equal quality. A dependable choice is **Original Murano Glass ♥♥** (Feb–Oct normally daily 9:30am–4:30pm; reserve 5€ tours and demonstrations at visitmuranoglassfactory.com), at the Ellegi Glass *fornaci,* Fondamenta San Giovanni dei Battuti 4, a few minutes' walk from the Murano Faro *vaporetti* stop. Almost all shops will ship their goods, although that often doubles the price. On the other hand, these pieces are instant heirlooms.

Murano is also graced with two worthy churches: the largely 15th-century **San Pietro Martire ♥♥** (free admission, 3€ museum and sacristy; Mon–Fri 9am–5pm [until 3:30pm Tues], Sat–Sun 11am–4:30pm), with paintings by Veronese and Giovanni Bellini, and the ancient **Santi Maria e Donato ♥♥** (3.50€; Mon–Sat 9am–5pm, Sun noon–5pm), with its intricate Byzantine exterior apse, 6th-century pulpit, stunning mosaic of Mary, and fantastic 12th-century inlaid floor. Look out also for the "dragon bones" hanging behind the altar—legend has it that the dragon was killed by St. Donatus of Euroea in the 4th century (the bones are actually thought be the ribs of a prehistoric mammal).

BURANO ♥♥♥

Lace is the claim to fame of tiny, historic Burano, a craft kept alive for centuries by the wives of fishermen waiting for their husbands to return from the sea. Sadly, most of the lace sold on the island these days is made by machine elsewhere. The local government continues its attempt to keep Burano's centuries-old lace legacy alive with subsidized classes. It's still worth a trip to stroll the back streets of the island, whose canals are lined with the brightly colored, simple homes of the Buranesi fishermen—quite unlike anything in Venice or Murano. **Butter biscuits,** known as *buranelli,* are another famous island product—expect to be offered them in almost every store. While you're here, visit the **Museo del Merletto** (Museum of Lace Making), Piazza Galuppi 187 (museomerletto.visitmuve.it; ✆ **041/730034**), to understand why something so exquisite should not be allowed to fade into extinction. It's open Tuesday to Sunday

Lacemakers ply their increasingly rare craft on the island of Burano.

10am to 5pm (Nov–Mar to 4pm); admission is 7€ adults, 3.50€ ages 6 to 14 and students 25 and under; it's included in the Museum Pass (p. 418).

TORCELLO ♥♥

Torcello is perhaps the most charming of the islands, though today it consists of little more than one long canal leading from the *vaporetto* landing to a clump of buildings at its center (a 10-min. walk). Hard to imagine this was once a thriving city in its own right, with at least 20,000 inhabitants in the 16th century. Torcello boasts the oldest Venetian monument, the **Basilica di Santa Maria dell'Assunta ♥♥♥**, whose foundation dates from the 7th century (✆ **041/2702464**). It's famous for its spectacular 11th- to 12th-century Byzantine mosaics—a *Madonna and Child* in the apse and a monumental *Last Judgment* on the west wall—rivaling those of Ravenna's and St. Mark's basilicas. Note that taking photos inside is forbidden. The cathedral is open daily 10:30am to 6pm (Nov–Feb to 5pm), and admission is 5€ (audioguide 2€). The bell tower, which is separate and closes 15 to 30 minutes earlier than the Basilica, is 5€, or 9€ combined with the Basilica, but is easily skipped. Of more interest is the adjacent 11th-century **Santa Fosca** (free admission; no photos; closes 30 min. before Basilica), a Byzantine brick chapel with a plain interior, and the **Museo di Torcello** (✆ **041/730761;** 3€; Tues–Sun 10:30am–5:30pm, Nov–Feb 10am–5pm), showcasing archaeological artifacts from the Iron Age to the medieval era, many found on the island. Buy tickets at the basilica entrance (all three attractions 12€).

Peaceful Torcello is now uninhabited except for a handful of families and is a favorite picnic spot. You'll have to bring the food from Venice—there are no stores on the island and only a handful of bars/trattorias along the canal plus one fabulous destination restaurant, the **Locanda Cipriani** ♥♥ (locandacipriani.com; ✆ **041/730150**), of Hemingway fame; Queen Elizabeth II, Winston Churchill, and Princess Diana all dined here too. Opened in 1935 by Giuseppe Cipriani (it's still owned by the family), this spot is definitely worth a splurge (reservations recommended). It reopened in 2026 after a major renovation (check website for opening times). Once the tour groups have left, the island offers a very special moment of solitude and escape.

THE LIDO

Although a convenient 15-minute *vaporetto* ride away from San Marco (see transport details p. 429), Venice's **Lido beaches** are not much to write home about and certainly no longer a chic destination (the Grand Hotel des Bains depicted in Thomas Mann's *Death in Venice* closed in 2010). For swimming and sunbathing there are much better beaches nearby—in **Jesolo,** to the north, for example. But the parade of wealthy Italian and foreign tourists and Venetian families who still frequent the Lido is an interesting sight indeed—in summer it feels more like the south of France than Venice.

The Lido has two main beach areas. **Blue Moon** (Piazzale Bucintoro) is at the opposite end of Gran Viale Santa Maria Elisabetta (the main drag, referred to as the Gran Viale) from the *vaporetto* station Santa Elisabetta. It's a 10-minute stroll; walk straight ahead along Gran Viale to reach the beach (Gran Viale is lined with seafood restaurants and bars). **San Nicolò,** about 1.5km (1 mile) north, can be reached by bus B from Santa Elisabetta. The beaches tend to get narrower to the south, though **Alberoni** at the southern tip is a wilder, less developed stretch backed by dunes. At the main beach areas, loungers and parasols can be rented for 10€ to 20€ per person (per day) depending on the time of year (it's just 1€ to use the public showers and bathrooms). Keep in mind that if you stay at any of the hotels on the Lido, most have some kind of agreement with the different *bagni* (private beach establishments). Also note that the restored **Ancient Jewish Cemetery** (Antico Cimitero Ebraico) on the Lido (established in 1386) is open to the public but best appreciated on a tour from the **Ghetto Venezia** (p. 427).

The Film Festival

The **Venice International Film Festival** ♥♥♥, in late August and early September, is the most respected celebration of celluloid in Europe after Cannes. Films from all over the world are shown primarily in the **Palazzo del Cinema** and **Palazzo del Casinò** on the Lido. Ticket prices vary, but those for the less-sought-after films are usually modest. For details visit **labiennale.org/en/cinema**.

carnevale A VENEZIA

Carnevale traditionally was the celebration preceding Lent, the period of penitence and abstinence prior to Easter; its name is derived from the Latin *carnem levare,* meaning "to take meat away." In Venice, the heyday of Carnevale was the 18th century; it was outlawed in 1797 and only revived in 1979 to boost winter tourism.

Today Carnevale in Venice builds for a whole month until the big blowout, Shrove Tuesday, when fireworks illuminate the Grand Canal, and Piazza San Marco becomes a giant open-air ballroom for the masses. The festival is a harlequin patchwork of cultural events, many free of charge, appealing to all ages, tastes, nationalities, and budgets. Musical events from reggae and zydeco to jazz and baroque are staged in dozens of *piazze.*

Book your hotel months ahead, especially for the 2 weekends prior to Shrove Tuesday. Check **carnevale.venezia.it/en** for details.

Organized Tours

Because of the sheer number of sights to see in Venice, some first-time visitors like to start out with an organized tour. Although few things can really be covered in any depth on these overview tours, they're somewhat useful for getting your bearings. **Avventure Bellissime** (tours-italy.com; ✆ **041/970499**) coordinates a plethora of tours (in English), by boat and gondola, though the walking tours are the best value, covering all the main sights around Piazza San Marco in 2 hours from 60€.

For those with more energy, learn to "row like a Venetian" (yes, standing up) at **Row Venice** (rowvenice.org; ✆ **347/7250637**), where 80-minute lessons take place in traditional, hand-built "shrimp-tail" or *batele coda di gambero* boats for 100€ for up to two people. Or you could abandon tradition altogether and opt for a **Venice Kayak** tour (venice kayak.com; ✆ **346/4771327**), a truly enchanting way to see the city from the water. The company offers 2½-hour day and night tours from April to early November (110€–140€). **SUP in Venice** (supinvenice.com; ✆ **389/9851866**) offers guided SUP ("stand-up paddleboard") tours in Venice (Apr–Oct), with 1-hour, 40-minute sessions starting at 70€.

Especially for Kids

It goes without saying that a **gondola ride** (p. 408) will be the thrill of a lifetime for any child (or adult). If that's too expensive, consider the far cheaper alternative: a **ride on the no. 1 *vaporetto*** (p. 403).

Judging from the squeals of delight, **feeding the pigeons in Piazza San Marco** could be the high point of your child's visit to Venice, and it's the ultimate photo op. Purchase a bag of corn and you'll be draped in fluttering and flapping pigeons in a nanosecond.

A jaunt to the neighboring **island of Murano** (p. 430) can be as educational as it is recreational—follow the signs to any *fornace* (kiln), where a glassblowing performance of the island's thousand-year-old art is free (or cheap) entertainment. But be ready for the sales pitch that follows.

Take the elevator to the **top of the Campanile di San Marco** (p. 414) for a scintillating view of Venice's rooftops and cupolas, or get up close and personal with the four bronze horses on the facade of the **Basilica di San Marco** (p. 410). The view from its outdoor loggia is something you and your children won't forget. Scaling the **Torre dell'Orologio** (p. 417) or the bell tower at **San Giorgio Maggiore** (p. 429) is also lots of fun.

The **winged lion,** said to have been a kind of good-luck mascot to St. Mark, patron saint of Venice, was the very symbol of the Serene Republic and to this day appears on everything from cafe napkins to T-shirts. Keep a running tab of who can spot the most flying lions—you'll find them on facades, atop columns, over doorways, as pavement mosaics, on government stamps, and on the local flag.

9

WHERE TO STAY IN VENICE

Few cities boast as long a high season as Venice, which begins with the Easter period—for most hotels it runs mid-March through November, includes weekends year-round, Christmas and New Year, and Carnevale. This leaves the few weeks between late November and mid-December, January, and the week or so after Carnevale in early March to capture low season rates. May, June, and September are the best months weather-wise, and therefore normally the most crowded. July and August are hot (few of the one- and two-star hotels offer air-conditioning; when they do, it usually costs extra). Hotels are normally more expensive here than in any other Italian city, with no apparent upgrade in amenities. The least special of those below are clean and functional; at best, they're charming and thoroughly enjoyable, with the serenade of a passing gondolier thrown in for good measure. Some may even be your best stay in all of Europe. You'll need to reserve lodging as far in advance as possible, even in the off-season.

Apartments & Room Rentals

Anyone looking to get into the local swing of things in Venice should opt for a short-term **rental apartment.** For the same price or less than a hotel room, you could have your own one-bedroom apartment with a washing machine, air-conditioning, and a fridge to keep your prosecco cold. That said, like many cities in Italy, Venice has been cracking down on short-term rentals in recent years to limit overtourism and housing shortages for locals (see Milan [p. 489] and Rome [p. 137]). The situation may change in the future, but for now, rentals are still available on sites like Airbnb.

In terms of **location,** San Marco is the most convenient part of the city, though anywhere near the Grand Canal will give you easy access to the best of Venice. Apartments in the farther reaches of Santa Croce, Cannaregio, Giudecca, and Castello may be slightly cheaper and allow a glimpse of residential life in the city, but getting to and from the main sights will take a lot of time.

For those renting apartments rather than staying in hotels, secure **luggage storage facilities** are available through Radical Storage from 5€ per day (radicalstorage.com). Radical Storage coordinates a network of various businesses throughout Venice prepared to look after your bags—check for the most convenient option on the website.

RECOMMENDED AGENCIES Until the rules change, **Airbnb** (airbnb.com) and **Vrbo.com** are still the major players in Venice, each with hundreds of properties listed. On Airbnb you can rent a room in someone's home from just 75€ per night. **Couchsurfing** (couchsurfing.com) is also popular and generally safe in Venice, though take the usual precautions (for those who don't know the company, it allows locals to offer free rooms to travelers). Established by a local, **Views on Venice** (viewsonvenice.com; ✆ **041/2411149**) specializes in luxury apartments in prime locations, ranging from 150€ to whole mansions for over 1,000€ a night.

It's standard practice for agencies to collect 40% to 50% of the total rental amount upfront to secure a booking (if your booking is less than 30 days ahead, you'll usually pay in full). The balance of your rental fee is normally payable when you check in, plus a cleaning fee and a refundable security deposit. Airbnb apartments usually take full payment a month before arrival, but at least a portion of this will be refundable if you cancel. Upon booking, the agency should provide you with detailed check-in procedures. Most apartments provide a list of nearby shops and services; beyond that, you're on your own, which is what makes an apartment stay a great way to do as the Venetians do.

San Marco

EXPENSIVE

B&B Bloom Settimo Cielo ♥♥♥ Right in the heart of San Marco, just off one of its most interesting squares, this boutique hotel is a romantic hideaway blending classical Venetian style and modern design. Each room is uniquely decorated in lavish color schemes that range from crimson to purple and includes exposed brick, baroque wallpaper, and lots of silky curtains—look at rooms carefully online if you have a preference. All are air-conditioned and feature a minibar and TV. The best feature is the rooftop terrace, with sensational city views, and the adjacent reading room. You may want to consider a first-floor room because there's no elevator.

Campo Santo Stefano 3470. bloom-settimocielo.com. ✆ **340/1498872.** 6 units. 142€–305€ double. Rates include breakfast. *Vaporetto:* Sant'Angelo (walk to tall brick building and go around it, turn right into Ramo Narisi; at small bridge turn left and follow Calle del Pestrin to Campiello Novo on your right—the hotel is opposite the church of Santo Stefano). **Amenities:** Concierge; room service (limited hours); free Wi-Fi.

Corte di Gabriela ♥♥♥ This gorgeous boutique hotel, just a short walk from Piazza San Marco, combines classical Venetian ceiling murals,

RESTAURANTS
Ai Mercanti 38
Al Covo 36
Alle Corone 28
Antico Forno 21
Bacareto da Lele 12
Bistrot de Venise 37
Cantina Arnaldi 10
Dal Moro's 29
Dama 17
Do Mori 23
Do Spade 22
Gam Gam 17
Gritti Terrace 40
Il Doge 8
La Bottiglia 14
La Mela Verde 39
La Palanca 2
Local 34
Locanda Montin 5
Osteria Alle Testiere 30
Osteria Al Squero 4
Osteria Enoteca Ai Artisti 6
Osteria La Zucca 19
Rosticceria Gislon 27
Wistèria 9
Zanze XVI 15
SANTA CROCE
SAN POLO
DORSODURO
Canàl Grande
Parco Savorgnàn
Campo S. Geremia
S. Geremia
Calle Priuli dei Cavaletti
Rio Terà Lista di Spagna
Riva da Biásio
Palazzo Giovanelli
Fond. d. Turchi
Ca' Tron
S. Stae
Ca' Pesaro
Stazione Venezia–Santa Lucia
S. Maria di Nazareth
Palazzo Donà-Balbi
S. Zan Degolà
Calle d. Tintòr
Pal. Mocenigo
S. Simeòn Piccolo
Palazzo Gradenigo
S. Simeòn Grande
Campo N. Sàuro
S. Giacomo dell'Orio
Campo S. Giacomo dell'Orio
S. Maria Màter Domini
Rio d. S. Cassiano
S. Cassian
Ferrovia
Ponte della Constituzione
Palazzo Soranzo-Cappello
Fond. Rio Marin
Pal. Zane
Pal. Grioni
Calle d. Chiesa
Giardini Papadopoli
Rio di S. Agostino
Scuola Grande di S. Giovanni
Pal. Zane Collalto
Pal. Muti Baglioni
Palazzo Albrizzi
Pal. Molin-Cappello
Pal. Molin
S. Giovanni Evangelista
Pal. Donà d. Rose
Rio di S. Polo
S. Nicolò di Tolentino
Palazzo Marcello
Ex Convento dei Frari
Palazzo Zen
Pal. Corner
Campo S. Polo
Pal. Soranzo
San Polo
S. Rocco
Frari
Campo d. Frari
Rio di San Polo
Scuola Grande di San Rocco
Pal. Papadopoli
Palazzo Centani (Museo Goldoni)
Pal. Dona
Pal. Layard
Pal. Grimani
Palazzo Barbarigo
S. Pantalòn
Rio d. Frescada
S. Tomà
S. Ángelo
Pal. Civràn-Grimani
Rio Ca' Foscari
Calle Foscari
Pal. Balbi
Pal. Cornèr Spinelli
Pal. Fortuny
Campo Santa Margherita
Ca' Foscari
Palazzo Mocenigo
Pal. Contarini d. Figure
Rio di S. Ángelo
Oratorio dell' Annunciata
Campo S. Ángelo
Palazzo Moro-Lin
Pal. Grassi
Saliz S. Samuele
Pal. Nani
Ca' Rezzonico
S. Samuele
San Samuele
S. Stefano
Campo S. Barnaba
S. Bárnaba
Ca' Rezzonico
Palazzo Malipiero
Campo S. Stefano
S. Maurìzio
Rio Malpaga
Pal. Stern
Ca' del Duca
Rio del Duca
C. Vetturi
Rio di S. Vidal
Pal. Morosini
Rio d. Santissimo
S. Maria d. Giglio
Pal. Loredan
Pal. Falier
Pal. Contarini degli Scrigni
Pal. Bàrbaro
Pal. Pisani
Palazzo Cornèr d. Ca' Granda
Accademia
Ponte dell'Accademia
Gallerie dell' Accademia
Palazzo Contarini dal Zaffo
S. Trovaso
Rio di S. Trovaso
Pal. Molin
Pal. Giustiniàn
Pal. Nani
Pal. Centani
Pal. Venièr dei Leoni (Guggenheim)
S. Maria d. Visitaz.
S. Agnese
Rio di S. Vio
Fond. Bragadin
Gesuati
Zàttere

Venice Hotels & Restaurants

HOTELS

Al Piave **31**
Al Ponte Antico **26**
Al Ponte Mocenigo **20**
American Dinesen **3**
Antiche Figure **16**
Arcadia **18**
B&B Bloom Settimo Cielo **42**
B&B San Marco **33**
Ca' San Rocco **13**
Casa Verardo **32**
Combo Venezia **25**
Corte Di Gabriela **41**
Generator Venice **1**
Locando Fiorita **43**
Metropole **35**
Moresco **11**
Pensione Accademia **7**
Pensione Guerrato **24**

Locando Fiorita's guest rooms make up in charm for what they lack in space.

marble pillars, and exposed brick with designer furniture and appliances (including free use of iPads, strong Wi-Fi, and satellite TV). The fully renovated property dates from 1870, once serving as the home and offices of Venetian lawyers. Breakfast is one of the highlights and well worth lingering over: fresh pastries made by the owners the night before, decent espresso, and crepes and omelets cooked on request.

Calle degli Avvocati 3836. cortedigabriela.com. ✆ **041/5235077.** 10 units. 220€–415€ double. Rates include breakfast. *Vaporetto:* Sant'Angelo. **Amenities:** Bar; babysitting; concierge; room service (limited hours); free Wi-Fi.

MODERATE

Locando Fiorita ♥♥♥ It's hard to imagine a more picturesque location for this little hotel, a charming, quiet *campiello* draped in vines and blossoms—no wonder it's a favorite of professional photographers. Most of the standard rooms are small (bathrooms are tiny), but all are furnished in an elegant 18th-century style, with wooden floors, shuttered windows, and richly patterned fittings (air-conditioning and satellite TV included). The helpful staff more than make up for any deficiencies, and breakfast is a real pleasure, especially when taken outside on the *campiello.*

Campiello Novo 3457a. locandafiorita.com. ✆ **041/5234754.** 10 units. 135€–250€ double. Rates include breakfast. *Vaporetto:* Sant'Angelo (walk to tall brick building and go around it, turn right into Ramo Narisi; at small bridge turn left and follow Calle del Pestrin to Campiello Novo on your right). **Amenities:** Babysitting; concierge; room service; free Wi-Fi.

Castello

EXPENSIVE

Metropole ♥♥ This behemoth with a waterfront location is part luxury hotel, part eclectic art museum, with antiques, Asian artworks, and tapestries dotted throughout. But this is no dusty grand dame; on the contrary, it's a chic boutique hotel with rooms opulently furnished in white, red, and gold color schemes. It began life in the Middle Ages as the Ospedale della Pietà, a charitable institution for orphans and abandoned girls, and later became a music school, where Vivaldi taught violin in the early 1700s. After it was converted into a hotel in 1895, Sigmund Freud was an early guest, along with Thomas Mann, who allegedly wrote parts of *Death in Venice* here. Note that it often closes in January for annual refurbishment.

Riva degli Schiavoni 4149. hotelmetropole.com. ✆ **041/5205044.** 67 units. 410€–630€ double. Rates include breakfast. *Vaporetto:* San Zaccaria (walk along Riva degli Schiavoni to right; hotel is next to La Pietà church). **Amenities:** Restaurant; bar; babysitting; concierge; room service; spa; free Wi-Fi.

MODERATE

Al Piave ♥♥ At this cozy, old-fashioned family-run hotel just 5 minutes from Piazza San Marco, rooms are simply but attractively furnished with richly woven rugs, marble floors, and some of the original wood beams exposed (some come with a terrace). Family suites are a good value for groups. Bathrooms are relatively big, and the air-conditioning is a welcome bonus in the summer. Ask for a room on a lower floor if climbing stairs is an issue; there's no elevator, and the hotel is four stories tall. Outside peak months (May, July, Sept), Piave offers exceptionally good value, given its proximity to the *piazza.* This is the only certified gluten-free hotel in Venice (breakfast comprises a decent range of gluten-free items).

Ruga Giuffa 4838. hotelalpiave.com. ✆ **041/5285174.** 20 units. 140€–370€ double. Rates include breakfast. Closed Jan 7–Carnevale. *Vaporetto:* San Zaccaria (find Calle delle Rasse beyond Palazzo Daniele; walk to end of street; turn left and then immediately right; continue to Ponte Storto, cross and continue to Ruga Giuffa—hotel is on left). **Amenities:** Babysitting; concierge; free Wi-Fi.

Casa Verardo ♥♥ Tucked away across a small bridge in the warren of central Castello, this enchanting property occupies a 16th-century *palazzo,* converted to a hotel in 1911. Rooms sport an old-fashioned Venetian style, with Florentine furniture, hand-painted beds, and colorful textiles (antiques and paintings are scattered throughout), but updated with air-conditioning and satellite TV. Some rooms have a view over a canal, others over the shady courtyard and the city.

Calle Drio La Chiesa 4765. casaverardo.it. ✆ **041/5286138.** 25 units. 140€–295€ double. Rates include breakfast. *Vaporetto:* San Zaccaria (walk straight on Calle delle Rasse to Campo SS. Filippo e Giacomo; cross *campo* to Calle della Sacrestia, then Calle Drio La Chiesa to Ponte Storto; look for hotel on left). **Amenities:** Bar; babysitting; concierge; room service; free Wi-Fi.

INEXPENSIVE

B&B San Marco ♥♥♥ With just three double rooms, this exquisite B&B in a peaceful residential neighborhood fills up fast, so book ahead. It's a comfortable, charming, yet convenient option, not too far from the main sights. Your hosts are the bubbly Marco and Alice Scurati, who live upstairs and are happy to provide help and advice. Rooms overlook the Scuola di San Giorgio degli Schiavoni and offer wonderful views of the canal. Two rooms share a bathroom; the third has private facilities. Breakfast is self-service in the shared kitchen, offering yogurts, pastries, espresso, cappuccino, juice, and tea. It's on the "third floor" (aka the fourth floor), with no elevator, so you'll need to carry your bags up.

Fondamenta San Giorgio dei Schiavoni 3385. realvenice.it. ✆ **041/5227589.** 3 units. 80€–140€ double (3-night min. stay). Rates include breakfast. Closed Aug and Jan 7 through Carnevale. *Vaporetto:* San Zaccaria (walk on Calle delle Rasse to Campo SS. Filippo e Giacomo; cross *campo* to Calle della Sacrestia, cross canal; turn left at Campo S Provolo on Fondamenta Osmarin; turn left at canal's end, walk to bridge that connects to Calle Lion; at street's end turn left along canal onto Fondamenta San Giorgio dei Schiavoni). **Amenities:** Babysitting; free Wi-Fi.

Dorsoduro

EXPENSIVE

American Dinesen ♥♥♥ Overlooking the San Vio Canal close to the Accademia, this 17th-century Venetian town house offers elegant rooms decorated in a classical Venetian style. All the "superior canal" rooms have picture-perfect vistas of the San Vio, many with a balcony (check if this is important to you), and even partial views of the Grand Canal. Cheaper, modern "dependence rooms" are in the annex next door and do not include breakfast.

San Vio 628 (on Fondamenta Bragadin). hotelamerican.it. ✆ **041/5204733.** 30 units. 180€–500€ double. Some rates include breakfast. *Vaporetto:* Accademia (veer left around Accademia, take first left turn, go straight to cross first small footbridge; turn right along Fondamenta Bragadin; hotel is on left). **Amenities:** Bar; babysitting; concierge; room service; free Wi-Fi.

Moresco ♥♥♥ An incredibly attentive staff, a decadent breakfast that includes prosecco (to mix with orange juice, ahem), and lavish 19th-century Venetian decor make this a popular choice away from the tourist hubbub. Rooms seamlessly blend Venetian style with modern design. Some have a terrace (with canal or garden views), while others have spa bathtubs. If the weather cooperates, take breakfast in the courtyard garden to really soak up the ambience. The hotel is a 5- to 10-minute walk from Piazzale Roma and the train station, but you'll have a number of bridges and stairs to negotiate along the way.

Fondamenta del Rio Novo 3499, Dorsoduro. hotelmorescovenice.com. ✆ **041/2440202.** 23 units. 165€–475€ double. Rates include breakfast. *Vaporetto:* Ferrovia/Piazzale Roma (from train station, walk southwest along Fondamenta Santa Lucia, cross Ponte della Costituzione, and turn left onto Fondamenta Santa Chiara; cross Ponte Santa Chiara and turn right onto Fondamenta Papadopoli; continue across Campiello Lavadori and then along Fondamenta del Rio Novo). **Amenities:** Bar; concierge; room service; free Wi-Fi.

Guests hang out in the relaxed lounge of the Pensione Accademia, a longtime favorite with many repeat visitors.

MODERATE

Pensione Accademia ♥♥♥ This spellbinding hotel with a tranquil, blossom-filled garden has a fascinating history. The Gothic-style Villa Maravege was built in the 17th century as a residence but served as the Russian Embassy between World Wars I and II before becoming a hotel in 1950. If that's not enticing enough, rooms are outfitted with Venetian-style antique reproductions, handsome tapestries, and air-conditioning, with views over the Rio San Trovaso or the garden. Breakfast is served in your room, in the dining hall, or on the patio.

Fondamenta Bollani 1058. pensioneaccademia.it. ✆ **041/5210188.** 27 units. 140€–305€ double. Rates include breakfast. *Vaporetto:* Accademia (turn right down Calle Gambara, which becomes Calle Corfu, which ends at a side canal; walk left over bridge, then turn right back toward Grand Canal to the hotel). **Amenities:** Bar; babysitting; concierge; room service; free Wi-Fi.

San Polo

MODERATE

Ca' San Rocco ♥♥♥ Off the Grand Canal but in the heart of the city, this elegant B&B is a short walk to just about anywhere in central Venice. It's another restored 18th-century property with a delightful summer terrace, lush gardens, and relatively spacious rooms (doubles or triples) decorated simply in shades of blue or red with old-fashioned wrought-iron beds (air-conditioning and satellite TV included). Ask for a room on a lower floor if climbing stairs is an issue; there's no elevator.

Ramo Cimesin 3078. casanrocco.it. ✆ **041/716744.** 6 units. 120€–255€ double (3-night min. stay in high season). Rates include breakfast. *Vaporetto:* Piazzale Roma (walk east across Ponte di Papadopoli, keep walking straight across Papadopoli Gardens and over another small bridge, Ponte dei Tolentini; turn left and walk along Calle Amai until you reach the Ramo Cimesin junction; turn right along Cimesin and ring bell at the fourth gate on left). **Amenities:** Room service; free Wi-Fi.

Pensione Guerrato ♥♥♥ Dating, incredibly, from 1227, this is definitely one of the city's most historic places to stay. The building's long history—it was once the "Inn of the Monkey," run by nuns, with the original structure mostly destroyed by fire in 1513—is worth delving into (the owners have all the details). Rooms are simply but classically furnished, with wood floors, exposed beams, air-conditioning, and private baths—many with original frescoes that may date from the medieval inn. Note that the cheapest rooms have shared bathrooms, and you may want to ask for a first-floor room since there's no elevator (and seven floors).

Calle Drio La Scimia 240a (near Rialto Market). hotelguerrato.com. ✆ **041/5227131.** 20 units. 95€–255€ double. Rates include breakfast. Closed Dec 22–26 and Jan 8 to early Feb. *Vaporetto:* Rialto (from north side of Ponte Rialto, walk through market to corner with UniCredit Banca; go 1 short block and turn right on Calle Drio La Scimia). **Amenities:** Babysitting; concierge; free Wi-Fi.

9

VENICE | Where to Stay in Venice

Santa Croce

EXPENSIVE

Al Ponte Mocenigo ♥♥♥ This gem of a hotel shows it is possible to live that Golden Age Venetian fantasy without breaking the bank (in the low season rates are practically a bargain for what you get). The especially spacious rooms are pure 18th-century Venice, with big beds, Murano glass chandeliers, and varnished furniture in pastel greens, creams, and golds. Traditional ceiling beams (in the second-floor rooms) and original Venetian wood and stone floors complete the effect. Breakfasts—served in an enchanting interior courtyard when weather allows—are substantial, with bacon, scrambled eggs, and sausage in addition to all the usual cheeses, fruits, and cold cuts. Another huge plus: It's steps away from the Stan Stae *vaporetto* stop, meaning easy transfers to/from the airport and elsewhere along the Grand Canal. Advance reservations highly recommended.

Fondamenta Mocenigo 2063. alpontemocenigo.com. ✆ **041/5244797.** 10 units. 210€–500€ double. Rates include breakfast. *Vaporetto:* San Stae. **Amenities:** Bar; babysitting; 24-hr. concierge; free Wi-Fi.

Antiche Figure ♥♥♥ The most convenient luxury hotel in Venice lies directly across the Grand Canal from the train station, a captivating 15th-century *palazzo* adjacent to an ancient gondola workshop. History aside, this is a very plush choice, its rooms decorated in neoclassical Venetian style with gold leaf, antique furniture, red carpets, silk tapestries, and Murano glass and chandeliers, but also LCD satellite TVs and decent Wi-Fi. There is an elevator, just in case you were wondering.

Fondamenta San Simeone Piccolo 687. hotelantichefigure.it. ✆ **041/2759486.** 22 units. 160€–415€ double. Rates include breakfast. *Vaporetto:* Ferrovia (from train station, cross Scalzi Bridge on left and take a right). **Amenities:** Bar; babysitting; concierge; room service; free Wi-Fi.

Cannaregio

EXPENSIVE

Al Ponte Antico ♥♥♥ Yes it's expensive, but this is one of the most exclusive hotels in Venice, steps from the Rialto Bridge, with a private wharf on the Grand Canal. To indulge your James Bond fantasy, look no further. Part of the attraction is its relatively small size; with just seven rooms, it feels far more intimate than most hotels in this price range, and service is always superior. Rococo wallpaper, rare tapestries, elegant beds, and Louis XV–style furnishings make this place seem like Versailles on the water. The building was originally a 16th-century *palazzo;* one of the many highlights is the charming balcony where breakfast is served, and where Bellinis are offered in the evenings.

Calle dell'Aseo 5768. alponteantico.com. ✆ **041/2411944.** 7 units. 270€–660€ double. Rates include breakfast. *Vaporetto:* Rialto (walk up Calle Large Mazzini, take second left to cross Campo San Bartolomeo; walk north on Salizada S.G. Grisostomo to Calle dell'Aseo on left). **Amenities:** Bar; concierge; room service; free Wi-Fi.

MODERATE

Arcadia ♥♥♥ This sensational boutique hotel set in a 17th-century *palazzo* has an appealing blend of old and new: The theme is Byzantium East-meets-West, a mix of Venetian and Asian style, but rooms are full of cool modern touches: rainfall showers, air-conditioning, flatscreen TVs, bathrobes, and posh toiletries, with a lobby crowned with a Murano glass chandelier. It's a 5-minute walk from the train station.

Rio Terà San Leonardo 1333. hotelarcadia.net. ✆ **041/717355.** 17 units. 140€–425€ double. Rates include breakfast. *Vaporetto:* Guglie (turn left into Rio Terà San Leonardo; Arcadia is 30m [98 ft.] on left). **Amenities:** Bar; concierge; room service; free Wi-Fi.

The charming breakfast room at the intimate, exclusive Al Ponte Antico.

INEXPENSIVE

Combo Venezia ♥♥♥ This excellent hostel is tucked away at the northern end of Cannaregio in the restored Ex Convento dei Crociferi. It's a quiet spot a little out the way, but only a 10- to 15-minute stroll from the Rialto and the Grand Canal. The elegant, cloistered courtyard is a tranquil place to hang out, while the on-site bar-restaurant usually offers good deals (especially on *cicchetti*). When it comes to the rooms, it's more like a budget boutique hotel than a traditional hostel. All of the rooms (singles, twins, doubles, and loft studios) have individual beds and an en-suite bathroom with shower, while some also have their own kitchenettes. Dorms are mixed or female-only, from 55€ per night in summer.

Campo dei Gesuiti 4878. thisiscombo.com/it/citta/venezia. ✆ **041/5286103.** 255 beds. 88€–145€ double. Rates include breakfast. *Vaporetto:* Fondamente Nove (walk straight up Campo dei Gesuit and it's on the left). **Amenities:** Restaurant; bar; concierge; self-service laundry; shared kitchen; free Wi-Fi in public areas only.

9

Giudecca

INEXPENSIVE

Generator Venice ♥♥ It's worth the trek over to the tranquil island of Giudecca to stay in this decent budget option, though amenities are basic and there can be long waits for the communal showers at busy periods. Set inside an old waterfront warehouse, Generator offers relatively stylish but cramped dorms with bunks (one dorm is female-only), as well as comfy en-suite doubles with air-conditioning and canal views. There are also private three-bed and four-bed rooms, with shared bathrooms, that work out a bit cheaper. The bar, restaurant, and waterside terrace are great places to hang out, with happy hour daily 6:30 to 8:30pm. Note that there is no communal kitchen or fridge (outside food is not allowed), and it's 5€ to rent a towel (1€ for shower gel).

Fondamenta Zitelle 86. staygenerator.com. ✆ **041/8778288.** 26 units. 110€–265€ double; 20€–48€ dorm. Breakfast 5€. *Vaporetto:* Zitelle (walk right along the canal side, Fondamenta Croce/Zitelle, for about 160m/525 ft., and the hostel is on the left, overlooking the water). **Amenities:** Bar; restaurant; concierge; bike rental; self-service laundry 4.50€, plus 3€ for detergent; free Wi-Fi (ground floor only).

WHERE TO EAT IN VENICE

Eating cheaply in Venice is not easy, though it's by no means impossible. The city's reputation for mass-produced menus, poor service, and overpriced food is, sadly, well warranted, and if you've been traveling in other parts of the country, you may be a little disappointed here. Having said that, everything is relative—this is still Italy, after all—and you'll find plenty of excellent dining options in Venice. In recent years there's been an explosion of cheap pizza slice shops (cheap means 5€ per slice in Venice) and fast-casual pasta-in-a-box joints with servings for around 10€—we recommend the better ones below. When it comes to sit-down restaurants, value for money tends to increase the farther you get from

BÀCARI & CICCHETTI

One of the essential culinary experiences of Venice is trawling the countless neighborhood bars known as ***bàcari,*** where you can stand or sit with *tramezzini* (small, triangular white-bread half-sandwiches filled with everything from thinly sliced meats and tuna salad to cheeses and vegetables) and ***cicchetti*** (tapas-like finger foods, such as calamari rings, fried olives, potato croquettes, or grilled polenta squares), traditionally washed down with a small glass of wine, Veneto Prosecco, or a spritz (a cocktail of prosecco and orange-flavored Aperol). All of the above will cost approximately 1.50€ to 6€ if you stand at the bar, as much as double when seated. Bar food usually sells out by late afternoon, so while it can make a great lunch, don't rely on it for dinner. A concentration of popular, well-stocked bars can be found along the **Mercerie** shopping strip that connects Piazza San Marco with the Rialto Bridge; on the always lively **Campo San Luca** (look for the character-filled Ostería Leon Bianco); and on **Campo Santa Margherita.**

Piazza San Marco, and anything described as a *menù turistico,* while cheaper than a la carte, is rarely any good in Venice (exceptions noted below). Note also that compared with Rome and other points south, Venice is a city of early meals: You should be seated by 7:30 to 8:30pm. Most kitchens close at 10 or 10:30pm, even though the restaurant may stay open later.

San Marco

EXPENSIVE

Bistrot de Venise ♥♥♥ VENETIAN/VEGAN It may look a bit like a wood-paneled French bistro, but the menu here is old-school Venetian, specializing in rare wines and historical recipes from the 14th to 18th centuries. It's gimmicky but it works; think fennel soup, homemade pasta with goose sauce and pine nuts, and almond-crusted sturgeon in a black grape sauce, with yellow garlic and almond pudding. The four-course "classic and historic" tasting menu is a splurge, but we recommend it as the best introduction, and there's a vegan option that's just as good (four courses for 90€). Lunch is much cheaper, with mains 18€ to 24€. There's a "smart casual and formal" dress code, and only children over 10 years old are permitted.

4685 Calle dei Fabbri. bistrotdevenise.com. ✆ **041/5236651.** Main courses 28€–48€, tasting menus 110€ and 180€. Daily noon–3pm and 7–11:30pm (bar 11am–11pm). *Vaporetto:* Rialto (turn right along canal, cross footbridge over Rio San Salvador, turn left onto Calle Bembo, which becomes Calle dei Fabbri; Bistrot is about 5 blocks ahead).

Gritti Terrace ♥♥♥ ITALIAN/VENETIAN One of the city's most famous restaurants remains one of its most magical experiences, despite the high prices. First-time Venice visitors in particular should not miss the chance to drink or dine on this venerable deck overlooking the Grand

Canal on a sunny day. The view across to Santa Maria della Salute is spectacular (the signature "Basil-i-ca" cocktail was inspired by the church). The lunch menu features light salads, pasta, risotto, and platters of seasonal seafood. In the evening the terrace becomes part of the posh Club Del Doge Restaurant offering a fuller menu of seasonal seafood and game (the deer tartare is especially prized). Reservations required and "smart casual" dress code encouraged.

Campo Santa Maria del Giglio 2467 (Gritti Palace Hotel). clubdeldoge.com. ✆ **041/794611.** Lunch main courses 38€–65€, dinner main courses 43€–70€. Apr–Oct daily 12:30–5:30pm and 7–10:30pm; closed Nov–Mar. *Vaporetto:* Santa Maria del Giglio.

MODERATE

Ai Mercanti ♥♥♥ VENETIAN/INTERNATIONAL Nadia Locatello's lauded restaurant pioneered the "gastrosteria" concept (based on the French "bistronomie"), where gourmet dishes are created from relatively simple (and cheap-ish) ingredients. Though it's not a budget restaurant, you'll definitely get your money's worth here, with creative dishes—such as croaker fish with cauliflower and candied lemon, cod in coconut and lemongrass spicy soup, and the signature "apparently crispy" egg—a little cheaper than they'd be at similarly feted spots. Dinner is served in two shifts: Tables are available at 7pm and 7:30pm for 2 hours, with a second sitting at 9pm and 9:30pm (reservations required online). Another plus: excellent wines by the glass, not just the "house" pours.

Corte Coppo 4346/a (off Calle dei Fuseri). aimercanti.it. ✆ **041/5238269.** Main courses 15€–26€. Tues–Sat 1–3pm and 7–10pm (closed Feb and mid-Aug). *Vaporetto:* Rialto.

Ai Mercanti's mission: to prove that creative cuisine doesn't need a stratospheric price tag.

tours **FOR FOODIES**

While it's relatively easy to explore Venice's culinary scene solo, it can be fun and enlightening to enlist the services of a local guide. **The Roman Guy** (theromanguy.com; ✆ **06/94804747**) offers focused evening food tours in various parts of Venice (from 79€ for 2½ hr.), while **Food Tours of Venice** (foodtoursofvenice.com; ✆ **393/1670961**) offers street food tours (from 45€ for 2½ hr.), as well as Rialto Market and Jewish Ghetto culinary tours (from 94€ for 4 hr.). **Cesarine** (cesarine.com), Italy's oldest network of home cooks, runs excellent cooking classes in Venice, as well as lunches in local homes, market tours, and wine tastings.

Rosticceria Gislon ♥♥ DELI/VENETIAN This no-frills spot is incredibly popular with locals, with a handful of small tables and barstools, plus bigger tables in the upstairs dining room known as Ristorante San Bartolomeo (which tends to be quieter but has a 10% service charge). Don't be fooled by appearances: The food is excellent, with a range of grilled fish and cheap seafood pastas and a tasty *mozzarella in carrozza* (fried cheese sandwich; 3€). Note that food displayed on the countertop is reheated to order but still tastes good. Otherwise just sit at the counter and soak up the animated scene, as cooks chop, customers chat, and people come and go.

Calle della Bissa 5424. ✆ **041/5223569.** Main courses 15€–24€ (pasta downstairs 8.50€–12€, *cicchetti* 2.50€–4€). Daily 9am–9:30pm. *Vaporetto:* Rialto (with bridge at your back on San Marco side, walk straight to Campo San Bartolomeo; take underpass to your left marked SOTTOPORTEGO DELLA BISSA; *rosticceria* is at 1st corner on right; look for GISLON above the entrance).

Castello

EXPENSIVE

Al Covo ♥♥ SEAFOOD/VENETIAN For years, this high-quality Venetian restaurant from Diane and Cesare Benelli has been deservingly popular with American food writers and TV chefs. It features two cozy dining rooms adorned with art (plus some outdoor seating in summer), but it's the food that takes center stage here: fresh fish from the lagoon or the Adriatic, fruits and vegetables from local farms, and meat sourced from the esteemed Fracassi butchery. The pasta, desserts, and sauces are all homemade. Begin with Venetian *saor* (sweet-and-sour fish and shellfish) or fried zucchini flowers, followed by veggie ravioli with red turnips, broccoli, and Parmesan, or the local catch of the day. Diane's desserts might include rustic pear and prune cake with a grappa-cinnamon sauce or green apple sorbet with Calvados. Shorts, sleeveless t-shirts, flip-flops, and sandals are discouraged for male guests.

Campiello della Pescaria 3968. ristorantealcovo.com. ✆ **041/5223812.** Reservations required. Main courses 15€–44€. Thurs–Mon 12:45–3:30pm (kitchen closes 2pm) and 7:30pm–midnight (kitchen closes 10pm). Closed usually Jan and 10 days in Aug. *Vaporetto:* Piazza San Marco (walk along Riva degli Schiavoni toward Arsenale, and take 3rd narrow street on left, Calle della Pescaria, after Hotel Metropole).

Alle Corone ♥♥♥ SEAFOOD/VENETIAN This is one of Venice's finest restaurants, an elegant 19th-century dining room overlooking the canal, inside the Hotel Ai Reali. Start with raw snapper with glasswort, raspberry, and ginger sauce before moving on to risotto, homemade ravioli stuffed with eggplant Parmesan, or main courses such as almond-crusted sea bass or guinea fowl leg with red onion, Roman cabbage, and tangerines. The homemade desserts are spectacular. Note that men's shorts, sleeveless shirts, and flip-flops are not permitted. Reservations recommended.
Campo della Fava 5527 (Hotel Ai Reali). ristoranteallecorone.com. ✆ **041/2410253.** Main courses 36€–45€; tasting menu 125€. Daily 7–10:30pm (closed Wed). *Vaporetto:* Rialto (walk east along Calle Larga Mazzini, turn left on Merceria, then right on Calle Stella to the hotel).

Local ♥♥♥ SEAFOOD/VENETIAN Local is one of several newish contemporary restaurants in Venice serving inventive seafood menus. In an elegant space with mint green walls and original timbered ceilings, Chef Salvatore Sodano serves a seven-course (160€) or nine-course seasonal menu (190€) that might feature traditional *cicchetti,* sushi, blue crab, and main courses such as spaghetti with hazelnut, sea urchin, and black tea, or duck with black cabbage and persimmon. The four-course lunch menu (70€) offers a cheaper introduction.
Salizada dei Greci 3303. ristorantelocal.com. ✆ **041/2411128.** Tasting menus 70€, 160€, or 190€. Mon and Fri–Sat noon–2pm and 7–10:30pm; Thurs and Sun 7–10:30pm (closed Tues–Wed and mid-Aug). *Vaporetto:* S. Marco–San Zaccaria A (walk north along Calle de la Pietà then Calle Bosello and turn right on Salizada dei Greci—restaurant is on left just before the canal).

Osteria Alle Testiere ♥♥♥ ITALIAN/VENETIAN This tiny nine-table restaurant is the connoisseur's choice (and an alleged favorite of Meryl Streep, Emily Blunt, and Stanley Tucci) for fresh fish and seafood, with a menu that changes daily. Dinner is served at two seatings (reservations are essential), where you choose from appetizers such as smoked burrata with Adriatic anchovies or grilled razor clams that seem to have been plucked straight from the sea. Fresh fish filets with aromatic herbs are always an exceptional main choice, but the seasonal pastas—like pumpkin-and-ricotta ravioli with prawns, or spaghetti with clams—are superb. Top things off with homemade peach pie or chestnut pudding. In peak season, make reservations at least 1 month ahead, and note that the second seating offers a less-rushed experience.
Calle del Mondo Novo 5801. osterialletestiere.it. ✆ **041/5227220.** Main courses 28€–32€; many types of fish sold by weight. Tues–Sat 12:30–3pm (last sitting 1:30pm), dinner seatings 7 and 9:30pm; closed first half of Jan. Vaporetto: Rialto or San Marco, look for Salizada San Lio (west of Campo Santa Maria Formosa), and from there ask for Calle del Mondo Novo.

INEXPENSIVE

Dal Moro's ♥♥ ITALIAN This tiny hole-in-the-wall is by far the best of the city's latest crop of fast-food "pasta-in-a-box" joints. Popular with students (older Venetians would rather jump in a canal than eat here) it knocks out surprisingly delicious and generous portions of bolognese, carbonara, pesto, chicken alfredo, and more creative options from an easy-to-read English menu. It's all freshly made for around 10€ a serving. The only issue is where to eat, as it's essentially take-out-only from a narrow alley: go to St. Mark's Square or the waterfront. Expect a long line at peak times, though it moves fast.

Calle de la Casseleria 5324. instagram.com/dalmoros. ✆ **041/4762876.** Daily noon–6pm. *Vaporetto:* Rialto or San Marco.

Dorsoduro

EXPENSIVE

Locanda Montin ♥♥ VENETIAN Montin was the famous ex-hangout of Peggy Guggenheim in the 1950s, and has been frequented by Jimmy Carter, Robert De Niro, and Brad Pitt, among many other celebs. Is the food still any good? Well, yes. Grab a table in the wonderfully serene back garden (completely covered by an arching trellis), itself a good reason to visit, and sample Venetian classics like sardines in *saor* (a marinade of vinegar, wine, onion, and raisins), and an exquisite creamed cod in polenta. For a main course, it's hard to beat the crispy sea bass (*branzino*) or legendary monkfish, while the lemon sorbet with vodka is a perfect tart conclusion to any meal.

Fondamenta di Borgo 1147. locandamontin.com. ✆ **041/5227151.** Main courses 24€–32€. Mon and Wed–Fri 7–10pm; Sat–Sun 12:30–2:30pm and 7–10pm (usually closed Nov to late Mar). *Vaporetto:* Ca'Rezzonico (walk straight along Calle Lunga San Barnaba, then turn left along Fondamenta di Borgo).

Try to score a table in the lovely back garden at Locanda Montin.

Osteria Enoteca Ai Artisi ♥♥♥ VENETIAN This unpretentious, family-owned *osteria* and *enoteca* is one of Venice's best dining experiences, with a menu that changes daily according to market offerings (the fish market is closed on Mondays, so no fish is served that day). Grab a canalside table and feast on octopus salad, braised beef, or an amazing deer filet with strawberry grape sauce, or opt for one of the wonderful pastas featuring curried prawns, beetroot and oysters, and many other inventive combos. It's a tiny place, so reservations are recommended. Fondamenta della Toletta 1169A. enotecaartisti.com. ✆ **041/5238944.** Main courses 22€–35€. Tues–Sat 12:45–2:45pm, dinner seatings 7–9pm and 9:30–11pm. *Vaporetto:* Accademia (walk around Accademia, turn right on Calle Gambara; at Rio di San Trovaso, turn left on Fondamenta Priuli; take first bridge onto road leading into Fondamenta della Toletta).

INEXPENSIVE

9

Where to Eat in Venice

VENICE

Osteria Al Squero ♥♥♥ WINE BAR/VENETIAN This enticing *osteria* with perhaps the most beguiling view in Venice is opposite the Squero di San Trovaso (p. 424). Sip coffee or wine and nibble *cicchetti* while observing the activity at the medieval gondola boatyard and workshop, on the other side of the Rio di San Trovaso (drinks served in glasses inside, in plastic cups if you want to stand outside). It's essentially a place for a light lunch or *aperitivi* rather than a full meal. Snack on delights such as Carnia smoked sausage, *baccalà* (cod) crostini, anchovies, blue cheese, tuna, and sardines in *saor* for a total of around 14€ to 16€ per person.

EATING cheaply IN VENICE

You don't have to eat in a fancy restaurant to enjoy good food in Venice. Prepare a picnic, and while you eat alfresco you can observe life in the city's *campi* or the aquatic parade on its main thoroughfare, the Grand Canal.

Mercato Rialto Venice's principal open-air market has two parts, beginning with the **produce section,** with many stalls unfolding north on the San Polo side of the Rialto Bridge. Vendors are here Monday to Saturday 7am to 1pm (some stay later). Behind these stalls a few permanent food stores sell cheese, cold cuts, and bread. At the market's farthest point, the covered **fish market** is still redolent of the days when it was one of the Mediterranean's great fish bazaars. The fish merchants take Monday off and work mornings only.

Campo Santa Margherita Every Tuesday through Saturday from 8:30am to 1pm, open-air stalls set up on this spacious Dorsoduro *campo,* selling fresh fruit and vegetables. A conventional supermarket, **Conad City** (Mon–Sat 7:30am–8:30pm, Sun 9am–7pm) is just off the *campo* in the direction of nearby Campo San Barnaba, at no. 3017.

San Barnaba Venice's heavily photographed **floating market** (mostly fruits and vegetables) now operates from just one boat moored off San Barnaba at the Ponte dei Pugni in Dorsoduro. This market is open daily 8am to 1pm and 3:30 to 7:30pm, except Wednesday afternoon and Sunday.

Spritz from 3.50€. If eating outside watch out for the seagulls, annoyingly adept at snatching food.

Fondamenta Nani 943–944. ✆ **335/6007513.** *Cicchetti* 2.50€–2.80€ per piece. Mon–Fri 10am–8:30pm; Sat 10am–3pm. *Vaporetto:* Zattere (walk west along water to Rio di San Trovaso and turn right up Fondamenta Nani).

San Polo

EXPENSIVE

Wistèria ♥♥♥ VENETIAN One of the city's newer batch of Michelin-starred restaurants, Wistèria was established by partners Andrea Martin and Massimiliano (Max) Rossetti in 2019, with Chef Valerio Dallamano in the kitchen and an outdoor space enhanced by blossoming wisteria in the spring. The menu is known for experimentation and innovation—expect lots of unusual shapes, colors, and ingredients and incredible flavors. For dinner there's usually a choice of two menus: the signature "Serendipity" eight-course menu and a slightly cheaper six-course tasting menu. Menus change seasonally but usually have a Venetian theme, with riffs on traditional *cicchetti* and *castradina* (a classic mutton soup) and creative dishes like "liquid ravioli Milanese style"; pink oyster and pomegranate; capon, hazelnut, and calamansi; and boiled salami, red chicory, and horseradish—you get the picture. No shorts or flip-flops.

Chefs meticulously plate courses for the creative tasting menus at Wistèria.

Fondamenta del Forner 2908. wisteria-restaurant.com. ✆ **041/5243373.** Tasting menus 160€ and 195€. Mon and Tues 7–9pm; Fri–Sun noon–1:30pm and 7–9pm (usually closed Jan). *Vaporetto:* San Tomà (with your back to Grand Canal, walk up Calle del Traghetto Vecchio, and turn left on Calle del Campanile; at canal turn right on Fondamenta del Forner, and the restaurant will be ahead on right).

MODERATE

Do Spade ♥♥ VENETIAN It's tough to find dining this authentic so close to the Rialto Bridge, but Do Spade ("Two Swords") has been around since 1448 (Casanova ate here). Most locals come for the *cicchetti,* with small plates (2€–3.50€) such as fried calamari, salted cod, or Do Spade's famed *polpetta di spianata calabra* (meatballs of Calabrian sausage, smoked cheese, and potatoes), and decent Italian wines (3.50€–6.50€ a glass). The more formal restaurant section is also worth a try, with seafood highlights including a delicately prepared monkfish, scallops served with fresh zucchini, and rich seafood lasagna. The seasonal pumpkin ravioli is one of the best dishes in the city.

Calle de le Do Spade 859. cantinadospade.com. ✆ **041/5210574.** Main courses 16€–26€. Daily 10am–3pm and 6–10pm. *Vaporetto:* Rialto Mercato (with your back to Grand Canal, walk up Ruga Vecchia San Giovanni, turn right on Ruga dei Spezieri; at end turn left on Calle de le Beccarie O Panataria, then take second right onto covered Sottoportego do Spade).

INEXPENSIVE

Antico Forno ♥♥♥ ITALIAN/PIZZA Venice is not known for pizza, partly because fire codes restrict the use of traditional wood-burning ovens, but the big, fluffy-crusted pies here are the best in the city. Little more than a hole-in-the-wall (takeout only), Antico Forno has been selling pizza by the slice since 2001, both thick- and thin-crust (as well as excellent craft beers). Its "La Pizzaccia-style" pizza is a soft focaccia topped with fresh chopped tomatoes, *mozzarella fior di latte* (from Treviso farms), and everything from Trevisan sausage to Gorgonzola and mushrooms.

Ruga Rialto 973. anticofornovenezia.it. ✆ **041/5204110.** Pizza slices 5.50€–12€. Daily 11:30am–10pm (usually closed Jan). *Vaporetto:* Rialto Mercato (walk into Campo de la Pescaria, follow Ruga Vecchia San Giovanni for around 300m/984 ft., just beyond Calle del Paradiso).

Do Mori ♥♥♥ WINE BAR/VENETIAN Serving good wine and *cicchetti* since 1462, Do Mori is above all a fun place to have a genuine Venetian experience, a small, dimly lit *bàcari* that can barely accommodate 10 people standing up. Sample the baby octopus and ham on mango, lard-smothered *crostini,* and pickled onions speared with salty anchovies, or

Where to Have a Picnic in Venice

You won't find much in the way of green space in Venice (if you are desperate for green, walk 30 min. past San Marco along the water to the **Giardini Pubblici,** Venice's only green park). But that doesn't mean you can't enjoy a meal alfresco. Just find one of the larger *campi* that have park benches, such as **Campo San Giacomo dell'Orio,** in the quiet *sestiere* of Santa Croce. The two most central are **Campo Santa Margherita** in Dorsoduro and **Campo San Polo** in San Polo.

Near La Salute Church in Dorsoduro, the **Punta della Dogana** (Customs House) is a prime viewing site at the mouth of the Grand Canal. Perch on the embankment here and watch the water activity against a canvaslike backdrop deserving of the Accademia Museum. In this same area, **Campo San Vio** (near the Guggenheim) is another superb spot directly on the Grand Canal; it boasts two benches and the option of sitting on an untrafficked small bridge.

A bit farther afield, you can take the *vaporetto* to Burano and then a 5-minute ride on no. 9 to the near-deserted island of **Torcello.** Bring a basketful of bread, cheese, and wine to reenact the romantic scene between Katharine Hepburn and Rossano Brazzi from the 1955 film *Summertime.*

opt for the *tramezzini* (tiny sandwiches). Local TV (and BBC) star Francesco da Mosto is a regular. This institution is very much on the well-trodden tourist trail—plenty of *cicchetti* tours stop by in the early evening. Local wine is 3.50€ to 7€ per glass. Cash only.

Calle Do Mori 429 (also Calle Galeazza 401). ✆ **041/5225401.** *Tramezzini* and *cicchetti* 2€–3.50€ per piece. Mon–Fri 8am–7:30pm; Sat 8am–3pm (June–Aug closed daily 2–4:30pm). *Vaporetto:* Rialto Mercato (with your back to Grand Canal, walk up Ruga Vecchia San Giovanni; turn right on Calle Galeazza).

Tiny La Bottiglia is all about the wine, with savory accompaniments.

La Bottiglia ♥♥♥ WINE BAR/VENETIAN This more contemporary *bàcari* features wonderful cheese and meat boards (6€–24€), a well-curated wine list (exceptional Amarone red wine is served here), and excellent panini sandwiches stuffed with prosciutto and cheeses. As you might expect, it's a tiny place, with a few tables outside near the Rio San Stin and just five barstools inside (most visitors stand).

Campo San Stin (Calle de la Chiesa) 2537. ✆ **041/4762426.** Sandwiches from 9€. Daily 11am–10:30pm (to 11:30pm Fri–Sat). *Vaporetto:* Ferrovia or San Tomà.

Santa Croce

EXPENSIVE

Zanze XVI ♥♥♥ ITALIAN/VENETIAN This contemporary *osteria* has an elegant dining room featuring exposed wood beams and woodblock tables. At the helm is Chef Giovanni Rigoni, whose dishes are created daily depending on fresh ingredients from local markets and gardens. The menu usually includes fresh fish, with dishes such as pilchard tortelli with chard and Pecorino cheese; risotto with oysters and prosecco; and sea bass in black squid ink.

Fondamenta dei Tolentini 231. zanze.it. ✆ **041/715394.** Main courses 35€. Tasting menus 75€ and 110€. Wed–Sun 12:30–2pm and 7:30–10pm. *Vaporetto:* Piazzale Roma (turn left and walk along Grand Canal, cross 2 bridges, then turn right on Fondamenta dei Tolentini).

MODERATE

Osteria La Zucca ♥♥ ITALIAN/VEGETARIAN Though not specifically a vegetarian restaurant, the romantic canalside dining room of La Zucca (aka "the pumpkin") does offer a huge range of high-quality vegetable dishes, from the signature pumpkin-and-ricotta flan and potato cakes to zucchini-and-almond lasagna. The seasonal menu (Italian only, but the staff speak English) also includes plenty of meat dishes, such as succulent rabbit with white wine and lamb with spices. End with one of the homemade cakes—pear cake with ginger or the "spices tart" with red wine and raspberry. Reservations are recommended, either by phone (Mon–Sat 10am–12:30pm and 6–7:30pm) or online, up 20 days in advance.

Calle dello Spezier 1762. lazucca.it. ✆ **041/5241570.** Main courses 12€–25€. Mon–Sat 12:30–2:30pm and 7–10:30pm (seatings at 7 and 9pm). *Vaporetto:* San Stae (walk down Salizada San Stae, turn right on Calle del Tentor; turn left at Calle Del Meglio and follow it as it turns right).

INEXPENSIVE

Bacareto da Lele ♥♥♥ WINE BAR/VENETIAN This tiny hole-in-the-wall *bàcaro* is worth seeking out for its cheap, fresh snacks, sandwiches, and *cicchetti.* Tiny glasses (*ombras*) of wine and prosecco are just 1.30€ to 2€—there are no seats, so do as the locals do and grab a space by the canal while you sip and nibble. Opt for a tiny porchetta or bacon and artichoke panini, antipasti plates (cheese and salami) or a freshly baked crostino. Expect long lines here in peak season—the secret is definitely out.

Campo dei Tolentini 183. bacaretodalele.it. ✆ **347/8469728.** *Cicchetti* 1.60€–2.50€ per piece. Mon–Fri 6am–8pm; Sat 6am–2pm. *Vaporetto:* Piazzale Roma (walk left along Grand Canal past Ponte della Costituzione into Giardino Papadopoli; turn right on Fondamenta Papadopoli, then left. Cross park at first bridge; next canal is Rio del Tolentini, with the *campo* across the bridge and Da Lele on the southwest corner).

Cantina Arnaldi ♥♥♥ WINE BAR/VENETIAN This welcoming *bàcari* offers some of the freshest snacks in the city, washed down with quality wines, spritz, and prosecco (6€–9.50€). The thing to order is the

Hunting for Venice's Best Gelato

Is the gelato any good in Venice? Italians might demur, but by international standards, the answer is most definitely yes. Of course, gelato parlors aimed exclusively at tourists are notorious for poor quality and extortionate prices; avoid places near Piazza San Marco altogether. One of our favorite spots in the city is **Il Doge** ♥♥ (facebook.com/ildogegelateria; ✆ **349/3507804;** daily 11am–10pm; vaporetto Ca'Rezzonico), conveniently located at the southern end of Campo Santa Margherita in Dorsoduro. These guys use only natural, homemade flavors and ingredients, from an exceptional spicy chocolate to the house specialty, Crema de Doge, a rich mix of eggs, cream, and oranges. Try a refreshing *granita* in summer. Our other favorite, **La Mela Verde** ♥♥♥ (✆ **349/1957924;** daily 11am–10:30pm; vaporetto San Zaccaria) is in Castello at Fondamenta de L'Osmarin 4977. The popular rival to Il Doge for best scoop in the city, it features sharp flavors and all the classics done sensationally well: pistachio, chocolate, *nocciola,* and the mind-blowing lemon and basil. The overall champions are *mela verde* (green apple), like creamy, frozen fruit served in a cup, and the addictive tiramisu. Note that both of these places close down in winter, Il Doge from late December through January, and La Mela Verde from late November to mid-February delicious board of cheese and cold cuts, all sourced from the region and enhanced with fresh fruits, fig jam, local bread, and a small pot of roasted potatoes. It's a small place, so reservations are recommended if you want a table (there are also a handful of barstools).

Salizada San Pantalon 35. facebook.com/cantinarnaldi. ✆ **041/718989.** *Cicchetti* 2.50€–6€ per piece. Thurs–Tues 11:30am–midnight. *Vaporetto:* San Tomà (walk up Calle Traghetto Vecchio Galeazza; turn left at Calle del Campanile and right on Fondamenta del Forner; turn left and cross canal on Calle Gozzi; follow to Calle Crosera; turn right and walk straight, crossing Rio de San Pantalon, and on to Salizada San Pantalon).

Cannaregio

EXPENSIVE

Dama ♥♥♥ VENETIAN/SEAFOOD Overlooking the busy Canale di Cannaregio in the historic Hotel Ca' Bonfadini (and a less than 10-min. walk from the station), this contemporary Venetian kitchen is one of the best in the city. Chef Lorenzo Cogo focuses on local seafood, using modern techniques and creative combinations; think langoustine with hazelnuts, miso, and sesame to start; black macaroni and spiked squid with ginseng and buffalo stracciatella for first course; and confit mullet with sweet and sour sauce, vermouth, plum, and rosemary for an entree. The long tables inside have been fashioned from old Venetian mooring posts.

Fondamenta Savorgnan 461. cabonfadini.com/dama-restaurant-venice. ✆ **041/0986297.** Main courses 24€–34€. Daily noon–3pm and 7:30–10pm. *Vaporetto:* Crea (walk left along canal with water on your left; the restaurant is around 200m/750 ft. on the right).

La Giudecca

MODERATE

La Palanca ♥♥♥ SEAFOOD/VENETIAN For simple, no-frills Venetian cuisine with a stellar view across to the spires of Dorsoduro, this Giudecca spot, well off the tourist trail, is hard to beat. Grab a table on the waterside for coffee and cake (most locals take breakfast standing at the bar), or have a sandwich, a more substantial lunch, or sunset spritz (meals usually served noon–2:30pm; it's just *cicchetti* and drinks thereafter).

Fondamenta Sant'Eufemia 448. ✆ **041/5287719.** Main courses 15€–24€. Mon–Sat 7am–9pm. Reserve for lunch. *Vaporetto:* Palanca (restaurant is 80m/262 ft. along canal to left).

Murano & Burano

The glass-making island of **Murano** isn't especially known for its food, though plenty of decent trattorias are scattered along the main streets. For a real treat, make for **La Fornace** ♥♥♥, Fondamenta Manin 1 (lafornacemurano.it; ✆ **041/5275408;** Mon noon–5pm, Wed–Sun noon–4pm and 6:30–10pm; usually closed Jan), a spacious restaurant in a restored glass furnace, with gorgeous views of the lagoon. It's best known for traditional Venetian dishes and fresh seafood.

The island of **Burano** makes a wonderful culinary excursion for its seafood restaurants, notably **Trattoria al Gatto Nero ♥♥**, the "Black Cat," Fondamenta della Giudecca 88 (gattonero.com; ✆ **041/730120;** Tues and Fri–Sat 12:30–5pm and 7:30–11pm, Wed–Thurs and Sun 12:30–5pm; usually closed Nov), around since the 1960s. Signature dishes include Burano-style risotto (made with *ghiozzi,* a small, long-bodied fish from the lagoon), local turbot and seabass, and tagliolini with spider crab. Another favorite is **Trattoria da Romano ♥♥**, Via Baldassarre Galuppi 221 (daromano.it; ✆ **041/730030;** Mon and Wed–Sun noon–3pm), its dining room adorned with over 400 artworks donated by visiting artists since the 1940s.

VENICE SHOPPING

Venice is famous for local crafts that have been produced here for centuries and are hard to get elsewhere: the **glassware** from Murano, the **delicate lace** from Burano, and the *cartapesta* (papier-mâché) **Carnevale masks** you'll find in endless *botteghe* (shops), where you can watch artisans paint amid their wares. Now here's the bad news: An overwhelming sea of cheap glass gewgaws has turned buying Venetian glass into something of a turnoff (shipping and insurance costs make most things unaffordable; the alternative is to hand-carry anything fragile); and with only a few women on Burano keeping alive the art of lace-making, any pieces not produced by machine in China are sold at stratospheric prices. The best place to buy glass is Murano itself—the **"Vetro Artistico Murano"** trademark guarantees its origin but expect to pay as much as 60€ for just a wineglass.

In a city that for centuries has thrived almost exclusively on tourism, remember this: **Where you buy cheap, you get cheap.** Venetians, centuries-old merchants, aren't known for bargaining. You'll stand a better chance of getting a good deal if you pay in cash or buy more than one item.

Shopping Streets & Markets

A mix of low-end trinket stores and midmarket-to-upscale boutiques lines the narrow zigzagging **Mercerie** running north between Piazza San Marco and the Rialto Bridge. More expensive boutiques make for great window-shopping on **Calle Larga XXII Marzo,** the wide street that begins west of Piazza San Marco and wends its way to the expansive Campo Santo Stefano near the Accademia. The narrow **Frezzaria,** just west of Piazza San Marco and running north–south, offers a grab bag of bars, souvenir shops, and tony clothing stores like Louis Vuitton and Versace. The non-produce part of the **Rialto Market** is as good as it gets for basic souvenirs, such as cheap T-shirts, glow-in-the-dark plastic gondolas, and tawdry glass trinkets.

The 3-day professional antiques market **Mercatino dell'Antiquariato** (mercatinocamposanmaurizio.it) takes place four to five times a year (usually Mar–Apr, May, Sept–Oct, and Dec; check website for dates) in Campo San Maurizio, San Marco.

Arts & Crafts

Atelier Segalin di Daniela Ghezzo ♥♥ Founded in 1932 by master cobbler Antonio Segalin and his son Rolando, this old leather shoe store is now run by Daniela Ghezzo (the star apprentice of Rolando), maker of exuberant handmade shoes and boots, from basic flats to crazy footwear designed for Carnevale (custom footwear from 650€–1,800€). Calle dei Fuseri 4365, San Marco. www.danielaghezzo.it/shoes.html. ✆ **041/5222115.** Mon–Fri 10am–1pm and 3–7pm; Sat 10am–1pm. *Vaporetto:* San Marco.

Il Grifone ♥♥♥ Toni Peressin's handmade leather briefcases, bound notebooks, belts, and soft-leather purses have garnered quite a following, and justly so—his craftsmanship is magnificent (he makes everything in the workshop out back). Items start at around 25€. Fondamenta del Gaffaro 3516, Dorsoduro. www.ilgrifonevenezia.it. ✆ **041/5229452.** Tues–Sat 10am–6pm. *Vaporetto:* Piazzale Roma.

Kartaruga ♥♥ Remember the creepy orgy scenes in Stanley Kubrick's film *Eyes Wide Shut?* The ornate masks used in the movie were made by the owners of this vaunted store. All manner of traditional, feathered, and animal masks are knocked out in their on-site workshop—it's worth visiting just to check out the craftsmanship (masks from 45€). Calle delle Bande 5369 (near Campo Santa Maria Formosa), Castello. kartaruga.it. ✆ **041/5210393.** Daily 10am–6pm. *Vaporetto:* San Zaccaria.

La Bottega dei Mascareri ♥♥ Brothers Sergio and Massimo Boldrin have been crafting high-quality, creative masks—some based on Tiepolo paintings—since 1984 (and also were involved in *Eyes Wide Shut*). Basic masks start at around 45€, but you'll pay over 75€ for a more innovative piece. The smaller, original branch lies at the foot of the Rialto

Four More Artisans Worth a Visit

In San Marco, **Rubelli ♥♥** (Ramo de la Piscina 3393; rubelli.com) shows off luxurious Venetian damask, brocade, velvet, and silk textiles and wall coverings, furniture, and accessories, while **Valese ♥♥** (Calle Fiubera 793; valese.it) is the place to shop for exquisite brass and bronze objects made by the city's last remaining foundry, including models of the Horses of St. Mark and Venetian lions.

Head to Castello to find **Scriba Venice ♥♥** (Salizada San Lio 5728; scribavenice.com), a treasure trove of fabulous stationery; hand-painted marbled paper, antique ink pens, leather-bound diaries, and more. And last but not least, in Cannareggio **Spezeria all'Ercole d'Oro ♥♥** (Salizada Santa Fosca 223; themerchantofvenice.com) is a 17th-century pharmacy with a beautifully restored wood-paneled section displaying artisan perfumes from local outfit The Merchant of Venice.

Bridge (San Polo 80; ✆ **041/5223857**). Calle dei Saoneri 2720, San Polo. www.mascarer.com. ✆ **041/5242887.** Both locations daily 9am–6pm. *Vaporetto:* Rialto.

Marco Polo International ♥♥ This vast showroom west of Piazza San Marco, displays Murano glass (although it's more expensive than if you buy on the island yourself), including some truly sensational pieces—it's like visiting an art gallery. The cheapest pieces tend to be rings and pendants (from 15€–25€). Frezzaria 1644, San Marco. marcopolointernational.it. ✆ **041/5229295.** Daily 10am–7pm. *Vaporetto:* San Marco.

Books

Libreria Acqua Alta ♥♥♥ Like a set on a Harry Potter movie, this venerable bookshop has become a tourist attraction as much for its museum-like atmosphere, its gondola filled with paperbacks, and its friendly cats as its books, though it's a great place to pick up rare and used tomes (especially in Italian). Get here early to avoid long lines, just to get in. Calle Longa Santa Maria Formosa 5176b. libreriacqualta.it. ✆ **041/2960841.** Daily 9am–7:15pm. *Vaporetto:* San Marco or Ospedale.

Food

Màscari ♥♥ Whether you're shopping for gifts or treating yourself, don't miss this local deli, in business since 1948. Here you'll find all sorts of tasty Venetian and Italian specialties, from Burano biscuits, heaps of chocolate, sweets, and dried pasta, to exotic herbs and spices. Calle Prima de la Donzella 306. www.imascari.com. ✆ 041/5229762. Mon–Sat 8am–1pm and 4–7:30pm (Wed morning only). *Vaporetto:* Rialto.

ENTERTAINMENT & NIGHTLIFE

If you're looking for serious nocturnal action, you're in the wrong town—Verona and Padua are far livelier. Your best bet is to sit in moonlit **Piazza San Marco** and listen to the cafes' outdoor orchestras, with the floodlit basilica before you—the perfect opera set—though this pleasure comes with a hefty price tag. Other popular spots include **Campo San Bartolomeo,** at the foot of the Rialto Bridge (a zoo in high season), and **Campo San Luca.** For low prices and low pretension, the absolute best place to go is **Campo Santa Margherita,** a huge open *campo* between the train station and the Accademia Bridge.

Visit one of the tourist information centers for current English-language schedules of the month's special events. The free website **Live Venice** (live-venice.it) is also extremely helpful, as is monthly magazine ***VeNews*** (venezianews.it).

Performing Arts & Live Music

Venice has a long and rich tradition of classical music; this was, after all, the home of Vivaldi. In heavily trafficked spots near San Marco and Rialto, people dressed in period costumes pass out brochures advertising

A classical concert at Teatro La Fenice.

classical music concerts, so you'll have no trouble finding up-to-date information.

Santa Maria della Pietà ♥♥ The so-called "Vivaldi Church," built between 1745 and 1760, holds concerts throughout the year, typically of the *Four Seasons* performed by the **Vivaldi Baroque Ensemble;** check the website for specific dates. Tickets are usually 32€ to 35€ (with discounts online). Riva degli Schiavoni 3701, Castello. vivaldichurchvenice.com. ✆ **041/5221120.** *Vaporetto:* San Zaccaria.

Teatro La Fenice ♥♥♥ The opera season runs late November through June, but there are also classical concerts and ballet. Tickets are expensive for the major productions (75€–210€ for the gallery and 190€–240€ for a decent seat); budget travelers can opt for obstructed-view seats (from 35€), but all the cheaper tickets sell out fast. Campo San Fantin 1965, San Marco. teatrolafenice.it. ✆ **041/2424.** *Vaporetto:* Giglio.

Cafes

For tourists and locals alike, Venetian nightlife mainly centers on the many cafes in one of the world's most beautiful public squares: Piazza San Marco. It is also a most expensive and touristed place to linger over a spritz (the Venetian classic cocktail of prosecco and orange-flavored Aperol), but it's a splurge that should not be dismissed too readily.

Caffè dei Frari ♥♥♥ Established in 1870, this inviting bar and cafe overlooking the Frari church has walls still adorned with the original Art Nouveau murals, an antique wooden bar, and cozy upstairs. The whole place morphs into **Il Mercante Cocktail Bar** in the evenings (Sun 6pm–midnight, Tues–Thurs 6pm–1am, Fri–Sat 6pm–1:30am). Fondamenta dei Frari 2564, San Polo. ilmercantevenezia.com. ✆ **041/5241877.** Tues–Sat 9am–5pm. *Vaporetto:* San Tomà.

Caffè Florian ♥♥ Occupying prime *piazza* real estate since 1720, this is one of the world's oldest coffee shops, with a florid interior of 18th-century mirrors, frescoes, and statuary. Sitting at a table ("*al tavolo*"), expect to pay 12€ for a cappuccino, 24€ for a Bellini (prosecco and fresh peach nectar in season), and 17€ for a spritz—add another 6€ per person if the orchestra plays (Mar–Nov). Standing at the bar ("*al banco*") is much cheaper (6€ for a cappuccino, 12€ for a Bellini, and so on). Piazza San Marco 57. caffeflorian.com. ✆ **041/5205641.** Sun–Thurs 9am–8pm; Fri–Sat 9am–11pm. *Vaporetto:* San Marco.

Il Caffè (Caffè Rosso) ♥♥ Open since 1913, Il Caffè has a history almost as colorful as its clientele—a mix of students, aging regulars, and lost tourists. This old-fashioned, no-nonsense cafe/bar with famously surly staff has reasonably priced drinks for Venice (spritz 5€, cappuccino 3.50€) and sandwiches, and lots of seating on the *campo* (plus a small seating area inside). Campo Santa Margherita 2963, Dorsoduro. ✆ **041/5287998.** Mon–Sat 7am–1am. *Vaporetto:* Ca'Rezzonico.

Pasticceria Tonolo ♥♥♥ This tiny bakery has enjoyed a cult following since 1886 thanks to its deep-fried sweet treats (*frittelle,* Italian-style doughnuts, plus a vast range of sumptuous cakes and cookies; *frittelle* 1.60€–1.80€). Coffee is served in charming, antique blue German porcelain cups (standing room only). Calle San Pantalon 3764, Dorsoduro. facebook.com/PasticceriaTonolo. ✆ **041/5237209.** Tues–Sat 7:30am–8pm; Sun 7:30am–1pm; often closed through Aug. *Vaporetto:* San Tomà.

Birreria, Wine & Cocktail Bars

Venice has never been a late-night clubbing hotspot. Evenings are better spent lingering over dinner, having a pint in a *birreria,* or nursing a glass of prosecco in one of the pricey outdoor bars and cafes in Piazza San Marco or Campo Santa Margherita.

Al Prosecco ♥♥♥ Get acquainted with all things bubbly at this smart *enoteca,* a specialist, as you'd expect, in Veneto Prosecco. It features tasty *cicchetti* and plenty of outdoor tables from which to observe the laid-back Campo San Giacomo dell'Orio, though it tends to close early. Most drinks run 6€ to 7€. Campo San Giacomo dell'Orio 1503, Santa Croce. ✆ **041/5240222.** Mon–Sat 10am–10:30pm (closes 8pm in winter; closed Aug and Jan). *Vaporetto:* San Stae.

A Legendary Watering Hole

Possibly the most famous bar in Venice (and now a global chain), **Harry's Bar ♥♥** (Calle Vallaresso 1323, San Marco; cipriani.com/harrys-bar; ✆ **041/5285777;** *vaporetto:* Vallaresso) was established in 1931 by Giuseppe Cipriani and frequented by the likes of Ernest Hemingway and Charlie Chaplin. The Bellini was invented here in 1948 (along with *carpaccio* 2 years later); you can sip the signature concoction of freshly squeezed peach juice and prosecco for a mere 22€. Go for the history but don't expect a five-star experience—most first-timers are surprised just how ordinary it looks inside (though the bow-tied waitstaff still look the part). It's more a restaurant than a bar these days, serving very expensive food (main courses 40€–50€, plus mandatory 10€ cover charge), but just stick to the drinks. No shorts after 7:30pm. It's open daily 11am to 11pm; usually closed in January.

Bar Dandolo ♥♥ Doge Dandolo built his glorious Venetian Gothic palace three doors down from the Palazzo Ducale in the 14th century, and current occupier Hotel Danieli has been one of the most sumptuous hotels in Venice since 1822. Nestled amid marble columns on the ground floor, this classic Venice bar serves everything from velvet-capped cappuccinos and a traditional afternoon tea (daily 3–6pm) to a decadent Vesper Martini cocktail. You can also opt for an alfresco drink on the rooftop **Bar Terrazza Danieli** (Apr–Oct daily 3–6:30pm). Riva degli Schiavoni 4196, Castello. hoteldanieli.com. ✆ **041/5226480.** Daily 10am–1am (pianist plays daily 7pm–12:30am); usually closed Jan. *Vaporetto:* San Zaccaria.

Bar Longhi ♥♥♥ The Gritti Palace Hotel really was the 16th-century palace of Doge Andrea Gritti, whose portrait graces one of the antiques-filled lounges (it remains the city's most expensive hotel since opening in 1895). Bar Longhi is the quintessential Venetian watering hole, with lavish decor (hand-sculptured mirrors, Murano glass appliqués, and a marble bar counter) plus paintings belonging to the school of the celebrated 18th-century Venetian artist Pietro Longhi. Afternoon tea, cocktails (featuring the bespoke "Martini Trolley"), and champagne are served. Campo Santa Maria del Giglio 2467 (Gritti Palace Hotel), San Marco. marriott.com. ✆ **041/794611.** Daily 11am–1am. *Vaporetto:* Santa Maria del Giglio.

Il Santo Bevitore ♥♥ Beer aficionados will be pleased to learn that Italy has a growing **craft beer** scene, and this local spot showcases the best brews from all over the country (many on tap). Sample brews from Milan's Birrificio Lambrate and Birrificio Extraomnes, Parma's Birra Toccalmatto, Udine's Borderline Brewery, and Veneto's very own Mesh Brewery. The small bar overlooks the Rio de Servi just off the main drag (Strada Nova), with a few benches outside for warmer weather. Fondamenta Diedo 2393, Cannaregio. ilsantobevitorepub.com. ✆ **335/8415771.** Daily 4pm–2am. *Vaporetto:* San Marcuola.

DAY TRIPS FROM VENICE

If you only have 3 days or so, you will probably want to spend them in the center of Venice. However, if you are here for a week—or on your second visit to the city—head over to the mainland to see some of the old towns that lie within the historic Veneto region.

Padua ♥♥♥

40km (25 miles) W of Venice

Tucked away within the ancient heart of Padua lies one of the greatest artistic treasures in all Italy, the precious Giotto frescoes of the **Cappella degli Scrovegni.** Although the city itself is not especially attractive (it was largely rebuilt after bombing during World War II), don't be put off by the urban sprawl that now surrounds it; central Padua is refreshingly bereft of tourist crowds, a workaday Veneto town with a large student population and a small but intriguing ensemble of historic sights.

ESSENTIALS

ARRIVING The most efficient way to reach Padua is to take the **train** from Venice's Santa Lucia station. Trains depart every 10 to 20 minutes and take 26 to 55 minutes depending on the class (4.90€–20€ one-way). Padua ("Padova" in Italian) station is a short walk north up Corso del Popolo from the Cappella degli Scrovegni and the old city.

VISITOR INFORMATION The **tourist office** at Piazza delle Erbe 52 is usually open daily 9am to 7pm (turismopadova.it; ✆ **049/5207415**). A kiosk at the train station (track 1) is open Monday to Saturday 9am to 7pm and Sunday 10am to 4pm.

EXPLORING PADUA

The one unmissable sight in Padua is the **Cappella degli Scrovegni** ♥♥♥ at Piazza Eremitani (cappelladegliscrovegni.it; ✆ **049/2010020;** daily 9am–7pm, late Mar–Oct until 10pm), an outwardly unassuming chapel commissioned in 1303 by Enrico Scrovegni, a wealthy banker. Inside, however, the chapel is gloriously decorated with a cycle of frescoes by Florentine genius **Giotto,** depicting the lives of the Virgin Mary and Jesus and culminating in the Ascension and Last Judgment. Seeing Giotto's work in the flesh is spine-tingling; this is where he makes the decisive break with Byzantine art toward the realism and humanism that would define the Italian Renaissance.

Frescoes by Giotto in the Capella degli Scrovegni, in Padua.

Entrance to the chapel is limited, involving small groups of visitors spending 15 minutes in a climate-controlled airlock, used to stabilize the temperature, before going inside for another 15 to 20 minutes. To visit the chapel, you must **make a reservation at least 24 hours in advance** (by phone or online) and arrive 30 minutes before the time on your ticket. Tickets cost 15€ (6€ for ages 6–17 and students under 27), plus 1€ if purchased online.

If you have time, try to take in Padua's other historic highlights. The vast **Palazzo della Ragione** ♥♥ on Piazza del Erbe (8€; Tues–Sun 9am–7pm) is an architectural marvel, a cavernous town hall completed in 1219 and decorated by frescoes by Nicola Miretto in the 15th century. The **Basilica di Sant'Antonio** ♥♥, on the Piazza del Santo (santantonio.org; ✆ **049/8225652;** free admission; daily 6:15am–6:45pm), is the stately resting place of **St. Anthony of Padua,** the Portuguese Franciscan best known as the patron saint of finding things or lost people. While the exterior of the church is a bizarre mix of Byzantine, Romanesque, and Gothic styles, the interior is richly adorned with statuary and murals. Don't miss **Donatello**'s stupendous equestrian statue of the Venetian *condottiere* Gattamelata (Erasmo da Narni) in the piazza outside, the first large bronze sculpture of the Renaissance.

WHERE TO EAT

Padua offers plenty of places to eat and drink (Aperol was created here in 1919), and you'll especially appreciate the overall drop in prices compared to Venice. It's hard to match the location of **Bar Nazionale** ♥♥, Piazza del Erbe 40 (Mon and Sat 7am–10:30pm, Tues and Thurs–Fri 7am–11:30am, Wed 7am–midnight, Sun 9am–9:30pm), on the steps leading up to Palazzo della Ragione, but it's best for drinks and snacks (excellent *tramezzini* from 3.50€, panini from 4.50€, spritz 4.50€, and glasses of wine 4€) rather than a full meal. For that, take a short walk from Piazza dei Signori to **Belle Parti** ♥♥♥, Via Belle Parti 11 (ristorantebelleparti.it; ✆ **049/8751822;** Mon–Sat 12:30–2:30pm and 7:30–10:30pm), one of Padua's best restaurants. Set within the historic Palazzo Prosdocimi, it serves classic Veneto dishes and seafood (main courses 26€–29€). For dessert head to venerable **Caffè Pedrocchi** ♥♥ at Via VIII Febbraio 15 (caffepedrocchi.it; ✆ **049/8781231;** daily 8am–midnight), an elegant institution since 1831 celebrated for its mint coffee ("*caffè alla menta*"), and mint, coffee, and chocolate cake.

Verona ♥♥

115km (71 miles) W of Venice

With its handsome red- and peach-colored medieval buildings and Roman ruins, the affluent city of Verona is one of Italy's major tourist draws, though its appeal is mostly due to William Shakespeare, who immortalized the city in his (totally fictional) *Romeo and Juliet*, *The Two Gentlemen of*

Verona, and partly, *The Taming of the Shrew*. In spite of its popularity with visitors, Verona is not Venice; it's a booming commercial center with vibrant science and technology sectors.

ESSENTIALS

ARRIVING The best way to reach Verona from Venice is by **train.** Direct services depart every 30 minutes and take anywhere from 1 hour and 10 minutes to 2 hours and 20 minutes, depending on the type of train you catch (one-way tickets cost 10.35€–29€). From Verona station (Verona Porta Nuova), it's a 15-minute walk to the historic center.

VISITOR INFORMATION The **tourist office** at Via Leoncino 61 (Palazzo Barbieri) in Piazza Bra (visitverona.it; ✆ **045/8068680;** July–Aug Mon–Sat 9am–7pm, Sun 10am–6pm; Mar–June and Sept–Oct Mon–Sat 9am–6pm, Sun 10am–5pm; Nov–Feb Mon–Sat 9am–5pm, Sun 10am–4pm) has maps and tour information.

EXPLORING VERONA

"Two households, both alike in dignity, in fair Verona…" So go the immortal opening lines of *Romeo and Juliet*, ensuring that the city has been a target for lovesick romantics ever since. Though Verona is crammed with genuine historic goodies, one of the most popular sites is the ersatz **Casa di Giulietta,** Via Cappello 23 (casadigiulietta.comune.verona.it; 12€ adults, 3€ ages 18–25, free for kids 17 and under; Tues–Sun 9am–7pm, also open Mon June–Sept; tickets must be reserved in advance at museiverona.com), a 14th-century house (with balcony, naturally), said to be the Capulets' home. In the courtyard, the chest of a bronze statue of Juliet has been polished to a gleaming sheen, thanks to a legend claiming that stroking her right breast brings good fortune. **Juliet's Wall,** at the entrance, is quite a spectacle, covered with the scribbles of star-crossed lovers (though the corridor is periodically scrubbed clean of graffiti and gum); love letters placed here are taken down and, along with 5,000 mailed letters annually, answered by the Club di Giulietta (locally based volunteers). There's not much to see inside the house (period bedrooms, costumes "worn" by Romeo and Juliet), though plenty of visitors line up for a chance of a selfie on the balcony.

Once you've made the obligatory Juliet pilgrimage, focus on actual historic sights. The 1st-century **Arena di Verona ♥♥♥** (12€; Tues–Sun 9am–7pm), in the spacious Piazza Bra, is the third-largest classical arena in Italy after Rome's Colosseum and the arena at Capua—it could seat some 25,000 spectators and still hosts performances today (arena.it).

To the northwest on Piazza San Zeno, the **Basilica di San Zeno Maggiore ♥♥♥** (chieseverona.it; 4€, includes audioguide; Mar–Oct Mon–Fri 9am–6:30pm, Sat 9am–6pm, Sun 1–6:30pm; Nov–Feb Mon–Fri 10am–5pm, Sat 9:30am–5:30pm, Sun 1–5:30pm) is the greatest Romanesque church in northern Italy. The present structure was completed around 1135 over a 4th-century shrine to Verona's patron saint, St.

Zeno (who died in 380). The church's massive rose window represents the Wheel of Fortune, while lintels above the portal represent the months of the year. The highlight of the interior is Mantegna's *Madonna and Saints* above the altar.

WHERE TO EAT

Even in chic Verona, you'll spend less on a meal than in Venice. The most authentic central restaurant is **Antica Bottega del Vino ♥♥**, Via Scudo di Francia 3 (bottegavini.it; ✆ **045/8004535;** daily 11am–midnight; restaurant daily 12:30–2:40pm and 7–10:40pm), open since 1890. Dishes range from risotto with Amarone wine and tortellini with black truffle and crispy Parmesan to pigeon with broccoli and Venetian-style veal liver with toasted polenta (18€–70€). Open since 1909, **Caffè Monte Baldo ♥♥**, Via Rosa 12 (osteriamontebaldo.com; ✆ **045/8030579;** Mon and Wed–Fri 11am–midnight, Sat–Sun 10am–midnight), an old-fashioned cafe transformed into a trendy *osteria,* serves classic pastas and scrumptious *crostini* with wine in the evenings.

Treviso ♥♥

30km (19 miles) N of Venice

Long overshadowed by Venice, **Treviso** is a small, prosperous city of narrow medieval streets, Gothic churches, and an enchanting network of canals, replete with weeping willows and waterwheels (it's known as "*piccola Venezia*" or "little Venice"). Giotto's follower **Tomaso da Modena** (1326–79), one of northern Italy's lesser-known artistic geniuses, frescoed many of its churches, and its maze of back streets makes for pleasant, often tourist-free exploring. Fashion giant Benetton was founded here in 1965; the city also claims to have invented tiramisu.

ESSENTIALS

ARRIVING The fastest way to reach Treviso from Venice is by **train** from Santa Lucia station (30–40 min.). Trains run two to four times an hour, and tickets start at 3.95€ one-way. From Treviso Centrale station, it's an easy 10- to 15-minute walk to Piazza dei Signori, north across the River Sile (follow signs to "Centro"). Note also that most Ryanair budget flights to Venice actually arrive at Treviso airport (p. 401).

VISITOR INFORMATION The **tourist office** at Piazza Borsa 4 (visit treviso.it; ✆ **0422/595780**) is open Monday to Saturday 9:30am to 1:30pm and 2pm to 6pm, and Sunday 10am to 3pm.

EXPLORING TREVISO

The **Piazza dei Signori ♥♥** is the historic heart of Treviso. The square is anchored by the **Palazzo del Podestà,** rebuilt in the 1870s with a tall clock tower, and the **Palazzo dei Trecento,** the 13th-century town council hall, now home to chic Bar Beltrame beneath the arches. Just beyond the

Canal in Treviso.

square, on adjacent Piazza San Vito, sits a handsome pair of medieval churches: **Santa Lucia ♥♥** (santaluciatreviso.it; ✆ **0422/5457200**), with a superb Tomaso da Modena fresco of the *Madonna del Pavegio* in the first shrine on the right, and **San Vito ♥♥**, with its Byzantine-style frescoes from the 13th century. Both are open daily 9am to noon, and Saturday and Sunday 3:30 to 6pm; admission is free. Historic **Via Calmaggiore,** lined with posh boutiques, runs northwest from Piazza dei Signori towards the cathedral. The relatively dull neoclassical facade of the **Duomo ♥♥** (free admission; Mon–Sat 7:30am–noon and 3:30–6pm, Sun 8am–1pm and 3:30–6:30pm) is from 1836, but it's flanked by Romanesque lions that, along with its seven Venetian-Byzantine-style green copper domes, are remnants of the cathedral's 12th-century origins. The crypt is the most compelling part of the interior, with the tombs of the city's bishops amid a forest of columns and fragments of 14th-century frescoes and mosaics. The highlight in the main body of the cathedral is a fine altarpiece, the *Malchiostro Annunciation* by Titian, from 1520.

A short stroll southwest from the Duomo, the massive brick 13th- to 14th-century Italian Gothic church of **San Nicolò ♥♥** (free admission; daily 8:30am–noon and 3:30–7:30pm) houses some intriguing Gothic frescoes. Tomaso da Modena and his school decorated the huge round columns with a series of saints, notably St. Jerome, St. Agnes, and St. Romuald. Antonio da Treviso painted the absolutely gargantuan St. Christopher—his .9m-long (3-ft.) feet strolling over biting fish—in 1410.

East of Piazza dei Signori, across the **Buranelli,** the most attractive of Treviso's canals, lies the wide Canale Cagnan Grande, whose island hosts a ***pescheria*** (fish market) Monday to Saturday.

Farther east on Piazzetta Mario Botter is a deconsecrated church that's now an enjoyable museum: **Museo di Santa Caterina ♥♥** (museicivicitreviso.it; ✆ **0422/658442;** 15€; Thurs–Tues 10am–6pm). Its highlight is another fresco cycle by Tomaso da Modena, the *Story of the Life of Saint Ursula* (detached from a now-destroyed church and preserved here). There's also a cache of local archaeological finds plus minor works by Titian, Lorenzo Lotto, and Francesco Guardi.

To the south, the 15th-century church of **Santa Maria Maggiore ♥♥** (free admission; daily 8am–noon and 3:30–6pm) houses a venerated image of Mary (the Madonna Granda), a frescoed *Madonna and Child* originally painted in Byzantine style (probably pre–9th c.), and later touched up by Tomaso and members of his school.

WHERE TO EAT

Treviso has some excellent restaurants, but its real claim to fame is as the home of **tiramisu.** Legend has it that the addictive dessert was first served at restaurant **Le Beccherie ♥♥**, Piazza Ancilotto 9 (lebeccherie.it; ✆ **0422/540871;** Wed–Mon 12:20–2:15pm and 7:20–10:15pm), in 1972. The claim has been disputed over the years, but the restaurant is still open and still knocks out an exceptional tiramisu (the "classico" is 9€). In fact, just about every menu in town features tiramisu, as well as Treviso's other culinary specialty, **radicchio** (bitter red lettuce).

The bars and cafes around the ***pescheria,*** particularly along Via Palestro, are always buzzing, and perfect for sampling good-value local cuisine. For atmosphere it's hard to beat the **Hostaria Dai Naneti ♥♥**, Vicolo Broli 2 (✆ **3403/783158;** Mon–Sat 9am–2:30pm and 5–9:30pm, Sun 11am–2pm and 5–8pm; closed Sun May–Sept), a cozy tavern, deli, and cheese shop where you can grab a delicious baguette and glass of wine, or just snack at the bar for around 6€ (standing room only).

For a full meal in the center, reserve a table at **Trattoria All'Antico Portico ♥♥**, overlooking the church at Piazza Santa Maria Maggiore 18 (✆ **0422/545259;** Mon 10:30am–3pm, Wed–Sun 10:30am–3pm and 6:30–11pm), which serves local specialties such as radicchio risotto and *baccalà alla veneziana* (salt cod); main courses are 19€ to 23€.

MILAN, PIEDMONT & THE LAKES

By Michelle Schoenung

10

Milan is the glitzy capital of Lombardy (Lombardia), Italy's most prosperous region. Its businesses largely fuel the Italian economy, and its attractions—high fashion, fine dining, world-class museums, and da Vinci's *Last Supper*—draw visitors in droves. But Lombardy is much more than just one sophisticated city. To the north, the region bumps up against craggy mountains in a romantic lake district, and the south spreads into fertile farmlands fed by the Po and other rivers.

Lombardy feels different from the rest of Italy. The *Lombardi* descended from one of the Germanic tribes that overran the Roman empire and have over the centuries been ruled by feudal dynasties from Spain, Austria, and France, so they tend to be a bit more Continental than their neighbors to the south—fast-talking, faster-paced, and more business-oriented. They even dine differently, with butter often used alongside olive oil, and polenta and risotto as common as pasta—though these days the Milanese are equally enamored of sushi and other imported cuisines.

Backed by the Alps and ringed by lush gardens and verdant forests, the Italian lakes have entranced writers from Catullus to Ernest Hemingway. While each lake has its own distinct charm, they are all ideal for short retreats: Lake Maggiore and Lake Como are both less than an hour from Milan, and Lake Garda is tantalizingly close to Venice.

DON'T LEAVE MILAN & THE LAKE DISTRICT WITHOUT . . .

Paying Homage to da Vinci & Michelangelo. In Milan, you'll find *The Last Supper* in Santa Maria delle Grazie (p. 483) and the *Pietà,* Michelangelo's first work, inside the medieval Castello Sforzesco (p. 474).

Climbing to the Roof of Milan's Gothic Duomo. Wander amid the buttresses and statue-topped spires for a citywide panorama. See p. 475.

Taking a Window-Shopping Spin. Browse the high-end boutiques in and around Milan's Via Montenapoleone, then go on a budget-shopping spree on Corso Buenos Aires. See p. 495.

Ferrying Among Lake Maggiore's Borromean Islands. You can tour the palaces of one of Lombardy's last remaining Renaissance-era noble families, and watch the peacocks wander their exotic gardens. See p. 519.

Visiting Lake Garda's Picturesque Sirmione. Despite plenty of summer tourists, this historic town—which has attracted visitors since the Romans discovered hot springs here—hasn't lost its charm. See p. 513.

FACING PAGE: **City views from amid the rooftop spires of Milan's Duomo.**

MILAN ♥♥♥

552km (342 miles) NW of Rome, 288km (179 miles) NW of Florence, 257km (159 miles) W of Venice, 140km (87 miles) NE of Turin, 142km (88 miles) N of Genoa

Milan—or Milano, as the Italians say it—is elegant, chaotic, and utterly beguiling. Traffic chokes the streets, and it can be bitterly cold in winter and stiflingly hot in summer, but it more than compensates with majestic architecture and robust Northern Italian cuisine. It's a world-class stop on the international fashion stage, the banking capital of Italy, and a wealthy city of glamorous people and stylish shopping streets. Milan is also rich in history, from its Roman ruins and soaring Duomo to a host of ancient churches, medieval castles, and Renaissance palaces.

Coming fresh off its role as host for the 2026 Winter Olympics, Milan has been riding a wave of urban revitalization for over a decade now, bringing a whole new energy to this northern Italian city along with ultra-modern skyscrapers, expanded parks, bike-sharing lanes, and a wider range of bars, restaurants, and hotels.

Essentials

ARRIVING

BY PLANE **Milan Malpensa (MXP)**, 45km (28 miles) northwest of the city, is Milan's major international airport. The Malpensa Express train (malpensaexpress.it; ✆ **02-7249-4949;** 13€ one-way, 20€ round-trip) leaves from both Terminal 1 and Terminal 2 with a 30-minute run half-hourly to Cadorna train station or hourly to Stazione Centrale (45 min.). Buses run directly to Stazione Centrale, a 50-minute journey, with five trips per hour, for 10€ one-way or 16€ round-trip; they're operated by **Malpensa Shuttle** (malpensashuttle.it; ✆ **02-5858-3185**) or **Autostradale** (autostradale.it; ✆ **02-3008-9000**). By taxi, the trip into town costs more than 100€ and takes the same amount of time as the bus—50 minutes. We don't recommend it, but it's the only option after midnight. Keep in mind that the two terminals are several miles apart; a shuttle bus between them runs frequently and takes about 15 minutes. Terminal 1 is the larger, newer terminal; most travelers will leave in and out of here. Older, smaller Terminal 2 mainly serves low-cost airlines for flights within Europe.

Milan Linate (LIN), 7km (4½ miles) east of the center, handles European and domestic flights. The city's subway network now reaches Linate, with the newly expanded blue line (also known as M4) connecting the airport to the city center for the cost of a regular ticket (2.20€). City bus no. 73 leaves about every 10 minutes during the day (less frequently after about 7pm) for the city center and takes 25 minutes. Tickets cost 2.20€. A trip into town by taxi costs roughly 25€.

BY TRAIN Milan is one of Europe's busiest rail hubs. Trains travel every half-hour to Bergamo (1 hr.), Mantua (2 hr.), and Turin (1 hr. by the AV high-speed train). Stazione Centrale is a half-hour walk northeast of the center, with easy connections to Piazza del Duomo by Metro, tram, and bus. The Metro stop is called Centrale F.S. To buy train tickets, use the multilingual automatic ticket machines, which accept cash, credit cards, and ATM cards (they even have a reader for contactless cards). Keep in mind that the credit-card and ATM functions are sometimes out of order; however, attendants are typically there to help (look for official attendants wearing a vest with the Trenitalia logo, and don't let "volunteers" help you—they will often badger you for a tip at the end of the transaction). You may need to validate your ticket in the machines at the beginning of the track as you get on your train, especially if you don't have an e-ticket.

While Stazione Centrale is Milan's major station, trains also serve **Stazione Cadorna** (Como and Malpensa airport) and **Porta Garibaldi** (Lecco and the north). All these stations are on the green Metro Linea 2; Cadorna is also on the red Metro Linea 1.

BY BUS Long-distance buses are useful for reaching the ski resorts in Valle d'Aosta. Most bus services depart from the Lampugnano bus terminal (Metro Lampugnano), although some originate in Piazza Castello (Metro Cairoli). **Autostradale** (autostradale.it; ✆ **02-3008-9000**) operates most of the bus lines and has a ticket office in front of Castello Sforzesco on Piazza Castello 1 (daily 9am–6pm); **Arriva** (arriva.it; ✆ **035/289-000**) runs five daily buses (sometimes more in winter) between Milan Lampugnano and Aosta (2½ hr.; 17€) or Courmayeur (3½ hr.; 19.50€).

BY CAR The A1 autostrada links Milan with Florence (3 hr.) and Rome (6 hr.), while the A4 connects Milan with Verona (2 hr.) and Venice (2½ hr.) to the east and Turin (1 hr.) to the west. That said, we don't recommend driving around Milan—it's a huge hassle. See p. 472 for more.

GETTING AROUND

BY PUBLIC TRANSPORT Milan's most famous sights are within walking distance of one another, but the public transport system, an integrated system of Metro, trams, and buses run by **ATM** (atm.it; ✆ **02-48-607-607**), is a cheap and effective alternative to walking. The Metro closes at midnight (Sat at 1am), but buses and trams run all night. Metro stations are well-signposted, and trains are speedy, safe, and frequent—they run every couple of minutes during the day and about every 5 minutes after 9pm. Tickets for 90 minutes of travel on Metro, trams, or buses cost 2.20€. A 24-hour unlimited travel ticket is a decent value at 7.60€. Tickets are available at newsstands and Metro stations (all machines have English-language options; the 24-hr. ticket option is listed under "Urban"). Stamp your ticket when you board a bus or tram—there is a 40€ fine (more if not paid on the spot) if you don't. Ticket cards with a microchip are in the process of being rolled out, allowing transit riders to "top up" and making for a more ecological, reusable option.

Lines 1 (red, with stops at Cairoli for Castello Sforzesco and Duomo for Galleria Vittorio Emanuele II and the Duomo) and **3** (yellow, with a stop at Via Montenapoleone) are the most useful for sightseeing. The recently expanded **Line 4** (blue) now connects Linate Airport directly to the city center, and crisscrosses Milan from east to west.

> ### Milano Discount Card
>
> The **MilanoCard** (milanocard.it) offers a great deal on sightseeing at 15€ for 24 hours, 22.50€ for 2 days, or 24€ for 3 days. You get quite a bit for your buck, including a 5€ credit toward taxi travel, free travel on all public transport, discounts in some stores and restaurants, a free drink at a bar in the city, discounted luggage storage, and free or reduced entry to some of Milan's best attractions. Cards can be purchased online with a credit card, and you will receive instructions for how to activate it for the public transportation system. You have 12 months from the time of purchase to use it.

BY CAR Driving and parking in Milan are not experiences to relish. First of all, you'll have to pay the Area C congestion charge of 7.50€ to enter the *centro storico* Monday to Friday 7:30am to 7:30pm. On top of that, the one-way system is complicated, some streets are reserved for public transport only, and there are many pedestrianized areas. Hotels will make parking arrangements for guests—take advantage of that.

BY TAXI While you can't hail a taxi on the street, taxi stands can be found in major *piazze* and by major Metro stops. Taxi stands are in Piazza del Duomo and outside Castello Sforzesco; a journey between the two will cost around 10€. Hotel staff can call a taxi for you; otherwise, a reliable company is **Taxiblu** at **✆ 02-4040.** Meters start at 4.10€ during the day (7.90€ at night), and prices increase by 1.32€ per kilometer. Expect surcharges for waiting time, luggage, late-night travel, and Sunday journeys. At press time, **Uber** was still operating legally in Milan.

BY BIKE With the streets of the *centro storico* largely pedestrianized, Milan is a good city for cycling, with a handy bike-sharing program, **BikeMi** (bikemi.com), that is so popular you can't always find bikes at some stations. The tariff for the pass is very convoluted: For 4.50€ a day or 9€ a week, you can buy a pass that allows 30 minutes of free travel between one station and the next. If you keep the bike longer, you are charged .50€ per 30 minutes (or part of it) up to 2 hours; thereafter you are charged 2€ per hour (or part of it). Once you return a bike, you have to wait 5 minutes before starting another rental. There are bike racks outside Castello Sforzesco and the Duomo as well as at tram, bus, and Metro stops. Buy your pass online, by phone (**✆ 02-48-607-607**), or at the ATM Points at Centrale, Cadorna, Garibaldi, and Duomo stations (Mon–Sat 7:45am–8pm).

ON FOOT The attractions of the *centro storico* are all accessible on foot. From Piazza del Duomo, Via Montenapoleone is a 10-minute walk through Piazza della Scala and along Via Manzoni, and it is a 10-minute walk to Castello Sforzesco. Santa Maria delle Grazie and *The Last Supper* are a 30-minute stroll from Piazza del Duomo.

VISITOR INFORMATION

The **main tourist office** (called **IAT,** for Informazione e Accoglienza Turistica) is in Piazza del Duomo 14 (✆ **02-8845-5555**). It's open Monday to Friday 9am to 7pm, Saturday 9am to 6pm, and Sunday 10am to 6pm (in winter, Sat–Sun hours are limited).

CITY LAYOUT

Milan developed as a series of circles radiating out from the central hub, **Piazza del Duomo.** Within the inner circle are most of the churches, museums, and shops of the *centro storico.* **Parco Sempione** and Leonardo's *The Last Supper* are to the west in a posh neighborhood. The slightly grungy yet hip, cafe-filled districts of **Porta Ticinese** and **Navigli** lie directly south. Genteel **Brera** and its classy stores, galleries, and restaurants are slightly north of the Duomo, with the mecca of Milanese fashion, the **Quadrilatero d'Oro** (Golden Quadrilateral), lying east of there. North of the center, there's a burgeoning financial district between Porta Garibaldi and Centrale stations, while the modern towers of the CityLife development rise northwest of Castello Sforzesco.

[Fast FACTS] MILAN

ATMs/Banks Banks with multilingual ATMs are all over the city center. Bank hours are roughly Monday to Friday 8:30am to 1:30pm and 3 to 4pm; major branches open Saturday morning for a couple of hours.

Business Hours Most stores in central Milan are open Tuesday to Saturday 9:30am to 7:30pm, with a half-day Monday (3:30–7:30pm). Most shops close on Sundays, and some still close for lunch between 12:30pm and 3:30pm.

Doctors/Dentists The **Centro Medico Santagostino** has several reasonably priced clinics throughout the city and a team of doctors and dentists with many different specialties. Call or make an appointment online; the website lists prices for most types of visits (www.cmsantagostino.it/en; ✆ **02/8970-1701**). You can also reserve via WhatsApp by messaging ✆ **345/398-8236** from 8am to 6pm Monday to Saturday.

Drugstores Pharmacies rotate 24-hour shifts. Signs in most pharmacies post the schedule. In Stazione Centrale, the **Farmacia Stazione Centrale** (✆ **02/669-0735**) keeps longer hours and is often open overnight; the staff speaks English.

Emergencies All emergency numbers are free. Call ✆ **112** for **police, medical, or fire emergencies.**

Hospitals The **Ospedale Maggiore Policlinico** (✆ **02/55-031**) is a 5-minute walk southeast of the Duomo at Via Francesco Sforza 35. Some of its medical staff speak English.

Internet The city purports to offer free Wi-Fi, but logging on can be a frustrating process involving codes sent to your mobile phone (not super-helpful if your phone is on airplane mode to avoid roaming charges). Many hotels, bars, and cafes offer free Wi-Fi, but the **Starbucks Reserve Roastery** (www.roastery.starbucks.it) is probably the best place in the city for free Wi-Fi and clean public bathrooms.

Police For police emergencies, dial ✆ **112.** A

police station is in Stazione Centrale; the **Questura** is at the main station, just west of the Giardini Pubblici at Via Fatebenefratelli 11 (✆ **02/62-261;** Metro: Turati).

Post Office The main post office, **Poste e Telecomunicazioni,** is at Via Cordusio 4 (✆ **02/7248-2508;** Metro: Cordusio). It's open Monday to Friday 8:20am to 7:05pm and Saturday 8:30am to 12:35pm. The post office in Stazione Centrale is open Monday to Saturday 8:20am to 7:05pm. Other branches are open Monday to Saturday 8:30am to 1:30pm.

Safety Milan has generally low levels of street crime, although public parks and the area around Stazione Centrale are best avoided at night.

Exploring Milan

The **Piazza del Duomo** has been the beating heart of Milan since the Romans took over in 222 B.C.E., naming it Mediolanum. This vast traffic-free piazza sees local life passing to and fro daily, while tourists peer up at the majestic **Duomo** (p. 475) and street sellers push cheap souvenirs. From here a tangle of narrow streets branch off in all directions through the city's *centro storico* (historic center). The square took on its present form following the Unification of Italy in 1861, when its medieval buildings were replaced by splendid neoclassical buildings designed by Giuseppe Mengoni (1829–77), also architect of the **Galleria Vittorio Emanuele II** (p. 478). Located around the piazza are the superb **Museo del Duomo** (p. 480), temporary art exhibitions in the **Palazzo Reale** (www.palazzorealemilano.it; ✆ **02/8844-5181**), and 20th-century Italian art in the **Museo del Novecento** (p. 480).

Note: Dress modestly when visiting Milan's churches: no short shorts for anyone. Shoulders must be covered, and skirts have to hit below the knee. The dress code at the Duomo is particularly strict.

Castello Sforzesco ♥ MUSEUM Although it has lived many lives under several different occupiers and been restored many times, this fortified castle is the masterpiece of Milan's two most powerful medieval and Renaissance dynasties, the Visconti and the Sforza. The Visconti built the castle (as well as the Duomo) in the 14th century; after the Sforzas married into the Visconti clan and eclipsed their power, they took the castle in the 1450s, transforming it into one of the most gracious palaces of the Renaissance. Sforza *capo* Ludovico il Moro and his wife, Beatrice d'Este, helped make Milan one of Italy's Renaissance centers by commissioning works by Bramante and da Vinci.

The castle was extensively restored by architect Luca Beltrami at the end of the 19th century, and restoration is always ongoing. It opened as a museum in 1905; today it contains a dozen museums, known collectively as the Musei del Castello Sforzesco. Many Sforza treasures are on view in the castle's labyrinthine courtyards and corridors, including a *pinacoteca* (painting gallery) with works by Bellini and Correggio plus Mannerists Ribera and Ricci. During recent cleaning and work done to the Filarete Tower—its distinctive look and shape make it a symbol of Milan—a list of wind types was found on the octagonal dome suggesting that Beltrami had conceived this as a Tower of Wind.

The area of the castle known as the Spanish Hospital (in the late 1500s, it was used as an infirmary by the castle's Spanish garrison) has been renovated to house Michelangelo's final work: the evocative, unfinished *Pietà Rondanini* marble sculpture, which was discovered in his Roman workshop after he died in 1564 at age 89 (✆ **02/8846-3700**).

Piazza Castello. milanocastello.it. ✆ **02/8846-3700.** Castle courtyards: Free admission. Daily 7am–7:30pm. Museums: 5€ adults, 3€ seniors and ages 18–25 (free on 2nd and 3rd Tues of month 2–5:30pm), free for ages 17 and under. Tues–Sun 9am–5:30pm (last entry 30 min. before closing). Metro: Cairoli.

Duomo di Milano ♥♥♥ CHURCH Although there has been a church here since at least C.E. 355, building began on Milan's magnificent Duomo—the last of Italy's great Gothic structures—in 1386 during the reign of the Visconti family. It took 5 centuries to complete; its mammoth cast-bronze doors were finally finished in 1965. Today it is the fourth-largest church in the world (after St. Peter's in Rome, Seville's cathedral, and a relatively new one on the Ivory Coast), with 135 marble spires, a stunning triangular facade, and 3,400-some statues flanking the massive yet surprisingly airy, fanciful exterior, which dominates the vast, traffic-free Piazza del Duomo.

Milan's Duomo, a masterwork of Gothic architecture.

The cavernous interior, lit by brilliant stained-glass windows, can hold 40,000 people but is usually quite serene, divided into five aisles by a forest of 52 columns. The poet Shelley used to sit and read Dante here, surrounded by monuments that include a gruesomely graphic **statue of St. Bartholomew** (who was flayed alive). Another British visitor, Alfred, Lord Tennyson, rhapsodized about the view from the roof (p. 478). In the crypt, the **Battistero di San Giovanni alle Fonti** reveals remains of the octagonal 4th-century foundations of an earlier church that stood here, which is almost certainly where Sant'Ambrogio—patron saint and bishop of Milan in C.E. 374—christened the great missionary St. Augustine. Pride of place in the crypt goes to the ornate gilded **tomb of San Carlo Borromeo,**

ATTRACTIONS

Basilica di San Lorenzo Maggiore **5**
Basilica di Sant'Ambrogio **11**
Basilica di Sant'Eustorgio **4**
Castello Sforzesco **17**
Conservatorio di Musica Giuseppe Verdi **31**
Duomo di Milano **29**
Galleria Vittorio Emanuele II **24**
Il Cenacolo Vinciano (The Last Supper) **15**
Museo Archeologico **10**
Museo del Duomo **30**
Museo del Novecento **28**
Museo di Storia Naturale **32**
Museo Nazionale Scienza e Tecnologia Leonardo da Vinci **12**
Museo Poldi Pezzoli **22**
Piazza del Duomo **26**
Pinacoteca Ambrosiana **8**
Pinacoteca di Brera **21**
Santa Maria del Carmine **19**
Santa Maria delle Grazie **13**
Teatro alla Scala **23**
Triennale di Milano **16**

HOTELS

Antica Locanda Leonardo **14**
BioCity Hotel **35**
Hotel Principe di Savoia **34**
Milano Suites **18**
nhow Milan **2**

RESTAURANTS

Contraste **3**
Joia **33**
La Pesa Trattoria dal 1902 **1**
Nerino Dieci Trattoria **7**
Osteria il Kaimano **20**
Panini De Santis **9**
Pizzeria Tradizionale **6**
Restaurant Giacomo Arengario **27**
Ristorante Cracco **25**

Milan
Stazione Centrale
Piazza S. Camillo de Lellis
Piazza S. Giochino
Piazzale Principessa Clotilde
Piazza della Repubblica
Repubblica
Piazza Cincinnato
Piazza S. Francesco Romana
Piazzale Lavaler
Piazza Otto Novembre
Piazza Guglielmo
Turati
Palazzo Dugnani
Giardini Pubblici
Planetario
Museo di Storia Naturale
Galleria d'Arte Moderna
Pinacoteca di Brera
BRERA
Museo del Risorgimento
Orto Botanico
Museo Bagatti Valsecchi
Palazzo Senato
QUAD D'ORO
Palazzo Serbelloni
Museo di Milano
Prefettura
Monte Napoleone
Teatro alla Scala
Piazza F. L. Meda
Municipio
S. Babila
Piazza S. Babila
Galleria Vittorio Emanuele II
Piazza Duomo
Duomo
Palazzo Arcivescovile
Palazzo Reale
Largo Augusto
Piazza S. Pietro in Gessate
Piazza Cinque Giornate
Piazza Fratelli Bandiera
Corso Concordia
Piazza Risorgimento
S. Stefano
Piazza G. Missori
Missori
Torre Velasca
Università degli Studi
Largo F. Richini
Palazzo di Giustizia
Rotonda della Besana
S. Nazaro
S. Eufemia
Crocetta
Piazza A. Ferrari
Porta Romana
Venice
Rome
0 1/4 mi
0 250 m

MILAN FROM on high

Take the trip up to the roof of the Duomo (duomomilano.it) for spine-tingling views across the rooftops of Milan and, on a clear day, to the Alps beyond.

Atop the Duomo, surrounded by Gothic pinnacles, saintly statues, and flying buttresses, you even get a close-up view of the spire-top gold statue of ***La Madonnina*** (the little Madonna), the city's beloved good-luck charm. You can either ascend by elevator (18€; go to the church's northeast corner, almost to the back of the Duomo) or climb the stairs (16€; stairs are on the church's north flank). A pass combining a roof-top visit with entrance to the cathedral and the Museo del Duomo (p. 480) costs 22€ if you take the stairs, 26€ if you opt for the elevator. The pass is good for 2 days, and there are discounts for children and seniors. The elevator is open daily 9am to 6:30pm (last ticket sold at 6pm).

Other sneaky viewpoints over the Duomo include the food market on the top floor of department store **La Rinascente** (p. 495) and the posh **Restaurant Giacomo Arengario** (p. 492) at the **Museo del Novecento** (p. 480).

archbishop of Milan and leader of the Counter-Reformation, who died in 1584. Entrance to the crypt is included in admission to the Museo del Duomo (p. 480), though opening times may be different.

Piazza del Duomo. duomomilano.it. ✆ **02/7202-2656.** Variety of ticket options starting at 10€. Daily 9am–7pm for visitors. Metro: Duomo.

Galleria Vittorio Emanuele II ♥♥ SHOPPING ARCADE The best place from which to admire the Duomo facade is from the cafe at the entrance of the Galleria, Milan's late-19th-century prototype of the modern shopping mall. No modern malls even come close to matching the Galleria for style and flair, however; this wonderful steel-and-glass-covered, cross-shaped arcade is a neoclassical beauty, with ornate marble flooring and a massive octagonal glass dome. Inside, the arcade is lined with grand cafes such as Biffi and Savini, where the local elite gather to dine after a night at the opera. Designer stores here include Gucci, Versace, Prada, and Louis Vuitton. Its span links the Piazza del Duomo with Piazza della Scala, site of the famous opera house.

The Galleria was the masterpiece of Bolognese architect Giuseppe Mengoni, who designed it in the 1870s to mark the unification of Italy under King Vittorio Emanuele II; mosaic and fresco decorations incorporate the patriotic symbols and coats of arms of various Italian cities. Mengoni never saw his magnus opus flourishing—he died in a fall from scaffolding the day before it opened in 1877. Today giggling visitors gather under the dome to spin around on one heel on the private parts of a little mosaic bull in the floor, a legendary good-luck ritual.

Piazza del Duomo. Open 24 hr. Metro: Duomo.

Museo Archeologico ♥♥ MUSEUM Milan's expertly curated archaeology museum is housed in a series of airy galleries among the cloisters, towers, and courtyards of the 8th-century convent of Monastero Maggiore of San Maurizio. As was common at the time, the convent was constructed atop an older structure, so part of the museum is built around the remains of an ancient villa and a section of 4th-century Roman walls, which fortified Milan—then called Mediolanum—in its heyday as capital of the Western Roman Empire. A 3rd-century defense tower has well-preserved medieval frescoes on its rounded walls portraying Jesus showing his stigmata to St. Francis. The inner cloister leads from the former convent to a more modern extension with Milanese, Greek, and Etruscan artifacts, some of which were excavated locally. Highlights of the collection include a 1st-century-B.C.E. mosaic pavement unearthed nearby in 1913; the stunning, gleaming 4th-century Trivulzio Diatreta Cup, made of the finest hand-blown glass and featuring the inscription BIBE VIVAS MULTIS ANNIS (drink so you can live many years); the Parabiago plate, an ancient Roman silver serving plate depicting mythological figures; and busts of various emperors from Caesar on. There is also an impressive collection of Gandhara art, originating from the ancient region corresponding to present-day northern Pakistan and northeastern Afghanistan, with

MILAN'S time-travel CHURCHES

Milan has been an important center of Christianity since Emperor Constantine sanctioned the faith in C.E. 313. The city has more than 100 churches, and, like the Duomo, many of them lie on pagan foundations. In these, layer upon layer of history can be stripped back to their early remains.

Two such churches are on Corso di Porta Ticinese. The **Basilica di San Lorenzo Maggiore** was built in the 4th century, using rubble removed from an ancient amphitheater (the row of 16 Corinthian columns outside are relics of the theater). The church now has a 16th-century facade, but inside, fragments of the original building survive: The octagonal Cappella di Sant'Aquilino retains pieces of the 4th-century gold mosaic that once covered all the walls, and to the right of this, stairs lead down to the foundations of the first basilica. Down the street, the **Basilica di Sant'Eustorgio** has undergone many face-lifts. The present Neo-Romanesque facade dates from 1865, but foundations of the original 4th-century church are behind the altar, and the ornate Cappella Portinari, a memorial to St. Peter of Verona, dates from the 15th century.

In Piazza Sant'Ambrogio, the sublime Lombard Romanesque **Basilica di Sant'Ambrogio** was built over a Roman cemetery and extensively remodeled from the 8th to 11th centuries. The remains of Milan's patron saint, Ambrogio, are housed here in the great gold altar, constructed in the 9th century; scenes from the saint's life are depicted in glittering mosaics in the apse and wall frescoes in the side chapels.

The church of **Santa Maria del Carmine** in Brera was built over the remains of a Romanesque basilica and partly remodeled in 1400; most of its present incarnation dates from 1447. Its baroque presbytery was added in the 17th century and the Gothic-Lombard facade in 1880, making the church a true stylistic mishmash.

exquisite sculptures and artifacts showcasing the meeting of Greco-Roman and Buddhist artistic traditions.

Corso Magenta 15. museoarcheologicomilano.it. ✆ **02/8844-5208.** Admission 5€ adults, 3€ seniors; free after 2pm on 1st Tues of month. Tues–Sun 10am–5:30pm. Metro: Cadorna.

Museo del Duomo ♥♥♥ MUSEUM Despite the name, this museum is actually located across the piazza from the Duomo, on the ground floor of Palazzo Reale. Captivating treasures from the cathedral are displayed here, offering a greater understanding of the famous Duomo. An imaginatively constructed exhibition serves as a chronological narrative of Milan and its cathedral. Highlights among the carved cherubs, angels, and Renaissance Madonnas displayed include a room full of startling gargoyles, ethereal 15th-century stained-glass works, scale models of the cathedral, and the original supporting structure of *La Madonnina* (p. 478), which has adorned the Duomo rooftop since 1774. The standout piece is *Christ Disputing in the Temple* by Tintoretto, rediscovered by happy accident in the Duomo sacristy after World War II.

Piazza del Duomo 12. duomomilano.it. ✆ **02/7200-3768.** Admission 10€ adults, 5€ seniors and ages 26 and under (ticket includes cathedral admission). Open daily 10am–7pm except Wed. Metro: Duomo.

Museo del Novecento ♥ MUSEUM Next door to the Palazzo Reale, Milan's museum of 20th-century art showcases Italian modern art from the Futurist movement to Pop art, making the case that Italy's contribution to the world of art did not end with the Renaissance. While that claim is only partially successful, you will see some brilliant bursts of genius like works by Amedeo Modigliani, such as *The Portrait of Beatrice Hastings* (1915), which marked his definitive return to painting after a period of working on sculpture, and the moving *Thirst* (1934) by sculptor Arturo Martini. There is a focus on Futurism here that emphasizes Italy's pioneering role in the development of modern art in the 20th century. Boccioni's *Unique Forms of Continuity in Space* (1913), for example, is an iconic work that embodies the movement's fascination with motion. One of the best things about this museum? The views of the Duomo and its famous square.

Via Marconi 1. www.museodelnovecento.org. ✆ **02/8844-0461.** Admission 5€ adults, 3€ seniors, free for kids 17 and under. Tues–Sun 10am–7:30pm (Thurs until 10:30pm). Metro: Duomo.

Museo Nazionale Scienza e Tecnologia Leonardo da Vinci ♥♥ MUSEUM The cavernous science museum occupies a former Benedictine monastery, and its picturesque cloister is seamlessly integrated with various modern additions. Make sure to pick up a brochure at the entrance in order to navigate the somewhat confusing layout. Parts of the museum have a certain endearingly nostalgic quality, but the Leonardo da Vinci galleries, for example, are more modern and interactive. Here you'll find more than 170 historical models, works of art, and ancient documents that bring the narrative to life—and make this the largest permanent exhibition in the world dedicated to da Vinci, the man, inventor, and humanist. There is also a hangar filled with planes, trains, and carriages. There's even a historic submarine to visit (tickets cost an extra 10€ for adults and 8€ for those 3–17; buy at the museum or online at museoscienza.org/toti). The museum often holds interactive science labs and has a tinkering zone and maker space for kids, but most activities are held in Italian.

Via San Vittore 21. museoscienza.org. ✆ **02/485-551.** Admission 13€ adults, 8€ seniors and ages 3–26, free for children 2 and under. Tues–Fri 9:30am–5pm; Sat–Sun 9:30am–6:30pm. Metro: Sant'Ambrogio.

Museo Poldi Pezzoli ♥♥ MUSEUM Aristocrat Gian Giacomo Poldi Pezzoli donated his cache of art and decorative objects to the city in 1879. This wonderfully eclectic collection is now elegantly displayed in the apartments of his luxurious 17th-century *palazzo,* one of Milan's several "house museums," giving visitors insight into how the upper class lived in previous centuries. The ornate rooms of the ground floor feature Oriental rugs, ancient armor, and rare books. Up the carved marble stairs the riches continue, through extravagant rooms adorned with family portraits, Murano glass, and Limoges china. Scenes from *The Divine Comedy* are featured in stained glass, and gilded pistols sit beside precious jewelry. Highlights include the Armillary Sphere, crafted by Flemish clockmaker Gualterus Arsenius in 1568 to illustrate contemporary theories of planetary movement, and Renaissance paintings by Botticelli and Piero della Francesca in the Golden Room. The clock room boasts more than 500 pieces from the Renaissance to the late 1800s.

Via Manzoni 12. museopoldipezzoli.it. ✆ **02/794-889.** Admission 15€ adults, 13€ seniors, 10€ students 11–18, free for children 10 and under. Audioguide 5€. Wed–Mon 10am–6pm; closed Tues. Metro: Montenapoleone.

cruising THE CANALS

Milan's **Navigli** area (*navigli* means "canals") is the perfect spot for a relaxed drink, people-watching, or a late-night supper. (To get there, take Metro Line 2 to Porta Genova.) Its streets are refreshingly casual in ambience as compared to the city center—it's one of the few places in Milan where you will see punks, hippies, and goths, and an abundance of vintage-clothing stores.

Construction of the canals started in the late 13th century, for defensive purposes and to transport marble slabs from quarries along Lake Maggiore (p. 518) to build the Duomo. The Naviglio Grande was Europe's first major canal and remains an engineering marvel of the medieval era. Used to import food, commodities, and trade goods, the canals were crucial to Milan's infrastructure until the 1970s, when road transport won out. Take a boat tour of the canals to peek into Milan's industrial heritage. **Navigami** (navigami.com; ✆ **02/867-131**) runs frequent tours, though lack of rain in recent years, especially during the summer, has led to low water levels in the canals. Check to make sure boats are running.

Pinacoteca Ambrosiana ♥♥ MUSEUM Founded in 1609 to display the collections of the pious Cardinal of Milan Federico Borromeo, this gallery is housed in Europe's second-oldest public library (after the Bodleian in Oxford). The space, which mostly features Italian art from the 15th to 20th centuries, has a confusing layout—a maze of courtyards, passageways, stairwells, and any number of tiny exhibition rooms—but it's worth persisting to find four outstanding artworks: the cartoon for *The School of Athens* by Raphael (1510), back in public viewing after a 4-year restoration; Caravaggio's charming *Basket with Fruit*, from around 1599; and Titian's *Adoration of the Magi* (ca. 1550). The fourth, the haunting *Portrait of a Musician* from sometime in the 1480s has been attributed to Leonardo da Vinci, although many scholars question whether the master only painted a part of it (most likely the figure's face) and was assisted with the rest of it by his students. If it is indeed a da Vinci, however, it's his only painting hanging in any Italian museum. You can hit most of the major works in the first eight rooms of the museum (there are about 24 in total).

Leonardo's original ***Codex Atlanticus*** is in the reading room of the Biblioteca Ambrosiana next door, along with other rare manuscripts. Leonardo's entire life as an artist and scientist can be found in this extraordinary collection. Drawings from the *Codex,* which consists of 1,750 drawings and jottings the master did between 1478 and 1519, can also be seen in the Sacristy of Bramante in **Santa Maria delle Grazie** (p. 483).

Piazza Pio XI. ambrosiana.eu. ✆ **02/806-921.** Pinacoteca 17€ (plus Codex Atlanticus 20€ adults), 13€ seniors, 5€ ages 6–14, free for kids 5 and under. Tues–Sun 10am–6pm. Metro: Duomo or Cordusio.

Pinacoteca di Brera ♥♥♥ MUSEUM Milan's, and indeed Lombardy's, premier art collection can be found in a 17th-century Jesuit college, wrapped around a two-story arcaded courtyard. This peerless collection leads the visitor through 38 roughly chronological rooms showcasing Italian art from medieval times to Surrealism. Along the way are splendid Renaissance altarpieces, Venetian School and baroque paintings, gloomy Mannerist works, and the odd piece by Carlo Carrà and Umberto Boccioni.

Although the collection is not immense, it is of exquisite quality; highlights include Piero della Francesca's sublime **Montefeltro Altarpiece** (1474); the ethereal ***Dead Christ*** by Andrea Mantegna (1480); Caravaggio's superb, mournful ***Supper at Emmaus*** (1601); and Raphael's ***Marriage of the Virgin*** (1504), expertly kept in glass-walled, temperature-controlled restoration rooms, which are also open to the public. More modern standouts include Francesco Hayez's ***The Kiss*** (1859) and artist Giovanni Fattori's pastoral scenes, which paved the way for the late-19th-century Macchiaioli School of Italian Impressionists. Moving the collection up to the present day are works by the Italian playboy artist Amedeo Modigliani and sculptor Marino Marini. Some of the Pinacoteca's

Gallery in the Pinacoteca di Brera.

contemporary works are now displayed in the nearby Palazzo Citterio, just a few doors away. This long-anticipated expansion has led to a dynamic, multi-site cultural complex known collectively as "Grande Brera."

Via Brera 28. pinacotecabrera.org. ✆ **02/722-632-30.** Admission 15€ adults, 2€ ages 18–25, 1€ seniors Tues–Wed, free for kids 17 and under. Tues–Sun 8:30am–7:15pm (until 10:15pm 3rd Thurs of month). Free every 1st Sun of month. Metro: Lanza.

Santa Maria delle Grazie ♥♥ CHURCH The delightful Lombard Renaissance church of Santa Maria delle Grazie is often ignored in the mad scramble to see Leonardo da Vinci's world-renowned *Last Supper* (see below) in the *cenacolo* (refectory) of the Dominican convent attached to the church. Started in 1465–82 by Guiniforte Solari (ca. 1429–81), the church was enlarged when the Sforza duke Ludovico il Moro (p. 474) decided to make it his family mausoleum. He commissioned Leonardo da Vinci to paint the *Last Supper,* and asked Donato Bramante, the leading architect of the Lombard Renaissance—who also helped design St. Peter's in Rome—to add the terra-cotta-and-cream-colored choir in 1492. Inside the church itself, note the clash of styles between Solari's frescoed Gothic nave and Bramante's airy, somber apse.

Piazza Santa Maria delle Grazie. legraziemilano.it. ✆ **02/467-6111.** Free admission. Mon–Sat 7am–noon and 3–7:30pm (4–7:30pm summer); Sun 7:30am–12:30pm and 4–9pm. Metro: Cadorna or Conciliazione.

Santa Maria delle Grazie, Il Cenacolo Vinciano (The Last Supper) ♥♥♥ CHURCH Milan's greatest art treasure is also one of the

To protect Da Vinci's fragile masterpiece *The Last Supper,* visitors are only allowed to enter in small groups with timed-entry tickets.

most famous on earth. Painted for Ludovico il Moro by Leonardo da Vinci between 1495 and 1497, *The Last Supper* adorns the back wall of the refectory in the Dominican convent attached to Santa Maria delle Grazie. Leonardo's masterpiece depicts Christ revealing that one of his disciples will soon betray him; horror and disbelief are etched into every face, while Jesus remains calm and resigned. As we look at the mural—often called a fresco, it was not painted using traditional fresco techniques—Judas sits to the left of Jesus, leaning away from him with the bag of silver in his right hand. Is that Mary Magdalene sitting between him and Jesus? (Most historians think it's St. John, who was typically depicted as a beautiful youth.) Wherever you stand on the issue, there's no doubt that *The Last Supper* is one of the world's most poignant works of art.

In experimenting with his painting technique, Leonardo applied tempera straight on to the walls of the refectory. As a result, his work began to deteriorate virtually as soon as it was completed. It suffered several botched restoration attempts in the 18th and 19th centuries and survived target practice by Napoleon's troops, not to mention a period exposed to the open air after Allied bombing in World War II. Over the years, the mural has been restored, and though the colors are muted, they are thought to resemble Leonardo's original. The famous painting is now climate-controlled for preservation; small groups are allowed in to view it, in pre-allocated periods of 15 minutes.

Piazza Santa Maria delle Grazie 2. cenacolovinciano.org. ✆ **02/9280-0360.** Admission 15€ adults, 2€ ages 18–25, free for kids 17 and under; 2€ booking fee for all tickets. Reservations essential. Tues–Sun 8:15am–7pm. Metro: Cadorna or Conciliazione.

Triennale di Milano ♥♥♥ MUSEUM Located at the north end of Parco Sempione by the Torre Branca, this cultural institution has been around since 1923, featuring on-trend temporary exhibitions and events focused on modern craftsmanship, fashion, theater, and photography. Some of the exhibitions are more interesting than others, but the garden and terrace restaurant (when open) are worth a visit.

Viale Alemagna 6. triennale.org. ✆ **02/724-341.** Depending on exhibition, tickets start at around 5€ adults, free for kids 15 and under. Tues–Sun 11am–8pm. Metro: Cadorna or Cairoli.

Outlying Attractions

Autodromo Nazionale Monza ♥♥ RACING CIRCUIT Located along the River Lambro, 15km (10¼ miles) northeast of Milan, Monza is an appealing city with a photogenic central core and a sprawling park that is famous throughout Europe. Sadly, the *centro storico* is usually bypassed in favor of this 10km (6.2-mile) Formula 1 racetrack, the epicenter of car-mad Italy's hopes and dreams. The home of the Italian Grand Prix since 1922, Monza track is now open to any and all who fancy being a racing driver for the day. Race-training sessions are held on a regular basis, with half-hour slots available for would-be champions to try out their skills on the track. Rallies, races, and special events take place all year round. Check the website for tickets and event details.

Via Vedano 5, Monza. monzanet.it. ✆ **039/24-821.** Ticket prices vary by race and event. Trains to Monza take about 15 min. from Centrale or Garibaldi station; park is a 15-min. walk from the town center.

Certosa di Pavia ♥♥♥ CHURCH Located a few miles north of the town of Pavia, this awe-inspiring Carthusian monastery was originally commissioned in 1396 as a mausoleum for Milan's ruling Visconti family

seeing ***THE LAST SUPPER***

Unsurprisingly, Leonardo's *The Last Supper* is on almost every tourist's Milan itinerary. As a maximum of 30 people are allowed into the Cenacolo Vinciano at a time, it is a challenge to get a ticket if you don't book well in advance. **Three months** or more before you are due to visit, try the official website first, cenacolovinciano.org, or call ✆ **02/9280-0360** (tickets are 15€ from the website, plus a 2€ booking fee; children 17 and under enter free but still pay the 2€ fee.

If you have purchased your tickets online (maximum of five tickets per order), go to the booking office outside the Cenacolo in Piazza Santa Maria delle Grazie at least 20 minutes before your allotted time slot. You will need to show identification that matches the name on the reservation. And remember that the Cenacolo is not in the church of Santa Maria delle Grazie itself, but in the refectory behind it, with a separate entrance of its own.

If you haven't been able to snag a ticket in advance, many tour companies guarantee admission to *The Last Supper* as part of their guided tours of the city, which range from 40€ to 70€ (see "Organized Tours," p. 486). You can also check the official website for last-minute tickets on Wednesdays around noon Italy time, when additional tickets are often released.

(p. 474). After their dynastic downfall, the Sforza family took over, refurbishing per their exorbitant tastes. The highly intricate Renaissance facade is the swan song of 15th-century master architect Giovanni Antonio Amadeo, who also worked on Bergamo's Basilica di Santa Maria Maggiore (p. 498). The monastery contains the ornate tombs (but not the bodies) of Ludovico del Moro and his wife, Beatrice, who together shaped the Milanese Renaissance. A tour takes in the peaceful cloisters, monks' cells, and refectory, but the highlight is the church, with its frescoes, the *pietra dura* altar, and the massive mausoleum of Gian Galeazzo Visconti, the first duke of Milan.

Via Del Monumento 4, Certosa di Pavia. museo.certosadipavia.beniculturali.it. ✆ **0382/925-613.** Admission and guided tours by donation. Tues–Sun 9–11:30am and 2:30–6pm (closes 5:30pm Apr and Sept, 5pm Mar and Oct, 4pm Nov–Feb). Metro Line 3 to Certosa, then a 10-min. walk.

Parks & Gardens

Milan is a densely populated urban sprawl where green space is rare and precious, though the city has worked hard in recent years to plant more trees and build and expand parks. The largest park is the 47-hectare (116-acre) **Parco Sempione** behind Castello Sforzesco, a favorite place for well-heeled Milanese to walk their dogs along shady pathways sheltered by giant chestnuts. The **Giardini Pubblici** at Porta Venezia is another haven, a firm favorite with families on the weekend for its playgrounds and proximity to the National History Museum. Joggers circle the park, and in winter there's ice skating.

The 1930s-era **Villa Necchi Campiglio** (fondoambiente.it/villa-necchi-campiglio-eng) is probably the most famous "house museum" in the city, especially considering it has been the setting for various films, including *House of Gucci* (though nobody in the Gucci family ever actually lived here). Its lush gardens and outdoor swimming pool make it an oasis of tranquility right in the heart of the city, between Porta Venezia and the Duomo. Sit in the garden and catch your breath from a busy day sightseeing, or come here for *aperitivo* and watch the sun go down poolside. It is free to enter the gardens.

Organized Tours

Among the scores of companies offering guided tours of Milan and Lombardy, here are a few of the best. **Zani Viaggi** (zaniviaggi.it; ✆ **02/867-131**) leads specialist tours to the revered turf of San Siro Stadium (p. 487) and the shopping outlets of northern Lombardy. **Opera d'Arte** (operadartemilano.it; ✆ **02/4548-7400**) offers guided tours of exhibitions, museums, and historic sites, including a special Castello Sforzesco tour with access to the battlements and underground areas that typically are not open to the public.

Risotto & Steel (risottoandsteel.com; ✆ **339/217-6067**) offers tours of Milan's best eating destinations starting at the Duomo, and with the

Match Day in Milan

Milan is also a prime destination for football, aka soccer, or *calcio* as it is called in Italy. To attend a soccer match at Milan's enormous **San Siro Stadium** (set to be demolished in the coming years to make way for a more modern venue by 2032), check the schedule on the official websites of the two local teams: **AC Milan** (acmilan.com) or **Inter Milan** (inter.it), which both have ticketing portals. It is best to avoid unofficial resellers. The most popular games (for example, the hotly contested "derby" match between the two hometown rivals) sell out quickly, so buy early. Keep in mind that sometimes the actual game time is not announced (or may change) until about 10 days before the event; in rare cases, the match may be held a day or two before or after what is listed on the schedule. On match day, make sure to bring a valid form of ID (even for children) to pass through the tight stadium security. When there are no matches scheduled, the stadium is also open for **tours** (sansirostadium.com; ✆ **02/4879-8201;** Metro: San Siro Stadio).

opportunity to explore other areas like the artsy Brera neighborhood and Navigli canal district. Run by American Elizabeth De Filippo-Jones, a culinary and culture producer, Risotto & Steel aims to allow visitors to experience immersive, convivial, and regional gastronomy.

Especially for Kids

Despite being world-renowned as a hub of high finance, fashion, and design, Milan is after all an Italian city—and all Italians dote on children. The city's rather formal facade belies its many family-friendly attractions, museums, *gelaterie,* and play parks. Everywhere you go, your *bambini* will be worshipped, hugged, and multilaterally adored.

Where to start? Chief among attractions is the **Duomo rooftop** (p. 478) for views of the city's red rooftops and the new skyscraper district, all the way to the Alps. The **Museo Nazionale Scienza e Tecnologia Leonardo da Vinci** (p. 480) is stuffed full of fun interactive activities for kids. Children ages 4 to 11 can enjoy workshops (usually in Italian) at the Sforzinda children's area in the 14th-century dungeons of **Castello Sforzesco** (p. 474) while parents explore the decorative arts. A picnic lunch and a jog in adjoining **Parco Sempione** is a welcome respite from cultural overload. The **Darsena,** the historic port of the canal network in the Navigli area, is a great place to watch boats go by, either in one of the seating areas or at waterside cafes.

The **Museo dei Bambini,** Via Enrico Besana 12 (muba.it; ✆ **02/4398-0402**), offers creative and educational workshops for children ages 2 and up (mostly in Italian, however). Opening times vary, as do the costs of workshops, which tend to run around 10€.

Another great green public space is the **Giardini Pubblici Indro Montanelli** (p. 486), which has playgrounds, roundabouts, and a little electric train that chugs around the park. On the Corso Venezia side of the park, you can take the kids to the **Museo di Storia Naturale** (museodistorianaturalemilano.it; ✆ **02/8846-3337;** Tues–Sun 9am–5:30pm; admission 5€ adults, 3€ seniors and students 18–25, free for kids 17 and under) to see dinosaur skeletons and the carcasses of massive bugs. Though the exhibitions are a bit dated, the museum is slowly being modernized.

Near Porta Romana, the **Bagni Misteriosi,** Via Carlo Botta 18 (bagnimisteriosi.com; ✆ **02/8973-1800**), is an outdoor swimming pool from the 1930s that was abandoned for decades and has been brought back to life. It's a great place to beat the heat in the torrid summer months, but make sure to arrive early to get a chair or a spot in the grass. Whatever you do, bring a swim cap (standard practice in most pools in Italy) or you'll be charged around 8€ for one. Full-day admission is typically 14€ (8€ half day).

Near Linate airport, just east of the city center, the park **Idroscalo,** Via Circonvallazione Idroscalo 29, Segrate (idroscalo.info; no phone; daily summer 7am–9pm, winter until 5pm), features a man-made lake that was originally created for seaplanes to land. The park offers every outdoor activity from sailing and swimming to climbing or tennis.

Most restaurants will happily rustle up a child's portion of pasta and tomato sauce, and if all else fails, it's usually easy to bribe any child with a visit to one of Milan's delicious ice cream shops. Try **Biancolatte,** Via

FUN IN THE theme parks

Italy's version of Disneyland, **Gardaland,** is located a couple of hours from Milan in Castelnuovo del Garda (p. 514), but plenty of other options lie closer to the city.

If you're looking to beat the summertime heat, the **Acquatica** waterpark, Via Gaetano Airaghi 61 (acquaticapark.it; ✆ **02/4820-0134**), on the far western outskirts of town has splashy waterslides, rides, and picnic areas. It opens at the end of May and closes at the end of August. To get there, take the subway's lilac line (also called MM5) to the San Siro stop, then either bus 80 (toward Quinto Romano) or bus 423 (toward Settimo Milanese), both of which stop directly in front of the waterpark. The park is open daily 10am to 7pm. An all-day ticket costs 28€ adults, 21€ for kids under 12. Children under 100cm (3 ft., 3 in.) tall enter for free. Enter after 2:30pm for slightly reduced tickets. Parking costs between 3€ and 5€ depending on the day of week.

About 30 minutes northeast of Milan in the direction of Bergamo, **Leolandia,** Via Vittorio Veneto 52, Capriate San Gervasio (leolandia.it) has rides and games for kids of all ages, as well as the delightful Minitalia, a replica of major cities and monuments in Italy. More compact and manageable than Gardaland, it may be better suited to smaller children, with features such as Peppa Pig World and Thomas the Tank Engine. Tickets purchased at the park cost 47.50€, but can be half that online. Children up to 89cm (about 3 ft.) enter free. Leolandia opens officially in March and stays open through Halloween. In late winter and fall, it's open weekends only; in the summer, it's open daily. The Z301 Milan-Bergamo bus, managed by **Nord Est Trasporti** (nordesttrasporti.it; ✆ **800/905-150**), stops near Leolandia, at Capriate San Gervasio.

Turati 30 (© **02/6208-6177**), for baked goods and ice-cream cakes, or **Chocolat,** Via Boccaccio 9 (© **02/3675-7819**), a gelateria near the castle and the church home to *The Last Supper*. True to its name, it has every imaginable type of chocolate gelato, in addition to other flavors.

See also "Fun in the Theme Parks," above, for more kid-pleasing attractions.

Where to Stay in Milan

Milan is northern Italy's largest commercial center, big on banking and industry, and for years its hotels have tended to chase expense-account customers, often to the detriment of tourists and families. The winds of change are blowing, however. A recent wave of cozy, independent *locandas* and *albergos,* as well as design-conscious boutique hotels, have come along to complement the grand old institutions.

Note that prices are often higher during the week than on the weekend, and room rates really soar when the fashion and design crowd hits town (in normal years, late Feb, mid-May, and late Sept).

APARTMENT & ROOM RENTALS

If you want to live like a real Milanese, self-catering rooms and apartments can be a great option, allowing you to shop at local markets, try your hand at cooking the local cuisine, or at least have a refrigerator where you can keep water, wine, and cheese. Some properties even have washing machines (due to high electricity costs, don't expect most to have dryers).

However, in recent years, many Italian municipalities have rolled out stricter regulations on short-term rentals like Airbnb (see also Rome, p. 137). Like many tourist destinations around the world, Milan has experienced how short-term rentals can contribute to rising housing costs for residents and alter the character of its neighborhoods. As such, some municipal governments are cracking down on Airbnbs—especially the lockboxes that allow guests to enter without having any contact with locals. Though we are not recommending any specific short-term rental properties for Milan, some travelers still prefer them. We have done our best to align the recommendations here with responsible tourism practices.

EXPENSIVE

Hotel Principe di Savoia ♥♥ At this grand Beaux Arts institution, part of the Dorchester Collection of hotels, every conceivable guest whim is impeccably addressed. A stay here is truly a respite from the bustling city outside; guests have access to serene gardens, a top-floor spa and fitness center, a fine-dining restaurant, the elegant Principe Bar, and opulent rooms and suites. (The presidential suite even has its own indoor swimming pool.) The newly renovated Il Salotto lobby lounge has been given a softer look in order to make it a cozier spot for gathering and lingering. This luxury comes at a price, but for a bit of old-fashioned glamour, there's nowhere else like it. This grande dame of a property is strategically

located near Stazione Centrale, the vibrant Brera arts district, and the modern Piazza Gae Aulenti, representing the new face of the city.
Piazza Della Repubblica 17. dorchestercollection.com. ✆ **02/623-01.** 301 units. 400€–1,000€ double. Metro: Repubblica. **Amenities:** Restaurant; bar; concierge; room service; babysitting; spa; gym; indoor pool; free Wi-Fi.

Milano Suites ♥♥♥ There are surprisingly few stand-out properties in Milan's historic center, so the location of Milano Suites can't be beat. This elegant, light-filled property on a cobblestoned street between the Duomo and the castle is in a charming 18th-century town house. One- and two-bedroom suites boast parquet floors and sleek white furnishings. All have separate living rooms; some have kitchenettes, but no laundry facilities. The property also has a lounge and communal area for breakfast, which is typically included in the room rate.
Via San Tomaso 6. milanosuites.it. ✆ **02/805-1023.** 5 units. 200€–300€ double. Metro: Cordusio or Cairoli. **Amenities:** Concierge; room service; free Wi-Fi.

MODERATE

Antica Locanda Leonardo ♥♥♥ This lovely family-run property located steps from where *The Last Supper* hangs in Santa Maria delle Grazie church feels more like a historic home. Housed in a 19th-century building, the Antica Locanda Leonardo overlooks a surprisingly tranquil courtyard garden. Brightly painted rooms retain a wonderfully traditional feel, with heavy antique headboards and dressers, gilt mirrors, and elegant draperies. Bathrooms, on the other hand, are quite modern. The cozy lounge and breakfast room retain a nostalgic, old-world ambience with modern touches here and there. The more expensive courtyard-facing rooms, many with tiny wrought-iron balconies, are buffered from the noise of trams rumbling down Corso Magenta.
Corso Magenta 78. anticalocandaleonardo.com. ✆ **02/4801-4197.** 26 units. 140€–360€ double. Rates include breakfast. Metro: Conciliazione, Cadorna. **Amenities:** Concierge; free Wi-Fi.

nhow Milan ♥♥ This boutique hotel in the Navigli canal district is popular with the fashion and design set who flock here during Milan's fashion weeks and the Salone del Mobile furniture fair. A sleek reception area sets the scene with quirky design elements and a vivid color scheme. nhow seeks to wow with what it calls "unconventional spaces": colorful corners for having a drink or admiring the various temporary art exhibitions. Glass elevators whiz guests up to rooms decorated in white with splashes of bright colors. Standard rooms can be a bit compact but have modern bathrooms with walk-in showers. Chic loft-style suites on the fourth floor have views over Milan's Zona Tortona fashion district along with unusual details like transparent glass tubs. The **Vertigo** rooftop cocktail bar offers refreshing drinks poolside in the warmer months.
Via Tortona 35. nhow-milan.com. ✆ **02/489-8861.** 246 units. 185€–300€ double. Rates include breakfast. Metro: Porto Genova. **Amenities:** Restaurant; bar; spa; gym; free Wi-Fi.

INEXPENSIVE

BioCity Hotel ♥♥♥ This fab little hotel in a brightly painted villa from the 1920s offers great value and is only a few minutes' walk from Stazione Centrale. BioCity is everything a budget hotel should be, and it's eco-friendly to boot. Common areas include a minuscule bar and breakfast room (serving a continental breakfast of cheeses, cold cuts, pastries, and yogurt, with many organic items on the menu), and a tiny terrace out back. Guest rooms are stylish with big bathrooms; some have small balconies with neighborhood views. The hotel has a small wellness area with sauna, aromatherapy showers, a relaxation zone, and herbal teas; the rate is 45€ an hour, robes and slippers included. The only time of year you won't find good value for money here is during the city's fashion weeks or the Salone del Mobile furniture fair in the spring.

Via Edolo 18. biocityhotel.it. ✆ **02/6670-3595.** 17 units. 110€–220€ double. Rates include breakfast. Metro: Sondrio. **Amenities:** Bar; free Wi-Fi.

Where to Eat in Milan

Milan has thousands of eateries, from pizzerias to grand old cafes, Michelin-starred restaurants in highfalutin surroundings to corner bars with a great selection of *aperitivo*-time tapas, *gelaterie,* and traditional *osterie.* Avoid obvious tourist traps—any place that has a menu showing photos of the dishes.

Cocktail hour starts around 6:30pm, all over town, as the Milanese magically appear from shopping or work to meet up for a bitter Campari or a glass of prosecco. By the time *aperitivo* hour is over, thoughts turn towards supper and restaurants start to fill up. Sadly, the lavish *aperitivo* spreads of the past—where you could fill up on olives, crudités, cold pasta dishes, rice, salads, salami, and breads—were suspended during the pandemic and may never return.

If you find yourself tiring of Italian cuisine, Milan now has quite a variety of restaurants serving the rest of the world's cuisines. Sushi and Chinese food are especially popular, and **Via Paolo Sarpi,** the main street of Milan's thriving Chinatown neighborhood, offers a variety of options.

EXPENSIVE

Contraste ♥♥♥ ITALIAN FUSION The "contrasts" are evident at this temple of modern Italian cuisine—from the graffiti-covered walls outside to the luxe space inside.. This Michelin-starred restaurant offers "wow factor" for the eyes and the taste buds, with spectacular dishes that are works of contemporary art, served in a space that mixes bold colors with historical elements. Chef Matias Perdomo has been likened to Willy Wonka, crafting dishes that impress with their daring combinations as well as their whimsical presentation. One dish combines lobster, mango, coffee, and olives, and another offers beef tendons, caviar, passionfruit, and peanuts presented as a "roast." Guests are given a choice of tasting menus that must be booked ahead of time.

Via G. Meda 2. contrastemilano.it. ✆ **02/4953-6597.** Tasting menus average 180€. Daily 7:30pm–midnight; Sat–Sun 12:30–3pm. On Tram 3 (7 stops from Duomo).

Joia ♥♥♥ VEGETARIAN Milan is not all bone-marrow risotto and osso buco. A pillar of the vegetable-forward dining scene here, Joia was the first vegetarian restaurant in Europe to earn a Michelin star. The decor, with light wood-paneled walls, is a nod to understated Eastern minimalism, but the real draw is Swiss chef Pietro Leemann's creative vegan and vegetarian food. He's known for dishes with philosophical inspirations: "The Enchanted Forest" is a stunning plate featuring wild mushrooms, chestnut puree, and herb-infused vegetable consommé, meant to evoke the essence of nature. Then there is "A Stone Falls," featuring a crunchy Indian-spiced potato and cauliflower sphere, saffron mayonnaise, chlorophyll, and wild-pea flower with daikon gently fermented in pomegranate juice. A special lunch tasting menu Tuesday to Friday changes daily, featuring four small courses presented in the style of a painting on a single plate for around 35€. Reservations recommended.

Artfully composed vegetarian dining at Joia.

Via P. Castaldi 18. joia.it. ✆ **02/2952-2124.** Main courses 30€–45€. Tues–Sat noon–2:30pm and 7:30–11pm. Closed Sun–Mon. Metro: Repubblica.

Restaurant Giacomo Arengario ♥♥♥ MODERN ITALIAN Deserving acclaim just for its Duomo views from the loggia and terrace, this restaurant is a top choice for ladies who lunch, businesspeople, and well-heeled Milanese. Set on the top floor of the Palazzo dell'Arengario, which also houses the **Museo del Novecento** (p. 480), it has a smart little bar for early-evening *aperitivo,* but the real point is to get a table near those plate-glass windows to gawk at the Duomo. The menu offers creatively presented Milanese classics like veal cutlet along with gourmet takes on dishes from around Italy, such as an Amalfi lemon risotto or tortelli filled with cheese and pepper, raw red prawns, lime, and bottarga. Finish off your meal with the house specialty dessert, the "Bomba," an artfully presented explosion of puff pastry, Chantilly cream, mascarpone, and wild strawberries. Not in the mood for a full meal but still want the spectacular terrace view? In warm weather, settle in at one of the umbrella-covered tables for coffee, dessert, or a sundowner.

Via Guglielmo Marconi 1. giacomomilano.com. ✆ **02/72-093-814.** Main courses 22€–60€. Daily noon–midnight. Aperitif on the terrace 4–6pm. Metro: Duomo.

Ristorante Cracco ♥♥ MODERN ITALIAN Situated in the Galleria, mere steps from the Duomo, celebrated chef Carlo Cracco's multitasking venue spans several floors, featuring a sophisticated cafe, a Michelin-starred fine-dining restaurant, an extensive wine cellar, a dedicated smoking room, and an exclusive private lounge. Patrons enter from the elegant cafe downstairs to reach the restaurant above, set up like a welcoming and elegantly appointed historic home. Cracco's cuisine is both traditional and innovative, and given that even the appetizers can be pricy, a meal here is certainly a splurge. Some of the dishes give a nod to local tradition with influences from around Italy, such as Milanese veal served with broccoli, Taggiasca olives, and grapes. The menu also includes elevated interpretations of classics like saffron risotto with grilled bone marrow. If you get a chance, choose a bottle from the wine cellar, which boasts more than 10,000 bottles.

Galleria Vittorio Emanuele II. ristorantecracco.it. ✆ **02/876-774.** Main courses 40€–70€. Tues–Fri lunch and dinner; Mon and Sat dinner only; closed Sun. Metro: Duomo.

MODERATE

La Pesa Trattoria dal 1902 ♥♥ LOMBARDY/NORTHERN ITALIAN With Milan being the most international city in Italy, it is sometimes easier to find Asian fusion or Lebanese cuisine here than traditional Milanese fare. La Pesa Trattoria, however, has been around since 1902, and it serves up all the Milanese classics, including saffron risotto, osso buco, polenta, and breaded veal cutlet. Start off with *sciatt,* crunchy fritters filled with Taleggio cheese, or the house specialty meatballs, called *mondeghili*, served with honey and a special mustard sauce. The atmosphere is intimate and rustic, with moss-green walls, beamed ceilings, and checkered tablecloths. A bit off the beaten path, near San Siro stadium, the restaurant is about a 15-minute walk from the nearest subway station.

Via Fantoni 26. trattorialapesa1902.it. ✆ **02/3651-4525.** Main courses 13€–25€. Mon–Sun noon–3pm and 7pm–midnight. Metro: Segesta, Bande Nere.

Osteria il Kaimano ♥♥ ITALIAN Don't be put off by the translated menu outside. This casual, boisterous *osteria* is a reliable choice in the artsy, cobblestoned Brera district, popular with locals and tourists alike. Standout dishes include zucchini flowers stuffed with ricotta, ravioli with smoked ham and radicchio, or the Neapolitan-style pizzas that continually slide out of the wood-burning oven. First courses (*primi*) are reasonably priced, but the second-course meat dishes (*secondi*) can be slightly more expensive. Milanese favorites like veal cutlet and saffron risotto are offered along with dishes from around Italy, ranging from spaghetti in

Bolognese sauce to Sicilian-style swordfish. There are quite a few dining options in the Brera neighborhood, but Kaimano stands out for its cozy atmosphere and pleasantly exuberant service. The owners often come around with free limoncello or other liqueurs at the end of the meal.

Via Fiori Chiari 20. il-kaimano.it. ✆ **02/8050-2733.** Main courses 15€–40€. Daily noon–2:30pm and 6–11:30pm. Metro: Lanza Brera.

INEXPENSIVE

Nerino Dieci Trattoria ♥♥ MEDITERRANEAN Call at least a month in advance for dinner reservations at this wildly popular family-run trattoria in the *centro storico.* Seasonal Italian cuisine is offered at relatively reasonable prices, complemented by surprisingly sophisticated presentation. The restaurant's cozy corners are perfect for a romantic dinner or even a business lunch, though some of the tables are a bit close together. Service is attentive. The menu changes with the seasons—seafood is one specialty here—with creative twists on traditional dishes, such as tagliolini pasta with clams and spicy salami or tuna and salmon tartare served with blueberry cream and olive mayonnaise. You can also find classic Milanese risotto and the famous cutlet here, and the spaghetti dish with fresh tomatoes prepared in a cheese wheel is especially popular.

Via Nerino 10. nerinodieci.it. ✆ **02/3983-1019.** Main courses 18€–28€. Mon–Fri noon–2:30pm and 7:30–11pm; Sat 7:30–11pm. Metro: Duomo, Missori.

Panini De Santis ♥♥ GOURMET SANDWICHES Located midway between the Duomo and the church that houses *The Last Supper*, this historic panini shop makes for a great on-the-go snack or meal. Many bars and cafes around town have pre-made panini wilting in showcases, but De Santis makes its sandwiches to order with quality ingredients, offering a wide variety of cold cuts, seafood options, cheeses, vegetables, and condiments. Vegetarians and vegans will find plenty of options beyond the standard mozzarella or grilled vegetables on plain bread. The original location in Corso Magenta has been there since 1964 and brims with old-school charm; customers spill out onto the cobbled street at all times of day, enjoying their panini (and even drinks at aperitivo hour) as the city's signature orange trams rumble past. There are newer outposts in the Brera neighborhood and inside the La Rinascente department store near the Duomo as well.

Corso Magenta 9. paninidesantis.it. ✆ **02/7209-5214.** Sandwiches 10€–16€. Mon–Sun 11am–11pm. Metro: Cairoli, Cordusio.

Pizzeria Tradizionale ♥♥ PIZZERIA This bustling canalside pizzeria in the Navigli neighborhood has been a local institution for decades. Given the location, this unpretentious spot is always busy, so you may want to reserve ahead of time. Patrons happily devour enormous crispy pizzas piled with cold cuts and mozzarella, as well as vast bowls of garlic-infused spaghetti alle *vongole* (clams). Pizzeria Tradizionale also offers a selection of Neapolitan-style seafood dishes. Make sure to get a table outside to soak up the buzzy Navigli atmosphere and for a front-row view of the boats gliding along the canals.

Ripa di Porta Ticinese 7. pizzeriatradizionale.com. ✆ **02/839-5133.** Main courses 10€–20€. Daily noon–2:30pm and 7pm–1am (no lunch Wed). Metro: Porta Genova.

Milan Shopping

Milan is known worldwide as a temple of high fashion, with the hallowed streets **Montenapoleone** and **Spiga** in the **Quadrilatero d'Oro** being the most popular places of wallet-stripping worship. Here D&G, Prada, Gucci, Hermès, Louis Vuitton, Armani, Ralph Lauren, Versace, and Cavalli all jostle for the attention of Milan's fashionistas. The area around Porta Nuova (at the top of **Corso Como**) is also starting to become a luxury-shopping district. More reasonable shopping areas include **Via Torino** and **Corso Buenos Aires,** where mid-range international brands proliferate; if you're clever you can snag a designer bargain at outlet store **Il Salvagente,** Via Fratelli Bronzetti 16 (✆ **02/7611-0328**). Milan is also a home design hub; if you want to take home a unique piece, stop in the three-story **Fornasetti Store,** Corso Venezia 21A (✆ **02/8416-1374**), which sells bold, whimsical creations (everything from coasters to ceramics to furnishings) based on the "practical madness" of the late Milanese designer Piero Fornasetti.

Upscale shopping at the Galleria Vittorio Emanuele II in Milan.

Fashion is one Milanese obsession; food is another, and the *centro storico* has many superb delis where you can purchase the purest of olive oils and the finest cheeses. **Peck,** Via Spadari 9 (✆ **02/802-3161**), still the number-one gourmet spot near the Duomo, has expanded to include several locations (near Porta Venezia and in the City Life district); it has keen competition in the **Eataly** megastore in Piazza XXV Aprile (eataly.it) for all Italian comestibles. The top floor of the **La Rinascente department store** in Piazza del Duomo is another haven for foodies, with its Obicà mozzarella bar, Moët & Chandon Champagne bar, a chocolate shop, a mini steak restaurant, and fine selection of packaged Italian goods (as an added bonus, you get a close-up view of the Duomo).

English-language books are sold at **Feltrinelli Librerie** (corner of Piazza del Duomo and Via Ugo Foscolo 1/3), **Mondadori Megastore**

(Piazza del Duomo, on the corner of Via Mazzini), **Rizzoli** (inside the Galleria Vittorio Emanuele II; see p. 478), and the **Feltrinelli Express** inside Stazione Centrale. English-language newspapers can be found on most major newsstands around the *centro storico.*

MILANO MARKETS

Everybody loves a bargain, and the colorful **Viale Papiniano market** (Metro Sant'Agostino) has plenty to offer savvy shoppers. Its sea of stalls is open Tuesday and Saturday; some sell designer seconds, others leather basics. **Flea markets** spring up on Saturdays along the Alzaia Naviglio Grande and Fiera di Sinigaglia (Metro Porta Genova for both), and on Sundays at San Donato Metro stop.

A large **food market** at the Piazza Wagner metro is open every morning except Sunday. A two-level food hall in Stazione Centrale known as **Mercato Centrale** (mercatocentrale.com/milan) has around 24 stalls and ample seating upstairs. Here you can find everything from empanadas to risotto to pizza to Chinese dumplings. Pop by the mercato to pick up bread or focaccia to take with you on the train.

During the Christmas season, **holiday markets** (complete with ice skating) pop up in different parts of the city, from Piazza Gae Aulenti (Metro Garibaldi) to the Castello Sforzesco (Metro Cairoli) to the area behind the Museum of Natural History (Metro Palestro) in the Giardini Pubblici Indro Montanelli.

Nightlife & Entertainment

Unless you're heading for the Ticinese and Navigli, Milan is a dressy city and generally looks askance at scruffy jeans and sneakers after dark. When many people don't dine until well after 9pm, it's not surprising that clubs and bars stay open until the very wee hours.

A couple of spots unique to Milan include the vine-covered cocktail terrace at **10 Corso Como** (the name is the address; 10corsocomo.com; ✆ **02/2901-3581**) and **Ceresio 7 Pools & Restaurant,** Via Ceresio 7 (ceresio7.com; ✆ **02/310-392-21**), which offers a novel setup: a chic, sleek rooftop lounge with two pools where one can enjoy a cocktail while taking in amazing views of the city.

A venerable Milan institution, the **Conservatorio di Musica Giuseppe Verdi** has two stages for classical concerts at Via Conservatorio 12 (www.consmi.it; ✆ **02/762-110**). Check the website for the latest schedules.

Milan is forever associated with the grand old dame of opera, **Teatro alla Scala ♥♥**, perhaps the world's favorite opera house, decked out with sumptuous red seats, boxes adorned with gilt, and chandeliers dripping crystal. It's a good idea to book well in advance of the opera season (Dec to late July and early Sept to Nov). Book online at teatroallascala.vivaticket.it or at the ticket office in Largo Ghiringhelli, Piazza della Scala (in between the theater entrance and the entrance to the La Scala Museum).

Tip: Two hours before each performance, unsold seats can typically be purchased at a discounted price online at teatroallascala.org, and you can also check the box office 1 hour before to see if any seats remain unsold. A limited number of obstructed-view balcony seats are available for most performances, but you must get on the list for these seats, which can be a somewhat complicated, ever-changing process. Keep in mind that to pick up tickets or be put on the list, you must bring a form of photo ID with you. For updated information, go to teatroallascala.org.

BERGAMO ♥♥

47km (29 miles) NE of Milan

Bergamo is a city of two distinct characters. The ancient **Città Alta** is a beautiful medieval and Renaissance town perched on a green hill. **Città Bassa,** mostly built in the 19th and 20th centuries, sits at the feet of the upper town and concerns itself with 21st-century life. Visitors tend to focus on the historic upper town, a place for wandering, soaking in the rarified atmosphere, and enjoying the lovely vistas from its belvederes.

Essentials

ARRIVING **Trains** arrive from and depart for Milan Stazione Centrale hourly (50 min.; 6.10€). If you are **driving,** Bergamo is linked to Milan via the A4. The trip takes under an hour if traffic is good. ***Note:*** It's difficult to park in the largely pedestrianized Città Alta—park instead in Città Bassa and take the **funicular** (see below) or walk up to the historic area.

VISITOR INFORMATION The Città Bassa tourist office is close to the train and bus stations at Piazzale Guglielmo Marconi (✆ **035/210-204**); it's open daily 9am to 12:30pm and 2 to 5:30pm. The Città Alta office is at Via Gombito 13 (✆ **035/242-226**), right off Via Colleoni, and is open daily 9am to 5:30pm. The **Visit Bergamo** official tourism website is visitbergamo.net.

GETTING AROUND Bergamo has an efficient bus system that runs throughout the Città Bassa and to points around the Città Alta; tickets are 1.70€ for 75 minutes of travel and are available from machines at the bus stops outside the train station or at the bus station opposite. To reach the Città Alta from the train station, take bus no. 1 or 1A (clearly marked Città Alta on front) and make the free transfer to the Funicolare Bergamo Alta, run by ATB Bergamo (Largo Porta Nuova; atb.bergamo.it), connecting the upper and lower cities. It typically runs every 7 minutes from 7am to 1:20am.

Exploring the Città Bassa

Most visitors scurry through Bergamo's lower town on their way to the Città Alta, but you may want to pause long enough to explore the main thoroughfare, **Corso Sentierone,** with its mishmash of architectural styles (16th-century porticos, the Mussolini-era Palazzo di Giustizia, and two mock Doric temples); it's a pleasant place to linger over espresso at a sidewalk cafe. The **Accademia Carrara,** Piazza Giacomo Carrara 82 (lacarrara.it; ✆ **035/234-396**), is worth a peek for its fine collection of more than 300 works spanning 5 centuries, including Raphaels, Bellinis, Botticellis, and Canalettos. Città Bassa's 19th-century **Teatro Gaetano Donizetti** (Piazza Cavour 15) is the hub of Bergamo's lively cultural scene, with a fall opera season and a winter-to-spring season of dramatic performances; for details, contact the theater at ✆ **035/4160-600** (teatrodonizetti.it).

Bergamo for Foodies

The countryside around Bergamo is famous for its award-winning cheeses and wines, such as Valcalepio DOP, Moscato di Scanzo DOCG, and world-renowned Franciacorta sparkling wines. To explore the region's gourmet side, you can schedule a **visit to local dairies or wineries** with a qualified expert (bergamovisit.com).

Exploring the Città Alta

Crammed with *palazzi,* monuments, and churches, the Città Alta centers on two hauntingly beautiful adjoining squares, **piazzas Vecchia** and **del Duomo.** The Città Alta is dissected by delightful cobblestoned **Via Colleoni** (named for the hard-nosed Bergamasco military leader Bartolomeo Colleoni; see p. 500), which is so narrow that in places you can almost touch the buildings on either side at once. It's lined with swank shoe shops, posh delis, and classy confectioners.

Piazza Vecchia (a 5-min. stroll from the funicular station along Via Gombito) looks like a set for one of local son Gaetano Donizetti's operas. This hauntingly beautiful square was the hub of Bergamo's political and civic life from medieval times. The 12th-century **Palazzo della Ragione** (Court of Justice) was built by the Venetians; its graceful arcades are embellished with the Lion of Saint Mark, symbol of the Venetian Republic, visible above the tiny 16th-century balcony and reached by a covered staircase to the right of the palace. Across the piazza is the **Biblioteca Civica** (Public Library).

Piazza Vecchia lies at the heart of Bergamo's Città Alta.

Walk through the archways of the Palazzo della Ragione to reach **Piazza del Duomo** and the **Basilica di Santa Maria Maggiore** ♥♥

Lombardy & the Lake District
0
20 mi
0
20 km
Milan
Venice
Rome
SWITZERLAND
TRENTINO-ALTO ADIGE
VENETO
LOMBARDY
PIEDMONT
EMILIA-ROMAGNA
Domodossola
Locarno
Lugano
Chiavenna
Sondrio
L. Maggiore
L. Lugano
L. Como
L. d'Iseo
Largo d'Idro
Lake Garda
Verbania
Isole Borromee
Stresa
Arona
Luino
Sasso del Fero
Sta. Caterina del Sasso Ballaro
Varese
Tremezzo
Lenno
Cernobbio
Como
Bellagio
Varenna
Bellano
Lecco
Erba
Cantu
Saronno
Seregno
Monza
Legnano
Busto Arsizio
Gallarate
Rho
Milan (Milano)
Melegnano
Certosa di Pavia
Pavia
Lodi
Bergamo
Seriate
Palazzolo
Rovato
Chiari
Treviglio
Crema
Codogno
Soresina
Cremona
Piacenza
Casalmaggiore
Darfo
Darfo Boario Terme
Brescia
Verolanuova
Leno
Asola
Limone sul Garda
Riva del Garda
Arco
Gardone Riviera
Salò
Desenzano del Garda
Rocca Scaligera
Sirmione
Verona
Mantua (Mantova)
Ostiglia
San Benedetto Po
Guastalla
Schio
Valdagno
Biella
Novara
Vercelli
Abbiategrasso
Vigevano
Mortara
Casale Monferrato
Voghera
Broni
Tortona
Alessandria
Asti
To Turin
To Parma
To Modena & Bologna
Sesia
Cervo
Ticino
Po
Adda
Serio
Oglio
Mincio
Adige
A4
A26
A9
A7
A1
A21
A22
E62
SS33
SS38
SS36
SS42
SS45
SS46
SS233
SS299
SS142
SS235
SS236
SS415
SS10
SS420
SS596
SS211
SS62
SS434
SR10

(fondazionemia.it; ✆ **035/211-355**). You'll enter the basilica through an ornate portico supported by Venetian lions; the interior is a masterpiece of baroque giltwork hung with Renaissance tapestries. Bergamo native Gaetano Donizetti, the famed composer, is entombed here in a marble sarcophagus that's as excessive as the rest of the church. The oft-forgotten **Tempietto di Santa Croce,** tucked to the left of the basilica entrance, is worth seeking out for its endearing frescoes depicting episodes in Jesus' life. The basilica is open Tuesday to Saturday 9am to 12:30pm and 2:30 to 6pm (Nov–Mar until 5pm); from April through October it's also open Sunday 9am to 1pm and 3 to 6pm. Mass is held at 10am during the week and 11am on weekends. Admission is free.

Most impressive, however, is the **Cappella Colleoni ♥♥♥**, Piazza del Duomo (free admission), to the right of the basilica doors, with its highly elaborate pink-and-white marble facade. Bartolomeo Colleoni, a Bergamasco *condottiero* (mercenary) who fought for the Venetians, was given Bergamo as a reward for his loyalty; it became his own private fiefdom in 1455. His elaborate funerary chapel was designed by Giovanni Antonio Amadeo, who created the Certosa di Pavia (p. 485). Colleoni lies surrounded by statuary beneath a ceiling frescoed by Tiepolo. Cappella Colleoni is open March to October daily 9am to 12:30pm and 2 to 6:30pm (Nov–Feb Tues–Sun 9am–12:30pm and 2–4:30pm).

Where to Stay & Eat in Bergamo

Hotel rooms in Bergamo's Città Alta are in great demand in summer, so make reservations well in advance if you plan to stay overnight (Bergamo is less than an hour's journey from Milan and easily visited on a day trip).

Al Donizetti ♥ CAFE This *enoteca* (wine bar) and restaurant in the heart of Bergamo Alta was previously a historic pastry shop, as evidenced by the faded lettering above the door. These days, Al Donizetti draws locals and tourists alike for *aperitivo,* a simple meal of wine with a charcuterie platter and small plates, or heartier fare. Come here for local specialties like *casoncelli* pasta (served Bergamo-style, filled with meat, cheese, and breadcrumbs) or buckwheat polenta heaped with mountain cheeses or a mushroom ragout. The menu can be heavy on meat dishes that some may find adventurous (pig's head or beef tongue), but vegetarians will also find a few options beyond the wide range of cheeses (there's even a dessert menu of *formaggi*), such as minestrone or the hummus plate. The extensive wine menu includes quite a selection of pricey options. Sit inside and enjoy rustic elegance or opt for the romantic atmosphere outside under the large porticos, perfect for watching people stroll the main drag.

Via Gombito 17a. donizetti.it. ✆ **035/242-661.** Main courses 19€–38€. Wed–Mon 11am–11pm.

Caffè del Tasso ♥ CAFE One of the oldest establishments of its kind in Italy, this charming spot on Città Alta's medieval main piazza has been in business since 1476. Today, it has the rather cozy air of a retro teashop, but Caffè del Tasso is more than just a casual spot for a snack. Here, you can start with a morning coffee, linger over lunch, return for an aperitif, or settle in for a dinner of dishes inspired by Italy's regions, presented with flair. A meal or an early-evening drink at one of the outdoor tables in the ancient piazza, which Le Corbusier is said to have described as one of the most beautiful squares in Europe, is a quintessentially Italian experience. Piazza Vecchia 3. caffedeltasso.com. ✆ **035/237-966.** Main courses 13€–25€. Daily 8am–midnight.

Hotel Le Funi ♥♥ Located in the shadow of the Venetian Walls in the Città Alta, this property in a historic building is in a great position for visiting the major sites of the old town. The overall aesthetic is minimalist and contemporary, with subtle references to the property's historic context. Light-filled rooms offer modern conveniences along with wonderful views of the nearby hills. In warm weather, a breakfast of pastries, croissants, and local specialties is provided on the panoramic terrace (otherwise, it is served indoors in the lounge, a characteristic old wine cantina with an arched stone ceiling). The funicular runs behind the five rooms in the hotel's annex, so if you are sensitive to noise, make sure to reserve in the main building.
Via S. Virgilio1. lefunihotel.it. ✆ **035/250-043.** 16 units. 140€–300€ double. Rates include breakfast. **Amenities:** Private parking (18€ per day); free Wi-Fi.

MANTUA ♥♥♥

158km (98 miles) E of Milan, 62km (38 miles) N of Parma, 150km (93 miles) SW of Venice

One of Lombardy's best-kept secrets, Mantua (*Mantova* in Italian) lies in the eastern reaches of the region, making it a fairly easy side trip from Milan. Like its neighboring cities in Emilia-Romagna, Mantua owes its handsome Renaissance monuments to one family, in this case the Gonzagas, who conquered the city in 1328 and ruled benevolently until 1707. Avid collectors, the Gonzagas ruled through the greatest centuries of Italian art, and today you can encounter their treasures in the **Palazzo Ducale;** in their summer retreat, the **Palazzo Te;** and in the churches and piazzas that grew up around their court.

Essentials

ARRIVING Six direct **trains** depart daily from Milan Stazione Centrale (1 hr. 50 min.; 12.50€); nine trains arrive daily from Verona (30–40 min.; 5.00€). The speediest **highway** connections from Milan are via the A4 autostrada to Verona, then the A22 from Verona to Mantua (about 2 hr.).

VISITOR INFORMATION The **tourist office** at Piazza Mantegna 6 (turismo.mantova.it; ✆ **0376/432-432**) is open Saturday and Sunday from 9am to 5pm; Monday to Friday hours are 9am to 1:30pm and 2:30 to 5pm (spring and summer until 6pm). It's just to the right of the basilica of Sant'Andrea.

CITY LAYOUT Mantua is tucked onto a fat finger of land surrounded on three sides by the Mincio River, which widens into a series of lakes, prosaically named Lago Superiore, Lago di Mezzo, and Lago Inferiore. Most sights are within an easy walk of one another in the compact center, a 15-minute walk northwards from the lakeside train station.

Exploring Mantua

Mantua is a place for wandering along arcaded streets and through cobbled squares with handsomely proportioned churches and *palazzi.*

The southernmost of these squares is **Piazza delle Erbe** ♥ (Square of the Herbs), so named for its produce and food market. Mantua's civic might is clustered here in a series of late-medieval and early Renaissance structures that include the **Palazzo della Ragione** (Courts of Justice) and **Palazzo del Podestà** (Mayor's Palace) from the 12th and 13th centuries, and the **Torre dell'Orologio,** topped with a 14th-century astrological clock. Also on this square is Mantua's earliest religious structure, the **Rotonda di San Lorenzo,** a miniature round church from the 11th century. The city's Renaissance masterpiece, **Basilica di Sant'Andrea** (see below), is off to one side on Piazza Mantegna.

Save €€€ with the Mantova Sabbioneta Card

If you're spending more than a few hours in Mantua, consider getting the **Mantova Sabbioneta Card** (www.mantovacard.it), which allows discounted or free access to 17 city museums plus several others in outlying Sabbioneta, as well as free bus transportation and bike sharing. Valid for 72 hours, it costs 25€ (13€ for ages 12–17 accompanied by at least one adult). Almost all of the museums listed here honor the card.

To the north, Piazza delle Erbe transforms into **Piazza Broletto** through a series of arcades; here a statue honors the poet Virgil, who was born in Mantua in 70 B.C.E. The next square, vast cobbled **Piazza Sordello,** is lined with medieval *palazzi* and the 13th-century Duomo. Most notable is the massive hulk of the **Palazzo Ducale** (p. 503), which forms the piazza's eastern wall. To enjoy lakeside views and walks, follow Via San Giorgio from Piazza Sordello and turn right onto Lungolago dei Gonzaga, which leads back along the lakeshore to the town center.

Basilica di Sant'Andrea ♥♥ CHURCH A graceful Renaissance facade fronts this 15th-century church by architect Leon Battista Alberti. The grandest church in Mantua, it is topped by a dome added by Filippo Juvarra in the 18th century. Inside, the vast classically proportioned space is centered on the church's single aisle. Light pours in through the dome, highlighting the carefully crafted *trompe l'oeil* painting of the coffered ceiling. The Gonzagas' court painter Andrea Mantegna—creator of the Camera degli Sposi in the Palazzo Ducale (see below)—is buried in the

Basilica of Sant'Andrea in Piazza Mantegna Square in Mantua.

first chapel on the left. The crypt houses a reliquary containing the blood of Christ, which was allegedly brought here by Longinus, the Roman soldier who thrust his spear into Jesus's side; this is processed through town on March 18, the feast of Mantua's patron, Sant'Anselmo.
Piazza Mantegna. Free admission. Daily 8am–noon and 3–7pm.

Museo di Palazzo Ducale ♥♥ PALACE The massive power base of the Gonzaga dynasty spreads over the northeast corner of Mantua, incorporating Piazza Sordello, the Duomo, Castello San Giorgio, and the Palazzo Ducale. Together they form a private city—making it Italy's largest architectural museum complex—connected by corridors, courtyards, and staircases filled with Renaissance frescoes and ancient Roman sculptures. Within the walls of this fortress palace lies the history of Mantua's most powerful family and what's left of the treasure trove they amassed over centuries. Between their skills as warriors and a knack for marrying into wealthier houses, the Gonzagas acquired power, money, and the services of some of the top artists of the time, including Pisanello, Titian, and Mantegna. The most fortunate union was in 1490 between Francesco II Gonzaga and aristocratic Isabella d'Este from Ferrara, who commissioned many of the complex's art-filled apartments. In this glorious maze of gilded, frescoed, marbled rooms, passageways, and secret gardens, some standouts are: the Arthurian legends adorning the Sala del Pisanello, painted by Pisanello between 1436 and 1444; the **Sale degli Arazzi** (Tapestry Rooms) hung with copies of Raphael's Vatican tapestries; the **Galleria degli Specchi** (Hall of Mirrors); **Appartamento dei Nani** (Apartments of the Dwarfs), with its miniature replica of the Vatican's

Holy Staircase; and the **Galleria dei Mesi** (Hall of the Months). In the north tower of the Castello San Giorgio, don't miss the incomparable **Camera degli Sposi,** the masterpiece of Andrea Mantegna, who took 9 years to complete it. Commissioned by Ludovico III Gonzaga, it features portraits of his family members, providing an intriguing glimpse into late-15th-century court life. (***Tip:*** Admission to the Camera degli Sposi is limited, so reserve a time slot for visiting it when you buy your tickets.)
Piazza Sordello 40. mantovaducale.beniculturali.it. ✆ **0376/352-100.** Admission 18€ for Castello San Giorgio, Corte Vecchia, Camera degli Sposi, and archaeological museum; 11€ without Camera degli Sposi and archaeological museum; free for ages 17 and under. Free admission 1st Sun every month. Tues–Sun 8:15am–7:15pm; last entry 6:20pm.

Palazzo Te ♥♥ PALACE This glorious Renaissance summer palace, designed by Giulio Romano between 1525 and 1535, was built for Federico II Gonzaga, the sybaritic son of Isabella d'Este. As his retreat from court life, it was designed to indulge his obsessions. A series of lavishly adorned apartments, decorated by the best artists of the day, reveal Gonzaga's enthusiasms for love and sex, astrology, and horses, from the almost 3-D effect in the Hall of the Horses to erotic frescoes by Romano in the elaborate Chamber of Amor and Psyche. The greatest room in the palace, however, is a metaphor for Gonzaga power: In the **Sala dei Giganti** (Room of the Giants), Titan is overthrown by the gods in a dizzying display of *trompe l'oeil* painting that surrounds the viewer on all sides (and overhead!). The Palazzo Te is also home to the Museo Civico, whose collections include the Gonzaga family's coins, medallions, and 20th-century portraits by Armando Spadini. While there are a few Egyptian artifacts here as well, the main focus is on the legacy of the Gonzaga family and Italian art from the Renaissance on. For those who don't want to trek out to the *palazzo* on foot—it is about a 20-minute walk from the city center—there is occasionally shuttle bus service available, but stops tend to change, so ask about it in the tourist office.

Arts & Culture in Mantua

Mantua is a cultured city with ample theater and classical concerts. There are regular recitals at **Teatro Bibiena,** Via Accademia 47 (opera-lirica.com) and a full program of films and concerts at **Mantova Teatro,** Piazza Cavallotti (teatrosocialemantova.it). A **chamber-music festival** is held every May, and the **Festivaletteratura** (festivaletteratura.it) literature festival is a popular draw in September.

Viale Te 13. centropalazzote.it. ✆ **0376/323-266.** Admission 15€ adults, 11€ seniors, 7€ ages 12–18 and students, free for children 11 and under. Mon 9am–7pm; Tues 1–7pm; Wed–Sun 9am–7pm (hours may be longer in summer or shorter in winter; ticket sales end 1 hr. before closing).

MORE MANTUA MUSEUMS

En route from the center of town to Palazzo Te, you'll pass **Casa del Mantegna** ♥, Via Acerbi 47, the house and studio of Andrea Mantegna, now an art gallery (casadelmantegna.it; ✆ **0376/360-506;** free admission; Tues–Sun 10am–1pm, Tues–Wed and Sat–Sun 3–6pm).

Just to the left of Palazzo Ducale's main entrance, in the old market hall at the corner of Piazza Sordello, the **Museo Archeologico Nazionale di Mantova** ♥ houses in one giant space all sorts of local discoveries of Bronze Age, Greek, Etruscan, and Roman pottery, glassware, and utensils (✆ **0376/320-003;** Tues–Sun 8:30am–7pm, Sun 2–7pm). Admission costs 18€ for adults, which also includes admission to the Palazzo Ducale and the Camera degli Sposi, or 11€ including Palazzo Ducale but not the Camera degli Sposi; it's free for ages 17 and under.

For a change of pace, the **Galleria Storica dei Vigili del Fuoco** ♥ (Fire Engine Museum) at Largo Vigili del Fuoco 1 (museovigilidelfuoco mantova.it; ✆ **0376/364-124;** free admission) has plenty of historic engines on display inside the Palazzo Ducale complex. The museum is typically open on Saturday afternoons and Sunday mornings and afternoons (it closes a couple of hours for lunch). Call or stop by to check opening hours.

Where to Stay in Mantua

Like Milan, Mantua sees mainly expense-account business travelers during the week, with families and tourists flocking in for the weekends and over summer, so book rooms in the town center well ahead of time.

Casa Poli ♥♥♥ Located about 15 minutes on foot from the center, this boutique gem hidden behind the facade of a 19th-century *palazzo* is popular with both business and leisure travelers. Spotless guest rooms have a chic minimalist style, with parquet floors, distinctive light fixtures, and bathrooms that prioritize practicality over luxury. Superior rooms are slightly larger, and there are also triple rooms that could work for families. This property stands out among other four-star hotels in town thanks to its friendly, accommodating staff, a lounge filled with arty books, and a delightful summer courtyard that serves as an idyllic spot for enjoying an evening drink. Casa Poli is also a good solution for those traveling by car because there is parking (18€ per day), and it is outside the restricted traffic zone for residents (entering that area by car unauthorized can lead to heavy fines).

Corso Garibaldi 32. hotelcasapoli.it. ✆ **0376/288-170.** 27 units. 120€–190€ double. Rates for all but the cheapest rooms include breakfast. **Amenities:** Bar; concierge; free Wi-Fi.

Residenza Bibiena ♥♥ Billing itself as the only B&B in Mantua with lake views, the cozy Residenza Bibiena is on a pretty corner of the *centro storico* near Palazzo Ducale. Housed in a traditional terra-cotta town house, Bibiena has a pleasing old-school charm. Warm color schemes and pretty linens enliven the simple but immaculately clean rooms named for historical figures or operas. In addition to the four double rooms in the main building, the Bibiena has a few triple rooms in another property a few doors down. A continental breakfast buffet includes cakes, pastries, yogurt, cold cuts, fresh fruit, and more. The property is situated along one of the main thoroughfares leading into the city, just outside the restricted traffic zone, which is an advantage for drivers. There is a public parking garage next door. Note that only some of the rooms have lake views.

Piazza Arche, 8. residenzabibiena.it. ✆ **331/508-0876.** 4 units. 100€ double. Rates include breakfast. **Amenities:** Free Wi-Fi.

Where to Eat in Mantua

Lo Scalco Grasso ♥♥ MODERN ITALIAN This contemporary bistro is light and bright, and a young, dynamic staff in the kitchen likes to push boundaries. It's a sophisticated choice, offering beautifully crafted dishes like thick "bigoli" pasta noodles with shrimp and sauce made of Roquefort and walnut cream, or beef tartare with a berry crumble, black truffle, and sauteed herbs. For dessert, try the local specialty known as *sbrisolona,* a crumbly almond-based cake, served with a rich, creamy custard. One tasting menu (called "Casa") features more traditional local dishes, while another seasonal menu is purely vegetarian (known as the "Natura"). The restaurant is about a 10-minute walk from the center. Reservations are highly recommended.

Via Trieste 55. loscalcograsso.it. ✆ **349/374-7958.** Main courses 18€–35€. Tues–Sat noon–2pm and 7:30–10pm (later on weekends); Sun noon–2pm; Mon 7:30–10pm.

Ortika ♥ CAFE/ECLECTIC Run by a young couple, this funky cafe sits on a quiet cobbled street in the center of town near Piazza delle Erbe. Chatty baristas serve up Italian coffee drinks and award-winning specialty brews all day long. The food menu includes appetizers as well as brunch and lunch items—everything from pastries to pancakes with fresh berries or chestnuts (depending on the season) to a wide variety of egg dishes or avocado toasts. Sit inside and enjoy the chill music and low-key atmosphere with wooden tables, mismatched chairs, and decorative greenery or grab a seat outside for streetside drinking and dining. Come early evening, settle in for an aperitif, a refreshing glass of wine, or a kombucha-infused drink accompanied by tasty nibbles.

Via Giovanni Battista Spagnoli, 20. instagram.com/ortika.mantova. No phone. Main courses 6€–16€. Mon–Tues 7:30am–7:30pm; Thurs 12:30–7:30pm; Fri–Sat 7:30am–7:30pm; Sun 9am–4pm. Closed Wed.

Osteria dell'Oca ♥♥♥ LOMBARDY Locals and tourists alike cram into this small family-run restaurant to enjoy vibrant cooking in a warm, rustic setting. Just a 10-minute walk from the center, this is the classic Italian *osteria* experience—loud, exuberant, and convivial. Start off sharing some *peccati di gola* ("delectable delights"), local salamis, pancetta, and lard served with warm polenta. Looking for true local specialties? Try "drunken" risotto with Lambrusco wine and bacon; or *tagliatelle alla* *baffo,* pasta in a meat sauce with beans and sausage, based on a family recipe. Wines are served in traditional copper carafes. The local Lambrusco is quite sweet, so keep that in mind if you prefer a drier wine. The generous outpouring of food ends with coffee served in small copper pots; you might even be asked if you'd like to taste a local liqueur. Book ahead, especially on weekends.

Via Trieste 10. osteriadelloca.it. ✆ **0376/327-171.** Main courses 14€–25€. Wed–Sat and Mon 12:15–2:30pm and 7:15–11:30pm; Sun 12:15–2:30pm.

Mantua Shopping

The favored shopping streets in Mantua radiate off Piazza delle Erbe, a delightful cluster of cobbled and arcaded streets sheltering delis stuffed with local cheeses, hams, fresh pasta, and olive oils. Posh boutiques, smart shoe shops, and bookstores line **Corso Umberto, Via Verdi,** and **Via Oberdan.** A **farmers' market** on Lungorio IV di Novembre on Saturday provides perfect fodder for a picnic in the lakeside gardens along Lungolago dei Gonzaga.

LAKE COMO ♥♥♥

Como (town): 65km (40 miles) NE of Milan; Menaggio: 35km (22 miles) NE of Como and 85km (53 miles) N of Milan; Varenna: 50km (31 miles) NE of Como and 80km (50 miles) NE of Milan

Life is slower around the northern Italian lakes than in fast-paced Milan. The city of Como is an ideal base for drawing breath and kicking back. Sitting on the southwestern tip of Lake Como, the city is essentially a center of commerce with a miniscule medieval quarter and a pretty waterfront. Tourists flock to Como for its ancient heritage, fine churches, and lake views. From here, frequent ferry service hops around the lake, visiting its many romantic lakeshore villas and villages.

Essentials

ARRIVING Frequent **trains** from Milan take 1 hour and cost 5.20€. Trains from Stazione Central and Porta Garibaldi arrive at Como San Giovanni; trains from Milan Cadorna arrive at Como Nord Lago, just off the lakefront promenade near the ferry point.

VISITOR INFORMATION The regional tourist office at Via Albertolli 7 (lakecomo.com; ✆ **031/449-3068**) has info on hotels, restaurants, and campgrounds around the lake. The office is open Monday to Saturday 9am to 1pm and 2 to 6pm. You'll also find tourist offices open in summer in several small towns around the lake; in Tremezzo at Via Regina 3 (✆ **0344/40-493**); in Varenna at Via IV Novembre 7 (varennaturismo.com; ✆ **0341/830-367;** usually closed Jan–Feb); and in Bellagio at Piazza della Chiesa 14 (bellagiolakecomo.com; ✆ **031/951-555**).

GETTING AROUND Como is the jumping-off point for most adventures on Lake Como, which is crisscrossed by regular ferry routes: It takes 4

hours to travel from one end to the other, with many stops along the way. The most popular are Tremezzo, Menaggio, Bellagio, and timeless Varenna. Single fares from Como are 10.40€ to Bellagio; a day pass costs 23.30€. Tickets cannot be purchased online. The ferry terminal, run by **Navigazione Lago di Como,** is on the esplanade at Via per Cernobbio 18 (navigazionelaghi.it; ✆ **800/551-801**).

Exploring Como ♥♥

Como's tiny *centro storico* is dominated by the impressively handsome **Duomo ♥♥** in Piazza Duomo (cattedraledicomo.it; ✆ **031/331-2275**), which combines Gothic and Renaissance architecture for two very different facades; long, narrow windows and a Gothic stained-glass rose window mark the western end, with an apse and baroque dome added in 1744 by architect Filippo Juvarra at the eastern end. The Duomo is free and open from Monday to Friday from 7:30am to 7:30pm (Sat–Sun tend to have shorter hours for tourist visits; check the official website for the latest information).

Taking a spin in a speedboat on Lake Como.

Two blocks south of the Duomo, the 12th-century **San Fedele ♥** basilica (parrocchiasanfedelecomo.it; free admission; daily 8am–noon and 3:30–7pm) stands above a charming square of the same name. Parts of the five-sided church, including the altar, date from the 6th century, and some fine frescoes are along the right-hand-side aisle.

Como's main street, **Corso Vittorio Emanuele II,** cuts through the medieval quarter and has plenty of upmarket boutiques and classy delis. If you have time, take the 10-minute **funicular ride** from Lungo Lario Trieste up to hilltop **Brunate ♥♥**, which has a cluster of excellent restaurants and bars. The funicular runs up a steep cliffside, with glorious views of Lake Como glinting below; at the top are wooded hiking trails that lead north to Bellagio. The funicular ticket office is at Piazza de Gasperi 4 (funicolarecomo.it; ✆ **031/303-608;** daily 6am–10:30pm; funicular runs until midnight on Sat and in summer). Tickets are 3.60€ adults, 2.40€ for kids 4 to 12, and free for children 3 and under. Trains depart from both ends of the line every 30 minutes.

Exploring Around Lake Como

The romantic waterfront villages of Lake Como, with their cute clusters of yellow and pink houses, majestic *palazzos,* and lush lakeside gardens, are easily explored by ferry (p. 507) or by car. Here are a few of the highlights, going clockwise around the lake from Como.

Lenno ♥♥♥ For centuries Lake Como was the playground of privileged Lombardian aristocrats, and quite honestly, not much has changed. **Villa del Balbianello** at Lenno, Via Comoedia 5 (fondoambiente.it/villa-del-balbianello-eng; ✆ **0344/56-110**), is one of the best-known of the fabulous villas, with ornate landscaped gardens and a 16th-century palace sitting high on a peninsula over the lake. (You may recognize it from *Star Wars: Episode II – Attack of the Clones* or the Bond movie *Casino Royale*.) The interior is full of priceless French furniture complemented by eclectic artwork from the travels of its former owner, explorer Guido Monzino, who died in 1988 and left the villa to the Italian National Trust. Garden entrance is 14€ adults, 11€ ages 6 to 18; garden and villa (with compulsory 1-hr. tour) is 25€ adults, 17€ ages 6 to 18. Admission is free for children 5 and under. It's open mid-March to mid-November 10am to 6pm (closed Mon and Wed). It is a bit of a walk to reach the villa from the center of Lenno, but you can take a taxi boat from Lenno and be let out right at the villa's dock, for about 8€ round-trip.

Tremezzo ♥♥ On the western side of Lake Como, Tremezzo was the 19th-century retreat of the Italian aristocracy; today it is lorded over by the exceptionally expensive **Grand Hotel Tremezzo** (grandhotel tremezzo.com; ✆ **0344/42-491**) and its wonderfully stylish beach. The plush gardens, museum, and rich art collections of the ornate 17th-century **Villa Carlotta** are open to the public (Via Regina 2; villacarlotta.it; ✆ **0344/404-05;** 15€ adults, 13€ seniors, 6€ students; late Mar to mid-Oct 9am–7:30pm [last entry 6pm] and late Oct to mid-Mar 10am–6pm [last entry 5pm]; hours can vary over holiday weekends).

Bellano ♥ Most people stop in Bellano on the eastern shore of Lake Como to visit the **Orrido** (discoveringbellano.eu/it/orrido-di-bellano; 8€ adults, 6€ seniors and ages 6–12, free for children 5 and under), a deep gorge cut out of the cliffs by the River Pioverna as it tears down the hillside. A nighttime trip down the floodlit gorge is a rare and eerie treat, and one that appears to be under threat from hydroelectric plans expected to reduce the flow of the torrent. Opening times vary seasonally. Check the website for more details.

Varenna ♥♥♥ Adorable Varenna gives Bellagio a run for its money as the prettiest village on Lake Como, a tumble of pink and terra-cotta houses in a labyrinth of narrow, cobbled streets, with smart villas clustered around the shoreline. Its winding lakeside path hangs over the water,

Varenna, one of Lake Como's prettiest villages.

with bars, shops, and art galleries looking over the lake. Linger a while over a glass of prosecco and watch the sun go down over the glittering water.

Bellagio ♥♥♥ Photogenic Bellagio is the most popular destination around Lake Como. The shady lakefront promenade is lined with chic hotels, bars, and cafes. Pretty medieval alleyways ascending steeply from the lake are lined with souvenir stores selling pricey handmade leather accessories. Regardless of the multitude of tourists, this is still a lovely place to linger for lunch overlooking the lake.

Where to Stay & Eat Around Lake Como

For such a popular destination, Como town suffers from a shortage of decent moderately priced hotels, although plenty of options can be found around the lake. If you're looking for a splurge, Cernobbio is home to one of Italy's most exclusive and expensive hotels, the **Villa d'Este ♥♥** (p. 512). The local cuisine draws heavily from the lake.

Casa du Lac ♥♥ Now part of the upmarket R Collection of hotels, this sophisticated lakeside property is an elegant 19th-century villa hidden away in Varenna's photogenic tangle of alleyways, with prized views of Lake Como. Each of the 13 rooms has been updated and modernized, relying on earth tones and natural textures to create welcoming lakeside boltholes. If you would like a terrace or sweeping lake view, make sure to book a suite or Deluxe category room. The restaurant, which boasts a lovely panoramic terrace, focuses on seafood and flavors inspired by the Amalfi Coast, reflecting the chef's southern Italian roots, while the wine

list showcases local labels alongside wines from all over Italy. Breakfast is served at sister property Hotel Royal Victoria, a 2-minute walk away.
Via del Prestino 11, Varenna. casadulac.it. ✆ **0341/830-238.** 13 units. 800€–1,100€ double. Rates include breakfast. Closed Nov to late April. **Amenities:** Restaurant; bar; free Wi-Fi.

Hotel Paradiso sul Lago ♥♥♥ Located in a little piazza at the top of the village of Brunate above Como town and near the famous Volta lighthouse (Faro Voltiano), this family-run property offers amazing hilltop views from the breakfast room and a panoramic terrace with swimming pool and Jacuzzi. Guest rooms are clean and functional, with ongoing upgrades and the addition of modern touches like Nespresso machines; some have great lake views, and there are triple and quadruple rooms for larger groups. The on-site **Mama Gina** cafe/bistro offers seasonal cuisine as well as sunset cocktails and snacks, and the property also now owns the nearby La Polenteria restaurant (see below), serving heartier local fare. The drive up the hill on a narrow road is tricky, but you can always take the cable car from Como. It's a challenging uphill walk from the funicular, but the hotel does run a shuttle service.
Via Scalini 7, Brunate. hotelparadisocomo.com. ✆ **031/364-099.** 13 units. 120€–169€ double. Rates include breakfast. **Amenities:** Restaurant; cafe; bar; outdoor pool; shuttle service; free Wi-Fi.

La Polenteria ♥♥♥ REGIONAL ITALIAN This out-of-the-way spot above Como in Brunate at the foot of the Faro Voltiano lighthouse has some of the best polenta around these parts. Now run by the same owners as the Hotel Paradiso sul Lago (see above), La Polenteria aims to highlight whatever is in season, such as chestnuts and porcini mushrooms in fall, or snails and fresh lake fish in spring. Vegetarians will find quite a selection on the menu—including pasta dishes and polenta (which is made with dairy products) with tomato sauce or cheese—but vegans may end up cobbling together a meal of sauteed vegetables and roasted potatoes. The restaurant is surprisingly light and bright but still has a rustic feel, plus outdoor tables. La Polenteria is almost always full, so you absolutely must reserve a table in advance before you make the trek up (if you don't feel like walking from the funicular, ask the restaurant about operating hours for the free round-trip shuttle).
Via Scalini, 66, Brunate. lapolenteria.it. ✆ **031/336-5105.** Main courses 14€–25€. Mon, Thurs–Sun 12:30pm–2:30pm and 7:30–10:30pm, Tues 7:30–10:30pm.

Nest on the Lake ♥♥ This gem of a B&B on the shores of Lake Como is in Lezzeno, a tranquil town just down the road from Bellagio. The views from this old fisherman's house from the early 1800s are some of the best on Lake Como. Each of the rooms—decked out in earth tones and calming pastel colors—have patios or wrought-iron balconies. Continental breakfast is served in a delightful stone-walled room on the ground floor. The location midway up the lake makes it a great base for hiking, waterskiing, and wakeboarding; guests can access a small beach with canoes that can be taken out onto the water. The property also has a variety of self-catering apartments for larger groups, but breakfast is not included, and there may be a cleaning fee.

Via Sostra 17/19, Lezzeno. nestonthelake.com. ✆ **031/914-372.** 4 rooms, 3 apartments. 180€–200€ double. Room rates include breakfast. **Amenities:** Solarium; free Wi-Fi.

Piazza Roma ♥♥ MODERN ITALIAN Tucked away on a nondescript side street behind the cathedral, this intimate *ristorante* serves contemporary takes on regional Italian classics. While there are a few tables outside, they lack lake vistas, so instead enjoy the rustic elegance indoors with stone walls, beamed ceilings, and refined candelabra-adorned tablescapes. The menu highlights fresh local ingredients, including fish from Lake Como and cheese and herbs from the nearby mountains. Tuck into ravioli filled with lake perch and topped with butter and sage, or roasted rack of lamb with an herbed anchovy sauce and charred onions. There is also a surprising selection of thoughtfully crafted and tasty vegan dishes, like an eggplant roll stuffed with beet "cream" and topped with bean sprouts and greens. Reservations are recommended.

Piazza Roma 43, Como. piazzaromacomo.com. ✆ **031/303-074.** Main courses 13€–29€. Mon, Wed–Sun noon–2:30pm and 7–10:30pm.

Splendide Ristorante ♥♥♥ REGIONAL ITALIAN You would be hard-pressed to find a prettier spot on the whole of Lake Como than the geranium-filled terrace of the Hotel Excelsior Splendide in Bellagio, but the view won't come cheap. Perched over the shimmering waters of the lake, the restaurant is a perfect place to watch boats pull into port while enjoying light dishes like steamed mussels in a spicy lemon sauce or heartier fare, such as homemade buffalo mozzarella lasagna with marinated prawns or filet mignon. Hit the **Lounge Bar** for a spritz at *aperitivo* hour or enjoy salads, panini, or one of the gourmet pizzas made with premium ingredients. The dramatic setting makes this a popular locale, and while the food is solid, service can be uneven.

Via Lungo Lario Manzoni 28, Bellagio. hsplendide.com. ✆ **031/950-225.** Main courses 18€–45€. Mar–Nov noon–2:30pm.

Villa d'Este ♥♥ Princes, princesses, and sultans have passed through the gates of this opulent Renaissance *palazzo* originally built as an exclusive summer residence in 1568. A hotel since 1873, today it welcomes a constant procession of major celebs and minor royalty arriving by speedboat or helicopter to luxuriate in an almost absurd level of grandeur. Villa d'Este is Lake Como at its finest, with stunning views of the water surrounded by verdant parklands. The property boasts a selection of fine-dining options (guests are expected to dress elegantly for dinner), while the Greenhouse lounge offers a more casual all-day menu and signature cocktails served during *aperitivo* hour. The wellness center and sports club are on par with the rest of the property, with a spa, gym, tennis courts, multiple pools, and running paths. The resort even has its own golf course. Those looking for a retreat away from the masses can rent out one of four large private villas (entire homes the resort calls "noble residences"), secluded in the resort's centuries-old park.

Via Regina 40, Cernobbio. villadeste.com. ✆ **031/3481.** 152 units. 900€–1,300€ double. Rates include breakfast. Closed Jan–Feb. **Amenities:** 3 restaurants; 3 bars; lounge, nightclub; indoor and outdoor pools; spa; concierge; free Wi-Fi.

LAKE GARDA ♥♥

Sirmione: 130km (81 miles) E of Milan, 150km (93 miles) W of Venice; Riva del Garda: 170km (105 miles) NE of Milan, 199km (123 miles) NW of Venice

Lake Garda is the largest and easternmost of the northern Italian lakes, with its western flanks lapping against the flat plains of Lombardy and its southern extremes in the Veneto. In the north, its deep waters are backed by Alpine peaks. Garda's shores are green and fragrant with flowery gardens, groves of olives and lemons, and forests of pines and cypress.

Essentials

ARRIVING Regular **trains** run from Milan Stazione Centrale, stopping at Desenzano del Garda (fares start at 10€). From here it's a 20-minute bus ride to Sirmione; buses make the trip every half-hour for 2€.

Hydrofoils and ferries operated by **Navigazione Laghi** (navlaghi.it; ✆ **800/551-801**) ply the lake waters. One to two hourly ferries connect Sirmione with Desenzano del Garda in season (20 min. by ferry; 3€), less frequently October to April.

Sirmione is just off the A4 between Milan and Venice. From Venice the trip takes about 1½ hours, and from Milan a little over an hour. Ample parking is in Piazzale Monte Baldo (though it can fill up early on weekends in spring and summer), which is about a 15-minute walk into the heart of town.

VISITOR INFORMATION **Sirmione's tourist office** is at Viale Marconi 8 (visitsirmione.com; ✆ **030/728-5327**). It includes a convenient bag drop-off service for a small fee. A tourism kiosk is across the street at Viale Marconi 2 just before the bridge into the old part of town. In **Riva del Garda,** the tourist office is on the lakefront at Largo Medaglie d'Oro 5 (gardatrentino.it/en; ✆ **0464/554-444**). In **Gardone Riviera,** the tourist office is located at Corso Repubblica 1 (rivieradelgarda.com). For all, hours vary depending on the season.

Exploring Around Lake Garda

SIRMIONE

Perched on a promontory swathed in cypress and olive groves on the southernmost edge of Lake Garda, photogenic Sirmione has been a popular spot since the Romans first discovered hot springs here. Despite the onslaught of summer visitors, this historic town manages to retain its charm. Sirmione has lakeside promenades and pleasant beaches and is small enough for everything to be accessible on foot. It is chiefly famous for its thermal springs, castle, and northern Italy's largest Roman ruins.

Rocca Scaligera castle in Sirmione.

Built on the peninsula's narrowest point, the moated, fortified **Rocca Scaligera** ♥♥♥ (✆ **030/916-468**) dominates the *centro storico.* Built in the 14th century by the Della Scala family, who ruled Verona and many of the lands surrounding the lake, the castle is worth a visit for its sweeping courtyards, turreted towers, dungeons, and views across Lake Garda. It's open Tuesday to Saturday 8:30am to 7:30pm, Sunday 8:30am to 1:30pm; admission is 6€ adults, 3€ ages 18 to 25, and is free for seniors and kids 17 and under.

From the castle, it's a 15-minute walk (or take the open-air tram from Piazza Piatti) along Via Vittorio Emanuele from the town center to the tip of Sirmione's peninsula and the **Grotte di Catullo** ♥♥ (✆ **030/916-157**), romantically placed ruins with views across the lake. Built around C.E. 150, the remains are thought to represent two sizeable aristocratic villas. A small museum of Roman artifacts from the site includes jewelry and mosaic fragments (Piazzale Orti Manara 4; 8€ adults, 4€ ages 18–25, free for ages 17 and under, free first Sun of month); hours are generally Tuesday to Saturday 8:30am to 7:30pm and Sunday 9:30am to 6:30pm, with shorter hours October to March.

The massive amusement park **Gardaland** (gardaland.it; ✆ **045/6449-777**) is half an hour's drive east of Sirmione at Castelnuovo del Garda. This huge resort includes several hotels, an aquarium, and LEGOLAND waterpark. It is generally busy during summer and school vacation periods.

GARDONE RIVIERA

Halfway up the western shore of Lake Garda, this little resort—easily accessible by ferry or bus from Desenzano del Garda—offers visitors a gorgeous backdrop for a little relaxation. Oleanders dot the paved promenade, and enticing bars and restaurants fill the charming *centro storico* (Gardone Sopra).

Uphill from the Gardone Riviera lakefront, the **Heller Garden ♥♥**, Via Roma 2 (hellergarden.com; ✆ **336/410-877**), is a tropical paradise founded by Arthur Hruska, a botanist who was also dentist to the ill-fated Tsar Nicholas II of Russia. Hruska planted this botanical haven in the 1900s, and thousands of rare palms, orchids, and tree ferns now thrive here, thanks to the town's mild, sheltered climate. The garden is open March to October daily 9am to 7pm; admission is 12€, 5€ for ages 6 to 11, and free for children 5 and under.

Gardone Riviera's other highlight is the **Vittoriale degli Italiani ♥♥**, Via Vittoriale 12 (vittoriale.it; ✆ **0365/296-511**), the wildly ostentatious and bizarrely decorated villa home of Gabriele d'Annunzio, the notorious Italian poet and sometime war hero. He bought this hillside estate in 1921 and died here in 1938; a visit pays tribute to d'Annunzio's hedonistic lifestyle rather than his fairly awful poetry. The claustrophobic rooms of this madcap mansion are stuffed with bric-a-brac and artifacts from his colorful life, including mementos of his long affair with actress Eleonora Duse. The patrol boat d'Annunzio commanded in World War I, a museum containing his biplane and photos, and his hilltop mausoleum are all found in the formal gardens that cascade down the hillside. The villa is open daily 9am until 8pm in summer and 5pm in winter. Admission ranges from 12€ to 18€, depending on which parts you visit. If your visit includes the house (with mandatory guided tour), you must show up at least 30 minutes before the scheduled time. Children 6 and under enter for free, and there are reduced prices for seniors and ages 7 to 18.

RIVA DEL GARDA

The northernmost settlement on Lake Garda is a thriving Italian town with medieval towers, Renaissance churches and *palazzi,* and narrow cobblestone streets where everyday business proceeds in its alluring way. Note that Riva del Garda becomes a cultural magnet in October, when the town hosts the international **Lago di Garda Musica Festival** (mrf-musicfestivals.com). If you want to see amateur choirs and orchestras perform classical music in magnificent villas and *palazzos,* with the lake as a breathtaking backdrop, make hotel reservations well in advance. Riva del Garda's **Old Town** is pleasant, although it has only two notable historic attractions. The 13th-century **Torre d'Apponale** (2€, free for ages 16 and under) in Piazza III Novembre is open in summer for visitors to climb its 165 steps for views across the lake. The town's moated lakeside castle, **La Rocca,** houses an unassuming civic museum (museoaltogarda.it; ✆ **0464/573-869;** 5€ adults, 4€ ages 15–26 and over 65, free for ages 14 and under; Tues–Sun 10am–6pm, typically closes Dec–Jan and sometimes Feb).

Where to Stay & Eat Around Lake Garda

Sirmione and Riva del Garda have a choice of pleasant, moderately priced hotels, all of which book up quickly in June, July, and August, when rates go up. The local cuisine features fish from the lake and lots of pasta.

RIVA DEL GARDA: watersports & more

Riva del Garda's main attraction is the lake itself, lined with plush hotels and a waterside promenade stretching for miles past parks and pebbly beaches. The water is warm enough for swimming May to October, and air currents fanned by the mountains make Riva and neighboring Torbole the windsurfing capitals of Europe. Kitesurfing, kayaking, and sailing are all popular pastimes.

A convenient point of embarkation for a lake outing is the beach next to **La Rocca** castle, where from March through October you can rent rowboats or pedal boats for about 10€ per hour; the concession is open daily 8am to 8pm.

Check out the sailing and windsurfing at **Sailing du Lac** (sailingdulac.com) at the luxurious **Hotel du Lac et du Parc** (below), where windsurf equipment can be rented for 66€ per day or 33€ per hour. Lessons start at 72€ for 2½ hours. A catamaran for two to four people can be rented for 85€ per hour; you must leave a 200€ deposit and show identification such as a passport. Catamaran lessons start at 85€ per 2-hour session. The school is open mid-April to mid-October from 8:30am to 6:30pm. Book ahead of time online for a small discount.

Lake Garda is also renowned for mountain biking; more than 80 routes circle around the lake and ascend the Alpine foothills. At **Happy Bike,** Viale Rovereto 72 (happy-bike.it; ✆ **347/943-1208;** daily 9am–7pm), you can rent a city bike for 16€ per day or a mountain bike for around 25€ per day. The staff is friendly and happy to offer detailed information on routes to take.

Hotel du Lac et du Parc ♥♥♥ The vast, lush gardens are one of the best parts of this massive, family-friendly Riva del Garda resort, which also boasts swimming pools, a modern spa, and every conceivable luxury. The grounds lead down to a little lakefront beach where you can windsurf, paddleboard, take sailing lessons, or join in the many other watersports at the **Sailing Du Lac** sailing school (see box above). Accommodation options include bungalows, luxurious suites in the villas, or rooms in the hotel in the heart of the resort. Despite the size of the property, service feels personal, and attention to detail can be seen everywhere. The gardens are immaculately manicured, hotel rooms are cheery and tasteful, and the breakfast is top-notch. The resort has three restaurants, including two upscale options and a more casual bistro/lounge; the massive breakfast buffet is a highlight. For much of the year, the **Paolino** mini-club is open to kids ages 3 to 10. While the little ones are occupied, parents can sneak away to the **Armonia Spa** to enjoy treatments as well as the sauna, steam room, Mediterranean bath, tropical showers, and whirlpool.

Via Rovereto 44, Riva del Garda. dulacetduparc.com. ✆ **0464/566-600.** 159 units in main hotel. 200€–400€ double. Rates include breakfast. Limited availability Dec–Mar. **Amenities:** 3 restaurants; 3 bars; 2 outdoor pools; indoor pool; gym; spa; sauna; babysitting; kids' club; water sports; concierge; room service; free Wi-Fi.

Hotel Eden ♥ This historic pink-stucco *palazzo* on the lake now operates as a modern hotel in the heart of Sirmione's *centro storico* mere steps

Sailing on Lake Garda with Sailing Du Lac.

from the castle. A favorite retreat for literary figures in the early 20th century, today the Eden is light and bright, with a neutral palette complemented by occasional splashes of bright colors. The vivid hues and modern touches continue in the immaculately clean guest rooms, with contemporary furnishings. The breakfast room leads to an outdoor terrace overlooking a pier jutting out into the water. Ask for a lakeview room, as the other side of the hotel can be somewhat noisy at night, given the prime location in the heart of the action. Guests have access to the hotel's lakeside solarium with sunbeds for relaxing while watching the boats drift by. The property can set up private boat tours, departing right from the dock outside.

Piazza Carducci 19, Sirmione. hoteledensirmione.it. ✆ **030/916-481.** 30 units. 160€–275€ double. Rates include breakfast. Closed Dec–Mar. **Amenities:** Lounge; bar; concierge; room service; free Wi-Fi.

Osteria Al Torcol ♥♥ ITALIAN Tucked away at the top of a little hill on a quiet side street, Torcol is consistently regarded as *the* standout restaurant in Sirmione and a welcome change from the tourist traps that dominate the main drag. The wood-beamed interior is packed with bottles of local wines (many available by the glass). Dishes at this high-end *osteria* are seemingly simple but are presented artfully and feature unique flavor combinations. Homemade spaghetti is sautéed in garlic and spicy olive oil, then topped with scallops and lime-infused breadcrumbs. Try a selection of grilled freshwater fish in a dill vinaigrette or grilled lamb chops served with cabbage salad, coconut sauce, and black sesame. If you have your heart set on views of the lake, this isn't the restaurant for you, but the vine-covered courtyard is a peaceful oasis. Make sure to book in advance.

Via San Salvatore 30, Sirmione. ✆ **030/990-4605.** Main courses 17€–32€. Thurs–Tues 12:30–3pm and 7:30–10:30pm. Closed some periods late Nov to late Feb.

Osteria Antico Brolo ♥ ITALIAN Located in the "upper" part of Gardone Riviera (about a 15-min. walk uphill from the center of town on winding Via Roma, or a 5-min. drive), this charming osteria serves updated Italian classics in a charming old-world setting. You can eat inside to enjoy the refined, yet informal atmosphere of this *palazzo* from the 1700s or outside in the stone-walled courtyard where the rumored "antico brolo" (ancient vegetable garden) would have been. The menu is a thoughtfully curated list of specialties that make the most of seasonal ingredients from around Italy. Try *gnocchi alla romana* (semolina dumplings) in a Bolognese sauce or parchment-baked cod in a light cherry tomato stew. The homemade breads served with meals are divine. Above the osteria are four well-appointed rooms for rent, some with lake views. Continental breakfast is included.

Via Carere 10, Gardone Riviera. ristoranteanticobrolo.it. ✆ **0365/214-21.** Main courses 16€–29€. Daily 12:30–2pm and 7:30–10pm; restaurant closed mid-Nov to mid-Feb.

LAKE MAGGIORE ♥♥

Stresa: 90km (56 miles) NW of Milan

To the west of Como lies Maggiore, a long, thin wisp of a lake protected by mountains and fed by the River Ticino, which flows on to Milan. Roughly a quarter of the lake (the northern end) lies in Switzerland, including the city of Locarno and its delightful satellite resort of Ascona. **Stresa** is the largest town on the Italian side, a timeless resort on the western shoreline, famed for its setting opposite the **Isole Borromee** (**Borromean Islands;** p. 519). Regular **ferries** span Maggiore, with frequent stops on the way from **Arona,** south of Stresa; two of the most popular stops are at **Luino,** known for its massive street market every Wednesday, and **Laveno,** which offers cable-car rides up to mountain peaks.

Essentials

ARRIVING Stresa is linked with Milan Stazione Centrale by 20 **trains** a day. Journeys take about an hour and cost 8.60€. Many lakeside spots can be reached from Stresa, with most boats on the lake operated by **Navigazione Laghi** (navlaghi.it; ✆ **800/551-801**); boats arrive at and depart from Piazza Marconi, Stresa. The main ferry office, however, is at the lake's southern tip in Arona, at Viale Baracca 1; from there, ferries to Stresa take 40 minutes and cost 6.20€.

By **car,** take the A8 west from Milan to Sesto Calende, near the south end of the lake; from there, follow Route SS33 up the western shore to

Stresa. The trip takes just over an hour, but it can be much longer in summer traffic.

VISITOR INFORMATION Stresa's **tourist office,** at the ferry dock on Piazza Marconi (stresaturismo.it; ✆ **0323/301-50**), is open daily 10am to 12:30pm and 3 to 6:30pm (mid-Oct to mid-Mar closed Sat afternoons and Sun).

Exploring Stresa & the Islands

The biggest town on the Italian side of Maggiore, elegant Stresa is the springboard to the Isole Borromee (Borromean Islands), the tiny baroque jewels of the lake. Now a genteel tourist town, Stresa captured the hearts of 19th-century aristocracy, who settled in grandiose villas strung along the promenade. Just back into the tangle of medieval streets, **Piazza Cadorna** is a mass of restaurants that spill out into the center of the square in summer. There's a food and craft market on summer Thursday afternoons on the promenade, and a lido and beach club on the lakefront.

The three **Isole Borromee** (terreborromeo.it) are named for the aristocratic Borromeo family (p. 520), who've owned them since the 12th century. Public **ferries** leave for the islands from Stresa's Piazza Marconi, with a more frequent schedule in the summer months.

ISOLA DEI PESCATORI ♥♥ Pescatori is stuck in a medieval time warp, with ancient fishermen's houses clustered together on every inch of the tiny island. As you wander the cobbled streets, you'll discover tiny churches, art galleries, souvenir shops, pizza and pasta restaurants, and, at every turn, a glimpse of the lake beyond. It's an entrancing place to explore, but be warned: The prices are extortionate, and it gets plenty of tourist traffic.

ISOLA BELLA ♥♥♥ The minute islet of Bella is dominated by the massive baroque **Palazzo Borromeo** with its formal Italianate gardens. The *palazzo* makes for an absorbing tour, with conspicuous displays of wealth evident in the rich decor and exquisite furnishings. Terraced gardens dotted with follies have spectacular views across Maggiore. Of special interest are the ornate grottoes where the Borromeos went to stay cool, and a painting gallery hung with 130 of the most important works the Borromeos collected over the centuries. Admission (23€ adults, 14€ ages 6–15, free for children 5 and under) includes entry to the gardens and the painting gallery. It's open mid-March through the end of October 9am to 5:30pm (it closes slightly earlier in spring and fall).

ISOLA MADRE ♥♥ The largest and most peaceful of the islands is Isola Madre (30 min. from Stresa), overspread with exquisite flora in the 3.2-hectare (8-acre) **Orto Botanico.** Pick up a map at the ticket office to identify all the rhododendrons, camellias, and ancient wisteria. Many a peacock and fancy pheasant stalk across the lawns of another 16th-century **Borromeo palazzo,** this one filled with family memorabilia and some interesting old puppet-show stages. Admission to the garden and

ITALY'S MEDIEVAL oligarchs

The all-powerful Borromeo family were Lombardian aristocrats who loomed large in Milanese politics and religion for 200 years. They regarded the vast tracts of land around the southern end of Lake Maggiore as their personal fiefdom, where they built castles, monuments, and palaces. The family spawned several archbishops of Milan, including Federico (1564–1631) and Carlo (1538–84), a singularly wily individual who was canonized in 1610 thanks to the leading role he took in the Counter-Reformation. A great bronze statue of Carlo stands in Arona, looking out across the lake to his former family home, **Rocca Borromeo** at Angera (terreborromeo.it), an imposing fortress that now offers visitors a medieval garden, a toy and doll museum, and exhibits of contemporary art. Like the other Borromeo properties, it's open mid-March through late October.

palace is 20€ adults and 11.50€ for ages 6 to 15 (free for children 5 and under). It's open March to late October 9am to 5:30pm (it closes slightly earlier in spring and fall).

Exploring Around Lake Maggiore

Beyond Stresa, Maggiore offers natural beauty and architectural wonders as well as lively towns, markets, and cable-car rides into the mountains.

Arona ♥♥ As well as having the lake's main ferry office (p. 518), this sophisticated town at the southern end of Lake Maggiore is a shopping magnet, with its charming **Via Cavour** lined with elegant boutiques and expensive delicatessens. The giant bronze **statue of Carlo Borromeo** (p. 475), who was born in Arona in 1538, is just outside of town. It's so huge you can even climb inside and gaze out at the lake through Carlo's eyes (statuasancarlo.it; ✆ **0322/249-669;** admission 10€ for the terrace and inside the statue, 5€ for terrace only, free for children 6 and under). It's open mid-March through October daily 9am to noon and 2 to 6pm (on Sun, it stays open continually 9am–6pm).

Luino ♥♥ On the western shore of Lake Maggiore just a few miles from the Swiss border, Luino is home to one of northern Italy's most popular **street markets,** with more than 350 stalls taking over the town every Wednesday. Here you'll find spices, piles of salami, *grappas,* and olive oils, as well as the hand-tooled leather belts and bags for which the region is famous. Extra ferries (navlaghi.it) serve the town every Wednesday, and many shoppers visit Luino directly by train from Milan's Stazione Centrale (2 hr.; 8.70€).

Santa Caterina del Sasso Ballaro ♥♥♥ Just south of the small town of Reno on the eastern shore of Maggiore, beneath an inconspicuous car park in Piazza Cascine del Quiquio, take an elevator or a 268-step staircase down to the magical hermitage of **Santa Caterina del Sasso Ballaro,** Via Santa Caterina 13, Leggiuno (www.santacaterinadelsasso.com;

The monastery of Santa Caterina del Sasso Ballaro clings to a cliff face high above Lake Maggiore.

(✆ **0332/647-014**). Founded in the 13th century, this Dominican monastery sits photogenically against a sheer rock face, clinging to an escarpment 15m (49 ft.) above the lake. The serene complex of soft-pink stone is embellished with Renaissance arches and pretty cobbled courtyards. Don't miss the chapel's 14th-century frescoes of biblical scenes, which were hidden under lime during the Italian suppression of the monasteries in the 1770s and only rediscovered in 2003. The gift shop sells honey, candles, and soaps made by the monks. It costs 5€ to enter, and the elevator costs 1€ (Apr–Oct 9am–noon and 2:30–6pm; Nov–Mar Sat–Sun 9am–noon and 2–5pm).

Sasso del Ferro ♥♥♥ Northeast of Laveno, Laveno Mombello is the terminus for a 16-minute **cable-car** ride (funiviedellagomaggiore.it; ✆ **0332/668-012;** 12€ round-trip) up the lush Val Cuvia to the Poggia Sant'Elsa viewpoint atop **Sasso del Ferro,** towering 1,062m (3,484 ft.) over Lake Maggiore. Each car is for one or two people. The truly breathtaking panoramas look west to the snow-capped Alps or south over the lakes Varese, Monate, and Comabbio; hiking trails traverse the hills. If the conditions are right, there'll be plenty of paragliders. Leave time to relax over a prosecco in the **Ristorante Albergo Funivia** (p. 521). Times vary according to weather and season, but the cable car generally runs March to November (Mon–Fri 11am–6:30pm, Sat–Sun 11am–10:30pm).

Where to Stay & Eat Around Lake Maggiore

There are many hotels scattered around Maggiore eager to grab the tourist dollar: some good, some bad, many indifferent. The two listed here, at opposite ends of the price spectrum, are exceptional. Similarly, food quality in the area varies wildly; in touristy Stresa, pick restaurants with care.

Albergo Funivia ♥♥ This no-frills hotel located on the Poggia Sant'Elsa lookout is only accessible by the Sasso del Ferro cable car (see above). What Albergo Funivia lacks in charm, it makes up for in beautiful views over Lake Maggiore and the Alps from the balconies in every room (where you can also choose to have breakfast). Rooms are quite basic, though some are gradually being updated, but they are clean and functional. Light sleepers should ask for rooms farther away from the cable car. Summer is the best time to come, with good weather almost guaranteed, though winters are milder than might be expected here "on top of the world." A restaurant/bar offers everything from simple salads to a selection of pastas and robust meat dishes. The food here is not gourmet, and prices reflect the enviable setting, with pasta dishes starting at around 20€. At night, it's a delight to sit here watching the lights around the lake glittering in the distance. The property typically closes from early November until the end of March.

Via Tinelli, 15, Località Poggio Sant Elsa, Laveno Mombello. funiviedellago maggiore.it. ✆ **0332/610-303.** 18 units. 130€–180€ double. **Amenities:** Restaurant; bar; free Wi-Fi.

Bistrot 76 ♥♥ NORTHERN ITALIAN Stresa's town center is full of anonymous pasta and pizza joints; this restaurant is certainly a cut above. It is owned by the Bellossi family, who are serious about food and wine. Start with a selection of regional antipasti—pâté, artichoke with *bagna cauda* (a sauce made of anchovies, olive oil, garlic, and herbs), and local cold cuts—and move on to creative first and second courses, such as grape risotto with Gorgonzola cheese and pecans, or marinated lake fish that is lightly fried and served with sweet-and-sour vegetables. Dine in the elegant wood-paneled main restaurant, which has an Art Deco feel, or, in warmer months, outside in a trellis-shaded courtyard, which is also the perfect spot for an aperitif.

Via Mazzini 25, Stresa. ristorantepiemontese.com. ✆ **0323/302-35.** Main courses 13€–35€. Tues–Sun 7:30–10:30pm. Closed Dec–Feb.

Grand Hotel des Iles Borromee ♥♥♥ Even from a distance, this majestic hotel—a vast, over-the-top example of Belle Epoque architecture, in Stresa—is a showstopper. The exquisitely manicured gardens lead into the impressive interior, where all is tastefully ornate and gilded, like a mini-Versailles. Rooms range from more traditional and opulent to clean and contemporary. Quirky "attic rooms" are slightly smaller and can be accessed from the sixth floor via a small staircase. These boltholes with sloped ceilings and dormer windows are the most budget-friendly option available. The fabulously glitzy Hemingway Suite (the famous writer actually stayed here twice) includes two bedrooms, a study, a living room, three bathrooms, and a terrace overlooking the lake. The hotel actually has a central role in *A Farewell to Arms*. The massive **Des Iles** wellness area offers everything from a Turkish bath and hammam to traditional Chinese medicine; it has a spa, two pools (indoor and outdoor), a medical and beauty lab, and a well-equipped gym.

Corso Umberto I 67, Stresa. borromees.it. ✆ **0323/938-938.** 172 units. 300€–600€ double. Rates include breakfast. **Amenities:** Restaurant; bar; concierge; spa; sauna; indoor pool; 2 outdoor pools; personal trainer; gym; helicopter pad; free Wi-Fi.

Il Verbano ♥♥ SEAFOOD While many restaurants on the Isole Borromee are overpriced and underwhelming, the fine food and sublime

The ornate lakeside Grand Hotel des Iles Borromee.

position of Hotel Verbano's restaurant on Isola Pescatori can't be beat. It offers breathtaking views of Isola Bella's Palazzo Borromeo (p. 519) and the nearby mountains, while lake waters lap around the terrace. Chef Marco Sacco (two Michelin stars) offers a variety of tasting menus that focus on delicacies from the lake and nearby mountains, along with a "tour of Italy" and a newer selection of vegan and vegetarian options. Some of the innovative and artfully presented dishes include pike-perch filet with peas, ponzu sauce, and salted orange, or gnocchi in a Castelmagno blue-cheese sauce with marinated zucchini and black truffle. The restaurant serves both lunch and dinner, but the atmosphere is quieter and more romantic at night when the day-trippers have left the island. Start with an aperitif as the sun goes down over the lake, with the sky taking on a distinctive reddish hue. Despite the sophisticated cuisine and price tag to match, the service can be quite low-key—don't expect white-glove service, even at these prices. If you don't come over by ferry, contact the restaurant to find out how you can zip here and back via private taxi boat, which feels like something out of a James Bond movie.

Via Ugo Ara 2, Isola Pescatori. ilverbano.com. ✆ **0323/312-26.** Main courses 28€–50€. Daily noon–2:30pm and 7–10pm. Closed Jan to mid-Mar.

TURIN ♥♥♥

669km (415 miles) NW of Rome, 140km (87 miles) E of Milan

It's often said that Turin (Torino in Italian) is the most French city in Italy. The reason is partly historical and partly architectural. From the late 13th century until Italy's unification in 1861, Turin was the capital of the **House**

of Savoy. These wealthy aristocrats were as French as they were Italian, with estates that extended into the present-day French regions of Savoy and the Côte d'Azur. Under the Savoys, Francophile 17th- and 18th-century architects razed much of the city and its Roman foundations, replacing them with broad avenues and grandiose buildings. As a result, Turin is one of Europe's great baroque cities, befitting a one-time capital of the nation. Though often overlooked, Turin is a vibrant, sophisticated city of museums, enticing cafes, beautiful squares, and designer shops.

Essentials

ARRIVING Domestic and international **flights** land at **Turin Airport (TRN;** aeroportoditorino.it; ✆ **011/567-6361**), about 13km (8 miles) northwest of Turin. Direct **trains** (gtt.to.it; ✆ **011/57-641**) run from the airport to GTT Dora commuter rail station every 30 minutes between 5am and 11pm; the 4€ trip takes 19 minutes. **Arriva buses** (torino.arriva.it) serve the airport and Turin's main train stations, Porta Nuova and Porta Susa (40 min.; 7.50€ from the ticket office, 8.50€ on board—though if you pay on board with a contactless credit card, the cost is 7.50€—and 11€ round-trip if you buy online). **Taxis** into town take about 30 minutes and cost 30€ to 50€, depending on the time of day.

Turin's main **train** station is **Stazione di Porta Nuova** on Piazza Carlo Felice. There is regular daily **Trenitalia** (trenitalia.com; ✆ **892-021**) service from Milan. The fastest trains take 1 hour, with fares averaging 29€ if purchased in advance. Slower trains take up to 2 hours, with fares of 12€ to 17€. **Stazione di Porta Susa** connects Turin with local Piedmont towns and is the terminus for the **TGV service to Paris;** two trains a day make that trip in under 6 hours for around 120€. To get a better fare, try to book well in advance.

Turin's main **bus terminal** is **Autostazione Bus,** Corso Vittorio Emanuele II 131 (autostazionetorino.it). Buses connect Turin to Courmayeur, Aosta, Milan, and many small towns in Piedmont. A 2-hour **Arriva** (torino.arriva.it) bus service to Milan Malpensa Airport costs 22€ each way (or 39€ round-trip if purchased online).

Turin is at the hub of the autostrade grid. The A4 connects Turin with Milan in 90 minutes. Journey time on the A5 to Aosta is around 90 minutes.

See Turin's Top Sights & Save

If you're planning to visit three or more attractions, you can save money by buying the **Torino+Piemonte Card** (turismotorino.org/card), which offers discounts or grants free admission to dozens of museums, monuments, castles, and royal *palazzi* throughout the Piedmont region. The card also includes discounts on public transportation. All of the attractions covered below are included. A variety of passes are available; a 24-hour pass valid for one adult costs 29€. Cheaper passes are available for families and people under the age of 18. Passes can be bought online or at the Piazza Castello tourist office or Stazione Porta Nuova.

GETTING AROUND All the main sights of Turin are well within walking distance of each other. There's also a vast network of **GTT** trams and buses as well as one Metro line (gtt.to.it; ✆ **011/57-641**). The historic Linea 7 tourist tram, known as a "museum on the move," trundles around a circular route from Piazza Castello. Public transport tickets, available at newsstands, cost 1.90€ for 100 minutes of travel for a digital ticket purchased via the app or online, or 2€ for a paper ticket. All-day tickets cost 3.70€ digitally and 4.50€ for a paper version; these are valid until the end of service that day. There is no need to drive in the city center.

You can find **taxis** at stands in front of the train stations and around Piazza San Carlo and Piazza Castello. To call a taxi, you can dial **Taxi**

Torino at ✆ **011/5730** or 011/5737, but all hotel reception desks will order a taxi for you. Meters start at around 4€ and increase by 1.50€ per kilometer up to 10€, after which the per-kilometer rate decreases based on how long you travel; there are surcharges for waiting, luggage, late-night travel, and Sunday journeys.

VISITOR INFORMATION The **tourist office** on the corner of Via Garibaldi and Piazza Castello (turismotorino.org; ✆ **011/535-181**) is open daily 9am to 6pm. There is also a branch across from Stazione Porta Nuova in Piazza Carlo Felice (same phone; same hours).

CITY LAYOUT Turin's glamorous spine is the arcaded **Via Roma,** lined with designer shops and grand cafes. Via Roma runs northwards through a series of ever-lovelier baroque squares until it reaches **Piazza Castello** and the palaces of the Savoy nobility. From here, a walk west on Via Garibaldi leads to the square-shaped **Quadrilatero Romano,** a mellow jumble of narrow streets that's the oldest part of the city. Or turn east from Piazza Castello along Via Po to one of Italy's largest squares, the **Piazza Vittorio Veneto,** and at the end of this elegant expanse, the River Po and Parco del Valentino.

Exploring Turin

In 1714, Filippo Juvarra designed the stately arcades of **Via Roma,** Turin's premier shopping street. Starting at the Porta Nuova train station, this chic thoroughfare runs from **Piazza Carlo Felice,** an ellipse of formal gardens ringed with outdoor cafes, north into **Piazza San Carlo** ♥♥, quite possibly

Turin's Piazza San Carlo.

Organized Tours

The nonprofit organization **Free Tour Turin** (freetourturin.com) offers a free 2½-hour guided tour of the city center (in English and Italian) Thursday through Monday at 10:30am. Tour groups meet outside the Porta Nuova Metro station in Piazza Carlo Felice next to the Tourist Info Point (look for the guide holding a sign or umbrella), but it is a good idea to book online on the official site.

Italy's most beautiful square. In summer, harmonious Piazza San Carlo is Turin's outdoor *salone,* its arcaded sidewalks lined with big-name fashion stores and elegant cafes, including the genteel **Caffé Torino** (caffetorino1903.it; ✆ **011/545-118**). In the center of the piazza prances a 19th-century equestrian statue of Duke Emanuele Filiberto of Savoy. Two 17th-century churches, **San Carlo** and **Santa Cristina,** face each other like bookends at the southern entrance to the square.

At the far north end of Via Roma, the **Piazza Castello** is dominated by **Palazzo Madama** ♥ (p. 531), named for its 17th-century inhabitant, Christine Marie of France, who married into the Savoy dynasty in 1619. Farther north still stands the massive complex of the **Palazzo Reale** ♥ (p. 531), residence of the Savoy dukes from 1646 to 1865.

Duomo di San Giovanni Battista ♥♥ CHURCH One of the few pieces of Renaissance architecture in baroque-dominated Turin, this otherwise uninspiring 15th-century cathedral is famous as the resting place

MYSTERY OF THE shroud of turin

One of the Christian world's most revered relics, the Shroud of Turin—displayed in Turin's **Duomo di San Giovanni Battista** (see above)—is said to be the very same piece of fabric in which Christ was wrapped when he was taken from the cross, which miraculously became imprinted with his image.

The image on the cloth does show a bearded face—remarkably similar to the depiction of Christ in Byzantine icons—and a body marked with bloodstains, in spots that match where a crown of thorns, a spear slash in the rib cage, and nail holes in the wrists and ankles would be, along with scourge marks on the back from flagellation.

So is the Shroud real? Carbon dating results are confusing; some suggest that the shroud was manufactured around the 13th or 14th centuries, while other tests imply that those results were thrown off by a fire that all but destroyed the shroud in December 1532.

But the mystery remains, at least in part because no one can explain how the haunting image appeared on the cloth. Skeptics have attempted to create replicas using lemon juice and the sun, mineral pigments, even aloe and myrrh (which were used in funerary traditions of Jesus' time). A 2015 study of DNA in the shroud's dust particles further confused the picture: It was shown to contain genetic material from plants across the globe—perhaps not surprising, considering how many people have come into contact with it over the years.

of the **Shroud of Turin** (p. 527). The linen cloth is preserved in an aluminum casket in the temperature-controlled, air-conditioned Cappella della Sacra Sindone and closed off from human contamination (and public view) with bulletproof glass. The casket is adorned with a crown of thorns; the faithful come in droves to worship at the chapel, which is the last one in the left-hand aisle. To learn about the history of the shroud, head for the **Museo della Sindone** (see below).

Piazza San Giovanni. Free admission. Mon–Fri 10am–12:30pm and 4–7pm; Sat–Sun 9am–12:30pm and 4–7pm. Bus: 11, 12, 51, 55, 56, 61, 68. Trams: 4, 13, 15, 18.

Mole Antonelliana & Museo Nazionale del Cinema ♥♥♥ MUSEUM Turin's most iconic building, dominating the skyline from all directions, was once the tallest in Europe. Building started in 1863 on what was originally meant to be a synagogue; later, city fathers decided to make it a monument to Italian unification. Set on a squat brick base, the Mole rises through tiers of windows and pseudo-Greek columns to a huge, ribbed cupola and needlelike spire, all of it looming 167m (548 ft.) above the streets.

The Mole is now home to Italy's National Film Museum, which houses more than 2 million objects, enhanced with interactive displays and hands-on activities. The first galleries track the intriguing development of moving pictures, from shadow puppets to risqué peep shows and flickering images of galloping horses filmed by Edward Muybridge in 1878. Other exhibits use clips, stills, posters, and props to illustrate aspects of movie production, such as the creepy steady-cam work in *The Shining*; a section of movie memorabilia includes jewels and shoes worn by Marilyn Monroe and Darth Vader's mask from *The Empire Strikes Back*. Aspiring filmmakers or die-hard movie buffs will appreciate some of the more technical exhibits, like the "Archaeology of the Cinema" section featuring early optical devices and equipment.

A major highlight of a visit includes a panoramic elevator ride through the roof of the museum's vast atrium and up 85m (279 ft.) inside the tower to the 360-degree observation platform at the top. The view of Turin and the surrounding countryside, backed by the Alps, is stunning. ***Note:*** You can bypass the museum and only do the panoramic elevator for a cost of 9€ (7€ with the **Torino+Piemonte Card;** see p. 524). Lines form on weekends, so try to come early or reserve your spot ahead of time by buying tickets online.

Via Montebello 20. museocinema.it. ✆ **011/8138-563.** Museum and elevator: 20€ adults, 17€ seniors and students up to age 26, 10€ ages 6–18, free for children 5 and under. Museum only: 15€ adults, 10€ seniors and students up to age 26, 4€ ages 6–18, free for children 5 and under. Elevator only: 9€ adults, 7€ students, seniors, and ages 6–18; free for children 5 and under. Wed–Mon 9am–8pm. Bus: 18, 55, 56, 61, 68. Tram: 13, 15, 16.

Museo della Sindone ♥♥ MUSEUM The Shroud of Turin is not actually kept here, but the endearing Holy Shroud Museum is still a hit, fully representing the shroud's status as one of the world's most famous religious relics (p. 527). A visit starts with a 15-minute film (offered in five languages) about the shroud, its provenance, and the various theories and mysteries surrounding it. Visitors then wander through a series of rooms chronicling the shroud's history, from its first mention in 1204 to the fire that nearly destroyed it in Chambéry in 1532 to its arrival in Turin with the House of Savoy in 1578 to modern-day carbon-testing efforts. The last stop is the richly ornamented chapel of Santo Sudario—a private place of worship for the Savoy dukes—where a copy of the shroud is displayed over the gleaming, gilded altar. Each of the displays is well marked in both English and Italian.

The **shroud** itself is kept nearby, in the royal chapel of the Duomo, usually out of public view (p. 527). It is, however, typically taken out for public viewing occasionally; the decision to do so is usually made by the reigning pope. The last time it was on display was 2015, though there was a "digital display" multimedia showing held during the Jubilee year of 2025. Check sindone.org to find out when the shroud will next be shown; advance reservations are required during these brief public displays.
Via San Domenico 28. sindone.it. ✆ **011/436-5832.** Admission 8€ adults, 6€ seniors and students, 3€ kids 6–12, free for children 5 and under. Daily 9am–noon and 3–7pm (during some periods, museum is open afternoons only).

Museo Egizio ♥♥ MUSEUM Turin attracts visitors from all over the world for its magnificent Egyptian Museum. It is one of the world's largest—no surprise, considering it was also the world's *first* Egyptian museum, with more than 200 years of history. This is thanks to the Savoy kings and their explorers Bernardino Drovetti and Ernesto Schiaparelli, who voraciously hoarded Egyptian ephemera until the early 1900s, when attitudes about cultural plundering changed. Some say this is the most

Museo Egizio has the world's largest collection of Egyptian art and artifacts.

important collection of Egyptian artifacts outside of Cairo. The museum offers a meticulous reconstruction of Egyptian cultural and funerary elements, capturing even the finest details. It also chronicles the history of archaeological expeditions. Here, one can find artifacts from all eras of ancient Egypt, including a papyrus *Book of the Dead* that is nearly 14m (45 ft.) long. One of the most captivating exhibits is the exquisitely painted wooden sarcophagi and mummies of Kha and Merit, an aristocratic couple whose tomb was discovered in 1906. A new exhibition has been unveiled, featuring a multimedia installation and 460 artifacts related to the life and burial of the elite Egyptians who lived over 3,500 years ago. In some cases, powerful X-ray technology has been used to digitally "unwrap" the mummies and showcase the types of artifacts they are buried with A visit to the museum finishes with the monumental statues in the spectacular "Gallery of Kings" designed by world-renowned production designer, costume designer, and art director Dante Ferretti. The "Writing Gallery" has hundreds of artifacts showcasing how ancient forms of writing evolved in Egypt. Bags larger than a purse are not allowed in the museum and will have to be left in the coat check. It's a good idea to reserve your visit ahead of time.

Via Accademia delle Scienze 6. museoegizio.it. ✆ **011/440-6903.** Admission 18€ adults, 3€ ages 15–18, 1€ ages 6–14, free for children 5 and under. Mon 9am–2pm; Tues–Sun 8:30am–7:30pm. Bus: 55, 56. Tram: 13.

Museo Nazionale del Risorgimento Italiano ♥♥♥ MUSEUM Located on majestic Piazza Carignano, the equally handsome red-brick *palazzo* of the same name acquired huge national importance as the occasional home of Italy's first king after the country's unification in 1861. Originally built between 1679 and 1685 by baroque maestro Guarino Guarini, the palace now houses the Museo del Risorgimento dedicated to the events that led to Italian unification. At the heart of Palazzo Carignano is the ornate circular chamber where Italy's first parliament met. Despite the museum's historical focus, the displays are quite innovative for an Italian museum, with multilingual signage and labeling, audioguides, video guides, and interactive touchscreens (the museum website also surprisingly has digital exhibitions to be enjoyed from home). A cinema room shows films that illustrate the importance of this building and of Turin during the era. More than 30 richly furnished rooms detail the military campaigns that led to unification; even non-Italians can easily appreciate the stirring drama of these years. Uniforms, paintings, weapons, maps, and correspondence testify to feats of great bravado, tracing a course through the Italy of the 19th century from Napoleon to Garibaldi.

Via Accademia delle Scienze 5. museorisorgimentotorino.it. ✆ **011/562-1147.** Admission 10€ adults, 8€ seniors, 6€ students 6–18, free for children 6 and under; free with the Torino+Piemonte Card (p. 524). Tues–Sun 10am–6pm. Bus: 11, 12, 27, 51, 51, 55, 56, 57. Tram: 13, 15.

Museo Nazionale dell'Automobile (MAUTO) ♥♥♥ MUSEUM Considering that Turin spawned auto giant Fiat, it is only fitting that the city would have a museum where the car is king. This innovative space just south of Parco del Valentino is a perfect place to bring kids who've traipsed around one too many dusty palazzos. Alfa Romeos and lots of bright-red Ferraris feature heavily among the displays, which start with vintage cars from the days when road travel was only for the very wealthy. The new Future of Mobility section looks ahead to how technology, design, and sustainability are set to reshape the way we move. A visit here will take about 2 to 3 hours depending on your level of interest.

Corso Unità d'Italia 40. museoauto.it. ✆ **011/677-666.** Admission 15€ adults, 12€ ages 18–25, 5€ ages 6–18 and seniors, free for kids 5 and under. Mon 10am–2pm; Tues–Sun 10am–7pm. Metro: Lingotto.

Palazzo Madama—Museo Civico di Arte Antica ♥ MUSEUM Don't be misled by the baroque facade on the Palazzo Madama, which was added by architect Filippo Juvarra in the 18th century—walk around this massive structure and you'll see that it also incorporates a medieval castle, a Roman gate, and several Renaissance additions. As you enter, take a moment to admire the monumental marble staircase, another Juvarra touch. The *palazzo* is now home to the Museo Civico d'Arte Antica, which takes up four mammoth floors, boasting more than 70,000 items from the Middle Ages to the baroque era.

Works from the medieval and Renaissance periods show off well against the building's austere, stony interior; on the top floor you'll also find one of Italy's largest collections of ceramics. Still, it can be rather disorganized—you'll have to hunt for the star of the show, Antonello da Messina's sublime *Portrait of a Man*, which is tucked away in the Treasure Tower at the back of the building on the ground floor.

Piazza Castello. palazzomadamatorino.it. ✆ **011/443-3501.** Admission 10€ adults, 8€ students and seniors; 5€ gardens only; free for ages 17 and under. Mon, Wed–Fri 10am–6pm; Sat 11am–7pm; Sun 10am–7pm. Bus: 11, 12, 51, 55, 56, 61, 68. Trams: 4, 13, 15, 18.

Palazzo Reale ♥♥ PALACE Dominating the north side of the Piazza Castello, the residence of the House of Savoy was begun in 1646; the family lived here until 1865. Designed by the architect Amedeo di Castellamonte, the palace's interiors reflect the ornate tastes of European ruling families of the time, while its sheer size proves their wealth. This Savoy palace gives the flamboyant frippery of Versailles a run for its money, its throne rooms, ballrooms, and apartments lavishly adorned with priceless Gobelins tapestries, silk walls, sparkling chandeliers, ornate wooden floors, and gilded furniture.

The east wing of the *palazzo* houses the **Armeria Reale,** one of Europe's most important arms and armor collections, especially of weapons from the 16th and 17th centuries. It also has a unique collection of stuffed horses, which look ready to leap into battle at any moment. Behind the palace are the formal **Giardini Reali** (Royal Gardens), laid out in part by André Le Nôtre, who designed the Tuileries in Paris and the gardens at Versailles.

The Savoy royal family had an even keener eye for paintings than for baroque decor, amassing a collection of 8,000 works of art. The collection's highlights are on display in the **Galleria Sabauda** in the Palazzo Reale's New Wing (a few minutes' walk from the main *palazzo*). The exhibition kicks off with early Piedmont and Dutch religious works, plus a moody Rembrandt self-portrait and two massive paintings by van Dyck: *The Children of Charles I* (1637) and a magnificent equestrian portrait of Prince Thomas of Savoy (ca. 1634). In the basement beneath the Galleria Sabauda, the **Museo Archeologico**'s thoughtfully designed exhibition tells the story of Turin's development from Roman through medieval times. Incorporated into its displays are a section of Roman wall, remnants from a theater nearby, and a mosaic only discovered in 1993.

A Glimpse into Roman Turin

Close to Turin's Duomo (p. 527) and partly incorporated into the Museo Archeologico (below) stand two landmarks of Roman Turin: the remains of a theater and fragments of wall, as well as the **Porta Palatina,** a Roman-era city gate, flanked by twin 16-sided towers on Piazza Cesare Augusto. The **Area Romana** west of the Piazza Castello is the oldest part of the city, a charming web of streets occupied since ancient times.

The **Biblioteca Reale** (Royal Library) is also part of the Palazzo Reale complex; it's free to enter, and you'll find it on the right of the main entrance. Founded in 1831, it houses 200,000 rare volumes as well as ancient maps and prints. On the opposite side of the gates is the fine **church of San Lorenzo,** designed by master architect Guarino Guarini in 1666. Its plain facade belies a lacy dome and frothy interior.

Piazzetta Reale 1. museireali.beniculturali.it/palazzo-reale. ✆ **011/436-1455.** Palazzo and all exhibitions: 15€ adults, 2€ ages 18–25, free for seniors and ages 17 and under. Free admission 1st Sun of month. Tues–Sun 9am–7pm; last admission 6pm. Museo Archeologico closed Sun morning. During some periods, museum complex closed Wed. Bus: 11, 51, 55, 56, 68. Trams: 4, 13, 15, 18.

Outlying Attractions

Basilica di Superga ♥♥ CHURCH Half the fun of a visit to this lovely basilica is the 6.5km (4-mile) journey northeast of the city center on a narrow-gauge railway through the lush countryside of the Parco Naturale della Collina di Superga. Occasionally, the *tranvia* is not operational, in which case buses will bring you here from the city center. The church was built as thanksgiving to the Virgin Mary for Turin's deliverance from the French siege of 1706. Prince Vittorio Amedeo II commissioned Filippo Juvarra, the Sicilian architect who designed much of Turin's elegant center, to build the magical baroque confection on a hill high above the city. The eye-catching exterior, with its beautiful colonnaded portico, elaborate dome, and twin bell towers, is actually more appealing than the ornate but gloomy interior, a circular chamber ringed by six chapels. Many scions of the House of Savoy are buried here in the Crypt of Kings beneath the main chapel.

Strada della Basilica di Superga, 73. basilicadisuperga.com. ✆ **011/899-7456.** Free admission to Basilica. Royal Tombs or Royal Apartment 6€ adults, 5€ students and seniors; dome 4€ adults, 3€ students and seniors. Free for children 11 and under. Mon–Fri 9am–noon and 3–6pm; Sat–Sun 9am–noon and 3–7pm (closes 1 hr. earlier in winter). Tram: Tranvia a Dentiera from Stazione Sassi (6€ round-trip weekdays, 9€ round-trip weekends or public holidays) to Superga stop. Bus: 61 from side of Ponte Vittorio Emanuele I opposite Piazza Vittorio Veneto.

Palazzina di Caccia di Stupinigi ♥ PALACE Yet another Savoy family home is found at Stupinigi, just a few miles southwest of Turin. Commissioned by the royal family in 1729, it's another winner by architect Filippo Juvarra, this time a sumptuous hunting lodge surrounded by lush forests. Built on a humungous scale, the palace's wings fan out from the main house, topped by a domed pavilion. Every bit as lavish as the apartments in the Savoys' city residence, **Palazzo Reale** (p. 531), the interior is stuffed with furniture, paintings, and bric-a-brac assembled from myriad Savoy residences; it's now the **Museo dell'Arte e Ammobiliamento** (Museum of Art and Furniture). Wander through the acres of apartments to understand why Napoleon chose this palace for his brief sojourn in Piedmont in 1805 while en route to Milan to be crowned emperor. Outstanding among the many, many frescoes are the scenes of a deer hunt in the King's Apartment and the triumph of Diana in the grand salon. The elegant gardens and surrounding forests provide lovely terrain for a jaunt. Keep in mind that you may find the ticket office closed for lunch between 1 and 2pm.

Piazza Principe Amedeo 7, Stupingi, Nichelino (8.5km/5¼ miles SW of Turin city center). ordinemauriziano.it/palazzina-di-caccia-stupinigi. ✆ **011/620-0601.** Admission 12€ adults, 5€ ages 6–18, free for kids 5 and under. Tues–Fri 10am–5:30pm; Sat 10am–6:30pm.

Reggia di Venaria Reale ♥♥♥ PALACE Completing the triumvirate of glitzy Savoy households around Turin, the Venaria was constructed in the mid-17th century to a design by Amedeo di Castellamonte, but sure enough Filippo Juvarra also had a hand in it. This massive complex, its stables, and the awesome formal gardens and parklands are a UNESCO World Heritage Site. Venaria makes for a great family-oriented day out with loads of outdoor activities as well as a glimpse into the extraordinarily privileged lives of the Savoy family. The Fountain of the Stag dances to music in the lake outside the *palazzo;* on the grounds are follies aplenty and the mock-Roman Fountain of Hercules.

Piazza della Repubblica 4, Venaria Reale (10km/6¼ miles NW of Turin city center). lavenaria.it. ✆ **011/499-2333.** Prices range from 25€ (palace, gardens, and exhibitions) to 5€ (gardens only). Hours change seasonally, but generally Tues–Fri 9am–5pm; Sat–Sun 9:30am–6:30pm (last admission 1 hr. before closing). Bus: 11 from Piazza Repubblica; also check schedule for Venaria Express bus (gtt.to.it/cms/turismo/venaria-express).

Reggia di Venaria Reale, a magnificent Savoy palace just outside of Turin (see p. 533).

Outdoor Activities

Turin's beautiful playground is **Parco del Valentino** ♥, which cradles the left bank of the River Po between Ponte Umberto I and Ponte Isabella. Its first incarnation was in 1630, when it was the private garden of the Savoy dukes, but the park was much extended in the 1860s and opened to the public. It's a romantic place to stroll among botanical gardens, flowerbeds, and manicured lawns. The park's massive **Castello del Valentino,** built in 1660, was once the pleasure palace of Christine Marie of France (p. 527); it is currently closed for renovations. The castle forms an incongruous backdrop to the **Borgo Medievale** (p. 535), a riverside replica of a 15th-century feudal village. It's a pleasant walk from the city center along Corso Emanuele Vittorio II, or you can hop on Tram 9.

Rowing on the Po is a popular pastime in Turin, with half a dozen rowing clubs, the oldest being Reale Società Canottieri Cerea. You can watch boats plying the water as you follow **jogging** and **cycling** routes along the riverside pathways.

Especially for Kids

There's plenty for kids to do in Turin. The **Parco del Valentino** ♥ (see above) has lots of open spaces to run around in, plus free admission to the open-air **Borgo Medievale,** the recreation of a feudal village built for the Italian General Exposition in 1884 (Viale Virgilio 107; borgomedievale torino.it; ✆ **011/4431-701;** daily 9am–7pm [summer until 8pm]). Most youngsters will be intrigued by the **Museum of Cinema** ♥ at the Mole Antonelliana (p. 528), or at least the trip up the Mole's tower to see the city far below. The **Museo Nazionale dell'Automobile** ♥♥♥ (p. 531) provides an antidote to Turin's baroque attractions. **Zoom Torino** (zoom torino.it) is an immersive zoo—no bars or cages—located about 35 minutes southwest of the city center by car in the town of Cumiana. You can also get there by train, getting out at the Piscina di Pinerolo station and taking the Zoom shuttle, though the shuttle is not offered at certain times of the year. Check the website for more details.

If all else fails, pop into **Alberto Marchetti,** Via Po 35 (alberto marchetti.it; ✆ **011/814-1160**), for some delicious local gelato. There are various locations throughout the city, and the Casa Marchetti hub in Piazza C.L.N. even offers gelato-making workshops.

Where to Stay in Turin

In recent years, Turin has seen an influx of different accommodation options, giving travelers an alternative to the faceless frumpery of many of the city's older hotels.

APARTMENT & ROOM RENTALS If you prefer to stay in an apartment, the charming **Mignon** flat (airbnb.com/rooms/17945654), located in the heart of the action mere steps from Piazza Castello, averages about 110€ a night (including fees) for two people. It has one bedroom, one bath, and a full kitchen; its historic beams blend well with the modern amenities.

Il Gioiellino ♥♥ With just three rooms, this B&B near the Porta Susa train station in one of Turin's most elegant neighborhoods truly lives up to its name—it's quite the gem. Il Gioiellino is in a lovely *palazzo* from the 19th century, known for its distinctive columns and other architectural flourishes. Spotlessly clean rooms come with parquet floors, modern amenities, and renovated bathrooms while maintaining a certain historic charm thanks to the antique furnishings. Room rates include breakfast, but each space also has its own refrigerator, coffeemaker, and tea kettle. Breakfast is served in a delightful dining room, and the hosts take pride in offering a beautifully set table each morning. Expect to find local pastries, traditional chocolate hazelnut biscuits, fresh baked goods, yogurt, a selection of jams, and fruit juices. The location is perfect for exploring the city on foot, but the Vinzaglio Metro stop is conveniently right downstairs.

Corso Vittorio Emanuele, II 100. gioiellino.com. ✆ **335/6889-932.** 3 units. 120€–190€ double; additional bed 30€ (15€ additional bed for children 4 and under). Rates include breakfast. **Amenities:** Free Wi-Fi.

Le Petit Hotel ♥♥ This great budget option in the center of the city is strategically positioned—it is a 10- to 15-minute walk from both the Porta Nuova and Porta Susa train stations, and very close to Palazzo Madama and the Egyptian museum. Rooms are simple and bathrooms are functional and clean. A colorfully furnished breakfast room offers a selection of bread, cheeses, fruit, and pastries. Plenty of dining options are nearby, but the hotel's restaurant, **Marechiaro,** is a solid choice if you don't feel like straying too far, serving pizza, traditional dishes from the Piedmont region, and Mediterranean favorites. In warm weather, the outdoor tables allow for prime people-watching on the pedestrian-only street. The hotel also has some slightly more modern self-catering apartments. Via San Francesco d'Assisi 21. lepetithotel.it. ✆ **011/561-2626.** 79 units. 140€–190€ double; 200€–240€ apartment. Rates include breakfast. **Amenities:** Restaurant; free Wi-Fi.

NH Hotels Torino Piazza Carlina ♥♥♥ Housed in a historic 17th-century palazzo, this hotel is perfectly positioned near the Po River and within easy reach of Turin's main attractions, just off a buzzing city piazza. Modern rooms have hardwood floors and come in muted shades of beige, cream, and rose, and some offer views of the square down below or the nearby Mole Antonelliana. There are even Family XL rooms for up to eight people and a selection of suites with contemporary touches, terraces, and some of the best views. Hotel guests can make use of two large terraces (including an herb garden) off the fifth floor, which is also home to a panoramic gym with Technogym machines. The sophisticated **Restaurant Carlina** offers modern Mediterranean cuisine with international flair; an abundant buffet breakfast, which includes hot dishes made to order, is served in an airy glass-walled room overlooking the inner courtyard. 15 Piazza Carlo Emanuele II. nh-hotels.com/en/hotel/nh-collection-torino-piazza-carlina. ✆ **011/860-1611.** 160 units. 200€–300€ double. Rates include breakfast. **Amenities:** Restaurant; bar; concierge; gym; free Wi-Fi.

Where to Eat in Turin

Turin's gourmet reputation outshines other Italian cities renowned for their gastronomy. Many restaurants are strong advocates of the Slow Food movement, with menus touting their local ingredients. Look for porcini mushrooms and truffles in season. Wine lists feature Barolo, Barbera, and Barbaresco reds and sparkling Asti whites. Turin is also home to one of the world's largest food and wine fairs, the **Terra Madre Salone del Gusto** (salonedelgusto.com), which runs every 2 years (even-numbered years) in September or October.

Almondo Trattoria ♥ MODERN ITALIAN You'll have to cross the Po to reach this contemporary establishment just over the Vittorio Emanuele I bridge (about a 15-min. walk from the center). Almondo Trattoria has a clean Italo-Scandinavian industrial aesthetic but with welcoming archways and plenty of greenery. The menu changes frequently, but the kitchen serves up bright plates of Italian specialty dishes from North to South—*pizzoccheri* pasta from the mountains, Roman *cacio e pepe,* Venetian-style liver, or *orecchiette* pasta with broccoli rabe, representing a classic dish from Puglia that the restaurant offers in a vegan version without anchovy. (The menu has several gluten-free and vegetarian options.) The wine list showcases vintages from the nearby Piedmont hills. The staff is cheerful and pricing is fair. Almondo looks out onto the Gran Madre di Dio church, an impressive example of neoclassical architecture to celebrate the defeat of Napoleon. There's a second Almondo outpost (called **Almondo Nuovo**) in lovely Piazza Bodoni in the city center, where the focus is on "Italian Sunday lunch" food with modern influences.

Piazza Gran Madre di Dio 2/L. almondotrattoria.it. ✆ **011/411-9684.** Main courses 12€–18€. Daily 12:30–2:30pm and 7:30–11:30pm.

A Moveable Feast on Two Wheels

Want to enjoy Turin's cuisine while keeping the calorie count in check? Local guide Roberto leads gourmet bike tours via **Easy-Torino** (easytorino.com). A variety of tours are available (from free tip-based excursions to longer journeys)—cycle through the city along the Po River or take to the hills where you can taste wine and products from small farms.

Cannavacciuolo Bistrot ♥♥ ITALIAN Don't let the word "bistrot" in the name fool you. One of the hottest fine-dining experiences in town is just across the Po River at Italian celebrity chef Antonio Cannavacciulo's elegant yet minimalist space. The chef hails from Italy's Campania region, a heritage that deeply shapes his cuisine, though he gives equal prominence to ingredients and flavors from Piedmont. Fassona beef tartare comes with a hazelnut mayonnaise and black truffle, while "plin" ravioli are filled with salt cod and served in an *acqua pazza* broth made up of water, tomatoes, olive oil, and garlic. The variety of tasting menus (120€–140€) includes a white-truffle menu and vegetarian option. Desserts are definitely a highlight—meals often end with a selection of Neapolitan pastries, a nod to the chef's origins.

Via Umberto Cosmo 6. cannavacciuolobistrot.it/torino. ✆ **011/839-9893.** Main courses 30€–40€. Tues 7:30–11pm; Wed–Sat 12:30–3pm and 7:30–11pm.

Cianci Piola ♥♥ ITALIAN REGIONAL With its in-your-face slogan—"life is short, free up the tables quickly"—and spirited decorations on the brick walls, this isn't your usual *piola* (a dialect term meaning an establishment that serves authentic Piedmontese cuisine at reasonable prices). Tables spill out onto a charming square, mere blocks from the Royal Palace. Given the location, prices are reasonable and portions are surprisingly large. The kitchen turns out creative and classic interpretations of *Piemontese* dishes, such as *tajarin* pasta prepared a variety of ways (with a rabbit ragù or with sausage and radicchio), and mustard-roasted pork is served with an apple salad. Finish off with *bounet* for dessert, a regional specialty similar to a chocolate custard served with *amaretti* biscuits. Reservations aren't taken over the phone, so you may want to pop by to reserve a table. In winter, Cianci Piola is sometimes closed for lunch Monday to Friday.

Via Largo IV Marzo 9/b. ciancipiola.it. ✆ **353/342-6322.** Main courses 7€–12€. Daily noon–midnight. Hours may be more limited in winter.

Trattoria Coco's ♥♥ ITALIAN Locals flock to this unassuming trattoria for the down-home cooking. With its wood-paneled walls and vintage sports photos on the wall, time seems to have stood still at this quintessential *piola* in the heart of the San Salvario neighborhood, about a 5-minute walk from Porta Nuova station. Coco's still makes things the way *nonna* used to—Italian comfort food like *pasta e fagioli* soup, *agnolotti* pasta in a sausage meat sauce, *vitello tonnato* (veal in creamy tuna sauce), and risotto with saffron and Toma cheese, all at incredibly reasonable prices. The restaurant now takes reservations in the evening, but you may have to wait in line outside, especially on weekends.

Via Bernardino Galliari 28. ✆ **011/657-465.** Main courses 9€–11€. Mon–Wed 7am–7pm; Thurs–Sat 7am–midnight.

Trattoria Spirito Santo ♥♥ SEAFOOD Located in a quaint piazza in the heart of the Quadrilatero Romano, Spirito Santo draws in locals and tourists alike for its seafood and fast, friendly service. It has been serving up vast platters of mussels, tuna carpaccio, simple grilled fish, and delicious fettucine with lobster for decades now. Portions are often huge—and the prices do reflect that to some extent—so don't be tempted to over-order. People come here for home cooking and fresh ingredients (try the smoked-fish appetizer, porcini mushroom ravioli, linguine with squid ink, or the special "Spirito Santo" grilled fish plate). In summer, tables take over the lovely square. Inside, space is tight and tables can be close together, but in winter, a cozy fire makes the atmosphere all the more convivial.

Largo IV Marzo 11. ✆ **011/4360-877.** Main courses 17€–42€; tasting menus 40€. Daily 12:30–3:30pm and 7:30pm–midnight.

Shaken, Not Stirred

Turin gave the world the aperitif vermouth, which was invented in 1786 by Antonio Benedetto Carpano; the brands Martini and Cinzano are still made in the Piedmont region. Order a glass at the gorgeous Art Nouveau **Caffè Mulassano** at Piazza Castello 15 (caffemulassano.com; ✆ **348/170-1696**) or come early to enjoy coffee and tempting cannoli or dainty fruit tarts at the ornate marble counter.

Turin Shopping

Turin's high-end shopping area is quite simply one of the most beautiful in the world. The arcaded **Via Roma** does full justice to the exquisite fashions of Gucci, Armani, Ferragamo, Max Mara, and so on. At the end of Via Roma, the glass-roofed **Galleria Subalpina,** Piazza Castello 27, which links Piazza Castello with Piazza Carlo, competes with Milan's Galleria Vittorio Emanuele II for sheer opulence in its three levels of art galleries, antiquarian bookstores, and cafes. For those whose pockets may not be quite so deep, **Via Garibaldi, Corso XX Settembre,** and their surrounding streets offer midrange brands at reasonable prices.

The windows of Italian food shops are always a thing of joy, and the specialist delis and confectioners of Turin are no exceptions. **Confetteria Stratta,** Piazza San Carlo 191 (stratta1836.it; ✆ **011/547-920**), and **Pasticceria Gerla,** Corso Vittorio Emanuele II 88, are known for their extravagant pastries, cakes, and *gianduiotti* (chocolate with hazelnuts). Turin is famous for its quality confectionery—the city and the Piedmont region are said to produce 40% of Italy's **chocolate.** Turin has two branches of the **Eataly** chain, the current megastore for gourmet Italian fare, one in the center in Via Lagrange 3 and another one in the Lingotto area at Via Nizza 230.

Most news agents in Turin have English-language newspapers, and the two branches of **Feltrinelli,** Piazza Castello 19 (✆ **011/541-627**) and Stazione Porta Nuova (✆ **02/9194-7777**), sell multilingual books.

The Markets of Turin

The **produce market** in and around Porta Palazzo takes over the gigantic Piazza della Repubblica Monday to Friday 7am to 2pm and Saturday until 7pm. A bustling **flea market** takes place in the warren of streets behind the Porta Palazzo every Saturday, among the antique shops on Via Borgo Dora. The second Sunday of every month, the same spot is the scene of an **antiques market,** the continuously expanding **Gran Balon** (balon.it), with more than 300 dealers from across northern Italy; a smaller version (called Balon) occurs every Saturday. Come December, a **Christmas market** sets out its stalls in Via Borgo Dora. Turin has many stores specializing in rare books and old prints, and these sell their wares from stalls along the Via Po.

The Arts & Nightlife

Dance, opera, theater, and musical performances (mostly classical) are on the agenda all year long—check visitatorino.com—but September is the month to really enjoy classical music in Turin, when more than 60 concerts are staged around the city during the month-long **Settembre Musica** festival (mitosettembremusica.it), hosted jointly with the city of Milan. Beyond the festivals you'll find classical concerts at **Auditorium della RAI,** Via Rossini 15 (raicultura.it/orchestrarai; ✆ **011/810-4653**), and dance performances and operas at the city's venerable **Teatro Regio** (teatroregio.torino.it; ✆ **011/8815-241**).

Nightlife in the city that invented the vermouth *aperitivo* is sophisticated and, as in Milan, starts in the cafes and bars and finishes very, very late. Squeeze in with the Torinese at **Caffè Platti,** Corso Vittorio Emanuele II 72 (platti1875.com; ✆ **011/454-6151**), for a vermouth, and pick from the plates of enticing little pizzas made on the premises.

THE PIEDMONT WINE COUNTRY ♥♥

South of Turin, the Po valley rises into the rolling hills of Langhe and Roero, flanked by orchards and vineyards. You'll recognize the region's place names from the labels of its first-rate wines, among them **Asti Spumanti, Barbaresco,** and **Barolo.** And vines are not all that flourish in this fertile soil—truffles top the list of the region's gastronomic delights, along with rabbit, game, and excellent cheeses.

Asti ♥♥♥

60km (37 miles) SE of Turin, 127km (79 miles) SW of Milan

The Asti of sparkling-wine fame is a bustling working city, but it has many treasures to uncover in its history-drenched *centro storico*—medieval towers (there were about 120 at one time), Renaissance palaces, and piazzas provide the perfect setting in which to sample the town's most famous product, which flows readily in the local *enoteche* and cantinas.

ESSENTIALS

ARRIVING Up to four **trains** per hour link Asti with Turin Porta Nuova (35 min.; 6.40€) via **Trenitalia** (trenitalia.com; ✆ **892-021**). By car, Asti can be reached in less than an hour from Turin via Autostrada 21.

VISITOR INFORMATION The APT tourist office is near the train station at Piazza Alfieri 34 (✆ **0141/530-357**). It's open Monday to Saturday 9am to 1pm and 2:30 to 6:30pm; Sunday 9am to 1pm and 1:30 to 5:30pm.

EXPLORING ASTI

Asti's historic heart is centered on three adjoining squares: **Piazza Libertá,** the vast **Campo del Palio,** and the grand arcaded **Piazza Alfieri.** Each year, in early September, the area is mobbed for the **Palio,** Asti's annual horse race (visit.asti.it; ✆ **0141/399-482**), now held in Piazza Alfieri (originally it was in Campo del Palio) and throughout the town's streets. Like the similar race in the Tuscan city of Siena (p. 235), Asti's Palio begins with a colorful medieval pageant through the town and ends with a wild bareback ride around the triangular piazza. First staged around

1275, the race often coincides with Asti's other great festival, the **Douja d'Or** (doujador.it), a weeklong bacchanal celebrating the grape harvest.

Behind Piazza Alfieri stands the Romanesque-Gothic **Collegiata di San Secondo** (✆ **0141/530-066;** daily 7:30am–7pm). This red-brick church has two distinctions: It houses the Palio Astigiano, the prestigious banner awarded to the winning jockey at the Palio; and it also contains the tomb of St. Secondo, patron saint of both the race and the town. A Roman officer who converted to Christianity in C.E. 119, Secondo was martyred for his faith, beheaded in roughly the spot where his tomb now stands.

PIEDMONT'S REGIONAL wines

The wines of Piedmont are of exceptional quality and distinctive taste. They're usually made with grapes unique to the region and grown on tiny family plots—making the countryside a lovely patchwork of vineyards and small farms.

Often called "the king of wines, wine of kings," **Barolo** is considered one of Italy's top wines, on par with Tuscany's Brunello and the Veneto's Amarone. It is the richest and heartiest of the Piedmont wines, and the one most likely to accompany game or meat. **Barbaresco,** like Barolo, is made solely from the red Nebbiolo grape, although it is less tannic. **Barbera d'Alba** is a bright, food-friendly red wine, the product of the delightful villages south of Alba (p. 543). **Dolcetto** is dry, fruity, mellow, and despite what its name might imply, not sweet. **Nebbiolo d'Alba** is rich, full, and dry.

As far as white wines go, **Spumanti DOCGs** are the sparkling wines that put Asti on the map. **Moscato d'Asti** is a delicious floral dessert wine, and the fiery local Piedmont **grappas** are none too shabby either.

From Piazza Alfieri, the charming and largely pedestrianized **Corso Alfieri** bisects the old town and is lined with Renaissance *palazzi.* At the eastern end is the church of **San Pietro in Consavia (© 0141/530-403;** Tues–Sun 10am–1pm and 3–6pm, summer until 7pm), with a 10th-century Romanesque baptistery that was once a place of worship for the Knights of the Order of St. John. At the western extreme of Corso Alfieri, you'll find the rotund **church of Santa Caterina,** abutting the medieval red-and-white-brick topped **Torre Rossa.**

Asti's 15th-century **Cattedrale di Santa Maria Assunta** (**© 0141/592-924;** daily 8:30am–noon and 3–7pm) is also at the western end of town in Piazza Cattedrale. Its austere exterior hides the gaudy excesses of the interior; every inch of the church is festooned with frescoes by late-15th-century artists, including Gandolfino d'Asti.

Being the agricultural and gourmet hotspot that it is, Asti is blessed with two **food markets.** The larger is held in the Campo del Palio on Wednesdays and Saturdays as part of a day-long street market with all kinds of wares; the food stands, however, are only there from 7:30am to 1pm. The market spills over into neighboring piazzas, with stalls selling cheeses, herbs, flowers, oils, and wines. The covered **Mercato Coperto** on Piazza della Libertà is open daily except Sunday (Tues–Fri 8am–1pm and 3:30–7:30pm, Mon and Sat 8am–7:30pm). Look for white truffles, *robiola* cheeses, *amaretti* biscuits, *nocciolata* (hazelnut and chocolate spread), and *bagna cauda* (a fondue-like warm dip made with olive oil, butter, garlic, and anchovies). The region's famous Asti Spumante DOCG sparkling wines can be bought from *enoteche* in the town center and direct from some vineyards—a list is available from the **tourist office** at Piazza Alfieri 34 (p. 540).

The Piedmont Wine Villages

Southwest of Asti lie some of the Piedmont's most enchanting wine villages, sitting on hilltops among orderly rows of vines. Many of these characteristic hamlets have their own local festivals (*sagre*), bringing people together to celebrate hyperlocal specialties like wine, chocolate, and seasonal delicacies. Most notably, the renowned **Alba International White Truffle Fair** in autumn (fieradeltartufo.org) is a celebration of the region's sought-after truffle. The best way to see these villages is to drive; hire cars in Turin from **Avis,** Via Giuseppe Giusti 1 (avisautonoleggio.it; ✆ **011/440-9231**), or **Hertz,** at Corso Turati 37 (hertz.it; ✆ **011/502-080**). Before you head out on the small country roads, get a list of vineyards from the tourist office in Asti (p. 540). A detailed map is also a good idea, in case you lose the satellite signal for your GPS.

The main road through the wine region is the SS231, which runs southwest from Asti. It is, however, a fast, busy, and unattractive highway; you'll want to turn off it to explore Piedmont's rustic backwaters among hazelnut groves and vineyards.

The village of Barolo and Castello Falletti.

Gastro-destination **Alba** ♥♥ (60km/37 miles south of Turin) is the jumping-off point for visiting the many vineyards of the Barolo wine-producing region. While it's a pleasure to walk along Via Vittorio Emanuele and the narrow streets of the old town center, wine and food are what Alba's all about. Wherever you go, you'll end up peering into store windows to admire displays of wines, truffles, and the calorific but exquisite *nocciolata* cake made of hazelnuts and chocolate. The streets are crammed with enough enticing restaurants to make gourmands very happy indeed (see below).

One enchanting drive heads south from Alba to the wine villages of the **Langhe hills** (follow signs out of town for Barolo on the SP3). After 8km (5 miles), take the right turn for **Grinzane Cavour,** a hilltop village built around a castle harboring the **Enoteca Regionale Piemontese Cavour** (castellogrinzane.com; ✆ **0173/262-159**), which is open daily 9:30am to 7pm (Nov–Mar until 6pm). Here you can sample local wines from a curated selection of labels. There is also a fine-dining restaurant on the premises.

Return to the main road, turn left, and after 4km (2½ miles) south, take the right fork to **La Morra,** perched among vineyards with panoramic views over the rolling, vine-clad countryside. La Morra has several cafes and restaurants in which to taste the local vintages. The **Cantina Comunale di La Morra** at Via Alberto 2 (cantinalamorra.com; ✆ **0173/509-204**) represents local growers, selling Barolo, Nebbiolo, Barbera, and Dolcetto. It's open daily (except Tues) 10am to 12:30pm and 2:30 to 6:30pm. La Morra's tourist office, Piazza Martiri 1 (lamorraturismo.it; ✆ **0173/209-664**), is open on Monday and Tuesday 9:30am to 1:30pm and Thursday to Sunday 10am to 6pm.

Barolo is a handsome little village dominated by two ancient castles; it's 5km (3 miles) along the SP58 from La Morra. Here, too, you'll find a choice of restaurants and shops selling world-renowned red wines from local vineyards. Among these is the **Enoteca del Barolo** (enotecadel barolo.it; ✆ **388/626-2864**), with a wine bar offering tastings in its cavernous cellars. They even offer Barolo and chocolate pairings.

WHERE TO STAY & EAT IN THE PIEDMONT WINE COUNTRY

The Barolo region is the land of *agriturismo,* with options to stay on wine estates in the hills of Langhe. You can find properties on agriturismo.it; search the Piedmont region or look for specific town names. There are also a few decent urban hotels. As for restaurants, the cuisine in Piedmont is rich and refined, known for hearty meat dishes, a wide variety of cheeses, and influences from nearby France. Truffles, hazelnuts, mushrooms, garlic, and rice also play an important role in this region's culinary repertoire.

Palazzo Finati ♥♥ This historic *palazzo* delivers old-world charm and a level of hospitality that exceeds expectations. Palazzo Finati is right in the heart of Alba, near the Piazza del Duomo and some of the town's best shops and gourmet restaurants. The nine individually designed rooms and suites have their own unique flourishes; some have romantic touches, frescoed ceilings, and terraces overlooking the inner courtyard. Works by local artists adorn the walls of common areas and rooms. A breakfast of fresh pastries, fruit, local cheeses, and cured meats is served in an elegant brick-ceilinged, barrel-vaulted dining room with details that go back to Roman times. Parking can be an issue—if you're coming by car, make sure to request access to the enclosed parking area.

Via Vernazza 8, Alba. palazzofinati.it. ✆ **348/008-0806.** 9 units. 160€–200€ double; 170€–250€ suite. Rates include breakfast. **Amenities:** Free Wi-Fi.

Star chef Marc Lanteri welcomes diners to his eponymous restaurant in the Piedmont wine country.

Ristorante Marc Lanteri ♥♥♥ GOURMET Having worked in some of the finest kitchens in France and Italy, Michelin-starred chef Marc Lanteri decided to set out on his own several years ago, opening a restaurant near Alba surrounded by rolling hills and vineyards. A French chef with Italian roots, Marc is committed to offering sustainable, local cuisine, and his dishes reflect his varied influences. A Piedmontese beef tartare is served with artichokes, hazelnut pesto, aromatic herbs, and olive-oil crackers, while a *hokkaido* pumpkin velouté comes with local mushrooms and crisp Parma ham. In the fall, the famous Alba white truffle takes center stage on the menu. The chef's American wife, Amy Marcelle Belloti, is the restaurant's sommelier and has put together a wine list full of labels meant to seamlessly pair with Lanteri's cuisine. The menu isn't vast, but vegetarians and vegans are also well taken care of here.

Via Serra 21/d, Castagnito d'Alba. marclanteri.it. ✆ **0173/262-172.** Main courses 18€–30€. Wed–Sun noon–2pm and 7–10pm. Closed Jan and sometimes Feb.

AOSTA ♥♥ & VALLE D'AOSTA ♥♥♥

Aosta: 113km (70 miles) N of Turin, 184km (114 miles) NW of Milan; Courmayeur: 35km (22 miles) W of Aosta, 148km (92 miles) NW of Turin

Tucked up against the French and Swiss borders in northwest Italy, the Aosta Valley is a land of harsh snowcapped peaks, lush pastures, thick forests, waterfalls cascading into mountain streams, and romantic castles clinging to wooded hillsides. A year-round stream of skiers, hikers, cyclists, and nature lovers flocks to this tiny Alpine region north of Turin for the scenery, outdoor adventure, and rustic gastronomy.

Aosta

ESSENTIALS

ARRIVING Aosta is served by 20 **trains** a day to and from Turin (2–3 hr.; change in Ivrea or Chivasso; tickets 10.50€) aboard **Trenitalia** (trenitalia.com; ✆ **892-021**). **Bus service** to Aosta has notoriously been less than reliable, but now **FlixBus** (flixbus.com) offers service between the two cities for as low as 9.50€. An **Arriva** (aosta.arriva.it) bus conveniently connects Aosta hourly to **Courmayeur** (1 hr.; 3.50€, 4€ if bought on board) and other popular spots in the valley.

Autostrada A5 from Turin shoots up the length of Valle d'Aosta en route to France and Switzerland via the Mont Blanc tunnel; there are numerous exits in the valley. The trip from Turin to Aosta normally takes about 90 minutes, but traffic can be heavy on weekends in ski season.

VISITOR INFORMATION The tourist office in Aosta, Piazza Porta Praetoria 3 (lovevda.it; ✆ **0165/236-627**), dispenses a wealth of information on hiking trails, ski lifts and passes, bike rentals, and rafting trips. It's open daily 9am to 7pm.

EXPLORING AOSTA

An appealing mountain town with an ancient heart, Aosta—nicknamed "the Rome of the Alps"—is surrounded by snowcapped peaks and steeped in a history that goes back to Roman times. Although you're not going to find much pristine Alpine quaintness here in the Valle d'Aosta's busy tourist center, you will find Roman ruins, medieval bell towers, and chic shops. Aosta's **weekly market** day is Tuesday, when stalls selling food, clothes, and crafts fill the Piazza Cavalieri di Vittorio Veneto.

Well-preserved city walls date from the days when Aosta was one of Rome's most important trading and military outposts. A **Roman bridge** spans the River Buthier, and two Roman gates arch gracefully across the Via San Anselmo. The **Porta Pretoria** forms the western entrance to the Roman town and the **Arco di Augusto** the eastern entrance. The **Teatro Romano** and the ruins of the **amphitheater** are north of the Porta Pretoria; the ruins of the **forum** are in an adjacent park. The theater and forum are open generally daily from 9am to 6pm (typically closed for a few hours in the afternoon in the winter), and admission is free. Architectural fragments found during excavations of these monuments are displayed in Aosta's **Archaeological Museum** at Piazza Roncas 12 (✆ **0165/275-902;** summer daily 9am–7pm, fall and winter Tues–Sun 10am–1pm and 2–5pm). The 5€ ticket (free for ages 17 and under) is valid for 6 months and allows you to visit four other sites of archaeological importance in the region.

The Valle d'Aosta

Most visitors to the Valle d'Aosta come here for outdoor activities rather than sightseeing; the region has some of Italy's best hiking trails and is a major skiing destination.

The little town of **Cogne** is the gateway to the **Parco Nazionale del Gran Paradiso** ♥♥, one of Europe's finest parcels of unspoiled wilderness. This national park, Italy's oldest, was once the hunting grounds of King Vittorio Emanuele II; it encompasses the jagged peaks of **Gran Paradiso** (4,061m/13,323-ft. high), five valleys, and some 703 sq. km (271 sq. miles) of forests and pastureland. Many Alpine beasts roam wild here, including the ibex (curly-horned goat) and the elusive chamois (small antelope), both of which are nearly extinct in Europe. Humans can roam these wilds via a vast network of well-marked hiking trails. The park's main **visitor center** is at Via Alpetta, Ronco Canavese (pngp.it/en; ✆ **0124/817-377**). Admission is free. In winter, the meadows and Alpine forests around Cogne boast 80km (50 miles) of challenging **cross-country (Nordic) skiing trails;** check cogneturismo.it for details.

Summer Alpine hiking in the Valle d'Aosta.

In winter, most visitors head for the **downhill skiing** and **snowboarding** destinations of **Courmayeur, Breuil-Cervinia,** and **Monte Rose,** a ski area around the resort towns of Champoluc and Gressoney. There are trails for all levels, from gentle nursery slopes to black diamond runs and mogul fields. Expert skiers are best off at high-altitude **La Thuile** for excellent off-trail powder and heli-skiing. Depending on conditions, the ski season kicks off in early November and runs through April. Altogether, 800km (500 miles) of ski runs are available under the **Valle d'Aosta ski pass.** In low season, multi-day passes range from a 3-day pass for 194€ to a 2-week pass for 665€; in high season, rates increase to 209€ for 3 days up to 730€ for 2 weeks. One child 7 and under skis free with each adult who buys the pass. For details, go to skilife.ski. Meanwhile, if you're looking for something a bit different, consider **dog sledding** (dogsledman.com) near Courmayeur.

Where to Stay & Eat in the Valle d'Aosta

In ski season, many Valle d'Aosta hotels expect guests to eat on premises and stay 3 nights or more, but they're more flexible outside busy tourist times.

The Valle d'Aosta is the land of mountain food—hams and salamis, creamy polenta—and buttery Fontina is the cheese of choice.

Hostellerie du Cheval Blanc ♥♥ It may not be a mountain chalet, but the Cheval Blanc (meaning "white horse") offers town-center convenience and an array of amenities. Thankfully, you still get some Alpine views. The contemporary-style hotel within walking distance of the ancient Roman heart of Aosta is designed around a massive atrium with stylish furnishings. The hotel has two restaurants: the fairly expensive **Le Petit** and the more casual **Brasserie.** Well-appointed rooms come with minimalist furnishings, a neutral color palette, and wood floors. Marble-lined bathrooms tend to have bathtubs as well as showers. Skiers will appreciate the winter shuttle to the cable car up to Pila (about a half-mile away), and the pool and sauna provide perfect après-ski relaxation before a night out in Aosta. Guests have access to a gym and wellness center with pools, Jacuzzi, and two saunas.

Rue Clavalité 20, Aosta. chevalblanc.it. ✆ **0165/239-140.** 55 units. 139€–200€ double. Rates include breakfast. **Amenities:** 2 restaurants; bar; children's playroom; indoor pool; gym; sauna; spa; room service; free Wi-Fi.

Osteria da Nando ♥♥ FONDUE This cheery *osteria* with terra-cotta-colored walls and rustic touches has been a family-run institution since 1957. Over the years, it has become one of Aosta's most popular restaurants for its hearty yet surprisingly sophisticated seasonal fare like Valdostan wild boar chops in a green herb breadcrumb crust, served with sautéed spinach and a mixed wild-berry coulis. Try different types of fondue, from *bourguignonne* served with tender beef filet to *raclette* served with creamy Fontina cheese and chunks of chewy bread, alongside the classic Piedmontese *bagna cauda* (an anchovy-based sauce with garlic, oil, and cream). The restaurant prides itself on being able to cater to celiacs and diners with food allergies—be sure to notify staff ahead of time of

UP & OVER mont blanc

Riding high over Mont Blanc—Europe's tallest mountain at 4,811m (15,784 ft.)—has to be one of the most awe-inspiring experiences in the Italian Alps. It's an enchanted journey passing over glaciers and steep ravines, mountain lakes, and snowy peaks on the Italian side of the Vallée Blanche.

For years, this trek involved three changes of cable car, starting from the little ski village of **La Palud** (3km/1¾ miles above Courmayeur) and ascending through **Le Pavillon** and **Rifugio Torino** to the viewing terrace at **Punta Helbronner** (3,462m/11,358 ft.), in the heart of the Mont Blanc Massif. From here it was possible to take the cable car down to **Aiguille de Midi** on the French side of Mont Blanc, and then the Panoramic Mont-Blanc Gondola on into the party-loving resort of **Chamonix.**

But all that changed in 2015 with the launch of a new, vastly improved cable-car service, **Skyway Monte Bianco** (montebianco.com). Run by Funivie del Monte Bianco, the system has sleek rotating gondolas departing from a swish station at **Pontal d'Entrèves** (near the entrance to the Mont Blanc tunnel) on a high-speed connection up to Punta Helbronner for a bird's-eye view of Monte Bianco and the surrounding peaks of Gran Paradiso and Monte Cervinia (Matterhorn).

Be prepared to pay for these breathtaking views: A round-trip ticket from Pontal to Punta Helbronner is 59€ if purchased online; a one-way ticket costs 45€. If you want to enjoy the views but may suffer from altitude sickness at the very top, you can opt to go just to the midway point, Pavillon du Mont-Fréty, which has a restaurant and shopping area; that ticket costs 25€ adults online (17€ one-way online). The journey is free for children 7 and under, and there are special deals for families with children.

You can still continue on from Punta Helbronner to Chamonix via cable car—and if you do so, you can return to Courmayeur via France's **SAT bus service** through the Mont Blanc tunnel. Buses run daily each way, and the journey takes 45 minutes (sat-montblanc.com; tickets 15€, discounts available for children 11 and under).

The Skyway Monte Bianco ascends Mont Blanc.

any special needs. Save room for one of the homemade desserts, like the delightful panna cotta with saffron custard, cinnamon, and licorice. The wine selection is impressively local.

Via Sant'Anselmo 99, Aosta. instagram.com/osteriadanando. ✆ **0165/44-455.** Main courses 12€–27€. Wed 7:30–10pm; Thurs–Mon noon–2pm and 7:30–10pm. Closed 2 weeks late June to early July.

Ristorante La Palud ♥♥ PIZZA/SEAFOOD Thanks to its proximity to the tunnel into France, this restaurant/pizzeria is a popular place to stop before crossing the border. Impressive Monte Bianco and glacier views make it a perpetual favorite. Decorated to look like an upscale mountain chalet, La Palud keeps diners coming back for enormous thin-crust pizzas, dishes typical of the Valle d'Aosta (like gnocchi in a fondue made from local cheese), deer steak with a sauce made of juniper and blueberries, and fresh fish brought up from the Ligurian coast on Fridays in the summer. In warm weather, sit outside on the flower-filled terrace; when it's cold outside, huddle around the open fire and admire the snowdrifts through the windows. End your meal with a sweet treat like the homemade *bounet* (a sort of custard made from Piedmontese chocolate and almond-flavored *amaretti* biscuits), although you can't go wrong with any of the desserts made by the in-house pastry chef.
Strada la Palud 17, Courmayeur. lapalud.it. ✆ **0165/89-169.** Main courses 13€–30€. Daily noon–3:30pm and 7:30–10:30pm.

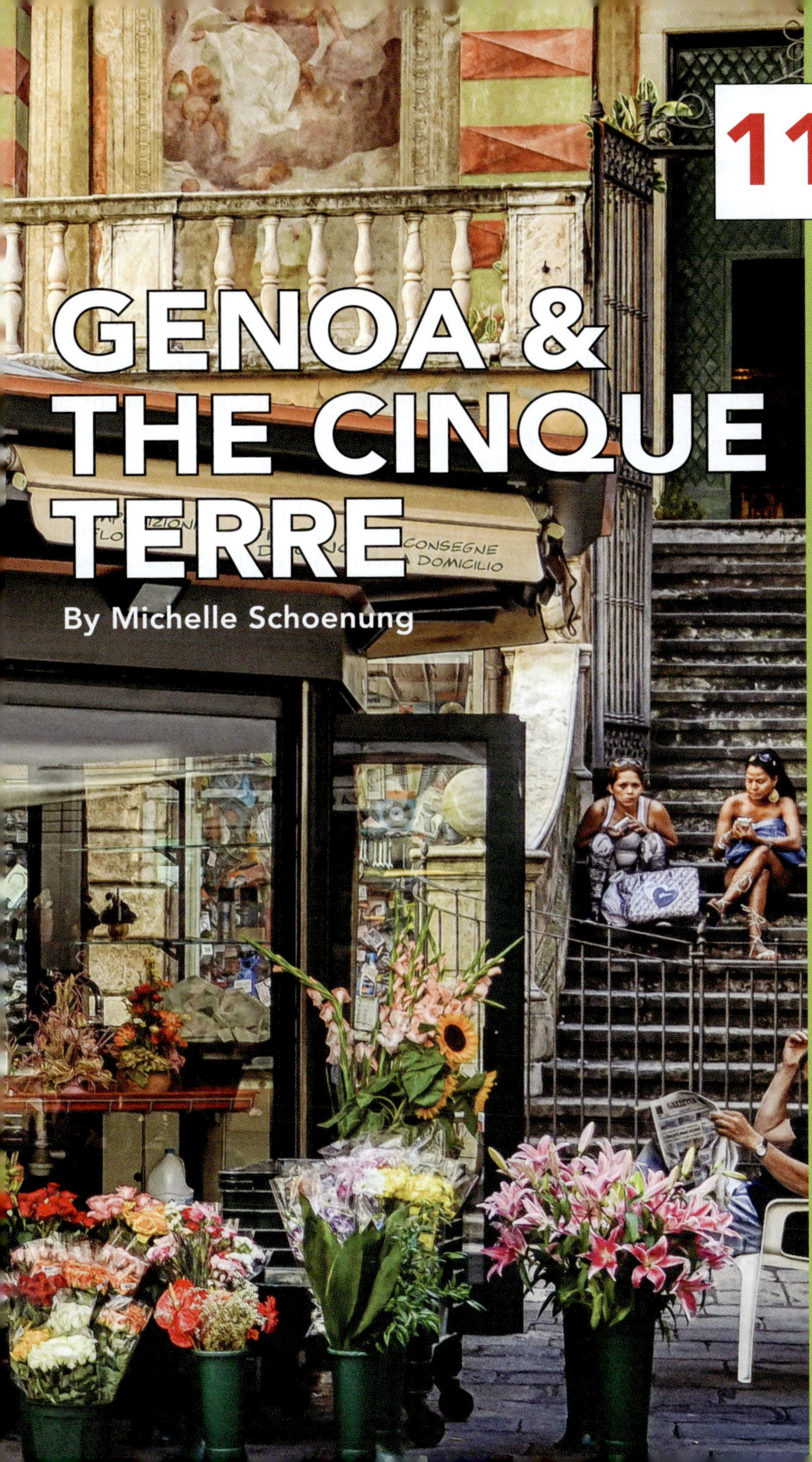

11

GENOA & THE CINQUE TERRE

By Michelle Schoenung

Hugging the Mediterranean coastline from the French border to the tip of Tuscany lies a crescent-shaped strip of land that makes up the region of Liguria. The pleasures of this area are no secret. Since the 19th century, world-weary travelers have been heading for Liguria's resorts, such as San Remo and Portofino, to enjoy balmy weather and the cliff-lined sea. Beyond the beach, fishing villages, small resort towns, and proud old port cities bake in the sun, and hillsides are fragrant with the scent of bougainvillea and pines.

Liguria is really two coasts. First, the "sandier" stretch west of Genoa known as the **Riviera di Ponente** (Riviera of the Setting Sun) is studded with fashionable resorts, many of which, like San Remo, have seen their heydays fade but continue to entice visitors with palm-fringed promenades and a gentle way of life. The rockier, more rugged, but also more colorful stretch southeast of Genoa, known as the **Riviera di Levante** (Rising Sun), extends past the posh harbor of Portofino to the ever-popular villages of the Cinque Terre.

The province's capital, Genoa, is one of Italy's busiest ports, an ancient center of commerce, and one of history's great maritime powers. Despite its rough exterior, it is an underrated gem filled with architectural delights, Italy's largest historic center, and a sense of "real Italy" that has become hard to come by in many of the country's more popular cities.

DON'T LEAVE GENOA & THE CINQUE TERRE WITHOUT . . .

Getting Lost in Genoa. Though it is more than 180 years since Charles Dickens described the pleasure of losing yourself in the labyrinth of Europe's largest preserved medieval city, the experience is still enthralling.

Toasting the Setting Sun. The Riviera di Levante is justifiably famous for its sunsets. Its sheer cliffs afford huge, humbling views of this blazing show. Raise a glass of the region's golden Sciacchetrà wine in tribute.

Seeing the Jewel of the Cinque Terre. Vernazza is the quintessential postcard-perfect seaside village, with tall, colorful houses (known as *terratetti*) clustered around a natural harbor where you can swim among the fishing boats. Best way to get here? Hike from Monterosso, along the most scenic, if arduous, leg of the famed Cinque Terre trail.

 FACING PAGE: **Genoa's atmospheric Old Town.**

The Italian Riviera
To Turin
To Milan
To Parma
Bra
Alba
Acqui Terme
Ovada
Busca
Cuneo
Mondovi
PIEDMONT
Millesimo
Cairo Montenotte
Masone
Busalla
Casella
Ligurian Apennines
LIGURIA
EMILIA-ROMAGNA
TUSCANY
FRANCE
MONACO
Maritime Alps
Montebruno
Torriglia
Rezzoaglio
Cabanne
Borgo Val di Taro
Borzonasca
Voltri
Pegli
GENOA
Arenzano
Varazze
Albisola
Savona
Spotorno
Noli
Varigotti
Finale Ligure
Loano
Toirano
Borghetto S. Spirito
Albenga
Alassio
Laigueglia
Andora
Cervo
Diano Marina
Oneglia
Imperia
Taggia
Arma di Taggia
San Remo
Bordighera
Ventimiglia
Giardini Botanici Hanbury
Menton
Nice
Monte Carlo
Dolceacqua
Baiardo
Triora
Pieve di Teco
Mendatica
Monesi
Nervi
Recco
Camogli
S. Fruttuoso
Portofino
Rapallo
S. Margherita Ligure
Chiavari
Sestri Levante
Moneglia
Deiva Marina
Varese Ligure
Brugnato
Levanto
Monterosso
Vernazza
Corniglia
Manarola
Riomaggiore
La Spezia
Portovenere
Lerici
Tellaro
Sarzana
Carrara
Gulf of Genoa
Ligurian Sea
Paradiso
Tigullio
Riviera di Levante
Cinque Terre
Riviera delle Palme
Riviera di Ponente
Riviera di Fiori
A26
E25
A7
E62
A6
E716
E74
SP428
SP1
A10
SP453
SP64
SP225
SP523
A12
E80
A15
E33
Venice
Genoa
The Italian Riviera
San Remo
Florence
Rome
0
20 mi
20 km

GENOA ♥♥

142km (88 miles) S of Milan, 501km (311 miles) NW of Rome, 194km (120 miles) E of Nice

With its dizzying mix of old and new, Genoa—or, as the Italians spell it, Genova—is as multilayered as the hills to which it clings. It was and is, first and foremost, a port city: an important maritime center for the Roman Empire, boyhood home of Christopher Columbus (whose much-restored house still stands near the medieval walls), and one of the largest and wealthiest cities of Renaissance Europe, fueled by seafaring trade that stretched to the Middle East.

Genoa began as a port of the ancient Ligurian people at least by the 6th century B.C.E., and by the early Middle Ages had become a formidable maritime power, conquering the surrounding coast and the mighty outlying islands of Corsica and Sardinia. Genoa established colonies throughout North Africa and the Middle East, and made massive gains during the Crusades. With bigger success came bigger rivals, and Genoa locked commercial and military horns with Venice, which eventually took the upper hand in the late 1300s. Genoa increasingly fell under the control of outsiders, and though self-government returned for a while in the 16th century, sea trade was shifting to Spain and eventually to its American colonies. Genoa's most famous son, Columbus, had to travel to Spain to find the financial backing for his exploration across the Atlantic.

It's easy to capture glimpses of Genoa's former glory days on the narrow lanes and dank alleys of the portside Old Town, where treasure-filled palaces and fine marble churches stand next to laundry-draped tenements and brothels. The other Genoa, the modern city that stretches for miles along the coast and climbs the hills, is a city of international business, parks, and breezy belvederes from which you can enjoy fine views of this colorful metropolis and the sea.

Essentials

ARRIVING

BY PLANE Flights to and from most European capitals serve **Cristoforo Colombo International Airport** (**GOA**), just 6.5km (4 miles) west of the city center (www.airport.genova.it; ✆ **010/60-151**). **Volabus** (amt.genova.it; ✆ **010/558-2414**) connects the airport with the Principe and Brignole train stations, with buses running the 30-minute trip once or twice an hour from 5am to 10pm; buy tickets on the bus (10€; includes 24 hr. of use on the local transportation system).

BY TRAIN Genoa has two major train stations: **Stazione Principe** (designated on timetables as Genova P.P.) near the Old Town and the port on Piazza Acquaverde, and **Stazione Brignole** (designated as Genova BR) in the modern city on Piazza Verdi. Many trains serve both stations; however, some stop only at one, so make sure you know which station

ATTRACTIONS

Acquario di Genova **3**
Cattedrale di San Lorenzo **10**
Galata Museo del Mare **2**
Galleria di Palazzo Bianco **6**
Galleria Nazionale di Palazzo Spinola **5**
Piazza Dante **11**
Via Garibaldi **6**

HOTELS

Best Western Hotel Metropoli **7**
Hotel Bristol Palace **12**
Hotel No Logo **13**
Ostello Bello **1**

RESTAURANTS

I Tre Merli **4**
La Cabotina **8**
Trattoria della Raibetta **9**

your train is scheduled to arrive at or depart from. Trains connect the two stations in 5 minutes and run about every 15 minutes.

Genoa is the hub for trains serving the Italian Riviera, with hourly trains arriving from and departing for **Ventimiglia** on the French border; trains for **La Spezia,** at the eastern edge of Liguria, run as often as three trains an hour during peak times. Check timetables: Regional trains stop at almost all the coastal resorts, while faster trains stop at only a few (for towns in this chapter, see individual listings for connections with Genoa). Lots of trains connect Genoa with major Italian cities: **Milan** (one or two per hour; 1½–2 hr.; a fast train is in the works that will connect the two cities in less than an hour), **Turin** (one per hour; 1¾–2 hr.), **Pisa** (hourly;

1½–3 hr.), **Florence** (hourly but with a change, usually at Pisa; 3 hr.), and **Rome** (hourly; 5–6 hr.).

BY BUS An extensive bus network connects Genoa with other parts of Liguria, and with other Italian and European cities, from the main bus station next to Stazione Principe. It's easiest to reach seaside resorts by the trains that run along the coast, but buses link to many small towns in the region's hilly hinterlands. For information about buses outside of town, check the **Genoa Transportation Authority** website (amt.genova.it) for "provincial service."

BY CAR Genoa is linked to other parts of Italy and to France by a convenient network of highways. Genoa has lots of pay parking around the port and the edges of the Old Town. It can be pricey (2€–2.50€ per hour).

BY FERRY Genoa connects by ferry to several other major Mediterranean ports, including Barcelona, Sardinia, and Sicily (www.traghettitalia.it). Most boats depart from the **Stazione Marittima** (✆ **010/089-8335**), which is on a waterfront roadway, Via Marina D'Italia, about a 5-minute walk south of Stazione Principe. For service to and from the **Riviera Levante,** check with **Tigullio** (traghettiportofino.it; ✆ **0185/284-670**) or **Golfo Paradiso** (golfoparadiso.it; ✆ **0185/772-091**); there's almost hourly service from 9am to 5pm daily in July and August.

VISITOR INFORMATION

The **main tourist office** is on **Via Garibaldi 12/R** across from the beautiful city hall (visitgenoa.it; ✆ **010/557-2903**), open daily 9am to 6:20pm. Other branches are near Porto Antico in **Via al Porto Antico 2,** open daily from about 9am to 6pm with longer hours in summer; and at **Cristoforo Colombo airport,** daily 9am to 1pm and 1:30 to 5:30pm.

GETTING AROUND

Given Genoa's labyrinth of small streets (many of which cannot be negotiated by car or bus), the only way to traverse much of the city is on foot—and you'll need a good map. The tourist office gives out terrific maps, but you can also buy an audioguide with map that really helps you navigate the small *vicoli,* or alleyways. Genovese are usually happy to direct visitors, but given the geography with which they are dealing, their instructions can be complicated.

BY BUS Bus tickets (2€) are available at newsstands and at ticket booths, *tabacchi* (tobacconists, marked by a brown-and-white T sign), and at the train stations; look for the symbol **AMT** (amt.genova.it; ✆ **010/558-2414**). You must stamp your ticket when you board; tickets are valid for 110 minutes. Bus tickets can also be used on the funiculars and public elevators that climb the steep hills surrounding the ancient core of the town. Tickets good for 24 hours cost 10€ and include travel throughout the city not just on Metro and bus but via Volabus, Navebus, and bus line 782 in Portofino as well.

BY TAXI A metered taxi, which you can find at cabstands, is your best bet for getting around Genoa at night. For instance, you may well want to consider taking one from a restaurant in the Old Town to your hotel or to one of the train stations (especially Stazione Brignole, which is a bit farther out). Cabstands at Piazza della Nunziata, Piazza Fontane Marose, and Piazza de Ferrari are especially convenient to the Old Town, or call **Radiotaxi** at ✆ **010/5966.** The meter starts at around 7€ and adds around 1€ every kilometer (or every minute if the taxi is traveling less than 30kmph). Additional fees are added at night or if one needs to leave city limits. There's a fixed price of 25€ to go from the city center to the airport.

Genoa Takes to the Sea

An ancient tradition continues when Genoa takes to the sea in the **Regata delle Antiche Repubbliche Marinare,** rowing against crews from its ancient maritime rivals, Amalfi, Pisa, and Venice. It's not always in Genoa—each city takes turns hosting the event, which happens between the end of May and the beginning of July. Another spectacular, though more modern, regatta is held every September: the **Millevele,** or Thousand Sails, when Genoa's bay is carpeted with the mainsails and spinnakers of nautical enthusiasts from around the world.

BY SUBWAY The city's nascent subway system is a work in progress, with only eight stops on a single line between the new Brignole station and a suburb to the northwest called Certosa (there are convenient stops in between at Stazione Principe and at Dinegro close to the ferry port). The tickets are the same as those used for the bus.

CITY LAYOUT

Genoa extends for miles along the coast, with neighborhoods and suburbs tucked into valleys and climbing the city's many hills. Most sights of interest are in the **Old Town,** a fascinating jumble of old palaces, shabby tenements, cramped squares, and tiny lanes and alleyways clustered on the eastern side of the old port. **Via Garibaldi,** lined with a succession of majestic *palazzi,* forms the northern flank of the Old Town and is the best place to begin your explorations. Many of the city's most important museums and monuments are on and around this street, and from here you can descend into the warren of little lanes, known as ***caruggi,*** that lead through the city down to the port. ***Note:*** These very small alleyways can feel a bit deserted at night. To be on the safe side, stay alert and navigate the *caruggi* by following the locals.

The city's two train stations are located on either side of the Old Town; wherever you are in the Old Town, you are only a short walk or bus or taxi ride from one of these two stations. **Stazione Principe** is the closest, just to the west; from Piazza Acquaverde, in front of the station, follow **Via Balbi** through **Piazza della Nunziata** and **Via Bensa** to **Via Cairoli,** which runs into Via Garibaldi (the walk will take at least 15 min.). From **Stazione Brignole,** walk straight across the broad, open space to Piazza della Vittoria/Via Luigi Cadorna and turn right to follow

Genoa's Old Port draws visitors with a cluster of attractions, including the Biosphere, the Acquario di Genoa, and the Galata Museo del Mare.

broad **Via XX Settembre,** one of the city's major shopping avenues, due west for about 15 or 20 minutes to **Piazza de Ferrari,** on the eastern edge of the Old Town. From here, **Via San Lorenzo** will lead you past Genoa's cathedral and to the port, or follow **Via XXV Aprile** north to Piazza delle Fontane Marose, the eastern end of Via Garibaldi.

Exploring Genoa

Acquario di Genova ♥♥♥ AQUARIUM Genoa boasts the largest aquarium in Europe, and it has undoubtedly been the city's biggest draw in its more than 30 years of existence. Like a huge freight ship, it presides over a pier in the Old Port, about a 15-minute walk from Stazione Principe and 10 minutes from Via Garibaldi. Visitors enter the Blue Planet room, which offers an overview of marine life from all bodies of water. Huge tanks recreate more than 70 marine ecosystems, including Red Sea coral reefs, pools in the tropical rainforests of the Amazon River basin, and many other habitats that provide homes for sharks, seals, dolphins, penguins, piranhas, and just about every other kind of water creature. The aquarium also offers behind-the-scenes tours, up-close encounters with marine animals, and expert-led explorations to discover the secrets of the underwater world, but these often must be reserved several days in advance. Afterward you can easily spend a day around the old harbor by also visiting the nearby **Galata Museo del Mare ♥♥** (p. 560), flying high over the harbor on the **Bigo Panoramic Lift,** and

A Cumulative Ticket

The **Genova City Pass** (www.genovacitypass.it) includes free public transport and can be personalized to visitors' interests (culture and heritage, edu-tainment, active, etc.), with specific itineraries over 24, 48, or 72 hours. It starts at around 20€.

walking through endangered tropical forests in the great glass globe of the **Biosphere.** The children's museum, **Città dei Bambini** ♥ (www.cittadeibambini.net), can also be found on the port. It is a great option for families if the aquarium is too busy, billing itself as an "experience museum" with interactive exhibits for children ages 2 to 12.

Ponte Spinola (at the port). acquariodigenova.it. ✆ **010/23451.** Admission 26€ and up adults, 20€ and up seniors, and 16€ and up children 4–12; prices vary depending on season or day of week; free for children 3 and under. Mon–Fri 9am–6pm, Sat–Sun 8:30am–7pm (July–Aug daily until 10:30pm). Bus: 1–8 and 12–15. Metro: Darsena.

Cattedrale di San Lorenzo ♥ CATHEDRAL Genoa's main cathedral has its own austere dignity, its black-and-white-striped 12th-century facade enlivened by fanciful French Gothic carvings over the main doorway and a pair of stone lions guarding the steps. A later addition is the bell tower, completed in the 16th century. In the frescoed interior, chapels house two of Genoa's most notable curiosities: Beyond the first pilaster on the right is a still-unexploded shell fired through the roof from a British ship during World War II; and in the **Cappella di San Giovanni** (left aisle), a 13th-century crypt contains what crusaders returning from the Holy Land claimed to be relics of John the Baptist. The adjoining treasury (**Museo del Tesoro**) seems to specialize in sacred tableware of doubtful provenance: the plate upon which Saint John's head was supposedly served to Salome, a bowl allegedly used at the Last Supper, and a bowl thought at one time to be the Holy Grail. Less storied but nonetheless magnificent gold and bejeweled objects reflect Genoa's medieval

Genoa's Gothic Cattedrale di San Lorenzo.

prominence as a maritime power. You can visit the treasury only by a half-hour guided tour in Italian, but it's still worth seeing what is inside, even if the extent of your Italian is *gelato* and *pizza*.

Piazza San Lorenzo. chiesadigenova.it. ✆ **010/254-1250.** Cathedral: Free admission. Treasury: 5€ adults, 4€ seniors and students. Included in Card Musei (www.visitgenoa.it). Mon–Sat 8am–noon and 3–7pm. Bus: 1, 7, 8, 17, 18, 19, 20.

Galata Museo del Mare ♥♥ MUSEUM Billing itself as the largest maritime museum in the Mediterranean, the Galata Museo del Mare offers 31 exhibits over five floors, and visiting it is like embarking on a voyage. Despite its modern appearance, the building is the oldest surviving construction of the dockyard from the old Republic, where Genovese galleys were built during the 17th century. Visitors enter through a gallery dedicated to the old port, with paintings and artifacts of the period, then it's on to a full-scale reproduction of a Genovese "attack ship," with fun items and props that will engage all ages. The museum's third floor is devoted to exploring immigration, highlighting the destinations Italians have migrated to around the world, such as the United States, Brazil, and Argentina. Certain exhibits (like the submarine *Nazario Sauro* docked in the waters alongside the museum) are offered at an additional cost. There is an "open air" section of the museum right out on the docks where visitors can learn more about the history of the shipyards and watch fishermen roll in with their fresh catches to be sold at the market right on the port.

Calata Ansaldo de Mari 1 (at the beginning of Porta Parodi). galatamuseodelmare.it. ✆ **010/234-5655.** Admission 17€ adults, 12€ seniors and students ages 7–17, free for children 6 and under. Mar–Oct daily 10am–7:30pm; Nov–Feb Tues–Fri 10am–6pm and Sat–Sun 10am–7:30pm (last entry 1 hr. before closing). Bus: 1–8 and 12–15. Metro: Darsena.

Galleria di Palazzo Bianco ♥♥ MUSEUM The White Palace is one of a string of magnificent *palazzi* along ritzy Via Garibaldi, the Strada Nuova created by the Genovese aristocracy during the Renaissance (and a UNESCO World Heritage Site). Although it was built during the mid-16th century by Luca Grimaldi, a scion of one of the most important Genovese families, the gorgeous white facade was reconstructed in the 18th century, making it both the "oldest and newest" of these mansions. Maria Durazzo Brignole-Sale de Ferrari donated the palace and her art collection to the city in 1884 to create Genoa's first public gallery. The collection is heavy on painters of the Spanish and Flemish schools, with significant works by masters such as Lippi, Murillo, Rubens, van Dyck, Veronese, and Zurbarán. One of the museum's most notable holdings is Caravaggio's *Ecce Homo*.

Via Garibaldi 11. museidigenova.it/it/content/palazzo-bianco. ✆ **010/557-2193.** Admission 9€ adults, includes entrance to Palazzo Rosso and Palazzo Tursi. Included in Card Musei (visitgenoa.it). Late Mar to early Oct Tues–Fri 9am–7pm and Sat–Sun 10am–7:30pm; rest of year Tues–Fri 9am–6:30pm and Sat–Sun 9:30am–6:30pm. Bus: 18, 20, 35, 37, 39, 40, 41, 42.

Galleria Nazionale di Palazzo Spinola ♥ MUSEUM Another prominent Genovese family, the Spinolas, donated their palace and magnificent art collection to the city in 1958. Not only is the art collection something to behold, but the circa-1593 palace, on historic Piazza Pellicceria, is a wonderful example of how Genovese aristocrats really lived, among frescoes and mirrored galleries. Lower floors fortunately escaped damage during World War II, though the two upper floors had to be completely rebuilt (and now host what is known as the National Gallery of Liguria with paintings, porcelain objects, and furnishings from over the centuries to display an array of local art). As in Genoa's other art collections, you will find masterworks ranging from native artists like Strozzi, da Messina, Reni, Giordano, and de Ferrari to van Dyck and other painters of the Dutch and Flemish schools, whose commissioned portraits were once a status symbol among Genoa's wealthy. The museum hosts occasional events to show how the *palazzo* looked when it was an aristocratic home, with, for example, the table set in the candlelit dining room as if for a sumptuous feast.

Piazza Pellicceria 1. palazzospinola.cultura.gov.it. ✆ **010/270-5300.** Admission 12€ adults, 2€ ages 18–25, free for seniors and kids 17 and under; includes admission to the National Gallery of Liguria and the museums of the Royal Palace. Included in Card Musei (visitgenoa.it). Free first Sun of month. Tues–Sat 8:30am–7:30pm; Sun 1:30–7:30pm. Bus: 1, 18, 20, 34.

Piazza Dante ♥ LANDMARK Though most of this square just south of Piazza de Ferrari is made up of 1930s-era office buildings, one end is bounded by the reconstructed **Porta Soprana** ♥♥, a twin-towered town gate built in 1155. The main draw, though, is the small **house** (rebuilt in the 18th c.), standing a bit incongruously in a tidy little park below the gate, said to have belonged to **Christopher Columbus's father,** a weaver and gatekeeper (whether young Christopher lived here is open to debate).

Bus: 14, 35, 42, 44.

A Market Cornucopia

The sprawling **Mercato Orientale** (moggenova.it), Genoa's boisterous indoor food market, evokes the days when ships brought back spices and other commodities from the ends of the earth. An excellent place to stock up on olives, herbs, fresh fruit, and other Ligurian products, the market is Monday to Wednesday 7:30am to 1pm and 3:30 to 7:30pm, and Thursday to Saturday 7:30am to 7:30pm. Entrances are on Via XX Settembre and Via Galata (about halfway between Piazza de Ferrari at the edge of the Old Town and Stazione Brignole). Inside the market are a few small eateries—from pasta and pizza to Peruvian and Kenyan food—but the district just north of here (especially Via San Vincenzo and Via Colombo) is a gourmand's dream, with many bakeries, *pasticcerie* (pastry shops), and stores selling pasta and cheese, wine, olive oil, and other foodstuffs.

Via Garibaldi ♥♥ ICON Many of Genoa's museums and other sights are clustered on and around this street, also known as Strada Nuova, one of the most beautiful in Italy. Here, Genoa's wealthy families built palaces in the 16th and 17th centuries that were the envy of all of Europe. Besides the **Galleria di Palazzo Bianco** (p. 560), the **Palazzo Podesta** (no. 7) features an ornate inner courtyard, and the **Palazzo Tursi** (no. 9), now partially used as municipal offices, displays artifacts of famous locals: letters written by Columbus and a Nicolo Paganini violin (still played on special occasions).

Palazzo Tursi entrance included in admission to Galleria di Palazzo Bianco; open same hours as Palazzo Bianco (p. 560). Bus: 20, 32, 33, 35, 36, 41, 42.

Where to Stay in Genoa

Despite the appeal of the aquarium and the intriguing Old Town, Genoa is still geared more toward business travelers and conference-goers. A pleasant boom of new quality accommodations has sprouted up, however, as the city becomes more tourist friendly. Keep in mind that Genoa books up solid in late September during its annual boat show, the world's largest, when hotel prices can jump as much as 25%.

APARTMENT & ROOM RENTALS If you want to feel like more of a local, self-catering apartments are definitely a great option. For example, **Virginia's Rooms** (which can be reserved via Booking.com for an average price of 120€ per night for a two-person deluxe room) are private rooms in a residential area within walking distance of the center. This property not only offers convenient parking but also modern bathrooms and colorful bedrooms with traditional furnishings.

EXPENSIVE

Hotel Bristol Palace ♥ This 19th-century *palazzo* has preserved its opulent curved staircase (legend has it that Alfred Hitchcock—twice a visitor here—found inspiration from this Art Nouveau marvel for his film *Vertigo*) and stunning stained-glass dome, establishing itself as one of Genoa's most regal hotels. The Bristol Palace's spacious rooms are continuously being updated to include modern comforts while preserving the property's old-world charm. Ristorante Giotto serves sophisticated local cuisine at lunch and dinner in a room with elegant, frescoed ceilings; an outdoor dining terrace adds even more appeal to this oasis-like lodging. In the middle of the city's shopping district and steps from Genoa's most famous museums, historic *palazzos,* and the opera house, it is surprisingly quiet and perfectly located for exploring the sights. Currently, the hotel doesn't have a gym or spa, which is sorely needed for a property of this stature, but a new wellness space is in the works.

Via XX Settembre 35. hotelbristolpalace.com. ✆ **010/592-541.** 133 units. 220€–500€ double. Rates include breakfast. **Amenities:** Restaurant; bar; babysitting; bikes; concierge; room service; free Wi-Fi.

MODERATE

Best Western Hotel Metropoli ♥♥ Located in the center of the action on one of the most beautiful squares in town, mere steps from Via Garibaldi's UNESCO-listed palaces, the Metropoli offers very good lodging with modern amenities, helpful service, and a robust breakfast buffet with local specialties like Genovese focaccia. Guest rooms are soundproof, clean, and comfortable, with refurbished bathrooms. Family rooms have bunk beds and game consoles (strollers, bottle warmers, and changing tables can also be provided for free). For travelers focused on location and clean lodgings rather than old-world charm or quiet surroundings, this hotel is a solid choice.

Piazza delle Fontane Marose. hotelmetropoli.it. ✆ **010/246-8888.** 48 units. 110€–2560€ double. Rates include breakfast. **Amenities:** Bar; room service; free Wi-Fi.

INEXPENSIVE

Hotel No Logo ♥♥ What No Logo lacks in frills, it makes up for in flair. Conveniently located near the Brignole train station, it is at the heart of a bustling neighborhood (with certain rough edges after dark, given the proximity to the train station). The property's brightly colored rooms all have music themes ("Rock," "Pop," "Reggae," "Blues"), and family rooms are big enough for up to six people. A simple breakfast buffet of coffee, tea, juice, croissants, focaccia, and fruit is offered for around 6€ per person. The second-floor terrace is a relaxing spot featuring sun loungers, a Jacuzzi, and a foosball table.

Via Sauli 5. hotelnologo.it. ✆ **010/089-8060.** 56 units. 75€–110€ double. **Amenities:** Bar; free Wi-Fi.

Ostello Bello ♥♥ Don't let the word "hostel" in the name put you off. Ostello Bello, which is near Genoa's Principe train station, is crisp and clean, offering dormitory beds in shared rooms as well as private rooms with en-suite bathrooms. The property also has a bar, a communal kitchen (guests can help themselves to free pasta, sauces, and vegetables from the rooftop garden), a large terrace with a grill, and hammocks. It has modern amenities like Wi-Fi throughout the property and USB plugs next to beds. There's also a small gym with a treadmill, a cycle, and free weights. Not only perfectly positioned for the train station, it's also a mere 10-minute walk to the city's famous alleyways and 15 minutes on foot from the Porto Antico and world-famous aquarium. An all-you-can-eat breakfast buffet—including coffee, tea, juice, cold cuts, brioches, and local focaccia—is available for 8.90€; American coffee and tea are on offer all day long. Ostello Bello has quickly made a name for itself as an expanding chain of modern hostels, with sister properties throughout Italy.

Via Balbi 38. ostellobello.com. ✆ **010/247-0800.** 25€ and up dormitory bed, 86€ and up twin room, 100€ and up triple room, 126€ and up family room. **Amenities:** Bar; luggage storage; free Wi-Fi.

FAST . . . & OH, SO good

All over Genoa you'll find shops selling **focaccia,** Liguria's answer to pizza, a thick flatbread often stuffed or topped with cheese, herbs, olives, onions, vegetables, or prosciutto. Many of these *focaccerie* also sell ***farinata,*** a chickpea fritter that usually emerges from the oven in the shape of a big round pizza. Just point and make a hand gesture to show how much you want. Prices are by weight, and in most cases a piece of either will cost about 1.50€ to 3€. Most focaccia (especially the ones with cheese) and all *farinata* are better warm, so if the piece you are getting looks like it's been there a while, ask them to warm it up (*scaldarla* in Italian).

A favorite spot for both snacks, near Stazione Principe, is **La Focacceria di Teobaldo ♥**, Via Balbi 115r (daily 8am–8pm), which also has a crunchy (*croccante*) focaccia that doesn't need to be warmed up and is great for taking on the go. In the heart of the Old Town, **Focacceria di Via Lomellini ♥**, Via Lomellini 57/59 (Mon–Sat 8am–7:30pm), has great *focaccia di Recco* (also called *focaccia al formaggio*), a super-thin focaccia filled with cheese and the specialty of the nearby town of Recco. Follow up with something sweet at **Fratelli Klainguti,** Piazza di Soziglia 98. At the Porto Antico, get your focaccia fix at **Il Localino,** Via Turati 8r (Tues–Mon 8am–8pm; closed Wed). You can also get pretty good focaccia at the **Eataly** emporium on the old port near the aquarium.

Where to Eat in Genoa

I Tre Merli ♥♥ LIGURIAN This stylish restaurant located right on the old port is all high ceilings, black-and-white columns, and exposed stone walls, in line with the local architecture. Opt for a table outside to enjoy prime views of the bustling Porto Antico. With a plethora of family-friendly attractions nearby, this spot is also a convenient choice for those travelling with children. Local seafood features heavily, in dishes such as *fritua* (fried fish, squid, and shrimp with crisp vegetables and fried sage) or Genovese-style stockfish with potatoes, black olives, and pine nuts. Pastas like cheese tortelli in a creamy walnut sauce or tiny ricotta-stuffed ravioli topped with a sea-bream ragout also pay homage to Genovese cuisine. The wood-burning oven continuously churns out thin, crispy pizzas. Vegetarians and vegans won't go hungry here. I Tre Merli also operates a small **wine bar** and *locanda* with rooms for rent in the seaside town of Camogli about 40 minutes south of Genoa (p. 572).

Calata Cattaneo 17. itremerli.it. ✆ **010/246-4416.** Main courses 16€–20€. Daily noon–3pm and 7:30–11pm.

La Cabotina ♥ GENOVESE/PIZZERIA Hidden in an alleyway (look for the sign outside advertising "vino, pizza, cucina") off Piazza delle Fontane Marose, this cozy family-run spot serves up thin, crispy pizzas, *farinata,* and abundant portions of Ligurian specialties at affordable prices. Try one of the savory tarts with herbs and cheese, "Portofino-style" spinach gnocchi, or a variety of local pastas in a walnut sauce or with pesto. The restaurant itself is quite small, and the tiny kitchen sometimes struggles to get dishes out in an orderly fashion, but the service is warm and welcoming. When the weather permits, guests can opt for a table outside along the quaint, sloping alleyway.

Vico della Loggia Spinola 6. ✆ **010/590-373.** Main courses 8€–15€. Tues–Sun noon–3pm and 7:30–10:30pm.

Trattoria della Raibetta ♥ GENOVESE Located in the maze of tiny streets not far from the port, this historic trattoria—dating back to the 1700s, making it one of the city's oldest restaurants—serves Ligurian favorites. Popular menu items include classics like *pasta al pesto* with green beans and potatoes, Genovese ravioli filled with meat and borage greens, and stuffed fried anchovies. The impressive wine list offers hundreds of labels, many of them local to the area. For a unique Genovese dessert, try the *canestrelli* shortbread cookies served with sweet Moscato wine. The atmosphere at Trattoria della Raibetta is warm and rustic, with brick archways and bright artwork. Reservations are highly recommended.

Vico Caprettari 12r. trattoriadellaraibetta.it. ✆ **010/246-8877.** Main courses 10€–22€. Tues–Sun noon–2:30pm and 7:30–10:30pm.

Entertainment & Nightlife

The Old Town, some parts of which have a gritty feel even in broad daylight, can be even more unwelcoming after dark; it's a good idea to always be aware of your surroundings and watch out for pickpockets. Late-hour prowls in this area should be confined to well-trafficked streets, such as Via San Lorenzo and Via Garibaldi. On the edges of the Old Town, good places to walk at night are around the waterfront, Piazza delle Fontane Marose, Piazza de Ferrari, and Piazza delle Erbe, where many bars and clubs are located.

Two of the most important cultural venues in Genoa include the restored **Teatro Carlo Felice** ♥, Piazza de Ferrari (operacarlofelicegenova.it; ✆ **010/538-1432**), home to Genoa's opera company, and the **Teatro Nazionale di Genova** ♥, formerly the Teatro Stabile (teatronazionalegenova.it; ✆ **010/53-421**), which hosts concerts, dance, and other programs around the city.

THE RIVIERA DI PONENTE: SAN REMO ♥♥

140km (87 miles) W of Genoa, 56km (35 miles) E of Nice

Gone are the days when Tchaikovsky and the Russian empress Maria Alexandrovna joined a well-heeled mix of *nobili* strolling along San Remo's palm-lined avenues. They left behind an onion-domed Orthodox church, a few grand hotels, and a casino, but **San Remo** is a different sort of town these days. It's still the most cosmopolitan stop on the Riviera di Ponente, as the coastal stretch west of Genoa is called, but now it caters mostly to sun-seeking Italian families in summer and, in winter, Milanese who come to escape the fog and chilly temperatures of their city.

If you've got a few extra days, base yourself in San Remo and explore farther along the coast, all the way to the French border. Train connections are good, and the coastal SS1 road links several charming towns. Highlights include the quiet resort town of **Bordighera** (12km/7½ miles west of San Remo); one of Europe's finest gardens, **Giardini Botanici Hanbury** (28km/20 miles west of San Remo, just past Ventimiglia); and the inland village of **Dolceacqua** (23km/14 miles northwest of San Remo), with its well-preserved medieval core and abandoned castle.

Essentials

ARRIVING **Trains** run hourly between San Remo and Genoa (about 2 hr.). If you're arriving by train, note that San Remo's newer rail station is a bit of a hike from the center of town and the old port. Trains from Genoa continue west for another 20 minutes to Ventimiglia on the French border. Some trains continue into France; at Ventimiglia you can change onto one of the frequent trains across the border to **Nice,** 50 minutes west.

The fastest **driving route** in and out of San Remo is Autostrada A10, which follows the coast from Genoa (about 45 min. away) to the French border (20 min. away). The slower coast road, SS1, cuts right through the center of town.

FESTIVALS Since the 1950s, the **Sanremo Festival** (mid- to late Feb; sanremo.rai.it) has been Italy's premier music fest, sort of an Italian Grammy Awards. Spread out over several days, it features live performances by Italian pop stars, international headliners, and plenty of up-and-comers. Hotels up and down the coast (and into France) get booked up months in advance.

A Day at the Beach

The pebbly strand below the **Passeggiata dell'Imperatrice** is lined with beach stations, where many visitors choose to spend their days: It's easy to linger here, because most provide showers, snack bars, beach chairs, lounges, and umbrellas. Expect to spend up to 20€ for a basic lounge and 25€ or more for a more elaborate sunbed arrangement with umbrella. ***Note:*** As is standard at most European resort towns without "public" sections of beach (which are usually not very nice anyway), you cannot go onto the beach in the main part of town without paying for at least a lounge chair in high season.

Exploring San Remo

San Remo's two main thoroughfares are **Via Roma** and **Corso Matteotti.** Corso Matteotti runs east–west between **Piazza Colombo,** with its flower market, and the **casino** (p. 567), passing through the heart of the bustling, pedestrian-only business district. Here you can shop, sit in cafes, and do a bit of Italian people-watching. Midway along Corso Matteotti, turn north on **Via Feraldi** to reach the charming older precincts of town. From **Piazza Mercato,** Via Montà leads into the medieval quarter, **La Pigna,**

San Remo's casino attests to the town's history as a fashionable resort.

set on a hill shaped like a pinecone (*la pigna* in Italian). Aside from a few restaurants, La Pigna is a residential quarter, with tall old houses overshadowing narrow lanes that twist and turn up the hillside, with the park-enclosed ruins of a **castle** at the top.

VISITING THE CASINO

San Remo's white palace of a **casino** (casinosanremo.it; ✆ **0184/5951**) is the hub of the local nightlife scene, set intimidatingly atop a long flight of steps just uphill from the old train station; Corso degli Inglesi curves up from Corso Matteotti to its entrance. You can't set foot inside without being properly attired (jacket for gents Oct–June; in general, avoid track suits, shorts, T-shirts, and flip-flops for the entire casino). You must show your passport to enter, and you must be 18 or older. Some of the poker tables start at just a few euros, but the more serious tables attract high rollers from the length of the Riviera. Gaming rooms are open 2:30pm to 2:30am (Fri–Sat 3pm–3:30am). Things are more relaxed in the rooms set aside for slot machines, where there is no real dress code. It's open Sunday to Thursday 10am to 2:30am and Friday and Saturday 10am to 3:30am.

Where to Stay & Eat in San Remo

Most restaurants and hotels in the "City of Flowers" are either along the promenade leading into town or in the streets and alleyways around the famous **Ariston Theater,** where the annual Sanremo music festival (p. 566) is held. Seafood specialties are featured in local restaurants, such as the upscale **Paolo & Barbara,** Via Roma 47, a San Remo favorite.

Hotel Villa Maria ♥♥ Originally three separate villas, this spacious, almost regal hotel recalls the golden eras of the 1920s, '30s, and '40s. Common areas lead to a nicely planted terrace. The Villa Maria offers comfort, friendly service, and a wonderful breakfast, served in the lush garden in warm weather. Perched on a hillside just above the casino, the property has a prime location near the beach and the Empress's Promenade. Room sizes and styles vary, with ongoing updates gradually modernizing the accommodations. Some rooms even feature balconies and sea views. Parking is at a premium in San Remo, so the fact that this hotel has its own lot available free to guests is a definite plus (contact the hotel ahead of time to guarantee your spot).
Corso Nuvoloni 30. villamariahotel.it. ✆ **0184/531-422.** 38 units, 2 w/shared bath. 60€–360€ double. Rates include breakfast. **Amenities:** Restaurant; concierge; room service; free Wi-Fi.

Ristorante L'Airone ♥ LIGURIAN/PIZZA In a quaint piazza halfway between the landmark Ariston Theater and the casino, this bustling restaurant serves consistently good food at decent prices. The ever-changing menu focuses on creative Mediterranean dishes—such as baked swordfish with asparagus or fish stew in a tomato and garlic broth—along with Ligurian and Italian classics like gnocchi with pesto or seafood risotto. Excellent thin-crust pizzas (gluten-free options available) are served at dinner but not always at lunch. The restaurant's decor is cute and characteristic, but tables inside can be a bit close together; in nice weather, opt for the small garden or the piazza. Reservations are recommended.
Piazza Eroi Sanremesi 12. ristorantelairone.it. ✆ **0184/531-469.** Main courses 12€–23€. Fri 7:30–11:30pm, Sat–Wed noon–2:30pm and 7:30–11:30pm.

Royal Hotel ♥♥♥ This sprawling, centuries-old seafront retreat on the edge of Old Town mixes timeless charm and luxury, boasting impeccable service. Many of the tastefully decorated rooms come with sea views. Along with the five-star designation, however, come jaw-dropping prices, even in the off-season. Families traveling in the warmer months will appreciate the kids' club, where children can play while parents relax or take advantage of the many activities on offer. The modern wellness center is an oasis of calm, and the outdoor pool—originally designed in 1948 by famed architect Giò Ponti but recently renovated—is the centerpiece of the spectacular gardens. The main restaurant serves seasonal cuisine from around the Mediterranean, with fusion influences; breakfast is particularly abundant. A new lounge bar in the lobby is a sophisticated space for enjoying creative cocktails with amazing sea views. The hotel closes for a few months in late fall and winter, usually reopening in mid-February.
Corso Imperatrice 80. royalhotelsanremo.com. ✆ **0184/5391.** 126 units. 354€–3,099€ double. Rates include breakfast. **Amenities:** 3 restaurants; 2 bars; saltwater pool; spa; babysitting; kid's club; concierge; 24-hr. room service; free Wi-Fi.

THE RIVIERA DI LEVANTE: CAMOGLI, SANTA MARGHERITA LIGURE & PORTOFINO ♥♥

Camogli: 26km (16 miles) E of Genoa; Santa Margherita Ligure: 31km (19 miles) E of Genoa; Portofino: 38km (24 miles) E of Genoa; Rapallo: 37km (23 miles) E of Genoa

Hugged by mountains that plunge into the sapphire-colored seas, the coast east of Genoa, the **Riviera di Levante** (Riviera of the Rising Sun), is more ruggedly beautiful and less developed than the Riviera Ponente. Three of the coast's most appealing towns are within a few kilometers of one another, clinging to the shores of the Monte Portofino Promontory east of Genoa: **Camogli, Santa Margherita Ligure,** and minute **Portofino.**

Essentials

ARRIVING One to three **trains** per hour ply the coastline, connecting Genoa with Santa Margherita (25–30 min.) and Camogli (30–45 min.); the trip between Camogli and Santa Margherita takes 5 minutes by train. To get to **Portofino,** take the train to Santa Margherita and then take a taxi or bus 782 (amt.genova.it; ✆ **848-000-030**), a 25-minute ride via a beautiful coastal road (bus service every 30 min. to 1 hr.). The one-way fare is 5€—buy it at any newsstand or the IAT office in Piazza Vittorio Veneto. Some buses and bus stops now have a credit-card reader, making purchasing tickets easier, but it's better to try to buy ahead of time.

In summer, **boats** operated by **Golfo Paradiso** (golfoparadiso.it; ✆ **0185/772-091;** round-trip tickets 6€–35€ depending on route) run from Camogli to Portofino and Genoa. **Tigullio ferries** (traghettiportofino.it; ✆ **0185/284-670**) make hourly trips from Santa Margherita to Portofino (15 min.; 16€ round-trip). In summer, a boat runs several days a week to the Cinque Terre (30€–45€). Hours of service vary considerably with the season; schedules are posted on the docks at Piazza Martiri della Libertà.

The fastest **car** route into the region is Autostrada A12 from Genoa (exit at Recco for Camogli), which takes about 40 minutes to either Camogli or Santa Margherita. Route SS1 along the coast from Genoa is much slower but more scenic. ***Note:*** Parking is a challenge in Camogli and Portofino in the summer, and traffic quickly gets clogged on the tiny road between Santa Margherita and Portofino. If you're coming by car, park in Santa Margherita and take the bus or boat to Portofino.

VISITOR INFORMATION Camogli's tourist office is across from the train station at Via XX Settembre 33 (welcomecamogli.it; ✆ **0185/771-066**). In Santa Margherita, the tourist office is in Piazza Vittorio Veneto (livesanta.it; ✆ **0185/287-485**). The Portofino tourist office is at Via Roma 35 (✆ **0185/269-024**). All are open daily in summer (Portofino's office is closed Mon); expect shorter hours in winter, and a lunchtime closure between noon and 3pm.

Camogli ♥

Camogli remains delightfully unspoiled, an authentic Ligurian fishing port with tall houses in pastel colors facing the harbor and a nice swath of beach. Given its excellent accommodations and eateries, Camogli is a lovely base for exploring the Riviera Levante. It's also a restful retreat from which to visit Genoa, which is only 30 minutes away. Some say Camogli's name comes from Genovese dialect and means "low lands." Others say it is derived from *"Ca de Mogge,"* or "House of the Wives" in the local dialect, so-named for the women who held down the fort while their husbands went to sea. Another possibility is that it comes from *"Ca a Muggi,"* or "clustered houses"—particularly apt when you're out swimming in the sea and turn to look up at the town's wonderful mass of colorful buildings.

EXPLORING CAMOGLI

Camogli is clustered around its delightful waterfront, from which the town ascends via steep, staircased lanes to Via XX Settembre, one of the few streets in the town proper to accommodate cars (the train station, tourist office, and many shops and other businesses are all here). Most visitors are drawn to the pleasant **seaside promenade** ♥ that runs the length of the town. You can swim from the pebbly beach below, and you can rent a lounge chair from one of the few beach stations for at least 20€—highly recommended in the summer months, when finding even a small piece of pebbly sand is nearly impossible.

The oldest part of Camogli juts into the harbor on a picturesque point (once an island). Here, ancient houses cluster around the little **Castello del Dragone** and the **Basilica di Santa Maria Assunta** (✆ **0185/770-130**), originally built in the 12th century but much altered through the ages; its dramatic baroque interior is open daily 7:30am to noon and 3:30 to 7pm.

WHERE TO STAY & EAT IN CAMOGLI

Hotel Cenobio dei Dogi ♥♥ Beautifully manicured grounds, old-world charm, and an incredible location right in the heart of Camogli

Getting Festive in Camogli

Camogli throws a well-attended annual party, the **Sagra del Pesce** ♥♥, on the second Sunday of May, when the town fries up thousands of sardines in a 3.6m-diameter (12-ft.) pan and passes them around for free.

The first Sunday of August, Camogli stages the lovely **Festa della Stella Maris** ♥, during which a procession of boats sails to Punta Chiappa, a spot of land about 1.5km (1 mile) down the coast, and releases 10,000 burning candles. Meanwhile, the same number of candles is set afloat from the Camogli beach. If currents are favorable, the burning candles will come together at sea, signifying a year of unity for couples who watch the spectacle.

Sweeping views of Camogli's seafront from a terrace at the Hotel Cenobio dei Dogi.

make this one of the most sought-after (and priciest) hotels along the Riviera Levante. The sweeping views over the Gulf of Camogli don't hurt either—make sure to grab a meal or a drink at one of the property's seaside restaurant terraces, which serve creative Ligurian cuisine. Watching the sun set from this spot is nothing short of magical. For a special occasion, you can even ask for a romantic "table for two on the pier." Rooms vary in shape and size but are tastefully decorated in neutral whites and beiges along with classic furnishings. The heated saltwater pool is especially inviting, as is the private beach of terraced stone and pebbles. The small but welcoming **Doge Beauty Spa** offers manicures, pedicures, facials, waxing, and various massages.

Via Cuneo 34. www.cenobio.it. ✆ **0185/7241.** 108 units. 200€–550€ double. Rates include breakfast and beach facilities. Free parking. **Amenities:** 3 restaurants; 1 bar; babysitting; concierge; outdoor saltwater pool; tennis courts; watersports rentals; free Wi-Fi.

La Camogliese ♥♥ What La Camogliese lacks in frills, it makes up for in location and friendly service. This affordable, family-run hotel is conveniently located at the end of the promenade, near the entrance to the old village, offering easy access to the beach as well as the nearby bus and train stations. Its large, bright rooms have simple furniture and comfortable beds; a few have balconies with partial sea views (the best views are from rooms 3 and 16B). Some bathrooms are small even by Italian standards, but they have everything you need. The property also has a few apartments with kitchenettes (daily cleaning and breakfast not included in rates). This hotel fills up fast, especially on weekends and in the summer, so book early. There's a restaurant of the same name nearby on the promenade, but the two businesses are not related.

Via Garibaldi 55. lacamogliese.it. ✆ **0185/771-402.** 21 units. 95€–160€ double. Rates include breakfast. 2- to 4-night required min. stay. **Amenities:** Babysitting; concierge; exercise room; room service; free Wi-Fi.

Locanda I Tre Merli ♥ This tiny property right on Camogli's charming harbor is part wine bar and part guesthouse, with five cozy, brightly colored rooms, each of which has views over the water. In warm weather, breakfast—freshly baked focaccia, yogurt, and other sweet and savory options—is served outside, offering a slice of true Italian seaside life, with fishermen unloading the day's catch and small children playing along the walkway. Ferries for Portofino, Genoa, and the Cinque Terre leave right from the port outside. The property has a compact wellness area with a hot tub overlooking the port and a Turkish bath with chromotherapy features. It is possible to rent out the entire space (for a small surcharge) and be provided with robes, slippers, and a special amenity kit. The staff can also set up massages at additional cost.

Via Scalo 5. locandaitremerli.com. ✆ **0185/776-752.** 5 units. 140€–275€ double. Rates include breakfast. **Amenities:** Bar; free Wi-Fi.

Osteria Xodò ♥ RESTAURANT Boasting a prime position along the *lungomare* (promenade), Xodò is a solid osteria turning out dependable Ligurian favorites. The small indoor dining room is homey and unpretentious, but try to sit outside if at all possible, to enjoy stunning views of the beach, the boats, and the nearby Church of Santa Maria Assunta. Typical dishes include Genovese fried anchovies, codfish-stuffed ravioli topped with an olive-pignoli sauce, and tuna steak served on arugula pesto. Finish a meal with Xodò's classic tiramisu. It's one of the better spots on the waterfront for honest, satisfying food with prices that won't break the bank.

Via Garibaldi 164. ✆ **0185/771-682.** Main courses 10€–25€. Thurs–Tues noon–3pm and 7pm–midnight. Closed Wed.

Vento Ariel ♥♥ SEAFOOD This rustic waterfront restaurant can be found just past the medieval archway leading from the main part of town to the old port. The charming location, with outdoor tables mere feet from the *gozzi* (traditional fishing boats), is nearly as impressive as the cuisine. Succulent seafood specialties include mussels in a spicy tomato sauce, "sea-to-table" *acciughe* (anchovies served in a variety of ways—with lemon juice, fried, or in a sweet-and-sour sauce), and homemade squid-ink gnocchi with crispy sautéed calamari, cherry tomatoes, and basil. The wine list is extensive and contains some local, hard-to-find bottles of Pigato along with other wonderful whites from around Liguria. Grab a table outside to take in the bustle of the port and breathe in the sea air. Reservations are highly recommended.

Calata Porticciolo 1. ventoariel.it. ✆ **0185/771-080.** Main courses 13€–25€. Daily noon–2:30pm and 8–11pm.

Santa Margherita Ligure ♥

Santa Margherita had one brief moment in the spotlight at the beginning of the 20th century, when it was an internationally renowned resort. Fortunately, the seaside town didn't let fame spoil its charm, and now that it's no longer as well-known as its glitzy neighbor Portofino, it could be the Mediterranean retreat of your dreams. A palm-lined harbor, a decent beach, and a friendly ambience make Santa Margherita a fine place to settle down for a few days of sun and relaxation.

EXPLORING SANTA MARGHERITA

Life in Santa Margherita centers on its palm-fringed **waterfront,** a pleasant string of marinas, docks for pleasure and fishing boats, and pebbly beaches, in some spots with imported sand of passable quality. Landlubbers congregate in the cafes that spill out into the town's two seaside squares, Piazza Martiri della Libertà and Piazza Vittorio Veneto.

The train station is above the waterfront, with a staircase in front of the entrance leading down into the heart of town. Santa Margherita's landmark of note is its namesake **Basilica di Santa Margherita** (daily 7:30am–noon and 3–6:30pm), on Piazza Caprera. It's well worth a visit to view the church's extravagant, gilded, chandeliered interior.

One of the more interesting daily spectacles in town is the **fish market** on Lungomare Marconi from 8am to 12:30pm. On Friday, Corso Matteotti, Santa Margherita's major street for food shopping, becomes an open-air **food market.**

WHERE TO STAY & EAT IN SANTA MARGHERITA LIGURE

Grand Hotel Miramare ♥♥♥ An impressive example of Art Nouveau architecture, this once-private villa is pure Riviera elegance. The Grand Hotel Miramare—known merely as "Mira" to those who frequent it—serves as a luxurious gateway to the Portofino Peninsula, and is positioned just beyond the heart of Santa Margherita Ligure (less than 10 min. away on foot). Every single room is said to have a history, but the large guest rooms still feel quite contemporary. Most have parquet floors,

Focaccia by the Seaside

It might be the perfect seaside setting, or perhaps there is something in the water, but no matter the reason, Camogli has some of the best focaccia in all of Liguria. Along Via Garibaldi, the promenade above the beach, there are many *focaccerie* to choose from. It's hard to go wrong with any of them, but one standout is family-run **Revello ♥** (revellocamogli.com; daily 10am–6pm, later in summer), at no. 183 (closest to the church), which has been serving up focaccia since 1964. Make sure to try their signature Camogliesi sweets, which are round choux pastries filled with everything from rum to cream to hazelnut and chocolate. You can enjoy your loot on the beach or on one of the many benches with sea views.

antique rugs, and charming stucco decorations on the walls and ceilings. Fifth-floor suites are larger, a bit more modern, and have balconies overlooking the Gulf of Tigullio. A lovely (but steep) park with terraced gardens rises behind the hotel toward Mount Portofino; it includes a pleasant hiking trail to Portofino with fantastic views of land and sea. You can relax at the small, private pebble beach, hit the state-of-the-art fitness center, or opt for a beauty or wellness treatment in the spa. Valet parking costs 50€ a day; reserve ahead of time, as space is limited.

Via Milite Ignoto 30. grandhotelmiramare.it. ✆ **0185/287-013.** 72 units. 265€–650€ double. Rates include breakfast. **Amenities:** 2 restaurants; 2 bars; babysitting; concierge; outdoor saltwater pool; room service; spa; watersports rentals; free Wi-Fi.

Hotel Metropole ♥♥ Set on a hill, with impressively landscaped gardens running down to the sea, this popular family-run hotel (now in its fifth generation) is at the beginning of Santa Margherita's promenade and a 5-minute stroll from the town center. Some accommodations are in the modern main building, while others are in the more appealing Villa Porticciolo, a dusty-red manor house right on the beach; rooms in the villa are smaller, but they're graced with 19th-century stuccoes and hand-carved furniture, and the sea practically laps up against the building. Some standard rooms in both buildings have small bathrooms and could use an

AN excursion TO SAN FRUTTUOSO

Much of the **Monte Portofino Promontory** can be approached only on foot or by boat (see below), making it a prime destination for hikers. Arm yourself with a map from the tourist offices in Camogli, Santa Margherita Ligure, Portofino, or Rapallo, and set out. You can explore the upper reaches of the promontory or aim for the **Abbazia di San Fruttuoso** (✆ **0185/772-703**), a medieval abbey surrounded by a tiny six-house hamlet and two beaches. It is at least a 90-minute hike from Portofino.

Once you reach San Fruttuoso, you may want to relax on the pebbly beach and enjoy a beverage or meal at a seaside bar. You can tour the stark interior of the abbey for 9€ (June to mid-Sept daily 10am–5:45pm, May Tues–Sun 10am–5:45pm, Mar–Apr and Oct Tues–Sun 10am–3:30pm, Nov–Feb Sat–Sun 10am–3:45pm). Despite these official hours, the abbey tends to close whenever the last boat leaves. Should you have scuba or snorkeling gear, you can take the plunge to visit **Christ of the Abyss,** a statue of Jesus erected 15m (49 ft.) underwater to honor sailors lost at sea. There are also boats that will take you close enough to view it from the surface.

In summer, boats to San Fruttuoso run almost every hour from Camogli (contact **Golfo Paradiso:** golfoparadiso.it; ✆ **0185/772-091**); a round trip costs 16€ (10€ one-way) and takes about 30 minutes. You can also get a boat from Portofino (10€–15€ round-trip), Santa Margherita (13€–10€ round-trip), or Rapallo (15€–22€ round-trip) with **Tigullio boats** (traghettiportofino.it; ✆ **0185/284-670**). Bear in mind that the seas are often too choppy to dock at San Fruttuoso; smaller private boats can be hired that are better suited to bad-weather landings, but these are expensive—from Portofino, you will likely be charged at least 100€ for up to 12 people.

update. Other amenities include a small private beach, a sunbathing terrace, a kids' club, and a private boat launch. An indoor swimming pool and wellness center make this property a good option year-round. The beach club restaurant serves typical Ligurian cuisine as well as dishes with international flair. The hotel has a secluded resort-like feel while still being close to everything. Parking is available for 30€ per day.
Via Pagana 2. metropole.it. ✆ **0185/286-134.** 57 units. 150€–425€ double. Rates include breakfast. **Amenities:** 2 restaurants; bar; babysitting; exercise room; indoor pool; sauna; watersports rentals; free Wi-Fi.

La Paranza ♥♥ GENOVESE/LIGURIAN Popular with tourists and locals alike, this light, bright, family-run restaurant near the port has a glass-enclosed veranda that offers partial views of the promenade and the sea. The menu includes Ligurian favorites like pasta with pesto or walnut sauce, but seafood is the star of the show, with tasty dishes like *bianchetti fritti* (fried baby sardines), Santa Margherita prawns, or grilled-to-perfection fresh lobster. There is also a raw fish menu. This is also a cozy spot for an *aperitivo* before dinner—stop in for a spritz and creative appetizers.
Via Jacopo Ruffini 46. laparanzasantamargherita.it. ✆ **0185/283-686.** Main courses 20€–35€. Daily 12:30–2:20pm and 7:30–10:30pm. Closed Nov.

Portofino ♥♥♥

Portofino is almost too beautiful for its own good. In practically any season, you'll be sharing Portofino's harborside quays with day-trippers, Italian industrialists, international celebrities, and rich-but-not-so-famous folks who consider this little town the epicenter of the good life. But if you make an appearance in the late afternoon when the promenades begin to empty a bit, you are sure to experience what remains so appealing about this enchanting place—its indelible beauty.

EXPLORING PORTOFINO

The one thing in Portofino that won't break the bank is the spectacular scenery. Begin with a stroll around the glamorous main square (the famed *piazzetta*) and stunning **harbor,** lined with expensive boutiques, eateries, and colorful houses.

A 10-minute scenic walk along a well-signposted path from the west side of town, just behind the harbor, takes you uphill to the **Chiesa di San Giorgio** (open daily 9am–7pm), built on the site of a sanctuary Roman soldiers dedicated to the Persian god Mithras. From there, continue uphill a few minutes more to Portofino's 15th-century **Castello Brown** (castellobrown.com; ✆ **375/791-8926**), which has a lush garden and great views of the town below. The castle is very popular for private events and is not always open to the public—check the website or call beforehand. For more scenic views of this stretch of coast, go even higher up through lovely pine forests to the ***faro*** (lighthouse).

From Portofino, you can set out for a longer hike on paths that cross the **Monte Portofino Promontory** to the Abbazia di San Fruttuoso (see "An Excursion to San Fruttuoso," p. 574). The tourist office provides maps.

Colorful, exclusive Portofino.

WHERE TO STAY & EAT IN PORTOFINO

Portofino's charms come at a price. Its few hotels are expensive enough to put them in the "trip of a lifetime" category, and the harborside restaurants can take a serious chunk out of a vacation budget. An alternative strategy is to enjoy a light snack at a bar or one of the many shops selling focaccia and wait to dine in Santa Margherita or one of the other nearby towns.

Belmond Hotel Splendido ♥♥♥ Perched on a hill in the heart of Portofino, this former monastery turned five-star hotel has been the Riviera's top resort for more than a century. Nearly all the guest rooms, including 35 suites, have balconies with scintillating views across the picturesque harbor. **La Terrazza,** the property's gourmet dining destination, features seasonal regional cuisine and a wisteria-covered terrace with breathtaking bay views (the **Pool Grill** is a more casual dining option). The hotel can set up a variety of local experiences, from a visit to an eco-farm, including a luxurious picnic overlooking the sea, to a night kayaking trip to Portofino's famous lighthouse. The Splendido's sister hotel, the **Belmond Hotel Mare,** is closer to the water and more intimate, with just 14 rooms, some of which offer views of the harbor and famous *piazzetta,* and two magnificent suites. The **Villa Beatrice,** another Belmond offshoot in Portofino, is a stunning historic cliffside retreat with a select number of suites and its own private butler. Be warned: All of this luxury comes at a price.

Salita Baratta 16. hotelsplendido.com. ✆ **0185/267-801.** 67 units. 600€–5,000€ double. Rates include breakfast. Closed mid-Nov to Apr. **Amenities:** 3 restaurants; piano bar; concierge; room service; wellness center; saltwater pool; tennis court; access to hotel's motorboat; free Wi-Fi.

Hotel Nazionale ♥♥ It isn't often that a hotel has the best spot in town—in this case, right on Portofino's famous square—and is relatively affordable. The rooms at this family-run property are clean and unfussy, but you are right on the harbor and paying less than most of the other options in the village. Several rooms are loft suites with bedrooms upstairs; we highly recommend splurging for one of the five junior suites, as they are a bit more colorful and offer harbor views. Breakfast is quite basic, but it is served on the wonderful veranda in warm weather. The hotel has no elevator, but luggage service is provided. The in-house restaurant, **Da Nicola,** offers delightful views of the *piazzetta* and water; it serves Ligurian standards and pizza, but the food is not particularly memorable.

Via Roma 8. nazionaleportofino.com. ✆ **0185/269-575.** 12 units. 200€–400€ double. Rates include breakfast. Closed mid-Dec to Mar. **Amenities:** Restaurant; bar; concierge; room service; free Wi-Fi.

Ristorante Puny ♥♥ LIGURIAN Although the famously gregarious "Puny" (owner Luigi Miroli) has passed away, his son still runs this harborfront restaurant, a longtime haunt of well-heeled locals and tourists (it's a favorite of Madonna and the Kardashians). Recently reopened after an extensive renovation, the restaurant has a fresh new look while remaining true to its culinary traditions. People go wild for the *pappardelle al Portofino* (large flat noodles served with a mix of tomato and pesto sauce), but fresh seafood is also a Puny trademark—try the heavenly *pesce al*

RIVIERA runners-up

While Portofino and the Cinque Terre get their accolades, it would be a shame to overlook some other lovely seaside destinations that also make a great base for exploring the area. When the Cinque Terre is drowning in tourists (a common occurrence in summer), these alternatives offer as much beauty, a bit more breathing room, and more options in terms of accommodations.

Set on opposites sides of the stunning Gulf of Poets lie the picturesque seaside medieval villages of **Portovenere** (tourist info portovenere.com) and **Lerici** (tourist info lericicoast.it; ✆ **0187/960-700**). Once archrivals—Portovenere belonged to Genoa and Lerici to Pisa—both built imposing fortresses to protect themselves from the enemy (and pirates). These incredible edifices still remain, along with charming, colorful homes backing up to olive tree–covered hills. The beautiful harbors hold local fishing boats and yachts, and a spectacular ferry ride will get you to the Cinque Terre from either in less than an hour.

To the north of the Cinque Terre and only a 5-minute train ride from Monterosso, the sunny seaside town of **Levanto** (tourist info visitlevanto.it; ✆ **0187/808-125**) has a large sand beach, lovely historic center, and lodging options ranging from campsites to four-star hotels. Heading west on the coast toward Santa Margherita Ligure, you'll also find nice beaches and colorful town centers at **Bonassola, Moneglia,** and **Sestri Levanto** (tourist info sestri-levante.net; ✆ **0185/478-530**). The beach along Sestri's breathtaking "Bay of Silence" is considered one of Italy's most beautiful strands.

forno baked in bay leaves, the famed *orata alla Genovese* (sea bream served Genovese-style with potatoes), or the curried rice with peas and shrimp. Be prepared to pay for the location, view, food, and being part of the scene. Given its popularity, this isn't a place to linger—expect to leave your table once you are done. Reservations are mandatory and can only be made by phone.

Piazza Martiri dell'Olivetta 5. ristorantepunyportofino.com. ✆ **0185/269-037.** Main courses 25€–50€. Fri–Wed 12:30–3:30pm and 7:30–11pm. Closed Jan–Feb.

THE CINQUE TERRE ♥♥♥

Monterosso: 93km (58 miles) E of Genoa

Rocky coves, dramatic cliffs, and Apennine ridges are the spectacular backdrop to the Cinque Terre (Five Lands), a region that consists of five fishing and wine-making villages dramatically perched along an 11-mile stretch of Italy's Ligurian coast. Terraced vineyards and olive groves climb slopes that are largely inaccessible by road but have become a hiker's haven, stretching southeast from Monterosso al Mare to Vernazza, Corniglia, Manarola, and Riomaggiore.

Not too surprisingly, these charms have not gone unnoticed. From May to October (weekends are worst), you are likely to find yourself in a long procession of like-minded, non-Italian-speaking trekkers making their way down the coast, including day-trippers from cruise ships. Two of the most popular trails now require you to buy a ticket during high season from about late March until November.

Essentials

ARRIVING Cinque Terre towns are served by local **trains.** Coming from Florence or Rome, you will likely have to change trains in nearby La Spezia, which has one or two local trains per hour. From Pisa, about six daily trains travel to La Spezia (1¼ hr.); from Genoa, there are a couple of trains per hour to the main town of Monterosso (takes about 90 min.). Some trains continue on to the other towns like Vernazza or Corniglia; you can also often transfer to the other villages from Monterosso, which is sort of the hub of the Cinque Terre.

The fastest **driving** route is via Autostrada A12 from Genoa. Get off at the Corrodano/Levanto exit for Monterosso. The drive from Genoa to Corrodano takes less than an hour, while the much shorter 15km (9¼-mile) trip from Corrodano to Monterosso (via Levanto) follows a narrow road and can take half an hour. Coming from the south or Florence, get off Autostrada A12 at La Spezia and follow CINQUE TERRE signs.

Navigazione Golfo dei Poeti (navigazionegolfodeipoeti.it; ✆ **0187/732-987**) runs a **ferry service** from the Riviera Levante towns, April to November, though these tend to be day cruises stopping for anywhere from 1 to 3 hours in Vernazza before returning.

GETTING AROUND Local **trains** make frequent runs (two or three per hour) between the five towns; some stop only in Monterosso and Riomaggiore, so check the posted *partenze* schedule at the station first to be sure you're catching the right one. One-way tickets (from around 5€–10€) between any two towns are available, and there is special pricing for children. It takes about 5 minutes to go from town to town.

From the port in Monterosso, **Navigazione Golfo dei Poeti** (navigazionegolfodeipoeti.it; ✆ **0187/732-987**) makes 8 to 10 **boat runs** a day between Monterosso and Riomaggiore (a 25-min. trip), all stopping in Vernazza and half of them stopping in Manarola as well. A daily pass for all of the Cinque Terre is 42€ (afternoon pass 28€), so you can ride as often as you like over the course of a day. Children 6 to 11 get a bit of a discount depending on the ticket. One-way tickets tend to cost 5€ to 15€, so decide how many trips you'll be taking before buying the pass.

A narrow, one-lane coast road hugs the mountainside above the towns, but all the towns' centers are closed to cars. **Parking** is difficult and, where available, expensive. Some people park along the side of the road, and there are areas where parking is free for a few hours (you will need a "parking disk" to show the time you arrived), but if you overstay your time, you risk a hefty fine. Riomaggiore and Manarola both have small public parking facilities just above their towns and, at times, minibuses to carry you into the center. In Monterosso, try to find a spot in the Loreto garage, located where Strada Provinciale 38 meets Via Roma just outside the pedestrian zone (there's another lot in an area of town called Fegina, but it's farther away); it costs 2.50€ per hour or 25€ per day, though prices go down for longer stays and are somewhat cheaper in the off-season (Nov–Mar).

VISITOR INFORMATION The Cinque Terre **tourist office** is underneath the train station of Monterosso, Via Fegina 38 (prolocomonterosso.it). It's open Easter through September daily 9am to 5pm; hours are reduced the rest of the year. Even when it's closed, there's usually a display of phone numbers and other information, from hotels to ferries, posted outside.

Useful websites for the region include **cinqueterre.it** and **parconazionale5terre.it**. Both sites are especially helpful in getting updated information about which trails are open, and which may be closed for maintenance or because of landslides or bad weather.

Exploring the Cinque Terre

Aside from swimming and soaking in the atmosphere of unspoiled fishing villages, the most popular activity in the Cinque Terre is **hiking from one village to the next ♥♥♥** along centuries-old goat paths, which are now maintained as a national park (see "The Cinque Terre Card," p. 580); two of the five trails require payment during high season. Trails plunge through

The Cinque Terre Card

Rules change year to year and depend upon the crowds, but if you plan to hike most or all of the trails of the Cinque Terre National Park, it is a good idea to purchase a **Cinque Terre Card,** available at welcome centers in each town. The **Cinque Terre Trekking Card** (15€ in high season, 7.50€ in low season; children 11 and under 9€ in high season, 4.50€ in low season) offers 1-day access to all of the trails, along with free use of pay bathrooms along the trails, bus service between towns, reduced-price admission to local museums, and use of Wi-Fi at public hotspots. The **Cinque Terre Treno Card** (20€–32€ for adults depending on the season, 12.50€–21€ for children 11 and under) offers all of the above plus unlimited second-class train travel between towns. If you only plan to hike one or two trails and return by train, it may be better to just pay for an individual town-to-town ticket, which averages around 2.70€. Train ticket prices go up during high season, so the Treno card typically is a better deal from March to November. Information about trail access changes frequently. Consult parconazionale5terre.it for the latest updates.

vineyards and groves of olive and lemon trees, hugging seaside cliffs and affording heart-stopping views of the coast and romantic little villages in the distance. The well-signposted walks from village to village range in difficulty and length, but as a loose rule, they get longer and steeper—and more rewarding—the farther north you go.

Depending on your pace, and not including eventual stops for focaccia and *Sciacchetrà,* the local sweet wine, you can make the trip between **Monterosso,** at the northern end of the Cinque Terre, and **Riomaggiore,** at the southern end, in about 4½ hours. You should decide whether you want to walk north to south or south to north. Walking south means tackling the hardest trail first, which you may prefer, because you'll get it out of the way and things will get easier as the day goes on. Heading north, the trail gets progressively harder between towns—a route you might prefer if you want to walk just until you tire and then hop on the train.

The walk from **Monterosso to Vernazza** is the most arduous and takes 1½ hours, on a trail that makes several steep ascents and descents (on the portion outside Monterosso, you'll pass beneath funicular-like cars that transport grapes down the steep hillsides). The leg from **Vernazza to Corniglia** is also demanding and takes another 1½ hours, plunging into some dense forests and involving some lengthy ascents, but it's probably the prettiest and most rewarding stretch. Part of the path between **Corniglia** and **Manarola,** about 45 minutes apart, follows a level grade above a long stretch of beach, tempting you to break stride and take a dip. From **Manarola** to **Riomaggiore,** it's easy going for about half an hour along a partially paved path known as the Via dell'Amore, so named for its romantic vistas (great at sunset).

The Via dell'Amore, a popular section of the Cinque Terre's network of walking paths, connects Manarola and Riomaggiore.

Because all the villages are linked by rail, you can hike as many portions of the itinerary as you wish and take the train (or a ferry) to your next destination. Trails also cut through the forested, hilly terrain inland from the coast, much of which is protected as a nature preserve. The tourist office in Monterosso can provide maps.

Monterosso ♥♥♥ The Cinque Terre's largest village seems incredibly busy compared to its neighbors, but it's not without its charms. Monterosso is actually two towns—a bustling, character-filled Old Town behind the harbor, and a relaxed resort that stretches west along the Cinque Terre's only **sand beach,** with the train station and regional tourist office nearby. Upon exiting the station, turn left and head through the tunnel for the Old Town; turn right for the newer town. You will find more modern conveniences in Monterosso, compared to the "rustic" experience of the other four villages. The region's most famous art treasure is in Monterosso's Old Town, in the **Convento dei Cappuccini** (daily 9am–noon and 4–7pm): a *Crucifixion* attributed to Anthony van Dyck, the Flemish master who worked for a time in nearby Genoa.

Vernazza ♥♥♥ Vernazza may just be the quintessential postcard-perfect seaside village. Tall, colorful houses (known as *terratetti*) cluster around a natural harbor, where you can swim among the fishing boats; above them a castle stands high atop a rocky promontory that juts into the sea (the **Doria Castle,** which is nothing special, though it offers great views; admission 2€; Mar–Oct daily 10am–6:30pm). The center of town is waterside **Piazza Marconi,** itself a sea of cafe tables. The only Vernazza drawback is that too much good press has turned it into the Cinque Terre's magnet for tourists from around the world.

Corniglia ♥ Midway down the coast, the quietest village in the Cinque Terre is isolated by its hilltop location, high above the open sea and the

Vernazza was built around a natural harbor.

hard-to-access harbor. Whether you arrive by boat or the trail from the south, you'll have to climb some 300 steps to reach the village proper (arriving by trail from the north is the one way to avoid these stairs), an enticing maze of little walkways shadowed by tall houses. (A shuttle bus runs from the train station to the town.) Once there, though, the views over the surrounding vineyards and up and down the coastline are stupendous—for the best outlook, walk to the end of the narrow main street to a belvedere that seems perched between sea and sky. Corniglia is the village most likely to offer a glimpse of Cinque Terre life as it was decades ago.

Manarola ♥ Manarola is a near-vertical cluster of tall houses that seem to rise piggyback up the hills on either side of the harbor. In a region with no shortage of heart-stopping views, one of the most amazing sights is the descent into Manarola on the path from Corniglia: From this perspective, the hill-climbing houses seem to merge into one another to form a row of skyscrapers. Despite that urban illusion, Manarola is a delightfully rural village where fishing and winemaking are big business. The region's major **wine cooperative,** Cooperativa Agricoltura di Riomaggiore, Manarola, Corniglia, Vernazza e Monterosso, made up of 300 local producers, is here; check cantinacinqueterre.com or call ✆ **0187/920-435** for information about tours of its modern (est. 1982) facilities or walking tours of the vineyards. Try to reserve at least 3 days before your visit. You can also pop into the cantina during opening hours to buy local wines directly from the source.

Riomaggiore ♥ Riomaggiore clings to the rustic ways of the Cinque Terre while making some (unfortunate) concessions to the modern world. As the old fishing quarter has expanded in recent years, Riomaggiore now has some sections of new houses and apartment blocks. The village center still looks like something from 50 years ago, bustling and prosperous in a charming setting, while the "new side" of town feels like a halfhearted effort to maintain the old, mostly in terms of color. From the parking garage, follow the main street down; from the train station, exit and turn right to head through the tunnel for the central part of town (or, from the station, take off left up the brick stairs to walk the Via dell'Amore to Manarola). That tunnel and the main drag meet at the base of an elevated terrace that holds the train tracks; from there, a staircase leads down to a tiny fishing harbor. To the left of the harbor, a rambling path leads to a pleasant little **beach** of large pebbles.

Where to Stay in the Cinque Terre

If you'd like to base yourself nearby but not technically in the five Cinque Terre villages, reasonably priced options are available in Portovenere (see "Riviera Runners-Up," p. 577), offering easy access to all of the Cinque Terre via boat. For example, **La Calata,** Via Capellini 57 (affittacamerelacalata.com; ✆ **380/450-9997**), is a small B&B right in the heart of town (and very close to the ferry port) renting out double, triple, and quadruple rooms with private bathrooms starting at around 95€. All rooms have sea views.

APARTMENT & ROOM RENTALS

There have always been quite a few *affittacamere* (room rentals) in the various Cinque Terre towns, but getting information on them meant having local contacts and relying on word of mouth. Now that local room and apartment owners have gotten more Internet savvy, finding rentals online has become much easier, even aside from **Airbnb.com**, which does have many listings in each of the five towns. For a room with private bathroom for two people, expect to pay anywhere from 70€ to 150€ per night depending on the season and the amenities offered. **Albergo Barbara** (albergobarbara.it) in Vernazza has clean rooms and apartments to rent—some with harbor views—but they are on the third and fourth floor of a building without an elevator, so keep that in mind before booking.

Hilltop balconies at La Torretta treat guests with lofty views of Manarola and the Ligurian Sea.

MANAROLA

La Torretta ♥♥♥ Located in an ancient tower in the center of Manarola, this charming "boutique lodge" has chic flair. A selection of lovely rooms and suites mix contemporary and traditional furnishings along with quirky details and boldly patterned wallpapers and textiles. Several rooms have sea or vineyard views and balconies, and all have nice in-room amenities, such as Nespresso machines, charging stations, luxurious toiletries, and a selection of wines. Our favorite rooms are the Design Suite in the main building and the Panoramic Suite in the annex, just a short walk from the main building. For the ultimate indulgence, opt for the two-bedroom tower suite with exposed stone walls and a stunning private terrace perched over the sea. Despite the fairly steep prices (and hilltop site), rooms book up quickly in high season, so reserve way ahead of time. This level of luxury includes a luggage transfer service from the town gate so guests don't have to lug their own bags up the hill. Breakfast is served on a panoramic terrace (*aperitivo* is often offered here as well).
Vico Volto 20, Manarola. torrettas.com. ✆ **0187/920-327.** 12 units. 400€–3,000€ double. Rates include breakfast. Closed Nov. **Amenities:** Solarium; free Wi-Fi.

MONTEROSSO

Hotel Porto Roca ♥♥ This four-star hotel is the Cinque Terre's one real resort, spectacularly positioned upon a cliffside overlooking the village and blue sea below. Guest rooms (especially suites) are gradually being updated, though entry-level standard options are still a bit outdated and low on frills. Most rooms in all classes have sea views; we suggest splurging on a better room to enjoy the experience fully. In addition to an infinity pool and Jacuzzi, there's a section of beach for hotel guests, with free umbrellas and deck chairs. The restaurant serves typical Ligurian dishes, and an abundant buffet breakfast is served on the panoramic terrace in warm weather. It is a 10-minute walk from the hotel into town, requiring an uphill climb on the way back, but the property also has a shuttle service. ***Note:*** Porto Roca is intended for guests 14 and older.

Via Corone 1, Monterosso al Mare (SP). portoroca.it. ✆ **0187/817-502.** 43 units. 370€–1,200€ double. Rates include breakfast. Closed Nov–Mar. **Amenities:** Restaurant; bar; concierge; spa; pool; room service; free Wi-Fi.

Il Giardino Incantato ♥♥ In the Cinque Terre's most bustling town, this "Enchanted Garden" makes a truly tranquil and relaxing refuge. Though it lacks sea views, this charming family-run B&B in a converted 16th-century Ligurian home does offer a prime location just off Via Roma in Monterosso's old village, a stone's throw from the town beach and the boat pier. The four guest rooms have traditional furnishings and are lovingly decorated with terra-cotta tiles, wood-beamed ceilings, and wrought-iron beds. Three rooms overlook the pedestrian street outside the property while the fourth opens onto a courtyard. The villa sits opposite a lovely garden with lemon trees, lavender, and colorful flowers, where breakfast (including Ligurian favorites like focaccia along with more typical options like cereal and eggs) is served in nice weather; it's also a wonderful place to sit and have drinks in the evening. The house is full of antiques and other precious objects, so the property does not allow pets or accept guests under the age of 14.

Via Mazzini 18, Monterosso al Mare (SP). ilgiardinoincantato.net. ✆ **0187/818-315.** 4 units. 220€–250€ double. Rates include breakfast. Closed Nov to early Apr. **Amenities:** Garden; free Wi-Fi.

VERNAZZA

Gianni Franzi ♥♥ This property near the Doria Castle is less of a hotel and more of a guesthouse spread across three different buildings connected by a common garden. Rooms vary in terms of size and decor, and some have amazing views over the water. When you arrive in town, stop by the trattoria of the same name (**Gianni Franzi**), in Piazza Marconi 5, or call ✆ **0187/812-228.** (The restaurant is closed on Wednesdays, but there's usually someone around to take care of new arrivals.) Breakfast is served on a rooftop deck designed to look like the bow of an ocean liner, offering wonderful sea views. Reaching most of the rooms requires a steep climb up alleyways and stairs, and there is no luggage service, but this is one of the few budget-friendly places to stay in the Cinque Terre's most coveted village.

Piazza G. Marconi 1, Vernazza (SP). giannifranzi.it. Hotel cell ✆ **393/900-8155.** 23 units. 90€–200€ double (some w/shared bath). Rates include breakfast (or ask for non-breakfast rates). Closed early Jan to mid-Mar. **Amenities:** Restaurant; bar; garden/terrace; free Wi-Fi.

La Mala ♥♥♥ There's a chic, beachy feel to this stylish four-room property (a converted Ligurian home). Rooms are not large, but they are contemporary and sunny, boasting gorgeous views of the sea, village, harbor, or Doria castle; bathrooms are clean and modern. Room 26 has a small living area that can accommodate two more beds, making it ideal for families. Room 31 is especially large and bright, seemingly suspended between sea and sky. The other two rooms are slightly smaller, with limited harbor views. La Mala is quite central, but it is set back so it really feels like a retreat, if you don't mind the sound of bells chiming from a nearby church. The communal seaside terrace is the perfect spot for a relaxing sunset *aperitivo.* Here, you can also take part in a personalized tasting of local wines and delicacies (at additional cost). When you arrive in town, someone will meet you to help you up the steep alleyways with your bags. Breakfast is not offered, but tea and coffee-making facilities are available.

Via San Giovanni Battista 29, Vernazza. www.lamala.it. ✆ **334/287-5718.** 4 units. 170€–350€ double. Closed Jan 10 to Mar. **Amenities:** Free Wi-Fi.

Where to Eat in the Cinque Terre

CORNIGLIA

Osteria a Cantina de Mananan ♥♥ LIGURIAN Set in an old wine cellar carved into the stone of an ancient house, this tiny yet lively eatery is always packed with locals and tourists. There are very few tables—be prepared to share one with other diners—and there's often only one or two seatings per meal, so be sure to call ahead for reservations. Arrive on time or someone else may nab your table! While the atmosphere is rustic, with paper placemats and walls adorned with an eclectic mix of quirky artwork, the true highlight is the food, featuring vegetables from local gardens and fresh seafood caught by the town's fishermen. Menu highlights include a unique Ligurian pasta dish with a sausage and meat sauce, tuna prepared by the chef's signature poaching method, and *testaroli* (a crepelike pasta said to date back to Etruscan times) in a traditional pesto sauce. Tiramisu made with ricotta and lemon is a delightful way to end the meal.

Via Fieschi 117, Corniglia. ✆ **0187/821-166.** Main courses 13€–25€. Wed–Mon 12:30–2:30pm and 7:30–9:30pm; closed Tues. Closed Mon–Fri in Dec and part of Jan–Feb.

MONTEROSSO

Ristorante Miky ♥ SEAFOOD This family-run restaurant on the waterfront in Monterosso has been a local institution since 1980. One of the finest—and most expensive—dining spots in the Cinque Terre, it boasts friendly service and artfully presented food. On warm days, you can dine in a lovely garden scented with lemon and rosemary. House specialties include the famous Monterosso anchovies, poached lobster, monkfish ravioli, and *pesce al sale,* fresh fish covered in coarse salt and slowly cooked in a wood-burning oven. The extensive wine list features local producers as well as prestigious vintages from all over Italy. Miky certainly isn't cheap, but the inventive food, elegant ambience, and overall experience make it worthwhile. Reserve well in advance. The owners also have a wine bar and cafe just a few doors down, the **Cantina di Miky,** Via Fegina 90 (cantinadimiky.it; ✆ **0187/802-525**), which offers more casual seaside dining as well as a bit of nightlife. The family has also opened an *agriturismo* spot just outside of town called **Radici** (radicibymiky.it; ✆ **335-761-1477**), on a farm surrounded by olive groves and vegetable gardens. The property has three contemporary guest rooms, a small restaurant, and spaces for cooking classes as well as olive-oil and wine tasting.

Via Fegina 104, Monterosso al Mare. www.ristorantemiky.it. ✆ **0187/817-608.** Main courses 25€–50€. Daily noon–3pm and 7:30pm–late. Closed Nov–Mar.

VERNAZZA

Ristorante Belforte ♥♥♥ LIGURIAN In a medieval watchtower overlooking the Mediterranean, this restaurant has been around for more than half a century. Tables are set on various terraces surrounding the stone tower or inside a well-appointed dining room. Seafood features heavily on the menu, and along with many Ligurian standards, such as different takes on the ever-present local anchovies, you can also find unique dishes like the signature curried rice with lobster. Vegetarians won't go hungry here—creative and artfully presented vegetable-forward options range from asparagus-and-Parmesan flan to spring rolls. Desserts include traditional Italian favorites like panna cotta and tiramisu as well as the house specialty: gelato served with sautéed strawberries. You'll need to reserve ahead of time and be persistent (reservations for four or more people require a deposit of 15€ per person)—if you manage to get the single table on a small balcony at sunset, you are in for a romantic treat!

Via Guidoni 42, Vernazza. ristorantebelforte.it. ✆ **0187/812-222.** Main courses 20€–30€. Wed–Mon noon–3:30pm and 7–10pm. Closed Nov to mid-Mar.

12

NAPLES & POMPEII

By Stephen Brewer

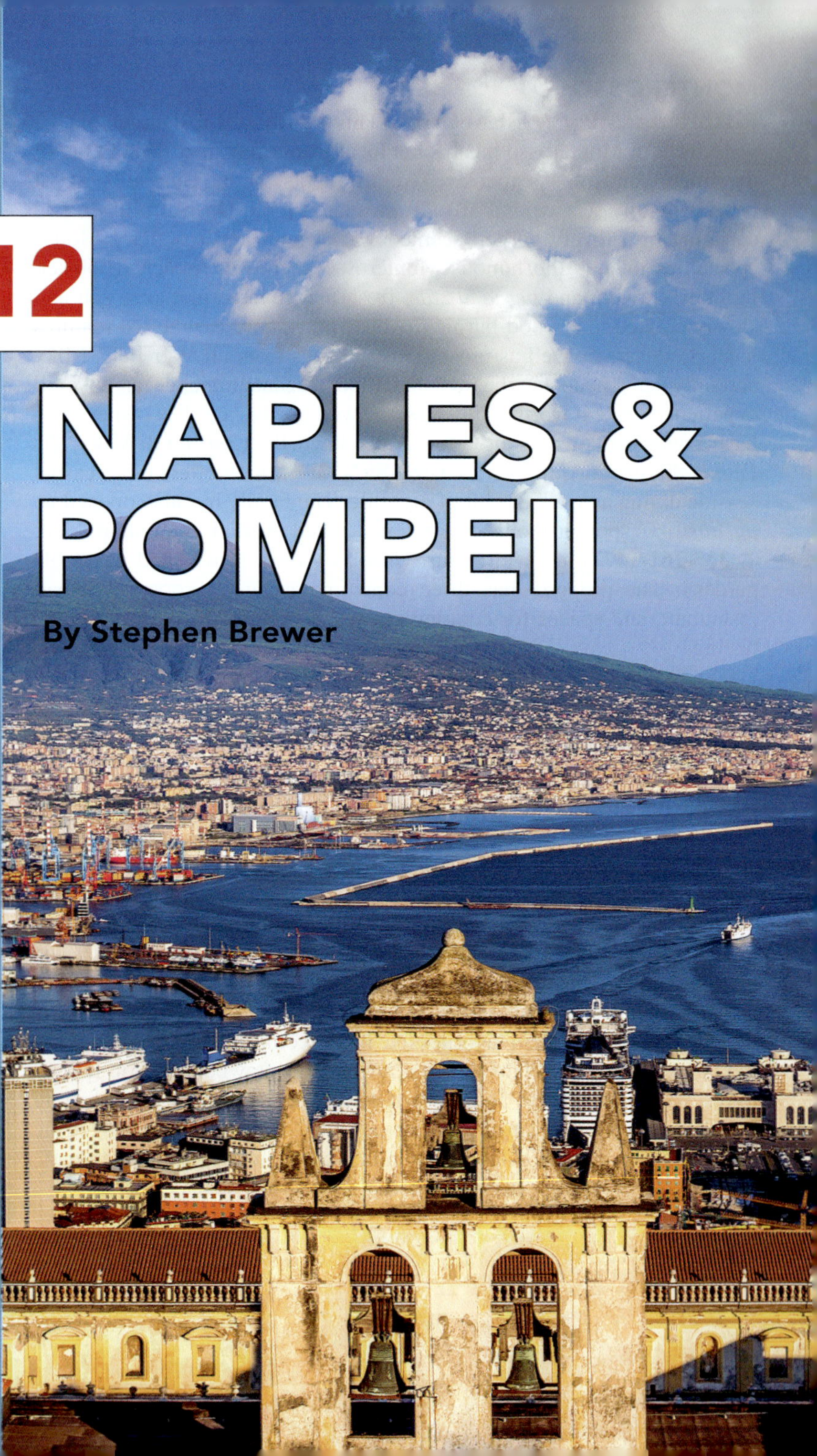

Your first encounter with southern Italy will probably be Naples. If you've enjoyed the grandeur of Venice, the elegance of Florence, and the awesomeness of monumental Rome, be prepared for a bit of a jolt: Everything seems a bit more intense in Italy's third-largest city, the capital of the South, noisy, crowded, chaotic, and a bit overwhelming. Though decidedly rundown in places, the city delights with its energy and genuine warmth, and surprises with the sophistication of the monuments, museums, and cultural and culinary scenes.

And Naples is just the beginning. Around the city are some of the ancient world's most extensive remains in Herculaneum and Pompeii, the ominous natural wonders of Mt. Vesuvius and the Campi Flegrei, and two of the world's most fabled islands, Capri and Ischia. It may help to think of the Naples area as Italy on overdrive, so *benvenuti al sud*—welcome to the South, and hang on and enjoy the ride.

DON'T LEAVE NAPLES & POMPEII WITHOUT . . .

Prowling Around the Attic of Antiquity. Among the prizes in the National Archaeology Museum, you'll find touchingly human statues of gods and goddesses, frescoes and mosaics from Pompeii and Herculaneum, and even some titter-inducing pornography.

Plunging into Neapolitan Street Life. Lively Via Tribunali provides a good taste of the city's color and clamor, from the magnificent church of San Lorenzo Maggiore to the pizzas emerging from the ovens at Sorbillo.

Soaking in Soothing Views. Hit the airy heights by riding the funicular up to the Certosa di San Martino. Admire the vista of Mt. Vesuvius looming over the bay from Castel dell'Ovo or the gardens of the Villa Comunale.

Stepping Back into Ancient Times in Herculaneum and Pompeii. It's eerily easy to imagine everyday life as it was 2,000 years ago along the streets of these accidentally preserved seaside towns.

Sampling Naples' Greatest Contribution to World Cuisine. You haven't eaten pizza until you've eaten it in Naples, the city where pizza was born. Pizza is just the gateway food when it comes to enjoying Neapolitan cuisine.

FACING PAGE: **Castel Sant' Elmo in Vomero offers a panoramic view of Vesuvius across the Bay of Naples.**

NAPLES ♥♥

219km (136 miles) SE of Rome

In Naples, Mt. Vesuvius looms to the east, the fumaroles of the Campi Flegrei hiss and steam to the west, and the isle of Capri (p. 687) floats phantomlike across the gleaming waters of the bay. For all the splendor and drama of this natural setting, one of Italy's most intense urban concoctions is the real show. Naples shoots out so many sensations that it takes a while for visitors to know what's hit them. Dark brooding lanes open to palm-fringed piazzas. Laundry-festooned tenements stand cheek by jowl with grand palaces. Medieval churches and castles rise above a grid of streets laid out by ancient Greeks. There's no denying that parts of the city are squalid, yet the museums are packed with riches.

It seems that most of life here transpires on the streets, so you'll witness a lot. The pace can be leisurely in the southern way, and amazingly hectic. When you partake—in a meal, in a *passeggiata,* or just in a simple transaction—you'll notice the warmth, general good nature, and a sense of fun. In more than a few places, you may be reminded of scenes from Elena Ferrante's bestselling quartet of Neapolitan novels. You get the idea—but you won't really, until you experience this fascinating, perplexing, and beguiling city for yourself.

Essentials

ARRIVING Naples is on the main southern rail corridor and is served by frequent and fast **train service** from most Italian and European cities. The trip between Rome and Naples on high-speed (Alta Velocità or AV) express trains takes only 87 minutes, making this by far the best way to travel between the two cities. Rail Europe and Eurail pass holders should note that AV trains require a reservation and an extra fee (10€). Contact **Trenitalia** (trenitalia.it; ✆ **892-021**) for information, reservations, and fares. High-speed **Italo** trains travel the route, too (italotreno.it; ✆ **060708;** p. 832). The central city's main rail terminal is **Stazione Centrale,** at Piazza Garibaldi, though many high-speed trains also stop at Napoli Afragola, an architectural showpiece designed by the late Zaha Hadid, about 3km (2 miles) north of the city center. Stazione Centrale is much more convenient for most visitors; it has a tourist office as well as baggage storage, operated by **Kibag** (kibag.it), open daily 8am to 8pm (8€ a bag). Transit connections at Stazione Centrale include Circumvesuviana trains to Pompeii and Sorrento as well as the Metro (the Piazza Garibaldi stop, in an adjacent arcade), and the city's terminal for long-distance buses is next to the station.

Although driving *in* Naples can be hair-raising, **driving** *to* Naples is easy. The city is linked by autostrada A2 to Rome and A3 to Reggio di Calabria, in the far south.

United Airlines (united.com) operates daily nonstop service from late-April through October between Newark Airport (EWR) and Naples'

Aeroporto Capodichino (**NAP;** aeroportodinapoli.it; ✆ **081/789-6111**), and many carriers, including low-cost Ryanair and easyJet, fly into Naples from Italian and European cities. From the airport, which is only 7km (4 miles) from the city center, you can take a taxi into town (make sure it is an official white taxi with the Naples municipal logo); the flat rate for the 15-minute trip to the train station is 18€ (20€–22€ to some other city center locations). **Alibus** bus service to the port (Piazza Municipio) and the train station (Piazza Garibaldi) is run by **ANM** (anm.it; ✆ **800/639-525;** 5€ one-way; buy tickets at machines in the arrivals hall, on board, or at bars and tobacco shops in the airport, or pay onboard with a contactless credit card or device). The bus runs every 30 minutes from a stop at the airport beyond the taxi stand outside the arrivals hall (6:30am–11:50pm) and from the beginning of the line at Piazza Municipio (6am–midnight).

Ferries between Naples and Palermo sail once or twice nightly and are operated by **Tirrenia Lines** (tirrenia.it; ✆ **089-2123**) and **Grandi Navi Veloci** (**GNV;** gnv.it; ✆ **010/209-4591**). You can buy tickets at travel agencies or at ferry offices in the port area: Tirrenia at Capannone Juta, Calata Porta di Massa; GNV in Piazzale Immacolatella. Accommodations for the 11-hour trip are in business-class-style reclining seats or cabins.

GETTING AROUND Most public transport in Naples comes under the auspices of **Azienda Napoletano Mobiltà,** usually referred to simply as **ANM** (anm.it; ✆ **800/639-525**). Its excellent website, with some English translations, is a helpful resource for planning your travels around the city, as is that of **Unico Campania** (unicocampania.it), the consortium that oversees integrated fares for various modes of transport. Metro line 1 connects the train station in Piazza Garibaldi with such central locations as the university (Università), Piazza Municipio (for the port), Via Toledo, Piazza Dante, Duomo, and the archaeological museum (Museo stop); Metro line 2 (a commuter line operated by Trenitalia) runs from Pozzuoli in the western suburbs through the city, with stops that include Mergellina, Piazza Amadeo, Montesanto, the archaeological museum (Museo stop), and Piazza Garibaldi. Several new stations have opened in recent years, with more on the way, including a planned and long-awaited expansion of line 1 to the airport. As you ride the system, you'll notice many stations decorated with art installations. Mosaic tiles and lights in the Toledo station are in shades of blue that become deeper and more intense as you descend; psychedelic colors and shapes in the Università station are intended to immerse you in the digital age.

There are also two urban railway networks that can be handy for getting to major attractions. The **Circumvesuviana train** leaves from a station adjacent to the main train station in Piazza Garibaldi and runs southeast around the Bay of Naples to Pompeii and Herculaneum (p. 629) and Sorrento (p. 644). The **Ferrovia Cumana** runs from Piazza Montesanto to Pozzuoli and other towns in the Campi Flegrei (p. 621).

HOTELS

Art Resort Gallery Umberto **16**
BnB Naples **26**
BnB Orsini46 **9**
Casa d'Anna ai Cristallini **51**
Chiaja Hotel de Charme **11**
Correra 241 **34**
Costantinopoli 104 **33**
Decumani Hotel de Charme **40**
Grand Hotel Parker's **2**
Grand Hotel Vesuvio **7**
Hotel Il Convento **18**
Hotel Piazza Bellini **32**
IStayinToledo **19**
San Francesco al Monte **22**
Tredici Boutique Rooms **28**

RESTAURANTS

Antica Pizzeria Port d'Alba **31**
Campagnola **37**
Da Nennella **20**
Europeo di Mattozzi **27**
I Buongustai **49**
L'Antica Pizzeria Da Michele **43**
La Locanda Gesù Vecchio **42**
Mimi alla Ferrovia **50**
Pescheria Azzura **25**
Pizzeria Brandi **12**
Pizzeria Gino e Toto Sorbillo **36**
Rosiello **1**
Tandem **41**
Trattoria A' Pignata **21**
Umberto **5**

ATTRACTIONS

Cappella Sansevero **38**
Castel dell'Ovo **8**
Castel Nuovo **14**
Castel Sant'Elmo **24**
Catacombe di San Gennaro Napoli **52**
Certosa e Museo di San Martino **23**
Chiesa del Gesù Nuovo **30**
Chiesa di San Gregorio Armeno **39**
Galleria Borbonica (Bourbon Tunnel) **6**
Galleria Umberto I **16**
Il Cattedrale di Santa Maria Assunta (Duomo) **47**
Monastero di Santa Chiara **29**
Museo Archeologico Nazionale **35**
Museo d'Arte Contemporanea Donnaregina (MADRE) **48**
Museo e Real Bosco di Capodimonte (Museum and Park of the Capodimonte) **53**
Napoli Sotterranea Percorso Ufficiale e Autorizzato **44**
Napoli Sotterranea Tour Ufficiale **10**
Palazzo Reale **13**
Palazzo Zevallos Stigliano **17**
Pio Monte della Misericordia **46**
San Lorenzo Maggiore **45**
Teatro San Carlo **15**
Villa Comunale **4**
Villa La Floridiana & Museo Nazionale della Ceramica Duca di Martina **3**

Naples
Capodimonte Park
CAPODIMONTE
Tangenziale di Napoli
To Rome, Milan (A1)
Salerno, Sorrento (A3)
Avellino, Benevento (A16)
Tondo di Capodimonte
A56
Piazza Ottocalli
Piazza G.B.Vico
Via Don Bosco
Osservatorio Astronomico
Palazzo Fuga
Orto Botanico
Piazza Carlo III
Corso A. di Savoia
Piazza Sanità
Via Miracoli
Via Foria
ARENACCIA
Via Arenaccia
Via F. Pignatelli
Stadio Albricci
Via Nuova Poggioreale
Piazza De Leva
Via Materdei
Via S. Teresa d. Scalzi
Piazza Pagano
Museo Archeologico Nazionale
Piazza S. Ferdinando
Via C. Rossaroli
Corso Garibaldi
Piazza Nazionale
Via Nazionale
Via M. R. Imbriani
Via Salvator Rosa
Porta S. Gennaro
Via S. Giovanni a Carbonara
Porta Capuana
Via Casanova
Piazza Museo
Via S. Rosa
Galleria Principe di Napoli
Duomo
Corso Meridionale
Piazza Leonardo
Piazza Mazzini
Via Correa
Via Pessina
Via Duomo
Via Tribunali
Castel Capuano
Piazza Garibaldi
Stazione Centrale
Porta Alba
Stazione Montesano
Piazza Dante
VOMERO
Corso Vittorio Emanuele
Via S. Biagio dei Librai
Corso Umberto I
Porta Nolana
Piazza Montesanto
Via Toledo
Via B. Croce
CITTÀ ANTICA
Via A. Lucci
Piazza D'Acquisto
Posta Centrale
Università di Napoli
Piazza Mercato
Via Nuova Marina
Via A. Vespucci
Piazza Bovio
Piazza Matteotti
QUARTIERI SPAGNOLI
Via Toledo
Via C. Colombo
Piazza Municipio
Calata Porta di Massa
Castel Nuovo (Maschio Angioino)
Stazione Marittima
V. d. Mille
Via Chiaia
Piazza del Plebiscito
Palazzo Reale
Molo Beverello
Piazza d. Martiri
SANTA LUCIA
Piazza Vittoria
Via S. Lucia
Via N. Sauro
Via Partenope
Castel dell'Ovo
Benevento
CAMPANIA
NAPLES
Salerno
Ischia
Sorrento
Capri
Tyrrhenian Sea
To Aeolian Islands, Sicily & Cagliari
Gulf of Naples
(Golfo di Napoli)
Ferry Terminal
Information
Funiculars
0
1/2 mi
0
0.5 km
To Sorrento
To Capri
To Ischia, Procida

Handy **bus** routes include the R lines (R1, R2, R3, R4), with frequent stops at major tourist attractions (the R4, for example, connects the archaeological museum and Catacombs of San Gennaro), and the electric minibuses (marked E) that skirt the historic district.

Be Prepared

It's a good idea to **carry extra transport tickets** with you when exploring the city. Lines at ticket-vending machines at Metro stations are often long (especially at Piazza Garibaldi), machines are commonly out of service (*fuori servizio*), and it can be hard to find ticket vendors near bus stops.

Four **funiculars** take passengers up and down the steep hills of Naples. The **Funicolare Centrale,** one of the world's longest (about a mile) and busiest funiculars, connects the central city to Vomero. Daily departures (6:30am–12:30am) are from the Augusteo station on the Piazzetta Duca d'Aosta just off Via Toledo.

One-way fare for subways, buses, and funiculars is 1.50€; daily tickets (Biglietto Giornaliero) cost 4.50€, valid until midnight the day they are validated; weekly tickets (Biglietto Settimanale) are 12.50€. You can buy tickets at some newsstands and tobacco shops, from machines in most Metro and funicular stations, and at some bus stops. Many Metro stations and some buses are equipped with terminals that allow you to pay with a contactless credit card or device for entrance. When riding the bus, you must validate tickets in the electronic ticket machines on board.

Taxis are a relatively inexpensive way to get around the city and are very reliable and strictly regulated. Official taxis are painted white and marked COMUNE DI NAPOLI. Inside, a sign lists official flat rates to the seaports, central hotels, and top attractions; don't fret if your driver doesn't use the meter—*not* using the meter is legal for all rides with established flat rates. Taxis don't cruise for street hails, but can be found at many taxi stands around town; for an extra 1€ surcharge, you can request a taxi by phone (✆ **081/8888** or 081/2222). You can also summon rides with the FreeNow (free-now.com) and Uber (uber.com) apps.

As for **driving** around Naples, we have one word: *Don't.* If you're tempted, take a look at the cars on the street. In the rest of Italy, even the simplest models are kept in pristine condition; here, cars look like they've been used in demolition derbies. Car theft is common—some rental companies won't extend theft protection coverage if you'll be driving in Naples. If you do bring a car into the city, a convenient place for long-term parking is **Parcheggio Brin,** Via Benedetto Brin at Via Volta (anm.it; ✆ **081/763-2855**), at the eastern edge of the center, easily reached from the Via Marina exit off the A3 autostrada. From 6am to midnight, parking costs 2€ for the first 4 hours, 0.50€ each additional hour to a maximum of 5€, then 5€ from midnight to 6am.

Walking is the best way to get around the city center, where sights are fairly close together, but remember: For Neapolitan drivers, red lights are mere suggestions; cross busy streets carefully. Always look both ways, too, since many drivers scoff at the notion of a one-way street. Zebra stripes (white lines) in the street, indicating where pedestrians have the right of way, mean absolutely nothing here.

VISITOR INFORMATION The **tourist office** in Stazione Centrale (Metro: Piazza Garibaldi) is open daily 9am to 6pm. Other **tourist information points** are located in Piazza del Gesù (✆ **342/677-9319**) and in the tourist port in Varco Immacolatella, both open daily (Mon–Sat 9am–7pm, Sun 9am–2pm). These offices can give you a free map, an essential piece of gear when navigating Naples, and advice on bus and subway routes.

Exploring Naples

Large as Naples is, it's easy to get to the sights you want to see on foot, letting you experience one of the city's greatest allures: its street life. From **Piazza Trieste e Trento,** with the magnificent Teatro San Carlo (p. 620) and Galleria Umberto I (p. 597), **Via Toledo** leads north. To the left as you head up the street is the **Quartieri Spagnoli,** a neighborhood of narrow, tightly packed lanes, while to the right, just behind Piazza Dante, is the atmospheric **historical center** of the city, also known as Spaccanapoli, where many of the churches you want to see face airy piazzas. Pizzeria- and shop-lined Via Tribunali is the main street through the quarter. At the northern end of Via Toledo, about a 10-minute walk beyond Piazza Dante, is Naples' celebrated archaeological museum.

> ### See the Sights for Less
>
> The confoundingly complex **Campania Artecard** can save you money if you plan to make the rounds of churches, museums, and archaeological sites. For most visitors, the most basic versions will suffice: The **Napoli Artecard** (27€), good for 3 days, gives you free admission to three attractions, a discount of 50% at others, and free use of public transport; the **Campania Artecard 3** (41€) provides free admission to two attractions and a 50% discount at others and includes Pompeii and Herculaneum, so it delivers a substantial discount if, for instance, you plan to see those two sites and the National Archaeological Museum. Cards are for sale at participating sites, at tourist information offices, and online at campaniartecard.it.

You'll probably be safe just about anywhere you wander along the well-worn tourist trail; the crime rate in Naples, despite the city's bad rap, is a lot lower than it is in many American cities. It's best to avoid the darker corners of the Spagnoli neighborhood and historical center at night, however, and pickpockets and purse-and-jewelry snatchers can be a menace, especially around the train station and in the Porta Nolana market; on **Via San Gregorio Armeno** (p. 619), people gawking at shop windows filled with Nativity scenes are easy targets.

SANTA LUCIA & THE SEAFRONT

Not surprisingly, some of the city's most magnificent squares and public monuments are clustered near the seafront. **Piazza del Plebiscito ♥♥**, the most beautiful square in Naples, is surrounded by an elegant assemblage

Sheltered by the curving colonnades of the basilica of San Francesco di Paola, beloved lion statues preside over the Piazza del Plebiscito.

of neoclassical landmarks. Among them is the **Palazzo Reale ♥♥** (Royal Palace), with 30 grandiose salons, along with a private theater and chapel, where Neapolitan royalty ruled and entertained in the 18th and 19th centuries. Among the more interesting objects on display are the gramophones, sheet music, recordings, and other mementos honoring Neapolitan-born tenor Enrico Caruso (palazzorealedinapoli.org; ✆ **081/580-8255;** admission 17€ adults, free for children 17 and under; daily 9am–8pm; gardens close at sunset; Museo Caruso Thurs–Tues 9am–2pm; bus R2 or R3). In the piazza, two Neapolitan kings survey the cobblestones on horseback: the forward-thinking Carlo III (1716–88) and the treacherous Ferdinando I (1423–94). It's said you will be blessed with good fortune if you face the Palazzo Reale, close your eyes, and walk backwards across the square between the two kings (much harder to do than you might think—local lore has it that condemned prisoners were once blindfolded and made to perform this feat, and few succeeded).

A short walk up the seafront, the airy **Piazza Municipio** is the best place to view

Getting to Know Napoli

A good way to get to know the city is on a free walking tour with **Napoli That's Amore** (napolithatsamore.org). Local professional guides lead highly informative and personalized walks: through the Old Town from Piazza Dante and a Best of Naples circuit beginning at Piazza Municipio. Go to the website to book; tour times vary throughout the year. There's no fee, but tips are appreciated and well deserved.

the towers and crenellations of **Castel Nuovo ♥♥**, also known as the Maschio Angioino, or Angevin Keep (New Castle; castelnuovo.comune.napoli.it; ✆ **081/795-7701**), with the white-marble Triumphal Arch of Alfonso I of Aragon squeezed between two of its turrets. You can forgo a visit to the castle's dank chambers and simply admire this medieval sea-girt beauty from the outside. (If you do want to step inside to see Roman ruins beneath a glass floor and, in the Cappella Palatina, fragments of a fresco by Giotto, the salons and galleries are open Mon–Sat 9am–6pm; admission 10€.) Gazing at the castle, you might consider the plight of former prisoners who shared their dungeons with crocodiles imported from Egypt to snack on the doomed souls. In Piazza Municipio you'll also see the water-spouting lions and sea monsters of the **Fontana del Nettuno ♥♥**, a 17th-century marble showpiece originally installed in front of the Palazzo Reale and carted around the city to several locations since then. It was partly the work of Pietro Bernini, whose greatest creation is the Fontana della Barcaccia at the bottom of the Spanish Steps in Rome (his more famous son, Lorenzo, designed the Fontana dei Quattro Fiumi in Rome's Piazza Navona).

From Giardini del Molosiglio, behind Piazza dei Plebiscito, the Lungomare follows the Santa Lucia seafront past sweeping views of Mt. Vesuvius, the bay, and the islands (all most photogenic at sunset). From a little islet rises the outrageously picturesque **Castel dell'Ovo ♥♥♥** (Castle of the Egg), on Borgo Marinari (off Via Partenope). As every Neapolitan knows, the ancient Roman poet Virgil placed an egg under the foundations of the castle; when it breaks, a great disaster will befall the city. Considering earthquakes, eruptions of nearby Mt. Vesuvius, plague outbreaks, and wars, it's probably safe to assume the egg is no longer intact. The castle is enchanting even without such legends, a royal residence from the 13th to 20th centuries squeezed onto a tiny island the Greeks first settled almost 3 millennia ago (comune.napoli.it/casteldellovo; ✆ **081/795-4593;** currently closed for restoration). The little lanes beneath the thick walls are lined with the fishermen's houses of Borgo Marinaro, now occupied by bars and pizzerias. For Neapolitans, a walk across the stout bridge onto the island is a favorite Sunday afternoon outing. Just behind the waterfront stretches the quirkily elegant **Chiaia** district, once the fashionable address for Bourbon nobility. Many palaces and villas from those days are slowly moldering, with the exception of the wonderful **Villa Pignatelli ♥♥** and attached carriage museum, its salons furnished in 19th-century gilded finery (Riviera di Chiaia 200; cultura.gov.it; ✆ **081/761-2358;** Wed–Mon 9:30am–4pm; 5€ adults, free for children 17 and under).

Galleria Umberto I ♥♥ SHOPPING MALL Shopping malls have only gone downhill since the late 19th century, when elegant glass-and-iron landmarks like this were all the rage. The cafe- and shop-lined gallery modeled after Milan's Galleria Vittorio Emanuele II (p. 478) saw its best days in the years before World War I, but Neapolitans still enjoy shopping beneath its glass dome and vaulted wings. If the place works its magic on you, dip into *The Gallery,* a poignant 1947 novel by John Horne Burnes about American GIs in Naples after World War II. Much of its action transpires in the Galleria.

Entrances off Via Toledo, Via Giuseppe Verdi, Via Santa Brigida, and Via San Carlo. Bus: R2 or 151 to Piazza Trieste e Trento. Metro: Municipio.

Villa Comunale ♥♥ PARK/GARDEN The public used to be allowed into the seaside gardens of the royal family on September 8 only, the Festa di Piedigrotta. That changed with the proletarian sentiments that swept in with the unification of Italy in 1869—and a good thing, too. One of the city's great delights is to follow the park's paths through greenery and past statues and fountains for a kilometer (½ mile) or so from Piazza Vittoria on the east to Piazza della Repubblica on the west. The Bay of Naples shimmers to the south, and many of its denizens—octopi, squid, and sea urchins—now reside within the park at the **Naples Aquarium** (fondazionedohrn.it/home/aquarium; ✆ **081/583-3442;** admission 10€ adults, 7€ students, seniors, and ages 4–12, free for children 3 and under; Tues–Sun 9am–5pm). A popular **antiques market** takes over a corner of Villa Comunale on the third and fourth weekends of each month from 8:30am to 1pm; contact the tourist office (p. 595) for info.

Piazza Vittoria. Daily 7am–midnight. Bus: C82 or R2.

CENTRO STORICO/SPACCANAPOLI

This warren of narrow lanes and boisterous piazzas is best known as Spaccanapoli (literally, "Naples Splitter," after the street that runs straight through the center of the neighborhood, as it has ever since the Greeks established a colony here). Roughly, the heart of Naples extends north from seaside Castel Nuovo to the Museo Archeologico Nazionale, and east from Via Toledo to the Porta Nolana Fish Market. West of Via Toledo, the Quartieri Spagnoli is a maze of laundry-strung lanes named for the Spanish troops once garrisoned here to subdue the rebellious population.

Cappella Sansevero ♥♥♥ MUSEUM Only in Naples would a room as colorful, fanciful, mysterious, beautiful, and macabre as this exist. Prince Raimondo di Sangro of Sansevero remodeled his family's funerary chapel in the 18th century, combining the then-fashionable baroque style with his own love of complex symbolism and intellectual quests. Neapolitan sculptor Giuseppe Sanmartino crafted *Christ Veiled Under a Shroud,* in which a thin, transparent covering seems to make Christ's flesh look even more tormented. When Venetian sculptor Antonio Canova came to Naples a century later, he said he would give 10 years of his life to have created something so beautiful. The prince's father lies beneath a statue of *Despair on Disillusion,* in which a man disentangling himself from a marble net suggests a troubled soul seeking relief—provided by the winged boy who represents intellect. Prince Raimondo's mother, who died at age

20, lies beneath a statue of *Veiled Truth,* in which a woman holds a broken tablet, symbol of an interrupted life. Raimondo himself is surrounded by colorful floor tiles arranged in a complex maze, symbol of the quest to unravel the secrets of life. Downstairs are the skeletal forms of a man and a woman in which the circulatory systems and musculature are brightly colored, allegedly with the injection of a substance the prince devised. Despite legend, the figures are not the prince's unwilling servants, scarified in the interest of science—they were fashioned from human skeletons and beeswax. The Museo Capella Sansevero sells out well in advance, and spots fill up quickly. Booking online is required.

Via Francesco de Sanctis 19 (near Piazza San Domenico Maggiore). museosansevero.it. ✆ **081/551-8470.** Admission 12€ adults, 8€ ages 18–26, 6€ ages 10–17, free for children 9 and under. Wed–Mon 9am–7pm. Audioguide 3.50€. Closed May 1 and Easter Mon. Metro: Dante.

Chiesa del Gesù Nuovo ♥♥ CHURCH The princes of Salerno built their palace in 1470, requesting that the facade be done in *bugnato a punta di diamante,* with stone blocks elaborately cut to create a pattern of projecting points, like cut diamonds. The princes lost the palace a century later as a result of their political intrigues, and the Jesuit order bought the property and converted its stately salons into a church. In due time they too were evicted, but not before enlivening the interior with opulent frescoes and marble work. Above the doorway inside is a dramatic fresco by Francesco Solimena (1657–1747), a mediocre baroque painter who compensated for his lack of genius with flamboyance—his *Expulsion of Heliodorus from the Temple* is a colorful swirl of flowing draperies and churning robes. The altar of the chapel of the Visitation is the final resting place of Naples' most popular modern saint, Giuseppe Moscati (1880–1927), a devout physician and biochemist famous for his ability to heal impossible cases. The so-called Holy Physician of Naples is believed to still be working miracles: His shrine is often thronged with the ill and injured, and it's said that many have been cured on the spot.

Piazza del Gesù. ✆ **081/557-8111.** Free admission. Mon–Sat 9am–12:30pm and 5–7:15pm; Sun 8:30am–1:30pm and 4:30–7:30pm. Bus: R1, R2, R3, or R4. Metro: Dante.

Chiesa di San Gregorio Armeno ♥♥ CHURCH When nuns fleeing persecution in Asia Minor came to Naples in the 8th century, they brought with them the relics of St. Gregory, an Armenian bishop. Over the centuries they built suitable surroundings for the saint, who now rests in a sumptuous baroque church bursting at the seams with gold leaf and elaborate marble carvings. Stepping into the church, described as "a room of paradise on earth," is like walking into one of the elaborate Nativity scenes, *presepi,* that vendors sell up and down the street outside (see box on p. 619). Seventeenth-century master of the baroque Luca Giordano tells the story of the nuns' flight with their precious cargo in a series of dramatic frescoes. Gregory, however, is upstaged by one of the nuns,

Santa Patrizia, whose body is on display in a glass coffin, in which her dried blood is said to liquefy every Tuesday. The beautiful cloisters, entered around the corner, are an oasis of tranquility; seek them out when the *centro storico* gets to be overwhelming.

Via San Gregorio Armeno 44. ✆ **081/552-0186.** Free admission to church; cloisters 7€ (cash only). Church Mon–Fri 10am–1pm, Sat–Sun 10am–7pm; cloisters Mon–Fri 9:30am–1pm, Sat–Sun 10am–1pm and 3–7pm. Metro: Cavour.

Il Cattedrale di Santa Maria Assunta (Duomo) ♥♥ CATHEDRAL Three times a year—the first Saturday in May, September 19, and December 16—all of Naples squeezes into the great cathedral that King Carlo I d'Angiò dedicated to San Gennaro, the city's patron saint, in the 13th century. On these dates the saint's dried blood is supposed to liquefy, though sometimes it doesn't—thus foretelling terrible events for Naples, such as an outbreak of the plague in 1528 or the 1980 earthquake that killed 2,000 residents. The rest of the year his blood is kept in a vault inside an altar in the **Cappella di San Gennaro (Chapel of San Gennaro)**, the baroque masterpiece of priest-architect Francesco Grimaldi, where a reliquary also houses Gennaro's head, severed from his body around 305. Decorating the chapel was a prize that set Neapolitan artists against one another, with Guido Reni fleeing the city when his assistant was stabbed and Domenichino dropping dead after a poisoning. The Spaniard Jusepe de Ribera (p. 602), a master of capturing human cruelty, survived to paint *St. Januarius Emerges Unscathed from the Furnace*, depicting another of San Gennaro's travails; he was also allegedly thrown to lions, who refused to eat him.

Within the cathedral are Naples' two oldest places of worship: the **Basilica di Santa Restituta (Basilica of Saint Restituta)**, entered from the left aisle, the city's 4th-century basilica, heavily renovated but still supported by a forest of columns from a Greek temple; and the **Cappella di San Giovanni in Fonte (Chapel of Saint John the Baptist)**, entered from the right aisle, a 5th-century baptistery; if you crane your neck and squint (binoculars or a telescopic lens come in handy) you can make out the extensive remnants of mosaic scenes in the dome.

The Museo del Tesoro di San Genaro, adjacent to the Duomo, houses the jewels and silver bestowed upon the church in honor of the saint. Genaro is also honored a few blocks south of the Duomo on Via Forcella, in a striking mural portrait by street artist Jorit Agoch.

Via del Duomo 147. chiesadinapoli.it; tesorosangennaro.it. ✆ **081/449097.** Free admission. Capella di San Genaro and Museo del Tesoro di San Genaro 14€ adults, 10€ seniors, free for children 11 and under. Battistero di San Giovanni in Fonte: 2.50€. Duomo: Mon–Sat 9:30am–1pm and 3–6pm, Sun 9am–1pm and 4:30–6pm. Museo del Tesoro di San Genaro: daily 9:30am–6pm. Bus R1. Metro: Cavour or Duomo.

Monastero di Santa Chiara ♥♥♥ CHURCH/GARDEN It's not a good sign in a marriage when a wife's only desire is to become a nun, but that's what Queen Sancha wanted, so Robert of Anjou founded Santa

Colorful tiled benches in the cloisters of the Monastero di Santa Chiara.

Chiara as a place for his wife to retreat. Their granddaughter, Joan, was crowned queen here in 1343, launching an enlightened reign nonetheless marred by plotting, intrigue, the murder of a husband, and her own demise at age 56, when she was smothered with pillows. Her body was thrown into a deep well on the grounds, and once retrieved, buried in an unmarked grave beneath the church floor. During World War II, Allied bombers laid waste to most of the church's frescoes, but a few fragments remain, including biblical scenes by Giotto. Other frescoes line the walls of the delightful lemon-scented cloisters, where columns and benches are covered in colorful Majorca tiles depicting landscapes, hunting parties, dancers, and other snippets of the good life in 18th-century Naples—surprisingly worldly and frivolous, considering that for 200 years or so the retreat was enjoyed only by cloistered nuns. This is one of the most refreshing corners of Naples, and well worth the admission fee if you've been walking around the city and need a little peace and quiet.

Via Santa Chiara 49. monasterodisantachiara.it. ✆ **081/797-1235.** Free admission to church; cloisters 7€ adults, 5€ seniors and students, free for children 6 and under. Church: Daily 7:45am–12:45pm and 4:40–8pm. Cloisters: Mon–Sat 9:30am–5pm; Sun 10am–2pm. Metro: Dante.

Museo Archeologico Nazionale (National Archaeological Museum) ♥♥♥ MUSEUM One of the world's great time-travel experiences takes visitors back to the ancient world. Two treasure troves in particular should not be missed.

BAD BOY of the baroque

The painter Caravaggio arrived in Naples in 1606, fleeing authorities in Rome after he killed a man in a fight over a debt. With his taste for gambling, prostitutes, young boys, rowdiness, and drunkenness, the tempestuous artist must have felt right at home in Naples. The city was then the second largest in Europe after Paris, with 350,000 inhabitants, more than a few of whom shared Caravaggio's reckless disposition. His sumptuous canvases, with their realistic human figures and dramatic use of light, have become emblematic of the city's emotion-filled baroque style.

Three major Caravaggio works are in Naples. The dark, moody, and chaotic *Seven Acts of Mercy* altarpiece is in the chapel of the **Pio Monte della Misericordia,** Via Tribunali 253 (piomontedellamisericordia.it; ✆ **081/446-944;** Metro: Duomo, Cavour), a fraternity founded by nobles in 1601 to loan money to the poor. Try to identify the various acts of mercy—St. Martin in the foreground giving his cloak to the beggar is easy (clothing the naked)—and you'll probably only detect six. But look again at the scene of the old man sucking at the breast of the young woman: That counts as two: visiting prisoners and feeding the hungry. (Classicists identify the pair as the Roman Cimon, who was sentenced to death by starvation, and his daughter, Pero, who secretly suckled him, an act of family honor that won him his release.) While you're here, look at the painting gallery upstairs: It features works by the so-called Cabal of Naples, a notorious trio of painters—Belisario Corenzio, Jusepe de Ribera, and Battistello Caracciolo—who were known to harass or even poison their competitors and destroy the works of rivals who won commissions they thought were rightfully theirs. Admission to the chapel and gallery is 10€ for adults, 8€ for youth 6 to 24, free for children 5 and under, 20€ for a family of two adults and two children 15 and under (Mon–Sat 10am–6pm, Sun 9am–2:30pm; last admissions 1 hr. before closing).

In the **Capodimonte gallery** (p. 607), Caravaggio's *Flagellation of Christ* depicts two brutish tormentors whipping a nearly naked Christ; a third one in the foreground is preparing his scourge to join in the action. Lighting emphasizes the flailing arms and Christ's twisted, suffering body; it's a visceral depiction of cruelty in action, and one of two flagellation scenes Caravaggio painted while in Naples.

The *Martyrdom of St. Ursula* hangs in the **Palazzo Zevallos Stigliano,** Via Toledo 185 (gallerieditalia.com; ✆ **800/167-619;** Metro: Montesanto), today the lavish headquarters of the Banco Intesa Sanpaolo. Ursula appears unfazed as the king of the Huns, whose marriage proposal she has just refused, shoots an arrow into her breast at point-blank range. (As legend has it, the 11,000 virginal handmaidens accompanying Ursula had just been beheaded, so she couldn't have been too surprised that her jilted suitor was displeased.) Caravaggio himself looks on from the background. This was his last painting and the last image we have of him—he died of fever while returning to Rome a couple months later. Admission to the Palazzo is 7€, 4€ seniors, free for children 17 and under (Tues–Fri 10am–7pm, Sat–Sun 10am–8pm).

On the mezzanine and upper floors are **mosaics, frescoes, and bronzes excavated from Pompeii and Herculaneum.** Seeing these everyday objects from villas and shops seems to bring the ruined cities to life. Most of the mosaics, on the first floor, are from the House of Faun, one of the largest residences in Pompeii. The million-plus-piece floor mosaic, *Alexander Fighting the Persians*, depicts the wavy-haired king of Macedonia astride Bucephalos, the most famous steed in antiquity, sweeping into battle against King Darius III of Persia, who's looking a bit concerned in his chariot. The **Gabinetto Segreto** (Secret Room; on the first floor) displays some of the erotica that was commonplace in Pompeii. Some works are from brothels, among them frescoes that show acts lively yet predictable and some bestial, and others include phallus-shaped oil lamps and huge phalluses placed at doorways to bring fertility and good fortune. We might titter at the bulges under togas, but they weren't necessarily intended to be pornography and rather suggest the libertine attitudes of the time.

The superb **Farnese Collection** of Roman sculpture shows off the pieces snapped up by the enormously wealthy Roman Cardinal Alessandro Farnese, later Pope Paul III (1543–49), who was at the top of the Renaissance game of antiquity hunting. His remarkable collection was inherited by Elisabetta Farnese, who married Philip V of Spain and whose son and grandson became kings of Naples and brought the collection here in the 18th century. Among Cardinal Farnese's great prizes was the **Ercole Farnese,** a huge statue of Hercules unearthed at the Baths of Caracalla in Rome. The superhero son of Zeus looks tuckered out, leaning on his club after completing his eleventh labor, and who can blame him? After slaying monsters and subduing beasts, he's just learned he has to go back into the fray, descend into Hell, and bring back Cerberus, the three-headed canine guardian. It's a magnificent piece, powerful and wonderfully human. Carved out of one piece of marble, the colossal ***Toro Farnese*** is 4m (13-ft.) high, the world's largest-known sculpture from antiquity; it was also unearthed at the Baths of Caracalla. Cardinal Farnese hired a team of Renaissance masters, Michelangelo among them, to restore it. The intricate and delicate work depicts one of mythology's most satisfying acts of revenge, when the twin brothers Amphion and Zethus tied Dirce—who had imprisoned and mistreated their mother, Antiope—to the horns of a bull that will drag her to her death. ***Note:*** Buying tickets online is optional, but doing so can eliminate a long wait. By 2027, more Vesuvian artifacts will be on view in new galleries in the massive Real Albergo dei Poveri, a Bourbon-era almshouse about a mile away on Piazza Carlo III.

Piazza Museo 19. museoarcheologiconapoli.it. ✆ **081/4422111.** Admission 20€, free for children 17 and under. Wed–Mon 9am–7:30pm. Metro: Museo or Cavour.

Museo d'Arte Contemporanea Donnaregina (MADRE) ♥♥

ART MUSEUM In the middle of medieval and baroque Naples, the **Palazzo Regina** provides a dramatic counterpoint with works by contemporary artists such as Andy Warhol and Richard Serra. Painter Francesco Clemente, who was born in Naples, decorated two rooms in colorful tile floors and frescoes replicating ancient symbols of the city. Conceptual sculptor Kapoor transformed a room into a white cube with rich blue pigments on the floor that seem to draw you into the bowels of the earth; he also designed the entrance to the Monte S. Angelo subway station to resemble Dante's entrance to the underworld (perhaps sympathizing with riders that commuting can be hell). Across town, the **Palazzo delle Arti Napoli (PAN;** Via dei Mille 60; comune.napoli.it; ✆ **081/795-8604)** houses rotating exhibits of contemporary art.

Via Settembrini 79. www.madrenapoli.it. ✆ **081/1931-3016.** Admission 8€ adults, 4€ ages 17 and under. Mon and Wed–Sat 10am–7:30pm; Sun 10am–8pm. Bus: E1. Metro: Cavour.

San Lorenzo Maggiore ♥♥ CHURCH The most beautiful of Naples' medieval churches seems to inspire great literature. Petrarch, the medieval master of Italian verse, lived in the adjoining convent in 1345, and it was here on Holy Saturday 1338 that Boccaccio (author of *The Decameron*) supposedly first laid eyes on his muse, Maria d'Aquino. The daughter of a count (but rumored to have been the illegitimate daughter of Robert of Anjou, king of Naples), Maria was married but preferred refuge in a convent to life with her debauched husband. For Boccaccio, it was love at first sight: He nicknamed her La Fiammetta (Little Flame), wooed her with his romantic epic *Filocolo*, and eventually convinced her to

underground NAPLES

Beneath Naples' city streets is a labyrinth of tunnels, age-old cisterns, and Greek and Roman ruins that you can explore on four tours. The **Galleria Borbonica ♥♥** (Bourbon Tunnel), usually entered through a parking garage at Via Morelli 61 (galleriaborbonica.com; ✆ **366/248-4151**), was engineered for mid-19th-century Bourbon royals as an escape route from the Palazzo Reale to military barracks near the port, maneuvering around ancient and medieval waterworks. The 1½-hour standard guided tour costs 10€ (5€ ages 10–13; free for children 9 and under) and runs Friday to Sunday at 10am, noon, 3pm, and 5pm. See website for other tours and prices. **Napoli Sotterranea Tour Ufficiale ♥♥**, usually leaving from the Gran Caffè Gambrinus on Piazza Trieste e Trento (lanapolisotterranea.it; ✆ **081/400-256**), explores the huge cisterns Romans dug beneath the city, which were used well into the 19th century, until cholera outbreaks necessitated purer sources. Parts of the cistern network were used as quarries and as World War II bomb shelters (some wartime furnishings and graffiti remain). Tours last about 1 hour and include English commentary. Exit points vary, but usually you climb out of the dark up a long staircase and emerge into the courtyard of an ordinary-looking apartment house—a good illustration of this city's age-spanning layers. Aside from climbing stairs, you'll also be asked to squeeze through a very tight passage (not recommended for the claustrophobic or the overweight). The guided tour, which is usually in English, costs 15€ (7€ ages 7–17, free for children 6 and under) and takes place daily at 10am, noon, 2pm, and 4:30pm (plus 6pm weekends). **Napoli Sotterranea Percorso Ufficiale ♥♥**, Piazza San Gaetano 58 (napolisotterranea.org; ✆ **081-296944**), shows off the diverse city that lies beneath the streets of the historic center with a tour of Greek waterworks, a Greco-Roman theater, and more World War II air-raid shelters. The guided tour costs 15€ (10€ children 10 and under), with tours in English at 10am, noon, 2pm, 4pm, and 6pm. Across the square, more ruins of Greco-Roman Neapolis can be explored beneath the church of **San Lorenzo Maggiore** (see above).

become his mistress (she jilted him for another man a few years later). Ponder 14th-century romance as you stroll the delightful cloisters and frescoed Chapter Hall, then descend a staircase to witness more of the city's multilayered history: Excavations have unearthed streets from the Greco-Roman city Neapolis, lined with bakeries and shops, a covered market, and an early Christian basilica.

Piazza San Gaetano, Via Tribunali 316. laneapolissotterrata.it. ✆ **081/211-0860.** Free admission to church. Subterranean Neapolis: 9€ adults, 7€ seniors, 6€ for ages 6 to 17, free for children 5 and under. Daily 9:30am–5:30pm. Free daily guided tours in English at 11am and 1:15, 3:15, and 5pm. Metro: Cavour.

VOMERO

Life in Naples never really becomes *too* gentrified, but it calms down a bit in the hilltop enclave of the Napoli *bene* (the city's middle and upper classes). **Castel Sant' Elmo,** a mighty fortress dating to the 13th century, commands the neighborhood's heights and affords spectacular views of the city and bay; admission (7€) includes the Museo Novecento, a collection of 20th-century Neapolitan art (daily 8:30am–7:30pm). The trip up from the center is on the Centrale, Montesanto, or Chaia funiculars, on the number 1 Metro line to the Medaglie d'Oro station, or, to be traditional, up the 414 steps of the **Pedamentina di San Martino,** a 14th-century staircase carved into the hillside leading to the Certosa di San Martino.

Certosa e Museo di San Martino (Carthusian Monastery) ♥♥♥

The Carthusian monks who took up residence high atop the Vomero hill in 1368 obviously knew something of the good life. Their view is still the best in Naples, across the city and the bay to Mt. Vesuvius (taking in the spectacle is reason enough to come up here), and over the centuries they hired the city's best artists to embellish their environs. Foremost among them, the fractious architect and sculptor Cosimo Fanzago (1591–1678) created the pièce de résistance, an enormous central courtyard/cloisters that is a masterpiece of the baroque, a grand assemblage of statue-lined porticoes facing a broad lawn. Lest the monks got too comfortable in their earthly surroundings, a gallery of skulls reminded them of their inevitable fate. As if to reinforce the point, in surrounding chapels the Spanish painter Jusepe de Ribera (1591–1652) executed ghoulish scenes of martyrdom and suffering,

A fancifully decorated ceiling at the Certosa di San Martino, once a monastery, now a museum.

so realistically portrayed with wounds, wrinkles, and writhing agony that he's been said to partake in "the poetry of the repulsive."

As you wander the vast monastery, now housing the **Museo Nazionale di San Martino ♥♥**, it's easy to see why royal administrators were so appalled by the monks' lavish lifestyle that they threatened to cut off state subsidies. The museum is a repository of all things Neapolitan: paintings, prints, sculpture, artifacts, and the *presepi* (Nativity scenes; p. 619) for which the city has an undying affection. None outshine the 750-piece Cuciniello Presepe, equipped with a lighting system that simulates the cycle of a day from dusk to nightfall. Even larger is the full-size model of the Great Barge used by King Charles of Bourbon in the 1700s, housed amid models and artifacts that honor the city's role as a maritime power. The Gothic cellars are filled with sculpture, including an astonishing St. Francis of Assisi by Giuseppe Sanmartino, who artfully crafted *Christ Veiled Under a Shroud* in the Cappella Sansevero (p. 598). A stroll in the pine-scented gardens on the hillside beneath the monastery is an ideal way to end a visit.

Largo San Martino 8. cultura.gov.it/luogo/certosa-e-museo-di-san-martino. ✆ **081/578-1769.** Admission 6€ adults, free for ages 17 and under. Thurs–Tues 8:30am–5pm; last admission 1 hr. earlier. Closed Jan 1 and Dec 25. Metro: Vanvitelli, then bus V1 to Piazzale San Martino. Bus: C28, C31, or C36 to Piazza Vanvitelli. Funicular: Centrale to Piazza Fuga or Montesanto to Morghen.

Villa La Floridiana & Museo Nazionale della Ceramica Duca di Martina ♥♥ MUSEUM When King Ferdinand I returned to Naples in 1815 after 10 years of exile, he brought with him an Italian/Spanish wife, Lucia Migliaccio, the duchess of Floridia. Their wedding, just months after the death of Ferdinand's first wife, Queen Marina Carolina of Austria, created an international scandal. The duchess did not care for court life or for Naples, and Neapolitans didn't care for her, so Ferdinand bought her this magnificent retreat on the Vomero hill with gardens and views that would make anyone surrender to the city's charms. The villa now houses the 6,000-plus ceramics collection of another noble Neapolitan, Placido de Sangro, the duke of Martina. Items of interest include King Ferdinand's walking stick, with a glass top that contains a portrait of Lucia; it was said this was the only way the queen would ever appear in court. Admission to the gardens is free, and though a bit ramshackle these days, they're green and luxuriant, and you can follow a path through them from the villa to a viewpoint overlooking the city.

Via Cimarosa 77. cultura.gov.it. ✆ **081/578-8418.** Museum 4€ adults, 2€ ages 17 and under; free admission to gardens. Wed–Mon 8:30am–5:30pm. Bus: C28, C32, or C36. Funicular: Chiaia to Cimarosa. Metro: Vanvitelli.

FARTHER AFIELD

Catacombe di San Gennaro Napoli (Catacombs of San Gennaro) ♥♥ RELIGIOUS SITE Naples' popular patron San Gennaro (St. Januarius) was once buried here, forever lending his name to this multistory underground cemetery, used from the 2nd through 11th centuries. Some of the city's earliest frescoes are here—look for a haloed San Gennaro with Mt. Vesuvius on his shoulders, and a charming 2nd-century scene with Adam and Eve. Guides (most speak English) will lead you past the frescoed burial niches and early basilicas carved from the tufa rock, with a special nod to Sant'Agrippino, a 3rd-century bishop once interred here (now under the altar of the Duomo), who is almost as popular among Neapolitans as San Gennaro. As you emerge from the lower level of this city of the dead, you'll be in the lively Rione Sanità quarter, until recently an infamous and dangerous haunt of the demimonde. Sanità was also at one time home to the well-to-do, among them early-18th-century architect Ferdinando San Felice, who built the elegant Palazzo dello Spagnolo at 19 Via Vergini; step inside the courtyard for a look at his magnificent double staircase.

Via Capodimonte 13. catacombedinapoli.it. ✆ **081/744-3714.** Admission 13€ adults, 9€ students and seniors, 6€ ages 6–17, free for children 5 and under. Tours (in English) daily on the hour 10am–5pm. Bus: 168, 178, C63, or R4 (from the Archaeological Museum).

Museo e Real Bosco di Capodimonte (Museum and Park of the Capodimonte) ♥♥ MUSEUM Italy has many better art collections, but there's plenty to lure you out to this former hunting preserve of the Bourbon kings. The *bosco reale* (royal woods) is one of the few parks in Naples, so you'll be sharing the greenery with picnicking families. The core of the collection is from Elisabetta Farnese, duchess of Parma, who handed down the family's paintings to her children and grandchildren after she became Queen of Spain; they in turn brought them back to Italy when they became kings of Naples. By the time the works got here, however, many of the best had found their way into other collections; what's left tend to be secondary works by a roster of Italian and Northern masters. In fact, the museum's two standout pieces have nothing to do with the Farneses: Caravaggio's dramatic *Flagellation of Christ* (p. 602), which was brought here in the 1970s, and in the contemporary galleries, Andy Warhol's *Mount Vesuvius*, a comic-book-like depiction of an eruption in gaudy modern colors. In the Royal Apartments are enough Sèvres and Meissen china to serve a royal feast of epic proportions. Most exuberant of all is the Porcelain Boudoir, entirely covered in tiles, 3,000 in all. Capodimonte ceramics were fired right here on the grounds throughout the 18th century.

Palazzo Capodimonte, Via Miano 1; also through the park from Via Capodimonte. capodimonte.cultura.gov.it. ✆ **081/749-9111.** Admission 15€ adults, ages 17 and under free. Thurs–Tues 8:30am–7:30pm. Bus: 168, 204, C63, and 3M (from the Archaeological Museum); the shuttle Capodimonte runs hourly from Piazza Trieste e Trento; 5€, buy tickets on board.

Reggia di Caserta (Royal Palace of Caserta) Museum & Gallery of the Capodimonte ♥♥♥ PALACE The 18th-century Bourbon kings of Naples intended their royal residence to impress, and the

> ### Local Hero
>
> One of Naples' most sainted figures, the Argentine soccer star Diego Maradona (1960–2020) arrived in Naples in 1984 and over the next years quickly became a legend, leading SSC Napoli to repeated victories. The city's stadium is named after him, and though he left Naples in 1992, his image has not diminished over the decades, despite numerous scandals. Maradona looks down on the narrow lanes from colorful murals (the largest is on Via Emanuele de Deo), and he's a popular figure among the Nativity statuettes for sale on Via San Gregorio Armeno. His shrine is **Bar Nilo,** Via San Biagio dei Librai (✆ **081/551-1709**), where mementoes of the beloved star include clippings from his hair and toenails.

largest palace in the world still awes visitors. The Royal Apartments in the 1,200-room showplace are reached by sweeping staircases and awash in marbles and frescoes, but the pièce de résistance lies beyond the tall windows: Versailles-like gardens stretch for 3km (2 miles) and are laced with pools, fountains, and forests of rare trees, the perfect setting for an easy day out from Naples.

Piazza Carlo di Borbone, Caserta, 35km (21 miles) north of Naples. reggiadicaserta.cultura.gov.it. ✆ **0823/448084.** Admission 12€ royal apartments; 9€ park and gardens; 18€ royal apartments and park and gardens; free for ages 17 and under. Daily 8:30am–7:30pm; Dec and Jan gardens until 3:30pm, Feb and Nov 4:30pm, Mar 5pm, Apr–Sept 7pm, Oct 5:30pm. Frequent train service from Naples Central Station to Caserta; the station is just outside the palace gates.

Where to Stay in Naples

Where you stay in Naples makes a difference. Our suggestions below meet the criteria of being in safe neighborhoods close to the sights.

EXPENSIVE

Grand Hotel Parker's ♥♥ Naples' oldest grand hotel has been welcoming guests since 1870, when Prince Grifeo decided to transform his palace into a posh stopover where travelers on the Grand Tour could enjoy a bit of Neapolitan luxury. The name comes from British naturalist George Parker Bidder, who bought the enterprise in 1899 while working on the gardens in the Villa Comunale (p. 598). Through wars, earthquakes, and other ups and downs the tradition continues, and this gracious old place on a hillside above the bay is still all about quiet refinement. Lounges are floored with rich marble and hung with a museum-worthy art collection, while the stylish guest rooms all open to balconies and are soothingly done with both traditional and contemporary touches. Choicest rooms overlook the bay, but all guests can enjoy the views from an airy top-floor lounge and dining area and an expansive roof terrace.

Corso Vittorio Emanuele 135. grandhotelparkers.it. ✆ **081/761-2474.** 82 units. 490€–600€ double. Rates include breakfast. Parking 25€. Bus: 128. Metro: Amedeo. Montesanto, or Centrale funiculars to Corso Vittorio Emanuele. **Amenities:** Restaurant; 2 bars; room service; spa; roof terrace; free Wi-Fi.

Grand Hotel Vesuvio ♥♥ Old-world glamour holds sway in this famed waterfront hostelry, which pampers the rich and famous with a Grand Tour–worthy experience plus all the 21st-century amenities, including a spa. Expanses of shiny parquet, handsome old prints, fine linens on firm beds, and classic furnishings give the large, very comfortable rooms sophisticated-yet-understated polish. The big perk, though, is the view of the bay, the Castel dell'Ovo, and Mt. Vesuvius through glass doors that open to balconies off many rooms. You'll get the same eyeful from the rooftop restaurant and the bright lounge where a lavish breakfast buffet is served.

Via Partenope 45 (off Via Santa Lucia by Castel dell'Ovo). vesuvio.it. ✆ **081/764-0044.** 160 units. 490€–550€ double. Most rates include breakfast. Bus: 152, 140, or C25. **Amenities:** 2 restaurants; bar; fitness center; indoor pool (fee); room service; spa; free Wi-Fi.

MODERATE

Art Resort Gallery Umberto ♥♥ The location, atop Galleria Umberto I (p. 597), is already dramatic enough, but these upper-floor accommodations in the city's 1890s Art Nouveau–style glass shopping arcade add plush, over-the-top interiors. The painted headboards, swag draperies, and gilded furniture may not be for minimalists, but it's hard to beat the theatricality and location. Many of the rooms face into the *galleria,* just below the glass roof, so they are quite bright; others look out over an adjoining piazzetta, while a choice few have little balconies. All guests can enjoy the large interior terrace high above the tile-floored arcades.

Galleria Umberto 1. artresortgalleriaumberto.com. ✆ **081/497-6224.** 16 units. 90€–150€ double. Rates include breakfast. Bus: R2. **Amenities:** Bar; concierge; free Wi-Fi.

BnB Orsini46 ♥♥♥ A stay in this pleasant little inn is like landing in a friend's beautiful home, and in a great location, too, in an old apartment block just off the Santa Lucia seafront. Hosts Gabrielle and Manuela are on hand to extend their generous hospitality, and they surround their guests with comfortable furnishings, including family antiques, in large, airy rooms (two with sea views) and a communal lounge where the day begins with a generous cooked breakfast.

Via Generale Giordano Orsini 46. orsini46.it. ✆ **081/764-3790**. 3 units. 115€–145€ double. Rates include breakfast. **Amenities:** Lounge; free Wi-Fi.

Casa d'Anna ai Cristallini ♥♥♥ One of the most beautiful small inns in Naples occupies an atmospheric old *palazzo* in the lively Sanità neighborhood, and the street life just beyond the door and proximity to many of the city sights add to the charm of a stay. Stylish and comfortable guest rooms face a quiet courtyard, and an elegant salon is perfect for lounging. A rooftop terrace is set up for warm-weather relaxation, and one of the rooms has its own little terrace.

Via dei Cristallini 138. casadanna.it. ✆ **081/446611.** 4 units. 100€–200€ double. Rates include breakfast. **Amenities:** Roof terrace; free Wi-Fi.

Aristocratic flourishes decorate rooms at the Chiaja Hotel de Charme.

Chiaja Hotel de Charme ♥♥ With its bright shops and bars, pedestrian-only Via Chiaia may be one of the city's most welcoming addresses, and this warmly decorated spot in an old noble residence does the location justice. Some smaller rooms face interior courtyards and have snug, shower-only bathrooms, while many larger ones on the street side (with double panes to keep the noise down) have large bathrooms with Jacuzzi tubs. Decor throughout is sufficiently traditional and regal to suggest the *palazzo*'s aristocratic provenance, and services are more wholesome than they were when the place was an upscale brothel. Pastries and snacks are laid out in the sitting room in the afternoon and evening, the buffet breakfast is generous, and the staff is adept at recommending restaurants and providing directions.

Via Chiaia 216. chiaiahotel.com. ✆ **081/415-555.** 33 units. 80€–170€ double. Rates include breakfast. Bus: R2. **Amenities:** Bar; concierge; Wi-Fi (free in lobby and some rooms).

Correra 241 ♥ Follow a narrow side street, enter the rear courtyard of an old *palazzo,* and walk up a ramp into a former factory tucked into a tufa cliff. Old workrooms and storage lofts have been converted into cheery lodgings done with quirky contemporary flair: yellow concrete floors, rock walls, colorful artwork, even an Etruscan-Greco aqueduct leading off the lobby. There are no standard accommodations: Some rooms are lit by skylights, others by windows high on double-height walls, and still others are two-story—ask about your room's distinct features when you book. You'll be only steps from the archaeological museum, but the rear courtyard setting lets you enjoy some quiet, a rare amenity in Naples.

Via Correra 241. correra.it. ✆ **081/1956-2842.** 21 units. 110€–200€ double (2- or 3-night minimum stay required some periods). Rates include breakfast. Parking 20€. Metro: Dante or Museo. **Amenities:** Bar; free Wi-Fi.

Costantinopoli 104 ♥♥ Set in a palm-shaded courtyard, this 19th-century Art Nouveau palace is mere steps from the archaeological museum but a world away from the noisy city—it even has a small swimming pool in the garden. Contemporary art and some stunning stained glass grace a series of salons; some rooms are traditionally done with rich fabrics and dark wood furnishings, others are breezily contemporary. The choicest are on the top floor and open onto a sprawling roof terrace that's a magical retreat above the rooftops; ask for these units when booking.
Via Santa Maria di Costantinopoli 104 (off Piazza Bellini). costantinopoli104.it. ✆ **081/557-1035.** 19 units. 150€–300€ double. Rates include breakfast. Metro: Museo. **Amenities:** Pool; room service; free Wi-Fi.

Decumani Hotel de Charme ♥♥ The heart-of-Naples neighborhood beyond the grand entrance can be gritty, but these are regal lodgings, on the *piano nobile* of the *palazzo* of the last Bourbon bishop, Cardinal Sisto Riario Sforza. Guest rooms surround a vast, frescoed ballroom–cum–breakfast room; all have plush draperies and fabrics and a few antiques complementing hardwood floors and timbered ceilings. Larger rooms include sitting areas and face the quiet courtyard, while many of the smaller, street-facing doubles share small terraces.
Via San Giovanni Maggiore Pignatelli 15 (off Via Benedetto Croce, btw. vias Santa Chiara and Mezzocannone). decumani.com. ✆ **081/551-8188.** 22 units. 100€–215€ double. Rates include breakfast. Metro: Dante. **Amenities:** Free Wi-Fi.

Hotel Il Convento ♥♥ If you want to experience a slice of Neapolitan life amid narrow Spagnoli streets teeming with neighborhood color and bustle, here's the place for you. This 17th-century former convent provides cozy ambience with lots of wood beams, brick arches, and terracotta floors. Two rooms have their own planted rooftop terraces, and two others spread over two levels. Main artery Via Toledo is just 2 short blocks

Decumani Hotel de Charme's elegant breakfast room.

away, simplifying comings and goings at night. An eager staff will steer you to neighborhood restaurants and shops. Small pets are allowed.

Via Speranzella 137/A. hotelilconvento.it. ✆ **081/403-977.** 14 units. 115€–135€ double. Rates include breakfast. Metro: Toledo or Municipio. **Amenities:** Bar; fitness room and sauna; room service; free Wi-Fi.

Hotel Piazza Bellini ♥♥♥ The archaeological museum and lively Piazza Bellini are just outside the door of this centuries-old palace, but a cool contemporary vibe softens the edges of city life. An outdoor living room fills the cobbled courtyard, and the rooms are minimalist chic with hardwood floors, sleek surfaces, neutral tones with warm-hued accents, and plenty of space for storage. Some rooms have terraces and balconies, a few are bi-level, and some with limited views are set aside as "economy"—but rates for any room in the house are a good value.

Via Costantinipoli 101. hotelpiazzabellini.com. ✆ **081/451-732.** 48 units. 115€–150€ double. Rates include breakfast. Metro: Dante or Cavour. **Amenities:** Bar; concierge; free Wi-Fi.

San Francesco al Monte ♥♥ This former Franciscan convent just above the Spanish quarter and halfway up the San Martino hill makes the monastic life seem pretty appealing. The friars left behind a chapel, a refectory, secret stairways, and lots of atmospheric nooks and crannies, while their cells have been combined into large, tiled guest rooms and sprawling suites. Views from all rooms and several airy lounges sweep across the city to the bay. In the sprawling rooftop garden, vine-shaded walkways are carved out of the cliffside, and a swimming pool and outdoor bar are welcome perks in summer. The hillside location is a handy refuge above the fray but an easy walk or funicular ride away from the sights.

Corso Vittorio Emanuele 328. sanfrancescoalmonte.it. ✆ **081/423-9111.** 45 units. 155€–240€ double. Rates include breakfast. Metro: Amedeo. Montesanto or Centrale funiculars to Corso Vittorio Emanuele. **Amenities:** Restaurant; bar; pool; room service; free Wi-Fi.

INEXPENSIVE

BnB Naples ♥♥ Native Neapolitan Elia has gone into the hospitality business with flair, converting his law offices on two upper floors of an old palace near the port into a welcoming little inn. His seven rooms are large and bright, with high ceilings, huge windows opening to balconies in some, and plenty of fine old woodwork and finishes; contemporary furnishings are sparse but comfortable and geared to convenience, with good workspaces, ample lighting, and room to spread out and lounge. Bathrooms are crisp and up to date. The location, just off Piazza Municipio, is prime for sightseeing, with the port, historic center, and Santa Lucia seafront all an easy walk away, and Elia is pleased to suggest ways to go about taking it all in. Modern conveniences aside, an old Neapolitan institution remains—the cage elevator operates on .10€ coins, so arrive with change in your pocket.

Via Medina 17. bnbnaples.com. ✆ **081/551-9978.** 7 units. 80€–100€ double. Rates include breakfast at nearby bar. Metro: Municipio. **Amenities:** Free Wi-Fi.

IStayinToledo ♥♥♥ Fabio and Dario's light-filled apartment-turned-guesthouse is a welcome retreat smack dab in the center of Naples. It's right above the stunningly designed Toledo metro station, a short subway ride from the main train station; much of what you want to see is within easy walking distance, and the brick 1920s-era Rationalist-style apartment and office block is itself a landmark. Commodious, light-filled rooms are immaculately kept and chicly furnished, each one named for its distinctive color scheme. All surround an airy lounge that opens to a corner balcony overlooking the comings and goings on Via Toledo. Breakfast, included in some rates, is served at a friendly cafe downstairs.

Via Amando Diaz 8. istayintoledo.it. ✆ **339/187-2920.** 6 units. 80€–110€ double. Most rates include breakfast. **Amenities:** Free Wi-Fi.

Tredici Boutique Rooms ♥♥♥ Brothers Andrea and Mattia Tredici fashioned their welcoming and luxurious guesthouse from an old apartment in the historical center, paying attention to every arch and beam to create comfortable and distinctive lodgings. The large, attractive rooms are equipped with minibars, excellent beds topped with down comforters and pillows, soothing lighting, plenty of storage, and spiffy bathrooms equipped with walk-in showers; one room sports a soaking tub. The brothers treat their guests with the same care they've lavished on the premises, and they are on hand with advice on dining, transport, sights, and anything else you need to know.

Via dei Carrozzieri a Monteoliveto 29. tredici-boutique.hoteldegollado.com. ✆ **339/694-0525.** 3 units. 80€–150€ double. Most rates include breakfast. **Amenities:** Free Wi-Fi.

Where to Eat in Naples

What's not to like about a cuisine in which pizza is closely entwined with city history? **Antica Pizzeria Port d'Alba ♥♥**, Via Port Alba 18 (anticapizzeriaportalba.com; ✆ **081/459713**), where rocks from Mt. Vesuvius line the ovens, claims to be the world's first pizzeria, established in 1738. D'Alba was once known for its generous (alas, erstwhile) *pizza a otto* payment system, by which patrons could pay 8 days after eating—making it *the* place to enjoy a free last meal if you were planning on dying before payment was due. **Pizzeria Brandi ♥♥**, Salita S. Anna di Palazzo 1/2 (pizzeriabrandi.com; ✆ **081/416928**), famously claims (with a plaque to back it up) to be the birthplace of the pizza Margherita, created in 1889 for Margherita, Queen of Savoy; topped with mozzarella, tomato sauce, and basil, its colors mimicked the Italian flag.

Neapolitan cuisine has plenty of other iconic dishes, too. Try *mozzarella in carrozza* (fried mozzarella in a "carriage"), in which mozzarella is fried between two pieces of bread and topped with a sauce of the chef's design, often with tomatoes and capers; *gnocchi alla sorrentina,* pockets of potato pasta filled with mozzarella and topped with tomato sauce; *ragù,* a meat sauce cooked for hours and served atop pasta; *Parmigiana di melanzane* (eggplant Parmesan), the ubiquitous dish of fried eggplant, tomato sauce, mozzarella, Parmigiano, and basil; *crocchè di patate* (fried potatoes), mashed with herbs, cheese, sometimes salami, lightly coated in breadcrumbs and fried; and *pasta e fagioli,* beans and pasta—nothing could be more Neapolitan. *Cozze* (mussels), often served *alla marinara* (simmered in tomato sauce), and *polpette,* succulent little meatballs, abound.

EXPENSIVE

Rosiello ♥♥ NEAPOLITAN/SEAFOOD It's a cab ride or long bus trip out to this retreat on a hilltop above the sea in swanky and leafy Posillipo, but a meal on the terrace here is one of the city's great occasions. Everything comes from the sea at your feet or the restaurant's extensive vegetable plots on the hillside; even the cheese is local. These ingredients find their way into feasts that might include risotto *alla pescatora* (with seafood) and *pezzogna all'acquapazza* (fish in a light tomato broth), but even a simple pasta here, such as *scialatielli con melanzane e provola* (fresh pasta with local cheese and eggplant), is elegant and simply delicious.
Via Santo Strato 10. ristoranterosiello.it. ✆ **081/574-2341.** Main courses 15€–35€. Thurs–Tues noon–4pm and 7pm–midnight. Closed 2 weeks Jan and Aug. Bus: C3 to Mergellina (end of line) and then 140.

MODERATE

Europeo di Mattozzi ♥♥ NEAPOLITAN/PIZZA/SEAFOOD Many Neapolitans rank this attractive center-of-town eatery as a favorite, and a meal here beneath walls covered with copper pots, framed photos, and oil paintings seems like a special event. Pizzas are traditional starters, while some excellent alternatives include *zuppa di cannellini e cozze* (bean and mussel soup) or *pasta e patate con provola* (pasta and potatoes with melted cheese). Seafood *secondi* are the house specialties, including *ricciola all' acquapazza* (a local fish in a light tomato and herb broth) and *stoccafisso alla pizzaiola* (dried codfish in a tomato, garlic, and oregano sauce). Reservations are a must on weekends.
Via Marchese Campodisola 4. instagram.com/ristorante_europeo_mattozzi. ✆ **081/552-1323.** Main courses 12€–24€. Mon–Sat noon–3:30pm and 7:30–11 (until 11:30pm Fri and Sat) Closed 2 weeks Aug. Bus: R2 or R3 to Piazza Trieste e Trento. Metro: Municipio or Dante.

La Locanda Gesù Vecchio ♥♥♥ NEAPOLITAN The warmth and flavors of old Naples take on a new twist in this attractive and stylish room in the historic center. Attentive service accompanies an innovative menu that presents standout pastas such as *paccheri ripieni e*

Pasta dishes are standouts at La Locanda Gesù Vecchio.

The Wines of Campania

The wines produced in the harsh, hot landscapes of Campania seem stronger, rougher, and, in many cases, more powerful than those grown in gentler climes. Ones to try are *Lacryma Christi* (Tears of Christ) reds and whites, from grapes that grow in the volcanic soil on the slopes of Mt. Vesuvius; *Taurasi,* a potent, full-bodied red also known as *Aglianico;* and *Greco di Tufo,* a pungent white laden with the odors of apricots and apples. *Falanghina,* one of the most popular white wine varieties, is produced from the famed Falernian grapes favored by the ancient Romans. Another varietal of special interest is fruity *Piedirosso,* a dark red grape that is famously grown on the slopes of Vesuvius and the isle of Capri.

fritti (stuffed pasta with cheese and pine nuts and simmered in a rich meat sauce) and excellent meat and fish dishes that include a couple of variations of fried *baccalà* (cod fish). A second location operates just down the street, at number 4; when making reservations, which are highly recommended, you may be assigned to one or the other.

Via Giovanni Paladino 26. lalocandagesuvecchionapoli.it. ✆ **081/461-3928.** Main courses 10€–22€. Tues–Sun noon–2:30pm and 7–11pm. Metro: Duomo.

Mimi alla Ferrovia ♥♥♥ SEAFOOD/NEAPOLITAN Emilio (Mimi) Giugliano must have been an optimist, opening what is now a beloved institution in 1943, when Naples was in the grip of World War II. Paintings from that time still adorn the elegantly plain rooms on a gritty side street near the train station, where a fourth generation now prepares variations of the original dishes, many of them almost legendary—ravioli with sea bass, a succulent *baccalà,* and to start any meal, roasted peppers stuffed with ham and cheese and lightly fried.

Via Alfonso D'Aragona 19–21. mimiallaferrovia.it. ✆ **081/553-8525.** Main courses 8€–20€. Mon–Sat 12:15–3:30pm and 7–11pm. Metro: Garibaldi.

Tandem ♥♥ NEAPOLITAN Take a seat in the simple dining room or on the pleasant little terrace on the lane outside and linger over the house specialty, ragù. A lot of locals stop by this friendly, funky little spot for their fix of the city staple, which comes with meat (three or four kinds, slow-cooked) or vegetarian (including a delicious version with smoky eggplant), served over a choice of pastas or by itself with thick slices of bread for dunking, along with carafes of the house wine. If there's a long wait, as there often is, you might have better chances of getting a table at the Tandem outlet a few blocks away on Piazza del Gesù Nuovo.

Via Giovanni Paladino 51. tandemnapoli.it. ✆ **081/1900-2468.** Main courses 8€–20€. Daily 12:30–3:30pm and 7pm–midnight. Metro: Dante.

Umberto ♥♥♥ NEAPOLITAN This Chiaia neighborhood favorite has been going strong for a century. Founder Umberto Di Porzio is commemorated in one of the many dishes his heirs continue to serve—*tubettoni 'do tre dita* ("three-finger") pasta with octopus, tomato, olives, and capers

(Umberto lost two fingers in a hunting accident). The family atmosphere befits such other homey classics as eggplant *Parmigiana* and spaghetti *con vongole,* while waistcoated waiters and exhibitions of contemporary art elevate a comfortable meal to a fine dining experience.

Vico Alabardieri 30. umberto.it. ✆ **081/418555.** Main courses 10€–24€. Tues–Sun 12:30–3pm and 7:15pm–11pm; Mon 7:15pm–11pm. Metro: Chiaia.

The Di Porzio family have been serving Neapolitan favorites to diners at Umberto since 1916.

INEXPENSIVE

Campagnola ♥♥ NEAPOLITAN Many students, professors, and neighborhood regulars eat almost every day at this plain, homey wine shop/trattoria, or at least stop by for a glass of the house wine and a plate of fried artichokes. The chalkboard menu changes daily, ranging through Neapolitan home-style favorites like *Parmigiano di melanzane* and *vitello limone.* Pizzas are perfect starters, and a meal usually ends with *zeppole* (fried doughnuts), courtesy of the house.

Via Tribunale 47. facebook.com/Campagnola1947. ✆ **081/457-663.** Main courses 7€–10€. Wed–Sat noon–3:30pm and 7–11pm and Sun–Mon noon–3pm. Metro: Dante.

Da Nennella ♥♥ NEAPOLITAN The guys at this Spagnoli favorite will make you feel like one of the regulars as you grab a seat on the covered terrace or in the plain white dining room for satisfying home cooking. Stick to the specials, listed on a board and recited by the busy waiters—*pasta e patate* (pasta and potatoes), maybe some fried fish or roasted pork, and salads of fresh greens. Even with wine, a meal here won't cost more than 12€ or 15€.

Piazza Carità. trattorianennella.it. ✆ **081/414338.** Main courses 6€–10€. Mon–Sat noon–3:30pm and 6:45–11pm. Metro: Toledo.

I Buongustai ♥♥ NEAPOLITAN/PIZZA To get away from the crowds on Via Tribunali, walk towards its eastern end, where a neighborhood vibe takes over. This local, no-frills lunchtime favorite is always busy, with a takeaway counter out front and a small dining room in the rear. A huge selection of pizzas, including one that can be made with your choice of toppings, is served alongside *fritturina* (fried vegetables and other bits), *bruschetti,* and choices from a *tavola calda* (hot table), with grilled sausages, meatballs, and whatever else the chef is making that day. Via Tribunali 201. trattoriaibuongustai.it. ✆ **081/446-768.** Pizzas and main courses 4€–18€. Mon–Sat 9am–5pm. Metro: Garibaldi.

Pescheria Azzurra ♥♥♥ SEAFOOD Fresh fish doesn't come to the table any fresher than it does in these unadorned surroundings in the picturesque Pignasecca market in Montesanto. It's a fishmonger by day, a low-key trattoria into the evening. A crowd of neighborhood regulars and Neapolitans in the know pack in for one of the city's best down-to-earth

GO OFF YOUR diet

To eat like a Neapolitan, you just may have to set healthy habits aside. Clam-shaped *sfogliatelle*, filled with ricotta cream, is the city's favorite pastry, available at bars and bakeries all over the city. *Il baba* are little cakes soaked in rum or limoncello syrup and often filled with cream; *delizia al limone* is sponge cake soaked with lemon or limoncello syrup, filled with lemon pastry cream, and iced with lemon-flavored whipped cream. Dark, flourless *torta* Caprese, topped with powdered sugar, is the chocolate cake of choice. For the classic coffee-and-a-pastry experience, try **Scaturchio ♥♥**, Piazza San Domenico Maggiore 19 (scaturchio.it; ✆ **081/551-7031**); **Sfogliatella Mary ♥♥** in the Galleria Umberto I (instagram.com/sfogliatellamary; ✆ **081/402-218**); and **Il Vero Bar del Professore ♥♥** at Piazza Trieste e Trento 46 (ilverobardelprofessore.com; ✆ **081/403-041**).

For some of Italy's best gelato, **Gelateria della Scimmia ♥♥**, Piazza Carità 4 (facebook.com/gelateriadellascimmia; ✆ **081/5520272**), is a mandatory stop. Naples' elegant temple of chocolate, **Gay-Odin ♥♥** (gay-odin.it), sells chocolate *cozze* (shaped like mussels) and chocolate-wrapped coffee beans at shops throughout the city; a convenient central location is at Via Toledo 427 (✆ **081/561-3491**).

Friggatorie shops focus on deep-fried snacks, like *panzarotti* (potato croquettes), *arancini* (fried rice balls), and *pizza fritte* (deep-fried pizza dough topped with sauce and cheese). Top stops are **Friggitoria Vomero ♥♥**, near the Vomero funicular stop at Via Domenico Cimarosa 44 (facebook.com/friggitoria.vomero; ✆ **081/578-3130**), and **1947 Pizza Fritta ♥♥**, in the historic center at Via Pietro Colletta 16 (1947pizzafritta.it; ✆ **333/400-8562**). **Di Matteo ♥♥**, a venerable pizzeria also in the historic center at Via Tribunali 94 (pizzeriadimatteo.it; ✆ **081/455-262**), sells fried food from a street-side counter. You'll sample many of these foods, accompanied by lively commentary, on a walk through the historic center on 2½-hour **Naples Street Food Tours ♥**, about 45€, from Viator (viator.com) and other companies; **Streaty ♥** tours (streaty.com; ✆ **0351/513-3552**) add a stop in the outdoor Pignasecca market and some drinks (59€). **Culinary Backstreets ♥♥** tours (culinarybackstreets.com) explore the city's iconic street foods as well as cheeses, wines, and other regional artisanal products, accompanied by an introduction to local culture and history (130€). Whatever tour you take, show up with an empty stomach, as the pizza, fried snacks, and sweets you'll sample add up to a hearty meal.

THE BEST pizza IN NAPLES

According to about half the residents of Naples, no-frills, zero-ambience **L'Antica Pizzeria Da Michele** ♥♥♥, Via Sersale 1 (damichele.net; ✆ **081/553-9204;** Metro: Piazza Garibaldi), serves the best pizzas in town—they come in just four varieties, *margherita, marinara,* a combo of the two, or *cosacca,* with Pecorino (toppings are for snobs, say aficionados). The other half would vote for **Pizzeria Gino e Toto Sorbillo** ♥♥♥, Via Tribunali 32 (sorbillo.it; ✆ **081/446-643;** Metro: Dante), where a long menu of pizzas with toppings is accompanied by a palatable house wine. At both, prepare to wait for a table, but not for long, as pizzas emerge from the ovens in a mere 20 seconds, an act of wizardry that keeps the tables turning quickly. At both, pizzas are 6€ to 7€; Michele is closed on Sunday.

dining experiences, enjoying spaghetti alla *vongole* (with clams), *cozze* (mussels, best in garlic-parsley sauce), and other simply done favorites. Via Portamedina 3/4. ✆ **081/1925-0591.** Main courses 10€–20€. Tues–Thurs 10am–9pm, Fri–Sat 10am–11:30pm, Sun 10am–3pm. Metro: Montesanto.

Trattoria 'a Pignata ♥♥♥ NEAPOLITAN This indoor/outdoor spot on a crowded alley in the Spagnoli, just off Via Toledo, is justly popular with Neapolitans and their visitors alike, and no one seems to mind waiting for a table while taking in the street life. A busy and friendly staff serves heaping plates of nicely done *gnocchi alla sorrentina,* eggplant *Parmigiana,* and other homey staples typical of the city's backstreet trattorias. Choices also include several pasta dishes topped with fresh-from-the market seafood. Vico Lungo del Gelso. www.trattoriapignata.it. ✆ **081/413-526.** Main courses 7€–12€. Tues–Sun noon–3:30pm and 7–11:30pm. Metro: Toledo.

Naples Shopping

Via Toledo and Galleria Umberto I hold their own as mainstays of Naples shopping, though the clothing and accessories shops in Chiaia tend to be a little more elegant these days. There, big Italian fashion names have outlets along the Riviera di Chiaia, Via Calabritto, Via dei Mille, Via Filangieri, and Via Poerio, and in Piazza dei Martiri.

Handmade **Marinella ties,** a symbol of luxurious quality for more than a century and worn by the likes of Bill Clinton and Aristotle Onassis, are showcased at the main store and workshop at Via Riviera di Chiaia 287 (emarinella.eu; ✆ **081/764-4212**).

The **Mercato di Porta Nolano** food market stretches around Piazza Nolano, south of the train station. Stalls burst with seafood and local produce and all manner of other foodstuffs, along with housewares and other goods; they operate Monday to Saturday until 6pm and Sunday until 2pm (pickpockets have a field day here, so watch your effects). **La Pignasecca,** above Via Toledo in hillside Montesanto, is the city's oldest market and specializes in sea creatures (daily 9am–2pm). The **Mercato di Antignano** spreads out along lanes beside medieval Castel Sant' Elmo in Vomero on weekdays from 7am to 1:30, with vendors selling food, housewares, and clothing. Every third Saturday and Sunday of each month from 8am to 2pm (except in Aug), a *fiera antiquaria* (**antiques fair**) is held in the Villa Comunale on Viale Dohrn.

Opening hours for stores in Naples are generally Monday to Saturday from 10:30am to 2pm and from 4 to 7:30pm, though some stay open continuously and keep longer hours. Many shops catering to tourists are open on Sunday as well.

Entertainment & Nightlife

Neapolitans make the best of balmy evenings by passing the time on cafe terraces. Top choice is the oldest cafe in Naples, with a Liberty-style interior from the 1860s, the elegant **Gran Caffè Gambrinus ♥♥**, Via Chiaia 1, in Piazza Trieste e Trento (grancaffegambrinus.com; ✆ **081/417-582**). Jean-Paul Sartre and Ernest Hemingway were among the luminaries who have lingered over coffee and drinks here, and the cafe observes the city's long-standing Suspended Coffee tradition—patrons who buy a coffee may pay for another and leave the receipt in an antique coffee pot so someone less fortunate can retrieve it and enjoy a cup, too.

OPERA & CLASSICAL MUSIC The great Naples-born tenor Enrico Caruso (1873–1921) appeared only once at his hometown's sumptuous opera house, in 1901, when he was booed off the stage and vowed never

EVERY DAY IS christmas

Among the many delights of Naples are the *presepi,* Nativity scenes that you can find everywhere, any time of the year, although they really come out in force around Christmas. St. Francis of Assisi is said to have commissioned the first *presepe* in the 13th century, but it was here in Naples that the scenes were elevated to high art, bolstered by the patronage of King Charles III in the 18th century. City craftsmen still go all out, carving figures in wood, firing them in ceramics, even fitting them with tailored clothing. Besides mainstays like Mary, Joseph, and the baby Jesus, the Neapolitan cast of characters often includes soccer stars and other celebrities, and settings can be a lot more elaborate than a humble manger: medieval town squares, rusticated villages with thatched cottages, elaborate caves that look like some troglodyte fantasy. On **Via San Gregorio Armeno,** dozens of shops sell figures beginning at about 15€. You can buy a complete scene for anywhere from 100€ to well into five digits, or have one made with figures of your own family and favorite celebrities (as many Neapolitans do). Be aware that pickpockets flock to the street like sheep to a Bethlehem hillside to prey on distracted window-shoppers. Among the most venerable shops are **Gambardella Pastoria e Presepi ♥♥**, Via San Gregorio Armeno 40 (gambardellapastori.com; ✆ **081/551-7107**); **Marco Giuseppe Ferrigno ♥♥**, Via San Gregorio Armeno 10 (arteferrigno.it; ✆ **081/552-3148**); and **Petrucciani ♥♥**, Via San Gregorio Armeno 51 (petruccianisangregorioarmeno.it; ✆ **081/551-2496**). Another shop selling handcrafted figurines is **La Scarabattola,** in the historic center at Via dei Tribunali 50 (lascarabattola.it; ✆ **081/291-735**), where the output includes traditional folk figures and contemporary ceramics.

The elegant Teatro Dan Carlo, opened in 1737, is the world's oldest opera house.

to return (these days he's honored with a museum in the Palazzo Reale; p. 596). The venerable **Teatro San Carlo ♥♥**, Via San Carlo 98 (teatrosancarlo.it; ✆ **081/797-2412** or 081/797-2331), has been kinder to other performers and composers. The world's oldest opera house, inaugurated on November 4, 1737, it has welcomed Rossini, Bellini, Verdi, Puccini, and a veritable who's who of opera greats. The house still stages world-class opera, along with dance and orchestral works, December to June Tuesday through Sunday. Tickets generally cost between 30€ and 100€, though prices can be much higher for some performances. Guided tours (9€, 7€ 29 and under) are available daily in English at 11:30am and 3:30pm.

The **Fondazione Pietà de' Turchini** music conservatory, Via Santa Caterina da Siena 38, at the base of the Vomero hill near the Vittorio Emanuele funicular stop (turchini.it; ✆ **081/402-395**), is renowned for concerts of early music, though the repertoire extends to other music as well. Concerts are held in the church of Pietà dei Turchini, beneath paintings by some of Naples' great baroque masters, and in a hall that was once an orphanage where young charges were instructed in singing and musical composition. Star pupils included Alessandro Scarlatti (1660–1725) and Giovanni Pergolesi (1710–36).

The **Associazione Alessandro Scarlatti,** Piazza dei Martiri 58 (associazionescarlatti.it; ✆ **081/406-011**), stages chamber music concerts at Castel Sant' Elmo and other locales; ticket prices range from 15€ to 25€. Student concerts are frequently staged at **San Pietro a Majella** (sanpietroamajella.it; ✆ **081/544-9255**), a former monastery and now a conservatory, at Via San Pietro a Majella 35, just off Via San Sebastiano, known for its many music shops.

Also known as the Teatro Della Canzone Napoletana, **Trianon Viviani,** near the Piazza Garibaldi train station at Piazza Vincenzo Calenda 9 (teatrotrianon.org; ✆ **081/225-8285**), focuses on traditional Neapolitan song and theater; the concert season usually starts in April, with performances Thursday through Sunday.

BARS & CLUBS **Piazza Bellini** ♥, near the university at the edge of the historical center, is an especially lively destination. With a lush terrace and rooms full of books and old photos, the deservedly popular **Intra Moenia** ♥♥, Piazza Bellini 7 (intramoenia.it; ✆ **081/290-988;** daily morning to late), is a gathering spot for coffee, light meals, and drinks. **Cammarota Spritz** ♥, in Spagnoli at Vico Lungo Teatro Nuovo 31 (facebook.com/cammarotaspritz), might be Naples' most popular bar, with outside service only for ridiculously inexpensive drinks served in plastic cups. **Archeobar** ♥, near the university at Via Mezzocannone 101/B (instagram.com/archeobarnapoli; ✆ **081/1917-8862**), is friendly to students and sightseers alike, with a lively downstairs room and a quieter, book-lined den upstairs where patrons chat quietly and even read.

Enoteche, or wine bars, provide wines by the glass and the bottle, Among the most pleasant and well-stocked are two stops in Chiaia: **Enoteca Belledonne** ♥♥, Vico Belledonne a Chiaia 18 (enotecabelledonne.eu; ✆ **081/403-162;** closed Sun), with a local vibe, and **Barril** ♥♥, Via Giuseppe Fiorelli 11 (barril.it; ✆ **081/4362**), serving wine and excellent cocktails, along with *cicchetti,* in chic rooms and a garden. In Vomero, **Archivio Storico** ♥, Via Alessandro Scarlatti 30 (instagram.com/archivio_storico_napoli; ✆ **375/608-9682**), mixes classic cocktails in refined surroundings.

AROUND NAPLES

To the west of Naples are the weird volcanic landscapes and evocative ancient ruins of the **Campi Flegrei,** the Phlegraean Fields. To the southeast are two of the world's most famous and well-preserved ancient cities, **Herculaneum** and **Pompeii,** and the volcano that doomed them, **Vesuvius.** You can visit any of these fabled places easily on a day trip and be back in Naples in time for a *passeggiata* and dinner.

Campi Flegrei (Phlegraean Fields) ♥♥

On this seaside peninsula just west of Naples, volcanic vents steam and hiss, and ruined villas testify to ancient accomplishments and no small amount of hedonism. Our alphabet was invented here, when the Latin language officially adopted the characters used for written communication in Cuma. Nero murdered his mother, Agrippina, outside Baiae, the Palm Beach of the ancient world, where Caesar relaxed and Hadrian breathed his last. Pozzuoli and other busy modern seaside towns provide some everyday drama, too, and beyond them, moonlike lava landscapes are interspersed with lush hillsides carpeted in olive groves and orange and lemon orchards, adding an eerie beauty to the mix.

ARRIVING & GETTING AROUND

A day exploring this strange, mythic landscape begins in seaside Pozzuoli, reached from Naples by Line 2 of the Metropolitana (subway) or via the **Cumana Railroad** (unicocampania.it; ✆ **800/053-939**), starting from Piazza Montesanto. The Metropolitana station in Pozzuoli is above the main town, near the Anfiteatro Flavio; the Cumana Railroad station is near the seafront and town center, just around the corner from the Serapeo ruins. From Pozzuoli, **EVA buses** (formerly SEPSA; eavsrl.it; ✆ **081/735-4965**) run to the Solfatara. The Cumana Railroad and bus connections will get you to Baia (change buses at Lucrina), Lago d'Averno, and Cuma (change buses in Torregaveta). Getting around the Campo Flegrei requires some logistics, but you can get a good sense of the area in just a day at Pozzuoli. ***Tip:*** If you plan to see several area sights, for just 10€ (5€ ages 18–25) you can get a **Campi Flegrei** combined ticket, valid for 2 days, which includes the Anfiteatro Flavio, Castello di Baia, Zona Archeologica in Baia, and Scavi di Cuma. Admission to any of these costs 5€ (but free for ages 17 and under), so if you visit more than two, it'll save you money. Purchase the ticket at any of the sites.

POZZUOLI ♥♥

23km (14 miles) W of Naples

Screen legend Sophia Loren was born in this seaside town in 1934, contributing more color to a place already steeped in lore. With its storied past, ancient monuments, volcanic landscapes, and sweeping views over the sea and the islands of Ischia and Procida, Pozzuoli is a lot more interesting and appealing than an otherwise scrappy suburban town has any right to be.

The Greek colony of Dicearchia, founded in 530 B.C.E., became the Roman Puteoli in 194 B.C.E. You will soon sniff out the origin of the name—from the Latin *putere,* "to stink," with the source being the sulfurous Solfatara, a dormant volcano at the edge of town where lunar landscapes hiss, steam, bubble, and spew (currently off-limits due to safety issues amid increased volcanic activity). More kindly, the name may also come from the Greek pyteolos, or "little well." Roman emperors preferred this harbor to the one at Partenope (Naples). Among them was Caligula, who performed a famous stunt at Puteoli: He rode his horse across a floating bridge of boats to Baia, defying the soothsayer who said he had "no more chance of becoming Emperor than of riding a horse across the Gulf of Baiae." The town also became famous for *pozzolana,* volcanic ash that reacts with water to form a concrete-like substance that allowed engineers to build the huge dome of Rome's Pantheon.

Puteoli was also a hub for cargo ships from all over the Roman world—dockworkers unloaded grain from Egypt, Sicily, and other outposts of the empire and reloaded them with marble, mosaics, and other exports. Among the voyagers who disembarked here was St. Paul, sometime around C.E. 60. He'd sailed across the Mediterranean from Caesarea, in present-day Israel, where he'd been imprisoned. From Puteoli he traveled up the Appian Way to Rome to stand trial for alleged crimes in Asia Minor and was later freed.

The barbarian Alaric destroyed the Roman town in C.E. 410, but the acropolis, on a tufa-stone promontory pushing into the sea, continued to be inhabited throughout the Dark Ages. A modern town grew up around the promontory in the following centuries, and the old city, known as the Rione Terra, remains. The quarter was inhabited until the 1980s, when "bradyseism," a settling and rising of unstable volcanic ground, rendered living in the district unsafe, especially after sewer lines burst, creating a public health issue. Beneath crumbling houses from the 16th and 17th centuries is the ancient town, with the foundations of shops, taverns, houses, and slave quarters intact. A magnificent Greek/Roman temple, incorporated into the baroque Duomo, is open Wednesday through Monday, 9:30am to 1:30pm and 2:30 to 6:30pm. The excavations are occasionally open for guided tours on weekends; for information, contact Puteoli Sacra, a local tourist organization (puteolisacra.com; ✆ **351/550-654**).

Anfiteatro Flavio ♥♥ RUINS More than 20,000 spectators could squeeze into the late-1st-century Flavian Amphitheater, the third-largest arena in the Roman world. So much remains that it seems as if a crowd is about to mill in for the next gladiatorial show. The theater's engineers, who also built the Colosseum in Rome, devised sophisticated subterranean staging areas with "mechanics" that hoisted wild beasts up to the field of slaughter and pumped in water to flood the arena for mock naval battles. Among the unfortunate victims of the spectacles staged here was Januarius, or San Gennaro, the patron saint of Naples. A painting by Artemisia Gentileschi (1593–1656), a surprisingly successful female artist of the Neapolitan baroque, shows the bishop calmly withstanding the attacks of a ferocious boar. (You can see Gentileschi's painting in Naples' Museo e Real Bosco di Capodimonte; see p. 607.) According to legend, however, the beasts released to devour him fell submissively at his feet. Alas, Gennaro was later beheaded on the crater floor of the nearby Solfatara volcano.
Via Nicola Terracciano 75. pafleg.cultura.gov.it. ✆ **081/526-6007.** Admission 5€ (10€ Campi Flegrei combined ticket; see p. 622), free for ages 17 and under. Hours vary but generally Wed–Mon 9am–4pm, sometimes later in summer.

Temple of Serapis ♥♥ RUINS The name refers to a statue of the Greco-Egyptian god Serapis, which once stood in a niche of this magnificent marketplace with a marble-floored arcaded courtyard; in the middle rose a *tholos,* a raised meeting hall decorated with sea creatures. In the 19th century, antiquarians noticed that columns in the marketplace were riddled with holes drilled by mollusks; subsequent investigations revealed that the culprit was bradyseism, where unstable ground settled under sea level for periods of time then rose above sea level again, shifting as much as 6 ft. in a decade—making living in Pozzuoli a shaky business. (A series of uplifts in the 1980s forced much of the town to be evacuated, damaged 8,000 buildings, and raised the seabed to the point that the harbor can no longer accommodate large craft.) As you circle around the site, try to spot the little holes in the marble columns once submerged in water.

Pozzuoli center. ✆ **081/526-6007.** Free admission. Viewed from surrounding sidewalk.

BAIA ♥

6km (4 miles) SW of Pozzuoli

Parco Archeologico di Terme di Baia.

Many of the villas and thermal baths of this ancient spa town are now underwater, though enough remains on terra firma to suggest the grandeur of **Ancient Baiae** (the modern town dropped the last "e"). Julius Caesar, Nero, and others of the Roman elite once relaxed and debauched in Baiae's large villas, equipped with swimming pools and other luxuries. Seneca the Younger, the 1st-century philosopher and man of letters, called the place a "vortex of luxury." The poet Ovid said it was "a favorable place for love-making," while Horace chimed in, "No bay on Earth outshines pleasing Baiae." The town—which takes its name from Baio, the navigator of Odysseus, said to be buried somewhere in Baia—was famed for its thermal baths, fed by sulfur springs believed to have medicinal properties.

Baiae had its share of salacious moments. According to legend, this is where emperor Nero tried to kill his mother, the ambitious and villainous Agrippina, by contriving to have a ceiling crash down on her bed. When that didn't work, he arranged to have her boat rammed at sea, but she swam ashore. The thwarted emperor finally sent a henchman to Baiae to stab the doomed woman. Poster girl for the town's debauchery may have been Messalina, third wife of the emperor Claudius, who was said to be sexually insatiable—gossip claimed she snuck out of her Baiae villa in disguise at night to work at the town's brothel under the name She Wolf.

Ruins of temples, villas, and bathing establishments litter three grassy terraces above the bay in the **Parco Archeologico delle Terme di Baia ♥♥**

(pafleg.cultura.gov.it). The ruins are not especially well marked nor well preserved. It's believed that a pile of stones near the top may have been the villa of Julius Caesar, who popped up to Rome from here for a meeting of the senate on the Ides of March 44 B.C.E. (the rest is history). His houseguest at the time was Cleopatra. Enough remains of the Terme di Baiae to show just how elaborate the bathing complexes were. Admission is 5€, free for ages 17 and under (10€ Campi Flegrei combined ticket; see p. 622); the park is open Tuesday through Sunday, 9am to sunset.

Much of the ancient town is underwater, preserved as the **Parco Archeologico Sommerso di Baiae ♥♥**, Via Sella di Baia 22, Bacoli (parcoarcheologicosommersodibaia.it; ✆ **815/232-739**). Mosaic flooring, statuary, fishponds, and other ruins litter the seabed amid bubbling geysers and flourishing flora. You can view this undersea world on dives, by snorkeling, or on trips on glass-bottom boats. Dive centers and boat tours operate out of the port and Via Lucullo in Baia; expect to pay about 25€ for a boat trip, 30€ for a snorkeling tour, and 40€ for a guided dive. The park office can provide a list of tour operators or go to GetYourGuide (getyourguide.com) or other major operators.

Castello di Baia ♥♥ HISTORIC SITE/MUSEUM One of the most impressive landmarks in a town steeped in legend is the work of the Aragonese kings of Naples of the 16th century. Their massive complex of thick walls and defensive moats rises from a wave-buffeted headland that was once topped with a villa of Emperor Nero. The sea-facing battlements were meant to deter Barbary pirates from North Africa, who would pillage coastal towns and take captives to sell into the Ottoman slave market. More important, the unassailable stronghold with its sweeping views of the bay also ensured protection against the French navy, whose ships didn't stand a chance of sailing past the lookouts to invade Naples. Some of the vast rooms now house the **Museo Archeological dei Campi Flegrei ♥♥**, showing off statuary and other artifacts from Baia and the surrounding region. Most enchanting are the two *nymphaeums,* delightful statue-lined porches that were once equipped with lavish fountains; one, rescued from the sea floor, is said to have been from the villa of Emperor Claudius.

Via Castello 39. pafleg.cultura.gov.it. ✆ **081/523-3797** or 848/800-288. Admission 5€ adults (10€ Campi Flegrei combined ticket; see p. 622), free for ages 17 and under. Tues–Sun 9am–8pm.

CUMA ♥

7km (4½ miles) NW of Lago d'Averno

The Greeks founded their first colony on mainland Italy at Cuma in the 8th century B.C.E., and Cuma grew into an important center of Greek farming operations in Campania. The settlers soon discovered they had a helpful neighbor: the Cumaean Sibyl, who, according to legend, passed on messages from Apollo. The god told the Sibyl he would grant her one wish. She took a handful of sand and said she wanted to live as many years as the number of grains she held. Then came the catch: Apollo wanted her virginity in return. Sibyl refused, so Apollo gave her long life but not eternal youth. Over the centuries she withered away, eventually becoming so small she could be kept in a jar, then only her voice remained—handy for uttering a last request, "I want to die." The **Sibyl's chamber**—a big draw for advice-seekers from around the ancient world and protected as the **Parco Archeologico di Cuma**—sits at the end of a long, narrow tunnel cut through volcanic stone, 131.5m (432 ft.) long, some 5m (16½ ft.) high, and as wide as 2.4m (8 ft.) across. That impressive entrance most likely assured supplicants they were about to hear something gravely important, and the long trapezoidal tunnel can still send chills down the spine.

The Sibyl is said to have ferried Aeneas, son of Aphrodite, across nearby **Lago d'Averno,** where he discovered the River Styx, the gateway to Hades. Legend claims that the lake's vaporous waters were once so lethal (possibly from gas-emitting underwater vents) that it was named after a Greek word meaning "without birds," because winged creatures flying over the waters would plunge to their deaths. In the 1st century B.C.E., Emperor Agrippa had a canal dug to connect the lake with the sea, providing safe harbor for Roman ships. He also ordered construction of the Grotta di Cocceio (Cocceio's Cave), a straight tunnel between the lake and Cuma, 1km (½ mile) long and wide enough for a chariot to pass. The tunnel was passable for almost 2,000 years, until World War II bombs caused a section to collapse.

Parco Archeologico di Cuma. Via Montecuma. pafleg.cultura.gov.it. ✆ **081/854-3060.** Admission 5€ adults (10€ Campi Flegrei combined ticket; see p. 622), free for ages 17 and under. Wed–Mon 9am until sunset.

PROCIDA ♥♥♥

15km (9 miles) W of Pozzuoli

The third of the trio of islands in the Bay of Naples is separated from Pozzuoli and other seaside suburbs only by a narrow channel. While not as glamorous as Capri nor as lush as Ischia, and less visited than these popular neighbors, the tiny island is a quiet beauty. The jumble of pastel-colored houses is a pleasure to explore on foot, wandering up and down the narrow alleys of Marina Grande into the old fishing village of Marina di Corricella. At the island's height is Terra Murrata, a medieval enclave rimmed with sea-facing viewpoints. Back at sea level are some much-appreciated beaches, including the sands around Marina di Chiaolella, and a pristine nature preserve, Isola di Vivara. Free electric buses make a circuit of the island. Frequent ferry service operated by **SNAV** (snav.it; ✆ **081/428555**) and **Caremar** (caremar.it; ✆ **081/189-66690**) connects Procida with Naples and Pozzuoli; go to ferryhopper.com for schedules.

Vesuvius ♥♥

Towering, pitch-black Mount Vesuvius looms menacingly over the Bay of Naples. The volcano has erupted periodically since C.E. 79, when it buried

Pompeii and Herculaneum in explosions that released 100,000 times the thermal energy of the Hiroshima bomb. Less violent eruptions occurred in 1631, 1906, and 1944. Mount Vesuvius is the only active volcano on mainland Europe, though another formidable volcanic peak, Mount Etna, is only 560km (335 miles) away, on the east coast of Sicily (p. 782).

The mountain still puffs steam every once in a while, just to keep everybody on their toes. Volcanologists and geologists say that, given the historic record, a major eruption is likely in the relatively near future—it's a question of *when* rather than *if* the mountain will blow its top again. With 3 million people living around the Bay of Naples, that makes Vesuvius one of the most potentially deadly volcanoes in the world.

ARRIVING The most convenient way to visit Vesuvius by public transportation from Naples or Sorrento is on the **Circumvesuviana train** (www.eavsrl.it; ✆ **800/211388** toll-free within Italy) to the Ercolano Scavi stop. From there you can catch **Vesuvio Express** (vesuvioexpress.info) vans to the parking lot below the summit. Fares are 10€ round-trip; you'll pay another 10€ (8€ 24 and under) for park admission. Vans run at least every 45 minutes daily from 9:30am; the last bus departs 2 hours before the park closes. **Busvia del Vesuvio** (busviadelvesuvio.com; ✆ **340/935-2616**) offers rides on a bumpy back road up the mountain from Pompeii Scavi in a 4×4 vehicle that drops you at the summit parking lot; round-trip fare is 22€, including park admission. The service runs April to October daily 9am to 3pm (sometimes later July–Aug). Buy tickets at a booth just outside the Pompei Scavi train station.

By **car,** take the Torre del Greco exit from the A3 autostrada and follow the signs to Vesuvio. The road ends in the parking lot below the summit, where you'll pay 6€ to park. From there it's an easy walk of 2km (about a mile) to the head of the trail to the cone; a shuttle bus also makes the ascent (1€). A taxi from Naples costs a flat rate of 100€ round-trip, including a 2-hour wait.

VISITOR INFORMATION The **Parco Nazionale del Vesuvio** (parconazionaledelvesuvio.it; ✆ **081/865-3911**) maintains trails and other visitor facilities. All transportation arrives below the park entrance at 1,017m (3,337 ft.) in altitude. You'll pay 10€ (8€ 24 and under) to climb the fairly steep trail to the summit or explore the mountainside on other trails, none of them wheelchair accessible. The entrance fee also includes admission to an observatory, the world's oldest seismological/volcanological institution, dating from 1841.

"Funiculì, Funiculà"

One way you won't be making the ascent up the mountain is on the Mt. Vesuvius Funicular, which once climbed to the summit from Pugliano, near Ercolano. It opened to great fanfare in 1880, when the song "Funiculì, Funiculà" was written to celebrate the event. Everyone from Connie Francis and the Grateful Dead to Luciano Pavarotti recorded the jaunty tune. The eruption of 1944 wiped out the tracks and sealed the railway's fate; the ascent by road was by then more practical.

KEEPING UP WITH THE pompeiians

All around the shores of the Bay of Naples, various towns reveal the good life wealthy Romans once enjoyed here. **Oplontis ♥♥**, a swanky seafront suburb of Pompeii (the very name means "opulence"), was wiped out in Vesuvius's eruption and subsequently buried beneath the highways, apartment blocks, and factories of grimy Torre Annunziata. You can still visit Oplontis' showplace, **Villa Poppea,** a huge spread that was the retreat of Poppea Sabina, second wife of Emperor Nero and an infamous schemer and plotter. Here she bathed in a milk filled pool beneath a fresco of Hercules and entertained in mosaic-floored rooms, sea-view gardens, and a massive swimming pool. Poppea allegedly met a gruesome end when her husband jumped on her stomach in a fit of rage and caused her to miscarry. Entrance to the villa is at Via Seplocri 12, Torre Annunziata (pompeiisites.org; ✆ **081/857-5347;** admission 8€, free for 17 and under; 26€ with a 3-day pass to Pompeii and other sites). The villa is open Wednesday through Monday 9am to 5pm (May–Oct until 7pm). It's a short walk from the Torre Annunziata Oplonti Circumvesuviana stop.

Stabia ♥♥ was another beautiful seafront enclave, long buried beneath **Castellammare del Stabia,** an industrial suburb known for shipbuilding. Excavations there include lavish **Villa di Arianna** and **Villa San Marco** (pompeiisites.org). Both have frescoed halls and atria, and the more lavish Villa San Marco has a massive swimming pool, a long colonnade, and a dining hall that could seat 125 guests. Entrances are off SS14; admission is free and the villas are open Wednesday through Monday 9am to 6pm (Nov–Mar until 4pm). Take the Circumvesuviana train to Castellammare di Stabia and get a taxi for the trip out to the villas; it's possible to walk from one to the other. A visit to Castellammare comes with a perk: From the station, a *funivia* (funicular) climbs the 1,100m (3,609-ft.) summit of Monte Faito, for sensational views across the Bay of Naples.

Boscoreale ♥♥, 3km (2 miles) north of Pompeii, was known for its fertile fields and productive vineyards. The sturdy Villa Regina (viewed only from the exterior) testifies to the relative comfort of a prosperous farmer, while the adjacent Antiquarium is a treasure house of farm implements, housewares, plants, and other remarkably preserved artifacts unearthed in the area. Admission is 8€, free for ages 17 and under; a ticket that also includes the Villa dei Misteri and Pompeii costs 22€ (free for 17 and under); and a 3-day pass that also includes Pompeii and Villa dei Misteri, Villa Oplontis, Villa Arianna, and Villa San Marco is 26€ (free for 17 and under). The Antiquarium is open daily 9am to 5pm (May–Oct until 7pm).

All these sites can be reached on a free shuttlebus from Pompeii; see pompeiisites.org for details.

The park opens daily at 9am, closing at 6pm July to August, 5pm April to June and September, 4pm March and October, and 3pm November through February. The trail to the crater closes in extreme weather.

EXPLORING VESUVIUS

The historic peak is the centerpiece of 8,482-hectare (20,959-acre) **Parco Nazionale del Vesuvio ♥♥♥** (Vesuvius National Park), where nine summit trails highlight the lava flows and other geology underfoot. Placards along the way explain the unique micro-environment of the volcanic summit, including many species of orchids and other amazingly tenacious vegetation. The ticket office hands out route maps (short versions are also on the website), which range from easy 1-hour strolls to strenuous 8-hour hikes. The number 5 trail, **Gran Cono,** is the classic ascent to the top: a moderately difficult uphill walk of about half a mile from the ticket office to the 230m-deep (754-ft.) crater. The walk takes about 20 minutes, but forego any notions of being alone in empty volcanic landscapes—cafes and souvenir stands line the route. A guide will lead you around the rim, but make sure the guide who approaches you is a bona-fide ranger and not a shill looking for a tip; guide service is free with the price of admission and mandatory if you want to explore the rim. Wear sneakers—the lava underfoot can be hard on the feet—and bring a sweater, because it can be surprisingly chilly in the heights. The mesmerizing view across Naples and the bay might just make you forget how menacing Vesuvius really is. As a reminder, consider that before the C.E. 79 eruption, the mountain was more than twice as tall as its current 1,282m (4,206 ft.).

POMPEII & HERCULANEUM ♥♥♥

On one fateful day in C.E. 79 the people of Pompeii, a prosperous fishing town, and Herculaneum, a resort just down the coast, watched Mount Vesuvius hurl a churning column of gas and ash high into the sky. It was only a matter of time before flows of superheated molten rock coursed through the streets of Herculaneum and ash and pumice buried Pompeii. In Herculaneum, volcanic debris quickly hardened into a layer of rock that fossilized everything—furniture, wooden beams, clothing, skeletons, graffiti, mosaics; in Pompeii, ash and rock fragments buried structures under a layer as deep as 12m (20 ft.), preserving everything beneath it through the centuries.

Pompeii is much more extensive than Herculaneum, with more to see, but Herculaneum provides an easier-to-manage experience. With its gridlike streets, Pompeii provides an overview of a large Roman town; Herculaneum's better-preserved houses and artifacts give an evocative glimpse into day-to-day life. It's possible to see both in 1 day, but get a good rest the night before, because seeing the sights involves lots of walking and possible sensory overload—you'll be taking in an enormous amount of information. If you have to choose between the two, Pompeii provides the more sensational experience.

Essentials

ARRIVING **Circumvesuviana** trains (www.eavsrl.it; ✆ **800/211-388** toll-free in Italy) run between Naples Piazza Garibaldi and Sorrento every half-hour (3.50€), with stops in Herculaneum and Pompeii. For

Herculaneum, get off at **Ercolano Scavi** (*scavi* means "archaeological excavation"). Herculaneum is 20 minutes from Naples and 50 minutes from Sorrento; the entrance is about 10 blocks, an easy downhill walk, from the station. For Pompeii, exit the train at **Pompei Scavi** (note that the modern spelling drops the last "i" of the ancient name). The main Porta Marina Superiore entrance is about 45m (150 ft.) from the station; the other two entrances, Piazza Esedra and Anfiteatro, are a trek from the station, but the Anfiteatro entrance is adjacent to parking (10€ per car). Pompeii is about 40 minutes from Naples and 30 minutes from Sorrento. The **Campania Express,** which runs between Naples Piazza Garibaldi and Sorrento four times a day from mid-March to mid-October, offers express service to the excavations; the trip from Naples to Herculaneum is only 10 minutes and the trip to Pompeii 30 minutes. **High-speed Frecciarossa trains** run from Rome directly to Pompeii in about 2 hours, but only on the third Sunday of the month; trains leave Roma Termini at 8:53am and return at 6:40pm. Service, which includes the screening of a video about Pompeii, may become more frequent; check **trenitalia.com** for schedules and updates.

To reach either by **car** from Naples, follow the *autostrada* A3 toward Salerno. If you're coming from Sorrento, head east on SS 145, where you can connect with A3 (marked NAPOLI). Then take the signposted turnoffs for Pompeii and Herculaneum.

LOGISTICS The **Herculaneum** excavations are open daily 8:30am to 7:30pm (mid-Mar to mid-Oct until 5pm), last admission 90 minutes before closing. Admission is 16€, 2€ for ages 18 to 25, free for 17 and under. The **Pompeii** excavations are open daily 9am to 7pm (closing at 5pm Nov–Mar), last admission 90 minutes before closing. Admission is 18€ (free for ages 17 and under); a ticket that includes the Villa dei Misteri and Boscoreale is 22€ (17 and under free); and a 3-day pass that includes Villa dei Misteri and Boscoreale as well as Villa Oplontis, Villa Arianna, and Villa San Marco is 26€ (17 and under free). You can purchase full-price tickets and the 3-day pass in advance online at ticketone.it for a 1.50€ fee or at the site. Note that EU citizens ages 18 to 25 pay only 2€, but those tickets may not be purchased online. Admission is limited to 20,000 entries a day, so an online advance purchase is well-advised in summer and on holidays. Admission is free the first Sunday of the month, but tickets must be reserved online in advance.

Both sites are busiest mid-mornings, when tour groups often arrive, especially in summer. They tend to be less crowded, and a bit cooler, in late afternoons. Ticket offices provide free maps, and you can rent audioguides at the Porta Marina Superiore entrance (8€, 5€ kids' version, 6.50€ for 2 people, though sharing is not a particularly good idea). Inside the entrances, bookstores sell guidebooks to the ruins (available in English), and licensed English-speaking guides await visitors. Guides are generally qualified and reliable, but establish a price before setting out (generally about 20€ a person, depending on the size of the group). Their services, or an audioguide, are a welcome asset, because labeling at both sites is extremely limited. An app, **MyPompeii,** provides a lot of background on stops within the excavations marked with QR codes, and also has updates on the number of visitors at any time so you can avoid crowds. Pompeii has a **cafeteria** inside the archaeological zone that's handy for sandwiches and drinks, and a number of restaurants and food carts are near the entrance (but note that you may not leave the site for a bite and then reenter). Herculaneum has a picnic area with vending machines, and several **cafes** are just outside the entrance. You can store your luggage at both sites (also at the train station in Pompeii), making it possible to work in a visit if you're en route between Naples and Sorrento or the Amalfi Coast. If you're visiting the sites on a sunny day, wear sunscreen and bring a bottle of water.

VISITOR INFORMATION For more information about Herculaneum, visit ercolano.cultura.gov.it or call © **081/777-7008;** for Pompeii, visit pompeiisites.org, an especially rich source of information that includes practical info along with news of ongoing excavations, or call © **081/857-5111.**

Herculaneum (Ercolano)

10km (6 miles) SE of Naples

Excavations began at Herculaneum in the early 18th century and continue to this day, with the fairly recent discovery of a beached boat full of desperate souls trying to escape by sea. Another 300 skeletons were found in vaulted stone boathouses on what would have been the town's beach; huddled there waiting to board boats and sail to safety, they were killed instantly by the poisonous vapors of a wall of heated gas and rock sweeping through the town at 100mph. Although many questions about Herculaneum remain unanswered, it's known for certain that this glitzy seaside resort for elite Romans was about a third the size of Pompeii, with a population of about 4,000. Herculaneum had little commerce or industry, and its streets were lined with elegant villas, along with a few apartment blocks for poor laborers and fishermen.

EXPLORING HERCULANEUM'S ARCHAEOLOGICAL AREA ♥♥♥

The ruins of Herculaneum give the unsettling impression of a ghost town from which residents have only recently walked away. Many of the houses retain their second floors, making them seem more like residences than ruins. The volcanic mud that covered Herculaneum during the eruption of Vesuvius in C.E. 79 quickly hardened to a rocklike material. While making excavations difficult, this semi-rock protected the structures underneath, and rather remarkably preserved wooden beams and floors along with

Houses at Herculaneum are more intact than those at Pompeii, giving visitors more of a sense of daily life in Roman times.

furnishings, clothing, and other household objects. The ruins provide a wealth of intriguing detail about building techniques, architecture, and domestic decoration in Roman times, and, of course, about daily life. The charred wood, staircases, and double-height houses here instill the sense of being in a real town, unlike the remote detachment you might experience in Pompeii and other ancient ruins.

The excavations stretch from the town's main street, Via IV Novembre, to what was once the shoreline (now a kilometer to the west); the rest of the Roman town remains inaccessible beneath the buildings of modern Ercolano. From the Ercolano-Scavi station, follow the signs for Scavi di Ercolano for 10 blocks down Via IV Novembre; the entrance is about a 10-minute walk from the station. Plan to spend at least 2 hours.

DECUMANUS MAXIMUS Decumanus Maximus is a street lined with shops, some of them still sporting advertisements and price lists. One of the discoveries along this street was a crucifix, proof that Christianity had already come to Herculaneum by the time of the eruption.

TERME DEL FORO Elegant mosaics of fish, dolphins, and other sea creatures decorate the town's largest and grandest bath complex, with

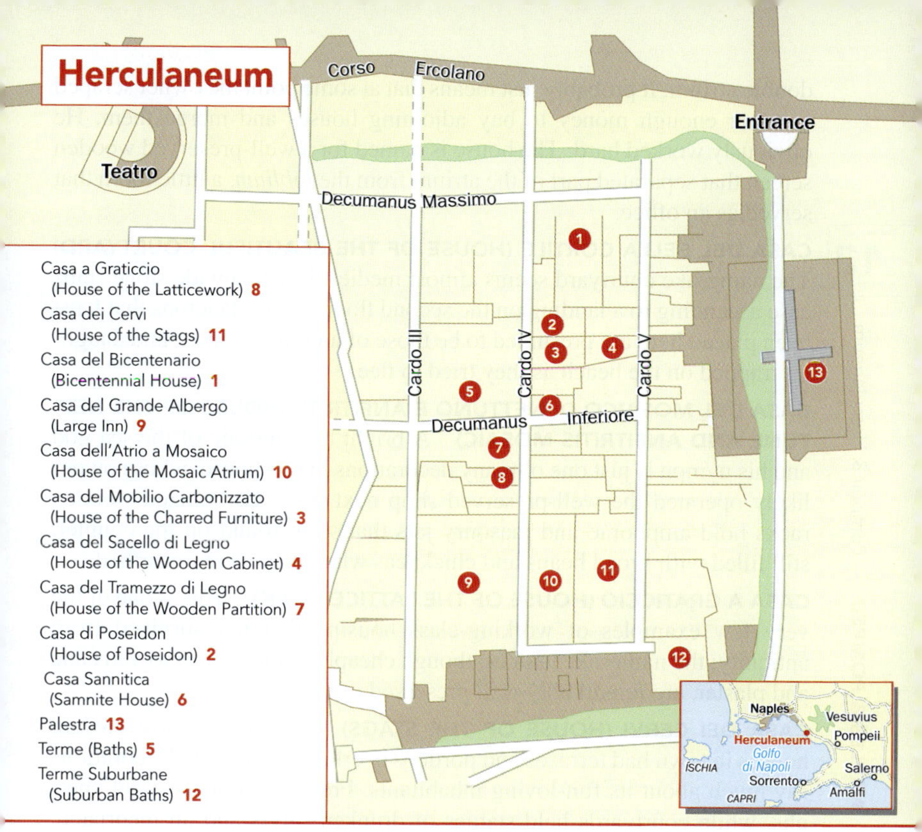

several entrances that include, of course, separate ones for men and women. Enough of the men's section, the **Terme Maschili,** remains to show the range of facilities: a latrine, a changing room lined with benches and shelves for stashing personal effects, and an exercise room. You can still make out the *frigidarium* (cold bath), to the left, and the *tepadarium* (tepid bath), to the right. Once patrons had gone through these ablutions, they could settle into the *caldarium* (hot bath) for a long, soothing soak. In the smaller but similarly elaborate **Terme Feminili,** a mosaic of a naked Triton decorates the floor of the changing rooms.

SEDES DEGLI AUGUSTALI (HALL OF THE AUGUSTALS) The Augustals were priests of a cult to Augustus, founder and first emperor of the Roman empire. These rooms with marble floors and elaborate wall paintings did justice to their elite status. Their custodian appears to have died in his sleep, in a small room that's still furnished with the bed where his skeleton was found.

CASA DEL TRAMEZZO DI LEGNO (HOUSE OF THE WOODEN PARTITION) Behind a perfect facade is a rarity in Roman houses: a double atrium. It probably just means that at some point the owner scraped together enough money to buy adjoining houses and merge them. He obviously worked hard: The house is named for a well-preserved wooden screen that separated part of the atrium from the *tablium,* a little room that served as an office.

CASA DEL BELLA CORTILE (HOUSE OF THE BEAUTIFUL COURTYARD) The namesake courtyard seems almost medieval, with a wide stone staircase ascending to a landing on the second floor. Three skeletons that have been placed here are presumed to be those of a mother, father, and daughter trapped on the beach as they tried to flee.

CASA DEL MOSAICO DI NETTUNO E ANFITRITE (HOUSE OF THE NEPTUNE AND ANFITRITIS MOSAIC) A bright blue mosaic of the sea god and his nymph is just one of many decorations in this house, whose owner likely operated the well-preserved shop next door. Carbonized wooden racks hold amphorae and masonry jars that were found on the counter, still filled with broad beans and chickpeas when they were unearthed.

CASA A GRATICCIO (HOUSE OF THE LATTICEWORK) This is one of the very few examples of working-class housing that has survived from antiquity; the namesake lattices, though cheaply made of interwoven cane and plaster, are remarkably well preserved.

CASA DEI CERVI (HOUSE OF THE STAGS) One of the most elegant houses in town had terraces and porticos overlooking the sea. Decorations say much about its fun-loving inhabitants: Frescoes depict playful cherubs, while courtyards held statues of drunken satyrs and an inebriated, peeing Hercules. The house is named for a statue of dogs attacking a pair of innocent, noble-looking deer, perhaps a commentary on the cutthroat politics and hard-edged social echelons of the Roman era.

VILLA DEI PAPIRI One of the grander seaside villas housed a huge library of 1,000-odd papyrus scrolls, badly charred but intact when they were uncovered during excavations (they're now in the library of the Palazzo Reale in Naples). The onetime home of Julius Caesar's father-in-law, consul Lucius Calpurnius Piso Caesoninus (100–43 B.C.E.), has also yielded a treasure trove of nearly 90 magnificent bronze and marble sculptures, Roman copies of Greek originals that are now housed in the Archaeological Museum in Naples (p. 601). Most famous among them is a sculpture of Pan, the half-man, half-goat god, caught in marble having sex with a nanny goat. The oddly humane scene was unearthed in the 18th century but was thought to be so licentious that it was locked away in the cellars of a royal palace. Since the early 19th century, randy Pan has been one of the Archaeological Museum's most cherished prizes.

TERME SUBURBANE (SUBURBAN BATHS) Another bath complex shows off state-of-the art sophistication, with marble floors and benches and an

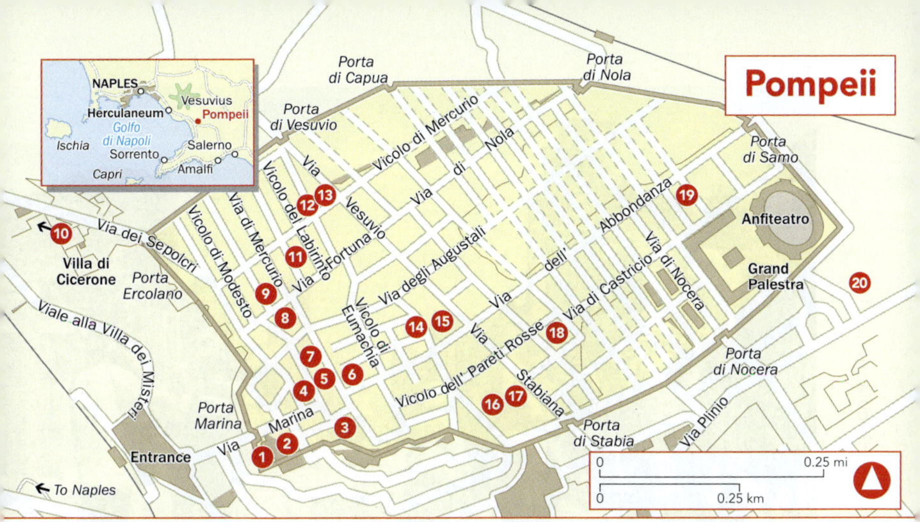

Antiquarium **1**
Basilica **3**
Casa degli Amorini Dorati (House of the Gilded Cupids) **13**
Casa dei Vettii (House of the Vettii) **12**
Casa del Fauno (House of the Faun) **11**
Casa del Menander (House of Menander) **18**
Casa del Poeta Tragico (House of the Tragic Poet) **9**
Casa di Venere in Conchiglia (House of Venus in the Shell) **19**
Cattedrale (Cathedral) **20**
Foro (Forum) **5**
Lupanare **14**
Odeon (Teatro Piccolo) **17**
Teatro Grande **16**
Terme del Foro (Forum Baths) **8**
Tempio di Apollo (Temple of Apollo) **4**
Tempio di Giove (Temple of Jupiter) **7**
Tempio di Venere (Temple of Venus) **2**
Tempio di Vespasiano (Temple of Vespasian) **6**
Stabian Thermae (Stabian Baths) **15**
Villa dei Misteri (House of the Mysteries) **10**

elaborate under-floor heating system in which heat generated by wood fires circulated through a maze of conduits. In the *caldarium* (hot bath), a few stucco friezes still look down on visitors as they did on bathers.

Pompeii

19km (11 miles) SE of Herculaneum, 30km (18 miles) SE of Naples

A visit to Italy's second-most-popular archaeological site (after the Colosseum in Rome) is a journey into a world locked in an ancient time. The 4 to 6m (13–20-ft.) layer of volcanic ash with which Vesuvius buried the city preserved shops, civic buildings, and private houses. Excavations began in 1748 and are still ongoing—a third of the city remains buried, and in Regio V, a section north of the current ruins, recent finds have included the remains of a horse being saddled for flight, an elaborately decorated ceremonial chariot, and frescoes, including one that depicts a plate of food that looks like a pizza and an erotic image of Leda and the Swan. While most of the section is closed to visitors, a recently excavated *thermopolium,* or snack bar, is open at limited times (check pompeiisites.

The ruins of Pompeii are extensive, and often rather crowded—be prepared for a lot of walking. Buy a good guidebook, rent an audioguide, or hire a tour guide to make the most of your visit.

org). The thermopolium, one of 80 such establishments unearthed in Pompeii, has a counter elaborately painted with images of the animals customers could likely consume there.

How many people were living in Pompeii at the time of the eruption is not known, nor is the exact date—based on ancient writings, it was long thought to be August 24, C.E. 79, but recent findings, including the seeds of autumn fruits and an inscription apparently dated in mid-October, suggest the event occurred later. A major earthquake in C.E. 62 had rocked the city, destroying temples, houses, and public works, and repairs were still underway in C.E. 79; many of the city's 11,000 recorded inhabitants had probably resettled elsewhere. The unfortunate Pompeiians who remained behind are the most haunting presence at the site. Their decaying bodies often left a mold inside the ash and lava that buried them, empty spaces that excavators filled with plaster. These eerie, lifelike casts lie in the Garden of the Fugitives and other spots around town.

The main entrance to the site, Porta Marina, is almost directly across from the train station. Allow at least 4 hours for even a superficial visit.

EXPLORING POMPEII'S ARCHAEOLOGICAL AREA ♥♥♥

Pompeii was a workaday town, and what stands out amid the ruins is a remarkable evocation of everyday life—streets, shops, bakeries, brothels, baths. Unlike Herculaneum, with its seafront district of lavish villas, in Pompeii the wealthy usually lived among the working classes. Houses are interspersed with shops, which were often combined with dwellings.

The first thing you'll notice is the typical Roman plan of gridlike streets, with stepping stones at every intersection. These were laid down to allow residents to cross the pavement even when the streets were being flushed with water, as they were at least once a day. Stones are spaced exactly to allow chariot wheels to roll past them. Also notice the remains of 25 street fountains, fed by a system of aqueducts, cisterns, and lead pipes that kept baths, businesses, and homes supplied with fresh water. Raised sidewalks conceal water and sewage pipes, while glittering bits of marble mixed in with the volcanic pavement reflected light to make walking easier at night.

PORTA MARINA The site's main entrance is an impressive gate that once faced the sea and was one of seven portals in the walls that surrounded the ancient city. Pompeii's docks did a brisk business importing and exporting goods that were often transported to and from Rome on the nearby Appian Way. The shimmering sea that once lapped the shoreline in front of the gate is nowhere to be seen: The sprawl of modern Pompei (one "i" in the modern spelling) now lies between the excavations and the sea, which has receded by about .5km (¼ mile) over the centuries. The **Tempio de Venere** (Temple of Venus), to the right of the entrance, has not fared as well as the gate; a lone column is all that attests to its onetime grandeur.

FORO (FORUM) Pompeii's marketplace, damaged in the C.E. 62 earthquake, had not been repaired when the final destruction rained down. Columns still line the portico that surrounded a large, rectangular open space on three sides and opened to a covered meat and fish market, the **Macellum.** Facing the Forum are the **Basilica** (the city's largest single structure), a law court, exchange, and civic hall. The **Temple of Apollo,** with its columned portico, was the city's most important religious building. The **Granai del Foro** (Forum Granary) is now the repository for many of the plaster casts of victims made by 19th-century excavators.

LUPANARE GRANDE (LARGE BROTHEL) Pompeii's most titter-inducing sight and prime photo op is just northeast of the Forum off Via degli Augustali. Graphic wall paintings reveal what certainly appears to be a libertine attitude toward sex. It's easy to see why, correctly or not, the city is often associated with easy virtue. In the nearby Basilica, where many travelers stopped on a visit to Pompeii, a bit of graffiti loosely read, "If anyone is looking for some tender love in this town, keep in mind that here all the girls are very friendly." A list of prices is inscribed on the wall near the brothel. It's believed that Pompeii may have had dozens of these establishments. Many of the graphic works that once covered the walls of this one, the city's grandest pleasure palace, have been carted off to the Archaeological Museum in Naples (p. 601), though many remain in place in 10 small rooms equipped with stone beds.

VIA DELL'ABBONDANZA The town's main commercial street is rightfully named: Surrounding fields and vineyards kept Pompeii supplied with an abundance of goods, as did a brisk trade with other Roman cities. This street was lined with shops, including **Fullonica Stephani** (Stephen's Laundry), and eateries where pots full of daily offerings were kept on counters that are still in place. In most houses on the street, a shop is on the ground floor and the owner's apartment is on the second level. Many of the painted signs for bars and shops remain; some have revealed the world's first known bit of advertising punditry, hawking Vesuvinum—a clever combo of Vesuvius and "vinum," the word for wine.

TRIANGULAR FORUM This large open area was the heart of the theater district. The beautiful **Teatro Grande,** carved out of a hillside of volcanic rock in the 2nd century B.C.E., could seat an audience of 5,000, while the smaller 1st-century-B.C.E. 1,000-seat **Odeion,** or Small Theater, was used for music and mime shows. Audiences could step out between acts for a stroll along the columned **Quadriportico dei Teatri,** though the breezy walkway was later enclosed to serve as a barracks for gladiators. Nearby is the **Tempio di Iside** (Temple of Isis), one of the best-conserved temples to this goddess to survive from antiquity.

CASA DEGLI AMANTI The House of the Lovers, recently reopened after sustaining damage in a 1980 earthquake, is named for a motto over the entrance ("Lovers like bees pass a sweet life like honey. I wish it were so."). The large dwelling at the edge of the theater district is built around a garden surrounded on the ground floor by a colonnaded portico, and has many frescoes of landscapes and domestic scenes.

TERME STABIANE One of Pompeii's many public baths, the Stabian Baths' arrangement of cold, tepid, and hot baths is a typical floor plan for such places, mainstays of all Roman towns, where people could cleanse, relax, and socialize. The vaulted *apodyterium* (changing room) was the showpiece here, with fanciful wall paintings of playful nymphs. Looking at them must have been a welcome perk for slaves as they waited for their masters in the vast chamber, with orders to keep an eye on their belongings.

CASA DI LOREIUS TIBURTINUS Election placards painted on the facade—"VOTE FOR LOREIUS" and "VOTE FOR TIBURNTINUS"—gave this large house its name. The owner, the well-off Octavius Quartio, entertained his guests in a gardenlike *triclinium,* or dining room, where a delightful fresco depicts Pyramis and Thisbe, the lovely maiden and handsome youth of myth who belonged to feuding families and inspired *Romeo and Juliet* centuries later.

GRANDE PALESTRA Sports events were held on this track and on the surrounding sports fields, while onlookers could escape the sun in the shade of an impressively long portico. A grandiose swimming pool was surrounded by plane trees (you can see the plaster casts of the stumps).

ANFITEATRO The oldest Roman amphitheater in the world (built in 80 B.C.E.) could seat 1,000 people and was the first to be constructed of stone. Especially enlightened were the entrances designed for crowd control, and the state-of-the-art latrines. The theater became known for its gladiatorial contests, and the ancient counterparts of soccer hooligans packed in for events. Games were banned for 10 years after a C.E. 59 brawl between Pompeiians and visitors from nearby Nuceria left 10 people dead.

TERME SUBURBANE Pompeii's bathhouses are some of the finest to survive from antiquity, and this one is unusual in that men and women

The richly colored frescoes at Villa dei Misteri.

shared the facilities. Vividly colored frescoes in the changing rooms depict graphic sex acts, a point of ongoing controversy: Were they simply amusing decorations, or did they advertise sexual services available on the upper floors? These scenes and other so-called pornography from Pompeii shocked Francis I, king of the Two Sicilies. Coming across erotic artifacts on an 1819 visit to the Archaeological Museum in Naples with his wife and daughter, he ordered many of them to be locked away in the museum's Gabinetto Segreto (Secret Cabinet), open only to "people of mature ages and respected morals."

CASA DEI VETTII Pompeii's most elegant patrician villa was the ultimate bachelor pad, the home of wealthy merchants, the Vettii brothers. The huge phallus resting on a pair of scales at the entrance was a sign of good fortune—which the black-and-red Pompeiian dining room with its frescoes of delicate cupids and colonnaded garden show the brothers had plenty of. Strongboxes embedded in the floor suggest that they might have made at least part of their fortune as money lenders.

CASA DEL FAUNO The sumptuous decor here is ancient proof that money and good taste can go together. Two of the great treasures of the Archaeological Museum in Naples (p. 601) come from this huge spread, covering an entire city block, the biggest house in town. A bronze statue of a dancing faun decorated the *impluvium* (rain tank) used to collect water for the household, and a much-celebrated *Battle of Alexander the Great* battle scene is one of many mosaics decorating the lavish rooms.

VILLA DEI MISTERI A layer of ash ensured that this 90-room villa near the Porto Ercolano, just outside the walls (follow Viale alla Villa dei Misteri; admission with the 22€ and 26€ tickets), retained its remarkable frescoes, the best still in place in Pompeii. Set against a background of a deep hue that's now known as Pompeiian red, figures in the Dionysiac Frieze are busy with elaborate rituals that, scholars say, may have been wedding preparations or initiation into a sect of Dionysus (Bacchus), one of many cults that flourished in Roman times.

13

SORRENTO & THE AMALFI COAST

By Stephen Brewer

The beautiful Sorrento peninsula and the Amalfi Coast have been tempting travelers ever since Ulysses sailed by, having filled his sailors' ears with wax and tied himself to the mast to withstand the Sirens' alluring call. Today, the pull of the sea and imposing rock-bound coast remain just as compelling. Graceful old Sorrento is perched high atop a cliff gazing across the sea toward the isle of Capri. The spectacular-if-nerve-racking Amalfi Drive heads vertiginously east, clinging to cliffs and rounding one bend after another until it comes to Positano, a tile-domed village hugging a near-vertical rock, then to Amalfi, a little seaside town that was once the center of a powerful maritime republic.

With transporting green hillsides, azure seas, and the enticing scent of lemon and frangipani, the charms of Sorrento and the Amalfi Coast are no secret. You'll do yourself a favor if you schedule a visit for the early spring or fall, before and after the peak summer season, and even then accept the fact that you will have to share this slice of paradise with others.

DON'T LEAVE SORRENTO & THE AMALFI COAST WITHOUT . . .

Floating Between Heaven & Earth in the Belvedere Cimbrone. In the gardens of Ravello's Villa Cimbrone, the coastal panorama of the shimmering Mediterranean meeting the blue sky just may be the most beautiful view in the world.

Strolling Along Capri's Via Tragara. With the sea twinkling far below, a warm breeze rustling the pines, and the legendary Faraglioni rock formations rising from the waves, you'll think you've found heaven on earth.

Taking a Bus down the Famed Amalfi Drive. Transport by public bus may not seem as glamorous as handling the hairpin curves in an Alfa Romeo, but the views are just as spectacular and you won't have to worry about keeping your eyes on the road.

Soaking on Ischia. Hot, mineral-rich waters bubble up everywhere on this beautiful island—on beaches, into the sea, and most hedonistically, in pleasure-geared thermal parks where luxuriant gardens are laced with soothing pools.

 PREVIOUS PAGE: **Coastal view from Ravello's Villa Rufolo.**

Campania & the Amalfi Coast
CAMPANIA
Gulf of Gaeta
(Golfo di Gaeta)
Gulf of Naples
(Golfo di Napoli)
Gulf of Salerno
(Golfo di Salerno)
Gulf of Pozzuoli
TYRRHENIAN SEA
The Amalfi Coast
Monti Lattari
VESUVIUS NATIONAL PARK
NATIONAL PARK OF THE CILENTO
Isola d'Ischia
Isola di Capri
I. di Procida
I. di Nisida
Bocca Piccola
Pta. Campanella
To Ponza
To Palermo, Cagliari
NAPLES
Benevento
Caserta
Caserta Vecchia
Avellino
Salerno
Capua
Santa Maria Capua Vetere
Maddaloni
Aversa
Pozzuoli
Nola
Pomigliano
Portici
Torre del Greco
Torre Annunziata
Castellammare di Stabia
Sorrento
Positano
Amalfi
Ravello
Atrani
Praiano
Cetara
Vietri sul Mare
Nocera Inferiore
Pagani
Pompei
Battipaglia
Eboli
Bellizzi
Pontecagnano
Capaccio
Roccadaspide
Altavilla Silentina
Campagna
Acerno
Montecorvino Rovella
Baronissi
Mercato San Severino
Cava de Tirreni
Gragnano
Vico Equense
Meta
Massa Lubrense
S. Agata sui Due Golfi
Anacapri
Capri
Ischia
Forio
Lacco Ameno
Casamicciola Terme
Barano d'Ischia
S. Angelo
Procida
Bacoli
Baia
Torregaveta
Arco Felice
Pianura
Marano
Qualiano
Mugnano
Afragola
Frattamaggiore
Casoria
Caivano
S. Antimo
Gugliano in Campania
Casal di Principe
Marcianese
Villa Literno
Castel Volturno
Mondragone
Cancello
Grazzanise
Marina di Lago di Patria
Licola Mare
San Angelo in Formis
S. Agata de Goti
Airola
Montesarchio
Cervinara
Pietrostornina
Avella
Baiano
Cicciano
Cancello
Acerra
Mercogliano
Monteforte Irpino
Moschiano
Palma Campania
Sarno
S. Guiseppe
Ottaviano
S. Anastasia
S. Giorgio a Cremano
Atripalda
Serino
Solofra
Volturara Irpina
Montella
Bagnoli Irpino
Nusco
Lioni
Sant'Angelo dei Lombardi
Paternopoli
Stumo
Grottaminarda
Ariano Irpino
Apice
S. Giorgio d. Sannio
Pratola Serra
Parolise
Herculaneum
Oplontis
Pompeii
Cuma
Liternum
Paestum
Vesuvius
M. Taburno
M. di Avella
Pizzo di Alvano
M. Mai
M. Cervialto
M. Raia
M. Faito
L. di Laceno
L. Patria
L. Fusaro
Regi Lagni
Volturno
Calore
Sele
Tusciano
A1
A3
A16
A30
E45
E842
SS6
SS7
SS18
SS88
SS90
SS163
SS164
SS264
SS265
SP1
0 10 mi
0 10 km
Venice
Florence
Rome
Sardinia
Sicily
Amalfi Coast

SORRENTO ♥♥♥

50km (31 miles) S of Naples

That old pop standard, *Come Back to Sorrento* sums it all up: *"Guarda il mare com'è bello"* ("See the sea, how beautiful it is"). The sea, scented gardens, and sun-drenched vistas have been luring travelers to this cliff-top resort since the days of the Grand Tour. Monuments are few and far between, but mingling with stylish crowds in Piazza Tasso or making the trek through atmospheric lanes down to Marina Grande, a fisherman's port, show off the town's irrepressible appeal. Sorrento provides easy access to Naples as well as such fabled places as Capri, Positano, Amalfi, and the ruins at Pompeii, and usually bustles with happy holidaymakers who, at their best, provide pleasant company. ***Note:*** As casual and easygoing as Sorrento can seem, keep your shirt on: The town recently enacted a law banning swimming suits in town and mandating that men wear tops in public.

Essentials

ARRIVING

BY TRAIN Sorrento is connected to Naples' Stazione Centrale by the **Circumvesuviana** railway (eavsrl.it; ✆ **800/211388,** toll-free in Italy); the ride takes about an hour and 15 minutes and trains run every half-hour or so. Its **Campania Express** trains run about four times a day from mid-March to mid-October, cutting the trip between Naples and Sorrento to less than 50 minutes. The train station is in the center of town, an easy walk from many hotels but quite a distance from others in the hills and along the coast; ask your hotel about transport options from the station.

BY BUS **Curreri Viaggi** (curreriviaggi.it; ✆ **081/946-0849**) offers frequent bus service between the airport in Naples and Sorrento, with at least

Leave the Driving to SITA Sud

SITA Sud buses (sitasudtrasporti.it) connect Sorrento, Positano, Amalfi, and other towns between them along the coast, with departures about every half-hour between 6:30am and 7pm, hourly until 10pm or so after that. Buses also travel between Amalfi and Salerno and the towns in between, with approximately the same frequency. Fares vary depending on destination, but expect to pay about 2.40€ for the trip between Sorrento and Positano and the same to get from Positano to Amalfi. The 24-hour **CostieraSita** pass gets you unlimited rides on SITA buses between all the towns along the Amalfi Coast, from Meta di Sorrento to Salerno, for 10€. You can buy tickets and passes at tobacco shops, newsstands, and bars, as well as at SITA ticket offices at the train stations. During peak summer months, agents sell tickets outside the bus in Amalfi and Sorrento. At these times, buses quickly fill to standing-room-only capacity—you're wise to get early and late buses to avoid daytime waits of an hour or even more and especially to avoid travel during the busiest times, such as the afternoon return trip from Positano to Sorrento. An easy-to-use source for travel info along the Amalfi Coast is **sorrentoinsider.com**.

ATTRACTIONS
Chiesa di San Francesco **11**
Largo Dominova **8**
Marina Grande **3**
Museo Correale di Terranova **23**
Villa Comunale **12**

HOTELS
Grand Hotel Cocumella **22**
Hotel Antiche Mura **18**
Hotel Rivoli **13**
La Badia **1**
Masseria Astapiana Villa Giusso **22**
Palazzo Marziale **10**
Parco di Principi **22**
Sorrento Relais **22**
Ulisse Deluxe Hostel **5**

RESTAURANTS
Davide **9**
Il Bagni Delfino **2**
Inn Bufalito **6**
Kebab Ciampa **17**
La Cantinaccia del Popolo **21**
Leone Rosso **20**
Pizzeria da Franco **21**
Primavera **16**
Ristorante Museo Caruso **15**
Ristorante o'Parrucchiano La Favorita **7**
Ristorante Pizzeria Tasso **19**
Star Pub Holy Burger **14**
Trattoria da Emilia **4**

eight trips in each direction every day; one-way fare is 13€. Once on the coast, the best way to get around is on **SITA Sud buses** (see box above).

BY BOAT In summer, ferries and hydrofoils operated by **NLG-Navigazione Libera del Golfo** (nlg.it; ✆ **081/552-0763**) and **Linee Lauro** (alilauro.it; ✆ **081/497-2206**) make daily runs to and from Sorrento, Naples, Ischia, Capri, Positano, and Amalfi, with limited service between Sorrento and Naples and Capri off-season.

BY CAR By **car** from Naples, take the A3, and exit at Castellammare di Stabia for the SS145 to Sorrento. Allow about 1 hour and 10 minutes for the drive. However, given the strict limitations on driving along the Amalfi Drive (p. 660), limited parking in most towns, and the excellent public transit options, it's a lot more convenient not to have a car in the region. The trip from Naples to Sorrento by **taxi** costs about 90€. The ride is metered, but drivers will usually establish a price before you set off.

VISITOR INFORMATION Sorrento's **tourist office** is at Via Luigi de Maio 35, off Piazza Tasso (✆ **081/807-4033;** summer daily 9am–7pm, rest of year Mon–Fri 9am–4pm). An **information office** outside the train station (daily 10am–1pm and 3–7pm) is run by a private company whose

choosing **A TOWN**

Just about everyone who visits Sorrento and the Amalfi Coast comes away with a favorite town to which they yearn to return. It's hard to go wrong in this beautiful part of the world, but you may want to take some practical considerations into account. **Sorrento** is best situated as a base for exploring, given its excellent train, bus, and boat connections to Capri, Naples, Pompeii, Herculaneum, and other towns. **Positano** is the most picturesque and resortlike, with the best (and most easily accessible) beaches, though the narrow streets are packed in summer, and getting in and out of town in high season on the traffic-choked coast road can be a nightmare (boats are a pleasant alternative). **Amalfi** provides small-town charm, easy access to hiking trails, and gives you a twofer—its beautiful neighbor **Ravello.** You can also avoid the worst of the coastal traffic by approaching and leaving Amalfi on buses from Salerno, with its excellent train connections to Naples.

interest is to book tours, but they are helpful with advice on transportation and other matters. The station newsstand sells bus tickets to points all along the Amalfi Coast. Informative web sources include **sorrentoinfo.com** and **sorrentoinsider.com**.

GETTING AROUND

BY BUS Just about everything you want to see in Sorrento is within walking distance, though **minibuses** (eavsrl.it) are a handy way to get to and from **Marina Piccola,** the commercial port where ferries and hydrofoils dock, especially if you're toting luggage. Buses also make the run to and from **Marina Grande,** the old fishing port below the town's western edge, and connect the center with the outlying seaside neighborhoods of Sant'Agnello, Piano, and Meta. Most single-fare tickets cost 1.20€ and can be purchased from tabacchi and newsstands. Convenient bus stops are on Piazza Tasso and in front of the train station. Taxis within Sorrento are exorbitantly expensive, so it's best to avoid using them if possible.

BY BOAT Boats connect Sorrento with Positano, Amalfi, Capri, and other ports along the coast and around the Bay of Naples. Not only do they provide a scenic ride, but traveling by sea is also a welcome alternative to the traffic-choked coastal roads in high season. From Sorrento it's about 50 minutes by sea to Naples, 30 minutes to Capri, 40 minutes to Positano, and an hour to Amalfi. See "Arriving" above for the companies that operate boats.

Exploring Sorrento

Sorrento is long and narrow, strung out along the top of seaside cliffs. The center of town is sunny **Piazza Tasso.** Amid the piazza's cafes and glossy shops stands a statue of namesake poet Tarquato Tasso, who was born into a noble family in Sorrento in 1544 and died in a madhouse at the age of 51. The piazza dramatically spans a deep gorge; the north end overhangs a steep hillside that descends to **Marina Piccola,** the city's main port, while to the south you can follow a walkway and look down into verdant **Vallone dei Mulini** (work is underway on a path into the valley). A small Greek settlement that became Roman Surrentum flourished in the valley as early as the 5th century B.C.E., and a stream that rushes out of the mountains powered *mulini,* flour mills, and sawmills that operated until the middle of the 20th century.

Corso Italia (closed to car traffic) bisects the old town. Along the Corso just west of the square is the privately owned **Palazzo Correale,** worth a stop to peer into the courtyard beautifully tiled with majolica. A few blocks along at Via Santa Maria della Pieta is Sorrento's **cathedral of San Giacamo e Filipo** (cattedralesorrento.it; ✆ **081/878-2248;** free admission; daily 8am–12:30pm and 4:30–8:30pm). Frequent rebuilding has rendered the facade rather plain except for an intriguing arcaded three-story campanile with embedded Roman columns; beyond doors inlaid with scenes of Sorrento life and a map of the town is an enormous *presepe* (Nativity scene), set on the streets of Naples with Mt. Vesuvius looming behind the manger, and, in the palatial interior, a forest of marble columns. The white **Villa Fiorentino,** just up the street at Corso Italia 59, was built in the 1930s by a family who made their fortune selling embroidered handkerchiefs (still a popular item on the Amalfi Coast). A few salons now host temporary exhibitions of art and photography, and the gardens are a welcoming spot in which to linger. The villa and gardens are open daily 9am to 1pm and 4 to 7pm; admission is free.

Corso Italia, in the heart of Sorrento town.

North of here are quieter precincts where artisan workshops turn out music boxes, picture frames, and large pieces of furniture with intricate design in wood inlays, or *intarsia,* for which Sorrento has long been known. You can see fine examples at the **Museo della Tarsia di Rolo,** Via San Nicola 28 (museodellatarsia.com; ✆ **081/877-1942;** Sat 3–6pm, Sun 10am–noon and 3–6pm); admission is free but donations are welcome. At the northern edge of the neighborhood, **Piazza della Vittoria** opens to sweeping views of the bay. A road west from Piazza Vittoria to **Marina Grande** (see below) eventually becomes a staircase and passes beneath a Greek gate—a reminder that

Marina Grande was once a separate town that was vulnerable to pirate raids, a much riskier place to live than fortified Sorrento.

Or head east from Piazza della Vittoria toward the **Villa Comunale** and nearby **Chiesa di San Francesco** (see below). Continue on Via S. Francesco to Piazza Sant'Antonino to visit a church dear to Sorrentines, the handsome **Basilica di Sant'Antonino** (✆ **081/878-1437;** free admission; Mon–Sat 7am–noon and 4–6:30pm, Sun 7am–noon). Antonino, who is interred in a crypt beneath the nave, was a miracle-working 7th-century abbot who is the town's patron saint. Two whale ribs near the entrance of the church commemorate the saint's most popular miracle, rescuing a little boy from the belly of a whale.

A filling way to get to know the town is with **Secret Walks of Sorrento,** from Tour Guide Naples (tourguidenaples.com; ✆ **338/888-4282**); you'll tour artisan workshops and quiet neighborhoods in the company of a local while stopping for coffee, gelato, and limoncello. The fee is 60€.

Chiesa di San Francesco ♥♥ CHURCH Top choice for the most charming spot in Sorrento goes to the 14th-century Moorish and Romanesque cloisters of this church and convent, where an old pepper tree shades tufa-rock arches interspersed with elaborately capped columns. In a painting above the altar Francis is shown, not in the usual pastoral scene surrounded by birds and animals, but in a transcendent moment when, after weeks of fasting and praying, wounds opened on his hands, sides, and feet, bringing him close to the suffering Christ in body as well as in spirit. Piazza Francesco Saverio Gargiulo. cattedralesorrento.it/chiesa-di-san-francesco. ✆ **081/878-1269.** Free admission. Daily 7am–7pm.

Largo Dominova ♥♥ SQUARE For Sorrentines, this little square in the old quarter at the intersection of Via San Cesareo and Via P. R. Giuliani is the real heart of town. The town council used to meet in the 16th-century Sedile Dominova, an arched loggia with a green-tile cupola; its richly frescoed interior of trompe l'oeil columns and scenes of aristocratic life is now a gathering spot for retired workers. The old gents are used to visitors popping in to admire their opulent surroundings, so don't be shy.

Marina Grande ♥♥ NEIGHBORHOOD Walking past a row of narrow houses squeezed along the quays between the steep hillside and the sea, you'll get a sense of Sorrento as an old-time fishing port. Even so, you'll have to contend with shills trying to lure you into restaurants with multi-language menus (a few restaurants here are excellent; see p. 653). You can take a dip here, but the small, pebbly beach is less than inviting; for better options, see p. 650. The scene is quite romantic in the evening, with moonlight illuminating a harbor full of bobbing boats. Should you have one *limoncello* too many or just can't face the trek up the stairs, hop on the minibus to get back up the hill. These run about hourly from the taxi stand on the quay, with the last bus at 8:25pm (eavsrl.it; 1.20€; purchase tickets from the *tabacchi* across from the stop).

Colorful Marina Grande in Sorrento.

Museo Correale di Terranova ♥ MUSEUM Counts Alfredo and Pompeo Correale donated their elegant 18th-century villa to the city of Sorrento, along with the collection that their family had amassed since 1500. The randomness of the assortment is its charm: Neapolitan paintings that capture scenic Sorrento views from the 17th through 19th centuries; inlaid intarsia furniture from studios right here in town; and porcelain fired in kilns on the grounds of the Capodimonte palace in Naples. It's all homey and charming, though the pieces in sum don't really warrant the stiff entrance fee. The payoff might be the enormous palm-shaded garden laced with paths that wind to a clifftop viewpoint with stunning coastal vistas.

Via Correale 50. museocorreale.it. ✆ **081/878-1846.** Admission 15€, free for children 10 and under. Tues–Sat 9am–2:30pm, Sun 9am–2pm.

Villa Comunale ♥♥ PARK/GARDEN Views from one side of this delightful, palm-studded patch of greenery take in the port far below and a broad sweep of the bay of Naples. A statue of St. Francis stands amid the cliffside gardens, looking contented to be in such pleasant surroundings. From the far side of the gardens, you can take an **elevator** (1.10€) or follow a well-marked lane and stairway down to a seaside promenade that leads past so-called beach clubs, where sun loungers line pier-like platforms, to Marina Grande.

Beaches

You can swim from pebbly patches at Marina Grande or Marina Piccola, or rent a sunbed at one of the many beach clubs beneath the cliffs below Villa Comunale and to the west of Marina Piccola, where umbrellas extend along piers onto the breakfront. These include **Leonelli's** (leonellis beach.com) and **Marameo** (marameobeach.com). Sunbed rentals are about 18€ a day; food and beverages are served. The nicest close-to-town beach is **Marinella,** below the cliffs in Sant'Agnello, an attractive seaside community that adjoins Sorrento to the east and a pleasant walk from the center. You can pay for a lounger at **Spiaggia la Marinella** (lamarinella sorrento.com), or perch for free on a concrete platform that extends onto a jetty. For real sand, take the Circumvesuviana train or the EAV bus (eavsrl.it; 1.20€; leaves from in front of the Sorrento train station) towards Naples to the beach at **Meta,** popular among Neapolitans out for a day in the sun. A slightly less crowded beach west of town, also reachable on the EAV bus from the station, is **Bagno della Regina Giovanna** (Queen Giovanna's Bath) at Punta del Capo, the northwestern tip of the Sorrento Peninsula. Here a small, rock-sheltered cove of clear water, reached on a path through citrus and olive groves, was once the private harbor of the ancient Roman Villa of Pollio Felice. Step through the ruins at the top of the cliff, where man of letters Pollio Felice once entertained guests with readings of Virgil and Horace. Just beyond, reached by the same bus, is **Marina di Puolo,** a little fishing port where you can swim from a sandy beach.

Set Sail

You can spend a pleasant day exploring the region on a boat tour, either cruising along the coast with stops in Positano and Amalfi, or sailing over to Capri, with time on the island. Rates are about 60€ for the Amalfi tour, 75€ for the Capri tour, including hotel pickup, on a boat that accommodates about 50 passengers. Among many companies offering the trip is **Jolly Rent,** Corso Italia 3 (jollyrent.com; ✆ **081/877-3450**).

Where to Stay in Sorrento

EXPENSIVE

Grand Hotel Cocumella ♥♥♥ This magical converted monastery is set amid lush gardens above the sea in Sant'Agnello, a residential enclave at the eastern end of town. Rooms created from combined monk's cells are chic and sophisticated, mixing antiques with nice contemporary touches, offset with gleaming white tile floors. Some have sea-view terraces while others hang over orange-scented gardens, where a pool is tucked into the greenery. An elevator descends to the sea and a swimming platform.

Via Cocumella 7, Sant'Agnello. cocumella.com. ✆ **081/878-2933.** 48 units. 450€–750€ double. Rates include breakfast. Closed Nov to mid-Apr. **Amenities:** Restaurant; bar; concierge; pool; beach; free Wi-Fi.

The blue of sea and sky is echoed everywhere in Parco di Principi's chic contemporary decor.

Parco di Principi ♥♥♥ On grounds where Jesuit friars once grew aphrodisiac plants, in the early 19th century Prince Leopold, Count of Syracuse, commissioned a villa in which he could lead a life wholeheartedly devoted to pleasure away from his fanatically religious wife. In the 1960s, architect Gio Ponti (designer of Milan's Pirelli Tower) redid the place, creating stunning surroundings that are all about blue: Blue sky and blue sea beyond the many terraces and huge windows, blue tiles covering the floors—even the upholstery on the impeccable Modernist chairs and couches is a blue that Ponti calibrated. The restful effect makes you feel, as Ponti intended, that you're floating between sea and sky, and earthbound views take in the sumptuous private park filled with exotic plants, equipped with a lavish swimming pool and laced with walkways.
Via Rota 44, Sant'Agnello. royalgroup.it/parcodeiprincipi. ✆ **081/878-4644.** 96 units. 255€–690€ double. Rates include breakfast; discounts for stays of 2 nights or more. Closed Dec–Mar. **Amenities:** 2 restaurants; bar; pool; beach; spa; gym; free Wi-Fi.

MODERATE

Hotel Antiche Mura ♥♥♥ This elegant Art Nouveau–style *palazzo* built atop the town's former defensive walls reveals many pleasant nooks and crannies, including a huge garden filled with lemon trees surrounding a pool, as well as precipitous views from many rooms into the deep gorge that runs through Sorrento. Attractive public lounges flow over a couple of floors and include a conservatory-like breakfast room. Guest quarters are bright and cheerful, with colorful Vietri tiles on the floors; many have balconies facing the gorge or town, while some are tucked into the garden. Service is as gracious and welcoming as the surroundings.

Via Fuorimura 7 (entrance on Piazza Tasso). hotelantichemura.com. ✆ **081/807-3523.** 46 units. 130€–420€ double. Rates include breakfast. Closed Jan to mid-Mar. **Amenities:** Bar; concierge; garage; pool; free Wi-Fi.

Hotel Rivoli ♥♥ Convenience comes with high style at this strikingly revamped convent right in the center of town. A dramatic glass staircase floats up to airy, smartly decorated guest rooms (no two alike), a rooftop breakfast room and terrace, and cozy, antique-filled reading nooks off the landings (there's also an elevator). You'll trade a pool and sea views for a center-of-town location—pedestrian-only lanes are just outside the soundproofed windows, and the train station, port, and bus stops are nearby, making this a very handy base for exploring the coast.

Via Santa Maria delle Grazie 16. sorrentorivoli.com. ✆ **081/365-4089.** 8 units. 70€–320€ double. Rates include breakfast. Discounts for longer stays. Closed Jan–Feb. **Amenities:** Free Wi-Fi.

La Badia ♥♥ A centuries-old monastery perched high on a hilltop above the city is an idyllic getaway, where extensive sea-view gardens of olive trees and pines surround guest quarters soothingly done with colorful tiles and light furnishings. Many units have balconies and private gardens. A huge panoramic terrace serves as a bar and outdoor living/dining room, and a pool is set amid the greenery. A footpath winds down the hillside to town, a 10-minute descent, and buses stop just outside the gates.

8 via Capodimonte. hotellabadia.it. ✆ **081/878-1154.** 28 units. 200€–250€ double. Rates include breakfast. Min. stay required at peak times. Closed Nov to mid-Apr. **Amenities:** Restaurant; bar; pool; gardens; free Wi-Fi.

Palazzo Marziale ♥♥♥ You can't help but feel a bit privileged in this character-filled old *palazzo* in the heart of town, as if you're visiting aristocratic relatives. In fact, this is the ancestral home of the proprietors, who've turned a stone-arched entrance court into a dramatic, glassed-in lounge and furnished the huge guest rooms with old family prints and antiques, adding designer touches with deep colors and rich fabrics. All have queen- or king-size beds, sofa beds, and enormous marble bathrooms.

Piazza Francesco Saverio Gargiulo 2. palazzomarziale.com. ✆ **081/807-4406.** 7 units. 250€–390€ double. Rates include breakfast. Parking 18€. Closed Nov to mid-Feb. **Amenities:** Restaurant; bar; free Wi-Fi.

INEXPENSIVE

Masseria Astapiana Villa Giusso ♥♥♥ An ancient monastery turned noble residence perched at the top of a hill outside Vico Equense is surrounded by parkland, olive groves, and vineyards, all set on 14 hectares (35 acres) overlooking the sea and the coast. Salons-turned-guest rooms in the atmospheric old house are comfortably and regally done with plump armchairs, antiques, and wrought-iron beds, with a smattering of original frescoes and arched ceilings throughout. Breakfast with lemons, walnuts, apples, and other bounty from the farm is served in a vast tiled kitchen, and the grounds are laced with woodland paths, sunny terraces, and other quiet hideaways. Sorrento is 10km (6 miles) west, so a car is a necessity. Via Camaldoli 51. astapiana.com. ✆ **081/802-4392.** 15 units. 110€–140€ double, discounts for longer stays and half-board available. Rates include breakfast. Closed Nov–Mar. **Amenities:** Restaurant; pool; free Wi-Fi.

Sorrento Relais ♥♥ No sea views, no balconies, no grand hotel atmosphere—but this small, modest inn on the lower levels of an apartment house across from the Museo Correale di Terranova is appealing, comfortable, and an extremely good value. Compact, contemporary-style rooms have excellent beds and good lighting (both a rarity in lower-priced Italian hotels) and are artfully decorated with striped fabrics, bright colors, and quirky wall coverings. Mood lighting in the showers changes with the touch of a remote control, adding an extra splash to the sleek bathrooms. Rooms on the ground floor are bright despite the lack of views—those in the rear are especially quiet—though some less desirable (and very inexpensive) accommodations are in the basement, where a decent breakfast is served in a large, convivial space.
Via Bernardino Rota 5. sorrentorelais.com. ✆ **081/1892-0834.** 7 units. 60€–140€ double. Rates include breakfast. **Amenities:** Lounge; free Wi-Fi.

Ulisse Deluxe Hostel ♥♥ Hostel life takes on a glossy sheen in these sprawling lounges and large, handsomely furnished guest rooms. A few quadruples remain true to the dormlike hostel image, but for the most part the emphasis is on quiet, hotel-standard comfort. Rooms lack thrills—no balconies or sweeping sea views—but white-tile floors shine, beds are firm (many are king-size), and extras include minibars and, for additional fees, a luxury spa and large pool. The hillside perch is at the edge of town on the road down to Marina Grande, just west of the historic center.
Via del Mar 22. ulissedeluxe.com. ✆ **081/877-4753.** 50 units. 55€–155€ double. Discounts for longer stays. Some rates include breakfast. **Amenities:** Bar; spa; pool; free Wi-Fi.

Where to Eat in Sorrento

For a quick meal, try the veal or chicken kebabs at **Kebab Ciampa ♥**, Via Pieta 23 (✆ **081/807-4595**), which also serves falafel and meatballs. **Star Pub Holy Burger ♥**, Via Luigi de Maio 17 (starpubholyburger.shop; ✆ **081/877-3618**), satisfies a hamburger craving, and also makes excellent salads, washed down with a well-curated selection of wine and beer. A local institution, **Pizzeria da Franco ♥**, Corso Italia 265 (facebook.com/daFrancopizzeriasorrento; ✆ **081/877-2066**), serves calzones, *piadine* (stuffed sandwiches), and pizzas in many varieties. Pizza aficionados also head 11km (7 miles) down the bay toward Naples to cliff-hugging Vico Equense (a 10-min. train ride), where **Pizza a Metro ♥** (pizzametro.it; ✆ **081/879-8309**) has been turning out pizzas by the meter since the 1930s.

Two gelato shops vie for the title of best in town: **Davide ♥♥**, Via Padre Reginaldo Giuliani 41 (gelateriadavidsorrento.it; ✆ **081/807-2092;** closed Wed in winter), and **Primavera ♥♥**, Corso Italia 142 (primavera sorrento.it; ✆ **081/807-3252**); flavors at both include deliciously creamy *noci di Sorrento* (Sorrento walnuts) and *delizia al limone* (a lemon cream).

EXPENSIVE

Ristorante Museo Caruso ♥♥ NEAPOLITAN/SORRENTINE The great tenor Enrico Caruso lived in Sorrento shortly before he died in his native Naples in 1921, and he's remembered in these elegant, shrinelike rooms by hundreds of photos and posters. Tasting menus show off the Neapolitan and Sorrentine classics he loved, with an emphasis on seafood. Ravioli is stuffed with octopus, and shrimp risotto and simple spaghetti with clams are seasoned with local lemons. A soundtrack of Caruso standards plays in the background.

Via Sant'Antonino 12. ristorantemuseocaruso.com. ✆ **081/807-3156.** Main courses 24€–60€; tasting menus 70€, 80€, and 100€. Daily noon–2:30pm and 6–11pm.

Ristorante Pizzeria Tasso ♥♥ SORRENTINE/SEAFOOD Casually elegant salons and a glassed-in veranda wrapping around a large garden set the stage for a festive meal that can include a celebratory Chateaubriand for two or a wood-fired pizza that seems like a gourmet feast in such refined surroundings. Meanwhile, clam-laden gnocchi and other pastas, many fish dishes, and a seven-course tasting menu spotlight the kitchen's focus on locally sourced seafood.

Via Correale 11d. ristorantetasso.com. ✆ **081/878-5809.** Main courses 25€–45€; pizza 10€–18€; tasting menu 90€. Daily 11:30am–11:30pm.

MODERATE

Il Bagni Delfino ♥♥ SORRENTINE A meal here comes with a perk: the chance to swim off the adjoining pier. That's a good incentive to eat lightly from the snack food menu, though the heaping platters of fresh seafood pastas are tempting. This is a popular Sunday afternoon lunch choice, when locals come down to take in the sun and indulge in excellent cooking and polished service.

Western end of beach off Via Marina Grande. ristoranteildelfinosorrento.com. ✆ **081/878-2038.** Main courses 15€–30€. Daily noon–2:30pm and 6:30–10pm. Closed Nov–Mar.

Inn Bufalito ♥♥ SORRENTINE The approach here is to use only local products, especially buffalo meats and cheeses (buffalo-milk mozzarella is one of the region's most prized specialties). You might think of the shaggy beasts in a whole new light after tasting such memorable creations as buffalo cheese baked in lemon leaves or pasta with a heavy sauce of buffalo *ragù*. The brown-toned room gives off a rustic vibe, and the polished service does justice to the distinctive menu.

Vico I Foro 21. innbufalito.com. ✆ **081/365-6975.** Main courses 15€–26€, steak by the weight. Daily noon–midnight. Closed Jan–Feb.

Ristorante o'Parrucchiano La Favorita ♥♥ SORRENTINE This old-time Sorrento landmark dates back to 1868, when a former priest decided to get into the restaurant business (the name means "Priest's Place"). The vast, multilevel, greenhouse-like space opens to a vine-covered garden planted with potted citrus trees, all geared to a festive dining experience. Tour groups pour in, but there's room for everybody, and while the cuisine doesn't quite do justice to the surroundings, the cannelloni is a standout, as well it should be—the baked crêpelike stuffed pasta dish with ricotta, mozzarella, and minced beef was invented here and is memorably delicious.

Corso Italia 71. parrucchiano.com. ✆ **081/878-1321.** Main courses 15€–25€. Daily noon–3pm and 7–10pm.

INEXPENSIVE

La Cantinaccia del Popolo ♥♥♥ SORRENTINE The hams hanging over your head and deli cases next to your table give you a good idea of what to expect at this town favorite on a back lane: a bounty of house-cured meats and local cheeses paired with garden-fresh vegetables, fresh fish, pasta served right from the pan, and grilled steaks. A front garden and homey paneled decor add to a sense that you've walked into a friend's barbecue party, and the house-made wine and limoncello enhance the feeling. This popular spot does not take reservations, so come early or late and expect a wait.

Vico Terzo Rota. ✆ **366/101-5497.** Main courses 7€–12€. Tues–Sun noon–3:30pm and 6:45–10:30pm (until 9pm on Sun).

Leone Rosso ♥♥ SORRENTINE/PIZZA Sorrentines fill the terrace and bright, rambling rooms for simple, straightforward seafood dishes, offered in many variations. Put down the huge menu and simply ask one of the friendly, English-speaking waiters to recite the daily specials—they'll likely include the day's fresh catch and heaping platters of *risotto alla pescatore* (seafood risotto) and *spaghetti alla vongole* (spaghetti with clams). Non-pescatarians can enjoy land-based classics and a big choice of pizzas.

Via Marziale 25. illeonerosso.it. ✆ **081/807-3089.** Main courses 10€–22€. Daily noon–11pm.

An Acquired Taste?

Lunch and dinner in Sorrento and on the Amalfi Coast often end with a *limoncello,* usually homemade and often complimentary. Almost every family in Campania has its own recipe, passed on for generations, for this potent and sweet liqueur. True *limoncello* is made from *sfusato di Amalfi,* a particular lemon that has obtained D.O.P. recognition (the stamp of controlled origin for produce, similar to D.O.C. for wine). The Amalfi lemon is large and light in color, with a sweet and very flavorful aroma and taste, almost no seeds, and very thick skin.

Trattoria da Emilia ♥♥ SORRENTINE The simple pleasures of this old boat shed in Marina Grande are well-known—even Sophia Loren was once a regular. Getting a table during the summer rush may require a long wait, but patience pays off with old-time classics such as *gnocchi alla Sorrentina* (potato dumplings with cheese and tomato sauce) along with their own variation with seafood, *gnocchi al frutti di mare.* The choicest tables, of course, are on the pier outside.

Via Marina Grande 62. daemilia.it. ✆ **081/807-2720.** Main courses 9€–18€. Daily noon–3pm and 6:30–10:30pm (closed Tues in winter). Closed Dec–Feb.

Sorrento Shopping

For a quick shopping fix, take a walk down Via San Cesareo, a narrow, souklike lane off Piazza Tasso into which spill stands full of leather goods, T-shirts, and bottles of the town's ubiquitous *limoncello* liqueur. The classiest of the *limoncello* vendors along the street is **Limonoro ♥♥**, Via San Cesareo 49 (limonorosorrento.com; ✆ **081/878-5348**), selling chocolate-covered limoncello balls, other candies, and, of course, their own limoncello, with ample tastings on offer. For a more rural experience, walk out to the touristic-yet-charming **Giardini di Cataldo ♥♥**, just off Corso Italia near the train station (igiardinidicataldo.it; ✆ **081/878-1888**); in a fragrant lemon and orange grove you can taste and buy *limoncello,* marmalade, and other products made on the premises. It's open daily 9am to 8pm, with some shorter hours out of season. Or head into the hills to the lemon-scented grounds of a former 14th-century Franciscan monastery, **Il Convento ♥♥**, at Via Lapurlo 12 outside the town of Massa Lubrense (ilconvento.biz; ✆ **081/878-9380**), where the Pollio family makes award-winning *limoncello,* along with *digestivi* from walnuts and fennel. It's open daily 9am to 6pm in season; a tasting and tour cost 25€.

Gargiulo & Jannuzzi ♥♥, Piazza Tasso 1 (gargiulo-jannuzzi.it; ✆ **081/878-1041**), sells beautiful inlaid wood designs known as intarsia, and you can visit the workshops for a demonstration. **Libreria Tasso ♥**, Via San Cesareo 96 (✆ **081/807-1639**), stocks a good selection of English-language titles, from the latest thrillers to guidebooks. **Gallery Raffaele Celentano ♥♥**, Via San Nicolo 21 (www.raffaelecelentano.com; ✆ **344/083-8503**), displays the work of this well-known photographer, whose engaging images capture iconic scenes of Italian life; prints are for sale.

The local craft specialty, inlaid wood (intarsia), fills shop shelves in Sorrento.

Sorrento Nightlife

The epicenter of nightlife in Sorrento is the lively terrace of the **Fauno Bar ♥♥**, Piazza Tasso 13 (faunobar.it; ✆ **081/878-1135**), popular for an *aperitivo* and people-watching throughout the day until late into the evening. **Guarracino ♥♥**, with a big terrace on Via Sant'Antonino 19 (guarracinosorrento.it; ✆ **081/878-1728**), a quiet little back lane off Piazza Tasso, is an especially pleasant place for a cocktail and snacks near the center of town. **Fuoro Caffè ♥**, Via Fuoro 19 (facebook.com/FuoroCaffe; ✆ **081/922-5971**), will introduce you to the *limoncello* spritz and a potent lemon granita infused with *limoncello,* served in from April through October in a little alleyway opposite the shop. **La Bottega della Birra ♥♥**, Via San Nicola 13 (labottegadellabirra.it; ✆ **340/591-6221**), stocks hundreds of beers from Italy and all over Europe. **Prosit,** Corso Italia 50 (prositsorrento.it; ✆ **081/1865-8716**), serves wine and cocktails in an attractive, bottle-lined room adjoining a salumeria, and accompanies drinks with a nice selection of appetizers. **Officina Wine Bar 82 ♥♥**, in a residential area east of the center at Viale Nizza 17 (officina82winebar.com; ✆ **340/069-8477**), has an extensive wine list (and art collection) assembled by its knowledgeable and affable owner Giacomo, who also serves huge platters of cheese and ham; closed January and February.

The **cloister of San Francesco,** Piazza Francesco Saverio Gargiulo, is the evocative setting for summertime concerts. Contact the tourist office (p. 645) for a schedule of events, including others staged at many restaurants and taverns in town.

THE SORRENTO PENINSULA

When Sorrento seems a little too crowded, you only need to travel a few miles into the southwestern stretches of the Sorrento peninsula, where lemon and olive groves blanket the steep hillsides.

Essentials

ARRIVING By **car,** SS145 leads west from Sorrento, then south for access to the peninsula. Both **EAV** and **SITA Sud buses** (p. 644) serve towns on the Sorrento Peninsula. EAV buses run more frequently, and fares (from 1.30€) are the same on both—specify which line you are using when you buy your ticket. ***Tip:*** To get the best views on the dramatic drive from Sorrento east along the coast, get a seat on the right-hand side of the bus.

VISITOR INFORMATION The **tourist office** in Sorrento (p. 645) has information on towns and activities, including hiking, on the Sorrento Peninsula. Another good source is the **tourist office** in the center of Massa Lubrense at Viale Filangieri 11 (massalubrenseturismo.it; ✆ **081/533-9021**), where the staff will provide info on hiking routes and help you sort out bus schedules for moving around the rest of the peninsula; it's open daily 9:30am to 1pm.

Sant'Agata sui Due Golfi ♥♥

7km (4½ miles) S of Sorrento

It won't take you too long to figure out where this hilltop village got the "two gulfs" part of its name. Look to the south, and you'll see the Gulf of Sorrento; turn your head to the north, and there's the Gulf of Naples. It's also easy to see why the town was already famous in the days of the Roman Empire as the junction of trading routes across the peninsula. Artisans working on the 17th-century church of **Santa Maria delle Grazie** matched the views with a ridiculously sumptuous altar of marble, mother of pearl, and lapis lazuli (daily 9am–1pm and 4–7pm). Nuns desiring less ostentatious surroundings settled in the **Monastero di San Paolo,** on a hillside 1km (half a mile) outside town; follow Corso Sant'Agata from the center to the pine-shaded drive. Few visitors are invited inside the formidable convent, but the attraction is the **view** from the tower-top terrace reached by a long staircase: You'll be able to see all the way to Ischia in the northwest and down the coast to Paestum in the east. Before the road to Positano and Amalfi opened in the late 1830s, this was a major stop on the Grand Tour, as far along the coast as view-seekers could get by land. The terrace is generally open April through September daily 8am to noon and 5 to 7pm; and October through March Monday to Friday 10am to noon and 3 to 5pm; a small donation is appreciated.

Marina del Cantone ♥

5km (3 miles) S of Sant'Agata sui Due Golfi

From Sant'Agata, follow the road down through Metrano then on to hillside Nerano and from there down to Marina del Cantone, on a cove cut into the cliffs. The beach (mostly pebbles) is the longest for miles around, packed solid in summer with sunbeds (any number of beach clubs rent them for about 15€ a day) and backed by houses and bars and cafes. Looming just offshore are **Li Galli,** an archipelago of tiny islets (p. 663).

Massa Lubrense ♥♥

5km (3 miles) W of Sant'Agata sui Due Golfi

Quiet hillside Massa Lubrense was once a powerful rival to Sorrento for dominance over this coast. These days the off-the-beaten-track position, along with considerable natural beauty, are the town's great assets. You'll want to pause long enough on Largo Vescovado to take in the dead-on view of the shimmering profile of Capri, just across the bay at this point, then step into the church of **Santa Maria delle Grazie** for a look at its colorful majolica floor; it's open daily 7am to noon and 5 to 7pm.

Massa's port, **Marina della Lobra,** is about 1km (half a mile) below town, reached on foot by following Via Roma until it ends at a centuries-old stone path that cuts through lemon and olive groves down to the sea (you might want to make the ascent by bus). With its pebbly beach and several low-key beach clubs, Marina della Lobra is one of the most pleasant seaside spots on the peninsula.

Punta Campanella ♥♥

9km (6 miles) S of Massa Lubrense

Land's End on the Sorrento Peninsula is this rocky point where a lighthouse guides ships through the treacherous Capri Narrows, the 3km (2 miles) of swift-moving waters between the peninsula and Capri. The name Punta Campanella refers to the "small bell" that once warned of pirate incursions from atop **Torre Minerva,** a 14th-century watchtower built next to the ruins of a temple dedicated to Athena (called Minerva by the Romans). With luck and divine guidance from the goddess, ancient sailors could just make it unscathed through the rock-strewn narrows.

Hiking in Punta Campanella, with a view of Capri across the narrows.

Hiking Around the Sorrento Peninsula

The peninsula is traversed by a network of 22 well-maintained **hiking paths** that crisscross valleys, meander atop seaside cliffs, and descend hillsides to secret coves for a total length of 110km (68 miles). The tourist offices in Sorrento (p. 645) and Massa Lubrense (p. 657) have maps.

One of the most scenic walks is from the village of **Torca** (2km/1 mile southeast of Sant'Agata sui Due Golfi), where Via Pedara becomes a dirt path that descends a cliff past the ruins of the 12th-century abbey of San Pietro, ending in a quiet cove. Just offshore are the Li Galli (the Rooster) islets.

Another walk descends from the village of **Termini** (5km/3 miles southwest of Sant'Agata sui Due Golfi) into the Vallone della Cala di Mitigliano, carpeted with olive groves and *macchia mediterranea,* typical Mediterranean vegetation that includes the beautifully scented *mirto.* The trail then crosses a plateau with large boulders and the ruins of Torre di Namonte, a medieval watchtower, before descending steeply toward the sea, with the profile of Capri looming ahead.

On the southwestern side of the peninsula, the seashore and offshore waters are protected as a marine park, **Area Marina Protetta di Punta Campanella** (www.puntacampanella.org; ✆ **081/808-9877**). A good way to see this unspoiled coast is on a snorkeling cruise with **Punta Campanella Diving,** on Via Fontanella in Massa Lubrense (puntacampanelladiving.com; ✆ **338/471-2360;** 4-hr. tours, including pickup in Sorrento, from 90€). **Masticiello Boat Service** (masticiello.com; ✆ **081/808-1443**) is one of many outfits in Marina del Cantone that rents motor launches on which you can explore the shoreline; prices begin at about 150€ a day for a motorized rubber boat that accommodates six.

Where to Eat Around the Sorrento Peninsula

Don Alfonso 1890 ♥♥ CREATIVE SORRENTINE The Iaccarino family has won international fame for their charming dining rooms, poolside terrace, and dishes infused with local flavors. Breads and pasta are made in-house, and almost everything else comes from the family garden or a network of local suppliers. Owner and former chef Alfonso Iaccarino grows the vegetables, shops, and orders; his wife, Livia, oversees the dining room. Homegrown tomatoes infuse a bouillabaisse with freshly caught fish and ravioli filled with farmhouse cheese. If you wish to prolong the experience, **Don Alfonso 1890 Relais** has nine elegant guest rooms, many with a glimpse of the sea and furnished with antiques (375€–405€ double). If you enjoy the food, you can sign up for a cooking class with the chefs (220€/session).

Corso Sant'Agata 11, Sant'Agata sui Due Golfi. donalfonso.com. ✆ **081/878-0026.** Main courses 35€–45€; tasting menus 150€–180€. Tues–Fri 8–10:30pm; Sat–Sun 12:30–2:30pm and 8–10:30pm. Closed Nov–Mar.

Leave the Car in the Garage

Driving along the Amalfi Drive, with its many twists and turns, bumper-to-bumper traffic, and near-impossible parking, is never a good idea, and at times it's even illegal. At certain times only cars with license plates ending in odd numbers may use the 22-mile stretch between Positano and Vietri sul Mare on odd-numbered dates, those with even-numbered plates other days. Taxis, buses, and residents' vehicles are exempt, as are those of visitors enroute to hotels where they've prebooked parking arrangements. Rules are in effect weekends from mid-June through September, all of August, and Easter week. Check with your hotel for updates, and be prepared to take advantage of the region's many public transport options.

POSITANO ♥♥

16km (10 miles) E of Sorrento

Hugging a semi-vertical rock formation, the first town of any size on the Amalfi Drive heading east from Sorrento is the very essence of picturesque—an enticing collection of pastel-colored houses and majolica domes that spill down a ravine to the sea. Novelist John Steinbeck, after a visit in 1953, described it in words that still ring true: "It is a dream place that isn't quite real when you are there and becomes beckoningly real after you have gone." It's not surprising that Positano was the retreat for *la dolce vita* set in the 1960s and '70s. In midsummer, visitors can seem like an invading horde, much like those that attacked the little kingdom

The beachfront promenade at Positano.

back in the 9th to 11th centuries, when it was part of the powerful Republic of the Amalfis, rival to Venice as a sea power.

Essentials

ARRIVING If you're driving down from Naples, take the A3 and exit at Castellammare di Stabia for the SS145 to Sorrento. The SS163 branches off the SS145 before you get to Sorrento and heads over the peninsula to Positano; drive time from Naples is about 2 hours. **SITA Sud** buses (see box on p. 644) connect Positano with other towns along the coast. In summer, ferries and hydrofoils operated by **NLG-Navigazione Libera del Golfo** (nlg.it; ✆ **081/807-552-0763**) and **Linee Lauro** (alilauro.it; ✆ **081/497-2206**) make daily runs to and from Sorrento, Naples, Ischia, Capri, Positano, and Amalfi.

VISITOR INFORMATION The **tourist office** is at Via Regina Giovanna 13 (aziendaturismopositano.it; ✆ **089/875067**), open Monday to Saturday 8:30am to 2pm, and also from 3:30 to 8pm in July and August.

Exploring Positano

Whether you arrive by boat or bus, you're in for an uphill or downhill climb along narrow lanes and steep lanes (wear comfortable walking shoes). At some point you'll want to stay put, probably along the sea at **Marina Grande,** where the town's few fishermen still haul up their boats, and ferries arrive and depart. The pebbly beach is backed by restaurants and bars in what were once shipyards and storehouses when Positano was a naval power. From Marina Grande, **Via Positanesi d'America,** a cliffside pedestrian promenade, stretches along the shore past the cape of

Start at the Top in Positano

SITA buses plying the coast make two stops in Positano: just above Piazza dei Mulini near the center of town and higher up, at the **Chiesa di Nuova** (it's the first stop if you're coming from Sorrento, the second from Amalfi). To explore this hill-clinging town while avoiding uphill climbs, get off at the Chiesa Nuova stop and, after taking a look at the church's colorful majolica tile floor, wander down from there. Stepped lanes lined with tiny houses stacked one atop the other will bring you down to the beach at Fornillo, where you can follow the waterfront into the main part of town, or with a little maneuvering take you down toward Spiaggia Grande.

Torre Trasita and a 13th-century lookout to the smaller and more relaxing beach of **Fornillo.**

If you wander up the steps from Marina Grande you'll soon find yourself amid a souklike sprawl of shops shaded by bougainvillea-laced trellises. The majolica-domed **Collegiata di Santa Maria Assunta ♥♥**, Piazza Flavio Gioia (✆ **089/875480;** daily 9:30am–noon and 4–8pm), is Positano's main church, founded as a Benedictine monastery in the 13th century and rebuilt in a grand baroque style in the 18th century. The *Madonna Nera* (Black Madonna), a Byzantine-style icon above the altar, allegedly gave the town its name when a 12th-century pirate ship carrying the icon sailed into a violent storm. Sailors heard the Madonna on the icon saying "Posa, Posa" ("Put me down") and they took their ship to safety in what would become the harbor of Positano. In fact, the monks most likely brought the icon from Constantinople, but the popular legend persists, and the icon is carried through the streets on August 15th, the feast of the Assumption of Mary; in the evening, illuminated boats come ashore to commemorate the fateful landing. A relief on the campanile outside shows a sea dragon and a wolf nursing seven fish, a clue to how the town once made its living. Excavations beneath the church have unearthed the remains of the large Roman Villa d'Ozio, a summer retreat that was buried by the eruption of Mt. Vesuvius in C.E. 79. The ruins are now on view as **MAR-Museo Archeologico Romano di Positano** (marpositano.it; ✆ **331/298-5821**), where a series of glass walkways lead into the triclinium, a large dining room decorated with colorful frescoes. The ruins are open April through October daily 9am to 9pm (Nov–Mar 10am–4pm); admission is 15€.

BEACHES & BOATING

Positano has two beaches: **Spiaggia Grande** and the slightly quieter **Fornillo.** You can swim for free at either or rent a lounger and umbrella for about 10€. Spiaggia Grande is backed by open-air beach bars and casual eateries, and a small string of open-air bar/cafes is at one end of Fornillo. To reach more idyllic settings, board any of the tour boats that set off from Spiaggia Grande for stops at coves along the coast, or rent a kayak and poke along the rocky shoreline at your own pace. **Kayak in Positano** (kayakinpositano.it/excursions.htm) rents kayaks, from 15€ an hour, and leads kayak excursions, from 80€.

Many day sailors set their sights on **Li Galli** ♥♥ (The Roosters), the four small islands visible to the west of Marina Grande. According to Homer, Sirens—birdlike creatures with human faces and the bodies of fish—who lived on the rocky outcroppings lured mariners to their deaths on the rocky shoals with their enchanting songs; the islands are also known as the Isole Sirenuse. If the light is right and you've had some wine on the voyage, it's easy to see how the fowl-shaped islets might have appeared to be Sirens rising out of the sea mist. The island to head for is **Gallo Lungo,** where a medieval watchtower rises above a little beach. This is where Russian dancer Rudolf Nureyev settled a few years before his death in 1993, transforming a villa built for another Russian ballet star, Léonide Massine (1896–1979), into an Aladdin's cave filled with rich mosaics and kilims. The public is not allowed to step ashore but may swim in the surrounding waters.

HIKING

The 8km-long (5-mile) **Il Sentiero degli Dei** ♥♥♥ (Path of the Gods) clings to a hillside above Positano, descending from Bomerano, part of the community of Agerola, to the little village of Nocelle, just above Positano. The relatively easy, well-signposted trail meanders through cultivated terraces and citrus groves and follows view-filled, vertigo-inducing heights along the way. To avoid the strenuous ascent from the coast, take the Sita Sud bus to Amalfi and switch there for a bus to Bomerano. From the village square there, it should take about 3 hours to make the gradual descent.

Where to Stay in Positano

Small, guesthouse-style rooms offer a way to beat Positano's sky-high lodging prices. The **tourist office** (p. 661) has a full list of bed-and-breakfasts, home stays, and other moderately priced accommodations.

A garden-view room at Palazzo Murat.

EXPENSIVE

Palazzo Murat ♥♥ Gioacchino Murat, Napoleon's brother-in-law and king of Naples, built this enticing and vaguely exotic 18th-century baroque palace near Positano's small port as a summer getaway. It's still a retreat of royal magnitude, set amid a vast garden and orchard swathed in flowering vines and scented with lemons and jasmine. Five especially large rooms, filled with handsome antiques, are in the original palace; others are in an extremely tasteful addition, where tile floors and traditional furnishings adhere to the historical ambience. Most rooms have balconies, some with sea views; others overlook the surrounding greenery and the tile-domed church of Santa Maria Assunta. Buffet breakfast is served in the garden in good weather.

Via dei Mulini 23. palazzomurat.it. ✆ **089/875177.** 31 units. 770€–1,100€ double (3-night min. stay for some summer dates). Rates include breakfast. Closed late Oct through the week before Easter. **Amenities:** Restaurant; concierge; pool; room service; free Wi-Fi.

San Pietro ♥♥♥ One of the world's most fabled getaways perches on its own promontory above the sea, providing the vacation experience of a lifetime. Opulently tiled terraces cascade down the cliff face, laced with shaded nooks and crannies (even if you're not staying here, the best setting in Positano for a cocktail, expensive but memorable). Facing the sea through huge windows and private balconies, the large accommodations are a gracious mix of antiques, stylishly informal pieces, and elaborate tiles and artwork. The pièce de résistance is the private beach, reached by an elevator that descends through the cliff. For those who want to venture farther, the hotel's private yacht takes guests on complimentary coast cruises, and a free shuttle plies the 2km (1 mile) to town. Many guests, however, choose to stay put in the hedonistic surroundings, relying on the glorious, view-filled terrace of **Il San Pietro** restaurant for exceptional sustenance.

Via Laurito 2. ilsanpietro.it. ✆ **089/812080.** 60 units. 900€–3,100€ double. Rates include breakfast. 3-night minimum stay in high season. Closed Nov–Mar. **Amenities:** 2 restaurants; 2 bars; concierge; health club; pool; room service; sauna; spa; tennis court; free Wi-Fi.

MODERATE

Hotel Buca di Bacco ♥♥ This former fisherman's hut, much expanded and glorified over the years, is right on Marina Grande. The beachfront perch puts you in the center of the action, so convenience comes with a bit of noise, along with endless sea views from colorfully tiled balconies and terraces. Even rooms with partial or no sea views are a bit of a treat, with handsome antiques and comfy upholstered pieces set on tile floors to create a casual, gracious elegance that's typical of the Amalfi Coast. Three generations of the Rispoli family look after guests with care. Excellent meals are served in a sea-facing dining room and an informal snack bar just off the beach below, a good stop for non-guests as well.

Via Rampa Teglia 4. bucadibacco.it. ✆ **089/875699.** 46 units. 370€–570€ double (2-night minimum stay for some summer dates). Rates include breakfast. Closed Nov–Mar. **Amenities:** Restaurant; bar; babysitting; concierge; room service; free Wi-Fi.

Hotel Dimora Fornillo ♥♥ It's hard to imagine a more dreamlike spot than this promontory several hundred feet above a beach of the same name. The simple decor and basic comforts don't match the grandeur of the setting, but rooms are large and airy and cheerfully decked out with bright tiles. Many guests happily forgo luxuries in an aerie like this, with

sweeping views over town and sea from all the rooms, which open to patios and the pine-shaded, edge-of-the-cliff garden beyond. Reaching this high-up perch requires maneuvering steps and narrow lanes, so notify the staff before you arrive to plan logistics and get help with your bags.
Via Fornillo 27. hoteldimorafornillo.it. ✆ **089/811422.** 7 units. 180€–320€ double. Rates include breakfast. 3-night minimum stay in high season. Closed Nov–Mar. **Amenities:** Garden; free Wi-Fi.

Hotel Savoia ♥♥ The old-fashioned ambience of this inn right in the heart of Positano comes with a provenance: The D'Aiello family has been running the place since 1936, when Positano was a getaway for a select few, and that's how they still treat their guests. Rooms are pleasantly done with bright tile floors, comfortable beds, and attractive traditional furnishings; some have sea views, while others take in the sweep of the old town climbing the hillside.
Via Cristoforo Colombo 73. savoiapositano.it. ✆ **089/875003.** 39 units. 365€–515€ double. Rates include breakfast. Up to 5-night minimum stay in high season. Closed Nov to mid-Mar. **Amenities:** Bar; babysitting; concierge; room service; free Wi-Fi.

Hotel Villa Yiara ♥♥♥ Imara and Silvio have converted their sun-drenched 18th-century villa into a welcoming bed-and-breakfast that combines the warmth of an artfully bohemian home with features found in more expensive Positano hotels: flower-filled terraces, endless sea views, and stylish decor awash in white furnishings set against colorful tiles. The town and beach are a 10-minute walk down the hill—a little bus makes the climb back up—and this privileged hillside locale seems a world removed from the bustle below.
Viale Pasitea 193. villayiara.it. ✆ **089/8122379.** 8 units. 310€–520€ double. Rates include breakfast. Closed Dec–Feb. **Amenities:** Free Wi-Fi.

La Rosa dei Venti ♥♥ Each of the simply furnished, tile-floored rooms in this house high on a hillside in a quieter part of Positano comes with a big perk: a large, planted terrace with a sea view. It's tempting to settle in here and stay put, but moving around town and the coast is easy to do. The beach at Fornillo is at the bottom of many flights of steps, shops and restaurants are nearby, and it's an easy climb up to the Chiesa di Nuova bus stop or along lanes into the heart of town and the harbor.
Via Fornillo 40. larosadeiventi.net. ✆ **089/875252.** 250€–350€ double. Rates include breakfast. **Amenities:** Free Wi-Fi.

INEXPENSIVE

La Fenice ♥♥♥ All the charm and beauty of Positano comes to the fore in this little parcel of heaven clinging to a cliff on the outskirts of town. A stay requires a bit of walking and climbing, to and from the town center (about a 10-min. stroll) and on the gorgeous property itself, along shaded walkways and stone stairways through gardens to the pool and private beach below—an amenity found in only a few much more expensive retreats along the coast. Simple whitewashed rooms, most with tiled terraces overlooking the sea, are tucked into villas and cottages that descend the hillside amid lemon groves and grapevines. Owner Constantino Marino and his family live on the property and make guests feel at home, carting bags up and down the stairs and serving informal meals made with produce from the garden (meals on request).

Via Giuglielmo Marconi 4. lafenicepositano.com. ✆ **089/875513.** 13 units. 140€–230€. Rates include breakfast. Closed Dec–Feb. **Amenities:** Pool; beach; free Wi-Fi.

Where to Eat in & Around Positano

The most popular place in Positano for cocktails and after-dinner drinks is the view-filled terrace at **Franco's,** Via Cristoforo Colombo 30 (francos bar.com; ✆ **089/812-189;** Apr–Oct). The more casual **Bar Paradise** (✆ **089/811-461;** Apr–Oct) serves drinks and snacks throughout the day on a terrace just above Spiaggia Grande.

EXPENSIVE

Next 2 ♥♥ AMALFITAN Step through iron gates into this softly lit courtyard with knockout sea views and a contemporary room of dazzling white table linens and bright cushions. You'll dine on refined takes on local favorites with fresh ingredients from the restaurant garden. Fried ravioli stuffed with ricotta and mozzarella are set on a bed of tomatoes plucked from the vine minutes before, while *fiori di zucchini* (zucchini flowers) are filled with ricotta, mozzarella, and basil and served with pesto sauce. Fresh fish is a specialty, paired with the same homegrown ingredients.

Via Pasitea 242. next2.it. ✆ **089/8123516.** Reservations recommended. Main courses 30€–45€, tasting menu 120€. Daily 6:30pm–11:30pm (closed Wed in off-season). Closed Jan–Mar.

MODERATE

Casa e Bottega ♥♥ ITALIAN A whitewashed room in the center of Positano is filled with sunlight and handsome wood furnishings to create an atmosphere as refreshing as the innovative menu. Options include a big choice of salads, along with eggs and pastries at breakfast, with juices and other drinks throughout the day. The light fare focuses on fresh produce and extends to a few daily fish and pasta dishes.

Viale Pasitea 100. casaebottegapositano.it. ✆ **338/709-7500.** Main courses 15€–28€. Daily 9am–3pm. Closed Nov–Mar.

Da Adolfo ♥♥ AMALFITAN/SEAFOOD One of Positano's old-time favorites, tucked away in a secluded cove east of town, is part beach club and part restaurant. The kitchen focuses on local specialties such as mozzarella *alla brace* (grilled on fresh lemon leaves), followed by a beautifully seasoned *zuppa di cozze* (mussel stew). Come for lunch and spend the afternoon, making use of the adjacent changing rooms, showers, and chair and umbrella rentals. Sooner or later, though, you'll have to face the 450 rugged steps up the hillside to the road—unless you take the free water-shuttle service back to town. Free boat service for customers leaves from Positano from 10am to 1pm; return trips begin at 4pm.

Via Spiaggia di Laurito 40. daadolfo.com. ✆ **089/875022.** Reservations (by phone only) recommended. Main courses 10€–22€. Daily 10am–8pm. Closed mid-Oct to early May.

Hostaria di Bacco ♥♥ SEAFOOD/AMALFITAN In 1948, director Roberto Rossellini and actress Anna Magnani, known affectionately as la Nannarella, lived in a simple fisherman's hut on the beach in Furore (18km/11 miles southeast of Positano; see p. 669). The couple dined regularly in what's still a local gathering spot, where one evening Rossellini broke the news to his lover that he was leaving her for Swedish actress Ingrid Bergman. The fiery Magnani replied by throwing a house specialty at Rossellini that has ever since been known as *Ferrazzuoli alla Nannarella,* pasta with swordfish, raisins, pine nuts, and sun-dried tomatoes. It's one of many straightforward local classics served in the view-filled dining room and on the terrace. Upstairs are nine pleasant guest rooms, with others scattered across the hillside village (from 180€–300€ double).

Via G.B. Lama 9, Furore. baccofurore.it. ✆ **089/830360.** Main courses 12€–22€. Daily 8:30am–11pm. Closed some winter periods.

INEXPENSIVE

Pupetto Cafe ♥♥ PIZZA The Pupetto hotel operates this bar on a shady deck just above the sand and rocks on Fornillo beach, serving sandwiches, salads, snacks, and drinks throughout the day. Service is friendly and attentive, and the staff encourages their clientele to hang around a long time, shuttling back and forth between the tables and the beach loungers below, enjoying one of the most pleasant experiences in Positano. Climb the stairs to the hotel's lemon-scented terrace for a more substantial lunch or dinner of grilled fresh fish, seafood pasta, or pizza (main courses 30€–35€, pizza 8€–14€; open daily 12:30–3pm and 7:30–10pm).

Via Fornillo 37. hotelpupetto.it. ✆ **089/875087.** Sandwiches and salads from 7€. Daily 9am–sunset. Closed Nov–Mar.

Photo Op

If you're traveling by car or taxi, just west of Positano on SS163 (that is, as you approach from Sorrento), keep an eye out for the renowned **Belvedere dello Schiaccone ♥♥♥**, the best lookout point on the Amalfi Drive, 200m (656 ft.) above sea level. The view extends across palm and citrus groves to the archipelago of Li Galli and Capo Sottile, with the splendid summit of Monte Sant'Angelo a Tre Pizzi in the background. According to the legend of Monte Sant'Angelo, the devil challenged the Virgin Mary to see who could pierce the rock face. The devil could only scratch the surface, but at the Virgin's touch the rock crumbled and the large opening that you see in one side of the peak appeared.

Positano Shopping

Positano sold its soul to the devils of commerce long ago. However, tucked among the endless rows of shops are some venerable standouts. Try **Sartoria Maria Lampo ♥**, Viale Pasitea 12 (marialampo.it; ✆ **089/875021**), a throwback to the '70s when Moda Positano casual wear was all the rage. The town is also famous for handcrafted sandals, often made while you wait. Top shoemakers are **La Botteguccia ♥♥**, Via Regina Giovanna 19 (✆ **089/811824**), and **Safari ♥♥**, Via della Taratana 2 (safaria.it).

BETWEEN POSITANO & AMALFI ♥♥

East of Positano, the famed Amalfi Drive swings into full gear, twisting and turning past a number of charming coastal towns. Parking for nonresidents is limited, however, so except for the winter months, you can't really explore them unless you're traveling by bus. SITA buses make stops at all communities along the Amalfi Drive.

With a profusion of porticos and domes, medieval **Praiano ♥♥** and its adjacent twin, **Vettica Maggiore ♥♥** (6km/4 miles east of Positano), sit 120m (394 ft.) above sea level on the slopes of Monte Sant'Angelo, draping seaward over the Capo Sottile promontory. (Urbino Positano minibuses, departing from Positano's Piazza dei Mulini, make regular runs to and from the mountainside center of Praiano.) It's said that "Whoever wants to live a healthy life spends the morning in Vettica and the evening in Praiano," which probably just means that this is a good place to spend an entire day, wandering up and down staired alleyways that meander through olive and lemon groves. The towns were the summer residence of the Amalfi doges, who loved the beautiful views over Positano, Amalfi, and the Faraglioni of Capri. The two settlements merge at a sea-facing, majolica-paved piazza in front of the **church of San Gennaro,** which seems more like a ship deck than a shelf of terra firma. From there, follow signs for "SPIAGGIA" (beach) on lanes tucked into the hillside to **Gavitella,** a tiny slip of pebbles on a cliff-enclosed cove. It's a pleasant 20-minute walk along shady lanes east from the church to picturesque **Marina di Praia,** at the bottom of a chasm below the stout Torre a Mare, a 13th-century watchtower. The pebbly beach is

The beautifully tiled dome of San Gennaro in Praiano.

The beach at Furore lies tucked at the head of a deep narrow fiord.

backed by a few fish trattorias and it's a short trek up to the SITA bus stop on the main road.

Residents of gravity-defying **Furore ♥♥♥**, 12km (7 miles) farther along the Drive (18km/11 miles southeast of Positano), might have the strongest legs in Italy, because it's a climb of more than 500m (1,600 ft.) from the waterfront to the top of the town. Down at sea level, where you'll probably spend most of your time, is the fjord of Furore, a deep cleft in the cliffs that provides a natural harbor. (From the bus stop, next to the bridge across the fjord, it's 944 steps down to the strip of pebbles along the harbor.) When water roars though the fjord with a fury, it's easy to see how the town got its name. You can sit in one of the little bars above the fjord and consider the perils of coastal life as you sip delicious wines from the highly acclaimed winery **Cantine Marisa Cuomo ♥♥**, Via Lama 14 (marisacuomo.com; ✆ **089/830348**); its tasting room is open Monday through Saturday by appointment from 9am to 5pm.

Rambling little **Conca dei Marini ♥**, 2km (1 mile) east of Furore, is really just a hamlet of houses perched along the coast road. It's hard to believe that the little harbor beneath Capo di Conca once bustled with boatbuilding and provided moorage for 27 galleons, making the town richer than Amalfi. Over the years Conca's views and out-of-the way quiet have lured privacy-seeking celebs, among them Jackie Onassis, Princess Margaret of England, Jennifer Lopez, and George Clooney.

Today Conca is best known as the jumping-off point for the touristy **Grotta dello Smeraldo ♥** (Emerald Grotto). Stalactites and stalagmites in this famous sea cave, discovered in 1932, produce transcendent light effects, and an otherworldly blue-green aura envelops the grotto when the

A Sweet Treat in Conca dei Marini

While you're in Conca, take time to try Sfogliatella di Santa Rosa, a delicious pastry invented by 17th-century nuns at the **Monastero Santa Rosa** (now a hotel). The enterprising sisters replaced the traditional ricotta-cheese filling of the popular Neapolitan *sfogliatella* with cream and a dash of *amarene*, candied sour cherries in syrup. And mamma mia!—the creation was a hit that you can still taste in pastry shops all along the coast.

sun is high and the sea is calm (it's open daily 10am–4:30pm; the light effects are best noon–3pm). You can reach the cave from the Amalfi Drive (SS163) via an elevator or a long series of steps, after which you climb into a rowboat for an all-too-short glide through the spectacle. You can also take a boat from Amalfi, just 5km (3 miles) down the coast (trips usually 17€, including admission to the grotto). Admission is 6€, including the rowboat ride through the grotto. The grotto often closes due to inclement weather and rough seas.

AMALFI ♥♥

19km (12 miles) E of Positano

From the 9th to the 11th century, the seafaring Republic of Amalfi rivaled the great maritime powers of Genoa and Venice. Nowadays, Amalfi is prominent mostly as an alluring resort town, set among lemon groves and olive trees between the Lattari Mountains and the Bay of Salerno. Despite its popularity, Amalfi doesn't seem crushed by tourism as Positano does—at least not in the early morning and evening hours before and after the tour buses and boats disgorge day trippers. The town is within easy reach of some of the coast's best stretches of sand and pebbles.

Essentials

ARRIVING If you're coming from Positano by land, you'll follow the famous Amalfi Drive (SS163) by car or take a **SITA Sud bus** (see box on p. 644). If you're driving directly from Naples, take autostrada A3 to Vietri sul Mare, then head west on SS163 from there; total travel time is about 1½ hours. **Taxis** offer a rate of about 130€ to Amalfi from Naples Airport (determine the price before you set out). By public transport from Naples, take the high-speed **train** to Salerno (p. 832) and from there head west up the coast on the SITA Sud bus (about 90 min. faster than taking the Circumvesuviana train to Sorrento and the SITA bus from there). A SITA Sud express bus (sitasudtrasporti.it) travels inland between Naples and Amalfi, with buses for the 2-hour trip operating from Naples mid-mornings and mid- and late afternoons on weekdays and Saturday, but the return bus to Naples from Amalfi is geared to locals and travels only in the early morning hours.

In summer, **ferries** and **hydrofoils** operated by **NLG-Navigazione Libera del Golfo** (nlg.it; ✆ **081/552-0763**) and **Linee Lauro** (alilauro.it; ✆ **081/497-2206**) make daily runs to and from Sorrento, Naples, Ischia, Capri, Positano, and Amalfi.

VISITOR INFORMATION The Amalfi Tourist Board provides a wealth of useful information, including itineraries for exploring the town and region, at visitamalfi.info.

Exploring Amalfi

Opening onto the harbor, **Piazza Flavio Gioia** commemorates the local navigator who some say invented the compass around 1300 (a dubious claim, because sailors used rudimentary compasses, likely introduced by Arab navigators, long before; it's more likely Gioia simply perfected the compass for marine use). It is fact that Amalfi sailors provided material for some of the Middle Ages' first nautical charts, and also developed the **Tavole Amalfitane,** a maritime code followed in the Mediterranean for centuries; the document, which covered everything from haulage terms to crew conditions, is on view in the **Arsenale della Repubblica** (see below).

Amalfi's former role as a world maritime power is illustrated in a pair of tile panels created in the 1950s by artist Renato Rossi, embedded in a wall along the harborfront by the **Porta della Marina.** To the east, on **Corso delle Repubbliche Marinare,** a 1970s-era ceramic piece tells more of Amalfi's history, from its founding by Romans to the arrival of relics of St. Andrew, Amalfi's patron saint, from Constantinople.

The medieval heart of Amalfi, a maze of covered walks and narrow streets, stretches from **Piazza Duomo,** a lively cathedral square near the seafront, into an increasingly narrow ravine. You can walk the length of town in 10 minutes or so, along Via Amalfi from Piazza Duomo up to the **Paper Museum** ♥♥ (p. 672). For much of the town's history, Via Amalfi was a rushing stream; you can still hear water gurgling beneath the pavement. To navigate the town as medieval residents once did, walk up the Ruga Nova Mercatorum, a tunnel-like alleyway east of Via Amalfi that ends in Piazza Santa Spirito. A fountain in the square, **Capo di Ciuccio** (Donkey's Head), is so called because the hardworking beasts could pause here and dip their muzzles into the cool water. A local family decorates every inch of the wall behind the basin with a year-round Nativity scene. From another tunnel, this one modern and off Piazza Municipio behind the cathedral (leading to the town's parking garage and Atrani; see below), an elevator whisks you to the cemetery at the top of town for a bird's-eye view over the cathedral's tiled dome, pastel-hued houses climbing steep hillsides, and the sea beyond; there's an easy walk back down along stepped lanes.

Arsenale della Repubblica (Museo della Bussola e del Ducato Marinaro) ♥♥ HISTORIC SITE The Republic of Amalfi's power in the Mediterranean was maintained in this medieval shipyard, where galleys up to 40m (131 ft.) long were built, to be powered by 120 oarsmen. The stone-vaulted boatsheds now house the solid-looking gold coins (*tarì*) that Amalfi once minted and the documents with which the republic wielded its considerable legal clout. The spotlight here is on the 66-chapter **Tavole Amalfitane,** a maritime code that more or less established the laws of the high seas from the 13th to 16th centuries.

Largo Cesareo Console 3. arsenalediamalfi.it. ✆ **089/873622.** Admission 3€, free for children under 13 (fees may vary with exhibitions on display). Apr–Oct daily 10am–8pm, Nov–Mar daily 10am–5pm.

Duomo di Sant'Andrea ♥♥♥ CHURCH This monument to Amalfi's rich past, covered in black-and-white marble and colorful mosaics, sits atop a monumental staircase just inland from the sea. The **Chiostro del Paradiso** (Cloister of Paradise) is decidedly Moorish, with a whitewashed quadrangle of interlaced arches and brightly colored geometric mosaics. Amalfi's medieval nobles are entombed in sarcophagi set around this exotic enclosure. The **Crypt** houses the remains of St. Andrew, Amalfi's protector saint. It was important for Amalfi to have a famous patron, just as Venice had St. Mark, so soldiers brought the head and other relics of Andrew back from Constantinople at the end of the Fourth Crusade, in 1206. Legend has it that Andrew has been working miracles ever since—such as in 1544, when the pirate Ariadeno Barbarossa's fleet, after attacking Amalfi, suddenly sank in a giant sea surge. Even now, on the saint's feast day, November 30, a miraculous thick ooze, reverentially called "manna," appears on his tomb. An 18th-century baroque restoration of the interior added lots of marble and mundane frescoes, but it's a disappointment after that wonderfully fanciful facade and cloisters. An austere medieval basilica next door holds a museum of gold chalices and other treasures.

Amalfi's imposing medieval Duomo testifies to the former power of this maritime republic.

Piazza del Duomo. ✆ **089/871059.** Free admission. Museum and cloister (✆ **089/871324**): 3€. June–Sept daily 9am–7:45pm; Oct–Feb 10am–1pm and 2:30–4:30pm; Mar–June 9am–6:30pm.

Museo della Carta (Paper Museum) ♥♥ HISTORIC SITE Among the many goods Amalfi's sailors and merchants brought back from their voyages was paper, a prized commodity throughout the Middle East. From the 13th through the mid–19th centuries, Amalfi was one of Europe's largest exporters of paper, produced in waterwheel-powered factories whose ruins dot the Valle dei Mulini (Valley of the Mills) at the inland end of town. In the remains of one of the mills, a museum shows off vintage machinery and paper that's still sold in Amalfi shops. A path through the valley (see "Hiking," below) takes you past several evocative factory ruins.

Palazzo Pagliara, Via delle Cartiere 24. museodellacarta.it. ✆ **089/830-4561.** Admission 4.50€ 3€ ages 5–18, free for children 4 and under; guided visit 7€ adults, 6€ children). Mar–Oct and Dec 27–Jan 6 daily 10am–7pm; Nov–Feb Tues–Sun 10am–5pm.

BEACHES & BOATING

Amalfi's **beaches** are two pebbly strips on either side of the harbor. However, the town of **Minori ♥♥**, 4km (2½ miles) east of Amalfi, has an asset that's the envy of almost every town on the Amalfi Coast: a long, sandy beach surrounded by citrus groves. Another Minori attraction is a lavish Roman holiday villa, with traces of frescoes and mosaics in rooms surrounding a garden; the entrance is at Via Capo di Piazza 28 (free admission; Tues–Sun 9am–4:30pm). **Maiori ♥♥**, separated from Minori by a rocky headland, has an even longer beach, backed by a palm-lined promenade. **Pasticceria Napoli,** in Maiori at Corso Regina 64 (✆ **089/853182**), serves ricotta-filled *sfogliatelle* and other pastries to savor on the beach. SITA Sud buses (see box p. 644) and ferries from Amalfi serve both towns. A pleasant and fairly easy walk between the two towns is through lemon groves along the 3-km (2-mile) long **Sentiero dei Limoni** (Path of the Lemons).

Off the coast road about 3km (2 miles) west of Amalfi (going toward Positano), a descent down 400 steps brings you to **Duoglio ♥**, a very nice stretch of sand backed by two beach bars that are good for snacks or drinks: **I Due Scugnizzi** (✆ **089/831-710**) and **Lido degli Artisti** (✆ **331/996-5635**). Boats from the pier in Amalfi shuttle back and forth to the beach (about 4€ for the round-trip). You can also take the coast-road bus to and from the top of the steps.

From the harbor at Amalfi's **Marina Grande ♥** you can rent **boats**—with or without a skipper—to explore the coast. **Cooperativa Sant'Andrea** (coopsantandrea.it; ✆ **089/873-190**) offers regular service to the beaches of Duoglio and Santa Croce, only a few minutes away; in summer, boats leave every 30 minutes between 9am and 5pm. **Amalfi Outdoor Experience ♥♥** (amalfioutdoorexperience.com; ✆ **331/315-9177**) leads kayak tours along the coast, from 50€.

HIKING

A popular hike from Amalfi is the walk along **Valle dei Mulini** (Valley of the Mills). Follow Via Amalfi through town until you come to a series of steps to the right as you head away from town; these climb the hillside to a well-signposted trail through lush countryside along the banks of the River Canneto to the **Mulino Rovinato** (Ruined Mill), about 1 hour away. Flour mills once thrived here, as did paper mills. If you continue to climb the hill, you'll come into the **Vallone delle Ferriere,** where now-ruined *ferriere* (iron mills) operated into the 19th century. At the top of the valley is a waterfall; allow 1½ hours to reach the falls from Amalfi. If you're really ambitious and have another 2 hours, continue from here up to Ravello (p. 678).

Paths crisscross **Capo d'Orso,** a wild, 1,235-acre headland near Maiori, just east of Amalfi. In Maiori, set off along Via Casale Alto, which becomes a flight of steps, then a mule path leading through vineyards, orchards, and meadows. An uphill trek of about 5km (3 miles) brings you to the Santuario di Maria Santissima Avvocata and sweeping coast views.

Where to Stay in & Around Amalfi

EXPENSIVE

Hotel Luna Convento ♥♥ St. Francis himself founded this seaside monastery in 1222, and the beautiful cloisters and transformed monks' cells and chapel also have a history of hospitality as one of the first grand hotels on the Amalfi Coast, receiving guests since 1822. American playwright Tennessee Williams spent time here, as did heads of state Otto von Bismarck and Benito Mussolini. Norwegian playwright Henrik Ibsen wrote *A Doll's House* here in 1879. Adding even more luster to the surroundings is a 15th-century Saracen watchtower, now housing a bar and standing guard over a private beach and large seawater pool. Most of the plain-yet-chic guest rooms, many carved out of former monks' cells, have sea views, and some have terraces. All are embellished with nice art and antiques to enhance the historic provenance. Lounging in the sunny gardens that once supplied the monks' kitchens is yet another experience to savor at this unusual retreat.

Via Pantaleone Comite 33. lunahotel.it. ✆ **089/871-002.** 48 units. 450€–550€ double. Rates include breakfast. Closed some winter months. **Amenities:** 2 restaurants; bar; babysitting; concierge; outdoor pool; room service; free Wi-Fi.

Hotel Santa Caterina ♥♥♥ One of the world's fabled getaways not only delivers the stay of a lifetime, but also makes guests feel right at home. Rooms and suites are wonderfully luxurious yet unpretentious, set in gardens and citrus groves hovering above the water. Colorful Vietri tiles and handsome antiques add notes of elegance, while balconies and terraces make the most of a cliffside location with the sea twinkling below. A glass elevator and winding garden paths descend to a private beach and saltwater swimming pool, where memorable meals are served in a vine-covered, glassed-in dining room or on a seaside terrace. Several private bungalows with private pools tucked into citrus groves provide the ultimate hideaways.

Via Nazionale 9. hotelsantacaterina.it. ✆ **089/871012.** 66 units. 510€–1,850€ double. Rates include breakfast. Closed Nov to mid-Apr. **Amenities:** 2 restaurants; 2 bars; beach; concierge; gym; pool; room service; spa; free Wi-Fi.

The seaview dining room at the Hotel Santa Caterina.

MODERATE

La Valle delle Ferriere ♥♥♥ Bad news first, and really the only less-than-glowing thing to say: This little oasis is beyond the reach of cars, at the top of 180 steps. While arriving with luggage can be a challenge, the Piscane family will meet you at the port with an electric buggy, drop you at the foot of the stairs, and help you up with your bags. Once there you'll be surrounded by lemon groves and away from it all at the head of the magical valley behind Amalfi. The bright rooms, handsomely furnished with iron bedframes and decorated with ceramics, share delightful terraces that, along with the thought of climbing all those stairs again, make it hard to leave.

Salita Grande Lughe. valledelleferriereamalfi.it. ✆ **320/880-906.** 4 units. 160€–220€ double. Rates include breakfast. Minimum stay required some periods. Closed Dec–Feb. Parking available. **Amenities:** Free Wi-Fi.

Residenza Luce ♥♥ Half of these attractive, bright, and comfortably furnished rooms have sleeping lofts tucked above living areas with majolica-tile floors and equipped with sleep sofas; many have balconies and all have tall (and soundproofed) windows opening onto Amalfi's medieval lanes and squares. A sunny rooftop breakfast room overlooks surrounding hills, while the beach and port are close at hand.

Via Fra Gerardo Sasso. residenzaluce.it. ✆ **089/871537.** 10 units. 170€–320€ double. Rates include breakfast. Minimum stay required some periods. Closed mid-Nov to mid-Mar. Parking 20€. **Amenities:** Free Wi-Fi.

INEXPENSIVE

Casa Amorino ♥♥♥ The friendly Amorino family's pleasant little bed-and-breakfast is set in a huge lemon garden in Minori, steps from the center of town and the beach and just 4km (2½ miles east of Amalfi. Soothing light-filled, tile-floored rooms, several large enough to accommodate families, come with perks that include a delicious buffet breakfast, the chance to relax over a glass of wine at the small garden bar, and the hospitable presence of the welcoming hosts.

Via Villamena. casaamorino.it. ✆ **089/853-373.** 5 units. 95€–140€ double. Rates include breakfast. Closed Dec–Feb. **Amenities:** Garden; free Wi-Fi.

Hotel Lidomare ♥ One of Amalfi's few bargains is set on a small square just beyond the main street, providing pleasant, old-fashioned ambience in a 13th-century *palazzo*. You might find the enormous, high-ceilinged, tile-floored guest rooms either charmingly authentic or a bit ramshackle, but many have sea views, and all are furnished with antiques and comfy old furnishings. Amalfi's beach is just steps away.

Largo Piccolomini 9. lidomare.it. ✆ **089/871-332.** 15 units. 90€–175€ double. Rates include breakfast. **Amenities:** Free Wi-Fi.

Where to Eat in & Around Amalfi

Pasticceria Pansa ♥♥, on Piazza Duomo (pasticceriapansa.it; ✆ **089/871065**), has been concocting delicious pastries since 1830; try the *torta* *caprese* or sticky, lemon-flavored *delizia al limone.* **Gelateria Porto Salvo ♥♥♥**, Piazza Duomo 22 (✆ **089/871-636;** closed Jan–Mar), is one of the best *gelaterie* on this part of the coast—try the *mandorla candita* (candied almond) flavor. **Gran Caffè di Amalfi ♥**, Corso Repubbliche Marinare (✆ **089/871-047**), overlooks the sea, making it a prime spot for an *aperitivo.*

EXPENSIVE

Da Gemma ♥♥ SEAFOOD/AMALFITAN Amalfi's old-time classic, in warm-hued rooms tucked behind the cathedral, has been in the hands of the Grimaldi family for several generations, and they hold high standards for the seafood they serve to their loyal and discerning clientele. The house *zuppa di pesce* is a meal in itself, prepared only for two. Equally memorable is the special pasta *paccheri all'acqua pazza,* with shrimp and monkfish. The dessert of choice is *crostata* (pie with jam), made with pine nuts and homemade marmalades of lemon, orange, and tangerine. Reservations, especially on weekends, are a must.

Via Frà Gerardo Sasso 11. trattoriadagemma.com. ✆ **089/871-345.** Main courses 25€–60€, tasting menus 70€, 75€, and 100€. Thurs–Tues noon–4pm and 7–10pm. Closed 6 weeks Jan to early Mar.

La Caravella ♥♥♥ MODERN AMALFITAN You'll leave today's world behind when you step into this 12th-century *palazzo* in medieval Amalfi. In romantic dining rooms, candlelight plays off stucco walls adorned with colorful frescoes, a stagelike setting for some of the best food on the coast. This was the first restaurant in Italy to earn a Michelin star, way back in 1967, and ever since, the *dolce vita* set has flocked to these linen-covered tables for Amalfi classics as simple as *scialatielli alla caravella* (handmade pasta in a tomato-seafood sauce) or *pezzogna* (fresh local fish) enlivened with local lemons and mountain herbs. Reservations are a good idea, especially in summer. Refined as the food and setting are, smart informal attire is acceptable; after all, this place is playful enough to embellish its tables with ceramic donkeys.

Via Matteo Camera 12. ristorantelacaravella.it. ✆ **089/871-029.** Main courses 35€–60€; tasting menus 170€ and 220€. Wed–Mon noon–2pm and 7–10pm. Closed Nov and Jan.

Ristorante Al Mare ♥♥ PIZZA/AMALFITAN The bamboo-roofed, alfresco dining terrace just above the beach at the **Hotel Santa Caterina ♥♥♥** (p. 674) is an alluring spot for a seaside lunch. The menu offers a nice choice of pizzas, grilled fish, and pastas, including the hotel specialty, *tagliolini limone,* homemade noodles with a lemon cream sauce. Prices aren't exactly in the beach-shack category, but it's hard to beat the magnificent surroundings for a dash of informal glamour.

Via Nazionale 9. hotelsantacaterina.it. ✆ **089/871-012.** Main courses 35€–45€, pizzas from 30€. May–Oct daily 12:30–3:30pm.

MODERATE

A'Paranza ♥♥ SEAFOOD/AMALFITAN The walk between Amalfi and Atrani (see below) is an excellent way to begin and end a meal, especially when the feast is as memorable as those served in this old-fashioned room off Atrani's main piazza. Seafood reigns right from the start, with antipasti of slices of fresh tuna, stewed octopus, and grilled razor clams. Other local favorites include *sarchiapone,* a long gourd stuffed with meat, or *melanzane con la cioccolata* dessert—eggplant with chocolate, deep-fried and topped with walnuts and dried fruit.

Via Dragone 1–2, Atrani. ristoranteparanza.com. ✆ **089/871-840.** Main courses 15€–35€. Wed–Mon 12:30–2:30pm and 7–10pm.

Il Tarí ♥♥ AMALFITAN/PIZZA The name (after the coin used in the days of the Amalfi Republic) and the setting (an old stable chicly redone with white walls and colorful artwork) harken back to older times in Amalfi, as does the simple menu of traditional favorites. *Scialatielli* (long, fettuccine-like noodles) comes laden with mussels and other seafood (a trio of pastas with various sauces is served as a starter), and the fish soup with pasta and beans is made from an old Amalfi recipe.

Via P. Capuano 9. amalfiristorantetari.it. ✆ **089/871-832.** Main courses 20€–28€. Daily noon–3pm and 6:30–10:30pm.

L'Abside ♥♥ SEAFOOD/AMALFITAN This delightful place deserves to be called a temple of gastronomy—after all, it occupies part of a former church. The arched, whitewashed room adds casual charm to a delicious meal (also served on a terrace out front in good weather). Seafood and vegetables are so fresh that even a simple bruschetta with anchovies is memorable, as are the homemade seafood pastas and risotto with shrimp and lemon.

Piazza dei Dogi. ristorantelabside.it. ✆ **089/873-586.** Main courses 20€–35€. Mon–Sat noon–3pm and 7–10pm.

Around Amalfi: Atrani ♥♥ & Beyond

Pretty little **Atrani ♥♥** is just 1km (half a mile) east along the coast, an easy 15-minute stroll from Amalfi. Leaving town, follow the main road around the headland until you come to a staircase signposted for Atrani; the stairs descend to a road leading to the town's beach and harbor. (To avoid walking on the busy road out of Amalfi, take the pedestrian tunnel from Piazza Municipio behind the Duomo; it leads to the town parking garage and will deposit you near the Atrani staircase.) From Atrani's beach, a maze of vaulted alleys and stepped streets leads through a labyrinth of white houses to **Piazza Umberto I,** where more than a few window boxes put the final flourishes on the charming tableau. M.C. Escher (1898–1972), the Dutch artist who depicted scenes filled with intricate geometric patterns and complex perspective, loved Atrani and often sketched the town; looking at the layer upon layer of connected whitewashed houses, it's easy to see Atrani's influence on his work.

By the 12th century, Atrani had become the preferred residence of Amalfi aristocrats, and Amalfi doges were crowned and buried in the 10th-century **church of San Salvatore de Bireto.** Inside, beyond bronze doors pillaged from Constantinople, a plaque shows off two peacocks, signs of vanity and pride, something this rich little town once had aplenty.

As the coast road continues east towards Salerno, after about 15km (9 miles) you'll come to **Cetara** ♥. The name refers to a tuna fishing net, and it's still one of the few remaining fishing ports on this coast, with boats bringing in large hauls of fresh tuna and anchovies. **Delfino Battista,** Via Rossini 1/3 (delfinobattistasrl.it; ✆ **0828/351028**), specializes in oil-packed tuna and *colatura,* an anchovy sauce the ancient Romans concocted. *Colatura* is made by layering anchovies and salt in wooden barrels and, after aging, applying a press to extract an amber-colored juice that's drizzled on fish, pasta, and vegetables.

In **Vietri sul Mare** ♥, another 7km (4 miles) east, the specialty is ceramics, made here since the 16th century, with massive furnaces firing pieces in bright Mediterranean colors. The most distinctive of Vietri's many outlets is **Ceramica Artistica Solimene,** Via Madonna degli Angeli 7 (ceramicasolimene.it; ✆ **089/210243**), built in the 1950s by Paolo Soleme, who fashioned the extraordinary-looking cooperative workshop out of glass and ceramics, arranged in conelike shapes.

RAVELLO ♥♥♥

7km (4 miles) N of Amalfi

Clinging to a mountainside high above Amalfi, Ravello can seem a world removed from the coastal towns below. This sense of escape, along with views and some of the world's most splendid gardens, has long made it a refuge for the rich and famous, including composer Richard Wagner, writers D.H. Lawrence and Gore Vidal, and actress Greta Garbo. Like they did, you'll come here to do not much else but stroll in the gardens, gaze at the coastline, and maybe relax for a few days in one of many villas converted into luxury hotels. Ravello is simply a beautiful, beautiful place, maybe more so than any other town in Italy.

Essentials

ARRIVING The most convenient way up to Ravello from Amalfi is the **SITA Sud bus** (see box p. 644). If you're going directly to Ravello from Naples, the quickest route is via high-speed train to Salerno (as quick as half an hour) and then the **SITA Sud** bus up the coast. If you're driving from Naples, take the A3 to a well-marked exit near Angri, then climb over the mountains on SP2b and SP1 before dropping into Ravello on the Valico di Chiunzi; total drive time is about 2½ hours. ***Tip:*** If you're driving, park as you approach town in a large public parking lot at Piazza Duomo (2.50€ an hour, 15€ a day); this is not an easy town to drive in.

VISITOR INFORMATION Ravello's **tourist office,** Piazza Fontana Moresca (✆ **089/857096**), is open daily 9am to 7pm (Nov–May until 5pm).

Exploring Ravello

Ravello is largely pedestrian, with steep lanes and many stairs. The heart of town is **Piazza del Vescovado,** a terrace overlooking the valley of the Dragone, and the adjacent **Piazza del Duomo.** From here Via Richard Wagner (behind the tourist office) climbs to reach **Via San Giovanni del Toro,** lined with some of Ravello's grandest medieval palaces, built as hilltop retreats for wealthy Amalfi Republic families and now home to some of Italy's most distinguished hotels. Two pockets of greenery open off the street—the public gardens of the Comune, or Town Hall, and the **Giardini Principessa di Piemonte,** which offers some sweeping views.

Auditorium Oscar Niemeyer ♥♥ LANDMARK Ravello's most controversial landmark was inaugurated in 2010 to critical architectural acclaim but the disdain of many residents and visitors. Naysayers find the sweeping, dazzling-white canopied roof of Brazilian architect Oscar Niemeyer's auditorium sorely out of keeping with Ravello's medieval ambience. It's hard, though, not to admire the way the sinuous curves tuck so naturally into the hillside, and no one can complain about the pleasure of enjoying a concert while viewing the spectacle of sea and sky through the huge eye-shaped window.

Via della Repubblica 12. ✆ **089/857096.** Open for concerts and film screenings (check tourist office for schedules).

Duomo ♥♥♥ CHURCH All the glories of Ravello's past seem to come to the fore in the cathedral that Orso Papiro, first bishop of Ravello, founded in 1086. The 54 embossed panels of the 12th-century bronze doors, cast in Constantinople, were designed to delight the faithful with stories of Christ's miracles and other familiar Bible stories. Another piece of scripture comes to life in the beautiful mosaics of the **Ambone dell'Epistola ♥♥**, a pulpit dating from 1130, depicting Jonah being swallowed by the whale. Opposite, another pulpit rests atop twisting columns that rise out of the backs of two regal-looking lions, with a mighty eagle perched atop the whole affair. Add to that a wonderful collection of Roman sarcophagi and columns, bits of medieval frescoes, and a floor that tilts gently toward the entrance, enhancing the perspective and visually enlarging the space. The **Cappella di San Pantaleone** honors the cathedral's patron, a physician saint who was beheaded in Nicomedia (in present-day Türkiye) on July 27, 305; the blood in his reliquary is said to liquefy and come to a boil every year on the anniversary of his death.

Piazza del Vescovado. ✆ **089/85831.** Duomo: Free admission. Museum: 3€. Duomo daily 9am–noon and 5:30–7pm; museum daily 9am–7pm (Nov–Mar until 6pm). Guided tours available.

Museo del Corallo ♥ MUSEUM/SHOP For centuries, craftspeople around the Bay of Naples carved precious cameos and other objects out of coral and shell. In fact, the earliest object in this stunning private collection is a C.E.-3rd-century Roman amphora with a coral formation inside it. The 600 pieces here are the possessions of cameo craftsman Giorgio Filocamo, whose Camo workshops are attached to the museum; the gallery testifies to his love for the art, with antique pieces, such as a 17th-century coral Christ on the Cross, which are coveted by museums around the world. Filocamo has carved cameos for Hilary Clinton, Pope John Paul II, and Princess Caroline of Monaco; you can pick up one of his creations for yourself in the adjoining shop.

Piazza Duomo 9. museodelcorallo.com. ✆ **089/857461.** Free admission. Mon 4:30–7:30pm, Tues–Sat 10:30am–2pm and 3:30–7:30pm.

Villa Cimbrone Gardens ♥♥♥ GARDEN Englishman Lord Grimthorpe—dilettante, gardener, and erstwhile banker—created this grand villa in 1904, embellishing a crumbling 14th-century farmhouse with towers, turrets, and exotic arabesque details (the villa is now a hotel). The lavish salons and gardens soon became associated with the 20th-century elite, few more elusive than Swedish actress Greta Garbo, who hid out here in 1937—not to be alone, but to be with her lover, the conductor Leopold Stokowski. The high point of the lavish gardens, quite literally, is the **Belvedere Cimbrone,** where you'll have the dizzying sensation of being suspended between sea and sky. Writer Gore Vidal, who for many years lived in a villa clinging to the cliff just below the gardens, called the outlook "the most beautiful view in the world."

The Villa Cimbrone's lavish gardens offer dizzying sea views.

Via Santa Chiara 26. ✆ **089/857459.** Gardens 10€. Daily 9am–sunset. Last admission 30 min. before closing.

Villa Rufolo ♥♥ GARDEN The 14th-century poet Boccaccio was so moved by this onetime residence of merchant prince Landolfo Rufolo that he included it as background in one of his tales. In the mid-19th century, Scotsman Sir Francis Reid transformed the house into an exotic fantasy, with Moorish cloisters. The palace's most famous visitor was Richard Wagner, who composed an act of his opera *Parsifal* here in 1880 and used the surroundings for his Garden of Klingsor, home of the Flower Maidens; the Norman tower was renamed Klingsor's Tower in his honor. Paths wind through beds of rare plantings to lookout points high above the coastline, where the surreal scene of sea meeting sky is as transporting as the house and gardens. The lower garden, known as the Wagner Terrace, is the setting for the Ravello Festival's **Concerti Wagneriani.**

Piazza Duomo. villarufolo.com. ✆ **089/857-621.** Admission 8€, 7€ ages 5–12, free for children 4 and under. Daily Nov–Mar 9am–5pm, Apr–Oct 9am–7:30pm. Last admission 30 min. before closing.

HIKING

Hikers can take heart in the fact that from Ravello it's all downhill—or mostly, since one popular hike goes up to the **Monastery of Saint Nicholas,** 486m (1,594 ft.) high. From the center of Ravello, take the road to Sambuco for 1km (half a mile) and from there the trail up to the monastery. Plan on 2 hours for the 9km (6-mile) round-trip. For a downhill hike, from the town center take another footpath—actually, a series of steps and alleys—that descends to seaside **Minori** (p. 673). Start from the alley to the left of Villa Rufolo, next to the small fountain. It will take you past the 13th-century Annunziata church, then the church of San Pietro, before you reach the hamlet of Torello. From there the path descends through olive trees to Minori. The hike down takes about an hour, the return trip at least double that (you may opt to take a bus back up!).

Where to Stay in Ravello

EXPENSIVE

Palazzo Avino ♥♥♥ A 12th-century patrician palace strikes just the right balance between comfort and opulence, with enough antiques, Vietri ceramic floors, and fine linens to satisfy the most discerning guest. Views extending for miles up and down the coast make the most of Ravello's aerie-like position. They're enjoyed through huge windows in just about every room, on a rooftop terrace with two Jacuzzis, from sumptuous gardens and pool that cascade partway down the cliff, and from the hotel's double-Michelin-starred, dinner-only **Rossellinis** (p. 683). A free shuttle takes guests to the **Clubhouse by the Sea** (May–Sept), the hotel's beach club, with a small outdoor pool, a waterside terrace with lounge chairs and umbrellas, and a casual restaurant.

The opulent Palazzo Avino.

Via San Giovanni del Toro 28. www.palazzoavino.com. ✆ **089/818181.** 43 units. 700€–1,200€ double. Rates include breakfast. Closed late Oct to Mar. **Amenities:** 2 restaurants; bar; concierge; gym; pool; room service; spa; free Wi-Fi.

MODERATE

Giordano Hotel ♥♥ Plenty of old-world charm, albeit slightly faded, prevails at this fine villa set right in the middle of town, with faux antiques and upholstered armchairs resting on tile floors and pretty gardens surrounding a swimming pool. Most of the rooms open to private or shared terraces, though none have sea views. For those, you need only step outside the door and into one of the nearby scenic overlooks.

Via Trinità 14. giordanohotel.it. ✆ **089/857255.** 33 units. 280€–550€ double. Rates include breakfast. Closed Nov–Apr. **Amenities:** Bar; pool; free Wi-Fi.

Hotel Parsifal ♥♥ A monastery-turned-holiday-getaway is hardly a rarity on the Amalfi Coast, but few offer good-value accommodations like these in such charming architectural surroundings. The cloisters, tiled hallways, fishpond, and flower-filled patios still exude contemplative peace, just as the original 13th-century residents intended. Whitewashed rooms fashioned from former monks' cells are plain and frugal enough to suit their former occupants, and the slightly rickety old-fashioned aura is enhanced with colorful tile floors and, from some rooms, sensational views. Meals in the friendly, sea-view dining room may remind you of the days when rooms came with board.

Via Gioacchino D'Anna. hotelparsifal.com. ✆ **089/857144.** 17 units. 115€–195€ double. Rates include breakfast. 2-night min. stay some periods. **Amenities:** Restaurant; bar; concierge; free Wi-Fi.

Hotel Rufolo ♥♥ Your postcards home might be a little more florid while staying at this ages-old villa in the heart of town, converted to a *pensione* for an arty set more than a century ago. D.H. Lawrence hid away in room 423 while writing *Lady Chatterley's Lover*, leading a monklike life despite the scenes erupting on his pages. It's hard to live here like a monk these days: Rooms and suites are filled with fine old furnishings set on gleaming Vietri tile floors, a large pool sparkles in the verdant garden, a hedonistic spa pampers guests, and the views are glorious.

Via San Francesco 1. hotelrufolo.com. ✆ **089/857133.** 34 units. 190€–330€ double. Rates include breakfast. Closed Nov–Mar. **Amenities:** Restaurant; bar; pool; spa; free Wi-Fi.

INEXPENSIVE

Cecco Rooms ♥♥ With Ravello's most lavish pleasure palace hotels as neighbors, these simple, lower-level rooms may seem a bit humble. But they place you in the best part of town at a fraction of the price of the luxury lodgings that line the street, and the prime real estate comes with views over the town and surrounding valleys. Gardens and the town center are just steps away, and the well-kept, low-key accommodations open to pleasant outdoor spaces.

Viale Gioacchino d'Anna 6. ✆ **389/545-8477.** 5 units. 90€–120€ double. Rates include breakfast. **Amenities:** Kitchens; high-speed Internet access.

Where to Eat in & Around Ravello

The garden-bar of the **Hotel Rufolo** ♥♥ (p. 682) is a choice spot to sit back, relax, and soak in Ravello's getaway ambience.

EXPENSIVE

Rossellinis ♥♥♥ CREATIVE AMALFITAN Meals in this elegant dining room and on the view-filled terrace come with a reputation as some of Italy's best, earning a Michelin star. Service is impeccable, and the menu showcases creative takes on local cuisine, with such sublime creations as ravioli stuffed with squid or cod in an olive crust. Meals are paired with local wines and followed with mountain cheeses and sweets that, like everything else here, satisfy without being overwhelming.

Via San Giovanni del Toro 28 (in Palazzo Avino; see p. 681). palazzoavino.com. ✆ **089/818181.** Main courses 40€–60€; tasting menus from 150€. Daily 7:30–11pm. Closed Nov–Mar.

> **The Mountain Cheeses of Ravello**
>
> The mountains behind Ravello are aptly named Monti Lattari, or "rich in milk" in Latin. Goats, sheep, and cows grazing the heights yield milk from which farmers make mozzarella, ricotta, provolone, and other cheeses, all scented with mountain herbs. In shops and restaurants along the coast look for *treccione,* a creamy mozzarella twisted into a braid, or hearty *caciocavallo,* the region's teardrop-shaped mountain cheese. About 15km (9 miles) north of Ravello off SP1, you can taste them at family-run dairy and shop **Antica Latteria di Tramonti,** in Gete on the flanks of Monte Finestre (anticalatteriaditramonti.it; ✆ **089/876920**).

MODERATE

Cumpa' Cosimo ♥♥ AMALFITAN Netta Bottone runs the restaurant her family started back in 1929, serving generous portions of pastas (including an extravaganza with seven types of noodles topped with seven different sauces) and big platters of *frittura di pesce* (fish fry) along with some lamb and veal dishes (Netta also runs the butcher shop next door). Artichokes and other vegetables are right out of nearby garden plots. Whatever you order, Netta herself may well serve it with a flourish and a kiss on the cheek.

Via Roma 44. ✆ **089/857156.** Main courses 12€–22€; pizza 7€–10€. Daily noon–3:30pm and 6–10:30pm. Closed Nov–Feb.

INEXPENSIVE

Pizzeria Vaccaro ♥♥♥ PIZZA Lemon groves and vineyards have long occupied residents of **Tramonti,** about 12km (8 miles) inland from Ravello, and in their spare time they invented a quick bite called pizza (a claim made by many others, for sure). The pizzas here, once baked in communal bread ovens, are undeniably delicious and make the village quite a culinary outpost. Local nuns added to the offerings when they came up with *concierto,* a bitter-sweet digestive liquor concocted from nine different mountain herbs and spices. Try these specialties at what many fans consider to be the best pizzeria on the Amalfi Coast. Delectable crusts are topped with ingredients from nearby farms: Salami and mozzarella are homemade, vegetables are homegrown, olive oil is from local groves, and the bread is fresh from the oven.

Via Vaccaro, Tramonti. ✆ **089/876140.** Main courses 8€–15€; pizza from 7€. Daily noon–3:30pm and 6:30–11:30pm. Closed lunch and weekends Nov–Mar.

Ristorante Vittoria ♥♥ PIZZA It's refreshing to know that life in Ravello can come down to earth, too, as it does in this friendly pizzeria near the Duomo. Thin-crust pies with a huge variety of toppings are the draw; even the classic margherita seems perfect, given that everything is fresh—tomatoes and basil from the garden, mozzarella from nearby farms, herbs from the mountains. Simple pastas, along with meat and fish dishes, are similarly well-done. The tile-floored rooms fill up quickly.

Via dei Rufolo 3. ristorantepizzeriavittoria.it. ✆ **089/857947.** Main courses 10€–22€; pizza from 8€. Daily 12:30–3pm and 7:30–10:30pm.

Ravello Shopping

In addition to the cameo handiwork that might tempt you at the **Camo** workshops at the Museo del Corallo (p. 680), you'll encounter some beautiful ceramics at **Ceramiche d'Arte Carmella,** Via die Rufolo 16 (ceramichedartecarmela.com; ✆ **089/857303**). **Profumi della Costiera,** Via Trinita 37 (profumi dellacostiera.cloud; ✆ **089/858-6492**), carries a remarkable selection of limoncello and other sweet liqueurs.

Colorful ceramics for sale in Ravello.

Nightlife

Ravello's entertainment scene ramps up considerably from July through September, when the town hosts the internationally famous **Festival di Ravello** (ravellofestival.com; ✆ **089/858422**). The focus is on classical music and includes concerts of Wagnerian works in the garden of **Villa Rufolo ♥♥** (p. 680). Tickets run from 15€ to 130€.

THE RUINS OF PAESTUM ♥♥♥

35km (22 miles) S of Salerno; 100km (62 miles) SE of Naples

Three honey-colored temples, some of the best-preserved remains of the ancient world, rise from the wide agricultural plain south of Salerno. The dramatic scene is especially picturesque in spring and early summer, when poppies and wildflowers surround the ruins. Adding to a sense of timelessness are huge Italian water buffalo, who have grazed the low-lying grasslands for the past 1,000 years or so, producing milk that yields the region's deliciously creamy *mozzarella di bufala.*

Essentials

ARRIVING **Trains** stop at two stations near the ruins: **Capaccio-Roccadaspide** and **Paestum,** only 5 minutes from each other. Either station is only about a 10- to 15-minute walk from the archaeological area, with Paestum being more convenient. Via Porta Sirena leads from Paestum station to Via Magna Grecia, which cuts through the middle of the archaeological site. The trip to either is about 30 minutes from Salerno, 90 minutes from Naples; to shorten the time from Naples, take the high-speed train to Salerno and connect to a local train there.

Paestum is well connected to Salerno by bus, via **BusItalia** (fsbusitalia.it; ✆ **089/252228** or 800/016659, toll-free within Italy), with regular service to Paestum from Naples and Salerno.

By **car,** take autostrada A3, exit at Battipaglia onto SS18, and follow the brown signs for Paestum.

Exploring the Ruins

While the forum and other parts of the town have been reduced to rubble, Paestum's three magnificent **temples,** excavated around 1750, are remarkably intact. So are parts of the circuit of massive defensive **walls,** 5m (16½ ft.) thick on average, 15m (50 ft.) high, and 4,750m (15,584 ft.) in length, with 24 square and round towers along their length. At the monumental western gate, **Porta Marina,** you can climb the walls and walk on the patrol paths, enjoying excellent views over the ruins and coast. Wear comfortable shoes and bring a hat and water. Allow at least an hour to see the temples and another hour for the museum (see below).

Archaeological Area of Paestum ♥♥♥ The wall-enclosed site contains the three temples (all built facing east) and a number of other ruins that were part of the sacred area at the center of the ancient Greek town. The **Via Sacra** (Sacred Street) runs arrow-straight through the length of the site, connecting all three temples, the Roman pavement laid over the original Greek road. When it was built, the road continued for about 12km (7½ miles) to connect the Greek town of Poseidonia with the Sanctuary of Hera, on the river Sele about 9km (5 miles) up the coast.

The Tempio di Nettuno, the best-preserved of Paestum's three remarkably intact Greek temples.

13

SORRENTO & THE AMALFI COAST | The Ruins of Paestum

TEMPIO DI HERA ♥♥♥ The oldest of Paestum's temples, the Temple of Hera was built in 550 B.C.E. with a massive portico that's still supported by 50 columns. Worshippers attended rites in front, gathering around a sacrificial altar (now partially ruined) and a square *bothros,* a sacrificial well where the remains were thrown. The temple is believed to have been part of a huge complex dedicated to Hera, wife and sister of Zeus and the goddess of fertility and maternity.

TEMPIO DI NETTUNO ♥♥♥ The world's best example of a Doric temple, the Temple of Neptune, which dates from around 450 B.C.E., is lined in travertine stone that glows a magical gold hue when struck by the sun's rays. Perfect proportions lend a slender elegance, while thick, closely spaced columns give the temple a sturdy, almost forceful presence. This is the best preserved of Paestum's temples: Only the roof and internal walls are missing. In front are two sacrificial altars; the smaller one is a Roman addition from the 3rd century B.C.E.

TEMPIO DI CERERE ♥♥ The smallest of the three temples, at the northern end of the site, was built at the end of the 6th century B.C.E., probably in honor of the goddess Athena. Under the Romans it was dedicated to Ceres, their goddess of agriculture and fertility; Christian tombs in the portico suggest later use as a church.

Main entrance Via Magna Grecia 917; secondary entrance Porta della Giustizia (Justice Gate) off Via Nettuno, for ticket holders only. parchipaestumvelia.cultura.gov.it. ✆ **0828/811023.** Admission Mar–Nov 15€, Dec–Feb 10€, family ticket 11€ (two adults plus children under 25), under 18 2€; includes admission to museum; free for children 11 and under. Daily May to late Sept 10am–7:30pm; check website for earlier closing hours rest of year. Last entry 1 hr. before closing.

Museo Archeologico Nazionale di Paestum (National Archaeological Museum of Paestum) ♥♥ MUSEUM Modern galleries near the entrance to the ruins feature the fresco of a young man taking a swan dive into a rushing stream, from the so-called Tomb of the Diver, probably dating to around 470 B.C.E. The meaning of the simple, powerful image has long been debated, though a good guess is that the diver is gracefully making the transition from earth into the other world. The young man was clearly an athletic sort—flasks filled with the oil he used to prepare himself for wrestling matches were found next to a skeleton assumed to be his. Four other frescoes from the same tomb complex depict scenes of a symposium—more or less a drinking bash—probably to give the deceased a good send-off. These images are unique, the only tomb frescoes from the ancient period that depict human figures.

A frieze from the nearby Sanctuary of Hera includes some mythological scenes that would have delighted a 6th-century-B.C.E. audience, such as the comical story of Hercules and the Kerkopes. As legend has it, the hero had fallen asleep when these two scamps snuck up and stole his weapons. Hercules awoke, captured the miscreants, and tied them upside down to a pole that he carried over his shoulder. The Kerkopes started laughing and Hercules demanded to know why. They told him they were laughing at his hairy backside, so he started laughing, too, and set the boys free (Zeus was less amused by their antics and later turned them into monkeys). Another delightful scene depicts two lithe and gleeful maidens running, their finely sculpted robes flowing around them—the joy of these images suggests just how lighthearted ancient Greek religion could be. Via Magna Grecia 918. parchipaestumvelia.cultura.gov.it. ✆ **0828/811023.** For admission and times, see Archaeological Area.

CAPRI ♥♥♥

5km (3 miles) W off the tip of the Sorrentine peninsula

Rugged, mountainous Capri (pronounced *Cap*-ry, not Ca-*pree*), just off the tip of the Sorrentine Peninsula, is one of the most glamorous and beautiful islands in the world. The legend-steeped, gossip-soaked outcropping of limestone, a mere 10 sq. km (4 sq. miles) in size, has beguiled a long list of admirers. Emperor Tiberius ruled the Roman Empire from these pine- and rosemary-scented cliffs, British music-hall star Gracie Fields belted out tunes for the likes of Maria Callas and Liz Taylor at her seaside hideaway on Marina Piccola, and poets Pablo Neruda and Rainer Maria Rilke took inspiration from the magical landscapes. The island is still a magnet for the rich, the famous, artists, eccentrics, and just plain folks. All delight in the same pleasures: stark-white villas, garden walls draped with bougainvillea and hibiscus, azure seas lapping rugged coasts, a chorus of birdsong, and a heady taste of the good life. Emperor Augustus was onto something when he called the island Apragopolis, or "City of Sweet Idleness."

Capri's popularity can sometimes make it difficult to soak in the island's beauty. An overnight stay lets you enjoy the quiet that descends when summer day-trippers have sailed away. To see the island at its best, you might want to visit in spring or early fall. Note that Capri shuts down almost entirely from November to May.

Essentials

ARRIVING You can easily reach Capri from either Naples or Sorrento, and in summer there's also regular ferry service from Amalfi and Positano. Don't let the profusion of companies confuse you: At tourist offices, docks, and most hotels along the Amalfi Coast, you'll find simplified listings of ferry schedules. From Naples' Molo Beverello dock (take a bus, the Naples metro, or a taxi from the train station), the **hydrofoil** (*aliscafo*) takes just 45 minutes and departs several times daily (some stop at Sorrento). Regular **ferry** (*traghetto*) service departing from Porta di Massa is cheaper but takes longer (about 1½ hr. each way). **Alillauro** (alilauro.it; ✆ **081/837-0819**) connects Capri with Salerno, Positano, Amalfi, and Ischia; **NLG-Navigazione Libera del Golfo** (nlg.it; ✆ **081/552-0763**) runs to Capri from Naples, Sorrento, and Castellammare di Stabia.

Caremar (caremar.it; ✆ **081/189-66690**) operates ferries to Capri from Naples and Sorrento; **SNAV** (www.snav.it; ✆ **081/428-555**) runs hydrofoils and catamarans to Capri from Mergellina and Naples (Molo Beverello) as well as to Ischia. In summer, Amalfi-based **Cooperativa Sant'Andrea** (santandrea.srl; ✆ **089/873190**) offers scheduled service from Amalfi, Capri, Minori, Salerno, and Sorrento; Positano-based **Lucibello** (lucibello.it; ✆ **089/875032**) also makes runs to and from Capri.

From the harbor, you can take a **taxi, bus,** or the **funicular** up to Capri Town and bus or taxi to Anacapri (see "Getting Around," below). Porters will approach you at the dock, and if you're taking a bus or funicular, *don't be in a hurry to shoo them away.* These fellows are trustworthy, and the charge is well worth the 10€ to 20€ per piece of luggage (depending on size). Your bags will soon appear in your hotel lobby, saving you the trouble of lugging them onto conveyances or dragging them along the island's pedestrian-only lanes. Many hotels will send a car to meet your boat, so ask when booking.

GETTING AROUND The island is served by funiculars, taxis, and buses; for schedules and other details, go to **capri.net** or **capritourism.com**. From the ferry dock in Marina Grande, take the funicular or a bus to **Capri Town** (2.40€ for the funicular and bus; buy tickets at the office near the funicular terminal or from newsstands or tobacco shops; note that drivers sometimes impose a 2.40€ luggage supplement). Buses also run between Capri and **Anacapri** about every 15 minutes throughout the day.

The **funicular** (✆ **081/837-0420**) is the picturesque means of transportation between Marina Grande—where the ferries and hydrofoils land—and the town of Capri. They depart every 15 minutes; the ride takes 5 minutes, arriving in the heart of town, off Piazza Umberto I.

The public **bus** system is excellent, but in high season, a ride in one of these diminutive vehicles can feel like being in the proverbial sardine can. Buses run between Marina Grande, Capri, Marina Piccola, Anacapri, the Faro (Lighthouse) at the far southwestern tip of the island, and the Grotta Azzurra on the northwestern coast.

Taxis, readily available at the port and at taxi stands outside the towns, are expensive but a welcome alternative when you encounter long lines to board buses and the funicular. Taxi fares are about 20€ for the short ride from the port up to Capri; 15€ between Capri and Anacapri; and 30€ between Marina Grande and Anacapri. There are supplements for more than one piece of baggage (2€–5€ per piece) and nighttime services. Many hotels provide pickup at the port, as well as shuttle service between Capri and Anacapri and other places on the island.

You'll do a lot of walking on Capri, where all but a few main roads are closed to cars, so wear comfortable shoes. You can hire an eco-friendly electric scooter at **Charlie Rent Scooter,** Via Roma 70 (www.capri rentscooter.com; ✆ **081/837-5863;** 50€ a day with return by 6pm or 65€

Capri
Gulf of Naples
(Golfo di Napoli)
To Ischia
To Naples, Sorrento
TYRRHENIAN SEA
Punta del Capo
Pta. dell' Arcera
Grotta Azzurra (Blue Grotto)
Damecuta
Torre Damecuta
GRADOLA
LINARO
ARTIMO
Bagni di Tiberio
MARINA GRANDE
Villa Jovis
LO CAPO
Grotta d. Tiberio
Via Tiberio
Grotta Meravigliosa
Grotta Bianca
Via Lo Capo
MONETA
S. Michele
Arco Naturale
LA CROCE
Grotta di Matermania
Grotta d. Massullo
Pta. Massullo
Via Matermania
Via Tragara
Piazzetta
CAPRI
Via Roma
Funicular
Via Marina Grande
S. Costanzo
Scala Fenicia
Castello Barbarossa
Via Lo Pozzo
Via G. Orlandi
Chair Lift
ANACAPRI
Via Tuoro
Via Pagliaro
ORRICO
Via Grotta Azzurra
Cala del Rio
MESOLA
Rio d. Cesa
CAPRILE
ANGINOLA
IL PASSETIELLO
Monte S. Maria 495 m
S. Maria Cetrella
Monte Solaro 589 m
Via Marina Piccola
Via Krupp
MARINA PICCOLA
Belvedere di Tragara
Grotta Porto di Tragara
Scoglio del Monacone
Faraglione di Terra
Faraglione di Mezzo (Stella)
Faraglione di Fuori
Pta. di Tragara
Via Nuova del Faro
MATERITA
Via Migliera
Antichi Pozzi
Torre di Materita
Cala di Mezzo
MIGLIERA
Belvedere Migliera
Pta. di Mulo
Pta. di Terita
Cala Ventroso
Pta. Ventroso
Grotta Verde
Cala Marmolata
LIMMO
Pta. Carena
Faro (Lighthouse)
0 1/2 mi
0 500 m
Grotto, Cave
Beach
Footpath
Ruins
NAPLES
Ischia
Salerno
Sorrento
Capri
ATTRACTIONS
Blue Grotto 2
Casa Malaparte 17
Certosa di San Giacomo 22
Chiesa di San Michele 6
Faraglioni 18
Monte Solaro 25
Villa Jovis 15
Villa Lysis 14
Villa San Michele 10
HOTELS
Casa Mariantonia 8
Hotel La Tosca 23
Hotel Punta Tragara 20
Jumeirah Capri Palace 9
San Nicola Guesthouse 7
Villa Brunella 21
Villa Ceselle 3
Villa Marina Capri 11
RESTAURANTS
Gelsomina 26
Il Riccio 1
La Canzone del Mare 24
La Fontelina 19
L'Angolo del Gusto 4
Le Grotelle 16
Pulalli Wine Bar 12
Ristorante Pizzeria Aurora 13
Ristorante-Pizzeria Materita 5

for 24 hr.), one of many scooter outlets clustered around the port in Marina Grande.

VISITOR INFORMATION The **tourist office** is in Capri Town on Piazzetta Italo Cerio (capritourism.com; ✆ **081/837-5308**), with a branch in Marina Grande. They are generally open Monday to Saturday 8:30am to 8:30pm and Sunday 8:30am to 2:30pm (Nov–Mar Mon–Sat 9am–1pm and 3:30–6:30pm). The website is a gold mine of information on the island, including bus, funicular, and boat schedules.

Exploring Capri

You'll soon discover that life on the island, quite literally, has its ups and downs. From **Marina Grande,** the main harbor, you'll go up, via road or funicular, to Capri Town. The white houses of the island's main settlement rise and dip across hilly terrain on a saddle between the twin peaks of Monte Tiberio and Monte Solaro. The easiest, and often only, way to get around is on foot, and it would be hard to find a more inviting place on the planet to walk. **Anacapri,** the island's other town, is even higher, tucked onto the slopes of Monte Solaro. Getting down to the sea from these towns, and elsewhere on the island, often means descending the formidable, grotto-laced cliffs that ring the shoreline. More often than not you do so via paths and steps, hundreds of them, that often lead to viewpoints where you can catch your breath and take in views.

CAPRI TOWN ♥♥

Most visitors approach Capri's mountainside main town on the funicular railway that climbs steep slopes just behind the harbor. A traffic-choked road also makes the ascent, as does a footpath for the hearty. However you make the climb, as soon as you step into the enticing warren of narrow lanes lined with walled villa gardens, you'll realize you're in a rather exotic place. Town life radiates from the **Piazzetta,** a small square that draws such a stream of visitors it's called the "world's living room." While the Gucci-dressed beauties and suave Lotharios suggest a certain see-and-be-seen glamour, you can escape the scene by popping into medieval **Palazzo Cerio** to visit the archaeology and natural history exhibits of the **Museo Caprense Ignazio Cerio** (centrocaprense.org; ✆ **081/837-6681;** admission 4€, free for ages 17 and under; Tues–Sat 11am–4pm). Overlooking the square, the pleasantly plain **Torre dell'Orologio** rises above the old city gateway; next to it is the homey **church of Santo Stefano.**

From the Piazzetta, the old town's narrow streets lead west past glittering shops along vista-filled, pine-scented walkways to the more sedate **Certosa di San Giacomo** (see below). Just beyond are the **Giardini di Augusto ♥♥**, terraced public gardens with panoramic views toward Monte Solaro, the Faraglioni, and Marina Piccola (admission 2.50€; daily 9am–8pm, Nov–Mar until 5pm; capriculturaeturismo.it). German steel manufacturer and longtime visitor Friedrich Alfred Krupp (1854–1902) laid out the gardens to show off the island's rich flora. An unexpected presence amid the flowerbeds is a statue of Vladimir Lenin (1870–1924), the first leader of the Soviet Union. In 1908 the great revolutionary was a guest of Russian writer Maxim Gorky, who lived here from 1906 to 1913. Gorky, a novelist and political activist, began his *Encyclopedia of Russian History* on Capri and lived in the villa opposite the gardens, now the Villa Krupp hotel.

Certosa di San Giacomo ♥ RELIGIOUS SITE The island's most imposing architectural landmark is this former monastery built in the 14th century by Count Giacomo Arcucci as a place to retire from the world. Arcucci's former employer, Queen Joanna I of Naples, provided the prime parcel of land and the funds, and the count became a Carthusian monk, ending his days in solitary contemplation. The monks were not popular with the islanders, who showed up at their gates seeking refuge from the plague of 1653 and were locked out. The suffering populace retaliated by throwing plague victims' corpses over the monastery walls. Ironically, the complex, perched poetically above the sea, is quite community-oriented these days, housing the island's public library and a high school. Its cloisters make an evocative setting for concerts, and the garden that looks out into azure infinity is a favorite spot for romantic tête-à-têtes. Also on the premises, the quirky **Museo Diefenbach** shows the work of painter Karl Wilhelm Diefenbach, a local character who lived on Capri from 1900 to 1913. An advocate of peace, free love, and nudism, he was often seen walking the paths barefoot in a white robe, his long gray hair flowing behind him.

Via Certosa. museiitaliani.it. ✆ **081/837-6218.** Admission 10€, 6€ ages 18–25, free for children 17 and under. No cash. Tues–Sun July–Sept 10am–6pm; Oct–Dec and Apr–May 10am–4pm; Jan–Mar 10am–2pm.

Dining alfresco on Piazza Umberto, aka the Piazzetta, in Capri Town.

Villa Jovis ♥♥ ARCHAEOLOGICAL SITE From Capri Town, a comfortable 45-minute stroll of about 2.5km (1½ miles) ends with a steep climb to the northeastern tip of the island and the most sumptuous and best-preserved of the 12 villas the Roman emperor Tiberius (ruled C.E. 14–37) built on Capri. The emperor spent the final 10 years of his reign on the island, partly because he was fond of the scenery and the views, but also because the sheer waterside cliffs and few closely guarded harbors made the island inaccessible to assassins. (The increasingly paranoid emperor even had his bread imported from Positano, afraid the islanders would poison him.) Eight levels of walls and many staircases remain to suggest the size of the villa, probably covering about 1.5 acres, with vast terraces and floors of reception halls and living quarters clinging to the craggy summit of Monte Tiberio. The covered Loggia Imperiale follows the cliff edge to the Salto di Tiberio, a 330m-high (1,083-ft.) precipice from which it was said Tiberius would hurl lovers who'd fallen out of favor with him. Whether or not you believe this—many historians consider it nothing more than grisly gossip—you can enjoy the views across the island and over the straits to the Sorrento Peninsula.

Via Tiberio. capri.it. ✆ **081/837-0381.** Admission 6€. No cash. Daily June–Sept 10am–7pm; Apr–May and Oct Wed–Mon 10am–6pm; Nov–Dec and Feb–Mar Wed–Mon 10am–4pm; closed Jan. Hours subject to change, so check with tourist office before making the trek up the hill.

Villa Lysis ♥♥ ARCHITECTURAL SITE Of the many eccentric foreigners who have sought refuge on Capri, Baron Jacques d'Adelswärd-Fersen (1880–1923) might be the most decadent character of all. When a scandal involving French schoolboys (and a subsequent prison stint) forced the dissolute baron to leave France in 1905, he came to Capri with his lover, Nino Cesarini, a young Roman model famous as the subject of erotic photographs. The house Fersen built on the heights just below Villa Jovis (see above) is a neoclassical fantasy of marble, columns, tile work, and gilt mosaics, with a motto etched in stone above the entrance proclaiming the premises to be a "shrine to love and sorrow." (The name Lysis, from the Socratic dialogues, is a reference to homosexual love.) The furnishings have long since been removed, but the blue-and-white majolica-tile lounge, the huge bedroom with three windows facing the Bay of Naples and three facing Monte Tiberio, and the many terraces and view-filled garden all suggest that Fersen drowned his sorrows in the good life. And more than that: In the Chinese room in the basement, specially built for smoking opium, he succumbed to an overdose of cocaine while sipping champagne.

Via Lo Capo. capriculturaeturismo.it. ✆ **081/838-6111.** Admission 2.50€. Thurs–Tues June–Aug 10am–7pm; Apr–May and Sept–Oct 10am–6pm; closed Nov–Mar.

MARINA PICCOLA ♥♥

The island's largest beach, on the southern shore, is nothing much, just a pebbly strip tucked picturesquely amid the rocky shorelines, but the water is clean and crystal clear. The pretty cove has been a focus of island life since the Romans harbored their boats here. In recent centuries fishermen have shared the space with beachgoers, who arrive in droves on summer weekends to frequent the many little bathing establishments perched on the rocks. It's said that the outcropping that divides Marina Piccola neatly into halves is the very rock from which the Sirens tried to lure Ulysses and his crew onto the shoals and wreck their ships, a tale that adds even more romance to an already picturesque setting.

While buses make frequent runs between Capri Town and Marina Piccola, the classic approach is on Via Krupp, a steep path that descends the cliffs in a series of giddy switchbacks from the Giardini di Augusto at the edge of Capri Town. Friedrich Alfred Krupp had the walkway built at the turn of the 20th century so he could easily travel between his two yachts at Marina Piccola and his suite at the Quisisana Hotel in Capri Town. Word leaked that Krupp also used the path to access the notorious Grotta di Fra Felice, a cave at the base of the cliff where gentlemen enjoyed the sexual favors of young island boys, and he was eventually forced to leave Italy and committed suicide soon after. The path is sometimes closed due to the risk of falling rock.

FARAGLIONI ♥♥♥

Among Italy's most famous natural sights are these three rock stacks rising as high as 100m (330 ft.) from the sea off of Capri's southeast coast. The outermost rock is home to a type of bright blue lizard, the *Podarcis sicula coerulea,* found nowhere else on the planet. It's believed that the blue color serves as camouflage that allows the little reptiles to blend in with the surrounding sky and water. Records suggest that ancient Roman aristocrats imported the colorful creatures from Greece to brighten up their island gardens. The middle stack, Faraglioni di Mezzo, is punctured with a poetic little archway where waves have worn away part of the base. It's a popular game for anyone at the helm of a boat to navigate the opening. A shale ledge connects the rock closest to shore, Stella, to the island, and the base shelters two famous beaches with bathing establishments, **La Fontelina** (p. 703) and **Da Luigi.** Boats ferry customers back and forth to Marina Piccola, but a far more sporting way to reach the base of the rocks is on the hundreds of steps that descend from Punta Tragara.

PUNTA TRAGARA ♥♥♥

Just 10 minutes beyond the Piazzetta, on pine-shaded paths, is a world far removed from the clamor and bling. The island's most dazzling walks are along this stretch of coastline on Via Tragara and its eastward continuation, Via Pizzolungo, skirting lush vegetation on the top of the cliffs and affording glimpses of spectacular seascapes through the trees. The enchanting paths intersect at the Punta Tragara lookout, a perch high above the sea and the Faraglioni. Among those who admired the views was Chilean poet-in-exile Pablo Neruda, who in 1953 stayed in a villa on Via Tragara as a guest of Edwin Cerio (see **Museo Caprense Ignazio Cerio,** p. 690). Steps leading down to the Faraglioni from the viewpoint are informally known as the Neruda path, and a plaque at the top honors the poet.

Isolated beyond Via Tragara atop Punta Massullo is **Casa Malaparte,** a boxlike villa that seems to grow out of the rock, with steps in the shape of an inverted pyramid leading to a rooftop terrace. It's the creation of the writer and filmmaker Curzio Malaparte, who curried favor with Fascists, communists, and even Italy's Allied liberators during the 1930s and World War II years. The house is still vilified by islanders for its harsh intrusion on protected lands, yet it is the star of Jean-Luc Goddard's 1963 film *Contempt*, in which cold, vast spaces and a vertigo-inducing perch high above the sea reflect the estrangement and sense of looming disaster between a couple, played by Brigitte Bardot and Michel Piccoli. The film might afford your only look at the interior; the house is now owned by the Ronchi Foundation and is open only occasionally for cultural events.

BLUE GROTTO (GROTTA AZZURRA) ♥♥♥

Italy's tourist-trap extraordinaire can be beguiling, despite all the hassle a visit entails—the frenzy of climbing off a motorboat into a small rowboat, waiting for your turn to be rowed in, lying back, squeezing through a narrow opening, and being rowed out again just as you are beginning to enjoy the experience. The magical colors of the water and walls of this huge grotto are extraordinary, even more so than they appear in countless photographs. Little wonder that postcard writers have rhapsodized about the cave since it became part of the tourist circuit in the 19th century. (Actually, a small, ancient Roman dock and some statues retrieved from the sea floor suggest that this outlet of a vast set of shoreline caverns was known long before then.) It's open daily 9am to 5pm (capri.com/en/e/la-grotta-azzurra). In summer, boats leave frequently from the harbor at Marina Grande, transporting passengers to the grotto's entrance for 21€ round-trip (that includes the fee for the rowboat that takes you inside). If you get to the entrance to the Blue Grotto under your own steam (via bus from Anacapri), you'll still pay 18€ to be rowed in. The boat trip out from Marina Grande is well worth a few extra euros, delivering sea-level views of the island's spectacular cliffs and rugged shoreline.

A motor launch takes visitors to the Blue Grotto, a touristy experience that is nevertheless beguiling.

ANACAPRI ♥♥♥

Capri's second town, perched on heights surrounded by vineyards, is a pleasant place where, once away from the main square, life transpires like you might have hoped it would on a small island in the Mediterranean.

Your first impression might be otherwise, as you arrive at the main squares, Piazza Della Pace and Piazza Vittoria, where folks gather to board buses down to the Blue Grotto, get onto the chairlift to be whisked up Monte Solaro, and make the short walk out to **Villa San Michele** (p. 696). Having ridden up here in the noisy little orange bus that zips along the island's narrow main road from Capri Town, grinding around switchbacks in first gear, you may be jostled by elderly housewives with sharp elbows and huge bags full of mysterious foodstuffs. (Before the bus, the only way to get between Capri's two towns was on the **Scala Fenicia,** or Phoenician Staircase, a steep 881-step path with many superb views.)

Wander off the square onto Via Orlandini, however, and you'll soon be passing tailor shops and shoemakers. Villagers sit on benches in front of the **church of Santa Sofia,** and from there you can meander along narrow lanes lined with vineyards, lemon groves, and flower-filled gardens. An easy 20-minute walk along Via Migliara takes you to **Philosophers Park ♥♥**, a parcel of hillside carpeted in scrub and broom, where 60 ceramic plaques bearing inscriptions from the great philosophers line the winding paths (philosophicalpark.org; free admission; open dawn–dusk). Just beyond the garden, the **Belvedere Migliara** overlooks the southern coast. Or follow Str. Faro di Carena out to Punta Carena, about 2km (1 mile) beyond Anacapri at the southwestern tip of the island, with its landmark **Faro** (lighthouse). A coastal path, the **Sentiero die Fortini,** or Path of the Forts, makes for some good hiking out here (see "Hiking," p. 697), and the little cove beneath the Faro is one of the nicest places on the island for a swim. From there, a bus takes you back to Anacapri.

Chiesa di San Michele ♥♥ CHURCH The 18th-century builders of this octagonal church made a wise decision when they decided to install a delightful **majolica floor,** now one of the island's most colorful manmade sights. Francesco Solimena (1657–1747), the undisputed master of Neapolitan baroque painting, did the design, full of his typical flamboyance, and Naples' finest ceramics master, Leonardo Chiaiese, executed the hand-painted tile work. Their minutely detailed assemblage re-creates the drama-filled moment when Adam and Eve are expelled from the Garden of Eden, as a unicorn, a goat, and other unlikely creatures look on. The final effect of the piece is so pleasing that no one's ever felt comfortable treading on the floor, creating some logistical problems. Pews were never installed, and worshippers and visitors are relegated to a wooden walkway around the perimeter. Those in the know head up the spiral staircase for a bird's-eye view of the multicolor scene.

Piazza San Nicola. chiesa-san-michele.com. ✆ **081/837-2396.** Admission 2€. Daily Apr–Sept 9am–7pm; Oct–Mar 10am–3pm.

Monte Solaro ♥♥♥ NATURAL WONDER Capri's highest peak soars to 590m (1,932 ft.), a magnet for view seekers who "ooh" and "ahh" at the island and the Bay of Naples unfolding at their feet. You can hike up along some fairly easy paths in about an hour (the easiest is a well-marked route that begins next to Villa San Michele). The chairlift **Seggiovia Monte Solaro** (capriseggiovia.it; ✆ **081/837-1428**) departs from Anacapri's Piazza Vittoria and whisks you to the top in just 12 minutes. Tickets cost 11€ one-way, 14€ round-trip, free for ages 8 and under; the lift runs daily May through October 9:30am to 5pm (Nov–Feb it stops at 3:30pm, Mar–Apr at 4pm). Emperor Augustus greets you at the top, right arm outstretched as if he's claiming everything below in the name of the Roman Empire, while also ushering you into the bustling, poetically named **Canzone del Cielo** (Song of the Sky) cafe.

Villa San Michele ♥♥♥ HISTORIC HOUSE Swedish doctor and writer Axel Munthe built this remarkable, gracious house in the 19th century on the ruins of one of Tiberius's villas. He had the funds and inspiration to fulfill his wish that "My home shall be open for the sun and the wind and the voices of the sea—like a Greek temple—and light, light, light everywhere!" Perched on a ledge at the top of the Scala Fenicia entrance to Anacapri (p. 695), the spacious, airy villa is filled with Munthe's art and antiques. An arbor-lined path leads to panoramic views across the bay. A sphinx looks out to sea—touching its well-worn hindquarters is said to bring good luck.

Munthe preferred San Michele to his residences in England and Sweden, though a devastating eye condition forced him to forgo Capri for a time in the 1920s. (In his absence he rented San Michele to the eccentric heiress Luisa Casati, who shocked the locals by walking around the island with leashed cheetahs and wearing live snakes as jewelry. Her lavish lifestyle left her $25 million in debt; she ended her days in relative poverty in London.) After successful eye surgery, Munthe returned to Capri, living many happy years here before returning to Stockholm during World War II as a guest of the royal family. Part of his legacy on Capri is the preservation of **Castello Barbarosa,** on the heights above the villa. Munthe purchased the mountainside to protect the island's many birds, once coveted and hunted for their valuable feathers; the castle is now headquarters of an ornithological research station.

Viale Axel Munthe 34. villasanmichele.eu. ✆ **081/837-1401.** Admission 12€, 8€ 18 and under and students. Daily May–Sept 9am–6pm; Apr and Oct 9am–5pm; Mar 9am–4:30pm; Nov–Feb 9am–3:30pm (closed Tues Dec–Feb).

Beaches

Inviting as Capri's waters are, getting into them can be bit of a challenge. The most convenient place for a dip is **Marina Piccola,** where the pebbly beaches are accessible by bus from Capri Town. Also near Capri Town, on the north side of the island is a nice, sandy stretch at **Bagni di Tiberio** (bagnitiberio.com), where the 20€ admission includes free transport to and from Marina Grande and use of the facilities; a deck chair costs 10€ and a lounger 15€. You can also enjoy the beach without making use of the club, but getting down (and especially back up) from the cliff path requires a bit of a scramble. Other beaches are **next to the Blue Grotto** (Via Grotta Azzurra), accessible by bus from Anacapri; below the Faro (lighthouse) at **Punta Carena,** at the southwest tip of the island, also reached by bus from Anacapri; and at the base of the **Faraglioni,** reached by hundreds of steps from Via Tragara or by boat from Marina Piccola. You can bring a towel and lounge on the beach and rocks at any of these places. Most are lined with **beach clubs** (*stabilimenti balneari*), usually open mid-March to mid-November 9am to sunset, which charge about 20€ a day for use of a changing room, chair or lounge, and towels; you'll find snack bars at most, excellent restaurants at some (see "Where to Eat on Capri," p. 700), and pools at a few.

Hiking

Capri is heaven for walkers. The island is laced with paths that beckon anyone with a good pair of walking shoes, a sun hat, and a bottle of water. Paths are indicated on most island maps, including those from the tourist office; you can also download them from the office's website, **capri tourism.com**. Some especially enticing routes just outside Capri Town take you across handsome, view-filled landscapes around Punta Tragara and to some of the island's most famous sights, including the Faraglioni and Villa Jovis. A less-traveled but no less exhilarating route is on the western side of the island, the **Sentiero die Forini** (Path of the Forts). This 5km (3-mile) walk between the Blue Grotto and Faro (lighthouse) at Punta Carena passes four small coastal fortresses erected over the centuries to keep pirates and foreign powers at bay. However busy the island might be, here you'll find yourself amid Mediterranean countryside and an almost inexhaustible supply of sparkling sea views.

You may opt to take the chairlift to the summit of Monte Solaro (p. 696) and hike down back to Anacapri through wooded countryside into the **valley of Cetrella.** You'll be following paths once used by the Carthusian monks of the Certosa di San Giacomo (p. 691), who came out here to check on their herds. The route passes the aptly named **Villa Solitaria,** the former home of British novelist Compton Mackenzie (1883–1972), who lived with his wife, Faith, on Capri from 1913 to 1920 and intermittently thereafter. The island's famous tolerance of homosexual foreigners, along with Faith's affair with the classical pianist Renata Borgatti, inspired Mackenzie's lesbian-themed 1928 novel *Extraordinary Women*. A less secular landmark is just down the path, where the little **hermitage of Cetrella** and its **church of Santa Maria** nestle in a verdant copse. The church is not often open, so check with the tourist office before setting out if you'd like to take a look inside at its unusual double nave.

Where to Stay on Capri

EXPENSIVE

Hotel Punta Tragara ♥♥ French architect le Corbusier designed this multilevel villa in the 1920s, and Winston Churchill and Dwight Eisenhower are among those who've enjoyed falling asleep to the sound of waves lapping on the shore far below. Stylish quarters are luxurious without being pretentious and open onto terraces, most offering views of the Faraglioni. You can descend to the sea via hundreds of steps outside the gate or take a dip in the two pools tucked into gardens.

Via Tragara 57, Capri Town. hoteltragara.com. ✆ **081/837-0844.** 45 units. 600€–1,480€ double. Rates include breakfast. Closed mid-Oct to mid-Apr. **Amenities:** Restaurant; bar; concierge; gym; 2 pools; room service; spa; free Wi-Fi.

13

Jumeirah Capri Palace ♥♥♥ At this delightful getaway in Anacapri on the slopes of Monte Solaro, an expanse of green lawn surrounds the swimming pool, chic lounges are quiet and welcoming, and guest rooms are done in restful creams with rose-colored tile floors and white linens. Some suites have private pools, and some rooms look across the sea all the way to Vesuvius, but even the outlooks from rear rooms over the green flanks of Monte Solaro are relaxing. A shuttle bus runs to the port, Capri Town, and a beach club with platforms that make it easy to dip into the Mediterranean.

Via Capodimonte 2, Anacapri. jumeirah.com. ✆ **081/978-0111.** 79 units. 650€–1,500€ double. Rates include breakfast. Closed mid-Oct to mid-Apr. No children 9 and under June–Aug. **Amenities:** 2 restaurants; bar; beach club (p. 702); pool; room service; spa; free Wi-Fi.

Villa Marina Capri ♥♥ On a view-filled hillside above Marina Grande, this late-19th-century villa has been converted into a romantic island getaway, set amid lush gardens and sunny terraces. Quietly glamorous rooms are named for artists and bohemians who have landed on Capri over the years, with decor firmly geared to soothing, contemporary comfort. Most rooms open to the outdoors and sea views. Among the pampering amenities are a spa, restaurant, and notably attentive service, as well as free shuttle to the port and Capri Town.

Via Prov, Marina Grande 191, Capri. villamarinacapri.com. ✆ **081/837-6630.** 21 units. 580€–1,090€ double. Rates include breakfast. Closed late Oct to Apr. **Amenities:** Restaurant; bar; pool; spa; free shuttle; free Wi-Fi.

MODERATE

Casa Mariantonia ♥♥ A gracious old villa near the Church of San Michele commands some of the best real estate in Anacapri—a shady lemon grove, lawns, gardens, and a big swimming pool all right in the center of town. Four generations have welcomed guests to the family home with its traditional island architecture, creating a relaxed but luxurious ambience. The family claims that great-grandmother Mariantonia invented *limoncello,* which may be a bit of a stretch, but sipping the

The lush gardens and pool area of the Villa Marina Capri.

house-made elixir on a terrace next to the trees from whence it comes is a great Capri experience.

Via Guiseppe Orlandi 180, Anacapri. casamariantonia.com. ✆ **081/837-2923.** 10 units. 240€–460€ double. Rates include breakfast. Closed mid-Oct to Mar. **Amenities:** Bar; pool; free Wi-Fi.

Villa Brunella ♥♥♥ Flower-filled terraces spilling down the hillside from Via Tragara pull you right into the magic of Capri, with eye-popping sea views from airy, tile-floored guest rooms and terraces. Ambience hovers between cozy old-fashioned Italian hospitality and romantic getaway, with some nice antiques and overstuffed armchairs in the bright rooms and bougainvillea-filled nooks on pine-shaded grounds. A pool sparkles on a patio, and guests have access to a beach club at Marina Piccola. **Terrazza Brunella** provides excellent food in an elegant setting when even the short walk to town seems an effort.

Via Tragara 24, Capri Town. villabrunella.it. ✆ **081/837-0122.** 20 units. 300€–550€ double. Rates include breakfast. Closed Nov to mid-Apr. **Amenities:** Restaurant; bar; pool; room service; free Wi-Fi.

INEXPENSIVE

Hotel La Tosca ♥♥ This stylish and pretty little retreat is tucked away among pines on the quiet side of Capri Town, near the Gardens of Augustus. Many of the bright, whitewashed rooms have sea views, some have terraces, and all look out over lush gardens. Arches, vaulted ceilings, and tile floors help create the ambience of a simple-yet-tasteful island house. Breakfast is served on a breezy sea-view terrace.

Via Dalmazio Birago 5, Capri Town. latoscahotel.com. ✆ **081/837-0989.** 11 units. 175€–330€ double. Rates include breakfast. Minimum stay required some periods. Closed Nov to mid-Apr. **Amenities:** Free Wi-Fi.

San Nicola Guesthouse ♥♥♥ Large, airy, tile-floored rooms tucked away on a little lane in Anacapri provide a quiet getaway and plenty of warm hospitality. Stylish contemporary furnishings are bright and comfortable, and bathrooms are commodious and up to date. Don't expect a view—high windows let the light stream in but have no outlooks—but a two-tiered shared terrace, well set up for outdoor lounging, looks over surrounding rooftops.

Via Prima Traversa Timpone 3A, Anacapri. sncapri.com. ✆ **338/831-8635.** 4 units. 100€–300€ double. Rates include breakfast. Closed mid-Oct to Mar. **Amenities:** Terrace; free Wi-Fi.

Villa Ceselle ♥♥ Pleasant and sunny rooms open to a large private garden, providing a getaway in the middle of Anacapri. The greenery, shady nooks for relaxing, and sea views are the most welcome amenities here, and guests have use of the pool at **Gelsomina,** a restaurant with rooms a short walk away (see below). A well-equipped apartment in a nearby annex accommodates six.

Via Monticello 1, Anacapri. villaceselle.com. ✆ **081/838-2236.** 14 units. 180€–200€ double. Rates include breakfast. Closed mid-Oct to Apr. **Amenities:** Garden; hot tub; use of nearby pool; free Wi-Fi.

Where to Eat on Capri

EXPENSIVE

Gelsomina ♥♥ CAPRESE The sparkling swimming pool is a tempting draw on a warm summer day at this countryside retreat outside Anacapri. Come for the day, to swim, have lunch, and maybe walk to the Belvedere della Migliera just down the road. This is also a popular evening spot, with dining on a sea-view terrace. The straightforward food is a perfect complement to the low-key setting, with many ingredients plucked straight from the surrounding gardens. Homemade *ravioli di caprese* is filled with delicious ricotta from a local producer. Anacapri is about 15 minutes away on foot, on lanes that slice through vineyards and gardens; a free shuttle is available. Five modest **guest rooms** (from 225€ double) are above the restaurant.

Via Migliara 72, Anacapri. dagelsomina.com. ✆ **081/837-1499.** Main courses 18€–30€. Daily noon–3:30pm and 7–11pm (from noon–11pm Fri–Sat; no dinner mid-Oct to Nov). Closed Nov to mid-Mar.

Le Grottelle ♥♥ CAPRESE A trek along the southern side of the island is rewarded with a stop at this out-of-the-way lair on a ledge above the Arco Naturale. A cave etched out of limestone cliffs and a panoramic terrace provide plenty of ambience, perhaps more memorable than the meal itself, though simple dishes like *zuppa di fagioli* (bean soup) and *spaghetti con pomodoro e basilica* (with fresh tomatoes and basil) are perfectly fine accompaniments to the views that extend across the sea to the Amalfi Coast. To find this delightful spot, wander east from Punta Tragara; it's about a 20-minute walk from the Piazzetta.

Via Arco Naturale 13, Capri Town. instagram.com/ristorantelegrottelle. ✆ **081/837-5719.** Main courses 15€–30€. Wed–Mon noon–3pm and 7–11pm. Closed Nov–Mar.

Ristorante Pizzeria Aurora ♥♥ CAPRESE You'll get a taste of Capri's high life at the island's oldest eatery, where photos of celebrities hang above the white banquettes. A few may also be sitting around you in the minimalist main dining room or on the terrace facing Capri Town's main thoroughfare. Despite all the glitz, the third generation of the D'Alessio family sticks to the basics, serving island classics like the trademark thin-crust *pizza all'acqua,* with mozzarella and hot peppers, *sformatino alla Franco* (rice pie in prawn sauce), and spaghetti *alle vongole* (clams).

Via Fuorlovado 18, Capri Town. auroracapri.com. ✆ **081/837-0181.** Main courses 16€–35€. Daily noon–3pm and 7–11pm. Closed Jan–Mar.

MODERATE

L'Angolo del Gusto ♥♥♥ CAPRESE/SEAFOOD Village life seems pretty idyllic when observed from this attractive terrace on a piazza in Anacapri, and not much dispels the mood—certainly not the excellent service, the delicious grilled fish, or the risotto with shrimp and just-plucked lemons. A simple whitewashed stone room is amply atmospheric when the terrace fills up, and you'll be encouraged to linger over dessert and *limoncello.*

Via Boffe 2, Anacapri. langolodelgustocapri.com. ✆ **081/837-3467.** Main courses 10€–28€. Daily noon–2:30pm and 6–10:30pm.

Pulalli Wine Bar ♥♥ CAPRESE To find a hideaway in the always-busy Piazzetta, just look up to this little terrace next to the clock tower. The bird's-eye view from this perch comes with wine, a selection of cheeses, or a full meal—the *risotto al limone* (lemon-flavored risotto) is especially memorable, served in a hollowed-out lemon. To secure one of the seven tables in this coveted spot, it's best to reserve well ahead.

Piazza Umberto I 4, Capri Town. capri.it/it/c/pulalli-wine-bar. ✆ **081/837-4108.** Main courses 10€–25€. Wed–Mon noon–3pm and 7–11pm. Closed Nov–Mar.

INEXPENSIVE

Ristorante-Pizzeria Materita ♥♥ PIZZERIA/CAPRESE All the warmth of little Anacapri comes to the fore in this busy local favorite on an animated square overlooking the church of Santa Sofia. Pizzas from the wood-fired oven and the palatable house wine are crowd pleasers, though the simple pastas are solidly tasty, too. Busy waiters are likely to come around with fresh fish that soon reappear grilled with island herbs.

Via Giuseppe Orlandi 140, Anacapri. ✆ **081/837-3375.** Main courses 8€–22€. Daily noon–3pm and 7–11pm (until 11:30pm Fri–Sun).

Beach Clubs

Some of Capri's most beloved institutions are the *stabilmenti balneari* (beach clubs) where you can eat well and begin or end a meal with a swim and some lounging. A day at one of these places is, like so much else about Capri, a simple pleasure with a glamorous twist.

Il Riccio ♥♥♥ SEAFOOD The cliffside pavilion that serves as the informal beach bistro of the Capri Palace hotel (p. 698) is done in soothing shades of blue and crisp white and hangs just above the Grotta Azzurra, bathed in the same mesmerizing light. The setting is so relaxing you won't want to leave after feasting on a fish lunch, and you don't have to—the top level is a sunning platform, filled with lounges and umbrellas, while stairs and a path descend to wave-washed swimming platforms below. Lunch draws patrons even from the mainland, and dinner is also served in summer, making this the prime spot on the island for a romantic splurge. The kitchen transforms what's said to be the freshest seafood on Capri into such creations as turbot baked in a salt crust, and a spaghetti with urchin roe that's so good you'll wonder why you've been missing out on this treat all your life. Buses from Anacapri to the Grotta Azzurra stop just outside the door, as do shuttles from the Capri Palace.

In the Capri Palace Hotel, Via Gradola 4, Grotta Azzurra. capripalace.com. ✆ **081/837-1380.** Main courses 55€–70€; sharing menus for two 95€–230€. Mon–Wed 12:30–3:30pm, Thurs–Sat 12:30–3:30pm and 7:30–10:30pm, Sun 12:30–6pm; lounge open throughout the day. Closed Nov to mid-Apr.

La Canzone del Mare ♥♥ SEAFOOD/CAPRESE The British music-hall star Gracie Fields came to Capri in the 1930s and decided she would be the happiest woman on earth if "one small blade of grass on this wonderful, gentle place could belong to me." She eventually bought Il Fortino, a house fashioned out of a ruined fort at Marina Piccola. Over the years she carved bathing platforms out of the rocks, installed a saltwater pool shaped like the island, and built terraces and lounges that would accommodate a restaurant, an American bar, and a few guest rooms, as well as living quarters that served as an informal retreat from life at her villa in Anacapri. Fields died of pneumonia after performing on the Royal Yacht anchored offshore, but her bathing establishment and restaurant still flourish. A meal of fresh vegetables and seafood pastas is a lot more expensive than you might expect from the simple surroundings, but the atmosphere is fun and eccentric, and Fields is still a presence. Five so-called Diva rooms named after famous former guests (like Elizabeth Taylor) provide sleeping quarters about as close to the sea as you'll find on Capri.

Via Marina Piccola 93. lacanzonedelmare.com. ✆ **081/837-0104.** Main courses 30€–45€. Daily noon–6pm; beach club daily 8:30am–7pm. Entry 70€ May to mid-June, 100€ mid-June to Sept, includes bar and restaurant credit. Diva rooms 300€–450€ double. Closed Oct to mid-Apr.

La Fontelina ♥♥ CAPRESE/SEAFOOD Many regular Capri visitors spend the winter months dreaming of a summertime lunch on the rocks at the base of the Faraglioni, where a meal comes with a swim in one of Europe's most legendary seaside settings. A fruit-loaded sangria is the house drink, the Caprese salad—with *mozzarella di bufala* and just-off-the-vine tomatoes—is legendary, and the fish is so fresh you might think it jumped right out of the sea onto your plate. Lunch is the only meal served, and it's necessary to reserve for either of the two seatings, at 1 and 3pm. Most guests come early and hang around long after a meal to lounge on the rocks and dip into the crystalline waters. You can reach this spot by following the Punta Tragara paths from Capri Town (p. 693), take a launch from and to Marina Piccola, for 10€ a person each way (operates from 3pm), or take a private water taxi.

Via Faraglioni. fontelina-capri.com. ✆ **081/837-0845.** Main courses 22€–40€. Daily 12:30–4pm, beach club until 6pm; beach club only entry from 40€. Closed Oct to late Apr.

ISCHIA ♥♥

30km (18 miles) NW of Capri; 42km (26 miles) SW of Naples; 20km (13 miles) W of Pozzuoli

While Capri is swathed in glamor and sophistication, Ischia (pronounced EES-kee-a) is scented with sulfur that rises off hundreds of hot springs. These wellsprings have been the island's calling card ever since ancient Greeks stepped ashore and discovered the pleasures of a long, soothing soak. **Monte Epomeo,** the island's 788m-high (2,585-ft.) dormant volcano, still has enough life in it to feed the mineral hot springs, producing therapeutic muds that supply the island's 150 spas. As a result, Ischia is often called the "island of eternal youth," a moniker that just as aptly describes the young Neapolitans who peacock around cafes and bronze themselves on the many beaches. Ischia is also known as the Isola Verde (Green Island), not, as some assume, for its verdant slopes, but for the green-tinged karst (limestone) that underlies much of the landscape. Yet Ischia *is* refreshingly green, with forests, orchards, and vineyards, and the towns along its 37km (23 miles) of shoreline are laid-back, pleasant places. They might lack the sophistication of Capri, but for many admirers they are all the better for that.

Essentials

ARRIVING Ischia's three main harbors—**Ischia Porto** (the largest), **Forio,** and **Casamicciola**—are well connected to the mainland. Both **ferry** and **hydrofoil** (*aliscafi*) services are frequent in summer but slow down during the winter, when the hydrofoil is sometimes suspended because of rough seas. **Caremar** (caremar.it; ✆ **081/189-66690**), **Medmar** (medmargroup.it; ✆ **081/333-4411**), and **SNAV** (snav.it; ✆ **081/428-555**) offer ferry service from Naples (both Mergellina Terminal Aliscafi and Stazione Marittima), Pozzuoli, Capri, and Procida to Ischia Porto and Casamicciola. **Alilauro** (alilauro.it; ✆ **081/497-2222**) runs hydrofoils from Naples (Molo Beverello) to Ischia Porto and to Forio. ***Note:*** In high season, car access to the island is restricted and car slots are limited; if you plan to bring your car, make your reservations well in advance.

GETTING AROUND Public transportation on Ischia is excellent, with a well-organized **bus** system, **EAV** (eavsrl.it; ✆ **800/0539-309** toll-free in Italy). One line circles the island in a clockwise direction (*circolare destra,* marked CD), and the other counterclockwise (*circolare sinistra,* marked CS). A number of other numbered lines crisscross the island. Tickets for point-to-point travel cost 1.70€; a Biglietto Orario, good for 100 minutes of travel with unlimited transfers, costs 2.10€, and a daily pass is 5.10€. Tickets can be bought at bars, tobacco shops, and news kiosks. The ticket office at the main bus station next to the harbor in Ischia Porto can provide bus schedules and tell you which bus goes where, or you can find the schedules online at **ischiareview.com**.

Taxis wait at stands around the island, including ones at Piazza degli Eroi (✆ **081/992550**) and Piazzetta San Girolamo (✆ **081/993720**) in Ischia Porto; Piazza Bagni (✆ **081/900881**) in Casamicciola; and Piazza Girardi (✆ **081/995113**) in Lacco Ameno.

You can **rent motor scooters, e-bikes, bicycles,** and **cars** on the island from a number of agencies, including **Calise** at Via Mazzella 116 in Forio (autonoleggio-ischia.com; ✆ **081/989486**).

VISITOR INFORMATION A good source of information for the island is **ischia.it**.

Exploring Ischia

Ischia is large as far as its neighbors in the Bay of Naples go, about 46 sq. km (18 sq. miles). Most of its main settlements—Ischia Porto, Casamicciola, and Lacco Ameno—are on the north, mainland-facing shore, with Forio on the west coast. The island's one great historic landmark, the **Castello Aragonese** (see below), is in Isola Ponte, adjoining Ischia Porto. The busy harbor of Ischia Porto was a landlocked volcanic crater until 1854, when Bourbon King Ferdinand II had a channel cut to the sea, creating one of the most thrilling sea entrances anywhere: Ferries and yachts navigate the impossibly narrow cut and emerge into a becalmed lake surrounded by waterside cafes and green hillsides carpeted with the island's distinctive white, flat-roofed houses.

Casamicciola, to the west of Ischia Porto, is a famous spa town, devoted to the healing arts since the 17th century. Among the arthritic, gouty, and otherwise ailing travelers who've stayed here, Norwegian playwright Henrik Ibsen came for a cure in the 1860s, writing his famous verse drama *Peer Gynt* between treatments. He's honored with a plaque in Piazza Marina, near a statue of King Vittorio Emanuele II. Just west of Casamicciola, the island's most sophisticated resort, **Lacco Ameno,**

Massive Castello Aragonese dominates Isola Ponte, a tiny island attached by causeway to Ischia.

became famous in 1963 when Richard Burton and Elizabeth Taylor arrived to shoot the barge scenes from the blockbuster film *Cleopatra*; the quiet little backwater became a jet-set hotspot when newspapers around the world ran paparazzi photos of the adulterous lovers yachting and swimming. Looming just offshore is the **Fungo,** a mushroom-shaped lump of wave-sculpted tufa that is as iconic to Ischia as the Faraglioni are to Capri. On the west coast, **Forio** compensates for its lack of beauty with spectacular stretches of sand, a lively resort scene, and some extremely palatable wines from the surrounding vineyards. Wherever you settle, you won't be too far from the island's main sights. A road follows the coast much of the way around the island, and buses make it easy to get from one town to the other.

Castello Aragonese ♥♥♥ HISTORIC SITE Greeks settled this rocky islet as early as the 5th century B.C.E., building watchtowers to keep an eye on enemy fleets. Alfonso I gave the walled complex its present form in the mid-15th century as a defense against pirate raids, shoring up watchtowers and walls and installing churches, terraces, and squares that give the compound a villagelike air. At one time some 17,000 people sheltered within the walls, among them nuns, monks, and soldiers. The British shelled the citadel during the Napoleonic Wars, and did a pretty good job of it, though enough remains to give an idea of the citadel's onetime might. Many churches still stand, in various states of repair. The frescoed crypt is about all that remains of the **Cattedrale dell'Assunta,** while the **Chiesa dell'Immaculata** and hexagonal **San Pietro a Pantaniello** are fairly intact. A somber if not downright macabre presence is the small **Cimitero delle Monache Clarisse,** attached to the island's convent. When the inhabitants breathed their last, they were left sitting on stone chairs as a reminder of what becomes of our earthly presence—the spooky-looking seating arrangement is still in place, minus the bones.

You can ponder all this as you make a circuit of the breezy ramparts, a vertigo-inducing lookout hundreds of feet above the crashing waves. An elevator whisks visitors up to the castle entrance, though the climb up the stairs and ramps provides a more authentic experience.

Piazzale Aragonese, Ischia Ponte. castelloaragoneseischia.com. ✆ **081/992834.** Admission 12€ adults, 6€ ages 10–18, free for children 9 and under. Daily 9am–sunset (last admission 1½ hr. before closing).

Villa La Mortella ♥♥♥ GARDEN Sir William Walton (1902–83), one of the greatest English composers of the 20th century, and his Argentine wife, Susana Walton (1926–2010), settled on Ischia in 1949. Walton found peace and light conducive to composition, and Susana became enchanted with the idea of creating a garden at their home, La Mortella (the Myrtles) on the west side of the Monte Vico promontory outside Forio. Working with the great landscape designer Russell Page, she created the Valley Garden, filling it with rare Mediterranean and South American species, great sweeps of orchids and other flowers, and fountains, ponds, and brooks. (Walton had valves in his study so he could turn off the jets when the gurgling disturbed him.) Lady Walton designed the sunny, view-filled Hill Garden as a tribute to her husband, working in the soil herself well into her later years. The exotic romance of the gardens are an apt tribute to the Waltons, who married just a few months after meeting in Buenos Aires; in a fit of spite, the bride's father spent his daughter's entire dowry on the champagne served at the wedding reception. It's customary on a walk along the garden paths to wave at the palms, following Lady Walton's belief that "you have to wave at them when you go by because they think you haven't paid attention."

Via Francesco Calise 39, Forio. lamortella.org. ✆ **081/986220.** Admission 12€ adults, 10€ 70 and older and ages 12–18, 6€ children 6–11, free for children 5 and under. Apr–Oct Tues, Thurs, and Sat–Sun 9am–7pm. Guided tour in Italian and English (15€, includes entry fee) Tues 10:30am and 4pm, Thurs 10:30am and 3:15pm, Sat 10:30am (limited tours offered in winter months); reservations required. Bus CS from Ischia Porto, Casamicciola, and Laco Ameno; CD from Forio.

Beaches

Ischia is ringed in places with long stretches of sand, which draw a mixed lot of islanders, day-tripping Neapolitans, and many Germans and Scandinavians. If you're staying in or near Ischia Ponte, your best bet is **Spiaggia dei Pescatori ♥♥**, where local fishermen beach their boats; it's just west of the Aragonese Castle. On the north coast, the scenic beach on the bay of **San Montano ♥♥** is set on the flanks of the Monte Vico promontory near Lacco Ameno. On the west coast, south of Forio, **Spiaggia Citara ♥♥** has hot mineral springs that flow out to sea at its southern edge. On the south coast, the island's most beautiful beach is 2km-long (1¼-mile) **Spiaggia dei Maronti ♥♥♥**. Also on the south coast, just east of the village of Sant'Angelo, is so-called **Fumarole beach,** where underground vapors heat the sand to such temperatures that islanders bury chicken and fish in aluminum foil, then take a swim as they wait for their food to cook. The sands are also sought out by arthritis sufferers, who plonk down and let the heat penetrate their aching joints. Just offshore, geysers bubble up to create natural hot-tub-like pools. A flotilla of little boats ferry passengers from the Sant'Angelo marina to this otherworldly seascape, about 5€ each way; the pools are also easy to reach on a seaside path.

Spas & Thermal-Mineral Baths

Ischia's elaborate *terme,* or thermal baths, have been popular ever since ancient Greeks soaked their weary bones in the natural hot springs. Most facilities offer slightly lower rates after midafternoon, so opt for a late entrance and a sunset soak. They also offer multi-day passes, for those who want to spend a lot of their time on Ischia quite literally in hot water.

Ischia has long been known for its thermal baths, such as this garden pool at Parco Termale Negombo.

Parco Termale Castiglione ♥♥ "Low-key" is not quite the right description for a place that splashes out with 10 pools, but they're set in tastefully designed seaside terraces laced with all sorts of quiet nooks and crannies. If the pool temperatures get to be too relaxing—they range from 28°C to 40°C (82°–104°F)—a stone jetty is poised for a dip in the sea. The lack of a beach, and the serious mud and thermal treatments, makes the park more popular with a sedate clientele than with families.

Shore Rd. btw. Ischia Porto and Casamicciola. termecastiglione.it. ✆ **081/982551.** Late Apr to May and late Aug to mid-Oct 49€ a day with lounger (37€ after 1pm), 29€ a day with deck chair (22€ after 1pm), 17€ ages 2–12 (13€ after 1pm); June to late Aug 55€ a day with lounger (41€ after 1pm), 33€ a day with deck chair (25€ after 1pm), 17€ ages 2–12 (13€ after 1pm). Free for infants age 1 and under. Mid-Apr to mid-Oct 9am–6pm.

Parco Termale Giardini Poseidon ♥ Everything about Ischia's largest spa is over the top, with 22 pools, a large private beach, tropical gardens, and several restaurants. The kitsch runs high, including toga-bedecked statues, yet it's hard not to feel like a figure of ancient legend in the complex's nicest feature, an eons-old natural thermal cave etched out of a cliff. The park is particularly popular with German and Italian families.

Via Giovanni Mazzella, Citara Beach, near Forio. giardiniposeidonterme.com. ✆ **081/908-7111.** Apr–May and Sept–Oct 45€ a day, 40€ after 1pm (after 12:30pm in Oct); Aug 50€ a day, 45€ after 1pm. Children ages 4–11 half price and free for ages 3 and under. Mid-Apr to Oct daily 9am–7pm (until 6:30pm in Oct).

Parco Termale Negombo ♥♥♥ If you only have time and/or the inclination to visit one thermal establishment on Ischia, make it this delightful spot on the island's most picturesque cove, San Montano. Gorgeous gardens, laid out by botanist Duke Luigi Camerini, surround 12 pools and facilities that include saunas, steam rooms, and massage cabins. Waterfalls and luxuriant plantings create a transporting getaway just as alluring as the beach of fine sand. You could happily spend a day shuttling between the warm pools and the refreshing sea, with some naptime in the shade beside one of the garden's beautiful ersatz waterfalls.

San Montano beach, on Monte Vico promontory near Lacco Ameno. terme.ischia.it/parco-termale-negombo. ✆ **081/9861.** Adult 70€, after 1:30pm 50€, after 3:30pm 40€; 2 adults 100€, after 1:30pm 85€, after 3:30pm 75€; children taller than 55 inches 30€, after 1:30pm 27€, after 3:30pm 25€. Late Apr to mid-Oct daily 8:30am–7pm.

Where to Stay on Ischia

Albergo Il Monastero ♥♥ The labyrinth of stone-walled, arched passageways, courtyards, and arbor-shaded seaside terraces of this former monastery are enticing in themselves, all the more so since the old premises are set within Ischia's spectacular **Castello Aragonese** (p. 705). Whitewashed guest rooms carved out of former monks' cells are spacious and welcoming, with simple yet handsome furnishings and knockout sea views from most. A huge panoramic terrace atop the castle walls is the setting for breakfast and delicious dinners, supplied by produce from the hotel's garden. Guests have access to the rest of the castle and the castle gardens.

Castello Aragonese, Ischia Ponte. albergoilmonastero.it. ✆ **081/992435.** 20 units. 120€–190€ double. Rates include breakfast. Closed mid-Oct to mid-Apr. **Amenities:** Restaurant; free Wi-Fi.

Hotel della Baia ♥♥ At this little getaway on a myrtle-clad hillside above San Montano Bay, lime trees shade a lounge, and simple-chic rooms open to bougainvillea-filled terraces. Just down the road are two delightful places to swim and lounge, a sandy beach in a lovely cove and **Negombo,** the nicest of Ischia's thermal parks (see above).

San Montano beach, on Monte Vico promontory near Lacco Ameno. hoteldellabaia.negombo.it. ✆ **081/986150.** 16 units. 125€–270€ double. Rates include breakfast/brunch. **Amenities:** Bar; pool; beach; free Wi-Fi.

Hotel Mandorla ♥♥ Maronti is the largest and to many beachgoers the best stretch of sand on Ischia, and the breezy terraces and gardens of this cheerful complex are right above the sands. All the simply furnished rooms open to outdoor spaces where greenery and patios surround pools for soaking in mineral-rich thermal waters. The easygoing ambience and a chance to soothe weary bones by lying in the sun are a big draw with many northern Europeans who return year after year to settle in for a week or so. Beachside restaurants and bars are just outside the door, as is a bus stop for the 20-minute ride to and from Ischia Porto.

Via Provinciale Maronti 57, Maronti. en.hotel-lamandorla.it. ✆ **081/990-046.** 36 units. 80€–205€ double. Rates include breakfast; A/C extra with some rates. Discounts for longer stays. Closed mid-Oct to mid-Apr. **Amenities:** Bar; pools; private beach; free Wi-Fi.

Mezzatorre Resort & Spa ♥♥♥ A former fortress at the end of a rocky promontory provides a sense of privileged escape and more than a whiff of *la dolce vita* amid 17 seaside acres of pine-scented gardens. Airy, view-filled accommodations in the dark-coral 15th-century watchtower and bungalows scattered among the garden are stylishly done in bright Mediterranean colors and a chic mix of antiques and contemporary pieces. Thermal pools on seaside terraces, a hot spring and spa, and a private beach ensure you can partake of a wellness regimen without leaving the property.

Via Mezzatorre, Forio. pellicanohotels.com. ✆ **081/986-111.** 60 units. 595€–1250€ double. Rates include breakfast. Free parking. Closed late Oct to Apr. **Amenities:** 2 restaurants; bar; babysitting; concierge; health club; 3 pools; room service; thermal spa; outdoor tennis courts; free Wi-Fi.

Where to Eat on Ischia

Da Ciccio ♥♥♥ SEAFOOD A seat on the terrace comes with killer views of the **Castello Aragonese ♥♥♥** (p. 705). That's about as showy as it gets at this little hole in the wall, where Ciccio and son Bruno focus on fresh seafood in delicious preparations: Thick mussel soup is steeped with mountain herbs and topped with fried bread; squid is stuffed with breadcrumbs, raisins, and chopped fish; and linguine is laden with clams.

Via Luigi Mazzella 32, Ischia Ponte. instagram.com/daciccio.ischiaponte. ✆ **081/991686.** Main courses 10€–25€. Daily noon–3pm and 7:30–11pm. Closed some winter months.

Ottomano ♥♥ ITALIAN/SEAFOOD A homey dining room and small terrace hang right over the sands of Maronti beach, making this a prime spot for a casual lunch or dinner. The small menu matches the easygoing ambience with a focus on *spaghetti alla vongole* and other nonfussy basics, as well as delicious pizzas from the oven.

Via Maronti, Barano D'Ischia. instagram.com/ristorante_ottomano. ✆ **328/902-9773.** Main courses 11€–20€. Daily 9am–9pm. Closed some winter months.

14

BASILICATA & PUGLIA

By Stephen Brewer

South of Naples, the Mezzogiorno begins in earnest. The name, which literally means "midday," evokes rugged sunbaked landscapes, but that doesn't begin to cover the riches you'll find in Basilicata and Puglia, the heel of the Italian boot. Some of Italy's unique architectural marvels are here: *sassi* cave dwellings in Matera, fantastical cone-shaped *trulli* in Alberobello, and Lecce's honey-colored baroque churches and palaces.

Outside the towns, the countryside is a sweep of groves, orchards, vineyards, and fields. It's estimated that more than 6 million olive trees carpet the southeast, yielding almost half of Italy's oil production, and almost any view may include gnarled trunks growing out of red earth. Where there's good olive oil, there's good wine and good food. Once you've tasted the region's simple, delicious *cucina povera* (peasant cooking), you'll never think of a fava bean with indifference again.

DON'T LEAVE BASILICATA & PUGLIA WITHOUT . . .

Climbing Through Matera. One of the oldest continually inhabited places on earth, Matera is a vertical maze of lanes and staircases connecting hill-clinging neighborhoods of *sassi* cave dwellings.

Gawking at the *Trulli.* Hundreds of these round, conical roofed houses line winding lanes in Alberobello, creating a fantasy-like townscape.

Being Dazzled by the White Cities. In the Valle d'Itria, the towns of Cisternino Locorotondo, Martina Franca, Ostuni, and Ceglie Messapica are so blindingly bright, you'll need sunglasses to wander their streets.

Going for Baroque in Lecce. The city is a showplace of extravagance from the 17th century, when craftsmen carved saints and sinners, gods and goddesses, and entire scenes into limestone as if it were butter.

MATERA ♥♥♥

254km (158 miles) SE of Naples, 73km (44 miles) SW of Bari, 136km (82 miles) W of Brindisi

In Matera, it's all about caves: A vast honeycomb of thousands of caverns riddles the chalk cliffs above the gorge of the Gravina River. It's estimated that these caves have been inhabited for at least 9,000 years, making Matera one of the oldest continuously inhabited places on earth. The rugged landscapes appear to have sheltered hunters and gatherers even long before then—the remains of a 150,000-year-old hominid have been found

FACING PAGE: ***Trulli* houses in Alberobello.**

in a nearby cave. Excavations have unearthed successive waves of occupation: 3,000-year-old ceramics, Greek and Byzantine coins, Roman houses, and the coffins of early Christians.

By the mid-20th century, however, some of Italy's poorest residents lived in Matera's caves, as many as 20,000 troglodytes eking out a miserable existence in what had become a vast, unsanitary underground slum. Man and beast shared the dank caves, a breeding ground for disease. As Carlo Levi observed in his 1945 autobiographical novel *Christ Stopped at Eboli*, "I have never in all my life seen such a picture of poverty."

Eventually the Italian government moved the cave dwellers to more sanitary housing on the ridge above the cliffs in modern Matera. By the mid-1980s, the rock-cut settlement was attracting attention for its unique beauty, a delightful warm-hued jumble of steep "streets" and meandering staircases running right over the rooftops of underlying houses. The unique cave city, now a UNESCO World Heritage Site, is so richly evocative of ancient Mediterranean civilization that it's been a location for many films, including Pier Paolo Pasolini's *The Gospel According to St. Matthew* (1964), Mel Gibson's *The Passion of the Christ* (2004), and the James Bond film *No Time to Die* (2020).

You can get a good sense of Matera and see the main sights in a full day, and the city makes a good overnight stop on the circuit south from Naples into Puglia.

Essentials

ARRIVING The closest airports are in Bari and Brindisi (for info on both, go to aeroportidipuglia.it). Bari is served by flights to and from hubs throughout Italy and the rest of Europe, as well as weekly nonstop service to and from New York's JFK airport on Neos (neosair.com) in summer. **Buses** operated by Cotrab (cotrab.it) make four or five trips between Bari airport and Matera throughout the day; travel time is about 75 minutes. Matera is about an hour's drive south of Bari via SP236; from Brindisi, it's 2 hours northeast via E90 and SS7.

Trains from Rome and other major Italian cities stop at Bari; to continue to Matera, switch to the narrow-gauge train operated by **Ferrovie Appulo Lucane** (**FAL;** ferrovieappulolucane.it), which runs almost hourly (no service Sun) and takes about 1½ hours. Trains leave from a terminal at the northeastern edge of Piazza Aldo Moro outside the main entrance to Bari Centrale and arrive at the Matera Centrale station; it's an easy walk down to the *sassi* from there. About a dozen trains (trenitalia.com) make the 3½- to 4-hour run daily (often with a change in Potenza or Salerno) between Naples and the town of Ferrandina-Scalo Matera, about 30km (18 miles) southwest of Matera, where you can catch a bus to Matera (fare around 3€). This trip shaves about 2 to 3 hours off train service from Naples to Matera Centrale, which often involves three or four changes.

Basilicata & Puglia
Milan
Venice
Rome
ADRIATIC SEA
Gulf of Manfredonia
Gulf of Taranto
Gulf of Salerno
PUGLIA
BASILICATA
CAMPANIA
CALABRIA
MOLISE
Gargano Peninsula
Salentine Peninsula
Le Murge
Appennino Lucano
Appennino Campano
Lago di Varano
Lago di Lesina
Ofanto
Bradano
Basento
Foggia
Bari
Brindisi
Lecce
Taranto
Matera
Potenza
Salerno
Avellino
Benevento
Vieste
Peschici
Rodi Garganico
San Nicandro Garganico
Apricena
Lesina
Torremaggiore
San Severo
Lucera
San Marco in Lamis
San Giovanni Rotondo
Monte Sant'Angelo
Manfredonia
Margherita di Savoia
Trinitapoli
San Ferdinando di Puglia
Cerignola
Orta Nova
Barletta
Trani
Andria
Canosa di Puglia
Bisceglie
Molfetta
Giovinazzo
Corato
Ruvo di Puglia
Castel del Monte
Bitonto
Bitetto
Grumo Appula
Cassano delle Murge
Santeramo in Colle
Altamura
Gravina in Puglia
Triggiano
Mola di Bari
Polignano a Mare
Monopoli
Egnazia
Fasano
Castellana Grotte
Alberobello
Locorotondo
Cisternino
Ostuni
Carovigno
San Vito dei Normanni
Martina Franca
Ceglie Messapica
Mesagne
San Pietro Vernotico
San Pancrazio Salentino
Oria
Manduria
Sava
Lizzano
Pulsano
San Giorgio Ionico
Grottaglie
Crispiano
Massafra
Mottola
Palagiano
Gioia del Colle
Castellaneta
Laterza
Ginosa
Montescaglioso
Bernalda
Policoro
Otranto
Maglie
Santa Cesarea Terme
Tricase
Ugento
Santa Maria di Leuca
Taurisano
Taviano
Racale
Matino
Gallipoli
Galatone
Nardò
Galatina
Copertino
Lavello
Venosa
Melfi
Rionero in Vulture
Avigliano
Volo dell'Angelo
Lauria
Maratea
Sapri
Sala Consilina
Capaccio
Agropoli
Campagna
Ariano Irpino
Sorrento
A14
A16
A3
A30
RA 2
RA 5
RA 9
SS7
SS16
SS17
SS89
SS96
SS99
SS106
SS172
SS379
SS407
SS655
SS691
SS87
SS18
SR1
SR6
SP231
SP430/a
SP430/b
0
25 mi
25 km

If you're traveling to Matera from Naples **by car,** follow the A3 south, then the E847 east through Potenza; the drive takes a little more than 2 hours. **Bus** service between Naples and Matera, run by Marino (marinobus.it; ✆ **080/3112335**), takes 4½ hours, with six buses a day. **Flixbus** (flixbus.it) and other companies operate **buses** several times a day to connect Matera with Bari in a little over an hour. Buses stop next to the train station. If you need to stash your bags in Matera, you can do so at **Self Bags** (self bags.it), near the train station at Vico Cappelluti 11; a locker costs 11€ a day.

Rising out of chalk cliffs, Matera is known for its maze of steep streets and homes carved out of ancient caves.

GETTING AROUND The only way to get around much of Matera is **on foot**—be prepared for a lot of climbing. Most of the *sassi* district is closed to car traffic; if you're arriving by car, arrange in advance with your hotel. Most hotels have agreements with lots and garages in the modern town where you can park for about 12€ a day, and garages will usually drop you off and pick you up at a point near your hotel for about 5€. At times it's possible to drive to the bottom of Sasso Barisano and continue along Via Madonna delle Virtù into the bottom of Sasso Caveoso, though this should be only to drop off bags; your hotel must give your license plate number to the police in advance. The dispatch number for **Matera taxi** is ✆ **334348.**

VISITOR INFORMATION The municipal **Matera Welcome tourist office** in the modern town across from the train station on Viale Aldo Moro (materawelcome.it; ✆ **0835/241-340**) is open Monday to Friday 9am to 2pm and Tuesday and Thursday 4 to 6pm. The website is a good source for tours, events, and other information. A regional tourist office, **APT Basilicata,** is at Via Antonio de Viti de Marco 9 (aptbasilicata.it; ✆ **0835/406-464**) and is open Monday to Friday 9:30am to 1:30pm. (Note that hours at both offices change frequently.) Your hotel will most likely provide you with a map, and beware, navigation apps go

A Crash Course on Cave Life

For some background on Matera, step into **Casa Noha,** Recinto Cavone 9 (fondo ambiente.it/luoghi/casa-noha; ✆ **0835/335-452**), where visual projections onto cave walls and a good soundtrack trace the city's history and its unique social and architectural heritage. It's open daily except Wednesday April through October 10am to 7pm (Feb–Mar and Nov–Dec 10am–5pm); admission is 6.50€, 3€ ages 6 to 18, 17€ families of two adults and two children, free for children 5 and under.

crazy in Matera. Private agencies abound, most in business to sell walking tours of the *sassi.* A good online source for tours is getyourguide.com, with 2½-hour excursions (from 30€) that shed light on life as it once was in the *sassi* and point out such details as charming frescoes by local artisans in the churches.

Exploring Matera

Matera is essentially divided into three districts. At the top of the ridge is the center of the modern town, or **Civita,** where the Duomo (p. 716) stands amid squares and palaces. Below Via Duomo spread the ***sassi*** (literally, "stones"), the cliff-hugging districts of cave dwellings. **Sasso Barisano,** to the north, has seen the most restoration, with many cave dwellings converted to hotels, restaurants, shops, and Airbnb rentals. **Sasso Caveoso,** to the south, is more authentically derelict, though renewal has begun.

The best way to appreciate the *sassi* is to plunge in and wander, following one of the well-marked stone staircases off Via Duomo. At the foot of the cliff in each *sasso* is one street with shops and cafes—in Sasso Barisano it's **Via dei Fiorentino,** in Sasso Caveoso, **Via Bruno Buozzi.** On the way down are wonky staircases, blind alleys, crumbling stone courtyards with bursts of greenery, and many remarkable vistas.

Trying to find a specific address in the *sassi* can be challenging, but a few sights are worth seeking out. In Sasso Caveoso, besides the **Casa Grotta di Vico Solitario** (p. 716), you'll be able to see some cave rooms in the **Museo della Scultura Contemporanea** (**MUSMA**) ♥♥, Via San Giacomo (musma.it; ✆ **0835/330-582**), housed in the Palazzo Pomarico, a 16th-century palace with frescoed salons displaying works by a roster of international contemporary sculptors. Admission is 10€ (5€ for ages 7–18, free for children 5 and under); it's open daily May through September

Strolling the mazelike streets of Matera.

10am to 8pm and the rest of the year until 6pm. Also in Sasso Caveoso are the ancient underground passages of **La Raccolta delle Acque ♥♥** (museimatera.it/raccolta-delle-acque; ✆ **329/063-1517;** enter at Via Purgatorio Vecchio), which carried the city's often-unhealthy water supply, channeling rainwater collected from streets and roofs into deep cisterns. Since streets were littered with human and animal waste, cholera and typhoid were rampant. The Raccolta is open daily 10am to 4pm. Admission is 2.50€ (free for ages 17 and under).

Lanes of the *sassi* are lined with *chiese rupestri* (rock churches), dug out of caves and often elaborately decorated with frescoes. One of Matera's best-preserved rock church complexes, **Santa Lucia alle Malve ♥♥**, in Sasso Caveoso (✆ **327/980–3776**), was a refuge for monks fleeing 8th-century persecution in the Middle East; it later became a convent for Benedictine nuns, who in the 13th century frescoed the caves in colorful scenes that include a breastfeeding Madonna. The church is open daily 10am to 4pm; admission is 4€.

Some of the best views of the *sassi* are from the **Parco della Murgia Materana ♥♥** (parcomurgia.it; ✆ **0835/336-166**), covering 70 sq. km (27 sq. miles) along the gorge of the Gravina River just below town. High ground affords sweeping views, while the ravines are riddled with caves that have been used as rock churches, stables, and shepherds' shelters. One of these churches, **La Cripta del Peccato (Crypt of the Original Sin) ♥♥♥** is known as the "Sistine Chapel of Cave Churches" for its vivid 9th-century frescoes of Adam and Eve and other biblical figures (criptadelpeccatooriginale.it; ✆ **320/334-5323**). The church is open daily, 9am to 6pm April to September (closes 4:30pm Oct and Mar, 3:30pm Nov–Feb); admission is 11€, 8.50€ youth 7 to 18, 6 and under free. Enter the park on trails off Via Madonna delle Virtù. Confusingly, this park is also known as Parco Archeologico Storico Naturale delle Chiese Rupestri del Materano; the names are used interchangeably.

Casa Grotta di Vico Solitario ♥♥ MUSEUM The past is brought to life in this re-created dwelling from the 1950s, when the government cleared out the *sassi* and moved residents up to modern Matera. The crude authentic furnishings include a ridiculously high bed that kept sleepers up off the frigid stone floor and provided storage space beneath. The cave and its alcoves are surprisingly spacious, but not as filthy as it must've been when residents shared the space with pigs and donkeys, as you'll see in accompanying film footage that conveys the district's former squalor.

Off Via Bruno Buozzi, Sasso Caveoso. casagrotta.it. ✆ **0835/310118.** Admission 5€, 3€ seniors and students, 2€ ages 11–18, free for children 10 and under. 9:30am–7pm (closing hours vary).

Duomo ♥♥ CHURCH The residents of the *sassi* are rarely out of sight of the city's soaring cathedral, completed in 1270 on high ground at the side of the cliff just above them. Carvings on the facade deliver a morality lesson to the faithful: A mermaid warns of the passions likely to steer us

off a path of righteousness; an eagle is poised to devour meeker animals, just as we are always prey to sin; the Archangel Michael battles a dragon (representing the forces of evil) before an audience of the town's medieval elite. Inside, to the right of the entrance, a terrifying 13th-century *Last Judgment* depicts the Archangel Michael wielding his sword in hell as serpents attack the damned—among them popes, monks, and kings, proof that no one escapes the final judgment. An antidote is the charming 16th-century Nativity scene in a side chapel, where shepherds and their flocks are set against a re-creation of Matera, looking just like it does today.
Piazza del Duomo. Free admission (audioguide 2€). Mon–Sat 9am–6:30pm; Sun 9–10:30am and 12:30–6:30pm.

Madonna delle Virtù e San Nicola dei Greci ♥♥♥ HISTORIC SITE In Sasso Barisano, this intriguing maze of 10th- and 11th-century chapels and living quarters once held a community of nuns on one level, monks on another. San Nicola has been frescoed in part by locals over the centuries and has some charmingly simple depictions of saints. Formerly abandoned and used as a dump, the cave church of Madonna delle Virtù, set beneath San Nicola, was one of the first of the *sassi* renewal projects, in 1967; its frescoes are more sophisticated.
Via Madonna delle Virtù, Sasso Barisano. caveheritage.it. ✆ **0377/444-8885.** Admission 12€ adults, 8€ ages 6–12, free for children 5 and under. June–Sept daily 10am–8pm; Oct and Apr–May daily 10am–1:30pm and 3–6pm; Nov–Feb Mon–Fri 10am–1:30pm; Mar daily 10am–1:30pm and Sat–Sun 3–5:30pm.

Museo Nazionale d'Arte Medievale e Moderna della Basilicata-Palazzo Lanfranchi ♥♥ MUSEUM Among the paintings and religious objects in this converted monastery are colorful canvases by painter/writer Carlo Levi (1902–75), who was exiled to this region in the 1930s for anti-Fascist activities. Levi's autobiographical novel, *Christ Stopped at Eboli*, brought the area's poverty and squalid living conditions to the world's attention, and these hard-hitting paintings capture the hardship of peasant life in the *sassi.*
Piazzetta Giovanni Pascoli, in the Civita. museonazionaledimatera.it. ✆ **0835/310058.** Admission 10€. Wed–Mon 9am–8pm; Tues 9am–2pm.

Where to Stay in Matera

Many Materani have converted caves into rentals, and a number of them are available through **Airbnb** (airbnb.com).

Corte San Pietro ♥♥♥ At this welcoming enclave in Sassi Caveoso, a cluster of cave dwellings surrounds a courtyard/outdoor lounge. Warmly hued walls, rustic antiques, and alcoves and crevices create a simple yet luxurious ambience, and the genuine warmth of the staff adds to the extraordinary experience of a stay.
Via Bruno Buozzi 97b. cortesanpietro.it. ✆ **0835/310-813.** 11 units. 175€–270€ double. 2-night minimum stay some periods. Rates include breakfast. **Amenities:** Bar; lounge; free Wi-Fi.

Fra I Sassi Residence ♥♥ At this beautiful enclave at the bottom of Sasso Barisano, well-designed and comfortably furnished cave rooms (some with sunken tubs) open onto a bright terrace—a front-row seat for a spectacular vista of dwellings clinging to the surrounding hillsides. Welcoming outdoor spaces are well supplied with loungers, the perfect perch for a drink, a nap, or just soaking in the views. The breakfast room does double duty as a bar/cafe.

Via D'Addozio 102. fraisassiresidence.com. ✆ **0835/336-020.** 18 units, plus 8-bed hostel. 120€–160€ double; hostel rates on request. 2- to 3-night minimum stay some periods. Rates include breakfast. **Amenities:** Bar; free Wi-Fi.

Matteotti Rooms ♥♥ This stylish little bed and breakfast is on level ground in the new town, so the comfortable rooms are well suited to travelers who don't want to lug their bags up and down the stepped streets of the *sassi* (though the entrance is one flight up from street level). The train and bus stations are just up the street, restaurants and shops are just outside the door, and the sights are an easy stroll away. Extremely comfortable, nicely furnished rooms come with coffeemakers and other thoughtful conveniences, and the welcoming staff dispenses advice on restaurants and attractions.

Via Roma 28. matteottiroomsmatera.com. ✆ **392/281-8752.** 5 units. 60€–80€ double. Rates include light breakfast in nearby cafe. **Amenities:** Free Wi-Fi.

San Giorgio Hotel ♥♥ You will feel like a bona-fide troglodyte—albeit a high-living one—in one of these well-equipped suite dwellings scattered throughout Sassi Barisano. Most have one or two bedrooms; many are multilevel and rich in arches, vaults, and other architectural details, including fireplaces and terraces in some. Accommodating staff serves breakfast in a pleasant room in the main house.

Via Fiorentini 259. sangiorgio.matera.it. ✆ **0835/334583.** 11 units. 100€–170€ double. 2- or 3-night minimum stay required some periods. **Amenities:** Free Wi-Fi.

Sextantio le Grotte della Civita ♥♥ If the Flintstones had hired a big-name decorator, they might have been treated to a design-magazine-worthy abode like these swanky cave sanctuaries overlooking the Gravina River gorge. Furnishings are rustic chic, with authentically old pieces scattered around cavernous spaces. Luxuries include freestanding tubs, fireplaces, heated floors, and (in many rooms) terraces overlooking green, rock-studded countryside. Breakfast, drinks, and some meals are served in an ancient church hewn out of the rock.

Via Civita 28. sextantio.it. ✆ **0835/332-744.** 18 units. 150€–250€ double. Rates include breakfast. **Amenities:** Bar; cafe; spa; free Wi-Fi.

Vetera Matera ♥♥♥ This luxurious enclave puts a romantic spin on cave life in richly refitted cave houses and some freestanding buildings. Cave accommodations, some multilevel and plunging deep into the hillside, provide an urbane experience with stylish furnishings, while more standard yet similarly comfortable hotel rooms come with expansive

Vetera Matera puts a luxury spin on cave dwelling.

views across Matera's extraordinary cityscape. All share access to a view-filled terrace, huge subterranean spa, a restaurant, and attentive service that includes carting luggage up and down the steps leading to the hotel. Rione Vetera 28. veteramatera.com. ✆ **0835/1670514.** 23 units. 250€–375€ double. Closed early Jan to Mar. **Amenities:** Bar; restaurant; spa; free Wi-Fi.

Where to Eat in Matera

Local pastas are made with local durum wheat and typically are ear-shaped *orecchiette* and *lagane* (similar to *tagliatelle*); sauces often use local **pork** and are seasoned with *peperoni* cruschi (fried red peppers) and fried breadcrumbs instead of Parmigiano. An atmospheric spot for a pre-dinner cocktail is **Zipa Café** ♥, 15 Via Madona dell'Idris (zipacafe.com; ✆ **370/323-4520**), where seating is on large stones outside a cave beneath the pinnacle-topping church of San Pietro Caveoso. **I Vizi degli Angeli Laboratorio di Gelateria Artigianale** ♥, Via Domenico Ridola 36 (ivizi degliangeli.it; ✆ **0835/310637**), serves organic *gelati* and *sorbetti.*

La Talpa ♥♥ BASILICATESE Matera's caves don't get much more inviting than these snug, white-walled rooms hung with old cooking implements and filled with gingham-topped tables. The homey setting is well-suited for such local dishes as *purea di fave con cicorielle di campo* (broad-bean puree with chicory) or *cavatelli* with chickpea puree, arugula, porcini mushrooms, and tomatoes. Lamb and veal are grilled to perfection, and pizzas emerge from a wood oven at the back of the cave. Via dei Fiorentini 167. latalparistorante.it. ✆ **0835/335-086.** Main courses 9€–18€. Mon–Sat 5–11:30pm, Sun 12:30–3pm and 5–11pm. Closed late Jan and early Feb.

The Bread of Life

Matera is known for its delicious breads, stuffed and topped with cheese and meat fillings. Bakeries around the city make *strazzata,* a type of focaccia, from local durum wheat, as well *pucce,* a sandwich bread based on pizza dough, and *panzerotti,* a crescent-shaped turnover that's like a calzone only thinner. **Panificio Perone il Forno di Gennaro ♥♥**, Via Nazionale 52 (ilfornodigennaro.com; ✆ **0835/385-656**), a long-standing Matera institution, moved out of the Sassi into the new town 60 years ago but still bakes its delicious bread, including focaccia, in wood-fired ovens; the bakery also offers 4-hour breadmaking workshops, from about 70€. **Bar Pasticceria Schiuma ♥♥**, near the Duomo at Via XX Settembre 10 (✆ **0835/331-862**), is another venerable favorite, serving snacks and sandwiches in polished surroundings, alongside an irresistible selection of cakes and pastries. **Panificio Paoluccio ♥♥**, Via del Corso 22 (✆ **0334/185-9799**), tops house-made focaccia with tomatoes, potatoes, garden vegetables, and other local ingredients, while **Quatro Quarti ♥♥**, Via Ascanio Persio 25 (✆ **393/966-2961**), stuffs *pucce* with pork sausage, local onions and eggplants, and smoked cheeses.

Oi Mari ♥♥ BASILICATESE/NEAPOLITAN This convivial spot in Sasso Barisano took its name from a famous Neapolitan serenade—and that's not the only way in which this cheery candlelit cave takes inspiration from Naples. The pizzas are the best in town, filling the cavernous space nightly with eager diners. You can nicely stretch out a meal with heaping platters of *antipasto di mare,* with octopus, squid, and *baccalà,* or choose from a wide array of seafood pastas and meat dishes.

Via dei Fiorentini 66. oimari.it. ✆ **0835/346-121.** Main courses 18€–22€; tasting menu 60€. Thurs 7:30–10:30pm, Fri–Tues noon–2:30pm and 7:30–10:30pm.

Ristorante Francesca ♥♥♥ BASILICATESE Simple contemporary furnishings and chic lighting highlight the atmosphere of a millennia-old dwelling, where a meal in soothing cave rooms or on a warm-weather terrace is steeped in Matera traditions. That means local *burratina* cheeses, herb-infused sausages and grilled lamb, and hand-rolled *orecchiette* and *cavatelli* with fava beans and fresh vegetables, all to be washed down with Aglianico, the inky local red wine.

Via Bruno Buozzi 9. ✆ **083/531-0443.** Main courses 10€–18€. Thurs–Sun 7:30–10pm; Sun 12:30–3pm and 7:30–11pm.

Trattoria del Caveoso ♥♥ BASILICATESE Bold contemporary art decorates this convivial multilevel cave in Sasso Caveoso, but the focus is on old-fashioned, wholesome, straightforward preparations that don't pretend to be anything other than *cucina povera*—poor man's grub. Fresh local produce brightens dishes like *strascinate con rape mollica fritta* (pasta topped with broccoli, chili peppers, and breadcrumbs) or lamb fried with onions, tomatoes, mushrooms, and wild onions.

Via Bruno Buozzi 21. ristorantedelcaveoso.it. ✆ **0835/312-374.** Main courses 8€–22€. Thurs–Tues 12:30–3pm and 7:30–11pm. Closed late Jan to early Feb.

PUGLIA'S EAST COAST ♥♥

Bari (see box on p. 722) is the gateway to the region: **Trains** operated by Trenitalia and Italo (italotreno.it) make the trip from Rome in about 4 hours, **buses** from Naples in about 4 hours (many operated by Marino [marino bus.it]). Bari's **airport** (aeroportidipuglia.it) handles flights to and from cities throughout Europe and even a weekly nonstop to and from New York's JFK airport in summer on **Neos** (neosair.com). For bus and train travel around Puglia, check schedules with **Ferrovie del Sud Est** (www.fseonline.it) or go to the Puglia tourism website, viaggiareinpuglia.it.

Trani

85km (51 miles) N of Matera, 51km (32 miles) NW of Bari

A bit off the beaten track, this once-thriving medieval seaport has twisting lanes and airy piazzas lined with palaces and churches, all hewn from golden limestone that glows with a tinge of pink in the sunshine. Sooner or later the maze untangles alongside the shimmering blue waters of the Adriatic, where one of Italy's most dramatic cathedrals seems to rise out of the waves. **Trani** is a jumping-off point for the remarkable **Castel del Monte** (p. 723) and the **Gargano peninsula** (p. 724).

ESSENTIALS

ARRIVING Trani is just off the E55 autostrada, which follows the Adriatic coast between Brindisi and Ravenna. If you're driving from Matera, head north to Altamura, then follow signs through Corato to Trani. Trani is 40 minutes by train from Bari; for schedules and tickets, go to trenitalia.com. The closest airports are in Bari and Brindisi (aeroportidipuglia.it).

GETTING AROUND Stash the car as soon as possible and navigate the old city on foot. You'll find park-and-display parking near the seafront next to the Duomo and Castello Svevo.

VISITOR INFORMATION Visit **viaggiareinpuglia.it** for information about the region. Trani's **tourist office** is at Piazza Trieste 10 (© **0883/588-830**).

fly LIKE AN ANGEL

To add some zip to a Matera visit, travel about 80km (49 miles) west via SS7 and E847 to Castelmezzano and Pietrapertosa, picturesque villages perched on adjacent mountainsides. The neighbors have linked themselves via the **Volo dell'Angelo** (Flight of the Angel) zipline, making it possible to get from one village to the other at a top speed of 120kph (74mph) along cables almost a mile long. You may also traverse the gorge between the two on the 2km (1¼-mile) **Percorso delle Sette Pietre** ("Walk of the Seven Stones"). The zipline operates May through early November: Sundays in May; Saturdays and Sundays from June through early July and mid-September through early November; Thursday to Tuesday from early July through mid-September. A round-trip costs 46€, 79€ for couples, 23€ and 39.50€ one way. For reservations and information, go to volodellangelo.com.

Bari: Gateway to Puglia & Home to Santa Claus

A 4th-century bishop of Myra, Türkiye, St. Nicholas—whose gift-giving habits gave rise to the Santa Claus tradition—lay at peace in his hometown until 1076, when pirates stole his bones and brought them to Bari, now the largest city in Puglia. Nicholas was a big prize, a top draw for pilgrims from all over Christendom, and Bari zealously built the almost fortresslike, twin-towered **basilica of San Nicola** (basilicasannicola.it) to house him. St. Nick's feast day, December 6, is a big event in Bari, especially the ceremony in which a flask is lowered into the crypt to extract a miraculous liquid said to be emitted by the saint's remains (they even sell it in little bottles). The basilica, on Largo Abate Elia (✆ **080/5737111**), is open Monday through Saturday 6:30am to 8:30pm and Sunday 6:30am to 10:30pm; admission is free. Around the basilica are the lanes and squares of **Bari Vecchia,** an intriguing old quarter that juts into the sea. Cafe-lined **Piazza del Ferrarese** is the liveliest corner; along atmospheric Arco Basso and Arco Alto, women sell homemade *orecchiette* and other goods from tables in front of their doors. Modern Bari, laid out in a grid around the historic quarter and a massive 12th-century castle (now government offices), is quite pleasant, inspiring the saying, "If Paris had the sea, it would be a little Bari."

EXPLORING TRANI

For most of Trani's history, travelers approached the city by sea. Today you'll likely enter town through its scruffy outskirts, but you'll still want to head to the port. The enormous 13th-century seafront **Castello Svevo** is proof of Trani's onetime power, street names like Via Synagoga testify to a large medieval Jewish population, and Via Cambio (Street of the Moneychangers) reveals Trani's role as a major Mediterranean trading center. During the Crusades, Trani was an embarkation port for Christian forces heading to the Middle East; soldiers of the elite Knights Templar order received blessings in the courtyard of the splendid **church of Ognissanti,** on Via Ognissanti (Fri 6–8pm, Sat 9:30am–12:30pm and 6–8pm).

Duomo ♥♥ CATHEDRAL For your first glimpse of this gleaming Romanesque-style masterwork, head for the east side of Trani harbor: You'll see the **campanile** (bell tower) stretching 59m-high (194-ft.) toward the sky, while the church's sheer limestone walls seem to be rooted not in the ground but in the sea. This dramatic union of sea and sky lifts the spirit, an effect no doubt intended by the architects and craftsmen who began work in 1097. Their singular mission was to outdo Bari, their neighbor just down the coast, which had just snatched the relics of St. Nicholas (see box above) and was building a basilica to house them, sure to draw crowds of pilgrims. Trani had a new saint of its own to promote, San Nicola Pellegrino (St. Nicholas the Pilgrim), an extremely pious Greek shepherd boy who, after a long sea voyage, collapsed and died from exhaustion in front of the 7th-century church of Santa Maria, which formerly occupied this site. (Nicola reputedly spent all his waking hours chanting the phrase "Kyrie Eleison" ["Lord, have mercy"], a habit that may have annoyed his shipmates but nevertheless won him almost instant sainthood.) The foundations of the Santa Maria church are still in the crypt, where the saint's tomb rests among a forest of columns. The main church is a soaring display of arches, columns, and vaults luminously fashioned from golden limestone. The heavy bronze doors (created by Barisano da Trani, whose most famous work is the doors in Monreale, Sicily; see p. 772) depict familiar biblical figures as well as dragons, lions, archers, and jugglers—look for the panel where the artist portrays himself, humbly at the feet of San Nicola.

Piazza Duomo 9. cattedraletrani.it. ✆ **0883/500-293.** Free admission. Apr–Oct daily 9am–12:30pm and 3:30–7pm (4–8pm Sun); Nov–Mar daily 9am–12:30pm and 3:30–6pm (4–7:30pm Sun).

Castel del Monte ♥♥♥

34km (21 miles) S of Trani

Topping a small mount above the fertile Puglian plains, this majestic castle comes into sight from miles away, just as the enlightened Frederick II, Holy Roman Emperor and King of Sicily, intended when he ordered it built in 1237. The distinctive octagonal shape may look familiar—it's reproduced on every 1-cent euro minted in Italy. What's not clear, however, is what this castle was built for. It has no moat or walls, so it wouldn't have been practical for defense, despite the strategic hilltop position. Frederick's passion for science and mathematics is reflected in the precision of the octagonal shape, with eight octagonal towers that blend Islamic

The octagonal citadel of Castel del Monte rises above the Puglian plains just south of Trani.

and Gothic influences and bear structural weight in lieu of the flying buttresses that supported the great cathedrals and other monuments of the time; it's been suggested the castle was built solely to show off this engineering innovation. Large rooms on two floors are warmed by fireplaces, implying a certain degree of luxury and suggesting also that the castle might have been built for entertaining or as a hunting lodge. A few fragments of mosaics, frescoes, and marble work remain, and an ingenious plumbing system fed by rainwater supplied baths and latrines. Frederick's successors converted the castle into a prison, where convicts languished in cold chambers. To get here from Trani, head southwest on SP130 to Andria, then south toward Spinazzola. From Matera, head to Altamura, then Gravina, and follow signs to Spinazzola. The **castle** (✆ **0883/569997**) is well signposted off Strada Statale 170, outside Andria. It is open daily April to September 10am to 6:45pm and October to March 9am to 5:45pm, and entrance is on the hour. Admission is 10€, 2€ ages 18 to 25, free for ages 17 and under.

Promontorio del Gargano

About 90km (55 miles) NW of Trani

The spur of the Italian boot is this thumb-shaped promontory northwest of Trani, mostly now protected as the **Parco Nazionale del Gargano.** Much of the peninsula's mountainous interior is carpeted with an ancient oak and beech forest, the Foresta Umbra, which once covered most of Central Europe, and the coast is a magical seascape of cliffs, rock formations, caves, islets, and sandy beaches. Come August, Italian families head to low-key summer resorts around the whitewashed towns of **Vieste** and **Peschici.** In centuries past, both towns continually fended off pirates and other invaders—in Vieste in 1554 the Turks beheaded more than 5,000 men, women, and children.

Rock outcroppings protect lovely sandy beaches along the coast of the Gargano peninsula.

The ever-popular **cave of St. Michael the Archangel** in hilltop Monte Sant'Angelo (santuariosanmichele.it) is the oldest shrine in Western Europe, founded in the 7th century (the archangel is believed to have appeared there three times). Admission to the chapels and rock-hewn sanctuary is free. It's open Monday to Saturday 7am to 1pm and 2:30 to 8pm (closes 7pm Nov–Mar), Sunday 7:30am to 12:30pm and 2:30 to 7pm; July through September, it stays open with no midday break and on Sunday until 8pm. Even more popular is the sanctuary of **Padre Pio** (conventosantuariopadrepio.it) in San Giovanni Rotondo, where the beloved mystic saint (canonized in 2002) served as priest from 1916 to 1968. Padre Pio's shrine includes architect Renzo Piano's stunning **Chiesa San Pio Da Pietrelcina** (daily 7am–7pm), built in 2004 and the second-most-visited Catholic pilgrimage site in the world (after Mexico City's Our Lady of Guadalupe) with 7 million pilgrims a year.

The Gargano gateway city is Manfredonia, about 80km (50 miles) northwest of Trani via SS16 and SP77. From there, SS89 skirts the peninsula; expect at least half a day of slow driving to make the circuit. You'll find **tourist offices** at Vieste, Piazza J.F. Kennedy (✆ **0884/708806**), and Peschici, Via Magenta 3 (✆ **0884/915362**). **Park headquarters** is in Monte Sant'Angelo, 90km (55 miles) NW of Trani (parks.it/parco.nazionale.gargano).

The Seacoast from Bari to Brindisi

The Adriatic washes up onto a long stretch of appealing coastline between Bari and Brindisi. One of the most picturesque seaside towns in Italy is **Polignano a Mare** ♥♥♥, 39km (24 miles) southeast of Bari (on the Bari–Ostuni–Lecce train line), where seaside cliffs are etched with coves and topped by the tall white houses of the intriguing old town; the cliffs are a venue for an international diving competition in July. Native son Domenico Modugno, who wrote the 1950s hit song "Volare," is honored with a statue on the seaside promenade named after him. Another local institution is the town's famous *caffè speciale,* a concoction of espresso, cream, lemon, and amaretto, served at **Il Super Mago del Gelo** on Piazza Garibaldi (ilsupermagodelgelo.it; ✆ **080/424-0025**). **Monopoli** ♥♥♥, 9km (5½ miles) southeast of Polignano a Mare and on the same train line, has a beautiful and evocative seaside old quarter packed with churches, palaces, and a 16th-century castle built around a string of harbors. Another 12km (7½ miles) down the coast, outside Fasano, lie the ruins of **Egnazia** ♥♥, a trading center that was settled around 1500 B.C.E. and flourished under the Romans. A well-preserved segment of the Trajan Way bisects the ancient city, where the Tomb of the Pomegranates (symbol of eternal life) is entered through huge old doors on which handles and hinges still function (open only on special occasions). The site is open Monday to Saturday 8:30am to 6:30pm and Sunday 8:30am to 1:30pm. Admission is 10€, 2€ ages 18 to 25, free for ages 17 and under.

East of Fasano, **Parco Naturale Regionale Dune Costiere** ♥♥ (parcodunecostiere.org) follows the coast for 8km (5 miles), its sandy beaches backed by dunes and centuries-old olive groves. Another half hour down the coast, the **Torre Guaceto** ♥♥ nature preserve (riservaditorreguaceto.it), 24km (13 miles) east of Ostuni, has miles of pristine sands, dunes, and marshes, and offshore coral formations are a lure for snorkelers.

Where to Stay & Eat on the Coast

Albergo Diffuso Monopoli ♥♥♥ Attractively furnished rooms and apartments are tucked into fishermen's houses and palaces scattered around Monopoli's intriguing old quarter, steps from a breakfast room and bar and office where a friendly staff is on hand throughout the day into the evening. Most units have terraces, many have kitchens, and all are only a short walk from the attractive seafront and old-town attractions.
Chiasso Carmelano 1, Monopoli. albergodiffusomonopoli.it. ✆ **0809/678-594.** 20 units. 65€–150€. 2- to 3-night minimum stay some periods. **Amenities:** Bar; free Wi-Fi.

B&B Palazzo Paciotti ♥♥ A restored palace in Trani's old quarter near the cathedral oozes history, but beyond the rich stone facade, large, high-ceilinged spaces on the third floor (with elevator) are spruce and modern. Low beds sit on tiled floors, and modern bathrooms gleam with mosaic tiles. Breakfast is served in an upper-floor sunroom with terrace, shared with the slightly more stylish **Le Dimore del Re** (✆ **393/019-2208**) on another floor of the palace.
Via della Giudea 41, Trani. bbtrani.com. ✆ **340/238-8121.** 5 units. 115€–125€ double. Rates include breakfast. **Amenities:** Free Wi-Fi.

Corteinfiore ♥♥ SEAFOOD A few outdoor rooms meander through the courtyard of an old palace near Trani's port, covered in winter and full of greenery offsetting chic white furnishings. The menu is a fish fancier's delight, with antipasti of fresh sashimi and sushi or a cooked chef's choice selection, depending on what's fresh; follow-ups are a few grilled choices and pastas and risottos laden with seafood.
Via Ognissanti 18, Trani. corteinfiore.it. ✆ **0883/508-402.** Main courses 25€–35€. Tues–Sat 12:30–2:15pm and 8–10:30pm, Sun 12:30–2:15pm.

Hotel Seggio ♥♥ The former 17th-century town hall of Vieste provides a picturesque clifftop perch for soaking in the drama and beauty of the Gargano region. Many of the basic but comfortable rooms take in the views from private balconies, while an elevator descends to a pool and private beach. The intriguing old town is just outside the door.
Via Vesta 7, Vieste. hotelseggio.it. ✆ **0884/708123.** 25 units. 220€–270€ double. Week-long stays may be required in summer; 2-night minimum other times. Rates include breakfast. Closed Dec to mid-Apr. **Amenities:** Bar; snack bar; pool; garage; free Wi-Fi.

THE VALLE D'ITRIA: *TRULLO* COUNTRY ♥♥

The Valle d'Itria is a magical place, where cone-shaped stone *trulli* houses poke above olive groves and instill a sense of wonder. *Trulli* are sprinkled over farms and fields throughout this part of Puglia, and more than 1,600 beehive houses line the hilly winding lanes of Alberobello, the town at the heart of the Valle d'Itria that's earned UNESCO World Heritage Site status for its architectural distinction. As if this weren't enough, roads heading south through the Valle d'Itria lead to a string of hilltop towns built of gleaming white stone.

Alberobello ♥♥♥

69km (43 miles) NE of Matera, 55km (34 miles) SE of Bari, 80km (50 miles) NW of Brindisi

Alberobello has 1,620 *trulli,* and the effect is whimsical, even a bit weird. Walking through the narrow streets, you can't help but feel you've stepped into the pages of a fairy tale or a scene from *The Hobbit.* You'll be forgiven for making a crack or two, in the vein of "These are *trulli* charming." Just don't think you're clever—the residents of Alberobello have heard it all.

Most of Alberobello's *trulli* (from the Greek *troulos,* "dome") date from the mid-16th century to the 19th century, when they proliferated for two reasons: They were easy to build, with stones put in place without mortar, and their design was flexible. At first the conical-roofed stone huts were shelters for farmers in the fields, but in Alberobello the *trullo* became the standard for homes. Local lore has it that the technique became popular because residents could swiftly dismantle their *trulli* when tax inspectors came around; more likely is the theory that since no mortar was used, the structures didn't qualify for full taxation. With thick stone walls supporting a conical roof, *trulli* could only be single-room structures—each roof corresponds with a single room below—but many *trulli* are clustered together to create multi-room residences.

A row of conical roofed *trulli* houses in Alberobello, a UNESCO World Heritage site.

ESSENTIALS

ARRIVING From Bari by **car,** head south on S100 and then east (signposted) on S172. A parking lot off Largo Martellotta charges about 2€ an hour; a machine dispenses a ticket to place on your dashboard. From Bari by **bus** and **train,** Ferrovia del Sud Est (FSE; fseonline.it) runs hourly (every 2 hr. Sun), taking about 1¾ hours; most trips are by bus, though some require a change to a train in Putignano.

VISITOR INFORMATION For many travelers, Alberobello offers a first taste of the Puglia region (for regional info, visit **viaggiareinpuglia.it**).

Alberobello's small municipal **tourist** office, in Via Brigata Regina, just off Largo Martellotta (comunealberobello.it; ✆ **080/432-1200**), is open daily 10am to 5:30pm (Sun until 8:30pm), with a midday closure from 1 to 2:30pm.

EXPLORING ALBEROBELLO

You need an hour or two to tour the *trulli,* starting from **Largo Martellotta,** an airy square that separates the two *trulli* zones. **Rione Monti,** to the south, is the larger and busier of the two; many of its *trulli* are now coffee bars and, of course, gift shops. It's hard to resist leaving Alberobello without a small-scale replica of a *trullo,* crafted in the same type of stone that the town's builders used. Once you've adjusted to the whimsy, cross the square and walk northeast up the hill into quiet, residential **Rione Aia Piccola,** which seems much more like a quaint village. From Aia Piccola's hillside, you'll get a great view across the valley to the spectacle of Monti's hundreds upon hundreds of densely packed *trulli.*

The most monumental house in town is the **Trullo Sovrano,** on the far northern edge of modern Alberobello at Piazza Sacramento 10 (trullosovrano.eu; ✆ **080/432-6030**). From Largo Martellotta, walk north into Piazza del Popolo and then follow Via Vittorio Emanuele north to Piazza Sacramento. This rare two-story *trullo* comprises 16 separate, joined structures surrounding a central *trullo* with a cupola. A prominent family built the compound, complete with stables, barns, and a farm court, in the late 18th century. It later became headquarters for a religious confraternity and today shows off *trulli* domestic life, with a bread-baking oven and quaintly furnished rooms. It's open daily 10am to 12:45pm and 3:30 to 6:30pm (until 6pm Nov–Mar). Admission is 2.50€.

In Trullo Sovrano, visitors can explore life inside a traditional *trullo* home.

As you walk around town, notice the sculpted pinnacles, or finials, atop many *trulli.* These probably advertised which *trullaro* (*trulli* craftsman) built the house. Some *trulli* have artwork on the sides of their roofs, often traditional pagan, Jewish, and Christian symbols—look for a radiant orb, representing the sun and Christ, or a heart with an arrow through it, depicting the heartache of the Virgin Mary.

Cooking Like a *Nonna* in Alberobello

Alberobello is an evocative setting in which to enjoy *cucina povera,* literally "poor kitchen," based on whatever ingredients are on hand. This often means pasta made with local durum wheat, sauces based on fresh vegetables, and a garnish of fried breadcrumbs instead of more expensive Parmigiano. For a hands-on experience with cucina povera, take a 1½-hour cooking class with Nonna Maria at **Trulli del Bosco** (trullidelbosco.com; ✆ **338/423-9369**) in the pleasant countryside just outside of town; classes start at 60€. The property also has accommodation in four *trulli,* each sleeping two to three people, set amid gardens equipped with a swimming pool (130€–150€ double, breakfast included).

WHERE TO STAY & EAT IN ALBEROBELLO

While it's easy to see the appeal of staying in a setting as unique as the *trulli* zone, remember that you will essentially be stepping onto a Disney-like stage set, with thousands of selfie-taking gawkers trooping up and down the narrow streets. On the other hand, once the day-trippers leave, having the strange townscape almost to yourself is a magical experience.

For a quick bite on the main square, step into **Braceria La Fontana 1914** at Largo Martellotta 55 (✆ **380/369-6969**), a butcher shop that also grills meat to order and serves *bombette,* pork shoulder wrapped around melted cheese and spiced with herbs. It's open daily 11am to 11pm.

La Cantina ♥♥ PUGLIESE The Lippolis family has been satisfying local appetites since 1958. Their homey, stone-walled eatery just outside the *trulli* district is such an institution that the street out front is named for them. Owner-chef Francesco usually sends out some delicious *bruschetta,* on thick local bread with rich olive oil and fresh tomatoes and mozzarella, perhaps followed by local *salumi* and *burrata.* The pork from nearby Martina Franca is grilled to perfection. La Cantina has only seven tables, so booking is essential, even in the winter.

Vico Lippolis 8. ✆ **080/432-3473.** Main courses 9€–15€. Wed–Mon 12:30–3pm and 8–10:30pm. Closed 2 weeks in Feb and 2 weeks in July.

Masseria Torre Coccaro ♥♥♥ You can jump from one architectural experience to another with a 45-minute drive northeast from Alberobello over to the coast, where this centuries-old *masseria,* a fortified farm compound, offers an experience as transporting as the *trulli.* Accommodations are tucked into haylofts and towers, and in the case of the cavernous Orange Garden suite, carved out of a rocky hillside. All surround citrus-scented gardens and a lake-like swimming pool. Dining is in an elegantly transformed stable block; cooking lessons are available.

Contrada Coccaro 8, Savelletri di Fasano. masseriatorrecoccaro.com. ✆ **080/482-9310.** 39 units. 325€–680€ double. Rates include breakfast. **Amenities:** Restaurant; bar; babysitting; bikes; exercise room; pool; room service; spa; free Wi-Fi.

Trulli e Puglia B&B ♥♥ A cluster of well-restored *trulli* in the heart of the Monti district shows off the stonework and conical beehive ceilings that make these dwellings so distinctive. Several are two stories, with sleeping lofts atop spiral staircases, and all sport rustic furnishings and wood finishes for a cozy atmosphere. All units have fridges and a few have kitchenettes, plus such modern conveniences as air-conditioning (not really necessary, given the thick walls and stone roofs) and surprisingly spacious, nicely appointed bathrooms. Innkeeper Mimmo and his staff provide a welcome that's as memorable as the architecture.

Via Monte San Michele 58. trulliepuglia.com. ✆ **080/432-4376.** 6 units. 105€–135€ double. Rates include breakfast. 2-night minimum stay. Closed Nov–Dec. **Amenities:** Bar; free Wi-Fi.

Trullo d'Oro ♥♥♥ PUGLIESE In a suite of warmly decorated *trulli,* chef Davide Girolamo presents a fresh take on *cucina povera.* His menu uses local seasonal ingredients, elevating the fava bean in many variations, and highlights such simple specialties as *burrata pugliese,* a soft, creamy mozzarella cousin encased in a skin of velvety curd, and *orecchiette* with a ragù of donkey. Seafood also comes into play, with a creamy *baccalà* and *puree di fave bianche con polpo,* steamed octopus served atop fava beans.

Via Felice Cavallotti 27. ristorantetrullodoro.com. ✆ **080/432-1820.** Main courses 14€–25€. Tues–Sat noon–2:30pm and 8–10:30pm; Sun noon–2:30pm.

A SIDE TRIP TO THE GROTTE DI CASTELLANA

The **Grotte di Castellana ♥♥**, 17km (11 miles) north of Alberobello via SS172 and SS237, is a vast network of caves, 3,350m (11,050 ft.) long and 125m (412 ft.) deep, carved out over centuries by water streaming through the limestone that underlies this part of Puglia. The caves' vastness and eerie light have given rise to all sorts of legends of demons and lost souls floating through the depths. A series of paths winds through underground rooms with names like the **Grave, Corridoio del Serpent,** and **Corridoio del Deserto,** filled with stalagmites and stalactites, and lead to the majestic **Grotta Bianca,** where walls gleam with white alabaster and the rock formations are translucent. Visits are only by guided tours, offered in Italian, English, French, and German; hours vary from 9am to noon in winter to 9am to 7pm in summer (grottedicastellana.it; ✆ **080/4998221**). From November to February, the caves are open by reservation only. Admission is 20€ for a 2-hour tour (17€ ages 6–14, free for children 5 and under); a slightly cheaper 1-hour tour does not include the Grotta Bianca. Bring an extra layer: It's 16° to 18°C (61°–64°F) in the caves year-round.

The White Cities

South of Alberobello lie a string of hill towns hewn out of light-colored stone, so glaringly bright in the sun that they're collectively known as the "white cities." **By car,** head south through the Valle d'Itria along SS172 to

Locorotondo and Martina Franca, and from there make short detours to Cisternino, Ostuni, and Ceglie Messapica; the towns are all well signposted, and you can easily visit all five in a couple of days. Ostuni is on the Adriatic **railway** line (trenitalia.com), while Locorotondo and Martina Franca are connected to Bari and Alberobello by frequent Ferrovie del Sud Est **bus** service (fseonline.it). Ceglie Messapica and Cisternino are both on the Martina Franca-Lecce train line. Service throughout the region is frequent, and the Ferrovie del Sud Est website makes planning fairly easy. Be forewarned, however, that various bus companies may use different bus stops, and finding the right one is not always easy. Bars, *tabacchi,* and travel offices that sell tickets can direct you to the right place, and tourist offices are also usually helpful in sorting out stops and schedules.

LOCOROTONDO ♥♥♥

8km (5 miles) SE of Alberobello

As you approach this cheerful little town you might think you're seeing a mirage: A ring of bright white houses with pointed gable roofs (called *cummerse*) crowns the top of a hill. From a distance the scene looks a little like a rimrock canyon from the American West, or the gabled skyline of a Hanseatic port on the Baltic Sea—except, of course, for the baroque church domes rising above the rooftops. Locorotondo means "round place," and once inside the gates you'll see why: Streets of light-colored stone are flanked by white houses that hug the contours of the hilltop in near-perfect concentric circles. Surrounding them are the old protective walls, skirted by a ring road from which you can see far across the plains

Locorotondo.

below—a view that earns Locorotondo the nickname "balcony of the Valle d'Itria."

Locorotondo is famous for its eponymous white wine, which you can sample in any of the restaurants and bars in town. The town's **tourist office,** at Piazza Vittorio Emanuele 27 (✆ **080/431-3099**), is usually open Tuesday through Sunday 9am to 1pm and 4 to 7pm.

MARTINA FRANCA ♥♥

6km (4 miles) S of Locorotondo, 14km (9 miles) S of Alberobello

This lively hill town with its baroque finery and whitewashed back alleys was founded in the 10th century by coastal residents fleeing Saracen attacks along the Adriatic and Ionian coasts. The *centro storico* is an intriguing tangle of medieval lanes that lead from one pretty piazza into another in a confusing fashion deliberately designed to confuse plunderers.

The **tourist office** at Piazza XX Settembre no. 3 (viaggiareinpuglia.it; ✆ **080/411-6554**) is usually open Monday through Friday 10am to 1pm and 5 to 8pm, and Saturday and Sunday 9:30am to 1pm and 4:30 to 8:30pm. You can't drive in Martina Franca's *centro storico,* but you can park a few blocks away on Via Giuseppe Aprile, Via Gabriele d'Annunzio, Piazza Francesco Crispi, Piazza Umberto, or Via Verdi.

At the center of town are two adjoining squares, Piazza Plebiscito and Piazza Immacolata. Rising above **Piazza Plebiscito** is the **Basilica di San Martino ♥♥** (basilicasanmartino.it; ✆ **080/4306536;** free admission; Apr–Oct daily 8am 11pm, Nov–Mar daily 8am–noon and 4pm–9pm), its facade richly adorned with baroque relief sculptures depicting episodes from the life of St. Martin. The most famous scene shows the saint, a Hungarian soldier in the Roman legions, meeting a poor beggar on a chilly November night and cutting his military cloak in half with his sword to keep the beggar warm. Martin's feast day on November 11th coincides with the grape harvest, earning him the honor of patron saint of wine. Also in the square is the **municipal clock tower,** erected in 1734, with a *meridiana* (sundial) inscribed on an eye-level plaque. In pretty **Piazza Immacolata,** a landmark beneath the gracefully elliptical arcades is century-old **Caffè Tripoli,** Via Garibaldi 12 (✆ **080/480-5260**), where the specialty is *granita di caffè* (espresso with

Martina Franca's baroque Basilica di San Martino.

whipped cream). **Via Cavour,** leading south from Piazza Immacolata, is the main street of the Lama, the old quarter. Lining the handsome street are baroque *palazzi,* with fanciful arches and balconies, often loaded with stone cherubs. On and off Via Cavour (and also north of the two piazzas) is a maze of whitewashed back streets, impossibly narrow passageways, and blind alleys.

The town's culinary specialty is *capocollo di Martina Franca,* cured pork cut from the top of the neck where it meets the shoulder, and dried with local wine, herbs, and wood smoke. Butcher/deli **Romanelli,** just off Piazza XX Settembre at Via Valle d'Itria 8–12 (macelleriaromanelli.it; ✆ **080/480-5385**), usually gives a tasting of its *capocollo,* and you can buy it sliced by the *etto* (100 grams).

CISTERNINO ♥♥

10km (6¼ miles) E of Locorotondo, 12km (7 miles) NE of Martina Franca

Like its near neighbor Locorotondo, this sunny whitewashed hilltop town is smaller and quainter than Martina Franca and Ostuni, without the spread of their modern outskirts. Before plunging into the labyrinth of medieval lanes that converge in central Piazza Vittorio, stop to enjoy the views over the Valle d'Itria from the base of the **Torre Normanno Sveva,** at the edge of the ridge on which the town is built.

Cisternino is famous for its Fornelli Pronti—literally, "ready ovens," holdovers from the times when butchers operated communal ovens where meat was grilled upon purchase. Shops all over town still do the honors, grilling *bombetti*—pork or veal crusted in breadcrumbs and Parmigiano and rolled around caciocavallo cheese—and serving them at outside tables, alongside other grilled meats and carafes of local red wine. One popular spot is **Zio Pietro,** Via Duca d'Aosta 3 (facebook.com/daziopietro; ✆ **080/444-8300**).

OSTUNI ♥♥

16km (10 miles) E of Martina Franca

Other nearby towns may bill themselves as "white cities," but they're positively beige compared to Ostuni. Practically blinding in the summer sun, perched atop a commanding hill 8km (5 miles) above the Adriatic coast, Ostuni makes it clear you're close to Greece. Ancient Greeks, in fact, are among the many invaders and occupiers who came here over the past 2,500 years, though the town's mazelike streets and arched steps tumbling down hillsides are mostly medieval. Especially beneficent to Ostuni over the ages were two female rulers, Isabella of Aragon and her daughter, Bona Sforza, who in the 16th century made the city a cultured outpost and added walls and lookout towers along the coast, where beacon fires were lit to warn of approaching pirates.

In **Piazza della Libertà,** at the foot of the hill to which the oldest part of town clings, look for the statue of Sant'Oronzo high atop La Colonna di Sant'Oronzo. The patron saint of nearby Lecce, Oronzo is honored here for allegedly saving Ostuni from the plague twice, in 1657 and 1771. On a warm weekend night, everyone from miles around gathers in the piazza beneath the saint to chat, stroll, and sit in the cafes. From Piazza della Libertà, **Via Cattedrale** winds up through *la città Bianca* to the hilltop Gothic **Duomo,** with its marble facade swooping into a gracious curve on one side; it's open daily 10am to noon and 3 to 6pm (admission 1€). Above a doorway to the left of the main entrance, Oronzo appears again, this time cradling Ostuni in his protective arms. For the best views of the town, follow Corso Vittorio Emanuele south from Piazza della Libertà to the overlook on one side of Piazza Martiri delle Foibe.

The narrow back streets of Ostuni resemble those of a charming Greek village.

The **tourist office** at Corso Mazzini 6 (comune.ostuni.br.it; ✆ **083/339627**) is open daily 10am to 1pm and 3pm to 6pm, keeping longer hours in summer.

CEGLIE MESSAPICA ♥♥

13km (8 miles) SW of Ostuni

A bit farther afield, this quiet town is older than the other White Cities, having been founded by seafaring Greeks in the 7th century B.C.E. The town flourished again in the 16th century under the kingdom of Naples, and a large hilltop castle, **Castello Ducale,** was enlarged, with the old town encircling it in a maze of narrow lanes. Surrounded by miles of rich farmland, vineyards, and olive groves, the town today is a prosperous-looking ensemble of three elegant squares surrounded by narrow streets lined with cubical whitewashed houses that look almost Moorish. The local bounty shows up in market stalls and restaurants around town; a staple is the *biscotto cegliese,* a biscuit made with almond paste and a hint of lemon. The helpful **tourist office** is in the oldest part of town, near the castle, at via G. Elia 16 (viaggiareinpuglia.it; ✆ **0831/371003**); it's open daily in summer 9am to 1pm and 4 to 9pm, with shorter hours the rest of the year.

WHERE TO STAY IN THE WHITE CITIES

A good source for stays in *masserie,* farmhouses near the White Cities and scattered around Puglia, is **masseriedimoresalento.com**.

La Sommità Relais ♥♥ A 16th-century fortified *palazzo* on a lane behind Ostuni's Duomo is full of hidden charms within thick stucco walls. On the ground floor, stylish lounges and an elegant restaurant occupy a maze of high arched rooms opening to a walled garden with a plunge pool; upstairs a sea-view terrace, a perfect spot for cocktails, sits on the ramparts. Some of the sleek, contemporary-styled, guest rooms, done in soothing cream tones with stone accents, have terraces facing the plain and seashore below, while others surround interior courtyards; most have deep soaking tubs and other luxuries (one has a fireplace). In summer a car shuttles guests to a private beach on the nearby coast

Via Scipione Petrarolo 7, Ostuni. relaischateaux.com. ✆ **0831/305925.** 15 units. 450€–650€ double. Rates include breakfast. Closed Nov–Mar. **Amenities:** Bar; restaurant; spa; free Wi-Fi.

Masseria Salinola ♥♥♥ A centuries-old walled olive estate outside Ostuni welcomes guests with stylish rooms and suites fashioned from an old salt warehouse; they're full of arches, stonework, and weathered beams, and enhanced with luxurious beds and well-curated family pieces. A former stable is now a character-filled, hearth-warmed lounge and dining room that spills onto a terrace in warmer months; a pool is set in lush gardens full of palm-shaded nooks. Though the historic town is just a short drive away, a family-style dinner of local favorites made with garden-fresh ingredients, served most evenings, is a good reason to stay put in such relaxing surroundings.

3km (2 miles) south of Ostuni off SP 29. masseriasalinola.it. ✆ **0831/308330.** 7 units. 220€–430€ double. Rates include breakfast. Closed Dec to mid-Mar. **Amenities:** Restaurant; bar; pool; free Wi-Fi.

Palazzo Camarda ♥♥ A meticulously renovated old palace high up in the historic district of Ceglie Messipica overlooks an airy piazza and the countryside beyond. The six large, beautifully furnished rooms and suites are each different; one has a balcony sitting room, and another is a cozy rooftop aerie that opens to a huge terrace. All come with an excellent breakfast served in a vaulted salon.

Largo Ognissanti 2, Ceglie Messipica. palazzocamarda.com. ✆ **0831/380-575.** 6 units. 90€–140€ double. **Amenities:** Bar; free Wi-Fi.

Sotto le Cummerse ♥♥♥ In welcoming Locorotondo, visitors can live like locals in distinctive lodgings tucked into houses around the old town. All are different, ranging from simple ground-floor studios to multilevel suites, and all are nicely furnished in traditional style and make the most of stone walls, fireplaces, and other vintage details. Many have terraces, and all have up-to-date bathrooms, some equipped with Jacuzzis. Breakfast is served in a welcoming room near the reception, where the accommodating staff is on hand well into the evening hours.

Via Vittorio Emanuele 138, Locorotondo. sottolecummerse.it. ✆ **080/431-3298.** 13 units. 100€–150€ double. Rates include breakfast. Closed part of Jan. **Amenities:** Free Wi-Fi.

WHERE TO EAT IN THE WHITE CITIES

La Tavernetta ♥♥ PUGLIESE Step down off the busy main street of Martina Franca into this arched, white-walled cellar and you're transported to old Puglia, where veteran waiters dispense one traditional Pugliese classic after another, at decidedly old-fashioned prices. House specialties include *fave e cicoria* (pureed fava beans with sautéed chicory), *orecchiette al ragù* (handmade ear-shaped semolina pasta with a robust sauce), and *braciole* (sliced veal stuffed with parsley, cheese, and garlic, simmered in tomato sauce).

Via Vittorio Emanuele 30, Martina Franca. ✆ **080/430-6323.** Main courses 9€–17€. Tues–Sun 12:30–2:45pm and 7:30–11:30pm.

Osteria del Tempo Perso ♥♥ PUGLIESE Even in its former guise as a bakery, the *osteria* "of lost time" must have been a charming presence in Ostuni, its rough-hewn walls carved out of a cave. Today, linen-topped tables spread into an atmospheric adjoining room, hung with old farm implements and beautiful local ceramics. In this colorful setting, just around the corner from the Duomo, the food sticks close to local tradition, with lots of Adriatic seafood. Try the house's special casserole, *tegamino di funghi,* with bread, mushrooms, and zucchini flowers. The kitchen shares its passion for local cuisine in frequent cooking classes.

Via G. Tanzarella Vitale 47, Ostuni. osteriadeltempoperso.com. ✆ **0831/304819.** Main courses 12€–28€. Tues–Sun 12:30–2:45pm and 7:30–11:30pm.

Pizzeria Casa Pinto ♥♥ PIZZERIA It's probably not much of an exaggeration to say that on weekend nights most of Locorotondo fills these tiny rooms, one of them taken up by a huge pizza oven. Tables are tucked into a cavelike vaulted cellar and a rooftop terrace, and the pizzas are almost as distinctive, made with local organic products. Some are topped so lightly with olive oil and cheese that they seem more like savory baked bread than pizza. Other toppings are more traditional, and any choice should be washed down with the town's signature white wine.

Via Aprile 23, Locorotondo. pizzeriacasapinto.it. ✆ **346/431-7510.** Pizzas 7€–12€. Wed–Mon noon–3pm and 7pm–midnight.

LECCE ♥♥

113km (68 miles) SE of Alberobello, 40km (25 miles) SE of Brindisi

Sophisticated Lecce combines baroque architecture and urbane elegance with typical southern Italian radiance. The handsome old city center is clad almost entirely in warm golden limestone, amplified by *il barocco leccese*—a particularly ebullient version of 17th-century Italy's fondness for architectural decoration. Because the local limestone is fairly soft and easy to chisel, sculptors covered church facades and civic palaces with saints, angels, and intricate details as if they were drawing on paper. While it's tempting to describe the stone as "buttery," "milky" is more apt—milk was applied to the final work, to seep into the stone's pores and harden it.

Lecce has more to show off than this flamboyant architecture. Founded by Greeks more than 2,200 years ago, the city has a Roman theater and amphitheater, the bastions of the 16th-century **Castello Carlo V** (Castle of Charles V, the Habsburg Holy Roman Emperor), and several proudly formidable city gates that boast of Lecce's longtime prominence in southern Italy. Lecce is often promoted as the "Florence of the South," but the city's identity is southern Italian through and through, and the local economy is still more reliant on agriculture—especially olive oil and wine—than on tourism. Lecce is a pleasant base for day trips around the rest of the Salento, the southernmost, seagirt region of Puglia that comprises the heel of the Italian boot.

Essentials

ARRIVING Six direct high-speed **trains** connect Lecce with Rome in about 5½ hours, 8½ to 11 hours by regular service, usually with a change or two. Lecce also has frequent train service to Bari (1½ hr.) and Brindisi (30 min.). Visit trenitalia.com for schedules and information. **Ferrovie del Sud Est** trains (fseonline.it) connect Lecce and other parts of Puglia, with runs to and from Ceglie Messipica, Cisternino, Martina Franca, Gallipoli, and other towns. Note that Lecce's train station is about 1.5km (1 mile) from the heart of the old quarter; from the train station, buses 11, 12, and 14 operated by Società Gestione Mobilità Lecce (sgmlecce.it) run to Porta Napoli at the edge of the *centro storico.* The fare is 1.20€ and tickets are sold at newsstands, or buy them on board for 1.50€. If you want to store your bags at the station, make arrangements with **radicalstorage.com** (5€ a bag per day).

If you're traveling by **car** from the north, follow signs to Brindisi, then take state highway SS613 south to Lecce (38km/24 miles). Most of the center is closed to car traffic and parking is extremely limited; it's best to leave your car in one of the large lots in Piazza Muratore or Piazza Giuseppe Libertini, where you'll pay about 1.50€ an hour. You can most likely make parking arrangements with your hotel for one of these lots in advance.

VISITOR INFORMATION A **tourist office** is at Piazza Duomo 2 (infolecce.it; ✆ **0832/521-877**); it's open daily 9am to 10pm. The office also operates an **info-point** in the Sedile, on Piazza Sant'Oronzo, open the same hours.

Exploring Lecce

A stroll around Lecce begins in monumental **Piazza Sant'Oronzo.** The **Colonna Romana,** the C.E.-2nd-century Roman column that rises above the square, once stood near its mate in Brindisi, where together they marked the end of the Appian Way. Lightning toppled this column in

Roman amphitheater in Lecce.

1528, and the Brindisians left it lying on the ground until 1661, when the citizens of Lecce bought it. Atop the capital is a statue of St. Oronzo, the city's patron saint, who miraculously delivered Lecce from a plague in 1658; his saint day is August 26, when the city shuts down for a festival that fills the streets with concerts, light displays, and food stalls. At the southern side of the piazza stand the remains of a **Roman amphitheater.** Archaeologists can't agree on its date—it's either Augustan (1st c. B.C.E., thus predating the Roman Colosseum) or Trajanic-Hadrianic (C.E. 2nd c.). It would have accommodated 25,000 fans, who came to watch bloody fights between gladiators and wild beasts. You can get a good view of the amphitheater from the square, and it's sometimes open for a closer look, usually in summer from 10am to noon and 3 to 7pm; admission is free. Wrapped around a curve of the amphitheater is the perfectly proportioned **Palazzo del Seggio,** or **Il Sedile,** built in 1592 as the seat (*sede*) of the city government. A tourist info-point is now set in its arched loggia.

You'll get a good overview of Lecce around the corner at **Museo Civico Citta di Lecce** (**MUST**), a wide-ranging collection that takes a look at the city's long history, along with showing off some stunning contemporary art and photography, in the Monastery of Santa Chiara at Via Ammirati 11 (mustlecce.it; ✆ **0832/241-067**); the museum is open Tuesday through Sunday 9am to 9pm (mid-Oct to mid-Apr it closes 7pm weekdays, 8pm weekends); admission is 8€ and free for children 9 and under.

Nearby is Lecce's **Roman Theater,** off Via Ammirati south of Piazza Sant'Oronzo, constructed sometime between the late 1st century B.C.E. and the early C.E. 2nd century. It holds about 5,000 spectators and is still used for plays and concerts. You can step into the theater as part of a visit to the adjacent **Museo del Teatro Romano** (itersalento.it/museo-teatro-romano; ✆ **0832/279196;** Tues–Sun 10am–6pm; admission 3€). To the west of Piazza Sant'Oronzo is a string of extravagantly baroque churches. To get an eyeful of them, follow Via Vittorio Emanuele and its continuation, Via Giuseppe Libertini, past the Duomo to the 18th-century Porta Rudiae. The first church you come to on Via Vittorio Emanuele, the **Chiesa di Sant'Irene,** dates to 1591; priest-architect Francesco Grimaldi designed it with the same flair he showed with his baroque landmarks in Naples and Rome, adorning the facade with columns, niches, statues, and a wolf from the town's coat of arms. St. Irene, who stands above the portal, was Lecce's patron saint before Oronzo. Lecce's first telegraph station was installed in the tower in the mid-19th century, while the nave became a community meeting hall during the unification of Italy. Farther up on Via Libertini, the 17th-century **Chiesa di Santa Teresa** (✆ **0832/332699**) has also served multiple humble purposes, as a police barracks, a school, and a tobacco warehouse, despite its fanciful facade by master sculptor Giuseppe Zimbalo (see the Duomo and Santa Croce, below). The facade, though unfinished, features an exuberance of columns and statuary, among them the two Saint Johns, the Baptist and the Evangelist. Inside is what might be the town's most macabre work of art, a lifelike statue of a bloodied, emaciated Christ lying in a coffinlike glass box. By comparison, the **Basilica di San Giovanni Battista,** a few steps up Via Libertini (✆ **0832/308-540**), is a joyful place, where cherubs float through the light-filled interior. Admission to most of Lecce's churches is free, and they're generally open daily from 7am to 1pm and 3:30 to 7pm.

For more layers of Lecce's history, descend through **Museo Faggiano,** Via Ascanio Grande (museofaggiano.it; ✆ **0832/300-528**), privately run by a family who bought a modest building and beneath it discovered ancient tombs, a Roman granary, and the embalming rooms of a Franciscan convent, now displaying a wealth of found artifacts. Admission is 5€, 3€ for ages 8 to 16, and free for children 7 and under; open daily 9:30am to 8pm.

Basilica di Santa Croce ♥♥ CHURCH The *barocco leccese* hits fever pitch at Santa Croce (Holy Cross) basilica, where sculptors crammed the facade with lions, angels, sea creatures, goddesses—hundreds of figures in all, crowding the columned tiers. Most significant might be the turbaned Turks, whose forces menaced Lecce and the rest of southern Europe for centuries before being defeated at the Battle of Lepanto in 1571. Beasts and figures on the lower tiers represent the Christian forces that conquered the Turks (the griffon stands for the Republic of Genoa; Hercules represents the dukes of Tuscany). It's okay if you don't understand much of the iconography—just stand out front and soak in the spectacle. The facade is the work of three generations of local masons; most notable is master Giuseppe Zimbalo (1620–1710), also known as Lo Zingarello, the "Tiny Gypsy." His son, Francesco, did the portals and some beautiful work in the interior, including his richly carved tomb of local saint Francesco di Paolo, an animal-loving hermit friar much like St. Francis of Assisi. You'll see scenes of his most acclaimed miracles, including restoring life to a roasted lamb and a fried trout; the envy of sailors, he could hoist up his robes to catch a breeze and sail across the sea.

Via Umberto I. basilicasantacrocelecce.it. ✆ **0832/241957.** Admission 11€ adults with Duomo (5€ ages 17 and under), 21€ adults (13€ ages 17 and under) with Duomo and Duomo Campanile. Daily 9am–9pm (until 6pm Oct–Mar).

Duomo ♥♥ CHURCH Lecce's cathedral stands in an almost completely enclosed square, a setting both dramatic and practical. In times of siege, residents would take refuge in the huge piazza, with its narrow entrances that could be completely closed off. Giuseppe Zimbalo, one of the creators of Santa Croce (above), also reworked the facade of the 12th-century cathedral, embellishing it with sculpted saints and other figures. Lecce's patron St. Oronzo makes another appearance high above the entrance. Zimbalo also designed the adjacent **campanile,** which towers 64m (210 ft.) above the piazza, ascending in tiers like a wedding cake.

St. Oronzo, Lecce's patron saint, presides over the Duomo's ornate facade.

The **seminary,** across the square, has a chiseled facade that could have been squirted out of a pastry tube, the work of Giuseppe Cino, a student of Zimbalo. The exuberant **Bishop's Palace** (Palazzo Vescovile), with its arches and saint-filled niches, is still home to Lecce's archbishops. The extravagance continues north up **Via Palmieri,** past a long line of sculpted palace facades to the triumphal arch of **Porta Napoli,** the main city gate, built in 1548 to honor a state visit from Holy Roman Emperor Charles V.

Piazza del Duomo. Via Vittorio Emanuele. cattedraledilecce.it. ✆ **0832/308557.** Admission 11€ with Santa Croce, 21€ with Santa Croce and Duomo Campanile. Daily 9am–9pm (until 6pm in winter).

Where to Stay in & Around Lecce

B&B Centro Storico ♥♥♥ Every inch of this beautifully restored lodging in a baroque palace in Lecce's historic center is carefully tended by the two proprietor brothers, Filippo and Alberto, who offer their guests the same attention. Centuries-old stone window frames were sculpted to capture maximum sunlight; baroque ceilings form *volte a stella,* star-shaped vaults; sleeping lofts rise above gleaming wood floors in salons-turned-suites. A mix of antiques and modern pieces add to the appeal of these character-filled, very comfortable spaces. Above is a rambling roof deck with a hot tub and a cottage-like guest room with private terrace. Breakfast is served in a nearby cafe.

Via A. Vignes 2, Lecce. centrostoricolecce.it. ✆ **0832/242-727.** 6 units. 100€–125€. Rates include breakfast. **Amenities:** Roof terrace; hot tub; free Wi-Fi.

B&B Corti Carmella ♥♥ Host Salvatore has meticulously restored an old mansion off the seafront in the historic center of Gallipoli (see p. 745). His guests are housed in character-filled, high-ceilinged, marble-floored rooms surrounding two courtyards that serve as shady lounges in pleasant weather. Salvatore's homemade breakfast is substantial, and restaurants, shops, and a strip of beach are an easy stroll away along the town's charming little lanes.

Via Franza 7, Gallipoli. corticarmela.it. ✆ **0833/262-100.** 5 units. 70€–180€. Rates include breakfast. **Amenities:** Bar; free Wi-Fi.

Hotel Residence Palazzo Baldi ♥♥ The three connected town houses that make up this unique inn do justice to the setting in charming

Galatina (see p. 745), a beautiful sleepy town about a half-hour south of Lecce. Lounges and terraces are welcoming, and each of the rooms and suites is different, furnished with antiques, full of arches and nooks and crannies, and overlooking courtyards and tranquil lanes.

Corte Baldi 2, Galatina. residence-palazzo-baldi.apuliahotelspage.com. ✆ **0836/568-345.** 14 units. 60€–95€ double. Rates include breakfast. **Amenities:** Bar; free Wi-Fi.

Palazzo dei Dondoli ♥♥♥ An elegant early-20th-century townhouse at the edge of the old city has been redone as a stylish retreat where rooms and suites surround a courtyard garden. Stone-walled guest quarters, including large ground-floor bedrooms and top-floor suites, are done with tasteful modern furnishings, warm wood trimmings, and luxurious amenities that include large walk-in showers; most open to outdoor spaces.

Via Sozy Carafa 20/a. palazzodeidondoli.it. ✆ **327/878-2456.** 7 units. 95€–180€. Rates include breakfast. **Amenities:** Courtyard lounge; free Wi-Fi.

Palazzo Rollo ♥♥ Stepping into the vine-covered courtyard of this 17th-century Lecce palace is like entering a world unto itself, the private domain of the Rollo clan for more than 200 years. In its current guise the old palace houses guests in a warren of suites that are more homey than luxurious, with tile floors, old-fashioned furnishings, and lots of nooks and crannies. Four ground-floor apartments off the courtyard were originally stone-vaulted storerooms. A luxuriant roof garden offers plenty of shade and a view over an adjacent bell tower and the *centro storico* rooftops.

Via Vittorio Emanuele II 14, Lecce. palazzorollo.it. ✆ **0832/3017152.** 4 suites, 4 apartments. 130€–190€ double. Rates include breakfast. **Amenities:** Free Wi-Fi.

Patria Palace Hotel ♥♥ Lecce's bastion of luxury has been pampering guests since 1797, and these days does so in richly upholstered and chicly appointed rooms to create a clublike lair that's especially popular with traveling business folk. Some windows of the old *palazzo* catch a glimpse of its flamboyant neighbor, the remarkably ornamented Santa Croce basilica. A few rooms have private terraces, while a roof garden is a perfect spot to enjoy a bottle of wine while admiring the baroque cityscape.

Piazzetta Riccardi 13, Lecce. patriapalace.com. ✆ **0832/245111.** 67 units. 225€–350€ double. Rates include breakfast. Closed mid-Jan to mid-Mar. **Amenities:** Restaurant; bar; concierge; room service; free Wi-Fi.

Where to Eat in Lecce

An almost mandatory stop in Lecce is **Natale,** at Via Trinchese 7A (natalepasticceria.it; ✆ **0832/202462**), for the town's best gelato and pastry. **Caffè Alvino,** on Piazza Sant'Oronzo (consolepsp.com/caffe-alvino; ✆ **0832/246-748**), is another popular *pasticceria* and bar. Both will introduce you to *pasticciotto*, the region's favorite sweet, a custard-filled pastry shell, as well as caffe Leccese, a shot of espresso combined with sweet almond syrup and served over ice. Lecce's large student population frequents pizzeria **La Succursale,** Viale dell'Università 15 (lasuccursale.it; ✆ **391/497-7749**), open Tuesday through Sunday 12:30 to 3:30pm and daily 6pm to midnight. **Quantobasta,** Via Marco Basseo 38 (quantobastalecce.com; ✆ **347/008-3176**), is an always-busy bar with a large choice of excellent cocktails.

Two local foods to look for are *puccia,* an oval sandwich stuffed with capers and dried or fresh tomatoes, cheese, and, among other fillings, tuna or anchovies that originated as a snack for Roman legionnaires, and *mariati,* pasta dressed with fresh tomato sauce and strong ricotta. For the most part, the food you'll encounter in trattorias is *cucina povera* (poor-man's cooking). That means a lot of fresh vegetables, with chickpeas (*ciceri*) and turnip greens (*rapa*) topping pasta. Horse meat, grilled and stewed, is a staple, but more appetizing is the bounty of fresh fish from the nearby seas. The **Awaiting Table** (awaitingtable.com; ✆ **347/676970**) offers day-long classes in Pugliese cooking, including a market visit and some sight-seeing; from 165€.

Alle Due Corti ♥♥♥ PUGLIESE These simple whitewashed rooms off two courtyards are a perfect backdrop for Pugliese cooking. The standout is *ciceri e tria,* a combination of pasta and chickpeas in which the pasta is lightly fried, a throwback to times when the added crunchiness compensated for a lack of meat. These days the kitchen, under the guidance of local gastronome Rosalba De Carlo, adds fresh seasonal vegetables and often seafood, and follows up with such simple concoctions as chicken baked in white wine and mussels with rice and potatoes. If you enjoy the meal, ask about Rosalba's cooking classes.

Corte dei Giugni 1. alleduecorti.com. ✆ **0832/242223.** Main courses 10€–18€. Mon–Sat 12:20–2pm and 7:20–10:30pm.

Doppiozero ♥ PUGLIESE Lecce shows off its hip, urbane side in this cafe/deli where repurposed bottles light long communal tables and local wines are stacked to the ceiling, alongside hams, long salamis, wheels of cheese, and vats of olive oil. These ingredients, also available for takeaway, find their way into sandwiches, deli boards, crostini, salads, soups, and a few daily pastas. The light fare is a hit with a crowd that doesn't seem to mind the rushed, indifferent service.

Via Paladini 2. facebook.com/doppiozerolecce. ✆ **0832/521-052.** Main courses 8€–14€. Daily 8:30am–12:30am.

Mamma Elvira Enoteca ♥♥ PUGLIESE The emphasis in this welcoming bar/shop is on wines, and you can introduce yourself to the production of the southeast from a selection of 250 vintages. You can also enjoy the cuisine of the region, with a nice choice of vegetable-rich pastas and seafood dishes made from traditional recipes.

Via Umberto I 19. mammaelvira.com. ✆ **0832/169-2011.** Main courses 9€–15€. Wed–Mon 12:30–3pm and 7–11:30pm.

Osteria Da Angiulino ♥♥ PUGLIESE These brightly tiled, vaulted rooms are Lecce's traditional outpost for *cucina povera.* Many of the dishes are vegetarian, including an appetizer of green beans and fava beans, parboiled to perfect crunchiness. The eggplant (*melanzane alla Parmigiana*) is a perfect meatless main-course follow-up. On the carnivorous side of the menu is horsemeat prepared in every way imaginable—as meatballs, chopped, filleted and topped with a green sauce, or in a savory stew. The house wine is as hearty and affordable as the cuisine.

Via Principe di Savoia 4. ✆ **0832/245146.** Main courses 7€–14€. Mon–Sat 12:45–3pm and 7:45–11pm.

Osteria Il Poeta Contadino ♥♥ PUGLIESE/SEAFOOD You'll be reminded that Lecce is almost on the Adriatic in this comfy little room with big glass windows facing a pretty little piazza. The freshest seafood shows up in a few well-done preparations each day, from sandwiches generously filled with filets of swordfish and fresh vegetables to *spaghetti alla vongole* (with clams). The name means "poet farmer," and true to the rural notion, there's a nice selection of land-based meat-and-vegetable-topped *bruschetta* and pastas with fresh vegetables, all accompanied by good local wines.

Piazzetta Castromediano 8. facebook.com/osteriailpoetacontadino. ✆ **392/540-2344.** Main courses 8€–16€. Tues–Sun noon–3pm and 6:30–11pm.

Trattoria Nonna Tetti ♥♥ PUGLIESE Warm and inviting, with lots of tile and stone, this is another outpost for local cooking. The big menu also expands into the rest of Italy, but the standouts are strictly Leccese, like *ricciarelle* pasta with cherry tomatoes, garlic, and cheese, or wild chicory with a purée of boiled fava beans.

Piazzetta Regina Maria 17. ✆ **0832/246036.** Main courses 8€–15€. Daily noon–3pm and 7:30–11pm.

Lecce Shopping

Cartoleria Pantheon Lecce, Via Giuseppe Libertini 69 (manufactuslecce.com; ✆ **0832/521312**), offers Florence-worthy leather and paper goods, from iPhone cases and datebooks to briefcases and bags. Papier-mâché is a local craft, and the material is often fashioned into Madonnas and saints. You'll find papier-mâché items in shops around town, and to see a true artisan at work, stop in the workshop of **Marco Epicochi** at Piazza Duomo 18 (✆ **327/282-4185**).

Lecce Beaches

The most popular beach for locals is at **San Cataldo,** 15km (9 miles) east on SP364, where a long stretch of sand borders the **San Cataldo reserve,** formerly malaria-infested swampland that's now green pine and eucalyptus forest. Another 8km (5 miles) south on SP366, the **Cesine nature preserve** (riservalecesine.it) has trails that lead across wetlands and through forests to remote beaches.

Side Trips from Lecce

GALATINA ♥♥

28km (16 miles) SW of Lecce

Deep in the sunbaked hinterland between Lecce and Gallipoli is the remarkably attractive little town of **Galatina,** 28km (16 miles) southwest of Lecce. Artisans of the *barocco leccese* went to work here, too, elaborately decorating the churches and palaces lining the narrow lanes and sunny squares to create a playful uniformity with the light stone. The town is also credited with inventing Puglia's ubiquitous pastry, the *pasticciotto,* a custard-filled shell. You can try one at **Pasticceria Ascalone** at Via Vittorio Emanuele 17 (instagram.com/ascalone_1740; ✆ **0836/566-009**) but go early, because they usually sell out.

GALLIPOLI ♥♥♥

52km (32 miles) E of Otranto, 30km (18 miles) SE of Lecce

The wave-washed old town of Gallipoli is a photogenic concoction of white houses and churches crammed onto a small island, connected by one bridge to the new town on the mainland. Greeks founded the once-thriving port, and Normans built a fortress on the islet's eastern edge. The old town's meandering lanes open into squares lined with baroque palaces and churches, and on the north side a sandy beach stretches beneath 14th-century seawalls.

Punta Prosciutto beach.

For many visitors, the real attractions are the beautiful beaches flanking Gallipoli. To the south, stretches of soft sand and rocky coves lie along **Baia Verde,** the least crowded spot being **Punta della Suina,** part of the **Punta Piazza nature preserve** 10km (6 miles) south of Gallipoli on SS274 and SS239. **Porto Selvaggio,** 19km (11 miles) north of Gallipoli on SP112 and SP286, is a rocky cove edged by a small sand beach and surrounded by a nature park that protects beautiful stands of pine and eucalyptus trees. The pretty fishing village of **Santa Maria al Bagno** is at the southern edge of the park. A long stretch of dune- and pine-backed white sands surrounds **Punta Prosciutto,** another 24km (15 miles) north.

OTRANTO ♥♥

45km (28 miles) SE of Lecce

It's said if you look hard enough on a clear day, you can see all the way to Albania from **Otranto,** the easternmost town in Italy. Two colors dominate here: the electric turquoise of the sea and the gleaming white of the old quarter. You can get here by **car** (45 min. from Lecce via SS16) or by **train** (Ferrovie Sud Est FSE; fseonline.it; travel time a little over an hour, often with a change to a bus at Lecce Via Don Bosco). The **tourist office** is at Piazza Castello 8 (✆ **0836/801436;** daily 9am–noon and 3–6pm).

Castello Aragonese ♥♥ FORTRESS Otranto's 15th-century sea-facing fortress, surrounded in part by a moat, looks mighty enough, but the thick fortifications failed to thwart Mehmet the Conqueror, who in 1480 took the city in just 2 weeks. Most of the garrison and townsfolk fled as the Turkish fleet approached, while those who hid in the fortress poured boiling water over the ramparts, to little avail. When the castle and town were overrun, more than 800 captives chose to die rather than renounce Christianity. The skulls of the Martyrs of Otranto are in the Duomo (see below). Don't expect to discover the settings of Horace Walpole's gothic novel *The Castle of Otranto*—the fortress looks nothing like its fictional self, though its underground tunnels are spooky indeed.

Piazza Castello. comune.otranto.le.it. ✆ **0836/210094.** Admission castle 3€ adults, 2€ ages 17 and under; underground passage 4€, 2€ ages 17 and under. June and mid- to late Sept 9am–10pm; July–Sept daily 9am–midnight; Oct–Nov daily 9am–9pm; other times Mon–Fri 10am–1pm and 3–6pm; Sat–Sun 10am–8pm.

Mosaic floors in the Cattedrale di Otranto are from the 12th century.

14

Lecce

BASILICATA & PUGLIA

Cattedrale di Otranto (Duomo di Santa Maria Annunziata) ♥♥♥ CHURCH Otranto's imposing 11th-century cathedral was built atop remains of a village founded by the Messappii tribe in the 8th century B.C.E.; a Roman villa; and an early Christian church. The remarkable **Tree of Life floor mosaic,** created in the 1160s by the monk-artist Pantaleone, covers the floor like a genealogy tree, telling a medieval version of history. Some figures are easy to identify—Adam and Eve, Noah, the goddess Diana, King Arthur—while others are mysterious (mermaids, couples riding fish). The *beati martiri,* the skulls of citizens beheaded after the 1480 Ottoman sack of the Castello (above), are preserved in a side chapel. Piazza Basilica. mosaicodiotranto.com. ✆ **0836/802720.** Free admission. Daily 8am–noon and 3–8pm.

BEYOND OTRANTO

Head south from Otranto on coastal SP87 for 17km (10 miles) to **Santa Cesarea Terme,** a spa town that's been attracting cure seekers for 500 years, thanks to the sulfuric waters rising from its underlying rock. Take a soak in thermal pools at the **Terme di Santa Cesarea** spa, Via Roma 40 (termesantacesarea.it; ✆ **0836/-944314;** from 55€ for treatment cycle; open 6am–6:30pm). **Castro,** 5km (3 miles) south, tops a seaside cliff, with a delightful fishing port below. At the peninsula's southern tip, **Santa Maria di Leuca** (58km/35 miles south of Otranto), you can climb up to the lighthouse and adjacent basilica, **Santa Maria de Finibus Terrae** (End of the World; basilicaleuca.it), for a bracing, almost 360-degree panorama of the Adriatic and Ionian Seas. Swing another 12km (7 miles) around the tip to **Pescolus** to enjoy its long white-sand beach. From here it's 55km (33 miles) back to Otranto or continue up the peninsula's east coast on SS274 to Gallipoli.

15

SICILY

By Stephen Brewer

The island of Sicily has been conquered, settled, and abandoned by dozens of civilizations, from the Phoenicians, Greeks, and Carthaginians in antiquity to the Arabs, Berbers, Moors, and Normans in the Middle Ages, to the Spanish and Bourbons in the Renaissance. With such an intricate, fascinating legacy, along with exuberant and wildly varying landscapes, Sicily can sometimes make you feel that you're visiting several different countries at once.

Though separated from the mainland only by the narrow Stretto di Messina (Strait of Messina), the 25,708-sq.-km (9,926-sq.-mile) island, the largest in the Mediterranean, has a captivating sense of otherness. Some Sicilians will refer to a trip to the mainland as "going to Italy." The descendants of many conquerors, Sicilians can be welcoming yet suspicious, taciturn yet garrulous, reverent of tradition yet determined not to be shackled by the past, and they can exude a warmth that makes even everyday transactions memorable.

Sicily offers the full package of Italian travel experiences: evocative towns, compelling art, impressive architecture, ancient ruins, wild mountains and beautiful beaches, and a robust culinary heritage. Alongside the jewels of Sicily's ancient past (Agrigento, Siracusa, Segesta, Piazza Armerina), you'll see baroque cities rebuilt after devastating earthquakes (Noto and Ragusa) and some hideous postwar concrete monstrosities (modern Agrigento). The island's geography ranges from the arid, chalky southeast to the brooding slopes of Mt. Etna to the brawny headlands of Palermo and the gentle agricultural landscapes of the east, surrounded by cobalt seas and beaches where you can swim from May to October.

As man of letters Johann von Goethe said of his visit in 1787, "The key to it all is here."

DON'T LEAVE SICILY WITHOUT . . .

Wandering Through a Palermo Market. The local bounty, from fresh tomatoes to huge tunas, is staggering, but the real treat is watching the shills and hagglers in action.

Gazing Skyward in Monreale's Cathedral. Biblical characters, saints, angels, and the heavenly pantheon look down from a sea of colorful mosaics.

Communing with the Ancient World. It's easy to do on an island so richly endowed with relics of the Greek and Roman past. Top stops are the

FACING PAGE: **Ballarò street market in Palermo.**

theaters in Taormina and Siracusa, the temples at Agrigento, Segesta, and Selinunte, and the mosaics in Piazza Armerina.

Hitting the Heights. Take in sweeping panoramic views from elegant, mountainside Taormina and aerie-like, medieval Erice. Highest and most dramatic of all: the summit of Mt. Etna.

Going for Baroque. Swaths of Noto, Ragusa, Siracusa, and other towns in the southeast are stage sets of honey-colored limestone fashioned into curvaceous facades and curling staircases.

PALERMO ♥♥♥

233km (145 miles) W of Messina, 721km (447 miles) S of Naples, 934km (579 miles) S of Rome

Palermo is Sicily's largest port, its capital, and a jumble of contradictions. Parts of some neighborhoods are still not yet fully rebuilt from World War II bombing, while others are rapidly gentrifying; unemployment, poverty, and crime are ever-present. Palermo's museums house some of Europe's greatest treasures, street markets evoke Middle Eastern souks, and famous monuments bear the exotic artistic signature of the Arab-Norman 12th century, when the city was one of Europe's greatest cultural and intellectual centers. Looming over it all is crown-shaped Monte Pellegrino, what Goethe called "the most beautiful headland on earth."

The mix of Byzantine mosaics, rococo stuccoes, Islamic red domes, and Catalonian-Gothic arches can be baffling. Yet there is magic in this madness, and those who embrace the city's chaotic charm discover architectural gems, some of the most exotic food to be had in Italy, and memorable vignettes of street life. You won't love every inch of this alluring yet hectic place, but you'll be swept away by much of the city, and you may come away with the travel experience of a lifetime.

Essentials

ARRIVING

BY AIR Palermo's dramatically situated **Falcone-Borsellino Airport (PMO,** aka Punta Raisi; gesap.it; ✆ **800/541880**) is on the sea among tall headlands 25km (16 miles) northwest of the city. Palermo is well served by flights from all over Italy and many European cities. **Neos** (neosair.com) and **United** (united.com) both operate summer-only nonstop service from New York three times a week.

All the major rental car companies have desks here (if you drive into Palermo with a rental car, get clear directions and parking information from your accommodation). An easier way to reach the center is on a **Prestia e Comandè** shuttle bus (prestiaecomande.it; ✆ **091/586351**), which runs every half-hour from 5am to 12:30am (service from Palermo begins at 4am and ends at 9:30pm)—the trip takes 45 minutes and costs 6.50€ one-way, 11€ round-trip; get tickets from a desk in the arrivals hall, on the bus, or online (.50€ discount each way if purchased online). In

Sicily
Venice
Florence
Rome
Sicily
Ustica
Stromboli
Panarea
Salina
Filicudi
Alicudi
Lípari
Vulcano
Aeolian Is.
TYRRHENIAN SEA
IONIAN SEA
MEDITERRANEAN SEA
Straits of Messina
Gulf of Castellammare
Gulf of Catania
Gulf of Avola
Parco Nazionale dell' Aspromonte
Parco Regionale dei Nebrodi
Parco Regionale delle Madonie
Mt. Etna
Villa San Giovanni
Reggio di Calábria
Messina
Milazzo
Barcellona Pozzo di Gotto
Capo d'Orlando
Castelmola
Taormina
Randazzo
Adrano
Acireale
Aci Trezza
Aci Castello
Paternò
Catania
Lentini
Augusta
Siracusa (Syracuse)
Buccheri
Avola
Noto
Ragusa
Módica
Íspica
Cómiso
Vittória
Caltagirone
Piazza Armerina
Gela
Licata
Canicattì
Agrigento
Porto Empédocle
Caltanissetta
Enna
Nicosia
Gangi
Petralias
Polizzi Generosa
Castelbuono
S. Stéfano di Camastra
Cefalù
Isnello
Caltavuturo
Alia
Bagheria
Palermo
Mondello
Monreale
S. Cipirello
Corleone
Prizzi
Chiusa Sclafani
Sambuca di Sicilia
Sciacca
Marinella
Selinunte
Castelvetrano
Salemi
Segesta
Érice
Trápani
Birgi
Marsala
Mazara d. Vallo
Marettimo
Levanzo
Favignana
Egadi Is.
A3
A18
A19
A29
S113
S114
S115
S117
S120
S121
S122
S186
S189
S192
S194
S284
S286
S514
S640
0
40 mi
0
40 km

central Palermo, buses stop at several points along Via Libertà, Teatro Politeama, the main train station, and Via Emerico Amari (port). A **train service,** the **Trinacria Express,** connects the airport with the main train station, but the "express" part is a bit of hyperbole: The train can take more than an hour, and the line is often nonoperational. Scheduled service from the airport begins at 5:30am and ends at 10:10pm; service operates every half-hour throughout most of the day and the fare is 5.90€ each way. You can purchase tickets at desks in the station and airport or from machines near the platform. **Taxis** are plentiful; expect to pay about 40€ to 45€ from the airport to town, but be sure to settle on a price before you set off. You can share a cab for about 10€—drivers depart from a well-marked "shared taxi" area outside the terminal and wait to leave until they have four or more passengers. This is a safe and reliable option, though you will have to slip the driver a little extra to take you all the way to your destination rather than dropping you at an intersection nearby.

BY TRAIN Trains to Palermo from mainland Italy come down through Calabria and across the Strait of Messina on ferries equipped with railroad tracks on the cargo deck. It's a novel way to arrive in Sicily, but takes some time (the Rome–Palermo trip is at least 11 hr., Naples–Palermo 9–10 hr.). Night trains between Palermo and Rome and other mainland cities usually have sleeping accommodations. All trains come into **Palermo Stazione Centrale,** at the edge of the historic center. Passenger rail service around the island is generally spotty and slow, but there's decent service on routes between Palermo and Messina, Catania, and Agrigento. For information, go to trenitalia.com or call ✆ **89/2021.**

BY BUS **Buses** from the mainland and elsewhere in Sicily arrive at a depot adjacent to the train station. Bus service in Sicily is excellent, with good connections between cities and many smaller towns. Coaches are clean and modern, with comfortable upholstered seats, air-conditioning, and smooth suspensions. Those on longer hauls often have toilets and stop for a snack break along the way. The main bus companies include **Interbus** (interbus.it; ✆ **06/164-160;** also known as **Etna Trasporti, Segesta,** or **Sicilbus,** depending on which part of Sicily you're in), and **Cuffaro** (www.cuffaro.info; ✆ **091/616-1510**), which operates buses between Palermo and Agrigento.

BY CAR The northeastern tip of Sicily is separated from mainland Italy by the 5km-wide (3-mile) Stretto di Messina (Strait of Messina), which is crossed by regular car ferries between the Calabrian port of Villa San Giovanni (just north of Reggio Calabria, on what is essentially the "toe" of the Italian peninsula's boot) and the Sicilian city of Messina. From Messina, which lies on the well-maintained A20 and A18 *autostrade,* it's a straight shot west to Palermo (233km/145 miles; about 2½ hr.). If you're driving down from Naples or Rome, prepare yourself for a long ride: 721km (448 miles) south from Naples or 934km (580 miles) south from Rome.

RESTAURANTS

Antica Focacceria San Francesco **29**
Antica Gelateria Patricola **43**
Antico Caffè Spinnato **12**
Arte e Tradizione **45**
Bar Rosanero **47**
Bar Touring **46**
Bisso Bistrot **20**
Casa del Brodo **27**
Cioccolateria Lorenzo **35**
Ferro di Cavallo **21**
I Segreti del Chiostro **22**
La Cambusa **30**
L'Acerba Osteria Dinamica **11**
La Galleria **10**
L'Ottava Nota **39**
Moltivolti **8**
Nni Franco U' Vastiddaru **31**
Osteria dei Vespri **25**
Palazzo Sambuca **34**
Pani câ Meusa **32**
Panineria Friggitoria Chiluzzo **44**
Quid Gusto Siciliano **36**
Sfrigola **3**

ATTRACTIONS

Catacombe dei Cappuccini **2**
Chiesa della Martorana/San Cataldo **23**
Duomo **9**
Galleria d'Arte Moderna **26**
Galleria Regionale della Sicilia/ Palazzo Abatellis **38**
Il Castello della Zisa **1**
Museo Archeologico Regionale Antonino Salinas **14**
Museo d'Arte Moderna e Contemporanea di Palermo **18**
Oratorio del Rosario di San Domenico **15**
Oratorio del Rosario di Santa Cita **16**
Oratorio di San Lorenzo **28**
Palazzo Butera **42**
Palazzo Chiaromonte Steri/ Museo dell'Inquisizione **37**
Palazzo dei Normanni and Cappella Palatina **4**
Palazzo Mirto **33**
San Giovanni degli Eremiti **5**
Stanze al Genio **49**

HOTELS

Bastione Spasimo Boutique Hotel **48**
B&B L'Olivella **13**
BB22 Charming Rooms and Apartments **17**
Butera 28 Apartments **41**
Eurostars Centrale Palace **19**
Grand Hotel Piazza Borsa **24**
Hotel Porta Felice **40**
Il Giardino di Ballarò **6**
Palazzo Brunaccini **7**

BY SEA Palermo's large port is served by passenger ferries from the Italian mainland ports of Naples, Civitavecchia (near Rome), and Genoa, and from the Sardinian city of Cagliari. Nearly all are nighttime crossings, departing between 7pm and 9pm and arriving the next morning between 6am and 8am. Some of these ferries are tricked out like miniature cruise ships, with swimming pools, beauty salons, discos, and cabins in many configurations, from four-bunk dorms to private rooms. Ferries from Naples are the most numerous, operating daily year-round. The Naples–Palermo route is run by **Tirrenia Lines** (tirrenia.it; ✆ **02/760-28132**) and **Grandi Navi Veloci** (**GNV;** gnv.it; ✆ **010/209-4591**). The trip takes 11 hours. **GNV** also operates overnight ferries to Palermo from Civitavecchia (the cruise ship port for Rome).

GETTING AROUND PALERMO

Walking is the best way to get around central Palermo, because distances are never great within the historic center. Bus service in the city and outlying areas, run by **AMAT** (✆ **091/350111**) is extensive but can be unreliable. Fare is 1.40€ per ride and 3.50€ for an all-day ticket; buses run from 5:30am to 11:30pm. Bus tickets are sold at *tabacchi,* some newsstands, and kiosks near some stops; if you buy them on board, you will pay 1.80€. Buses are not equipped for contactless payments. Four tram lines, with the same fare, serve outlying districts; tickets are available from machines on the platforms. A free shuttle bus runs around the historic center, from Porta Felice near the waterfront up Via Allora to Via Maqueda.

VISITOR INFORMATION

A municipal **tourist information office** (turismo.comune.palermo.it) is located in the city center at Piazza Bellini (✆ **091/740-8873;** Mon–Fri 8:30am–1:30pm and 2:30–5:30pm; afternoon hours only on Tues and Thurs in winter). **Wonderful Italy** at Via Torremuzza 15 in the Kalsa district (wonderfulitaly.eu; ✆ **091/783-8185;** Mon–Sat 10am–1pm and 2:30–5:30pm, Sun 10am–2pm) rents bikes and arranges accommodation and kayaking, hiking, and other excursions, as well as offbeat tours, such as walks showing off sites in Palermo where anti-Mafia activity has centered.

SAFETY

Palermo is quite safe for tourists, though the city is home to some of the most skilled pickpockets on the continent. Police squads operate mobile centers throughout the town to help combat street crime, but **your best defense is common sense.** Don't flaunt expensive jewelry, cameras, or wads of bills, and be especially careful in busy street markets and on buses; routes to Monreale and Mondello, popular sightseeing destinations, are fertile ground for pickpockets. Thieves on scooters are adept at snatching jewelry and handbags. Do not carry a wallet anywhere accessible, even in an inside jacket pocket, where someone (or a pair, as is often the case) brushing against you can easily get to it. When traveling around Sicily, don't leave documents, cash, credit cards, expensive electronics, and other valuables in an unattended car, even out of sight in the trunk. Stash them safely at your hotel or, if you're on the move and stopping at an attraction en route, carry them with you.

Neighborhoods in Brief

Palermo is divided into four historical districts, or *mandamenti,* that spread out from **Quattro Canti,** or Four Corners. (Time was, and not too long ago, that it was unthinkable for Palermitani from one district to marry someone from another.) The square (officially Piazza Vigliena, after the viceroy who commissioned the elegant assemblage) marks the intersection of north–south **Via Maqueda** and east–west **Corso Vittorio Emanuele.**

One of the four "corners" of Quattro Canti, where Palermo's four historic districts meet.

ALBERGHERIA Southwest of the Quattro Canti, the oldest of the four *mandamenti* is also referred to as Palazzo Reale because the royal palace was set here, in the highest part of the city. The Albergheria is filled with narrow, dimly lit alleyways and decaying buildings, though there are some exquisite corners—especially the splendid **Piazza Bologni,** with its noble palaces and statue of Charles V, and the historic **Il Ballarò** market extending from Piazza Bologni to Corso Tukory.

IL CAPO The neighborhood northwest of the Quattro Canti, enclosed within Via Maqueda, Corso Vittorio Emanuele, Via Papireto, and Via Volturno, is a warren of tiny winding streets and alleyways spread out behind the Teatro Massimo. At its heart is the largest of Palermo's markets, **Il Capo** (p. 771), once the headquarters of the secret society of the Beati Paoli, who robbed from the rich and gave to the poor. Pickpockets still adhere to this age-old principle, so watch your wallet.

CASTELLAMMARE Named after the castle that once overlooked the sea, this northeastern quadrant is bordered by Corso Vittorio Emanuele, Via Cavour, Via Roma, and Via Crispi. Though heavily bombed in World War

II, the neighborhood still has some spectacular *palazzi* and churches, such as the **Oratorio del Rosario di Santa Cita** and the **Oratorio di San Lorenzo** (p. 759). The centuries-old **La Vucciria** market, once the beating heart of Palermo, is here (p. 771), with a few remaining butcher shops, fishmongers, and hole-in-the-wall eateries; it's now a nightlife scene, too.

LA KALSA Settled a thousand years ago by Arabs, this southeast quadrant, bounded by Via Lincoln, Via Roma, Corso Vittorio Emanuele, and the seaside Foro Italico, still has an exotic aura. Some patches were never rebuilt after 1943 Allied air raids, and the never-completed church **Santa Maria dello Spasimo** (Via dello Spasimo; ✆ **091/616-1486**) is a skeleton of broken Gothic vaults. Even 10 years ago, walking down La Kalsa's narrow lanes was risky business (it's still wise to avoid empty areas after dark), but a rash of hip restaurants and bars have recently opened in old *palazzi.* The neighborhood's renewal has come into full flower with the recent opening to the public of the vast, 300-year-old **Palazzo Butera ♥♥♥** (p. 760). The excellent **Galleria Regionale della Sicilia ♥♥♥** (p. 758) is also here, as is a shady park in the middle of Piazza Marina, cooled by sea breezes. At the southern end of the neighborhood, off Via Lincoln, you'll find the city's lush botanical garden, **Orto Botanico di Palermo.**

NEW CITY The monumental **Teatro Massimo** at Piazza Verdi roughly marks the division between the Old City and the New City. Head northwest up Via Ruggero Séttimo to the massive double squares at Piazza Politeama, site of the **Teatro Politeama Garibaldi.** North of there, swanky **Via della Libertà** runs up to the Giardino Inglese (the English Gardens). This is Palermo's Art Nouveau quarter, though many streamlined beauties were torn down to make way for ugly cement behemoths, marring the neighborhood's elegance.

Exploring Palermo

Most of everything you want to see is within walking distance of the Quattro Canti, where Via Maqueda, running north–south through the city, meets Corso Vittorio Emanuele, running east–west. The seaside entrance to Corso Vittorio Emanuele is the Porta Felice and the landside entrance, near the Duomo and Palazzo dei Normanni, is the Porta Nuova.

Catacombe dei Cappuccini ♥♥ CEMETERY In 1599, the occupants of the adjoining Capuchin monastery discovered that the bodies of the brothers they placed in their catacombs soon became naturally mummified (albeit with the aid of chemical infusions), and Sicilians began demanding to be buried along with them. Which is why the corpses of some 8,000 people in various stages of preservation now hang from walls and recline in open caskets. Wearing their Sunday best, the ghoulish assemblage is grouped according to sex and rank—men, women, virgins, priests, nobles, professors (possibly including the painter Velasquez), and children. This last grouping includes the most recent resident, 2-year-old

Rosalia Lombardo, who died in 1920 and whom locals have dubbed "Sleeping Beauty."

Piazza Cappuccini 1. catacombefraticappuccini.com. ✆ **091/212-117.** Admission 5€, 3€ ages 17 and under. Mon–Sat 9am–12:30pm and 3–5:30pm. Bus: 327 from Piazza Indipendenza.

Chiesa della Martorana/San Cataldo ♥♥ CHURCH These two Norman churches stand side by side, separated by a little tropical garden. George of Antioch—Sicilian king Roger II's Greek admiral—founded Santa Maria dell'Ammiraglio in 1141; the church was later renamed **Chiesa della Martorana** for Eloisa Martorana, who established a nearby Benedictine convent. The nuns earned the everlasting appreciation of Palermitans when they invented marzipan, and *frutta di Martorana*—in which marzipan is fashioned into the shape of little fruits—has outlived the order. George of Antioch, for his part, loved Byzantine mosaics and hired North African craftsmen to cover the church's walls, pillars, and floors with stunning examples of the craft. Christ crowns Roger II, George appears in a Byzantine robe, and Christ appears again in the dome, circled by angels. The Arab geographer/traveler Ibn Jubayr visited Palermo in 1166 and called the church "the most beautiful monument in the world." In 1266 Sicilian nobles met here and agreed to offer the crown to Peter of Aragon, ending a bloody uprising against French rule known as the Sicilian Vespers. A baroque redo has rendered the interior a little less transporting than it was then, but it's still beautiful.

The Fountain of Shame

Near Chiesa della Martorana in Piazza Pretoria, naked nymphs, gods, and goddesses romp over the 16th-century **Fontana Pretoria,** created by Florentine sculptor Francesco Camilliani for the garden of a Tuscan villa and sold to Palermo in 1574 to show off the city's new waterworks. Palermitans call the nude-encrusted fountain the "Fountain of Shame," and nuns from a nearby convent used to clothe the statues. They went so far as to lop off the noses of the naked males (you can still see some clumsy reattachments)—the sisters could not bring themselves to touch the members that really offended them.

Maio of Bari, chancellor to William I, began the tiny **Chiesa di San Cataldo** next door in 1154; after he died in 1160, the church was left unfinished. The red domes and the lacy crenellation around the tops of the walls are decidedly Moorish, while the stone interior, with three little cupolas over the nave, evokes the Middle Ages.

Piazza Bellini 2, adjacent to Piazza Pretoria. La Martorana (✆ **345/828-8231**) admission 2€; Mon–Sat 10am–1pm. San Cataldo (✆ **091/782-9684**) admission 2.50€; daily 10am–2pm and 2:30–6pm. Bus: 101 or 102.

Duomo ♥♥ CATHEDRAL All those who came, saw, and conquered in Palermo left their mark on the city's cathedral, a remarkable architectural pastiche begun in 1184, a counterpart to the cathedral that was beginning to rise high above Palermo in Monreale (p. 772). In 1771, architect

Palermo's Duomo is an intriguing mix of architectural styles.

Ferdinando Fuga, a favorite of the Naples-based Bourbon royalty who then ruled Sicily, undertook a clumsy restoration in a neoclassical style, adding a cupola that rises impressively but incongruously above the original Norman design. Some earlier and better elements remain, including large swaths of the elegant Gothic-Catalan exterior and a beautifully carved 15th-century entry portico. The church is the final resting place of Roger II, the first king of Sicily (died 1154), and other Norman–Swabian royalty who lie in splendid canopied-and-columned sarcophagi.
Piazza Cattedrale. ✆ **091/334373.** Free admission to Duomo; royal tombs 2€; tombs, crypt, treasury, and terraces 7€. Church: Mon–Sat 7am–7pm, Sun 10am–7pm. Crypt, treasury, and terraces: Mon–Fri 9am–2pm, Sat 9am–5:30pm, and Sun 9am–1pm. Bus: 101, 104, 105, 107, 139.

Galleria Regionale della Sicilia/Palazzo Abatellis ♥♥♥
MUSEUM Competing for attention with this fine art collection is the late-15th-century *palazzo* that houses it, built around two courtyards and beautifully restored in the 1950s. On display is an array of Sicilian art from the 13th to the 18th centuries. You can't miss the gallery's most celebrated work, the ***Trionfo della Morte*** (Triumph of Death), prominently displayed in a two-story ground-floor gallery (climb the stairs to the balcony for an overview). Dating from 1449 and of uncertain attribution, this huge study in black and gray depicts Death as a fearsome skeletal demon astride an undernourished steed, brandishing a scythe as he leaps over his victims (allegedly members of Palermo aristocracy, who were none too pleased with the portrayal); the poor and hungry look on, having escaped this gruesome fate for now. The precision of this astonishing work, including details of the horse's nostrils and the men and women in the full flush

of their youth, juxtaposed against such darkness, suggests the Surrealism movement that arose 500 years later.

The second masterpiece of the gallery, in room 4, is a refreshing antidote, and also quite modern-looking. Francesco Laurana's white-marble, slanted-eyed bust of **Eleonora di Aragona** captured the likeness of the daughter of King Ferdinand I of Naples shortly before she married Ercole d'Este in 1468 and became the duchess of Ferrara. Another highlight is in room 11: Antonello da Messina's ***Annunciation***, probably the artist's most famous work, completed in 1476 in Venice. He depicts the Virgin as an adolescent girl, sitting at a desk with a devotional book in front of her, clasping her cloak modestly to her chest. She raises her hand, seemingly to us viewers but probably to Gabriel, who has just announced that she is to be mother to the son of God. Considering that news, her expression is remarkably serene. It's one of the most calming, lovely works anywhere. Via Alloro 4, Palazzo Abatellis. facebook.com/abatellis. ✆ **331/658-1788.** Admission 8€ adults, 4€ ages 17 and under; 10€ adults, 5€ ages 17 and under combined with Palazzo Mirto (p. 762). Tues–Sat 9am–6:30pm; Sun 9am–1:30pm. Bus: 103, 105, 139.

THE oratories OF GIACOMO SERPOTTA

Some of Palermo's most delightful places of worship are oratories, private chapels funded by societies and guilds and usually connected to a larger church. As you explore Palermo, seek out these three oratories that were decorated in the early 18th century by Giacomo Serpotta, a native master of sculpting in stucco.

Serpotta was a member of the Society of the Holy Rosary, and he decorated the society's **Oratorio del Rosario di San Domenico ♥♥**, Via dei Bambinai, with delightfully expressive *putti* (cherubs), who are locked forever in a playground of happy antics. His 3-D reliefs depict everything from the *Allegories of the Virtues* to the *Apocalypse of St. John* to a writhing *Devil Falling from Heaven.* The Dutch master Anthony van Dyck, who spent time in Palermo in the 1620s, did the *Madonna of the Rosary* over the high altar (turismo.comune.palermo.it; ✆ **091/332779;** 6€ or 9€ with Santa Cita; Mon–Sat 10am–1:30pm and 2–5:30pm).

The all-white **Oratorio del Rosario di Santa Cita ♥♥♥**, Via Valverde 3, houses Serpotta's crowning achievement: a detailed relief of the 1571 Battle of Lepanto, in which a coalition of European states defeated the Turks, more or less preventing the expansion of the Ottoman Empire into Western Europe. Serpotta's cherubs, oblivious to international affairs, romp up and down the walls and climb onto window frames (ilgeniodi palermo.com; ✆ **091/332779;** 4€ or 9€ with San Domenico; Wed–Mon 10am–1:30pm and 2–5:30pm).

Serpotta also worked on the **Oratorio di San Lorenzo ♥♥**, Via dell'Immacolatella, creating what critics have admiringly called "a cave of white coral." In his panels on the lives of St. Francis and St. Lawrence, some of the most expressive stuccoes depict the martyrdom of Lawrence, who, being roasted to death, nonchalantly told his tormentors, "I'm well done. Turn me over." Caravaggio's last large painting, a Nativity, once hung over the altar, but it was stolen in 1969 and never recovered (amicimuseisiciliani.it; ✆ **091/611-8168;** 3€; daily 10am–6pm).

Il Castello della Zisa ♥♥ PALACE Few places in Palermo evoke the Arab past as evocatively as this palace of pleasure-loving Norman king William I. Arriving in Palermo, the 12th-century ruler adapted to the contemporary style, hiring craftsmen to create his summer retreat—Zisa translates as "splendid"—in Moorish style. Arches, niches, fountains, towers, and ingenious cooling systems (contrived from breezes flowing over pools and through interior vents) were all geared to creating an exotic retreat. Despite a rather clumsy recent restoration, just enough remains of the once-derelict palace to suggest its original glory.

Piazza Guglielmo il Buono (near Piazza Camporeale at end of Via Dante). ✆ **091/652-0269.** Admission 8€ adults, free for ages 17 and under. Tues–Sat 9am–6:30pm. Bus: 106, 124, 134.

Museo Archeologico Regionale Antonino Salinas (Regional Archaeological Museum) ♥♥♥ MUSEUM A head-spinning repository of artifacts from Sicily's many inhabitants and invaders—Phoenicians, Greeks, Saracens, Romans—is set in the former convent of the Filippini. The most important treasures are *metopes* (temple friezes) from Selinunte (p. 819), sumptuous, detailed marbles depicting Perseus slaying Medusa, the Rape of Europa by Zeus, Actaeon being transformed into a stag, and other scenes that bring these myths vividly to life. Among the other artifacts—anchors from Punic warships and mirrors used by the Etruscans—is a rare Egyptian find: the **Pietra di Palermo** (Palermo Stone), a black slab dating from 2700 B.C.E. that is known as the Rosetta stone of Sicily. Discovered in Egypt in the 19th century, it was in transit for the British Museum in London when it was shuffled off to the corners of a Palermo dock. Hieroglyphics reveal the inscriber's attention to detail: a list of pharaohs, details of the delivery of 40 shiploads of cedarwood to Snefru, and flood levels of the Nile.

Piazza Olivella 24. ✆ **091/611-6805.** Admission 8€, free for ages 17 and under. Tues–Sat 9am–7pm; Sun 9am–1:30pm. Bus: 101, 102, 103, 104, 107.

Palazzo Butera ♥♥♥ MUSEUM Art collectors Francesca and Massimo Valsecchi have restored one of Palermo's grandest yet long-crumbling *palazzos* and filled its salons with works by artists ranging from Renaissance masters to Andy Warhol, along with objects from African vases to Arts and Crafts furniture. Much of the charm

Art from all eras hangs in the salons of the restored Palazzo Butera.

is the randomness of the collection, placed in no chronological order and displayed without labels, allowing viewers to make one discovery after another. MadoniEAT, a friendly cafe and shop specializing in Sicilian food, especially that from the Madonie mountains, is on the ground floor. Via Butera 8. palazzobutera.it. ✆ **091/752-1754.** 10€ adults, free for ages 17 and under. Tues–Sun 10am–8pm.

Palazzo Chiaramonte Steri/Museo dell'Inquisizione ♥♥ PALACE/MUSEUM The Inquisition held sway in Sicily from about 1600 to 1780, allowing the Roman Catholic church to stifle the aristocracy and control the populace. The accused (essentially anyone who expressed beliefs outside the church's teachings) were held in this palace, built in 1307 for the powerful Chiaramonte family, when it was headquarters of the Aragonese/Spanish viceroys of Sicily. The lower floors housed prisoners from all levels of society in miniscule cagelike cells that were left untouched through the centuries, preserving a wealth of graffiti: hearts, caricatures, maps, initials, and verse inscribed by the hapless souls who were left here to rot or, worse, tortured and hanged. An antidote to all this misery is a bright gallery housing *Le Vucciria*, an exuberant scene of the nearby market saturated with color and realism, by Palermitano painter Renato Guttuso (1912–87). Even more refreshing are views of the sea and the old city from the top-floor **Sala Magna,** with its elaborately painted ceiling depicting scenes from the Bible and mythology. You can only visit on guided tours, offered in English.
Piazza Marina 61. musei.unipa.it/steri.html. ✆ **091/607-5306.** Admission 8€ adults, 5€ seniors 70 and over and ages 10–25, free for children under 10. Mar–Oct daily 9am–8pm; Nov–Feb 9am–6pm.

Palazzo dei Normanni ♥♥ and Cappella Palatina ♥♥♥ PALACE The cultural influences of Sicily collide in this palace dating back to the 8th century B.C.E., when Punic administrators set up an outpost in the highest part of the city. In the C.E. 9th century, the Arabs built a stronghold here for their emirs and their harems, and in the 12th century the Normans turned what was essentially a fortress into a sumptuous royal residence. Here Frederick II presided over the early-13th-century court of minstrels and literati that founded the Scuola Poetica Siciliana, marking the birth of Italian literature. In 1555, Spanish viceroys moved in, and today most of the vast maze of rooms houses Sicily's regional government.

Arab-Norman cultural influences intersect most spectacularly in the **Cappella Palatina,** a chapel covered in glittering Byzantine mosaics from 1130 to 1140. Work was finished in time for the coronation of Roger II, who proved to be as enlightened as he was powerful. High in the cupola at the end of the apse is Christ Pantocrator (holding the New Testament in his left hand and making the blessing with his right hand), surrounded by biblical characters, some interpreted a little less piously than usual—Adam and Eve blithely munch on the forbidden fruit and greedily reach for a second piece. (Shame prevails in the next scene, when God steps in reproachfully and the naked couple cover themselves.) The mosaics are vibrant in the soft light, an effect especially powerful in scenes depicting water—in the flood and the Baptism of Christ, the water actually appears to be shimmering.

Scenes on the wooden ceiling were done in a 3-D technique using small sections of carved wood, known in Arabic as *muqarnas.* A team of Egyptian carpenters and painters created the playfully secular scenarios of dancers, musicians, hunters, drinkers, and banqueters in a harem. They're best seen with binoculars or a telephoto lens.

The **Royal Apartments** are open to the public when the Sicilian parliament is not in session. Among them is the **Salone d'Ercole,** where the legislators often meet Tuesdays through Thursdays; it is named for its mammoth 19th-century frescoes of the 12 labors of Hercules (an apt emblem for legislators wading through government bureaucracy). Adjoining rooms from the years of Spanish rule are fairly pompous, but remnants of earlier eras are fascinating. The **Sala dei Presidenti,** a stark medieval chamber hidden in the bowels of the palace for centuries, was completely unknown until it was exposed by a 2002 earthquake. The **Torre Gioaria** (Tower of the Wind) provided a 12th-century version of air-conditioning: A fountain in the middle of the tower (since removed) spouted water that cooled the breezes coming from the four hallways. Much less hospitable are the **Segrete,** or dungeons, where cold stone walls are etched with primitive scenes of Norman warships. The otherwise enlightened Frederick II allegedly took his interest in science to perverse lengths in these chambers, shutting prisoners in casks to see if their souls could be observed escaping through a small hole at the moment of death. Frederick was also fascinated by the stars and brought many astronomers and astrologers to his court. His Bourbon successors shared the interest and in 1790 added a still-active astronomical observatory at the top of the **Torre Pisana.** From these heights in 1801 the priest Fra Giuseppe Piazza discovered Ceres, the first asteroid known to mankind.

Piazza del Parlamento. federicosecondo.org. ✆ **091/626-833.** Cappella Palatina, Royal Apartments, Royal Gardens, and exhibitions 19€ adults, 15€ seniors and ages 14–17; Cappella Palatina, Royal Gardens, and exhibitions 15.50€ adults, 13.50€ seniors and ages 14–17. Children under 13 free. Mon–Sat 8:30am–4:30pm; Sun 8:30am–12:30pm. Bus: 104, 105, 108, 109, 110, 118, 304, 309.

Palazzo Mirto ♥♥ HISTORIC SITE The streets of old Palermo are lined with palaces, and though some are decrepit and/or abandoned, many are still the homes of aristocrats. Few are as beautifully maintained as the home of the princes of Lanza Filangieri, one of Sicily's oldest families. The last of the princes bequeathed his 17th-century home to the city in the 1980s, leaving behind the trappings of his privileged lifestyle: furnishings, statues, rococo fountains that splash on hidden patios, and elaborate tableware (including plates given away as party favors, decorated with

State-of-the-Art Art

Palermo also has a rich contemporary art scene anchored in the beautiful 18th-century Palazzo Riso, home to the permanent collection and rotating exhibitions of contemporary artists in the **Museo d'Arte Moderna e Contemporanea di Palermo,** Via Vittorio Emanuele 365 (museoartecontemporanea.it; ✆ **091/778-3343;** 7€ adults, free for ages 17 and under; Tues–Sat 9am–6:30pm, Sun 9am–1pm). Works by late-19th- and 20th-century Sicilian artists fill a 15th-century Franciscan convent and an adjoining church housing the **Galleria d'Arte Moderna** (**GAM**), in the Kalsa at Via Sant'Ana 21 (gampalermo.it; ✆ **091/843-1605;** 10€ adults, 8€ seniors and ages 19–25, 1.50€ ages 6–18, free for children under 6; Tues–Sun 9:30am–6:30pm). The excellent English-language audioguides enhance the experience.

images of the costumed nobs who once danced the night away in the over-the-top ballroom). It's hard to imagine that life in the grandiose, tapestry-hung salons was very comfortable or relaxed, especially for the 20th-century princes and princesses whose photos appear casually on ornate side tables. Then again, it would have been transporting to while away an evening in the smoking room, decorated in painted-silk scenes of everyday life in China as a 19th-century artisan imagined it.

Via Merlo 2. ✆ **331/661-6927.** Admission 8€ adults, 4€ ages 17 and under; 10€ adults, 5€ ages 17 and under combined with Galleria Regionale (p. 758). Tues–Sat 9am–6:30pm; Sun 9am–1:30pm. Bus: 103, 105, 139.

San Giovanni degli Eremiti ♥♥ CHURCH Palermo's most romantic landmark is a simple affair, part Arab, part Norman, with five red domes atop a portico, a single nave, two small apses, and a squat tower. As befits the humble Spanish recluse it honors, St. John of the Hermits, the church is almost devoid of decoration, though surrounding citrus blossoms and flowers imbue the modest structure with an otherworldly aura. Adding to the charm of the spot is a Norman cloister, part of a Benedictine monastery that once stood here.

Via dei Benedettini 3. turismo.comune.palermo.it. ✆ **091/651-5019.** Admission 8€. Mon–Sat 9am–7pm; Sun 9am–1:30pm. Bus: 109 or 318.

Where to Stay in Palermo

Palermo has many excellent hotels, with rates that in general are much lower than those in Rome or Florence. For convenience and atmosphere, don't stay too far beyond the neighborhoods in the old center (p. 755).

EXPENSIVE

Bastione Spasimo Boutique Hotel ♥♥♥ In the early 16th century, the Viceroy of Sicily commissioned the Bastione dello Spasimo and other defenses around Palermo to protect the city from invasion by sea. The well-preserved fort and garrison, which has been a spice warehouse and a cart factory, is in its current incarnation an exotic and welcoming

House of Tiles

One of Palermo's delightful hidden treasures is the **Stanze al Genio, Museo delle Maioliche** ♥♥, a collection of 2,300 historic tiles of Neapolitan and Sicilian manufacture, covering every inch of a private apartment on the *piano nobile* of an old palace in the Kalsa district. An informative guide will walk you through the kitchen, dining room, and living room, explaining the glorious ceramics carpeting the walls and floors. The museum is at Via Garibaldi 11 (stanzealgenio.com; ✆ **380/367-3773**); open Tuesday 4 to 6:30pm and Wednesday through Sunday from 10am to 12:30pm and 4 to 6:30pm. Reserve by phone or e-mail in advance. Admission is 10€.

small hotel, with stone-walled rooms tucked into the original defenses and on an airy upper floor. All are handsomely and comfortably furnished, and many have balconies and terraces opening to a garden full of lush plantings surrounding a swimming pool—a rarity in the old Kalsa quarter, and covered with glass in winter for year-round use.

Via Filippo Evola 1. bastionespasimo.com. ✆ **091/649-7212.** 13 units. 140€–220€ double. Rates include breakfast. **Amenities:** Pool; free Wi-Fi.

Grand Hotel Piazza Borsa ♥♥ A conglomeration of three historic buildings (the old stock exchange, a monastery, and a centuries-old *palazzo*) have been transformed into atmospheric public areas that include a cloister, open-roofed atrium, paneled dining rooms, and frescoed salons. Guest rooms are a bit more businesslike, though they are large and comfortable, with hardwood floors and handsome furnishings that cross tradition with contemporary style; the best have balconies overlooking nearby churches and palaces. A spa and exercise area includes a sauna and steam room.

Via dei Cartari 18. piazzaborsa.com. ✆ **091/320075.** 103 units. 125€–230€ double. Rates include breakfast. Bus: 103, 104, 105, 118, 225. **Amenities:** Restaurant; bar; babysitting; concierge; spa; gym; free Wi-Fi.

Palazzo Brunaccini ♥♥ Princess Lucrezia Brunaccini probably wouldn't recognize the home from which she reigned over 18th-century Palermo society, but her dignified old *palazzo* still commands a beautiful and tranquil piazza just steps from the madness of the Ballarò market. Salons and the airy guest rooms are a pleasant mix of traditional grandeur and clean-lined touches, with oil paintings, wall hangings, and antiques thrown into the mix. Many of the high-ceilinged rooms overlook the piazza and surrounding neighborhood from small terraces.

Piazza Lucrezia Brunaccini. palazzobrunaccini.it. ✆ **091/586904.** 18 units. 160€–215€ double. Rates include breakfast. Bus: 104, 105, 108, 109, 110, 118. **Amenities:** Restaurant; bar; free Wi-Fi.

MODERATE

Butera 28 Apartments ♥♥♥ Charming duchess Nicoletta Polo Lanza Tomasi welcomes guests in 12 short-stay apartments tucked throughout the 17th-century Palazzo Lanza Tomasi, which she lovingly

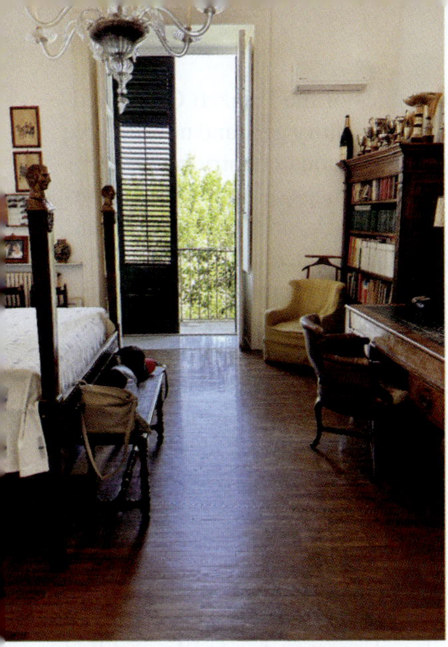

The Butera 28 Apartments have a comfy, home-like decor.

restored over the years with her late husband, Duke Gioacchino Lanza Tomasi, adopted son of Prince Giuseppe Tomasi di Lampedusa (author of the great modern Italian novel *The Leopard*). Apartments have one or two bedrooms; some have sea views and terraces, others are multilevel, and all have beautiful hardwood or tile floors and other detailing. They're furnished with family pieces and all the modern conveniences, including commodious bathrooms, many with lavish showers, and well-equipped kitchens with washing machines. The duchess is also host of her popular "A Day Cooking with the Duchess" experience (p. 768), and she and her hospitable assistants provide a wealth of advice on where to eat, drink, shop, and in other ways get the most out of Palermo.

Via Butera 28. palazzolanzatomasi.it. ✆ **333/316-5432.** 12 units. 100€–260€ double. Bus: 103, 104, 105, 118, 225. **Amenities:** Kitchens; free Wi-Fi.

Eurostars Centrale Palace ♥♥ A convenient location steps from the Quattro Canti puts this much-redone yet still grand *palazzo* within easy reach of most sights. The vast frescoed salon where breakfast is served evokes the 1890s Belle Epoque when the 17th-century *palazzo* was first converted to a hotel, while the good-size guest rooms are comfortably functional, with rich fabrics, mosaic-tiled bathrooms, and other luxe touches; double-pane windows in the front rooms keep the street noise at bay. A rooftop terrace with an airy dining room has views extending to Monte Pellegrino and is a great spot for cocktails on a warm night.

Via Vittorio Emanuele 327 (at Via Maqueda). eurostarshotels.it. ✆ **091/336666.** 104 units. 70€–220€ double. Breakfast included in most rates. Bus: 103, 104, 105. **Amenities:** 2 restaurants; bar; exercise room; sauna; room service; babysitting; free Wi-Fi.

Hotel Porta Felice ♥♥ A force behind the old Kalsa district's gentrification, this elegant and subdued retreat has risen amid a once-neglected block of buildings just off the seafront. Marble-floored public areas are coolly soothing, while sleek guest rooms are embellished with traditional touches such as antique pieces and expanses of hardwood. A rooftop bar and terrace is an airy oasis; downstairs, guests can enjoy a spa and wellness club, with a sauna and steam room.

Via Butera 35. hotelportafelice.it. ✆ **091/617-5678.** 33 units. 110€–160€ double. Rates include breakfast. Bus: 103, 104, 105, 118, 225. **Amenities:** Bar; spa; free Wi-Fi.

Il Giardino di Ballarò ♥♥♥ The stables of the Palazzo Conte Federico were converted to a bakery more than a century ago, and now they've been revamped in the style of a casually luxurious country house steps from the Ballarò market. In the downstairs lounges, plump couches surround a fireplace against a backdrop of old brick, arches, and columns, while a breakfast lounge and several guest rooms face a rear garden filled with banana trees and other exotic plantings. Two rooms are tucked under the eaves beneath huge skylights, and the large family rooms have two bathrooms. The distinctive decor is enhanced with splashes of color, kilims, and contemporary art, all reflecting the refined taste of proprietor Annalise Correnti, whose two daughters are gracious and capable hosts. Via Porta di Castro 75/77. ilgiardinodiballaro.it. ✆ **091/212215.** 7 units. 100€–150€ double. Rates include breakfast. Bus: 104, 105, 108, 109, 110, 118. **Amenities:** Bar; garden; Jacuzzi (use by arrangement); free Wi-Fi.

INEXPENSIVE

B&B L'Olivella ♥♥♥ Elena Ciccero welcomes guests in an Art Nouveau *palazzo* that's been in her family for four generations. A stay here comes with the sense of being a privileged guest in her heirloom-filled home, and the surroundings are probably just what you'd expect of a Sicilian palace, with sunlight streaming through French doors onto tiled floors beneath high frescoed ceilings, plant-filled balconies, and the welcoming presence of Elena and her family. The excellent location in a warren of streets puts you near the Archaeological Museum and Teatro Massimo, along with many restaurants and shops. Via Bara All'Olivella 67. olivellabb.it. ✆ **347/694-8662.** 5 units. 80€–100€ double. Rates include breakfast. **Amenities:** Free Wi-Fi.

BB22 Charming Rooms and Apartments ♥♥♥ A stay in this 17th-century *palazzo* puts you in the heart of old Palermo, near the Vucciria market and Piazza San Domenico, and that means many restaurants and sights are just outside the door. You'll be staying in style in large rooms and suites soothingly done with chandeliers, gilt mirrors, and carefully chosen antiques. The many amenities include an honesty bar and an airy, glassed-in terrace, an ideal place to relax after a day of sightseeing. Self-catering apartments are available in another restored *palazzo* nearby. Via Pantelleria 22. bb22.it. ✆ **091/326-214.** 7 units. 90€–145€ double. Rates include breakfast. **Amenities:** Lounge; free Wi-Fi.

Where to Eat in Palermo

The opulent **Antico Caffè Spinnato ♥**, Via Principe di Belmonte 115, established in 1860, is the place to linger over a pastry and coffee (spinnato.it; ✆ **091/329220**). In the Kalsa quarter, **Cioccolateria Lorenzo ♥**, Via Quattro Aprile 7 (instagram.com/cioccolaterialorenzo; ✆ **091/549486;** closed Mon), has a wonderful selection of cakes and the best hot chocolate in Palermo. For a huge selection of elaborate pastries, head to the corner of Via Lincoln and Via Nicolo Cervello, across from the botanical

Fast Food, Palermo-Style

Sicily's *cucina povera* (literally "poor man's cuisine"), sold by street vendors and simple eateries, is a delicacy in itself. For a flavorful introduction, take a fun and wonderfully informative food tour with **Streaty ♥♥** (streaty.com; ✆ **351/513-3552**), which includes a market visit, many tastings, and a picnic of local delicacies from shops along the route; tours run daily and cost from 64€.

Among the street classics are *cazzilli* (potato croquettes), *panelle* (chickpea fritters), and *arancini* ("little oranges," saffron-flavored rice balls, usually filled with meat ragù or ham and mozzarella, rolled in breadcrumbs, and fried). A venerable stop for *arancini* is **Sfrigola ♥**, just outside the Porta Nuova at Corso Calatafimi 11, with a branch at Via Maqueda 223 (sfrigola.it; ✆ **091/271-0460;** Mon–Fri 10am–10pm, Sat–Sun 9am–10pm).

Commanding a side of Piazza Kalsa, **Panineria Friggitoria Chiluzzo ♥♥**, Piazza della Kalsa 10 (✆ **329/061-5929;** Mon–Sat 8am–4pm), is Palermo's go-to spot for street food. Even in the heat of summer, a big vat of boiling oil turns out *panelle* and *pane e panelle* (in which the fritter is tucked between heavenly pieces of sesame bread), eaten at shared tables overlooking the palm-studded square and the wonderfully arabesque 16th-century Greek Gate.

Nni Franco u Vastiddaru ♥, Via Vittorio Emanuele 21 (✆ **091/325987**), masters the art of deep frying and also serves *pani ca meusa* (bread roll stuffed with slices of boiled spleen and melted cheese) from a takeout window or in a bare-bones room and terrace overlooking Piazza Marina; the buzzing spot is open daily 9am to 1am, Tuesdays until 11pm. Another popular spleen-stop is **Pani câ Meusa Porta Carbone ♥**, facing the marina at Via Cala 62 (✆ **091/323433;** Mon–Fri 7:30am–10pm, Sat until midnight, Sun 11am–10pm). The master of *pani ca meusa*, though, is Rocky Basile, a longtime fixture of the Vucciria market, where most days he sells sandwiches from a cart.

gardens, where neighboring **Bar Touring ♥**, 38 Via Lincoln (✆ **091/616-7242**), and **Bar Rosanero ♥**, Piazzetta Porta Reale 6 (barrosanero.com; ✆ **091/616-4229**), outdo each other with their displays of homemade sweets. The Riso di Paradise, a concoction of chocolate, rice, and whipped cream, will bring you back daily to **Antica Gelateria Patricola ♥♥**, on the waterfront at Foro Umberto 1 (✆ **379/1781738**). Next to the cloisters of the Monastero Santa Caterina d'Alessandria, the treats at **I Segreti del Chiostro ♥♥**, Piazza Bellini 1 (isegretidelchiostro.com; ✆ **0327/588-2302;** daily 9am–4:30pm), are based on recipes gathered from convent bakeries throughout Sicily and made with the purest ingredients; many of them, including marzipan fruits and many types of *cassata,* are almost too beautiful to eat, but you should. While there, step into the exquisite baroque church and climb to the rooftop terrace for views over Palermo (terrace 7€).

EXPENSIVE

L'Ottava Nota ♥♥♥ SICILIAN "New Sicilian" is in full force at the most exciting of the restaurants that have opened in recent years in the once-derelict Kalsa district, where a sleek black-on-gray decor is the setting for

DINE LIKE A duchess

The best lunch in Palermo is a banquet in the Palazzo Lanza Tomasi, part of a **Day Cooking with the Duchess ♥♥♥** (palazzolanzatomasi.it; ✆ **333/316-5432**). Duchess Nicoletta Polo Lanza Tomasi introduces students to the art of Sicilian cookery in the colorfully tiled kitchens of the palace (p. 764) that she and her late husband, Gioacchino Lanza Tomasi, the Duke of Palma, restored in the Kalsa (the duke was the adopted son of Prince Giuseppe Tomasi di Lampedusa, author of the modern classic *The Leopard*, who lived here at the end of his life). Sessions include a market visit and a stop on the palace's seaside terrace to pick herbs; participants are guided through preparations of typical Sicilian dishes, stroll through stately rooms with a stop in the library where Lampedusa's original manuscript for *The Leopard* enjoys pride of place, and enjoy a meal served by footmen in the regal dining room. Classes are 200€.

creative takes on Sicilian classics. Duck, beef, and fish are market-fresh and beautifully prepared, and you may want to make a meal solely of the innovative pastas with fresh seafood—linguine with scallops, risotto with shrimp, tagliatelle with sea urchins, risotto laced with leeks and tuna caviar. Despite the chic vibe, the friendly service is strictly old-school; a meal often begins with a complimentary glass of prosecco.

Via Butera 55. ristoranteottavanota.it. ✆ **091/616-8601.** Main courses 25€–30€, set menus 90€ and 110€. Mon–Sat 7:30–11pm. Bus: 103, 104, 105, 118, 225.

Osteria dei Vespri ♥♥ SICILIAN On a beautiful square in the Kalsa, several small, simple rooms occupy the lower floor of the Palazzo Valguarnera-Gangi (film buffs take note: The ballroom scene in *The Leopard* was filmed upstairs). Menus change frequently, but they reliably focus on fresh seasonal ingredients and include such innovative house creations as ravioli stuffed with potato cream and gnocchi topped with mussels, as well as gently roasted tuna, pasta with sea urchins, cuttlefish couscous, and other Sicilian seafood classics. In summer the main dining scene moves to the romantic terrace out front.

Piazza Croce dei Vespri. osteriadeivespri.it. ✆ **091/617-1631.** Main courses 28€–35€; tasting menus 95€, 115€, 130€, and 150€. Mon–Wed and Fri–Sat 12:30–2:45pm and 7:30–10:30pm, Thurs 12:30–10:30pm. Bus: 103, 104, 105, 118, 225.

Palazzo Sambuca ♥♥ SEAFOOD/SICILIAN The beautifully restored Palazzo Sambuca in the Kalsa quarter is one of Palermo's great baroque landmarks, and this ground-floor namesake is white and chicly contemporary, with a couple of small, intimate, and elegant dining rooms. A mother-and-son team oversees the kitchen while father and daughter tend to guests, serving Sicilian classics on a daily-changing menu. Seafood is the focus, in dishes such as lightly fried baby squid, simply grilled and baked fresh fish, seafood risottos, and many pasta dishes.

Via Alloro 26. ✆ **091/507-6794.** Main courses 18€–30€. Mon–Sat noon–3pm and 7–11pm. Bus: 103, 104, 105, 118, 225.

MODERATE

Casa del Brodo ♥♥♥ SICILIAN This local institution became deservedly beloved in the early 1900s, when the kitchen dispensed the namesake *brodo* (broth) for free to indigent residents during a cholera epidemic; these days the rich and healthful concoction is served several ways, best as *tortellini in brodo,* with house-made pasta. Many regulars come to these plain rooms on the edge of the old Vucciria market to enjoy other vintage Sicilian specialties that you might not encounter outside of home kitchens, such as *fritelle di fava,* fava beans fried with vegetables and cheese; *carni bollite,* a tantalizing assortment of tender, herb-flavored boiled meats; and *macco di fave* (meatballs and tripe), a carnivore's delight.

Corso Vittorio Emanuele 175. casadelbrodo.it. ✆ **091/321655.** Main courses 12€–18€. Wed–Mon 12:30–3pm and 7:30–10:30pm. Bus: 103, 104, 105, 118, 225.

La Cambusa ♥♥ SICILIAN/SEAFOOD Palermitani have been coming to "The Galley" for decades to enjoy Sicilian favorites, in good weather on a terrace facing the beautiful Piazza Marina and at other times in one of two plain dining rooms warmly decorated with paintings by local artists. The city's ties to the sea come to the fore in deep dives into such Sicilian classics as *zuppe di cozze* (mussels soup), *bucatini con sarde* (homemade bucatini with fresh sardines), and *couscous di pesce alla Trapanese* (fish and seafood simmered in stock and served over hand-rolled semolina couscous).

Piazza Marina. lacambusa.it. ✆ **091/584574.** Main courses 14€–22€. Wed–Sun 11am–10pm; shorter hours Jan–Feb. Bus: 103, 104, 105, 118, 225.

L'Acerba Osteria Dinamica ♥♥♥ SICIILIAN/SEAFOOD This informal and welcoming haven for seafood lovers is tucked away in a charming courtyard amid the Capo market, just off lanes lined with stalls overflowing with the local catch. Grilled sardines, thick tuna steaks, and seafood-rich pastas are served by a friendly staff, followed by wonderfully innovative and delicious takes on Sicilian desserts, including a memorable semifreddo with Marsala wine.

Vicolo Maestro Cristofaro 9/10. ✆ **091/732-1100.** Main courses 12€–25€. Daily 12:30–3pm and 7–11pm.

La Galleria ♥♥ SICILIAN Despite the city-center surroundings behind the cathedral, the food in this rustic dining room and pretty terrace on a little alley is inspired by rural Sicily. Rich sauces of wild boar and grilled *caciocavallo,* an earthy southern cheese, make unexpected appearances here in the heart of the city, and the rich caponata and seafood-laden pastas are traditional Palermo cooking at its best.

Piazza Sett'Angeli 3. facebook.com/lagalleria2014. ✆ **329/981-5433.** Main courses 13€–18€. Tues–Sat 12:30–3pm and 6–11pm, Sun 1–3pm and 6–11pm.

Quid Gusto Siciliano ♥♥ SICILIAN/PIZZA Classic Sicilian recipes are given a modern twist in a memorably Palermo setting—a terrace shadowed by the huge banyan tree in atmospheric Piazza Marina. The handsomely sparse white interior is welcoming, as are such home-style dishes as *mezzemaniche* (half sleeves) pasta with clams in a white bean sauce and squid served Palermitana-style, in red anchovy sauce. A huge pizza menu is available, too.

Piazza Marina 52. quidgustosiciliano.com. ✆ **091/729-6996.** Main courses 15€–24€. Daily noon–3pm and 7–11pm.

INEXPENSIVE

Antica Focacceria San Francesco ♥♥ SICILIAN/SNACKS If you've shied away from buying a *pani câ meusa* (bread roll stuffed with slices of boiled spleen and melted cheese) from a street vendor, you might want to initiate yourself to the Palermo specialty in this atmospheric, marble-floored institution that opened up shop in a disused chapel in 1834. You can also snack or dine on *arancini* (rice balls stuffed with tomatoes and peas or mozzarella), *panelle* (deep-fried chickpea fritters), and *focaccia farcita* (flat pizza with fillings), all curtly dispensed from a busy counter.

Via A. Paternostro 58. afsf.it. ✆ **091/321655.** Main courses 6€–18€. Daily noon–3pm and 7–11pm. Bus: 103, 105, 225.

Arte e Tradizione ♥♥ PIZZA One of the city's favorite pizza parlors might be the liveliest spot in the Kalsa quarter. In the large, bright room, and on the terrace facing a scrappy patch of greenery, you'll likely dine with students and huge extended families. Aside from some appetizers, you won't find much but pizza, with choices running to the dozens, including some decadent dessert concoctions. Reservations are essential on weekends, when you're unlikely to get a table without one.

Via Santa Teresa 2. arteetradizione.it. ✆ **091/252-4451.** Pizzas 6€–14€. Tues–Sun 7–11pm. Bus: 107, 224.

Bisso Bistrot ♥♥♥ SICILIAN It's a sign of Palermo's renewal that you can now sit down and enjoy a meal right on the Quatro Canti, in character-filled rooms that were once the Libreria Dante bookstore. Pastas, including a classic alla Norma (with eggplant), swordfish *involtini,* and other Sicilian classics are served at communal tables that are always bustling with patrons enjoying sustenance from morning coffee to late-night snacks.

Via Maqueda 172a. bissobistrot.it. ✆ **328/131-4595.** Main courses 8€–13€. Daily 8am–11pm.

Ferro di Cavallo ♥♥♥ SICILIAN Bright red walls seem to rev up the energy to high levels in this ever-busy favorite, but the buzz is really about the good, simple food served at very reasonable prices. A decent *antipasti* platter offers a nice sampling of *panelle* (fried chickpea fritters) and other street food, and the daily specials give the full flavor of the

Do Some Market Research

You can't do justice to Palermo without swinging through one of its street markets. Nowhere is Palermo's multicultural pedigree more evident than at the stalls of the **Ballarò** ♥♥ (in Piazza Ballarò), **Capo** ♥ (from Via Porta Carini south toward the cathedral), and even the sadly declined **La Vucciria** ♥ (on Via Argenteria, north of Via Vittorio Emanuele and east of Via Roma). These open-air souks go on for blocks, with vendors hawking everything from spices to seafood to handicrafts to electronics. Delve even deeper into Palermo's market culture at the neighborhood **Borgo Vecchio** ♥ market (along Via Ettore Ximenes to Via Principe di Scordia) in the newer part of the city, northwest of Piazza Politeama. Antiques vendors with many unusual offerings congregate at the **Mercato delle Pulci** ♥ (Flea Market) along the Piazza Peranni, off Corso Vittorio Emanuele.

Tempting food stalls at Il Ballarò market.

kitchen. The preference is for beans and celery, broad beans and vegetables, meatballs in tomato sauce, boiled veal, and other simple staples, most of which have been on the menu since the grandfather of present-day owner Giuseppe Cimmina founded "The Horseshoe" in 1944. Service hovers between nonchalant and brusque, but the jovial atmosphere compensates, and you'll pay very little for your homey meal.

Via Venezia 20. ferrodicavallopalermo.it. ✆ **091/331835.** Main courses 8€–12€. Mon–Tues 9am–3pm; Wed–Sat 9am–3pm and 6:30–10:30pm. Bus: 103, 104, 105, 118, 225.

Moltivolti ♥♥♥ MIDDLE EASTERN/NORTH AFRICAN/MEDITERRANEAN The name means "many faces," and these colorful mural-decorated rooms in the Ballarò neighborhood function as an all-day cafe, bar, restaurant, social enterprise, and shared workspace for humanitarian groups, creating a vibrant cultural hub that focuses on Palermo's migrant culture. The international staff, many from North Africa and the Middle East, prepare a similarly eclectic and excellent menu of couscous, *mafe* (a stew of lamb in peanut sauce), moussaka, and some Sicilian standards, served at communal tables and accompanied by dips, salads, and a few desserts.

Via Giuseppe Mario Puglia. moltivolti.org. ✆ **091/271-0285.** Main courses 10€–14€. Daily 9am–midnight. Bus: 104, 105, 108, 109, 110, 118.

Palermo Entertainment & Nightlife

Palermo is a cultural center of some note, with an opera and ballet season running from November to July. The principal performance venue is the restored **Teatro Massimo ♥♥**, Piazza G. Verdi (teatromassimo.it; ✆ **091/605-3111**), which boasts the third-largest indoor stage in Europe. (Francis Ford Coppola shot the climactic opera scene here for *The Godfather Part III.*) Built between 1875 and 1897 in a neoclassical style, the theater was restored in 1997 to celebrate its centennial. Tickets range from 10€ to 125€. The box office is open Tuesday to Sunday 10am to 3pm. Guided tours (12€, 6€ under 26) in English are given daily 9:30am to 5:30pm. Watch your step on the monumental staircase leading up to the entrance: Legend has it that the ghost of a nun whose convent was displaced to build the theater takes her revenge by tripping operagoers.

The old **Vucciria market,** no longer the lively shopping souk it once was, is reemerging as a nightlife scene. **Via Chiavettieri,** leading into the neighborhood off Via Vittorio Emanuele, is lined with bars where your aperitivo comes with free *cicchetti* (snacks). Street-food outlets and bars line the decrepit old market square and surrounding lanes; the square also fills with tables on weekends and during soccer matches, broadcast on a huge outdoor screen. **Via Maqueda,** in the blocks just north of the Quattro Canti, is also a nightlife strip with many bars and restaurants.

Side Trips from Palermo

A popular summertime escape from Palermo is **Mondello Lido ♥**, 12km (7½ miles) west, where Belle Epoque Europeans once came to winter. Their Art Nouveau villas face a sandy beach that stretches for about 2km (1¼ miles), though there's little or no elbow room in July and August. Bus no. 806 makes the 45-minute trip from Piazza Francesco Crispi and along Via Libertà. Many other sights are within easy reach of Palermo.

MONREALE ♥♥♥

10km (6 miles) S of Palermo

On Monte Caputo overlooking the fertile Conca d'Oro (Golden Valley), Monreale would be just another pretty hilltop village if it weren't for the majestic Duomo, one of Italy's greatest medieval treasures, sheathed in shimmering mosaics. The locals have a saying, "To come to Palermo without having seen Monreale is like coming in like a donkey and leaving like an ass."

ARRIVING **AMAT bus 389** (✆ **091/350111**) leaves approximately every 1 hour and 15 minutes throughout the day from a stop near Palazzo dei Normanni, on Piazza Indipendenza. If you are **driving** (it's about a 30-min. trip), leave your vehicle at the car park at Via Ignazio Florio. From there walk up the 99 steps that lead to the cathedral.

Duomo ♥♥♥ CATHEDRAL Legend has it that the idea for a cathedral came to William II in a dream when, during a hunting expedition, he

Gleaming mosaics inside the Cathedral of Monreale.

fell asleep under a carob tree. In his slumber, the Virgin Mary appeared to him, indicating where a treasure chest was located and telling him that with this loot he was to build a church in her honor. Closer to fact, William's ambition to leave his mark was the force behind the last and greatest of Sicily's Arab-Norman cathedrals, begun, like the one in Palermo, in 1184. The cathedral in Monreale never underwent the "improvements" that were applied to the cathedral of Palermo, so its original beauty has been preserved.

Mosaics carpet the vast interior and comprise 130 individual scenes depicting biblical and religious events, covering some 6,400 sq. m (68,890 sq. ft.), and utilizing some 2,200 kg (4,850 lb.) of gold. The shop in the arcade outside the entrance sells a plan of the mosaics with a legend detailing what's what, a mandatory aid to enjoying the spectacle; binoculars are also handy.

Episodes from the Old Testament are in the central nave (a particularly charming scene shows Noah's Ark riding the waves) while the side aisles illustrate scenes from the New Testament. Christ Pantocrator, the Great Ruler, looks over it all from the central apse; actually, he gazes off to one side, toward scenes from his life. Just below is a mosaic of the Teokotos (Mother of God) with the Christ child on her lap, bathed in light from the window above the main entrance. Among the angels and saints flanking Teokotos is Thomas à Becket, Archbishop of Canterbury, who was murdered on the order of William's father-in-law, Henry II (he is the second from the right). William is buried here and honored with a mosaic showing him being crowned by Christ.

The cloisters adjacent to the cathedral are an arabesque fantasy, surrounded by 228 columns topped with capitals carved with scenes from Sicily's Norman history. A splendid fountain in the shape of a palm tree adds to the romance of the place.

Piazza Guglielmo il Buono. duomomonreale.com. ✆ **091/640-4413.** Free admission; 10€ north transept Roano chapel (with Norman floors), cloisters, Diocesan Museum, and roof. Mon–Sat 9am–1pm and 2:30–5pm, Sun 2–5pm (cloisters Mon–Sat 9am–7pm, Sun 9am–1:30pm).

CEFALÙ ♥♥

81km (50 miles) E of Palermo

If you saw the Oscar-winning film *Cinema Paradiso*, you've already been charmed by the former fishing village of Cefalù, now a popular resort. The filmmakers wisely left out the swarm of white-fleshed northern Europeans who roast themselves on its crescent-shaped **beach,** one of the best along the northern coast, which stretches beneath the tall white houses of the old town. Towering 278m (912 ft.) above the beach and town is **La Rocca,** a massive and much-photographed crag. The Greeks thought this mountain evoked a head, so they named the village Kephalos, which in time became Cefalù. It's a vigorous climb up to the top of La Rocca, but once there, the view is panoramic, extending all the way to Palermo's skyline in the west, Capo d'Orlando in the east, and across the Madonie mountains to the south.

ARRIVING From Palermo, some three dozen daily **trains** (trenitalia.com; ✆ **892021**) head east to Cefalù (trip time: 1 hr.). It's about a 10-minute walk from the station to Piazza Garibaldi, at the entrance to the old town. By **car,** follow Route 113 east from Palermo to Cefalù; count on at least 1½ hours of driving time. Once in Cefalù, park along either side of Via Roma for free, or pay 1€ per hour for a spot within one of the two lots signposted from the main street; both are within an easy walk of the town's medieval core.

The Norman-era Duomo di Cefalù sits at the foot of the towering crag La Rocca, which gives the town its name.

VISITOR INFORMATION The **Cefalù tourist office,** Piazza Duomo 9 (✆ **327/196-5559**), is open daily 9am to 1pm and 3 to 7pm.

Exploring Cefalù

Getting around Cefalù on foot is easy, and no cars are allowed in the historic core. The city's main street, **Corso Ruggero,** starts at Piazza Garibaldi, one of four historic gateways to the town. Well marked off Via Vittorio Emanuele in the town center, the river Cefalino flows through a series of large basins in the communal laundry, with a channel carrying dirty rinse water into the sea below. On the north end of town, remains of medieval bastions skirt a rocky shoreline.

Duomo ♥♥♥ CHURCH Anchored on a wide square at the foot of towering La Rocca, the twin-towered facade of Cefalù's Duomo forms a landmark visible for miles around. Legend has it that Roger II ordered the construction of this mighty church in the 12th century after his life was spared in a violent storm off the coast. In reality, he probably built the cathedral to flex his muscle with the papacy and show the extent of his power in Sicily. This being a Norman church, shimmering mosaics in the apse depict Christ as a blonde, not a brunette. In his hand is a Bible, a standard fixture in images of Christ the Pantocrator (the Ruler), with the verse, "I am the light of the world; he who follows me shall not walk in darkness." The 16 columns in the nave are said to be from the ruined Temple of Diana halfway up La Rocca. A 10€ ticket also gives you access to the towers for thrilling views of the cathedral interior and mosaics on the way up and over the town and sea from the top. A more comprehensive 13€ ticket also includes the beautiful and transporting cloisters, where ancient Greek columns support exotic Arab-Norman arches.

Piazza del Duomo. duomocefalu.it. ✆ **0921/926366.** Free admission to Duomo; 10€ towers, 13€ towers, cloister, and cathedral treasury. Daily 8:30am–1pm and 3:30–6pm.

Monumento per Un Poeta Morto (Monument to a Dead Poet) ♥♥ SCULPTURE PARK This extraordinary art installation on the coast east of Cefalù commemorates the late painter Tano Festa (1938–88) with a huge blue concrete frame facing the sea. You may or may not see the work as representing the limitations that prevent us from soaring to our potential (as the expanse of sea and infinite horizon beyond suggest), but it's a compelling and provocative presence nonetheless. To see more contemporary art, continue on to **Fiumara d'Arte,** 23km (14 miles) south on SP176, Europe's largest sculpture park, where labyrinths, pyramids, arcs, and other conceptual creations appear among the stark landscape of the Nebrodi mountains.

Lungomare Colonna, Villa Margi, 36km (22 miles) east of Cefalù. Free admission.

Museo Mandralisca ♥ MUSEUM There is only one real reason to step into this small museum, and it's a compelling one: *Ritratto di un Uomo Ignoto* (*Portrait of an Unknown Man*), a 1470 work by the Sicilian painter Antonello da Messina. Seeing this young man with a sly smile and twinkling eyes—some say he was a pirate from the island of Lipari—is an experience akin to seeing the *Mona Lisa*, and you won't have to fight your way through camera-wielding crowds to do so.

Via Mandralisca 13. fondazionemandralisca.it. ✆ **0921/421-547.** Admission 8€ adults, 6€ ages 11–15, 3€ ages 6–10, free for children 5 and under. Mon–Sun 9am–7pm (to 9pm July–Aug; closed Mon Nov–Mar).

Where to Stay & Eat in Cefalù

B&B Siroco ♥♥♥ Friendly host Nicole's sunny and attractive top-floor guesthouse shows off Cefalù in all its beauty, quite literally so, as the town and seafront spread out below the large windows and roof terrace, with La Rocca as a backdrop. Handsomely furnished rooms are accented with colorful wall coverings and filled with views, two from private balconies. In all but the chilliest weather a homemade breakfast is served beneath a canopy high above town on the terrace. The station is a short walk away, but travel light—these views come with a climb up several flights of stairs.

Piazza Garibaldi 8. sciroccobeb.com. ✆ **392/644-4131.** 4 units. 70€–130€ double. **Amenities:** Free Wi-Fi.

Osteria del Duomo ♥♥ SICILIAN/SEAFOOD A prime spot across from the Duomo with great views of that imposing facade with La Rocca behind makes this a worthy stop, and the fresh seafood does justice to the locale. Seafood salads are a perfect choice for lunch on a summer's day, and fish-lovers will appreciate the *carpaccio de pesce* (raw, thinly sliced fish). Carnivores can tuck into the similarly excellent carpaccio of beef. Reserve on weekends.

Via Seminario 3. ✆ **0921/421838.** Main courses 8€–16€. Daily 10:30am–11:30pm. Closed mid-Nov to Jan.

SEGESTA ♥♥♥

75km (47 miles) SW of Palermo

The **Tempio di Segesta,** one of the best-preserved ancient Doric temples in Italy, proves yet again that the Greeks had a remarkable eye for where to build. Part of the ruined ancient city of Segesta, for millennia this beautiful structure in a lonely field overlooking the countryside has been delighting those lucky enough to gaze upon it. The temple was especially popular with 18th-century artists traveling in Sicily, whose paintings usually included flocks of sheep and herds of cattle surrounding the temple.

ARRIVING By **car,** take the *autostrada* (A29) running between Palermo and Trapani. The exit at Segesta is clearly marked. The journey takes a little under an hour from Palermo. The only easy way to visit the temple by public transportation is by bus from **Trapani** (p. 809). Buses operated by **Tarantola** (tarantolacuffaro.it; ✆ **092/431-020**) make a trip from Palermo to Segesta, but infrequently and at inconvenient hours, and not to the site but to the town of Calatafimi. **Tours of Sicily** (tourofsicily.com;

© **091/626-9685**) and numerous other tour companies include Segesta on their day-trip itineraries from Palermo.

Exploring the Archaeological Park

The archaeological site, which is outside the modern town of Calatafimi, is still the subject of study by archaeologists from around the world. There's a small, canopied eating area opposite the only cafe, where visitors can unwind or rest during their visit.

Area Archeologico Segesta ♥♥♥ RUINS The **Tempio di Segesta** (Temple of Segesta) stands on a 304m (997-ft.) hill, on the edge of a deep ravine carved by the Pispisa River. Built in the 5th century B.C.E., the temple was never finished, its columns left unfluted and its roof missing. It's been suggested that the temple was actually a ruse, begun to impress diplomats from Athens who, it was thought, would see the project as a sign of the city's wealth and therefore ally with Segesta against Selinunte. Construction, it's been suggested, halted as soon as the delegation left town. Segesta's other great sight is the perfectly preserved **Teatro** (Theater), hewn out of rock at the top of 431m (1,414-ft.) Mount Barbaro (accessible by a hike of 4km/2½ miles or by buses that run every half-hour; 1.50€ round-trip). The *cavea* of 20 semicircular rows could seat 4,000 spectators, who enjoyed views across the surrounding farmland to

The Greek Theater of Segesta.

AEOLIAN ISLAND escapes

The **Aeolian Islands** can seem like exotic getaways, even as close as they are to Sicily's civilized north coast (they're reached by ferries and hydrofoils from the port of **Milazzo,** a 45-min. drive west of Messina, 2½ hr. east of Palermo). The seven islands share sparkling waters and lava-etched landscapes, and each has its own devotees. Especially popular are **Vulcano,** a stomping ground for summertime partiers and known for black-sand beaches and thermal baths, and **Stromboli,** whose volcano sends red-hot lava tumbling down its slopes to meet the sea with a loud hiss. For more information, go to **visitsicily.info/en/aeolian-islands**.

the Gulf of Castellammare. Those stunning views surely competed with any performance—and still do, during summertime stagings of operas, concerts, and plays.

Parco Archeologico Segesta. parcodisegesta.com. ✆ **0924/952-356.** Admission 12€ adults, free for ages 17 and under. Apr–Sept daily 9am–6pm; Mar and Oct 9am–5pm; Nov–Feb 9am–3:30pm. Ticket office closes 1½ hr. before park closes.

TAORMINA ♥♥♥

53km (33 miles) N of Catania, 53km (33 miles) S of Messina, 250km (155 miles) E of Palermo

The Roman poet Ovid loved Taormina, and 18th-century German man of letters Wolfgang Goethe put the town on the Grand Tour circuit when he extolled its virtues in his widely published diaries. Oscar Wilde was one of the gentlemen who made Taormina, as writer and dilettante Harold Acton put it, "a polite synonym for Sodom," and Greta Garbo is one of many film legends who have sought a bit of privacy here. A recent depiction in the television series *The White Lotus* as an enchanted playground for the rich and entitled (and those who prey on them) has put Taormina in the spotlight yet again. Many contemporary visitors would no doubt agree with Guy de Maupassant, the 19th-century French short-story writer, who summed up the city as having been "created to seduce the eyes, the mind and the imagination."

With its beauty and sophistication, Taormina has a surfeit of star quality. The town seems more international than Sicilian, with visitors often outnumbering locals. Then again, perched precariously on a cliff between the sinister slopes of Mount Etna and the glittering Ionian Sea, with captivating alleyways lined with churches and *palazzi,* Taormina is almost over-the-top beautiful, and what could be more Sicilian than that?

Essentials

ARRIVING If you plan to arrive by **air,** the most convenient airport for Taormina is Catania's **Fontanarossa airport** (CTA; aeroporto.catania.it), which has numerous connections to mainland Italy and major European

ATTRACTIONS

Teatro Greco 10
Villa Comunale 7

HOTELS

Excelsior Palace 1
Hotel Bel Soggiorno 8
Hotel del Corso 2
Villa Carlotta 9
Villa Ducale 12
Villa Paradiso 6

RESTAURANTS

Al Duomo 3
Osteria da Rita 5
Tischi Toschi 4
Trattoria da Nino 11

cities, as well as daily service on **Delta** (delta.com) to and from New York's JFK airport between May and late October. Hourly **buses** operated by **Etna Trasporti** (etnatrasporti.it; ✆ **06/164160**) run up the coast from there to Taormina (trip time about 1½ hr.; tickets 5€ one-way). A taxi costs 70€ to 80€.

If you're arriving by **car,** the A18 highway connects with Messina from the north (45 min.; take Taormina exit) and Catania from the south (50 min.; exit at Giardini Naxos and follow signs uphill to Taormina). If your hotel offers parking, get very clear instructions about how to arrive—Taormina is a mind-boggling maze of tiny one-way streets and hairpin turns. Otherwise, take advantage of the large public parking garages just outside the old town, both clearly signposted with blue "P"s on all roads that approach Taormina. On the north side of town, **Parking Lumbi** (✆ **0942/24345**) charges 2€ to 3€, depending on season, for first 1½ hour, 6€ to 9€ for 3 hours, 1€ an hour after that, and 20€ to 23€ a day, and has a free shuttle from the garage to the Porta Messina gate of Taormina proper. On the south end of town, the multilevel garage **Parking Porta Catania** (✆ **0942/620196**) has the advantage of being practically in town, just 100m/328 ft. from the Porta Catania city gate, and charges 3€ to 5€ for first hour, depending on season, 7€ to 10€ for 2 hours, 1€ an hour after that, and 25€ to 28€ per day. Down by the beach at Mazzarò, in the vicinity of the lower cable-car station, is **Parking Mazzarò** (6€–10€, depending on season, for 3 hr., 1€/hr. after that, and 25€–30€ per day). For more info on parking, go to **taorminaservizipubblici.it**.

Taormina is well served by **buses** from the rest of Sicily, usually connecting through Catania (visit etnatrasporti.it for schedules). Taormina's bus station is on Via Pirandello, near Porta Messina, on the north end of town. **Trains** to Taormina run on a line between Messina and Catania, each between 40 minutes and 1½ hours away, depending on the speed of your train. Go to trenitalia.com (✆ **89/2021**) for schedules; service on Sundays is infrequent. Taormina's train station is shared with the seaside town of Giardini-Naxos, so it's 1.6km (1 mile) below town—you'll have to take a taxi (about 15€–20€) or a bus up the hill to Taormina (buses run infrequently 9am–9pm; 1.50€ one-way; asmtaormina.com for schedules).

VISITOR INFORMATION The **tourist office** is in Palazzo Corvaja, Piazza Santa Caterina (✆ **0942/23243;** Mon–Thurs 8:30am–2pm and 4–7pm, Fri 8:30am–2pm). Here you can get a free map, hotel listings, bus and rail timetables, and a schedule of summer cultural events staged at the **Teatro Greco** (Greek Theater; below).

Exploring Taormina

Just about everything to see in Taormina unfolds from the main drag, **Corso Umberto I,** which slices through town from Porta Messina, in the north, to Porta Catania, in the south. It only takes 15 minutes to walk the length of the Corso.

The evening *passeggiata* along Corso Umberto I.

Teatro Greco (Teatro Antico) ♥♥♥ RUINS With their penchant for building in beautiful settings, the Greeks perched the second-largest ancient theater in Sicily (after Siracusa's; see p. 792) on the rocky flanks of Mount Tauro. The backdrop of smoldering Mount Etna and the sea crashing far below certainly provided as much drama as any theatrical production. Romans rebuilt much of the theater, adding the finishing touches on what we see today in the C.E. 2nd century, and put the arena to use for gladiatorial events. In ruin, but with much of the hillside *cavea* (curved seating area) intact, the theater is still the setting for performances and film screenings, greatly enhanced by columns and arches framing the sea and volcano in the background. Check with the **TaorminaArte** headquarters, Corso Umberto 19 (taoarte.it; ✆ **391/746-2146**), or at the tourist office for performance dates and ticket info.

Via del Teatro Greco. traveltaormina.com. ✆ **0942/21142.** Admission 14€; audioguide 5€; guided tours 12€. Daily 9am–7pm (early Sept to 6:30pm, late Sept to 6pm, early Oct to 5:30pm, late Oct to 5pm, Nov to mid-Feb to 4pm, late Feb to Mar to 4:30pm, Apr to 6:30pm).

Villa Comunale ♥♥♥ PARK/GARDEN Of all the colorful characters who have spent time in Taormina, the one leaving the biggest mark may have been Lady Florence Trevelyan, who in the late 19th century created these beautiful gardens, now also known as Parco Duca di Cesarò. Lady Trevelyan allegedly was asked to leave Britain after an entanglement with Edward, Prince of Wales, son of Queen Victoria. She settled in Taormina, married, and lived quite happily in the lovely adjacent villa, now the hotel **Villa Paradiso** (p. 784). Her liaison with a farmer, much of it conducted amid these groves and terraces, supposedly inspired D.H. Lawrence's *Lady Chatterley's Lover*. Lady Trevelyan built the stone and brick pavilions in the park for birdwatching and entertaining, and 3 hectares (7½ acres) of groomed terraces are filled with luxuriant vegetation, cobblestone walkways, picturesque stone stairways, and a sinuous path lining the park's eastern rim with superb views over the sea.

Via Bagnoli Croce. No phone. Free admission. Daily 8:30am–7pm (winter 'til 6pm).

MEET mighty MOUNT ETNA

Looming menacingly over the coast of eastern Sicily, Mount Etna is the highest and largest active volcano in Europe. Taormina is a handy base for trips to Mount Etna—the high-altitude visitor areas on the south slope are only about 1 hour away by car. ***Warning:*** Always get the latest report from the tourist office before setting out for a trip to Mount Etna, one of the world's most active volcanoes. In 1928, the little village of Mascali was buried under lava, and powerful eruptions in 1971, 1992, 2001, and 2003 caused extensive damage to facilities nearby. Episodes of spectacular but usually harmless lava fountains are not uncommon, creating ash clouds that sometimes force the airport in Catania to close.

Etna has played a role throughout history and Greek mythology. Hephaestus, god of fire, made his headquarters in Etna, and it was under Etna that Zeus crushed the multiheaded dragon Typhoeus, thereby securing domination over Olympus. Empedocles, the 5th-century-B.C.E. Greek philosopher, is said to have jumped into its crater in the belief that he would be delivered directly to Mt. Olympus to take his seat among the gods.

Etna is easy to reach by car from Taormina. The fastest way is to take the E45 *autostrada* south to the Acireale exit. From here, follow the brown ETNA signs west to Nicolosi, passing through several smaller towns along the way. From Nicolosi, keep following the ETNA signs up the hill toward **Rifugio Sapienza** (1,923m/6,307 ft.), the starting point for expeditions to the crater. The faux-Alpine hamlet here has tourist services and cheap and ample parking, and it is the base station of the **Funivia del Etna** cable car (funiviaetna.com; ✆ **095/914141;** daily winter 8:30am–4:10pm, summer 'til 5:15pm), which takes you to the **Torre del Filosofo** (Philosopher's Tower) station at 2,900m (9,514 ft.). You can also hike up to the station, but it's a strenuous 5-hour climb. The final ascent to the authorized crater areas (as close to the summit as visitors are allowed) is via *Star Wars*–ish off-road vehicles over a scrabbly terrain of ash and dead ladybugs (dead ladybugs are everywhere on Mount Etna). Conditions at the crater zone are thrilling, but the high winds, exposure, and potential sense of vertigo are not for the faint of heart.

The round-trip cable-car ride is 52€. Getting all the way to the top of Etna, including the cable car, off-road vans, and the requisite authorized guide at the crater zone, costs about 80€.

If you'd prefer to go with a tour, Taormina is chock-full of agencies that organize Etna day trips. Some operators also approach the mountain from the less-visited north slope, leading guided hikes through birch forests and across the lava fields near the wine village of Linguaglossa.

Where to Stay in Taormina

Hotels in Taormina are some of the best in Sicily. Quite a few close in the winter, but those that remain open offer rates at a fraction of summertime tariffs. If you're driving to Taormina, call ahead to see what arrangements can be made for your car.

EXPENSIVE

Villa Carlotta ♥♥ Tucked away at the edge of town, this castellated 1920s stone villa is another creation of Andrea and Rosaria Quartucci, who work their magic at **Villa Ducale** (below). A wall of Byzantine catacombs adds an air of mystery, but what wins you over is the classic-yet-contemporary style and wonderful sense of privacy and comfort. Most of the warm-hued, stylish rooms have terraces and sea views, and many overlook the luxuriant rear gardens, with a swimming pool set amid the greenery. Service is personalized and attentive. Villa Carlotta also houses guests in luxury apartments up the street.

Via Pirandello 81. hotelvillacarlottataormina.com. ✆ **0942/626-058.** 23 units. 280€–650€ double. Rates include breakfast. 2-night minimum stay some periods. Parking 30€. Closed Nov to early Mar. **Amenities:** Restaurant; concierge; health club; pool; free Wi-Fi.

Villa Ducale ♥♥♥ Andrea and Rosaria Quartucci have fashioned a family villa into a warm and stylish getaway perched high on a hillside above the town, with flower-planted terraces, Mediterranean gardens, and extraordinary eagle's-nest views that extend as far as Calabria. Distinctive rooms and suites, in the villa and a house across the road, are done in Sicilian chic, with extremely comfortable furnishings set against warm hues that play off terra-cotta floors. Beams, arches, and other architectural details enliven the rooms, which are equipped with luxurious baths and fitted out with fine linens and works by local artists. Service is warm and personal. A lavish buffet breakfast and complimentary sunset cocktails, accompanied by a spread of Sicilian appetizers, are served on a living-room-like terrace. A shuttle runs to and from town.

A room with a killer view at hillside Villa Ducale.

Via Leonardo da Vinci 60. villaducale.com. ✆ **0942/28153.** 15 units. 410€–520€ double. Rates include breakfast. Parking 20€. Closed Jan–Mar. **Amenities:** Restaurant; bar; pool; Jacuzzi; room service; free Wi-Fi.

MODERATE

Excelsior Palace ♥ Though this sprawling pink landmark behind the Duomo, welcoming guests since 1904, is often filled with groups, service is attentive and old-world, with waiters in ties and jackets serving cocktails in frumpy lounges full of overstuffed couches and armchairs. Rooms are a bit outdated but conventionally comfortable and well maintained, and all have views, many of Mt. Etna and the coastline; several have tiny balconies with just enough room for two chairs. The best amenity is the magnificent garden, draped over a view-filled promontory with a superbly perched pool, making this a top summertime choice.

Via Toselli 8. excelsiorpalacetaormina.it. ✆ **0942/23975.** 85 units. 140€–275€ double. Rates include breakfast. **Amenities:** Restaurant; bar; concierge; pool; free Wi-Fi in public areas.

Hotel Bel Soggiorno ♥♥ You could be nowhere but Sicily in this rather grand old villa surrounded by lush gardens that tumble down a hillside, filled with lemon and orange trees, exotic flowers, and sweeping coastal vistas. Tile-floored guest rooms are plain but comfortable, with handsome iron bedsteads and simple wooden furniture. All open through French doors to balconies and, in many cases, huge terraces. A friendly staff serves breakfast, with some cooked choices, in a beautiful *orangerie* and on an adjoining patio. As bucolic as the surroundings are, the center of town is an easy 10-minute walk away.

Via Luigi Pirandello 60. belsoggiorno.com. ✆ **0942/23342.** 120€–180€ double. Rates include breakfast. Closed Dec to mid-Mar. **Amenities:** Bar; free Wi-Fi.

Villa Paradiso ♥♥♥ Lady Florence Trevelyan, who created the beautiful gardens that are now the Villa Comunale (p. 781), lived in this villa until her death in 1907. The elegant house then passed to the Martorana family, three generations of which have proven to be outstanding hoteliers and avid renovators, adding entire floors to the original house. Family antiques, comfy armchairs and couches, and paintings (many presented by guests over the years) fill lounges and bright, handsomely decorated guest rooms, where balconies and sun-drenched sitting alcoves face the sea. Breakfast and dinners are served in a top-floor, glassed-in restaurant, **Settimo Cielo** (Seventh Heaven), which it really seems to be. Between June and October, the hotel offers shuttle service and free entrance to the Paradise Beach Club, about 6km (4 miles) to the east, in the seaside resort of Letojanni.

Via Roma 2. hotelvillaparadisotaormina.com. ✆ **0942/23921.** 37 units. 190€–335€ double. Rates include breakfast. Parking 20€. **Amenities:** Restaurant; bar; room service; free Wi-Fi.

INEXPENSIVE

Hotel del Corso ♥♥ You'll forgo spas, pools, and other chic luxuries in these basic lodgings in the heart of town near the Duomo, but you won't give up views of the sea and Mt. Etna. They fill the windows of many of the rooms and spread out below the top-floor lounge, breakfast room, and sun terrace; some rooms have less dramatic but pleasing views of the town. Black-and-white terrazzo floors, iron bedsteads, and soothing neutral colors add a lot of spark to the comfortable guest rooms, a few of which have small balconies. Book well in advance, especially for weekends, when this good-value property fills up fast.

Corso Umberto 328. del-corso.taorminahotelsweb.com. ✆ **0942/628-698.** 15 units. 100€–150€ double. Rates include breakfast. **Amenities:** Free Wi-Fi.

Where to Eat in Taormina

The ultimate Sicilian summer refreshment, sorbetlike *granita,* is perfect at **Bam Bar ♥♥**, not far from the Grand Hotel Timeo at Via di Giovanni 45 (✆ **0942/24355**). Specialties are the almond (*mandorla*) or white fig (*fico bianco*), but usually you'll have a dozen or more flavors to choose from. Wines to enjoy in Taormina are those from vineyards on a wine route around the village of Linguaglossa on the north slope of Mount Etna. Reds and whites are slightly fruity with an underlying mineral quality.

Dine overlooking the namesake cathedral at Al Duomo.

Al Duomo ♥♥ SICILIAN/SEAFOOD Take a table near the large window overlooking the namesake landmark or, in good weather, on the side terrace. Then enjoy traditional Sicilian cooking with some well-conceived modern twists, with many fish- and shellfish-laden pasta dishes. This might be the best place in town to try pasta *con sarde* (with sardines and breadcrumbs), fresh fish accented with capers, tomatoes, and olives.

Vico Ebrei (at Piazza Duomo). ristorantealduomotaormina.com. ✆ **0942/625-656.** Main courses 18€–30€. Daily noon–midnight.

Osteria da Rita ♥♥ SICILIAN/PIZZA Taormina needs more easygoing eateries like this pleasant little place tucked away between the Corso and Villa Comunale. Pizzas, sandwiches, salads, omelets, and a few pasta dishes—including heaping platters of spaghetti carbonara and *pasta alla Norma*—are served in a small, plain room and on a picture-perfect piazzetta out front. Service is friendly and prices are reasonable.

Via Calapitrulli 3. instagram.com/osteriadarita. ✆ **0942/681015.** Main courses 15€–22€. Daily 11am–11pm. Closed Dec–Jan.

Tischi Toschi ♥♥♥ SICILIAN/SEAFOOD A warm-hued yellow room facing a little piazza and decorated with old ceramics is the setting for creative takes on old Sicilian classics. Even the ubiquitous *pasta alla Norma* (with eggplant and ricotta) seems like a work of art here, topped with grilled eggplant. Venture further and sample some dishes you might not find many other places, such as *insalata di pesce stocco,* a salad made from dried cod, raw fennel, and tomato dressed with olive oil and parsley, or *sarde a beccafico,* sardines stuffed with pine nuts and fennel and served with lemon and orange. Don't miss the delicious fried artichokes, or, to top off a meal, the heavenly, refreshing lemon jelly.

Via F. Paladini 3 (off Corso Umberto). tischitoschitaormina.com. ✆ **339/364-2088.** Main courses 15€–25€. Mon–Thurs 7–10pm; Fri–Sun 1–2pm and 7–10pm.

Trattoria da Nino ♥♥ SICILIAN Good, no-nonsense Sicilian *cucina casalinga* (home cooking) is the recipe for success in this unpretentious, brightly lit room (with an airy terrace in warm weather) across from the upper station of the cable car. Pastas are house-made (deliciously delicate gnocchi, little potato dumplings, are served *alla Norma,* with eggplant and ricotta), and the fish is served simply grilled. Nino's is a local institution, a 50-plus-year veteran of the Taormina dining scene, and it's always busy. They don't take reservations for groups of fewer than six.

Via Pirandello 37. trattoriadaninotaormina.com. ✆ **0942/21265.** Main courses 15€–25€. Thurs–Tues 12:30–3pm and 6:30–11pm.

Beaches near Taormina

You can reach Taormina's best and most popular beach, **Lido Mazzarò,** via a cable car (taorminaservizipubblici.it; ✆ **0942/23906**) that in theory—but not always in practice—leaves from Via Pirandello every 15 minutes (6€ one-way, 10€ round-trip; spring and summer only) between 8am and 8pm. The soft, finely pebbled beach is one of the best equipped in Sicily, with bars, restaurants, and hotels. You can rent beach chairs, umbrellas, and watersports equipment at kiosks from April to October. South of Lido Mazzarò, past the Capo Sant'Andrea headland, is the region's prettiest cove, where twin crescents of beach sweep out to the minuscule **Isola Bella** islet. South of Isola Bella, the large resort beach of **Giardini** can get crowded. North of Mazzarò, you'll find fewer people at the long, wide beaches at **Spisone** and **Letojanni.** A local bus leaves Taormina for Mazzarò, Spisone, and Letojanni; another heads down the coast to Giardini.

Lido Mazzarò.

Taormina Shopping

Shopping is all too easy in Taormina—just walk along **Corso Umberto I.** Ceramics are one of Sicily's most notable handicrafts, and Taormina's shops are among the best places to buy them on the island, as the selection is excellent. **Di Blasi Ceramiche,** Corso Umberto I 103 (✆ **0942/24671**), has a nice range of designs and specializes in the highly valued "white pottery" from Caltagirone (p. 803).

Side Trips from Taormina

CASTELMOLA ♥♥

Taormina gets high praise for its gorgeous views, but for connoisseurs of scenic outlooks, the real show takes place in the village of Castelmola, 3km (2 miles) northwest of Taormina, and about 300m (1,000 ft.) higher. The Ionian Sea seems to stretch to the ends of the earth from up here, and you'll be staring right into the northern flanks of Mt. Etna. For the full experience, make the trip up on foot, following routes that begin at Taormina's Porta Catania and Porta Messina (the tourist office or any hotel desk can give you directions); the Porta Messina trail passes a section of the Roman aqueduct and the Convento dei Cappuccini, where you can pause for a breather. Either route involves an hour or so of fairly strenuous walking. Once at the top, stop at Castelmola's **Bar Turrisi,** Piazza Duomo 19 (✆ **0942/28181;** daily 9am–1am), for a glass of *vino alla mandorla* (almond wine) and a look at its peculiar phallus-themed art collection. If that's more walking than you care to do, you can also drive up to Castelmola (park below the village and walk in) or take an orange bus that runs more or less hourly from Porta Messina (1.80€ one-way).

CATANIA ♥♥♥

If any place can outdo Palermo for chaos and exuberance it would be Catania, Sicily's second-largest city, founded by the Greeks on the island's east coast. Most travelers move on quickly from the airport, with its convenient connections to the rest of Europe and the U.S., bypassing the scruffy outskirts as they shuttle between Taormina and Siracusa. Yet a stopover, or a day trip from either of those cities (both less than an hour away by train or car), shows off baroque architecture, Sicilian workaday life, and a lot of youthful energy (Catania's university was founded in 1434). By car, it's an easy trip between Taormina and Catania on autostrada A18 and between Siracusa and Taormina on SS114; trains run between Taormina, Siracusa, and Catania as often as twice an hour.

First stop is **Piazza Duomo,** a graceful expanse surrounded by palaces built in part from the lava that Mount Etna, only 25 miles north, has supplied over the centuries. (On March 11, 1669, one of Etna's most violent eruptions ever nearly buried Catania, followed by a catastrophic earthquake in 1693, which is why so much of the city is built in the 18th-century baroque style.) After visiting the elegant **Cattedrale di Sant'Agata,** check out the charming black-lava Fontana dell'Elefante, fashioned by the Romans, at the center of the square. The exuberant Fontana dell'Amenano, on the seaward side, marks the entrance to the **Pescaria,** a raucous fish market that introduces onlookers to all the sea creatures of the Mediterranean. From the north side of Piazza Duomo, **Via Etna** leads directly toward the mountain that looms on the near horizon, adding even more drama to this lively and appealing city.

GOLE DELL'ALCANTARA ♥♥

In a series of narrow gorges (*gole*) on the Alcantara (Al-*cahn*-ta-rah) river, rushing ice-cold water fed by Mt. Etna snowmelt dashes over fantastically twisted volcanic rock, creating a scenic spectacle that's especially refreshing on a hot day. The gorges, 21km (13 miles) northwest of Taormina, are protected as **Parco Fluviale dell'Alcantara** (parcoalcantara.it; ✆ **0942/985010**), though ticket booths, turnstiles, and elevators into the gorge lend an amusement-park aura. Get away from the crowds with a hike along the riverbed, stopping now and then to lounge on flat riverside rocks and wade and even swim in the chilly water. From October to April, only the upper area of the park, with an overlook trail above the gorge, is open. It costs 13€ to enter the park via elevator in summer, from 7€ to 10€ other times, and 2€ via long flights of steps (daily 8am–7pm, shorter hours in winter). Amenities include a gift shop, cafeteria, picnic areas, and toilets. You can reach the Gole dell'Alcantara by car from Taormina in 35 minutes, or you can take **Interbus** (interbus.it; ✆ **0942/625301**), a 1-hour trip with several daily runs from Taormina (6.40€ round-trip). Organized excursions (from 25€) are also offered by tour operators in Taormina, often in conjunction with a visit to Mount Etna.

SIRACUSA ♥♥♥

120km (75 miles) S of Taormina, 70km (43 miles) S of Catania, 280km (174 miles) SE of Palermo

This small, out-of-the-way southern city packs a one-two punch. Siracusa was one of the most important cities of Magna Graecia (Greater Greece), rivaling even Athens in power and influence. The still-functioning Teatro Greco, where Aeschylus debuted his plays, is one of many landmarks of this ancient metropolis. Ortigia, the quaint historical center spreading over its own island, belongs to a much later time, when palaces and churches were built in baroque style after the earthquake that destroyed much of the southeast in 1693.

> **Every Drop Counts**
>
> Southeast Sicily is currently experiencing one of the worst droughts in Sicilian history, and water resources are severely limited. Wherever you travel in this corner of the island, keep showers short, don't let taps run unnecessarily, and in other ways be mindful of conservation and local restrictions regarding usage.

Siracusa might seem far removed from most of the rest of Europe, but in visiting the southeast coast you'll follow the illustrious footsteps of the scientist Archimedes, statesman Cicero, evangelist St. Paul, martyr St. Lucy, painter Caravaggio, and naval hero Admiral Lord Horatio Nelson, all of whom left a mark on this remarkable place. According to myth, Leto gave birth here to Artemis, one of the twins she conceived with Zeus, before continuing on to deliver Apollo on the Greek island of Delos.

Essentials

ARRIVING The most convenient airport for Siracusa is Catania's **Fontanarossa airport (CTA;** aeroporto.catania.it), which has numerous connections to mainland Italy and many European cities. **Interbus buses** (etnatrasporti.it) run almost hourly for the 45-minute trip from the airport to Siracusa.

By **car,** Siracusa is 1½ hours south of Taormina on the A18, and about 2 hours south from Messina. Driving time to Palermo or Agrigento is about 3 hours. Siracusa is well connected with the rest of Sicily by **bus,** 3½ hours from Palermo and 2 hours from Taormina (interbus.it). It's 5 to 6 hours from Palermo and 2 hours from Taormina by **train,** usually with a change in Catania (trenitalia.com; ✆ **89/2021**); bus service throughout the south is more efficient and frequent than train service. Both trains and buses arrive in Siracusa at the station on Via Francesco Crispi, between the archaeological park and Ortigia Island.

GETTING AROUND You won't need a car, just your own two feet and perhaps a few bus or cab rides to see the best of Siracusa proper. **Buses** (saisautolinee.it) run between the train station and Ortigia (a fairly easy 15-min. walk), and also serve the archeological park from Ortigia; tickets, from newsstands and tobacco shops, are 1.20€, day ticket 3€.

If you're traveling by car, ask your hotel before arriving about the best place to park. Ortigia Island is ringed with public lots, including the large **Talete** complex at the northern end, near the bridge to the mainland. Parking is 1.50€ an hour, 15€ a day, payable in machines. You can also pay from your phone or other device through the EasyPark app (easypark.com). Much of Ortigia, with the exception of a few main thoroughfares, is off limits to nonresidents' cars and monitored with cameras, so pay close attention to signs.

VISITOR INFORMATION A **tourist office** near the archeological park at Via San Sebastiano 43 (✆ **0931/481232**) is open Monday to Friday 8:30am to 1:30pm and 3 to 6pm, Saturday 8:30am to 1:30pm (closed in winter). There's a regional tourist office in Ortigia at Via della Maestranza 33 (✆ **0931/464255**); it's open Monday through Friday 8:30am to 1:30pm. A good online source for information on what to see and do is **siracusaturismo.net**.

Exploring Siracusa

Ortigia Island is Siracusa's *centro storico,* a mostly pedestrian zone where narrow alleys lined with romantic 18th-century *palazzi* spill onto Piazza del Duomo. The ancient ruins are a good half-hour walk north of Ortigia along Corso Gelone.

ORTIGIA ISLAND ♥♥♥

The historic center of Siracusa is an island only about 1 sq. km (¾ sq. mile), with breezy, palm-shaded seaside promenades fringing its shores. Although Ortigia was settled in ancient times, most of the island today is baroque, with grandiose palaces and churches lining narrow lanes and flamboyant piazzas.

The first landmark you'll come to after you cross Ponte Umbertino from the mainland is the **Temple of Apollo,** the oldest Doric temple in Sicily. The temple would have measured 58m×24m (190×79 ft.) when it was built in the 6th century B.C.E. It later served as a Byzantine church, then a mosque, then a church again under the Normans; it's now an evocative ruin, with the temple platform, a fragmentary colonnade, and an inner wall rising in the middle of Piazza Pancali.

The **Piazza del Duomo,** certainly one of the most beautiful squares in Italy, is all about theatrics—a sea of white marble softened by pink oleander, surrounded by beautiful palaces with elaborate stone filigree work and wrought-iron balconies. Similarly fanciful are the frothily baroque **Duomo** and the pretty church of **Santa Lucia alla Badia,** where the facade is equipped with a wrought-iron balcony from which cloistered nuns once watched goings-on in the piazza.

South of Piazza del Duomo, on the waterfront, is the **Fonte Aretusa,** a basin where papyrus grows in a shallow pool that supplied Siracusa with fresh water for millennia. Classical myth, however, tells a different story: The nymph Aretusa was bathing in a river in Greece when the river god

Fonte Aretusa, a landmark with a mythological twist, on Ortigia Island, Siracusa's historic quarter.

SIRACUSA'S virgin SAINT

St. Lucia, a plucky 4th-century Siracusan virgin, is the city's patron. Born of wealth, Lucy decided to give her worldly goods to the poor from an early age. Her piety and generosity so annoyed the young man to whom she'd been betrothed that out of spite he denounced her to Roman authorities.

Lucia was condemned to prostitution but refused to be dragged off to a brothel. Authorities tied her to a pillar and lit a fire beneath her, and she proved to be flame-resistant. Finally, a soldier plunged a sword into her throat. Later embellishments have Lucy gouging her eyes out to defy a lustful brute who admired them or soldiers removing them—these details have earned her a place as the patron saint of those suffering from eye ailments.

You'll see depictions of the saint and her gruesome martyrdom throughout Siracusa and the rest of Sicily, often holding her eyes on a plate. She is the subject of Siracusa's prize painting, Caravaggio's ***Burial of St. Lucia,*** commissioned in 1608 when the artist had escaped prison in Malta and fled to Sicily. The masterpiece now hangs above the altar in the **Basilica Santuario Santa Lucia al Sepolcro,** off of Ortigia on the site of the saint's 4th-century martyrdom on Piazza Santa Lucia (basilicasantalucia.com; ✆ **0931/67946**); the walk from Ortigia takes about 15 minutes. With his characteristic lighting, Caravaggio highlights the muscular gravediggers, showing their brute strength, while the mourners seem small and meek in the background. A shaft of light falling on Lucia's face and neck highlights the stab wound that killed her; she is a study in serenity, having entered the heavenly kingdom. Lucia's sepulcher is next to the church, though a few centuries ago her remains were spirited away to Venice and remain there. The complex is open daily 9am to 12:45pm and 3:30 to 7pm; admission is free.

Alpheus took a liking to her. She asked the goddess Artemis, protectress of young women, for help in avoiding his advances; Artemis turned Aretusa into a river that emerged here. Not to be thwarted, Alpheus followed suit, and the two of them bubble forth for eternity.

One of Siracusa's most poignant artworks, an *Annunciation* by Antonello da Messina, is in the elegant 13th-century **Galleria Regionale Palazzo Bellomo,** on Ortigia at Via Capodieci 16 (✆ **0931/69511**). Damaged yet still moving, the work is an intricate study in light and detail. The gallery is open Tuesday through Saturday 9am to 7pm and Sunday 9am to 1:30pm. Admission is 8€,

Duomo ♥♥ CHURCH Despite a frothy baroque facade, Siracusa's main church has ancient roots. Two tiers of Doric columns that define the entrance were once part of the 5th-century-B.C.E. Temple of Athena, one of the best-known sights of the ancient world, built to mark a Greek victory over the Carthaginians. Cicero, the Roman orator and traveler, reported that the temple was filled with gold, the doors were made of gold and ivory, and a statue of Athena atop the pediment was visible for miles out to sea. Romans made off with much of the gold, alas, and 9th-century

A Gigantic Teardrop

The tallest building in Siracusa is the bizarre **Santuario della Madonna delle Lacrime** (Our Lady of Tears Sanctuary, Via Santuario 33; madonnadellelacrime.it; ✆ **0931-21446**), a monstrous cone of contemporary architecture (built in 1993) halfway between Ortigia and the archaeological zone. Meant to evoke a sort of angular teardrop and rising 74m (243 ft.) with a diameter of 80m (262 ft.), the showy edifice houses a statue of the Madonna that supposedly wept for 5 days in 1953. Alleged chemical tests showed that the liquid was similar to that of human tears. Pilgrims flock here, and you'll see postcards of the weepy Virgin around Siracusa. In the interior, vertical windows stretch skyward to the roof. A charlatan TV evangelist and his congregation would not look out of place here. Admission is free and the sanctuary is open daily 7:30am to 12:30pm and 3:30 to 7:30pm (Sun 7:30am–1pm and 3:30–8:45pm).

Arab marauders took the rest. The church was first fashioned from the temple ruins around the 7th century, and a statue of the Virgin now stands atop the pediment as Athena once did. Other ancient columns line the aisle in the church's strikingly simple interior, while a silver statue in a side chapel protects an arm of Santa Lucia, Siracusa's patron saint (p. 791).

Piazza Duomo. ✆ **389/550-3267.** Admission 2€, free on Sun. Mon–Sat 7:30am–7pm; Sun 7:30am–12:30pm and 4–8pm.

THE ANCIENT RUINS ♥♥♥

Of all Sicily's Greek cities of antiquity, Siracusa was the most important, a formidable competitor of Athens. In its heyday, the city dared take on Carthage and even Rome. To reach the sprawling ruins, walk north along Corso Gelone or take a minibus or cab from Ortigia's Piazza Pancali or from Siracusa's central train station and other mainland stops.

Area Monumentale della Neapolis ♥♥♥ RUINS Many of Siracusa's ancient ruins are clustered in this archaeological park at the western edge of town, immediately north of Stazione Centrale.

The **Teatro Greco ♥♥♥** (Greek Theater) was hewn out of bedrock in the 5th century B.C.E., with 67 rows that could seat 16,000 spectators. Reconstructed in the 3rd century B.C.E., the seating and other elements appear now much as they did then, and the theater is still the setting for ancient drama in spring and early summer.

Gladiators sparred in the **Anfiteatro Romano,** created around 20 B.C.E. A square hole in the center of the arena suggests that machinery was used to lift wild beasts from below. Historical evidence also suggests that the arena could be flooded for mock sea battles called *naumachiae;* pumps could also have flooded and drained a reservoir in which crocodiles are said to have fed on the corpses of victims killed in the games. The Spanish carted off much of the stonework to rebuild city fortifications when they conquered Siracusa in the 16th century, but some seats remain—the first rows would have been reserved for Roman citizens, those right above for wealthy Siracusans, and the last rows for the hoi polloi.

What is now a lush grove of lemon and orange trees, the **Latomia del Paradiso** (Quarry of Paradise) was at one time a fearsome place, vast, dark, and subterranean—until the cavern's roof collapsed in the great earthquake of 1693. Originally prisoners were worked to death here to quarry the stones used in the construction of ancient Siracusa. What is certainly the most storied attraction in the park is here: the **Orecchio di Dionisio** (Ear of Dionysius), a tall and vaguely ear-shaped cave dug into the cliff by the Greeks to expand the limestone quarry for water storage. This huge cavern has inspired many dramatic accounts, such as the legend (completely unfounded) that the cave was once a prison for Athenians captured by Siracusan ruler Dionysius' mercenaries in the Peloponnesian Wars; supposedly he liked how the cave's acoustics amplified their screams as they were tortured. Almost as fascinating is the well-documented purpose of the **Ara di Ierone** (Altar of Heron): 5th-century-B.C.E. Greeks built the altar, 196m (636 ft.) long and 23m (75 ft.) wide and approached by gigantic ramps, to sacrifice 450 bulls at one time.

The ancient cave known as the Ear of Dionysius.

Via Del Teatro (off intersection of Corso Gelone and Viale Teocrito), Viale Paradiso. parchiarcheologici.regione.sicilia.it. ✆ **0931/66206.** Admission 13€, 18€ with archaeological museum (see below), under 18 free. Apr–Sept daily 8:30am–7:45pm (until 4:30pm on performance evenings); Mar daily 8:30am–6pm; Oct–Feb Mon–Sat 8:30am–4:40pm and Sun 8:30am–1:40pm. For performance tickets (30€–70€), contact **INDA,** Corso Matteotti 29, Siracusa (indafondazione.org; ✆ **0931/487248**).

Castello Eurialo ♥♥ RUINS This evocative 4th-century-B.C.E. ruin overlooking the Siracusan plain is the best-preserved Greek castle in the Mediterranean. Part of a massive, 27km-long (16-mile) defense system, the fortress is surrounded by three trenches connected by underground tunnels. These supposedly impregnable defenses were never put to the test: Siracusa fell to the Romans in 212 B.C.E. without a fight, because the entire garrison was celebrating the feast of Aphrodite. It was here, legend has it, that the Greek mathematician Archimedes famously cried "Eureka!"

having discovered the law of water displacement while taking a bath. The defenses are at the far end of the archaeological zone, about 5km (3 miles) outside the city center near a village called Belvedere; buses 25 and 26 pass the entrance.

Piazza Eurialo 1, off Viale Epipoli. parchiarcheologici.regione.sicilia.it. ✆ **0931/481111.** Admission 6€, free for ages 17 and under. Wed and Sun 8:30am–1:40pm; Sat 8:30am–4:40pm (hours vary; verify with tourist office before making the trip).

Catacombe di San Giovanni ♥♥ RUINS Spooky subterranean chambers, installed in underground aqueducts that had been abandoned by the Greeks, contain some 20,000 ancient Christian tombs. They are entered through the Church of San Giovanni, now in ruin but holy ground for centuries; this was the city's cathedral until the church was more or less leveled by the 1693 earthquake. St. Paul allegedly preached here when he stopped in Siracusa around C.E. 59, and a church was erected in the 6th century to commemorate the event. The Cripta di San Marciano (Crypt of St. Marcian) honors a popular Siracusan martyr, a C.E.-1st-century bishop who was tied to a pillar and flogged to death on this spot.

Piazza San Giovanni, at end of Viale San Giovanni (on mainland, just east of the Parco Archeologico). ✆ **0931/64694.** Admission 8€ adult, 5€ seniors and ages 15 and under. Tues–Sun 9:30am–12:30pm and 2:30–4:30pm. Closed part of Jan.

Museo Archeologico Regionale Paolo Orsi ♥♥♥ MUSEUM One of Italy's finest archaeological collections shows off artifacts from southern Sicily's prehistoric inhabitants through the Romans, showcasing pieces in stunning modern surrounds. The museum's most celebrated piece is the **Landolina Venus,** a Roman copy of an original by the great classical Greek sculptor Praxiteles. The graceful and modest goddess, now headless, rises out of marble waves; French writer Guy de Maupassant called her "the perfect expression of exuberant beauty."

Amid the other artifacts are the skeletons of a pair of dwarf elephants, as intriguing to us as they were to the ancients: It's believed that the large central hole in these skeletons' faces—actually a nasal passage—inspired the myth of the one-eyed Cyclops. Look for the often-reproduced grinning terra-cotta Gorgon, originally part of the frieze of the Greek temple of Athena (see Duomo on p. 791), where it was placed to ward off evil. You'll also see votive cult statuettes devoted to Demeter and Persephone, mother and daughter goddesses linked to fertility and the harvest. Legend has it that Hades, god of the underworld, abducted Persephone in Sicily and carried her down to his realm; her angry mother, Demeter fought for her return, and the gods struck a deal—Persephone could return to earth every spring and summer, making nature bloom, but she had to resume her duties as queen of the underworld in fall and winter, causing the lands above to wither and die.

In the gardens of Villa Landolina in Akradina, Viale Teocrito 66. parchiarcheologici.regione.sicilia.it. ✆ **0931/464-022.** Admission 10€, 18€ with archaeological park (see above), ages 17 and under free. Tues–Sat 9am–7pm; Sun 9am–2pm.

Where to Stay in Siracusa

The choice place to stay in Siracusa is Ortigia, with enough character, charm, and comfortable accommodations to keep the most discerning traveler happy. For villas, **The Thinking Traveller** (thethinkingtraveller.com) has a carefully edited list of well-equipped properties in and around Siracusa, and elsewhere in Sicily.

EXPENSIVE

Algilà Ortigia Charme Hotel ♥♥ A slightly exotic air pervades this old stone palace at the edge of the sea. Interiors surrounding a peaceful inner courtyard with a splashing fountain are accented with carefully restored stonework and wooden beams, offset by multicolor tiles and other rich details. Rooms combine conventional luxury with all the modern amenities, plus a surfeit of four-poster beds, antiques, and tribal kilims. Many rooms have sea views. The in-house restaurant serves Sicilian classics and seafood beneath a beautiful wooden ceiling.

Via Vittorio Veneto 93. algila.it. ✆ **0931/465-186.** 30 units. 150€–230€ double. Rates include breakfast. Closed mid-Jan to late Feb. **Amenities:** Restaurant; room service; free Wi-Fi.

Henry's House ♥♥♥ The namesake Henry, a now-departed friend of the owners, could not have a nicer legacy than this distinctive seaside *palazzo* at the southern edge of Ortigia. Several terraces, including a few private spaces off some rooms, look over the sea, while salons filled with antiques and artifacts are homily atmospheric. Guest quarters set on several floors have beams, tile floors, and character-filled furnishings that further enhance the sense that you're staying with a cultured Sicilian friend.

Via del Castello Maniace 68. www.hotelhenryshouse.com. ✆ **0931/21361.** 14 units. 200€–350€. Rates include breakfast. Closed Jan–Mar. **Amenities:** Bar; room service; free Wi-Fi.

MODERATE

Apollo Suite ♥♥♥ At this extremely attractive guesthouse on the upper floors of an old apartment house (reached by an elevator), the large, high-ceilinged, light-filled rooms open to small balconies, most of them overlooking the ruins of the temple of Apollo. Stylish furnishings include comfortable beds, and bathrooms are very well done with large showers. Friendly service extends to a small but ample breakfast of pastries, eggs, and fruit, accompanied by fresh-squeezed orange juice.

Via Salvatore Chindemi 7. apollosuiteortigia.it. ✆ **0347/665-4399.** 5 units. 120€–230€ double. Rates include breakfast. **Amenities:** Free Wi-Fi.

Domus Mariae Benessere Guest House ♥♥ The Ursuline sisters who still occupy a wing of this seaside convent have found their calling as innkeepers. The large, bright rooms border on vaguely luxurious, with plush headboards on extremely comfortable beds, attractive rugs on tile floors, and lots of counter and storage space in the large bathrooms. Some rooms have sea views, while others face an atrium-like courtyard. Surprising indulgences include a roof terrace and a lower-level spa, with a small pool and Jacuzzi. An in-house restaurant serves a monastic buffet breakfast.

Via Veneto 89. domusmariaebenessere.com. ✆ **0931/60087.** 21 units. 120€–140€ double. Most rates include breakfast. Closed part of Jan. **Amenities:** Restaurant; bikes; pool; spa; free Wi-Fi.

INEXPENSIVE

Hotel Gutkowski ♥♥ Two old houses facing the sea at the edge of Ortigia have been redone as warm and hospitable lodgings that capture the essence of southern Italy, with Sicilian hues on the walls, colorful floor tiles, and views of the blue water or sunbaked roofs of the old city. Each room is different, some with balconies, some with terraces; furnishings and decor are geared to stylish simplicity, with old Sicilian and vintage mid-century pieces offset by contemporary tables and bedsteads. A rooftop terrace becomes an outdoor living room for much of the year, and the bar serves regional wines and one or two well-prepared dishes in the evenings.

Lungomare Vittorini 26. guthotel.it. ✆ **0931/465861.** 25 units. 75€–125€ double. Most rates include breakfast. 2-night (or more) minimum stay required some periods. Closed Jan to early Feb. **Amenities:** Restaurant; bar; free Wi-Fi.

L'Approdo delle Sirene ♥♥ This bright, stylish little inn occupies two floors of a seaside apartment house, beautifully refashioned as light-filled quarters with a slightly nautical flair, as befits the sparkling blue water just beyond the tall windows. In the contemporary guest rooms, polished wood floors offset handsome furnishings, striped fabrics, and bold colors. Several rooms have French doors opening to small balconies, though some rooms are sky-lit only—flooded with light but without views. The sunny breakfast room/lounge and terrace provide plenty of panoramas, however. The hosts, mother Fiora and son Friedrich, are a hospitable on-the-scene presence and can arrange all kinds of tours and excursions. Free bikes are available for guests' use.

Riva Garibaldi 15. approdods dellesirene.com. ✆ **0931/24857.** 8 units. 80€–110€ double. 2-night minimum stay required some periods. Rates include breakfast. Closed Jan–Feb. **Amenities:** Bikes; free Wi-Fi.

Where to Eat in Siracusa

Apollonion Osteria da Carlo ♥♥♥ SEAFOOD Though the bustling rooms are on an inland street, the emphasis is on the bounty of the sea: huge platters of fish *capriccio,* orecchiette topped with shrimp and other sea creatures, many kinds of fish fried, baked, and grilled—all fresh from boats docked nearby. Meals are served in a six-course set menu that includes at least one pasta and many variations of seafood, accompanied by house wine or another beverage.

Via Carmelo Campisi 18. facebook.com/osteriapollonion. ✆ **0931/483362.** Set menus from 40€. Mon–Sat 12:30–2:30pm and 7:30–10:30pm. Closed Feb to early Mar.

Don Camillo ♥♥♥ SIRACUSAN/SEAFOOD A longtime Siracusa favorite, Don Camillo is decked out with polished antiques offsetting handsomely tiled floors, rows of wine racks, and vintage photos of Ortigia. House specialties, including spaghetti *delle Sirene* (with sea urchin and shrimp in butter) and *tagliata al tonno* (with sliced tuna), have drawn regulars for years, and on weekend evenings the vaulted medieval rooms fill with Siracusan families out for a special meal.
Via Maestranza 96. ristorantedoncamillosiracusa.it. ✆ **0931/67133.** Main courses 25€–40€, tasting menus 80€–120€. Mon–Sat 1–2:30pm and 8–10:30pm. Closed part of Jan and Feb.

L'Osteria da Seby ♥♥ SIRACUSAN/SEAFOOD Oil paintings, linen tablecloths, and exposed stone create a warm and inviting setting at this friendly place, a favorite of guests staying at hotels on the nearby waterfront. The straightforward *osteria* fare includes seafood pastas and risottos, mixed grills, and well-done standards such as scallopini in lemon sauce.
Via Mirabella 19. sebylosteria.it. ✆ **0931/181-5619.** Main courses 16€–28€. Tues–Sun 12:30–2:30pm and 7–11:30pm.

Osteria Sveva ♥♥ SIRACUSAN/SEAFOOD Escape the crowds with a walk out toward the Castello Maniace at the tip of Ortigia, where a breeze-cooled terrace facing a cobbled square is the perfect setting for a summer meal of classic vegetable and seafood pastas and fresh fish. In cooler weather, the hospitality moves to a simple, rich-hued room that sets the stage for perfectly grilled steaks. Indoors or out, land-based or from the sea, meals are served at rough-hewn tables on hand-painted ceramics that lend just the right touch for the honest cooking.
Piazza Federico di Svevia. instagram.com/osteriasveva. ✆ **0931/24663.** Main courses 12€–24€. Thurs–Tues 10:30am–3:30pm and 7pm–midnight.

Ristorante La Darsena ♥♥ SEAFOOD "Darsena" means dock, and the town piers line the harbor just across the street from this brightly lit room with a terrace out front. Several generations of Siracusans have counted on Darsena for the freshest fish in town, displayed on ice in cases

Market Feasting

Tucked in among piles of fresh fish in Ortigia's morning market, **Caseificio Borderi ♥♥**, Via die Benedictis 6 (✆ **329/985-2500**), is a required stop on the food circuit for its huge selection of house-made cheeses, cured meats, olives, and wine. The staff hands out samples and makes delicious sandwiches and crostini platters (from 4€), paired with excellent wines by the glass, and eaten in the piazza out front; it's open Monday through Saturday 7am to 4pm. Another market stop is **Fratelli Burgio ♥**, Piazza Cesare Battista 4 (fratelliburgio.com; ✆ **0931/60069**), where a *tagliere* (platter of cheeses and other antipasti, from 8€) is a meal in itself; it's open Thursday through Tuesday 7am to 9pm.

near the entrance. A waiter will bring some of the just-caught offerings around for your inspection, then take it back to the kitchen to be grilled or roasted to your preference. *Riccio,* sea urchin, and other local specialties are served raw and in a long, long list of seafood pastas.

Riva Giuseppe Garibaldi. instagram.com/ladarsenasiracusa. ✆ **0331/342-2000.** Main courses 11€–28€. Thurs–Tues 12:30–3:30pm and 7:30–11pm. Closed mid-Nov to mid-Dec.

Beaches near Siracusa

Some of the best, most unspoiled shoreline in all of Italy is on Sicily's southeastern coast. (You don't even have to leave Ortigia to get into the water: From July into September, the city maintains wooden swimming platforms near the Fonte Aretusa and off the rocks on the east side of the island.) **Fontane Bianche** is the closest beach to Siracusa, 15 minutes away by car or frequent train service. It's an almost-square bay with laid-back beach clubs and luxurious deep sand. **Lido di Noto,** 15 minutes from the baroque hill town of Noto (see below), is a lively beach strip with great waterfront restaurants. Half the beach is taken up with private beach clubs (where you pay around 10€ for day use of a lounge chair, umbrella, and shower facilities), and half is free public access.

Between Noto and Pachino, the beautiful **Vendicari Nature Reserve ♥♥♥**, 11km (7 miles) south of Noto on SP19, is set amid acres of fragrant citrus groves growing behind beaches backed by wetlands, a refuge for exotic migratory birds. Vendicari's most popular beach is **Calamosche,** on an intimate cove framed by rock cliffs and sea caves; from the Calamosche parking area it's about a 15-minute walk along a path to the beach.

Isola delle Correnti ♥♥, a little over an hour south of Siracusa at Sicily's southeastern tip, is one of the best beaches on the island, though it's a bit windier and more wave-swept than the other spots. On a clear day, you can see Malta, just 100km (60 miles) to the south.

Day Trip to Noto ♥♥

31km (19 miles) SW of Siracusa

This beautiful little town is a baroque stage set, with rich-looking buildings of golden stone lining its main street, Corso Vittorio Emanuele. Noto sits on a high plateau surrounded by olive groves and almond trees, and the town heights provide splendid vistas of the Asinaro Valley.

ESSENTIALS

ARRIVING Take the A18 south from Siracusa for 27km (17 miles), then exit and head north up a hill, following blue signs toward Noto. Near town, follow yellow signs to Noto's *centro storico* (brown NOTO ANTICA signs lead to the ruins of the old city, outside town). It's about a 35-minute drive. Trains run throughout the day from Siracusa, a 35-minute trip, though the station is about a 15-minute walk outside the center. You can also reach Noto from Siracusa by **AST** bus (www.aziendasiciliana trasporti.it; ✆ **0932/681-818**); about 10 buses per day make the 80-minute trip from Siracusa train station, arriving at the edge of the *centro storico.*

VISITOR INFORMATION The **tourist office,** at Corso Vittorio Emanuele 135 (✆ **339/481-6218**), is open daily 10am to 6pm.

EXPLORING NOTO

This hill town on the flanks of Mount Alviria was a flourishing place in the late 17th century, having outgrown its medieval core and expanded into streets lined with palaces and convents. On January 11, 1693, all came tumbling down when the strongest earthquake in Italian history leveled Noto and much of the rest of southeastern Sicily.

The Duomo in Noto.

The good to come of such a devastating tragedy is that Noto was rebuilt—not on the same site but on the banks of the River Asinaro, and not haphazardly but in splendid, unified baroque style. Noto is all honey-colored limestone, with curved facades, curling staircases, and wrought-iron balconies. You will be surrounded by this theatricality on a walk down **Corso Vittorio Emanuele;** things hit an architectural high note on a side street, **Via Nicolaci,** with the beautiful elliptical facade of the **Chiesa di Montevergine** and playful **Palazzo Villadorata,** where expressive maidens, dwarves, lions, and horses support the balconies.

Almost as stunning as Noto's baroque architecture are the creations at richly atmospheric, old-fashioned **Caffè Sicilia,** Corso Vittorio Emanuele 125, purveyor of Sicily's best granita and gelato (caffesicilia.it; ✆ **0931/835013**).

Excursion to Ragusa ♥♥♥

79km (49 miles) SW of Siracusa

Like Noto (see above), Ragusa was all but obliterated by the powerful earthquake of 1693, and also like Noto, was rebuilt as a planned city in exuberant baroque style. The wary residents decided to relocate to an adjacent ridge, separated by a deep ravine, the Valle dei Ponti. Today,

Piazza Duomo in Ragusa Ibla looks like a set piece of "Sicilian baroque" architecture.

Ragusa Superiore is the modern center of the sprawling, bifurcated town, while baroque Ragusa Ibla is a place to wander on quiet lanes and through big piazzas overlooked by flamboyant 18th-century churches. Some top-notch dining and lodging options (see below) make Ragusa worth more than a hurried day trip.

ESSENTIALS

ARRIVING The quickest option from Siracusa is by **car,** which takes a little over an hour, driving through Noto and then southwest along Route 115 to the town of Ispica, at which point the highway swings northwest toward Ragusa. Parking lots ring the old town and include a handy one outside the Giardino Ibleo. Three **trains** a day make the 2-hour trip to Ragusa from Siracusa, and **AST buses** (www.aziendasicilianatrasporti.it; ✆ **091/620-8111**) make the 3-hour run seven times daily. The train and bus stations are in Ragusa Superiore on Piazza del Popolo and adjoining Piazza Gramsci.

VISITOR INFORMATION Ragusa has two **tourist offices** (www2.comune.ragusa.it), one on Piazza San Giovanni in Ragusa Superiore (✆ **0932/676550**), the other in Ragusa Ibla on Piazza Repubblica (✆ **366/874621**); both are usually open Monday through Friday 9am to 7pm.

EXPLORING RAGUSA IBLA

The most scenic way to reach historic Ragusa Ibla from modern Ragusa Superiore is by taking the 242 steps of the Salita Commendatore down the hillside. (Otherwise, take city bus no. 3 from Piazza del Popolo.) You can take a breather along the way on a landing in front of **Santa Maria delle Scale** (St. Mary of the Steps), enjoying views of the ochre-colored houses of Ragusa Ibla spreading out at your feet. The path eventually winds down and around to **Piazza del Duomo,** where a dramatically curved staircase leads to the sumptuous facade of **Duomo di San Giorgio** ♥♥♥ (✆ **0932/220085;** daily 10am–12:30pm and 4–6:30pm). The three tiers of columns and balconies are the pièce de résistance of architect Rosario Gagliardi, master of the Sicilian baroque. Gagliardi's second-best work is just east, **Chiesa di San Giuseppe** ♥♥, Via Torre Nuova 19 (✆ **0932/621-779;** Fri–Sun 9am–noon and 3–7pm), with its tall, three-tiered facade embellished with columns and statues of saints. Inside, above a striking floor of black asphalt interspersed with majolica tiles, is one of Ragusa's most beloved paintings, an altarpiece of the Holy Family—see how Mary holds cherries in her apron, offering them to passersby.

Just down the street are Ragusa's beautiful public gardens, **Giardino Ibleo** ♥♥. The long avenues lined with palms are idyllic places to stroll, with stone benches tucked into shady alcoves. At the edge of the gardens, a terrace opens to views across the Valley of Irminio. The gardens are free and open daily 8am to 8pm.

EXPLORING MARINA DI RAGUSA ♥♥

Ragusa's seaside getaway, 25km (15 miles) southwest, is a pleasant collection of houses facing a sandy beach and marina. Smaller, quieter, and more famous these days is adjacent **Punta Secca,** fictional home to Inspector Montalbano of the popular Italian TV series; fans will recognize his house near the lighthouse. The series is also filmed on location in Ragusa, Modica, Scicli, and other towns in this corner of the southeast.

WHERE TO STAY & EAT IN RAGUSA

A sign of a new wave of gentrification sweeping over Ragusa Ibla is **I Banchi** ♥♥, Via Orfanotrofio 39, a stylish bakery, food shop, wine bar, and casual eatery that would seem trendy even in Rome (ibanchiragusa.it; ✆ **0932/655-000;** Mon 6–10:30pm; Tues–Sat 10am–2:30pm and 6–10:30pm; closed Jan–Feb).

Ciccio Sultano Duomo ♥♥♥ NEW SICILIAN/SEAFOOD This famed spot is the creation of Chef Ciccio Sultano. His stylish, parlor-like dining rooms suggest an experience as extravagant as Ragusa's baroque architecture, and nothing that emerges from the kitchen dispels that notion. Regional ingredients and age-old Sicilian traditions form the foundation for dishes that combine homemade pastas, local seafood, and fresh garden produce in remarkably innovative ways, such as a *cannolo* of crème fraîche, raw shrimp, and caviar, or in relatively down-to-earth preparations, such as fresh pasta with *bottarga* (fish roe). Leave frugality at the door: The best way to indulge in the extravagance is with one of the tasting menus. Reserve well in advance.

Via Capitano Bocchieri 31, Ibla. cicciosultano.it. ✆ **0932/651-265.** Choice of 2 to 4 dishes from tasting menus, 90€–180€; tasting menus 150€–250€. Tues–Sat 12:30–2pm and 7:30–10:30pm (daily in Aug). Closed Jan to mid-Mar.

Hotel Antico Convento dei Cappuccini ♥♥ The Capuchin monks who settled this convent in the 16th century had a good eye for location, at the edge of town atop the Irminio valley. The setting was later enhanced even more with the addition of the town's beautiful public gardens, the Giardino Ibleo, which now surround the stone walls. Small monks' cells converted to guest rooms remain simple though not austere, with bright stone floors and handsome wooden built-ins, overlooking the peaceful cloister, the gardens, or the valley below. A bar/restaurant spills into the cloister in warmer months.

Giardino Ibleo. Via Margherita 41. anticoconventoibla.it. ✆ **347/147-2915.** 24 units. 105€–145€. Rates include breakfast. **Amenities:** Restaurant; bar; free Wi-Fi.

La Bettola ♥♥ SICILIAN The 1940s-era decor suggests simpler times, and Sicilian classic dishes keep that throwback ambience going strong, arriving at tables bedecked with red-checked tablecloths in the homey dining room and large front terrace. Daily offerings are listed on a chalkboard and include generous servings of such homey favorites as house-made caponata, octopus salad, platters of spaghetti *alla Norma,* or simple grilled pork cutlets topped with fresh herbs.

Largo Camerina 7. www.trattorialabettola.it. ✆ **0932/081189.** Main courses 10€–18€. Fri–Wed noon–4:30pm and 7–11pm.

Locanda Don Serafino ♥♥ Accommodations in two medieval *palazzi* on a narrow lane above Piazza Duomo are reached by a gloriously primitive rock-hewn staircase, and the wonderful quirks continue from there, in poshly outfitted cave rooms and dramatic two-floor vaulted suites. Many guests come to enjoy dining in the locanda's offsite **restaurant** (on Via Avvocato Giovanni Ottaviano), serving memorable meals in a strikingly decorated maze of stone-vaulted rooms and caves at the edge of town (✆ **0932/248778;** two plates 90€, three plates 130€, set menus 130€–150€; Thurs–Mon 12:45–2:30pm, Wed–Mon 8–10:30pm). The food is innovative yet down-to-earth, relying on a bounty of fresh local ingredients that come to the fore in such signature dishes as *zuppa di pesce don Serafino* (a rich fish soup). The adjoining guest accommodations are the hotel's splashiest, with private gardens and plunge pools.

Via Via XI Febbraio 15. locandadonserafino.it. ✆ **0932/22006.** 11 units. 125€–155€ double. Rates include breakfast. Closed mid-Feb to mid-Mar. **Amenities:** Restaurant; free Wi-Fi.

WHERE TO STAY & EAT IN SCICLI

The lovely baroque town of Scicli, about 30km (18 miles) south of Ragusa, offers some outstanding dining and lodging options as well.

La Gioie Posto Siciliano ♥♥♥ SICILIAN You'll have one of the standout meals of your travels in Sicily when you step into this 10-table restaurant in the center of Scicli, where chef/owner Fiorenzo set up shop almost a decade ago to pursue his passion for Sicilian flavors. He shops

Modica: A Sweet Stop in the Southeast

Chocoholics and other sweet-tooths should head to nearby **Modica** ♥♥, 35km (21 miles) west of Noto, 16km (20 miles) south of Ragusa, noted as much for its chocolatiers as for its baroque architecture. The chocolate here is grainy, made straight from cocoa beans, and is often flavored with vanilla, cinnamon, and pepperoncino. Local Katia Amore teaches chocolate-making techniques, as well as other Sicilian cookery, in **Love Sicily** ♥♥ sessions in her grandmother's kitchen overlooking the town's domes (lovesicily.com; from 110€). You may also taste the local product at nearby **Antica Dolceria Bonajuto** ♥♥, Corso Umberto I 159, Sicily's oldest chocolate maker (bonajuto.it; ✆ **0932/941225**).

daily for fresh ingredients, and the dishes he lists on a blackboard lean heavily toward fresh fish and seafood, including an especially memorable linguine with tuna. The house wine is local, and dessert is homemade gelato or biscotti dipped in Fiorenzo's special elixir.

Via Aleardi 5, Scicli. instagram.com/legioie_postosiciliano. ✆ **340/547-9265.** Main courses 13€–18€. Daily noon–3pm and 7pm–midnight.

Scicli Albergo Diffuso ♥♥♥ Fans of the *Inspector Montalbano* series will recognize Scicli as the backdrop of the opening credits of one of Italy's most popular TV shows. In fact, breakfast at this unique inn, comprised of accommodations scattered around town, is served in a cafe room across from the police station where the fictional detective supposedly works. Even without these media associations, the hotel is charming, with rooms scattered among a palace and character-filled old houses along sunbaked streets and squares. All rooms are stylish (some of the palace rooms are especially grand), many have outdoor space, and all provide a comfortable, independent stay in an exotic Sicilian town. A willing staff is on hand with advice on what to see and do.

Piazza Italia 28, Scicli. sciclialbergodiffuso.it. ✆ **0932/185-5555.** 15 units. 65€–85€ double. Rates include breakfast. **Amenities:** Free Wi-Fi.

PIAZZA ARMERINA ♥♥♥

134km (83 miles) NW of Siracusa, 158km (98 miles) SE of Palermo

Many travelers make a big effort to get to this dusty, sunbaked hill town in the center of Sicily, and you should be one of them. Here is the world's richest collection of Roman mosaics, in a near-miraculous state of preservation, at the **Villa del Casale,** in the countryside 5km (3 miles) outside of town. Piazza Armerina itself is a friendly, handsome, hilly town, well worth walking around from the hilltop Duomo through the 13th-century center. If you're arriving from the southeast, a worthy stop is **Caltagirone,** 30km (18 miles) southeast of Piazza Armerina, famous for its ceramics; check out the 142 steps of the Scalinata di Santa Maria del Monte, all colorfully tiled.

Essentials

ARRIVING From Taormina, Siracusa, or anywhere in the east, take the A19 west from Catania, exit at Dittaino, and head south following blue signs for Piazza Armerina. From Palermo, take the A19 east and south, exit at Caltanissetta, then immediately look for signs for Piazza Armerina. (The route is SS626 south to SS122 east to SS117bis.) You can reach Piazza Armerina from Palermo (a 2-hr. trip) via **SAIS bus** (saisautolinee.it; ✆ **091/616-6026;** five buses a day, three on weekends); coming from Siracusa or other east coast towns, your best bet is to take a bus to Enna and switch there for Piazza Armerina (40 min.; eight buses a day). Once in Piazza Armerina, take local bus B to the site (15 min.; runs daily 9am–noon and 3–6pm); taxis also eagerly await visitors.

Intricate mosaics at the Villa Romana del Casale in Piazza Armerina.

Exploring Villa Romana del Casale

Built between 310 and 340, this enormous villa of a rich and powerful landowner was the center of a vast agricultural estate. The villa was almost completely covered by a landslide in the 12th century, a natural disaster that turned out to be a blessing, because the mud preserved almost 38,000 square feet (3,500 sq. m) of mosaic flooring. Rediscovered in the 19th century, the villa was excavated and restored starting in the early 20th century.

The place must have been magnificent, more a palace than a mere villa, with 40 rooms, many of them clad in marble, frescoed, and equipped with fountains and pools. *Terme,* or steam baths (rooms 1–7), also heated the villa, with steam circulating through cavities in the floors and walls. The ostentation reached its zenith with mosaics of mythology, flora and fauna, and domestic scenes carpeting most of the floors. Given the style and craftsmanship, these were likely the work of North African master artists.

The 40 rooms are arranged around a garden courtyard, or peristyle. Take time as you wander through the rooms on elevated walkways above the mosaic flooring to enjoy the expressions, colors, and playfulness of the scenes. They were intended to delight visitors, and they are still entertaining, like a film in glorious Technicolor. Of special note:

Peristyle (room 13): A bestiary of birds, plants, wild animals, horses, and other domesticated creatures covers the floor of this colonnaded walkway.

Palestra (Exercise Area, room 15): Mosaics depict a chariot race at Rome's Circus Maximus.

Sala degli Eroti Pescatori ♥♥ (Room of the Fishing Cupids, room 24): In what was probably a bedroom, one could drift off to a scene of four boatloads of winged cupids harpooning, netting, and trapping various fish and sea creatures.

Sala della Piccola Caccia (Room of the Small Hunt, room 25): Hunters in togas pursue deer, wild boar, birds, and other small game as Diana, goddess of the hunt, looks on.

Corridoio della Grande Caccia ♥♥♥ (Corridor of the Great Hunt, room 28): Men capture panthers, leopards, and other exotic animals, loading them onto wagons for transport, and finally onto a ship bound for Rome, where they will be part of the games in the Colosseum.

Vestibolo di Ulisse e Polifemo (Vestibule of Ulysses and Polyphemus, room 47): The Homeric hero proffers a *krater* of wine to the Cyclops (here with three eyes instead of one, and a disemboweled ram draped casually over his lap) in hopes of getting him drunk.

Cubicolo con Scena Erotica (Bedroom with Erotic Scene, room 46): A seductress with a side gaze and a nicely contoured rear end embraces a young man.

Sala delle Palestrite ♥♥♥ (Room of the Gym Girls, room 30): Girls engaged in various exercises—curling dumbbells, tossing a ball, running—are dressed in skimpy strapless bikinis that would fit right in on any 21st-century beach. Ancient literary sources suggest that these were standard workout apparel 1,700 years ago—the bandeau top was called the *strophium,* and the bikini bottom the *subligar.*

Triclinium (room 33): A large dining room is decorated with a magnificent rendition of the Labors of Hercules. In the central apse of the room, mosaics depict the Gigantomachy (Battle of the Giants), in which five mammoth creatures are in their death throes after being pierced by Hercules' poison arrows.

Villa Romana, Strada Provinciale 15. villaromanadelcasale.it. ✆ **0935/680036.** Admission 14€ adults, 7€ ages 18–24, free for ages 17 and under. Late Mar to Oct daily 9am–7pm; Nov to late Mar daily 9am–5pm. Parking 3€.

AGRIGENTO & THE VALLEY OF THE TEMPLES ♥♥♥

129km (80 miles) SE of Palermo, 208km (125 miles) W of Siracusa

The evocative skeletons of seven temples of honey-colored stone, arranged on a long ridge with commanding views of the sea, comprise one of the most memorable sights of the ancient world. Colonists from Crete or Rhodes established Akragas in the 7th century B.C.E., and by the 5th century B.C.E. the city was one of the great Mediterranean powers. The

Greek poet Pindar described Akragas as the most beautiful city "inhabited by mortals" but commented that its citizens "feasted as if there were no tomorrow." The city poured part of its enormous wealth into these temples, their bright pediments becoming well-known landmarks along southern sea routes. Carthage and Rome fought over the city for centuries until Akragas became part of the Roman Empire in 210 B.C.E. Tumbled by earthquakes, plundered for marble, and for centuries overgrown from neglect, today the temples are proud remnants of ancient grandeur.

Essentials

ARRIVING Agrigento is about 2½ hours by **car** from either Palermo or Siracusa. From Palermo, cut southeast on the SS121, which becomes SS189 before it reaches Agrigento. From Siracusa, take the A18 *autostrada* north to Catania and the A19 west toward Enna; just past Enna, exit the A19 and follow signs south through Caltanissetta and down to Agrigento. (The "coastal route" from Siracusa—taking the SS115 all the way—may look more direct on the map but is much more time-consuming, up to 5 hr. on an often very curvy two-lane road.) Well-marked **parking** areas are below the temples, near the entrances to the western section (Zeus) and eastern section (Collina dei Templi); 3€ an hour. A well-marked path leads along the ridge past the temples. A shuttle bus (1.20€ from kiosks near parking areas, 1.70€ on the bus, each way, 3.40€ day ticket) connects the parking areas with the top of the site, though the walk up and through the site is not terribly strenuous. However, it's quite a hike out to the Templo di Juno from the west entrance. Entering from the west, you may want to walk as far as the Tempio della Concordia, then return to the entrance and take the shuttle bus to the east entrance for the Templo di Juno.

Bus connections between Palermo and Agrigento are fairly convenient: **Cuffaro** (cuffaro.info; ✆ **0922/403-150**) runs as many as six buses per day on weekdays, five on Saturday, and three on Sunday to stops right in front of the entrance to the archaeological site; the 2-hour trip costs about 13€ round-trip. Bus service does run from Siracusa, but it's at least 4 hours each way.

A **train** from Palermo takes 2 hours; 12 trains run daily. From Siracusa, trains take 6 hours, with a change in Catania. For information, visit trenitalia.it or call ✆ **89/2021.** Agrigento's rail station, **Stazione Centrale,** is at Piazza Marconi; from there, take a cab or local bus (lines 1, 2, or 3) to the temples, 10 minutes away (1.20€ from machines or newsstands, 1.70€ on the bus, 3.40€ for a day ticket that includes the shuttle bus at the site).

VISITOR INFORMATION Ticket offices at the site can provide any info you need on transport and other matters. For online info, go to **lavalledeitempli.it**.

Exploring the Ruins

As you enter the valley surrounded by hills planted with olive and almond trees, you'll see that "valley of the temples" is a misnomer, as the temples

The Temple of Hercules is the oldest ruin in the Valley of the Temples, Agrigento.

are perched along a ridge. The park is divided into eastern and western zones, with entrances at each.

Parco Valle dei Templi ♥♥♥ RUINS In the eastern zone are Agrigento's three best-preserved temples. The **Tempio di Ercole** (Temple of Hercules) is the oldest, dating from the 6th century B.C.E. At one time, the temple sheltered a celebrated statue of Hercules, long since plundered. Eight of thirty-six columns have been resurrected, while the others lie romantically scattered in the tall grass and wildflowers; they still bear black sears from fires set by Carthaginian invaders. The **Tempio della Concordia** (Temple of Concord), surrounded by 34 columns, has survived almost intact since its completion in 430 B.C.E. and is one of the best-preserved remnants of the Greek world. The temple was shored up as a Christian basilica in the 6th century, so it was never plundered, and its foundations rest upon soft soil that absorbs the shock of earthquakes. The **Templo di Juno** (Temple of Juno, also known as the Temple of Hera Lacinia), at the eastern end of the ridge, had no such structural resiliency and was partly destroyed in an earthquake, though 30 columns and sections of the colonnade have been restored. A long altar was used for wedding ceremonies and sacrificial offerings.

The western zone would have been the setting of the largest temple in the Greek world, if the **Tempio di Giove** (Temple of Jove, also known as the Temple of Olympian Zeus) had ever been completed—and if what was built had not been toppled in earthquakes. A copy of an 8m-tall (26-ft.) *telamon* (sculpted figure of a man with arms raised) lies on its back amid the rubble; the original is the pride of the site's Museo Archeologico.

Several such figures were used as column-like supports on the temple. The nearby **Tempio di Castore e Polluce** (Temple of Castor and Pollux, also called Tempio di Dioscuri), with four Doric columns intact, honors Castor and Pollux, the twins who were patrons of seafarers; Demeter, goddess of marriage and the fertile earth; and Persephone, the daughter of Zeus and the symbol of spring.

For more detailed explanations, in both Italian and English, of the many artifacts unearthed here, stop by the **Museo Archeologico,** Via dei Templi (✆ **0922/40111;** Mon 9am–7pm), between the ruins and Agrigento town. However, after a long and dusty outing at the ruins, this isn't a mandatory stop.

A refreshing way to end a tour is to walk along shaded paths through the **Giardino della Kolymbethra,** a grove of citrus and olive trees and other lush Mediterranean vegetation in the valley beneath the temples; the garden fills what was once a large basin that supplied the city with fresh fish.

Parco Valle dei Templi. parcovalledeitempli.it. ✆ **0922/621-611.** Admission 17€ temples only, 22€ combined with museum, 23€ with Giardino della Kolymbethra (7€ for Giardino alone); free for ages 17 and under. Timed-entry tickets available online in advance. Mid-July to mid-Sept Mon–Fri 7–10pm and Sat–Sun 7pm–11pm; rest of year daily 8:30am–8pm (Giardino della Kolymbethra daily 10am–6pm, until 6:30pm July–Sept, until 3pm Jan–Feb).

Where to Stay & Eat in Agrigento

Hotel Villa Athena ♥♥ An 18th-century villa set in gardens within the Valley of the Temples might be the best-located hotel in all of Italy. Looking at the Temple of Concord illuminated at night is one of Sicily's great travel experiences and can be enjoyed from the balconies and even the beds of many of the rooms, strikingly done with handsome furnishings and rich fabrics. The beautiful garden, surrounding a pool, is also a prime spot to savor the view while enjoying a glass of wine.

Via Passeggiata Archeologica 33. hotelvillaathena.it. ✆ **0922/596-288.** 27 units. 150€–650€ double. Rates include breakfast. Bus: 2. **Amenities:** Dining room; 2 bars; outdoor pool; room service; free Wi-Fi.

A Nearby Natural Attraction

Vying with the ruins for popularity is the **Scala dei Turchi (Stairway of the Turks) ♥♥**, the stunning, glaringly white stepped limestone cliffs on the coast near Porto Empedocle, 13km (8 miles) southwest of the Valley of the Temples. Two beautiful beaches are at the foot of the cliffs, named for the stepped appearance and the Saracen pirates who once raided this coast. Follow signs along the coast from Porto Empedocle through Lido Marnella to parking areas. Visitors are asked to be respectful and tread gently in this fragile natural area, avoid climbing the cliffs, and leave no trash behind. The seascape is a candidate for UNESCO protection and may be closed at times to limit access. Tour-boat operators on the docks in Porto Empedocle lead excursions past the cliffs.

L'Ambasciata di Sicilia ♥♥ SICILIAN One of the few reasons to venture into modern Agrigento is a chance to enjoy a meal at this old-fashioned favorite, a city institution since 1919. True to its name, the kitchen makes a point of being a Sicilian ambassador, introducing diners to the island's finest cuisine, with delicious preparations of fresh fish, along with *linguine al'Ambasciata* (prepared with meat sauce, bacon, calamari, and zucchini). Meals are served in a small dining room crammed to the ceiling with marionettes and other colorful artifacts; a breezy terrace overlooks the surrounding rooftops.
Via Gianbertoni 2, off Via Atenea. ✆ **0392/976-7278.** Main courses 10€–18€. Thurs–Tues noon–3pm and 7–11:30pm. Closed 2 weeks Nov.

SICILY'S WEST COAST ♥♥

On its western shores, Sicily is both dazzling and fascinating, as intriguing as the rest of the island. Gleaming white salt pans, protected as a nature reserve and populated by migratory birds, line the coast between the storied port towns of Trapani and Marsala. A winding uphill half-hour drive (or a funicular ride from Trapani), will take you to the austerely medieval mountaintop town of Erice. At the southern end of the coast is the vast archaeological park of Selinunte, flecked with Greek temples and other evocative ruins, while to the north are the beautiful headlands and beaches around San Vito Lo Capo.

Arriving

BY PLANE **Vincenzo Florio Airport (TPS)** at Birgi, 15km (9 miles) from the center of Trapani (airgest.it; ✆ **0923/610-111**), is the island's third-largest airport and the main Ryanair hub for Sicily from the U.K. From here, **AST** buses (www.aziendasicilianatrasporti.it; ✆ **091/620-8111**) run hourly into Trapani (fare 3€); a taxi from the airport into Trapani costs about 35€. If you're headed farther afield, **Salemi** buses (autoservizisalemi.it; ✆ **0923/981120**) make the trip to and from central Palermo for 11€.

BY CAR From Palermo, the A29 autostrada is the fastest route southwest into Trapani, about a 1½-hour drive. Marsala is another 45 minutes south on Route 115; the drive from Trapani up to Erice takes about half an hour. Selinunte is a 2-hour drive from Palermo via A29 and E90 (exit at Castelvetrano); the drive between Trapani and Selinunte takes a little over an hour.

BY BUS & TRAIN The train journey from Palermo to Trapani takes as long as 4½ hours, usually with a change, and it's another 30 minutes on to Marsala, so the bus to either is a much better option. From Palermo, **Salemi** (autoservizisalemi.it; ✆ **0923/981120**) has service to Trapani and Birgi airport (1½ hr.), Marsala (2½ hr.), and Selinunte (1¾ hr.; change buses at Castelvetrano for another 20-min. trip to the ruins). **Segesta Autolinee** (segesta.it; ✆ **06/164160**) operates hourly buses between Pal-

Windmills among the salt fields between Trapani and Marsala.

ermo and Trapani (70 min.). **AST** buses (www.aziendasiciliana trasporti.it; ✆ **0921/620-8111**) run between Marsala and Trapani (Piazza Montalto) four times a day, a 35-minute journey; they also go from Trapani's Piazza Montalto to historic Erice (daily 6:40am–7:30pm), a winding, uphill 50-minute trip, and to San Vito Lo Capo, with as many as eight buses a day making the 80-minute trip. One convenient **train** route in the region runs hourly between Trapani and Marsala (trenitalia.it; ✆ **89/2021**), a 30-minute trip.

BY BOAT Trapani is a major embarkation point for **ferries** and **hydrofoils.** Most depart for the Egadi Islands of Marettimo, Levanzo, and Favignana. Service is also available to the islands of Ustica and Pantelleria and to the mainland ports of Civitavecchia near Rome and Tunisia in North Africa. Ferries depart from the docks near Piazza Garibaldi. Service is offered by **Liberty Lines** (libertylines.it; ✆ **0923/022022**) or **Grimaldi** (grimaldi-lines.com; ✆ **081/496444**).

Trapani ♥♥

100km (62 miles) SW of Palermo, 14km (9 miles) SW of Erice, 31km (19 miles) N of Marsala

Wedged between two especially scenic stretches of shoreline, Trapani spreads along the coastal plain below Mount Erice. The historic center, on a sea-girt promontory, is an atmospheric maze of gridlike medieval streets and squares, chockablock with baroque churches and palaces that testify to the city's prominence on Mediterranean trading routes. To the northeast is the dramatic headland at San Vito Lo Capo, with fine beaches and the

Zingaro nature reserve. Stretching south of Trapani are coastal salt pans that have been harvested since antiquity.

VISITOR INFORMATION **Trapani Infopoints,** at Via Torrearsa 69 (trapanistruzioniperluso.com; ✆ **0923/031701**) and Via Garibaldi 120 (✆ **0923/24459**), provide maps and info on exploring Trapani and other places on the west coast; they're open daily 8am to 7pm.

EXPLORING TRAPANI

The old town extends westward out to sea, with a North African feel to the labyrinth of narrow streets that lead toward the **Torre di Ligny,** a watchtower built in 1671 on the tip of the peninsula. Many elegant baroque landmarks line **Corso Vittorio Emanuele,** sometimes called Rua Grande, as it extends west from the **Palazzo Senatorio,** the 17th-century pink-marble town hall.

Adjacent 18th-century **Via Garibaldi** (also known as Rua Nova, or "New Road") is flanked by palaces and churches. One of them, the 17th-century baroque **Chiesa del Purgatorio,** houses the single greatest treasure in Trapani: the ***Misteri,*** 20 life-size wooden figures from the 18th century depicting Christ's Passion. Every year they are carried through town for Good Friday's **Processione dei Misteri** (Procession of the Mysteries). The church is officially open daily 8:30am to 12:30pm and 4 to 8pm but is often closed.

Pedal Across Sicily

Trapani is the western terminus of the 285-mile **Sicily Divide,** a bike route that crosses the island, passing through age-old villages and striking countryside before skirting the flanks of Mount Etna (p. 782) and dropping down to Catania. For more information, go to **sicilydivide.it**.

Via Torrearsa leads down to a bustling *pescheria* (fish market) on the northern edge of town, where tuna is traded; the valuable commodity is caught in nearby waters and traded with buyers from as far off as Japan. A popular sandy beach skirts the shore below the market. **Villa Margherita,** public gardens stretching between old and new Trapani, is an inviting oasis with fountains, banyan trees, and palms rustling in the sea breeze.

Santuario dell'Annunziata/Museo Regionale Agostino Pepoli ♥♥ CHURCH/MUSEUM The cloisters of a 14th-century convent, about 2km (a mile or so) outside the center on the eastern edge of town, enclose a collection of archaeological finds, art, and a crowd pleaser, a guillotine used by the island's Bourbon rulers. Much of the collection was salvaged by a local aristocrat, Count Pepoli, who found the best examples of coral carving, a popular Trapani tradition that local craftspeople pursued up until the early 20th century, when nearby coral beds were depleted. Many of the works, in which coral is often intermingled with silver filigree, are by local artisans Andrea and Alberto Tipa. Among their creations is a spectacularly elaborate *presepe* (Nativity scene).

Before leaving the premises, step into the convent's **Cappella della Madonna** to see a graceful, sculpted scene of the Virgin and Child, attributed to the 14th-century Tuscan master Nino Pisano.

Via Conte Agostino Pepoli 200. regione.sicilia.it/beniculturali/museopepoli. ✆ **0923/553269.** Admission 8€ adults, ages 17 and under free. Tues–Sat 9am–6pm; Sun 9am–1pm. Bus: 224, 225, or 230 from Piazza Vittorio Emanuele.

Erice ♥♥♥

96km (60 miles) SW of Palermo, 14km (9 miles) NE of Trapani, 45km (28 miles) NW of Marsala

Medieval Erice, high atop Mount Erice (743m/2,438 ft.), is all about views. On a clear summer day, you can see west to the Egadi Islands, east to Mount Etna, and, some sharp-eyed observers claim, south to Africa, but the town puts on a good show even in the mists and fogs that frequently roll in, with towers and craggy rocks poking through a hazy blanket of gray. In any kind of weather Erice is an atmospheric place, where you'll stop to admire an arch, a door, or a bell tower as you wander its steep cobblestone streets, flanked by churches and stone houses with elaborate baroque balconies packed with cascading geraniums. The city is famous throughout Sicily for its pastries, so be sure to sample such delights as tangy *dolci di badia* cakes, made from almond paste and citron juice.

From Trapani, you can either take an AST bus (p. 809) or choose a more scenic option: the ***funivia*** (cableway; funiviaerice.it; ✆ **0923/560023**). From the station on Via Capua at the eastern edge of Trapani, cable cars whisk you up to Erice in about 12 view-filled minutes at a cost of 11€ round-trip, 6.50€ one-way (wheelchair accessibility available). To get to the funicular, take **ATM Trapani** bus no. 201 or 203 from Trapani's Piazza Garibaldi, leaving half-hourly (atmtrapani.it; ✆ **0923/559575;** fare 1.20€). ***Note:*** The cableway closes Monday mornings for general maintenance, does not operate in inclement weather, and often isn't running when you want it to be; check before going, but generally the service operates Monday 2pm to 8pm, Tuesday to Friday 8:30am to 8pm, and Saturday and Sunday 9:30am to 8:30; from mid-July to early September, the cableway operates until 1am, 1:30am on weekends, and until 11pm on weekdays and midnight on weekends the rest of September.

EXPLORING ERICE

Whether you come up to Erice by road or cable car, you will arrive at **Porta Trapani,** one of three entrance gates (the other two are Porta Spada and Porta Spagnola, farther north). The 12th-century Porta Trapani is imbedded in the Elymian-Punic walls, an extensive defense barrier laid out by the Elymians (the ancient inhabitants of western Sicily) around 1200 B.C.E. and later fortified by the Carthaginians from North Africa to guard the city from attackers coming from the west.

Steep cobblestoned **Via Vittorio Emanuele** leads past churches and monasteries to the town's high point and central square, **Piazza Umberto I.**

Approaching Erice's 12th-century Castle of Venus.

From there, Via Guarnotti leads through Piazza San Giuliano to the beautiful **Giardino del Balio,** surrounding the Norman-era **Castello di Venere.** A cliffside promenade beneath the castle affords the most spectacular views in western Sicily, on a clear day all the way to Tunisia (or some locals claim), a distance of 170km (106 miles). The gardens are always open.

Castello di Venere (Castle of Venus) ♥ RUINS The Normans who conquered Sicily in the 12th century built a massive mountaintop castle, a majestic show of might, on the site of an ancient temple to Venus, goddess of love. Medieval towers and the ruins of walls still surround the compound, and through defensive slits and other openings you can look out over the plains of Trapani and the Egadi Islands, showing off the site's defensive advantage. Still visible are the foundations of the temple and precincts that housed a cult whose young female devotees serviced male worshippers sexually. This was deemed such an honorable profession that when the women ended their duties at age 21, they were considered especially desirable brides.

East end of Giardano del Balio. fondazioneericearte.org. ✆ **366/671-2832.** Admission (includes Chiesa Matrice tower) 5€ adults, 2€ ages 11–16, free for ages 10 and under. Daily July–Sept 10am–7pm (Aug until 8pm); Apr–June and Oct 10am–6pm; Nov–Mar Sat–Sun 10am–4pm.

Chiesa Matrice (Royal Duomo of Erice) ♥♥ CHURCH Erice's 14th-century Duomo was constructed with stones from the ancient Temple of Venus, and the *campanile* (bell tower) that rises 28m (92 ft.) next to the church also has an ancient past, built in the late 15th century atop a watchtower from the 2nd century B.C.E. Frederick of Aragon, who eventually lost Sicily to the Spanish, built the bell tower so his sentries could watch for invading troops in the sea lanes far below, a view that's still

Sicily's Pastry Capital

Erice is renowned throughout Sicily for its pastries, refined by cloistered nuns from the 14th to the 18th century. Maria Grammatico, raised under austere conditions in the nearby San Carlo convent, became famous in Italy when she wrote her autobiography, *Bitter Almonds.* Her famed crunchy almond cookies, rum- or orange-filled marzipan balls, and confections fashioned from chocolate-covered almond paste are sold at **Pasticceria Maria Grammatico ♥♥♥**, Via Vittorio Emanuele 14 (mariagrammatico.it; ✆ **0923/869390**). **Pasticceria San Carlo ♥♥**, Via S. Domenico 18 (✆ **0923/869586**), may not have the same celebrity status, but its offerings are also beautiful and tempting.

worth the climb. The church's porch, dubbed the "Gibbena" (from the Latin *agi bene,* meaning "act well"), is a later addition, built to accommodate penitents who weren't allowed to partake in the Mass. Inside, a vaulted arabesque ceiling soars over an enormous altarpiece of Carrara marble, depicting the life of Christ.

Piazza Umberto I. ✆ **0923/869123.** Church, tower, nearby churches of San Marino and San Giuliano 6€. Daily Jan–Mar 10am–4pm; Apr–June and Oct to 6pm; July and Sept to 7pm; Aug to 8pm; Nov–Dec to 1:30pm.

Along the West Coast

From the headlands north of Trapani down to Mazara delle Valo, the stunning natural beauty of western Sicily is on full display.

RISERVA NATURALE DELLO ZINGARO & SAN VITO LO CAPO ♥♥

A 45-minute drive east from Trapani across the island's northwest tip, the tiny town of **Scopello** is the beginning of the most beautiful stretch of coastline in Sicily, running north for 12km (7½ miles) to the dramatic bluffs around the resort town of **San Vito Lo Capo.** Beaches here can be overly busy in summer, but they're paradisiacal, alternating sand and pebble strands washed by waters as clear and warm as those of the Caribbean. At the edge of Scopello, the **Tonnara di Scopello**—an abandoned 13th-century tuna-processing plant—is an especially idyllic spot to swim, a sparkling cove surrounded by wind-sculpted rocks. Much of the land is set aside as the **Riserva Naturale Orientata Zingaro** (riservazingaro.it; ✆ **0924/35108**), the first designated wildlife area in Sicily, covering nearly 1,600 hectares (3,954 acres) of Mediterranean maquis and coastline. Within the reserve, the **Grotta dell'Uzzo,** a cave that served as a dwelling 12,000 years ago in Paleolithic/Mesolithic times, is now a refuge for six different types of bats (off-limits to all but sanctioned naturalists). Motorized vehicles are prohibited within the reserve—the only transport is by foot and mule.

AST buses (www.aziendasicilianatrasporti.it; ✆ **091/620-8111**) make regular runs between Trapani and San Vito Lo Capo. Excursion

A lively summertime beach at San Vito Lo Capo.

boats departing from the dock in San Vito Lo Capo offer the best way to reach Scopello and the Zingaro reserve's coastline.

THE SALT MARSHES ♥♥♥

Stretching from Trapani south to Marsala along route SP21, the salt pans skirting the coast have been harvested since antiquity (see box on p. 816). For millennia, salt was used as a preservative for perishable food and for the Romans as payment for mercenaries (the word *salary* is from the Latin *salaries,* meaning "soldier's allowance for the purchase of salt"). The area is now protected as the **Riserva Naturale Orientata Saline di Trapani e Paceco** (wwfsalineditrapani.it; ✆ **0923/867700**), covering 1,000 hectares (2,471 acres). The horizon is broken by red-and-white stone windmills, and in the late afternoon migrating birds perform spectacular in-flight choreographies. One of these windmills, **Mulino delle Saline Infersa** (seisaline.it; ✆ **0923/733003**), has a museum and salt tasting room and organizes walks through the salt pans. It's open daily, April to May and October 9am to 7pm; June to September 9am to 8pm; November 9am to 5pm; December and March 9:30am to 3:30pm; and by appointment only January and February. To get to the reserve by public transportation from Trapani, take an **AST bus** (www.aziendasiciliana trasporti.it; ✆ **0923/21021**) to Nubia, a village 7km (4 miles) south in the middle of the pans.

MOZIA ♥♥♥

A mere kilometer offshore from the northern outskirts of Marsala, the tiny island of **San Pantaleo** lies in the Stagnone, a lagoon and nature reserve. Owned by the prominent Marsala winemaking family the Whitakers, the

Salt of the Earth

When the Carthaginians first landed in the area from North Africa, they saw the potential for salt production and created basins from which to harvest the valuable commodity. The process exploits the high level of salinity in the seawater and the wind and sun that contribute to the evaporation process. In mid- to late winter, water is pumped into the pans through a canal. Over the next few months the water is left to evaporate to a point at which it assumes a reddish color and is dense with mineral pigment. Around July, just as the water reaches a sluggish consistency, the salt is raked, harvested, and brought onto dry land to complete the exsiccation process. What look like little salt huts line the road, covered in protective terra-cotta tiles. Once completely dry, the salt is cleansed of debris and packaged.

islet is a wonderful place to observe pink flamingoes, curlews, and egrets; in summer the sparse landscape is abloom with white sea daffodil and sea lavender. On San Pantaleo, footpaths meander among the scattered ruins of the ancient city of Motya (today's **Mozia**), a 6th-century-B.C.E. Phoenician stronghold. In its heyday, the island settlement was surrounded by nearly 2.5km (1½ miles) of defensive walls. In 397 B.C.E., Dionysius the Elder of Syracuse mounted a massive attack on the inhabitants, who retreated to Lilybaeum (now Marsala). Today, little is left but crumbling low walls. Most intact are the **Casa dei Mosaici** (House of Mosaics), with scenes of animal life dating to the 4th to 3rd centuries B.C.E., and the **Tophet,** a Phoenician burial ground for victims of child sacrifice, with intricately carved gravestones. The small **Museo Whitaker** (fondazione whitaker.it/isola-e-museo-di-mozia; ✆ **349/625-6508**) displays excavated artifacts, including a sensual marble statue of a young man in a wet tunic, the **Giovane di Mozia** ♥♥♥ (Young Man of Mozia), dating to around 440 B.C.E. Admission to the island, including the museum but not the boat trip over, is 10€ (6€ 17 and under); it's open daily April to October 9am to 6:30pm and November to March 9am to 3pm.

Ferries operated by **Arini and Pugliese** (ariniepugliese.com; ✆ **347/779-0218**) and the **Mozia Line** (mozialine.com) run daily year-round to Mozia from docks outside Marsala, reached by infrequent bus service from Piazza del Popolo. A round-trip costs 5€ (2.50€ for children 4–14, free for children 3 and under). Be sure to pick up a free island map at the boat landing—it's essential for making sense of the littered ruins and remains.

THE EGADI ISLANDS

Served by ferry and hydrofoil from Trapani and Marsala, the archipelago of Favignana, Levanzo, and Marettimo forms the westernmost point of Sicily. The islands are popular summertime retreats for swimming and scuba diving, but the rest of the year their 4,600 inhabitants are left to live from the fruits of the sea, especially tuna, as they have done for centuries.

A pleasant way to enjoy the beauty of the islands is on boat trips operated by **Egadi Boating** (egadiboating.com; ✆ **327/677-2824**) and other companies leaving from the Trapani docks. These trips usually include some time ashore and stops for swimming and snorkeling, and cost about 80€ for a day's outing.

Marsala ♥♥

124km (77 miles) SW of Palermo, 31km (19 miles) S of Trapani, 48.5km (30 miles) SW of Erice

This thriving little port on Cape Boéo, the western tip of Sicily overlooking the Egadi Islands and Tunisia, is where the world-famous Marsala sweet wine is produced. You can sample some amber yellow Marsala in one of the town's wine shops, or head through the hills along roads lined with prickly-pear cacti to vineyards nearby. Townspeople sip the dark, vintage Marsala as a dessert wine with hard piquant cheese, fruit, or pastries. Famous product aside, Marsala is an elegant town with baroque palaces and churches, Roman ruins, a lively fish market, and a long, sandy coastline stretching to the north and south.

VISITOR INFORMATION The **tourist office,** Via 11 Maggio 100 (✆ **0923/714097**), is open Monday to Saturday 9am to 1pm and 3:30 to 7:30pm.

EXPLORING MARSALA

Enter the city from the **Porta Garibaldi,** a massive 17th-century arched gateway crowned by an eagle. Garibaldi is honored because it was at Marsala that the 19th-century freedom fighter and his red-shirted volunteers overthrew the Bourbon regime, paving the way for the independence of southern Italy. From the gate, Via Garibaldi leads to busy **Piazza della Repubblica,** the heart of the city. The square's 18th-century Palazzo Senatorio, now the Town Hall, is nicknamed "The Loggia" for its row of elegant arcades.

Leading north from Piazza Repubblica, the main thoroughfare **Via 11 Maggio** is flanked by many splendid baroque palaces. One of them, at Via Garraffa 57, houses the **Museo degli Arazzi Fiamminghi** (Flemish Tapestry Museum). Darkened salons display eight magnificent Flemish tapestries, woven between 1530 and 1550, depicting the wars against the Jews when the Romans occupied Jerusalem (museionline.info/musei/museo-degli-arazzi-fiamminghi; ✆ **0923/711327;** admission 2.50€; Mon–Sat 10am–6pm, Sun 9am–1pm). To the northwest, facing the sea on the **Lungomare Boéo,** the archaeological museum (see below) stands amid old *bagli,* Marsala wine warehouses.

Museo Archeologico Lilibeo Marsala–Baglio Anselmi ♥♥ MUSEUM A former wine warehouse (*baglio*) houses gold jewelry from ancient Mozia (p. 815), as well as the museum's showpiece, a relatively well-preserved **Punic ship** (*punicus* being a Latin term referring to

Carthage, the ancient kingdom in what is today Tunisia). It's believed the ship, discovered in shallow waters in 1971, was constructed for the Battle of the Egadi Islands during the First Punic Wars between Rome and Carthage in 241 B.C.E. and sank on its maiden voyage; some scholars argue that the vessel was not a warship but a cargo ship. Measuring 35m (115 ft.) long, the ship was manned by 68 oarsmen. Large sections remain, enough to suggest the sleekness and power of the wooden shell covered with sheets of lead fixed with bronze nails. They're displayed along with bowls, plates, animal bones, cannabis leaves, and other material carried on board. Behind the museum (included with admission) are the excavations of ancient Lilybaeum, as Marsala was known in Roman times. Among the relics are the remains of a villa with a steam room and still-glittering mosaics.

Lungomare Boéo. turismocomunemarsala.com. ✆ **0923/952535.** Admission 4€ adults, 2€ ages 18–24, ages 17 and under free. Daily 9am–7:30pm (archaeological area until 5pm).

San Tomaso di Canterbury (Chiesa Madre) ♥♥ CHURCH It's only fitting that Marsala's most imposing church is dedicated to Britain's St. Thomas à Becket, given the English connections that brought the city such wealth over the centuries (see box below). Legend has it that a ship headed for England, carrying materials to build a church dedicated to Becket, was forced by a storm to seek haven at Marsala, and the crew simply built the church here instead. It's more likely that the cultlike popularity of the saint, murdered in Canterbury cathedral in 1170, had spread as far as Sicily by the 13th century, when the church was founded. The most impressive decorative pieces in the three-aisle interior are also by outsiders—the Gaginis, a 15th-century family of Swiss sculptors who worked their way down the Italian boot until they reached Sicily, undertaking commissions in Palermo and elsewhere around the island. Their best work here, by Domenico Gagini, is the lovely *Madonna del Popolo* in the right transept.

Piazza della Repubblica. ✆ **0923/716295.** Free admission. Daily 9am–7pm.

NEAR MARSALA: MAZARA DEL VALLO & CRETTO DI BURRI

One of the most exotic cities in Sicily, Mazara del Vallo, 25km (15 miles) south of Marsala, is not only Italy's largest fishing port but was also once a hub of the island's Arab culture, and is now home to a large Tunisian population. A mazelike kasbah clusters near the port, and Norman churches and baroque palaces surround the central Piazza della Repubblica. On the delightfully baroque Piazza Plebiscito, surrounded by domed towers and arched loggias, the **Museo del Satiro Danzante ♥♥♥** in the church of Sant' Egidio (parchiarcheologici.regione.sicilia.it; ✆ **0923/933917**) displays the namesake "dancing satyr." The bronze from the 4th century B.C.E., attributed by some scholars to Greek sculptor Praxiteles, catches a young male in a state of ecstatic frenzy, head thrown back and arms wide,

A TASTE FOR marsala

On a dark and stormy night in 1770, English trader John Woodhouse was forced to anchor in Marsala. He headed for a tavern, downed some local wine, discovered it tasted similar to the Portuguese "Porto," and realized the commercial potential. Woodhouse began to mass-produce and export the wine, and he got a big break when Admiral Horatio Nelson developed a taste for Marsala and decided that the British Navy should allot sailors a glass per day.

Around the same time, Joseph Whitaker, another English entrepreneur, inherited a vast vineyard in Marsala and expanded the wine's reputation by exporting it to the United States. He also bought the island of **Mozia** (p. 815), where he founded an archaeological museum and published important studies of Tunisian birds.

One more businessman entered the scene in the mid-19th century: Vincenzo Florio, from Palermo, who purchased the Woodhouse wine empire and refined Marsala grapes. The Florios, who also exported tuna, were one of Sicily's most prominent families well into the 20th century.

Sample Marsala at **Enoteca La Ruota** on Via Scipione l'Africano near the archaeological museum (enotecalaruota.it; ✆ **0347/925-8451**), while admiring the Stagnone lagoon in front of you.

and he remained that way on the bottom of the sea for millennia until fishermen dredged him up in their nets in 1998. The museum is open daily 9am to 7:15pm, and admission is 6€. Trains make the 25-minute trip between Marsala and Mazara throughout the day, and it's about a 25-minute drive on the SS115.

Another manmade phenomenon here in the southwest is **Cretto di Burri,** also known as Il Grande Cretto, or "Great Crack." This sprawling work of concrete "landscape art" spreads across the ruins of the village of Gibellina, destroyed in an earthquake in 1968, serving as a memorial to the 400 villagers who died and hundreds of others who survived but suffered enormous hardship in the aftermath. The installation, begun by Alberto Burri in 1985 and completed after the artist's death in 2015, is about 50km (30 miles) northeast of Mazara delle Vallo on SS119.

Selinunte ♥♥♥

122km (76 miles) SW of Palermo, 55km (34 miles) SE of Marsala, 73km (45 miles) SW of Trapani

This Greek colony on Sicily's southwest coast was once one of the most powerful cities in the world, with a population estimated to have been close to 50,000. Then the great Carthaginian general Hannibal virtually destroyed Selinunte in 409 B.C.E. Even in the context of those brutal times the wrath of the Carthaginians was abhorrent—an army of 100,000 men descended on the city with battering rams, and in an orgy of destruction raped, looted, plundered, and butchered most of the inhabitants and enslaved the rest. Hannibal spared only the temples—not out of respect for the deities, but to preserve the loot they housed.

Today this vast park is Europe's largest archaeological site, covering 270 hectares (670 acres). Selinunte is not just large, however, it's also a bucolic spot where you can walk amid the ruins, gaze out to sea, and ponder what life was like millennia ago. As you stroll amid the wildflowers and smell the wild herbs, remember that the town name comes from the Greek word *selinon,* meaning parsley.

Tip: Selinunte is doable as a day trip from Palermo—it's about a 2-hour drive via the A29/E90 autostrada (exit at Castelvetrano)—but try to leave early in the morning. You'll need at least 4 hours to explore the ruins, and you don't want to do that in the full heat of midday.

VISITOR INFORMATION You can enter the park at two points, with ample parking near each: from Via Selinunte in the village of Marinella di Selinunte and from Via Mediterraneo in the village of Triscina di Selinunte.

EXPLORING THE ARCHAEOLOGICAL PARK

Given the enormity of the area, allow yourself at least 4 hours to visit. Bring drinks, as it can get hot under the sun. If you're not up to extensive walking, you can hop on an electric train that makes a circuit through the ruins; tickets cost 12€ (6€ children 4–9, under 3 free) for a full circuit to Sanctuary of Demeter Malophoros; 8€ and 3€ for a trip to the Acropolis.

Parco Archeologico Selinunte ♥♥♥ RUINS The archaeological grounds have three designated zones: the East Hill and temples, the Acropolis and ancient city, and the Sanctuary of Demeter Malophoros. You will likely start your visit from the East Hill, adjacent to the main entrance.

The **East Hill** was the sacred district of the city, with three temples surrounded by an enclosure. Archaeologists are still trying to determine which deity each of the Doric temples was dedicated to—for now, they are simply denoted by letters of the alphabet. Temple E, which was in all probability dedicated to Hera, was built between 490 and 480 B.C.E. and has a staggering 68 columns. The Metopes (reliefs) that are the pride and joy of the archaeological museum in Palermo (p. 760) are from this temple. Temple F is the oldest of the trio, built between 560 and 540 B.C.E.; in its original state, the temple had a double row of six columns at the eastern entrance and 14 columns on either side. Temple G, now an impressive heap of rubble except for a lone standing column, was destined to be of colossal proportions, but it appears that construction was halted, probably because of ongoing raids from Carthage.

The **Acropolis,** a district of gridlike streets surrounded by defensive walls, was the center of social and political life. Here atop a plateau stood most of Selinunte's important public and religious buildings, as well as the residences of the town's aristocrats. Temple C, the earliest surviving

Among the Greek ruins at Selinunte, Temple E still has 68 columns standing.

temple of ancient Selinus, was built here in the 6th century B.C.E. and is still surrounded by 14 of its resurrected 17 columns. From the Acropolis, you cross the now-dry Modione River to the **Sanctuary of Demeter Malophoros,** the ruins of several shrines to Demeter, goddess of fertility (p. 794). The custom was for worshipers to place stone figurines in the shrines to honor Demeter, and as many as 12,000 such figurines have been unearthed.

Via Selinunte. ✆ **0349/625-6508.** Admission 14€ adults, ages 17 and under free. Daily May to mid-Sept 9am–7pm, mid-Sept to Oct 9am–5pm, Nov to mid-Mar 9am–3:30pm, mid-Mar to Apr 9am–6pm.

Where to Stay & Eat on Sicily's West Coast

Fresh fish is plentiful, especially locally caught tuna (grilled and topped Sicilian style, with capers, olives, tomatoes, and spices). Look for North African influences in spices and such staples as seafood couscous, which often supplants pasta. Speaking of pasta, the most common here is *busiati,* the oldest handmade pasta in the world. The curly, eggless noodles have a firm texture and mealy taste and are usually topped with pesto made Trapanese-style, with an uncooked sauce of cherry tomatoes, basil, pecorino, and almonds, often sprinkled with toasted breadcrumbs for a little extra crunch.

ERICE

Hotel Elimo ♥♥ A 400-year-old *palazzo* in the heart of Erice's historic core welcomes guests in stone-walled lounges where in the chilly months a fire blazes in a hearth beneath beamed ceilings. Guest quarters are a bit more conventional, though comfortable, and some have views over the plains below, as do the restaurant and terrace.

Via Vittorio Emanuele 75, Erice. hotelelimo.it. ✆ **0923/869377.** 22 units. 75€–125€ double. Rates include breakfast. Closed Dec–Feb. **Amenities:** Restaurant; bar; free Wi-Fi.

Hotel Moderno ♥ The "moderno" dates to the conversion of a 19th-century Erice house just after World War II, though old-fashioned charm prevails. Antiques, brass, and wicker pieces lend a homey touch. About a dozen rooms open onto private balconies, some with stunning views, like that from the breakfast terrace.

Via Vittorio Emanuele 67, Erice. hotelmodernoerice.it. ✆ **0923/869300.** 40 units. 70€–100€ double. Rates include breakfast. **Amenities:** Restaurant; bar; free Wi-Fi.

Il Carmine ♥♥ This refurbished 15th-century convent still shows traces of monastic living in simple, no-frills rooms and shower-only bathrooms. Yet the spartan surroundings are loaded with character, and views into the gardens are as soothing as they were intended to be. A separate entrance ensures that you won't disturb convent life.

Piazza del Carmine, Erice. ilcarmine.com. ✆ **0923/869069.** 6 units. 80€–110€ double. Rates include breakfast. Closed Jan–Mar. **Amenities:** Restaurant; free Wi-Fi.

Ristorante Monte San Giuliano ♥♥♥ SICILIAN You'll navigate some steps and stone alleyways to reach this restaurant, where a table on the terrace or in the rustic dining room seems, like much of medieval Erice, far away from the modern world. The menu shows off Arab influences in the flavorful seafood couscous, with many nods to such local favorites as lamb with a pistachio crust. Choice pasta dishes are the ones served with *sarde* (sardines) or *pesto alla Trapanese,* with garlic, basil, fresh tomatoes, and almonds.

Vicolo San Rocco 7, Erice. montesangiuliano.it. ✆ **0923/869595.** Main courses 13€–27€. Tues–Sun 12:30–2:15pm and 7:30–10pm. Closed part of Jan.

MARSALA

Grand Hotel Palace ♥♥ The 19th-century estate of an English wine importer in Marsala has been heavily redone, but the premises retain a luxurious, old-world aura, so hushed and quiet you feel that even the statues might doze off and topple over. The most character-filled rooms are in the old house, but those in the new annex are also spacious and outfitted with traditional furnishings; many have sea views. In the gardens, stately trees are a backdrop for the swimming pool.

Lungomare Mediterraneo 57, Marsala. grandhotelpalace.eu. ✆ **0923/719492.** 56 units. 120€–155€ double. Rates include breakfast. **Amenities:** Restaurant; bar; outdoor pool; room service; babysitting; free Wi-Fi.

Trattoria Garibaldi ♥♥ SICILIAN/SEAFOOD At this 60-year-old institution near Marsala's cathedral, four arched, colorful dining rooms serve local seafood favorites with a well-deserved reputation for freshness.

Fish and shrimp, simply grilled with spices or served atop couscous, has a decidedly North African flair, while the homemade local pasta *busiati* with fresh fish is a specialty you probably won't find beyond the west coast.

Piazza dell'Addolorata 35, Marsala. instagram.com/trattoriagaribaldimarsala. ✆ **0923/953-006.** Main courses 8€–22€. Mon–Sat 12:30–2:45pm (until 3:30pm Mon) and 7:30–10:30pm; Sun 12:30–2:45pm.

Villa Favorita ♥♥ An early 19th-century hunting lodge is tucked into lush gardens at the edge of historic Marsala. The most appealing guest rooms and suites are on the upper floors of an elegant villa, with wide-oak and tile floors and arched loggias opening onto a courtyard. Others are garden bungalows that resemble stone igloos—they're unusual but attractive, sort of an Italian take on glamping, and divided into small sitting rooms and bedrooms with a cramped bathroom; they're scattered among greenery and shaded lanes surrounding a beautiful swimming pool. The atmosphere is casual, and the grounds are full of many corners for relaxing. A pizza oven is fired up for summer dining in the garden, and throughout the year the restaurant serves well-done Sicilian dishes. From the center of Marsala, take SS115 north toward Trapani; the hotel is signposted.

Via Favorita 23, Marsala. villafavorita.com. ✆ **0923/989-100.** 29 bungalows, 13 units in main building. 90€–120€ double. Rates include breakfast. **Amenities:** 2 restaurants; bar; outdoor pool; tennis court; free Wi-Fi.

TRAPANI

For the past 75 years, the favorite stop in town for a quick bite has been **Calvino Pizzeria dal 1946 ♥♥**, Via Nunzio Nasi 71, with slices and pies to take out or eat in, in several atmospheric rooms (✆ **0923/21464;** Wed–Mon 7pm–midnight). **12 Chiavi ♥**, Corso Vittorio Emanuele 74 (✆ **331/925-6610**), serves a good selection of Sicilian wines by the glass; hours are variable, but it's open most evenings.

Ai Lumi ♥♥ SICILIAN The narrow, arched ground floor of a *palazzo,* filled with heavy rustic tables and chairs, is a cool retreat in which to enjoy Trapanese classics. Seafood is plentiful, as are such meat specialties as roast lamb in a citrus sauce and *busiati,* the thick local pasta, topped with *pesto trapanese.* The front terrace is one of the nicest places in Trapani to spend a summer evening. Upstairs are 12 pleasant, well-furnished rooms, some with kitchenettes (85€–110€ double).

Corso Vittorio Emanuele 75, Trapani. ailumi.it. ✆ **0923/872-418.** Main courses 8€–18€. Daily 1–11pm.

B&B Terrazze Villanova ♥♥♥ A stay in this bright, spacious apartment puts you in modern Trapani, a 15-minute walk from the old city in one direction and 15 minutes in the other to the cable car that whisks you up to Erice. Beaches, shops, and restaurants are within easy walking distance, and the bus from Palermo stops outside the door. The large, well-appointed, and immaculately kept rooms share two terraces along with the hospitality of hosts Elda and Vitto, who dispense advice, help with reservations for meals and tours, and on occasion offer free transport to the port and nearby sights.

Vicolo Villanova 33. terrazzevillanova.it. ✆ **347/320-4730.** 5 units. 65€–140€ double. Rates include breakfast in nearby cafe. Closed mid-Nov to mid-Dec and mid-Jan to mid-Mar. **Amenities:** Free Wi-Fi.

Cantina Siciliana ♥♥♥ SEAFOOD/TRAPANESE Colorful tiles, Sicilian puppets, and welcoming service enliven this Trapani institution on an old street in the Jewish quarter. The kitchen focuses on local classics: Trapani-style fish couscous, swordfish with capers, and *busiata* pasta topped with Trapanese pesto, accompanied by carefully chosen wines and served with polish.

Via Giudecca 36. cantinasiciliana.it. ✆ **0923/28673.** Main courses 7€–22€. Thurs–Tues 1–3pm and 7:45–11pm.

Osteria La Bettolaccia ♥♥♥ SICILIAN Trapani's longtime favorite never disappoints, drawing a steady stream of diners (reserve if you can) to a couple of rambling, tile-floored rooms near the seafront. The kitchen prepares what many regulars claim is the best seafood couscous in Sicily, laden with calamari and a spicy sauce. Another standout is spaghetti with swordfish, tuna, tomatoes, herbs, and breadcrumbs.

25 Via Enrico Fardella, Trapani. labettolaccia.it. ✆ **0923/21695.** Main courses 12€–20€. Daily 12:45–3pm and 7:45–11pm.

16

PLANNING YOUR TRIP TO ITALY

By Donald Strachan

This chapter has many tips and tools for planning your trip to Italy, including information on how to get there, how to get around in safety and comfort, and the inside track on local resources for up-to-date advice. If you do your homework, pick the right place for the season, and pack for the climate, preparing for a trip to Italy should be pleasant and uncomplicated. See also "When to Go," p. 37.

ARRIVING

By Plane

If you're flying across an ocean, you'll likely land at Rome's upgraded **Leonardo da Vinci–Fiumicino Airport (FCO;** adr.it/fiumicino), 40km (25 miles) from the center, or **Milan Malpensa (MXP;** milanomalpensa-airport.com/en), 45km (28 miles) northwest of central Milan. These are Italy's intercontinental hubs; it is usually cheapest to fly long-haul to one or the other.

Rome's much smaller **Ciampino Airport (CIA;** adr.it/ciampino) and Milan's **Linate Airport (LIN;** milanolinate-airport.com) serve low-cost airlines connecting to European cities and other destinations in Italy. For information on getting to central Rome from its airports, see p. 63; for Milan, see p. 470. Three times a day, travelers can board a direct high-speed train from Rome's Fiumicino Airport to Florence (2¼ hr.) or Venice (4¼ hr.) **without** changing in Rome.

FLYING DIRECTLY TO VENICE, BOLOGNA, PISA, NAPLES, BARI, OR SICILY

If you are arriving in Italy from elsewhere in Europe, it is often good value to fly direct to one of the smaller cities. Among the most convenient are Venice's **Marco Polo Airport** (VCE; veneziaairport.it/en), Bologna's **Marconi Airport** (BLQ; bologna-airport.it), Pisa's **Galileo Galilei Airport** (PSA; pisa-airport.com/en), **Naples International Airport** (NAP; aeroportodinapoli.it/en), **Bari International Karol Wojtyła** (BRI; bari.airports.aeroportidipuglia.it/en), Catania's **Vincenzo Bellini Airport** (CTA; aeroporto.catania.it/en), and Palermo's **Punta Raisi Airport** (PMO; aeroportodipalermo.it/en). For information on getting into central Venice from the airport, see p. 401; for reaching Florence from Pisa, see p. 165; for reaching central Naples from the airport, see p. 590. For information on arriving in Sicily via Palermo's airport, see p. 750.

 PREVIOUS PAGE: **Rent a sporty Vespa to zip around Italian cities in style.**

ETIAS: EUROPE'S NEW entry REQUIREMENT

Travelers planning to visit Italy from late 2026 onward will encounter a new hoop to jump through: the **European Travel Information and Authorization System** (**ETIAS**). This electronic visa waiver is essentially the European Union equivalent to the USA's Electronic System for Travel Authorization (ESTA). ETIAS registration will be mandatory for travelers who don't need a visa to enter 30 European countries, a list that includes 26 European Union member states (all except Ireland) plus Iceland, Liechtenstein, Norway, and Switzerland. It applies to the citizens of around 60 visa-exempt countries, including the U.S., Canada, Mexico, U.K., Australia, Japan, much of the Caribbean, and most of South America.

The online application process includes the following requirements: personal data (including name, date of birth, address); passport info; name of first country of intended stay; and answers to background questions about criminal record, any past deportations, and past travel to zones experiencing conflict or infectious disease epidemics.

Unless the applicant is flagged on one of the EU's watch lists, e-mail approval of ETIAS should arrive within minutes. As of now, the proposed fee for ETIAS registration is 20€ (about $23.70) per applicant between the ages of 18 and 70. All travelers, regardless of age, must register with ETIAS, but those under 18 and over 70 are exempt from paying the fee.

Once approved, ETIAS registration is valid for 3 years. However, if your passport expires during that time, you'll need to apply for a new ETIAS waiver. Consistent with current tourist visa rules, ETIAS is intended for stays of 90 days or less within a 180-day period.

When should travelers planning a trip to Italy apply for ETIAS status? Although the EU promises nearly instant approval for most travelers, in some cases processing can take up to 30 days. So, it's best to play it safe and secure your ETIAS status a few weeks before your trip. And keep in mind: If you show up for your international flight to Italy without a valid ETIAS document, you will be denied boarding or entry.

For complete information, go to **travel-europe.europa.eu/etias**.

Italian tour operator **Neos** (neosair.com), **United** (united.com), and **Delta** (delta.com) often run summer-season nonstop services from New York to regional hubs including Palermo and Catania (Sicily), Naples, and Bari.

By Train

Italy's major cities are well connected to Europe's rail hubs. You can arrive in Milan or Turin on direct trains from **France** (Paris, Lyon) by **TGV** (sncf-connect.com), or in Milan from **Switzerland** (sbb.ch/en). Connect there for Venice, Florence, or Rome (see "Getting Around," p. 829). Several routes connect **Vienna** with Italy via a comfortable overnight Austrian sleeper train. These **Nightjet** (nightjet.com) services visit Verona, Bologna, Florence, Rome, and Venice, among other places. Flexible cabin options include booking out a whole couchette for a family—one to three adults and up to four children ages 14 and under (six people

TURNING TO THE internet or apps FOR A HOTEL DISCOUNT OR EXTRAS

Before going online, it's important that you know what "flavor" of discount you're seeking. Here are several types of discounts, plus advice on booking strategies:

1. **Discounts available via virtual private networks (VPNs).** There's more and more evidence that online consumers get different prices based on what the average income is in the area they live. By disguising your identity and locale with a VPN, and picking a less affluent region to search from, you will likely be shown lower prices on hotel rooms. Note that you will have to get a VPN subscription, but they tend to be quite reasonably priced.
2. **Extreme discounts on sites where you bid for lodgings without knowing which hotel you'll get.** You'll find these on such sites as **Priceline.com** ("Express Deals") and **Hotwire.com**, and they can be money-savers, particularly if you're booking within a week of travel (that's when the hotels resort to deep discounts to get beds filled). As these companies use only major chains, you can rest assured that you won't be put up in a dump. For more reassurance, install the Chrome extension **HotelCanary** on that browser. It will identify what hotel is being shown on both Priceline and Hotwire. I think you'll be pleasantly surprised by the quality of many of the hotels that are offering these "secret" discounts.
3. **Discounts on chain hotel websites.** Not long ago, all of the major chains announced they'd be reserving special discounts for travelers who booked directly through the hotels' websites (usually in the portion of the site reserved for loyalty members). They weren't lying: These are the lowest rates at the hotels in question some 80% of the time, though discounts can range widely, from as little as $1 to as much as $50. Our advice: Search for a hotel that's in your price range and ideal location (see below for where to do that) and then, if it is a chain property, book directly through the online loyalty portal.
4. **Savings found by using the right hotel search engine.** They're not all equal, as we at Frommers.com learned after putting the top 20 sites, and 6 AI services, to the test around the globe. We discovered that **Trivago.com** and **Google Travel** both listed the lowest rates most consistently.
5. **Last-minute discounts.** Booking last minute can be a great savings strategy, as prices sometimes drop in the week and days before travel as hoteliers scramble to fill their rooms. But you won't necessarily find the best savings through companies that claim to specialize in last-minute bookings. Instead, use the sites recommended in point 2 of this list.

It's a lot of surfing, I know, but in the hothouse world of hotel pricing, this sort of diligence can pay off.

maximum). The latest generation of Nightjet trains also offer mini-cabins for solo travelers. Seats open up **180 days ahead of travel;** you will need to be sharp to bag the best prices. Similar services also connect Munich, Germany with Venice or Florence/Bologna/Rome.

You can book international rail travel online directly or via **Rail Europe** (raileurope.com); see p. 834.

GETTING AROUND

By Car

Much of Italy is accessible by public transportation, but to explore vineyards, countryside, and smaller towns, you need a car. You'll get the **best rate** if you book your car far ahead of arrival—car rental search companies usually report the lowest rates available between 6 and 8 weeks ahead of arrival. Rent the smallest car possible and request a diesel (*gasolio* or *diesel* in Italian) rather than a gasoline (*benzina*) engine, to minimize fuel costs. You must be 25 or older to rent from many agencies, although some accept ages 21 and up, at a premium price.

You also must have nerves of steel, a sense of humor, a valid domestic driver's license, and strictly speaking (for non-EU citizens), an **International Driving Permit** (see below). Insurance on all vehicles is compulsory.

Note: If you're planning to rent a car in Italy during high season, **book farther in advance than you usually would.** It's not unheard of to arrive at an airport in July to find every agent out of cars, perhaps for the week.

It can sometimes be tricky to get to the *autostrada* (fast highway) from a city center or airport, so consider renting or bringing a GPS-enabled device, or installing an offline sat-nav app on your phone. In bigger cities you often first have to get to the *tangenziale,* or beltway, which will eventually lead to your highway of choice. The beltway in Rome is known as the Grande Raccordo Anulare, or "Big Ring Road."

The going can be slow almost anywhere, especially on Friday afternoons leaving the cities and Sunday nights on the way back into town, and rush hour around any city can be epic. Driving long-distance for a day or so on either side of the busy *Ferragosto* (Aug 15) holiday is to be avoided *at all costs.* See **autostrade.it** for live traffic updates and a road-toll calculator.

Autostrada tolls can get expensive, costing around 1€ for every 13km (8 miles), which means it would be about 23€ for a trip from Rome to Florence. Fuel prices have remained high now for a few years: Gas cost approximately 1.70€ *per liter* at the time of writing (diesel around .05€ less). The **PrezziBenzina app** (prezzibenzina.it) finds the lowest-priced local gas station. Add in the price of the vehicle rental, and it's often cheaper to travel by train, even for two people.

Before leaving home, you can apply for an **International Driving Permit** from the American Automobile Association (AAA; aaa.com; ✆ **800/622-7070** or 650/294-7400). You should apply at least a month before travel; the license costs $20. In Canada, the permit is available from the Canadian Automobile Association (CAA; caa.ca; ✆ **800/222-4357**).

Technically, you need this permit and your actual driver's license to drive in Italy. Traffic police can fine you for driving without an IDP. Visitors from within the EU need only carry a domestic driver's license.

Italy's equivalent of AAA, the **Automobile Club d'Italia** (ACI; aci.it), will respond if you place an emergency call to ✆ **803-116** for road breakdowns (✆ **800/000-116** from an overseas cellphone). You'll be charged for this service if you're not a member.

DRIVING RULES Italian drivers aren't all maniacs; most of them only *appear to be.* Spend any time on a highway and you will have the experience of somebody driving up from behind insanely close, headlights flashing. Take a deep breath and don't panic: This is the aggressive signal for you to move to the right so he (invariably, it's a "he") can pass. Until you do, he will stay mind-bogglingly close. On a two-lane road, the idiot who swerved into your lane to pass someone in oncoming traffic expects you to veer obligingly over toward the shoulder so three lanes of traffic can fit. He would do the same for you. Probably. Many Italians seem to think blinkers are optional, so assume a car in front could be ready to turn at any moment. When traveling outside of towns, it is compulsory to keep your headlights illuminated—set to dip—even during the day.

Autostrade are toll highways, denoted by **green signs** and prefaced with an *A,* like the A1 from Milan to Florence, Rome, and Naples. A few fast highways aren't numbered and are simply called a *raccordo,* a connecting road between two cities (such as Florence–Siena and Florence–Pisa).

Strade statali (singular: *strada statale*) are state roads, often without a center divider and two lanes wide (although they may be a divided four-way highway), indicated by **blue signs.** Their route numbers are prefaced with an *SS,* as in the SS11 from Milan to Venice. On signs, however, these official route numbers are used infrequently. Usually, you'll just see blue signs listing destinations by name with arrows pointing in appropriate directions. It's impossible to predict which of all the towns that lie along a road will be shown on a particular sign. Sometimes a sign gives only the first minuscule village past the turnoff. At other times it lists the first major town down that road. Some signs mention only the major city where the road eventually terminates, even if it's hundreds of kilometers away. It pays to study the map before coming to an intersection or to carry a GPS device or download an offline GPS app for your smartphone. A *strada statale* can be frustratingly slow thanks to traffic, traffic lights, and the fact that it bisects countless towns: If you're in a hurry, pay for the autostrada.

The **speed limit** on roads in built-up areas around towns and cities is 50kmph (31 mph). On two-lane roads it's 90kmph (56 mph), and on the highway it's 130kmph (81 mph). Italians have an astounding disregard for these limits. Know that police can ticket you and collect any fine on the spot. The **blood-alcohol limit** in Italy is .05%, generally achieved with just two regular-size drinks; driving above the limit can result in a fine of up to 6,000€, a driving ban, or jail. The blood-alcohol limit is zero for commercial drivers and for anyone who has held a driver's license for less than 3 years.

Seat belts are obligatory in both front and back seats; ditto child seats or special restraints for minors under 1.5m (5 ft.) in height, although this latter regulation is often flouted. Drivers may not use a handheld cellphone while driving—yet another law that locals treat as optional.

PARKING Even savvy locals struggle to find convenient parking in Italy's cities. Urban hotels rarely have parking facilities, but many do negotiate a deal with a private city lot. Your hotel should be a first point of contact if you plan to park and leave the car for the duration of a stay. Should you prefer driving to the high-speed train, this is the only sensible option in big cities. On streets, **white lines** indicate free public spaces, **blue lines** are public pay spaces, and **yellow lines** mean only residents are allowed to park. Meters don't line the sidewalk; rather, there's usually one machine on the block where you punch in coins corresponding to how long you want to park. The machine spits out a ticket to leave on your dashboard. Many machines accept card payment.

If you park in an area marked *parcheggio disco orario,* root around in your glove compartment for a cardboard parking disc. With this device, you dial up the hour of your arrival and display it on the dash. You're allowed *un'ora* (1 hr.), *due ore* (2 hr.), or whatever the sign advises. If you do not have a disc, write your arrival time on a sheet of paper and leave it clearly visible.

Parking lots have ticket dispensers, but exit booths are not usually staffed. When you return to the lot to depart, first visit the office or payment machine to exchange your ticket for a paid receipt or exit token, which you then use to pass the exit barrier. Again, cards are widely accepted.

ROAD SIGNS A **speed limit** sign is a black number in a red circle on a white background. The **end of a speed zone** is just black and white, with a black slash through the number. A red circle on white, a black arrow pointing down, and a red arrow pointing up means **yield to oncoming traffic,** while a red-and-white triangle pointing down means **yield ahead.**

Many city centers are closed to traffic: A simple white circle with a red border, or the words *zona pedonale* or *zona traffico limitato,* denotes a **pedestrian or restricted zone** (you can often prearrange to drop off baggage at your hotel inside the zone); a white arrow on a blue background is used for Italy's many **one-way streets;** a mostly red circle with a horizontal white slash means **Do Not Enter.** Any image in black on a white background surrounded by a red circle means that image is **not allowed** (for instance, if the image is two cars next to each other, it means no passing; a motorcycle means no Harleys permitted; and so on). A circular sign in blue with a red circle-slash means **no parking.** You **may be fined for infringements,** including via automatic traffic camera. The fine may be

SHOPPING IN ITALY: chain stores you can trust

Not every store can be hyperlocal or artisanal. Italy has several **homegrown retail chains** to rely on for everyday essentials or something to take home. If you're traveling with teens, direct them here to help their hard-saved euros stretch a little further:

- **OVS** (ovsfashion.com): Value clothes with character, especially for kids and for every season
- **Carpisa** (carpisa.it): Well-made, affordable bags, wallets, luggage, and accessories
- **Goldenpoint** (goldenpoint.com): Swimsuits, bikinis, PJs, and underwear, mostly for women, with big sale discounts if you time it right
- **Pinalli** (pinalli.it): Vast range of brand-name cosmetics, perfumes, and beauty products at good prices; most common in the North
- **Legami** (legami.com): Design-forward pens, cute stationery including diaries, and seasonal gifts such as Christmas ornaments
- **Il Papiro** (ilpapirofirenze.it): Born in Florence but now with branches in Rome and Venice selling high-quality paper products including leather-bound journals
- **Tigotà** (tigota.it): Hygiene is a national pastime in Italy, and here you'll find cleaning products and scents for both you and your home; Acqua & Sapone (acquaesapone.it) is similar

automatically deducted from a credit card you provided to your rental agency—occasionally many weeks later.

Gasoline (*benzina*) is sold from gas stations along major roads and on the outskirts of town, as well as in 24-hour stations along the autostrada. Almost all stations are closed for the *riposo* and on Sundays (except on the autostrada), but most have machines that accept bills and often cards. All gas is unleaded. Diesel is *gasolio* (or simply *diesel*).

By Train

Italy, especially its northern half, has one of the best train systems in Europe with most destinations connected by rail. Almost all lines are run by state-owned **Ferrovie dello Stato,** aka **Trenitalia** (trenitalia.com; ✆ **892021**). A private operator, **Italo** (italotreno.com; ✆ **060708** or 892020) serves key stations on a many long-distance routes: the Turin–Milan–Florence–Rome–Naples–Salerno high-speed line; on branches north from Bologna, including to Ferrara–Padua–Venice and Verona–Trento–Bolzano; between Turin and Venice via Milan and Verona; and from Rome southeast to Bari, in Puglia. Prices on Italo tend to be a few euros lower in standard class, but it is always worth checking both.

Travel durations and ticket prices vary considerably depending on the type of train you choose. The country's principal north–south high-speed line links Turin and Milan to Bologna, Florence, Rome, Naples, and Salerno. Milan to Rome, for example, takes just over 3 hours on the quick train, and costs around 105€ in standard class—although you can find tickets for under 30€ if you buy way in advance and travel in off-peak hours. Rome to Naples takes 70 minutes and costs 52€ (walk-up fare) on the fast train, or you can spend 14€ for a slower train that takes more than twice as long. To bag the cheapest fares on high-speed trains, aim to **book around 100 to 120 days before your travel dates.** Our advice: Book ahead for the best prices, but do not buy until you are certain you will travel. The **Italo newsletter** (and home page) regularly advertises limited-time promo code discounts of up to 50% off advance fares, making them crazy cheap. You can also book rail travel on both Trenitalia and Italo via **Trainline** (thetrainline.com/trains/italy).

TYPES OF TRAIN The speed and overall quality of Italian trains vary widely. The high-speed **Frecciarossa,** along with **Italo**'s rival high-speed service, is the fastest of the fast. These trains mostly operate on the Turin–Milan–Florence–Rome–Naples–Salerno line and run up to 300kmph (186 mph); new FS equipment (Frecciarossa 1000) has a potential top speed of 400kmph (249 mph). Frecciarossa services also run along Italy's east coast (Milan–Rimini–Ancona–Bari–Lecce) and connect Turin with Venice (with stops in Milan, Verona, and Vicenza). The cheapest class on both operators is perfectly comfortable, even on long journeys (although Business class on the Frecciarossa is well worth the extra cost if you can find a cheap advance fare). These are Italy's premium rail services.

The **Frecciargento** uses lower-grade hardware and travels a little slower; it links Rome with Puglia (Bari and Lecce) at speeds of up to 250kmph (155 mph). There are also Rome–Naples–Reggio Calabria, Rome–Rimini–Ravenna, and Rome–Florence–Pisa–Genoa Frecciargento services. Frecciargento trains have the usual two classes, First and Second. The **Frecciabianca** service isn't a genuine high-speed service, merely a slightly upgraded train running on standard track.

Speed and cleanliness come at a price: Tickets for high-speed trains usually cost around three times what you'd pay for a slower "regional"

Travel Times Between the Major Cities

CITIES	DISTANCE	(FAST) TRAIN TRAVEL TIME	DRIVING TIME
Florence to Venice	281km/174 miles	2 hr.	3 hr.
Florence to Milan	298km/185 miles	1 hr., 40 min.	3½ hr.
Milan to Venice	267km/166 miles	2 hr.	3¼ hr.
Milan to Rome	572km/355 miles	2 hr., 55 min.	5½ hr.
Rome to Florence	277km/172 miles	1½ hr.	3 hr.
Rome to Naples	219km/136 miles	1 hr., 10 min.	2½ hr.
Rome to Bari	425km/264 miles	4 hr., 20 min.	5 hr.
Rome to Turin	669km/415 miles	3 hr., 50 min.	6½ hr.
Rome to Venice	528km/327 miles	3hr., 25 min.	5½ hr.

train. With the *Frecce* you **must make a seat reservation** when you buy a ticket. If you are traveling with a rail pass (see below), you pay a 13€ supplementary fee to ride them and reserve a seat. Passes are not accepted on Italo trains.

InterCity (IC) trains are another step down, in both speed and comfort; as with *Le Frecce,* seat reservations are compulsory on IC trains. These are the top-level trains in Sicily. The slower ***Regionale*** (R) and ***Regionale Veloce*** (RV) make many stops and can occasionally be on the shabby side, but they are also very cheap: A Venice–Verona second-class ticket will put you back only 10€, compared with 29€ on the high-speed service. There is no advantage in booking R or RV services ahead of travel; just turn up, get a ticket, and ride. Old *Regionale* rolling stock is slowly being replaced and comfort is improving. However, overcrowding has long been a problem on these services on Friday evenings, weekends, and holidays, especially in and out of big cities, or just after a strike.

TRAIN TRAVEL TIPS **Rail apps** for both Italo and Trenitalia offer paperless e-ticketing and easy in-app payment via credit card or PayPal. These represent the simplest way to buy and carry rail tickets—for both high-speed and regular services. They are available, in English, from the usual app stores. You can also show a copy (paper or electronic) of an online booking confirmation with its unique PNR code. Tickets are valid for the specific service booked. In big cities (especially Milan and Rome) and tourist destinations (above all Venice and Florence), ticketing lines in stations can be dreadfully long. If you are reluctant to embrace the apps, don't be scared of **automatic ticket machines.** They are easy to navigate, provide instructions in English, accept cash and credit cards, and save you the stress of waiting in a slow line. (***Note:*** You can't buy international tickets at automatic machines.)

If you board a train without a ticket, you have to pay a hefty fine on top of the ticket or supplement, which the conductor will sell you. If you realize once aboard that you have the wrong type of ticket, your best bet is to search out the conductor, who is likely to be more forgiving because you found her and made it clear you weren't trying to ride for free.

At small local stations, **schedules** for all trains leaving a given station are still often printed on yellow posters tacked up on the station wall (a similar white poster lists all the arrivals). These are good for general guidance. Keep your eye on electronic boards and screens, which update with delays and track (*binario*) changes. You can also get official schedules (and more train information, also in English) and buy tickets at trenitalia.com or italotreno.com, or via an agent such as **Rail Europe** (raileurope.com).

RAIL PASSES & DISCOUNTS To buy the **Eurail Italy Pass,** available only outside Europe and priced in U.S. dollars, contact **Rail Europe** (raileurope.com) or **Eurail** (eurail.com). You have 1 month in which to use the train for a set number of days (the base number of days is 3, and you can add up to 5 more). For adults, the first-class pass costs $250, second-class is $196. Each additional day costs around $35 to $45 for first class, $30 to $35 for second class. Up to two children ages 4 to 11 are entitled to a child pass free with any adult pass purchase. For youth travelers (27 and under), a 3-day second-class pass is $148 and additional days about $25 each.

Buying your rail pass early is sometimes rewarded with an extra day's travel at no additional cost (such as pay for 3 days, get 4) or seasonal discounts (we have seen up to 25% off Eurail Italy passes). The **Eurail Global Pass** covers rail travel in Italy, all its neighbors, and most of the rest of Europe (33 countries).

Note: Booking every rail journey online ahead of arrival may beat a rail pass on price, especially if you factor in the cost of compulsory seat reservations on Italy's high-speed trains. However, because the cheapest online fares are usually nonrefundable, you gain flexibility with a pass. The **Trenitalia Pass** works out around $30 cheaper than Eurail, plus seat reservations are free, but it offers less flexibility in the choice of days and validity period. You can buy it in Italy or online at trenitalia.com.

Children 14 and under ride half-price on long-distance trains; on regional (R or RV) trains, it's children 11 and under. Kids under 4 don't pay, although they also do not have the right to their own seat. Some state railway services offer free tickets for children 14 and under traveling with an adult; ask about *"Bimbi gratis"* fares when buying (ticket machines offer this option automatically, if it's available). The **Italo Family** fare, available at least 3 days before travel at a station or online, includes free travel for up to three kids ages 13 and under accompanying an adult (in Smart class only).

By Bus

Although trains are quicker and easier, you can get just about anywhere in Italy on a network of local, provincial, and regional bus lines. Keep in mind that in smaller towns, buses mainly shuttle workers and schoolchildren, so most runs are Monday to Friday (*feriali* on timetables, which includes Sat), early in the morning, and usually again from midafternoon.

In a big city, the **bus station** for intercity trips is usually near the main train station. A small town's **bus stop** is generally in the main square, on the edge of town, or just outside the town gate. You should always try to find the local ticket vendor—if there's no office, this is invariably the nearest newsstand or *tabacchi* (look for a sign with a white T), or occasionally a bar—but you can usually buy tickets on the bus. Buses in cities and on major routes increasingly accept **fare payment via contactless card or mobile phone.** You can sometimes flag down a passing bus on a country road but try to find an official stop (a small sign, sometimes tacked onto a tree or pole). Tell the driver where you're going and ask politely if he'll let you know when to get off. When he says, *"È la prossima* *fermata,"* that means yours is the next stop. *"Posso scendere a...?"* is "Can I get off at...?"

For details on urban bus transportation, see individual chapters. Perhaps the only intercity bus you will take in Italy is the efficient **Florence–Siena** service; see "Siena," p. 229. However, if you are traveling on a tight budget, check **FlixBus** (flixbus.it) intercity fares. They often significantly undercut train prices. For comparing times and prices across different modes of transport in Italy, **rome2rio.com** is useful. A long-distance bus in Italian is *un pullman.*

By Plane

These days, the only internal air connection you will likely make is to **Sicily.** Direct Sicily routes from mainland airports are operated by **Ryanair** (ryanair.com); **easyJet** (easyjet.com); **ITA** (ita-airways.com); **AeroItalia** (aeroitalia.com/en); **Volotea** (volotea.com/en); and **Wizz Air** (wizzair.com).

[FastFACTS] ITALY

Area Codes The **country code** for Italy is **39. City codes** (for example, Florence 055, Venice 041, Milan 02, Rome 06) are incorporated into the numbers themselves. Therefore, you must dial the entire number, ***including the initial zero,*** when calling from *anywhere* outside or inside Italy and even within the same town. For example, to call Milan from the United States, you must dial **011-39-02,** then the rest of the phone number. Phone numbers in Italy can range anywhere from 6 to 12 digits in length.

ATMs The easiest and best way to get cash is from an ATM, referred to in Italy as ***un bancomat.*** ATMs are easy to find in Italian cities; smaller towns usually have one, but it's good practice to fuel up on cash in urban centers before heading to villages or rural areas. Only use ATMs which are connected to, or clearly affiliated with, a bank. Standalone ATMs found in shops and even in the street often charge very high fees (or worse).

Before traveling, confirm that your card is valid for international withdrawals and that you have a four-digit PIN. Some ATMs in Italy will not accept any other number of digits. Also, be sure you know your daily withdrawal limit before you depart. ***Note:*** Many banks impose a fee when you use a card at another bank's ATM, and this fee can be higher for international transactions (up to $5 or more) than for domestic ones. In addition, the bank from which you withdraw cash may charge its own fee, although this is not common practice in Italy.

If at the ATM you get an on-screen message saying your card isn't valid for international transactions, don't panic: It's most likely the bank can't make an electronic connection (occasionally this can be a city-wide epidemic). Try another ATM or another town.

Business Hours **Banks** tend to be open Monday through Friday 8:30am to 1:30pm and 2:45 to 4:15pm. General opening hours for **stores, offices,** and **churches** are from 9:30am to noon or 1pm, and again from 3 or 3:30pm to 7:30pm. The early afternoon shutdown is the *riposo,* the Italian siesta (in downtown areas of large cities, stores don't usually close for a *riposo*). Most small stores close all day Sunday and some also on Monday (morning only or all day). Some public services and business offices are open only in the morning.

Traditionally, **state (i.e., national) museums** are closed Mondays. Most large museums stay open all day long otherwise, although some smaller or private collections close for *riposo* or are only open in the morning (9am–2pm is common). **Churches,** including many that are art-stuffed and firmly on the tourist trail, often close for a long lunch break.

Cellphones Pretty much any phone with **4G/LTE** or **5G** capability will work in Italy, as long as international service is allowed on the account—contact your service provider before leaving. But—and it's a *big* but—using roaming can be expensive, especially if you access the Internet on your phone. It's often much cheaper, once you arrive, to buy an Italian SIM card. This is a particularly good idea if your stay in Italy is more than a week. You can **buy a SIM card** at cellphone shops in every city: The main service providers are **TIM** (tim.it), **Vodafone** (privati.vodafone.it), **WINDTRE** (windtre.it), and **Iliad** (iliad.it). With a prepaid Italian SIM card in your phone, local and national calls may be unlimited and incoming calls are free. Value prepaid data packages are available—usually with data inclusive—as are prepaid data bundles for iPads and other tablets. Not every network allows **tethering:** Ask if you need it. ***Note:*** U.S. contract cellphones are often "locked" and only work with a SIM card from your home service provider, so check whether you have an unlocked phone before buying an Italian SIM card.

Buying a phone is another option, and you shouldn't have trouble finding one for about 20€. Use it, then recycle it when you get home. It will save you a fortune versus alternatives such as roaming or using hotel telephones, as will using Wi-Fi to call on Teams, Zoom, or FaceTime.

Credit Cards The evolution of international computerized banking has led to the triumph of plastic throughout Italy. It's still a good idea to carry some cash—small businesses occasionally accept only cash. **Visa** and **Mastercard** are almost universally accepted, and some businesses, typically at the luxe end, take **American Express. Diners Club** tends not to be accepted in Italy. Be sure to let your bank know you'll be traveling abroad to avoid having your card blocked after a few days of big purchases far from home. ***Note:*** Many banks assess a 1% to 3% "transaction fee" on **all** charges you incur abroad, whether you're using the local currency or your native currency. Research card providers to see which offer better rates for travelers. ***Tip:*** If a store clerk gives you a choice, **pay in local currency** (euro), not your home currency. Their system's exchange rates will invariably be poor compared with your bank or card provider. The same applies at ATMs.

Customs Foreign visitors arriving by air can bring in most items for personal use, including new merchandise bought duty-free for up to 430€. Returning to the United States, U.S. citizens can bring with them up to $800 of goods, including 1 liter of alcohol, but no meats or fresh fruits and vegetables. Vinegars, oils, jams, chocolates, and many cheeses are permissible (vacuum-packed soft and hard cheeses, yes; "runny" cheeses, no).

Drinking Laws People of any age can legally consume alcohol in Italy, but a person must be 16 years old to be served alcohol in a restaurant or bar. Bars generally close by 2am, although alcohol is often served in clubs after that. Supermarkets and convenience stores sell beer, wine, and liquor.

Electricity Italy operates on a 220-volt AC (50 cycles) system, as opposed to the U.S. 110-volt AC (60 cycles) system. A simple adapter plug makes American flat pegs fit the Italian round holes and, unless your appliance is dual-voltage (as some hair dryers, travel irons, and almost all electronics are), an electrical converter will be necessary. You can pick up the hardware at electronics stores, travel specialty stores, luggage shops, and airports. Buy **before** you travel.

Embassies & Consulates The **U.S. Embassy** is in Rome at Via Vittorio Veneto 121 (it.usembassy.gov; ✆ **06/46-741**). There are also **U.S. Consulates General** in Florence, at Lungarno Vespucci 38 (✆ **055/266-951**); in Milan, at Via Principe Amedeo 2/10 (✆ **02/290-351**); and in Naples, in Piazza della Repubblica (✆ **081/583-8111**).

The **Canadian** Embassy is in Rome at Via Zara 30 (travel.gc.ca; ✆ **06/85444-1**). There is also a **Consulate General** in Milan, at Via Verziere 11.

The **Australian Embassy** is in Rome at Via Antonio Bosio 5 (italy.embassy.gov.au; ✆ **06/852-721**). The **Australian Consulate-General** is in Milan at Via Borgogna 2 (✆ **02/7767-4200**). The **New Zealand Embassy** (mfat.govt.nz/italy; ✆ **06/853-7501**) is in Rome at Via Clitunno 44. The **U.K.** Embassy (www.gov.uk/world/italy; ✆ **06/4220-0001**) is in Rome at Via XX Settembre 80a. The **British Consulate-General** is in Milan at Via San Paolo 7.

Emergencies The best number to call in Italy with a **general emergency** is ✆ **112,** which connects you to the ***Carabinieri*** who will transfer your call as needed. For the **police,** dial ✆ **113;** for a **medical emergency** and to call an **ambulance,** the number is ✆ **118;** for the **fire department,** call ✆ **115.** All are free calls. For roadside assistance, a paid service, see "Getting Around," p. 829.

Family Travel Italy is a family-oriented society. A crying baby at a dinner table is greeted with a knowing smile, rather than a stern look. Children can almost always request discounted smaller portions, and sometimes even get a special treat from the waiter, but the availability of such accoutrements as child seats for dinner tables is more the exception than the norm. For cars, however, this is a legal requirement: Ask your rental company to provide one. There are plenty of parks, offbeat museums, markets, ice-cream parlors, and vibrant street-life scenes to amuse even the youngest children. Child discounts apply on public transportation, and at public and private museums.

Healthcare Italy offers universal healthcare to its citizens and those of fellow European Union countries. Others should be prepared to pay medical bills upfront. Before leaving home, find out what medical services your **health insurance** covers. You will be treated in any emergency in Italy, irrespective of whether you have travel insurance. The country's public healthcare system is generally well regarded. The richer North tends to have better **hospitals** than the South.

Insurance Italy may be one of the safer places you can travel in the world, but accidents and setbacks can and do happen, from lost luggage to car crashes. We recommend looking at the following online marketplaces for insurance: **SquareMouth.com**, **InsureMyTrip.com**, and **TravelInsurance.com**. All three allow users to quickly and easily compare policies from different, vetted travel insurance companies. We find the user interface at SquareMouth to be more intuitive, but all three are excellent resources.

Internet Access You will find reliable Wi-Fi in almost every accommodation, but if it is essential for your stay, make sure to ask before booking. Don't always expect to find a connection in a rural *agriturismo*—digital detox is sometimes part of their appeal. In a pinch, hostels, libraries, and many cafes and bars have public access. Several spots around Venice, Florence, Rome, and other big cities are covered with free Wi-Fi access provided by the local government, but at these and other Wi-Fi spots around Italy, antiterrorism laws make it obligatory to register before you can browse. **High-speed trains** often have free Wi-Fi (but throttle Facetime, video streaming, file sharing, and similar data-hungry services). **Airports** generally offer fast, free Wi-Fi.

LGBT+ Travelers Italy as a whole, and northern Italy in particular, is

WHAT THINGS COST IN ROME (HOTEL PRICES ARE HIGH SEASON)

Bus ticket (from/to anywhere in the city)	1.50€
Double room at Inn at the Spanish Steps (expensive)	160.00€–500.00€
Double room at Lancelot (moderate)	150.00€–225.00€
Double room at Mimosa (inexpensive)	85.00€–250.00€
Continental breakfast (cappuccino and croissant standing at a bar)	3.00€–4.50€
Tasting menu for one at Pipero Romano (expensive)	100.00€–220.00€
Dinner for one, with wine, at La Barrique (moderate)	25.00€–30.00€
Piza dinner for one, with wine, at Li Rioni (inexpensive)	13.00€–18.00€
Small gelato at Fatamorgana	2.50€–5.00€
Glass of wine at a bar	3.50€–8.00€
Coca-Cola (standing/sitting in a bar)	2.50€/5.00€
Cup of espresso (standing/sitting in a bar)	1.00€/2.50€
Admission to the Colosseum and Forum	20.00€–26.00€ online

LGBT-friendly. Homosexuality is legal and the age of consent is 16. Same-sex civil unions became legal in 2016; the Meloni government (p. 18) has said these hard-won rights will remain but will not be extended. Italians tend to be more affectionate than North Americans in all their friendships, and even straight men occasionally walk down the street with their arms around each other—however, kissing anywhere other than on the cheeks may draw attention in some places. As you may expect, small towns can be less permissive than cities and beach resorts.

Italy's national associations and support networks for gays and lesbians are **ArciGay** (arcigay.it) and **ArciLesbica** (arcilesbica.it). Most cities have a local office: See **arcigay.it/en/sedi** for a directory.

Mail & Postage Sending a postcard or letter up to 20 grams, or a little less than an ounce, costs 1.30€ to European countries, 2.45€ to North America, and a whopping 3.20€ to Australia and New Zealand. Full details on Italy's postal services are available at **poste.it** (some of it in English).

Mobile Phones See "Cellphones" above.

Money & Costs Frommer's lists prices in the local currency. The currency conversions quoted below were correct at press time. However, rates fluctuate, so before departing, consult a currency exchange website, such as **oanda.com/currency-converter**, to check up-to-the-minute rates.

THE VALUE OF THE EURO VS. OTHER POPULAR CURRENCIES

€	US$	Aus$	Can$	NZ$	UK£
1	1.18	1.68	1.61	1.95	0.86

Like many European countries, Italy uses the **euro** as its currency. Euro coins are issued in denominations of .01€, .02€, .05€, .10€, .20€, and .50€, as well as 1€ and 2€; bills come in denominations of 5€, 10€, 20€, 50€, 100€, 200€, and 500€. You'll get the best rate if you **exchange money** at a bank or bank ATM. The rates at "cambio/change" exchange booths are less favorable but still better than what you'd get exchanging money at a hotel or shop (a last-resort tactic only). **Traveler's checks** have gone the way of the Stegosaurus.

Newspapers & Magazines *The New York Times International Edition* and *USA Today* are available at newsstands in big cities, and sometimes even in smaller towns. At larger kiosks in big cities, you may find the *Wall Street Journal Europe, The Economist,* and major European newspapers and magazines.

Pharmacies Italian pharmacies offer essentially the same range of generic drugs available in North America and internationally. They are ubiquitous (look for the green cross) and serve almost like mini clinics, where pharmacists diagnose and treat minor ailments with over-the-counter drugs. Carry the generic name of any prescription medicines in case a local pharmacist is unfamiliar with the overseas brand name. Pharmacies in cities take turns doing the 24-hour night shift. For health, beauty products, and over-the-counter meds at fair prices, look for a branch of **dm** (www.dm-drogeriemarkt.it), a CVS-style chain with branches in the North. They cannot fill prescriptions.

Police In any emergency, call ✆ **112.** The *Carabinieri* (✆ **112;** www.carabinieri.it) normally concern themselves only with serious crimes but point you in the right direction. The *Polizia* (✆ **113;** poliziadistato.it), whose city headquarters is called the *questura,* is the place for help with lost and stolen property or petty crimes.

Safety Italy is a remarkably safe country in terms of street crime. The worst threats you'll likely face are pickpockets who sometimes frequent touristy areas and public buses: Keep your hands on your camera at all times and valuables in an inside zip-pocket. Don't leave anything valuable in a rental car overnight and leave nothing visible inside at any time. If you are robbed, you can fill out paperwork at the nearest police station (*questura*), but this is mostly for insurance purposes or to get a new passport issued—don't expect them to hunt down the perpetrator. In general, avoid public parks at night. Areas around rail stations are often shabby but rarely threatening.

Senior Travel Seniors and older people are treated with deference in Italy, but few specific programs exist. One exception is at museums and sights, where those aged 60 or 65 and older often pay a reduced admission. As a senior in Italy, you're *un anziano,* or if you're a woman, *un'anziana,* "elderly"—it's a term of respect. Let people know you're one if you think a discount may be in order.

Smoking Smoking has been eradicated from inside restaurants, bars, and most hotels, so smokers tend to take outside tables. If you're keen to eat or drink alfresco, you are essentially choosing a seat in the smoking section; requesting that your neighbor not smoke may not be politely received.

Student Travelers An **International Student Identity Card** (ISIC) qualifies students for savings on travel tickets, entrance fees, and more. The card is valid for 1 year. You can apply for the card online at **isicusa.com**. If you're not a student but are aged 30 and under, you can get an **International Youth Travel Card** (IYTC) from the same agency, which entitles you to some discounts. Teachers can apply for an **International Teacher Identity Card** (ITIC), although your work I.D. card should suffice at museums and the like. Students will find that many university cities offer ample student discounts and inexpensive youth hostels.

Taxes No sales tax is added onto purchases at checkout, but a 22% value-added tax (in Italy: **IVA**) is automatically included in just about everything, except some foods and a few specific goods and services, where rates of 4%, 5%, or 10% apply. Local transportation, hotels, and dining are among a group of goods taxed at 10%. For large purchases, non–E.U. residents can get IVA refunded at the airport: Look out for signage in store windows or ask the cashier. Several city governments have also introduced an **accommodation tax.** For example, in Florence you may be charged between 3.50€ and 8€ per person per night, depending on the government star rating of the hotel, guesthouse, or rental apartment. Children 11 and under are exempt. Venice, Rome, and many other popular localities also levy their own taxes. This tax is not usually included in any published room rate, even rates prepaid online. Many places prefer to take payment for this tax in cash.

Tipping In **hotels,** service is usually included in your bill. In family-run operations, additional tips are unnecessary. In fancier places with a hired staff, however, you may want to leave a 2€ per day tip for the housekeeper and pay the bellhop or porter 2€ per bag, but it is not expected. In **restaurants,** a 2€ to 4€ per person "cover charge" is automatically added to the bill, and in some tourist areas, especially Venice, another 10% to 15% service is tacked on. Except in the most unscrupulous places, this will be noted on the menu somewhere; if unsure, you should ask, *è incluso il servizio?* It is not necessary to leave extra money on the table, although it is not uncommon to leave up to 10€, especially for good service. Locals often leave nothing. At **bars and cafes,** you can leave small change on the counter for the barman (maybe 1€ or 2€ if you have had a few drinks), although it is not expected. There is no need to leave anything extra if you sit at a cafe table, as they are likely already charging you double or triple the price of standing at the bar. It is not necessary to tip **taxi** drivers, although it is common to round up a euro or two.

Toilets Public toilets are few and far between, aside from train stations, where they cost .50€ or 1€ to use, and gas stations, where they are free (with perhaps a basket seeking gratuities for cleaners). In an emergency, standard procedure is to enter a cafe, make sure the bathroom is not *fuori servizio* (out of order), and then order a cup of coffee before bolting to the facilities. It is advisable to always make use of the facilities in a hotel, restaurant, or museum before a long walk around town. Public toilets—and often those in bars, too—can be dirty, with no seat or toilet paper. It's best to carry a pack of tissues and some hand sanitizer.

Travelers with Disabilities Most of the top museums and churches have ramps at their entrances, and several hotels have converted rooms into accessible units. Other than that, you may find some parts of Italy tricky. Builders in the Middle Ages didn't have wheelchairs in mind when they fashioned narrow doorways or spiral staircases, and preservation laws make it tricky to do much about this in some places.

Public transportation is much improved, however, with better access for passengers using wheelchairs, particularly on high-speed trains, modern local buses, and new transit infrastructure like Florence's tram. There are usually dedicated seats or spaces for those with disabilities, and Italians are quick to give up their place for somebody who appears to need it. **Trenitalia** has a special number for disabled travelers to call for assistance on the rail network: ✆ **02/323232. Italo** has dedicated wheelchair spaces on every train: Call ✆ **060708** for station assistance.

Websites Following are some of our favorite sites to help you plan your trip: **italia.it/en** is the official English-language tourism portal for visiting Italy, although regional and city tourism websites are usually more comprehensive and up-to-date (see individual chapters); **arttrav.com** is excellent for cultural travel, exhibitions, and openings, especially in Florence and Tuscany; **ansa.it** and **thelocal.it** supply you with Italian news in English; and naturally, **frommers.com/destinations/Italy** offers more expert advice on the country.

MOLTO ITALIANO

Basics

USEFUL ENGLISH-ITALIAN PHRASES

English	Italian	Pronunciation
Thank you	Grazie	***graht**-tzee-yey*
You're welcome	Prego	***prey**-go*
Please	Per favore	***pehr** fah-**vohr**-eh*
Yes	Si	**see**
No	No	**noh**
Good morning or Good day	Buongiorno	**bwohn-*djor*-noh**
Good evening	Buona sera	***bwohn**-ah **say**-rah*
Good night	Buona notte	***bwohn**-ah **noht**-tay*
It's a pleasure to meet you.	Piacere di conoscerla.	**pyah-*cheh*-reh dee *koh*-nohshehr-lah**
My name is ____.	Mi chiamo ____.	**mee *kyah*-moh**
And yours?	E lei?	**eh lay**
Do you speak English?	Parla inglese?	***pahr*-lah een-*gleh*-seh**
How are you?	Come sta?	***koh*-may *stah***
Very well	Molto bene	***mohl*-toh *behn*-ney**
Goodbye	Arrivederci	**ahr-ree-vah-*dehr*-chee**
Excuse me (to get attention)	Scusi	***skoo*-zee**
Excuse me (to get past someone)	Permesso	**pehr-*mehs*-soh**

GETTING AROUND

English	Italian	Pronunciation
Where is . . . ?	Dov'è . . . ?	***doh**-vey*
the station	la stazione	**lah stat-tzee-*oh*-neh**
a hotel	un albergo	**oon ahl-*behr*-goh**
a restaurant	un ristorante	**oon reest-ohr-*ahnt*-eh**
the bathroom	il bagno	**eel *bahn*-nyoh**
I am looking for . . .	Cerco . . .	***chehr*-koh**
a porter	un facchino	**oon fahk-*kee*-noh**
the check-in counter	il check-in	**eel check-in**
the ticket counter	la biglietteria	**lah beel-lyeht-teh-*ree*-ah**
arrivals	l'area arrivi	***lah*-reh-ah ahr-*ree*-vee**
departures	l'area partenze	***lah*-reh-ah pahr-*tehn*-tseh**
gate number	l'uscita numero	**loo-*shee*-tah *noo*-meh-roh**
the waiting area	l'area d'attesa	***lah*-reh-ah daht-*teh*-zah**
the men's restroom	la toilette uomini	**lah twa-*leht* *woh*-mee-nee**
the women's restroom	la toilette donne	**lah twa-*leht* *dohn*-neh**
the police station	la stazione di polizia	**lah stah-*tsyoh*-neh dee poh-lee-*tsee*-ah**
a security guard	una guardia di sicurezza	***ooh*-nah *gwahr*-dyah dee see-koo-*ret*-sah**
the smoking area	l'area fumatori	***lah*-reh-ah foo-mah-*toh*-ree**
the information booth	l'ufficio informazioni	**loof-*fee*-choh een-*fohr*-mah-*tsyoh*-nee**
a public telephone	un telefono pubblico	**oon teh-*leh*-foh-noh *poob*-blee-koh**
an ATM/cashpoint	un bancomat	**oon *bahn*-koh-maht**
baggage claim	il ritiro bagagli	**eel ree-*tee*-roh bah-*gahl*-lyee**
a luggage cart	un carrello portabagagli	**oon kahr-*rehl*-loh *pohr*-tah-bah-*gahl*-lyee**
a currency exchange	un cambiavalute	**oon *kahm*-byah-vah-*loo*-teh**
a cafe	un caffè	**oon kahf-*feh***
a bar	un bar	**oon bar**
a bookstore	una libreria	***oo*-nah lee-breh-*ree*-ah**
a duty-free shop	un duty-free	**oon duty-free**
To the left	A sinistra	**ah see-*nees*-tra**
To the right	A destra	**ah *dehy*-stra**
Straight ahead	Avanti (*or* sempre diritto)	**ahv-*vahn*-tee (*sehm*-pray dee-*reet*-toh)**

DINING

English	Italian	Pronunciation
Breakfast	Prima colazione	**_pree_-mah coh-laht-tzee-_ohn_-ay**
Lunch	Pranzo	**_prahn_-zoh**
Dinner	Cena	**_chay_-nah**
How much is it?	Quanto costa?	**_kwan_-toh _coh_-sta**
The check, please	Il conto, per favore	**eel kon-toh _pehr_ fah-_vohr_-eh**

A MATTER OF TIME

English	Italian	Pronunciation
When?	Quando?	**_kwan_-doh**
Yesterday	Ieri	**ee-_yehr_-ree**
Today	Oggi	**_oh_-jee**
Tomorrow	Domani	**doh-_mah_-nee**
What time is it?	Che ore sono?	**kay _or_-ay _soh_-noh**
It's one o'clock.	È l'una.	**_eh loo_-nah**
It's two o'clock.	Sono le due.	**_soh_-noh leh _doo_-eh**
It's two-thirty.	Sono le due e mezzo.	**_soh_-noh leh _doo_-eh eh _mehd_-dzoh**
It's noon.	È mezzogiorno.	**_eh_ mehd-dzoh-_johr_-noh**
It's midnight.	È mezzanotte.	**_eh_ mehd-dzah-_noht_-teh**
It's early.	È presto.	**_eh prehs_-toh**
It's late.	È tardi.	**_eh tahr_-dee**
in the morning	al mattino	**ahl maht-_tee_-noh**
in the afternoon	al pomeriggio	**ahl poh-meh-_reed_-joh**
at night	alla notte	**dee _noht_-the**

DAYS OF THE WEEK

English	Italian	Pronunciation
Monday	Lunedì	**loo-nay-_dee_**
Tuesday	Martedì	**mart-ay-_dee_**
Wednesday	Mercoledì	**mehr-cohl-ay-_dee_**
Thursday	Giovedì	**joh-vay-_dee_**
Friday	Venerdì	**ven-nehr-_dee_**
Saturday	Sabato	**_sah_-bah-toh**
Sunday	Domenica	**doh-_mehn_-nee-kah**

NUMBERS

English	Italian	Pronunciation
1	uno	***oo*-noh**
2	due	***doo*-ay**
3	tre	**tray**
4	quattro	***kwah*-troh**
5	cinque	***cheen*-kway**
6	sei	**say**
7	sette	**set-tay**
8	otto	***oh*-toh**
9	nove	***noh*-vay**
10	dieci	**dee-ay-chee**
11	undici	***oon*-dee-chee**
20	venti	***vehn*-tee**
21	ventuno	**vehn-*toon*-oh**
22	venti due	***vehn*-tee *doo*-ay**
30	trenta	***trayn*-tah**
40	quaranta	**kwah-*rahn*-tah**
50	cinquanta	**cheen-*kwan*-tah**
60	sessanta	**sehs-*sahn*-tah**
70	settanta	**seht-*tahn*-tah**
80	ottanta	**oht-*tahn*-tah**
90	novanta	**noh-*vahnt*-tah**
100	cento	***chen*-toh**
1,000	mille	***mee*-lay**
5,000	cinque milla	***cheen*-kway *mee*-lah**
10,000	dieci milla	**dee-ay-chee mee-lah**

ITALIAN MENU TERMS

Abbacchio Roast haunch or shoulder of lamb baked and served in a casserole and sometimes flavored with anchovies.

Agnolotti A crescent-shaped pasta shell stuffed with a mix of chopped meat, spices, vegetables, and cheese; when prepared in rectangular versions, the same combination of ingredients is identified as ravioli.

Amaretti Crunchy, sweet almond-flavored macaroons.

Anguilla alla veneziana Eel cooked in a sauce made from tuna and lemon.

Antipasti Succulent tidbits served at the beginning of a meal (before the pasta), whose ingredients might include slices of cured meats, seafood (especially shellfish), and cooked and seasoned vegetables.

Aragosta Lobster.

Arrosto Roasted meat.

Baccalà Dried and salted codfish.

Bagna cauda Hot and well-seasoned sauce, heavily flavored with anchovies, designed for dipping raw vegetables; literally translated as "hot bath."

Bistecca alla fiorentina Florentine-style steaks, coated before grilling with olive oil, pepper, lemon juice, salt, and parsley.

Bocconcini Veal layered with ham and cheese, then fried.

Bollito misto Assorted boiled meats served on a single platter.

Braciola Pork chop.

Bresaola Air-dried spiced beef.

Bruschetta Toasted bread, heavily slathered with olive oil and garlic and often topped with tomatoes.

Bucatini Coarsely textured hollow spaghetti.

Busecca alla milanese Tripe (beef stomach) flavored with herbs and vegetables.

Cacciucco alla livornese Seafood stew.

Calzone Pizza dough rolled with the chef's choice of sausage, tomatoes, cheese, and so on, and then baked into a kind of savory turnover.

Cannelloni Tubular dough stuffed with meat, cheese, or vegetables and then baked in a creamy white sauce.

Cappellacci alla ferrarese Pasta stuffed with pumpkin.

Cappelletti Small ravioli ("little hats") stuffed with meat or cheese.

Carciofi Artichokes.

Carpaccio Thin slices of raw cured beef, sometimes in a piquant sauce.

Cassatta alla siciliana A richly caloric dessert that combines layers of sponge cake, sweetened ricotta cheese, and candied fruit, bound together with chocolate buttercream icing.

Cervello al burro nero Brains in black-butter sauce.

Cima alla genovese Baked filet of veal rolled into a tube-shaped package containing eggs, mushrooms, and sausage.

Coppa Cured morsels of pork filet encased in sausage skins, served in slices.

Costoletta alla milanese Veal cutlet dredged in breadcrumbs, fried, and sometimes flavored with cheese.

Cozze Mussels.

Fagioli White beans.

Fave Fava beans.

Fegato alla veneziana Thinly sliced calves' liver fried with salt, pepper, and onions.

Focaccia Ideally, concocted from potato-based dough left to rise slowly for several hours and then garnished with tomato sauce, garlic, basil, salt, and pepper and drizzled with olive oil; similar to a deep-dish pizza most popular in the deep south, especially Bari.

Fontina Rich cow's-milk cheese.

Frittata Italian omelet.

Fritto misto A deep-fried medley of whatever small fish, shellfish, and squid are available in the marketplace that day.

Fusilli Spiral-shaped pasta.

Gelato (produzione propria) Ice cream (homemade).

Gnocchi Dumplings usually made from potatoes *(gnocchi alla patate)* or from semolina *(gnocchi alla romana),* often stuffed with combinations of cheese, spinach, vegetables, or whatever combinations strike the chef's fancy.

Gorgonzola One of the most famous blue-veined cheeses of Europe—strong, creamy, and aromatic.

Granità Flavored ice, usually with lemon or coffee.

Insalata di frutti di mare Seafood salad (usually including shrimp and squid) garnished with pickles, lemon, olives, and spices.

Involtini Thinly sliced beef, veal, or pork, rolled, stuffed, and fried.

Minestrone A rich and savory vegetable soup usually sprinkled with grated Parmigiano and studded with noodles.

Mortadella Mild pork sausage, fashioned into large cylinders and served sliced; the original lunchmeat bologna (because its most famous center of production is Bologna).

Mozzarella A nonfermented cheese, made from the fresh milk of a buffalo (or, if unavailable, from a cow), boiled, and then kneaded into a rounded ball, served fresh.

Mozzarella con pomodori (also Caprese) Fresh tomatoes with fresh mozzarella, basil, pepper, and olive oil.

Nervetti A northern Italian antipasto made from chewy pieces of calves' foot or shin.

Osso buco Beef or veal knuckle slowly braised until the cartilage is tender and then served with a highly flavored sauce.

Pancetta Herb-flavored pork belly, rolled into a cylinder and sliced—the Italian bacon.

Panettone Sweet, yellow-colored bread baked in the form of a brioche.

Panna Heavy cream.

Pansotti Pasta stuffed with greens, herbs, and cheeses, usually served with a walnut sauce.

Pappardelle alle lepre Pasta with rabbit sauce.

Parmigiano Parmesan, a hard and salty yellow cheese usually grated over pastas and soups but also eaten alone; also known as *granna.* The best is Parmigiano-Reggiano.

Peperoni Green, yellow, or red sweet peppers (not to be confused with pepperoni).

Pesci al cartoccio Fish baked in a parchment envelope with onions, parsley, and herbs.

Pesto A flavorful green sauce made from basil leaves, cheese, garlic, marjoram, and (if available) pine nuts.

Piccata al Marsala Thin escalope of veal braised in a pungent sauce flavored with Marsala wine.

Piselli al prosciutto Peas with strips of ham.

Pizza Specific varieties include *capricciosa* (its ingredients can vary widely, depending on the chef's culinary vision and the ingredients at hand), *margherita* (with tomato sauce, cheese, fresh basil, and memories of the first queen of Italy, Marguerite di Savoia, in whose honor it was first made by a Neapolitan chef), *napoletana* (with ham, capers, tomatoes, oregano, cheese, and the distinctive taste of anchovies), *quattro stagione* (translated as "four seasons" because of the array of fresh vegetables in it; it also contains ham and bacon), and *siciliana* (with black olives, capers, and cheese).

Pizzaiola A process in which something (usually a beefsteak) is covered in a tomato-and-oregano sauce.

Polenta Thick porridge or mush made from cornmeal flour.

Polenta e uccelli Assorted small birds roasted on a spit and served with polenta.

Polenta e coniglio Rabbit stew served with polenta.

Polla alla cacciatore Chicken with tomatoes and mushrooms cooked in wine.

Pollo all diavola Highly spiced grilled chicken.

Ragù Meat sauce.

Ricotta A soft, bland cheese made from cow's or sheep's milk.

Risotto Italian rice.

Risotto alla milanese Rice with saffron and wine.

Salsa verde "Green sauce," made from capers, anchovies, lemon juice and/or vinegar, and parsley.

Saltimbocca Veal scallop layered with prosciutto and sage; its name literally translates as "jump in the mouth," a reference to its tart and savory flavor.

Salvia Sage.

Scaloppina alla Valdostana Escalope of veal stuffed with cheese and ham.

Scaloppine Thin slices of veal coated in flour and sautéed in butter.

Semifreddo A frozen dessert; usually ice cream with sponge cake.

Seppia Cuttlefish (a kind of squid); its black ink is used for flavoring in certain sauces for pasta and also in risotto dishes.

Sogliola Sole.

Spaghetti A long, round, thin pasta, variously served: *alla bolognese* (with ground meat, mushrooms, peppers, and so on), *alla carbonara* (with bacon, black pepper, and eggs), *al pomodoro* (with tomato sauce), *al sugo/ragù* (with meat sauce), and *alle vongole* (with clam sauce).

Spiedini Pieces of meat grilled on a skewer over an open flame.

Strangolaprete Small nuggets of pasta, usually served with sauce; the name is literally translated as "priest-choker."

Stufato Beef braised in white wine with vegetables.

Tagliatelle Flat egg noodles.

Tonno Tuna.

Tortelli Pasta dumplings stuffed with ricotta and greens.

Tortellini Rings of dough stuffed with minced and seasoned meat served either in soups or as a full-fledged pasta covered with sauce.

Trenette Thin noodles served with pesto sauce and potatoes.

Trippe alla fiorentina Beef tripe (stomach).

Vermicelli Very thin spaghetti.

Vitello tonnato Cold sliced veal covered with tuna sauce.

Zabaglione/zabaione Egg yolks whipped into the consistency of a custard, flavored with Marsala, and served warm as a dessert.

Zampone Pigs' feet stuffed with spicy seasoned port, boiled and sliced.

Zuccotto A liqueur-soaked sponge cake, molded into a dome and layered with chocolate, nuts, and whipped cream.

Zuppa inglese Sponge cake soaked in custard.

Index

B

C

M

U

Accommodations

Restaurants

PHOTO CREDITS

p. i: Courtesy of Castello di Volpaia; p. iii: Meghan Lamb; p. 1: Meghan Lamb; p. 3, top: Smit / Shutterstock; p. 3, bottom: Resul Muslu / Shutterstock; p. 4: Courtesy of Da Nello al Montegrappa; p. 5: Meghan Lamb; p. 7: Courtesy of Agriturismo La Bruciata / Sara Cencetti; p. 8: Andrea Bonfanti / Shutterstock; p. 9: Ragemax / Shutterstock; p. 10: Framarzo / Shutterstock; p. 11: Kirill Skorobogatko / Shutterstock; p. 12: PhotoSunnyDays / Shutterstock; p. 13: Courtesy of Alba International White Truffle Fair / Lavezzo Studio; p. 14: Giuseppe Strafaci / Shutterstock; p. 15: Andrew Angelov / Shutterstock; p. 16: Stefano Cellai / Shutterstock; p. 19: Meghan Lamb; p. 20: Paolo Gallo / Shutterstock; p. 23: Paolo Gallo / Shutterstock; p. 27: Nejdet Duzen / Shutterstock; p. 28: Meghan Lamb; p. 29: Michelangeloop / Shutterstock; p. 30: Renata Sedmakova / Shutterstock; p. 32: Paolo Bona / Shutterstock.com; p. 33: Cabuscaa / Shutterstock; p. 36: Rostislav Glinsky / Shutterstock; p. 39: Adisa / Shutterstock; p. 41: Shaiith / Shutterstock; p. 44: F11photo / Shutterstock; p. 46: DaLiu / Shutterstock; p. 50: AS photo family / Shutterstock; p. 55: Courtesy of Bologna Welcome / Meridiana; p. 56: Ray Zacek / Shutterstock.com; p. 60: Mix Tape / Shutterstock; p. 61: RossHelen / Shutterstock; p. 67: Muratart / Shutterstock; p. 70: Boris-B / Shutterstock; p. 78: Iakov Kalinin / Shutterstock; p. 84: Igor Link / Shutterstock; p. 86: Juan Antonio Orihuela / Shutterstock; p. 91: Kavalenkava / Shutterstock.com; p. 94: Viacheslav Lopatin / Shutterstock; p. 103: Ivan Moreno sl / Ivan Moreno sl; p. 109: Andrei Nekrassov / Shutterstock; p. 110: Mistervlad / Shutterstock; p. 111: Liz Heath; p. 114: Richard A. McGuirk / Shutterstock; p. 126: Courtesy of Villa Laetitia; p. 129: Courtesy of Chapter Roma / Giulia Venanzi; p. 131: Courtesy of Hotel L'Orologio; p. 132: Courtesy of The Inn at the Spanish Steps / Max Littera; p. 136: Courtesy of Donna Camilla Savelli / Diego De Pol; p. 139: Courtesy of Taverna Angelica; p. 144: Courtesy of La Barrique; p. 145: Liz Heath; p. 147: Courtesy of Imàgo; p. 158: Courtesy of Salotto42; p. 161: ValerioMei / Shutterstock; p. 163: Bernd Rehorst / Shutterstock; p. 168: Umberto Shtanzman; p. 177: TTphoto / Shutterstock.com; p. 181: WhyNotChannel / Shutterstock; p. 183: Ivan Moreno sl / Shutterstock; p. 186: Nataly Reinch / Shutterstock.com; p. 189: Paolo Gallo / Shutterstock; p. 190: Federico Magonio / Shutterstock; p. 193: Todamo / Shutterstock; p. 195: Radiokafka / Shutterstock; p. 197: D.Bond / Shutterstock; p. 201: Anna Pakutina / Shutterstock; p. 211: Courtesy of Grand Hotel Minerva / Andrea Getuli; p. 213: Courtesy of Riva Lofts / ALESSANDRO MICHELAZZI; p. 214: Courtesy of Coquinarius; p. 217: Courtesy of Cantinetta dei Verrazzano; p. 221: Courtesy of Osteria dell'Enoteca / Olga Makarova; p. 224: Courtesy of Scuola del Cuoio; p. 227: Richard Semik / Shutterstock; p. 234: Courtesy of Museo Civico / Palazzo Pubblico / Caroverna Fotógrafa; p. 236: Pargabriele / Shutterstock; p. 248: Courtesy of Castello di Volpaia; p. 254: Courtesy of Agriturismo La Bruciata / Sara Cencetti; p. 257: Katuka / Shutterstock; p. 263: Courtesy of Abbazia di Monte Oliveto Maggiore; p. 267: Courtesy of Visit Arezzo / ICASTICA Arte e Culture della comunicazione; p. 271: Marcobrivio.gallery / Shutterstock; p. 273: Courtesy of Museo dell'Accademia Etrusca (MAEC); p. 278: Travelview / Shutterstock; p. 284: StevanZZ / Shutterstock; p. 286: Courtesy of Volterra Walking Tour; p. 293: AlmacUK / Shutterstock; p. 301: Fokke Baarssen / Shutterstock; p. 305: Ragemax / Shutterstock; p. 307: Dima Moroz / Shutterstock; p. 310: ValerioMei / Shutterstock; p. 312: Davide Zanin / Shutterstock.com; p. 315: Courtesy of Castello di Monterone; p. 319: Buffy1982 / Shutterstock.com; p. 323: © MiC / Palazzo Ducale di Urbino / Direzione Regionale Musei Nazionali Marche / Photo Claudio Riplati; p. 326: Pecold / Shutterstock; p. 329: Tanialerro.art / Shutterstock; p. 336: Lauravr / Shutterstock; p. 343: ermess / Shutterstock; p. 346: Courtesy of Six Keys Guesthouse / Liz Heath; p. 349: Trabantos / Shutterstock; p. 351: Courtesy of Bologna Welcome / Marco Augusto Ghilardi; p. 357: Courtesy of Bologna Welcome / Marco Augusto Ghilardi; p. 360: Courtesy of Bologna Welcome / Wildlab Multimedia; p. 368: Courtesy of Da Nello al Montegrappa; p. 378: Trabantos / Shutterstock; p. 381: Vivida Photo PC / Shutterstock; p. 382: Kooroh / Shutterstock; p. 386: Courtesy of Casa Masoli; p. 390: Courtesy of Comune di Parma; p. 395: Courtesy of Da Nello al Montegrappa; p. 397: Catarina Belova / Shutterstock; p. 400: ColorMaker / Shutterstock; p. 406: Kamira / Shutterstock; p. 410: Cristi Croitoru / Shutterstock.com; p. 415: Yasonya / Shutterstock; p. 421: Maziarz / Shutterstock; p. 424: Arndale /

Shutterstock; p. 426: Stefano Politi Markovina / Shutterstock; p. 428: Lois GoBe / Shutterstock; p. 431: Simone Padovani / Shutterstock; p. 438: Courtesy of Locando Fiorita / Andrea Sarti; p. 441: Courtesy of Pensione Accademia; p. 443: Courtesy of Al Ponte Antico; p. 446: Courtesy of Ai Mercanti; p. 449: Courtesy of Locanda Montin; p. 451: Courtesy of Wistèria; p. 453: Courtesy of La Bottiglia; p. 459: © Fondazione Teatro La Fenice / Michele Crosera; p. 462: EQRoy / Shutterstock; p. 466: Triff / Shutterstock; p. 468: Zevana / Shutterstock; p. 475: Saiko3p / Shutterstock; p. 483: Jaroslav Moravcik / Shutterstock.com; p. 484: Posztos / Shutterstock; p. 492: Courtesy of Joia; p. 495: George Wirt / Shutterstock; p. 498: Ecstk22 / Shutterstock; p. 503: Roman Babakin / Shutterstock.com; p. 508: Courtesy of Grand Hotel Tremezzo; p. 510: Gaspar Janos / Shutterstock; p. 514: Mikolajn; p. 517: Courtesy of Sailing du Lac; p. 521. ElisabettaCavagnino / Shutterstock; p. 523: LizCoughlan / Shutterstock; p. 526: MikeDotta / Shutterstock.com; p. 529: Courtesy of Museo Egizio / Mauro Ujetto; p. 534: Consorzio delle Residenze Reali Sabaude / Michele D'Ottavio; p. 543: Rostislav Glinsky / Shutterstock.com; p. 545: Courtesy of Ristorante Marc Lanteri; p. 547: Fabio Lamanna / Shutterstock.com; p. 549: Julia Kuznetsova / Shutterstock; p. 551: Petru Stan / Shutterstock; p. 558: Saiko3p / Shutterstock; p. 559: Stella Photography / Shutterstock; p. 567: Minoli / Shutterstock; p. 571: Courtesy of Hotel Cenobio dei Dogi / Janos Grapow; p. 576: Monticello / Shutterstock; p. 581: SeaRain / Shutterstock; p. 582: Iryna1; p. 584: Courtesy of La Torretta; p. 588: Sergii Figurnyi / Shutterstock; p. 596: Meghan Lamb; p. 601: Felix Lipov / Shutterstock; p. 605: Ivo Antonie de Rooij / Shutterstock; p. 610: Courtesy of Chiaja Hotel de Charme / Francesco Squeglia; p. 611: Courtesy of Hotel Decamuni de Charme / Marco Baldassarre; p. 614: Courtesy of La Locanda Gesù Vecchio / Andreina Nacca; p. 616: Courtesy of Umberto; p. 620: Paradise at risk / Shutterstock; p. 624: Stefano Tammaro / Shutterstock.com; p. 632: Brenda Kean / Shutterstock; p. 636: Letchik-34 / Shutterstock; p. 639: BBA Photography / Shutterstock; p. 641: Meghan Lamb; p. 647: Stephan Schlachter / Shutterstock; p. 649: Nicola Pulham / Shutterstock; p. 651: Courtesy of Parco di Principi / Janine Pereira Alves; p. 656: Todamo / Shutterstock; p. 659: Massimo Buonaiuto / Shutterstock; p. 661: Brunocoelho / Shutterstock; p. 663: Meghan Lamb; p. 668: Boris Stroujko / Shutterstock; p. 669: My Personal Legend / Shutterstock; p. 672: Julia Chan Kar Wai / Shutterstock; p. 674: Meghan Lamb; p. 680: SilkeW; p. 681: Courtesy of Palazzo Avino; p. 684: Meghan Lamb; p. 685: Sirio Carnevalino; p. 691: Roman Babakin / Shutterstock.com; p. 694: Meghan Lamb; p. 699: Meghan Lamb; p. 705: trabantos / Shutterstock; p. 707: AWP76 / Shutterstock.com; p. 710: Meghan Lamb; p. 714: StevanZZ / Shutterstock; p. 715: ValerioMei / Shutterstock; p. 719: Courtesy of Vetera Matera; p. 723: Lev Levin / Shutterstock; p. 724: Maurizio De Mattei / Shutterstock; p. 727: Meghan Lamb; p. 728: Meghan Lamb; p. 731: Zedspider / Shutterstock; p. 732: Nejdet Duzen / Shutterstock; p. 734: Meghan Lamb; p. 738: Emily Marie Wilson / Shutterstock.com; p. 741: www.marcobrivio.photo / Shutterstock; p. 745: PannaPhoto / Shutterstcok; p. 746: Igor Zuikov / Shutterstock; p. 748: Meghan Lamb; p. 755: Meghan Lamb; p. 758: Meghan Lamb; p. 760: Meghan Lamb; p. 765: Meghan Lamb; p. 771: Meghan Lamb; p. 773: Meghan Lamb; p. 774: Yury Dmitrienko / Shutterstock.com; p. 777: Essevu / Shutterstock.com; p. 781: Meghan Lamb; p. 783: Meghan Lamb; p. 785: Meghan Lamb; p. 786: Meghan Lamb; p. 790: DaLiu / Shutterstock; p. 793: Mkos83 / Shutterstock; p. 799: Meghan Lamb; p. 800: Saiko3p / Shutterstock; p. 804: Adwo / Shutterstock; p. 807: Meghan Lamb; p. 810: Ecstk22 / Shutterstock; p. 813: Avillfoto / Shutterstock.com; p. 815: Roman Babakin / Shutterstock; p. 821: Meghan Lamb; p. 825: Ragemax / Shutterstock.